Lecture Notes in Artificial Intelligence 5816

Edited by R. Goebel, J. Siekmann, and W. Wahlster

Subseries of Lecture Notes in Computer Science

Luís Seabra Lopes Nuno Lau
Pedro Mariano Luís M. Rocha (Eds.)

Progress in Artificial Intelligence

14th Portuguese Conference
on Artificial Intelligence, EPIA 2009
Aveiro, Portugal, October 12-15, 2009
Proceedings

Springer

Series Editors

Randy Goebel, University of Alberta, Edmonton, Canada
Jörg Siekmann, University of Saarland, Saarbrücken, Germany
Wolfgang Wahlster, DFKI and University of Saarland, Saarbrücken, Germany

Volume Editors

Luís Seabra Lopes
Nuno Lau
Pedro Mariano
Departamento de Electrónica, Telecomunicações e Informática
Universidade de Aveiro
Aveiro, Portugal
E-mail: {lsl, nunolau, plsm}@ua.pt

Luís M. Rocha
School of Informatics & Computing
Cognitive Science Program
Indiana University, Bloomington, IN, USA
E-mail: rocha@indiana.edu

Library of Congress Control Number: 2009935766

CR Subject Classification (1998): I.2, J.4, H.3, H.5.2, I.5, I.4, K.4, K.3

LNCS Sublibrary: SL 7 – Artificial Intelligence

ISSN 0302-9743
ISBN-10 3-642-04685-1 Springer Berlin Heidelberg New York
ISBN-13 978-3-642-04685-8 Springer Berlin Heidelberg New York

springer.com

Printed in Germany

Typesetting: Camera-ready by author, data conversion by Scientific Publishing Services, Chennai, India
Printed on acid-free paper SPIN: 12767465 06/3180 5 4 3 2 1 0

Preface

The 14th Portuguese Conference on Artificial Intelligence, EPIA 2009, took place at Hotel Meliá Ria, in Aveiro, Portugal, in October 12–15, 2009. This international conference was organized by the University of Aveiro and, as in previous years, was held under the auspices of the Portuguese Association for Artificial Intelligence (APPIA). The purpose of EPIA 2009 was to promote research in all areas of Artificial Intelligence (AI), covering both theoretical/foundational issues and applications, and to encourage the scientific exchange among researchers, engineers and practitioners in related disciplines.

To promote discussions among participants, EPIA 2009 was structured as a set of thematic tracks proposed by the international AI research community. Thematic tracks are intended to provide an informal environment that fosters the active cross-fertilization of ideas between researchers within specific subareas of AI, including theoretical/foundational, integrative, application-oriented and newly emerging areas. The proposals received in response to a public Call for Thematic Tracks were evaluated by the Program Chair and the General Chairs in consultation with the Advisory Committee. The following tracks were selected and included in the conference program:

AITUM – Artificial Intelligence in Transportation and Urban Mobility
ALEA – Artificial Life and Evolutionary Algorithms
CMBSB – Computational Methods in Bioinformatics and Systems Biology
COLA – Computational Logic with Applications
EAC – Emotional and Affective Computing
GAI – General Artificial Intelligence
IROBOT – Intelligent Robotics
KDBI – Knowledge Discovery and Business Intelligence
MASTA – Multi-Agent Systems: Theory and Applications
SSM – Social Simulation and Modelling
TEMA – Text Mining and Applications
WNI – Web and Network Intelligence

Each track was coordinated by an Organizing Committee composed of, at least, two researchers in the field, from different institutions. An international Program Committee, with recognized researchers within the track's scientific areas, was created.

In response to the Call for Papers, a total of 163 paper submissions were received from 21 countries, namely Australia, Austria, Belgium, Brazil, Bulgaria, Cuba, France, Germany, Hungary, India, Iran, Italy, Kuwait, The Netherlands, Portugal, Singapore, Spain, Taiwan, Tunisia, UK and USA. All submissions were evaluated by at least three members of the Program Committees of the respective tracks and were selected for presentation at the conference on the basis of quality and relevance to the issues addressed in the track. The present volume contains a selection of higher quality full papers presented in the different tracks. These papers are organized in chapters, one for each track. The numbers of submitted papers in each track and the respective numbers of papers accepted for this volume are given in Table 1. The overall acceptance rate for this volume was 33.7%. All remaining papers presented at the conference are included in a separate proceedings volume published by the University of Aveiro.

Table 1. Numbers of submitted and selected papers.

	submitted	selected
AITUM	11	3
ALEA	12	3
CMBSB	5	2
COLA	10	5
EAC	7	3
GAI	11	3
IROBOT	27	10
KDBI	17	7
MASTA	22	7
SSM	10	4
TEMA	25	7
WNI	6	1
Total	163	55

This edition of EPIA featured, for the first time, a *Nectar Track*, that is, a set of plenary sessions with a selection of top-quality papers accepted in the different tracks. The Nectar Track aims to promote the dissemination of information between research groups with different interests within the AI field, as well as the cooperation between different research groups and the development of integrative research projects. The Nectar Track also aims to provide increased visibility to some of the best papers in the conference program and, in so doing, provide a general view of the AI field and its current hot topics. After consultation with the EPIA 2009 Advisory Committee, the following papers were included in the Nectar Track:

- "A Data-Based Approach to Integrating Representations of Personality Traits, Values, Beliefs and Behavior Descriptions", by Boon-Kiat Quek, Kayo Sakamoto, and Andrew Ortony
- "Comparing Different Properties Involved in Word Similarity Extraction", by Pablo Gamallo Otero
- "Constraint-Based Strategy for Pairwise RNA Secondary Structure Prediction", by Olivier Perriquet and Pedro Barahona

- “Cost-Sensitive Learning Vector Quantization for Credit Scoring”, by Ning Chen, Armando S. Vieira, João Duarte, Bernardete Ribeiro, and João C. Neves
- “Efficient Coverage of Case Space with Active Learning”, by Nuno Filipe Escudeiro and Alípio Mário Jorge
- “How Much Should Agents Remember? The Role of Memory Size on Convention Emergence Efficiency”, by Paulo Urbano, João Balsa, Paulo Ferreira Jr., and Luis Antunes
- “Roles, Positionings and Set Plays to Coordinate a RoboCup MSL Team”, by Nuno Lau, Luís Seabra Lopes, Nelson Filipe, and Gustavo Corrente
- “Semantic Image Search and Subset Selection for Classifier Training in Object Recognition”, by Rui Pereira, Luís Seabra Lopes, and Augusto Silva
- “Sensitivity Analysis of a Tax Evasion Model Applying Automated Design of Experiments”, by Attila Szabó, László Gulyás, and István János Tóth
- “Type Parametric Compilation of Algebraic Constraints”, by Marco Correia and Pedro Barahona
- “Using Operator Equalisation for Prediction of Drug Toxicity with Genetic Programming”, by Leonardo Vanneschi and Sara Silva

In addition to the parallel sessions for the different tracks and the plenary nectar sessions, the program of EPIA 2009 included plenary talks by distinguished researchers in the AI field, namely:

- Hod Lipson, from Cornell University, with a talk on “The Robotic Scientist: Mining Experimental Data for Dynamical Invariants, from Cognitive Robotics to Computational Biology”.
- Marie-Francine Moens, from the Katholieke Universiteit Leuven, with a talk on “More than Just Words: Discovering the Semantics of Text with a Minimum of Supervision”.
- Demetri Terzopoulos, from the University of California, Los Angeles, with a talk on “Artificial Life Simulation of Humans and Lower Animals: From Biomechanics to Intelligence”.

Finally, the program of EPIA 2009 also included the 2nd Doctoral Symposium on Artificial Intelligence (SDIA).

EPIA 2009 was organized in cooperation with the Special Interest Group on Artificial Intelligence of the Association for Computing Machinery (ACM-SIGART) and the Portuguese Chapter of the IEEE Computational Intelligence Society. The conference was co-sponsored by the Portuguese Research Foundation (FCT) and IEEE Portugal Section. The participation of Demetri Terzopoulos as invited speaker was funded by the Organizing Committee of the ALEA Thematic Track. We highly appreciate and thank the collaboration of the members of all committees, namely the Advisory Committee, the Organizing Committees and the Program Committees of the different tracks and the Organizing Committee of SDIA. We also thank invited speakers, authors, referees and session chairs for their contributions to the conference program. Thanks are also due to Microsoft Research, for their Conference Management Service

(CMT), which was freely used for managing the paper submission and evaluation processes in EPIA 2009. Last but not least, we thank Springer for publishing this volume.

October 2009

Luís Seabra Lopes
Nuno Lau
Pedro Mariano
Luís M. Rocha

EPIA 2009 Conference Organization

Conference Chairs

Luís Seabra Lopes	Universidade de Aveiro, Portugal
Nuno Lau	Universidade de Aveiro, Portugal
Pedro Mariano	Universidade de Aveiro, Portugal

Program Chair

Luís M. Rocha	Indiana University, USA

Advisory Committee

Salvador Abreu	Universidade de Évora, Portugal
Pedro Barahona	Universidade Nova de Lisboa, Portugal
Pavel Brazdil	Universidade do Porto, Portugal
Luís Camarinha-Matos	Universidade Nova de Lisboa, Portugal
Amílcar Cardoso	Universidade de Coimbra, Portugal
Hélder Coelho	Universidade de Lisboa, Portugal
Luís Correia	Universidade de Lisboa, Portugal
Ernesto Costa	Universidade de Coimbra, Portugal
Gaël Dias	Universidade da Beira Interior, Portugal
Pedro Rangel Henriques	Universidade do Minho, Portugal
Gabriel Pereira Lopes	Universidade Nova de Lisboa, Portugal
José Manuel Machado	Universidade do Minho, Portugal
José Maia Neves	Universidade do Minho, Portugal
Arlindo Oliveira	Universidade Técnica de Lisboa, Portugal
Eugénio Oliveira	Universidade do Porto, Portugal
Luís Moniz Pereira	Universidade Nova de Lisboa, Portugal
José Carlos Príncipe	University of South Florida, USA
Carlos Ramos	Instituto Politécnico do Porto, Portugal
Manuel Filipe Santos	Universidade do Minho, Portugal
Manuela Veloso	Carnegie Mellon University, USA

Thematic Track Chairs

AITUM

Rosaldo Rossetti	Universidade do Porto, Portugal
Ronghui Liu	University of Leeds, UK
Elisabete Arsénio	Laboratório Nacional de Engenharia Civil, Portugal
Jorge Lopes	BRISA S.A., Portugal

ALEA

Agostinho Rosa	Universidade Técnica de Lisboa, Portugal
Luís Correia	Universidade de Lisboa, Portugal

CMBSB

Miguel Rocha	Universidade do Minho, Portugal
Rui Camacho	Universidade do Porto, Portugal
Florentino Fdez-Riverola	Universidad de Vigo, Spain

COLA

Carlos Viegas Damásio	Universidade Nova de Lisboa, Portugal
Fernando Silva	Universidade do Porto, Portugal

EAC

Goreti Marreiros	Instituto Politécnico do Porto, Portugal
Andrew Ortony	Northwestern University, Chicago, USA
Ana Paiva	Universidade Técnica de Lisboa, Portugal
Luis Antunes	Universidade de Lisboa, Portugal

GAI

Luís Seabra Lopes	Universidade de Aveiro, Portugal
Nuno Lau	Universidade de Aveiro, Portugal
Pedro Mariano	Universidade de Aveiro, Portugal
Luís M. Rocha	Indiana University, USA

IROBOT

Luís Paulo Reis	Universidade do Porto, Portugal
Luís Correia	Universidade de Lisboa, Portugal
António José Neves	Universidade de Aveiro, Portugal

KDBI

Nuno Marques	Universidade Nova de Lisboa, Portugal
Paulo Cortez	Universidade do Minho, Portugal
João Moura Pires	Universidade Nova de Lisboa, Portugal
Luís Cavique	Universidade Aberta, Portugal
Manuel Filipe Santos	Universidade do Minho, Portugal
Margarida Cardoso	ISCTE, Portugal
Robert Stahlbock	University of Hamburg, Germany
Zbigniew Michalewicz	University of Adelaide, Australia

MASTA

Ana Paula Rocha	Universidade do Porto, Portugal
Paulo Urbano	Universidade de Lisboa, Portugal
César Analide	Universidade do Minho, Portugal

SSM

Luis Antunes	Universidade de Lisboa, Portugal
Marco Janssen	Arizona State University, USA
Antônio Rocha Costa	Universidade Católica de Pelotas, Brazil
Laszlo Gulyas	Lorand Eotvos University, Hungary

TEMA

Joaquim Ferreira da Silva	Universidade Nova de Lisboa, Portugal
Gabriel Pereira Lopes	Universidade Nova de Lisboa, Portugal
Gaël Dias	Universidade da Beira Interior, Portugal
Vitor Jorge Rocio	Universidade Aberta, Portugal

WNI

Alípio M. Jorge	Universidade do Porto, Portugal
Alneu de Andrade Lopes	Universidade de São Paulo, Brazil
Solange Rezende	Universidade de São Paulo, Brazil

Program Committee

AITUM

Ana Almeida, Portugal
Constantinos Antoniou, USA
Ana Bazzan, Brazil
Moshe Ben-Akiva, USA
Carlos Bento, Portugal
João Bento, Portugal
Eduardo Camponogara, Brazil
Hussein Dia, Australia
Alberto Fernandez, Spain
Franziska Klügl, Sweden
Henry Liu, USA
Kai Nagel, Germany
Luís Nunes, Portugal
Eugénio Oliveira, Portugal
Luís Osório, Portugal
Sascha Ossowski, Spain
Francisco C. Pereira, Portugal
Luís Paulo Reis, Portugal
Giovanna Di Marzo Serugendo, UK
Agachai Sumalee, Hong Kong
Shuming Tang, China
José Telhada, Portugal
Harry Timmermans, The Netherlands
Giuseppe Vizzari, Italy
Fei-Yue Wang, USA
Geert Wets, Belgium
Danny Weyns, Belgium
Chris Zegras, USA

ALEA

Helio Barbosa, Brazil
Ernesto Costa, Portugal
Peter Eggenberger, Denmark
Carlos M. Fernandes, Portugal
Carlos M. Fonseca, Portugal
Inman Harvey, UK
Francisco Herrera, Spain
Colin G. Johnson, UK
Fernando Lobo, Portugal
Pedro Mariano, Portugal
Fernando M. Melicio, Portugal
José Ferreira Mendes, Portugal
Juan Julián Merelo, Spain
Francisco B. Pereira, Portugal
José A. Pereira, Portugal
Vitorino Ramos, Portugal
Marc Schonenauer, France
Sara Silva, Portugal
Miroslav Snorek, Czech Republic

CMBSB

Alexessander Alves, UK
Paulo Azevedo, Portugal
Pierre Baldi, USA
Lourdes Borrajo, Spain
Philip Bourne, USA
Pavel Brazdil, Portugal
Chris Bystroff, USA
André Carvalho, Brazil
Vítor Santos Costa, Portugal
Francisco Couto, Portugal
Luc Dehaspe, Belgium
Fernando Diaz-Gomez, Spain
Inês Dutra, Portugal
Timothy Ebbels, UK
Fazel Famili, Canada
Eugénio C. Ferreira, Portugal
Nuno Fonseca, Portugal
Elaine Holmes, UK
Eva Iglesias, Spain
Hasan Jamil, USA
Alípio M. Jorge, Portugal
Rosalia Laza, Spain
Rui Mendes, Portugal
José Mendez-Reboredo, Spain
Kiran Patil, Denmark
Reyes Pavon, Spain
Enrique C. Pelaez, Spain
Yonghong Peng, UK
Arlo Zan Randall, USA
Isabel Rocha, Portugal
Luís M. Rocha, USA
Marie-France Sagot, France
Santiago Schnell, USA
Mário Silva, Portugal
Jorge Vieira, Portugal
Mohammed Zaki, USA

COLA

Salvador Abreu, Portugal
Manuel Ojeda Aciego, Spain
José Júlio Alferes, Portugal
Grigoris Antoniou, Greece
Vítor Santos Costa, Portugal
Bart Demoen, Belgium
Inês Dutra, Portugal
Paulo Gomes, Portugal
Gopal Gupta, USA
Pascal Hitzler, Germany
Priscila Lima, Brazil
Frank Pfenning, USA
Enrico Pontelli, USA
Nuno Silva, Portugal
Umberto Straccia, Italy
Terrance Swift, Portugal
David Warren, USA
Gregory Wheeler, Portugal

EAC

César Analide, Portugal
Luis Antunes, Portugal
Robert Axtell, USA
Win Burleson, USA
Lola Canamero, UK
Amílcar Cardoso, Portugal
Cristiano Castelfranchi, Italy
Hélder Coelho, Portugal
Nigel Gilbert, UK
Samer Hassan, Spain
Jennifer Healey, USA
Ian Horswill, USA
Eva Hudlicka, USA
José Machado, Portugal
Goreti Marreiros, Portugal
Stacy Marsella, USA
José Maia Neves, Portugal
Paulo Novais, Portugal
Andrew Ortony, USA
Ana Paiva, Portugal
Juan Pavón, Spain
Paolo Petta, Austria
Boon Kiat Quek, Singapore
Carlos Ramos, Portugal
Ricardo Santos, Portugal
Michelle See, Singapore
Juan Velásquez, USA
Yinping Yang, Singapore

GAI

Salvador Abreu, Portugal
Michael Anderson, USA
Francisco Azevedo, Portugal
Pedro Barahona, Portugal
Carlos Bento, Portugal
Luís Camarinha-Matos, Portugal
Amílcar Cardoso, Portugal
Hélder Coelho, Portugal
Jonathan Connell, USA
Juan Corchado, Spain
Luís Correia, Portugal
Anna Really Costa, Brazil
Ernesto Costa, Portugal
Manuel Delgado, Spain
Gaël Dias, Portugal
Inês Dutra, Portugal
Florentino Fdez-Riverola, Spain
Cipriano Galindo, Spain
Pedro Rangel Henriques, Portugal
João Leite, Portugal
Gabriel Pereira Lopes, Portugal
Inês Lynce, Portugal
José Machado, Portugal
Rui Mendes, Portugal
Bernd Neumann, Germany
Arlindo Oliveira, Portugal
Eugénio Oliveira, Portugal
Luis Moniz Pereira, Portugal
José Carlos Príncipe, USA
Ricardo Rabelo, Brazil
Carlos Ramos, Portugal
Fariba Sadri, UK
Manuel Filipe Santos, Portugal
Paulo Urbano, Portugal
Zita Vale, Portugal
Rosa Vicari, Brazil
Michael Witbrock, USA

IROBOT

César Analide, Portugal
Gabriella Sanniti Di Baja, Italy
Stephen Balakirsky, USA
Jacky Baltes, Canada
Reinaldo Bianchi, Brazil
Hans-Dieter Burkhard, Germany
Carlos Carreto, Portugal
Xiaoping Chen, China
Luís Correia, Portugal
Augusto Loureiro da Costa, Brazil
Jorge Dias, Portugal
Marco Dorigo, Belgium
Paulo Gonçalves, Portugal
Huosheng Hu, UK
Nuno Lau, Portugal
Luís Seabra Lopes, Portugal
António Paulo Moreira, Portugal
António José Neves, Portugal
Urbano Nunes, Portugal
Paulo Oliveira, Portugal
Fernando Osório, Brazil
Enrico Pagello, Italy
Fernando Lobo Pereira, Portugal
Armando J. Pinho, Portugal
Mikhail Prokopenko, Australia
Luís Paulo Reis, Portugal
Fernando Ribeiro, Portugal
Maria Isabel Ribeiro, Portugal
Martin Riedmiller, Germany
Jose Miguel Sanchiz, Spain
Eduardo Silva, Portugal
Armando Sousa, Portugal
Guy Theraulaz, France
Flavio Tonidandel, Brazil
Paulo Urbano, Portugal

KDBI

António Abelha, Portugal
Vasilis Aggelis, Greece
Victor Alves, Portugal
Carlos Alzate, Belgium
Orlando Belo, Portugal
Agnès Braud, France
Rui Camacho, Portugal
Logbing Cao, Australia
Emilio Carrizosa, Spain
André Carvalho, Brazil

Ning Chen, Portugal
José Costa, Brazil
Mário Figueiredo, Portugal
Cristian Figueroa-Sepulveda, Chile
João Gama, Portugal
Peter Geczy, Japan
Paulo Gomes, Portugal
Pascal Hitzler, Germany
Beatriz De La Iglesia, UK
Wolfgang Jank, USA
Stéphane Lallich, France
Philippe Lenca, France
Stefan Lessmann, Germany
Wolfram-M. Lippe, Germany
Victor Lobo, Portugal
José Machado, Portugal
Ernestina Menasalvas, Spain
Armando Mendes, Portugal
Patrick Meyer, France
João Pedro Neto, Portugal
José Maia Neves, Portugal
Fátima Rodrigues, Portugal
Joaquim Ferreira da Silva, Portugal
Carlos Soares, Portugal
Murat Caner Testik, Turkey
Theodore Trafalis, USA
Armando Vieira, Portugal
Gregory Wheeler, Portugal

MASTA

César Analide, Portugal
Luis Antunes, Portugal
João Balsa, Portugal
Ana Bazzan, Brazil
Reinaldo Bianchi, Brazil
Luis Botelho, Portugal
Amílcar Cardoso, Portugal
Hélder Coelho, Portugal
Antônio Rocha Costa, Brazil
Yves Demazeau, France
Virginia Dignum, The Netherlands
Edmund Durfee, USA
Michael Fisher, UK
Graça Gaspar, Portugal
Marie-Pierre Gleizes, France
Wojtek Jamroga, Germany
Nuno Lau, Portugal
Paulo Leitão, Portugal
Jorge Louçã, Portugal
Luis Macedo, Portugal
José Machado, Portugal
Andreia Malucelli, Brazil
Carlos Martinho, Portugal
John-Jules Meyer, The Netherlands
Jörg Müller, Germany
Paulo Novais, Portugal
Luís Nunes, Portugal
Oliver Obst, Australia
Eugénio Oliveira, Portugal
Andrea Omicini, Italy
Julian Padget, UK
Paolo Petta, Austria
Isabel Praca, Portugal
Mikhail Prokopenko, Australia
Luís Paulo Reis, Portugal
Ana Paula Rocha, Portugal
Rosaldo Rossetti, Portugal
Jordi Sabater, Spain
Jaime Sichman, Brazil
Paulo Urbano, Portugal

SSM

Frederic Amblard, France
Pedro Andrade, Brazil
Robert Axtell, USA
João Balsa, Portugal
Ana Bazzan, Brazil
Pedro Campos, Portugal
Amílcar Cardoso, Portugal
Claudio Cioffi-Revilla, USA
Hélder Coelho, Portugal
Nuno David, Portugal
Paul Davidsson, Sweden
Guillaume Deffuant, France
Alexis Drogoul, France
Julie Dugdale, France
Bruce Edmonds, UK
Nigel Gilbert, UK

Nick Gotts, UK
Samer Hassan, Spain
Rainer Hegselmann, Germany
Wander Jager, The Netherlands
Michel Klein, The Netherlands
Jorge Louçã, Portugal
Fernando Neto, Brazil
Mario Paolucci, Italy
Juan Pavón, Spain
Carlos Ramos, Portugal
Juliette Rouchier, France
Keith Sawyer, USA
Jaime Sichman, Brazil
Carles Sierra, Spain
Elizabeth Sklar, USA
Ron Sun, USA
Keiki Takadama, Japan
Jan Treur, The Netherlands
Klaus Troitzsch, Germany
Harko Verhagen, Sweden

TEMA

António Branco, Portugal
Pavel Brazdil, Portugal
Eric de la Clergerie, France
Guillaume Cleuziou, France
Luisa Coheur, Portugal
Walter Daelemans, Belgium
Gaël Dias, Portugal
Antoine Doucet, France
Tomaz Erjavec, Slovenia
Pablo Gamallo, Spain
Pablo Gervás, Spain
Adam Kilgarriff, UK
Mark Lee, UK
Gabriel Pereira Lopes, Portugal
Belinda Maia, Portugal
Nuno Mamede, Portugal
Nuno Marques, Portugal
Veska Noncheva, Bulgaria
Maria das Graças Volpe Nunes, Brazil
Manuel Palomar, Spain
Paulo Quaresma, Portugal
Vitor Jorge Rocio, Portugal
Irene Rodrigues, Portugal
Antonio Sanfilippo, USA
Frédérique Segond, France
Joaquim Ferreira da Silva, Portugal
Aline Villavicencio, Brazil
Spela Vintar, Slovenia
Christel Vrain, France
Katerzyna Wegrzyn-Wolska, France
Pierre Zweigenbaum, France

WNI

Sarabjot Anand, UK
Paulo Azevedo, Portugal
José Luís Borges, Portugal
Pavel Brazdil, Portugal
Pedro Campos, Portugal
Gaël Dias, Portugal
Alípio M. Jorge, Portugal
José Paulo Leal, Portugal
Alneu de Andrade Lopes, Brazil
Nuno Marques, Portugal
Maria Carolina Monard, Brazil
Maria Cristina F. de Oliveira, Brazil
Thiago Pardo, Brazil
Lubos Popelinsky, Czech Republic
Solange Rezende, Brazil
Eduarda Mendes Rodrigues, UK
Giovanni Semeraro, Italy
Mário Silva, Portugal
Carlos Soares, Portugal
Maarten van Someren, The Netherlands

External Reviewers

Susana Aguiar, UK
Bettina Berendt, Belgium
Anders Christensen, Portugal
Ruth Cobos, Spain
Debora Donato, Spain
Grzegorz Dziczkowski, France

Table of Contents

Chapter 1: AITUM – Artificial Intelligence in Transportation and Urban Mobility

Chapter 2: ALEA – Artificial Life and Evolutionary Algorithms

Chapter 3: CMBSB – Computational Methods in Bioinformatics and Systems Biology

Chapter 4: COLA – Computational Logic with Applications

Chapter 8: KDBI – Knowledge Discovery and Business Intelligence

Chapter 9: MASTA – Multi-Agent Systems: Theory and Applications

Chapter 10: SSM – Social Simulation and Modelling

Chapter 11: TEMA – Text Mining and Applications

Chapter 12: WNI – Web and Network Intelligence

Chapter 1

AITUM – Artificial Intelligence in Transportation and Urban Mobility

Genetic Algorithm for the Calibration of Vehicle Performance Models of Microscopic Traffic Simulators

André Luiz Cunha, José Elievam Bessa Jr., and José Reynaldo Setti

Universidade de São Paulo, São Carlos School of Engineering
Dept. of Transport Engineering
Av. Trabalhador São-carlense, 400 – S. Carlos, SP, Brazil – 13566-590
{acunha,jebessa}@sc.usp.br, jrasetti@usp.br

Abstract. A genetic algorithm was used to search for optimum calibration parameter values for the vehicle performance models used by two well-known microscopic traffic simulation models, CORSIM and Integration. The mean absolute error ratio between simulated and empirical performance curves was used as the objective function. Empirical data was obtained using differential GPS transponders installed on trucks travelling on divided highways in Brazil. Optimal parameter values were found for the "average" truck for each truck class and for each vehicle in the sample. The results clearly show the feasibility of the proposed approach. The simulation models calibrated to represent Brazilian trucks individually provided average errors of 2.2%. Average errors around 5.0% were found when using the average truck class parameters.

Keywords: Genetic algorithm, performance curve, traffic simulation.

1 Introduction

Microscopic traffic simulation models have become a very useful tool for planning, design and operation of transport systems. The greatest advantage of using such tools is the ability to evaluate alternatives prior to their implementation. However, the adequate use of simulation models requires calibration of the model parameters to ensure a proper representation of the real traffic behavior [1].

The accuracy of the results provided by a simulation model is highly dependent upon its calibration parameters [2]. The values adopted for those parameters are used by the model's internal logic to govern the movement of vehicles and driver behavior. The vehicle performance model is one of the logics used to represent the movement of vehicles and thus its travel speed along the modeled network. It is especially important in links where heavy vehicles climb steeper grades and other situations where the available engine power is fully utilized.

Most users simply use the default values for the vehicle performance calibration parameters. The accuracy of simulations involving networks in mountainous or hilly terrain with traffic containing a significant fraction of heavy vehicles can,

L. Seabra Lopes et al. (Eds.): EPIA 2009, LNAI 5816, pp. 3–14, 2009.

however, be compromised and could be improved by a properly conducted calibration of the performance model for the typical trucks in the traffic stream. The calibration of such models, however, is not a simple task given the complexity of the models and the difficulties in obtaining optimal parameter values empirically. This paper proposes a genetic algorithm approach for this task and presents an application of the proposed approach to two widely different traffic simulation models based on truck performance data collected on Brazilian highways.

2 Traffic Simulation Models

Traffic simulation models are efficient and powerful tools for the operational analysis of traffic streams. Their main advantage is to allow for the evaluation of alternatives prior to their implementation or under conditions that would be very difficult to observe in the real world, without submitting the users to any inconveniences that such tests might cause [1,2]. Simulation models are now widely used for the planning, design and management of highway networks and intelligent transportation systems. For instance, in the development of procedures within the Highway Capacity Manual, traffic flow computer simulation was extensively used [3,4]. The use of simulation, however, requires an extensive knowledge about the model itself and its limitations, as well as an excellent understanding of the traffic flow theories upon which the model is based [5]. Two microscopic simulation models were used in this study: CORSIM, one of the most used traffic simulators, and Integration, which uses a more sophisticated vehicle performance model. The next section briefly discusses the relevant aspects of them.

2.1 CORSIM

CORSIM (CORridor SIMulation), developed by US FHWA in the late 1970s, consists of two integrated microscopic simulators, NETSIM, which simulates traffic flow on arterials and roads with interrupted flow, and FRESIM, which simulates freeways and other roads with uninterrupted flow [6]. It is one of models most used by practitioners and researchers, due to its ability to simulate all types of road, from freeways to local streets, subjected to all types of control, in addition to having a friendly user interface and high-quality graphical representation of the simulated traffic flow [7,8].

CORSIM is an stochastic model that assigns random attributes to drivers, vehicles and decision-making processes, allowing for a realistic representation of the road network [6]. Driver behavior is defined by random attributes (varying degrees of aggressiveness); vehicle performance (acceleration and speed) is randomly defined in a similar fashion. Vehicle movement in the network is based on the Pitt car-following behavior [9], which is based on the distance headway and speed differential between the leading vehicle and follower. The model updates position, speed and acceleration for all vehicles in the network every second.

Thus, vehicular locomotion is determined by the car-following and acceleration behavior.

CORSIM's heavy vehicle performance model is based on average accelerations that may be achieved based on the vehicle's instantaneous speed. The performance model adopted assumes fixed acceleration values for speeds ranging from 0 to 110 ft/s (120 km/h), for four truck types (light, medium, heavy and extra-heavy). The user manual does not explain how the default values were obtained. However, these values are stored in RT173 (*Maximum Acceleration Table*) and may be modified by the user to better reflect the performance of the trucks being simulated.

The calibration of this performance model requires the collection of speed and acceleration data for trucks representative of the four truck types. Compared to Integration's, this approach is less sophisticated, but is computationally less intensive – something that made sense at the time the model was originally developed.

2.2 Integration

Integration is a model capable of simulating from freeways to local roads using the same logic. Created by Michel Van Aerde in the late 1980s, Integration is not as widely used as CORSIM but is widely recognized as a very sophisticated model capable of modelling a wide range of traffic conditions [10]. While Integration is a microscopic simulation model, its car-following model parameters can be calibrated macroscopically, from speed-flow data [11]. Vehicle movement along the links is controlled by three logics: car-following, lane-changing and acceleration (as a function of vehicle performance). Vehicle position, speed and acceleration are updated every 0.1 s.

Integration stores parameters for its vehicle performance model in a file called `maxi_acc.dat`. The logic calculates acceleration from the resultant of the forces acting on the vehicle and assumes that engine power is constant. The acceleration a is

$$a = \frac{F - R}{m} (\text{m/s}^2), \tag{1}$$

where F is the tractive force (N), R is the total resistance (N) and m is the vehicle mass (kg). The tractive force F (N) produced by the engine is

$$F = \min \begin{cases} 3600\,\eta\, P/V \\ W_{ta}\,\mu \end{cases} (\text{N}), \tag{2}$$

where η is the transmission efficiency ($0 \leq \eta \leq 1$); P is the nominal engine power (kW); V, the vehicle speed; W_{ta}, the weight on the tractive axles (N); and μ the tyre-pavement friction. The total resistance R is the sum of three components – drag (R_a), rolling resistance (R_r) and grade resistance (R_g):

$$\begin{aligned} R &= R_a + R_r + R_g \text{ (N)}, \quad \text{with} \\ R_a &= c_1\, C_D\, C_h\, A\, V^2 \text{ (N)} \\ R_r &= C_r\, (c_2\, V + c_3)\, W/1000 \text{ (N)} \\ R_g &= W\, i \text{ (N)} \end{aligned} \tag{3}$$

where c_1 is constant and equal to 0.047285; c_2 and c_3 are constants reflecting the tyre characteristics; C_D is the drag coefficient; C_h is the correction due to altitude; A is the cross-section area (m^2); V, the speed (km/h); C_r is the rolling resistance coefficient; and i is the grade (m/m).

Due to the number of parameters involved, calibration of this model is more complicated than CORSIM's. The complexity of the calibration process and the number of calibration parameters involved suggests that a genetic algorithm would be an efficient approach to the calibration of these models, perhaps with an edge over other possible approaches, as the literature suggested [1,2,12,13]. The next sections present a brief review on the use of genetic algorithms for calibration of simulation models.

3 Calibration of Traffic Simulation Models Using Genetic Algorithm

Calibration is the process through which the user fine tunes model parameters, compares simulation results to empirical data and verifies the ability of the simulation model to represent adequately the observed traffic stream [2,12,14]. Model developers provide default values for model parameters that reflect the data used in the validation of the software. Users applying the model to other regions should ideally recalibrate model parameters to improve the representation of local vehicle and driver peculiarities by the simulation.

Genetic algorithm (GA), which were first created by Holland [15], is a search method based on the principles of evolution and natural selection. One of its advantages is to search for solutions from multiple points, increasing the probability of finding a global, instead of a local, optimum [1]. Thus, it is particularly useful for problems with a complex search space – as in the case of traffic flow simulation. GAs have been successfully applied to many aspects of transportation engineering: traffic flow simulation modelling [1,2,12,13,16,17], traffic signal timing [18] and even infrastructure maintenance planning [19].

GAs simulate the process of natural evolution, with the possible solutions (in this case, the set of calibration parameter values) representing individuals in a population. An initial population is randomly generated, with the individual level of adaptation to the environment (the quality of the solution) measured by a fitness function. Individuals are represented by strings – called chromosomes – which represent the individual characteristics, genes. Each gene represents one of the calibration parameters.

The search consists in creating successive generations of individuals. At each new generation, new individuals are created from the previous generation using selection and reproduction processes to exchange genetic material. One of these processes, elitism, consists in selecting the individuals who are best adapted to the environment for reproduction, to assure that the best traits are propagated to their descendants. Other genetic operators, predation and mutation, are used to introduce variability (new solutions) into the gene pool. The former consists in replacing the less adapted individuals in the population by new chromosomes, randomly generated. Mutation is used to randomly modify some of the genes in a population.

A literature survey shows that most of the previous applications of GA to traffic flow simulation models have focused on the calibration of car-following parameters [9,13,16,20,21]. Schultz and Rilett [16], however, emphasize that the use of default parameters for the performance model might affect the quality of the simulation results for networks with a large number of trucks, as it is the case in Brazil. The need for a method to calibrate the vehicle performance models used by CORSIM and Integration was identified. The next section explains the adopted approach.

4 The Proposed Approach

The proposed approach consisted in using a GA to find the best values for the parameters of CORSIM and Integration performance models using empirical performance data collected on divided highways. The accuracy of the simulation was evaluated comparing empirical and simulated performance curves (speed vs. distance travelled along a grade). Initially, the GA was used to find parameter sets to best represent the performance each truck observed during the data collection. This step was the validation of the process. Subsequently, the GA was modified to obtain parameter sets representative of the performance of typical vehicles for four classes: light, medium, heavy and extra-heavy trucks.

4.1 Field Data Collection

Data for the observed performance curves were collected on a divided highway in the state of São Paulo, Brazil. Total truck mass, nominal engine power, as well as axle number and configuration data were collected at a mobile weigh station. With the agreement of the driver, a differential GPS receiver was installed in the truck to collect kinematic speed and position data. The trucks were monitored along a section of approximately 10 km. The GPS data provided vertical and horizontal alignment and truck speed at 1-s intervals. From this data, performance curves were constructed for all vehicles in the sample.

Trucks were grouped in 4 classes according to the number of axles: light (two-axle rigid trucks), medium (three-axle rigid trucks), heavy (five- and six-axle articulated trucks) and extra-heavy (seven- to nine-axle articulated trucks). The sample consisted of 62 trucks (light: 5; medium: 13; heavy: 22; extra-heavy: 22) travelling on grades varying from 0.6% to 5.2%, although most of the observations were made on 1.8% (22 trucks), 2.9% (13 trucks) and 3.4% (14 trucks) grades.

4.2 Genetic Algorithm

The genetic algorithm was coded in Microsoft Excel's Visual Basic for Application. Figure 1 shows a simplified flowchart of the GA's main components. In the next sections the main features of the GA are explained.

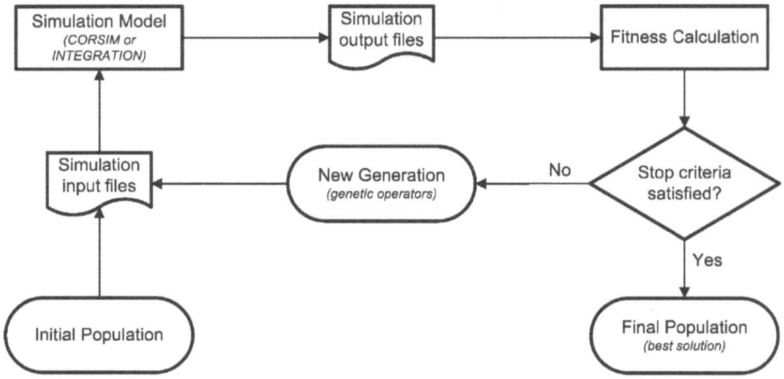

Fig. 1. Simplified flowchart of the genetic algorithm used

Initial Population. An initial population of 40 individuals was used. The population size was chosen after a sensitivy analysis using light trucks, whose results suggested that the best combination would be 40 individuals and 50 generations.

Each individual in the population is a string (chromosome) containing model parameter values (genes). Parameter values for the initial population were generated randomly, within predefined search space limits. For CORSIM, the genes are the acceleration for 10 ft/s speed intervals, from 0 to 110 ft/s, and search spaces are shown in Table 1. The search spaces were established assuming that the upper and lower limits should follow a monotone decrescent function. Special care was also taken to avoid acceleration ranges that could result in the truck not being able to climb a steep grade.

Table 1. Search space for CORSIM calibration parameters

	Speed (ft/s)										
Acceleration (ft/s^2)	0	10	20	40	50	60	70	80	90	100	110
Minimum	2	1.5	1	0	0	0	0	0	0	-1	-1
Maximum	20	15	10	6	4	3.5	3	2.5	2	1.5	1.5

The chromosome used for Integration's calibration was made of 8 genes, containing the parameters listed in Table 2, which also lists the search spaces for each truck class. The search spaces for mass W and nominal engine power P were defined as the confidence interval ($\alpha = 5\%$) for the sample mean, for each class. Search spaces for the other parameters were defined from the literature [11]. An additional parameter, η_2, was included in the chromosome to represent driver aggressiveness and is a multiplier of the nominal power.

Simulation Input Files. The next step is the preparation of the input files for the simulation of each chromosome. For CORSIM, a `.trf` file is created, in

Table 2. Search spaces for Integration calibration parameters

	Truck class			
Parameter	Light	Medium	Heavy	Extra-heavy
W (kg)	5,998–12,510	19,222–23,464	42,164–44,074	58,844–59,401
P (kW)	95–110	115–158	252–264	281–292
η	0.7000–0.9000	0.7000–0.9000	0.7000–0.9000	0.7000–0.9000
C_D	0.5000–12.000	0.5000–12.000	0.5000–12.000	0.5000–1.2000
c_2	0.0100–0.0500	0.0100–0.0500	0.0100–0.0500	0.0100–0.0500
c_3	20.000–90.000	2.0000–90.000	2.0000–90.000	2.0000–9.0000
C_r	10.000–20.000	1.0000–20.000	1.0000–20.000	1.0000–2.0000
η_2	0.5000–15.000	0.5000–15.000	0.5000–15.000	0.5000–1.5000

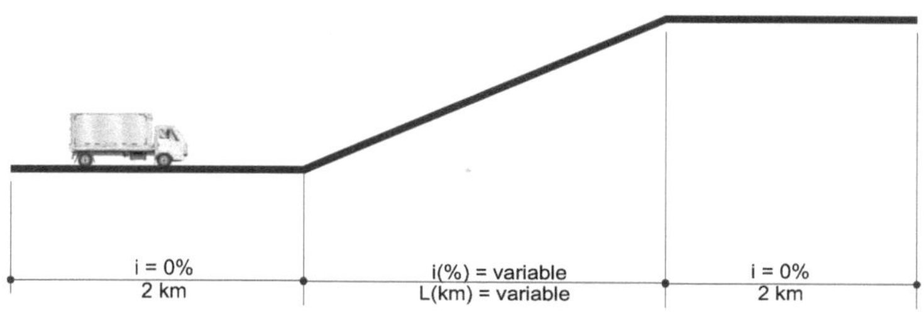

Fig. 2. Vertical alignment of the simulated road network

which the line corresponding to RT173 contains the parameter values for that individual. For Integration, a `maxi_acc.dat` file is created for each individual in the population, containing the corresponding parameter values.

Simulation Runs. In this step, the model is called to run the simulation for each chromosome in the population. The simulation experiments used an hipotetical road section composed of three segments, as shown in Figure 2: an initial 2-km level segment, an intermediate segment with variable grade and length, and a final 2-km level segment. The initial segment was used to adjust the vehicle speed to the initial speed of the observed truck. This assured that both the simulated and observed performance curves had the same entry speed. The grade magnitude for the second segment was set to the observed grade magnitude. The simulated traffic flow was set to 10 veic/h to avoid interaction between vehicles and the consequent effects of the car-following logic on the acceleration. The simulation time used was 30 min and just one type of truck was used in each simulation. The simulation results are then used in the next step.

Simulation Output Files. The simulation results are used to create performance curves, which were built using instantaneous speeds at every 100 m along the grade. The data were extracted from the simulation output files, `.tsd` for CORSIM and `detector.out` for Integration. At the end of this step, the observed and simulated performance curves were available to be compared.

Fitness Calculation. In this step, the quality of the solution provided by each chromosome is evaluated using a fitness function which, in this case, was the mean absolute error ratio (*MAER*). The fitness function measures the chromosome's ability to represent faithfully the behavior of all trucks in a class and is given by:

$$MAER_{jk} = \frac{1}{N_k} \sum_{l=1}^{N_k} IMAER_{jkl} \tag{4}$$

in which $MAER_{jk}$ is the average *MAER* for the k-th truck class using chromosome j; and N_k is the number of trucks in the k-th truck class. $IMAER_{jkl}$ is a measure of the discrepance between the simulated and observed speeds, which are determined at every 100 m along the grade:

$$IMAER_{jkl} = \frac{1}{m} \sum_{i=0}^{m} \left| \frac{VSIM_{kl}(i) - VOBS_{kl}(i)}{VOBS_{kl}(i)} \right| \tag{5}$$

in which $IMAER_{jkl}$ is the *MAER* for l-th truck in the k-th truck class using chromosome j; $VSIM_{kl}(i)$ is the simulated speed at the i-th station along the grade for the l-th truck in the k-th class; $VOBS_{kl}(i)$ is the observed speed at the i-th station along the grade for the l-th truck in the k-th class; and m is the number of speed observation stations along the grade. The values of the observed speed used to calculate *IMAER* were "raw" — i.e., they were not filtered to remove any observational noise.

The smaller $MAER_{jk}$ is the better the quality of the solution provided by chromosome j; the greater $MAER_{jk}$ is the poorer the solution provided by this parameter set.

Stop Criteria. Two stop criteria were adopted for the GA used to find the calibration parameters for truck classes: $MAER \leq 3.0\%$ or 50 generations. For the calibration for individual trucks in the sample, the criteria were $MAER \leq 0.1\%$ or 10 generations. Once one of these criteria is reached, the best solution is provided by the chromosome with the smallest *MAER*.

New Generation. If the stop criteria is not satisfied, a new generation is created from the current population, through the use of genetic operators. Different strategies were adopted for each model. The one used for CORSIM was more aggressive, given the paucity of information about its performance logic and how the default values were found [16]. For Integration, however, a less agressive strategy was utilized because ranges of values for the parameters used in its performance model can be easily found in the literature [11].

For CORSIM, at the end of each generation, *predation* is used to cull from the gene pool that half of the population with the highest *MAER*. These least fit individuals are replaced by randomly generated chromosomes. Next, the best fit individual of that generation – the chromosome with the smallest *MAER* – is selected (*elitism*) to exchange genetic material with the remainder of the population (*crossover*). The chromosomes thus created are then subjected to *mutation*, which is a random change in one of the genes; the mutation rate used was 30%. The resulting population is the new generation, which is subjected to all steps until one of the stop criteria is satisfied.

For Integration, elitism was used to select the chromosome to crossover genetic material with the remainder of the population. The main difference is that predation and mutation are applied only after five generations. The mutation rate used was 10% and the predation rate, 30%. The new generation is made of the chromosomes thus obtained and the process repeats until one of the stop criteria is met.

5 Analysis of the Results

Initially, the GA was used to obtain calibration parameters for each truck observed, to validate the proposed approach. The calibration results are illustrated in Figure 3, which shows the simulated (GA individual) and "raw" observed performance curves (GPS) for one of the heavy trucks in the sample. Also shown in the figure is the simulated performance curve using the calibration parameters obtained for the heavy truck class (GA category), which are discussed next.

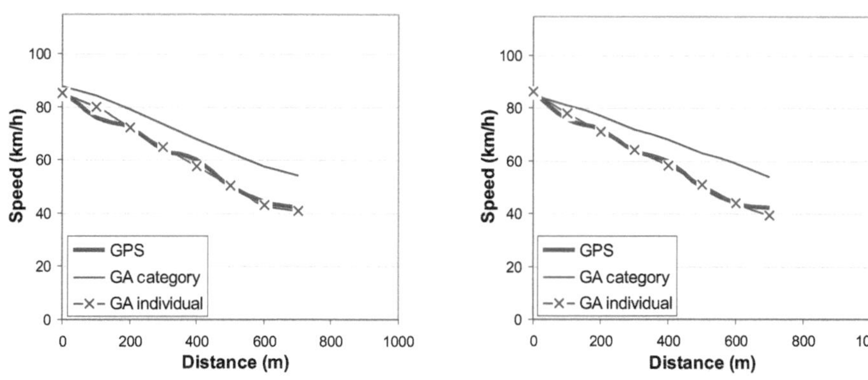

Fig. 3. Simulated and unfiltered observed performance curves for one of the heavy trucks in the sample (CORSIM on the left; Integration on the right)

The histograms in Figure 4 show the distribution of *MAER* found in the calibration of each model. *MAER* was greater than 5% in only 7 of the 62 trucks observed for the CORSIM calibration; for Integration, 5 trucks had *MAER* greater than 5%, which clearly demonstrates the efficiency of the proposed approach.

5.1 Calibration for Truck Classes

Once the proposed approach was tested and validated, the GA was used to find calibration parameter sets for typical trucks that would represent each of the four truck classes adopted. The results for this are summarized in Figure 5, which shows the improvement obtained with the use of the new parameter values to replace the default values. It can be easily noticed that the default values could not simulate the performance of Brazilian trucks adequately and that the models recalibrated using the GA are able to provide better results. The recalibrated parameters are shown in Tables 3 and 4, which show the best results (least *MAER*) produced by the GA. The last generation, however, had several individuals that provided solutions only marginally worse than the best, for both CORSIM and Integration.

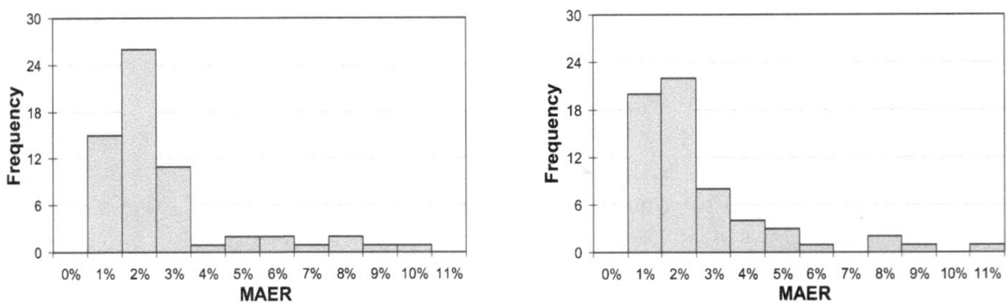

Fig. 4. Mean absolute error ratio distributions found in the calibration of the models (CORSIM on the left; Integration on the right)

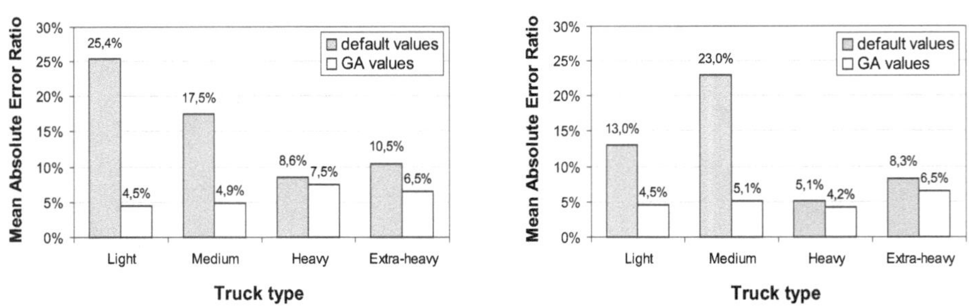

Fig. 5. Mean absolute error ratios disaggregated by truck class, before and after the calibration of the models (CORSIM on the left; Integration on the right)

Table 3. New values found for Integration's performance model parameters by the GA

Truck class	W (kg)	P (kW)	η	C_D	c_2	c_3	C_r	η_2
Ligth	11,383	106.1	0.7486	0.6632	0.0150	3.1638	1.6049	1.0372
Medium	21,974	142.5	0.7227	0.7584	0.0212	2.5301	1.3168	0.7153
Heavy	43,954	253.8	0.7515	0.8217	0.0108	5.1679	1.8076	1.1992
Extra-heavy	59,076	284.9	0.8062	0.8210	0.0426	3.6663	1.2803	0.7507

Table 4. New values of acceleration (ft/s^2) found for CORSIM by the GA

	Truck class			
Speed (ft/s)	Light	Medium	Heavy	Extra-heavy
0	12.56	12.95	11.76	16.29
10	10.25	4.32	6.36	1.68
20	5.76	1.94	3.11	1.60
30	3.09	0.65	2.30	0.75
40	2.24	0.35	1.79	0.50
50	1.20	0.35	0.84	0.48
60	0.73	0.28	0.54	0.35
70	0.31	0.23	0.46	0.06
80	0.27	0.02	0.45	0.00
90	0.15	0.02	0.06	0.01
100	−0.05	0.01	0.02	−0.84
110	−0.13	−0.10	−0.10	−0.97

6 Concluding Remarks

This research has shown that a GA can be used to calibrate the performance models used by two traffic flow simulators, CORSIM and Integration. Specifically, new parameters were found for Brazilian trucks using empirical speed data collected with a differential GPS. Furthermore, the GA was able to find parameters to represent the average performance of trucks in four classes: light, medium, heavy and extra-heavy. When using truck class parameters found by the GA, the differences between observed and simulated speeds, measured as the mean absolute error ratio, for trucks climbing grades from 0.6% to 5.2% ranged from 4.5% (light trucks) to 7.5% (heavy trucks) for CORSIM. For Integration, the differences ranged from 4.2% (heavy trucks) to 6.4% (extra-heavy trucks).

The vehicle performance models used in CORSIM and Integration, while very different, proved capable to represent the climbing performance of most trucks in the sample with high fidelity. When using parameters found by the GA for individual trucks, the difference between simulated and observed speeds was greater than 5% for only 7 of the 62 trucks for CORSIM and 5 out of 62, for Integration. The average $MAER$ was 2.2%.

Acknowledgments. The research reported in this paper was funded by CNPq, the Brazilian National Council for Scientific and Technological Development. The support given by Centrovias Sistemas Rodoviários S.A. and its personnel during the data collection is also gratefully acknowledged.

References

1. Kim, K.-O., Rilett, L.R.: Genetic-Algorithm-Based Approach for Calibrating Microscopic Simulation Models. In: 2001 IEEE Intelligent Transportation Systems Conference Proceedings, pp. 698–704. IEEE Press, New York (2001)

2. Ma, T., Abdulhai, B.: Genetic Algorithm-Based Optimization Approach and Generic Tools for Calibrating Traffic Microscopic Simulation Parameters. Transp. Res. Rec. 1800, 6–15 (2001)
3. Elefteriadou, L., Torbic, D., Webster, N.: Development of Passenger Car Equivalents for Freeways, Two-Lane Highways, and Arterials. Transp. Res. Rec. 1572, 51–58 (1997)
4. Harwood, D., May, A., Anderson, I., Leiman, L., Archilla, R.: Capacity and Quality of Service of Two-Lane Highways. NCHRP, Transportation Research Board (1999)
5. Halati, A., Lieu, H., Walker, S.: CORSIM – Corridor Traffic Simulation Model. In: Traffic Congestion and Traffic Safety in the 21st Century, pp. 570–576. ASCE, Chicago (1997)
6. CORSIM User's Guide. Federal Highway Administration, U.S. Department of Transportation, Washington, D.C. (2001)
7. Owen, L.E., Zhang, Y., Rao, L., McHale, G.: Traffic Flow Simulation Using CORSIM. In: Proc. of the 2000 Winter Simulation Conference, pp. 1143–1147 (2000)
8. Milam, R.T., Choa, F.: Recommended Guidelines for the Calibration and Validation of Traffic Simulation Models. In: 8th TRB Conference on the Application of Transportation Planning Methods, pp. 178–187. Transportation Research Board, Washington (2002)
9. Rakha, H., Crowther, B.: Comparison and Calibration of FRESIM and INTEGRATION Steady-state Car-following Behavior. Transp. Res. A 37, 1–27 (2003)
10. May, A.D.: Traffic Management from Theory to Practice: Past, Present, Future. Transp. Res. Rec. 1457, 1–14 (1994)
11. Demarchi, S.H.: Heavy Vehicle Effects on Capacity and Level of Service of Divided Highways (in Portuguese). Ph.D. thesis, Univ. de São Paulo, Brazil (2000)
12. Egami, C.Y., Setti, J.R., Rilett, L.R.: Calibration of a Two-Lane Highway Traffic Simulator Using Genetic Algorithm (in Portuguese). Transportes 12, 5–14 (2004)
13. Cheu, R., et al.: Calibration of FRESIM for Singapore Expressway Using Genetic Algorithm. J. Transp. Engg. 124, 526–535 (1998)
14. Hellinga, B.R.: Requirements for the Calibration of Traffic Simulation Models. In: Proc. of the Canadian Society for Civil Engineering, vol. IVb, pp. 211–222 (1998)
15. Goldberg, D.E.: Genetic Algorithms in Search, Optimization and Machine Learning. Addison-Wesley, Reading (1989)
16. Schultz, G.G., Rilett, L.R.: Calibration of Distribution of Commercial Motor Vehicle in CORSIM. Transp. Res. Rec. 1934, 246–255 (2005)
17. Araújo, J.J., Setti, J.R.: Analysis of Heavy-Vehicle Impacts on a Bridge Using Microsimulation (in Portuguese). In: Transporte em Transformação XII, pp. 23–42. Positiva, Brasília (2008)
18. Teklu, F., Sumalee, A., Watling, D.: A Genetic Algorithm Approach for Optimizing Traffic Control Signals Considering Routing. Computer-Aided Civil and Infrastructure Engineering 22, 31–43 (2007)
19. Liu, C., Hammad, A., Itoh, Y.: Maintenance Strategy Optimization of Bridge Decks Using Genetic Algorithm. J. Transp. Engg. 123, 91–100 (1997)
20. Payne, H.J., et al.: Calibration of FRESIM to Achieve Desired Capacities. Transp. Res. Rec. 1591, 23–30 (1997)
21. Chundury, S., Wolshon, B.: Evaluation of CORSIM Car-Following Model by Using Global Positioning System Field Data. Transp. Res. Rec. 1710, 114–121 (2000)

Simulating Communication in a Service-Oriented Architecture for V2V Networks

João F.B. Gonçalves, Edgar F. Esteves, Rosaldo J.F. Rossetti, and Eugénio Oliveira

Department of Informatics Engineering
Artificial Intelligence and Computer Science Laboratory (LIACC)
Faculty of Engineering, University of Porto (FEUP)
Rua Dr. Roberto Frias, S/N, 4200-465 Porto, Portugal
{ee02123,edgar.esteves,rossetti,eco}@fe.up.pt

Abstract. A framework based on the concept of service-oriented architectures (SOA) to support the assessment of vehicular *ad-hoc* networks (VANET) is herein presented. Concepts related to SOA, as well as technologies that allow real-time data acquisition and dissemination within urban environments, and simulation tools to aid the simulation of VANET were preliminarily studied. A two-layered architecture was specified on the basis of the requirements for our simulation framework resulting in the specification of a multi-agent system formed of vehicle entities that are able to communicate and interact with each other and with their surrounding environment as well. A prototypical application was implemented, which was used to demonstrate the feasibility of the approach presented through experimental results.

Keywords: Intelligent Transportation Systems, Service-Oriented Architectures, Vehicle-to-Vehicle Communication and Simulation, Multi-Agent Systems.

1 Introduction

Most urban areas all over the globe have increased considerably in the last few decades, giving rise to important mobility issues. Unfortunately, virtually all people tend to opt for using private car instead of public transport. This trend has turned infrastructures unable to cope with the ever increasing demand, which work most of the time in saturation regime. This problem motivates the scientific community that strives to devise different solutions. Some approaches suggest the physical improvement of infrastructure by means of increasing road capacity. Others try to enhance the control systems responsiveness, with relative success. More recently, though, researchers have experimented promising innovative information technologies to aid driving tasks and traveller decision-making. The latter underlie the concept of intelligent transportation systems (ITS), which attempts at integrating contemporary and breakthrough computer and information technologies to better managing and controlling modern urban transportation systems. ITS is intended to turn future urban transport (FUT) into greener, cheaper, reliable, secure, and sustainable systems, functionally, energetically and environmentally efficient.

L. Seabra Lopes et al. (Eds.): EPIA 2009, LNAI 5816, pp. 15–26, 2009.

Indeed, high-class vehicles will very soon be equipped with short-range wireless communication interfaces, bringing about major concerning issues as well. Thus, simulation tools will need to be adapted to support the assessment of V2V communication infrastructures and performance. This work is based on our study of the communication technologies underlying vehicle-to-vehicle interactions then. We aim at studying concepts related to SOA and ways in which such concepts can be adapted to VANET. The work started by the specification and implementation of a simulation framework on the basis of the concept of multi-agent systems, and preliminary results allowed us to gain further insight into such motivating and challenging new arena.

2 Related Technologies

ITS-based technologies have proven a great impact and influence on future urban transport scenarios. As the automotive industry starts marketing vehicles equipped with wireless communication capabilities, some technologies are being deemed be potentially applicable and beneficial.

2.1 Service Oriented Architectures

Service-oriented architectures are devised as software architectures whose main goal advocates that application functionalities must be made available in form of services. Thus, services from SOA's point of view are functions of a computational system that are made available to other systems. Such a novel approach might be well represented by the "find-bind-execute" paradigm, which is analogous to the Deming's cycle applied to services, involving planning, execution, monitoring and pro-active decision-making phases to improve systems' performance. The "find-bind-execute" paradigm allows a consumer of a service to ask for registering in a service provider that suits its criteria and requirements. If the service of interest is found, the provider sends the consumer a contract and the address in which the service can be found. Such a mechanism is depicted in Figure 1.

According to [1], the entities that support such a service infrastructure are service consumers, providers, registry and contract.

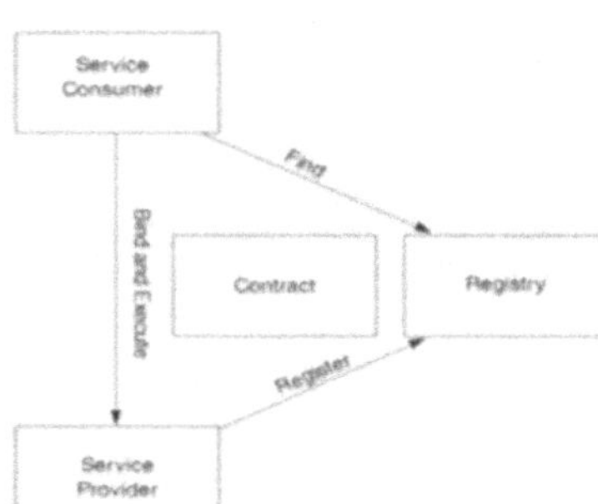

Fig. 1. Find-bind-execute paradigm (adapted from [1])

Service consumers are basically an application, a service, or another type of software requiring a service. This is the entity who initiates the process, looking for a service capable of supplying its requirements. The consumer executes the service by sending a request formatted in accordance with the contract.

Service providers are addressable entities that accept and execute services. These entities might be a mainframe, a component or another type of software that executes a requested service. Service providers publish their contract in the service registry for other potentially interested consumers to access them.

The *service registry* is a sort of network directory that "knows" the available services. It accepts and stores contracts of providers and provides consumers with these service options. Finally, a *service contract* is a kind of specification of the way in which a service consumer must interact with the provider. This entity rules the protocol for requests and respective answers from services. A contract may require a set of pre- and post-conditions representing the state of a service to be deemed acceptable to execute certain functions. Contracts may also contain information on quality of services, as well as conditions to which consumers must comply.

2.2 Vehicle-to-Vehicle Networks

Vehicle-to-vehicle communication networks are, as its designation suggests, networks formed by several vehicles equipped with wireless communication devices that can communicate with each other. In V2V networks, each vehicle analyses, within a certain radius, other vehicles that are in range, and can inform its position, velocity, direction and other characteristics. This kind of communication has been one of the fields of interest in telecommunications that grew very quickly lately. Thus, vehicles with such capabilities can form a special type of mobile *ad-hoc* network with particular applications, known as Vehicular Ad-hoc Networks (VANET). VANET are a special type of Mobile Ad-hoc Networks (MANET) that supports communications between vehicles. According to [2], VANET inherit some characteristics from the MANET, but also improve the former with new features, which differentiate it from other *ad-hoc* mobile networks. These characteristics include high mobility, open network with dynamic topology, limited connectivity, potential to achieve larger scale, all nodes are providers, forwarders and consumers of data and the wireless transmission can suffer from much noise and interferences.

These characteristics make VANET sufficiently different from other networks and significantly affect their properties. For example, in [3] it is demonstrated that the movement of vehicles has a significant effect on the latency of messages delivery. Most applications that can be implemented on a MANET require a certain type of data dissemination. Studies argue, however, this must be implemented through specific routing protocols, as long as VANET are concerned, basically due to their particular characteristics, such as in [4]. Nonetheless, there are other studies that suggest it is possible to use the available MANET protocols. Some of those protocols are designed to support dedicated short range communications (DSRC), which is already implemented in USA, such as VITP and PAVAN. Due to its topology, the MANET already have a large set of protocols.

There are several ways to classify routing protocols for such networks, some of which are listed below:

- According to the range, they can be either unicast or multicast.
- According to the route discovery, they can be either pro-active, reactive or hybrid.
- According to the search algorithm they are based on, they can be either Distance Vector, Link State, based on geographic information, or Zone based.

In Figure 2, the protocols previously mentioned are related, as well as are their classification according to the characteristics presented above.

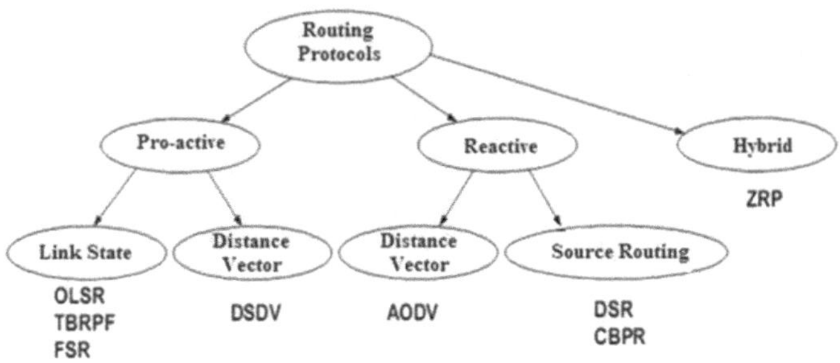

Fig. 2. MANET routing protocols classification

2.3 Simulation Tools for VANET

The development of applications and protocols associated to VANET can be studied through simulation, especially when a real traffic network in urban environments, which must involve a large number of nodes, is subject to study. Through simulation models, the performance of V2V networks, as well as other characteristics can be assessed and improved. Indeed, conducting experiments and studies on such a large scale within the real scenario has proven extremely difficult and expensive. Thus, simulation has become an indispensable and even an imperative tool.

Basically, simulation of V2V networks requires two different components, namely a communication networks simulator, capable of simulating the properties of a wireless network, and a vehicular traffic simulator, able to monitor and represent the kinematic aspects of mobility through the VANET nodes. Recent studies [5] suggested that the vehicular mobility model is very important to obtain significant results and should be well integrated with the wireless communication networks model. Other authors further suggested that the use of an inappropriate model, such as the popular "random waypoint model" (which can work very well for some mobile *ad-hoc* networks, but very likely is not an appropriate representation of mobility in wireless vehicular networks) can lead to erroneous results [5], [6].

Nevertheless, traffic simulators have been subjected to enormous developments and greatly improved in recent years to include communication between vehicles. Several ways to achieve such an advanced feature have been proposed and actually implemented. The greatest trend in most studies moves towards the creation of simulators that include traffic and wireless communication simulation models in one single simulation tool. Some examples of such tools include GrooveNet and Divert.

However, other studies prefer to use two independent simulators, combining stand-alone traffic and communication networks simulators, which are interconnected by an application that ensures the exchange of information between them. Among traffic simulators used for this purpose, one can mention the popular SUMO, as well as VISSIM and CARISMA. Wireless communication networks simulators include GloMoSim, QualNet and the NS2. The interested reader is referred to [7] for a more detailed discussion on the above simulation tools, including their respective references.

3 Coupling SOA and V2V Communication

Currently, services that both drivers and travellers in general can use on-board in journey time demand a great deal of hardware and software. Each new feature must be implemented in a new device to be embedded in the car. Such an approach has proven very expensive, with little flexibility, which contradicts the increasing trend of services made available on-demand, for instance. On the other hand, services made available as software to be executed in an on-board unit (OBU) based on an embedded computer with considerable processing and memory, as well as communication capabilities seem to be very promising and present great potentials and advantages. According to such not-so-much futuristic scenario, we intend to specify and implement an extensible architecture based on OBU computers and featured with communication capabilities to the level of services.

Bearing in mind that such architecture was intended to promote services throughout V2V communication networks, we opted for a layer-based structure. Thus, the proposed architecture is divided into two main levels, namely the network services level and the end-user services level. This approach is illustrated in Figure 3, in which the two different levels are identified. The first level in such a structure is responsible for network-related tasks, such as building network topology, as well as discovering and exchanging services among vehicles (the nodes of the communication network). The second level, on the other hand, implements the necessary basis underlying the management of the so called high-level services, to be made available to end-users.

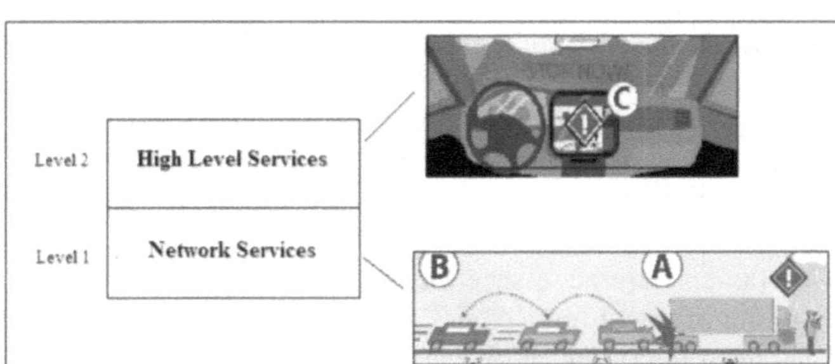

Fig. 3. SOA layered architecture for V2V networks

3.1 The Network Services Layer

For the first level, and accounting for its functions within the proposed structure, we adopted the solution suggested in [8]. The scenario illustrated in Figure 4 is a good representation of the adopted solution, as explained below.

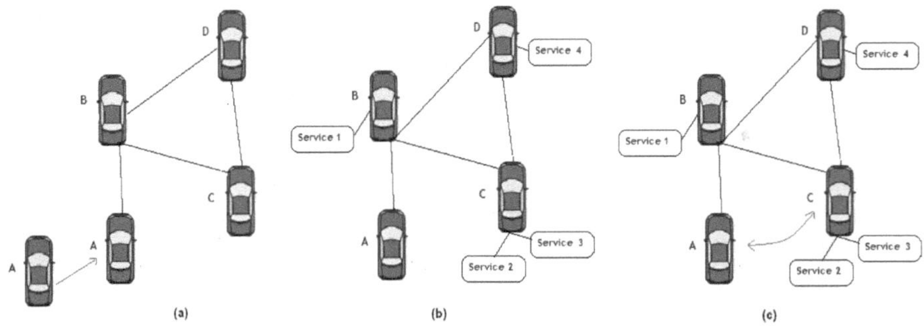

Fig. 4. SOA-based V2V communication interactions

Let us consider the communication network formed up by vehicles as illustrated in Figure 4. In (a), the network is actually set-up. All nodes (A to D) are vehicles equipped with mobile wireless V2V communication devices. Initially, A node is not connected for there is no other vehicle within its range vicinity. As soon as it finds other vehicles within its range, then they get connected. All connected nodes thus form a VANET, allowing V2V communication. After all the necessary automatic configurations are set up, the VANET is ready for routing any messages sent by any node and addressed to any other node of the network.

After the VANET is ready, the SOA-based features must be deployed too. All nodes that provide any service must publish it alongside a comprehensible description, so that other nodes will be able to discover the service and use it as needed. The service discovering capabilities of each node must be implemented in such a way that the node may be able to find the needed service throughout the VANET which every configuration must apply. Thus, in (b), provider nodes publish their services, whereas any consumer will be able to find them whenever necessary.

An illustrative service use example is demonstrated in (c). A node gets connected to the service interface of service whose ID is 3, hosted in C node. All information necessary to message exchange between consumer (A node) and provider (C node) is available in the description of service 3, needing A no further information about C. As A and C nodes are not directly connected to each other, messages must be routed through B node.

Two basic components are necessary for the example presented above to be possible, namely a routing protocol for VANET and the implementation of SOA functionalities. One of the most important SOA features is the service discovering mechanism. Two approaches are then possible for us to implement such a mechanism. First, we can integrate it within a VANET routing protocol or, alternatively, we can implement it on top of the network layer, as a separate functionality. In the current work we opted for the first solution, and integrated it in the VANET routing mechanism. Such a decision proved advantageous as both the routing tables and protocol routing techniques are used in the service discovering process. For this purpose, we chose the optimised like state routing protocol (OLSR) for it is a pro-active protocol, which facilitates the propagation of services description throughout a network of known topology. Among pro-active protocols, OLSR has the advantage of using multi-points relaying (MPR) and offers an open source application (OLSR *Daemon*) allowing it to be extended.

Routing in MANET is based in the cooperation of participating nodes; all nodes must run the protocol in such a way they collectively achieve routing goals. Such a behavior is also desirable in VANET, as all nodes are expected to collaborate in services discovery as well. In practice, it means all nodes manage message routing even though they may not know its contents. This way all service provider nodes may use the entire network and routing protocol.

A node intending to publish its services must generate and propagate SOA messages periodically, carrying the service information, according to certain transmission interval. Whenever a node receives a SOA message, it must resend it and, if it supports SOA services, process it too.

The format of a SOA message has two basic fields, namely the message length and the service description, which describes the service as a unique service (no other service will have the same description). This sort of message is carried within OSLR packages and propagated throughout the network. Nonetheless, there is no specific format for the content of a service descriptor, which will depend on the type of service and the way it is implemented. XML might be used for this purpose, though.

3.2 The High Level Services Layer

The second layer of the proposed architecture consists of the necessary structure to adequately manage the high level services to users. In other words, high level services can be seen as final applications presenting some degree of interaction with users, most of the time through a graphical user interface (GUI), which can be accessed from inside the vehicle. Thus, all hardware and software components somehow necessary to effectively run such services are specified in this level. Some examples include traffic jams detection, collision avoidance and emergency calls among others.

Once again, we consider that vehicles are equipped with some sort of OBU as discussed earlier. Figure 5 depicts the main components of this level in a UML development diagram, illustrating the distribution of components both embedded in a vehicle and those that are present in the surrounding environment, and eventually in other vehicles.

Before we can go a bit further into the description of each component, the service concept must be clarified in this context. In this architecture, *services* are abstract resources able to carry out tasks that are coherent both from provider and from request entities' point of view, and are classified according to their abstraction level. Thus, *low level* services are basically pieces of software that access physical devices of a vehicle. On the contrary, *high level* services are responsible to carry out tasks that are expected to transform information somehow. Such a hierarchical structure of services has a two-fold purpose. Firstly, it offers a modular programming infrastructure that is extensible and scalable. Secondly, it seems to be adequate to overcome synchronisation issues while a variety of devices are accessed. Indeed, for the latter case, the *vehicle* component can be actually seen as an agent, whereas multiple vehicles interacting within an urban network environment form a multi-agent system. This metaphor becomes quite intuitive when we consider that vehicles are equipped with sensors, are able to determine their geographical location and to interact with the surrounding environment, as well as with other vehicles. From this standpoint, the OBU is their reasoning kernel that executes tasks of both levels.

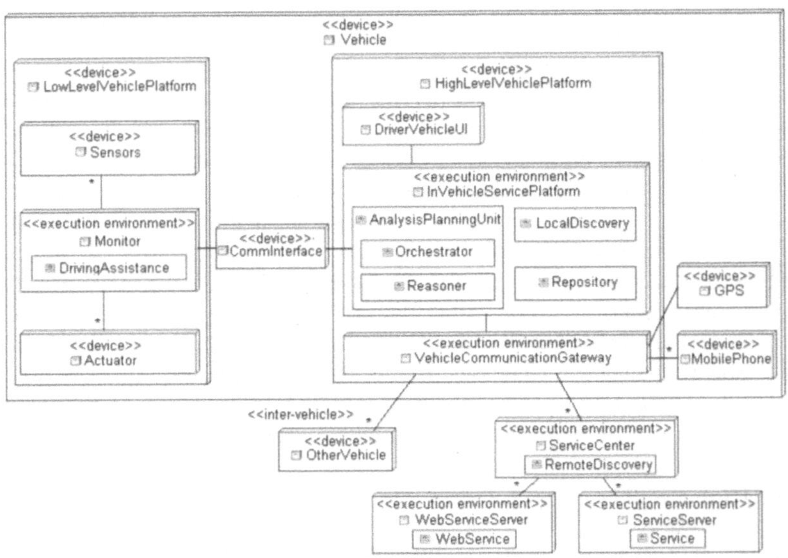

Fig. 5. UML development diagram of a vehicle service-oriented architecture

As for the *low level platform*, it contains the hardware and software elements of a vehicle in charge of critical services such as driving aids (e.g. ABS and ESP). Also, it features a number of diverse actuation software pieces reacting to vehicle's sensors to ensure a minimum answer time and meet real-time constraints. Thus, *sensors* components represent the necessary interface for vehicles to define their current state with regard their surrounding environment and neighbouring counterparts. *Actuators*, on the other hand, automatically trigger assisted driving capabilities whenever they are needed. The relationship between sensors and actuators is basically implemented through *monitors*. These components manage sensors and are constantly observing their activities. Whenever sensors accuse an event, monitors give the appropriate warning and evaluate the situation. Critical events are then reported to actuators so as they can react accordingly, while others are submitted to the *analysis and planning* unit. *Assisted driving* elements contain all functionalities to aid the low level driving tasks triggered by actuators and managed by monitors, after sensors' events have been evaluated.

Drivers and passengers alike interact with active services in the *high level platform*. They can receive information and select commands to trigger, stop or adapt services through the *driver-vehicle interface*. The *service platform* is a subcomponent accessible from the vehicle that contains a service repository and features the necessary functionalities to manage services' specificities, such as service discovery and orchestration. An *analysis and planning* unit evaluates events reported by other elements such as the monitor, the driver-vehicle interface and the communication gateway, and other current plans to define the appropriate course of actions accordingly. We intend to extend this feature with a BDI-like (belief, desire, intention) architecture, as initially proposed in [9].

The *service repository* is the place where services and other necessary applications are locally stored in the vehicle. This element can be inquired by certain services, local or remote, and asked for a specific function or action. It features functions such as service registry, discovery and update as well. *Local service discovery* allows local services to be found. In this structure, an *orchestrator* is responsible for pursuing and achieving a given goal through the invocation of one or more services combined, whereas a *selector* analyses and selects services based on certain criteria that are set in advance.

Both platforms, namely the low level and the high level as discussed so far, are features of the vehicle element and interact through the *communication interface*. Nonetheless, vehicles can also interact with external services, hosted in other remote elements. The *vehicular communication gateway* is responsible for that, sending messages to external components (e.g. other vehicles or servers), on an abstract basis firstly. Then the most appropriate communication technique is selected (e.g. GSM, GPRS or VANET) and the message is effectively sent. Mobile phones and PDA, for instance, are used to build long range communication connections, and can be embedded in vehicles or borne by drivers and/or passengers that normally use them in other environments. A global positioning system (GPS) receiver, on the other hand, keeps track of the vehicle's position.

Apart from vehicles, services can be executed in other environments, which is a more classical perspective. The beauty behind vehicular *ad-hoc* networks is their great potential to provide transport systems with a great number of diverse services as people move. The *services centre* is a remote execution platform that offers services discovery and other applications that support active services' requests in a more traditional way, but now including requests from VANET. It also features a *remote discovery* function that finds appropriate services throughout the network, which can be present in diverse environments such as web servers (e.g. web services on the Internet) or traditional service providers implementing private client-server environments.

4 Experimental Set-Up and Results

The experimental framework carried out was based on a simple network. Despite its simplicity, results showed promising potentials of the proposed approach. The network was coded in the XML format supported in the simulation engine of MAS-T^{2}er Lab, as defined in [10, 11, 12], which was extended to support the current prototypical implementation. Readers are referred to [7] for more details.

4.1 Scenarios Definition

Three different traffic flow configurations were set up, which allowed us to test the system behaviour under different flow regimes. The effects of these flow regimes on the V2V communication performance were analysed then.

A low traffic flow regime was implemented in the *first scenario*, in which source nodes were set to yield 100 to 250 vehicle/hour traffic flows, representing a free-flow regime. The *second scenario* is intended to represent an average traffic flow regime. In this case, source nodes were set to yield 250 to 850 vehicle/hour traffic flows, allowing us to analysis V2V performance under average conditions. Finally, in the *third scenario* source nodes were set to yield 850 to 1300 vehicles/hour traffic flows, representing traffic under saturation conditions. Such a scenario is quite common in must urban areas, during peak hours, for instance, or during the occurrence of some incidents strangulating road capacity, such as accidents.

Each simulation run was set to last for 10 minutes' time, corresponding to 30 minutes in real time. To test the communication interaction between vehicles, a car approaching an intersection sends a message (this is done with a 2 minutes' frequency). Intersections are selected sequentially, following a clockwise order. Allowing cars to send messages at intersections is required as an attempt at maximizing the neighbouring cars within the range of the sender's wireless range. Indeed, as intersections are spots of converging traffic streams, then it is very likely the number of cars at intersections, especially in the second and third scenarios, will be considerable.

4.2 Preliminary Results

Preliminary results are plotted in the graph of Figure 6. The graph shows how much of the network is covered by the V2V communication mechanism over time. The results are very interesting and demonstrate the ability of the implemented prototype to cope with both communication and vehicular traffic simulation. As we expected, the results of different scenario set-ups suggest different behaviours for the system under varying traffic conditions.

In the low traffic flow scenario, message dissemination through the V2V infrastructure é quite poor, basically due to the discontinued coverage of the network. Only a small part of the network, *circa* 27%, can be affected by the message propagation. In such circumstances, it is possible that even none of the vehicles will receive the message sent.

Scenarios in which traffic flow follows an average flow regime, such as in the second experimental set-up above, a larger part of the network can be easily covered. In our case, about two thirds of the network was covered in the most appropriate circumstances, meaning the increasing number of cars propitiated a better coverage and improved communication.

Only in the third scenario it was possible to achieve a full coverage of the network, which is quite expectable too. Indeed, in nearly saturated traffic conditions, network links tend to work in their full capacity, meaning the density is very high and vehicle headways tend to the average vehicle unit. In these circumstances, it is most probable that neighbouring vehicles will be within the range of other vehicles' wireless sensors, improving the connectivity of the network.

In all simulation scenarios, nonetheless, coverage increases as time evolves, which can be associated to the small network used and to the semaphore control at all junctions. Indeed, controlled intersections tend to group vehicles together at red lights, especially if traffic flow is higher than the saturation flows of each phase of the control plan. In such a situation, intersections will never be empty improving the connectivity of the V2V communication network.

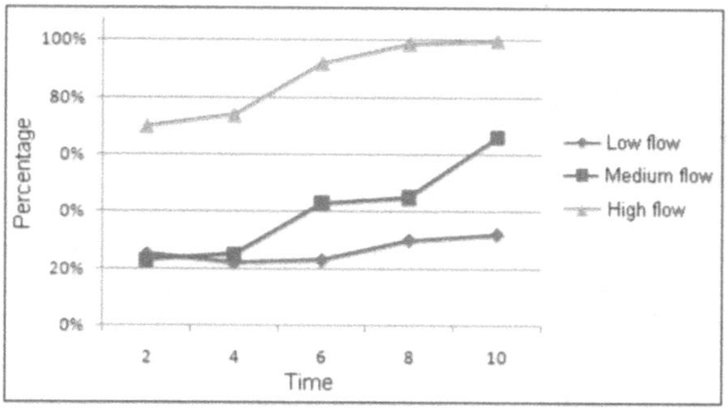

Fig. 6. Comparison of the three different scenarios, relating simulation time and the percentage of network covered by the V2V communication

The three different scenario set-ups were inspired in a typical daily flow profile of a urban network, in which the first scenario might represent a free flow regime, at high night and dawn, the second scenario might represent average situation of off-peak hours during the day, and the third one the morning and afternoon peak hours. Nonetheless, the first scenario might also be associated to rural areas, whereas the third scenarios might well be representative of a bottleneck caused by an incident, such as accident, for instance.

In either case, results corroborate the idea that V2V communication presents a great potential and is a promising technology of future urban transport, whereas implementing SOA beneath such communication infrastructure can contribute a great deal for a better transport service and quality of life in urban areas.

5 Conclusions

In this work, a V2V architecture based on the concept of services was specified. A layered architecture based on different levels of abstractions of services providing SOA in V2V networks was devised in terms of a multi-agent system, as well as was a prototype implemented for testing and evaluating the approach proposed. For the first level of our architecture, we have implemented a SOA-based feature that allows services discovering within the routing protocol of VANET networks. This resulted in the specification of a dynamic and adaptable routing structure compliant with the abstract nature inherent in any SOA-based applications. For the second level, on the other hand, we presented a modular and easily extensible architecture that allows services to be made available in vehicles, based on the concept of multi-agent systems. We have specified the vehicular architecture that underlies the implementation of on-board services, as well as the adequate means to request services from exogenous sources and other vehicles too. In general terms, the developed prototype and experimental results demonstrated the feasibility of the proposed approach. The simulation environment resulted from the improvements implemented is an important asset for testing and experimenting new generation intelligent transportation systems, which will strongly rely on V2V communication capabilities. Further developments will also include implementation of more complex scenarios and adequate tools to support the assessment of a whole urban network.

References

1. McGovern, J., Tyagi, S., Stevens, M., Mathew, S.: Java Web Services Architecture. Morgan Kaufmann, San Francisco (2003)
2. Mello, H., Endler, M.: Identificação de Região de Congestionamento através de Comunicação Inter-veicular. Monografias em Ciência da Computação 26 (2006)
3. Chen, Z.D., Kung, H., Vlah, D.: Ad hoc relay wireless networks over moving vehicles on highways. In: 2nd ACM International Symposium on Mobile Ad Hoc Networking and Computing, pp. 247–250 (2001)
4. Blum, J.J., Eskandarian, A., Hoffman, L.J.: Challenges of inter-vehicle ad hoc network. IEEE Transactions on Intelligent Transportation Systems, 347–351 (2004)
5. Choffnes, D.R., Bustamante, F.E.: An Integrated Mobility and Traffic Model for Vehicular Wireless Networks. In: 2nd ACM International Workshop on Vehicular Ad Hoc Networks (VANET), pp. 65–78 (2005)
6. Saha, A., Johnson, D.: Modelling Mobility for Vehicular Ad-hoc Networks. In: ACM International Workshop on Vehicular Ad Hoc Networks (VANET), pp. 91–92 (2004)
7. Gonçalves, J.: Arquitectura baseada em serviços para redes veículo-a-veículo. Master's Dissertation. FEUP, Porto (2009)
8. Halonen, T., Ojaja, T.: Cross-Layer Design for Providing Service Oriented Architecture in a Mobile Ad hoc Network. In: 5th international Conference on Mobile and ubiquitous multimedia, paper 11 (2006)
9. Rao, A.: AgentSpeak(L): BDI agents speak out in a logical computable language. In: Perram, J., Van de Velde, W. (eds.) MAAMAW 1996. LNCS (LNAI), vol. 1038, Springer, Heidelberg (1996)
10. Rossetti, R.J.F., Oliveira, E.C., Bazzan, A.L.C.: Towards a specification of a framework for sustainable transportation analysis. In: 13th Portuguese Conference on Artificial Intelligence, Guimarães, Portugal (2007)
11. Ferreira, P.A.F., Esteves, F.E., Rossetti, R.J.F., Oliveira, E.C.: A Cooperative Simulation Framework for Traffic and Transportation Engineering. In: 5th International Conference on Cooperative Design, Visualization, and Engineering, pp. 89–97 (2008)
12. Ferreira, P.A.F.: Specification and Implementation of an Artificial Transport System. Master's Dissertation. FEUP, Porto (2008)

Applying Event Stream Processing on Traffic Problem Detection

Oliver Pawlowski[1], Jürgen Dunkel[1], Ralf Bruns[1], and Sascha Ossowski[2]

[1] Hannover University of Applied Sciences and Arts, Computer Science Department,
Ricklinger Stadtweg 120, 30459 Hannover, Germany
[2] CETINA, University of Rey Juan Carlos,
Calle Tulipán s/n, 28933 Mostoles (Madrid), Spain
{juergen.dunkel,oliver.pawlowski,ralf.bruns}@fh-hannover.de,
sascha.ossowski@urjc.es

Abstract. Sensor-based traffic management systems have to cope with a high volume of continuously generated events. Conventional software architectures do not explicitly target the efficient processing of continuous event streams. Recently, Event-Driven Architectures (EDA) have been proposed as a new paradigm for event-based applications. In this paper we propose a reference architecture for event-driven traffic management systems, which enables the analysis and processing of complex event streams in real-time. In particular we are going to outline the different stages of traffic event processing and present an approach based on event patterns to diagnose traffic problems. The usefulness of our approach has been proven in a real world traffic management scenario.

Keywords: Event Stream Processing (ESP), Event-Driven Architecture (EDA), Complex Event Processing (CEP).

1 Introduction

Current traffic control systems are mostly sensor-based: loop-detectors installed in the roads emit data in form of events when cars pass by and thus making traffic data available in real-time [1]. The sensors provide a very high volume of events that must be processed for analyzing the current traffic situation and for triggering appropriate control actions. There are several key issues sensor-based traffic management systems have to cope with:

- *Fine-grained and uncorrelated sensor data*: Traffic control systems are not interested in a single sensor event, but in correlated events to build temporal and spatial granules [2]. For instance, data of all the sensors located in one road segment must be correlated to evaluate average traffic density and occupancy. In a subsequent processing step, the calculated traffic data must be interpreted to diagnose emerging traffic problems, like jams or accidents.
- *Continuous event streams*: Sensor-based systems have to deal with continuously arriving data, i.e. infinite data streams [3]. Therefore, data must be continuously processed, and data analysis cannot be applied in retrospect.

L. Seabra Lopes et al. (Eds.): EPIA 2009, LNAI 5816, pp. 27–38, 2009.

- *Short latency*: A key issue in traffic management is short latency. Despite of its high volume, sensor data must be processed in short latency. The gap between the time the sensor data is emitted and the time the analysis results are available should be as short as possible in order to react immediately on traffic jams or accidents. Appropriate systems must provide real-time decision support [4] or "zero latency" responsiveness as proposed by Gartner Group [5].

Current software architectures do not target on sensor-based systems, i.e. they cannot deal with the efficient processing of continuous event streams. Instead, they are based on a process-oriented control flow, which is not appropriate for event-driven systems. Due to the high volume of events and their complex dependencies it is not possible to specify a predefined process flow. Other approaches, such as mainstream, AI-based multi-agent architectures ([6], [7], [8], [9]) focus on knowledge processing, but do not explicitly target the problems associated to real-time high-volume event processing. Furthermore, they lack inherent concepts for describing temporal dependencies between events, which are crucial to react appropriately on specific situations [10].

In recent years, Event-Driven Architecture (EDA) has gained significant attention and is emerging as a new architectural paradigm for event-based applications [11]. The main idea lies in the processing of events as the central architectural concept. The key concept is to use Complex Event Processing (CEP) as the general process model. Event streams generated by sensors contain a large volume of different events, which must be transformed, classified, aggregated, and evaluated to initiate suitable actions.

In this paper, we propose a reference architecture for event-driven traffic control systems, which enables the analysis and processing of complex event streams in real-time. In particular, our architecture shows the different stages of traffic event processing. Furthermore, we introduce a general approach for deriving and classifying event patterns suitable for diagnosing traffic problems. We have successfully applied our approach to model to a real-world traffic management scenario similar to [21].

The remainder of the paper is organized as follows. In the next section, we briefly introduce the key concepts of event stream processing. In section 3 we show an event-driven architecture for sensor-based traffic management systems. In this section, we present a general event hierarchy for traffic management and explain the different building blocks of event stream processing. Additionally, event pattern and rules appropriate for traffic diagnosis are classified and discussed. Section 4 shows the usefulness of the approach presenting a real world scenario as well as some simulation experiments. Finally, we summarize the most significant features of our approach and provide a brief outlook on future lines of research.

2 Event-Driven Architecture – Overview

Event-Driven Architecture provides an architectural concept for dealing with event streams using Complex Event Processing as the event processing model [11]. Because sensor-based traffic management systems emit continuously a high volume of data they can be considered as event-driven systems. Consequently, they are particularly suited for CEP. Figure 1 illustrates the main CEP concepts:

- *Events*: Each event emitted by a sensor contains general metadata (event ID, timestamp) and event specific information, e.g. sensor ID and certain traffic data.

- *Event Patterns*: The main task of CEP is *Event Pattern Matching*, i.e. to identify in a huge event cloud those patterns of events that are significant for the application domain. In traffic management millions of sensor-emitted events must be analyzed to discover event patterns signifying upcoming traffic problems. In particular, event patterns must take temporal dependencies between events into account.

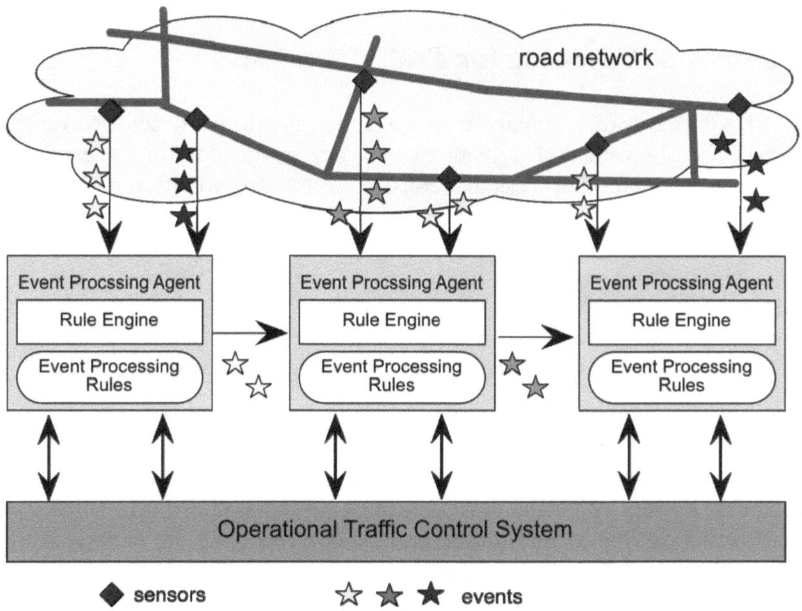

Fig. 1. Complex Event Processing components in traffic management system

- *Event Processing Rules* consist of two different parts: event patterns specify a certain situation of events; and event actions are executed when the event pattern is fulfilled. Essentially, event processing rules are used to filter, split, aggregate, transform, and enrich events [8]. In particular, new events can be generated within the event action part. Essentially, the event processing rules should transform simple sensor events into more abstract and sophisticated domain events for evaluating the actual traffic situation and initiating appropriate traffic control actions.
- *Event Processing Languages (EPL)*: The rules are expressed by event processing languages (EPLs) based on event algebras [14] and processed by a corresponding rule engine. Basically, two different kinds of EPLs can be distinguished: ECA rules (event condition actions) [12], [13] or SQL-like continuous queries over event streams [14]. Therefore, the pattern matching is characterized by *continuous queries* that are issued once and then run continuously over the data stream.
- *Sliding Windows*: Due to the continuously arriving data, the event processing has to cope with the infinite number of data. For that reason, *sliding windows* are used, where only the set of the least recently occurred events is considered. Therefore, each event has a certain lease time and is deleted when it has expired. An appropriate rule language should allow the specification of sliding windows.

- *Event Processing Agents*: Pattern matching and event processing can be distributed among the so-called event processing agents (EPAs), which are connected to an *event processing network* (EPN) [15]. The events processing agents can access the operational traffic control system to enrich the sensor events. For instance, they use knowledge about the road structure and sensor locations for deriving appropriate event rules.

3 Event Stream Processing for Traffic Analysis

Basically, EDA-based traffic management systems transform raw sensor events into more abstract and sophisticated domain events. For traffic control systems, Fig. 2 illustrates the transformation process that consists of mainly two different steps:

Fig. 2. Event stream transformation in traffic control systems

A stream of continuously arriving *Raw Sensor Events* emitted by the loop detectors must be transformed into a *Traffic Event* stream. The *Traffic Events* contain traffic indices as traffic density or occupancy characterizing the actual traffic situation in a certain road section during a certain time period. *Traffic Events* are generated by aggregating *Raw Sensor Events*. Subsequently, the stream of *Traffic Events* must be analyzed to identify upcoming traffic problems. This is achieved by applying event patterns on the *Traffic Event* stream that diagnose traffic problems. If a problem detection pattern matches a corresponding *Problem Event* is created specifying a certain problem like traffic jams or accidents. When a problem is identified, an action-planning step is needed, which yields a sequence of appropriate actions. Traffic rerouting to bypass a blocked road is an example of a possible action. In the following section we will derive a more-detailed event model for traffic management systems.

3.1 Event Hierarchies

Obviously, events are the key concept of EDA. Therefore, they should be defined precisely by a formal event model, which provides a complete understanding of the different event types, its properties, constraints, and dependencies. A semantically rich event model is the indispensable basis to derive the software architecture of an EDA-based system [16].

All events can be structured in a layered hierarchy: fine-grained events processed by the sensors are aggregated and correlated to more meaningful events (here: *Traffic Events* or *Problem Events*). Furthermore, the hierarchy of events reflects the sequence of event processing steps. For traffic control systems, Fig. 3 shows the relevant event types, which split the types of Fig. 2 into appropriate sub types.

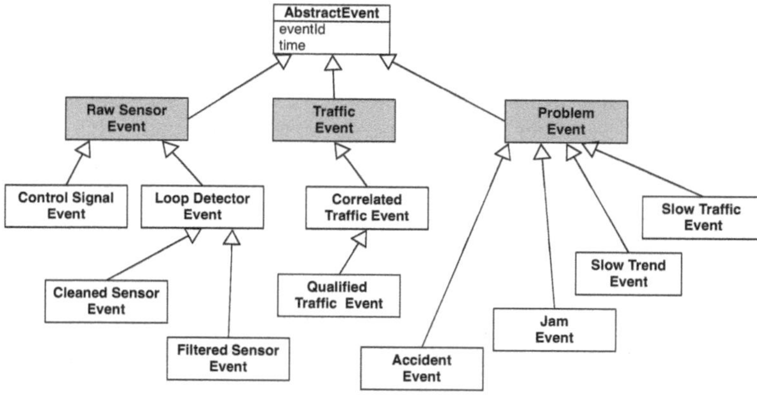

Fig. 3. Fine-grained event hierarchy in traffic control systems

Abstract Event is an abstract event class that contains meta data, which is common to all events types, i.e. the occurrence time and an event Id. All event types inherit from this class to make use of these properties.

Raw Sensor Events are the events directly produced and emitted by the different sensors incorporated in the road network. These events contain the raw and unmodified sensor data. We can distinguish the following subtypes:

- *Loop Detector Event* is the general class of sensor events emitted when cars pass a loop detector. Depending on the sensor type the events contain different traffic data, as the number of passed cars or velocity. *Loop Detector Events* contain data related to a single car or aggregated data of a certain period of time.
- *Cleaned Sensor Events:* Due to technical problems sensor data is often inconsistent. Missed or duplicated readings, as well as unreliable readings causing outliers must be treated to overcome these inconsistencies [17] [18]. *Cleaned Sensor Events* fulfill all the constraints defined for the sensor data. Event constraints can be specified by constraint languages, for instance OCL [19]. The following OCL invariant defines that two *Loop Detector Events* emitted from the same sensor with a difference in their occurrence time smaller than 0.01 are identical.

```
context Loop Detector Event inv:
    forAllInstances(e1, e2 |
        (e1.time - e2.time) < 0.01 AND
        e1.sensorID == e2.sensorID
        implies e1 == e2)
```

  Note that *Cleaned Sensor Events* do not add any new information to the original events.
- *Filtered Events:* To accelerate event processing the high volume of sensor events should be reduced as early as possible. Therefore, all irrelevant events must be filtered out. For instance, some sensors emit events periodically, even

if no cars have passed. Thus, the stream of *Filtered Events* can be considered as the stream of *Cleaned Sensor Events* reduced by all unnecessary events.
- *Control Signal Events* are all the further sensor events available in the road network, which are not related to car data. Examples are events emitted by traffic lights, weather stations, emergency telephone calls, etc.

Traffic Events: A single sensor event is not sufficient for deriving a meaningful state of the actual traffic situation. In general, sensor data is uncorrelated and too fine-grained, and therefore must be aggregated and correlated.

- *Correlated Traffic Events:* Traffic management systems are not interested in individual readings in time or individual devices in space, but rather in correlating events on base of temporal and spatial observations [13]. For instance, a *temporal correlation* aggregates the data at a certain sensor over a period of time for calculating average traffic measures, like average velocities or average densities. *Spatial correlations* combine the data of several sensors at a certain time instant; for instance to calculate the traffic behavior in a certain road segment, where numerous sensors are located.
- *Qualified Traffic Events*: Traffic engineers use symbolic rather than numerical values in their knowledge representation of problem detection patterns; e.g. low speed, high density. Numerical measures, e.g. an average velocity of 50 km/h, have no significance if not related to the characteristics of the road network (here the allowed speed limit). *Qualified Traffic Events* map numerical values to meaningful qualitative statements by enriching the sensor data with structural road network information.

Problem Events: In a problem identification step the *Qualified Traffic Events* are analyzed and in case of an undesirable situation a *Problem Event* is created and emitted. Identified accidents and traffic jams result in *Accident Events* or *Jam Events*, respectively. Furthermore, two different preliminary stages of traffic jams are considered. If the traffic has slowed down under a certain threshold a *Slow Traffic Event* is emitted; if the traffic is continuously slowing down a *Slow Trend Event* is created.

3.2 Event Processing

The hierarchy of events reflects the traffic analysis process, which can be understood as a sequence of event processing steps. The system transforms the *Raw Sensor Events* into more abstract *Traffic Events*, which are used to analyze the actual situation and to identify emerging problems described by *Problem Events*.

The event transformation steps are processed by corresponding event processing agents (EPA), which are connected to an event processing network (EPN) [15]. Each event processing agent consists of a rule engine with a set of event processing rules. The distribution of the processing rules on different agents has two advantages: each agent has a definitive task with a relative small number of rules and, as a result, yielding high cohesion. Furthermore, the agents can be distributed on different processing components achieving a scalable architecture.

The event processing network connecting the event processing agents is shown in Fig. 4. It is a refinement of the Complex Event Processing components in Fig. 1. This EPN has much in common with the processing models used in Data Fusion [20].

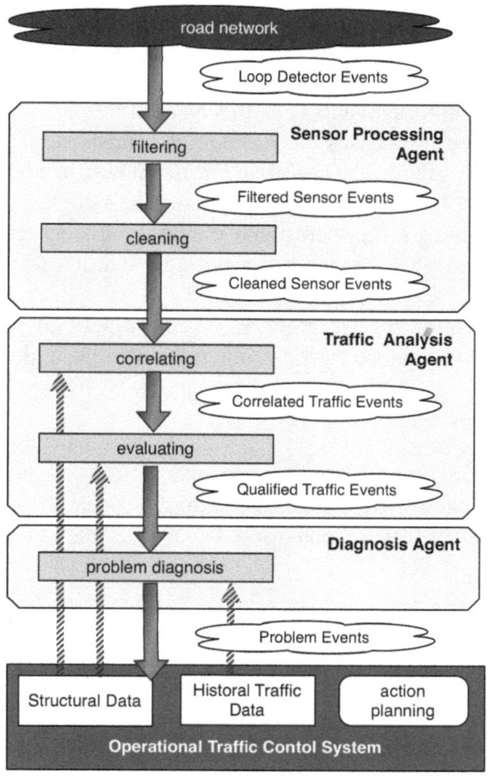

Fig. 4. Event Processing Network for traffic problem diagnosis

However, EDA and CEP focus on real-time processing of arbitrary events instead of defining generic approaches for combining incoherent sensor data.

The ***Sensor Processing Agent*** processes the *Raw Sensor Events,* especially the *Loop Detector Events* to reduce the number of events and to achieve consistency. Firstly, in a filtering step all unnecessary events, e.g. no-car events are filtered out from the event stream. Secondly, the *Filtered Sensor Events* are cleaned to cope with events that violate the constraints defined in the event model. For instance, duplicate events or outliers are corrected. The *Sensor Processing Agent* emits a stream of *Cleaned Sensor Events* that contains only problem-relevant and consistent data.

The ***Traffic Analysis Agent*** tries to extract meaningful measurements from the *Cleaned Sensor Event* stream. At first, the agent correlates the fine-grained sensor events on base of the spatial or temporal characteristics. To derive *spatial correlation* rules structural information of the road network is required, e.g. about sensor proximity. These rules are often structurally identical, so that they can be generated on base of the road network topology. *Temporal correlations* consider the traffic behavior over a longer period of time regarding a certain sensor. In current event processing languages appropriate sliding windows can be defined and arithmetic operations for calculating average and covariance are available. Note, that such average traffic measurements characterize the normal traffic behavior and can be used to identify abnormal problematic situations.

At second, the *Traffic Analysis Agent* transforms numerical event data into meaningful qualitative statements, like FAST or SLOW velocity instead of absolute values. This step is some kind of data enrichment, because additional knowledge of the road network is integrated into the events (e.g. the speed limits).

The ***Diagnosis Agent*** processes the problem diagnosis step: it applies problem detection patterns on the stream of *Qualified Traffic Events* to identify upcoming traffic problems. When a problem detection pattern matches, a corresponding *Problem Event* will be created and send to the operational traffic control system that triggers an appropriate control action. Possible actions are road blocking, traffic rerouting, modifying speed limits, etc.

In the following section we are going to discuss a general approach on how event patterns can be used to diagnose traffic problems in the emitted event streams.

3.3 Traffic Diagnosis

Generally speaking, traffic problems are unusual yet critical situations resulting from unusual behavior in road traffic. Thus, traffic diagnosis can be understood as identifying deviations from usual traffic behavior.

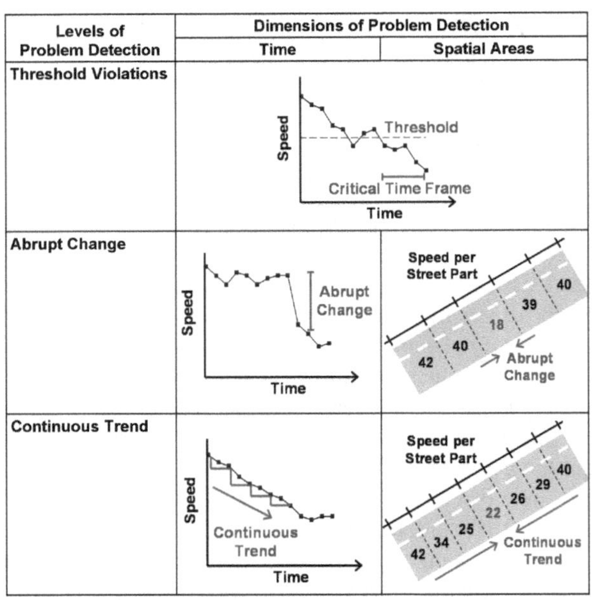

Fig. 5. Levels and Dimensions of Problem Detection

Abnormal traffic situations can be detected according to different dimensions as illustrated in Fig. 5. Basically, temporally or spatially correlated events can be distinguished: This means to analyze individual traffic events over a period of time or across street sections.

Threshold violations: The easiest case is considering just one street section at a certain point in time. A traffic problem is identified when the current traffic measure violates a threshold, e.g. the average speed falls below a specific value (see Fig.5, first row). In a pseudo language, rules for detecting these problems look as follows.

```
rule "slow traffic"
for TrafficEvent as t
if t.speed < 20 and t.streetSectionID = 4711
```

Usually, applying rules in such an atomic and instantaneous manner is not sufficient. The state that indicates "slow traffic" must last for a certain period of time or the average speed within a certain time frame must not rise above the given threshold value. Time is an inherent concept of CEP and can be expressed in event processing languages by using sliding windows. Consequently, the previous rule may be adapted as follows.

```
rule "slow traffic"
for TrafficEvent.within(30 seconds) as t
if t.speed.average() < 20 and t.streetSectionID = 4711
```

The thresholds defining normal behavior can either be defined statically with help of expert knowledge or determined dynamically by applying long-term rules on the streams of traffic events. Note, that the Traffic Analysis Agents, which continuously observe the traffic behavior, can calculate traffic measures characterizing normality.

Abrupt Changes: Apart from those simple comparisons against a threshold, traffic problems can be identified by means of abrupt changes or significant contrasts in subsequent time instants or adjacent street sections. This includes, for example, sudden drops in speed and discrepancies in recorded data between sections of the same street (see Fig. 5 second row). This rule reflects the experience that severe problems like accidents cause abrupt changes.

A rule that detects a sudden drop in speed possibly indicating an accident looks as follows in a pseudo language. Note that event sequence operators like `followed-by` allow expressing temporal relations in a very natural manner.

```
rule "sudden drop in speed"
for TrafficEvent.within(15 seconds) as t1 followed-by
     TrafficEvent.within(15 seconds) as t2
if t2.speed.average() < t1.speed.average() / 2.0 and
   t2.time - t1.time < 20 seconds and
   t2.streetSectionID == t1.streetSectionID
```

Local discrepancies between adjacent street sections can be detected with this rule.

```
rule "local discrepancy"
for TrafficEvent.within(15 seconds) as t1,
     TrafficEvent.within(15 seconds) as t2,
     TrafficEvent.within(15 seconds) as t3
if t2.speed.average() < t1.speed.average() / 2.0 and
   t2.speed.average() < t3.speed.average() / 2.0 and
   isAdjacent(t2.streetSectionID, t1.streetSectionID) and
   isAdjacent(t2.streetSectionID, t3.streetSectionID)
```

Continuous Trends: Other traffic problems as jams evolve rather slowly. Some kind of trend prediction is thus required in order to identify them. Again, this can be performed in the dimensions of both time and space. A prediction that is evolved over a period of time may continuously analyze changes of the average speed. A problem will be reported when a progressive decrease in speed is detected within a certain time frame. Spatial trends include, for example, successive decrease of speed across adjacent street sections and help identifying bottlenecks from a global point of view.

Regarding the different dimensions and levels of problem detection illustrated in Fig. 5 we can observe similarities to analysis of functions and their derivatives. While problem detection via threshold value react to discrete values of the "speed function" itself, detection of significant changes takes the slope of the speed progression (either temporally or spatially) into account. Trend analysis even involves the development of the speed progression over a longer period of time or across several spatial areas.

4 Case Study and Implementation Issues

In recent years, EDA has been used successfully applied for implementing event-based applications. Several products, both open source and commercial, supporting EDA are available. We have implemented a prototype of an EDA-based Decision Support System for traffic control [21] on the base of Esper, an open source CEP engine.

Esper provides an SQL-like event processing language that enables developers to perform continuous queries on streams of events. The Esper engine is implemented in Java and both languages integrate into each other.

As stated before, the syntax of Esper's EPL is quite similar to SQL. For instance, it makes use of `SELECT` and `WHERE` statements for event instance selection. However, while SQL processes rigid table data, EPL statements are applied permanently on continuous event streams. Additionally, the Esper EPL introduces the concept of sliding windows which provide views on a certain number of consecutive events or on those events that occurred within a specific time frame. Esper also offers a powerful pattern matching language that allows complex correlations of events. An Esper rule that detects slow traffic within a certain time frame (see the second rule in section 3.3) can be expressed as follows.

```
SELECT streetSectionID, avg(speed)
FROM TrafficEvent.win:time( 30 sec )
WHERE streetSectionID = 4711
GROUP BY streetSectionID
HAVING avg(speed) < 20;
```

This rule uses the `GROUP BY` and `HAVING` statements in order to correlate the average speed of the given street section within the past 30 seconds. If the average speed is less than 20 km/h, the respective street section ID and the actual average speed are returned. In similar way, the other rules presented in section 3.3 can be implemented in Esper.

The applicability of Esper and the usefulness of our problem detection rules have been evaluated by simulating several scenarios. It has shown up that Esper is able to cope with quite a large volume of events in real-time. Language concepts of CEP like sliding windows and event sequence operators assist developers in writing rules that refer to temporal constraints.

5 Conclusion

Sensor-based traffic control systems generate continuous streams of low-level data at a very high volume. The challenge is to utilize this ever growing data flow to analyze the current traffic situation and to release suitable control actions if necessary.

In this paper, the Event-Driven Architecture (EDA) has been presented as a novel approach for intelligent traffic management. The approach is different from other approaches in that it is based on the detection of patterns of events in the streams of sensor data leading to a deep understanding of the current traffic situation. A concrete reference architecture for event-driven traffic management systems has been proposed, which is implemented by a network of communicating (lightweight) rules engines. The different steps of event processing have been discussed by identifying the involved event types and event processing agents. Especially, we proposed a general approach for deriving event patterns for traffic problem diagnosis. Problem detection patterns may use temporal and spatial correlations to identify abnormal traffic behavior characterized by threshold violations, rapid changes or traffic trends.

By means of a case study with real-world traffic data the applicability of the approach has been investigated with the result, that event processing can significantly improve the real-time analysis and control capabilities of a traffic control system.

While the Event-Driven Architecture provides promising benefits for event-driven business processes, some severe challenges need still to be overcome before the benefits can be realized. One important obstacle in order to exploit the full power of Event-Driven Architecture is still the lack of standardization. At the moment, no generally accepted standards exist for event definition, event pattern languages, and rule engines. However, some promising efforts in the standardization process are in progress.

Next steps for future research are the investigation of design patterns and architectural guidelines for the development of event-driven systems in practice.

Acknowledgement

This work was supported in part by the European Community (Europäischer Fonds für regionale Entwicklung – EFRE) under Research Grant EFRE Nr. 2-221-2007-0042.

References

1. Cuena, J., Hernández, J., Molina, M.: Knowledge-Oriented Design of an Application for Real Time Traffic Management. In: Proc. Europ. Conf. on Artificial Intelligence (1996)
2. Dunkel, J.: On Complex Event Processing for Sensor Networks. In: IEEE 9th International Symposium on Autonomous Decentralized Systems (ISADS), Athens (Greece), March 2009, pp. 249–255 (2009)
3. Babu, S., Widom, J.: Continous queries over Streams. SIGMOD Record (2001)
4. Delic, K., Douillet, L., Dayal, U.: Towards an Architecture for Real-Time Decision Support Systems: Challenges and Solutions. In: Intern. Symposium on Database Engineering & Applications, pp. 303–311 (2001)

5. GARTNER GROUP, Introducing the Zero-Latency Enterprise. Research Note COM-04-37770, (June 1998)
6. Ossowski, S., Hernández, J., Iglesias, C., Fernández, A.: Engineering agents systems for decision support. In: Tolksdorf, P., Zambonelli (eds.) Engineering Societies in an Agent World III. LNCS (LNAI), pp. 234–274. Springer, Heidelberg (2002)
7. Bandini, S., Bogni, D., Manzoni, S.: Alarm Correlation in Traffic Monitoring and Control Systems: A Knowledge-Based Approach. ECAI 2002, 638–642 (2002)
8. Dresner, D., Stone, P.: Multiagent Traffic Management: An Improved Intersection Control Mechanism. In: Proceedings of the fourth international joint conference on Autonomous agents and multiagent systems, pp. 471–477 (2005)
9. Roozemond, D.A.: Using intelligent agents for urban traffic control systems. In: Proceedings of the International Conference on Artificial Intelligence in Transportation Systems and Science, pp. 69–79 (1999)
10. Lamport, L.: Time, clocks, and the ordering of events in a distributed system. Commun. ACM 21(7), 558–565 (1978)
11. Luckham, D.: Power of Events. Addison-Wesley, Reading (2002)
12. Zimmer, D., Unland, R.: On the semantics of complex events in active database management systems. In: ICDE, pp. 392–399 (1999)
13. Paton, N., Díaz, O.: Active Database Systems. ACM Computing Surveys 31(9), 63–103 (1999)
14. Arasu, A., Babu, S., Widom, J.: CQL A language for continuous queries over streams and relations. In: 9th Intern. Conf. on Data Base Programming Languages (DBPL), pp. 1–19 (2003)
15. Sharon, G., Etizon, O.: Event-processing network model and implementation. IBM Systems Journal 47(2), 321–334 (2008)
16. Dunkel, J., Fernández, A., Ortiz, R., Ossowski, S.: Injecting Semantics into Event-Driven Architectures. In: 11th International Conference on Enterprise Information Systems (ICEIS), Milano, Italy, May 6-10 (2009)
17. Bickel, P., Chen, C., Kwon, J., Rice, J., van Zwet, E., Varaiya, P.: Measuring Traffic. Statistical Science 22(4), 581–597 (2007)
18. Jeffrey, S., Alonso, G., Franklin, M., Hong, W., Widom, J.: A pipelined framework for online cleaning of sensor data streams. In: ICDE 2006, pp. 140–142 (2006)
19. Object Management Group (OMG), UML 2.0. OCL Specification (2003), `http://www.omg.org/docs/ptc/03-10-14.pdf`
20. Veloso, M., Bento, C., Câmara Pereira, F.: Multi-Sensor Data Fusion on Intelligent Transport Systems. University of Coimbra, Working Paper (2009)
21. Dunkel, J., Fernández, A., Ortiz, R., Ossowski, S.: Event-Driven Architecture for Decision Support in Traffic Management Systems. In: Proc. of the IEEE 11th International Conference on Intelligent Transportation Systems, pp. 7–13 (2008)

Chapter 2

ALEA – Artificial Life and Evolutionary Algorithms

Instability in Spatial Evolutionary Games

Carlos Grilo[1,2] and Luís Correia[2]

[1] Dep. Eng. Informática, Escola Superior de Tecnologia e Gestão, Instituto Politécnico de Leiria Portugal
[2] LabMag, Dep. Informática, Faculdade Ciências da Universidade de Lisboa, Portugal
grilo@estg.ipleiria.pt, luis.correia@di.fc.ul.pt

Abstract. We investigate the aspects that influence the instability of spatial evolutionary games, namely the Prisoner's Dilemma and the Snowdrift games. In this paper instability is defined as the proportion of strategy changes in the asymptotic period of the evolutionary process. The results show that with the Prisoner's Dilemma, when the level of noise present in the decision process is very low, the instability decreases as the synchrony rate decreases. With the Snowdrift this pattern of behavior depends strongly on the interaction topology and arises only for random and scale-free networks. However, for large noise values, the instability in both games depends only on the proportion of cooperators present in the population: it increases as the proportion of cooperators approaches 0.5. We advance an explanation for this behavior.

1 Introduction

Spatial evolutionary games are used as models to study, for example, how cooperation could ever emerge in nature and human societies [14]. They are also used as models to study how cooperation can be promoted and sustained in artificial societies [12]. In these models, a structured population of agents interacts during several time steps through a given *game* which is used as a metaphor for the type of interaction that is being studied. The population is structured in the sense that each agent can only interact with its neighbors. The underlying structure that defines who interacts with whom is called the *interaction topology*. After each interaction session, some or all the agents, depending on the *update dynamics* used, have the possibility of changing their strategies. This is done using a so called *transition rule* that models the fact that agents tend to adapt their behavior to the context in which they live by imitating the most successful agents they know. It can also be interpreted as the selection step of an evolutionary process in which the least successful strategies tend to be replaced by the most successful ones.

Spatial evolutionary games were created by Martin Nowak and Robert May in a seminal work in 1992 [11]. They showed that cooperation can be maintained when the Prisoner's Dilemma game is played on a regular 2-dimensional grid. This is not possible in well-mixed populations, in which each agent can play the game with any other player in the population. Since then, a large number of

L. Seabra Lopes et al. (Eds.): EPIA 2009, LNAI 5816, pp. 41–52, 2009.

works have been published about how different input conditions influence both the level of cooperation and the evolutionary dynamics. For example, in [13] and [7] the influence of the interaction topology is examined. Also, in [16] the influence of the interaction topology, the transition rule and the update dynamics in the Hawk-Dove or Snowdrift game are studied. The influence of the update dynamics is addressed, for example, in [8] and [9]. We also studied the influence of the update dynamics and found that, in general an asynchronous dynamics supports more cooperators than a synchronous one [3, 4, 5, 6].

In this paper we address the problem of how different conditions influence the instability of the system. That is, once the system enters an asymptotic phase, where the proportion of cooperators in the population stabilizes, we are interested in knowing how much agents change their strategies, from cooperation to defection and vice-versa and what are the factors that influence this phenomenon. The proportion of surviving cooperators is undoubtedly a relevant measure of interest and this is why it has captured almost all the attention in previous works. However, the proportion of cooperators in an asymptotic phase rarely is a constant value: it varies within an interval. Even if nearly constant, it may be the result of agents changing strategies from cooperator to defector an the other way around. Instability is an important measure because a volatile society, where agents often change their strategies, turns it difficult to identify defecting agents and, therefore, to undertake measures for the promotion of cooperation. It can also be interpreted as a measure of the level of dissatisfaction in the population since unsatisfied agents tend to change their way of acting. As far as we know, until now instability was only studied by Abramson and Kuperman [1]. They studied the Prisoner's Dilemma game played on small-world networks under the best-neighbor transition rule (see Section 2). They found that instability grows as the interaction topology approaches a random network.

We apply the study of instability to the Prisoner's Dilemma and the Snowdrift games, which are the two most used games in this area. There are at least two good reasons to use more than one game in this type of investigation. The first one is that both the similarities and the differences in the results achieved with different games can lead us to a better understanding of the problem. The second reason follows from the difficulty that field researchers frequently experience in the evaluation of the relative value of the payoffs involved in concrete real situations [7]. Different payoff relations may define different games and that reinforces the need to experiment with several games. Frequently in this area, conclusions are driven based only on a limited number of tested conditions. Here, we use a broad number of conditions so that a better identification of how each aspect influences the behavior of the model is achieved. Namely, different interaction topologies, noise levels and synchrony rates are used.

The paper is structured as follows: in Section 2 we describe the model used in our experiments and the experimental setup. In Section 3 we present and discuss the results and, finally, in Section 4 some conclusions are drawn and future work is advanced.

2 The Model

2.1 The Games

The Prisoner's Dilemma (PD) and the Snowdrift (SD) are two-player games in which players can only cooperate (C) or defect (D). The payoffs are the following: R to each player if they both play C; P to each if they both play D; T and S if one plays D and the other C, respectively. These games differ in the relations existing between the payoff values: while in the PD game these values must obey $T > R > P > S$, in the SD game they must obey $T > R > S > P$. Given these conditions, it follows that, in the PD game, D is the best action to take regardless of the opponent's decision. In the SD the best action depends on the opponent's decision: the best thing to do is to take the opposite action the opponent takes. For practical reasons, it is common to rescale the payoffs such that the games can be described by one parameter only [13]. The PD's payoffs are defined as $R = 1, T = b > 1$ and $S = P = 0$, where b represents the advantage of D players over C ones when they play the game with each other. It was shown that with this payoffs the game keeps its essential properties [11]. In the SD game, payoffs are defined as $T = \beta \geq 1$, $R = \beta - 1/2$, $S = \beta - 1$ and $P = 0$ which leads to a cost-to-benefit ratio of mutual cooperation $r = 1/(2\beta - 1), 0 \leq r \leq 1$.

2.2 Interaction Topology

We used two types of interaction topologies: *small-world networks* (SWNs) [17] and *scale-free networks* (SFNs) [2]. In order to build SWNs, first a toroidal regular 2D grid is built so that each node is linked to its 8 surrounding neighbors by undirected links; then, with probability ϕ, each link is replaced by another one linking two randomly selected nodes. We do not allow self or repeated links nor disconnected graphs. Networks built this way have the property that, even for very small ϕ values, the average path length is much smaller than in a regular network, maintaining a high clustering coefficient. Both these properties are very commonly observed in real social systems. As $\phi \to 1$, we get random networks with both small average path lengths and clustering coefficients.

SFNs have a power law degree distribution $P(k) \sim k^{-\gamma}$ that is also very common in real social networks[1]. SFNs are built in the following way: the network is initialized with m fully connected nodes. Then, nodes are added, one at a time, until the network has the desired size. Each added node is linked to m already existing nodes so that the probability of creating a link with some existing node i is equal to $\frac{k_i}{\sum_j k_j}$, where k_i is the degree of i, that is, the number of nodes to which it is connected. After t time steps, the network has $m + t$ nodes and mt links (plus the links connecting the initial set of nodes). The resulting γ exponent is approximately 2.9 and is independent of m in large networks. This method of link creation is called *preferential attachment*, since the more links a node has, the greater is the probability of creating links to it. This has the effect that a

[1] $P(k)$ is the probability of a node with k neighbors.

small proportion of nodes has a big connectivity while a large majority has a very low connectivity.

2.3 Interaction and Strategy Update Dynamics

On each time step, agents first play a one round PD or SD game with all their neighbors. Agents are pure strategists which can only play C or D. After this interaction stage, each agent updates its strategy with probability α using a *transition rule* (see next section) that takes into account the payoff of the agent's neighbors. The update is done synchronously by all the agents selected to engage in this revision process. The α parameter is called the *synchrony rate* and is the same for all agents. When $\alpha = 1$ we have a synchronous model, where all the agents update at the same time. As $\alpha \rightarrow \frac{1}{n}$, where n is the population size, the model approaches sequential dynamics, where exactly one agent updates its strategy at each time step.

2.4 The Strategy Update Process

The strategy update process is done using a transition rule that models the fact that agents tend to imitate the most successful agents they know. In this work, we used the generalized *proportional* transition rule (GP) proposed in [10]. Let G_x be the average payoff earned by agent x, N_x be the set of neighbors of x and c_x be equal to 1 if x's strategy is C and 0 otherwise. According to this rule, the probability that an agent x adopts C as its next strategy is

$$p_C(x, K) = \frac{\sum_{i \in N_x \cup x} c_i (G_i)^{1/K}}{\sum_{i \in N_x \cup x} (G_i)^{1/K}}, \qquad (1)$$

where $K \in]0, +\infty[$ can be viewed as the noise present in the strategy update process. Noise is present in this process if there is some possibility that an agent imitates strategies other than the one used by its most successful neighbor. Small noise values favor the choice of the most successful neighbors' strategies. Also, as noise diminishes, the probability of imitating an agent with a lower payoff becomes smaller. When $K \rightarrow 0$ we have a deterministic best-neighbor rule such that i always adopts the best neighbor's strategy. When $K = 1$ we have a simple proportional update rule. Finally, for $K \rightarrow +\infty$ we have random drift where payoffs play no role in the decision process. Our analysis considers the interval $K \in]0, 1]$.

2.5 Experiments Setup and Instability Measure

All the experiments were performed with populations of $50 \times 50 = 2500$ agents, randomly initialized with 50% of cooperators (Cs) and 50% of defectors (Ds). When the system is running synchronously, i.e., when $\alpha = 1$, we let it first run during a transient period of 900 iterations. After this, we let the system run for 100 more iterations during which the proportion of cooperators varies around a value that depends on the input conditions. During this asymptotic period, we measure the instability of the system as described in the next paragraph. When $\alpha \neq 1$ the number of selected agents at each time step may not be equal to the size of the population and it may vary between two consecutive time steps. In order to guarantee that these runs are equivalent to the synchronous ones in what concerns the total number of individual updates, we let the system first run until 900×2500 individual updates have been done. After this, we let the system run during more 100×2500 individual updates. Each experiment is a combination of b or r (for the PD and the SD, respectively), ϕ or m (for SWNs and SFNs, respectively), α, and K parameters. All the possible combinations of the values shown in Table 1 were tested. For each combination, 30 runs were made and the average instability values of these runs is taken as the output, as well as the standard-deviation. For each run, a different random number seed is used, including the generation of the interaction topology.

Table 1. Parameter values used in the experiments

Parameter	**Values**
b (PD)	1, 1.1, 1.2, 1.3, 1.4, 1.5, 1.6, 1.7, 1.8, 1.9, 2
r (SD)	0, 0.1, 0.2, 0.3, 0.4, 0.5, 0.6, 0.7, 0.8, 0.9, 1
ϕ (SWNs)	0 (regular), 1 (random), SW: 0.01, 0.05, 0.1
m (SFNs)	2, 4, 8
α	0.1, 0.2, 0.3, 0.4, 0.5, 0.6, 0.7, 0.8, 0.9, 1
K	0, 1/100, 1/10, 1/8, 1/6, 1/4, 1/2, 1

In this paper we consider the instability of the system as a measure of how much agents change their strategies in the asymptotic period. The instability of the system is, therefore, measured as follows:

$$\text{Instability} = \frac{\text{Number of strategy changes in the asymptotic period}}{\text{Number of individual updates in the asymptotic period}}, \tag{2}$$

where a strategy change means that an agent changed its strategy from C to D or vice-versa. Instability could be interpreted, instead, as the level of variation of the proportion of cooperators present in the population. We have also considered this in the experimental work by measuring the average standard-deviation of the proportion of cooperators. All the values are, however, very small, never exceeding 0.05 and rarely exceeding 0.01, which means that the level of cooperation is very stable in the asymptotic period.

3 Results

The first observation that can be made from the results is that the noise level, K, has not a direct consistent influence on the instability of the model. By this we mean that, other parameters being constant, we do not observe a direct

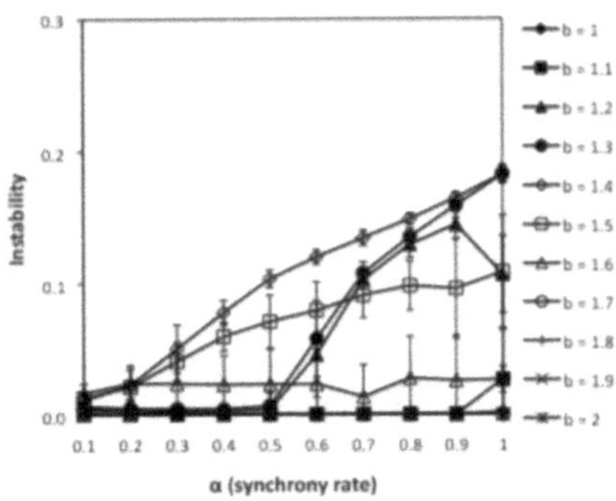

(a)

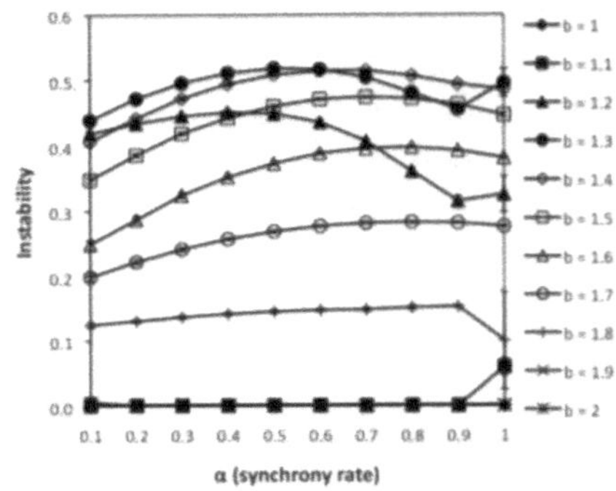

(b)

Fig. 1. Instability as a function of α when the PD (a) and the SD (b) are played without noise ($K = 0$) on SWNs ($\phi = 0.1$)

dependency of instability on the noise level. However, there is a kind of second order type of influence. We observe that in the PD game, when the noise level is very small ($K = 0$ and $K = \frac{1}{100}$), the instability decreases as the synchrony rate (α) decreases. Saying it another way, the model becomes more stable, or less dynamic, as α decreases. Fig. 1(a) shows an example of this for the PD game. This pattern is common to all the interaction topologies we experimented with.

In the SD game, this pattern is, however, strongly dependent on the interaction topology: on SFNs, instability slightly increases as α is changed from 1.0 to 0.8. Then, from $\alpha = 0.8$ to $\alpha = 0.1$ it decreases, as in the PD game. On networks generated with the SWNs model, instability decreases with α only when $\phi = 1$ (random networks). As ϕ is decreased it becomes more difficult to identify a pattern of influence of the synchrony rate. Fig. 1b) shows an example for $\phi = 0.1$, where one can see that for some r values the instability decreases with α and that it increases for others.

The results described above apply only to small noise values. For larger noise values the synchrony rate plays no role on the instability of the model. Instead, as the noise level is increased, it turns out that instability becomes progressively dependent on the proportion of cooperators. More specifically, with large noise values, instability grows as the proportion of Cs approaches 0.5. This pattern is common to both games and is not dependent on the interaction topology that is used. Figs. 2 and 3 shows examples of this behavior for the PD and SD games, respectively.

This result means that for noise values close to 1, the input parameters seem to play no direct influence on the instability of the model. We can talk only about an indirect influence in the sense that both b/r, ϕ/m, K and α influence the level of cooperation, which in turn determines how unstable are these games in the asymptotic period. It remains, however, to explain why, for K values near 1, the instability grows as the proportion of Cs approaches 0.5.

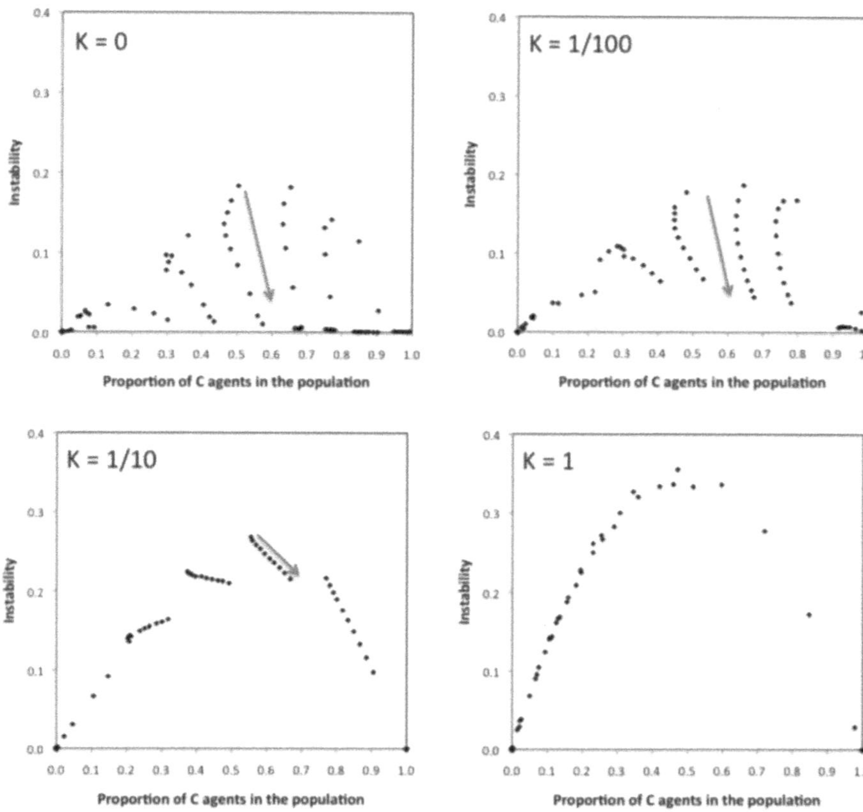

Fig. 2. Instability as a function of the proportion of cooperators in the population for different noise (K) values in the PD game played on SWNs ($\phi = 0.1$). In the charts corresponding to $K = 0, \frac{1}{100}, \frac{1}{10}$ and 1, one may observe that some points organize into line-like shapes. Each "line" corresponds to the instability values obtained for a given b value. The arrows point the direction of decreasing α. The chart for $K = 0$, corresponds to the situation of Fig. 1(a).

As a starting point, we may look for situations in which the asymptotic proportion of Cs is close to 0. In these situations, there is a large majority of D-D links, and a small number of C-C and C-D links. Given that a C agent can only change its strategy to D if it has at least one D neighbor and vice-versa, this explains why the average number of strategy changes is small in these situations. The same reasoning can be done for situations in which the proportion of C agents is very close to 1. As the proportion of Cs approaches 0.5, it is expectable that the number of C-D links per agent gets larger on average. In complete networks, where each agent is connected to all the other agents of the population,

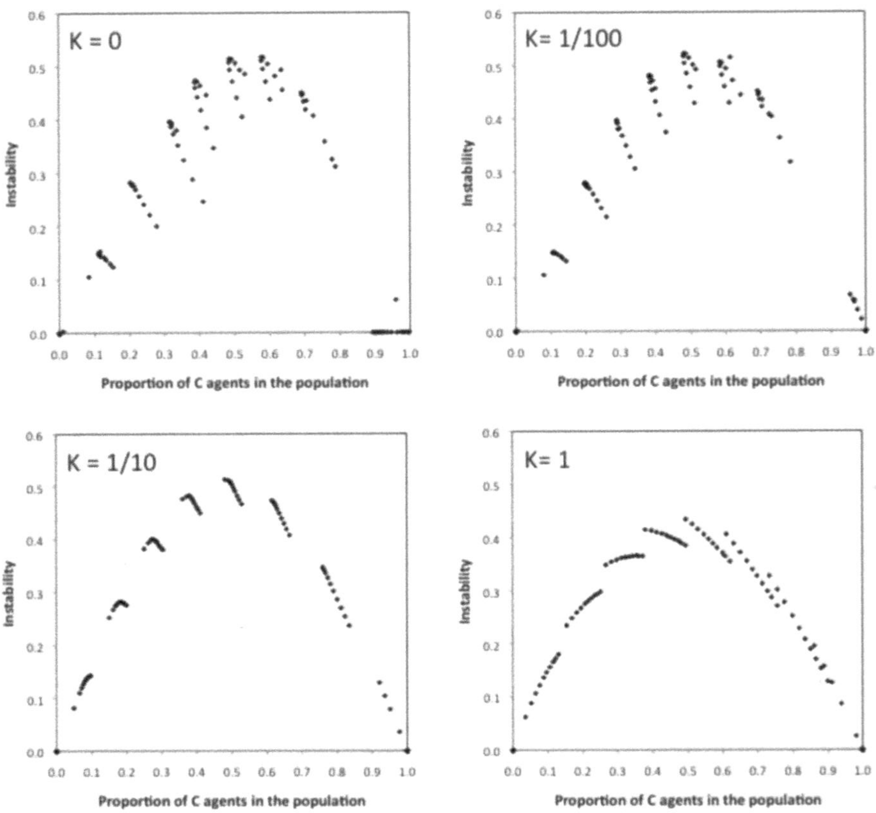

Fig. 3. Instability as a function of the proportion of cooperators in the population for different noise (K) values in the SD game played on SWNs ($\phi = 0.1$). The chart for $K = 0$, corresponds to the situation of Fig. 1(b).

it is straightforward to compute the proportion of C-D links in the population. It is equal to

$$p_{CD}(n,k) = \frac{k(n-k)}{\sum_{i=1}^{n-1} i}, \quad (3)$$

where n is the size of the population and k is the number of C agents. In structured networks the value of $p_{CD}(n,k)$ depends on the shape of the network and on how the agents are distributed over the nodes. We numerically computed the average value of $p_{CD}(n,k)$ for the networks used in this work as described next. First, an interaction topology was generated. SWNs and SFNs were used, respectively with the ϕ and m values described in Table 1. Then, for each interaction topology all the possible configurations of the population were generated (populations of 36 agents were used). For each configuration we measured the proportion of C-D links between agents and their neighbors. That is, for each possible configuration, we measured the proportion of links per agent that may

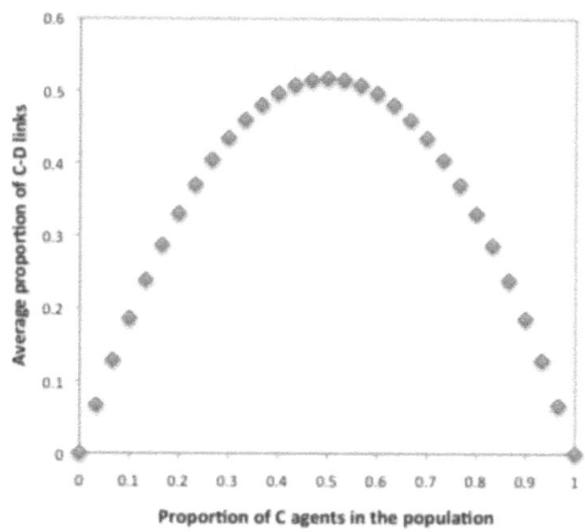

Fig. 4. Average proportion of C-D links per agent as a function of the proportion of Cs in the population over all possible configurations of 36 agents. The shape of the curve is exactly the same for complete networks.

lead to strategy changes. Notice that these were static populations. In this setting, we were only interested in knowing how the proportion of C agents in the population influences the potential for strategy changes (proportion of C-D links). The resulting chart in the Fig. 4 shows the average proportion of C-D links as a function of the proportion of Cs in the population. It shows that the average proportion of C-D links grows as the proportion of C agents approaches 0.5, exactly as for complete networks. The shape of the curve does not depend on the type of interaction topology. This curve strongly resembles the instability curves of both games when $K = 1$ (Figs. 2 and 3), specially for the PD game. This is an additional evidence that, in this regime, the instability depends mainly on the proportion of C agents in the population.

In order to understand why this pattern is absent for very small noise values and why it arises as the noise level gets larger, we must examine the GP transition rule and how K influences agents' decisions. As we have seen in Section 2.5, when $K \approx 0$, an agent always imitates the strategy of its wealthiest neighbor. In this regime there is not a direct correlation between the imitated strategy and the most common strategy in the neighborhood of an agent. For example, a C agent that has 7 C neighbors and 1 D neighbor will imitate the D one if this one has the highest payoff. However, as K approaches 1, the difference between the payoffs (powered to $\frac{1}{K}$) becomes smaller. This means that, as the noise level grows, the relative proportion of Cs and Ds in the neighborhood becomes an important factor in the decision process. For example, if there are more C agents in the neighborhood than D agents, the sum of their payoffs may exceed the sum of the D payoffs even if the C agents have smaller payoffs individually. This does not guarantees that the strategy with the larger payoff sum will be imitated since the stochastic nature of the rule allows less successful strategies to be selected when $K \neq 0$. However, as K approaches 1, the decision process will tend to reflect more and more the

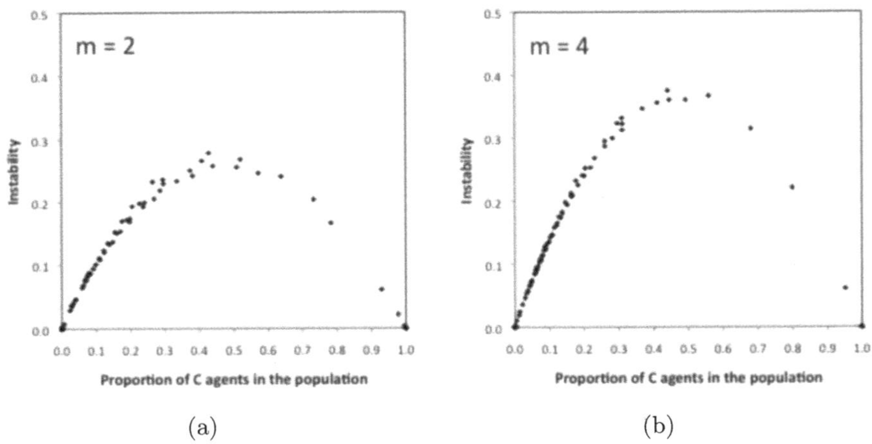

Fig. 5. Instability as a function of the proportion of cooperators in a population PD players. Conditions: a) SFNs ($m = 2$), $K = 1$; b) SFNs ($m = 4$), $K = 1$.

composition of the neighborhood. The effect it impinges on the instability is the following: when there is a clear difference in the proportion of Cs and Ds in the neighborhood, there will be a tendency to imitate the most frequent strategy. In subsequent updates, the agent will tend to keep its strategy since the most part of its neighbors has the same strategy it has. This contributes to less strategy changes and, hence, less instability in the system. On the other side, situations where there is an equilibrium between Cs and Ds in the neighborhood will lead, on average, to more uncertainty in the strategy to imitate. This leads to more strategy changes, which means more instability.

In what concerns the dependency of the instability level on the interaction topology, we found that, for SFNs, instability grows as m is increased (see example in Fig. 5). This is a natural result since the larger m the more links exist between the agents and, therefore, the greater the potential for strategy changes. For SWNs, we confirmed the results of Abramson and Kuperman [1] for the PD game: instability grows with ϕ. This effect is, however, absent in the SD game.

Finally, Figs. 2 and 3 also illustrate that instability is bigger for the SD game than for the PD game. As stated in Section 2.1, in the SD game, it is better to play C if the other player plays D and vice-versa. On the other side, playing D is always the best option in the PD game. This means that a C agent in the SD game is more resistant to the presence of D neighbors. In general, this leads to the formation of smaller and less compact clusters in the SD game than in the PD game. This, in turn, means that, on average, there are more C-D links in a population of SD players than in a population of PD players, which is a possible explanation for more instability in the SD game.

4 Conclusions and Future Work

In this work we identified the features that determine the instability of the Spatial Prisoner's Dilemma and Snowdrift games. Stability is here defined as the proportion of strategy changes that happen in the asymptotic period of the evolutionary process. As far as we know, this is one of the first works where such issue is investigated in the context of spatial evolutionary games. Besides the two games, a big number of conditions were tested: different interaction topologies, noise levels and synchrony rates were used.

The results can be summarized in the following way: As the noise level is increased, the instability becomes increasingly dependent on the composition of the population only. More specifically, instability increases as the proportion of cooperators in the population approaches 0.5. This means that in situations where there is a significant noise level, the identification of defecting agents becomes more difficult as the proportions of cooperating and defecting agents are similar. On the other side, for very small noise values, the instability decreases as the synchrony rate is decreased in the Prisoner's Dilemma game. In the Snowdrift this happens only for random networks and in scale-free networks for synchrony rates bellow $\alpha = 0.8$.

Trying to explain the effect of the synchrony rate for small noise values in both games and the behavior differences between them in this regime will be one of the main future directions of this work. In further extensions we will also explore other transition rules. The generalized proportional transition rule used in this work models a situation of complete neighborhood monitoring. This means that each agent analyses the payoffs of all its neighbors in order to decide which strategy to adopt next. As the noise level increases, the relative proportion of cooperators and defectors in the neighborhood assumes a relevant role in the decision process. This aspect is determinant in the instability level for significant noise values. Hence, it makes sense to experiment with transition rules that model just a partial neighborhood monitoring, while allowing variable noise levels. The *sigmoid* transition rule [15] is a good candidate for this test because it allows varying degrees of noise and only the payoff of one neighbor, randomly selected, is taken into account in the decision process. Finally, we will also explore n-player games such as the Public Goods game in order to verify if the results achieved so far are generalizable to these situations.

Acknowledgements

This work is partially supported by FCT/MCTES grant SFRH/BD/37650/2007.

References

[1] Abramson, G., Kuperman, M.: Social games in a social network. Physical Review E 63, 30901 (2001)
[2] Barabási, A.-L., Albert, R.: Emergence of scaling in random networks. Science 286(5439), 509–512 (1999)
[3] Grilo, C., Correia, L.: Asynchronous stochastic dynamics and the spatial prisoner's dilemma game. In: Neves, J., Santos, M.F., Machado, J.M. (eds.) EPIA 2007. LNCS (LNAI), vol. 4874, pp. 235–246. Springer, Heidelberg (2007)

[4] Grilo, C., Correia, L.: The influence of asynchronous dynamics in the spatial prisoner's dilemma game. In: Asada, M., Hallam, J.C.T., Meyer, J.-A., Tani, J. (eds.) SAB 2008. LNCS (LNAI), vol. 5040, pp. 362–371. Springer, Heidelberg (2008)
[5] Grilo, C., Correia, L.: What makes the spatial prisoner's dilemma game sensitive to asynchronism. In: Proceedings of the 11th International Conference on the Simulation and Synthesis of Living Systems, Alife XI, pp. 212–219. MIT Press, Cambridge (2008)
[6] Grilo, C., Correia, L.: The influence of the update dynamics on the evolution of cooperation. International Journal of Computational Intelligence Systems, Special Issue on Computational Intelligence Issues in Systems Experiencing Nonlinear Dynamics and Synchronization 2(2), 104–114 (2009)
[7] Hauert, C., Doebeli, M.: Spatial structure often inhibits the evolution of cooperation in the snowdrift game. Nature 428, 643–646 (2004)
[8] Huberman, B., Glance, N.: Evolutionary games and computer simulations. Proceedings of the National Academy of Sciences 90, 7716–7718 (1993)
[9] Newth, D., Cornforth, D.: Asynchronous spatial evolutionary games: spatial patterns, diversity and chaos. In: Proceedings of the 2007 IEEE Congress on Evolutionary Computation, pp. 2463–2470 (2007)
[10] Nowak, M., Bonhoeffer, S., May, R.M.: More spatial games. International Journal of Bifurcation and Chaos 4(1), 33–56 (1994)
[11] Nowak, M., May, R.M.: Evolutionary games and spatial chaos. Nature 359, 826–829 (1992)
[12] Oh, J.C.: Cooperating search agents explore more than defecting search agents in the internet information access. In: Proceedings of the 2001 Congress on Evolutionary Computation, CEC2001, pp. 1261–1268. IEEE Press, Los Alamitos (2001)
[13] Pacheco, J.M., Santos, F.C.: Network dependence of the dilemmas of cooperation. In: Mendes, J.F.F. (ed.) Science of Complex Networks: From Biology to the Internet and WWW, CNET 2004. vol. 776, pp. 90–100. AIP Conference Proceedings (2005)
[14] Smith, J.M.: Evolution and the Theory of Games. Cambridge University Press, Cambridge (1982)
[15] Szabó, G., Fáth, G.: Evolutionary games on graphs. Physics Reports 446, 97–216 (2007)
[16] Tomassini, M., Luthi, L., Giacobini, M.: Hawks and doves on small-world networks. Physical Review E 73(1), 16132 (2006)
[17] Watts, D., Strogatz, S.H.: Collective dynamics of small-world networks. Nature 393, 440–442 (1998)

Agent-Based Model of *Aedes aegypti* Population Dynamics

Carlos Isidoro, Nuno Fachada, Fábio Barata, and Agostinho Rosa

Evolutionary System and Biomedical Engineering Lab
Systems and Robotics Institute
Instituto Superior Técnico
Av. Rovisco Pais, 1049-001 Lisboa, Portugal
cisidoro@laseeb.org, nfachada@laseeb.org, fbarata@laseeb.org, acrosa@laseeb.org

Abstract. The paper presents an agent based model of the *Aedes aegypti* mosquito and it is focused on simulations of population dynamics and population control strategies. The agents model the main aspects of mosquito's ecology and behavior, while the environmental components are implemented as layer of dynamic elements obeying to physical laws. The main objective of this approach is to provide realistic simulations of insect biologic control strategies, namely population suppression by releasing large amounts of sterile males, such as Sterile Insect Technique (SIT) or Release of Insects carrying a Dominant Lethal gene (RIDL). Model verification is done through simulations analysis of parameters variation and qualitative assessment with existing models and simulations. The use of LAIS simulator proved to be a valuable tool allowing efficient agent based modeling (ABM) and simulations deployment and analysis.

Keywords: Artificial Life, Agent Based Modelling, Aedes aegypti, Dengue, RIDL, SIT.

1 Introduction

The dengue is a dangerous disease which still lacks a cure, and it is spread through a specific type of vector, the *Aedes aegypti* mosquito. Currently, the most affected areas are the ones with tropical climates since factors like high temperature and frequent precipitation are favorable to *Aedes aegypti* growth. However, if current predictions about climate change happen, many new areas might start facing the dengue threat [1].

Since an effective treatment is yet to be found, it is particularly important to focus on prevention, keeping the mosquito population under transmission threshold. Various strategies have been developed and used for this purpose, ranging from releasing large amounts of sterile mosquitoes into the environment to clearing areas with still water that might be used as mosquito breeding sites. However, for these defensive measures to be as effective as possible, it is necessary

L. Seabra Lopes et al. (Eds.): EPIA 2009, LNAI 5816, pp. 53–64, 2009.

to devise ways of predicting their impact, taking into account evolution of the mosquito population and the spread of the disease.

In this paper an agent based model and simulation of *Aedes aegypti* populations is presented. To effectively control the mosquito population, it is crucial that its evolution can be predicted. That is the aim of this model; while it still does not implement the spread of the dengue virus, it is already a functional model that simulates mosquito behavior and how the mosquito population evolves over time. The model can be used to determine the best approaches to contain the population size. In particular, the effect of the RIDL strategy as a containment method was studied.

In section 2 the state-of-the-art on mosquito population modeling is presented. The methods and materials used for developing the mosquito model, namely the ABM approach and the LAIS simulator, are discussed in section 3. The model itself is described in greater detail in section 4. In section 5 simulations and results are presented and discussed. Finally, in section 7 we conclude the presented work, underlining the model's potential and proposing future improvements.

2 State of the Art

There have been numerous models of mosquitoes and mosquito-borne disease, beginning with the classic Ross-Macdonald malaria models [2,3,4] and extending to present day models of vectors populations or aspects of vector biology, not directly considering disease [5,6,7,8].

One example of modeling the dengue vector mosquito population dynamics is by Focks and colleagues [9,10], examining the biology of *Aedes aegypti*. This is an exceptionally detailed model, with numerous types of containers for larval development. Hydrology (water levels and drying), temperature-dependent larval development, food availability and survival are explicitly tracked in each container type. Detailed weather data are used to drive the hydrological and biological functions. This level of detail has both costs and benefits; it enables consideration of detailed aspects of the mosquito biology, but also makes true sensitivity analysis of the model difficult or impossible. Thus, to develop a model with this level of detail, it is necessary to have extensive data available for parameter estimates and validation.

The use of ABM methodologies to model *Aedes aegypti* populations has been scarce at best. Some interesting ideas are presented in a work by Deng *et. al* [11], namely the use of an utility function to determine mosquito movement, taking into account factors such as population, wind direction, land use type and landscape roughness. However, the practical implementation of the model is very limited, with coarse spatial discretization (30x30) and a small number of agents representing a large number of model components and their behaviors.

Models can be useful to evaluate different strategy of mosquito control. Recently, techniques like releasing genetic modified mosquitoes have been considered as an enhanced SIT to control the mosquito population, as the genetic manipulation in insects result in sterility or lethal genes [12,13]. Although there wasn't any genetic modified mosquito open field release conducted yet, a couple of mathematical modeling works have been done to assess the control efficacy [14,15,16]. But none of those could provide a tool to simulate the interaction between mosquito individuals such as mating behavior, spatial distribution, and immigration etc. All these are important for the evaluation and guidance of genetic control approach.

3 Methods and Materials

ABM is well suited for describing complex systems in general and disease transmission in particular, providing a way to represent the true diversity of intervening components, such as environmental factors, disease vectors and disease hosts. Other advantages include the possibility to determine spatial behavior distribution, rapid insertion of new components and natural consideration of non-linear interactions between agents. This approach is not without problems of its own: it requires considerable computational power to simulate individual agents; parameter tuning is not trivial; and, being a relatively recent modeling methodology, lacks the formal framework provided by other approaches, such as differential equation modeling (although work concerning ABM formalism already exists [17]). Nonetheless, for explicitly spatial models, such as the one presented here, the advantages of ABM clearly outweigh its limitations.

The model was developed using the LAIS simulator, a multithreaded agent-based simulation platform, offering a modeling paradigm and a set of tools for the simulation of complex systems [18]. The platform is implemented in Java and makes use of several open source libraries which provide tools for spatial organization and visualization, event scheduling, simulation output (e.g., charts, CSV files, movies) and simple class development and instantiation using XML. Simulations are performed in discrete time and two-dimensional discrete space. As such, space is divided into blocks, which are independently processed by different threads, making LAIS scalable on modern multiprocessor systems.

There are two main actors in the LAIS framework: *agents* and *elements*. Agents are typical ABM discrete and independent decision-making entities. When prompted to act, each agent analyzes its current situation (e.g. what resources are available, what other agents are in the vicinity), and acts accordingly, based on a set of rules. These rules incorporate knowledge or theories about the respective low-level components. On the other hand, elements are real-valued objects which obey predetermined rules, such as physical laws (e.g., diffusion).

4 Model Description

The *Aedes aegypti* LAIS model implements a square topology where each spatial block has 8 neighbors. Five different agents are considered: Wild Male Mosquitoes (WM), Wild Female Mosquitoes (WF), Sterile Male Mosquitoes (SM), Humans (H) and Oviposition spots (OS). Five different elements are also used, and they fall into one of the following categories: mosquito attractors (of

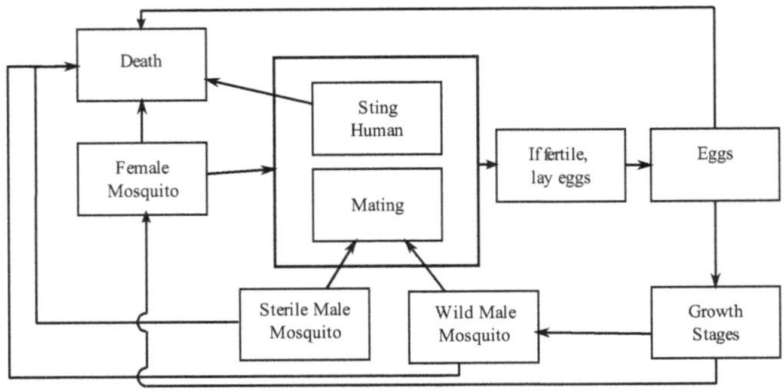

Fig. 1. Model overview

Table 1. Base mortality and maturing chances for mosquitoes

Parameter	Egg	Larva	Pupa	Adult
WF Base Mortality Rate	0.15	0.05	0.05	0.05
WF Maturing Chance	1	0.99	0.6	-
WM Base Mortality Rate	0.15	0.15	0.15	0.15
WM Maturing Chance	1	0.99	0.7	-
SM Base Mortality Rate	0.15	0.15	0.15	0.15

which there are three kinds), mosquito density measure and observable mosquito properties.

The interactions between the various agents are represented in a simplistic way in fig. 1. Table 1 shows various parameters related to the agents.

4.1 Agents

Female Mosquito (WF). The Female Mosquito (WF) is by far the most complex agent in the simulation. Adult females try to find humans nearby (by following the concentration of the *body heat* element) and attempt to sting them in order to obtain blood. Exposure to humans is a risky activity however, and might result in the death of the mosquito. If the female succeeds, it then starts moving randomly waiting for a male to mate with, and then looks for an Oviposition Spot (by moving to areas with a higher concentration of the *humidity* element). If it has already found a mate before finding a Human it goes directly to the OS after stinging the Human. During the first two steps, looking for humans and mates respectively, the female regularly deposits pheromones for the males to follow. When it reaches the Oviposition spot it lays its eggs if the mate was fertile, and then starts looking for another human, resuming the cycle.

The female has a certain chance to die at each iteration (table 1), and that chance will vary with the density of other mosquitoes in the area. New females start as eggs, and then go through a number of growth stages (currently larvae

Table 2. More parameters related to the WF

Parameter	Value
Chance to die when meeting a Human	0.5
Chance to successfully sting a Human	0.9
Number of male eggs laid	16
Number of female eggs laid	11
Chance to mate with wild males	0.7
Chance to mate with sterile males	0.7

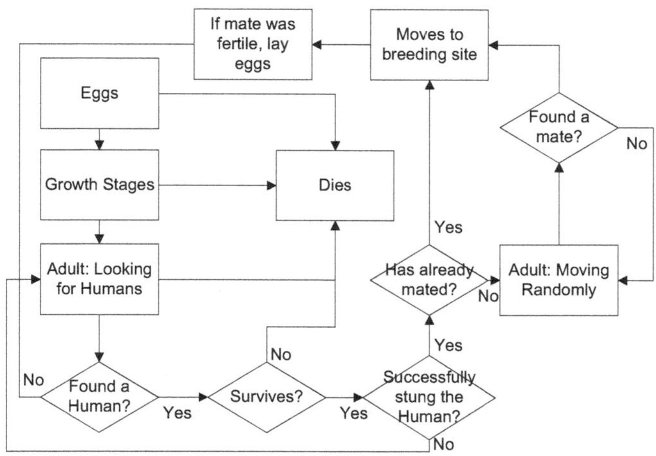

Fig. 2. WF mosquito model

and pupa), before maturing into an adult (maturing chances for each stage can also be found on table 1). Table 2 provides various parameters related to the WF and figure 2 shows a summary of the WF sequence of actions.

Male Mosquito (WM). The Wild Male Mosquito (WM) is much simpler when compared to the female version. Adult males follow the pheromone released by females, trying to find one to mate with, and continue with this behavior until they die. Like females, males always have an intrinsic chance to die that increases with the amount of mosquitoes in the area, and new males also start as eggs and go through some growth stages before reaching the adult state.

Sterile Male Mosquito (SM). Sterile Male Mosquitoes (SM) act in exactly the same way as WM. It is the females that check whether their mates were sterile or not. Sterile males do not have growth stages because they are never generated by the mosquitoes, they have to be inserted manually. The parameters associated with the SM in this model are the same as the ones for the WM. This makes this particular implementation of the SM closer to the RIDL approach than the SIT one, since the competitiveness of the SM is the same as the WM.

Oviposition spot. This agent is also extremely simple. It is immobile and only executes two different actions: It is constantly releasing humidity for the females to find them, and it clears the toxicity (*density* element) in its spatial block to ensure they do not become deadly to mosquitoes (since there will be a large number of mosquitoes in such spatial blocks - eggs, growing mosquitoes, females, and the occasional male that wanders into it in search of females).

Human. Humans are perhaps the most basic agent in the model. They simply move randomly in the environment, releasing body heat that the WF follow. They provide the blood that the WF need to lay eggs.

4.2 Elements

Most of these elements have already been presented in the previous section, while describing the agents that use them. It should be noted that elements are used to model mosquito behavior and might not correspond to the exact process the mosquitoes use to follow their targets. For example, females might not track humans based on their body heat, but through other means, be it vision, or some other property the female identifies.

Element diffusion and degradation is performed using a simple method where element concentration in each local block is determined by eq. 1. In this equation, C^n is the substance concentration at tick n, C_i is the substance concentration at neighbor i, N is the number of neighbor blocks (8 in this case) and α and β are the diffusion and evaporation coefficients, respectively. The parameters related to each element are presented on table 3

$$C^{t+1} = \beta \left(C^t + \alpha(\sum_{i=1}^{N} C_i^t - C^t) \right) \tag{1}$$

Attractive Elements: Pheromone (Ph), Body Heat (BH) and Humidity (Hu). These three elements are quite similar, differing only on the agents that release them and the agents that react to them. Pheromone (Ph) is released by WF and attracts males (WM and SM). Body Heat (BH) is released by Humans and attracts WF that are seeking blood. Humidity is released by OS and attracts WF that are looking for a place to lay their eggs.

Table 3. Elements Parameters

Element	Diff. Rate	Evap. Rate	Qty. released	Attractive influence
Ph	0.3	0.05	1	0.5
BH	0.3	0.05	1	0.9
Hu	0.3	0.05	1	0.5
De	0.001	0.2	0.0041	-

Adult Pheromone. This element is placed by WM on themselves when they become adults. This is simply a way for WF to identify them as suitable mates.

Density. This element is released by all types of mosquitoes, and is consumed by Oviposition spots. It is used to model the impact a high density of mosquitoes has on their mortality rate. The reason it is consumed in Oviposition spots is to ensure that they do not become a deadly site for mosquitoes due to the high amount of mosquitoes that will be there.

5 Experiments and Results

This section details the various tests and simulations performed with the LAIS *Aedes aegypti* model. Table 4 shows the default model parameters used for all tests. The 100x100 default size for the test area was chosen because it was a good compromise between the quality of the results and the processing time required for each simulation. Excluding test 5.1 (which just shows the basic evolution of the mosquito population over time), all graphics were determined by averaging the population values of 20 similar simulations. Each block represents around 100 square meters, and each iteration corresponds to a single day.

Table 4. Model default parameters

Parameter	Value
Model width (blocks)	100
Model height (blocks)	100
Initial number of Male Mosquitoes	1250
Initial number of Female Mosquitoes	750
Number of Humans	700

5.1 Default Model

This test is a basic simulation to show the normal evolution of the mosquito population with no treatment (fig. 3). The number of OS used was 300. The mosquito population seems to reach a steady state between 1000 and 2000 individuals from each gender, values that are independent of their initial number. These variations suggest the presence of homeostasis and limit cycles that depend on the various WF and WM parameters.

5.2 Varying Number of Oviposition Spots

In this test the impact of OS availability was studied (fig. 4). As was expected, the final population increases in a linear fashion with the number of OS, since more places to breed makes it easier for more females to lay their eggs. There is probably a maximum number of OS that still significantly affects the number of mosquitoes, as there are other factors that limit their growth, namely death by density and the number of available humans.

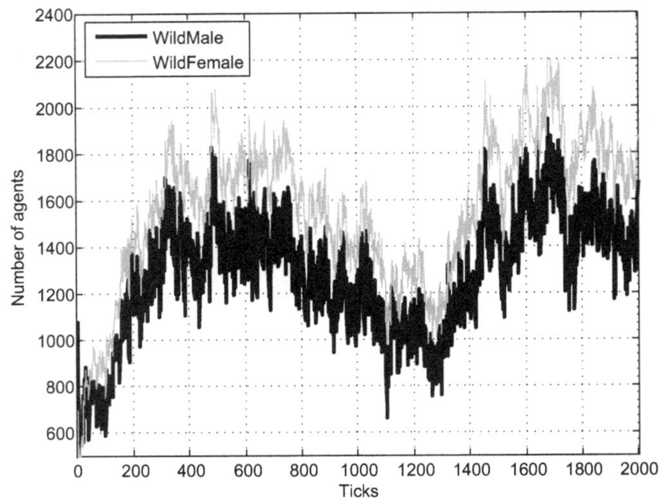

Fig. 3. Mosquito population over a period of 2000 iterations with no treatment applied (300 OS)

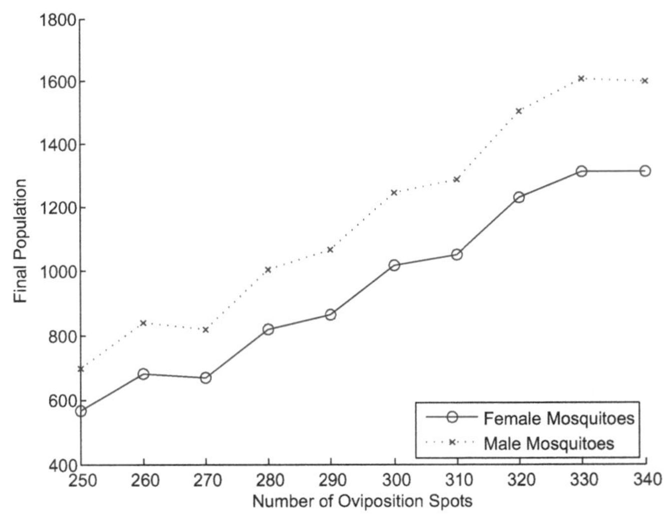

Fig. 4. Final Mosquito Population as a function of the number of Oviposition Spots

5.3 Efficiency of Sterile Mosquitoes

As has already been said in the introduction, this model was used to study the effect of a specific population control strategy, the RIDL method. Tests were performed to show the impact of two factors on the efficacy of the treatment: a) the amount of SM released, in the form of the sterile to wild ratio SM/WM (fig. 5), and b) the width of the time frame in which the release occurred, T

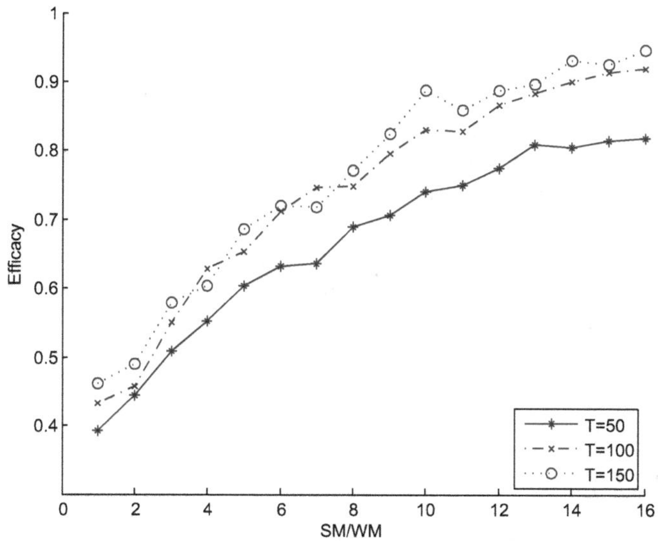

Fig. 5. Efficacy as a function of the SM/WM ratio (300 OS)

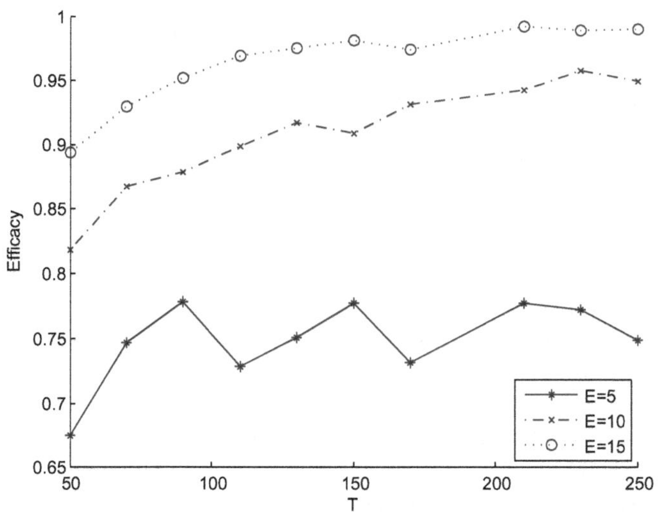

Fig. 6. Efficacy as a function of T (300 OS)

(fig. 6). The efficacy of the treatment is given by eq. 2, where P_i is the population value when the treatment starts, and P_f the minimum population value obtained during the period encompassing the duration of the treatment and a short time after the treatment ends.

$$\text{Efficacy} = \frac{P_i - P_f}{P_i} \tag{2}$$

This kind of simulations are extremely important in order to find the best release strategy and amount of SM to produce, information that is necessary for any control program. The number of OS for all these tests was 300. Fig. 5 shows a sigmoid-like increase of efficacy with SM/WM, with saturation starting for values of SM/WM above 12. There is no significant difference for distinct release periods, but larger values of T tend to yield higher efficacies. The results presented in fig. 6 are consistent with the ones from fig. 5, demonstrating that for values of T above 100 the change in efficiency is negligible, and a higher SM/WM results in higher efficacies.

6 Discussion

The results obtained regarding the effectiveness of this particular population control strategy concerning SM/WM ratio, and the ones related to the width of the time frame of the release are quite similar (from a qualitative point of view) to the ones obtained in [19].

It is also important to comment that these were not the only results that could be obtained from the LAIS simulator, but only the ones that were found to be most important. The LAIS simulator can also yield information about the concentration of all elements for each iteration, the number of agents in a given state (larvae, pupas, adults, etc.), and the 2D representation of the environment gives the possibility of checking the contents of any given block.

7 Conclusions and Future Work

The model presented in this paper is far from complete, since it is missing certain important factors, most noticeably environmental factors like temperature, precipitation and wind. The various parameters also need to be fine-tuned to get a model as close to the real population as possible (in particular, some parameters might not be entirely correct in relation to the amount of time associated with each iteration). The possibility to have infected mosquitoes and humans will also be an important improvement to the model, since then it can also be used to directly predict the spread of the dengue disease.

Other strategies to contain the population could also be studied, and even variations on this particular control strategy, like PRP (Prevention Release Program), regularly releasing a lower number of sterile mosquitoes after the population has been reduced below the transmission threshold, in order to keep the population controlled.

Nevertheless, the model presented here can be the basis of an important tool to: a) help in the comprehension of *Aedes aegypti* population dynamics; b) predict the efficacy of mosquito population control strategies; and c) assess the best courses of action to contain the spread of the dengue disease.

Acknowledgements

This work was partially supported by Fundação para a Ciência e a Tecnologia (ISR/IST plurianual funding) through the POS_Conhecimento Program that includes FEDER funds. The authors C. Isidoro and F. Barata acknowledge their grant BII-2009 to Fundação para a Ciência e Tecnologia (FCT). The author N. Fachada acknowledges its grant SFRH/BD/48310/2008 to Fundação para a Ciência e Tecnologia (FCT).

References

1. Senior, K.: Climate change and infectious disease: a dangerous liaison. The Lancet Infectious Diseases 8(2), 92–93 (2008)
2. Ross, R.: The Prevention of Malaria (1911)
3. Macdonald, G.: The analysis of equilibrium in malaria. Trop Dis Bull 49(9), 813–829 (1952)
4. Macdonald, G.: The epidemiology and control of malaria (1957)
5. Eisenberg, J., Reisen, W., Spear, R.: Dynamic model comparing the bionomics of two isolated Culex tarsalis (Diptera: Culicidae) populations: model development. Journal of Medical Entomology 32(2), 83–97 (1995)
6. Eisenberg, J., Reisen, W., Spear, R.: Dynamic model comparing the bionomics of two isolated Culex tarsalis (Diptera: Culicidae) populations: sensitivity analysis. Journal of medical entomology 32(2), 98–106 (1995)
7. Alto, B., Juliano, S.: Precipitation and temperature effects on populations of Aedes albopictus (Diptera: Culicidae): implications for range expansion. Journal of medical entomology 38(5), 646–656 (2001)
8. Ahumada, J., Lapointe, D., Samuel, M.: Modeling the population dynamics of Culex quinquefasciatus (Diptera: Culicidae), along an elevational gradient in Hawaii. Journal of medical entomology 41(6), 1157–1170 (2004)
9. Focks, D., Haile, D., Daniels, E., Mount, G.: Dynamic life table model of a container-inhabiting mosquito, Aedes aegypti (L.)(Diptera: Culicidae). Part 1. Analysis of the literature and model development. Journal of Medical Entomology 30, 1003–1017 (1993)
10. Focks, D., Haile, D., Daniels, E., Mount, G.: Dynamic life table model of a container-inhabiting mosquito, Aedes aegypti (L.)(Diptera: Culicidae). Part 2. Simulation results and validation. Journal of Medical Entomology 30, 1018–1028 (1993)
11. Deng, C., Tao, H., Ye, Z.: Agent-based modeling to simulate the dengue spread. 7143, 714310 (2008)
12. Thomas, D., Donnelly, C., Wood, R., Alphey, L.: Insect population control using a dominant, repressible, lethal genetic system. Science 287(5462), 2474–2476
13. Atkinson, M., Su, Z., Alphey, N., Alphey, L., Coleman, P., Wein, L.: Analyzing the control of mosquito-borne diseases by a dominant lethal genetic system. Proceedings of the National Academy of Sciences 104(22), 9540–9546 (2007)
14. Esteva, L., Mo Yang, H.: Mathematical model to assess the control of Aedes aegypti mosquitoes by the sterile insect technique. Mathematical biosciences 198(2), 132–147 (2005)
15. Li, J.: Simple mathematical models for interacting wild and transgenic mosquito populations. Mathematical biosciences 189(1), 39–59 (2004)

16. Maiti, A., Patra, B., Samanta, G.: Sterile insect release method as a control measure of insect pests: A mathematical model. Journal of Applied Mathematics and Computing 22(3), 71–86 (2006)
17. Helleboogh, A., Vizzari, G., Uhrmacher, A., Michel, F.: Modeling dynamic environments in multi-agent simulation. Autonomous Agents and Multi-Agent Systems 14(1), 87–116 (2007)
18. Fachada, N.: Agent-based Simulation of the Immune System. Master's thesis, Instituto Superior Técnico, Lisboa (July 2008)
19. Ferreira, C., Yang, H., Esteva, L.: Assessing the suitability of sterile insect technique applied to Aedes aegypti. Journal of Biological Systems 16(4), 565–577 (2008)

Using Operator Equalisation for Prediction of Drug Toxicity with Genetic Programming

Leonardo Vanneschi[1] and Sara Silva[2]

[1] Dipartimento di Informatica, Sistemistica e Comunicazione (D.I.S.Co.),
University of Milano-Bicocca, Milan, Italy
[2] CISUC, Department of Informatics Engineering,
University of Coimbra, Polo II, Coimbra, Portugal

Abstract. Predicting the toxicity of new potential drugs is a fundamental step in the drug design process. Recent contributions have shown that, even though Genetic Programming is a promising method for this task, the problem of predicting the toxicity of molecular compounds is complex and difficult to solve. In particular, when executed for predicting drug toxicity, Genetic Programming undergoes the well-known phenomenon of bloat, i.e. the growth in code size during the evolutionary process without a corresponding improvement in fitness. We hypothesize that this might cause overfitting and thus prevent the method from discovering simpler and potentially more general solutions. For this reason, in this paper we investigate two recently defined variants of the operator equalization bloat control method for Genetic Programming. We show that these two methods are bloat free also when executed on this complex problem. Nevertheless, overfitting still remains an issue. Thus, contradicting the generalized idea that bloat and overfitting are strongly related, we argue that the two phenomena are independent from each other and that eliminating bloat does not necessarily eliminate overfitting.

1 Introduction

Because of recent advances in high throughput screening, pharmaceutical research is currently changing. In the drug discovery process, when a target protein is identified and validated, the search of lead compounds begins with the design of a structural molecular fragment with therapeutic potency. Libraries of millions of chemical compounds similar to the identified effective fragment are then tested and ranked according to their specific biological activity. This biological activity is usually measured according to the value of so called *pharmacokinetic parameters*. In this paper, we are interested in the prediction of a particular pharmacokinetic parameter called Median Lethal Dose (represented by LD50 from now on), that measures the toxicity of a given compound. Being able to reliably predict the LD50 value for a potential new drug is outstandingly important, given that the majority of failures in compound development from the early nineties to nowadays are due to a wrong prediction of this pharmacokinetic parameter during the drug discovery process (see [10, 26] for detailed discussions).

In [1, 2] various machine learning methods have been investigated for LD50 predictions, including Support Vector Machines, Artificial Neural Networks, Linear and Least

L. Seabra Lopes et al. (Eds.): EPIA 2009, LNAI 5816, pp. 65–76, 2009.

Square Regression methods, and Genetic Programming (GP) [17]. Those contributions suggest that GP is a valuable technique for predicting LD50, given that its results are more accurate than the ones returned by the other machine learning methods. Nevertheless, those results also give a clear indication of the complexity of the studied problem. In particular, this application emphasizes one of the most well-known and widely investigated negative features of GP, called *bloat*, i.e. the growth in code size during the evolutionary process without a corresponding improvement in fitness. Indeed, after few GP generations executed for LD50 prediction, the population is composed by huge potential solutions, each one characterized by several thousands of nodes, while no significant improvement of fitness is observed. According to the so called minimum description length principle (see for instance [19]), generally accepted in machine learning, we hint that the excessive solutions complexity is a limit to the GP generalization ability and one possible cause of overfitting.

For this reason, we apply one of the newest and most recognized methods for counteracting bloat in GP to the same dataset as in [1, 2], with the goal of producing simpler solutions. The study of the performance of those solutions on out-of-sample testing data will also allow us to make useful inferences about the relationship between bloat and overfitting. Thus, the main contributions of this paper are: (1) deepening the study of LD50 prediction, using new and promising GP methods and thus generating simpler and more readable solutions than the ones returned by canonical GP; (2) shedding a light on the relationship between bloat and overfitting, by comparing the generalization ability of these solutions with the one of the solutions returned by canonical GP.

The method we use to counteract bloat is the recently defined *operator equalisation* [5, 24]. Developed alongside the crossover bias theory [3, 4, 15, 16] (the most recent bloat theory, that explains code growth in tree-based GP by the effect that standard subtree crossover has on the distribution of program lengths in the population), the operator equalisation is one of the few bloat control methods based on a precise theoretical study. By filtering which individuals are accepted in each new generation, this technique allows accurate control of the distribution of program lengths inside the population, easily biasing the search towards smaller or larger programs. In the first published version of operator equalisation [5], the user had to specify the desired length distribution, called *target*, as well as a maximum allowed program length. Both remained static throughout the entire run. Each newly created individual was accepted or rejected for the new generation based on its length and the target distribution. This first implementation was recently followed by a dynamic version of operator equalisation (here called DynOpEq) [24], where both the target and the maximum allowed program length are self adapted along the run. In DynOpEq, the acceptance or rejection of the newly created individuals is based not only on their length, but also on their fitness. In [24] DynOpEq has been experimented on four well-known GP benchmark problems (symbolic regression, artificial ant, even-parity and multiplexer), while in [25] DynOpEq has been executed for the first time on a real-life application (prediction of another pharmacokinetic parameter, human oral bioavailability). Furthermore, in [25] a new version of the operator equalisation has been defined. Contrarily to DynOpEq, it does not reject any individuals, and instead transforms them by slightly mutating their genotype until they reach the desired length. This new implementation has been called MutOpEq.

In this paper, for the first time, we test both DynOpEq and MutOpEq on LD50 prediction, which is a much more complex problem than the one studied in [25], as confirmed in [1, 2].

The paper is structured as follows: in Section 2 we present the problem of LD50 prediction; Section 3 describes the operator equalisation and both its variants studied here; in Section 4 we present the experimental setting used; Section 5 contains the obtained experimental results and a discussion of them; finally, Section 6 concludes the paper and offers ideas for future research.

2 Toxicity of Drugs: Median Lethal Dose

Pharmacokinetics prediction tools are based on two approaches: *molecular modeling*, which uses intensive protein structure calculations and *data modeling*. Methods based on data modeling are widely reported in literature, and all belong to the category of Quantitative Structure Activity Relationship (QSAR) models [9]. The goal of such models is defining a quantitative relationship between the structure of a molecule and its biological activity. To obtain a QSAR model, it is necessary to collect a training set of drugs for which biological activity parameters are known. A wide spectrum of features, called molecular descriptors, are calculated from the structural representation of each compound. Descriptors are computed from a graph based representation of molecules, in which labelled nodes refer to atoms and labelled edges represent bonds between atoms. Two main categories of features are generally used in QSAR procedures: 2D-chemical descriptors, based on a bi-dimensional representation of compounds and 3D-chemical descriptors, whose computation is time-consuming since they are calculated from a tri-dimensional molecular structure. For a detailed discussion on molecular descriptors, see for instance [18]. After molecular features calculation, it comes natural to try to formalize a mathematical relationship between them and the biological target parameter, applying statistical or machine learning procedures.

The pharmacokinetic parameter studied in this paper (Median Lethal Dose (LD50)) is one of the parameters measuring the toxicity of a given compound. More precisely, LD50 refers to the amount of compound required to kill 50% of the test organisms (cavies). It is usually expressed as the number of milligrams of drug related to one kilogram of mass of the model organism (mg/kg). Depending on the specific organism (usually rat, mouse, dog, monkey, or rabbit), and on the precise way of supplying (generally intravenous, subcutaneous, intraperitoneal, or oral) that are chosen in the experimental design, it is possible to define a spectrum of LD50 protocols. In our work we consider only the Median Lethal Dose measured in rats with the compound orally supplied, which represents the most used protocol.

Drug toxicity prediction is a very difficult and challenging task: because of the complexity of possible interactions between the organism and the pharmacological molecule, similar compounds may undergo different toxic behaviors. A benchmark of mathematical methods, including recursive partitioning (RP) and Partial Least Square regression (PLS) among others, has been tested by Feng and co-workers [12]. Multivariate linear regression and Artificial Neural Networks have been applied for building a model of LD50 in fathead minnow (*Pimephales promelas*) for 397 organic chemicals [27]. A technique called Genetic Function Approximation (GFA) considering 107 molecular descriptors has been proposed in [8].

GP has been used in pharmacokinetics for instance in [30], where it is used to classify molecules in terms of their bioavailability, but to the best of our knowledge, it has not intensively been used for toxicity predictions yet, except for the contributions presented in [1, 2]. These references show that GP is a promising method, but code growth and overfitting of training data still remain important issues.

3 Operator Equalisation

Developed alongside the crossover bias theory [3, 4, 15, 16], operator equalisation is a recent technique to control bloat that allows an accurate control of the program length distribution during a GP run. To better explain how it works, we use the concept of a histogram. Each bar of the histogram can be imagined as a bin containing those programs whose length (i.e., total number of nodes) is within a certain interval. The width of the bar determines the range of lengths that fall into this bin, and the height specifies the number of programs allowed within. We call the former *bin width* and the latter *bin capacity*. All bins are the same width, placed adjacently with no overlapping. Each length value, l, belongs to one and only one bin b, identified as follows:

$$b = \left\lfloor \frac{l-1}{bin\_width} \right\rfloor + 1 \tag{1}$$

For instance, if $bin\_width = 5$, bin 1 will hold programs of lengths 1,..,5, bin 2 will hold programs of lengths 6,..,10, etc. The set of bins represents the distribution of program lengths in the population. Operator equalisation biases the population towards a desired target distribution by accepting or rejecting each newly created individual into the population (and into its corresponding bin). The original implementation of operator equalisation, where the user was required to specify the target distribution and maximum program length, rapidly evolved to a self adapting implementation where both these elements are automatically set and dynamically updated to provide the best setting for each stage of the evolutionary process. There are two tasks involved in operator equalisation: calculating the target (in practical terms, defining the capacity of each bin) and making the population follow it (making sure the individuals in the population fit the set of bins). The first task is common to both implementations described here. The second task differs between DynOpEq and MutOpEq.

Calculating the Target Distribution. Provided with a simple and effective method for biasing the search towards the desired program lengths, the question immediately arises: what is the best program length distribution? Preliminary steps were taken in this direction [5] and evidence has shown that (1) it depends on the problem and (2) it depends on the stage of the run. In both DynOpEq and MutOpEq the dynamic target length distribution simply follows fitness. For each bin, the average fitness of the individuals within is calculated, and the target is directly proportional to these values. Bins with higher average fitness will have higher capacity, because that is where search is proving to be more successful. Formalizing, the capacity, or target number of individuals, for each bin b, is calculated as: $bin\_capacity_b = round(n \times (\bar{f}_b / \sum_i \bar{f}_i))$, where $\bar{f}_i$ is the average fitness in the bin with index i, $\bar{f}_b$ is the average fitness of the individuals in b, and n is the number of individuals in the population.

Initially based on the first randomly created population, the target is updated at each generation, always based on the fitness measurements of the current population. This creates a fast moving bias towards the areas of the search space where the fittest programs are, avoiding the small unfit individuals resulting from the crossover bias, as well as the excessively large individuals that do not provide better fitness than the smaller ones already found. Thus the dynamic target is capable of self adapting to any problem and any stage of the run.

Following the Target Distribution. In operator equalisation, every newly created individual must be validated before eventually entering the population. The details differ between the two implementations used in our study, here designated as DynOpEq and MutOpEq. The main difference resides on the fact that DynOpEq rejects the individuals that do not fit the target, and MutOpEq mutates the individuals until they fit the target.

In both implementations, individuals from the population are selected for mating and the application of genetic operators allow us to create new individuals, as in canonical GP. After that, the length of each new individual is measured, and its corresponding bin is identified using Equation 1. If this bin already exists and is not full (meaning that its capacity is higher than the number of individuals already there), the new individual is immediately accepted. If the bin still does not exist (meaning it lies outside the current target boundaries) the fitness of the individual is measured and, in case we are in the presence of the new best-of-run (the individual with best fitness found so far), the bin is created to accept the new individual, becoming immediately full. Any other non-existing bins between the new bin and the target boundaries also become available with capacity for only one individual each. The dynamic creation of new bins frees the operator equalisation technique from the fixed maximum program length that was present in the very first implementation. The criterion of creating new bins whenever needed to accommodate the new best-of-run individual is inspired by a successful technique to control code growth based on dynamic limits [22, 23].

The differences between DynOpEq and MutOpEq are revealed when the intended bin exists but is already at its full capacity, or when the intended bin does not exist and the new individual is not the best-of-run. In the first case, DynOpEq evaluates the individual and, if we are in the presence of the new best-of-bin (meaning the individual has better fitness than any other already in that bin), the bin is forced to increase its capacity and accept the individual. Otherwise, the individual is rejected. Permitting the addition of individuals beyond the bin capacity allows a clever overriding of the target distribution, by further biasing the population towards the lengths where the search is having a higher degree of success. In the second case, when the bin does not exist and the individual is not the best-of-run, rejection always occurs. There is an obvious computational overhead in evaluating so many individuals that end up being rejected[1]. MutOpEq, on

[1] This subject has been extensively addressed in previous work [24] where the main conclusion was that most rejections happen in the beginning of the run and refer to very small individuals.

the other hand, never rejects individuals. In both cases mentioned above, this new implementation performs the same action: it searches for the closest existing non-full bin, and then mutates the new individual until its length fits this bin. The mutations used are "weak" mutations in the sense that they modify the least possible amount of code each time they are applied. Loosely based on the shrink and grow mutations defined in [29], our weak mutations can be informally described as follows: (1) *Shrink*: chooses a terminal branch (a minimum-depth branch containing only one function whose arguments are all terminals) and replaces it with one of its terminal nodes (one of the arguments of the function); (2) *Grow*: chooses a terminal node and replaces it with a terminal branch where one of the arguments is the replaced terminal. We use one or the other, depending on whether we need to reduce or enlarge the individual. Whenever there is a tie (i.e., there are two existing non-full bins at the same distance), the preferred option is to reduce. The same individual will undergo several mutations until it reaches the desired length. We expect that, by iteratively inserting or removing only terminal elements, instead of inserting or removing a larger branch in a single operation, we minimize the impact on the fitness of the individual [11, 13].

4 Experimental Setting

Here we describe how the data for the problem described in Section 2 was collected and prepared, and what parameters and tools were used in our experiments. The techniques tested were both operator equalisation versions (DynOpEq and MutOpEq) and a standard non-equalising version of GP (StdGP).

We have obtained a set of molecular structures and the corresponding LD50 values using the same data as in [6] and a public database of food and drug Administration (FDA) approved drugs and drug-like compounds [20]. Chemical structures are all expressed as SMILES code (Simplified Molecular Input Line Entry Specification), i.e. strings coding the 2D molecular structure of a compound in an extremely concise form. The resulting libraries of molecules contained 234 molecules with measured LD50 values. SMILES strings belonging to the LD50 dataset have been used to compute 627 bi-dimensional molecular descriptors using the on-line DRAGON software [28]. Thus, data have been gathered in a matrix composed by 234 rows (instances) and 627 columns (features). Each row is a vector of molecular descriptors values identifying a drug; each column represents a molecular descriptor, except the last one, that contains the known values of LD50. This dataset can be downloaded from the webpage: http://personal.disco.unimib.it/Vanneschi/toxicity.txt. Training and test sets have been obtained by randomly splitting the dataset: at each GP run, 70% of the molecules have been randomly selected with uniform probability and inserted into the training set, while the remaining 30% form the test set.

A total of 30 runs were performed with each technique. All the runs used populations of 500 individuals allowed to evolve for 100 generations. Tree initialization was performed with the Ramped Half-and-Half method [17] with a maximum initial depth of 6. The function set contained the four binary operators $+$, $-$, $\times$, and $/$, protected as in [17]. The terminal set contained all 234 variables and no random constants. Because the cardinalities of the function and terminal sets were so different, we have explicitly imposed functions and terminals the same probability of being chosen. Fitness was calculated as the root mean squared error between outputs and targets. Selection for reproduction used Lexicographic Parsimony Pressure [14] tournaments of size 10. Very similar to a regular tournament, the lexicographic tournament chooses smaller individuals when their fitness is the same. Tested in different problems, it appears like this tournament is advantageous or, in the worst case, does not affect the performance of the search process. The reproduction (replication) rate was 0.1, meaning that each selected parent has a 10% chance of being copied to the next generation instead of being engaged in breeding. Standard tree mutation and standard crossover (with uniform selection of crossover and mutation points) were used with probabilities of 0.1 and 0.9, respectively. The new random branch created for mutation has maximum depth 6. Selection for survival was not elitist. Regarding the parameters specific to each technique, standard GP used a fixed maximum depth of 17, and both operator equalisation techniques used a bin width equal to 1.

All the experiments were performed using a modified version of GPLAB [21], a Genetic Programming Toolbox for MATLAB. Statistical significance of the null hypothesis of no difference was determined with pairwise Kruskal-Wallis non-parametric ANOVAs at $p = 0.01$. A non-parametric ANOVA was used because the data is not guaranteed to follow a normal distribution. For the same reason, the median was preferred over the mean in all the evolution plots shown in the next section. The median is also more robust to outliers.

5 Results and Discussion

The criteria to evaluate the performance of a given optimization heuristic may depend on the goals and particularities of the application being studied. In this work, program length (i.e. the number of nodes contained in a solution) will be one of our main concerns, a par with fitness, in particular the fitness measured on the test set. In fact, in our application it is very important that results are accurate and general, but they must also be simple and "human readable", if we want our computational tool to have a real impact on pharmaceutical industry.

Figure 1 contains three boxplots[2]. The first one (a) refers to the best fitness achieved on the final generation, measured on the training set; the second (b) shows the fitness achieved by the same individuals when measured on the test set; the third (c) shows the average program length measured on all the generations.

All the fitness differences are statistically significant on the training set (a), where DynOpEq is the technique that reaches better fitness, followed by StdGP, and finally MutOpEq. On the test set (b), a significant difference is observed between DynOpEq and MutOpEq, where MutOpEq maintains a better generalization ability. The three techniques present behavioral differences in terms of variability of the test fitness. Both in StdGP and DynOpEq there are several outliers not shown in the plot, as hinted by the magnitude of the mean values. In contrast, MutOpEq exhibits a fairly constrained and predictable behavior. Interestingly, all the differences in the average program length (c)

[2] In the boxplots each technique is represented by a box and pair of whiskers. Each box has lines at the lower quartile, median, and upper quartile values, and the whiskers mark the furthest value within 1.5 of the quartile ranges. Outliers are represented by +, and × marks the mean.

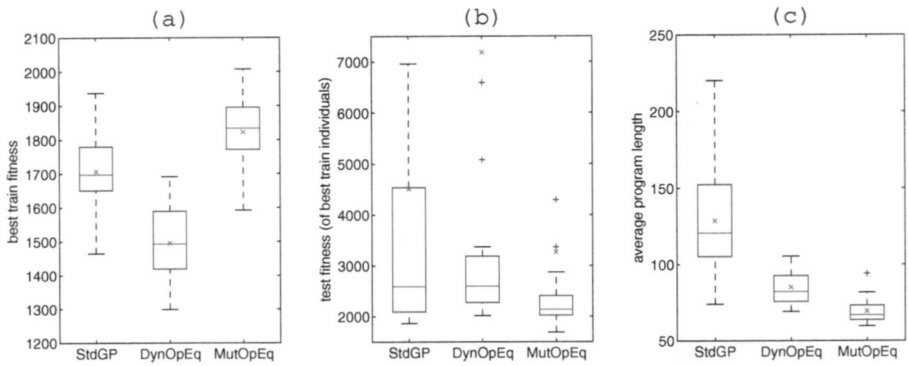

Fig. 1. Boxplots of (a) best training fitness, (b) test fitness of best training individuals, and (c) average program length

are statistically significant, with StdGP producing the largest individuals. Among the equalisation techniques, MutOpEq produces shorter individuals than DynOpEq. Already from these first results we can say that, in the context of our application, MutOpEq seems the technique producing the most desirable results. In fact, the quality of the solutions found by MutOpEq on the test set is better than the one of the solutions found by the other methods, in terms of fitness *and* program length.

Now we take a closer look at fitness and program length and we observe how they evolve along the runs. Figure 2 contains six plots. Let us focus first on plots (a) and (b) containing best training fitness and test fitness of best training individuals respectively. Because of the large differences observed in the average program length of the different techniques, and because we are particularly interested in program length, we plot fitness against a rough estimate of computational effort, calculated as the total number of nodes used by all the individuals that were once part of the population. This measure of computational effort clearly also depends on the population size. The suitability of plotting fitness against total number of nodes visited by GP populations, instead of fitness against generations, has been deeply explained in previous studies (see for instance [7, 24]) and will not be further discussed here. We observe that StdGP requires substantially more effort than the equalisation techniques, and MutOpEq requires less effort than DynOpEq. This, as well as the training and test fitness recorded at the end of the run, was already known from the observation of the previous figure. The interesting information provided by these plots is that on the training set all the techniques show a similar steady improvement of fitness along the run, while on the test set all the techniques show a fast improvement in the beginning followed by a worsening tendency from early in the run until the end. We deduce that all the techniques overfit the training data. This confirms that the problem we are studying is a very complex and difficult one, as already observed in [1, 2]. We can only observe that overfitting is less marked in MutOpEq than in StdGP and DynOpEq. Once again, MutOpEq seems the preferable method, given that it finds better fitness values on the test set all along the run with less computational effort.

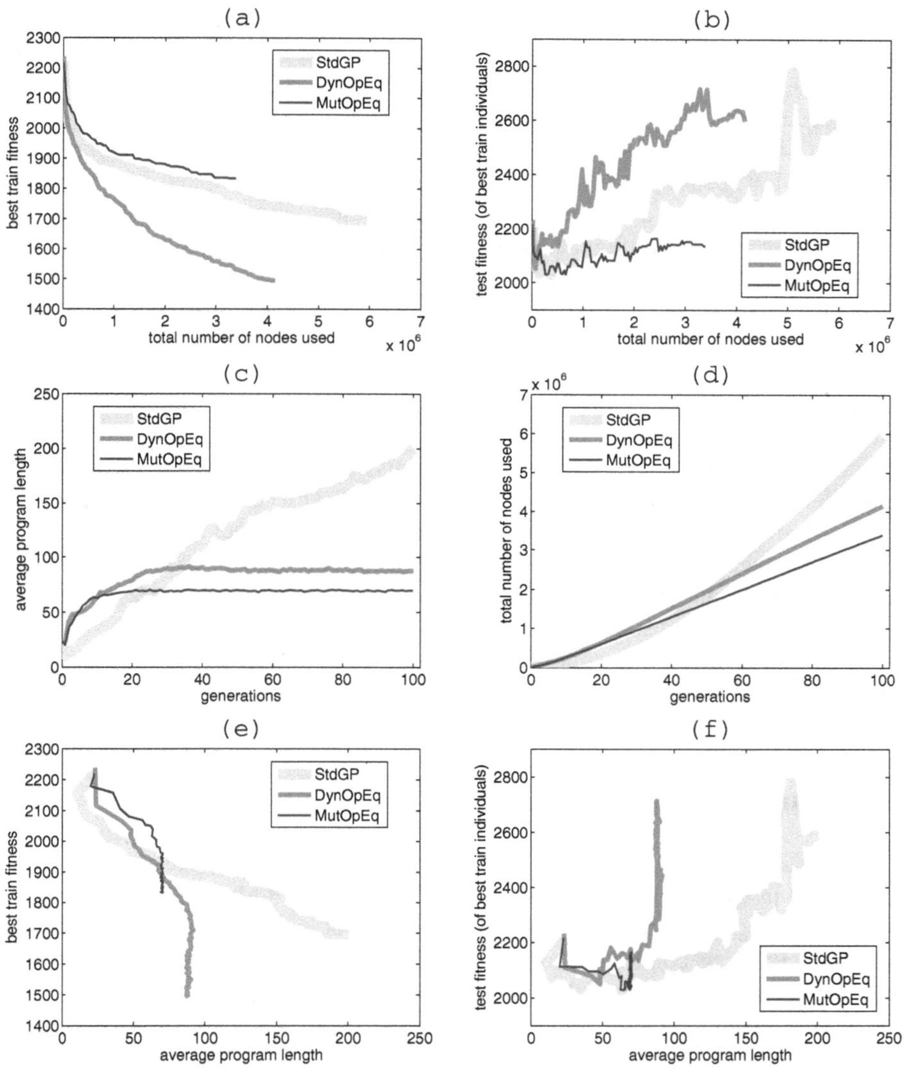

Fig. 2. Evolution plots of (a) best training fitness and (b) test fitness of best training individuals, both against computational effort; (c) average program length and (d) computational effort, both against generations; and (e) best training fitness and (f) test fitness of best training individuals, both against average program length

We now shift our attention to the evolution of program length and computational effort, regardless of fitness. Plot 2(c) reports the average program length in each generation. The difference between StdGP and the equalisation techniques is striking: StdGP exhibits a marked increase all along the run, while for both DynOpEq and MutOpEq the average program length increases very rapidly in the first few generations, and then stabilizes rather suddenly on a relatively low value. MutOpEq stabilizes sooner, and on a slightly lower value, than DynOpEq. Plot 2(d) shows the computational effort, roughly expressed as the total (cumulative) number of nodes used so far, in each generation. Directly related to the previous plot, it is not surprising to see that, unlike in StdGP, in operator equalisation the computational effort rises linearly.

In synthesis, while plots 2(a) and 2(b) show that all methods overfit training data, plots 2(c) and 2(d) show that only StdGP bloats, while DynOpEq and MutOpEq are completely bloat free. As a consequence, we can state that when we have bloat we may have overfitting, but preventing bloat does not necessarily avoid overfitting.[3]

This result is confirmed by plots 2(e) and 2(f). They report fitness against average program length (plot 2(e) referring to the training set and plot 2(f) to the test set). Depending on how fast the fitness improves with the increase of program length, the lines in the plot may point downward (south), or they may point to the right (east). Lines pointing south represent a rapidly improving fitness with little or no code growth. Lines pointing east represent a slowly improving fitness with strong code growth. Lines pointing southwest (bottom left) represent improvements in fitness along with a reduction of program length. We want our lines to point as south (and west) as possible. Only plot (e) (the one based on the training set) should be used to make inferences about bloat. Plot (f) can be used to make inferences about overfitting. As can be seen, in the training set both equalisation techniques point south, while StdGP points south-east. Once again, we can safely say that both equalisation techniques are bloat free. In the test set, all the methods point north or northeast, thus confirming that they all overfit. The speed of overfitting seems to be directly related to the speed of learning, regardless of the amount of code growth.

6 Conclusions and Future Work

We have tested two recently defined versions of the operator equalisation method for bloat control in Genetic Programming (called DynOpEq and MutOpEq) on the problem of predicting the value of Median Lethal Dose of a set of drug-like molecular compounds. Previous contributions have shown that when standard Genetic Programming (StdGP) is used to mine this dataset, the phenomenon of bloat is particularly relevant, causing the generation of huge and poorly general solutions. The presented results have shown that both equalisation techniques are completely bloat free, producing much smaller individuals than StdGP. Nevertheless, overfitting is still present in all the three techniques (even though its negative effects are less important in MutOpEq). Contradicting the generalized idea that bloat and overfitting are strongly related, we have argued that the two phenomena seem to be independent from each other, by showing that eliminating bloat does not eliminate overfitting, and recalling previous results [25] where the occurrence of bloat did not cause overfitting.

As future work, we plan to develop new methods to limit overfitting for LD50 predictions. We would also like to deepen and broaden this study in order to further clarify the relationship between bloat and overfitting. We also plan to test new implementations of operator equalisation and apply them to many more complex real-life problems in the field of drug discovery. Furthermore, we plan to compare DynOpEq and MutOpEq

[3] Previous results presented in [25] have also shown that bloat can happen without overfitting.

with multi-objective approaches and with other techniques that do not bloat (such as Cartesian GP) or that counteract bloat (such as Dynamic Limits, Tarpeian or Double Tournament methods).

Acknowledgments. Sara Silva acknowledges grant SFRH/BPD/47794/2008 from Fundação para a Ciência e a Tecnologia, Portugal.

References

1. Archetti, F., Lanzeni, S., Messina, E., Vanneschi, L.: Genetic programming and other machine learning approaches to predict median oral lethal dose (LD_{50}) and plasma protein binding levels (%PPB) of drugs. In: Marchiori, E., Moore, J.H., Rajapakse, J.C. (eds.) EvoBIO 2007. LNCS, vol. 4447, pp. 11–23. Springer, Heidelberg (2007)
2. Archetti, F., Messina, E., Lanzeni, S., Vanneschi, L.: Genetic programming for computational pharmacokinetics in drug discovery and development. Genetic Programming and Evolvable Machines 8(4), 17–26 (2007)
3. Dignum, S., Poli, R.: Generalisation of the limiting distribution of program sizes in tree-based genetic programming and analysis of its effects on bloat. In: Thierens, D., et al. (eds.) GECCO 2007: Proceedings of the 9th annual conference on Genetic and evolutionary computation, vol. 2, pp. 1588–1595. ACM Press, New York (2007)
4. Dignum, S., Poli, R.: Crossover, sampling, bloat and the harmful effects of size limits. In: O'Neill, M., Vanneschi, L., Gustafson, S., Esparcia Alcázar, A.I., De Falco, I., Della Cioppa, A., Tarantino, E. (eds.) EuroGP 2008. LNCS, vol. 4971, pp. 158–169. Springer, Heidelberg (2008)
5. Dignum, S., Poli, R.: Operator equalisation and bloat free GP. In: O'Neill, M., Vanneschi, L., Gustafson, S., Esparcia Alcázar, A.I., De Falco, I., Della Cioppa, A., Tarantino, E. (eds.) EuroGP 2008. LNCS, vol. 4971, pp. 110–121. Springer, Heidelberg (2008)
6. Yoshida, F., Topliss, J.G.: QSAR model for drug human oral bioavailability. Journal of Medicinal Chemistry 43, 2575–2585 (2000)
7. Fernandez, F., Tomassini, M., Vanneschi, L.: An empirical study of multipopulation genetic programming. Genetic Programming and Evolvable Machines 4(1), 21–51 (2003)
8. Colmenarejo, G., Alvarez-Pedraglio, A., Lavandera, J.L.: Chemoinformatic models to predict binding affinities to human serum albumin. Journal of Medicinal Chemistry 44, 4370–4378 (2001)
9. Van de Waterbeemd, H., Rose, S.: In: Wermuth, L.G. (ed.) The Practice of Medicinal Chemistry, 2nd edn., pp. 1367–1385. Academic Press, London (2003)
10. Kola, I., Landis, J.: Can the pharmaceutical industry reduce attrition rates? Nature Reviews Dug Discovery 3, 711–716 (2004)
11. Igel, C., Chellapilla, K.: Investigating the influence of depth and degree of genotypic change on fitness in genetic programming. In: Banzhaf, W., et al. (eds.) Proceedings of the Genetic and Evolutionary Computation Conference, vol. 2, pp. 1061–1068. Morgan Kaufmann, San Francisco (1999)
12. Feng, J., Lurati, L., Ouyang, H., Robinson, T., Wang, Y., Yuan, S., Young, S.S.: Predictive toxicology: benchmarking molecular descriptors and statistical methods. Journal of Chemical Information Computer Science 43, 1463–1470 (2003)
13. Luke, S.: Modification point depth and genome growth in genetic programming. Evolutionary Computation 11(1), 67–106 (2003)
14. Luke, S., Panait, L.: Lexicographic parsimony pressure. In: Langdon, W.B., et al. (eds.) GECCO 2002: Proceedings of the Genetic and Evolutionary Computation Conference, pp. 829–836. Morgan Kaufmann Publishers, San Francisco (2002)

15. Poli, R., Langdon, W.B., Dignum, S.: On the limiting distribution of program sizes in tree-based genetic programming. In: Ebner, M., et al. (eds.) Proceedings of the 10th European Conference on Genetic Programming, Valencia, Spain, April 11 - 13, pp. 193–204. Springer, Heidelberg (2007)
16. Poli, R., McPhee, N.F., Vanneschi, L.: The impact of population size on code growth in GP: analysis and empirical validation. In: Keijzer, M., et al. (eds.) GECCO 2008: Proceedings of the 10th annual conference on Genetic and evolutionary computation, pp. 1275–1282. ACM, New York (2008)
17. Poli, R., Langdon, W.B., McPhee, N.F.: A field guide to genetic programming (2008) (Published), `http://lulu.com`, `http://www.gp-field-guide.org.uk`, (With contributions by J. R. Koza)
18. Todeschini, R., Consonni, V.: Handbook of Molecular Descriptors. Wiley-VCH, Weinheim (2000)
19. Rissanen, J.: Modeling by shortest data description. Automatica 14, 465–471 (1978)
20. David, S., Wishart, Knox, C., Guo, A.C., Shrivastava, S., Hassanali, M., Stothard, P., Chang, Z., Woolsey, J.: DrugBank: a comprehensive resource for in silico drug discovery and exploration. Nucleic Acids Research, 34 (2006), doi:10.1093/nar/gkj067
21. Silva, S.: GPLAB – a genetic programming toolbox for MATLAB, version 3.0 (2009) `http://gplab.sourceforge.net`
22. Silva, S., Almeida, J.: Dynamic maximum tree depth. In: Cantú-Paz, E., et al. (eds.) Genetic and Evolutionary Computation – GECCO-2003, pp. 1776–1787. Springer, Heidelberg (2003)
23. Silva, S., Costa, E.: Dynamic limits for bloat control in genetic programming and a review of past and current bloat theories. Genetic Programming and Evolvable Machines 10(2), 141–179 (2009) (Published Online January 13, 2009)
24. Silva, S., Dignum, S.: Extending operator equalisation: Fitness based self adaptive length distribution for bloat free GP. In: Vanneschi, L., et al. (eds.) Proceedings of the 12th European Conference on Genetic Programming, EuroGP2009, pp. 159–170. Springer, Heidelberg (2009)
25. Silva, S., Vanneschi, L.: Operator Equalisation, Bloat and Overfitting - A Study on Human Oral Bioavailability Prediction. In: Rothlauf, F., et al. (eds.) Proceedings of GECCO-2009, ACM Press, New York (to appear, 2009)
26. Kennedy, T.: Managing the drug discovery/development interface. Drug Discovery Today 2, 436–444 (1997)
27. Martin, T.M., Young, D.M.: Prediction of the Acute Toxicity (96-h LC50) of Organic Compounds to the Fathead Minnow (Pimephales promelas) Using a Group Contribution Method. Chemical Research in Toxicology 14(10), 1378–1385 (2001)
28. Tetko, I.V., Gasteiger, J., Todeschini, R., Mauri, A., Livingstone, D., Ertl, P., Palyulin, V.A., Radchenko, E.V., Zefirov, N.S., Makarenko, A.S., Tanchuk, V.Y., Prokopenko, V.V.: Virtual computational chemistry laboratory - design and description. Journal of Computer Aided Molecular Design 19, 453–463 (2005)
29. Vanneschi, L., Tomassini, M., Collard, P., Clergue, M.: Fitness distance correlation in structural mutation genetic programming. In: Ryan, C., Soule, T., Keijzer, M., Tsang, E.P.K., Poli, R., Costa, E. (eds.) EuroGP 2003. LNCS, vol. 2610, pp. 455–464. Springer, Heidelberg (2003)
30. Langdon, W.B., Barrett, S.J.: Genetic Programming in data mining for drug discovery. In: Evolutionary computing in data mining, pp. 211–235 (2004)

Chapter 3

CMBSB – Computational Methods in Bioinformatics and Systems Biology

Syntactic Parsing for Bio-molecular Event Detection from Scientific Literature

Sérgio Matos[1], Anabela Barreiro[2], and José Luis Oliveira[1]

[1] IEETA, Universidade de Aveiro, Campus Universitário de Santiago, 3810-193 Aveiro, Portugal
[2] Faculdade de Letras, Universidade do Porto, Via Panorâmica, 4150-564 Porto, Portugal
{aleixomatos,jlo}@ua.pt, barreiro_anabela@hotmail.com

Abstract. Rapid advances in science and in laboratorial and computing methods are generating vast amounts of data and scientific literature. In order to keep up-to-date with the expanding knowledge in their field of study, researchers are facing an increasing need for tools that help manage this information. In the genomics field, various databases have been created to save information in a formalized and easily accessible form. However, human curators are not capable of updating these databases at the same rate new studies are published. Advanced and robust text mining tools that automatically extract newly published information from scientific articles are required. This paper presents a methodology, based on syntactic parsing, for identification of gene events from the scientific literature. Evaluation of the proposed approach, based on the BioNLP shared task on event extraction, produced an average F-score of 47.1, for six event types.

Keywords: Biomedical literature, information extraction, bio-molecular events, syntactic parsing, semantic properties.

1 Introduction

Recent advances in biotechnology, namely the widespread use of high-throughput methods for gene analysis, have originated vast amounts of published scientific literature. While much of the data and results described in these studies are being annotated in the various existing biomedical databases, these are not easily kept up-to-date. As a result, many relevant research outcomes are still enclosed as free-text in the scientific literature, which remains the major source of information for researchers [1]. It is therefore increasingly difficult for researchers to keep track of the quickly expanding biomedical knowledge to support their experiment planning and analysis of results [2][3].

Researchers are currently faced with issues such as (i) how to identify the most relevant articles for their specific study, (ii) how to identify the mentioned concepts (genes, proteins, diseases and so on) and relations between them, and (iii) how to integrate the extracted information with the existing knowledge in a simple, efficient, and user-friendly manner [2][4]. This integrated view of information extracted from literature, in the framework of more systematized and formalized knowledge annotated in databases and ontologies, is an important requisite for biological data analysis [3].

L. Seabra Lopes et al. (Eds.): EPIA 2009, LNAI 5816, pp. 79–85, 2009.

To address these issues, several tools have been developed in the past years that combine Information Extraction (IE), Text Mining (TM) and Natural Language Processing (NLP) techniques with the domain knowledge available in resources such as the Entrez Gene, UniProt, GO or UMLS [1][2][4][5]. Such tools process text titles and abstracts from the MEDLINE/PubMed [6] literature database and present the extracted information in different forms. The iHOP tool [7] identifies genes and proteins in PubMed abstracts and uses them as links, allowing the navigation through sentences and abstracts. The AliBaba system [8] is based on pattern matching and co-occurrence statistics to find associations between biological entities such as genes, proteins or diseases, and presents the search results in the form of a graph. EBIMed [9] also finds associations between protein/gene names, GO annotations, drugs and species in PubMed abstracts resulting from a user query. The results are displayed in a table with links to the sentences and abstracts that support the corresponding associations. A similar tool, FACTA [10] retrieves abstracts from PubMed and identifies biomedical concepts (e.g. genes/proteins, diseases, enzymes and chemical compounds) co-occurring with the user query term. The concepts are presented to the user in a tabular format and ranked based on the co-occurrence statistics or on pointwise mutual information.

More recently, there has been some focus on applying more detailed linguistic processing in order to improve information retrieval and extraction. Chilibot [11] retrieves sentences from PubMed abstracts related to a pair or a list of proteins, genes, or keywords, and applies shallow parsing to classify these sentences as interactive, non-interactive or simple abstract co-occurrence. The identified relationships between entities or keywords are then displayed as a graph. MEDIE [12] uses a deep-parser and a term recognizer to index abstracts based on pre-computed semantic annotations, allowing for real-time retrieval of sentences containing biological concepts associated with the terms specified in the user query.

Interest in the application of more advanced methods of linguistic processing is also evident in the recent information extraction evaluation challenges, namely the BioNLP shared task on event extraction [13] and the BioCreAtIvE II.5 challenge [14], which investigate the extraction of gene events from literature. In this paper, we describe a methodology based on syntactic parsing to detect and annotate bio-molecular events, such as protein production and breakdown, localization or binding events. We present results from our participation in the BioNLP shared task and discuss the main difficulties and further developments required in this area.

2 Methods

The method described in this paper to identify bio-molecular events is based on syntactic grammars that process texts and detect the occurrence of linguistic patterns that describe such events. Syntactic parsing was implemented using NooJ [15], a freely available development environment and linguistic processing engine that includes tools for inflectional and derivational morphology, syntactic grammars and semantics.

NooJ uses dictionaries and grammars to produce formalized descriptions of natural language and contains a system of inflectional and derivational paradigms, which interacts with the dictionary. Inflectional rules apply to a dictionary entry (lemma) to recognize and generate inflected forms, including gender, number and tense. Derivational rules apply to a dictionary entry to recognize and generate derived forms, such as nominalizations (predicate nouns morphosyntactically related to a verb) as adopted in [16]. Lemmas can also have semantic information included. Semantic properties allow, for example, adding the characteristic of a particular named entity, such as 'ORGANISM', 'PROTEIN' or 'DISEASE'. These properties are illustrated in Table 1.

Table 1. Dictionary entries in NooJ

Lemma	PoS	FLX	Semantic properties	ID	TAXID
human	N	TABLE	ORGANISM		9606
Homo sapiens	N		ORGANISM		9606
Breast cancer type 1 susceptibility protein	N		PROTEIN	P38398	9606
BRCA1	N		PROTEIN	P38398	9606
BRCA1	N		PROTEIN	P48754	10090
BRCA1	N		GENE	672	9606
RNF53	N		GENE	672	9606

To create the dictionaries used in this method, we adapted the verb dictionary from the biomedical resource BioLexicon [17][18]. BioLexicon includes verbs that occur frequently in the biomedical literature and that usually describe a specific event, such as "express", "bind" and "transcribe". We enhanced the BioLexicon dictionary with inflectional ("FLX") and derivational ("DRV") attributes and with semantic properties, as shown in Table 2. For example, ION:TABLE represents the derivational and inflectional paradigms for the nominalization "expression" (which inflects as the word TABLE), and ABOLISH represents the inflectional paradigm for the verb "express".

The semantic properties in NooJ dictionaries were used to assign specific event types to the verbs in the literature that describe those events. In Table 2, the verb "stimulate", for example, is assigned a semantic property "EventType" with a value "Positive_Regulation". This semantic property is then used in the syntactic grammars, which add an annotation to that type of event whenever it is detected in texts.

Table 2. Definition of verbs in the dictionary

Lemma	PoS	DRV	FLX	EventType
express	V	ION:TABLE	ABOLISH	Gene_expression
ligate	V	TION:TABLE	SMILE	Binding
stimulate	V	TION:TABLE	SMILE	Positive_regulation

The inflectional and derivational paradigms are described in terms of re-write rules. For example, the noun inflectional paradigm "TABLE", defines that the plural of the dictionary word associated with this rule is formed by adding an "s" to the lemma. Hence, the plural of any word associated with the attribute "+FLX=TABLE" (ex. "human") will be obtained in the same way. In the case of verbs, inflectional rules describe the conjugation of the verb. For example, the inflectional paradigm "SMILE" defines re-write rules in terms of person, number and tense for verbs that conjugate like the verb "to smile". Similarly, the derivational system allows the derivation of a word, as defined by the derivational rule. This allows, for example, obtaining nouns and adjectives from verb entries. The derived word maintains the semantic properties of the word from which is derived (lemma). Thus, the predicate noun "stimulation" is produced and linked to a positive regulation event, through its inherited semantic properties from the verb "stimulate".

In order to define the type of events linked to each verb, we used the training data in the BioNLP shared task. Based on the manual linguistic annotations, we extracted the sentences corresponding to each event, and assigned the event type to the verbs found on those sentences. We then manually checked this list and selected only those verbs showing a specific link to a type of event. In case verbs were linked to more than one event type, only the most frequent event type was selected, and the remaining ones removed.

In NooJ, syntactic grammars can be used to process sequences of tokens to recognize and annotate multiword expressions. In the approach used, our aim was to detect linguistic patterns, based on named entities (genes and proteins) and on biologically relevant verbs and verb nominalizations referencing some type of bio-molecular event. These entities, verbs and nouns are automatically annotated by NooJ when the dictionaries and grammars are applied to texts.

In order to create the relevant grammars, we first used NooJ to extract general concordances from the texts that included an annotated gene or protein and a verb or nominalization. We then identified, in the examples provided by the concordances, specific grammatical constructions describing different types of events. For example, we were able to identify a simple pattern composed of a nominalization, the particle 'of' and a named gene or protein, as in "expression of p53" or "stimulation of CD4". These patterns were described in terms of syntactic grammars, as illustrated in Fig. 1. The output of the grammar (shown below the connecting lines) identifies the protein ("CD4"), the expression referencing the event ("stimulation") and the type of event.

Construction and refinement of the syntactic grammars is an iterative process. After creating a baseline grammar to describe a particular construction, we try to incorporate syntactic-semantic variants (paraphrases) in order to achieve better recall, without compromising precision. For example, the grammar used to identify the construction "expression of p53" should also be able to identify "expression of gene p53" or "expression of the human gene p53". The training and development data sets of the shared task were used during this iterative process.

The semantic properties included in the dictionary are used in the syntactic grammars to specify the event type in the annotation. Example 1 shows the output of the grammar in Fig. 1: "CD4" is the named entity and "stimulation" is the expression identifying the bio-molecular event. The event type, "positive regulation", is obtained directly from the expression's semantic properties.

Example 1. Grammar output used to annotate the expression in texts

```
Stimulation of human CD4
<EVENT+PROTEIN=CD4+EXP=Stimulation+TYPE=Positive_regula
tion>
```

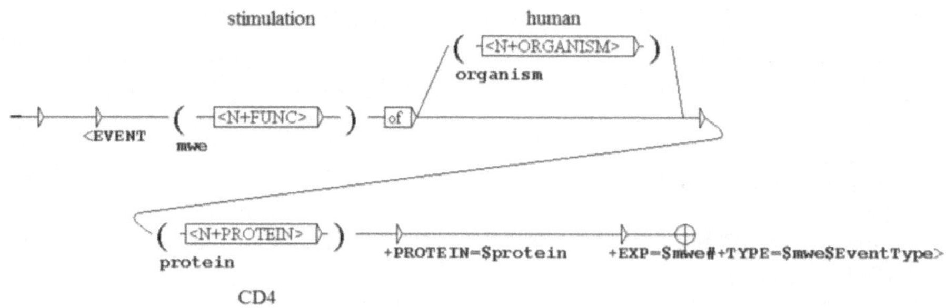

Fig. 1. Grammar to detect phrases, such as "stimulation of CD4"

3 Results

The application of the grammars described in the previous section allowed the extraction of phrases that reference gene related events. Table 3 shows some examples of the patterns described by these grammars and the corresponding concordances found in texts. Although these are relatively simple patterns, they can model a large portion of the language used to present such events.

Table 3. Patterns detected by the grammars

Pattern	Concordance in text
<entity> [<entity_type>] <nominalization>	*HSP gene expression*
<nominalization> "of" [<entity_type>] <entity>	*upregulation of Fas*
<entity> [<entity_type>] <be> ["not"] [<adverb>] <verb>	*IL-2R stimulation was totally inhibited*
<verb> <preposition> <entity>	*binding of TRAF2*
<verb> <nominalization> "of" <entity>	*suppressing activation of STAT6*

This section presents the evaluation results of the proposed method, obtained using the test data from the BioNLP shared task on event extraction. This data set was not used for defining the semantic properties to include in the dictionary or for creating the syntactic grammars. The aim of the shared task was to detect gene events in PubMed abstracts and create the corresponding annotations, including the protein(s) involved, the referencing expression or trigger and the type of event. The data for the BioNLP task was derived from the GENIA event corpus and comprised 800 abstracts in the training set, 150 in the development set, and 260 in the test set. Details on the annotation procedure and evaluation metrics are described in [13].

The BioNLP shared task divided events into nine types. The regulatory events were not included in this study due to time constraints and to the more complex structure of those events. Results for the remaining six event types are displayed in Table 4. These results were achieved using six grammars similar to the one exemplified in Fig. 1. An average F-score of 47.11 was obtained. Except for binding events, the results are promising and show that a good performance can be obtained using this simple approach. In

Table 4. Performance of the event detection method (test data)

Event type	Recall	Precision	F-score
Localization	35.63	70.45	47.33
Binding	13.54	34.06	19.38
Gene Expression	46.40	78.45	58.31
Transcription	33.58	41.07	36.95
Protein Catabolism	35.71	62.50	45.45
Phosphorylation	49.63	79.76	61.19
Average	36.76	65.58	47.11

the case of binding events, the participation of two proteins creates extra difficulty in describing such events, and the results are still poor.

4 Discussion

We have described an approach which uses syntactic grammars to detect and annotate gene events from the scientific literature. The proposed method takes advantage of the inflectional and derivational morphology and the semantic properties established in dictionaries and grammars developed with NooJ, which allow to associate terminological verbs and their derivations to specific event types. This approach provides a general and flexible solution for information extraction from biomedical texts.

The results illustrated in Table 4 indicate that this approach can be used to process the literature and extract networks of events and interactions. These networks are valuable for literature search and navigation, as proposed in MEDIE or Chilibot tools, but require much less processing. However, some shortcomings need to be considered and improved. The first limitation is related to named entity recognition. In the BioNLP shared task, participants were supplied with the names and positions in text of mentioned genes and proteins. In such a setup, recognizing linguistic patterns where these entities occur is significantly simplified. In a more realistic task, the processing pipeline would not have the list of mentioned entities as an input and a named entity recognizer with a very good performance needs to be included in the processing steps.

Another limitation concerns the identification of patterns and creation of grammars. Although a manual procedure such as the one taken can identify the most salient linguistic patterns, it would be interesting to investigate the possibility to generate and assess new patterns automatically. In this study, we have not included the gene regulatory events because these are frequently referenced by more complex constructions which are not yet covered by our grammars. Describing and extracting these events is of great importance and will become a future direction of our work.

Finally, it is important to assess the advantages and disadvantages of the proposed approach for identifying relations and events, when compared to other methods based on shallow or deep parsing.

Methods such as the one proposed in this paper can be used to help database curators identify the most relevant facts in the literature and speed-up the annotation process. Tools based on these methods can also provide alternative querying and browsing of facts cited in the literature and be useful for researchers. However, before these methods can be truly useful, they must be included in user-oriented tools that offer robust and reliable performance while hiding the complexity of the linguistic processing. It is also of major importance that these tools keep links to the reference databases so that users can navigate from the literature to these resources and back, in a simple and fluid way.

References

1. Rebholz-Schuhmann, D., Kirsch, H., Couto, F.: Facts from text: is text mining ready to deliver? PLoS Biol. 3, e65 (2005)
2. Altman, R.B., Bergman, C.M., Blake, J., Blaschke, C., Cohen, A., Gannon, F., Grivell, L., Hahn, U., Hersh, W., Hirschman, L., Jensen, L.J., Krallinger, M., Mons, B., O'Donoghue, S.I., Peitsch, M.C., Rebholz-Schuhmann, D., Shatkay, H., Valencia, A.: Text mining for biology - the way forward: opinions from leading scientists. Genome Biology 9(suppl. 2), S7 (2008)
3. Jensen, L.J., Saric, J., Bork, P.: Literature mining for the biologist: from information retrieval to biological discovery. Nat. Rev. Genet. 7, 119–129 (2006)
4. Shatkay, H.: Hairpins in bookstacks: Information retrieval from biomedical text. Briefings in Bioinformatics 6(3), 222–238 (2005)
5. Weeber, M., Kors, J.A., Mons, B.: Online tools to support literature-based discovery in the life sciences. Briefings in Bioinformatics 6(3), 27–286 (2005)
6. PubMed, `http://www.ncbi.nlm.nih.gov/pubmed/`
7. Hoffmann, R., Valencia, A.: iHOP - A Gene Network for Navigating the Literature. Nature Genetics 36, 664 (2004)
8. Plake, C., Schiemann, T., Pankalla, M., Hakenberg, J., Leser, U.: Ali Baba: PubMed as a graph. Bioinformatics 22(19), 2444–2445 (2006)
9. Rebholz-Schuhmann, D., Kirsch, H., Arregui, M., Gaudan, S., Riethoven, M., Stoehr, P.: EBIMed–text crunching to gather facts for proteins from Medline. Bioinformatics 23(2), 237–244 (2007)
10. Tsuruoka, Y., Tsujii, J., Ananiadou, S.: FACTA: a text search engine for finding associated biomedical concepts. Bioinformatics 24(21), 2559–2560 (2008)
11. Chen, H., Sharp, B.M.: Content-rich biological network constructed by mining PubMed abstracts. BMC Bioinformatics 5, 147 (2008)
12. Miyao, Y., Ohta, T., Masuda, K., Tsuruoka, Y., Yoshida, K., Ninomiya, T., Tsujii, J.: Semantic Retrieval for the Accurate Identification of Relational Concepts in Massive Textbases. In: Proceedings of COLING-ACL 2006, Sydney, pp. 1017–1102. (2006)
13. Kim, J.-D., Ohta, T., Pyysalo, S., Kano, Y., Tsujii, J.: Overview of BioNLP 2009 Shared Task on Event Extraction. In: Proceedings of Natural Language Processing in Biomedicine (BioNLP) NAACL 2009 Workshop (2009)
14. BioCreAtIvE - Critical Assessment of Information Extraction Systems in Biology, `http://www.biocreative.org/`
15. NooJ, `http://www.nooj4nlp.net/`
16. Barreiro, A.M.: Make it simple with paraphrases: Automated paraphrasing for authoring aids and machine translation. PhD dissertation. Faculdade de Letras da Universidade do Porto, Porto (2008)
17. Sasaki, Y., Montemagni, S., Pezik, P., Rebholz-Schuhmann, D., McNaught, J., Ananiadou, S.: BioLexicon: A Lexical Resource for the Biology Domain. In: Proceedings of the Third International Symposium on Semantic Mining in Biomedicine (2008)
18. BOOTStrep Bio-Lexicon, `http://www.nactem.ac.uk/biolexicon/`

Constraint-Based Strategy for Pairwise RNA Secondary Structure Prediction

Olivier Perriquet and Pedro Barahona

CENTRIA - Centre for Artificial Intelligence - Dep. de Informática,
FCT/UNL - Quinta da Torre 2829-516 CAPARICA - Portugal
Tel.: (+351) 21 294 8536; Fax: (+351) 21 294 8541
olivier@perriquet.net, pb@di.fct.unl.pt

Abstract. RNA secondary structure prediction depends on context. When only a few (sometimes putative) RNA homologs are available, one of the most famous approach is based on a set of recursions proposed by Sankoff in 1985. Although this modus operandi insures an algorithmically optimal result, the main drawback lies in its prohibitive time and space complexities. A series of heuristics were developed to face that difficulty and turn the recursions usable. In front of the inescapable intricacy of the question when handling the full thermodynamic model, we come back in the present paper to a biologically simplified model that helps focusing on the algorithmic issues we want to overcome. We expose our ongoing developments by using the constraints framework which we believe is a powerful paradigm for heuristic design. We give evidence that the main heuristics proposed by others (structural and alignment banding, multi-loop restriction) can be refined in order to produce a substantial gain both in time computation and space requirements. A beta implementation of our approach, that we named ARNICA, exemplify that gain on a sample set that remains unaffordable to other methods. The sources and sample tests of ARNICA are available at http://centria.di.fct.unl.pt/~op/arnica.tar.gz

1 Introduction

The interest for RNA secondary structure prediction in the last decades may be driven by the combination of two reasons, a biological one and a theoretical one. From the biological viewpoint, RNA secondary structure prediction is a challenging problem to help bridging the gap between the different levels of description of the structure [CMR08, SYKB07]. The discovery of new families of non-coding RNA (ncRNA) demands adapted tools to predict or at least provide information about their structure, and the programs that compute secondary structure naturally organize themselves along several noticeable directions that implicitly depend on their context of use. When the family of sequences under consideration is large enough and the sequences not too divergent, a good multiple alignment is obtained by sequence alignment methods ([OH98] assess the reliability of such methods for rRNA) or by semi-automated methods. The structure

L. Seabra Lopes et al. (Eds.): EPIA 2009, LNAI 5816, pp. 86–97, 2009.

prediction programs based on covariation analysis [ED94, KH03] can then handle the alignment and they have proven to be very accurate in guessing the structure in that context. With a small family of poorly conserved RNA sequences, a good starting alignment can hardly be constructed, resulting usually in the inapplicability of the methods based on pre-alignment. In that second context it makes sense to search for the alignment and the structure at the same time. Sankoff [San85] pioneered the field by exhibiting a set of recursions to optimally compute the best structural alignment of two RNA sequences when the structure is not known a priori. These recursions can be straightforwardly extended to N sequences and can also handle the energy parameters traditionally used for energy minimization [MSZT99]. Although the time and space complexities for two sequences remains polynomial (resp. $O(n^6)$ and $O(n^4)$ if their lengths are the same order of magnitude n), the algorithm is not applicable without heuristic adaptations. From this more abstract point of view, RNA structural alignment becomes a challenging problem in terms of algorithmic issues. Diverse heuristic ideas were applied in able to turn the recursions usable. The first implementation of the Sankoff recursions was DYNALIGN [MT02, HSM07] that reduced the complexity to $O(M^2n^2)$ in space and $O(M^3n^3)$ in time, where M is a (tunable) hard constant which bounds the shift allowed between the two sequences. [HLSG05, HTG07] investigated further (FOLDALIGN) by combining other different restrictions, namely:

- **alignment banding:** like in DYNALIGN the maximal shift between the sequences is bounded by a constant δ
- **structural banding:** the default behavior for the program is to perform a local alignment and the maximal size for a common motif is bounded by λ
- **multi-loop restriction:** the structure bifurcativity is limited in multi-loops

The resulting space and time complexities in FOLDALIGN become $0(n^2\lambda\delta)$ and $0(n^2\lambda^2\delta^2)$. The Vienna RNA Package also proposes an alternative attempt PMComp [HBS04] which is implemented as part of the RNAfold program and makes use of the McCaskill algorithm to compute the probabilities of base pairings for a single sequence [McC90]. The authors of FOLDALIGN then revisited the idea by integrating their banding heuristic to PMComp [THG07].

Although these heuristics allow the application of the algorithm of Sankoff on natural RNA sequences, some recalcitrant contexts still remain where the method stays inapplicable. When the sequences under consideration show a large difference of length, poor conservation at the primary level or important structural variations, all Sankoff-based method either do not apply or – if they do – the banding heuristics prevent the algorithm from finding the correct structure, while the memory and time consumption explodes. One of the main drawbacks of this kind of heuristics is their global nature: they cannot take advantage of local similarities in the sequences. When performing a global structural alignment, the shift restriction δ should be at least the difference of length between the sequences. FOLDALIGN bypasses the later difficulty by doing local alignment as a default behavior. In this paper we prove that the banding can be local, which results in a huge gain, both in memory and time consumption. We also propose a strategy to guarantee optimality in our framework even if we are using a heuristic. The strategy is presented in terms of constraints, as we believe indeed that the constraint paradigm (already in use for other kind of methods, like CONSAN [DE06] or STEMLOC [Hol05]) is helpful and relevant to model the forthcoming improvements of our method. We observe that the recursions of Sankoff are a natural combination of the two kinds of recursions it is supposed to extend: sequence alignment and secondary structure prediction. Likewise, a structural alignment may be modeled as a subgraph of a combination of two graphs - an alignment graph and a folding graph. Imposing structural constraints on those graphs may lead to efficient heuristic design. The authors of FOLDALIGN already proposed a combination of constraints on each of these graphs, namely alignment banding and structural banding ; the next section proposes a framework that allows for the integration of more accurate constraints. Experimental results are given in the last section.

2 Applying Constraints on the Recursions of Sankoff

Alignments – An alignment of two sequences may be seen as a subgraph of the full bipartite graph where the nodes are the respective positions in each sequence. Such a subgraph (see Figure 1) is said to be an alignment if the following conditions hold: (1) the arity of each node is at most one, and (2) there is no crossing edge (we assume the nodes are placed in the sequence order). Moreover, we impose the extra restriction of maximality (3) no edge can be added without breaking one of the two former requirements. If the graph were not maximal in the sense of (3), it would mean that somewhere a deletion followed by an insertion would be preferred to a substitution. When the edges and remaining free bases are weighted according to the usual scoring schemes for two sequences, with linear or affine gap penalties [NW70, EGG88, EGGI92b, EGGI92a] such an alignment is automatically disqualified, since an appropriate shift of the corresponding bases would result immediately in an alignment of better score.

Secondary structure – Once again we consider the sequence as a list of nodes drawn in increasing order. Following the usual definition, a secondary structure is a subgraph of the full graph on these nodes with no crossing edge when drawn in a half plane (a so called outerplanar graph) and for which the node arities are at most one.

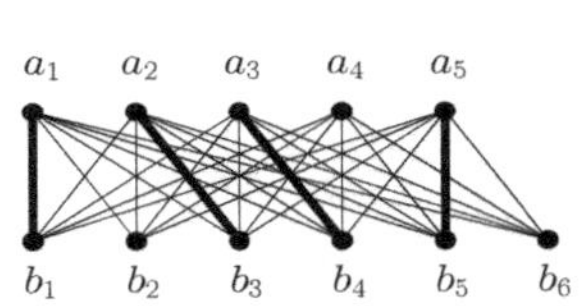

a_1 $-$ a_2 a_3 a_4 a_5 $-$
b_1 b_2 b_3 b_4 $-$ b_5 b_6

Fig. 1. An alignment can be seen as a subgraph of the full bipartite graph, we highlighted here the subgraph corresponding to a sample alignment

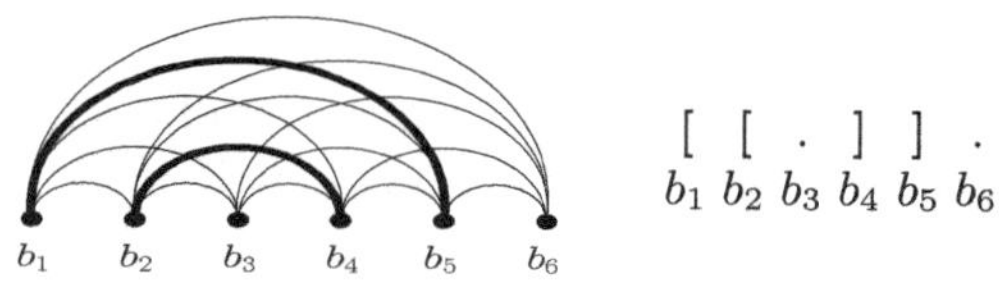

Fig. 2. A secondary structure and the corresponding subgraph

In our framework, a structural alignment of two sequences can be represented as a combination of three graphs: an alignment graph and two structure graphs, like in Figure 3. In the following, we will call **structural envelope** any graph that contains the structural alignment we are searching for. In practice, the structural envelope is not the full graph. For instance the steric constraints of the molecule imply that the minimal size for a loop should be three bases, consequently we can already remove all the edges that do not fulfill that constraint. In the next section, we investigate how the efficiency of the algorithm can be improved when extra constraints are imposed on the structural envelope.

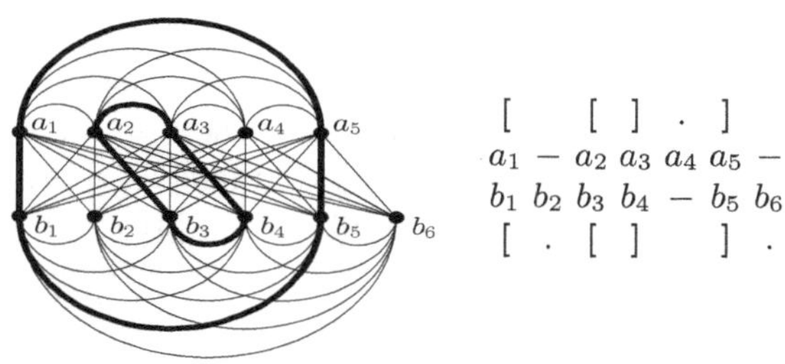

Fig. 3. Example of a structural alignment seen as a subgraph of its structural envelope. The structural envelope holds no constraint here.

The recursions of Sankoff – The recursion set used in RNA prediction methods based on free energy minimization [JTZ89, ZMT99, Zuk03, Hof03] is a more complex version of the Nussinov formulas [NJ80]. We express here the recursions given by Sankoff in the simplified model of Nussinov and we discuss later how far they can be extended to a more sophisticated model with no loss in complexity. While, for Nussinov, two indices are needed to represent any segment of the sequence under consideration, in the case of Sankoff, four indices are requiered to represent any pair of segment. We note $seq_0 = seq_0[1..n]$ and $seq_1 = seq_1[1..m]$ the two sequences in use. The Sankoff recursions call for the computation of a four-dimensional matrix where a cell $\mathbf{e}\ [i, j, k, l]$ stores the score of the best structural alignement of the pair of segments $seq_0[i..j]$ and $seq_1[k..l]$.

$$
\mathbf{e}\ [i,j,k,l] := \mathbf{MAX} \begin{cases} \mathbf{e}\ [i,j-1,k,l-1] + \mathbf{align\_base}(seq_0[j], seq_1[l]) \\ \mathbf{e}\ [i,j,k,l-1] + \mathbf{gap\_penalty}() \\ \mathbf{e}\ [i,j-1,k,l] + \mathbf{gap\_penalty}() \\ \mathbf{e}\ [i,x-1,k,y-1] + \mathbf{e}\ [x+1,j-1,y+1,l-1] + \\ \quad \mathbf{match\_pair}(seq_0[x], seq_0[j], seq_1[y], seq_1[l]) \\ \qquad [i \leqslant x \leqslant j] \qquad [k \leqslant y \leqslant l] \end{cases}
$$

The value $\mathbf{e}\,[1, n, 1, m]$ gives the best score for a structural alignment in that model. Any of the corresponding best alignments can be retrieved in linear time by tracing back into the dynamic programming matrix if the corresponding pairings that maximize the score were stored during the search, which would require only $\mathrm{O}(n^2)$ space. In that form, the Sankoff recursions may be considered, in a certain sense, a combination of the recursions for sequence alignment [SW81] and the recursions for secondary structure prediction of Nussinov. The Sankoff algorithm can integrate any Boolean restraints imposed (by the user or by automated methods) on the structural envelope by simply assigning an infinite score to the forbidden matches. What we show is that these constraints can be used to reduce both memory and time consumption.

Constraining the alignment – Two bases, belonging to each sequence (or their index in the respective sequence) are said to be **alignable** if they are allowed to participate in the final alignment. We call the resulting subgraph the **alignment envelope**, as termed by Eddy and Holmes [Hol05, DE06] (Dowell and Eddy use a series of highly reliable single anchor points that they call *pins* to restrain the alignment. In our case, we do not adopt the same perspective: rather than anchoring the sequence alignment, we simply restrict it by constraints). In Figure 4, we show such an alignment envelope where we only represented the edges for one index in each sequence. For a given index i of arity M_i in the first sequence, we note $a_i = a_i[0 \,..\, M_i] = \{\ a_i[0]\ ,\ ..\ ,\ a_i[M_i]\ \}$ the list of alignable bases, and for k in the second sequence, of arity N_k, we note b_k the list of its alignable bases in the first sequence. The sequence banding heuristic used in DYNALIGN and FOLDALIGN gives for any index a list of contiguous bases of fixed length δ where the value for δ is a global constant. In our case, alignable bases in a list do not need to be contiguous in the sequence.

If a linear gap penalty is used and a double indel is assumed to be always worse than a substitution, only a reduced 4D-matrix needs to be allocated (Figure 5). Like for the banding heuristic, only the indices corresponding to the admissible pairs of segments need to be allocated but in our case, we are far more flexible on the possible indices, as discussed in the last paragraph. We prove that when a

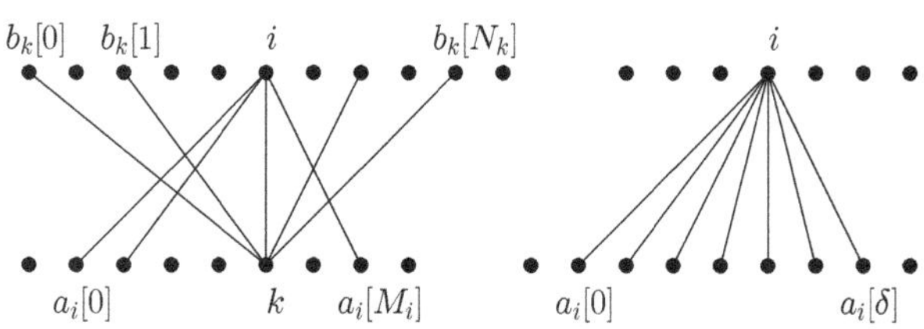

Fig. 4. On the left are represented the lists a_i and b_k of alignable bases for some indices i and k. We note M_i the length of a_i and N_k the length of b_k. The figure on the right shows the list of contiguous indices for an arbitrary index i when using a sequence banding heuristic with a fixed global constant δ, like in DYNALIGN and FOLDALIGN.

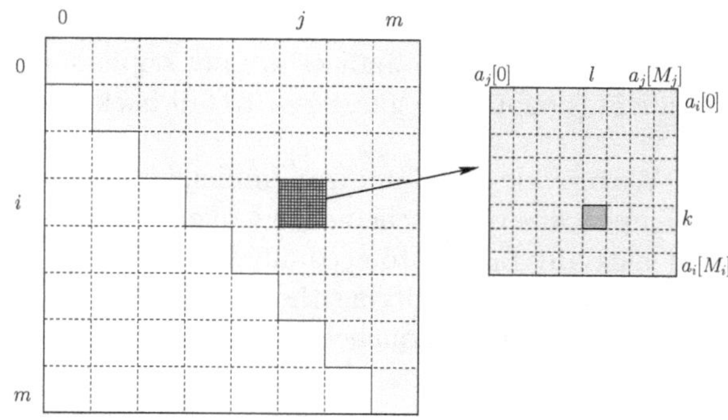

Fig. 5. The 4-dimensional matrix used for the computation of the best structural alignment can be represented as a bi-dimensional matrix, each cell being a bi-dimensional matrix. The value in the cell $[i, j, x, y]$ stores the score for the best structural alignment between the segments $seq_0[i..j]$ and $seq_1[a_i[x]..a_i[y]]$.

recursive call falls out of that allocated matrix during the computation process, the best structural alignment between any segments $seq_0[i..j]$ and $seq_1[k..l]$ can be retrieved in constant time from the allocated part of the 4D-matrix. The demonstration of that result may not be valid for more sophisticated scoring schemes and would also have to be adapted for more than two sequences, where the second assumption about the preference of a substitution over a double indel is not always true in an optimal multiple alignment.

To prove that the score $\mathbf{e}\ [i, j, k, l]$ can be retrieved in constant time from the reduced matrix of Figure 5, let's assume that during the computation $\mathbf{e}\ [i, j, k, l]$ falls out of the matrix. This means that either i and k are not alignable and/or j and l are not alignable. We detail the right hand case, the other one is symmetric. Given two non-empty segments $[i..j]$ and $[k..l]$, belonging to each sequence, if j and l are not alignable then either j align with some base in $[k..l]$, or l with some base in $[i..j]$. Otherwise j and l would both create an indel and the optimal alignment of the two segments would then result in a double indel which was previously assumed to be more expensive than a substitution. Let's assume first that l aligns with a base in $[i..j]$. Consequently $[i..j] \bigcap b_l \neq \emptyset$. Let's call $\beta_l = max([i..j] \bigcap b_l)$. Every base of the segment $[\beta_{l+1}..j]$ has no alignable partner in $[k..l]$ or it would contradict the maximality of β_l. The remaining sequence $seq_0[\beta_{l+1}..j]$ has no other possibility than being deleted, resulting in a $(j - \beta_l)$ long gap in the alignment. This gives:

$$\mathbf{e}\ [i, j, k, l] = \mathbf{e}\ [i, \beta_l, k, l] + (j - \beta_l) * \textbf{gap\_penalty}$$

If l does not align, then j must align with some base in $[k..l]$ and we pose $\alpha_j = max([k..l] \bigcap a_j)$. In that case we must have:

$$\mathbf{e}\ [i, j, k, l] = \mathbf{e}\ [i, j, k, \alpha_j] + (l - \alpha_j) * \textbf{gap\_penalty}$$

Note that α_j and β_l depend only on three indices and can be precomputed in cubic time so that the former retrieval can then be managed in constant time when the routines are calling an index out of the matrix. The left hand case with indices i and k is symmetric. As the indices are not dependent, a single test on each of the four indices is enough to guarantee to fall back in the allocated part.

Implementation – We provide and discuss an implementation (named ARNICA) based on a rather empirical scoring scheme for sequence alignment and a reduced energy model that partially takes into account the stabilizing effect of base pair stacking in stems, aimed at exemplifying the gain both in space and time consumption when running on live sequences. ARNICA proceeds in three steps, detailled below:

- **1. Setting alignment constraints** - we build the graph of alignable bases by computing all the alignments within a user-specified distance of the optimum alignment value
- **2. Setting structural constraints** - we compute all the pairing probabilities for each sequence and filter with a threshold
- **3. Computing common folding and alignment** - we compute the optimal structural alignment with the recursions of Sankoff

1. Setting alignment constraints – This first phase uses a variant of the standard alignment with affine gap penalty (open_cost = -80, elongation_cost = -30) reminiscent of the algorithm of Waterman [Wat83] that gives for each pair of positions (i, j) the score of the best alignment when the bases at position i in the first sequence and j in the second one are imposed to be aligned. The variant of the algorithm has the same algorithmic complexities than for standard alignment methods. Then we build the adjacency matrix of the alignment envelope by simply applying a threshold (thd): a pair i, j will be allowed to align if there exists at least one alignment passing by this coordinate with a global score exceeding the best alignment score by less than thd.

2. Setting structural constraints – In the second phase, the pairing probabilities are computed for each sequence with the McCaskill algorithm [McC90] and the graph of possible pairings is filtered: two bases for which the pairing probability is less than 1% are not allowed to pair. This has no consequence on the computation space/time but simply increases the quality of the solutions found by discarding spurious base pairs.

3. Computing common folding and alignment – The optimal folding and alignment is computed with the recursions of Sankoff. The alignment part of the score uses a linear gap penalty scheme and the structural part a probability-based score. The combination of two scores of different nature (an alignment score and a structure score, here based on probabilities) is a difficult issue and a full problem in itself, related to the paradox of structural alignment, not discussed in the present paper. The model in use takes into account only indirectly (via the algorithm of McCaskill) the stabilizing and destabilizing effects of stacking. Integrating the full thermodynamic model would provide results more accurate biologically but also call for non-straightforward developments and adaptations. The folding computed by ARNICA is optimal with regard to our model. The

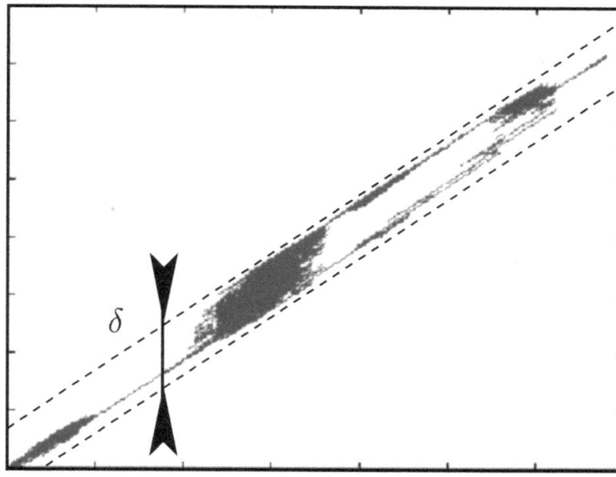

Fig. 6. Suboptimal alignments of two RNase P RNA (D.desulfuricans vs A.eutrophus) showing alternative alignment paths resulting from large zones of deletion. To reach any of these suboptimal alignments with a banding heuristic, the value chosen for the allowed shift δ has to encompass all the possible paths.

next section demonstrate that the method already appears competitive despite the simplicity of the model and that it clearly outperforms other programs based on the same recursions when the data presents uneasy features.

Discussion on complexity – The size of the 4-dimensional matrix to be allocated in the last step obviously increases with the alignment threshold chosen in the first step. If the threshold chosen is infinite, then the alignment envelope is the full bipartite graph and there is no gain over the complexities of the Sankoff recursions. In practice however, our framework is quite effective and far more efficient than any alignment banding heuristic, which is no more than a peculiar case of it. The algorithmic complexities for a Sankoff-based pairwise secondary structure alignment with alignment banding δ are $O(\delta^2 n^2)$ in space and $O(\delta^3 n^3)$ in time (we suppose that $m \sim n$). They can be reformulated as $O(\alpha^2)$ and $O(\alpha^3)$, where $\alpha \sim \delta n$ is the size of the diagonal band corresponding to the alignment envelope induced by the banding heuristic. More precisely, α is the size of the *true* zone in the adjacency matrix of the alignment envelope. As shown on Figure 6, this zone is an exact diagonal band in the banding heuristic, whereas it can be a tunable zone in our framework.

3 First Experimental Results

As our main focus is the difficult context of few poorly conserved RNA sequences, we have selected 7 RNase P RNA of the alpha subdivision taken in the database of Brown [Bro99], showing deep variations in structure, which make them difficult candidates for all Sankoff-based methods, as mentioned by [GG04]. The

Table 1. Average performance of ARNICA and FOLDALIGN on a set of RNase P (alpha subdivision) ; specificity = number of true predicted pairings / total number of predicted pairings ; sensitivity = number of true predicted pairings /number of pairings in the known structure

	option	specificity	sensitivity	time (sec)	space (Mb)
FOLDALIGN	local	56.2%	40.5%	1107	142.1
ARNICA	thd 0	73.6%	43.3%	6	16.5
	thd 10	74.1%	45.9%	7	16.7
	thd 30	75.7%	51.0%	10	17.5
	thd 50	76.2%	55.0%	20	19.1
	thd 80	75.7%	58.3%	77	23.7
	thd 100	74.7%	58.7%	148	29.0
	thd 150	73.9%	60.5%	536	46.5
	thd 200	73.2%	61.0%	1079	64.4

sequences are around 400 bases long with an average identity rate of 64%. A wider performance assessment will be proceeded along with the next improvements on ARNICA. In this paper, we only compared to FOLDALIGN for simplicity, as it is one of the prominent Sankoff-based structural alignment method. The program FOLDALIGN does not allocate the whole needed memory at once: in the comparisons, we always display the maximum amount of memory in use by the program during the computation. To keep in reasonable space and time limits, and given that a memory allocation of several hundreds of Mb would usually result in hours of computation, we stopped the computation whenever the estimated needed resources for memory were above 300Mb. All the tests were run on an IBM thinkpad T40 (pentium 1.5GHz - RAM 512Mb). Table 1 gives the average performances of ARNICA with different values for the threshold, compared to FOLDALIGN ; the results for a medium threshold of 100 are detailed in Table 2. For FOLDALIGN (version 2.1.0), we use the default parameters and the default option of performing a local alignment, as the global option can seldom be chosen, the difference of length being too important between the sequences. However, we indicate in Table 2 the percentage of sequence covered by the structural alignment predicted. When this coverage is close to 100%, the difference between local and global is weak and comparing the performances is meaningful.

On this data set, FOLDALIGN seems to be limited by its heuristic restrictions whereas ARNICA performs better from any point of view (specificity, sensitivity, time and memory usage) remaining fast and low memory consuming. The average gain in computational time and memory with a threshold 100 is by a factor 7 and 5, and the correctness of ARNICA is neighboring 75%. This globally stable behavior despite the divergence of structure is a promising advantage for the integration of a more complete model.

Table 2. Performance of ARNICA and FOLDALIGN on a set of RNase P (alpha subdivision). Each sequence is folded together with each other. We display their percentage of identity and their difference in length (their average length is around 400 bases) [spec1 and spec2 (specificity for each of the two sequences) - sens1 and sens2 (sensitivity) - time is in seconds - mem is in Mb - cov is the percentage of sequence covered by the local alignment given by FOLDALIGN (ARNICA is global)].

				ARNICA						FOLDALIGN						
sequence 1	sequence 2	id	δl	**spec1**	**sens1**	**spec2**	**sens2**	**time**	**mem**	spec1	sens1	spec2	sens2	time	mem	cov
C.crescentus	A.tumefaciens	68%	4	**70%**	**69%**	**74%**	**73%**	**46**	**22.7**	69%	66%	65%	62%	1428	170.5	99%
R.capsulatus	A.tumefaciens	67%	3	**83%**	**81%**	**82%**	**84%**	**31**	**21.4**	59%	54%	74%	71%	1647	181.4	99%
R.capsulatus	C.crescentus	67%	7	**77%**	**58%**	**73%**	**58%**	**55**	**23.6**	49%	33%	45%	32%	1090	169.9	71%
R.palustris	A.tumefaciens	75%	77	**77%**	**59%**	**77%**	**78%**	**87**	**30.1**	36%	17%	42%	26%	1329	200.6	58%
R.palustris	C.crescentus	65%	81	**83%**	**57%**	**77%**	**71%**	**114**	**32.1**	19%	12%	27%	23%	1840	226.5	87%
R.palustris	R.capsulatus	67%	74	**82%**	**61%**	**78%**	**74%**	**287**	**42.4**	24%	16%	27%	23%	2326	262.7	91%
R.prowazekii	A.tumefaciens	60%	17	**75%**	**50%**	**74%**	**48%**	**37**	**21.3**	70%	59%	66%	53%	516	79.0	87%
R.prowazekii	C.crescentus	56%	13	**84%**	**52%**	**80%**	**49%**	**66**	**24.1**	65%	52%	61%	48%	423	76.1	84%
R.prowazekii	R.capsulatus	56%	20	**80%**	**47%**	**83%**	**45%**	**39**	**21.5**	61%	51%	61%	48%	585	75.4	86%
R.prowazekii	R.palustris	60%	94	**78%**	**53%**	**81%**	**41%**	**161**	**31.6**	35%	28%	40%	24%	554	83.9	76%
R.rubrum	A.tumefaciens	74%	27	**70%**	**57%**	**71%**	**65%**	**43**	**23.2**	46%	43%	62%	65%	1991	208.6	98%
R.rubrum	C.crescentus	69%	31	**60%**	**51%**	**64%**	**61%**	**28**	**21.3**	62%	57%	63%	64%	2030	214.4	97%
R.rubrum	R.capsulatus	68%	24	**77%**	**63%**	**81%**	**71%**	**46**	**24.0**	68%	63%	75%	74%	2253	252.2	96%
R.rubrum	R.palustris	74%	50	**80%**	**68%**	**83%**	**60%**	**167**	**34.5**	34%	30%	43%	32%	2960	299.5	91%
R.rubrum	R.prowazekii	55%	44	**39%**	**26%**	**59%**	**45%**	**728**	**57.7**	66%	47%	77%	64%	588	94.4	80%
Wolbachia-sp	A.tumefaciens	60%	54	**67%**	**65%**	**72%**	**59%**	**71**	**23.2**	69%	35%	69%	29%	277	65.8	51%
Wolbachia-sp	C.crescentus	56%	50	**72%**	**49%**	**76%**	**44%**	**95**	**25.3**	56%	36%	61%	33%	309	66.0	64%
Wolbachia-sp	R.capsulatus	59%	57	**77%**	**73%**	**78%**	**60%**	**87**	**24.8**	81%	39%	81%	31%	265	62.9	48%
Wolbachia-sp	R.palustris	58%	131	**81%**	**78%**	**85%**	**53%**	**744**	**54.5**	33%	10%	57%	11%	274	69.2	28%
Wolbachia-sp	R.prowazekii	67%	37	**61%**	**42%**	**70%**	**42%**	**77**	**23.3**	70%	39%	79%	34%	195	55.0	58%
Wolbachia-sp	R.rubrum	60%	81	**79%**	**76%**	**68%**	**49%**	**97**	**25.6**	62%	42%	51%	26%	376	79.0	61%
	average			**74%**	**59%**	**76%**	**59%**	**148**	**29.0**	54%	39%	58%	42%	1107	142.1	

4 Conclusions

This paper proposes a refinement of the heuristics commonly used by the Sankoff-based pairwise secondary structure RNA prediction methods. The strategies for heuristic design are conceptualized and refined using the constraints paradigm in a simpler model, that actually constitutes the core of these methods, for which we proved that our framework is valid. Our ongoing developments aim at incorporating a more complete thermodynamic model while refining even further the method by allowing dynamic restraints on the graphs, the promising behavior of ARNICA on poorly conserved structures being its major asset.

References

[Bro99] Brown, J.W.: The Ribonuclease P database. NAR 27(314) (1999), `http://www.mbio.ncsu.edu/RNaseP/`

[CMR08] Capriotti, E., Marti-Renom, M.A.: Computational RNA structure prediction. Current Bioinformatics 3(1), 32–45 (2008)

[DE06] Dowell, R.D., Eddy, S.R.: Efficient pairwise RNA structure prediction and alignment using sequence alignment constraints. BMC Bioinformatics 7, 400 (2006)

[ED94] Eddy, S.R., Durbin, R.: RNA sequence analysis using covariance models. NAR 22, 2079–2088 (1994)

[EGG88] Eppstein, D., Galil, Z., Giancarlo, R.: Speeding up dynamic programming. In: Proceedings of the29th IEEE Annual Symposium on Foundations of Computer Science, White Plains, NY, pp. 488–496. IEEE Computer Society Press, Los Alamitos (1988)

[EGGI92a] Eppstein, D., Galil, Z., Giancarlo, R., Italiano, G.F.: Sparse dynamic programming I: linear cost functions. J. ACM 39(3), 519–545 (1992)

[EGGI92b] Eppstein, D., Galil, Z., Giancarlo, R., Italiano, G.F.: Sparse dynamic programming II: convex and concave cost functions. J. ACM 39(3), 546–567 (1992)

[GG04] Gardner, P.P., Giegerich, R.: A comprehensive comparison of comparative RNA structure prediction approaches. BMC Bioinformatics 5(1) (September 2004)

[HBS04] Hofacker, I.L., Bernhart, S.H., Stadler, P.F.: Alignment of RNA base pairing probability matrices. Bioinformatics 20(14), 2222–2227 (2004)

[HLSG05] Havgaard, J.H., Lyngsø, R.B., Stormo, G.D., Gorodkin, J.: Pairwise local structural alignment of RNA sequences with sequence similarity less than 40%. Bioinformatics 21(9), 1815–1824 (2005)

[Hof03] Hofacker, I.L.: Vienna RNA secondary structure server. Nucleic Acids Res 31(13), 3429–3431 (2003)

[Hol05] Holmes, I.: Accelerated probabilistic inference of RNA structure evolution. BMC Bioinformatics 6(1) (2005)

[HSM07] Harmanci, A.O., Sharma, G., Mathews, D.H.: Efficient pairwise RNA structure prediction using probabilistic alignment constraints in dynalign. BMC Bioinformatics, 8 (April 2007)

[HTG07] Havgaard, J.H., Torarinsson, E., Gorodkin, J.: Fast pairwise structural RNA alignments by pruning of the dynamical programming matrix. PLoS Computational Biology 3(10), e193 (2007)

[JTZ89] Jaeger, J.A., Turner, D.H., Zuker, M.: Improved predictions of secondary structures for RNA. PNAS 86, 7706–7710 (1989)

[KH03] Knudsen, B., Hein, J.: Pfold: RNA secondary structure prediction using stochastic context-free grammars. Nucleic Acids Res. 31(13), 3423–3428 (2003)

[McC90] McCaskill, J.S.: The equilibrium partition function and base pair binding probabilities for RNA secondary structure. Biopolymers 29, 1105–1119 (1990)

[MSZT99] Mathews, D.H., Sabina, J., Zuker, M., Turner, D.H.: Expanded sequence dependence of thermodynamic parameters improves prediction of RNA secondary structure. JMB 288, 911–940 (1999)

[MT02] Mathews, D.H., Turner, D.H.: Dynalign: An algorithm for finding the secondary structure common to two RNA sequences. JMB (in press, 2002)

[NJ80] Nussinov, R., Jacobson, A.B.: Fast algorithm for predicting the secondary structure of single stranded RNA. PNAS 77, 6309–6313 (1980)

[NW70] Needleman, S.B., Wunsch, C.D.: A general method applicable to the search for similarities in the amino acid sequence of two proteins. J. Mol. Biol. 48(3), 443–453 (1970)

[OH98] O'Brien, E.A., Higgins, D.G.: Empirical estimation of the reliability of ribosomal RNA alignments. Bioinformatics 14(10), 830–838 (1998)

[San85] Sankoff, D.: Simultaneous solution of the RNA folding, alignment and protosequence problems. SIAM J. Appl. Math. 45(5), 810–825 (1985)

[SW81] Smith, T.F., Waterman, M.S.: Identification of common molecular subsequences. JMB 147, 195–197 (1981)

[SYKB07] Shapiro, B.A., Yingling, Y.G., Kasprzak, W., Bindewald, E.: Bridging the gap in RNA structure prediction. Curr. Opin. Struct. Biol. 17(2), 157–165 (2007)

[THG07] Torarinsson, E., Havgaard, J.H.H., Gorodkin, J.: Multiple structural alignment and clustering of RNA sequences. Bioinformatics (February 2007)

[Wat83] Watermann, M.S.: Sequence alignments in the neighborhood of the optimum with general application to dynamic programming. Applied Mathematical Sciences 80, 3123–3124 (1983)

[ZMT99] Zuker, M., Mathews, D.H., Turner, D.H.: Algorithms and thermodynamics for RNA secondary structure prediction. A practical guide. RNA Biochemistry and Biotechnology (1999)

[Zuk03] Zuker, M.: MFOLD web server for nucleic acid folding and hybridization prediction. NAR 31(13), 1–10 (2003)

Chapter 4

COLA – Computational Logic with Applications

A Logic Programming System for Evolving Programs with Temporal Operators

José Júlio Alferes, Alfredo Gabaldon, and João Leite

CENTRIA, Universidade Nova de Lisboa, Portugal

Abstract. Logic Programming Update Languages were proposed as an extension of logic programming that allows modeling the dynamics of knowledge bases where both extensional (facts) and intentional knowledge (rules) may change over time due to updates. Despite their generality, these languages do not provide a means to directly access past states of the evolving knowledge. They are limited to so-called Markovian change, i.e. changes entirely determined by the current state.

We remedy this limitation by extending the Logic Programming Update Language EVOLP with LTL-like temporal operators that allow referring to the history of the evolving knowledge base, and show how this can be implemented in a Logic Programming framework.

1 Introduction

While belief update in the context of classical knowledge bases (KBs) has traditionally received significant devotion [1], only in the last decade have we witnessed increasing attention to this topic in the context of non-monotonic KBs, notably using logic programming (LP) [2,3,4,5,6,7,8,9,10,11,12]. Chief among the results of such efforts are several semantics for sequences of logic programs (dynamic logic programs) with different properties, and the so-called LP Update Languages: LUPS [11], EPI [4], KABUL [3] and EVOLP [10].

LP Update Languages are extensions of LP designed for modeling dynamic, non-monotonic KBs represented by logic programs. In these KBs, both the extensional part (a set of facts) and the intentional part (a set of deductive rules) may change over time due to updates. In these languages, special types of rules are used to specify updates to the current KB leading to a subsequent KB. LUPS, EPI and KABUL offer a very diverse set of update commands, each specific for one particular kind of update (assertion, retraction, etc). On the other hand, EVOLP follows a simpler approach, staying closer to traditional LP.

A generalization of EVOLP with temporal operators, called EVOLP_T, was introduced in [13] and its usage illustrated in the context of multi-agent systems. In this paper we present a simplified reformulation of the definition of the semantics (Sec. 2) and introduce an implementation of EVOLP_T programs[1] (Sec. 3).

[1] Freely available from `http://centria.di.fct.unl.pt/~jja/updates/`

L. Seabra Lopes et al. (Eds.): EPIA 2009, LNAI 5816, pp. 101–112, 2009.

1.1 Intuitions and Motivating Example

EVOLP (Evolving Logic Programming) generalizes Answer Set Programming [14] by allowing the specification of a program's own evolution, arising both from self (i.e. internal to the program) updating and from external updating originating in the environment. From a syntactical point of view, evolving programs are just generalized logic programs extended with (possibly nested) assertions appearing in the heads and bodies of rules. From a semantic point of view, a model-theoretic characterization is offered of the possible evolutions of such programs by means of the so-called *evolving stable models*, which are sequences of interpretations. Each interpretation in the sequence describes, at the corresponding evolution step, what is true and the possible next-step evolutions.

Despite their generality, none of the update languages available provides means to directly access past states of an evolving KB. These languages were designed for domains where updates are Markovian, that is, entirely determined by the current state. There are many scenarios, however, where the update dynamics are non-Markovian and EVOLP_T was proposed for such cases where non-Markovian control is required. The following example illustrates this.

Consider a KB of user access policies for a number of computers at different locations. A login policy may say, e.g., that after the first failed login a user is warned by sms and if there is another failed login the account is blocked. This policy could be expressed by the following two rules:

$$sms(User) \leftarrow \Box(not\, sms(User)), fLogin(User, IP).$$
$$block(User) \leftarrow \Diamond(sms(User)), fLogin(User, IP).$$

where $fLogin(User, IP)$ represents an external event of a failed login. The ability to represent such external influence on the contents of a KB is one of the features of EVOLP (and of EVOLP_T). The symbols $\Diamond$ and $\Box$ represent Past Linear Temporal Logic (Past LTL) like operators. $\Diamond\varphi$ means that there is a past state where φ was true and $\Box\varphi$ means that φ was true in all past states.

Now suppose that we want to model some updates made by the system administrator. For example, adding a new policy consisting in blocking a user after the first failed login attempt if the user has an IP address from a "bad domain", and that an sms is not sent him. This is captured by the rules:

$$block(User) \leftarrow fLogin(User, IP), domain(IP, BadDom).$$
$$not\, sms(User) \leftarrow fLogin(User, IP), domain(IP, BadDom).$$

with *BadDom* instantiated to the domain in question. Whether a domain is bad or not, however, depends on the particular machine. In this case, the sys admin may want to send an update to all machines so that the above rules are added to each machine's policy only for domains which are bad according to the machines' current history. The sys admin issues the following update to every machine, saying that the above new rules are to be asserted if the domain has been considered a bad one since the last failed attempt:

$$\begin{aligned}
&assert(\ block(User) \leftarrow fLogin(User, IP), domain(IP, Dom)\ ) \leftarrow \\
&\qquad \mathbf{S}(badDomain(Dom),\ fLogin(Usr2, IP2)), \\
&\qquad domain(IP2, Dom). \\
&assert(\ not\, sms(User) \leftarrow fLogin(User, IP), domain(IP, BadDom)\ ) \leftarrow \\
&\qquad \mathbf{S}(badDomain(Dom),\ fLogin(Usr2, IP2)), \\
&\qquad domain(IP2, Dom).
\end{aligned}$$

where *badDomain*(*Dom*) is machine specific. The symbol **S** represents an operator similar to the Past LTL operator "since". The intuitive meaning of $\mathbf{S}(\psi, \varphi)$ is: at some point in the past φ was true, and ψ has always been true since then. The *assert* construct is one of the main features of EVOLP. It allows one to specify updates to a KB, leaving to its semantics the task of dealing with contradictory rules such as the one that specifies that an sms should be sent if it is the first failure, and the one that specifies otherwise if the domain is bad.

2 Evolving Logic Programs with Temporal Operators

EVOLP [10] is a logic programming language for specifying dynamic KBs. Change is specified through two constructs: a special predicate *assert*/1 for adding new rules to the KB, and negated rule heads which have the effect of invalidating previously added rules in the KB. EVOLP$_T$ extends EVOLP with Past LTL like operators $\bigcirc(G)$, $\Diamond(G)$ $\Box(G)$, and $\mathbf{S}(G_1, G_2)$, which intuitively mean, respectively: G is true in the previous state; there is a state in the past in which G is true; G is always true in the past; and G_2 is true at some state in the past, and since then until the current state G_1 is true.

Arbitrary nesting of these operators as well as negation-as-failure in front of their arguments is allowed. On the other hand, unlike *not*, the temporal operators are not allowed to appear in the head of rules. The only restriction on the body of rules is that negation is allowed to appear in front of atoms and temporal operators only. The formal definition of the language and programs in EVOLP$_T$ is as follows.

Definition 1 (EVOLP$_T$). Let $\mathcal{L}$ be any propositional language not containing symbols *assert*, $\bigcirc$, $\Diamond$, **S** and $\Box$. The EVOLP$_T$ *b-literals*, *t-formulae*[2] and rules are inductively defined as follows:

1. Propositional atoms in $\mathcal{L}$ are (atomic) b-literals.
2. If G_1 and G_2 are b-literals then so are $\bigcirc(G_1)$, $\Diamond(G_1)$, $\mathbf{S}(G_1, G_2)$ and $\Box(G_1)$. These b-literals are the t-formulae.
3. If G is a t-formula or an atomic b-literal, then $not\, G$ is a b-literal.
4. If G_1 and G_2 are b-literals, then (G_1, G_2) is a (conjunctive) b-literal.
5. If L_0 is an atomic b-literal, A, or its negation, $not\, A$, and $G_1, \ldots, G_n$ are b-literals, then $L_0 \leftarrow G_1, \ldots, G_n$ is a *rule*.

[2] b-literal stands for "body literal" and t-formula for "temporal-formula".

6. If R is a rule, then $assert(R)$ is an atomic b-literal.
7. Nothing else is a b-literal, t-formula, or rule.

Atomic b-literals will simply be called *atoms*. A b-literal is called *objective* if *not* does not appear in it. An EVOLP$_T$ program is a (possibly infinite) set of rules.

The following is a 'legal' EVOLP$_T$ rule:

$$assert(a \leftarrow not\,\Diamond(b)) \leftarrow not\,\Box(not\,\Diamond(b, not\,assert(c \leftarrow d))).$$

Notice the nesting of temporal operators and the appearance of negation, conjunction and assert under the scope of the temporal operators.

The following are not 'legal' EVOLP$_T$ rules:

$$assert(\Box(b) \leftarrow a) \leftarrow b. \qquad a \leftarrow \Diamond(not\,(a, b)). \qquad a \leftarrow not\,not\,b.$$

In the first rule, $\Box(b)$ appears in the argument rule $\Box(b) \leftarrow a$, but temporal operators are not allowed in the head of rules. The second rule applies negation to a conjunctive b-literal, and the third rule has double negation. But negation is only allowed in front of atomic b-literals and t-formulae.

The definition of the semantics of EVOLP$_T$ is based on sequences of interpretations (sets of atoms), $\langle I_1, \ldots, I_n\rangle$, called *evolution interpretation.* Each interpretation I_i contains the atoms that hold at state i of the evolution, and a sequence represents a possible evolution of an initial program after the given n evolution steps.

Satisfaction of b-literals by an evolution interpretation is defined as follows.

Definition 2 (Satisfaction of b-literals). Let $\mathcal{I} = \langle I_1, \ldots, I_n\rangle$ be an evolution interpretation of a program P and let G and G' be b-literals. Then

$$\begin{array}{lll}
\langle I_1, \ldots, I_n\rangle \models A & \text{iff} & A \in I_n \text{ and } A \text{ is an atom.}\\
\langle I_1, \ldots, I_n\rangle \models not\,G & \text{iff} & \langle I_1, \ldots, I_n\rangle \not\models G.\\
\langle I_1, \ldots, I_n\rangle \models G, G' & \text{iff} & \langle I_1, \ldots, I_n\rangle \models G \text{ and } \langle I_1, \ldots, I_n\rangle \models G'.\\
\langle I_1, \ldots, I_n\rangle \models \bigcirc(G) & \text{iff} & n \geq 2 \text{ and } \langle I_1, \ldots, I_{n-1}\rangle \models G.\\
\langle I_1, \ldots, I_n\rangle \models \Diamond(G) & \text{iff} & n \geq 2 \text{ and } \exists i < n : \langle I_1, \ldots, I_i\rangle \models G.\\
\langle I_1, \ldots, I_n\rangle \models \mathbf{S}(G, G') & \text{iff} & n > 2,\ \exists i < n : \langle I_1, \ldots, I_i\rangle \models G' \text{ and}\\
 & & \forall i < j < n : \langle I_1, \ldots, I_j\rangle \models G.\\
\langle I_1, \ldots, I_n\rangle \models \Box(G) & \text{iff} & \forall i < n : \langle I_1, \ldots, I_i\rangle \models G.
\end{array}$$

Given an evolution interpretation, an *evolution trace* represents one of the possible evolutions of the KB.

Definition 3. The *evolution trace* associated with an evolution interpretation $\mathcal{I}$ of a program P is the sequence of programs $\langle P_1, P_2, \ldots, P_n\rangle$ where:

$$P_1{=}P \textit{ and } P_i{=}\{R \mid assert(R) \in I_{i-1}\} \quad \textit{for each } 2 \leq i \leq n.$$

Our first step towards defining the semantics of EVOLP$_T$ programs consists in defining an operator that eliminates t-formulae from a program by evaluating them against an evolution interpretation.

Definition 4 (Elimination of Temporal Operators). Let $\mathcal{I} = \langle I_1, \ldots, I_n \rangle$ be an evolution interpretation and $L_0 \leftarrow G_1, \ldots, G_n$ a rule. The rule resulting from the elimination of temporal operators given $\mathcal{I}$,

$$El(\mathcal{I}, L_0 \leftarrow G_1, \ldots, G_n)$$

is obtained by replacing by *true* every t-formula G_t in the body such $\mathcal{I} \models G_t$ and by replacing all remaining t-formulae by $false$, where constants $true$ and $false$ are defined, as usual, such that the former is true in every interpretation and the latter is not true in any interpretation.

The program resulting from the elimination of temporal operators given $\mathcal{I}$, $El(\mathcal{I}, P)$ is obtained by applying El to each of the program's rules.

Before we define the models of a program, we need to introduce some notation. Let $\mathcal{P} = \langle P_1, ..., P_n \rangle$ be a sequence of programs. For $1 \leq s \leq n$, $\rho_s(\mathcal{P})$ denotes the multiset of all the rules appearing in the subsequence $P_1, ..., P_s$. For a set atoms I, $\hat{I} = I \cup \{not\_A \mid A \notin I\}$. If r is a rule $L_0 \leftarrow L_1, \ldots, L_n$, then $H(r) = L_0$ (dubbed the head of the rule) and $B(r) = L_1, \ldots, L_n$ (dubbed the body of the rule). We say r and r' are *conflicting rules*, denoted by $r \bowtie r'$, iff $H(r) = A$ and $H(r') = not\, A$ or $H(r) = not\, A$ and $H(r') = A$. Let $\mathcal{P}$ be a program, I an interpretation, and $1 \leq s \leq n$. The following sets originate form the semantics of Dynamic Logic Programs [2].

$$\begin{aligned} Def_s(\mathcal{P}, I) &= \{not\, A \mid A \text{ is an objective atom}, \\ &\qquad\qquad \nexists r \in \rho_s(\mathcal{P}), H(r) = A, I \models B(r)\}. \\ Rej_s(\mathcal{P}, I) &= \{r \mid r \in P_i, \exists r' \in P_j, i \leq j \leq s, r \bowtie r', I \models B(r')\}. \end{aligned}$$

Intuitively, $Def_s(\mathcal{P}, I)$ is the set of 'default' b-literals, $not\, A$, such that A has never held at any state up to s. $Rej_s(\mathcal{P}, I)$ is the set of rules that are 'rejected' (i.e. disabled) at state s because a conflicting rule whose body is satisfied was added in a more recent or the same state than the state where the rejected rule was added.

Finally, $least(P)$ denotes the least model of the definite program obtained from a program P without t-formulae by replacing every b-literal $not\, A$, where A is an atom, by a new atom not_A.

Definition 5 (Dynamic Stable Models). Let $\mathcal{P} = \langle P_1, \ldots, P_n \rangle$ be a sequence of EVOLP$_T$ programs and I an interpretation. I is a *dynamic stable model* of $\mathcal{P}$ at state s, $1 \leq s \leq n$ iff

$$\hat{I} = least\left([\rho_s(\mathcal{P}) - Rej_s(\mathcal{P}, I)] \cup Def_s(\mathcal{P}, I)\right).$$

Definition 6 (Evolution Stable Models). Let $\mathcal{I} = \langle I_1, \ldots, I_n \rangle$ be an evolution interpretation of an EVOLP$_T$ program P and $\mathcal{P}$ be the corresponding evolution trace. Then $\mathcal{I}$ is an *evolution stable model* of P iff for every $1 \leq s \leq n$, I_s is a dynamic stable model of $El(\mathcal{I}, \mathcal{P})$ at s.

In addition to allowing the specification of updates in the KB itself, EVOLP$_T$ also allows, as does its predecessor EVOLP, incorporating changes caused by external events. These events may be facts/rules representing observations made at some stage of the evolution or assertion commands specifying new update directives to be added to the KB. Both types of event can be represented as EVOLP_T rules: the former by rules without the assert predicate in the head, and the latter by rules with it. Formally, a sequence of such events is just a sequence of programs over the same language:

Definition 7. Let L be the language of an evolving program P. An *event sequence* over P is a sequence of evolving programs over L.

Definition 8 (Evolution Stable Models with Events). Let $\mathcal{I} = \langle I_1, \ldots, I_n \rangle$ be an evolution interpretation of an EVOLP_T program P and $\langle P_1, \ldots, P_n \rangle$ be the corresponding evolution trace. Then $\mathcal{I}$ is an *evolution stable model* of P given event sequence $\langle E_1, E_2, \ldots, E_n \rangle$ iff for every s, $1 \leq s \leq n$, I_s is a dynamic stable model of $El(\mathcal{I}, \langle P_1, P_2, \ldots, (P_s \cup E_s) \rangle)$ at s.

Since multiple different evolutions of the same length may exist, evolution stable models alone do not determine a truth relation. But one such truth relation can be defined, in the usual way, based on the intersection of models:

Definition 9 (Stable Models after n Steps given Events). Let P be an EVOLP_T program. We say that a set of atoms M is a *stable model of P after n steps given the sequence of events $\mathcal{E}$* iff there exist $I_1, \ldots, I_{n-1}$ such that $\langle I_1, \ldots, I_{n-1}, M \rangle$ is an evolution stable model of P given $\mathcal{E}$.

We say that an atom A is:

- *true after n steps given $\mathcal{E}$* iff all stable models after n steps contain A;
- *false after n steps given $\mathcal{E}$* iff no stable model after n steps contains A;
- *unknown after n steps given $\mathcal{E}$* otherwise.

It is worth noting that basic properties of Past LTL operators carry over to EVOLP_T. In particular, in EVOLP_T, as in LTL, some of the operators are not strictly needed, since they can be rewritten in terms of the others:

Proposition 1. *Let $\mathcal{I} = \langle I_1, \ldots, I_n \rangle$ be an evolution stable model over a set L of b-literals. Then, for every $G \in L$:*

- $\mathcal{I} \models \Box(G)$ *iff* $\mathcal{I} \models not\, \Diamond(not\, G)$,
- $\mathcal{I} \models \Diamond(G)$ *iff* $\mathcal{I} \models \mathbf{S}(true, G)$.

Moreover, it should also be noted that EVOLP_T is a generalization of EVOLP in the sense that when no temporal operators appear in the program and in the sequence of events, then evolution stable models coincide with those of EVOLP. A further, immediate consequence of this fact is that if the sequence of events is empty and predicate $assert/1$ does not occur in the program, evolution stable models as defined for EVOLP_T coincide with answer-sets.

3 EVOLP$_T$ Implementations

We have developed two implementations of EVOLP$_T$. One follows the evolution stable models semantics defined above, while the second one computes answers to existential queries under the well-founded semantics [15]. The implementations rely on two consecutive program transformations: the first transforms an EVOLP$_T$ program into an EVOLP one, i.e. temporal operators are eliminated. The second transformation, which is based on previous work [16], takes the result of the first and generates a normal logic program.

We start by defining the first program transformation, then give some intuitions on the second transformation. That is followed by a description of the actual implementation and its usage and then some details about the other implementation.

3.1 Program Transformations

The transformation of EVOLP$_T$ programs and sequences of events into EVOLP mainly consists in eliminating the t-formulae by introducing new propositional atoms and rules that encode the dynamics of the temporal operators. We start by defining the target language of the resulting EVOLP programs.

Let P be an EVOLP$_T$ program and $\mathcal{E}$ a sequence of events in a propositional language $\mathcal{L}$. The target language is obtained from $\mathcal{L}$ by adding a new propositional variable for every non-atomic b-literal that appears in P and $\mathcal{E}$. Recall that atomic b-literals are the propositional atoms and atoms of the form $assert(R)$. Formally:

Definition 10 (EVOLP Target language). Let P and $\mathcal{E}$ be an EVOLP$_T$ program and a sequence of events, respectively, in a propositional language $\mathcal{L}$. Let $\mathcal{G}(P, \mathcal{E})$ be the set of all non-atomic b-literals that appear in P or $\mathcal{E}$.

The EVOLP target language is $\mathcal{L}_E(\mathcal{L}, P, \mathcal{E}) = \mathcal{L} \cup \{'L' \mid L \in \mathcal{G}(P, \mathcal{E})\}$, where by $'L'$ we mean a propositional variable whose name is the (atomic) string of characters that compose the formula L (which is assumed not to occur in $\mathcal{L}$).

The transformation takes the rules in both program and events, and replaces all occurrences of t-formulas and conjunctions in their bodies by the corresponding new propositional variables in the target language. Moreover, extra rules are added to the program for encoding the behaviour of the operators.

Definition 11 (Transformed EVOLP program). Let P be an EVOLP$_T$ program and $\mathcal{E} = \langle E_1, E_2, \ldots, E_n \rangle$ be a sequence of events in a propositional language $\mathcal{L}$. Then $Tr_E(P, \mathcal{E}) = (T_P, \langle T_{E_1}, \ldots, T_{E_n} \rangle)$ is a pair consisting of an EVOLP program (i.e., without temporal operators) and a sequence of events, both in language $\mathcal{L}_E(\mathcal{L}, P, \mathcal{E})$, defined as follows:

1. **Rewritten program rules.** For every rule r in P (resp. each of the E_i), T_P (resp. T_{E_i}) contains a rule obtained from r by replacing every t-formula G in its body by the new propositional variable $'G'$;

2. **Previous-operator rules.** For every propositional variable of the form $'\bigcirc(G)'$, appearing in $\mathcal{L}_E(\mathcal{L}, P, \mathcal{E})$, T_P contains:

   $assert('\bigcirc(G)') \leftarrow' G'.$ $\qquad$ $assert(not' \bigcirc (G)') \leftarrow not'G'.$

3. **Sometimes-operator rule.** For every propositional variable of the form $'\Diamond(G)'$, appearing in $\mathcal{L}_E(\mathcal{L}, P, \mathcal{E})$, T_P contains:

   $assert('\Diamond(G)') \leftarrow' G'.$

4. **Since-operator rules.** For every propositional variable of the form $'\mathbf{S}(G_1, G_2)'$, appearing in $\mathcal{L}_E(\mathcal{L}, P, \mathcal{E})$, T_P contains:

   $assert('\mathbf{S}(G_1, G_2)') \leftarrow' G_1',' \bigcirc(G_2)'.$
   $assert(assert(not'\mathbf{S}(G_1, G_2)') \leftarrow not'G_1') \leftarrow assert('\mathbf{S}(G_1, G_2)').$

5. **Always-operator rules.** For every propositional variable of the form $'\Box(G)'$, appearing in $\mathcal{L}_E(\mathcal{L}, P, \mathcal{E})$, T_P contains:

   $'\Box(G)' \leftarrow' G', \ not \bigcirc true.$ $\qquad$ $assert(not'\Box(G)') \leftarrow not'G'.$

6. **Conjunction and negation rules.** For every propositional variables of the form $'not\, G'$, or of the form $'G_1, G_2'$ appearing in $\mathcal{L}_E(\mathcal{L}, P, \mathcal{E})$, T_P contains, respectively:

   $'not\, G' \leftarrow not'G'$
   $'G_1, G_2' \leftarrow' G_1',' G_2'.$ $\qquad$ $'G_1, G_2' \leftarrow' G_2',' G_1'.$

The correctness of this transformation is established by the theorem:

Theorem 1 (Correctness of the EVOLP transformation). Let P and $\mathcal{E} = \langle E_1, \ldots, E_k \rangle$ be, respectively, an EVOLP$_T$ program and a sequence of events in a propositional language $\mathcal{L}$, and let $Tr_E(P, \mathcal{E}) = (T_P, \langle T_{E_1}, \ldots, T_{E_k} \rangle)$. Then $M = \langle I_1, \ldots, I_n \rangle$ is an evolution stable model of P given $\mathcal{E}$ iff there exists an evolution stable model $M' = \langle I_1', \ldots, I_n' \rangle$ of T_P given $\mathcal{E}$ such that $I_1 = (I_1' \cap \mathrm{L}), \ldots, I_n = (I_n' \cap \mathrm{L})$.

Proof. (Sketch) The proof, that can only be sketched here due to lack of space, proceeds by induction on the length of the sequence of interpretations, showing that the transformed atoms corresponding to t-formulae satisfied in each state, and some additional assert-literals guarantying the assertion of t-formulae, belong to the interpretation state.

For the induction step, the rules of the transformation are used to guarantee that the new propositional variables belong to the interpretation of the transformed program whenever the corresponding temporal b-literals belong to the interpretation of the original EVOLP$_T$ program. For example, if some $G \in I_i$ then, according to the EVOLP$_T$ semantics, for every $j > i$ $\Diamond(G) \in I_j$; by induction hypothesis, $'G' \in I_i'$ and the "sometime-operator rule" guarantees that $'\Diamond(G)'$ is added to the subsequent program and so, since no rule for $not'\Diamond(G)'$ is added in the transformation, for every $j > i$ $'\Diamond(G') \in I_j'$. As another example, note that the first "previous-operator" rule is similar to the "sometime-operator rule" and the second adds the fact $not' \bigcirc (G)'$ in case $not'G'$ is true; so, as in the EVOLP$_T$ semantics, $' \bigcirc (G)' \in I'_{i+i}$. A similar reasoning is applied also for the since-operator and always-operator rules.

To account for the nesting of temporal operators first note that the transformation adds the above rules for all possible nestings. Since this nesting can be combined with conjunction and negation, as per the definition of the syntax of EVOLP$_T$ (Def. 1), care must be taken with the new propositional variables that stand for those conjunctions and negations. This is taken care the the conjunction and negation rules, which guarantee that a new atom with a conjunction is true in case the b-literals in the conjunction are true, and that a new atom with the negation of a b-literal is true in case the negation of the b-literal is true. □

As explained above, the implementation proceeds by transforming the resulting EVOLP program into a normal logic program. This is done by using the results of [16]. In a nutshell[3], for a program P and a sequence of events $\langle E_1, \ldots, E_n \rangle$ in $\mathcal{L}$, the language is first extended with, for every proposition $A \in \mathcal{L}$, new propositional variables A^j and A^j_{neg} for every $j \leq n$, and $rej(A^j, i)$ and $rej(A^j_{neg}, i)$ for every $j \leq n$ and $i \leq j$. Intuitively, these new variables stand for, respectively: the truth (resp. falsity) of A in P_j, and the rejection of rules with head A at I_j due to the existence of a rule in P_i.

All rules $L \leftarrow Body$ in P and in each E_i are transformed in this extended language into, resp., $L^j \leftarrow Body^j, not\, rej(L^j, 1)$ for every $j \leq n$, and $L^i \leftarrow Body^i, not\, rej(L^j, i)$. Further rules are added to account for the semantics of EVOLP. For example, for every rule $r = (L \leftarrow Body)$ and all $1 < i \leq j$ s.t. $(assert(r))^{i-1}$ is the head of some transformed rule, add also the rule

$$L^j \leftarrow Body^j, (assert(r))^{i-1}, not\, rej(L^j, i)$$

As another example, to account for default negation, for every $j \leq n$ and for every A, add $A^j_{neg} \leftarrow not\, rej(A^j_{neg}, 0)$. Other rules are added (see [16]) to account for rejection, and for guaranteeing that in every interpretation I^j either A^j or A^j_{neg} belong to it (and not both).

Given the results of [16], proving a one to one relation between the stable models of the so transformed normal program and the stable models of the original EVOLP program, and the result of Theorem 1, it is clear that the composition of these two transformation is correct, i.e. the stable models of the obtained normal logic program correspond to the stable models of the original EVOLP$_T$ program plus events.

3.2 Implementations and Usage

Our implementation relies on the above described composed transformation. More precisely, the basic implementation takes an EVOLP$_T$ program and a sequence of events and preprocesses it into a normal logic program.

[3] For details see [16].

The preprocessor that is available at `http://centria.di.fct.unl.pt/~jja/updates/` is implemented in Prolog. It takes a file that starts with an EVOLP$_T$ program, where the syntax is just as described in Def. 1, except that the rule symbol is `<-` and the temporal operators are `previous/1`, `sometime/1`, `since/2`, `always/1` standing for the temporal operators $\bigcirc(G)$, $\Diamond(G)$, $\mathbf{S}(G_1, G_2)$ and $\Box(G)$, respectively. The EVOLP$_T$ program is ended by a fact `newEvents`. The rules after this fact constitute the first set of events, and is again ended by a fact `newEvents`, after which the rules for the second set of events follow, etc.

The preprocessing is done by combining the two transformation in a single step, rather than having them in sequence as described in the previous subsection. This is done for efficiency of the preprocessors, and the combination simply combines in sequences each of the rules in both transformations. Moreover, instead of creating new atomic names, as done in both transformations, the preprocessor uses Prolog terms for the new propositions accounting for the b-literal (e.g. it uses a term `sometime(a)` instead of $'\Diamond(p)'$ or $'sometime(p)'$), which eases the processing of nested temporal operators; it adds new arguments to predicates $A(j)$, instead of creating new propositions of the form A^j, as in the second transformation.

The programs obtained by the Prolog preprocessor can then run in any answer-set solver to obtain the set of the stable models of the original EVOLP$_T$ program and events. We have tested the implementation using the lparse grounder and the smodels solver(`http://www.tcs.hut.fi/Software/smodels/`). The implementation can also take advantage of the implementation of EVOLP and interface described in [17]. For this, we provide a version that one performs the first transformation, that is to be fed to the (java-based) implementation of [17] which, in turn, performs the second transformation and computes the stable models (using smodels).

Instead of computing the stable models of the resulting normal program, one may compute its well-founded model [15]. This provides a (3-valued) model which is sound, though not complete, w.r.t. the intersection of all stable models. I.e. if an atom $A(n)$ belongs to the wf-model then A is true in all stable models of the program and events after n steps; if *not* $A(n)$ belongs to the wf-model then A belongs to no stable models after n steps; if neither $A(n)$ nor *not* $A(n)$ belong to the wf-model, then nothing can be concluded.

Despite the incompleteness, the wf-model has the advantage of having polynomial complexity and allowing for (top-down) query-driven procedures. With this in mind, we have done another implementation, also available online, that besides the preprocessor also includes a meta-interpreter that answers existential queries under the well founded semantics. The meta-interpreter is implemented in XSB-Prolog, and relies on its tabling mechanisms for computing the wf-model. For top-down querying we provide a top goal predicate `G after I in (N1,N2)` which, given a goal `G` and two integers `N1` and `N2`, returns in `I` all integers between `N1` and `N2` such that in all stable models after `I` steps, `G` is true. This XSB-Prolog implementation also allows for a more interactive usage, e.g. allowing to add events as they occur (and adjusting the transformation on the fly), separately from the initial programs, and querying the current program (after as many steps as the number of events given).

4 Related Work and Conclusions

The language EVOLP_T generalizes its predecessor EVOLP by providing rules that, via Past LTL like modalities, may refer to past states in the evolution of a KB. Here, in addition to a simplified reformulation of its semantics, we have presented a provably correct transformation of EVOLP_T programs and two implementations based on it.

The use of temporal logic in computer science is widespread. Here we would like to mention some of the most closely related work. Eiter et al. [5] present a very general framework for reasoning about evolving knowledge bases. This abstract framework allows the study of different approaches to logic programming knowledge base update, including those specified in LUPS, EPI, and KABUL. For the purpose of verifying properties of evolving knowledge bases in this language, they define a syntax and semantics for Computational Tree Logic (CTL), a branching temporal logic, modalities. While in [5] temporal logic is only used for verifying meta-level properties, in EVOLP_T temporal operators are used in the object language to specify the behavior of an evolving knowledge base.

In the area of reasoning about actions, [18] describes an extension of the action language $\mathcal{A}$ with Past LTL operators, which allows formalizing actions whose effects depend on the evolution of the described domain. On a similar vein but in the more expressive situation calculus, [19] shows a generalization of Reiter's Basic Action Theories for systems with non-Markovian dynamics. Both of these formalisms provide languages that can refer to past states in the evolution of a dynamic system. However, the focus of these formalisms is on solving the *projection problem*, i.e., reasoning about what will be true in the resulting state after executing a sequence of actions. On the other hand, the focus in the EVOLP_T language is specifying updates to the system's knowledge base itself due to internal or external influence. For example, a system formalized in EVOLP_T would be able to modify the description of its own behavior, which is not possible in $\mathcal{A}$ or in Basic Action Theories.

Also designed for specifying dynamic systems using temporal logic is MetateM [20]. A program in this language consists of rules of the form $P \Rightarrow F$, where P is a Past LTL formula and F is a Future LTL formula. Intuitively, such a rule evaluated in a state specifies that if the evolution of the system up to this state satisfies P, then the system must proceed in such a way that F be satisfied. EVOLP_T does not include Future LTL connectives (our future work) so MetateM is more expressive in that sense. On the other hand, MetateM does not have a construct for updates and it is monotonic, unlike EVOLP_T. In [21] the authors propose a non-monotonic extension of LTL with the purpose of specifying agent's goals. Whereas [21] share with our work the use of LTL operators and non-monotonicity, like MetateM it provides future operators, but the non-monotonic character in [21] is given by limited explicit exceptions to rules, thus appearing to be less general than EVOLP_T.

References

1. Gabbay, D., Smets, P. (eds.): Handbook of Defeasible Reasoning and Uncertainty Management Systems, vol. 3. Kluwer, Dordrecht (1998); Belief Change
2. Alferes, J.J., Leite, J.A., Pereira, L.M., Przymusinska, H., Przymusinski, T.C.: Dynamic updates of non-monotonic knowledge bases. Journal of Logic Programming 45(1-3), 43–70 (2000)
3. Leite, J.A.: Evolving Knowledge Bases. IOS Press, Amsterdam (2003)
4. Eiter, T., Fink, M., Sabbatini, G., Tompits, H.: On properties of update sequences based on causal rejection. Theory and Practice of Logic Programming 2(6) (2002)
5. Eiter, T., Fink, M., Sabbatini, G., Tompits, H.: Reasoning about evolving non-monotonic knowledge bases. ACM Trans. Comput. Log. 6(2), 389–440 (2005)
6. Šefránek, J.: Irrelevant updates and nonmonotonic assumptions. In: Fisher, M., van der Hoek, W., Konev, B., Lisitsa, A. (eds.) JELIA 2006. LNCS (LNAI), vol. 4160, pp. 426–438. Springer, Heidelberg (2006)
7. Zhang, Y., Foo, N.Y.: Updating logic programs. In: Procs. ECAI (1998)
8. Sakama, C., Inoue, K.: Updating extended logic programs through abduction. In: Gelfond, M., Leone, N., Pfeifer, G. (eds.) LPNMR 1999. LNCS (LNAI), vol. 1730, p. 147. Springer, Heidelberg (1999)
9. Marek, V., Truszczynski, M.: Revision programming. Theor. Comput. Sci. 190(2), 241–277 (1998)
10. Alferes, J.J., Brogi, A., Leite, J., Moniz Pereira, L.: Evolving logic programs. In: Flesca, S., Greco, S., Leone, N., Ianni, G. (eds.) JELIA 2002. LNCS (LNAI), vol. 2424, pp. 50–61. Springer, Heidelberg (2002)
11. Alferes, J.J., Pereira, L.M., Przymusinska, H., Przymusinski, T.C.: LUPS – a language for updating logic programs. Artificial Intelligence 138(1& 2) (June 2002)
12. Alferes, J.J., Banti, F., Brogi, A., Leite, J.A.: The refined extension principle for semantics of dynamic logic programming. Studia Logica 79(1), 7–32 (2005)
13. Alferes, J.J., Gabaldon, A., Leite, J.A.: Evolving logic programming based agents with temporal operators. In: IEEE/WIC/ACM Int'l Conf. on Intelligent Agent Technology (2008)
14. Gelfond, M., Lifschitz, V.: Logic programs with classical negation. In: Procs. of ICLP 1990, pp. 579–597 (1990)
15. Gelder, A.V., Ross, K.A., Schlipf, J.S.: The well-founded semantics for general logic programs. Journal of the ACM 38(3), 620–650 (1991)
16. Slota, M., Leite, J.: Evolp: Tranformation-based semantics. In: Sadri, F., Satoh, K. (eds.) CLIMA VIII 2007. LNCS (LNAI), vol. 5056, pp. 117–136. Springer, Heidelberg (2008)
17. Slota, M., Leite, J.: Evolp: An implementation. In: Sadri, F., Satoh, K. (eds.) CLIMA VIII 2007. LNCS (LNAI), vol. 5056, pp. 288–298. Springer, Heidelberg (2008)
18. Mendez, G., Lobo, J., Llopis, J., Baral, C.: Temporal logic and reasoning about actions. In: 3rd Symp. Logical Formalizations of Commonsense Reasoning (1996)
19. Gabaldon, A.: Non-markovian control in the situation calculus. In: Procs. AAAI, pp. 519–524. AAAI Press, Menlo Park (2002)
20. Barringer, H., Fisher, M., Gabbay, D., Gough, G., Owens, R.: Metatem: An introduction. Formal Aspects of Computing 7(5), 533–549 (1995)
21. Baral, C., Zhao, J.: Non-monotonic temporal logics for goal specification. In: Procs. IJCAI, pp. 236–242 (2007)

On Improving the Efficiency of Deterministic Calls and Answers in Tabled Logic Programs

Miguel Areias and Ricardo Rocha

DCC-FC & CRACS
University of Porto, Portugal
{miguel-areias,ricroc}@dcc.fc.up.pt

Abstract. The execution model on which most tabling engines are based allocates a choice point whenever a new tabled subgoal is called. This happens even when the call is deterministic. However, some of the information from the choice point is never used when evaluating deterministic tabled calls with batched scheduling. Moreover, when a deterministic answer is found for a deterministic tabled call, the call can be completed early and the corresponding choice point can be removed. Thus, if applying batched scheduling to a long deterministic computation, the system may end up consuming memory and evaluating calls unnecessarily. In this paper, we propose a solution that tries to reduce this memory and execution overhead to a minimum. Our experimental results show that, for deterministic tabled calls and tabled answers with batched scheduling, it is possible not only to reduce the memory usage overhead, but also the running time of the execution.

Keywords: Tabling, Deterministic Calls and Answers, Implementation.

1 Introduction

Tabling [1] is an implementation technique that overcomes some limitations of traditional Prolog systems in dealing with redundant sub-computations and recursion. Implementations of tabling are now widely available in systems like XSB Prolog, Yap Prolog, B-Prolog, ALS-Prolog, Mercury and more recently Ciao Prolog. The increasing interest in tabling led to further developments and proposals that improve some practical deficiencies of current tabling execution models in key aspects of tabled evaluation like re-computation, scheduling and memory recovery. The discussion we address in this work also results from practical deficiencies that we have found in the execution data structures and algorithms used to deal with deterministic tabled calls and answers if applying batched scheduling [2].

The execution model on which most tabling engines are based allocates a choice point whenever a new tabled subgoal is called. This happens even when the call is deterministic, i.e., *defined by a single matching clause.* This is necessary since the information from the choice point is crucial to correctly implement some tabling operations. However, some of this information is never used when

L. Seabra Lopes et al. (Eds.): EPIA 2009, LNAI 5816, pp. 113–125, 2009.

evaluating deterministic tabled calls with batched scheduling. Moreover, when an answer found for a deterministic tabled call is known to be a deterministic answer, i.e., *be the single matching answer for the call*, then the call can be completed early [3] and the corresponding choice point can be removed.

Thus, if tabling is applied to a long deterministic computation, the system may end up consuming memory and evaluating calls unnecessarily. In this paper, we propose a solution that tries to reduce this memory and execution overhead to a minimum. We will focus our discussion on a concrete implementation, the YapTab system [4], an efficient suspension-based tabling engine that extends the state-of-the-art Yap Prolog system to support tabled evaluation for definite programs, but our proposal can be generalized and applied to other suspension-based tabling engines. Our experimental results show that, for deterministic tabled calls and tabled answers with batched scheduling, it is possible not only to reduce the memory usage overhead, but also the running time of the execution.

The remainder of the paper is organized as follows. First, we briefly introduce the main background concepts about tabled evaluation. Next, we discuss in more detail how YapTab compiles and dynamically indexes deterministic tabled calls and how deterministic tabled answers can be handled. We then describe how we have extended YapTab to provide engine support to efficiently deal with deterministic tabled calls and answers. Finally, we present some experimental results and we end by outlining some conclusions.

2 Basic Tabling Concepts

Tabling consists of storing intermediate answers for subgoals so that they can be reused when a repeated subgoal appears[1]. Whenever a tabled subgoal is first called, a new entry is allocated in an appropriated data space, the *table space*. Table entries are used to collect the answers found for their corresponding subgoals. Moreover, they are also used to check whether calls to subgoals are repeated. Repeated calls to tabled subgoals are not re-evaluated against the program clauses, instead they are resolved by consuming the answers already stored in their table entries. During this process, as further new answers are found, they are stored in their tables and later returned to all repeated calls. Within this model, the nodes in the search space are classified as either: *generator nodes*, corresponding to first calls to tabled subgoals; *consumer nodes*, corresponding to repeated calls to tabled subgoals; or *interior nodes*, corresponding to non-tabled subgoals.

The YapTab design follows the seminal SLG-WAM design [3]: it extends WAM's execution model with a new data area, the *table space*; a new set of registers, the *freeze registers*; an extension of the standard trail, the *forward trail*; and four new operations for definite programs:

Tabled Subgoal Call: this operation checks if the subgoal is in the table space. If so, it allocates a consumer node and starts consuming the available answers. If not, it allocates a generator node and adds a new entry to the table space.

[1] A subgoal repeats a previous subgoal if they are the same up to variable renaming.

New Answer: this operation checks whether a newly found answer is already in the table, and if not, inserts the answer. Otherwise, the operation fails.

Answer Resolution: this operation checks whether extra answers are available for a particular consumer node and, if so, consumes the next one. If no answers are available, it suspends the current computation and schedules a possible resolution to continue the execution.

Completion: this operation determines whether a tabled subgoal is completely evaluated. A subgoal is said to be completely evaluated when the set of stored answers represents all the conclusions that can be inferred from the set of facts and rules in the program. When this is the case, the operation closes the subgoal's table entry and reclaims stack space. Otherwise, control moves to a consumer with unconsumed answers.

During tabled evaluation, at several points, we can choose between continuing forward execution, backtracking to interior nodes, returning answers to consumer nodes, or performing completion. The decision on which operation to perform is determined by the *scheduling strategy*. Different strategies may have a significant impact on performance, and may lead to a different ordering of solutions to the query goal. Arguably, the two most successful tabling scheduling strategies are batched scheduling and local scheduling [2]. YabTab supports both batched scheduling, local scheduling and the dynamic intermixing of batched and local scheduling at the subgoal level [5]. Local scheduling does not have any relevance for this work, so we will not consider it.

Batched scheduling schedules the program clauses in a depth-first manner as does the WAM. It favors forward execution first, backtracking next, and consuming answers or completion last. It thus tries to delay the need to move around the search tree by batching the return of answers. When new answers are found for a particular tabled subgoal, they are added to the table space and the execution continues. For some situations, this results in creating dependencies to older subgoals, therefore enlarging the current SCC (*Strongly Connected Component*) [3] and delaying the completion point to an older generator node. By default in YapTab, tabled predicates are evaluated using batched scheduling [5].

3 Deterministic Tabled Calls and Answers in YapTab

In this section, we discuss how tabled predicates are compiled in YapTab and, in particular, we show how YapTab uses the Yap compiler to generate compiled and indexed code for deterministic tabled calls. We then discuss how deterministic tabled answers for deterministic tabled calls can be handled in YapTab.

3.1 Compilation of Tabled Predicates

Tabled predicates defined by several clauses are compiled using the `table_try_me`, `table_retry_me` and `table_trust_me` WAM-like instructions in a manner similar to the generic `try_me`/`retry_me`/`trust_me` WAM sequence. The `table_try_me` instruction extends the WAM's `try_me` instruction to support the tabled subgoal call operation. The `table_retry_me` and `table_trust_me` differ from the generic WAM instructions in that they restore a generator choice point rather than a standard WAM choice point. Tabled predicates defined by a single clause are compiled using the `table_try_single` WAM-like instruction, a specialized version of the `table_try_me` instruction for deterministic tabled calls. We next show YapTab's compiled code for a tabled predicate `t/1` defined by a single clause and for a tabled predicate `t/3` defined by several clauses.

```
% predicate definitions
:- table t/1, t/3.
t(X) :- ...
t(a1,b1,c1) :- ...
t(a1,b2,c2) :- ...
t(a1,b1,c3) :- ...
t(a2,b2,c4) :- ...

% compiled code generated by YapTab for predicate t/1
t1_1:  table_try_single t1_1a
t1_1a: 'WAM code for clause t(X) :- ...'

% compiled code generated by YapTab for predicate t/3
t3_1:  table_try_me t3_2
t3_1a: 'WAM code for clause t(a1,b1,c1) :- ...'
t3_2:  table_retry_me t3_3
t3_2a: 'WAM code for clause t(a1,b2,c2) :- ...'
t3_3:  table_retry_me t3_4
t3_3a: 'WAM code for clause t(a1,b1,c3) :- ...'
t3_4:  table_trust_me
t3_4a: 'WAM code for clause t(a2,b2,c4) :- ...'
```

As `t/1` is a deterministic tabled predicate, the `table_try_single` instruction will be executed for every call to this predicate. On the other hand, `t/3` is a non-deterministic tabled predicate, but some calls to it can be deterministic, i.e., defined by a single matching clause. Consider, for example, the calls `t(a2,X,Y)` and `t(X,Y,c3)`. These two calls are deterministic as each of them matches with a single `t/3` clause, respectively, the 4th and 3rd clause. We next describe how YapTab uses the demand-driven indexing mechanism of Yap to dynamically generate `table_try_single` instructions for this kind of deterministic calls.

3.2 Demand-Driven Indexing

Yap implements *demand-driven indexing* (or *just-in-time indexing*) [6] since version 5. The idea behind it is to generate flexible multi-argument indexing of Prolog clauses during program execution based on actual demand. This feature is implemented for static code, dynamic code and the internal database. All indexing code is generated on demand for all and only for the indices required. This is done by building an indexing tree using similar building blocks to the WAM but it generates indices based on the instantiation of the current goal, and expands indices given different instantiations for the same goal.

This powerful optimization allows YapTab to execute some calls to non-deterministic tabled predicates like deterministic tabled predicates. This happens when Yap's indexing scheme finds that for a particular call to a non-deterministic tabled predicate, there is only a single clause that matches the call. We next show an example illustrating the indexed code generated for a non-deterministic call and two deterministic calls to the previous `t/3` tabled predicate.

```
% indexed code generated by YapTab for call t(a1,X,Y)
table_try   t3_1a
table_retry t3_2a
table_trust t3_3a

% indexed code generated by YapTab for call t(a2,X,Y)
table_try_single t3_4a

% indexed code generated by YapTab for call t(X,Y,c3)
table_try_single t3_3a
```

The call `t(a2,X,Y)` is non-deterministic as it matches the 1st, 2nd and 3rd clauses of `t/3`, so a `table_try/table_retry/table_trust` sequence is generated. The other two calls, `t(a3,X,Y)` and `t(X,Y,c3)`, are both deterministic as they only match a single `t/3` clause, so a `table_try_single` instruction can be generated. Note however, that there are situations where a call can be deterministic, but Yap's indexing scheme cannot detect it as deterministic in order to generate the appropriate `table_try_single` instruction [6]. In such cases, we cannot benefit directly from our approach, but we can take advantage of the similarities between the `table_try_single` instruction and the *last matching clause* of a non-deterministic tabled call to apply our approach later.

3.3 Last Matching Clause

When evaluating a tabled predicate, the last matching clause of a call to the predicate is implemented either by the `table_trust_me` instruction or by the `table_trust` instruction. The former situation occurs when we have a generic call to the predicate (all the arguments of the call are unbound variables) and the latter situation occurs when we have a more specific call (some of the arguments are at least partially instantiated) optimized by indexing code. In a WAM-based implementation, the last matching clause of a call is implemented by first restoring all the necessary information from the current choice point (usually pointed to by the WAM's `B` register) and then, by discarding the current choice point (by updating `B` to its predecessor). In a tabled implementation, the `table_trust_me` and `table_trust` instructions also restore all the necessary information from the current choice point `B`, but instead of updating `B` to its predecessor, they update the next clause field of `B` to the `completion` instruction. By doing that, they force completion detection when the computation backtracks again to `B`, i.e., whether the clauses for the subgoal call at hand are all exploited.

Hence, the computation state that we have when executing a `table_trust_me` or `table_trust` instruction is similar to that one of a `table_try_single` instruction, that is, in both cases the current clause can be seen as deterministic as it is the last (or single) matching clause for the subgoal call at hand. Thus, we can view the `table_trust_me` and `table_trust` instructions as a special case of the `table_try_single` instruction. This means that the approach used for the `table_try_single` instruction to efficiently deal with deterministic tabled calls can be applied to the `table_trust_me` and `table_trust` instructions. We discuss the implementation details for these instructions in the next section.

3.4 Deterministic Tabled Answers

A tabled answer is deterministic when it is the single matching answer for the corresponding tabled call. Determining when an answer is deterministic is important because the tabled call can be completed early and the corresponding choice point can be removed. Taking into account the formulation discussed above for the last matching clause, we can also extend the definition of being a deterministic tabled answer and say that a tabled answer is deterministic when we can safely conclude that no more answers will be found, i.e., when the current answer is the last (or single) matching answer for the corresponding tabled call.

However, during execution time, it is not always possible to conclude beforehand that no more answers will be found for a particular tabled call. This is a safe conclusion only when the tabled call is deterministic, i.e., the clause being executed for the tabled call at hand is the last (or single) matching clause, and the choice point for the tabled call is the topmost choice point, i.e., no alternative paths exist for evaluating the tabled call at hand. In what follows, we will thus assume that a tabled call is deterministic when the clause being executed for the call is the *last matching clause* and that a tabled answer is deterministic when the answer is the *last matching answer* for the corresponding tabled call.

4 Implementation Details

In this section, we describe in detail how we have extended YapTab to provide engine support to efficiently deal with deterministic tabled calls and answers.

4.1 Generator Nodes

In YapTab, a generator node is implemented as a WAM choice point extended with some extra fields. The format of a generic generator choice point in YapTab is depicted in Fig. 1(a). Fields that are not found in standard WAM choice points are coloured gray. A generator choice point is divided in three sections. The top section contains the usual WAM fields needed to restore the computation on backtracking plus two extra fields [5]: `cp_dep_fr` is a pointer to the corresponding dependency frame, used by local scheduling for fix-point check, and `cp_sg_fr` is a pointer to the associated subgoal frame where answers should be stored. The middle section contains the argument registers of the subgoal and the bottom section contains the *substitution factor* [7], i.e., the set of free variables which exist in the terms in the argument registers. The substitution factor is an optimization that allows the new answer operation to store in the table space only the substitutions for the free variables in the subgoal call.

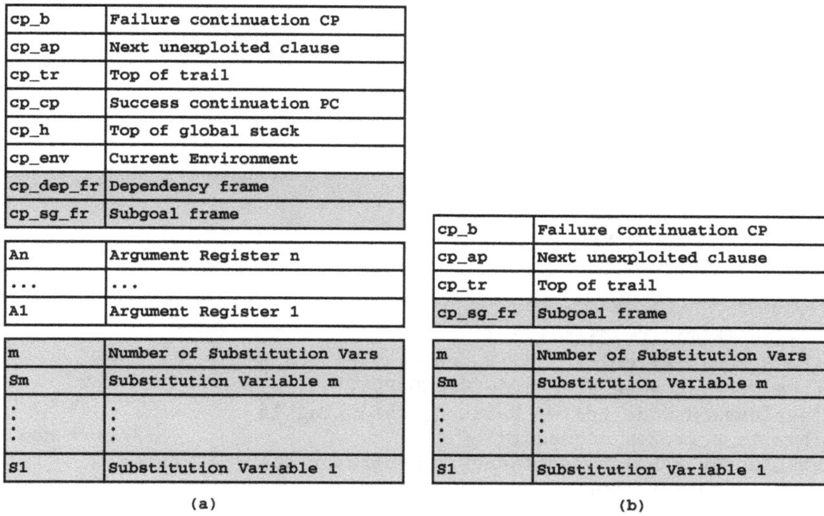

Fig. 1. (a) Generic and (b) deterministic generator choice points in YapTab

If we now turn our attention to how generator choice points are handled during evaluation, we find that some of this information is never used when evaluating deterministic tabled calls with batched scheduling. This happens mainly because, with batched scheduling, the computation is never resumed in a deterministic generator choice point. This allows us to remove the argument registers and the standard `cp_cp`, `cp_h` and `cp_env` fields. The `cp_dep_fr` field can also be removed because it is only necessary with local scheduling [5].

Figure 1(b) shows the new format of a deterministic generator choice point in YapTab. The `cp_b` field is needed for failure continuation; the `cp_ap` and `cp_tr` are required when backtracking to the choice point; the `cp_sg_fr` is required by the new answer and completion operations; and the substitution factor fields are required by the new answer operation. This optimization is similar to the *shallow backtracking* optimization as introduced by Carlsson [8]. The main difference to our approach is that, instead of delaying the initialization of some choice point fields, here we can safely ignore and remove them as they are never used.

Considering that N is the number of arguments registers and that M is the number of substitution variables, the ratio of memory usage in the choice point stack between the new and the original representation of deterministic generator choice points can be expressed as follows:

$$\frac{4+1+M}{8+N+1+M}$$

4.2 Tabling Operations

Dealing with deterministic tabled calls and answers required small changes to the tabled subgoal call, completion and new answer operations. Figure 2 shows

```
table_try_single(TABLED_CALL tc) {
  sg_fr = subgoal_check_insert(tc)    // sg_fr is the subgoal frame for tc
  if (new_tabled_subgoal_call(sg_fr)) {
    if (evaluation_mode(tc) == batched_scheduling)          // *** new ***
      store_deterministic_generator_node(sg_fr)
    else                                                 // local scheduling
      store_generic_generator_node(sg_fr)
    ...
  }
  ...
}


table_trust_me(TABLED_CALL tc) {
  // the B register points to the current choice point
  restore_generic_generator_node(B, COMPLETION)
  if (evaluation_mode(tc) == batched_scheduling &&
      not_in_a_frozen_segment(B) {                          // *** new ***
    subs_factor = B + sizeof(generic_generator_cp) + arity(tc)
    gen_cp = subs_factor - sizeof(deterministic_generator_cp)
    gen_cp->cp_sg_fr = B->cp_sg_fr
    gen_cp->cp_tr = B->cp_tr
    gen_cp->cp_ap = B->cp_ap
    gen_cp->cp_b  = B->cp_b
    B = gen_cp
  }
  ...
}
```

Fig. 2. Pseudo-code for the `table_try_single` and `table_trust_me` instructions

in more detail the changes (blocks of code marked with a '`// *** new ***`' comment) made to the `table_try_single` and `table_trust_me`[2] instructions.

The `table_try_single` instruction now checks whenever the subgoal being called is to be evaluated using batched or local scheduling. If batched, it allocates a deterministic generator choice point. If local, it proceeds as before and allocates a generic generator choice point.

The `table_trust_me` instruction now checks if the current tabled call is being evaluated using batched scheduling and if the current choice point is not in a frozen segment[3]. If these two conditions hold, we can recover some memory space by transforming the current generator choice point into a deterministic generator choice point (we assume that the choice point stack grows upwards). To do that, we need to copy the `cp_sg_fr`, `cp_tr`, `cp_ap` and `cp_b` fields in the current choice point to their new position, just above the substitution factor variables.

Deterministic generator choice points can be accessed later when executing the completion and/or new answer operations. Since both generator types have different sizes, we need to distinguish which is the type of the generator in

[2] The changes made to the `table_trust` instruction are identical.

[3] The YapTab system uses frozen segments to protect the stacks of suspended computations [4]. Thus, if the current choice point is trapped in a frozen segment it is worthless to try to recover memory from it using our approach.

```
completion() {
  ...                                              // fixpoint check loop
  // subgoal completely evaluated
  if (is_deterministic_generator_cp(B)) {                 // *** new ***
    gen_cp = deterministic_generator_cp(B)
    sg_fr = gen_cp->cp_sg_fr
  } else {                             // generic generator choice point
    gen_cp = generic_generator_cp(B)
    sg_fr = gen_cp->cp_sg_fr
  }
  complete_subgoal(sg_fr)
  ...
}


new_answer(TABLED_CALL tc, CHOICE_POINT cp, ANSWER ans) {
  // cp is the generator choice point for the tabled call tc
  if (is_deterministic_generator_cp(cp)) {                // *** new ***
    gen_cp = deterministic_generator_cp(cp)
    sg_fr = gen_cp->cp_sg_fr
    subs_factor = gen_cp + sizeof(deterministic_generator_cp)
  } else {                             // generic generator choice point
    gen_cp = generic_generator_cp(cp)
    sg_fr = gen_cp->cp_sg_fr
    subs_factor = gen_cp + sizeof(generic_generator_cp) + arity(tc)
  }
  insert = answer_check_insert(sg_fr, subs_factor)
  if (insert == FALSE || evaluation_mode(tc) == local_scheduling) {
    fail()                         // repeated answer or local scheduling
  } else {                          // new answer and batched scheduling
    if (is_deterministic_generator_cp(gen_cp) &&
        topmost_choice_point(gen_cp) {                    // *** new ***
      // the new answer is deterministic, thus the tabled call can be ...
      mark_as_completed(sg_fr)          // ... completed early and the ...
      B = gen_cp->cp_b    // .. corresponding choice point can be removed
    }
    ...
  }
}
```

Fig. 3. Pseudo-code for the `completion` and `new_answer` instructions

order to correctly access the fields required by each operation. The completion operation needs to access the `cp_sg_fr` field and the new answer operation needs to access the `cp_sg_fr` and substitution factor fields. Figure 3 shows in more detail the changes made to the `completion` and `new_answer` instructions. For the `new_answer` instruction, we also show the pseudo-code that determines when an answer is deterministic. Remember from section 3.4 that we can conclude that an answer is deterministic when the tabled call is deterministic and the choice point for the tabled call is the topmost choice point[4].

[4] Detecting if a choice point is the topmost choice point is implemented by comparing it against the `B` register (that points to the topmost choice point on the current branch) and the `B_FZ` register (that points to the topmost frozen choice point).

5 Experimental Results

We next present some experimental results comparing YapTab with and without the new support for deterministic tabled calls and answers. The environment for our experiments was an Intel(R) Core(TM)2 Quad CPU Q9550 2.83GHz with 2 GBytes of main memory and running the Linux kernel 2.6.24-24 with YapTab 5.1.3. To put the performance results in perspective and have a well-defined starting point comparing the memory ratio between the new and the original representation of deterministic generator choice points, first we have defined three deterministic tabled predicates, respectively with arities 5, 11 and 17, that simply call themselves recursively:

```
:- table t/5, t/11, t/17.

t(N,A2,A3,A4,A5) :- N>0, N1 is N-1, t(N1,A2,A3,A4,A5).

t(N,A2,A3,A4,A5,A6,A7,A8,A9,A10,A11) :-
  N>0, N1 is N-1, t(N1,A2,A3,A4,A5,A6,A7,A8,A9,A10,A11).

t(N,A2,A3,A4,A5,A6,A7,A8,A9,A10,A11,A12,A13,A14,A15,A16,A17) :- N>0,
 N1 is N-1, t(N1,A2,A3,A4,A5,A6,A7,A8,A9,A10,A11,A12,A13,A14,A15,A16,A17).
```

The first argument `N` controls the number of times the predicate is executed. It thus defines the number of generator choice points to be allocated (we used a value of 200,000 in our experiments). In order to have specific combinations of argument registers (column ***Args***) and substitution variables (column ***Subs***), we have run each predicate with three different sets of free variables in the arguments. Table 1 shows the local stack[5] memory usage, in KBytes, and the running time, in milliseconds, for YapTab without (column ***YapTab***) and with (column ***YapTab+Det***) the new support for deterministic tabled calls and answers. A third column shows the memory and running time ratio between both approaches. For the memory ratio, we show in parentheses the ratio given by the formula introduced at the end of section 4.1.

As expected, the results in Table 1 confirm that memory reduction increases when the number of argument registers is bigger and the number of substitution variables is smaller. This is consistent with the formula presented in section 4.1. The small difference between our experiments and the values obtained when using the formula came from the fact that, in the formula, we are considering a local stack without environment frames and, in the experiments, for each generator choice point we are also allocating an environment frame[6]. The results in Table 1 also suggest that this memory reduction can have an impact in the running time of the execution.

Next, we tested our approach using two well-know problems: the *fibonacci* problem (using lists of integers to represent arbitrary numbers) and the *sequence*

[5] In YapTab, the local stack contains both choice points and environment frames [9]. Other systems, like XSB Prolog, have separate choice point and environment stacks.

[6] As these experiments do not store permanent variables [9] for environments, this corresponds to adding the size of an environment frame to both parts of our formula.

Table 1. Local stack memory usage (in KBytes) and running times (in milliseconds) for YapTab without and with the new support for deterministic tabled calls and answers

Args	*Subs*	*YapTab* *Memory*	*YapTab* *Time*	*YapTab+Det* *Memory*	*YapTab+Det* *Time*	*YapTab+Det/YapTab* *Memory*	*YapTab+Det/YapTab* *Time*
5	**4**	18,751	224	11,719	160	0.62 (0.50)	0.71
5	**2**	17,188	216	10,157	148	0.59 (0.44)	0.69
5	**0**	15,626	216	8,594	152	0.55 (0.36)	0.70
11	**10**	28,126	332	16,407	240	0.58 (0.50)	0.72
11	**5**	24,219	256	12,501	268	0.52 (0.40)	1.05
11	**0**	20,313	232	8,594	184	0.42 (0.25)	0.79
17	**16**	37,501	444	21,094	340	0.56 (0.50)	0.77
17	**8**	31,251	436	14,844	300	0.47 (0.38)	0.69
17	**0**	25,001	312	8,594	236	0.34 (0.19)	0.76
Average						**0.52 (0.39)**	**0.76**

comparisons problem[7]. For both problems, we used a standard implementation (tabled predicates `fib/2` and `seq/3`) and a transformed implementation (tabled predicates `fib_t/2` and `seq_t/3`) that forces all tabled calls to use the `table_try_single` instruction. The Prolog code for the main predicates that implement both problems are presented next.

```
:- table fib/2, fib_t/2, seq/3, seq_t/3.

fib(0,[1]).
fib(1,[1]).
fib(N,L) :- N>1, N1 is N-1, N2 is N-2,
  fib(N1,L1), fib(N2,L2), sum_lists(L1,L2,L).

fib_t(N,L):- (N=<1 -> L=[1] ; (N1 is N-1, N2 is N-2,
  fib_t(N1,L1), fib_t(N2,L2), sum_lists(L1,L2,L))).

seq(0,0,0).
seq(0,M,M).
seq(N,0,N).
seq(N,M,C) :- N>0, M>0, N1 is N-1, M1 is M-1,
  seq(N1,M,C1), seq(N,M1,C2), seq(N1,M1,C3), min(N,M,C1,C2,C3,C).

seq_t(N,M,C) :- (N==0 -> M=C ; N>0, (M==0 -> C=M ; N1 is N-1, M1 is M-1,
  seq_t(N1,M,C1), seq_t(N,M1,C2), seq_t(N1,M1,C3), min(N,M,C1,C2,C3,C))).
```

We experimented the *fibonacci* problem with sizes 1000, 2000 and 4000 and the *sequence comparisons* problem with sequences of length 500, 1000 and 2000. Table 2 shows the local stack memory usage, in KBytes, and the running time, in milliseconds, for YapTab without (column ***YapTab***) and with (column ***YapTab+Det***) the new support for deterministic tabled calls and answers. Again, a third column shows the memory and running time ratio between both approaches.

[7] In the *sequence comparisons* problem, we have two sequences A and B, and we want to determine the minimal number of operations needed to turn A into B.

Table 2. Local stack memory usage (in KBytes) and running times (in milliseconds) for YapTab without and with the new support for deterministic tabled calls and answers

Program	Size	YapTab		YapTab+Det		YapTab+Det/YapTab	
		Memory	Time	Memory	Time	Memory	Time
	1000	250	984	203	884	0.8120	0.8984
fib/2	2000	375	2,880	305	2,804	0.8133	0.9736
	4000	500	6,492	407	6,420	0.8140	0.9889
	500	45,914	792	39,079	448	0.8511	0.5657
seq/3	1000	183,625	8,108	156,282	3,272	0.8511	0.4036
	2000	734,438	135,580	718,813	117,483	0.9787	0.8665
	1000	250	988	125	368	0.5000	0.3725
fib_t/2	2000	375	3,040	188	1,268	0.5013	0.4171
	4000	500	6,516	250	2,828	0.5000	0.4340
	500	45,914	804	78	252	0.0017	0.3134
seq_t/3	1000	183,625	8,844	157	952	0.0009	0.1076
	2000	734,438	131,904	313	7,048	0.0004	0.0534

The results in Table 2 show improvements on the local stack memory usage and in the running time of the execution for all experiments. In particular, for the standard predicates, `fib/2` and `seq/3`, our approach shows, on average, a slightly worse tendency to memory and running time reduction, if compared with the results on Table 1. This happens mainly because of the existence of permanent variables in the body of the tabled clauses. However, on average, our approach is able to improve the performance of the execution for all `fib/2` and `seq/3` experiments. This suggests that it is possible to take advantage of our approach by using the last matching clause optimization when a program do not contains deterministic tabled predicates.

For the transformed predicates, `fib_t/2` and `seq_t/3`, our approach shows very good performance. For the `fib_t/2` experiments, it decreases, on average, memory usage to 50% and running time to 40%. For the `seq_t/3` experiments, it shows impressive gains. In particular for sequences of length 2000, it uses 2500 times less memory on the local stack and executes 19 times faster. This shows that our approach can be quite effective when we have deterministic tabled answers for deterministic tabled calls.

6 Conclusions and Further Work

We have presented a proposal for the efficient evaluation of deterministic tabled calls and answers with batched scheduling. A well-known aspect of tabling is the overhead in terms of memory usage compared with standard Prolog. This suggested to us the question of whether it was possible to minimize this overhead when evaluating deterministic tabled computations. Our initial results are quite promising, they suggest that, for deterministic tabled calls and tabled answers with batched scheduling, it is possible not only to reduce the memory usage overhead, but also the running time of the execution for certain applications.

Further work will include exploring the impact of applying our proposal to more complex problems, seeking real-world experimental results allowing us to improve and expand our current implementation.

Acknowledgements

This work has been partially supported by the FCT research projects STAMPA (PTDC/EIA/67738/2006) and JEDI (PTDC/EIA/66924/2006).

References

1. Chen, W., Warren, D.S.: Tabled Evaluation with Delaying for General Logic Programs. Journal of the ACM 43(1), 20–74 (1996)
2. Freire, J., Swift, T., Warren, D.S.: Beyond Depth-First: Improving Tabled Logic Programs through Alternative Scheduling Strategies. In: Kuchen, H., Swierstra, S.D. (eds.) PLILP 1996. LNCS, vol. 1140, pp. 243–258. Springer, Heidelberg (1996)
3. Sagonas, K., Swift, T.: An Abstract Machine for Tabled Execution of Fixed-Order Stratified Logic Programs. ACM Transactions on Programming Languages and Systems 20(3), 586–634 (1998)
4. Rocha, R., Silva, F., Santos Costa, V.: On applying or-parallelism and tabling to logic programs. Theory and Practice of Logic Programming 5(1 & 2), 161–205 (2005)
5. Rocha, R., Silva, F., Santos Costa, V.: Dynamic mixed-strategy evaluation of tabled logic programs. In: Gabbrielli, M., Gupta, G. (eds.) ICLP 2005. LNCS, vol. 3668, pp. 250–264. Springer, Heidelberg (2005)
6. Santos Costa, V., Sagonas, K., Lopes, R.: Demand-driven indexing of prolog clauses. In: Dahl, V., Niemelä, I. (eds.) ICLP 2007. LNCS, vol. 4670, pp. 395–409. Springer, Heidelberg (2007)
7. Ramakrishnan, I.V., Rao, P., Sagonas, K., Swift, T., Warren, D.S.: Efficient Access Mechanisms for Tabled Logic Programs. Journal of Logic Programming 38(1), 31–54 (1999)
8. Carlsson, M.: On the Efficiency of Optimising Shallow Backtracking in Compiled Prolog. In: International Conference on Logic Programming, pp. 3–16. The MIT Press, Cambridge (1989)
9. Aït-Kaci, H.: Warren's Abstract Machine – A Tutorial Reconstruction. MIT Press, Cambridge (1991)

On Just in Time Indexing of Dynamic Predicates in Prolog

Vítor Santos Costa

DCC-FCUP & CRACS-INESC Porto LA
Universidade do Porto, Portugal
vsc@dcc.fc.up.pt

Abstract. Prolog is the most well-known and widely used logic programming language. A large number of Prolog applications maintains information by *asserting* and *retracting* clauses from the database. Such dynamic predicates raise a number of issues for Prolog implementations, such as what are the semantics of a procedure where clauses can be retracted and asserted while the procedure is being executed. One advantage of Logical Update semantics is that it allows indexing. In this paper, we discuss how one can implement just-in-time indexing with Logical Update semantics. Our algorithm is based on two ideas: stable structure and fragmented index trees. By *stable structure* one means that we define a structure for the indexing tree that not change, even as we assert and as we retract clauses. Second, by *fragmented index tree* we mean that the indexing tree will be built in such a way that the updates will be local to each fragment. The algorithm was implemented and results indicate significant speedups and reduction of memory usage in test applications.

1 Introduction

Prolog is the most well-known and widely used logic programming language. Prolog is based on Horn Clauses, a subset of First Order Logic for which a refutation-complete procedure exists. Definite Horn clauses have a single positive literal, the head, and zero or more negative literals. Clauses are called facts, if they have no negative literals, or rules, otherwise. Prolog programs rely on a static data-base of facts and procedures, but a large number of applications maintains information by *asserting* and *retracting* clauses from the database. In modern Prolog systems, predicates where one can assert and retract clauses are named *dynamic*.

A major issue for Prolog implementers is what are the *semantics* of a procedure where clauses can be retracted and asserted while the procedure is being executed. Originally, Prolog systems implemented what is called *immediate* updates, where a new clause or a retracted clause was immediately visible to a new execution. Unfortunately, these semantics can be hard to capture. Indexing also becomes impossible, as we may need to backtrack to a newly added clause.

L. Seabra Lopes et al. (Eds.): EPIA 2009, LNAI 5816, pp. 126–137, 2009.

Lindholm and O'Keefe [5] proposed what is nowadays called the *Logical Update semantics.* In these semantics, a call to a dynamic predicate operates on a snapshot of the clauses defining a predicate at the time of the call. In other words, adding or removing clauses will not change the clauses seen by a call to a predicate. The approach allows indexing and is intuitive. On the other hand, one problem is that deleted clauses need to be stored until all calls that use them terminate; moreover, the current goal should not be allowed to backtrack into "future" clauses. Lindholm and O'Keefe use time-stamps to control access to clauses, and garbage collection to remove dead clauses.

Logical Update semantics have become very popular. They are enforced by the ISO Prolog standard and they are implemented in most Prolog systems [2] (although not all [6]). As discussed above, one advantage of LU semantics is that it allows indexing (in contrast with immediate semantics). In this paper, we discuss how one can implement just-in-time indexing with logic update (LU) semantics. Just-in-time indexing [8] was motivated by the observation that the performance of Prolog programs strongly depends on the ability of the Prolog engine to find sets of clauses to match against sub-goals. Unfortunately, most Prolog systems have very limited indexing, usually by default just on the first argument. Extensions, such as multi-argument indexing [12], require user intervention and are designed to optimize a single mode of usage. *Just in Time Indexing (JITI)*, can address larger databases, allowing for different modes of usage. JITI relies on two key ideas. First, indexing should be performed *late*, when we know how the actual queries are instantiated. Second, different queries may have different modes. Thus, the indexing code should be able to change and *grow* to support different moded queries.

Dynamic predicates present a challenge to JITI: the indexing code can grow both because we have new modes of usage, and because we have new clauses. Moreover, the code can now *contract* as we retract clauses. Next we contribute over prior work [8] by extending the JITI algorithm to index dynamic predicates. The new algorithm is based on two ideas: stable structure and fragmented index trees. By *stable structure* one means that we define a structure for the indexing tree that not change, even as we assert and as we retract clauses. Second, by *fragmented index tree* we mean that the indexing tree will be built in such a way that the updates will be local to each fragment. The algorithm was implemented on the YAP Prolog system and results indicate significant speedups and reduction of memory usage in test applications.

The paper is organized as follows. First, we briefly review the JITI through an example. Next, we discuss the updating algorithm. We present performance results next. Last, we present some conclusions and suggest further work.

2 The JITI by Example

The JITI extends David H. D. Warren's WAM design. Figure 1(a) shows the WAM code for a small database fragment from a well-known machine learning

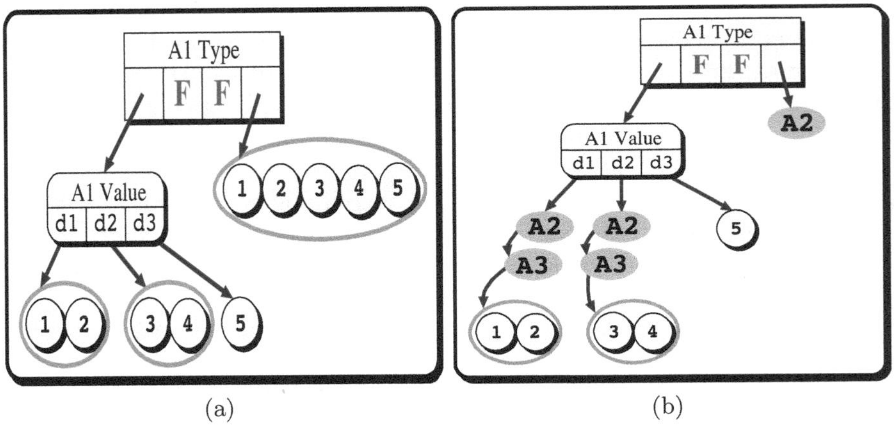

Fig. 1. WAM and JITI Code for `has_property/3`. The "Type" nodes have four children: constant, compound term, list or unbound term. Sets of clauses are grouped as ovals.

dataset, *Carcinogenesis*, which contains information on the carcinogenic properties of several chemical compounds in mice [10]:

```
has_property(d1, salmonella, p).
has_property(d1, salmonella_n, p).
has_property(d2, salmonella, p).
has_property(d2, cytogen_ca, n).
has_property(d3, cytogen_ca, p).
```

Figure 1(a) shows WAM indexing code as a tree, with *switch* nodes, and *clause chain* nodes. The WAM has two different switches: *switch_on_type* selects according to the first argument, A_1, being unbound, constant, pair or structure; *switch_on_constant* selects according to a value. The WAM also separates *clause chain* nodes with a single clause, that are implemented as a jump, and sets of clauses, that are implemented as `try`, `retry`, `trust` sequences of instructions.

In the original WAM one only considers A_1. This is not always optimal, as shown in the following queries:

```
?- has_property(d1, _, _).
?- has_property(d1, salmonella, _).
?- has_property(_, salmonella_, _).
?- has_property(_, cytogen_ca, p).
?- has_property(_, _, n).
```

The WAM would only generate ideal code for the first example. In all the other cases it would backtrack through every clause in the procedure, even though the queries are deterministic.

Unfortunately, generating indexing code for every combination of arguments can be quite expensive: with arity 3 and no sub-arguments, we have $2^3 = 8$ different input-output combination. The JITI approaches this task by assuming that all calls will have the same mode of usage: it generates multi-argument indices based on the indexing patterns for the *first* call of a predicate.

Figure 1(b) shows JITI code for our example procedure, if the first query was:

```
?- a(d1,Prop,Type).
```

The JITI algorithm generates the code at the first call. The code is based on the WAM code, but it differs as follows:

- If A_1 = `d1` or A_1 = `d2` the JITI cannot commit to a single clause. In order to achieve determinacy, it thus adds extra code to test whether A_2 is instantiated. If the test succeeds, it tries generating a new index for the remaining clauses on A_2. This is not the case, so the JITI again adds code to test whether A_3 is instantiated. In the example, A_3 is unbound, so the JITI has no choice but to generate a `try-trust` chain.
- If A_1 = `d3` there is no need to perform further indexing: the goal is already determinate so the JITI transfers control to clause 5.
- The WAM generates a sequence of `try_me`, `retry_me`, `trust_me` instructions for the case A_1 is unbound. In the purest version of the JITI this is not necessary: the JITI just leaves code to check for the next argument, A_2.

We call the nodes that wait until an argument instantiates to generate code for the argument *wait* nodes, because the JITI is waiting on a chance to increase the trees. The usefulness of wait nodes becomes clear when consider the next example goal:

```
?- a(d1,salmonella,Type).
```

In this case, we have A_2 bound. Going back to Figure 1(b), we execute the `switch_on_type` instruction, next the `switch_on_cons`, and enter the wait node for A_2. At this point, the indexing code expands `d1`'s sub-tree using the same algorithm we used to build the indexing code for A_1. It first generates a `switch_on_type`, and then a `switch_on_cons`. The new tree replaces the A_2 wait node, resulting in the tree shown in Figure 2(a). Notice that we only expand the case for `d1`: we could be aggressive and also expand for `d2`, but our reference implementation tries to generate code as lazily as possible.

Last, imagine we run a call where only the second argument is bound:

```
?- a(Compound,salmonella,Type).
```

again we will execute the top `switch_on_type`, but now we will proceed to the rightmost wait node. The JITI builds a new indexing tree for A_2, shown in Figure 2(b).

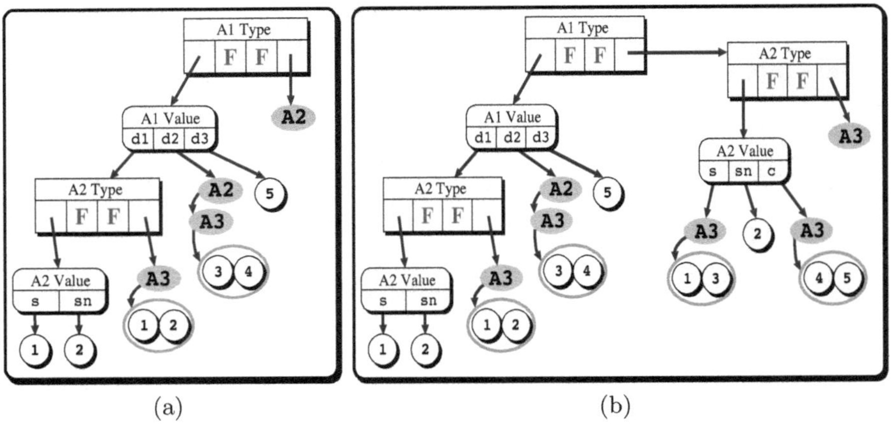

Fig. 2. Expanding JITI Code for `has_property/3`: A_1, A_2 bound and A_2 bound

3 Dynamic Procedures

We have explained the key ideas in the JITI. Before we proceed, it is important to understand how the YAP Prolog system implements dynamic predicates. Dynamic procedures are sets of dynamic clauses. Each dynamic clause is always allocated *independently* (in contrast to static clauses [7]). The main fields in the clause's header are:

- `ClFlags`: every clause has a set of flags; important flags indicate whether the clause has been deleted, and whether it is in use.
- `ClRefCount`: how many external pointers to the clause; most of these pointers will be from indexing code.
- `ClSource`: a data-structure containing the original source of the clause.
- `ClPrev, ClNext`: pointers to a doubly linked list.

The `assert/1` procedure stores a clause with three components: the header, the compile term, and a term containing the source-code.

The `retract/1` and `erase/1` procedures remove a clause from a list immediately, but do not try to recover space. Space is only recovered when `ClFlags` does not have `in-use` set, and if the `ClRefCount` is 0. Actually recovering space is the performed either at backtracking or when recovering space in the indexing code.

Our system implements a few optimizations of interest to dynamic code:

- Facts do not have source code: source code is actually recovered by executing the code;
- The Prolog Internal Data-Base is implemented as dynamic clauses with a single instruction, that unifies the second argument with a copy of the data in the `ClSource` field.

4 Indexing Dynamic Procedures

We have so far presented the JITI assuming the code is static. Dynamic procedures introduce several complications. The key ideas in our implementation are as follows: **(a)** try to keep the code as simple as possible; **(b)** try to make as little changes to the current tree as possible; **(c)** try to make changes local at each node. We discuss these principles next.

Simplicity. Our discussion so far assumes that indexing code is always a simple tree, rooted at a `switch_on_type` node, with switch on value nodes below, and where leaves are wait nodes, jumps to clauses, or sequences of clauses. We shall always follow this structure for dynamic procedures, even though this is not always true in the WAM and in the JITI for static procedures. For example indexing code on A_1 for

```
has_property(_, salmonella, p).
has_property(d1, salmonella_n, p).
has_property(d2, salmonella, p).
has_property(d2, cytogen_ca,n).
has_property(_, cytogen_ca, p).
```

first *tries* the clause, then *retries* and enters a switch, and last *trusts* the fifth clause. Updating such sequences is difficult, and not typical of the code most often found with dynamic procedures.

Structure Preservation. For simple trees, asserting a clause will not affect the *structure* of the tree: we just expand switch on values nodes, and add new leaves, but we do not need to build any *new* type and value switches tables. Retracting a clause is more complex: if a clause is the only clause for a sub-tree, we can (and should) recover space for the whole sub-tree.

Notice that the term *last* clause in a sub-tree must be understood in the context of LU semantics: we can only remove a clause from a `try–trust` when we are sure the code will not backtrack there.

Locality. Last, given that the tree structure is preserved, adding a clause can be seen as a set of independent updates to non-structure nodes: we just need to visit the tree and apply an operation at each node. Retracting follows similar principles, but with the caveat that we must remove empty sub-trees.

4.1 Asserting Clauses

We can now present a clause insertion algorithm, $Insert(p, C, B)$, where p is the predicate, C the new clause, and B a boolean saying whether we want to insert as the *first* or as the *last* clause.

Our algorithm performs a pre-order walk of the indexing tree. Throughout, it maintains two stacks: the *label stack* includes pointers to all the branches we

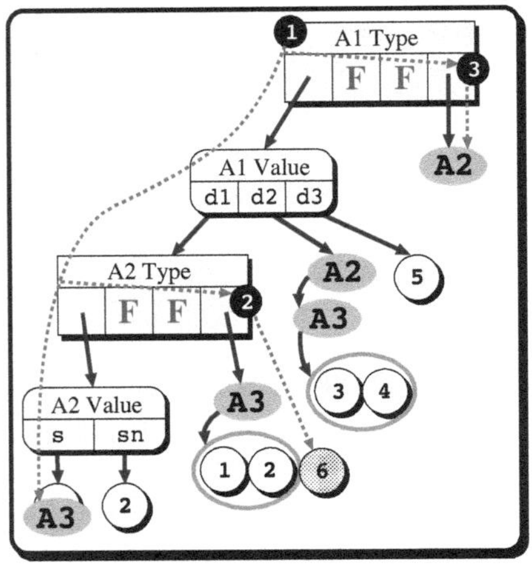

Fig. 3. Assert on `has_property/3`

have yet to visit; the *block stack* contains the node's parents. Both stacks are initially empty. The algorithm proceeds as follows:

1. If the current node is a `switch_on_type` node on argument A_i, then:
   (a) check what constraints the new clause imposes on A_i.
   (b) If the clause imposes no constraints or if A_i can match different types (e.g., $number(A_i)$), remove the sub-tree rooted at this node, replacing it by a `wait` node. One could add a `try` before/or a `trust` after the `switch_on_type` but doing so would break simplicity, as discussed above.
   (c) Otherwise, the clause must be added to two of the four cases in the `switch_on_type`: the case that matches the type, and the unbound case. The label stack allows us to process this case: we push the unbound label to the *label stack*, and jump to the bound case.
2. If the current node is a `switch` on value node, say `switch_on_constant`, then there must be a `switch_on_type` above, and that node ensured there is a constraint of the form $A_i = V$ in the clause:
   (a) if V is not in the table, one must expand the table. Our system follows the WAM and has a number of different cases: if the table is small, it use sequential search; otherwise, it uses a hash table. In either the case, if there is room in the table, one simply can insert the new entry. If there is no room, a new table is allocated. The system guarantees that value tables are only pointed from the current instruction, so the old table can be removed immediately. The algorithm than proceeds by popping the next instruction from the label stack.
   (b) if V is in the table, and matches a single clause (leaf), replace V's code by a wait node. Again, pop the next instruction from the label stack.
   (c) Otherwise, push the current block on the block stack and follow the table entry.

3. If the current node is a `try-retry-trust` chain (TTT): add a pointer to the clause to the chain. Our algorithm represents TTT nodes as lists of clauses [1], so we simply need to update the predicate's time-stamp and add the instruction to the list.
4. If the current node is a childless `wait` node: pop next instruction from label stack if childless. Otherwise, proceed to the node's child.

The algorithm terminates when the label stack empties.

Figure 3 shows an example of how the algorithm works, given the tree in Figure 2(a).

```
?- assert(atm(d1, salmonella, n)).
```

The algorithm starts by visiting the top `switch_on_type` node. The algorithm detects the constraint A_1 = `d1`, hence it takes the constant label (shown as path 1) and pushes the unbound pointer to the label stack. Next, it visits the value node for A_1. The `d1` case points to a tree, so there is no need to update the node. Next, it visits the `switch_on_type` for A_2. It detects the constraint A_2 = `salmonella`, hence the code will do as for A_1. It takes the leftmost branch, and pushes the rightmost pointer to the stack. The next `switch_on_constant` has two cases, `salmonella` and `salmonella_n`. The `salmonella` case pointed to a single clause, which must be replaced by a pointer to a `wait` node.

The next step is to pop the label stack and enter path 2. The algorithm first meets a wait node $\mathcal{T}_2$ with a child. It follows the child and meets the TTT chain node. At this point, it simply adds the new clause as a last `trust` in the chain, and replaces the previous `trust` clause 6 and the `trust 2` by a `retry 2`. We pop again and enter path 3. We only find a `wait`, pop again and exit.

4.2 Retracting Clauses

The first difference between the retracting and asserting, is that when retracting *we know that the clause must be consistent with the indexing tree.* Again, we start by emptying the two stacks, and enter at a `switch_on_type` node. The algorithm then does a pre-order walk in a fashion similar to the previous algorithm:

1. If the number of clauses for the predicate was 2, remove the whole tree.
2. If the current node is a `switch_on_type` node on some argument A_i, we must have a constraint of the form $A_i = V$. Push the unbound label to the label stack, and jump to the label matching V's type.
3. If the current node switches on value, then either:
   (a) V matches a single clause, replace the entry with `fail`.
   (b) Otherwise, jump to the label in the table, pushing the previous block on the block stack.
4. If the current node is a TTT node we have a number of possibilities:
   (a) 2 nodes in the chain: mark the TTT chain as deleted and replace the entry above by a pointer to the last clause.
   (b) else, if the TTT chain is not in use: remove the clause;
   (c) else, mark the TTT chain as *dirty*.

As usual, the algorithm terminates when the label stack empties.

Purging Dynamic Indices. Dynamic nodes are purged after retracting clauses or after backtracking. Reclaiming a node is only performed after detaching all children; decrease reference to other clauses, and decrease the parent's reference counter.

5 Performance

The performance of JITI has been discussed in [8]. Previous results [3] show that for an ILP system the benefits of indexing are partly derived from indexing dynamic procedures. Next, we present in more detail some time and performance results on two real applications typical of dynamic updates, one from van Noord's FSA utilities [11], and the other from the ILP system Aleph [9].

The experiments were performed using on a Max Powerbook Pro with a 2.5GHz Intel Core Pro Duo and 4GB of memory, running OSX Leopard in 32 bit mode. The experiments consisted of running applications with the JITI totally enabled and only enabled for the main functor of the first argument. They therefore always apply the JITI.

Kiraz and Grimley-Evans. The FSA toolkit includes a number of algorithms for finite-state automata. One of these algorithms is based on Kiraz and Grimley-Evans' algorithm for automata minimization [4]. The algorithm maintains a state table as dynamic procedures, and operates by manipulating this table, therefore it strongly depends on indexing.

Table 1 shows an advantage of using full versus first argument indexing in this case: there is a 10% speedup, at the cost of a 20% increase in index space. On the other hand, index space is still much smaller than clause compiled space.

A more detailed analysis finds that the difference essentially comes from two predicates, `symbol_state_/2` and `class_state_/2`. If one uses multiple argument, indexing execution is deterministic, and no choice-points are created. If one just uses first argument indexing, execution is non-deterministic. Execution thus becomes slower for two reasons: the system has to create choice-points, and it has to maintain a TTT chain for `symbol_state_/2` and `class_state_/2`. At the end of execution, the application erases all clauses for `symbol_state_`.

Table 1. Running Time and Space Usage for Dynamic Predicates in the Kiraz/Grimley-Evans benchmark at the end of forward execution. Sizes refer to total size spent in dynamic clauses and in indices. Indexing code is divided into code for `switch_and_type` and `switch_on_value` instructions, sequences of `try-retry-trust` instructions, `wait` nodes, and indexing tables.

	Time (msec)	Dynamic Code (in KB)					
		Clauses	*Indices*	*Switches*	*TTT*	*Wait*	*Tables*
1st **Arg**	211	998	126	7	85	18	14
Full	181	998	165	10	98	44	20

Table 2. Running Time and Space Usage for a possible Aleph execution where we first saturate example 1, reduce, saturate example 2, reduce, saturate example 3, and reduce

Experiment		Time (msec)	Dynamic Code (in KB)					
			Clauses	*Indices*	*Switches*	*TTT*	*Wait*	*Tables*
`sat(1)`	1st **Arg**	23	1066	25	4	4	9	7
	Full	21	1066	36	11	2	17	4
`reduce`	1st **Arg**	4385	12170	238	5	4	139	7
	Full	4100	12107	1495	12	91	148	23
`sat(2)`	1st **Arg**	34	12182	158	4	6	139	7
	Full	28	12182	291	16	94	153	27
`reduce`	1st **Arg**	4710	11471	162	5	6	143	7
	Full	4270	11471	378	17	155	157	49
`sat(3)`	1st **Arg**	17	11437	154	4	4	137	7
	Full	14	11437	369	13	153	147	46
`reduce`	1st **Arg**	4980	10713	284	5	4	267	7
	Full	4090	10713	595	13	242	277	61

Using multiple arguments results in deeper and larger trees. The results show that *Switches*, the space spent on `switch_on_type` and the space spent on the non-table code in the `switch_on_cons` instructions, grows to 10KB from 7KB. The last interesting data concerns the sizes of the tables used to store hash tables and other chains. The results show *Table* size of 20KB for multiple argument, whereas when using the first argument usage is negligible. The `wait` node space corresponds to the space spent to support quick expansion of indexing trees. This space will grow as we generate deeper trees.

In a second experiment we use the *Aleph* Inductive Logic Programming System running the `Carcinogenesis` benchmark [10]. We run saturation and reduction three times, for three different examples. Because the Carcinogenesis database strongly benefits from multiple indexing, the 1st argument experiment only disables indexing on the dynamic predicates.

Table 2 shows performance for a possible Aleph run where one saturates the first example, reduces, the second example, reduce. The results are quite similar to the previous dataset. There is a speedup in using multiple argument indexing, at the cost of using more memory, but the total amount of memory is still quite low compared to the compiled code. A detailed analysis shows again two predicates dominating execution in the multiple-argument case: `$aleph_search_expansion/4` and `$aleph_search_node/8`. The latter predicate performs well with first argument indexing, but the second one creates very large TTT chains.

6 Discussion

We discuss the implementation of dynamic updates for just-in-time indexing. Although the key ideas have been presented previously, our contribution provides a detailed explanation of the actual algorithms, given wide experience in using the system.

Experience has forced a number of changes over the initial implementation. Arguably, the main change was that the original implementation maintained TTT chains as a single block. Extra space was reserved at the beginning and end in case clauses would be asserted. Instead of using time-stamps, blocks were copied. Unfortunately, experience showed that copying was just too expensive for larger applications.

In general, TTT chains have shown to be the source for most of the complexity of in the system. Note that the WAM always has a TTT chain, where each instruction is stored just before a clause [13]. By default, our system has no TTT chains, both on static and dynamic procedures. Clauses are linked by an single chain, for static procedure, and by a doubly linked lists, for dynamic procedures. One advantage of using a default chain is that it is straightforward to enumerate every clause. In contrast, enumerating clauses requires generating a new index, which is expensive for predicates with large number of clauses. In the worst case, calling a built-in such as `listing/0` might overflow the system. The system chose not to support a default TTT chain in order to save space in large databases [7].

Indexing dynamic clauses can be seen as a "light" version of the static indexing algorithm. This "simplicity" principle is based on experience: updating in the original WAM algorithm was complex because it is not always very clear where a TTT chain ends, and thus, what is a real `trust` instruction.

There is relatively little work on indexing dynamic procedures. Some inspiration to our work comes from the way indexing is implemented in SICStus Prolog [1]: SICStus uses very dynamic data-structures to support logical updates. One interesting alternative to our approach would be to support a single mode: XSB supports indexing dynamic data through tries [6]. Tries are a compact representation, and are clearly much more space efficient than our approach. On the other hand, they cannot support logical updates and multiple modes.

7 Conclusions and Future Work

We present in detail an indexing algorithm for Prolog that can support Just-In Time Compilation and that can support Logical Update Semantics. The algorithm was motivated by experience with user programs, and has been successfully applied in practice. The major advantage of this approach is that it supports the main benefits of the JITI in applications such as updatable data-bases of ground terms. The main cost in our experience is that it can be relatively expensive in terms of memory usage: namely, allocating independently each instruction in a TTT chain is quite costly space-wise.

Our implementation includes a number of design decisions that were based on particular applications. We expect that new applications will require further improvements. Ultimately, though, the question is whether one should invest on alternate data-structures that can provide the functionality of dynamic procedures in a more disciplined and efficient fashion.

Acknowledgments

This work has been partially supported by projects JEDI (PTDC/EIA/66924/2006) and STAMPA (PTDC/EIA/67738/2006) and funds granted to CRACS through the Programa de Financiamento Plurianual, Fundação para a Ciência e Tecnologia and Programa POSC.

References

1. Carlsson, M.: Freeze, Indexing, and Other Implementation Issues in the Wam. In: ICLP 1987, May 1987, pp. 40–58 (1987)
2. Deransart, P., Ed-Dbali, A., Cervoni, L., Ed-Ball, A.A.: Prolog, The Standard: Reference Manual. Springer, Heidelberg (1996)
3. Fonseca, N.A., Santos Costa, V., Rocha, R., Camacho, R., Silva, F.M.A.: Improving the efficiency of inductive logic programming systems. Softw., Pract. Exper. 39(2), 189–219 (2009)
4. Kiraz, G.A., Grimley-Evans, E.: Multi-Tape Automata for Speech and Language Systems: A Prolog Implementation. In: Wood, D., Yu, S. (eds.) WIA 1997. LNCS, vol. 1436. Springer, Heidelberg (1998)
5. Lindholm, T.G., O'Keefe, R.A.: Efficient implementation of a defensible semantics for dynamic Prolog code. In: Lassez, J.-L. (ed.) Proceedings of the Fourth International Conference on Logic Programming, University of Melbourne, MIT Press Series in Logic Programming, pp. 21–39. MIT Press, Cambridge (1987)
6. Sagonas, K.F., Swift, T., Warren, D.S., Freire, J., Rao, P.: The XSB programmer's manual. Technical report, State University of New York at Stony Brook (1997), `http://xsb.sourceforge.net/`
7. Santos Costa, V.: Prolog performance on larger datasets. In: Hanus, M. (ed.) PADL 2007. LNCS, vol. 4354, pp. 185–199. Springer, Heidelberg (2007)
8. Santos Costa, V., Sagonas, K., Lopes, R.: Demand-driven indexing of prolog clauses. In: Dahl, V., Niemelä, I. (eds.) ICLP 2007. LNCS, vol. 4670, pp. 305–409. Springer, Heidelberg (2007)
9. Srinivasan, A.: The Aleph Manual (2001)
10. Srinivasan, A., King, R., Muggleton, S., Sternberg, M.: Carcinogenesis predictions using ilp. In: Džeroski, S., Lavrač, N. (eds.) ILP 1997. LNCS, vol. 1297, pp. 273–287. Springer, Heidelberg (1997)
11. van Noord, G.: FSA Utilities: A Toolbox to Manipulate Finite-State Automata. In: WIA: International Workshop on Implementing Automata. LNCS. Springer, Heidelberg (1997)
12. Van Roy, P., Demoen, B., Willems, Y.D.: Improving the execution speed of compiled Prolog with modes, clause selection and determinism. In: Ehrig, H., Levi, G., Montanari, U. (eds.) CAAP 1987 and TAPSOFT 1987. LNCS, vol. 249, pp. 111–125. Springer, Heidelberg (1987)
13. Warren, D.H.D.: An Abstract Prolog Instruction Set. Technical Note 309, SRI International (1983)

Intention Recognition via Causal Bayes Networks Plus Plan Generation

Luís Moniz Pereira and Han The Anh

Centro de Inteligência Artificial (CENTRIA)
Universidade Nova de Lisboa, 2829-516 Caparica, Portugal
lmp@di.fct.unl.pt, h.anh@fct.unl.pt

Abstract. In this paper, we describe a novel approach to tackle intention recognition, by combining dynamically configurable and situation-sensitive Causal Bayes Networks plus plan generation techniques. Given some situation, such networks enable recognizing agent to come up with the most likely intentions of the intending agent, i.e. solve one main issue of intention recognition; and, in case of having to make a quick decision, focus on the most important ones. Furthermore, the combination with plan generation provides a significant method to guide the recognition process with respect to hidden actions and unobservable effects, in order to confirm or disconfirm likely intentions. The absence of this articulation is a main drawback of the approaches using Bayes Networks solely, due to the combinatorial problem they encounter.

Keywords: Intention recognition, Causal Bayes Networks, Plan generation, P-log, ASCP, Logic Programming.

1 Introduction

Recently, there have been many works addressing the problem of intention recognition as well as its applications in a variety of fields. As in Heinze's doctoral thesis [5], intention recognition is defined, in general terms, as the process of becoming aware of the intention of another agent, and more technically, as the problem of inferring an agent's intention through its actions and their effects in the environment. According to this definition, an approach to tackle intention recognition is by reducing it to plan recognition, i.e. the problem of generating plans achieving the intentions and choosing the ones that match the observed actions and their effects in the environment of the intending agent. This has been the main stream so far [5,8].

One of the main issues of that approach is that of finding an initial set of possible intentions (of the intending agent) that the plan generator is going to tackle, and which must be come up with by the recognizing agent. Undoubtedly, this set should depend on the situation at hand, since generating plans for all intentions one agent could have, for whatever situation he might be in, is unrealistic if not impossible.

In this paper, we propose an approach to solve this problem using so-called *situation-sensitive Causal Bayes Networks* (CBN) - That is, CBNs [15] that change according to the situation under consideration, itself subject to change. Therefore, in some given situation, a CBN is configured, dynamically, to compute the likelihood of intentions

L. Seabra Lopes et al. (Eds.): EPIA 2009, LNAI 5816, pp. 138–149, 2009.

and filter out the much less likely intentions. The plan generator then only needs to deal with the remaining (relevant) intentions. Moreover, it being one of the important advantages of our approach, on the basis of the information provided by the CBN the recognizing agent can see which intentions are more likely and worth addressing first, and thus, in case of having to make a quick decision, focus on the most relevant ones.

CBNs, in our work, are represented in P-log [1,3,2], a declarative language that combines logical and probabilistic reasoning, and uses Answer Set Programming (ASP) as its logical and CBNs as its probabilistic foundations. Given a CBN, its situation-sensitive version is constructed by attaching to it a logical component to dynamically compute situation specific probabilistic information, which is forthwith updated into the P-log program representing that CBN. The computation is dynamic in the sense that there is a process of inter-feedback between the logical component and the CBN, i.e. the result from the updated CBN is also given back to the logical component, and that might give rise to further updating, etc.

In addition, one more advantage of our approach, in comparison with those using solely BNs [6,7] is that these just use the available information for constructing CBNs. For complicated tasks, e.g. in recognizing hidden intentions, not all information is observable. The approach of combining with plan generation provides a way to guide the recognition process: which actions (or their effects) should be checked for whether they were (hiddenly) executed by the intending agent. We can make use of any plan generators available. In this work, for integration's sake, we use the ASP based conditional planner called ASCP [10], re-implemented [11] in XSB Prolog using the XASP package [4,22] for interfacing with Smodels [20] – an answer set solver.

The rest of the paper is organized as follows. Section 2 briefly recalls CBNs and describes how they are used for intention recognition. This section also briefly introduces P-log. Section 3 proceeds by illustrating P-log with an example and discusses situation-sensitive CBNs. Section 4 describes the ASCP planner and shows how it is used for generating plans achieving hypothesized intentions. The paper ends with conclusions and directions for the future.

2 Causal Bayes Networks in P-Log

2.1 Causal BN

Humans know how to reason based on cause and effect, but cause and effect is not enough to draw conclusions due to the problem of imperfect information and uncertainty. To resolve these problems, humans reason combining causal models with probabilistic information. The theory that attempts to model both causality and probability is called probabilistic causation, better known as Causal Bayes Networks (CBN).

A Bayes Network is a pair consisting of a directed acyclic graph (dag) whose nodes represent variables and missing edges encode conditional independencies between the variables, and an associated probability distribution satisfying the assumption of conditional independence (Causal Markov Assumption - CMA), saying that variables are independent of their non-effects conditional on their direct causes [15].

If there is an edge from node A to another node B, A is called a parent of B, and B is a child of A. The set of parent nodes of a node A is denoted by $parents(A)$. Ancestor nodes of A are parents of A or parents of some ancestor nodes of A. If A has no parents ($parents(A) = \emptyset$), it is called a top node. If A has no child, it is called a bottom node. The nodes which are neither top nor bottom are said intermediate. If the value of a node is observed, the node is said to be an evidence node.

In a BN, associated with each intermediate node of its dag is a specification of the distribution of its variable, say A, conditioned on its parents in the graph, i.e. $P(A|parents(A))$ is specified. For a top node, the unconditional distribution of the variable is specified. These distributions are called Conditional Probability Distribution (CPD) of the BN.

Suppose nodes of the dag form a causally sufficient set [14], i.e. no common causes of any two nodes are omitted, then implied by CMA [14], the joint distribution of all node values of the set can be determined as the product of conditional probabilities of the value of each node on its parents

$$P(X_1, ..., X_N) = \prod_{i=1}^{N} P(X_i|parents(X_i))$$

where $V = \{X_i | 1 \leq i \leq N\}$ is the set of nodes of the dag.

Suppose there is a set of evidence nodes in the dag, say $O = \{O_1, ..., O_m\} \subset V$. We can determine the conditional probability of a variable X given the observed value of evidence nodes by using the conditional probability formula

$$P(X|O_1, O_2, ..., O_m) = \frac{P(X, O)}{P(O)} = \frac{P(X, O_1, ..., O_m)}{P(O_1, ..., O_m)} \tag{1}$$

where the numerator and denominator are computed by summing the joint probabilities over all absent variables w.r.t. V as follows

$$P(X = x, O = o) = \sum_{av \in ASG(AV_1)} P(X = x, O = o, AV_1 = av)$$

$$P(O = o) = \sum_{av \in ASG(AV_2)} P(O = o, AV_2 = av)$$

where $o = \{o_1, ..., o_m\}$ with $o_1, ..., o_m$ being the observed values of $O_1, ..., O_m$, respectively; $ASG(Vt)$ denotes the set of all assignments of vector Vt (with components are variables in V); AV_1, AV_2 are vectors components of which are corresponding absent variables, i.e. variables in $V \setminus \{O \cup \{X\}\}$ and $V \setminus O$, respectively.

In short, to define a BN, one needs to specify the structure of the network, its CPD and, finally, the prior probability distribution of the top nodes.

2.2 Intention Recognition with Causal Bayesian Networks

The first phase of the intention recognition system is to find out how likely each possible intention is, based on current observations such as observed actions of the intending agent or the effects its actions, either observed or unobserved, have in the environment. It is carried out by using a CBN with nodes standing for binary random variables that represent causes, intentions, actions and effects, and adopts the following structure.

Intentions are represented by intermediate nodes whose ancestor nodes represent causes that give rise to those intentions. Intuitively, we extend Heinze's tri-level model [5] with a so-called pre-intentional level that describes the causes of intentions, which are used to estimate prior probabilities of the intentions. This additional level also guarantees the causal sufficiency condition of the set of nodes of the dag. However, if these prior probabilities can be specified without considering the causes, intentions are represented by top nodes. Top nodes reflect the problem context or the intending agent's mental state.

Observed actions are represented as children of the intentions that causally affect them. Observable effects are represented as bottom nodes. They can be children of observed action nodes, of intention nodes, or of some unobserved actions that might cause the observable effects that are added as children of the intention nodes.

The above causal relations (e.g. which causes give rise to an intention, which intentions trigger an action, which actions have an effect) among nodes of the BNs, as well as its CPD and the distribution of the top nodes, are specified by domain experts. However, they are also possible to learn automatically. Finally, by using formula 1 the conditional probabilities of each intention on current observations can be determined, X being an intention and O being the set of current observations.

Example 1 (The Fox-Crow story - adapted from Aesop's fable). There is a crow, holding a cheese. A fox, being hungry, approaches the crow and praises her, hoping that the crow will sing and the cheese will fall down near him. Unfortunately for the fox, the crow is very intelligent, having the ability of intention recognition.

The Fox's intentions CBN is depicted in the Figure 1. The initial possible intentions of Fox that Crow comes up with are: Food - $i(F)$, Please - $i(P)$ and Territory - $i(T)$. The facts that might give rise to those intentions are how friendly the Fox is ($Friendly\_fox$) and how hungry he is ($Hungry\_fox$). Currently, there is only one observation which is: Fox praised Crow ($Praised$).

2.3 P-Log

The computation in CBNs can be automated by using P-log, a declarative language that combines logical and probabilistic reasoning, and uses ASP as its logical and CBNs as its probabilistic foundations.

The original P-log [1,3] uses ASP as a tool for computing all stable models of the logical part of P-log. Although ASP has been proved to be a useful paradigm for solving a variety of combinatorial problems, its non-relevance property [4] makes the P-log system sometimes computationally redundant. Newer developments of P-log [2] use the XASP package of XSB Prolog [22] for interfacing with Smodels [20] – an answer set solver. The power of ASP allows the representation of both classical and default negation in P-log easily. Moreover, the new P-log uses XSB as the underlying processing platform, allowing arbitrary Prolog code for recursive definitions. Consequently, it allows more expressive queries not supported in the original version, such as meta queries (probabilistic built-in predicates can be used as usual XSB predicates, thus allowing full power of probabilistic reasoning in XSB) and queries in the form of any XSB predicate

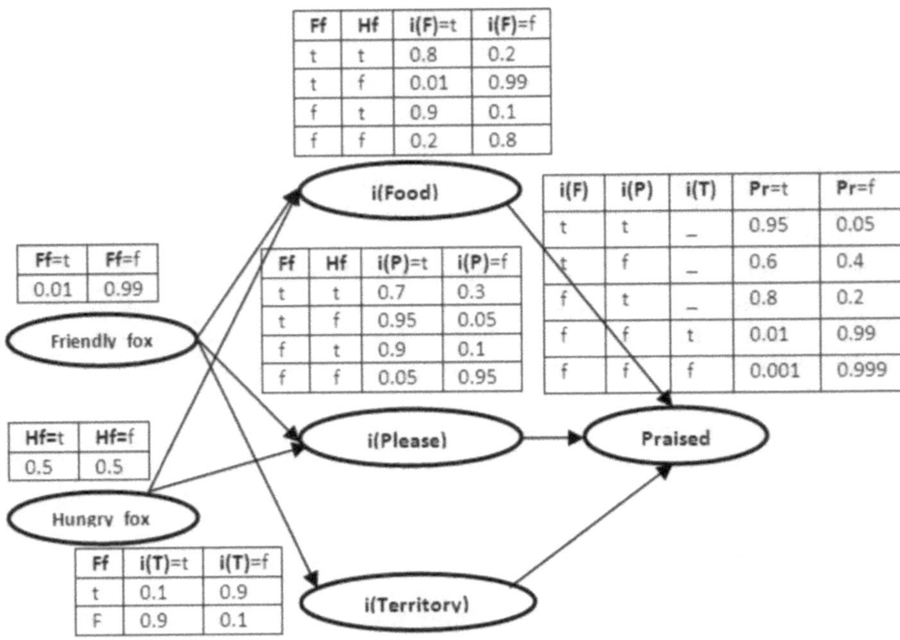

Fig. 1. Fox's intentions CBN

expression [2]. Moreover, the tabling mechanism of XSB [21] significantly improves the performance of the system.

In general, a P-log program Π consists of a sorted signature, declarations, a regular part, a set of random selection rules, a probabilistic information part, and a set of observations and actions.

Sorted signature and Declaration. The sorted signature Σ of Π contains a set of constant symbols and term-building function symbols, which are used to form terms in the usual way. Additionally, the signature contains a collection of special function symbols called attributes. Attribute terms are expressions of the form $a(\bar{t})$, where a is an attribute and $\bar{t}$ is a vector of terms of the sorts required by a. A literal is an atomic statement, p, or its explicit negation, neg_p.

The declaration part of a P-log program can be defined as a collection of sorts and sort declarations of attributes. A sort c can be defined by listing all the elements $c = \{x_1, ..., x_n\}$, by specifying the range of values $c = \{L..U\}$ where L and U are the integer lower bound and upper bound of the sort c

Attribute a with domain $c_1 \times ... \times c_n$ and range c_0 is represented as follows:

$$a : c_1 \times ... \times c_n \texttt{ --> } c_0$$

If attribute a has no domain parameter, we simply write $a : c_0$. The range of attribute a is denoted by $range(a)$.

Regular part. This part of a P-log program consists of a collection of XSB Prolog rules, facts and integrity constraints (IC) formed using literals of Σ. An IC is encoded as a XSB rule with the `false` literal in the head.

Random Selection Rule. This is a rule for attribute a having the form:

$$random(RandomName, a(\bar{t}), DynamicRange) \; :- \; Body$$

This means that the attribute instance $a(\bar{t})$ is random if the conditions in $Body$ are satisfied. The $DynamicRange$ allows to restrict the default range for random attributes. The $RandomName$ is a syntactic mechanism used to link random attributes to the corresponding probabilities. If there is no precondition, we simply put $true$ in the body. A constant $full$ can be used in $DynamicRange$ to signal that the dynamic domain is equal to $range(a)$.

Probabilistic Information. Information about probabilities of random attribute instances $a(\bar{t})$ taking a particular value y is given by probability atoms (or simply pa-atoms) which have the following form:

$$pa(RandomName, a(\bar{t}, y), d\_(A, B)) :- \; Body.$$

meaning that if the $Body$ were true, and the value of $a(\bar{t})$ were selected by a rule named $RandomName$, then $Body$ would cause $a(\bar{t}) = y$ with probability $\frac{A}{B}$.

Observations and Actions. These are, respectively, statements of the forms $obs(l)$ and $do(l)$, where l is a literal. Observations are used to record the outcomes of random events, i.e. random attributes and attributes dependent on them. The statement $do(a(t, y))$ indicates that $a(t) = y$ is enforced true as the result of a deliberate action.

3 Recognizing Fox's Intentions – An Example

Example 2 (Fox-Crow). The Fox's intentions CBN can be coded with the P-log program in Figure 2.

Two sorts *bool* and $fox\_intentions$, in order to represent boolean values and set of Fox's intentions, are declared in part 1. Part 2 is the declaration of four attributes $hungry\_fox$, $friendly\_fox$, $praised$ and i which state the first three attributes have no domain parameter and get boolean values, and the last one maps each Fox's intention to a boolean value. The random selection rules in part 3 declare that these four attributes are randomly distributed in their ranges. The distributions of the top nodes ($hungry\_fox$, $friendly\_fox$) and the CPD corresponding to the CBN in Figure 1 are given in part 4 and parts 5-8, respectively, using the probabilistic information pa-rules. For example, in part 4 the first rule says that fox is hungry with probability $1/2$ and the second rule says he is friendly with probability $1/100$. The first rule in part 5 states that if Fox is friendly and hungry, the probability of him having intention Food is $8/10$.

Note that the probability of an atom $a(\bar{t}, y)$ will be directly assigned if the corresponding $pa/3$ atom is in the head of some *pa-rule* with a true body. To define probabilities of the remaining atoms we assume that by default, all values of a given attribute which are not assigned a probability are equally likely. For example, first rule in part 4 implies that fox is not hungry with probability $1/2$. And, actually, we can remove that rule without changing the probabilistic information since, in that case, the probability of fox being hungry and of not being hungry are both defined by default, thus, equal to $1/2$.

```
1. bool = {t,f}.     fox_intentions = {food,please,territory}.
2. hungry_fox : bool.                 friendly_fox : bool.
   i : fox_intentions --> bool.       praised : bool.
3. random(rh, hungry_fox, full).      random(rf, friendly_fox, full).
   random(ri, i(I), full).            random(rp, praised, full).
4. pa(rh,hungry_fox(t),d_(1,2)).      pa(rf,friendly_fox(t),d_(1,100)).
5. pa(ri(food),i(food,t),d_(8,10)):-friendly_fox(t),hungry_fox(t).
   pa(ri(food),i(food,t),d_(9,10)):-friendly_fox(f),hungry_fox(t).
   pa(ri(food),i(food,t),d_(0.1,10)):-friendly_fox(t),hungry_fox(f).
   pa(ri(food),i(food,t),d_(2,10)):-friendly_fox(f),hungry_fox(f).
6. pa(ri(please),i(please,t),d_(7,10)):-friendly_fox(t),hungry_fox(t).
   pa(ri(please),i(please,t),d_(1,100)):-friendly_fox(f),hungry_fox(t).
   pa(ri(please),i(please,t),d_(95,100)):-friendly_fox(t),hungry_fox(f).
   pa(ri(please),i(please,t),d_(5,100)):-friendly_fox(f),hungry_fox(f).
7. pa(ri(territory),i(territory,t),d_(1,10)):-friendly_fox(t).
   pa(ri(territory),i(territory,t),d_(9,10)):-friendly_fox(f).
8. pa(rp, praised(t),d_(95,100)) :- i(food, t), i(please, t).
   pa(rp, praised(t),d_(6,10)) :- i(food, t), i(please, f).
   pa(rp, praised(t),d_(8,10)) :- i(food, f), i(please, t).
   pa(rp, praised(t),d_(1,100)):-i(food, f),i(please,f),i(territory,t).
   pa(rp, praised(t),d_(1,1000)):-i(food,f),i(please,f),i(territory,f).
```

Fig. 2. Fox's intentions CBN

The probabilities of Fox having intention Food, Territory and Please given the observation that Fox praised Crow can be found in P-log with the following queries, respectively,

$? -$ $\mathbf{pr(i(food, t)\ '|'\ obs(praised(t)), V_1)}$. The answer is: $V_1 = 0.9317$.
$? -$ $\mathbf{pr(i(territory, t)\ '|'obs(praised(t)), V_2)}$. The answer is: $V_2 = 0.8836$.
$? -$ $\mathbf{pr(i(please, t)\ '|'\ obs(praised(t)), V_3)}$. The answer is: $V_3 = 0.0900$.

From the result we can say that Fox is very unlikely to have the intention Please, i.e. to make the Crow pleased since its likelihood is very much less than the others. Thus, the next step of Crow's intention recognition is to generate conceivable plans that might corroborate the two remaining intentions. The one with greater likelihood will be discovered first.

Situation-sensitive CBNs. Undoubtedly, CBNs should be situation-sensitive since using a general CBN for all specific situations (instances) of a problem domain is unrealistic and most likely imprecise. For example, in the Fox-Crow scenario the probabilistic information in Crow's CBN about the Fox's intention of getting Crow's territory very much depends on what kind of territories the Crow occupies. However, consulting the domain expert to manually change the CBN w.r.t. each situation is also very costly.

We here provide a way to construct situation-sensitive CBNs, i.e. ones that change according to the given situation. It uses Logic Programming (LP) techniques to compute situation specific probabilistic information which is then updated into a CBN general for the problem domain.

The LP techniques can be deduction with top-down procedure (Prolog) (to deduce situation-specific probabilistic information) or abduction (to abduce probabilistic information needed to explain observations representing the given situation). However, we do not exclude various other types of reasoning, e.g. including integrity constraint satisfaction, abduction, contradiction removal, preferences, or inductive learning, whose results can be compiled (in part) into an evolving CBN.

The issue of how to update a CBN with new probabilistic information can take advantage of the advance in LP semantics for evolving programs with updates [17,18,19]. However, in this work we employ a simpler way, demonstrated in the following example.

Example 3 (Fox-Crow (cont'd)). Suppose the fixed general CBN is the one given in Figure 2. The Prolog program contains the following two rules for updating the probabilistic information in part 7 of the CBN:

```
pa_rule(pa(ri(territory),i(territory,t),d_(0,100)),[friendly_fox(t)])
        :- territory(tree).
pa_rule(pa(ri(territory),i(territory,t),d_(1,100)),[friendly_fox(f)])
       :- territory(tree).
```

Given a P-log probabilistic information pa-rule, then the corresponding so-called situation-sensitive $pa\_rule/2$ predicate takes the head and body of the pa-rule as its first and second arguments, respectively. A situation is given, in this work, by asserted facts representing it. In order to find the probabilistic information specific for the given situation, we simply use the XSB built-in $findall/3$ predicate to find all true $pa\_rule/3$ literals.

In the story the Crow's territory is a tree, thus the fact $territory(tree)$ is asserted. Hence, the following two $pa\_rule/3$ literals are true

```
pa_rule(pa(ri(territory),i(territory,t),d_(0,100)),[friendly_fox(t)])
pa_rule(pa(ri(territory),i(territory,t),d_(1,100)),[friendly_fox(f)])
```

The CBN is updated by replacing the two pa-rules in part 7 of the CBN with the corresponding two rules

```
pa(ri(territory),i(territory,t),d_(0,100)) :- friendly_fox(t)
pa(ri(territory),i(territory,t),d_(1,100)) :- friendly_fox(f)
```

This change can be easily made at the preprocessing stage of the implementation of P-log(XSB) (more details about the system implementation can be found in [2]).

In this updated CBN the likelihood of the intentions $i(food, t)$, $i(territory, t)$, $i(please, t)$ are: $V_1 = 0.9407$; $V_2 = 0.0099$; $V_3 = 0.0908$, respectively. Thus, much likely, the only surviving intention is $food$.

4 Plan Generation

The second phase of the intention recognition system is to generate conceivable plans that can achieve the most likely intentions surviving after the first phase. Any appropriate planners, though those implemented in ASP and/or Prolog are preferable for integration's sake, might be used for this task, e.g. $DLV^{\mathcal{K}}$ – a declarative, logic-based planning system built on top of the DLV [9] and ASCP – an ASP based conditional planner [10].

In our system, plan generation is carried out by a new implementation of ASCP in XSB Prolog using XASP package [11]. It has the same syntax and uses the same transformation to ASP as in the original version. It might have better performance because of the relevance property and tabling mechanism in XSB, but we will not discuss that here. Next we briefly recall the syntax of ASCP necessary to represent the example being considered. Semantics and the transformation to ASP can be found in [10].

4.1 Action Language A_K^c

ASCP uses A_K^c - a representation action language that extends $\mathcal{A}$ [12] by introducing new types of propositions called *knowledge producing proposition* and *executability condition*, and *static causal laws*.

The alphabet of A_K^c consists of a set of actions **A** and a set of fluents **F**. A *fluent literal* (or *literal* for short) is either a fluent $f \in \mathbf{F}$ or its negation $\neg f$. A fluent formula is a propositional formula constructed from the set of literals using operators $\wedge$, $\vee$ and/or $\neg$. To describe an action theory, 5 kinds of propositions used: (1) **initially**(l); (2) **executable**(a, ψ); (3) **causes**(a, l, ϕ); (4) **if**(l, φ); and (5) **determines**(a, θ).

The initial situation is described by a set of propositions (1), called v-propositions. (1) says that l holds in the initial situation. A proposition of form (2) is called executability condition. It says that a is executable in any situation in which ψ holds. A proposition (3), called a dynamic causal law, saying that performing a in a situation in which ϕ holds causes l to hold in the successor situation. A proposition (4), called a static causal law, states that l holds in any situation in which φ holds. A knowledge proposition (5) states that the values of literals in θ, sometimes referred to as sensed-literals, will be known after a is executed.

A *planning problem instance* is a triple $\pi = (D, I, G)$ where D is a set of propositions of types from (2) to (5), called domain description; I is a set of propositions of type (1), dubbed initial situation; and G is a conjunction of fluent literals.

With the presence of sensing actions we need to extend the notion of plans from a sequence of actions so as to allow conditional statements of the form **case-endcase** (which subsumes the **if-then** statement). A conditional plan can be empty, i.e. containing no action, denoted by []; or sequence [a; p] where a is a non-sensing action and p is a conditional plan; or conditional sequence $[a; cases(\{g_j \rightarrow p_j\}_{j=1}^{n}]$ where a is a sensing action of a proposition (5) with $\theta = \{g1, ..., gn\}$ and p_j's are conditional plans; Nothing else is a conditional plan.

To execute a conditional plan of the form $[a; cases(\{g_j \rightarrow p_j\}_{j=1}^{n}]$, we first execute a and then evaluate each g_j w.r.t. our current knowledge. If one of the g_j's, say g_k holds, we execute p_k.

ASCP planner works by transforming a given planning problem instance into an ASP program whose answer sets correspond to conditional plans of the problem instance (see [10] for details).

4.2 Representation in the Action Language

We now show how the Crow represents Fox's actions language and two problem instances corresponding to the two Fox's intentions, gathered from the CBN: $Food$ (not to be hungry) and $Territory$ (occupy Crow's tree) in A_K^c. The representation is inspired by the work in [13].

Example 4 (Fox-Crow (cont'd)). The scenarios with intentions of getting food and territory are represented in Figure 3 and 4, respectively. The first problem instance has the conditional plan:

$[praise(fox, crow), \mathbf{cases}(\{$
$\quad \mathsf{accepted(crow)} \rightarrow [sing(crow), grab(fox, cheese), eat(fox, cheese)];$
$\quad \mathsf{declined(crow)} \rightarrow \bot\})]$ (where $\bot$ means no plans appropriate)

```
1.animal(fox). bird(crow). object(cheese). edible(cheese).
  animal(X) :- bird(X).
2.executable(eat(A,E),[holds(A,E)]) :- animal(A), edible(E).
  executable(sing(B),[accepted(B)]) :- bird(B).
  executable(praise(fox,A), []) :- animal(A).
  executable(grab(A,O),[holds(nobody,O)]) :- animal(A),object(O).
3.causes(sing(B),holds(nobody,O),[holds(B,O)]) :- bird(B),object(O).
  causes(eat(A,E),neg(hungry(A)),[hungry(A)]) :- animal(A), edible(E).
  causes(grab(A,O),holds(A,O),[]) :- animal(A), object(O).
4.determines(praise(fox,B),[accepted(B),declined(B)]) :- bird(B).
5.initially(holds(crow,cheese)). initially(hungry(fox)).
6.goal([neg(hungry(fox))]).
```

Fig. 3. Fox's plans for food

i.e. first, Fox praises Crow. If Crow accepts to sing, Fox grabs the dropped cheese and eats it. Otherwise, i.e. Crow declines to sing, nothing happens. The second problem instance has the conditional plan:

$[praise(fox, crow), \mathbf{cases}(\{$
$\quad \mathsf{accepted(crow)} \rightarrow [sing(crow), approach(fox, crow), attack(fox, crow)];$
$\quad \mathsf{declined(crow)} \rightarrow \bot\})]$

Thus, with the only current observation (Fox praised) Crow cannot decide which is the real intention of Fox. Since the only way to identify is an acceptance to sing, which in both cases leads to a bad consequence, losing the cheese and/or the territory, Crow can simply decline to sing. However, being really smart and extremely curious, she can first eat or hide the cheese in order to prevent it from falling down when singing, then she starts singing, keeping an eye on Fox's behaviors. If Fox approaches her, she flies, knowing Fox's real intention is to get her territory (supposing Crow does not get injured by a Fox attack, she can revenge on Fox to get back the territory). Otherwise, if Fox does nothing or simply goes away, Crow knows that Fox's real intention was to get the cheese.

```
1.place(tree).
2.executable(attack(fox,A),[]) :- bird(A), near(fox,A).
  executable(approach(fox,A), [happy(A)]) :- animal(A).
3.causes(attack(fox,A),occupied(fox,P),[occupied(A,P)]) :-
       animal(A),place(P).
  causes(approach(A,B),near(A,B), []) :- animal(A),animal(B).
  causes(sing(A),happy(A),[]) :- bird(A).
4.occupied(crow, tree).
5.goal([occupied(fox,tree)]).
```

Fig. 4. Fox's plan for territory

5 Conclusions and Future Work

We have shown a novel approach to intention recognition, by combining situation-sensitive CBNs and a plan generator. Based on the situation at hand and a starting CBN default for the problem domain, its situation-sensitive version is dynamically reconfigured, using LP techniques, in order to compute the likelihood of intentions w.r.t. the situation given, then filter out those much less likely than others. The computed likelihoods enable the recognizing agent to focus on the more likely ones, which is especially important for when having to make a quick decision. Henceforth, the plan generator just needs to work on the remaining relevant intentions. In addition, we have shown how generated plans can guide the recognition process: which actions (or their effects) should be checked for whether they were (hiddenly) executed by the intending agent. We have illustrated all these features with an example.

There are currently several possible future directions to explore. First of all, we can employ an interplay between CBNs and the planner. Besides being a consumer of CBNs as shown, the planner can also be a producer for the CBN in the following ways. Firstly, its feedback about the final intention of the intending agent may increase the corresponding probabilistic relations of the confirmed intention in the CBN; Secondly, when new actions (or their effects) of the intending agent, not being observable before, become confirmed, the CBN is updated again, which might rule out more intentions, not yet explored or able to be confirmed or denied. Moreover, the planner might do real experiments, or even thought experiments, where values of nodes may be enforced true. The thought experiments may involve hypothetical or even counterfactual reasoning (possibly prospecting the future [16]).

In addition, the advance in LP semantics for evolving program with updates [17] should be used to give more flexibility in updating CBNs with new information. This is essential when more dynamic reasoning processes, e.g. in the above CBNs-Planner interplay, are employed.

References

1. Baral, C., Gelfond, M., Rushton, J.N.: Probabilistic reasoning with answer sets. In: Lifschitz, V., Niemelä, I. (eds.) LPNMR 2004. LNCS (LNAI), vol. 2923, pp. 21–33. Springer, Heidelberg (2004)

2. Anh, H.T., Kencana Ramli, C.D.P., Damásio, C.V.: An implementation of extended P-log using XASP. In: Garcia de la Banda, M., Pontelli, E. (eds.) ICLP 2008. LNCS, vol. 5366, pp. 739–743. Springer, Heidelberg (2008)
3. Baral, C., Gelfond, M., Rushton, N.: Probabilistic reasoning with answer sets. TPLP 9(1), 57–144 (2009)
4. Castro, L., Swift, T., Warren, D.S.: XASP: Answer set programming with xsb and smodels, `http://xsb.sourceforge.net/packages/xasp.pdf`
5. Heinze, C.: Modeling Intention Recognition for Intelligent Agent Systems, Doctoral Thesis, the University of Melbourne, Australia (2003), `http://www.dsto.defence.gov.au/publications/scientific_record.php?record=3367`
6. Tahboub, K.A.: Intelligent Human-Machine Interaction Based on Dynamic Bayesian Networks Probabilistic Intention Recognition. Journal of Intelligent Robotics Systems 45(1), 31–52 (2006)
7. Schrempf, O.C., Albrecht, D., Hanebeck, U.D.: Tractable Probabilistic Models for Intention Recognition Based on Expert Knowledge. In: Procs. 2007 IEEE/RSJ Intl. Conf. on Intelligent Robots and Systems (IROS 2007), pp. 1429–1434 (2007)
8. Kautz, H.A., Allen, J.F.: Generalized plan recognition. In: Procs. 1986 Conf. of the American Association for Artificial Intelligence (1986)
9. Eiter, T., Faber, W., Leone, N., Pfeifer, G., Polleres, A.: A Logic Programming Approach to Knowledge State Planning, II: The $DLV^{\mathcal{K}}$ System. Artificial Intelligence 144, 157–211 (2003)
10. Tu, P.H., Son, T.C., Baral, C.: Reasoning and Planning with Sensing Actions, Incomplete Information, and Static Causal Laws using Answer Set Programming. TPLP 7(4) (July 2007)
11. An implementation of ASCP using XASP, `http://centria.di.fct.unl.pt/lmp/software/cataplan-online.zip`
12. Gelfond, M., Lifschitz, V.: Representing actions and change by logic programs. Journal of Logic Programming 17(2,3,4), 301–323 (1993)
13. Kowalski, B.: How to be Artificially Intelligent, `http://www.doc.ic.ac.uk/~rak/`
14. Glymour, C.: The Mind's Arrows: Bayes Nets and Graphical Causal Models in Psychology. MIT Press, Cambridge (2001)
15. Pearl, J.: Causality: Models, Reasoning, and Inference. Cambridge U.P, Cambridge (2000)
16. Pereira, L.M., Anh, H.T.: Evolution Prospection. In: Procs. First KES Intl. Symposium on Intelligent Decision Technologies (KES-IDT 2009), Himeji, Japan, April 2009. Engineering Series, Springer, Heidelberg (2009)
17. Alferes, J.J., Brogi, A., Leite, J., Moniz Pereira, L.: Evolving logic programs. In: Flesca, S., Greco, S., Leone, N., Ianni, G. (eds.) JELIA 2002. LNCS (LNAI), vol. 2424, pp. 50–61. Springer, Heidelberg (2002)
18. Alferes, J.J., Banti, F., Brogi, A., Leite, J.A.: The Refined Extension Principle for Semantics of Dynamic Logic Programming. Studia Logica 79(1), 7–32 (2005)
19. Alferes, J.J., Leite, J.A., Pereira, L.M., Przymusinska, H., Przymusinski, T.C.: Dynamic updates of non-monotonic knowledge bases. J. Logic Programming 45(1-3), 43–70 (2000)
20. Niemelã, I., Simons, P.: Smodels: An implementation of the stable model and well-founded semantics for normal logic programs. In: Fuhrbach, U., Dix, J., Nerode, A. (eds.) LPNMR 1997. LNCS (LNAI), vol. 1265, pp. 420–429. Springer, Heidelberg (1997)
21. Swift, T.: Tabling for non-monotonic programming. Annals of Mathematics and Artificial Intelligence 25(3–4), 201–240 (1999)
22. The XSB System Version 3.0 Volume 2: Libraries, Interfaces and Packages (July 2006)

An ILP System for Learning Head Output Connected Predicates

José C.A. Santos, Alireza Tamaddoni-Nezhad, and Stephen Muggleton

Department of Computing, Imperial College London
{jcs06,atn,shm}@doc.ic.ac.uk

Abstract. Inductive Logic Programming (ILP) [1] systems are general purpose learners that have had significant success on solving a number of relational problems, particularly from the biological domain [2,3,4,5]. However, the standard compression guided top-down search algorithm implemented in state of the art ILP systems like Progol [6] and Aleph [7] is not ideal for the Head Output Connected (HOC) class of learning problems. HOC is the broad class of predicates that have at least one output variable in the target concept. There are many relevant learning problems of this class such as arbitrary arithmetic functions and list manipulation predicates which are useful in areas such as automated software verification[8]. In this paper we present a special purpose ILP system to efficiently learn HOC predicates.

1 Introduction

Inductive Logic Programming (ILP) [1] systems are general purpose machine learners that have had significant success on solving a number of relational problems particularly from the biological domain [2,3,4,5].

However, the standard compression guided top-down search algorithm implemented in state of the art ILP systems like Progol [6] and Aleph [7] is not ideal for the Head Output Connected (HOC) class of learning problems. HOC is the broad class of predicates that have at least one output variable in the target concept.

The reason compression or coverage guided searchs are not suitable for this class of problems is because it really only makes sense to evaluate the clause when the head output variable has been instantiated in the body of the clause. In the HOC class of problems knowning the coverage of the intermediate clauses, besides computationally expensive, is useless and cannot guide the search as often all the intermediate clauses cover all the examples or the coverage bears no relation to the target concept.

Thus, unfortunately, recent significant performance improvements [9] to general purpose ILP systems that focus on more efficient algorithms and datastructures to process the hypotheses and their coverages, albeit very useful in general, are of little help for the HOC class of problems.

The HOC class is a special case of relational path finding which was first studied by Richards and Mooney [10]. More recently, Ong et al. [11] extended Richards and Mooney's work to make use of mode declarations and bottom clauses. Our work also uses the mode declarations to specify the call modes

L. Seabra Lopes et al. (Eds.): EPIA 2009, LNAI 5816, pp. 150–159, 2009.

(input or output) for predicate variables and the bottom clause to anchor one end of the search space but proposes an efficient algorithm for the case when there is at least one head output variable in the target concept to be induced.

The HOC class of problems may seem too specific at first but several important problems belong to it. Perhaps the most evident one are arbitrary arithmetic functions (e.g. polynomials, factorial, fibonnaci, ...). Being able to efficiently induce arithmetic functions is important in software verification, for instance, to find loop invariants [8].

This paper is organized as follows. In section 2, the minimal background in ILP is provided in order for this paper to be self contained. In section 3, the algorithm to efficiently learn problems in the HOC class is presented. In section 4 an empirical evaluation is presented. Finally we conclude on section 6.

2 ILP Background

We assume the reader to be familiar with the basic concepts from logic programming [12] and inductive logic programming [13]. This section is intended as a reminder of some of concepts used in definitions in this paper.

Several ILP systems, including Progol [6] and Aleph [7], use mode declarations to constrain the search space. Mode declaration (M), definite mode language ($\mathcal{L}(M)$) and depth-bounded mode language ($\mathcal{L}_i(M)$) used in these systems are defined as follows.

Definition 1 (Mode declaration M). *A mode declaration has either the form modeh(n,atom) or modeb(n,atom) where n, the recall, is either an integer, $n > 1$, or '*' and atom is a ground atom. Terms in the atom are either normal or place-marker. A normal term is either a constant or a function symbol followed by a bracketed tuple of terms. A place-marker is either +type, -type or #type, where type is a constant. If m is a mode declaration then $a(m)$ denotes the atom of m with place-markers replaced by distinct variables. The sign of m is positive if m is a modeh and negative if m is a modeb.*

Definition 2 (Definite mode language $\mathcal{L}(M)$). *Let C be a definite clause with a defined total ordering over the literals and M be a set of mode declarations. $C = h \leftarrow b_1, .., b_n$ is in the definite mode language $\mathcal{L}(M)$ if and only if 1) h is the atom of a modeh declaration in M with every place-marker +type and -type replaced by variables and every place-marker #type replaced by a ground term and 2) every atom b_i in the body of C is the atom of a modeb declaration in M with every place-marker +type and -type replaced by variables and every place-marker #type replaced by a ground term and 3) every variable of +type in any atom b_i is either of +type in h or of -type in some atom b_j, $1 \leq j < i$.*

Definition 3 (Depth of variables). *Let C be a definite clause and v be a variable in C. Depth of v is defined as follows:*

$$d(v) = \begin{cases} 0 & \textit{if } v \textit{ is in the head of } C \\ (max_{u \in U_v} d(u)) + 1 & \textit{otherwise} \end{cases}$$

where U_v are the variables in atoms in the body of C containing v.

Definition 4 (Depth-bounded mode language $\mathcal{L}_i(M)$). *Let C be a definite clause with a defined total ordering over the literals and M be a set of mode declarations. C is in $\mathcal{L}_i(M)$ if and only if C is in $\mathcal{L}(M)$ and all variables in C have depth at most i according to Definition 3.*

Progol and Aleph search a bounded sub-lattice for each example e relative to background knowledge B and mode declarations M. The sub-lattice has a most general element which is the empty clause, $\square$, and a least general element $\bot_i$ which is the most specific element in $\mathcal{L}_i(M)$ such that

$$B \wedge \bot_i \wedge \overline{e} \vdash_h \square$$

where $\vdash_h \square$ denotes derivation of the empty clause in at most h resolutions. The following definition describes a bottom clause $\bot_i$ for a depth-bounded mode language $\mathcal{L}_i(M)$.

Definition 5 (Most-specific clause or bottom clause). *Let h, i be natural numbers, B be a set of Horn clauses, $e = a \leftarrow b_1, .., b_n$ be a definite clause, M be a set of mode declarations containing exactly one modeh m such that $a(m) \succeq a$ and $\hat{\bot}$ be the most-specific (potentially infinite) definite clause such that $B \wedge \hat{\bot} \wedge \overline{e} \vdash_h \square$. $\bot_i$ is the most-specific clause in $\mathcal{L}_i(M)$ such that $\bot_i \succeq \hat{\bot}$. C is the most-specific clause in $\mathcal{L}$ if for all C' in $\mathcal{L}$ we have $C' \succeq C$.*

3 Head Output Connected Learning

In this section we introduce some definitions needed to present the HOC learning algorithm.

Definition 6 (IO consistent). *A definite clause $h \leftarrow b_1, .., b_n$ is said to be IO consistent iff the input variables for each body atom b_i, are either a subset of the head input variables or are found in a previous body atom b_j, with $1 \leq j < i$.*

Example 1. Given the predicate signatures c(+int), a(+int,-int), b(+int, -int), $c(X) \leftarrow a(X,Y), b(Y,Z)$ is IO consistent but $c(X) \leftarrow a(X,Y), b(Z,Y)$ is not because Z is an input variable for $b/2$ but is not connected to the head input variables.

An ILP system only generates IO consistent clauses as valid hypotheses. By construction the bottom clause ensures it.

Definition 7 (Head Output Connected (HOC)). *A definite clause C is said to be Head Output Connected iff it is IO consistent and all its head output variables are instantiated in the body (i.e. there is a chain of literals connecting the head input variables to the head output variables).*

Example 2. Given the predicate signatures c(+int,-int), a(+int,-int), b(+int, -int), $c(X,Y) \leftarrow a(X,Z), b(Z,Y)$ is Head Output Connected as there is a chain of literals from variable X to variable Y.

Note that a general purpose ILP system does not distinguish HOC clauses from non-HOC clauses.

Definition 8 (Support clause at depth D). *A clause C' is a support clause (SC) for a clause C at depth D iff, C' subsumes C, C' has D literals, is Head Output Connected and has itself no shorter support clause (i.e. $SC(C') = C'$).*

Support clauses are an important concept in the context of head output variable connectness. They are, at a given depth, the shortest clauses that minimally connect the clause's head input variables to its head output variables.

Note that the support clause at a given depth is not necessarily unique as Example 3 illustrates.

Example 3. Let $Clause = a(A,B) \leftarrow b(A,C), b(A,B), c(A,D), c(C,B), c(D,B)$ and the mode declarations are:

$\{a(+t,-t), b(+t,-t), c(+t,-t)\}$, with t an arbitrary type shared by all predicates (e.g. int), then:
$SC_{Clause,1} = \{\{a(A,B) \leftarrow b(A,B)\}\}$
$SC_{Clause,2} = \{\{a(A,B) \leftarrow b(A,C), c(C,B)\}, \{a(A,B) \leftarrow b(A,D), c(D,B)\}\}$
$SC_{Clause,3} = \{\}$

Note that HOC learning is robust to both determinate and non-derminate predicates, both in head or in the body of a clause (b/2 and c/2 are non-determinate in the above example).

In order to search for the Head Output Connected clauses we need to define an ordering of clauses from the Head to the most specific clause, $\bot$. It is useful to first define the concept of subclause 9.

Definition 9 (Subclause of another clause). *Let $C = h \leftarrow b_1, .., b_n$ be an arbitrary IO consistent clause. C' is a subclause of C iff it is of the form $h \leftarrow b'_1, .., b'_{n'}$, where $b'_1, .., b'_{n'}$ is a subsequence of $b_1, .., b_n$ and C' is also an IO consistent clause.*

Example 4. Let $C = c(X) \leftarrow a(X), b(X), d(X)$, $C' = c(X) \leftarrow a(X), b(X)$ and $C'' = c(X) \leftarrow b(X), a(X)$, then C' is a subclause of C but C'' is not because its literals are not a subsequence of C.

Definition 10 (Successors of a subclause with respect to a parent clause). *A clause C_{suc} is the sucessor of a clause C_{sub} with respect to a clause C, iff C_{sub} is a subclause of C, C_{sub} is a subclause of C_{suc} and C_{suc} is one of the subclauses of C obtained by adding a single atom from the body of C to C_{sub}. The set of successors of a subclause C_{sub} with respect to a parent clause C (i.e. $S_{C_{sub},C}$), are all the C_{suc} clauses that can be generated from this definition.*

Example 5. Let $C = c(X,Y) \leftarrow a(X,A), b(A,B), d(A,D), e(D,Y)$ and $C_{sub} = c(X,Y) \leftarrow a(X,A)$, then $C_{suc_1} = c(X,Y) \leftarrow a(X,A), b(A,B)$ and $C_{suc_2} = c(X,Y) \leftarrow a(X,A), d(A,D)$. Thus $S_{C_{sub},C} = \{C_{suc_1}, C_{suc_2}\}$. Notice that $S_{C_{suc_1},C} = \{\}$ and $S_{C_{suc_2},C} = \{c(X,Y) \leftarrow a(X,A), d(A,D), e(D,Y)\}$.

3.1 Algorithms

The algorithm to compute all the sets of support clauses for the head output variables until depth D is given in Figure 1. It is essentially a breadth-first search over the implicit hypotheses space defined by the bottom clause. This space is traversed using the successor subclauses of the current subclauses to visit. The initial clause to visit is the head. Notice that the main difference to Progol and Aleph is that no coverage computation needs to take place during the search.

Set of support clauses for a clause, C, until a given max depth, D

```
Input: Clause C and depth D
Let ClausesToVisit = C's head
Let SuppClauses = {}
Let Depth = 1
while ClausesToVisit≠ {} and Depth < D do
  ClausesToVisitNext = {}
  for each clause c ∈ ClausesToVisit do
    Let SuccClauses = Successors of c with respect to C
    Let CurSuppClauses = Head Output connected clauses ∈ SuccClauses
    SuppClauses = SuppClauses ∪ CurSuppClauses
    ClausesToVisitNext = ClausesToVisitNext ∪ SucessorClauses - CurSuppClauses
  end for
  ClausesToVisit = ClausesToVisitNext
  Depth = Depth + 1
end while
Output: SuppClauses
```

Fig. 1. Algorithm to generate the set of support clauses for a single clause at depth D

Head Output Connected special purpose ILP system

```
Input: Positive examples E+, mode declarations M, settings S
         and background knowledge B
Let Hyps = {}
for each example e ∈ E+ do
  Let C = ⊥e
  Let Hype = support set of clauses for C until depth=max. clause length
  Hyps = Hyps ∪ Hype
end for
Let Theory = Greedy search on Hyps for the highest scoring clauses
Output: Theory
```

Fig. 2. Main loop of the Head Output Connected special purpose ILP system

Figure 2 presents the main cycle of the Head Output Connected special purpose ILP system. Notice that this algorithm is robust to the order of the examples as it processes all the examples. Only at the end, after all HOC clauses from all the examples are known, it performs a greedy search to find the set of HOC clauses that maximizes a clause evaluation function.

By default the clause evaluation function is compression. The compression of a clause is given by: $Pos - Neg - Len$, where Pos is the number of positive examples covered, Neg is the number of negative examples covered and Len the number of literals in the clause. The related coverage evaluation function is identical except that it does not take into account the length of the clause.

4 Empirical Evaluation

In this section we perform an empirical evaluation of the HOC learning algorithm. We implemented the algorithm in YAP 6 [14] inside GILPS, our ILP system developed from scratch publicly available at http://www.doc.ic.ac.uk/~jcs06, and compare it against both Progol and Aleph.

4.1 Materials

Aleph 5 [7], Progol 4.4 [6] and our implementation of the HOC learner were used to solve two well known math problems: Fibonnaci and Binomial Coefficient. Note that, obviously, these problems have both one output variable.

In the Fibonnaci problem we are trying to learn the ith element of the series. That is, we want the ILP system to induce a predicate that returns the correct Fibonnaci function value for an arbitrary index $i > 1$ in the series. For instance, $Fib_8 = 21$.

$$Fib_n = \begin{cases} 0, & n = 0 \\ 1, & n = 1 \\ Fib_{n-1} + Fib_{n-2}, & n \geq 2 \end{cases} \tag{1}$$

In the Binomial Coefficient the aim is identical, although the problem looks a bit more difficult as there are two input variables. We want the ILP system to induce a predicate that, given distinct non zero n and k, returns the correct Binomial Coefficient. For instance, $\binom{6}{2} = 15$.

$$\binom{n}{k} = \begin{cases} 1, & n = k \vee k = 0 \\ \binom{n-1}{k-1} + \binom{n-1}{k}, & otherwise \end{cases} \tag{2}$$

Note that these are notouriously difficult problems for an ILP system to learn as the layer of new variables (parameter i in Aleph and Progol) must be set to 3 and 4 (see 4.3), thus yielding a very large search space.

Figures 3 and 4 show the background knowledge and mode definitions used in Aleph. For the other ILP systems the same background knowledge and mode definitions were used apart from minor syntactic changes.

For both problems we provided, to all ILP systems, the base, non recursive cases, as part of the background knowledge. Only positive examples were given

```
:- modeh(1, fib(+int,-int)).
:- modeb(1, pred(+int,-int)).
:- modeb(1, fib(+int,-int)).
:- modeb(1, plus(+int,+int,-int)).
:- commutative(plus/3).

:- determination(fib/2, pred/2).
:- determination(fib/2, fib/2).
:- determination(fib/2, plus/3).

pred(A, B):- B is A-1.
plus(A, B, C):- C is A+B.

fib(0, 0):-!.
fib(1, 1):-!.
```

Fig. 3. Fibonnaci problem definition in Aleph

```
:- modeh(1, binomial(+int,+int,-int)).
:- modeb(1, pred(+int,-int)).
:- modeb(1, binomial(+int,+int,-int)).
:- modeb(1, plus(+int,+int,-int)).
:- commutative(plus/3).

:- determination(binomial/3, pred/2).
:- determination(binomial/3, binomial/3).
:- determination(binomial/3, plus/3).

pred(A, B):- B is A-1.
plus(A, B, C):- C is A+B.

binomial(_, 0, 1):-!.
binomial(N, N, 1):-!.
```

Fig. 4. Binomial Coefficient problem definition in Aleph

in both cases. When there are output variables in the head of the target concept, negative examples play a less important role as maximizing recall (i.e. just covering the positives) may be enough to find the correct definition.

The positive examples given were, for Fibonnaci: fib(7,13), fib(8,21), fib(9,34) and for Binomial: binomial(6,2,15), binomial(6,3,20) and binomial(7,3,35).

4.2 Methods

The three systems were run with identical settings for all parameters: number of nodes (5,000), depth of new variables (i=4 for Fibonnaci and i=3 for binomial), noise (0%) and maximum clause length (6).

Since we provide few examples the evaluation function was set to coverage in both Aleph and the HOC learner. In Progol, since it is not possible to have other evaluation function other than compression, the examples were inflated 5 times to achieve an effect identical to the usage of coverage as the evaluation function.

Progol was asked to generate a theory using the 'generalise' command and Aleph with the 'induce' command.

4.3 Results

Only the HOC ILP system was able to successfully learn the target concept. It took 0.4s to learn Fibonnaci and 2.1s to learn Binomial. Progol, even when nodes was later set to 100,000 could not learn either and took several hours to report it. Aleph crashed in both problems, after a few seconds[1].

```
fib(A,B) :-
    pred(A,C),    % i=1
    pred(C,D),    % i=2
    fib(C,E),     % i=3
    fib(D,F),     % i=3
    plus(F,E,B).  % i=4
```

```
binomial(A,B,C) :-
    pred(A,D),           % i=1
    pred(B,E),           % i=1
    binomial(D,B,F),     % i=2
    binomial(D,E,G),     % i=2
    plus(G,F,C).         % i=3
```

Fig. 5. Induced Fibonnaci and Binomial Coefficient predicates

Figure 5 shows the induced predicates by the HOC ILP system. They are the intended definitions. We also added the i setting, the layers of new variables introduced, which is a direct measure of the concept depth and an indirect measure of its complexity.

Notice that by default $i = 2$ in both Aleph and Progol, which is enough for typical classification problems [2,3,4,5] but insufficient to many HOC problems.

5 Discussion and Future Work

The HOC learning algorithm only solves one of the problems general purpose ILP systems have with this class of problems: it does not have to compute the coverage of the intermediate, non head output connected, clauses. However this approach still shares two problems: 1) computing the bottom clause which, depending on the mode declarations and background knowledge, can be quite large and 2) do a breadth-first search to find the support clauses for the head output variables.

[1] It was an "Instantiation error" while evaluating recursive clauses like "fib(A,B) :- pred(A,C), fib(C,D), pred(D,E)." We suppose this is a bug in Aleph while learning recursive clauses where the last literal is not the recursive call. We believe that even without this error Aleph would not be able to learn the target concepts as it uses essentially the same algorithm as Progol.

The breadth-first search could be relaxed and replaced by an heuristic that returns support clauses. However, in doing so, we could not guarantee that the shortest set of support clauses for a given clause length would be returned. Furthermore, while the breadth-first search is robust to any number of head output variables in the target concept, such an heuristic would not be.

As for the potentially very large bottom clauses, a problem shared with other mode directed inverse entailment ILP systems, it might be possible to avoid its generation at the start of the search if we perform a depth-first search and dynamically compute the sucessors of a clause, trading space by time.

Finally, it is worth pointing out that a simple inspection on the mode declarations is enough to automatically decide if the HOC learning algorithm should be used instead of the general purpose one. Therefore this algorithm can be easily integrated in general purpose ILP learners.

6 Conclusions

In this paper we presented a special purpose ILP algorithm to efficiently solve the class of problems where the concept to be learned has at least one output variable. This is an important class of problems that deserves special attention. We presented and implemented an algorithm that efficiently learns problems from this class. We showed two examples, Fibonnaci and Binomial coefficient, that can be learned in a coupple of seconds by our system but cannot be easily learned by a general purpose ILP system. The proposed approach is an initial step in handling more efficiently this class of problems in ILP systems.

Acknowledgments

The first author thanks Wellcome Trust by the financial support for his Ph.D. scholarship. The second author was supported by the BBSRC CISBIC grant BB/C519670/1. The third author thanks the Royal Academy of Engineering and Microsoft for funding his present 5 year Research Chair. We are also indebted to three anonymous referees for valuable comments.

References

1. Muggleton, S.: Inductive logic programming. New Generation Computing 8(4), 295–318 (1991)
2. Finn, P., Muggleton, S., Page, D., Srinivasan, A.: Pharmacophore discovery using the inductive logic programming system progol. Machine Learning 30, 241–271 (1998)
3. Srinivasan, A., King, R.D., Muggleton, S.H., Sternberg, M.: Carcinogenesis predictions using ilp. In: Džeroski, S., Lavrač, N. (eds.) ILP 1997. LNCS(LNAI), vol. 1297, pp. 273–287. Springer, Heidelberg (1997)
4. Srinivasan, A., Muggleton, S., King, R., Sternberg, M.: Theories for mutagenicity: a study of first-order and feature based induction. Artificial Intelligence 85(1,2), 277–299 (1996)

5. Turcotte, M., Muggleton, S.H., Sternberg, M.J.E.: Protein fold recognition. In: Page, D.L. (ed.) ILP 1998. LNCS, vol. 1446, pp. 53–64. Springer, Heidelberg (1998)
6. Muggleton, S.: Inverse entailment and Progol. New Generation Computing, Special issue on Inductive Logic Programming 13(3-4), 245–286 (1995)
7. Srinivasan, A.: The Aleph Manual. University of Oxford (2007)
8. Flanagan, C., Qadeer, S.: Predicate abstraction for software verification. In: POPL, pp. 191–202 (2002)
9. Fonseca, N.A., Costa, V.S., Rocha, R., Camacho, R., Silva, F.: Improving the efficiency of inductive logic programming systems. Softw., Pract. Exper. 39(2), 189–219 (2009)
10. Richards, B.L., Mooney, R.J.: Learning relations by pathfinding. In: AAAI, pp. 50–55 (1992)
11. Ong, I.M., de Castro Dutra, I., Page, D.L., Santos Costa, V.: Mode directed path finding. In: Gama, J., Camacho, R., Brazdil, P.B., Jorge, A.M., Torgo, L. (eds.) ECML 2005. LNCS (LNAI), vol. 3720, pp. 673–681. Springer, Heidelberg (2005)
12. Lloyd, J.W.: Foundations of Logic Programming, 2nd edn. Springer, Berlin (1987)
13. Nienhuys-Cheng, S.-H., de Wolf, R.: Foundations of Inductive Logic Programming. LNCS(LNAI), vol. 1228. Springer, Heidelberg (1997)
14. Santos Costa, V.: The life of a logic programming system. In: de la Banda, M.G., Pontelli, E. (eds.) ICLP 2008. LNCS, vol. 5366, pp. 1–6. Springer, Heidelberg (2008)

Chapter 5

EAC – Emotional and Affective Computing

A Data-Fusion Approach to Representing Personality Traits, Values, Beliefs and Behavior Descriptions

Boon-Kiat Quek[1], Kayo Sakamoto[1], and Andrew Ortony[1,2]

[1] Computational Cognition for Social Systems, Institute of High Performance Computing, Agency for Science, Technology and Research, Singapore
[2] Northwestern University, Evanston, Illinois, USA
{quekbk,sakamotok}@ihpc.a-star.edu.sg, ortony@northwestern.edu

Abstract. Starting with currently available data sets that capture the relationships between different pairs of personality-related constructs (for instance, descriptions of behaviors and personality traits), we describe a way of representing personality traits, human values, beliefs, and behaviors in one integrated network-centric model. We propose that such a unified representation can contribute to the making of predictions from one type of construct to another, for example, between personality characteristics and value preferences. Using a spreading activation mechanism, we show how, in principle, such a model can be used to make inferences about the plausibility of unobserved characteristics of an individual, given a very limited initial set of known characteristics.

Keywords: Personality, values, network, spreading activation, inference.

1 Introduction

Understanding other people (indeed, perhaps even understanding ourselves) requires that we constantly make inferences from what we know (the given) to what we don't know (beyond the given). Sometimes these inferences are made consciously, and sometimes unconsciously, but one way or the other, they are made. So when, for example, we encounter someone who subscribes to the value *Conservatism*, we might (among other things) infer that he or she may not be very open to new ideas. Inferences of this kind are by no means a "sure thing." Rather, they serve as a kind of social information processing heuristic. Without them, we'd be constantly surprised by the words and deeds of those in our social world. The goal of the work described here is to develop a comprehensive representational system that allows inferences of this kind to be made in computational contexts by taking advantage of relevant empirical data from personality psychology [e.g., 7, 8] and the psychology of human values [e.g., 16, 19]. The primary objective of such studies has been to uncover the underlying structure of personality or of value systems, typically using factor analysis or multidimensional scaling. However, extant research tends to treat the two domains (personality and value systems) independently, whereas we view them as comprising one underlying representational system that people draw upon in the course of understanding and interacting with other social agents.

L. Seabra Lopes et al. (Eds.): EPIA 2009, LNAI 5816, pp. 163–173, 2009.

We begin by first focusing on existing correlational data relating personality trait words (for instance, those found in [7, 8, 11]), the Big Five personality factors, and personality inventory items. Our assumption is that by using known relationships between some of the elements of a substantial set of traits, behavior descriptions and other inventory items, and the five factors identified in the so-called Five-Factor model of personality [5], it would be feasible, given only partial or sparse personological information about an individual, to draw plausible probabilistic inferences about other characteristics of that individual. Furthermore, by exploiting known correlations between the five personality factors and human value dimensions as discussed by Renner [16], it might be possible to make interesting inferences from traits, behaviors, etc. to human values, and *vice versa*.

With this motivation, the rest of this paper is organized as follows. First, we describe our approach to integrating representations from existing data sources. Then, a mathematical formulation showing how such information is represented in a network, and mechanisms for making inferences from the integrated representation are described. Finally, as a proof of concept, we demonstrate the use of the integrated network representation in a selection of cases in which limited information about an individual (for example, a few observed traits) can be used to predict additional characteristics about that individual.

2 Representation and Modeling

The purpose of the integrated representation we describe is to make it possible to understand and exploit existing relationships between different psychological and behavioral constructs in potentially new and interesting ways. We view this as contributing to the development of comprehensive computational models which incorporate representations of personality and values, as well as goals, motivation, affect, and action [e.g., 14].

2.1 Obtaining Data Sources

There are many sources of empirical data that might help in the development of computational models, but the best candidates are those derived from ratings on items on inventories for assessing individual differences. From these one can get loadings of, for example, trait descriptors [7, 8, 17] or self and peer reported behaviors [e.g., 2, 9] on the Big Five factors of personality (*Extraversion*, *Agreeableness*, *Conscientiousness*, *Emotional Stability*, and *Openness to Experience*). In addition to the domain of personality, correlational data are also available in the domain of human values, and Renner [16] has recently explored the relationship between human values (including Schwartz's Values Inventory [19]) and the Big Five. The following is a selection of some of the data used in our work:

Personality Inventories. These are collections of items (or markers) on personality questionnaires that describe behaviors and beliefs that are used for personality assessment and which can be obtained from, for example, the International Personality Item Pool (IPIP) [2, 9]. For instance, on the Big Five Markers scale by Buchanan et al. [2], the following behavior descriptions are found to have loadings on *Extraversion*: (i) *Am* *the life of the party*. (ii) *Feel comfortable around people*. (iii) *Start conversations*. (iv) *Talk to a lot of different people at parties*. (v) *Don't mind being the centre of attention*. In fact, some of the items in [2] (e.g., "*believe that others have good intentions*," "*believe in the importance of art*") are beliefs rather than behavior descriptions, as are most of the items used in instruments to assess values.

Personality Traits. These are a list of adjectives describing a characteristic of an individual. Goldberg [8] uses a list of 100 such adjectives, including, for example, *extraverted, talkative, assertive, verbal, energetic, bold* (all of which load primarily on *Extraversion*). So far, for the sake of simplicity, our own work has been based on a shorter list of (40) trait terms (Saucier's Mini Markers [17]).

Human Values and Personality Factors. Work by Renner [16] reports correlations between five Human Value factors and the Big Five personality factors, as well as the value domains from Schwartz's Values Inventory [19]. Renner's value factors, namely, *Balance*, *Intellectualism*, *Conservatism*, *Salvation*, and *Profit*, were derived from a German lexicon of 383 nouns. Renner also reports correlations between these factors and Schwartz's value domains of *Conformity*, *Tradition*, *Benevolence*, *Universalism*, *Self-Direction*, *Stimulation*, *Hedonism*, *Power*, *Achievement*, and *Security*. The correlations between Renner's value factors, the Big Five personality factors, and the Schwartz's value domains can be viewed as providing a bridge between the personality and value domains.

2.2 Constructing an Integrated Representation

The data sets described above comprise correlational relationships between collections of concepts. So, essentially, what we have is a graph or network in which the nodes represent concepts and the edges correspond to the correlations between them. Mathematically, each data set G comprising concepts and correlations can be represented as a graph:

$$G = \{ V, E \}\ , \tag{1}$$

where V and E represent the sets of concepts and correlations, respectively.

To generate such a graphical representation, a node for each item in the data set G is created, with each node v_i being a tuple containing a label $name_i$ (e.g. *talkative*) and a placeholder for a numerical quantity $0 \le x_i \le 1$ which is subsequently used to represent the activation level of v_i:

$$v_i = < name_i\ , x_i > \ ;\ v_i \in V\ . \tag{2}$$

Similarly, correlations between pair-wise items in the data sets are represented as edges, each taking the following form:

$$\varepsilon_{i,j} = < v_i\ , v_j\ , w_{i,j} > \ ;\ \varepsilon_{i,j} \in E\ , \tag{3}$$

where $w_{i,j}$ is the correlation between nodes v_i and v_j. These correlation values are obtained from the data sets in question. For instance, <"*shy*", "*extraversion*", -0.79> represents the negative correlation (and in this case, the factor loading) between *shy* and *Extraversion*, with a magnitude of 0.79. Since the nature of the relationships in question is only known to be correlational (without further evidence as to whether they could in fact be causal, or time-dependent), edges are deemed to be undirected, i.e. $\varepsilon_{i,j} = \varepsilon_{j,i}$.

Given a collection of n different data sets $\{G_1, G_2, G_3, \dots, G_n\}$, they can be fused into an integrated graph representation $G_{1:n}$ with the set union operation:

$$\begin{aligned} G_{1:n} &= G_1 \cup G_2 \cup \dots \cup G_n \\ &= \{ V_1 \cup V_2 \cup \dots \cup V_n, E_1 \cup E_2 \cup \dots \cup E_n \} . \end{aligned} \tag{4}$$

As an illustration, let $G_{traits\text{-}big5}$ represent the data set comprising personality trait words and the Big Five factors [17], where its nodes $V_{traits\text{-}big5}$ contain both a set of trait nodes V_{traits} and a set of personality factor nodes V_{big5}. The edges $E_{traits\text{-}big5}$ are the correlations between trait and personality factor pairs, i.e.:

$$G_{traits\text{-}big5} = \{ V_{traits} \cup V_{big5}, E_{traits\text{-}big5} \} . \tag{5}$$

In addition, a personality inventory comprising behavior descriptions and beliefs, and Big Five factors as depicted in [2] can be represented as:

$$G_{behaviors\text{-}big5} = \{ V_{behaviors} \cup V_{big5}, E_{behaviors\text{-}big5} \} , \tag{6}$$

where $V_{behaviors}$ is the set of nodes representing behavior descriptions, and $E_{behavior\text{-}big5}$ is the set of correlations between behavior-descriptions and Big Five factors. Both $G_{traits\text{-}big5}$ and $G_{behaviors\text{-}big5}$, are bipartite, because edges $E_{traits\text{-}big5}$ and $E_{behaviors\text{-}big5}$ only connect traits to personality factors, or behaviors to personality factors, respectively. An integrated representation can be generated by fusing both data sets as in (7):

$$\begin{aligned} G_{traits\text{-}big5\text{-}behaviors} &= G_{traits\text{-}big5} \cup G_{behaviors\text{-}big5} \\ &= \{ V_{traits} \cup V_{big5} \cup V_{behaviors}, E_{traits\text{-}big5} \cup E_{behavior\text{-}big5} \} . \end{aligned} \tag{7}$$

The result is that there now exist paths between nodes in V_{traits}, V_{big5}, and $V_{behaviors}$, such that traits and behaviors are now indirectly connected via the Big Five factors. As illustrated in Fig. 1, behavior descriptions and personality traits are mediated by the Big Five which act as intersection points between the two otherwise disparate data sets.

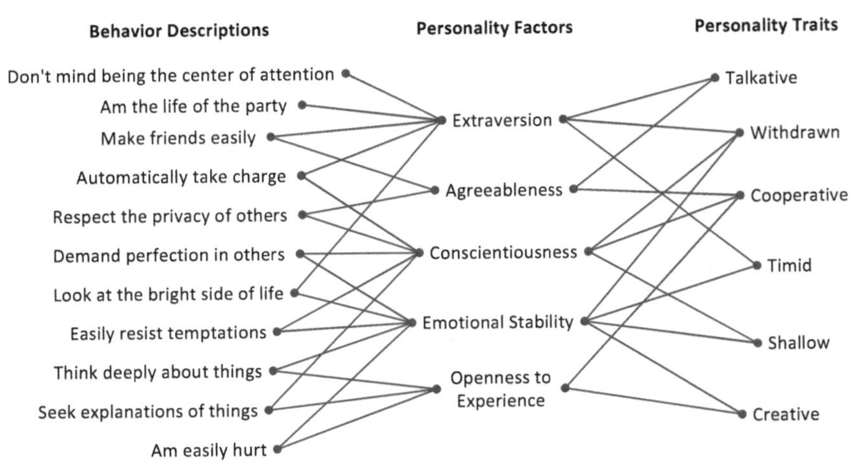

Fig. 1. Example of a network formed between behavior descriptions, personality factors, and personality trait words (The hypothetical links are for illustration only)

In addition to $G_{traits\text{-}big5}$ and $G_{behaviors\text{-}big5}$, our study incorporates the known correlations between the Big Five personality factors and Renner's value factors, and those between the latter and human value dimensions on Schwartz's Value Inventory. These data sets are obtained from [16], and represented as $G_{big5\text{-}Renner}$ and $G_{Renner\text{-}Schwartz}$ respectively:

$$G_{big5\text{-}Renner} = \{ V_{big5} \cup V_{Renner} , E_{big5\text{-}Renner} \} ; \tag{8}$$

$$G_{Renner\text{-}Schwartz} = \{ V_{Renner} \cup V_{Schwartz} , E_{Renner\text{-}Schwartz} \} . \tag{9}$$

Fusing all the data sets gives us the following integrated representation:

$$\begin{aligned} G_{traits\text{-}big5\text{-}behaviors\text{-}Renner\text{-}Schwartz} &= G_{traits\text{-}big5} \cup G_{behaviors\text{-}big5} \cup G_{big5\text{-}Renner} \cup G_{Renner\text{-}Schartz} \\ &= \{ V_{traits} \cup V_{big5} \cup V_{behaviors} \cup V_{Renner} \cup V_{Schwartz} , \\ &\quad E_{traits\text{-}big5} \cup E_{behavior\text{-}big5} \cup E_{big5\text{-}Renner} \cup E_{Renner\text{-}Schwartz} \} . \end{aligned} \tag{10}$$

The above representation is depicted in Fig. 2 which shows the relationships between the different data sets. Paths between personality traits and behavior descriptions are possible because each data set incorporates the Big Five factors as described in equation (7). Similarly, the bipartite relationships between Renner's value factors with both the Big Five personality factors and the value dimensions on Schwartz's value inventory result in the availability of paths connecting all these data sets together, including personality traits and behavior descriptions. To demonstrate this visually, Fig. 3 depicts a network representation of the above data sets. (For the sake of clarity, the lengthier behavior descriptions have not been included).

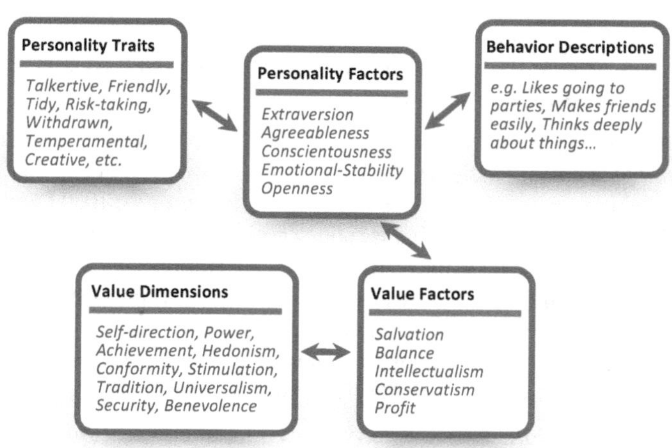

Fig. 2. Sources of data and their relationships with one another. The Big Five *Personality Factors* serve as intersection points between the disparate sets of data, resulting in a connected graph between *Personality Traits* [17], *Personality Factors* [8], descriptions of *Behaviors* [2], *Value Factors* [16], and *Value Dimensions* [19].

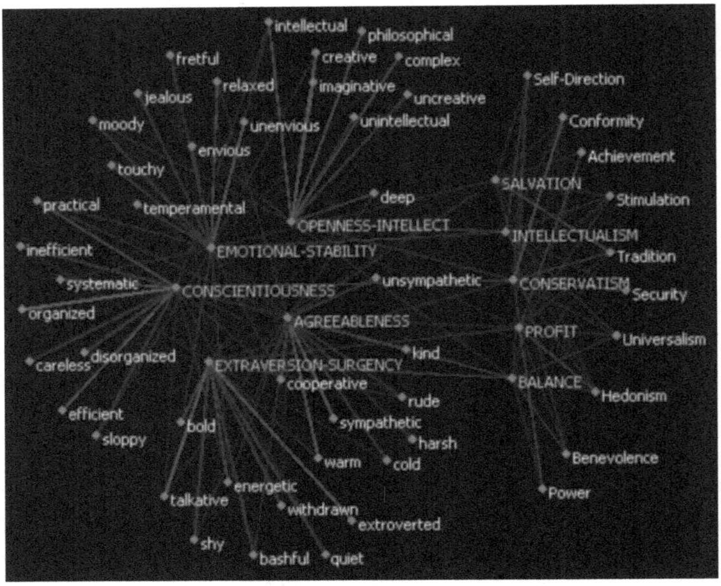

Fig. 3. Network-based representation integrating *Personality Traits* [17], *Personality Factors* [8], *Value Factors* [16], and *Value Dimensions* [19]. Green edges represent positive correlations, and red edges represent negative correlations. The thickness and brightness of each edge indicates its magnitude.

2.3 Making Inferences with Integrated Representations

The generation of inferences using the kind of integrated representation described above requires us to specify rules for propagating information through the network. In this section we discuss an approach to doing this.

Initialization of network and input nodes. Nodes in the network are connected if and only if one of the data sets includes the correlation between the concepts those nodes represent. Activation levels of all nodes have values in the range [0, 1] and first initialized to 0.5. However, input nodes, that is, nodes corresponding to properties taken to be the starting points of inferences, have their initial activation levels set higher. For instance, to represent an individual known for his creativity and intellect, but who is quiet, the nodes representing the traits *creative*, *intellectual*, and *quiet* may be configured with activation values closer to 1. The actual activation levels can be thought of as being a reflection of the extent to which the traits are cognitively accessible.

Propagation of activation. With the activation of input nodes set to initial values, the process of propagation is directed at determining the activation levels of all the other nodes in the network. To achieve this, we make use of the following weighted sum rule for each node v_i to determine its activation x_i at each time step:

$$x_i(k+1) = \alpha\, x_i(k) + (1-\alpha)\,\varphi\left(\frac{\beta}{\deg(v_i)} \sum_{\varepsilon_{i,j} \in G} (x_j(k) - \mu)\, w_{i,j}\right) \tag{11}$$

where α is a constant (set to 0.5), β is a scaling factor (set to 30) to spread the output over a wider range, deg(v_i) denotes the degree of v_i (i.e., number of edges connected to v_i), μ is an offset (set to 0.5) that re-centers (via a vertical translation of) all x from the range [0, 1] down to [-0.5, 0.5], and the function $\varphi(.)$ is a sigmoid function [13] that is defined as:

$$\varphi(y) = \frac{1}{1+e^{-\lambda y}} \quad ; \quad \varphi : \Re \rightarrow [0,1] \tag{12}$$

where λ is a constant (set to 1.0) which determines the shape of the sigmoid, and hence its sensitivity to values of x_i closer to 0.5. For each node v_i, a weighted sum of the activation levels of every node v_j that is correlated (i.e., for which an edge $\varepsilon_{i,j}$ exists) with v_i is first computed; this result is transformed into the range [0, 1] with the sigmoid function $\varphi(.)$ in equation (12), and used in an update rule that modifies the activation x_i in the subsequent time step (k+1). In this manner, previous activation levels can be taken into account in the computation of the current level.

The iterative nature of equation (11) allows time for input activations to spread throughout the rest of the network, at the same time, permitting new information to be introduced into the network as and when it is available. Thus, changes in activations due to a new input can modify the values of other nodes, which is analogous to the manner in which knowledge can be updated which new observations. Of course, equation (11) is one of many possibilities in which activation can be propagated in a coherent manner. We are currently experimenting with other functions.

Interpreting the results. After activation levels in all nodes have stabilized (to three decimal places), they can be queried and analyzed. While the activation level of a node is not an exact measure of the actual probability or likelihood of the concept being applicable, it does allow different concepts to be compared with one another in a relative manner. One of the many ways of achieving this is to identify for a set of input nodes those nodes with the highest activations, overall or in a domain. This can answer, for example, queries such as *What are the most plausible behaviors of an individual given some observed traits,* or *To what values might an individual with certain observed traits plausibly subscribe?*

3 Making Predictions between Constructs

In this section, we present three cases of how, given some small number of characteristics of an individual, the integrated network representation can be used to make plausible inferences about other characteristics of that individual. The first example demonstrates the plausibility of inferences from a small set of traits to other traits. In the second example, observed traits are used to make inferences about (presumed) likely behaviors (or behavioral tendencies). Finally, the third demonstrates the process of inferring human values priorities or preferences from traits.

3.1 Inferring from Observed to Unobserved Traits

This example demonstrates how, given only two known traits, predictions about unobserved traits can be generated in a manner that is consistent with their factor loadings on a specific Big Five personality factor. Two personality trait words, *warm* and *kind*, which load primarily on *Agreeableness*, are selected and each initialized with an activation level of 1.0. As shown in Table 1, after activation levels have stabilized, traits with stronger positive loadings on *Agreeableness* are found to possess higher activation levels. Similarly, lower activation levels are observed in traits having stronger negative correlations with the same factor. The results suggest the in-principle feasibility of making trait-trait inferences.

Table 1. Activation levels generated from input traits *warm* and *kind* for other traits which load primarily on *Agreeableness*. Factor loadings of selected traits are shown as a comparison.

Traits	Activation Levels	Factor Loadings on *Agreeableness* [17]
Cooperative	0.811	0.52
Sympathetic	0.753	0.72
Rude	0.232	-0.55
Unsympathetic	0.243	-0.64
Harsh	0.241	-0.54
Cold	0.167	-0.65

3.2 Inferring Expected Behaviors from Observed Personality Traits

In this second example, a list of behavior descriptions [2] is integrated with a set of personality traits [17] so that inferences about expected behaviors can be made from a small set of observed traits. Two pairs of traits ("*energetic*, *talkative*", and "*shy, quiet*") are selected for their primary loadings on *Extraversion* and initialized with activation levels of 1.0. Expected behavior predictions generated for each of the two independent runs are shown in Table 2.

Table 2. Activation levels of behavior descriptions with primary loadings on *Extraversion* as a function of input trait pairs ("*energetic, talkative*" and "*shy, quiet*"). Factor loadings are shown for purposes of comparison.

Behavior Descriptions	Input Traits		Factor Loadings on *Extraversion* [2]
	Energetic, Talkative	*Shy, Quiet*	
Am the life of the party	0.815	0.180	0.76
Make friends easily	0.857	0.140	0.71
Am skilled in handling social situations	0.870	0.127	0.75
Feel comfortable around people	0.849	0.149	0.67
Know how to captivate people	0.813	0.182	0.70
Don't like to draw attention to myself	0.386	0.626	-0.57
Would describe my experiences as somewhat dull	0.332	0.671	-0.37
Have little to say	0.280	0.728	-0.61
Keep in the background	0.267	0.741	-0.66
Don't talk a lot	0.248	0.760	-0.70

For input traits having positive loadings on *Extraversion* (i.e., *energetic, talkative*), correspondence is observed between the activation levels of the behaviors, and their factor loadings on *Extraversion.* Conversely, lower activation levels are observed for behavior descriptions with stronger loadings on *Extraversion* when subject to input traits with negative loadings on the same factor (i.e., *shy*, and *quiet*). Thus we see here how the fusion of multiple data sets onto the same representation can provide a feasible platform for making inferences across different constructs (for instance, between personality traits and behaviors).

3.3 Inferring Value Preferences from Personality Traits

Correlations between value factors identified from a German lexicon and the Big Five personality factors have recently been identified [16]. For instance, *Openness* reportedly has a positive correlation (0.39) with *Intellectualism* (a value factor identified in the same paper), while having a negative correlation (-0.42) with *Conservatism* (another identified value factor). While such reported relationships are derived from the German edition of the NEO-FFI [1], our attempt to replicate similar results with the integrated representation is based on Big Five data from a distinctly different source – a fact which we consider to strengthen rather than weaken our case.

In this example, two pairs of traits ("*creative, imaginative*", and "*uncreative, unintellectual*") are selected respectively for their high positive and high negative loadings on *Openness*. Each pair is used as input for a separate pass. As shown in Table 3, and consistent with Renner's findings, with input traits that load primarily on *Openness* (i.e., *creative* and *imaginative*), activation for the value factor *Intellectualism* is observed to be high, while *Conservatism* shows the highest level of activation in response to traits negatively correlated with *Openness* (i.e., *uncreative* and *unintellectual*). These predictions of value preferences concur with Renner's observations, despite employing different data sources, thus lending some support for the feasibility of our approach.

Table 3. Activation levels of value factors with primary loadings on *Openness* as a function of input trait pairs ("*creative, imaginative*" and "*uncreative, unintellectual*"). Correlations between value factors and *Openness* are shown for purposes of comparison.

Value Factors	Input Traits		Correlation with *Openness* [16]
	Creative, Imaginative	*Uncreative, Unintellectual*	
Intellectualism	0.732	0.269	0.39
Conservatism	0.157	0.843	-0.42

4 Discussion

So far we have focused on exploring the way in which an integrated network-centric representation can be constructed, and on demonstrating its feasibility in producing intuitively plausible results. However, what we have described amounts to little more than a proof of concept, with a great deal of work remaining to be done. Nevertheless, we think that our preliminary results are sufficiently promising to warrant further work.

It is clear that the utility of the data-fusion approach to generating integrated representations that we are proposing will be enhanced with both the quantity and quality of data that these representations incorporate. To this end, an appealing milestone would be to augment or replace the data sets with much richer ones, especially if these already exist, as they do in the personality domain. Thus, for example, we might replace the 40-item Mini-Markers data set with the 300-item Adjective Checklist [10], as well as perhaps incorporating the 240-item NEO PI-R (behavior descriptions) inventory [3].

In addition to increasing the size of the network, its richness may be enhanced by augmenting it with data collected specifically for this purpose. As the network is currently constructed, it comprises disparate data sets collected from different sets of individuals. For example, the data relative to value preferences come from different respondents than the data derived from personality inventories. Collecting large amounts of reliable data on traits, behaviors, beliefs, and values from a large number of respondents, while easy in principle, is a long arduous task in practice, requiring many hours of respondent participation. On the other hand, having some subsets of data of this kind might be a viable compromise. Other kinds of data from human participants would also be valuable as a means of testing the predictions of the model. For instance, suppose that given input (of known) characteristics a, b, and c, the model predicts additional characteristics w, x, y, and z with their respective activation levels. One could then ask participants to judge how likely they though it would be that an individual with characteristics a, b, and c would indeed possess other characteristics, including (but not limited to) w, x, y, and z.

Apart from enhancing the data richness and scope of the unified representational network, we plan to refine the activation propagation mechanisms operating over it by exploring other mechanisms such as those used in conjunction with fuzzy cognitive maps [12], Bayesian belief networks [15], or evidence accumulation mechanisms characterized by Dempster-Shafer's theory [20].

As far as applications are concerned, one place to start, and the one with the lowest cost for what will inevitably be frequent erroneous or low probability inferences, is in the design for interactive gaming systems of non-player characters with some degree of personological coherence. It is our hope however, that a well-designed and rich network of the kind we have outlined could provide a useful computational infrastructure for a variety of applications in the general domain of what might be called computational social cognition.

References

1. Borkenau, P., Ostendorf, F.: NEO Five Factor Inventory (NEO-FFI) by Costa and McCrae (in German). Hogrefe, Göttingen (1993)
2. Buchanan, T., Johnson, J.A., Goldberg, L.R.: Implementing a Five-Factor Personality Inventory for Use on the Internet. European Journal of Psychological Assessment 21, 115–127 (2005)

3. Costa Jr., P.T., McCrae, R.R.: NEO PI-R Professional Manual. Psychological Assessment Resources, Inc., Odessa (1992)
4. Davison, M.: Multidimensional Scaling. Willey, New York (1983)
5. Digman, J.M.: Personality structure: Emergence of the five-factor model. Annual Review of Psychology 41, 417–440 (1990)
6. Fiske, S.T., Neuberg, S.L.: A Continuum of Impression Formation, from Category-Based to Individuating Processes: Influences of Information and Motivation on Attention and Interpretation. In: Zanna, M.P. (ed.) Advances in Experimental Social Psychology, vol. 23, pp. 1–74. Academic Press, New York (1990)
7. Goldberg, L.R.: An Alternative "Description of Personality": The Big-Five Factor Structure. Journal of Personality and Social Psychology 59, 1216–1229 (1990)
8. Goldberg, L.R.: The Development of Markers for the Big-Five Factor Structure. Psychological Assessment 4, 26–42 (1992)
9. Goldberg, L.R., Johnson, J.A., Eber, H.W., Hogan, R., Ashton, M.C., Cloninger, C.R., Gough, H.C.: The International Personality Item Pool and the Future of Public-Domain Personality Measures. Journal of Research in Personality 40, 84–96 (2006)
10. Gough, H.G., Heilbrun, A.B.: The Adjective Check List Manual. Consulting Psychologists Press, Palo Alto (1983)
11. Hofstee, W.K.B., de Raad, B., Goldberg, L.R.: Integration of the Big-Five and Circumplex Approaches to Trait Structure. Journal of Personality and Social Psychology 63, 146–163 (1992)
12. Kosko, B.: Fuzzy Cognitive Maps. International Journal of Man-Machine Studies 24, 65–75 (1986)
13. Mitchell, T.: Machine Learning. WCB-McGraw-Hill, New York (1997)
14. Nelissen, R.M.A., Dijker, A.J.M., de Vries, N.K.: Emotions and Goals: Assessing Relations between Values and Emotions. Cognition and Emotion 21(4), 902–911 (2007)
15. Pearl, J.: Fusion, Propagation, and Structuring in Belief Networks. Artificial Intelligence 29(3), 241–288 (1986)
16. Renner, W.: Human Values: A Lexical Perspective. Personality and Individual Differences 34, 127–141 (2003)
17. Saucier, G.: Mini-Markers: a Brief Version of Goldberg's Unipolar Big-Five Markers. Journal of Personality Assessment 63(3), 506–516 (1994)
18. Schedler, J., Western, D.: Dimensions of Personality Pathology: An Alternative to the Five-Factor Model. American Journal of Psychiatry 161(10), 1743–1754 (2004)
19. Schwartz, S.H.: Universals in the Content and Structure of Values: Theory and Empirical Tests in 20 Countries. In: Zanna, M. (ed.) Advances in Experimental Social Psychology, vol. 25, pp. 1–65. Academic Press, New York (1992)
20. Shafer, G.: Perspectives on the Theory and Practice of Belief Functions. International Journal of Approximate Reasoning 4(5-6), 323–362 (1990)

A Formal Model of Emotion-Based Action Tendency for Intelligent Agents*

Bas R. Steunebrink, Mehdi Dastani, and John-Jules Ch. Meyer

Department of Information and Computing Sciences, Intelligent Systems Group, Utrecht University, The Netherlands
{bass,mehdi,jj}@cs.uu.nl

Abstract. Although several formal models of emotions for intelligent agents have recently been proposed, such models often do not formally specify how emotions influence the behavior of an agent. In psychological literature, emotions are often viewed as heuristics that give an individual the tendency to perform particular actions. In this paper, we take an existing formalization of how emotions come about in intelligent agents and extend this with a formalization of action tendencies. The resulting model specifies how the emotions of an agent determine a set of actions from which it can select one to perform. We show that the presented model of how emotions influence behavior is intuitive and discuss interesting properties of the model.

1 Introduction

There has recently been increasing interest in bringing emotions to Artificial Intelligence, in particular to model intelligent agents [1,2,3,4,5,6,7,8,9,10]. There are (at least) three important reasons for this. First, an obvious application of emotions is to make artificial agents and robots more believable to human users (both in the actions that they select and the affective expressions they show based on emotions) [1,4,5]. Second, from a more theoretical perspective, it is investigated what the role of emotions is in models of human decision-making and how they may be employed to make them more accurate and effective [11,2,12]. Third, there exists psychological [13,14,15,16] and neurological [17] evidence that emotions are not only relevant but even necessary for rational behavior.

Although several formal models of emotions for intelligent agents have recently been proposed, these models often only specify when emotions are triggered, but not how they affect the behavior of an agent. In psychological literature, emotions are often viewed as heuristics that give an individual the tendency to perform particular actions [16,13]. Viewed from this perspective, emotions can be used to determine a set of actions that an agent tends to perform in a certain situation, which is typically a subset of all possible actions it can perform. Moreover, action tendency can provide a measure to order this subset, thereby indicating which action(s) an agent tends to perform most. Thus, a model of emotion-based action tendency can help limiting and ordering options in an agent's action selection process.

* This work is supported by SenterNovem, Dutch Companion project grant nr: IS053013.

L. Seabra Lopes et al. (Eds.): EPIA 2009, LNAI 5816, pp. 174–186, 2009.

In this paper, we incorporate a notion of action tendency in an existing formalization of emotions which is tailored to (artificial) goal-directed agents [9,10]. The resulting model allows us to reason about situations in which tendencies arise with respect to particular emotions.

Outline: In section 2 we give an overview of psychological literature on emotions and their behavioral effects. A formal model of emotions is presented in section 3 so that a notion of action tendency can be incorporated in section 4. Section 5 discusses alternatives and extensions of the presented model, while section 6 discusses related work.

2 Emotion and Action Tendency in Psychology

There is little consensus among psychologists as to what exactly constitutes an emotion and how it differs from related affective processes. However, this does not mean that making broad classifications is impossible or useless. Following Gross [18], *emotions* typically have specific objects and give rise to action tendencies relevant to these objects. Moreover, emotions can be both positive and negative. Emotions are often distinguished from *moods*, which are more diffuse and last longer than emotions. Other affective processes include *stress*, which arises in taxing circumstances and produces only negative responses; and *impulses*, which are related to hunger, sex, and pain and give rise to responses with limited flexibility. Of these four types of affective processes, we will focus on *emotions* in this paper.

With respect to emotions, usually three phases are distinguished. First, the perceived situation is *appraised* by an individual based on what it thinks is relevant and important (e.g., gratitude is triggered for Alice towards Bob for giving her a necklace). Second, the appraisal of some situation can cause the triggered emotions, if exceeding some threshold, to create a conscious awareness of emotional feelings, leading to the *experience* of having emotions (e.g., Alice's gratitude towards Bob will have a certain intensity, depending on the desirability of receiving a necklace from Bob). Third, emotional feelings need to be *regulated* (e.g., Alice may tend to be nicer to Bob so that he will give her more presents). In fact, some emotion theories posit that the main purpose of emotions is to function as a heuristical mechanism for selecting behaviors [17,16,14].

Following Frijda [13] (see also Table 1), *action tendencies* are "states of readiness to execute a given kind of action, [which] is defined by its end result aimed at or achieved" (p70). In the case of negative emotions, reaching the associated end state should mitigate its experience (e.g., fear subsides once one believes the object of one's fear cannot reach oneself anymore), whereas positive emotions generally put an individual in a "mode of relational action readiness" (e.g., joy can put one in a mode of readiness for new interactions). In this paper, we will restrict our investigation to action tendencies related to negative emotions, because these signal that some things are not as they should be, making it possible to identify actions that can fix the situation. Indeed, in our formalization, the experience of negative emotions will be constrained such that for some actions, reaching their end state removes the emotional experience. Action tendencies will then follow naturally in response to emotional experience. It should be noted that action tendencies differ from intentions in that they are not goal-directed, but rather stimulus-driven [13]; e.g., fear does not (necessarily) spawn a goal to flee *towards* safety, but rather gives the urge to flee *away* from the perceived danger.

Table 1. A classification of several relational action tendencies. Adapted from a table on page 88 of Frijda [13].

Emotion	Function	Action tendency	End state
Desire	Consume	Approach	Access
Joy	Readiness	Free activation	—
Anger	Control	Agonistic	Obstruction removed
Fear	Protection	Avoidance	Own inaccessibility
Interest	Orientation	Attending	Identification
Disgust	Protection	Rejecting	Object removed
Anxiety	Caution	Inhibition	Absence of response
Contentment	Recuperation	Inactivity	—

3 Language and Semantics

In this paper, we build on an existing formalization by Steunebrink *et al.* [9,10] of the psychological "OCC model" of emotions [19]. The logic of rational agency that underlies this formalization of the OCC model is KARO [6,20], which is a mixture of dynamic logic, epistemic logic, and several additional operators for dealing with the motivational aspects of artificial agents.

The OCC model describes a hierarchy classifying 22 emotion types. The hierarchy contains three branches, namely emotions concerning aspects of objects (e.g., Alice loves Bob), actions of agents (e.g., Alice admires Bob for helping with her homework), and consequences of events (e.g., Alice pities Bob having lost his job). Additionally, some branches combine to form a group of compound emotions, namely emotions concerning consequences of events *caused* by actions of agents (e.g., Alice is grateful towards Bob that his help resulted in a good grade). It should be noted that emotions are not used to describe the entire cognitive state of an agent (as in "Alice is happy"); rather, emotions are always relative to individual objects, actions, and events. So Alice can be joyous about receiving her new furniture and at the same time be distressed about the height of the accompanying bill.

The OCC model defines both qualitative and quantitative aspects of emotions. Qualitatively, it defines the conditions that trigger each of the emotions. Quantitatively, it describes how an intensity is associated with each triggered emotion and what are the variables affecting emotional intensity. For example, the compound emotion *gratitude* is qualitatively specified as "approving of someone else's praiseworthy action and being pleased about the related desirable event," whereas the variables affecting its (quantitative) intensity are (1) the degree of judged praiseworthiness, (2) the unexpectedness of the event, and (3) the degree to which the event is desirable. It should be noted that in [9,10], qualitative and quantitative aspects of emotions (of the OCC model) have been formalized, respectively, corresponding to the first two phases described in section 2. In this paper we build upon their work, focusing on action tendencies, which corresponds to the third phase as described in section 2.

In order to formalize the OCC model in an agent specification language, the concepts of *objects*, *actions*, and *events* must be translated to notions common in agent specification languages, which is done as follows. The agent specification language is based on dynamic logic, so the concept of *actions* is directly available. For goal-directed agents, important *events* pertain to the accomplishment of (sub)goals and the undermining of subgoals (i.e. the undoing of previously accomplished subgoals). Therefore, an event is defined as the *accomplishment* of a set of subgoals (from a single goal) or the *undermining* of a set of subgoals (from a single goal). The *objects* to which an agent can have an affective attitude include all agent names.

The formalization by Steunebrink *et al.* distinguishes between the conditions that trigger emotions and their actual experience. The satisfaction of the triggering conditions of an emotion is seen as merely a property of one moment in time, whereas emotional experience is something that endures over time. This means that an emotion that has been triggered does not necessarily have to be experienced, either because it was triggered some time in the past and its intensity has since dropped to zero, or because it was assigned zero intensity to begin with.

To cater for this distinction, two sets of emotional fluents are defined: *emotion triggering fluents* and *emotional experience fluents*:

$$ETrig = \{\, \mathbf{emotion}^{\mathbf{T}} \bar{o} \mid \mathbf{emotion}\, \bar{o} \in EExp \,\} \tag{1}$$

$$\begin{aligned} EExp = \{\, & \mathbf{gratification}_i(\alpha, \varphi), && \mathbf{remorse}_i(\alpha, \varphi), \\ & \mathbf{gratitude}_i(j, \alpha, \varphi), && \mathbf{anger}_i(j, \alpha, \varphi), \\ & \mathbf{pride}_i(\alpha), && \mathbf{shame}_i(\alpha), \\ & \mathbf{admiration}_i(j, \alpha), && \mathbf{reproach}_i(j, \alpha), \\ & \mathbf{joy}_i(\varphi), && \mathbf{distress}_i(\varphi), \\ & \mathbf{happy\text{-}for}_i(j, \varphi), && \mathbf{resentment}_i(j, \varphi), \\ & \mathbf{gloating}_i(j, \varphi), && \mathbf{pity}_i(j, \varphi), \\ & \mathbf{hope}_i(\pi, \varphi), && \mathbf{fear}_i(\pi, \neg\varphi), \\ & \mathbf{satisfaction}_i(\pi, \varphi), && \mathbf{disappointment}_i(\pi, \varphi), \\ & \mathbf{relief}_i(\pi, \neg\varphi), && \mathbf{fears\text{-}confirmed}_i(\pi, \neg\varphi), \\ & \mathbf{love}_i(x), && \mathbf{hate}_i(x) \,\} \end{aligned} \tag{2}$$

where i and j are agent names ($i \neq j$), α is an atomic action, π is a plan (i.e. atomic actions and sequential compositions thereof), φ is a goal formula, and x is an agent name or object name. The definition of *ETrig* should be read as follows: if $\mathbf{emotion}\,\bar{o}$ refers to, e.g., $\mathbf{joy}_i(\varphi)$, then $\mathbf{emotion}^{\mathbf{T}}\bar{o}$ is $\mathbf{joy}_i^{\mathbf{T}}(\varphi)$. The informal reading of, e.g., $\mathbf{joy}_i^{\mathbf{T}}(\varphi)$ is "joy is triggered for agent i with respect to event φ", whereas $\mathbf{joy}_i(\varphi)$ is read as "agent i experiences joy with respect to event φ." By convention, we write $\epsilon^{\mathbf{T}} \in ETrig$ and $\epsilon \in EExp$. With slight abuse of notation, the 'T' is also used to convert between *ETrig* and *EExp*, e.g., if $\epsilon = \mathbf{joy}_i(\varphi)$ then $\epsilon^{\mathbf{T}} = \mathbf{joy}_i^{\mathbf{T}}(\varphi)$ in the same context.

Definition 1 (Agent specification language). *Let $\mathcal{P}$ be a set of atomic propositions, $\mathcal{A}$ a set of atomic actions, and $\mathcal{G}$ a set of agent names. Plans is the smallest set such that $\mathcal{A} \subseteq Plans$ and if $\alpha \in \mathcal{A}$ and $\pi \in Plans$ then $\alpha;\pi \in Plans$. The agent specification language $\mathcal{L}_{PAG}$ is the smallest set closed under:*

- $\{\bot, \top\} \cup \mathcal{P} \cup ETrig \cup EExp \subseteq \mathcal{L}_{PAG}$.
- *If* $\varphi_1, \varphi_2 \in \mathcal{L}_{PAG}$ *then* $\neg\varphi_1, (\varphi_1 \wedge \varphi_2) \in \mathcal{L}_{PAG}$.
- *If* $\varphi \in \mathcal{L}_{PAG}$, $i \in \mathcal{G}$ *then* $\mathbf{B}_i\varphi, \mathbf{G}_i\varphi \in \mathcal{L}_{PAG}$.[1]
- *If* $\pi \in Plans$, $\varphi \in \mathcal{L}_{PAG}$, $i \in \mathcal{G}$ *then* $\mathbf{A}_i\pi, \mathbf{Com}_i(\pi), [i:\pi]\varphi \in \mathcal{L}_{PAG}$.

[1] For simplicity, we deviate slightly from [9,10] by allowing arbitrary goal formulas.

With respect to the semantics of $\mathcal{L}_{PAG}$, the belief (**B**) and action ($[\cdot]$) operators are modeled in a standard way using Kripke semantics, while using sets for goals, abilities, commitments, and emotional fluents. The modal logic KD45 is used for belief models, having the form $\mathrm{M} = \langle S, R, V \rangle$, where S is a set of states (or 'possible worlds'), R is a set of relations on S (one for each agent), and V is a valuation on S. The semantics of actions are defined *over* the Kripke models of belief, as actions may change the mental states of agents. Action models have the form $\mathcal{M} = \langle \mathcal{S}, \mathcal{R}, \mathrm{Emo}, \mathrm{Aux} \rangle$, where $\mathcal{S}$ is the set of possible model–state pairs (where models are of the form M as above and states are from S therein) and $\mathcal{R} = \{ \mathcal{R}_{i:\alpha} \mid i \in \mathcal{G}, \alpha \in \mathcal{A} \}$ is a set of relations on $\mathcal{S}$ (one for each agent–action combination). $\mathcal{R}$ is required to produce a branching future and a single history, allowing its converse $\mathcal{R}^{-1}$ to be used as a history function. Notation: $(\mathrm{M}', s') \in \mathcal{R}_{i:\alpha}(\mathrm{M}, s)$ iff $\mathcal{R}^{-1}(\mathrm{M}', s') = \langle (\mathrm{M}, s), (i, \alpha) \rangle$.

$\mathrm{Emo} = \{ \mathit{Gratification}, \ldots, \mathit{Hate} \}$ is a set of 22 functions designed to define the semantics of the emotion triggering fluents [10]. $\mathrm{Aux} = \langle \Gamma, \mathcal{C}, \mathit{Agd}, T, \mathit{int} \rangle$ is a structure of auxiliary functions, where Γ is a function returning the set of goals an agent has per model–state pair; $\mathcal{C}$ is a function that returns the set of actions that an agent is capable of performing per model–state pair; Agd is a function that returns the set of actions that an agent is committed to (are on its 'agenda') per model–state pair. An external clock function $T : \mathcal{S} \to \mathbb{R}_{\geq 0}$ is used (only) to calculate actual emotion intensity values. Therefore, it is assumed it assigns the same time to each state s of a belief model M, so we will (sloppily) express the time at a model–state pair (M, s) simply as T_{M}. It is also assumed that all actions take time, i.e., $\forall (\mathrm{M}', s') \in \mathcal{R}_{i:\alpha}(\mathrm{M}, s) : T_{\mathrm{M}'} > T_{\mathrm{M}}$.

We say that an emotion ϵ is *triggered* in state (M, s) iff $\mathrm{M}, s \models \epsilon^{\mathbf{T}}$ (see Definition 2). An emotion's triggering conditions often cease to hold when a transition to a next state is made, but emotional *experience* is supposed to be able to endure. Therefore, an *emotional memory EMem* is kept containing all newly triggered emotions (i.e. $\{ \epsilon \in \mathit{EExp} \mid \mathrm{M}, s \models \epsilon^{\mathbf{T}} \}$) plus all previously triggered ones ($\mathit{EMem}^*(\mathrm{M}', s')$). Thus, *EMem* makes previously triggered emotions available for assigning current intensities to them. We also define an extended emotional memory EMem_i^* as the union of all *EMems* in an agent's belief model, because it is desirable that emotional experience is the same in all belief states.

$$\begin{aligned}
\mathit{EMem}(\mathrm{M}, s) &= \{ \epsilon \in \mathit{EExp} \mid \mathrm{M}, s \models \epsilon^{\mathbf{T}} \} \\
&\quad \cup \{ \epsilon \in \mathit{EMem}^*(\mathrm{M}', s') \mid \mathcal{R}^{-1}(\mathrm{M}, s) = \langle (\mathrm{M}', s'), _ \rangle \} \\
\mathit{EMem}^*(\mathrm{M}, s) &= \textstyle\bigcup_{i \in \mathcal{G}} \mathit{EMem}_i^*(\mathrm{M}, s) \\
\mathit{EMem}_i^*(\mathrm{M}, s) &= \textstyle\bigcup_{s' \in \mathrm{GS}(R_i \cup R_i^{-1}, s)} \mathit{EMem}(\mathrm{M}, s')
\end{aligned}$$

where $\mathrm{M} = \langle S, R, V \rangle$ and $\mathrm{GS}(R', s)$ returns all states in the *generated submodel* starting from s and following the relation R'. Thus, with slight abuse of notation, $\mathrm{GS}(R_i \cup R_i^{-1}, s)$ denotes all states reachable from s if R_i were an equivalence relation.

As previously stated, an emotion that is triggered is not necessarily *experienced*. To model emotional experience, the function $\mathit{int} : \mathcal{S} \to \mathit{EExp} \to \mathcal{I}$ is used, which assigns, per model–state pair, an intensity function to an emotional experience fluent. Each intensity function, as returned by $\mathit{int}(\mathrm{M}, s)(\epsilon)$, is a monotonically decreasing function of time. So $\mathcal{I}$ denotes the class of monotonically decreasing functions of type $\mathbb{R}_{\geq 0} \to \mathbb{R}_{\geq 0}$ (negative intensities are not allowed). As will be formally specified below, the idea is that an emotion ϵ that has been triggered now or in the past (i.e. $\epsilon \in EMem^*(\mathrm{M}, s)$) is currently experienced (i.e. in (M, s)) iff the intensity function f currently associated with ϵ (i.e. $int(\mathrm{M}, s)(\epsilon) = f$) returns a value greater than zero for the current time (i.e. $f(T_\mathrm{M}) > 0$). It is desirable that emotional experience is the same in all belief states, so the function int is constrained as follows: $\forall(\mathrm{M}, s) \in \mathcal{S}, i \in \mathcal{G}, s' \in \mathrm{GS}(R_i, s) : int(\mathrm{M}, s) = int(\mathrm{M}, s')$. It is also assumed for all $(\mathrm{M}, s) \in \mathcal{S}$ and $\epsilon \in EExp$ that $int(\mathrm{M}, s)(\epsilon) = f_0$ if $\epsilon \notin EMem^*(\mathrm{M}, s)$, where $f_0(x) = 0$ for all x. It is crucial to note that the main idea of assigning intensity *functions* to triggered emotions (as opposed to directly assigning intensity *values*) is that we can then say that 'usually', performing an action does not change the way emotion intensities behave, i.e., for 'most' α, $(\mathrm{M}', s') \in \mathcal{R}_{i:\alpha}(\mathrm{M}, s)$ implies $int(\mathrm{M}', s') = int(\mathrm{M}, s)$. For certain actions we can then put useful constraints on int such that these actions can be said to influence emotions by changing the intensity functions that are assigned to these emotions. Indeed, this is exactly what we will do in section 4.

Definition 2. *(Interpretation of formulas).*
Let $\mathrm{M} = \langle S, R, V \rangle$ *and* $\mathcal{M} = \langle \mathcal{S}, \mathcal{R}, \mathrm{Emo}, \mathrm{Aux} \rangle$ *be structures defined as above. Formulas in language* $\mathcal{L}_{\mathcal{PAG}}$ *are interpreted in model–state pairs as follows:*

$$
\begin{array}{lcl}
\mathrm{M}, s \models p & \Leftrightarrow & p \in V(s) \quad \textit{for } p \in \mathcal{P} \\
\mathrm{M}, s \models \neg\varphi & \Leftrightarrow & \mathrm{M}, s \not\models \varphi \\
\mathrm{M}, s \models \varphi_1 \wedge \varphi_2 & \Leftrightarrow & \mathrm{M}, s \models \varphi_1 \ \&\ \mathrm{M}, s \models \varphi_2 \\
\mathrm{M}, s \models \mathbf{B}_i\varphi & \Leftrightarrow & \forall s' \in R_i(s) : \mathrm{M}, s' \models \varphi \\
\mathrm{M}, s \models \mathbf{G}_i\varphi & \Leftrightarrow & \varphi \in \Gamma(i)(\mathrm{M}, s) \\
\mathrm{M}, s \models \mathbf{A}_i\pi & \Leftrightarrow & \pi \in \mathcal{C}(i)(\mathrm{M}, s) \\
\mathrm{M}, s \models \mathbf{Com}_i(\pi) & \Leftrightarrow & \pi \in Agd(i)(\mathrm{M}, s) \\
\mathrm{M}, s \models [i{:}\pi]\varphi & \Leftrightarrow & \forall(\mathrm{M}', s') \in \mathcal{R}_{i:\pi}(\mathrm{M}, s) : \mathrm{M}', s' \models \varphi \\
\mathrm{M}, s \models \mathbf{emotion}_i^{\mathbf{T}}\bar{o} & \Leftrightarrow & \bar{o} \in Emotion(i)(\mathrm{M}, s) \\
\mathrm{M}, s \models \mathbf{emotion}_i\bar{o} & \Leftrightarrow & \mathbf{emotion}_i\bar{o} \in EMem_i^*(\mathrm{M}, s)\ \& \\
 & & \quad int(\mathrm{M}, s)(\mathbf{emotion}_i\bar{o})(T_\mathrm{M}) > 0
\end{array}
$$

The last two lines abbreviate 2×22 lines; e.g., $\mathrm{M}, s \models \mathbf{joy}_i^{\mathbf{T}}(\varphi) \Leftrightarrow \varphi \in Joy(i)(\mathrm{M}, s)$ and $\mathrm{M}, s \models \mathbf{joy}_i(\varphi) \Leftrightarrow \mathbf{joy}_i(\varphi) \in EMem_i^*(\mathrm{M}, s)\ \&\ int(\mathrm{M}, s)(\mathbf{joy}_i(\varphi))(T_\mathrm{M}) > 0$.

Whenever we focus on a single-agent situation, we omit agent indices to ease notation. As explained before, we will write $\epsilon^{\mathbf{T}}$ for $\mathbf{emotion}_i^{\mathbf{T}}\bar{o}$ and ϵ for $\mathbf{emotion}_i\bar{o}$ henceforth. Finally, we use the following abbreviations that are common in KARO:

$\mathbf{P}(\alpha, \varphi) \equiv \mathbf{A}\alpha \wedge \langle\alpha\rangle\varphi$: An agent has the *practical possibility* to perform an action/plan α to bring about φ iff it has the ability to perform α and doing so can bring about φ.
$\mathbf{Can}(\alpha, \varphi) \equiv \mathbf{BP}(\alpha, \varphi)$: An agent *can* perform α to bring about φ iff it believes it has the practical possibility to do so.
$\mathbf{I}(\alpha, \varphi) \equiv \mathbf{Can}(\alpha, \varphi) \wedge \mathbf{BG}\varphi$: An agent has the *possible intention* to perform α to accomplish φ iff it *can* do so and it believes φ is one of its goals.

4 Emotion-Based Action Tendency Formalized

In this section, we add a formal notion of action tendency. We write $\mathbf{T}_i(\alpha, \epsilon)$, meaning that agent i has the tendency to perform action α due to negative emotion ϵ:

$$\mathrm{M}, s \models \mathbf{T}_i(\alpha, \epsilon) \quad \Leftrightarrow \quad (\alpha, \epsilon) \in \mathit{RelTen}(i)(\mathrm{M}, s)$$

where the function $\mathit{RelTen} : \mathcal{G} \times \mathcal{S} \rightarrow \wp(\mathcal{A} \times \mathit{EExp})$ formalizes (relative) action tendency as follows. We examine each negative emotion in the emotional memory of an agent; if there exists an action of which it believes that it is capable of performing the action and doing so may result in a state in which the emotion has strictly less intensity, then it tends to perform this action. Formally, this is written as:

$$\begin{aligned}\mathit{RelTen}(i)(\mathrm{M}, s) = \{\, (\alpha, \epsilon) \mid \epsilon \in \mathit{EMem}_i^*(\mathrm{M}, s),\ \mathit{neg}(\epsilon),\ \forall s' \in R_i(s) : [\alpha \in \mathcal{C}(i)(\mathrm{M}, s')\ \& \\ \exists(\mathrm{M}', s'') \in \mathcal{R}_{i:\alpha}(\mathrm{M}, s') : \mathit{int}(\mathrm{M}', s'')(\epsilon)(T_{\mathrm{M}'}) < \mathit{int}(\mathrm{M}, s)(\epsilon)(T_{\mathrm{M}})] \,\}\end{aligned}$$

where $\mathrm{M} = \langle S, R, V \rangle$ and $\mathit{neg}(\epsilon)$ is true iff ϵ is in the right-hand column of formula (2). It should be noted that, although there is no consensual definition of action tendency in the literature, our formalization is general enough to capture the basic concept.

With these definitions, we obtain the following propositions:

$$\not\models \epsilon^{\mathbf{T}} \rightarrow \epsilon \tag{3}$$
$$\not\models \epsilon \rightarrow \epsilon^{\mathbf{T}} \tag{4}$$
$$\models \epsilon \leftrightarrow \mathbf{B}\epsilon \tag{5}$$
$$\models \epsilon \wedge \mathbf{Can}(\alpha, \neg\epsilon) \rightarrow \mathbf{T}(\alpha, \epsilon) \qquad \text{(for negative emotions)} \tag{6}$$
$$\models \mathbf{T}(\alpha, \epsilon) \rightarrow \epsilon \wedge \mathbf{Can}(\alpha, \top) \tag{7}$$

The first proposition (which abbreviates, e.g., $\not\models \mathbf{joy}_i^{\mathbf{T}}(\varphi) \rightarrow \mathbf{joy}_i(\varphi)$) states that a newly triggered emotion is not necessarily experienced, whereas the second proposition (e.g., $\not\models \mathbf{joy}_i(\varphi) \rightarrow \mathbf{joy}_i^{\mathbf{T}}(\varphi)$) means that an emotion that is currently experienced is not necessarily a newly triggered one (as it may have been triggered in the past). The third proposition states that an agent is 'conscious' of each emotion it experiences (but not of emotion triggering, i.e. $\epsilon^{\mathbf{T}} \rightarrow \mathbf{B}\epsilon^{\mathbf{T}}$ is *not* valid). The fourth proposition states that an agent has the tendency to perform action α for emotion ϵ if ϵ is a currently experienced negative emotion and it 'can' perform α to mitigate the experience of ϵ. Note that the antecedent is slightly stronger (hence no bi-implication) than action tendency as formalized by RelTen, as RelTen does not require the intensity of ϵ to become zero, but just less than before. The fifth proposition states that action tendency $\mathbf{T}(\alpha, \epsilon)$ requires that ϵ be currently experienced and that α 'can' be performed.

Next we show how, for certain types of actions, constraints can be put on the framework, such that specific emotions can be shown to lead to action tendencies.

4.1 Idling

Consider the most basic emotion regulation strategy: letting feelings subside by themselves. Since time is supposed to "heal all wounds" (and negative emotions in particular), the presented formalization of action tendency should straightforwardly capture tendency towards idling (e.g., 'count till ten before acting when feeling angry').

Let `idle` denote the action that has no effects other than the passage of time. (Here it does not matter how long an agent will actually be idling.) It is not unreasonable to assume that an agent always has the *practical possibility* of idling, i.e., for all states $(\mathrm{M}, s) \in \mathcal{S}$ and agents $i \in \mathcal{G}$ we have that $\mathtt{idle} \in \mathcal{C}(i)(\mathrm{M}, s)$ and $\mathcal{R}_{i:\mathtt{idle}}(\mathrm{M}, s) \neq \emptyset$.

Furthermore, let int be constrained such that performing `idle` does not cause any changes in intensity functions:

$$\forall(\mathrm{M}', s') \in \mathcal{R}_{i:\mathtt{idle}}(\mathrm{M}, s) : \forall \epsilon \in EMem_i^*(\mathrm{M}, s) : int(\mathrm{M}', s')(\epsilon) = int(\mathrm{M}, s)(\epsilon)$$

Now we have that for all negative emotions ϵ: if for all (M, s), $int(\mathrm{M}, s)(\epsilon)$ is *strictly*[2] monotonically decreasing, then:

$$\models \epsilon \leftrightarrow \mathbf{T}(\mathtt{idle}, \epsilon) \tag{8}$$

Obviously, idling is only a valid strategy for negative emotions whose intensities actually decrease over time, hence the added requirement of strict monotonicity for this proposition.

4.2 Social Tendencies

In the following, it should be kept in mind that in the framework of [10], pity or resentment can be triggered when an agent believes that another agent's (sub)goal has been undermined (undone) or accomplished, respectively, and the agent views this as undesirable for itself. The (sub)goal that has been undermined or accomplished is denoted as φ, as in $\mathbf{pity}_i^{\mathbf{T}}(j, \varphi)$. Moreover, gratitude or anger can be triggered when a (sub)goal has been accomplished or undermined, respectively, by an action of another agent.

A reasonable constraint on int would now be to require that the intensity of a pity emotion is decreased if the agent believes that the action it performs re-accomplishes the (sub)goal of the other agent that it pitied, which is exactly the case when gratitude is triggered in the other agent. Formally, we constrain int such that for all states $(\mathrm{M}, s) \in \mathcal{S}$, agents $i \in \mathcal{G}$, actions $\alpha \in \mathcal{A}$, and all $(\mathrm{M}', s') \in \mathcal{R}_{i:\alpha}(\mathrm{M}, s)$:

$$int(\mathrm{M}', s')(\mathbf{pity}_i(j, \varphi)) = \begin{cases} f_0 & \text{if } \mathrm{M}', s' \models \mathbf{B}_i\mathbf{gratitude}_j^{\mathbf{T}}(i, \alpha, \varphi) \\ int(\mathrm{M}, s)(\mathbf{pity}_i(j, \varphi)) & \text{otherwise.} \end{cases}$$

Since the same reasoning applies to resentment and anger, we repeat the above with $\mathbf{pity}_i(j, \varphi)$ / $\mathbf{gratitude}_j^{\mathbf{T}}(i, \alpha, \varphi)$ replaced by $\mathbf{resentment}_i(j, \varphi)$ / $\mathbf{anger}_j^{\mathbf{T}}(i, \alpha, \varphi)$. Furthermore, this constraint for resentment and anger can be made more generic by dropping the φ, so we add a third constraint as above with $\mathbf{hate}_i(j)$ / $\mathbf{reproach}_j^{\mathbf{T}}(i, \alpha)$.

With these constraints the following propositions are valid:

$$\models \mathbf{pity}_i(j, \varphi) \wedge \mathbf{Can}_i(\alpha, \mathbf{B}_i\mathbf{gratitude}_j^{\mathbf{T}}(i, \alpha, \varphi)) \rightarrow \mathbf{T}_i(\alpha, \mathbf{pity}_i(j, \varphi)) \tag{9}$$

$$\models \mathbf{resentment}_i(j, \varphi) \wedge \mathbf{Can}_i(\alpha, \mathbf{B}_i\mathbf{anger}_j^{\mathbf{T}}(i, \alpha, \varphi)) \rightarrow \mathbf{T}_i(\alpha, \mathbf{resentment}_i(j, \varphi)) \tag{10}$$

$$\models \mathbf{hate}_i(j) \wedge \mathbf{Can}_i(\alpha, \mathbf{B}_i\mathbf{reproach}_j^{\mathbf{T}}(i, \alpha)) \rightarrow \mathbf{T}_i(\alpha, \mathbf{hate}_i(j)) \tag{11}$$

The first proposition states that if an agent pities another agent because its (sub)goal φ has been undermined, then it has the tendency to perform any action with which it can

[2] Intensity functions are supposed to reach zero within a finite amount of time but not to return negative values, so "strictly" should in this case be interpreted as: $int(\mathrm{M}, s)(\epsilon) = f$ where $f(x) = \max(g(x), 0)$ and g is (truly) strictly monotonically decreasing.

trigger, in the other agent, gratitude towards itself with respect to φ. Similar readings apply to the other propositions. It should be noted that the third proposition is like the second proposition but without relating α to a goal φ. Applying the same generalization to the first proposition yields the formula $\mathbf{love}_i(j) \wedge \mathbf{Can}_i(\alpha, \mathbf{B}_i\mathbf{admiration}_j^{\mathbf{T}}(i, \alpha)) \rightarrow \mathbf{T}_i(\alpha, \mathbf{love}_i(j))$. The problem with this formula is that it expresses action tendencies resulting from positive emotions (i.e. love), whereas action tendency so far has only been defined with respect to negative emotions. Indeed, with a suitable definition of 'positive' action tendency, this proposition will be worth investigating.

4.3 Reconsideration

In this section, we investigate a specific *class* of actions, namely reconsideration actions. For actions of this type, we formulate specific constraints and study their implications.

According to [9], hope to accomplish a goal by performing a plan is triggered when an agent has the possible intention to perform the plan for the goal and is committed to the plan, i.e., $\mathbf{I}(\pi, \varphi) \wedge \mathbf{Com}(\pi) \rightarrow \mathbf{hope}^{\mathbf{T}}(\pi, \varphi)$. Conversely, fear is triggered when the agent believes the plan may fail to accomplish the goal hoped for, i.e., $\mathbf{hope}^{\mathbf{T}}(\pi, \varphi) \wedge \mathbf{B}\langle\pi\rangle\neg\varphi \rightarrow \mathbf{fear}^{\mathbf{T}}(\pi, \neg\varphi)$. Note that these are propositions that are provable given suitable definitions of the functions *Hope*, *Fear* $\in$ Emo (see section 3).

Positive emotions are often associated with a tendency to proceed as planned, whereas negative emotions can cause reconsideration or trying harder [16]. Viewed from this perspective, an agent should have the tendency to reconsider if it fears a current (possible) intention may fail to accomplish its goal. We will first specify in more detail what we mean by reconsidering, and then show how this tendency can be modeled.

More specifically, reconsideration can be done when an agent has the (possible) intention $\mathbf{I}(\pi, \varphi)$ to perform some plan π for some goal φ, with the result that π or φ is dropped and possibly a new plan towards φ is found. It is assumed there exists a set of special reconsideration actions. An example is *uncommitting* (intention reconsideration), i.e., the special action $\texttt{uncommit}(\pi)$. (It is special in the sense that it is not supposed to be nested [20].) The result of this action is that π is removed from the agent's agenda. Another example is *replanning* (plan reconsideration), i.e. $\texttt{replan}(\pi, \varphi, \pi')$, which generates a (new) plan π' to accomplish goal φ and replaces π for π' on the agent's agenda. Alternatively, the agent can *drop* its goal φ or substitute it for another (similar) goal (goal reconsideration). In the following, we will write a reconsider action as $\mathit{reconsider}(\pi, \varphi)$. Each formula containing this expression should actually be viewed as a set of formulas; one for each instance of reconsider action.

As a first constraint we specify that an agent has the *practical possibility* of reconsidering a plan toward a goal if it has the possible intention to perform the plan for the goal:

$$\mathrm{M}, s \models \mathbf{I}(\pi, \varphi) \Rightarrow \mathit{reconsider}(\pi, \varphi) \in \mathcal{C}(\mathrm{M}, s) \ \&\ \mathcal{R}_{\mathit{reconsider}(\pi,\varphi)}(\mathrm{M}, s) \neq \emptyset$$

Next, we constrain int such that reconsidering causes all hope and fear with respect to the old plan to be assigned an intensity function that always returns zero (i.e. f_0). So we specify: if $\epsilon \in \{\mathbf{hope}(\pi, \varphi), \mathbf{fear}(\pi, \neg\varphi)\}$, then $\forall(\mathrm{M}, s) \in \mathcal{S} : \forall(\mathrm{M}', s') \in \mathcal{R}_{\mathit{reconsider}(\pi,\varphi)}(\mathrm{M}, s) : \mathit{int}(\mathrm{M}', s')(\epsilon) = f_0$. The result of this is that any old fear (with respect to π possibly failing to accomplish φ) is guaranteed to be gone after reconsidering π for φ. With these constraints, the following proposition is valid:

$$\models \mathbf{I}(\pi,\varphi) \wedge \mathbf{fear}(\pi,\neg\varphi) \rightarrow \mathbf{T}(\mathit{reconsider}(\pi,\varphi), \mathbf{fear}(\pi,\neg\varphi)) \tag{12}$$

for any type of reconsider action. In other words, an agent has the tendency to reconsider a plan towards a goal if it has the possible intention to perform the plan for the goal but fears the plan may fail to accomplish the goal.

5 Discussion

Several noteworthy variations on the presented formalization of action tendency are possible. For example:

'Strict' action tendency. The definition of *RelTen* can be made stricter by replacing the inequality by $\mathit{int}(\mathrm{M}', s'')(\epsilon)(T_{\mathrm{M}'}) < \mathit{int}(\mathrm{M}, s)(\epsilon)(T_{\mathrm{M}'})$. The (subtle) difference is that both intensity functions are evaluated at time $T_{\mathrm{M}'}$, so that the function returned by $\mathit{int}(\mathrm{M}', s'')(\epsilon)$ must really be different *and* better than the old one $\mathit{int}(\mathrm{M}, s)(\epsilon)$.

'Long-term' action tendency. The formalization of 'strict' action tendency can be made even stronger by adding: $\ldots \;\&\; \forall t > T_{\mathrm{M}'} : \mathit{int}(\mathrm{M}', s'')(\epsilon)(t) \leq \mathit{int}(\mathrm{M}, s)(\epsilon)(t)$. This means that the new intensity function $\mathit{int}(\mathrm{M}', s'')(\epsilon)$ for emotion ϵ must be better than the old one in all future time points (although it is possible that a future action replaces the intensity function for emotion ϵ again with a worse one).

'Overall' action tendency. So far we have only dealt with action tendency *relative* to a single (negative) emotion. However, it is possible to formalize a kind of action tendency that takes into account *all* negative emotions of an agent and specifies that an agent tends to perform some action if the sum of the intensities of its negative emotions in the state after performing the action is less than this sum was before. So the inequality in the definition of *RelTen* would then be replaced by $\sum_{\epsilon} \mathit{int}(\mathrm{M}', s'')(\epsilon)(T_{\mathrm{M}'}) < \sum_{\epsilon} \mathit{int}(\mathrm{M}, s)(\epsilon)(T_{\mathrm{M}})$ where the summations are over all negative emotions $\epsilon \in \mathit{EMem}_i^*(\mathrm{M}', s'')$ and $\epsilon \in \mathit{EMem}_i^*(\mathrm{M}, s)$, respectively.

It may be interesting to note that these alternative specifications of action tendency can be formally compared. Let the three kinds of action tendency as described above be formalized as $\mathbf{T}^{\mathrm{s}}(\alpha,\epsilon)$, $\mathbf{T}^{\mathrm{l}}(\alpha,\epsilon)$, and $\mathbf{T}^{\mathrm{o}}\alpha$, respectively. Then:

- $\mathbf{T}^{\mathrm{l}}(\alpha,\epsilon)$ implies $\mathbf{T}^{\mathrm{s}}(\alpha,\epsilon)$ implies $\mathbf{T}(\alpha,\epsilon)$;
- $\mathbf{T}^{\mathrm{o}}\alpha$ implies that there exists an ϵ such that $\mathbf{T}(\alpha,\epsilon)$.

It is easy to see that an agent would never 'strictly' tend to perform the action `idle` as above, i.e., $\models \neg\mathbf{T}^{\mathrm{s}}(\mathtt{idle},\epsilon)$ for any ϵ. Moreover, the reconsideration result can be strengthened as follows. If it is assumed that the intensities of corresponding hope and fear emotions always sum to a constant,[3] that reconsidering does not change an agent's beliefs, and that any new plan or goal, if found, does not cause more new fear than new hope, then we would have that $\models \mathbf{I}(\pi,\varphi) \wedge \mathbf{hope}(\pi,\varphi) < \mathbf{fear}(\pi,\neg\varphi) \rightarrow \mathbf{T}^{\mathrm{o}}\mathit{reconsider}(\pi,\varphi)$, where $<$ compares emotions by intensity. Indeed, as is evident from the previous sentence, there are usually a lot of constraints that have to be placed in order to attain an 'overall' tendency towards some (type of) action.

[3] This is not unreasonable; in fact, it is argued for by OCC [19]. Details on how to model this assumption can be found in [10].

It should be emphasized that the presence of action tendencies still does not specify which action will actually be chosen by an agent. However, an ordering can easily be defined on the subset of actions that an agent tends to perform by comparing their 'gain', i.e., the difference in intensity that the agent believes to obtain by performing an action. Then one can determine which action an agent tends to perform most and is thus most likely to be selected. Moreover, properties such as $\mathbf{T}(\alpha_1, \epsilon) \wedge \neg \mathbf{T}^{\mathbf{s}}(\alpha_1, \epsilon) \wedge \mathbf{T}^{\mathbf{s}}(\alpha_2, \epsilon) \rightarrow \alpha_1 \prec \alpha_2$ can then be investigated, where $\alpha_1 \prec \alpha_2$ means that the agent in question strictly prefers to perform α_2 over α_1 to regulate emotion ϵ.

6 Related Work

Meyer [6] formalized four basic emotion types (i.e., happiness, sadness, anger, and fear) inspired by the psychological work of Oatley & Jenkins [16]. In addition to formalizing their triggering conditions, a heuristic is associated with each emotion type, indicating how an agent should act on it. However, lacking a formalization of quantitative aspects, it is left unspecified how executing such a heuristic influences the experience of the associated emotion. Moreover, in our approach, any number of 'heuristics' can be defined; the action tendency operator will pick up on any action that can improve the situation.

Adam [8] proposed a purely qualitative formalization of the OCC model also incorporating emotion regulation. However, only the regulation of negative event-based emotions (i.e., distress, disappointment, fear, fears-confirmed, pity, and resentment) is investigated. To this end, seven coping strategies are defined. Some coping strategies (e.g., denial, resign) change the beliefs or desires of an agent such that the triggering conditions for the negative emotion cease to hold. Other coping strategies (e.g, mental disengagement, venting) lead to the adoption of intentions to bring about new positive emotions that "divert the individual from the current negative one" [8]. However, in contrast to our approach, quantitative aspects of emotions are not taken into account, so it is left unspecified how these coping strategies actually mitigate the experience of negative emotions. Moreover, it is not clear how Adam measures whether the situation after coping is better than before.

Gratch & Marsella [4] have been working on a computational framework for modeling emotions inspired by the OCC model, among others. An implementation, named EMA, is used for social training applications. Like Adam, their framework incorporates a number of coping strategies. However, in EMA, the link from appraisal to coping is rather direct. In contrast, we put a notion of action tendency in between emotions and regulatory actions, on which an agent can decide to act or not. Moreover, few formal details about the logic underlying EMA are provided.

7 Conclusion

In this paper, we have formalized a notion of action tendency and incorporated it into an existing formalization of emotions. This formalization is based on the psychological OCC model of emotions and grounded in the KARO framework of rational agency. However, so far it only incorporated the appraisal and experience phases of emotions. What is lacking in this (and several other) formalizations of emotions is a specification of how emotions influence behavior. In psychology, emotions are often seen as learned and innate heuristics that give an individual the tendency to prefer certain actions over others, based on its current emotional state. Thus by incorporating action tendency in a formal model of agency, we have introduced a mechanism for limiting and ordering options in an agent's action selection process. In line with the general view of action tendency in psychology, our formalized notion of action tendency is based on reducing negative emotion intensity. To this end, a goal may be adopted or reconsidered (as shown in section 4.3), but not necessarily so.

It should be noted that the presented formalization of action tendency is only defined with respect to negative emotions. Moreover, due to space limitations, only action tendencies with respect to several of the emotion types in the formal emotion model have been presented. For future work, responses to positive emotions as well as the remaining negative emotions have to be investigated. Because there are several ways of formalizing action tendency, the implications of choosing any particular 'flavor' have to be explicated. As shown, it is also possible to incorporate multiple notions of action tendency and study their relations.

References

1. Picard, R.W.: Affective Computing. MIT Press, Cambridge (1997)
2. Johns, M., Silverman, B.G.: How emotion and personality effect the utility of alternative decisions: A terrorist target selection case study. In: 10th Conference On Computer Generated Forces and Behavioral Representation, SISO (2001)
3. Sloman, A.: Beyond shallow models of emotion. Cognitive Processing 2(1), 177–198 (2001)
4. Gratch, J., Marsella, S.: A domain-independent framework for modeling emotions. Journal of Cognitive Systems Research 5(4), 269–306 (2004)
5. Marinier, R.P., Laird, J.E.: Toward a comprehensive computational model of emotions and feelings. In: Proceedings of the International Conference on Cognitive Modeling (ICCM 2004), Pittsburgh, PA, pp. 172–177 (2004)
6. Meyer, J.-J.C.: Reasoning about emotional agents. International Journal of Intelligent Systems 21(6), 601–619 (2006)
7. Dastani, M., Meyer, J.-J.C.: Programming agents with emotions. In: Proceedings of the 17th European Conference on Artificial Intelligence (ECAI 2006), pp. 215–219 (2006)
8. Adam, C.: The Emotions: From Psychological Theories to Logical Formalization and Implementation in a BDI Agent. PhD thesis, Institut National Polytechnique de Toulouse (2007)
9. Steunebrink, B.R., Dastani, M., Meyer, J.-J.C.: A logic of emotions for intelligent agents. In: Proceedings of the 22nd Conference on Artificial Intelligence (AAAI 2007). AAAI Press, Menlo Park (2007)
10. Steunebrink, B.R., Dastani, M., Meyer, J.-J.C.: A formal model of emotions: Integrating qualitative and quantitative aspects. In: Proceedings of the 18th European Conference on Artificial Intelligence (ECAI 2008), pp. 256–260. IOS Press, Amsterdam (2008)
11. Elster, J.: Rationality and the emotions. Economic Journal 106(438), 1386–1397 (1996)
12. Coppin, G.: Emotion, personality and decision-making: Relying on the observables. In: Proceedings of the 3rd International Conference in Human Centered Processes, HCP-2008 (2008)
13. Frijda, N.H.: The Emotions. Studies in Emotion and Social Interaction. Cambridge University Press, Cambridge (1987)

14. LeDoux, J.E.: The Emotional Brain: Mysterious Underpinnings of Emotional Life. Simon & Schuster (1996)
15. Ekman, P., Davidson, R.J. (eds.): The Nature of Emotion: Fundamental Questions. Series in Affective Science. Oxford University Press, Oxford (1994)
16. Oatley, K., Jenkins, J.M.: Understanding Emotions. Blackwell Publishing, Oxford (1996)
17. Damasio, A.R.: Descartes' Error: Emotion, Reason and the Human Brain. Grosset/Putnam, New York (1994)
18. Gross, J.J., Thompson, R.A.: Emotion regulation: Conceptual foundations. In: Gross, J.J. (ed.) Handbook of Emotion Regulation. Guilford Press, New York (2007)
19. Ortony, A., Clore, G.L., Collins, A.: The Cognitive Structure of Emotions. Cambridge University Press, Cambridge (1988)
20. Meyer, J.-J.C., Hoek, W.v.d., Linder, B.v.: A logical approach to the dynamics of commitments. Artificial Intelligence 113, 1–40 (1999)

An Emotional and Context-Aware Model for Adapting RSS News to Users and Groups

Eugénia Vinagre[1], Goreti Marreiros[1,2], Carlos Ramos[1,2], and Lino Figueiredo[1,2]

[1] Institute of Engineering – Polytechnic of Porto
Porto, Portugal
{1000318}@dei.isep.ipp.pt, lbf@isep.ipp.pt
[2] GECAD – Knowledge Engineering and Decision Support Group
Porto, Portugal
{goreti,csr}@dei.isep.ipp.pt

Abstract. The exhibition of information does not always attend to the preferences and characteristics of the users, nor the context that involves the user. With the aim of overcoming this gap, we propose an emotional context-aware model for adapting information contents to users and groups. The proposed model is based on OCC and Big Five models to handle emotion and personality respectively. The idea is to adapt the representation of the information in order to maximize the positive emotional valences and minimize the negatives. To evaluate the proposed model it was developed a prototype for adapting RSS news to users and group of users.

Keywords: Affective computing, Context-aware computing.

1 Introduction

We live in the technology era. Today, with rare exceptions, we all have direct or indirect contact with technology and access to more or less intelligent devices. Society in general is more and more critic. We do not just want to enjoy the features of a given device, but we think also, that the device should be intelligent enough to understand our needs and adapt its behaviour in order to answer our needs. For instance, if we are in an unknown place and we are hungry we want that our PDA (Personal Digital Assistant) help us in the process of choosing a restaurant according to our gastronomic preferences. For doing this it is necessary to give to the devices the ability to interact with the environment and at the same time the ability to search for information. These features are related with areas like ubiquitous computing and context-aware computing.

Ubiquitous computing aims the creation of intelligent environments, equipped with computational resources whose goal is to support user's daily tasks. The idea is that computers should adapt to man and not man to computers. The involved research areas are:

- Natural interfaces;
- Automated capture of information;
- Context-aware computing.

L. Seabra Lopes et al. (Eds.): EPIA 2009, LNAI 5816, pp. 187–198, 2009.

A context-aware system is a system that uses context to provide relevant information or services to its users [1]. In [2] context awareness means that the system has conscience about the current situation we are dealing with. An example is the automatic detection of the current situation in a Control Centre. Are we in presence of a normal situation or are we dealing with a critical situation, or even an emergency?

This paper is organized as follows. Section 2 provides a general approach to affective computing. Section 3 presents the model that we propose to address the representation of emotional and context-aware information. Section 4 describes the implementation of the prototype and finally section 5 presents some conclusions.

2 Affective Computing

An emotion is characterized as a set of reactions that a human being has when facing several situations. These reactions, which vary from individual to individual, are influenced by his personality, by the way he observe the world around him as well as by his emotional state at the time when those situations take place. An emotion causes physical (e.g. change in facial expression, tone of voice, heartbeat) and psychological reactions (e.g. change in cognitive capacity, decision-making capacity, memory, behaviour). Emotions have an important influence on the life of the human being, influencing many aspects of biological functioning, psychological functioning and social behaviour.

Neurology studies point out that reason and emotion are indissoluble and that the emotional state is decisive at the cognitive process. If emotions affect the cognitive capacity of human beings and if we want to develop more real and credible systems, able to replace or help the human beings in some situations, then we must bring them closer to the way of thinking and feeling of the human being, i.e., reason alone is not enough.

Having these objectives in mind, several studies were performed aiming recognizing and simulating emotions in computer systems [3,4,5,6,7]. Rosalind Picard defines affective computing as the area dedicated to the investigation of affection on non biological systems, i.e., studies the use of emotions in informatics systems from the recognition, representation and simulation to the research that involves emotions in human-machine interactions [8].

The cognitive approach of emotions has been influencing the research in the area of affective computing resulting in some models for the treatment of emotions in computing environments such as the OCC model and the big five model.

OCC Model

In 1988 Andrew Ortony, Clore and Collins developed a model of emotions known as OCC whose main objective is to specify a structure based on the description of personal and interpersonal situations as a way to infer emotions. The model is composed by 22 emotions and they are grouped into categories according to the conditions that generate them [9]:

- *Events* – According with their objectives, the agents classify the events as desirable or not. The fact that an event is a lot or little pleasant/unpleasant, contributes significantly to the intensity of emotions such as happiness/anguish.

The forecast of future events can cause emotions such as hope/fear, whose intensity comes from the fact that the future event can be a lot or little pleasant/unpleasant for the objectives that the agent proposes to achieve;

- *Actions* – the agents' actions can be approved or disapproved in agreement with their judgement of values (set of beliefs about itself and about others), originating emotions of pride/shame or admiration/reproach;
- *Objects* – The objects are appreciated by the agent in agreement with their preferences and personal tastes. The fact that the agent approaches (i.e., thinking, imagining or observing) an object that he likes or dislikes, can cause situations in which relations of friendship or antipathy (i.e., emotions) are developed.

The OCC model defines the following factors for the variation of the emotional intensity [9]:

- *Sense of reality* – i.e., the importance that an agent attributes to an event, action or object in a certain context;
- *Proximity* – i.e., the amplitude time elapsed between the moment when the emotion is felt until the moment that the event that caused the emotion occurred;
- *Surprise* – i.e., the degree of unpredictability contained in a certain occurrence;
- *Incentive* – i.e., the expectation created by the agent when facing a certain situation.

Big Five Model

In 1966 Gordon Allport proposed a theory of traits. For Allport, there are traits that characterize the human behaviour in many situations. The observation of these traits in a person can predict what he will probably do, even in situations never observed [10].

From this approach several studies were made to reduce the personality traits. In this context it appears the Big Five model (Five Great Factors) [11]. The model defines the Big Five factors of personality in the following way:

- *Extroversion* – The extroversion evaluates the quantity and intensity of interpersonal interactions, the level of activity, the stimulation needs and the capacity to express the happiness. This factor characterizes people guided for the external world, sociable, impulsive, assertive, optimistic, energetic, they love the fun and enjoy the interaction with others. They like to be in a group and among the crowds. They are usually lively and cheerful. People with low scores on this factor, show a more reserved behaviour, sober and more calm, not very exuberant, distant, shy, quiet and more oriented to the task.
- *Agreeableness* – The agreeableness evaluates the quality of the interpersonal orientation in a continuous way, varying from the compassion to the antagonism in the thoughts, feelings and actions. Similarity to what was said relatively to the Extroversion, this factor evaluates also the interpersonal tendencies, but whose existence is focused in others. Persons with a high index in this factor are altruistic, helpful, accurate, reliable and friendly towards others. They manifest an unequivocal will to help the neighbour and they believe that others

will be equally nice. On the contrary way, a low index identifies unpleasant, egocentric, cynic, simple, suspicious, not very cooperative, revengeful, irritable, manipulators, sceptics in relation to the interests of the others and usually more competitive people.

- *Conscientiousness* – This factor evaluates the organizational degree, persistence and motivation in the behaviour guided for a certain objective, i.e., it characterizes the individuals according with his will and desire of realization. On both ends of the scale there are, on one side, scrupulous people and trustworthy and, on the opposite end, lazy and careless people. A conscientious individual has willpower, he is determined, scrupulous, punctual, organized, hard-working, disciplined, neat, an ambitious person, tenacious and of trustworthy. A not very conscientious person is less obstinate in achieving their own objectives, lazier, reckless and negligent.
- *Neuroticism* – Neuroticism evaluates the emotional instability. It is more accentuated in anxious, nervous, emotionally insecure, hypochondriac people, with propensity to pessimistic behaviour with unrealistic, desires and needs excessive. A high index in this factor identifies persons with a tendency to experiment negative emotions such as sadness, fear, embarrassment, anger, guilt and rejection. On the contrary, the opposite a low index in Neuroticism identifies persons emotionally stable, calm, relaxed, safe, happy with themselves and constant mood.
- *Openness* – The Openness tries to evaluate the enjoyment of the existence and exploration of new experiences. The active imagination, the aesthetic sensibility, the intellectual curiosity and the independent judgement, are components of this factor. People with high level of openness are curious about the inner and outer world and their repertoire of life experiences is very rich. They are available to accept new ideas and unconventional values and experience a wide range of positive and negative emotions. In contrast, people with a low level of openness are more conventional, more conservatives, they prefer the usual to the innovation. Their range of interests is more limited and they show less tendency for the arts.

It is important to make the distinction between the concepts of personality, feelings, emotions and emotional state. According to some authors, an emotion is an experience, with greater or lesser intensity, of short duration (seconds or minutes) triggered by an event. The emotional state (also called state of mind or mood) is characterized by lasting hours or days. It is caused by the existence of one or more factors such as emotions, environmental changes or physical conditions [5]. Unlike emotions and emotional states, feelings can persist along an individual's life. Feelings are related to the emotions that an individual expects to experience interacting with an entity, i.e. the set of values and judgments about the world around him (e.g. like or not like a football team). Finally, according to psychologists David Krech and Richard Crutchfield [12] the personality is a permanent feature of the individual which shows itself in consistent behaviour against a wide variety of situations.

3 Proposed Model

Before describing the proposed model we will give a brief idea of the test scenario. The idea is to have a visualization device (e.g. a LCD) adapting information to be exhibited (e.g. RSS news) to one or more users, identified by RFID tags. The main goal is to adapt the exhibited information to the emotional state and personality of the user or group of users.

The proposed model is composed by the context model, emotional model and user model. In this section we detail each one of the models.

3.1 Context Model

The context model is composed by three layers (Fig. 1):

- The context information capture layer - which is responsible for acquiring information using RFID (Radio-Frequency Identification) and RSS (Really Simple Syndication) technologies;
- The interpretation layer - constituted by the interpreters;
- The context manager layer.

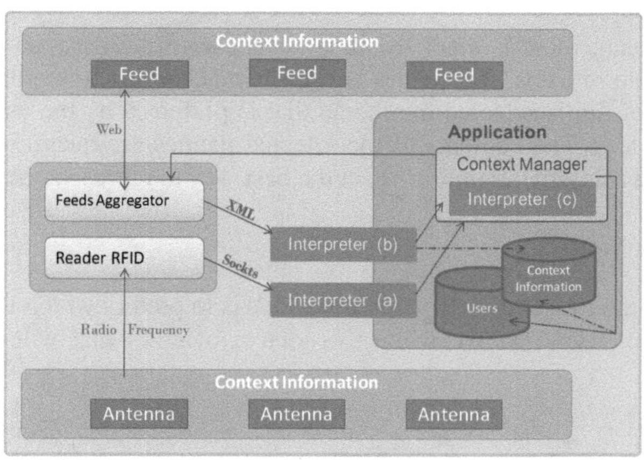

Fig. 1. Context Model

Context Information Capture

This layer is responsible for capturing two types of context information:

- ID of the users – The identification of users is made by RFID. The users have an RFID card that stores an ID (identifier) allowing the identification by the application.
- News contents – The news contents were selected in this work as the information to be presented to users according to their themes. The news is acquired by the feeds aggregator. The aggregator is responsible to subscribe, receive and update the contents. Whenever a new user appears the aggregator is requested

to subscribe the themes of his preference. The aggregator performs the updating of these subjects according to the time configured in the system.

Interpretation of Context Information

The interpretation layer is composed by the three interpreters represented in Fig.1 whose function is to decode and interpret the context information which they are sent by the capture layer.

- *Interpreter (a)* – It is a socket permanently listening for new messages sent by the RFID system and has the function of decode the information. After interpreting the message, it adds or removes from a list the identified users. Whenever a change occurs in the list an event is generated and captured by the Context Manager whose mission is to rebuild the visualization scenario.
- *Interpreter (b)* – Its function is to decode the information sent to it by the news aggregator (i.e. interpret the information contained in files feed). The interpreter extracts information about the title and details of each file contents.
- *Interpreter (c)* – Its function is to do an interpretation at the highest level. Its aim is to select the type and the form of representation (i.e. what should be showed and how to do it).

Context manager

The context manager must select the themes of user preference in this scenario of view. For a group of users, the themes are selected according to the preference of the group. In case of tie, is selected the theme that is preferred by the user who first arrived to the system. The contents of the selected themes are quantified emotionally. According to this classification it is select the best way to represent the themes.

3.2 Emotional Model

The purpose of the model developed in this work is to predict which will be the emotional reaction of users from viewing the content of news that will be shown. The

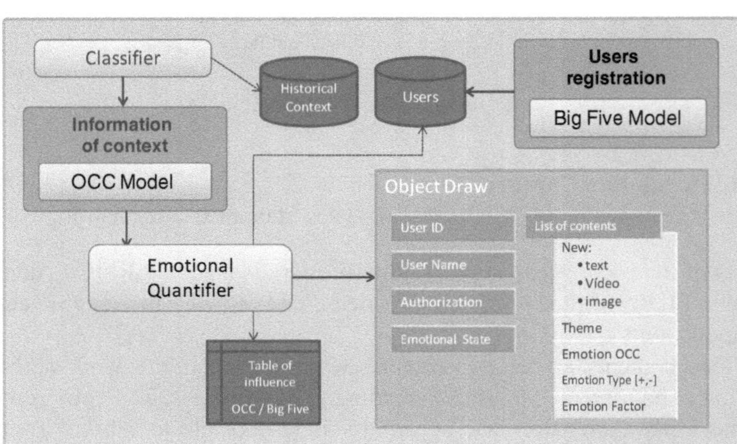

Fig. 2. Emotional Model

prediction of that reaction will allow the system to readjust the representation of content (displayed information) in order to reduce negative impacts and increase the positive ones. In Fig. 2 it is possible to see the proposed emotional model.

The emotional model proposed for the referred objectives, uses the OCC model to classify the content of news and the Big Five model to infer users' personality.

The emotional model is composed by two components to predict the intensity of emotions: the *Classifier* and the *Emotional Quantifier*.

Classifier

Its function is to classify the news content, obtained by a news feed, according to the OCC model. The classification consists on identifying which is the type of emotion and its intensity.

The type of emotion in news is directly related to the theme. For example, the sentence "*Team A beat team B*" may generate opposite emotions. It depends on the theme assigned to the news. If we consider that the theme is *"Team A"*, the type of emotion will be "Happiness", but if we consider that the theme is *"Team B"* the type of emotion will be "Sadness". I.e., to assign a type of emotion to the news, first the classifier must assign a theme to the news. In the example the classifier should generate two news contents, one for each of these two themes and to classify them according to the type of emotion involved.

It is considered that the value assigned to news content is the minimum of the emotional intensity of the news. For example, the new "*Air accident in Madrid killed 120 people*" has a much higher intensity than the new "*Died today at age of 85 the writer xpto victim of prolonged disease*". There are several factors that influence the value of the intensity of the emotions of the OCC model, such as the expectation created on a particular event. If something of good that was not planned happened, then we will have an explosion of happiness. But if a good thing, was expected and does not happen then we will suffer a great disappointment. I.e., the news by themselves are not enough. First, the component should acquire knowledge on the domain to get which is the type and value of the emotion in the news. This component is also responsible for maintaining a history of the contents so that it can classify correctly the news.

Emotional Quantifier

In real time the application use this component to quantify the emotional intensity of the news. In agreement with that value and with the profile of the users it makes the selection of the best way to represent the information. There are several factors that influence the emotional intensity in news for a certain user:

- Personality – It is considered that personality traits have a certain degree of influence on each of the emotions in OCC model (e.g. a user with a high index of extraversion will be less influenced by sad news that's a user with a high index in neuroticism). In this work the emotions *pride* and *remorse* of the OCC model [13] were not considered. In the current context these emotions only make sense if the users are viewing news about yourself. The probability of this happening is very rare. However in future work we can assess which personality traits influence of these emotions (e.g. to consider the viewing of news for known people). In this case the classifier should add the feature to identify if the news is or is not related with the user that will visualize her.

The degree of influence of personality traits on the emotions is set in a 10x5 matrix (10 emotions of the OCC model an 5 personality traits from the Big Five model), represented by $EP, \forall ep_{ij} \in [-0.5, 0.5]$

Being $E_{occ} = \{e_1, e_2, ..., e_{10}\}$ the set that defines the emotions of the OCC model [13], $P_{BF} = \{p_1, ..., p_5\}$ the set that defines the personality traits according to the Big Five model [6] and $P_{user} = \{up_1, ..., up_5\}$ the set that defines personality traits of one user, then

$$\text{Influence of traces}(ITe_i) = \sum_{j=1}^{5} up_j * EP_{ij} \qquad , \forall up_j \in [0,1]$$

- Preference - It is considered that the preference for the six themes has a weight on the intensity of emotions.

  $$\text{Weight Preference } (WP) = \{0.1,\ 0.05,\ 0.04,\ 0.03,\ 0.02,\ 0.01\},$$

  where the value *0.1* represents the weight of the themes of greater choice and *0.01* for the weight of lower preference.
- Emotional State - It is considered that the intensity of emotion varies between 0 and 1. When the value of emotional intensity is greater than 0.75 causes a weight of 0.1 in the user's emotional state. The emotional state will influence the intensity of the next emotion.

  $$\text{Emotional State } (S_{em}) = S_{em-1} + 0.1 * t_e, \qquad \forall t_e \in \{1, -1\},$$

  where t_e represents the type of emotion (i.e. positive or negative)

Therefore, the Emotional Intensity of news content can be quantified in the following way:

$$\text{Emotional Intensity}(EI_i) = N_e + ITe_i + WP + S_{em} \qquad ,$$

where N_e represents the value assigned by the Classifier to the news content and *i* the type of OCC emotion.

In the case of a users group the emotional intensity is:

$$\text{Emotional Intensity}(EI_i)_g = N_e + \left[\left(\sum_{u=1}^{n} ITe_{iu} + WP_u \right) / n \right] + S_{em} \qquad ,$$

where *u* represents the user and *n* the number of users in the group.

3.3 User Model

The purpose of this model is to store knowledge about the users' profile. The following elements are considered in user model:

- Basic information - basic data about the user, e.g. age, occupation and sex.
- Preferences - represents the user's preferences on the news themes.

- Personality - The users answer to an inquiry, when they make their registration in the system, from which can get their personality traits according to the Big Five model. The proposed inquiry was based on BFI (*Big Five Inventory*) [14]. In agreement with the result of this inquiry the system can infer about the user's personality.

4 Prototype

The prototype was developed using the development platform .Net and the programming language C#. It was used the API ASPRSSToolkit for the collection and interpretation of news content and ActiveX ITDC for the management and control of RFID system.

The architecture of the developed system uses RFID technology for recognition of users in the visualization scenario, and RSS technology to get informative contents in agreement with the interests of users.

For the classification of the informative contents it was used the OCC model and for the characterization the user's emotional profile it was used the Big Five model.

The following figure shows the architecture of the prototype

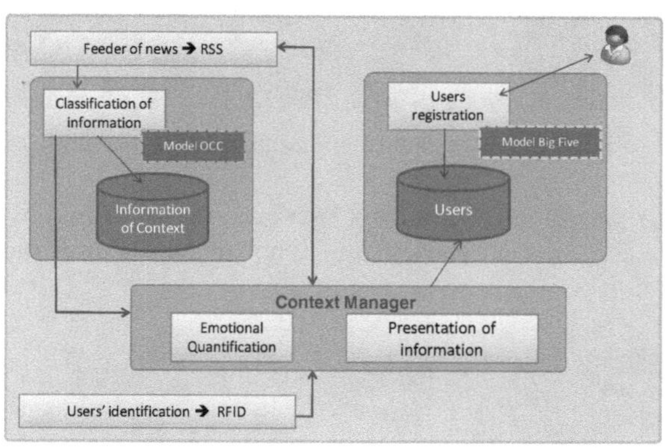

Fig. 3. Architecture of prototype

The developed prototype allows the configuration of the visualization of contents in the following way:

- Visualization considering or not the emotional factor;
- Individual or group visualization.

Among other settings the prototypes allows the configuration of the best representation of news according to the emotional intensity towards the objective of reducing the negative impact of news and reinforce positive emotions. In the following figure we can see the screen of the system configuration.

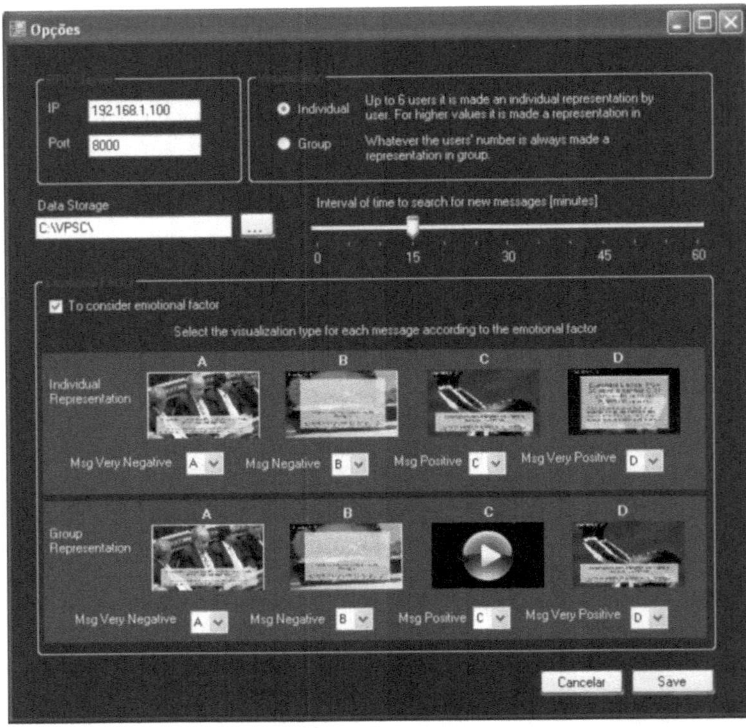

Fig. 4. Display system configuration of visualization

When in the visualization environment users are not identified by system, the display shows the latest news on each theme. The figure 5 shows the scenario of the default representation.

Fig. 5. Default visualization

In the default representation the photos deals with topics and not with new itself. This is also the way chosen to display news with emotional intensity very negative. The forms used to represent the news are: text, images and videos. We assumed that the text is a form of representation that have less emotional impact and the video is one that causes a greater impact. Like this, different scenarios were prepared for viewing on the same news in order to reduce or increase their emotional intensity. All these ways of representing the news can be configured as shown in Fig.4.

5 Conclusions

In this work it was developed a model and a prototype that allows the visualization of personalized information of news contents. These contents are shown in agreement with the preferences of specific user or group users. With the goal of minimizing the negative impact of the news and to maximize positive emotions, the representation of contents is made taking in consideration the emotional state of each user.

An example of the application of this work can be the placement of informative screens in common areas of a company. These screens will show the news so carefully in order to maintain the motivation, whenever possible, of their employees.

Predict user's reaction to displayed contents is not an easy task. Each human being is unique and often unpredictable. However it is possible to find patterns of behaviour. The more fitting and refined these patterns are lower is the margin of error in predicting the users' reaction to the contents visualized.

At this stage the classification of news is made manually, as future work we will develop an automatic classifier of news, i.e. a classifier that classify news, in real time, according OCC model of emotions.

As further work we will still need test the application with different users groups, and study the results.

References

1. Dey, K.A.: Providing Architectural Support for Building Context-Aware Applications, PhD thesis. Georgia Institute of Technology, Georgia (November 2000)
2. Ramos, C.: Ambient Intelligence — a State of the Art from Artificial Intelligence Perspective. In: Neves, J., Santos, M.F., Machado, J.M. (eds.) EPIA 2007. LNCS (LNAI), vol. 4874, pp. 285–295. Springer, Heidelberg (2007)
3. Gratch, J., Marsella, S.: Evaluating a computational model of emotion. Journal of Autonomous Agents and Multiagent Systems 11(1), 23–43 (2006)
4. Prada, R., Paiva, A.: Teaming up humans with autonomous synthetic characters. Artificial Intelligence 173(1), 80–103 (2009)
5. Marreiros, G.: Agentes de Apoio à Argumentação e Decisão em Grupo, Tese de Doutoramento. Universidade do Minho, Portugal (2008)
6. Hudlicka, E.: Depth of feelings: Alternatives for modeling affect in user models. In: Sojka, P., Kopeček, I., Pala, K. (eds.) TSD 2006. LNCS (LNAI), vol. 4188, pp. 13–18. Springer, Heidelberg (2006)

7. Cañamero, L., Avila-García, O.: A Bottom-Up Investigation of Emotional Modulation in Competitive Scenarios. In: Paiva, A.C.R., Prada, R., Picard, R.W. (eds.) ACII 2007. LNCS, vol. 4738, pp. 398–409. Springer, Heidelberg (2007)
8. Picard, R.: Affective Computing, M.I.T Media Laboratory Perceptual Computing Section Technical Report N° 321, (November 26, 1995), http://vismod.media.mit.edu/tech-reports/TR-321.pdf [September 21, 2008]
9. Ortony, A., Clore, G., Collins, A.: The cognitive structure of emotions. Cambridge University Press, Cambridge (1988)
10. Allport, G.: Traits revisited. American psychologist 21, 1–10 (1966)
11. McRae, R.R., Costa, P.T.: Validation of the five-factor model of personality across instruments and observers. Journal of Personality and Social Psychology 52, 81–90 (1987)
12. Krech, D., Crutchfield, R.: Elementos da Psicologia. Livraria Pioneira, SP (1971)
13. Ortony, A.: On making believable emotional agents believable. In: Trapple, R., Petta, P., Payr, S. (eds.) Emotions in humans and artefacts. MIT Press, Cambridge (2003)
14. John, O.P., Srivastava, S.: The Big Five Trait Taxonomy: History, Measurement, and Theoretical Perspectives. In: Pervin, L.A., John, O.P. (eds.) Handbook of personality: Theory and research, vol. 2, pp. 102–138. Guilford Press, New York (1999)

Chapter 6

GAI – General Artificial Intelligence

Type Parametric Compilation of Algebraic Constraints

Marco Correia and Pedro Barahona

Centro de Inteligência Artificial, Departamento de Informática,
Universidade Nova de Lisboa, 2829-516 Caparica, Portugal
{mvc,pb}@di.fct.unl.pt

Abstract. This paper addresses the problem of propagating constraints involving arbitrary algebraic expressions. We formally describe previous approaches to this problem and propose a new model that does not decompose the expression thus avoiding introducing auxiliary data structures. We show how this compilation model fits naturally in a popular programming language supporting type parametricity, yielding significant speedups with respect to previous models.

1 Introduction

One of the key features in constraint programming is the ability to exploit problem structure. Traditionally, this has been achieved by designing efficient filtering algorithms for common constraints, and making them available to the user as modeling primitives. These algorithms remove inconsistent values from the domains of the variables subject to a constraint, often enforcing generalized arc-consistency (GAC) [13].

Unfortunately, enforcing GAC on an algebraic constraint is NP-complete in general [17]. In practice, constraints involving arbitrary algebraic expressions are decomposed into primitive subexpressions for which weaker filtering algorithms are available. However, since the decomposition consists of introducing auxiliary variables and propagators for each subexpression, propagating a large algebraic constraint may still be space and time inefficient.

This paper focuses on compiling (as opposed to decomposing) arbitrary algebraic expressions. We present two compilation models based on an abstraction called *view* [14,6] which overcome the limitations of decomposition based methods. The first model was first used in [12], but as far as we know, never formally described. The second model is original and improves over the first in a number of ways.

The output of the compilation process is a filtering algorithm which enforces some consistency on the entire expression. We will consider bounds(R) consistency algorithms [2], although the method works with other weak consistency types, namely node consistency.

The structure of the paper is the following. In section 2 we introduce the terminology used throughout the paper. Section 3 describes the classical approach to algebraic expression decomposition based on auxiliary variables and propagators. In section 4 we introduce views as the key for compiling expressions, and describe the compilation models for two different types of views. Theoretical and empirical comparisons of models using views and the classical decomposition are detailed in section 5 and 6 respectively. Section 7 points related work in the literature and state-of-the-art solvers, and the main conclusions are summarized in section 8.

L. Seabra Lopes et al. (Eds.): EPIA 2009, LNAI 5816, pp. 201–212, 2009.

2 Background and Notation

We will consider sentences from a first-order language $\mathcal{L}(\Sigma, V)$ involving the standard set of arithmetic and logical operators Σ and domain variables V (denoted by lowercase letters and the suffix : dvar). Additionally, we refer to subsets of $\mathcal{L}$ using *expression templates*, defined as follows:

Definition 1. [Expression template] *An expression template is an expression* $t \in \mathcal{L}(\Sigma, V')$ *where* V' *is* V *augmented with term variables (denoted by uppercase letters). It represents the largest language subset* $\mathcal{L}^t \subseteq \mathcal{L}$ *where for all* $i \in \mathcal{L}^t$, i *may be obtained from* t *by instantiating the term variables.*

The compilation process will be defined declaratively by means of action rules:

Definition 2. [Action Rule, Rule repository] *An action rule associated with a language* $\mathcal{L}$ *takes the form*

$$\frac{t}{e}\begin{bmatrix} a_1 \\ \vdots \\ a_n \end{bmatrix}$$

and defines the rewriting of any input expression $i \in \mathcal{L}^t$ *(i.e. matched by the template expression* t*) into output expression* $e \in \mathcal{L}$*, performing actions* $a_1, \ldots, a_n$ *(the rule actions) as a side effect. A rule repository* $\mathrm{R}(\mathcal{L})$ *is a collection of action rules associated with language* $\mathcal{L}$.

Rule repositories will be used to perform derivations of expressions.

Definition 3. [Derivation] *A derivation (written* $R[e]$*) denotes the output of applying the most specific rule in the repository* R *matching* e*. A rule* $r_1 \equiv \frac{t_1}{e_1}$ *is more specific than a rule* $r_2 \equiv \frac{t_2}{e_2}$ *if* $\mathcal{L}^{t_1} \subset \mathcal{L}^{t_2}$*. For simplification, we will assume that there is no ambiguity for selecting the most specific rule for a given expression. In practice this can be enforced by adding extra rules to the repository.*

The following definition introduces the formalism for indexed collections, which will be used extensively.

Definition 4. [Indexed collection] *An indexed collection is a tuple* $\langle C, X, M \rangle$ *where* C *is a collection of arbitrary objects,* X *is a collection of indexing objects, and* $M : X \rightarrow C$ *is a mapping. We will denote an indexed collection by* $C\langle X \rangle$ *and will use* $C[x]$ *to refer to the element of the collection* $c \in C\langle X \rangle$ *mapped to by element* $x \in X$.

The following definitions introduce notions and standard terminology from the field of constraint programming. For detailed information see for example [13].

A constraint network is a tuple $\langle X, D, C \rangle$, consisting of a set of variables X, a set of domains D, and a set of constraints C. Every variable $x \in X$ has an associated domain $D(x)$ representing its possible values. A $k-$ary constraint c over the set of variables $X(c) = \{x_1, \ldots, x_k\}$ defines the subset of the cartesian product $\mathrm{D}(c) = D(x_1) \times \ldots \times D(x_k)$ that satisfy the constraint. The constraint satisfaction problem consists of finding an assignment of values to variables which satisfy all constraints.

A propagator associated with a constraint c is a contracting and monotone function $\pi : \wp(\mathrm{D}(c)) \rightarrow \wp(\mathrm{D}(c))$ ($\wp(X)$ is the powerset of X) which removes inconsistent values from the domains. The application of a propagator to a constraint network is called propagator execution.

Given a network $\langle X, D, C\rangle$ and a constraint $c \in C$, a bound support τ on c is a tuple that satisfies c and such that for all $x_i \in X(c)$, $\lfloor D(x_i)\rfloor \leq \tau[x_i] \leq \lceil D(x_i)\rceil$.

- A constraint c is bound(Z) consistent iff for all $x_i \in X(c)$, there exists two bound supports τ_1, τ_2 such that $\tau_1[x_i] = \lceil D(x_i)\rceil$ and $\tau_2[x_i] = \lfloor D(x_i)\rfloor$, and $\tau_1, \tau_2 \in \mathbb{Z}^k$.
- A constraint c is bound(R) consistent iff for all $x_i \in X(c)$, there exists two bound supports τ_1, τ_2 such that $\tau_1[x_i] = \lceil D(x_i)\rceil$ and $\tau_2[x_i] = \lfloor D(x_i)\rfloor$, and $\tau_1, \tau_2 \in \mathbb{R}^k$.

3 Auxiliary Variables

The decomposition process for the auxiliary variables model recursively rewrites an expression bottom-up, starting with higher precedence subexpressions. It is defined by the following repository, where the first rule appears for every $\oplus \in \Sigma$, and $\texttt{post}\,\pi$ inserts propagator π in the constraint store:

$$\mathrm{R}_{\mathrm{AUX}}(\pi) = \left\{ \begin{array}{l} \bigvee_{\oplus\in\Sigma} \dfrac{X \oplus Y}{z : \mathsf{dvar}} \left[\begin{array}{c} z \leftarrow \mathsf{new\,dvar}, \\ \texttt{post}\ \pi\left[\mathrm{R}_{\mathrm{AUX}}[X] \oplus \mathrm{R}_{\mathrm{AUX}}[Y] = z\right] \end{array} \right] \\ \dfrac{x : \mathsf{dvar}}{x : \mathsf{dvar}} [] \end{array} \right\}$$

We first remark that a constraint is a special case of an expression, specifically a comparison or logical expression. The decomposition process for an arbitrary constraint $e \in \mathcal{L}$ is triggered by the addition of the following propagator to the constraint store:

$$\pi\left[\mathrm{R}_{\mathrm{AUX}}[e] = \texttt{true}\right] \tag{1}$$

Note that, in the decomposition process, auxiliary variables are introduced for any subexpression, possibly using reification in the case of logical or comparison subexpressions.

Example 1. The decomposition of the constraint $a \times b + c \leq d$ using repository $\mathrm{R}_{\mathrm{AUX}}$ yields the following derivation:

$$\dfrac{\dfrac{\dfrac{a : \mathsf{dvar} \times b : \mathsf{dvar} + c : \mathsf{dvar} \leq d : \mathsf{dvar}}{t_3 : \mathsf{dvar} + c : \mathsf{dvar} \leq d : \mathsf{dvar}}}{t_2 : \mathsf{dvar} \leq d : \mathsf{dvar}}}{t_1 : \mathsf{dvar}} \left[\begin{array}{c} t_1 \leftarrow \mathsf{new\,dvar} \\ t_2 \leftarrow \mathsf{new\,dvar} \\ t_3 \leftarrow \mathsf{new\,dvar} \\ \texttt{post}\ \pi\left[a : \mathsf{dvar} \times b : \mathsf{dvar} = t_3 : \mathsf{dvar}\right] \\ \texttt{post}\ \pi\left[t_3 : \mathsf{dvar} + c : \mathsf{dvar} = t_2 : \mathsf{dvar}\right] \\ \texttt{post}\ \pi\left[(t_2 : \mathsf{dvar} \leq d : \mathsf{dvar}) = t_1 : \mathsf{dvar}\right] \\ \texttt{post}\ \pi\left[t_1 : \mathsf{dvar} = \texttt{true}\right] \end{array} \right]$$

This method requires a predefined repository of propagators for basic expressions involving domain variables, more specifically it assumes the existence of a collection of propagators $\pi \langle \mathcal{L}' \rangle$ indexed by expressions of a bounded language $\mathcal{L}' \subset \mathcal{L}$, typically defined as

$$\mathcal{L}' = \bigcup_{\oplus \in \Sigma} x : \mathsf{dvar} \oplus y : \mathsf{dvar} = z : \mathsf{dvar}$$

Since rules in $\mathrm{R}_{\mathrm{AUX}}$ may only generate $x : \mathsf{dvar}$ expressions, created propagators will always have $x : \mathsf{dvar}$ operands, i.e. $\mathrm{R}_{\mathrm{AUX}} (\pi) [e]$ only requires propagators in $\pi \langle \mathcal{L}' \rangle$, for any $e \in \mathcal{L}$.

Assuming a method like hashing is used to index elements of the rule and propagator repositories, the runtime cost of the compilation algorithm $\mathrm{R}_{\mathrm{AUX}}$ for an arbitrary constraint is linear on the number of binary operators in the constraint.

4 View Stores

Definition 5. [View store] *A view store $\lambda \langle X \rangle$ is an indexed collection of objects which provides a common interface (a view) to each element of the entity X being viewed. We call $\lambda \langle X \rangle$ a view store λ over X, and $\lambda [x]$ the λ view for x.*

For illustration purposes, we will detail a view store $\mathsf{bnd} \langle \mathcal{L} \rangle$ over expressions from language $\mathcal{L}$. Specifically, all members of the bnd view store must expose the following interface[1]:

$$\mathsf{bnd} : \left\{ \begin{array}{c} \text{GETMIN} : \mathsf{func}[\rightarrow r], \text{GETMAX} : \mathsf{func}[\rightarrow r], \\ \text{UPDMIN} : \mathsf{func}[i \rightarrow], \text{UPDMAX} : \mathsf{func}[i \rightarrow] \end{array} \right\} \tag{2}$$

Defining a view store is achieved by defining views for concrete viewed objects, in our case expressions $e \in \mathcal{L}$. The bnd view for a domain variable is as follows, where i and r are respectively the input and output parameters of the functions defined above:

$$\mathsf{bnd}[x : \mathsf{dvar}] = \left\{ \begin{array}{l} \text{GETMIN} = \{r \leftarrow \lfloor D(x) \rfloor\} \\ \text{GETMAX} = \{r \leftarrow \lceil D(x) \rceil\} \\ \text{UPDMIN} = \{D(x) \leftarrow D(x) \setminus [-\infty \ldots i-1]\} \\ \text{UPDMAX} = \{D(x) \leftarrow D(x) \setminus [i+1 \ldots +\infty]\} \end{array} \right\}$$

Defining the full set of views for a collection of infinite size, such as language $\mathcal{L}$, is clearly infeasible. We now turn to this problem and present two possible solutions with a different compromise regarding efficiency as we will see later.

4.1 Finite View Stores (FVS)

The first solution follows from the fact that all views in a store have a common interface. They can all therefore be represented by a single semantic $x : \mathsf{bnd}$ object which exposes the views's interface while abstracting its syntactic identity.

[1] This corresponds to the set of functions $\{\varphi, \varphi^{-}\}$ as defined in [15].

The compilation algorithm follows an approach similar to the auxiliary variables method, where the introduction of an auxiliary variable is replaced by the introduction of a $x : \mathsf{bnd}$ object. This means that all bnd views may safely assume a finite set of operands, which in this case are $x : \mathsf{bnd}$ objects.

Example 2. The following is a specialization of the bnd view for the addition of two arbitrary expressions:

$$\mathsf{bnd}\left[x : \mathsf{bnd} + y : \mathsf{bnd}\right] : \left\{ \begin{array}{l} \text{GETMIN} = \{r \leftarrow x.\text{GETMIN}() + y.\text{GETMIN}()\} \\ \text{GETMAX} = \{r \leftarrow x.\text{GETMAX}() + y.\text{GETMAX}()\} \\ \text{UPDMIN} = \left\{ \begin{array}{l} x.\text{UPDMIN}(i - y.\text{GETMAX}()) \\ y.\text{UPDMIN}(i - x.\text{GETMAX}()) \end{array} \right\} \\ \text{UPDMAX} = \left\{ \begin{array}{l} x.\text{UPDMAX}(i - y.\text{GETMIN}()) \\ y.\text{UPDMAX}(i - x.\text{GETMIN}()) \end{array} \right\} \end{array} \right\}$$

The compilation algorithm is fully described by the following rule repository:

$$\mathrm{R}_{\mathrm{BND}} = \left\{ \begin{array}{l} \bigvee_{\oplus \in \Sigma} \dfrac{X \oplus Y}{z : \mathsf{bnd}} \left[z \leftarrow \mathsf{new\,bnd}\left[\mathrm{R}_{\mathrm{BND}}[X] \oplus \mathrm{R}_{\mathrm{BND}}[Y]\right]\right] \\ \dfrac{x : \mathsf{dvar}}{z : \mathsf{bnd}} \left[z \leftarrow \mathsf{new\,bnd}\left[x : \mathsf{dvar}\right]\right] \end{array} \right\}$$

and may be used to define a specific propagator for an arbitrary constraint:

$$\pi[X] = \{\mathrm{R}_{\mathrm{BND}}[X].\text{UPDMIN}(\mathtt{true})\} \tag{3}$$

Propagator $\pi[e]$ instantiates the view for the constraint e and propagates it by setting its value to `true`.

Example 3. The compilation of the expression $a \times b + c \leq d$ using repository $\mathrm{R}_{\mathrm{BND}}$ yields the following derivation:

$$\dfrac{\dfrac{\begin{array}{c} a : \mathsf{dvar} \times b : \mathsf{dvar} + c : \mathsf{dvar} \leq d : \mathsf{dvar} \\ v_1 : \mathsf{bnd} \times v_2 : \mathsf{bnd} + c : \mathsf{dvar} \leq d : \mathsf{bnd} \\ v_3 : \mathsf{bnd} + v_4 : \mathsf{bnd} \leq v_6 : \mathsf{bnd} \end{array}}{v_5 : \mathsf{bnd} \leq v_6 : \mathsf{bnd}}}{v_7 : \mathsf{bnd}} \left[\begin{array}{c} v_1 \leftarrow \mathsf{new\,bnd}\left[a : \mathsf{dvar}\right] \\ v_2 \leftarrow \mathsf{new\,bnd}\left[b : \mathsf{dvar}\right] \\ v_3 \leftarrow \mathsf{new\,bnd}\left[v_1 : \mathsf{bnd} \times v_2 : \mathsf{bnd}\right] \\ v_4 \leftarrow \mathsf{new\,bnd}\left[c : \mathsf{dvar}\right] \\ v_5 \leftarrow \mathsf{new\,bnd}\left[v_3 : \mathsf{bnd} + v_4 : \mathsf{bnd}\right] \\ v_6 \leftarrow \mathsf{new\,bnd}\left[d : \mathsf{dvar}\right] \\ v_7 \leftarrow \mathsf{new\,bnd}\left[v_5 : \mathsf{bnd} \leq v_6 : \mathsf{bnd}\right], \\ \pi = \{v_7.\text{UPDMIN}(\mathtt{true})\} \\ \mathtt{post}\ \pi \end{array} \right]$$

Like the previous model, this method requires a predefined collection of objects indexed by members of a bounded language $\mathcal{L}' \subset \mathcal{L}$. The difference is that these objects are now bnd views instead of propagators, and $\mathcal{L}'$ is defined as:

$$\mathcal{L}' = \{x : \mathsf{dvar}\} \cup \bigcup_{\oplus \in \Sigma} x : \mathsf{bnd} \oplus y : \mathsf{bnd}$$

4.2 Infinite View Stores (IVS)

The decomposition model described above assumes the existence of a finite indexed collection of views. Replacing subexpressions by x : bnd objects guarantees the existence of a view for each generated subexpression.

The present method takes the direct approach: it defines an infinite indexed collection of views. For this, it makes two key requirements. Firstly, a view $\lambda\langle X\rangle$ may be defined by providing specializations for partially instantiated members $x \in X$, also called *partial specializations*. Secondly, new specializations may be created not only in the compilation process as before, but also in the body of any specialization.

Example 4. The following is a partial specialization of the bnd view for addition of two arbitrary expressions:

$$\mathsf{bnd}\,[\mathsf{X}+\mathsf{Y}] =$$
$$\left\{\begin{array}{l} \textsc{getMin} = \{r \leftarrow \mathsf{bnd}\,[X]\,.\textsc{getMin}\,() + \mathsf{bnd}\,[Y]\,.\textsc{getMin}\,()\} \\ \textsc{getMax} = \{r \leftarrow \mathsf{bnd}\,[X]\,.\textsc{getMax}\,() + \mathsf{bnd}\,[Y]\,.\textsc{getMax}\,()\} \\ \textsc{updMin} = \left\{\begin{array}{l} \mathsf{bnd}\,[X]\,.\textsc{updMin}\,(i - \mathsf{bnd}\,[Y]\,.\textsc{getMax}\,()) \\ \mathsf{bnd}\,[Y]\,.\textsc{updMin}\,(i - \mathsf{bnd}\,[X]\,.\textsc{getMax}\,()) \end{array}\right\} \\ \textsc{updMax} = \left\{\begin{array}{l} \mathsf{bnd}\,[X]\,.\textsc{updMax}\,(i - \mathsf{bnd}\,[Y]\,.\textsc{getMin}\,()) \\ \mathsf{bnd}\,[Y]\,.\textsc{updMax}\,(i - \mathsf{bnd}\,[X]\,.\textsc{getMin}\,()) \end{array}\right\} \end{array}\right\}$$

In this model, the compilation algorithm involves the recursive instantiation of views. This can be done simply by instantiating the view for the full expression:

$$\pi\,[X] = \{\mathsf{bnd}\,[X]\,.\textsc{updMin}\,(\mathtt{true})\} \tag{4}$$

Given that now the full expression is known to the view (i.e. operands are not abstractions like before), it is easy to design an algorithm which, for a specific instantiation, replaces all function calls with the corresponding definitions.

Example 5. Simplification of the GETMIN function of the bnd view over the $a+b+c$ expression:

$$\begin{array}{l} \mathsf{bnd}\,[a:\mathsf{dvar}+b:\mathsf{dvar}+c:\mathsf{dvar}]\,.\textsc{getMin} = \\ \quad = \{r \leftarrow \mathsf{bnd}\,[a:\mathsf{dvar}+b:\mathsf{dvar}]\,.\textsc{getMin}\,() + \mathsf{bnd}\,[c:\mathsf{dvar}]\,.\textsc{getMin}\,()\} = \\ \quad = \{r \leftarrow \mathsf{bnd}\,[a:\mathsf{dvar}]\,.\textsc{getMin}\,() + \mathsf{bnd}\,[b:\mathsf{dvar}]\,.\textsc{getMin}\,() + \lfloor D(c)\rfloor\} = \\ \qquad\qquad = \{r \leftarrow \lfloor D(a)\rfloor + \lfloor D(b)\rfloor + \lfloor D(c)\rfloor\} \end{array}$$

In the present context, views are used very much like macros, effectively allowing creating specific propagators for arbitrary expressions which do not make use of function calls at execution.

Example 6. Propagator for the expression $a+b+c=d$ using repository R_{BND}:

$$\pi = \left\{\begin{array}{r} D(d) \leftarrow D(d) \setminus [-\infty \ldots \lfloor D(a)\rfloor + \lfloor D(b)\rfloor + \lfloor D(c)\rfloor - 1] \\ D(d) \leftarrow D(d) \setminus [\lceil D(a)\rceil + \lceil D(b)\rceil + \lceil D(c)\rceil + 1 \ldots +\infty] \\ \textit{etc.} \end{array}\right\}$$

5 Model Comparison

For the memory and runtime analysis below we will consider an arithmetic constraint involving n variables with uniform domain size d, with an unbalanced syntax tree, i.e. where each operator in the expression involves at least one variable. Figure 1 shows a fragment of the expression syntax tree.

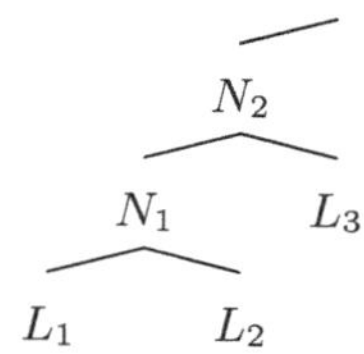

Fig. 1. A subtree of an unbalanced expression syntax tree. The internal nodes $N_1 \ldots N_{n-1}$ represent operators and leafs $L_1 \ldots L_n$ represent variables.

5.1 Memory

A view can be designed to expose just the subset of the expression's domain which is required for the view's client (e.g. the bounds of the expression). In contrast, a variable maintains the full domain of the expression, possibly containing regions which will always be ignored for propagation. For an expression containing $n-1$ operators such as the expression in fig. 1, the auxiliary variables memory overhead is in $O(nD)$ compared to any of the views model, where D is the size of the largest domain of an auxiliary variable. For some expressions, namely an expression containing only multiplications, we can have $D = d^{n-1}$. In practice, the use of intervals to store the auxiliary variable's domains (i.e. $D = 2$) eliminates this problem.

5.2 Runtime

There is a fundamental operational difference between the views and the auxiliary variables model. A view computes its domain *on demand*, that is, it never updates its domain before it is needed by the view's client. This is the opposite of what happens in the auxiliary variable model, as the posted propagators will act on the auxiliary variable's domains independently.

This analysis focuses on the cost of accessing and updating the bounds of an expression, which may correspond to accessing/updating an auxiliary variable or a view, depending on the model. The cost is measured in terms of number of propagators executed, number of function calls, number of arithmetic operations, and number of domain updates.

We first note that enforcing bounds(R) consistency to an algebraic expression requires $O(nd)$ steps. As an example, consider a CSP with the constraint $x \times 2 = y \times 2 + 1$, where $D(x) = D(y) = [1 \ldots d]$. See also [17].

We will first focus on the costs of updating the bounds of an expression whose syntax tree resembles fig. 1. The auxiliary variables model associates a propagator and an auxiliary variable with each internal node N_i of the expression syntax tree. The propagator for a node N_1 involving two leafs may execute $O(2d)$ times and cause the same number of updates in the domain of the corresponding auxiliary variable. This means that the propagator for N_2 may execute $O(3d)$ times and so on for all the $n-1$ internal nodes. The number of propagators executed for the auxiliary variables model is therefore $O\left(n^2 d\right)$. Since each propagator execution requires a constant number of arithmetic operations, the number of operations for this model is also $O\left(n^2 d\right)$. Finally, given that each propagation implies the update of the domain of an auxiliary variable, the number of domain updates is $O\left(n^2 d\right)$.

Both models using views have only one propagator for the entire expression, which can be executed at most $O(nd)$ times. Unfortunately, a single update of the expression is now more costly because it may require evaluating the full tree, which is $O(n)$. This means that the total number of operations is still $O(nd \times n)$. However, given that there are no auxiliary variables in these models, the number of domain updates is only $O(nd)$. We remark that the only difference between both views is in the number of function calls.

Accessing the bounds of an expression is cheaper in the auxiliary variables model. This is because the domain of each subexpression is *cached* in the associated auxiliary variable. In contrast, both models involving views require evaluating the expression. Table 1 summarizes these results.

Table 1. Cost of accessing and updating an arbitrary expression represented by each of the described models

model	propagators		functions		operations		updates	
vars	-	$O\left(n^2 d\right)$	$O(1)$	-	$O(1)$	$O\left(n^2 d\right)$	-	$O\left(n^2 d\right)$
fvs	-	$O(nd)$	$O(n)$	$O\left(n^2 d\right)$	$O(n)$	$O\left(n^2 d\right)$	-	$O(nd)$
ivs	-	$O(nd)$	$O(1)$	-	$O(n)$	$O\left(n^2 d\right)$	-	$O(nd)$

5.3 Propagation

The consistency level achieved by view based propagators is detailed in [15], namely in terms of bounds(Z) and bounds(R). Here, we remark that using a variable decomposition may improve propagation w.r.t. views, in particular, to achieve a pruning between bounds(Z) and bounds(R). This may be seen in the following example:

Example 7. Consider the constraint $x \times y \times 2 = z$, where $D(x) = D(y) = [2 \ldots 3]$, and $D(z) = [9 \ldots 15]$. Given that $x = z/(y \times 2)$, $y = z/(x \times 2)$, we have

$$D(x) = D(y) = [2 \ldots 3] \cap [9/(3 \times 2) \ldots 15/(2 \times 2)] = [2 \ldots 3]$$
$$D(z) = [9 \ldots 15] \cap [2 \times 2 \times 2 \ldots 3 \times 3 \times 2] = [9 \ldots 15]$$

which means that the constraint is at a fixpoint according to bounds(R) (note that a bounds(Z) propagator for this constraint infers $z = 12$). Now let us assume the decomposition $e \equiv x \times y$ and $e \times 2 = z$, with $D(e) = [4 \ldots 9]$. Propagating the latter constraint infers

$$D(e) \leftarrow [4 \ldots 9] \cap \left[\frac{9}{2} \cdots \frac{15}{2}\right] = \left[\frac{9}{2} \cdots \frac{15}{2}\right]$$

Using the auxiliary variables model associates an integer variable with e, imposing an additional restriction: it must be an integer. This allows more pruning from the domain of z:

$$D(t_1) \leftarrow [4 \ldots 9] \cap [5 \ldots 7] = [5 \ldots 7]$$
$$D(z) \leftarrow [9 \ldots 15] \cap 2 \times [5 \ldots 7] = [10 \ldots 14]$$

Even if stronger propagation leads to smaller search spaces, in our experiments it did not compensate the inefficiencies of the variable decomposition model.

6 Experiments

The first experiment applies previous compilation models to a system of linear equations. This problem is usually solved in constraint programming by using a specific propagator for linear equations. The goal of the experiment is therefore to assess the overhead of decomposing/compiling expressions using the presented models compared to a decomposition which uses a special purpose algorithm. The second experiment considers systems of nonlinear equations. These problems arise often in practice, and since the decomposition to special purpose propagators is not so direct as in previous case, it provides a realistic opportunity to apply the previously discussed models. The last experiment consists in solving the Golomb ruler problem (prob6 in [11]), a common benchmark for CSP solvers.

The code for all the following experiments was compiled with the gcc-4.2.3 C++ compiler, and executed on an Intel Core 2 Duo @ 2.20GHz, using Linux-2.6.24. Each experiment was repeated until the standard deviation of the runtime was below 1% of the average time, and then the minimum runtime was used. The search trees explored by all models are the same for each instance.

All previously described models were implemented in CaSPER [6]. Additionally, we used Gecode-2.2.0 [9] on one problem as a reference.

6.1 Modeling

Each system of linear equations is described by a tuple $\langle n, d, c, a, s|u\rangle$ where n is the number of variables in the problem, d is the uniform domain size, c is the number of linear equations, a is the number of terms in each equation, and the last term denotes if the problem is (s)atisfiable or (u)nsatisfiable. Problems were generated randomly, and the most difficult instances were selected (based on number of fails). In addition to the previously described models (vars,fvs, and ivs) for this problem we also tested a model using a propagator for linear equations (linear). Table 2 shows the results.

Each system of nonlinear equations is described by a tuple $\langle n, d, c, a_1, a_2, s|u\rangle$ where a_1 is the number of terms in each equation, each term is composed of a product of a_2 factors, and all remaining variables have the same meaning as before. In this experiment we also tested a model where each product is decomposed using auxiliary variables, projected to a variable x_i, and a linear propagator is used to enforce $\sum_{i=1}^{a_1} x_i$ for each equation (linear+vars). Table 3 show the results.

In the Golomb ruler problem, the use of views allows saving a quadratic number of variables (one for each difference between marks). The results are shown in table 4.

Table 2. Runtime for finding all solutions or proving that no solution exists for problems consisting of systems of linear equations. For each result the table presents the runtime in seconds and the speed up compared to the worst performing model in that problem.

	20-7-7-4-s		20-30-6-8-u		40-7-12-20-u		40-7-10-40-u	
casper-vars	21.1	1.00	135	1.00	128	1.00	137	1.02
casper-fvs	20.5	1.03	90.9	1.48	87.0	1.47	140	1.00
casper-ivs	19.5	1.08	40.0	3.37	17.4	7.34	13.2	10.6
casper-linear	19.5	1.08	43.7	3.09	18.8	6.81	13.3	10.5

Table 3. Runtime for finding the first solution or proving that no solution exists for problems consisting of systems of nonlinear equations

	20-20-10-4-2-s		50-10-19-4-2-s		50-10-28-4-3-u	
casper-vars	49.1	1.00	126	1.00	85.2	1.37
casper-fvs	48.4	1.01	117	1.08	117	1.00
casper-ivs	22.9	**2.14**	55.7	**2.26**	43.1	**2.70**
casper-linear+vars	40.1	1.22	106	1.19	93.4	1.25
gecode-vars	36.6	1.34	98.2	1.28	72.7	1.60
gecode-linear+vars	26.8	1.83	70.2	1.79	65.7	1.77
	50-5-20-4-3-u		50-6-26-4-4-u		60-4-24-4-4-5-u	
casper-vars	47.1	1.05	63.4	1.84	1.29	1.86
casper-fvs	49.6	1.00	116	1.00	2.40	1.00
casper-ivs	18.8	**2.64**	31.2	**3.73**	0.68	**3.52**
casper-linear+vars	49.3	1.01	66.4	1.75	1.46	1.64
gecode-vars	40.4	1.23	52.2	2.23	1.18	2.03
gecode-linear+vars	32.4	1.53	47.2	2.47	1.11	2.16

Table 4. Number of propagations (x1000) (p), runtime (t), and speedup (s) for finding the solution to the Golomb ruler problem

	golomb-10			golomb-11			golomb-12		
	p	t	s	p	t	s	p	t	s
casper-vars	0.38	0.14	1	2.12	0.73	1	116	40.3	1
casper-fvs	0.05	0.11	1.26	0.24	0.65	1.11	11.9	35.8	1.13
casper-ivs	0.05	0.1	1.36	0.24	0.5	1.46	11.9	30.19	1.33

6.2 Discussion

As expected, the FVS model has a good performance on small problems, but it degrades for larger expressions. It can be one order of magnitude slower than IVS on linear equations, and two times slower than the auxiliary variables decomposition on other problems. The performance of the IVS model is significantly better than the other methods. In fact it achieves similar performance of the model using global propagators on linear equations (table 2), which shows the potential of the IVS model to seamingly derive propagators for other global constraints over algebraic expressions.

Comparing to Gecode we notice a small difference regarding the runtimes for the same models favoring the Gecode implementation. We think this discrepancy is probably due to some optimization of Gecode not present in CaSPER, and that applying the IVS model to Gecode should yield similar gains in performance. We note that the IVS model still outperforms the best model we could implement in Gecode using the available modeling primitives in some instances.

7 Related Work

The idea of using type polymorphism for defining generic propagators is incipient in [6] and [14]. The former presents a general overview of a constraint solver incorporating type polymorphism, and gives a first description on some of the data structures required for creating generic propagators from arbitrary expressions. The latter coins the term *view* (we originally called them *polymorphic constraints*), and describes how it can be used for creating generic propagator implementations, that is, propagators which can be reused for different constraints. [15] provides further analysis, in particular, it is shown for which consistencies using views achieves less pruning than a specialized propagator.

[1] focus on the complexity of propagation for different decomposition models, specifically through symbolic manipulation of expressions, such as replacing common subexpressions and factorizing. In this context, the authors show that the propagation resulting from the decomposition using auxiliary variables is stronger than propagation on the original expression. It turns out that introducing auxiliary variables may strenghten propagation also without any symbolic manipulation (see section 5.3).

Constraint solvers deal with constraints over arbitrary algebraic expressions in different ways. Most prolog systems [16,8,7] automatically decompose them, apparently using the auxiliary variables model. The use of indexicals and goal expanded constraints [3] is advised as a way to avoid introducing auxiliary variables, and should be comparable to the IVS model (without the optimizations available to strongly typed languages). ILog Solver processes arbitrary expressions bottom-up, converting its subexpressions to *constrained expressions* [12], following the FVS model. Choco [5] features automatic decomposition using auxiliary variables.

The problem of creating propagators for arbitrary expressions has been approached in a different way using knowledge compilation techniques [10,4]. These methods create a compact extensional representation of the set of solutions to the constraint and apply a general propagation algorithm which filters tuples not found in this set. Applying these algorithms for arithmetic expressions is possible, and not so inefficient in practice concerning runtime. However even the most compact extensional representation is exponential in the number of variables in the worst case, while all the decompositions we presented above are linear.

8 Conclusion

This paper presents an approach for creating view based propagators for arbitrary algebraic expressions *at the modeling phase*. The performance of the resulting model compares favourably, both theoretically and experimentally, with models resulting from other decomposition/compilation methods. The method may be integrated in any constraint solver implemented in a type parametric programming language, which is often the case (e.g. [5,12,9]).

References

1. Apt, K.R., Zoeteweij, P.: A comparative study of arithmetic constraints on integer intervals. In: Apt, K.R., Fages, F., Rossi, F., Szeredi, P., Váncza, J. (eds.) CSCLP 2003. LNCS(LNAI), vol. 3010, pp. 1–24. Springer, Heidelberg (2003)
2. Bessiere, C.: Constraint Propagation. In: Handbook of Constraint Programming. Foundations of Artificial Intelligence, pp. 29–83. Elsevier Science, Amsterdam (2006)
3. Carlson, B.: Compiling and executing finite domain constraints. PhD thesis, Uppsala University (1995)
4. Cheng, K.C.K., Yap, R.H.C.: Maintaining generalized arc consistency on ad hoc r-ary constraints. In: Stuckey, P.J. (ed.) CP 2008. LNCS, vol. 5202, pp. 509–523. Springer, Heidelberg (2008)
5. Choco. Choco constraint programming system (2003), `http://www.emn.fr/x-info/choco-solver/doku.php?id=`
6. Correia, M., Barahona, P., Azevedo, F.: Casper: A programming environment for development and integration of constraint solvers. In: Azevedo, F. (ed.) Proceedings of the First International Workshop on Constraint Programming Beyond Finite Integer Domains, BeyondFD 2005 (2005)
7. Diaz, D., Codognet, P.: Design and implementation of the gnu prolog system. Journal of Functional and Logic Programming 2001(6) (October 2001)
8. ECLiPSe. ECLiPSe prolog (2008), `http://www.eclipse-clp.org/`
9. Gecode. Gecode: Generic constraint development environment (2006), `http://www.gecode.org`
10. Gent, I.P., Jefferson, C., Miguel, I., Nightingale, P.: Data structures for generalised arc consistency for extensional constraints. In: AAAI, pp. 191–197. AAAI Press, Menlo Park (2007)
11. Gent, I.P., Walsh, T.: Csplib: a benchmark library for constraints. Technical report, APES-09-1999 (1999), `http://www.csplib.org/`
12. ILOG. Ilog solver 6.0: Reference manual, 2003.
13. Rossi, F., Van Beek, P., Walsh, T. (eds.): Handbook of Constraint Programming. Foundations of Artificial Intelligence. Elsevier Science, Amsterdam (2006)
14. Schulte, C., Tack, G.R.: Views and iterators for generic constraint implementations. In: Hnich, B., Carlsson, M., Fages, F., Rossi, F. (eds.) CSCLP 2005. LNCS (LNAI), vol. 3978, pp. 118–132. Springer, Heidelberg (2006)
15. Schulte, C., Tack, G.R.: Perfect derived propagators. In: Stuckey, P.J. (ed.) CP 2008. LNCS, vol. 5202, pp. 571–575. Springer, Heidelberg (2008)
16. SICStus. SICStus Prolog 3.12 User's Manual, 3.12 edn. (October 2006), `http://www.sics.se/sicstus/`
17. Yuanlin, Z., Yap, R.H.C.: Arc consistency on n -ary monotonic and linear constraints. In: Principles and Practice of Constraint Programming, pp. 470–483 (2000)

Colored Nonograms: An Integer Linear Programming Approach

Luís Mingote and Francisco Azevedo

Faculdade de Ciências e Tecnologia
Universidade Nova de Lisboa
2829-516 Caparica, Portugal

Abstract. In this paper we study colored nonogram solving using Integer Linear Programming. Our approach generalizes the one used by Robert A. Bosch which was developed for black and white nonograms only, thus providing a universal solution for solving nonograms using ILP. Additionally we apply a known algorithm to find all solutions to a puzzle. This algorithm uses a binary cut to exclude already known solutions. Finally we compare the performance of our approach in solving colored nonograms against other approaches, namely the iterative and the brute-force ones, pointing to a research direction of developing a hybrid method combining the iterative approach with ILP.

1 Introduction

Nonograms are a popular kind of puzzle whose name varies from country to country, including Paint by Numbers and Griddlers. The goal is to fill cells of a grid in a way that contiguous blocks of the same color satisfy the clues, or restrictions, of each line or column. In black and white nonograms these clues indicate the sequence of contiguous blocks of cells to be filled (e.g. the clue 3,1,2 indicates that there is a block of 3 contiguous cells, followed by a sequence of one or more empty cells, then a block of one cell filled, followed by another sequence of one or more empty cells, finally followed by a sequence of two filled cells in that row or column).

In colored nonograms the clues are composed of pairs that indicate the size and color of each sequence of blocks to be filled. For example, the clue <(3,Red), (1,Green), (2,Blue)> indicates that there is a block of 3 contiguous cells of red, followed by a block of one green cell separated or not by a sequence of empty cells, followed by a sequence of two blue cells separated or not from the green block by a sequence of empty cells, in that row or column. The general rule for separating blocks is that if a block is of the same color of the previous one in the respective sequence then they must be separated by at least an empty cell. Otherwise (i.e., the two blocks have different colors), they may have no cells in between, i.e., they may be adjoining blocks. Note that in the particular case of black and white nonograms this means that blocks in a sequence must always be separated by at least one empty cell. Figure 1 represents an example of a colored nonogram with 10 lines by 8 columns with 3 colors.

L. Seabra Lopes et al. (Eds.): EPIA 2009, LNAI 5816, pp. 213–224, 2009.

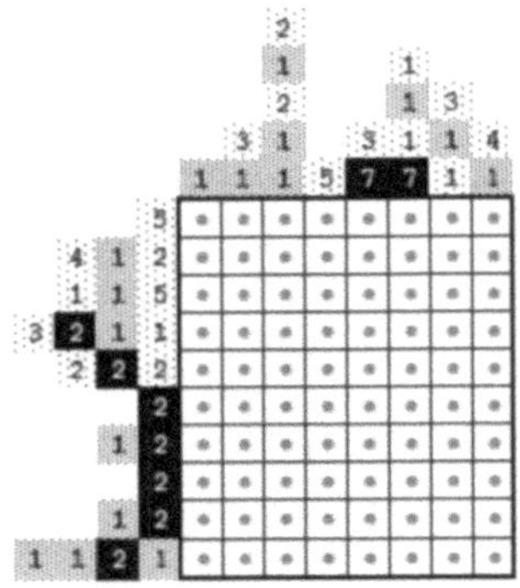

Fig. 1. Colored Nonogram Example

As described in [1,4,5], one way to solve this kind of puzzles is by iteratively analyzing the clues in each row or column and paint cells in the grid according to the information we can infer. For the example given in Figure 1, a first pass through the rows allows us to paint 10 cells light grey and one cell black, as shown in Figure 2(a). For instance, in row 2 we can paint for sure cells of columns 2, 3, and 4, in light grey, since its first block (of size 4) can only start at columns 1 or 2 due to the next blocks, in both cases occupying those 3 pixels.

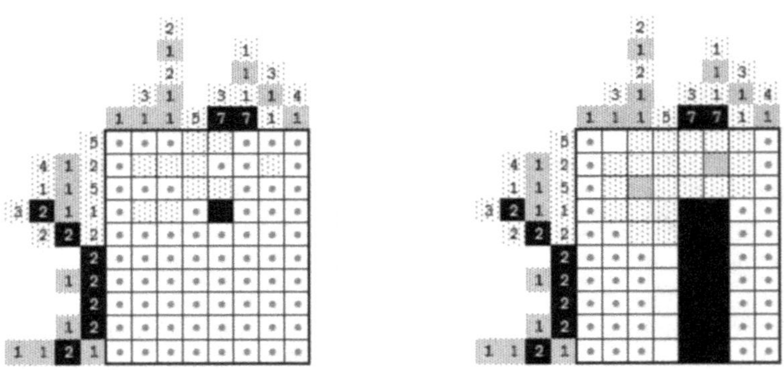

(a) After first pass on rows

(b) After first pass on rows and columns

Fig. 2. Colored Nonogram Example (partially solved)

A subsequent pass through the columns allows us to paint 10 more cells light grey, two dark grey, 13 more black and 6 white, as shown in Figure 2(b). Some additional passes through the rows and columns and we paint all 80 cells of the puzzle as shown in Figure 3. For such simple puzzles this is enough to solve them, but for more complex puzzles one may reach a fixed-point where no more

Fig. 3. Colored Nonogram Example (solved)

inferences can be made and with a number of cells yet to be colored. At this point a guess is needed to proceed, leading to a search process with possible backtracking on wrong choices made along the way.

There are a number of nonogram solvers listed in [6] that are compared by Jan Wolter in [7]. The best ones are *pbnsolve* [8], *Olšák* [10] and *Simpson* [5], but only *pbnsolve* and *Olšák* can solve colored nonograms. These three algorithms try to logically (iteratively) solve the puzzles and, when they stall, they begin a search process with possible backtracking. Wolter also states that the use of an optimizing compiler makes a significant difference in performance (approximately twice as fast, for C-language ones).

In this paper we generalize the ILP approach by Bosch in [1] to solve colored nonograms, and is organized in the following way. In Section 2 we describe the ILP model we developed to solve colored nonograms. Then, in Section 3 we demonstrate that our approach corresponds to the one by Bosch in [1] for black and white nonograms. In Section 4 we show how to apply a simple technique in order to find additional solutions in case the first solution obtained for a puzzle is not unique. In Section 5 we present the results of our approach and compare it with the iterative and the brute-force ones. Finally, in Section 6 we present our conclusions.

2 Model Description

In this section we describe the ILP model we developed to solve colored nonograms. As in [1], our approach is to think of a colored nonogram as a problem comprised of two interlocking tiling problems: one involving the placement of the row blocks, and the other involving the placement of the column blocks. If a cell is painted (we will assume that unpainted cells are painted white) then it must be covered by both a row block and a column block; if it is painted white (not painted) then it must be left uncovered by the row blocks and the column blocks.

2.1 Notation

The notation used here is similar to the one used by Bosch in [1], as follows.

$m =$ the number of rows,
$n =$ the number of columns,
$o =$ the number of colors excluding white (We use a sequence of natural numbers to identify colors, starting at 1 $(1, 2, \ldots, o)$.),
$b_i^r =$ the number of blocks in row i, $1 \leq i \leq m$,
$b_j^c =$ the number of blocks in column j, $1 \leq j \leq n$,
$s_{i,1}^r, s_{i,2}^r, \ldots, s_{i,b_i^r}^r =$ the block-size sequence for row i,
$s_{j,1}^c, s_{j,2}^c, \ldots, s_{j,b_j^c}^c =$ the block-size sequence for column j,
$c_{i,1}^r, c_{i,2}^r, \ldots, c_{i,b_i^r}^r =$ the block-color sequence for row i,
$c_{j,1}^c, c_{j,2}^c, \ldots, c_{j,b_j^c}^c =$ the block-color sequence for column j.

In addition, let

$e_{i,t}^r =$ the smallest value of j such that row i's t^{th} block can be placed in row i with its leftmost pixel occupying cell j,
$l_{i,t}^r =$ the largest value of j such that row i's t^{th} block can be placed in row i with its leftmost pixel occupying cell j,
$e_{j,t}^c =$ the smallest value of i such that column j's t^{th} block can be placed in column j with its topmost pixel occupying cell i,
$l_{i,t}^c =$ the largest value of i such that column j's t^{th} block can be placed in column j with its topmost pixel occupying cell i.

These are constants valid for the empty puzzle. (The letters "e" and "l" stand for "earliest" and "latest"). In our example puzzle, second row's first block must be placed so that its leftmost pixel occupies cell 1 or 2, the second block must be placed so that its leftmost pixel occupies cell 5 or 6, and the third block must be placed so that its leftmost pixel occupies cell 6 or 7. In other words

$$e_{2,1}^r = 1, l_{2,1}^r = 2, e_{2,2}^r = 5, l_{2,2}^r = 6, e_{2,3}^r = 6 \quad \text{and} \quad l_{2,3}^r = 7.$$

These values are obtained by iteratively placing the blocks in their leftmost or topmost possible cells and then placing them in their rightmost or bottommost possible cells. In our example, the first block's first cell is 1 and, since the first block's size is 4 and the color of both blocks is different, the second block's first possible cell is 5. Then, since the color of the third block is also different from the second one and the size of the second block is 1, the third block's first possible cell is 6. Now, we push the third block to its rightmost cell (7) and we find out that the second block's last possible cell is 6 and the first block's last possible cell is 2.

Note that the rules for determining these values are the same for colored or black and white nonograms. Of course, in black and white puzzles all the blocks are of the same color, which means they have to be separated by at least one empty cell.

2.2 Variables

As in the approach by Bosch in [1], in our approach there are three sets of variables. One set specifies the color of each cell:

$$\forall_{1\leq i\leq m,1\leq j\leq n} \quad z_{i,j} = \begin{cases} 1 \leq c \leq o & \text{; if row } i\text{'s } j^{th} \text{ cell is painted with color } c \\ 0 & \text{; if row } i\text{'s } j^{th} \text{ cell is not painted} \end{cases} \tag{1}$$

The other two sets of variables are concerned with placements of the row and column blocks.

$$\forall_{1\leq i\leq m,1\leq t\leq b^r_i,e^r_{i,t}\leq j\leq l^r_{i,t}} \quad y_{i,t,j} = \begin{cases} 1 & \text{; if row } i\text{'s } t^{th} \text{ block is placed in row } i \text{ with its leftmost pixel occupying cell } j \\ 0 & \text{; if not} \end{cases} \tag{2}$$

$$\forall_{1\leq j\leq n,1\leq t\leq b^c_j,e^c_{j,t}\leq i\leq l^c_{j,t}} \quad x_{j,t,i} = \begin{cases} 1 & \text{; if column } j\text{'s } t^{th} \text{ block is placed in column } j \text{ with its topmost pixel occupying cell } i \\ 0 & \text{; if not} \end{cases} \tag{3}$$

2.3 Block Constraints

To ensure that row i's t^{th} block appears in row i exactly once, we impose

$$\forall_{1\leq i\leq m,1\leq t\leq b^r_i} \quad \sum_{j=e^r_{i,t}}^{l^r_{i,t}} y_{i,t,j} = 1 \tag{4}$$

For line 2 of our example we have

$$y_{2,1,1} + y_{2,1,2} = 1,$$

$$y_{2,2,5} + y_{2,2,6} = 1,$$

$$y_{2,3,6} + y_{2,3,7} = 1.$$

For the next two constraints we define the auxiliary function (5) that returns the value 1 if the two arguments are the same, and 0 otherwise, which will be useful to compare colors of two contiguous blocks.

$$eq(c_1, c_2) = \begin{cases} 1 & \text{; if } c_1 = c_2 \\ 0 & \text{; otherwise} \end{cases} \tag{5}$$

To ensure that row i's $(t+1)^{th}$ block is placed to the right of its tth block, we impose

$$\forall_{e^r_{i,t}+1\leq j\leq l^r_{i,t}} \quad y_{i,t,j} \leq \sum_{j'=j+s^r_{i,t}+eq(c^r_{i,t},c^r_{i,t+1})}^{l^r_{i,t+1}} y_{i,t+1,j'} \tag{6}$$

In line 2 of our example we have

$$y_{2,1,2} \leq y_{2,2,6},$$

$$y_{2,2,6} \leq y_{2,3,7}.$$

To ensure that column j's t^{th} block appears in column j exactly once, we impose

$$\forall_{1 \leq j \leq n, 1 \leq t \leq b^c_j} \sum_{i=e^c_{j,t}}^{l^c_{j,t}} x_{j,t,i} = 1 \tag{7}$$

To ensure that column j's $(t+1)^{th}$ block is placed under its tth block, we impose

$$\forall_{e^c_{j,t}+1 \leq i \leq l^c_{j,t}} \quad x_{j,t,i} \leq \sum_{i'=i+s^c_{j,t}+eq(c^c_{j,t},c^c_{j,t+1})}^{l^c_{j,t+1}} x_{j,t+1,i'} \tag{8}$$

2.4 Double Coverage Constraints

To guarantee that each painted cell is covered by both a row block and a column block, we impose the following pair of inequalities:

$$\forall_{1 \leq i \leq m, 1 \leq j \leq n} \quad z_{i,j} \leq \sum_{t=1}^{b^r_i} \sum_{j'=max\{e^r_{i,t}, j-s^r_{i,t}+1\}}^{min\{l^r_{i,t}, j\}} y_{i,t,j'} \times c^r_{i,t} \tag{9}$$

$$\forall_{1 \leq i \leq m, 1 \leq j \leq n} \quad z_{i,j} \leq \sum_{t=1}^{b^c_j} \sum_{i'=max\{e^c_{j,t}, i-s^c_{j,t}+1\}}^{min\{l^c_{j,t}, i\}} x_{j,t,i'} \times c^c_{j,t} \tag{10}$$

Without these restrictions the model would allow having cells painted by row blocks, but not painted by any column block, or vice versa. The first inequality (9) states that if row i's j^{th} cell is painted, then at least one of row i's blocks must be placed in such a way that it covers row i's j^{th} cell. (The upper and lower limits of the second summation make sure that j' satisfies the two pairs of inequalities $e^r_{i,t} \leq j' \leq l^r_{i,t}$ and $j - s^r_{i,t} + 1 \leq j' \leq j$. The first pair holds if, and only if, row i's t^{th} cell is covered when row i's t^{th} block is placed in row i with its leftmost pixel occupying cell j'. The second pair holds if and only if row i's j^{th} pixel is covered when row i's t^{th} block is placed in row i with its leftmost pixel occupying pixel j'). The other inequality (10) makes sure that if row i's j^{th} cell is painted, then at least one of column j's blocks covers it. For line 2 in our example we have for cell $z_{2,4}$ that

$$z_{2,5} \leq y_{2,1,2} \times c^r_{2,1} + y_{2,2,5} \times c^r_{2,2},$$

$$z_{2,5} \leq x_{5,1,1} \times c^c_{5,1} + x_{5,1,2} \times c^c_{5,1}$$

If $z_{2,5}$ is painted, the right hand terms of these inequalities will yield exactly its color value in a solved puzzle. Otherwise (empty cell), the terms hold value 0. Ideally, the model should express this disjunction directly, allowing only those 2 values. However, in order to allow ILP solving, we keep it as a linear inequality. Nevertheless, below we prove that this is sufficient for a correct and complete model, in the presence of the other constraints.

Finally, we include constraints that prevent unpainted cells from being covered by the row blocks or column blocks — inequalities (11) and (12).

$$\forall_{1\leq i\leq m,\ 1\leq j\leq n,\ 1\leq t\leq b_i^r,\ j-s_{i,t}^r+1\leq j'\leq j,\ e_{i,t}^r\leq j'\leq l_{i,t}^r} \quad z_{i,j} \geq y_{i,t,j'} \times c_{i,t}^r \tag{11}$$

$$\forall_{1\leq i\leq m,\ 1\leq j\leq n,\ 1\leq t\leq b_j^c,\ e_{j,t}^c\leq i'\leq l_{j,t}^c,\ i-s_{j,t}^c+1\leq i'\leq i} \quad z_{i,j} \geq x_{j,t,i'} \times c_{j,t}^c \tag{12}$$

In line 2 of our example we have that

$$z_{2,5} \geq y_{2,1,2} \times c_{2,1}^r, \quad z_{2,5} \geq y_{2,2,5} \times c_{2,2}^r,$$

$$z_{2,5} \geq x_{5,1,1} \times c_{5,1}^c, \quad z_{2,5} \geq x_{5,1,2} \times c_{5,1}^c.$$

One might think that we have to ensure that each painted cell must be covered by one row block and one column block of the same color. However, the remaining constraints ensure that we only need to guarantee that a painted cell must be covered by one row block and one column block. In order to prove it, let us explore all the possibilities regarding the coverage of some cell z:

1. No block covers cell z;
2. Only one block covers cell z and it is of the same color;
3. Only one block covers cell z and its color is smaller than the color of z;
4. Only one block covers cell z and its color is greater than the color of z;
5. More than one block covers cell z;

Of these five possibilities, only the first two are possible in real puzzles. The last three are the ones that our model has to avoid. In sake of simplicity, but with no loss of generality, only inequality (9), for lines, of the double coverage constraints will be used in our case analysis for these five possibilities:

Possibility 1: The only way to satisfy this possibility is with an empty cell z, with value 0, which, by inequality (9), will guarantee that no block covers it (forcing the respective $y_{i,t,j'}$ variables to be 0), i.e.

$$\sum_{t=1}^{b_i^r} \sum_{j'=min\{e_{i,t}^r, j-s_{i,t}^r+1\}}^{max\{l_{i,t}^r, j\}} y_{i,t,j'} \times c_{i,t}^r = 0.$$

Possibility 2: This possibility fully satisfies inequality (9), corresponding to the equality of both terms.

Possibility 3: If a single block of smaller color than the color of cell z covers it then inequality (9) is not satisfied, thus disallowing such possibility, as desired.

Possibility 4: In the case that there may be one block that covers cell z, and which color is greater than the color of z, then inequality (9) would be satisfied. However, this would violate inequality (11) thus turning the solution invalid.

Possibility 5: If more than one block covers cell z, inequality (9) could only be satisfied if the sum of the colors of the covering blocks is less than or equal to the color of cell z. But this would violate equation (4) thus turning the solution invalid.

2.5 Objective Function

Since this is a satisfaction problem there is no need for an objective function, but since ILP solvers need one, we include the following (note that this function is a constant and we already know its value):

$$minimize/maximize \sum_{i=1}^{m} \sum_{j=1}^{n} z_{i,j} \tag{13}$$

2.6 Pre-conditions

We also include in our approach one pre-condition in order to verify whether the puzzle is trivially impossible to solve, before even trying to search for a solution (another improvement with respect to [1]). This is a necessary, but not sufficient condition that will save us the time of trying to solve a puzzle that is impossible, and that also helps us determining whether there is any error in the definition of the puzzle. This condition, shown by equation (14), checks whether the sum of the sizes of all blocks of each color is the same for both the rows and columns clues.

$$\forall_{c \in \{1..o\}} \quad \sum_{i=1}^{m} \sum_{t=1}^{b_i^r} f(s_{i,t}^r, c_{i,t}^r, c) = \sum_{j=1}^{n} \sum_{t=1}^{b_j^c} f(s_{j,t}^c, c_{j,t}^c, c) \tag{14}$$

where $f(s, c_1, c_2) = s$ if $c_1 = c_2$, and 0 otherwise.

3 Instantiation to Black and White Nonograms

If we set $o = 1$, thus allowing only black and white in a puzzle, our model becomes the one provided by Bosch in [1], i.e., equation (1) becomes

$$z_{i,j} = \begin{cases} 1 & \text{; if row } i\text{'s } j^{th} \text{ cell is painted} \\ 0 & \text{; if row } i\text{'s } j^{th} \text{ cell is not painted} \end{cases} \tag{15}$$

Equations (2) and (3) are kept from the approach provided by Bosch. Equation (4) is equal to the one in the approach by Bosch, but inequality (6) was extended so block $t+1$ can follow block t immediately, due to possible contiguous blocks of different colors. For black and white puzzles it corresponds exactly to the formulation in [1] since all blocks have the same color which leads the *eq* function to always yield value 1. Inequalities (7) and (8) are similar, but regard columns. Finally, since the only possible color takes value 1, the double coverage constraints set by inequalities (9) and (10) become

$$\forall_{1\leq i\leq m, 1\leq j\leq n} \quad z_{i,j} \leq \sum_{t=1}^{b_i^r} \sum_{j'=max\{e_{i,t}^r, j-s_{i,t}^r+1\}}^{min\{l_{i,t}^r, j\}} y_{i,t,j'}, \tag{16}$$

$$\forall_{1\leq i\leq m, 1\leq j\leq n} \quad z_{i,j} \leq \sum_{t=1}^{b_j^c} \sum_{i'=max\{e_{j,t}^c, i-s_{j,t}^c+1\}}^{min\{l_{j,t}^c, i\}} x_{j,t,i'}, \tag{17}$$

$$\forall_{1\leq i\leq m, 1\leq j\leq n, 1\leq t\leq b_i^r, j-s_{i,t}^r+1\leq j'\leq j, e_{i,t}^r\leq j'\leq l_{i,t}^r} \quad z_{i,j} \geq y_{i,t,j'} \tag{18}$$

and

$$\forall_{1\leq i\leq m, 1\leq j\leq n, 1\leq t\leq b_j^c, e_{j,t}^c\leq i'\leq l_{j,t}^c, i-s_{j,t}^c+1\leq i'\leq i} \quad z_{i,j} \geq x_{j,t,i'} \tag{19}$$

as in [1] (where the *min* and *max* functions are incorrectly swapped in the summation limits).

4 Finding Multiple Solutions

The described ILP model allows finding a single solution to a puzzle, which actually is the best one, although in this case all solutions are alike since the optimizing function is a constant.

Nonograms are satisfaction problems, which in ILP must be modeled as optimization problems. Since it is possible that the obtained solution is not unique, we also try to find additional solutions to a puzzle. For that, we first considered the algorithm developed by Jung-Fa Tsai et al. described in [2], using an integer cut to exclude the previously found solution, extending the ILP model to a Mixed ILP model (MILP), which is the general approach to finding additional solutions in ILP. But, in fact, we used a much simpler approach applying a binary cut similar to the one proposed by Balas and Jeroslow in [3].

Since our binary variables (either $y_{i,t,j}$ or $x_{j,t,i}$) are enough to provide the solution (they completely determine the filled puzzle, since clues are constant), a binary cut is enough.

The cut we need to apply to exclude an existing solution is shown in (20) using the y set of variables (the x set of variables could also be used).

$$\sum_{(i,t,j)\in A} y_{i,t,j} - \sum_{(i,t,j)\in B} y_{i,t,j} \leq |A| - 1, \quad \begin{array}{l} A = \{(i,t,j) \mid y_{i,t,j} = 1\}, \\ B = \{(i,t,j) \mid y_{i,t,j} = 0\} \end{array} \tag{20}$$

Basically, after finding a solution to the problem, the constraints in inequality (20) are added to the problem and another try is made to find another solution.

5 Results

In order to test the performance of our model (without the use of Balas and Jerowlow's algorithm) we tested our approach against three algorithms: one adaptation (the original program solves only black and white nonograms) of an implementation in Prolog of a brute force search by Werner Hett [9], an optimized variant of this implementation (by altering the ordering of the line tasks), and an implementation in C of the iterative approach by Mirek Olšák and Petr Olšák available in [10].

We used four puzzles for the purpose of our tests: the "Fall" puzzle from Griddlers.net [11] (10x8x3, i.e. a 10 by 8 grid with 3 colors) used as an example in this article, the "Fish" and the "AtoZ" puzzles (16x16x2) from Ali Corbin's web page [12], and the "Time" adapted from the copyrighted Sunday Telegraph & Aenigma Design and colored by Brian Grainger (35x30x5) [13].

The times were measured on a 2.4 GHz Intel© Centrino© vPro™with 2 GB of RAM running Microsoft© Windows©. The Prolog program was run in ECLiPSe [14] and the generated ILP problems were run on SCIP [15]. Results are shown in table 1, where NPC stands for "Number of Painted Cells".

Table 1. Experimental Results (in seconds)

Puzzle	R×C×Col	NPC	Brute-force (Prolog)	Brute-force opt (Prolog)	Iterative	ILP
Fall	10x8x3	47	1,050.70	0.03	0.07	0.03
Fish	16x16x2	164	(too long)	0.08	0.07	0.21
AtoZ	16x16x2	50	(too long)	0.92	0.10	23.04
Time	35x30x5	520	(too long)	(out of memory)	0.21	3.51

As shown in table 1 the first puzzle was solved almost instantly by both the iterative implementation and our ILP approach. The brute-force implementation took about 17 minutes to return the results. With some optimization applied to the brute-force approach, namely by re-sorting the line tasks, the puzzle is also solved almost instantly. The "Fish" puzzle is a little harder to solve. The brute-force approach was not able to solve it in a timely fashion although all other approaches solved it pretty quickly. The other 16x16 puzzle — "AtoZ" — is even harder to solve. This was the hardest puzzle to solve by the ILP approach. The fourth (and biggest) puzzle could not be solved by the brute-force algorithms. The iterative approach found all 14 solutions to the puzzle in less than half a second and the ILP approach took about 3.5 seconds.

In order to try to improve the ILP approach we added equation (21) to the set of constraints, where the right-hand term is a constant.

$$\sum_{i=1}^{m}\sum_{j=1}^{n} z_{i,j} = \sum_{i=1}^{m}\sum_{t=1}^{b_i^r} s_{i,t}^r \times c_{i,t}^r \tag{21}$$

Table 2. Results of adding equation (21) to ILP (in seconds)

Puzzle	ILP	ILP w/ AC
Fall	0.03	0.03
Fish	0.21	0.11
AtoZ	23.04	33.58
Time	3.51	2.45

The results are shown in table 2.

Only the performance on the hardest puzzle was not improved which turns out to be inconclusive as to the advantages of adding this extra constraint.

6 Conclusions and Future Work

In this paper we presented a new ILP approach to model the Colored Nonograms problem, which generalizes a known approach which was limited to black and white Nonograms. We demonstrated its correctness and, additionally, we also showed how to efficiently find possible additional solutions by a simple adaptation of a known technique using a binary cut, by taking advantage of the specificities of this problem.

Nonogram problems are usually developed as toy puzzles for people to fill the grid presented in a magazine or newspaper in an enjoyable session. As such, the available clues allow quickly filling many cells using simple inferences. This is why even naive techniques may easily find a solution, since with simple tests there remain little or no options left for cells to color.

Thus, for the tests and comparisons performed on some available puzzles (which so far we have to convert their format 'by hand' in a cumbersome manner), the Iterative approach (performing successive simple inferences) and even an optimized 'brute-force' Prolog approach, provide in general already good results, since there is not much search involved.

ILP approaches are usually much more efficient than other techniques when there is much search involved, which was not the case, and so could only present competitive results if run with a commercial tool such as CPLEX (which we had not available).

The ILP approach presented here starts from scratch with an empty grid and, in general, could not improve the Iterative method for the available tests, although already presented similar results using a non commercial tool.

Our initial idea when developing the ILP model, in addition to the new theoretical results, was to use it together with the Iterative method, which we knew was efficient to quickly fill many cells of the grid using simple inferences on the rows and columns clues. That is precisely what we intend to do next, by applying the ILP model only after the Iterative technique already filled many cells, thus reducing a lot the model complexity by converting many variables to constants.

The search phase that is left then is hopefully much more efficiently solved with ILP than with any other method, which we will have to test with more challenging puzzles.

We thus believe that the approach can be optimized by trying to infer more information from the clues and using that information to enhance our model. We can go further and deduce all information there is to deduce from the clues and then build our model as described in this paper with the addition of the constraints obtained by the deduction step. In this way we substitute the search part of the Iterative algorithm — when no more information can be deduced from the clues and we have to try one color on an empty cell — with the ILP approach.

Therefore, in future research we intend to develop an hybrid model (Iterative/ILP) for Colored Nonograms. To test it more thoroughly we will need to have more puzzles with different parameters. We will search available challenging puzzles and develop some tool to easily convert them to our model, and we also intend to automatically generate random puzzles providing different parameters such as density, average block size and standard deviation, in addition to the grid size and the number of colors.

References

1. Bosch, R.A.: Painting by Numbers. Optima 65, 16–17 (2001)
2. Tsai, J.-F., Lin, M.-H., Hu, Y.-C.: Finding multiple solutions to general integer linear programs. European Journal of Operational Research 184(2), 802–809 (2008)
3. Balas, E., Jeroslow, R.: Canonical Cuts on the unit hypercube. SIAM Journal of Applied Mathematics 23(1), 61–69 (1972)
4. Nonogram, `http://en.wikipedia.org/wiki/Nonogram`
5. Simpson, S.: Nonogram Solver, `http://www.comp.lancs.ac.uk/~ss/nonogram/`
6. Simpson, S.: Nonogram Solver - Solvers on the Web, `http://www.comp.lancs.ac.uk/~ss/nonogram/list-solvers`
7. Wolter, J.: Survey of Paint-by-Number Puzzle Solvers, `http://webpbn.com/survey/`
8. Wolter, J.: The 'pbnsolve' Paint-by-Number Puzzle Solver, `http://webpbn.com/pbnsolve.html`
9. Hett, W.: P99: Ninety-Nine Prolog Problems, `https://prof.ti.bfh.ch/hew1/informatik3/prolog/p-99/`
10. Olšák, M., Olšák, P.: Griddlers solver, nonogram solver, `http://www.olsak.net/grid.html#English`
11. Griddlers Net, `http://www.griddlers.net/`
12. Corbin, A.: Ali Corbin's Home Page, `http://www.blindchicken.com/~ali/`
13. Grainger, B.: Pencil Puzzles and Sudoku, `http://www.icpug.org.uk/national/features/050424fe.htm`
14. The ECLiPSe Constraint Programming System, `http://www.eclipse-clp.org/`
15. SCIP: Solving Constraint Integer Programs, `http://scip.zib.de/`

Learning Visual Object Categories with Global Descriptors and Local Features

Rui Pereira[1] and Luís Seabra Lopes[1,2]

[1] Transverse Activity on Intelligent Robotics, IEETA, Universidade de Aveiro
[2] DETI, Universidade de Aveiro

Abstract. Different types of visual object categories can be found in real-world applications. Some categories are very heterogeneous in terms of local features (broad categories) while others are consistently characterized by some highly distinctive local features (narrow categories). The work described in this paper was motivated by the need to develop representations and categorization mechanisms that can be applied to domains involving different types of categories. A second concern of the paper is that these representations and mechanisms have potential for scaling up to large numbers of categories. The approach is based on combinining global shape descriptors with local features. A new shape representation is proposed. Two additional representations are used, one also capturing the object's shape and another based on sets of highly distinctive local features. Basic classifiers following the nearest-neighbor rule were implemented for each representation. A meta-level classifier, based on a voting strategy, was also implemented. The relevance of each representation and classifier to both broad and narrow categories is evaluated on two datasets with a combined total of 114 categories.

1 Introduction

Category learning is a core problem in cognitive science and artificial intelligence. Visual category learning and recognition are capabilities relevant for a wide range of applications, from digital libraries and the semantic web to manufacturing systems and robotics. Different types of visual categories can be found in real-world applications. Some are very heterogeneous in terms of local features while others are consistently characterized by several highly distinctive local features.

Given the different characteristics of categories, different representations can be more suited to some categories than to others. Based on this fact, Wardhani and Thomson [19] divide images into several very abstract categories, such as natural scenes, people, etc.., and use different methods according to this division. This way, they obtain better results than using a single method. However, it appears that most successful results reported in the literature come, not from using multiple classifiers according to the type of images, but from their combination, be it by using voting [5][18][16] or other approaches [1][6][16].

This paper also explores multiple representations and classification mechanisms to address domains where different types of categories must be processed.

L. Seabra Lopes et al. (Eds.): EPIA 2009, LNAI 5816, pp. 225–236, 2009.

For that purpose, visual object categories are divided into two main groups: if a category exhibits a high variation among its members, then it is said to be a *broad* (or *general*) category; on the other hand, if a category exhibits small variations between its members and they display a high number of unique local features, the category is said to be *narrow* (or *specific*). Broad categories usually are named by common nouns like "cup", "chair", "apple", etc., while narrow categories are named by proper nouns, including brand names, book titles, etc..

Previous work in our group [16] already explored the geometrical analysis of objects to compute multiple object representations, based on divisions of the object in layers and slices. In that work, the combination of the different representations is achieved through a multi-classifier architecture. The final categorization of an object is delivered by a classifier combination. With this approach, it was possible to learn over 70 categories. However, the approach was only tested with broad categories, in the sense explained above. Sarfraz and Rhida [14] also use multiple representations derived from divisions of the objects in slices and layers: one based on three concentric layers and another based on eight slices around the centre of the object. In addition, several other different types of features, such as moment invariants and the so-called "simple shape descriptors", were also used. All features of an object were gathered in a feature vector and objects were compared with Euclidean distance. The approach was applied to the problem of learning 12 broad object categories.

To enhance performance, several projects have been exploring representations combining global and local features. Murphy et al. [9] used global and local features to detect and localize objects in images. Patches around interest points are converted to codewords. Because this type of features is sometimes ambiguous, the coarse texture and spatial layout of the image are also used to help overcoming this difficulty. Once global features are computed, an approximate location and scale of the object are predicted and a local detector is applied to refine this prediction.

Lisin et al. [7] developed a system for object classification and inquired on two different types of combinations of local and global features: stacking, in which outputs of the individual classifiers are used as input features for a meta-classifier; and hierarchical classification, in which classes that are not separable by global features, are clustered and a local feature classifier determines to which class they belong. SIFT [8] is used for computing local features and three shape properties (area, perimeter and compactness) are used as global features. The authors concluded that stacking is superior to hierarchical classification, using images of plankton from a total of 14 categories.

Neumann et al. [10] researched the use of local and global features for logo classification. Logos are analyzed as sets of connected components. Local shape information is extracted from these components, such as eccentricity, circularity, etc.. Global shape information is retrieved by computing the horizontal and vertical projections of the logo's binary image (i.e., counting the number of white pixels for each row and column). A vector describing the logo (its signature) is then obtained using a wavelet transformation. A combined classifier works by

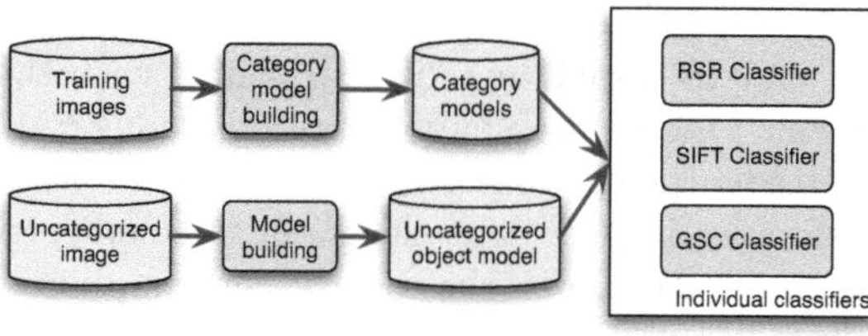

Fig. 1. System overview

adjusting the weights of individual classifiers while classifying a logo. Tests were carried out on the UMD-Logo-Database, containing 123 logos.

In the context of human-robot interaction, some recent approaches explore the combination of incremental learning and interaction with teachers to ground vocabulary about physical objects [16][15][13][17]. This type of approach to category learning naturally raises the problem of scalability: How many visual categories can an artificial system learn? What are the main features of an incremental and open-ended category learning process?

The work described below in this paper was motivated by two of the main problems identified above. First, the need to combine different types of representations to support the acquisition of different types of categories. Second, the need to develop powerful representations and categorization mechanisms enabling to scale up to larger numbers of categories. The work was carried out in the framework of the development of UA@SRVC, a team for participation in the *2nd Semantic Robot Vision Challenge, SRVC'2008* (Anchorage, Alaska, June 2008), an event sponsored by NSF and Google. Other aspects of UA@SRVC are presented in a separate paper[11].

Figure 1 provides an overview of the developed category learning and recognition system. Three basic classifiers, using different representations, are the base of the categorization system. Two of the representations are global shape representations and the third is based on SIFT local features. A meta-level classifier is also included. This classifier combines the decisions of three basic classifiers through voting. The approach is tested on a large number of categories (68 broad categories and 46 narrow categories, for a total of 114 categories).

The paper is organized as follows: Section 2 describes the representations used for objects and categories. Section 3 describes the categorization mechanisms. Section 4 describes the performance evaluation approach and obtained results. Section 5 summarizes conclusions and future work.

2 Representations

As mentioned before, different representations can be more suited to some categories than to others. This section presents the alternative object and category representations used in this work. A global shape context was designed and implemented. For comparison, the shape representation proposed by Roy [13] was also implemented and used. For handling the specificities of narrow categories, local features extracted with SIFT [8] are also used.

Global Shape Context. The edges of an object are usually representative of its shape. For a human, it is usually easy to associate a "line drawing" with the object that it is supposed to represent. One of the shape representations used in this work is a polar histogram of edge pixels that we call a "global shape context" (GSC). A polar frame of reference is located at the geometric centre of the object. Then, the space around the centre up to the most eccentric pixel is divided into a slices (angle bins) and d layers (distance bins)[1]. The intersection of slices and layers results in a polar matrix (Fig. 2)(a) that will be mapped to a 2D histogram counting the number of edge pixels in each cell. This histogram is finally normalized by dividing the counts by the total number of edge pixels.

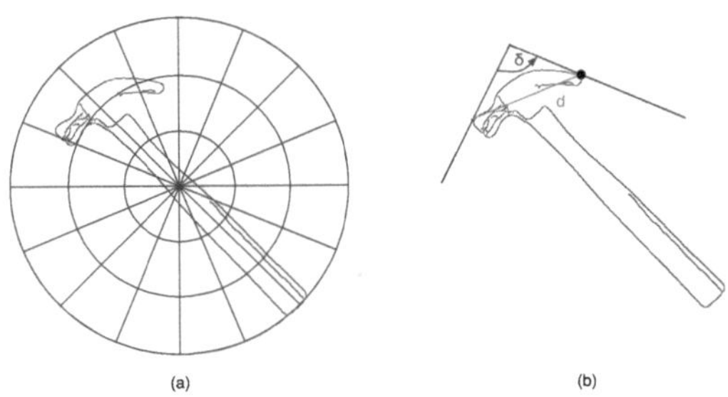

Fig. 2. Shape representations: (a) Global shape context (GSC). (b) Roy's shape representation (RSR).

In most real-world applications, rotation-, translation- and scale-invariance are necessary. The proposed GSC is translation invariant, since it is computed in a frame of reference centered in the geometric centre of the object. It is also scale invariant because the image region mapped to the histogram is delimited by the minimal circle enclosing the object. The histogram itself is not invariant to rotation, but similarity between any two objects can be computed in a rotation-invariant way, as explained in section 3.

The histogram here proposed is similar to the shape context of Belongie et al. [2]. However, in their approach, the shape context itself is used as a local feature, and thus a logarithmic distance scale is used. For each edge pixel, a different shape context is computed. In contrast, the histogram here proposed is used as a global shape descriptor. In terms of computational complexity, building the GSC takes $O(n)$ time, n being the number of edge pixels, whereas building the shape representation proposed by Belongie et al. involves building shape contexts for all pixels, which takes $O(n^2)$ time. The GSC can also be related to the binary shape matrix of Goshtasby [4], derived from a polar raster sampling also centered in the object's geometric center. The shape matrix, whose cells represent the points of intersection between the circles and radial lines in the polar raster are mapped to the cells in the shape matrix. The value in a cell is 1 if the corresponding intersection point is inside the object and 0 otherwise. Similarity between two objects is given by the percentage of matrix cells with the same value for both objects. While the shape matrix is

[1] a=40 and d=10 were used.

a very light representation, the proposed global shape context contains much more information on shape-related details of an object, such as internal edges. The GSC can be seen as a compromise between the computational lightness of the shape matrix and the high expressivity of the Belongie et al.'s approach.

Roy's Shape Representation. Roy [13] proposed a shape representation based on tangents to object edges. It will be refered here as "Roy's shape representation" (RSR). A Canny edge detector is used to obtain the edges from an object. Then, for all pairs of edge pixels, the distances between them, D, and the angles between the respective tangents, δ, are computed (Fig. 2)(b). The tangent at a pixel is approximated by the linear regression line of the neighboring pixels and its orientation is estimated from the regression line [12]. All this information is summarized through a two-dimensional histogram with a angle bins on one dimension and d distance bins on the other[2]. In each cell, the histogram counts the number of edge pixel pairs in the corresponding distance and angle bins.

To obtain scale invariance, distances are normalized by dividing each of them by the maximum distance between any two edge points. Since the angle calculated between the tangents at two edge points is a relative measurement, rotation invariance is also achieved.

For an object with n edge points, $\frac{n(n-1)}{2}$ distances and angles have to be determined, giving a complexity of $O(n^2)$ for the process of building a RSR.

SIFT. SIFT (Scale Invariant Feature Transform [8]) produces highly distinctive features that can be used for matching objects with different scales, positions and orientations, as well as with some variations in illumination. A Difference-of-Gaussians function is used to detect keypoints, based on scale-space extrema. Local gradients sampled in a grid in the vicinity of a keypoint are summarized through a histogram that becomes the keypoint descriptor, as illustrated in Figure 3. From an *8×8* grid centered in the keypoint, gradients are grouped *4* by *4* forming a *2×2* descriptor with *8* directions. The length of the arrows in the right represents the sum of the magnitudes of the gradients, which were nearer to each of the *8* directions, weighted by a Gaussian window. In the work of this paper, a *4×4* descriptor with also *8* directions is computed from a grid of *16×16*, where gradients are grouped *4* by *4*, forming a vector of 128 features per keypoint.

Category Models. An instance-based approach was adopted for category representation. Three alternative category models are used: (1) The category is represented by the set of global shape contexts of the respective training images; (2) The category is represented by the set of Roy's shape representations of the respective training images; (3) The category is represented by the concatenation of the lists of SIFT keypoints extracted from the respective training images.

---

[2] a=32 and d=32 were used in the implementation [12]. This was decided based on experimentation showing it was better for our objectives than the 8×8 suggested by Roy [13].

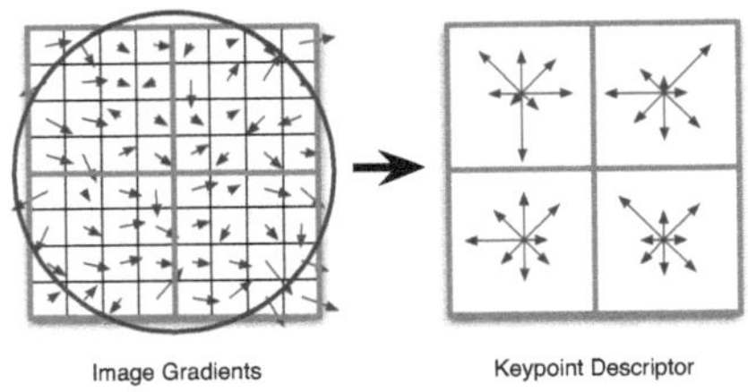

Fig. 3. SIFT keypoint descriptor creation

3 Classification

The goal of the classification (or categorization) module is to categorize objects in the context of an application. This module is composed of three basic classifiers, each based on one of the object representations presented above, and a meta-level classifier. In the basic classifiers, categorization is done by computing a representation of the target object and comparing it to the category models. Categories are ranked in descending order of similarity to the target object. A nearest neighbor strategy is adopted, in which the similarity of the target object to a category is given by the highest similarity between the target object and one instance of the category. The highest ranked category will be the category predicted by the classifier. The ranking itself is used by the meta-level classifier.

GSC-Based Classifier. This classifier follows the general nearest-neighbor scheme just outlined. The χ^2 distance is the base for assessing similarity between any two objects.

$$D_{pq} = \frac{1}{2} \sum_{i=1}^{a} \sum_{j=1}^{d} \frac{[h_p(i,j) - h_q(i,j)]^2}{[h_p(i,j) + h_q(i,j)]} \tag{1}$$

where p and q are two objects, h_p and h_q are the respective histograms (GSCs), a is the number of angle bins, d is the number of distance bins, i is an angle bin and j is a distance bin.

Finally, the similarity between p and q is given by $S_{pq} = 1/D_{pq}$.

As mentioned before, the global shape context is not invariant to rotation. To make rotation invariant matching possible, the histograms are rotated and compared a times (where a is the number of angle bins). The angle displacement that results in the lowest distance is the one used to calculate the similarity between the two shapes.

For $a \times d$ histograms, computing the similarity between two histograms has a complexity of $O(a\times(a\times d))$, since we calculate the χ^2 distance a times (for each histogram rotation). Being independent of the number of edge pixels, this is far more efficient than object matching with the shape representation of Belongie et al. [2], which is based on local shape contexts centred in edge pixels. In this case, most of the steps of the similarity computation algorithm run in time quadratic to cubic in the number of edge pixels.

RSR-Based Classifier. Follows the general nearest-neighbor scheme just outlined and also uses the χ^2 distance as the base for assessing similarity. Since RSR is rotation-invariant, a single comparison is enough. So, for $a \times d$ histograms, computing the similarity between two histograms has a complexity of $O(a \times d)$.

SIFT-Based Classifier. In this case, a category is represented by the concatenation of the lists of SIFT keypoints of all training images that belong to the category. When comparing two objects, the features (keypoints) in each of them are paired according to a nearest-neighbor criterion. Instead of using a global threshold to discard matches, the distances to the two nearest neighbors are computed and compared. If the ratio between them is greater than 0.35, the pair of features is rejected. Finally, similarity between the two objects is given by the number of accepted pairs of features.

Voting System. The performance of a combination of classifiers is often superior to their individual performance [3][6]. A voting approach makes the system very scalable, because it is possible to insert any number of additional classifiers, as long as they vote according to the same rules. In this work, the following voting scheme was implemented. Each classifier determines the 3 most likely categories of an object, i.e., the categories with the higher similarity scores to the object, and casts a variable number of votes to these top ranked categories. For the shape-based classifiers, the first category in the ranking gets 3 votes, the second gets 2 and finally the third gets 1 vote. In the case of the SIFT-based classifier, the three top categories get 6, 4 or 2 votes, respectively. This is done to balance the weight of global (shape-based) and local (SIFT) features in the final voting. In the end of the voting process, the category with more votes is selected. The maximum number of votes a category can have is 12, meaning that all classifiers agree on the best category for the image.

4 Performance Evaluation

Datasets. To evaluate the performance of the classifiers, two sets of images are used. For the evaluation with broad categories, a set of 6914 images of 109 objects belonging to 68 different categories[3] was used. These images have been collected in experiments in the framework of the LANGG project[16] and do not have background noise, occlusion or deformation. However, images were captured under different illumination conditions (artificial / natural, morning / afternoon / evening, etc.) and therefore there is some variability between them.

[3] Letter a; battery; bottle top; box; box2; boy; cd; cigbox; circle; circuit board; coffee cup; coffee mug; coffee spoon; cup; duster; floppy; glove; glue bottle; horse; icetea can; ink remover bottle; key; key1; lighter; mobile; mouse; nail; number one; passbook; pen; pencil; penguin; penguin sitting; postit; remote; screw; sd; sf; stapler1; stapler2; stapler3; staple remover; sugar packet; table fork; table knife; table spoon; tape; teddy bear; number three; tilted coffee mug; tilted cup; tilted tractor; toy bike; toy car; toy jeep; toy mobile; toy saw; toy scissor; toy screw; toy sd; toy tractor; toy train; train top; twenty cent; ubuntu cd cover; usb pen; water bottle; water cup.

In case of narrow categories, a set of 459 images of 46 different categories[4] was used. Many of these images were obtained from the *SRVC* (*Semantic Robot Vision Challenge*) datasets, while others were mannualy collected on the Internet. Objects can have any orientation or localization inside the image and can have a small quantity of noise, variations in 3D viewpoint and occlusion. For fair comparison between shape-based and SIFT-based classifiers, care was taken to not include images with significant clutter, occlusion or background noise, since this can ruin the performance of shape-based classification.

Experimental Approach. The evaluation of the developed system on a particular dataset is carried out as a series of training and testing experiments, for increasing number of categories. For a given number of categories, N, the same basic experiment is repeated 5 times. In each basic experiment, a set of N categories is randomly generated (from the categories in the dataset) and then training and test sets are created as follows:

- Training set: A set of randomly chosen images is used to build the model of the category. In the performed experiments, 4 training images were used for each category.
- Test set: Another set of randomly chosen images is used for testing the category models. In the experiments, the test set contains 3 images from each category.

Broad Categories. Experiments with the broad categories dataset were carried out for the number of categories varying between 5 and 40, with a step of 5. This results in a total of $5 \times 180 \times 3 = 2700$ object classifications with each method. Figure 4 shows the average percentages of correct classifications for each number of categories and each method. While for a small number of categories there isn't a big gap in the performance of the classifiers, this is not true when more categories are added. The SIFT classifier has a faster and more evident degradation in the number of correct classifications. Shape-based classifiers, on the other hand, are more suitable for these types of objects. Both shape-based

[4] Aerius Allergy; book "Artificial Intelligence: a Modern Approach"; book "Big Book of Concepts"; book "Harry Potter and the Deathly Hallows"; book "Lonely Planet Walking in Italy"; book "Paris to the Moon" by Adam Gopnik; Butterfinger logo; Cadbury Caramilk; CD "Begin to Hope" by Regina Spektor; CD "Hey Eugene" by Pink Martini; CD "Introducing Joss Stone"; CD "Look-Alikes Jr." by Joan Steiner; CD "Retrospective" by Django Reinhardt; Cheerios cereal box; "Coca-cola" can; Colgate Fresh; Crayola Crayons box; Dasani bottle; Doritos Blazin' Buffalo Ranch; DVD "Gladiator"; DVD "I, Robot"; DVD "Madagascar"; DVD "Shrek"; Fanta orange can; "Gears of War" box; Gillette Mach3; Head & Shoulders shampoo; Ikea logo; Kellogg's Corn Flakes; "Lucky charms"; Nescafe Tasters Choice; Nintendo Wii box; "Pirates of the Caribbean" dvd; Portugal flag; Pringles; Red Bull can; Ritter Sport Marzipan; Ritz crackers; Snickers wrapper; Star Wars logo; Tide detergent; Toblerone; Twinings Earl Grey Tea; Twix Candy Bar; Vodafone logo; Whiskas logo was used.

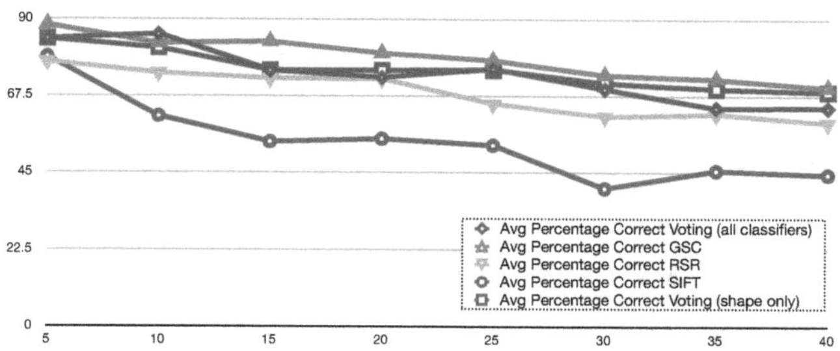

Fig. 4. Classifier performance on broad categories versus number of categories

classifiers clearly outperform the SIFT-based classifier. In fact, while the SIFT-based classifier had an average accuracy of 53.9% in the experiments, the RSR-based classifier had an average accuracy of 68.0% and GSC was even better, with an average accuracy of 78.3%. The difference between these strategies becomes more noticeable with the increase on the number of categories.

Two voting strategies were tested, one combining only the two shape-based classifiers and the other combining all classifiers. No significant difference on their performance was noticed. In fact, the first had an average accuracy of 74.8% and the second 73.6%. They both performed worse than the best basic classifier (GSC), but closer to this one than to any of the others.

We can therefore conclude that, for broad categories, because of high intra-category variance and few distinctive keypoints, shape-based classification provides much better results than SIFT-based classification. We can also conclude that including the SIFT-based classifier in the voting system doesn't degrade performance significantly.

Narrow Categories. In narrow categories, a similar set of experiments was carried out, i.e. from 5 to 40 categories, with a step of 5. Figure 5 shows the average classification accuracies for each method. According to these experiments, the best method for this type of categories is the one based on SIFT, with an average accuracy of 92.1%. In contrast, RSR has an average accuracy of 64.4% and GSC has an average accuracy of only 45.1%.

SIFT is a very good method for this type of categories. Their richness in local features makes it possible to achieve good classification results with SIFT, while at the same time (together with variations in 3D viewpoint, occlusion, etc.) confuses the classifiers based on shape.

The voting system, combining the three basic classifiers, reached an average accuracy of 89.0%, i.e. performed only slightly worse than the best basic classifier.

Mixed Categories. In the previous experiments, it could be observed that the voting system performed only slightly worse than the basic classifiers more suited for the type of categories (either broad or narrow) present in the dataset.

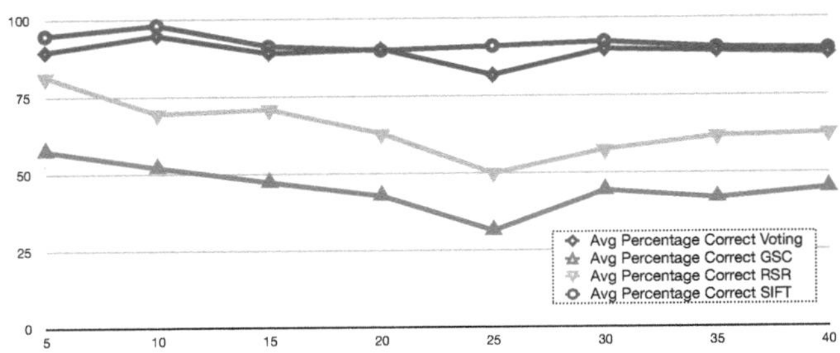

Fig. 5. Classifier performance on narrow categories versus number of categories

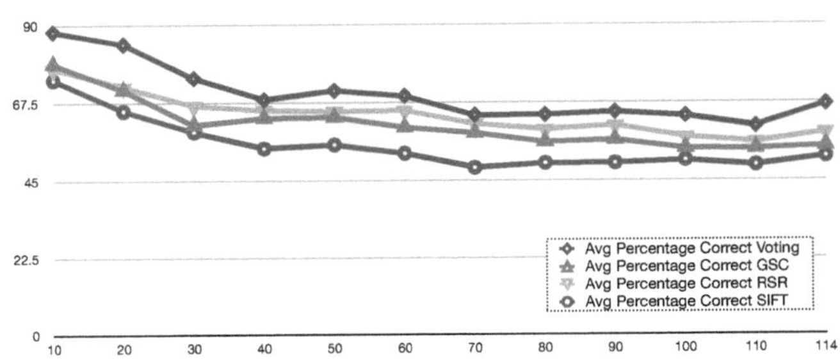

Fig. 6. Classifier performance on mixed categories versus number of categories

Therefore, it becomes interesting to find out how the voting system behaves in a dataset where both types of categories are present. For that purpose, the two mentioned datasets were united producing a new dataset with 7373 images of 114 different categories. Experiments on this united dataset were carried out starting with 10 categories and going up to 110 categories with a step of 10. Experiments were also conducted for the complete set of 114 categories. This results in a total of $5 \times 774 \times 3 = 9288$ classifications with each method.

Figure 6 shows the results. Given the presence of both broad and narrow categories, no major differences in performance were observed between the three basic classifiers: 60.3% for RSR, 57% for GSC and 50.9% for SIFT. The superior performance of GSC reflects, at least in part, the fact that there are more broad categories (for which GSC is the most suited) than narrow categories. The average accuracy of the voting system was 65.3%. The fact that the voting system improves on the individual classifiers is inline with previous observations [3][5][18][16][6].

With respect to scalability, the obtained results seem promising. In fact, while the average accuracy of the best classifier (voting) degradates visibly (from 90% to 67.5%) between 10 and 40 categories, it nearly stabilizes between 40 and 114 categories. We therefore have reasons to expect that the approach will easily scale up to larger numbers of categories.

5 Conclusions

The work described in this paper was motivated by the need to develop representations and categorization mechanisms that can be applied to domains involving different types of categories. The approach is based on combinining global shape descriptors with local features. A new shape representation was proposed, the global shape context (GSC). Two additional representations were used. One is Roy's shape representation (RSR). The other is based on sets of SIFT local features. Basic classifiers following the nearest-neighbor rule were implemented for each representation. In tests with up to 40 broad categories, GSC performed clearly above the other two classifiers, and SIFT delivered the worse results. By contrast, in similar tests with narrow categories, SIFT delivered the best results, far above the other two classifiers. RSR had intermediate performance on both domains. In a mixed domain combining 68 broad categories and 46 narrow categories (114 categories in total), the three classifiers had a more balanced performance. In this case, GSC was the best, which also reflect the fact that broad categories were in majority.

A meta-level classifier, based on a voting strategy, was also implemented. In tests on domains with only one of the types of categories (either broad or narrow), the meta-level classifier performed only slightly worse than the best basic classifier for those domains. In tests with the mixed domain, the meta-level classifier produced the best results.

Another concern of this work was to assess the scalability of the developed/implemented representations and classification mechanisms. In this respect, the obtained results seem promising. In the largest tests (with 114 categories), the average accuracy of the best classifier (voting) degraded visibly between 10 and 40 categories, but stabilized between 40 and 114 categories, so it's possible that the approach will easily scale up to larger numbers of categories.

Acknowledgments

The first author is currently with a research grant funded by Aveiro University. The participation of the UA@SRVC team in SRVC'2008 was partially funded by Google. The used implementation of SIFT was developed by Rob Hess and is publicly available. The implementation also used OpenCV extensively.

References

1. Al-Ani, A., Deriche, M.: A new technique for combining multiple classifiers using the dempster-shafer theory of evidence. Journal of Artificial Intelligence Research 17, 333–361 (2002)
2. Belongie, S., Malik, J., Puzicha, J.: Shape matching and object recognition using shape contexts. IEEE Transactions on Pattern Analysis and Machine Intelligence 24, 509–522 (2002)
3. Dietterich, T.G.: Ensemble methods in machine learning, pp. 1–15. Springer, Heidelberg (2000)

4. Goshtasby, A.: Description and discrimination of planar shapes using shape matrices. IEEE Trans. Pattern Anal. Mach. Intell. 7, 738–743 (1985)
5. Huang, Y.S., Suen, C.Y.: A method of combining multiple experts for the recognition of unconstrained handwritten numerals. IEEE Trans. Pattern Anal. Mach. Intell. 17(1), 90–94 (1995)
6. Kittler, J., Hatef, M., Duin, R., Matas, J.: On combining classifiers. IEEE Transactions on Pattern Analysis and Machine Intelligence 20(3), 226–239 (1998)
7. Lisin, D., Mattar, M., Blaschko, M., Learned-Miller, E., Benfield, M.: Combining local and global image features for object class recognition. In: IEEE Computer Society Conference on Computer Vision and Pattern Recognition - Workshops, 2005. CVPR Workshops, p. 47 (2005)
8. Lowe, D.G.: Distinctive image features from scale-invariant keypoints. International Journal of Computer Vision 60, 91–110 (2004)
9. Murphy, K.P., Torralba, A.B., Eaton, D., Freeman, W.T.: Object detection and localization using local and global features. In: Ponce, J., Hebert, M., Schmid, C., Zisserman, A. (eds.) Toward Category-Level Object Recognition. LNCS, vol. 4170, pp. 382–400. Springer, Heidelberg (2006)
10. Neumann, J., Samet, H., Soffer, A.: Integration of local and global shape analysis for logo classification. Pattern Recognition Letters 23(12), 1449–1457 (2002)
11. Pereira, R., Seabra Lopes, L., Silva, A.: Semantic image search and subset selection for classifier training in object recognition. In: Seabra Lopes, L., et al. (eds.) EPIA 2009. LNCS(LNAI), vol. 5816, pp. 338–349. Springer, Heidelberg (2009)
12. Ribeiro, L.S.: Object recognition for semantic robot vision. Master's thesis, Universidade de Aveiro (2008)
13. Roy, D.K.: Learning Words from Sights and Sounds: A Computational Model. PhD thesis, MIT (2000)
14. Sarfraz, M., Ridha, A.: Content-based image retrieval using multiple shape descriptors. In: IEEE/ACS International Conference on Computer Systems and Applications, AICCSA 2007, pp. 730–737 (2007)
15. Seabra Lopes, L., Chauhan, A.: How many words can my robot learn? an approach and experiments with one-class learning. Interaction Studies 8(1), 53–81 (2007)
16. Seabra Lopes, L., Chauhan, A.: Open-ended category learning for language acquisition. Connection Science 8(4) (2008)
17. Steels, L., Kaplan, F.: Aibo's first words: the social learning of language and meaning. Evolution of Communication 4(1), 3–32 (2002)
18. van Erp, M., Vuurpijl, L., Schomaker, L.: An overview and comparison of voting methods for pattern recognition. In: 8th International Workshop on Frontiers in Handwriting Recognition (IWFHR-8), pp. 195–200 (2002)
19. Wardhani, A., Thomson, T.: Content based image retrieval using category-based indexing. In: IEEE International Conference on Multimedia and Expo, ICME 2004, vol. 2, pp. 783–786 (2004)

Chapter 7

IROBOT – Intelligent Robotics

Analysis and Forecast of Team Formation in the Simulated Robotic Soccer Domain

Rui Almeida[1], Luís Paulo Reis[2,4], and Alípio Mário Jorge[3,5]

[1] FEP - Faculty of Economics of the University of Porto, Portugal
[2] FEUP - Faculty of Engineering of the University of Porto, Portugal
[3] FCUP - Faculty of Science of the University of Porto, Portugal
[4] LIACC – Artificial Intelligence and Computer Science Lab., University of Porto
[5] LIAAD – Artificial Intelligence and Decision Support Lab. - INESC Porto L.A.
ruifigueiredoalmeida@gmail.com, lpreis@fe.up.pt, amjorge@fc.up.pt

Abstract. This paper proposes a classification approach to identify the team's formation (formation means the strategical layout of the players in the field) in the robotic soccer domain for the two dimensional (2D) simulation league. It is a tool for decision support that allows the coach to understand the strategy of the opponent. To reach that goal we employ Data Mining classification techniques. To understand the simulated robotic soccer domain we briefly describe the simulation system, some related work and the use of Data Mining techniques for the detection of formations. In order to perform a robotic soccer match with different formations we develop a way to configure the formations in a training base team (FC Portugal) and a data preparation process. The paper describes the base team and the test teams used and the respective configuration process. After the matches between test teams the data is subjected to a reduction process taking into account the players' position in the field given the collective. In the modeling stage appropriate learning algorithms were selected. In the solution analysis, the error rate (% incorrectly classify instances) with the statistic test t-Student for paired samples were selected, as the evaluation measure. Experimental results show that it is possible to automatically identify the formations used by the base team (FC Portugal) in distinct matches against different opponents, using Data Mining techniques. The experimental results also show that the SMO (Sequential Minimal Optimization) learning algorithm has the best performance.

Keywords: Data Mining, Classification, Weka, Sequential Minimal Optimization, Formation Detection, Simulated Robotic Soccer.

1 Introduction

The RoboCup initiative is an international project aiming to promote (Distributed) Artificial Intelligence and Intelligent Robotics [1] research. For many years, chess was the main area for the application of artificial intelligence methodologies but, after

L. Seabra Lopes et al. (Eds.): EPIA 2009, LNAI 5816, pp. 239–250, 2009.

the victory of Deep Blue computer over the human Gary Kasparov (world champion at the time), an era was closed. It was necessary to find more challenging domains and more complex problems for the scientific community.

One of those domains was the robotic soccer – RoboCup. The robotic soccer requires the application and integration of a wide range of technologies to enable the setting and programming of a team with real or virtual robots able to participate in a soccer match with a certain set of pre-specified rules. Soccer is a highly complex domain, opening new research horizons in the areas of Distributed Artificial Intelligence, Intelligent Robotic, Decision Support Systems, Knowledge Extraction, Forecasting Methods, among others.

The RoboCup initiative aims at stimulating research and cooperation between the scientific community and the business world, by organizing an annual international competition. Therefore it is possible to get the attention of the media and of the general public. It also serves to evaluate the scientific contribution in this domain.

Soccer was one of the initial inspirations for the RoboCup, resulting on RoboCup Soccer. It is as a very popular sport and presents relevant scientific challenges, both at the collective level (strategies, tactics, formations, among others) and individual level (shoots, positioning, among others).

Simulated robotic soccer is one of the RoboCup Soccer competitions and it is played in two and three dimensions leagues. In the simulation 2D league, teams of simulated robots are organized with eleven players competing with rules and strategies very similar to a real soccer match.

This paper presents a Data Mining methodology to predict the formations used by a simulated robotic soccer team (2D simulation league).

The selected base team (FC Portugal) obtained excellent results in the RoboCup competition. This team won five European championships and three World Cup championships of Simulated Robotic Soccer [2], [3] in distinct leagues. These achievements motivated the use of FC Portugal for the forecast of team formation in simulated robotic soccer, in order to develop a methodology for classification in this research. Additionally the team was selected mainly due to its very flexible strategy that enables to completely change the collective behavior and formation just changing parameters on a configuration file.

For the identification of formations, a special agent (the coach) of a robotic soccer team is able to make a strategic analysis of the field situation. But the time spent by the coach in this analysis is costly. So the automation of the formations forecast allows the reduction of that time and gives the chance to the coach to analyze more matches. Thereby, this study contributes to the RoboCup initiative by providing a flexible tool for formation forecast, not limited only to the simulation 2D league.

This paper has the following structure: section 2 presents simulated robotic soccer composition, some works related and the importance of Data Mining in the detection of the teams formations; section 3 presents the selection of the teams that participated in the construction of the log files, the formations selected and the data set creation process; section 4 shows the experiments and the results obtained and finally section 5 shows the conclusion and a future work.

2 Simulated Robotic Soccer Features

SoccerServer is a soccer simulation system based on a set of modules – usually three separate modules: simulation, visualization and video. The simulator module uses client-server architecture, provides a virtual soccer field and simulates the movement of all objects, controlling the match according to a set of pre-specified rules. The simulator receives the commands of the agents, executes them simulating the movement of all objects and sends sensor information to the agents [2].

Fig. 1. The Visualizator Soccer Monitor

The screens with 3D capabilities or traditional monitors work with the help of the simulator. There is a possibility of connection of several monitors to the server that runs the match, regardless of the platform on which the visualization is done. The Soccer Monitor is an application to watch the matches that the simulator Soccer Server makes (see Figure 1).

Video - LogPlayer - is an application that enables log files visualization and has all the movements of the players (agents) in the simulated soccer field. In this application it is possible to view the simulated match in slow, fast and cycle to cycle motion, among others.

3 Related Work

The task of recognizing team formation in robotic soccer has been a subject of study, given its importance in this domain. Visser et al. [4] emphasize the importance of the online coach within the simulation league because this agent has information about the objects in the field and is able to send messages to their players during any break in the match. For recognizing formations Visser et al. [4] propose a model based in an artificial neural network. In this model a set of default formations supply information about the opponent team to the online coach.

Another study by Ramos and Ayanegui [5] points the difficulty in managing the dynamics of a soccer match. The solution proposed by these authors is a model that allows the building of topological structures based on triangular planar graphs, able to manage the constant changes in the match. This approach enables multiple relations between the agents.

4 Detection of Formations in the Simulated Robotic Soccer

The techniques of Data Mining for classification problems can be used to solve the problem of formations detection within the simulated robotic soccer environment.

All the matches in simulated robotic soccer are saved in log files. Thus, it is possible to create a repository of data containing the historical records of certain teams. A team can be studied in detail, because all its activities carried out in official RoboCup matches are saved in log files. Using specialized software, such as Soccer Scope2 or Soccer Monitor, the log files can be used to provide a visual perception of the behavior of virtual players in the field. When necessary it can lead to analyze the behavior of the team, forecasting the actions or players positions, using information from past matches.

Therefore it will be possible for a team in a simulated robotic soccer tournament competition to previously study its opponents through Data Mining techniques. The extracted information in this study may be used for future matches allowing to configure the match processes and better face the opponent.

5 Selection of Test Teams and Test Formations

Teams naturally don't change their formation so often, which makes it difficult for building and evaluating an approach for automatic team formation. For that reason we have chosen teams with different levels of performance to play against the FC Portugal team. Based on the flexible configuration abilities of the FC Portugal team we developed a configuration file. It enabled us to get ten different formations during a robotic soccer match, in order to create a data set with diversified formations and then proceed to the modeling and evaluation of the learning algorithms.

To perform the analysis, we have used several versions of teams that participated in RoboCup 2007 Atlanta, who could face the team on this study: FC Portugal. Thus, the selected teams were: Brazil (Brasil2D), AT Humboldt (ATH07) and Helios (Helios2007), as test teams.

Brazil team is based on the Bahia Robotics Team which started its work for this category in 2006. This team had relatively weak results in the tournament when comparing with other teams.

AT Humboldt team is from Humboldt University of Berlin, created in 1997, world champion in 1997 and vice-champion in 1998. They reached sixth place in the RoboCup 2007 Atlanta, and obtained average competitive results.

The Helios team came from the National Institute of Advanced Industrial Science and Technology in Japan, and reached the third place in the RoboCup Atlanta 2007. Today, it is one of the strongest teams.

The different performances of these teams in Atlanta were the basis for team selection. Following this basis we selected a superior, a similar and an inferior team comparatively to FC Portugal. So, it was expected balanced matches with AT Humboldt and unbalanced with opposite signs in the matches against Helios and Brazil.

After the test team selection a version of FC Portugal team was trained to be able to play in one match with ten (10) different formations. This procedure enabled to acquire a data repository for the formations' study.

From the Pro Evolution Soccer PlayStation game [6], we have chosen the following typical soccer formations for analysis: 325, 442, 343, 352, 541, 532, 361, 451, 334 and 433. These formations are graphically represented in Figure 2 and Figure 3 by the yellow team (the light team, playing from the left to the right side).

Table 1 shows the correspondence between formations and classes.

Table 1. Correspondence between formations and classes

Class	1	2	3	4	5	6	7	8	9	10
Formation	433	442	343	352	541	532	361	451	334	325

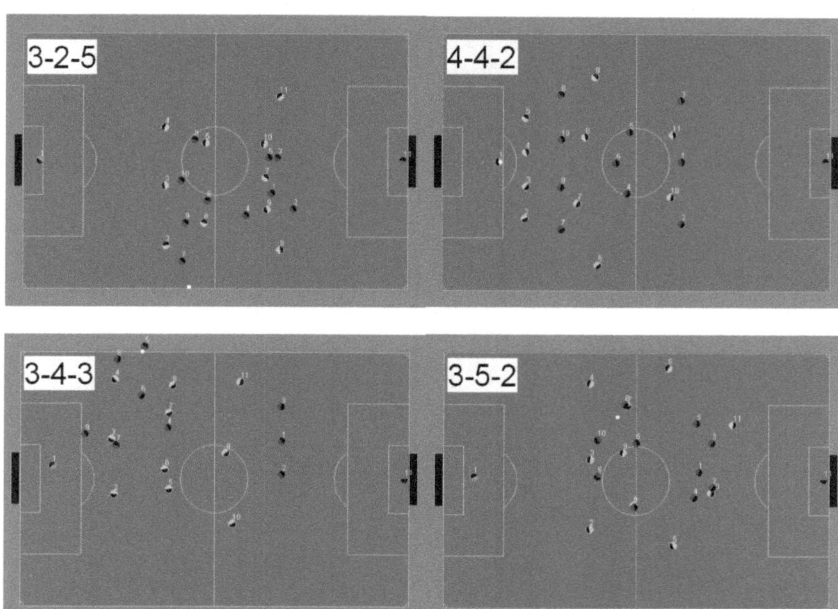

Fig. 2. Formations: 325, 442, 343 and 352

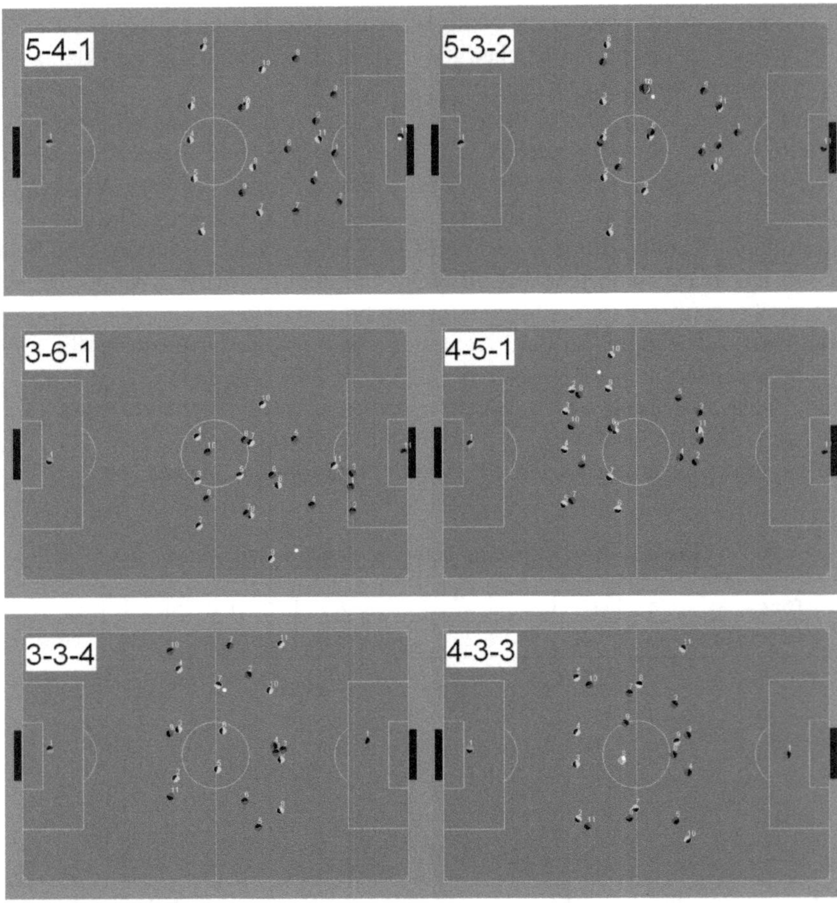

Fig. 3. Formations: 541, 532, 361, 451, 334 and 433

Since a simulated soccer match has the duration of six thousand (6000) cycles, we have divided the match duration so that each part corresponds to a specific formation, as shown in Table 2.

Table 2. Formations for each part of the match

Cycles	Class
[0, 599]	10
[600, 1199]	2
[1200, 1799]	3
[1800, 2399]	4
[2400, 2999]	5
[3000, 3599]	6
[3600, 4199]	7
[4200, 4799]	8
[4800, 5399]	9
[5400, 6000]	1

After selecting the formations, the FC Portugal team played two games with each test team. The results of these matches appear on Table 3.

Table 3. Results of the matches to analyze

Teams	Result
FC Portugal x ATH07	0 x 0
ATH07 x FC Portugal	0 x 1
FC Portugal x Helios	0 x 4
Helios x FC Portugal	4 x 0
FC Portugal x Brazil	7 x 0
Brazil x FC Portugal	0 x 8

6 Data Set Construction

To construct the data set we have converted the log files into text files, through the getWState software built in C++ language. Each text file generated by getWState software contained all the attributes [players positions (x, y), ball position (x, y), speed of each player, stamina of each player, among others], which may be exported from the Soccer Server. The attributes considered relevant for the problem under study were the position of the players (x, y) of the FC Portugal team. This decision was based on domain knowledge.

To take into account the dynamics of the players and how they coordinate and interact we have added two new variables (x, y) from the available data, which represent the center of mass of the team's formation. This is a summary of players' positions. The two new variables were calculated from the positions (x, y) of the players from FC Portugal team without the goalkeeper (see Eq. 1 and Eq. 2). The center of mass for coordinate x and y;

$$\bar{x} = \sum_{i=1}^{10} (x_i)/10, \quad \bar{y} = \sum_{i=1}^{10} (y_i)/10 \qquad \text{(Eq. 1, 2)}$$

After calculating the center of mass of FC Portugal team, the next step was the data standardization of the players' positions to the center of mass (see Eq. 3 and Eq. 4). Standardized positions x' and y' of the players;

$$x_i' = x_i - \bar{x}, \quad y_i' = y_i - \bar{y} \qquad \text{(Eq. 3, 4)}$$

The attributes for analysis have become the standard positions of the virtual players and the center of mass. Next we have included the Class variable with the respective result for all cases in the six matches, according to Table 2.

To create a data repository all data has been merged into a single file for further processing according with the experiments.

7 Experiments and Results

To perform the detection of the formations the software Waikato Environment for Knowledge Analysis (WEKA) [7] was chosen because it includes a diversity of learning algorithms able to assist in the forecast of the teams formations in the domain of robotic soccer, and has an easy graphical interface to use.

The pool of learning algorithms was chosen on the basis of popularity and known experimental results: J48, Naive Bayes, K-Nearest Neighbor (IBK), PART, Multilayer Perceptron and Sequential Minimal Optimization (SMO) [8] [9].

The main indicators for evaluating learning algorithms were the error rate (% incorrectly classify instances) and the test t-Student [10].

7.1 Experiments Performed

We made some experiments of which we highlight two of them. One had some parts of matches for training and other parts for testing. The other experiment had subsets of one match for training and another match of the same team for testing as well as subsets of one match for training and two matches from different teams for testing. These experiments were performed to choose the most appropriate learning algorithm for the forecast of team formation.

The first experiment was made in a proportional way, one match for training and five matches for testing (1-5); two matches for training and four matches for testing (2-4); three matches for training and three matches for testing (3-3) and so on, as shown in Figure 4.

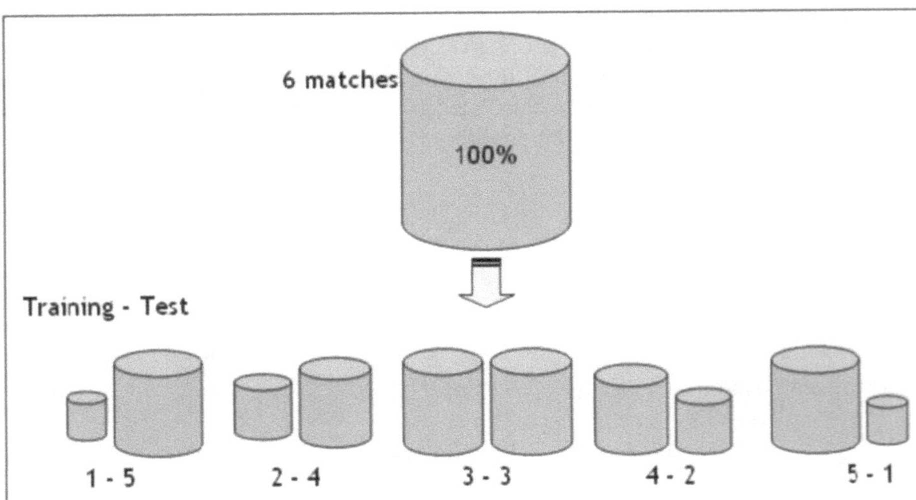

Fig. 4. Subsets of x matches for training with y matches for testing

The second experiment was made with subsets of one match for training/testing with the same team, as well as subsets of one match for training and two matches for testing with different teams. It meant the unfolding of the entire data set in matches for training and in matches for testing. For instance, FC Portugal team played against AT Humboldt one match for training and one match for testing; next, one match for training with AT Humboldt and two matches for testing with team Helios team; and finally, one match for training with AT Humboldt and two matches for testing with team Brazil. The same rational was applied, for this second experiment, with Helios and Brazil teams. Each of these cases experiments were performed with the mentioned learning algorithms. The total number of unfolding was nine, as shown in Figure 5.

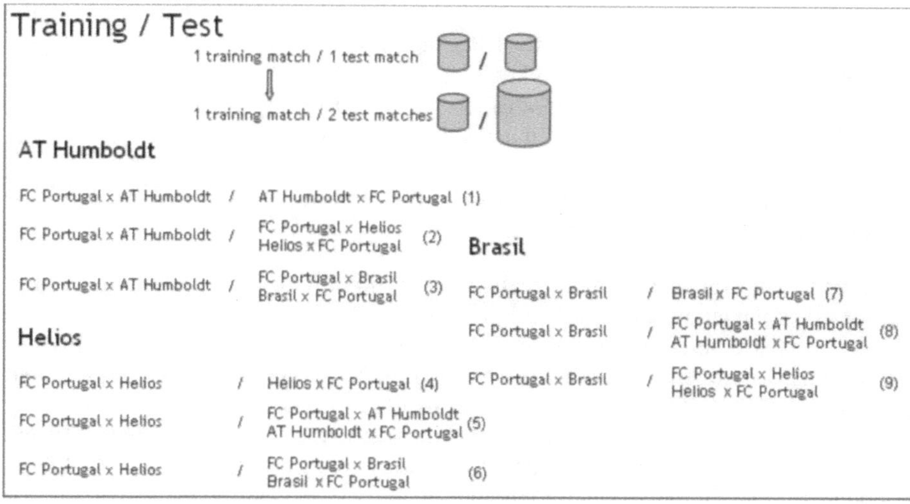

Fig. 5. Subsets of one match training/test of the same team and one match training/tests of different teams

7.2 Subsets of x Matches for Training with y Matches for Testing

This experiment aims to examine the error rate evolution as the subset for training grows as well as identify the best performing learning algorithms. Figure 6 shows the

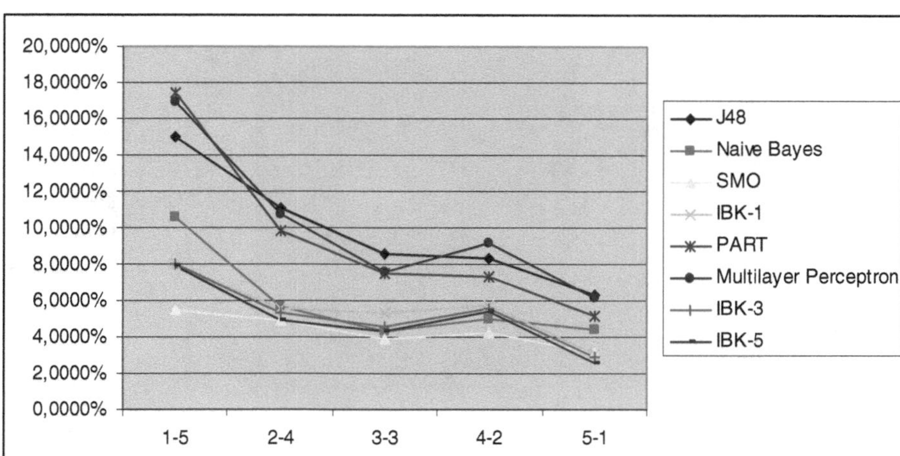

Fig. 6. Graphic of error rates of x matches for training and y matches for testing

error rate in the proportion for different numbers of games for training and testing (1-5, 2-4, 3-3, 4-2 and 5-1). SMO had three times the lowest error rate and IBK-5 had the lowest error rates two times in the experiments of x matches for training and y matches to test.

The t-Student test assumes that data should follow a normal distribution. Using the Shapiro-Wilk [10] test in the Statistical Package for the Social Sciences (SPSS) we have observed, for a significance level of 5%, that SMO-IBK5 has normal distribution. This enables the use of t-Student. For this test, we have used significance level of 5%.

For SMO-IBK5 the result showed that the differences are not statistically significant.

7.3 Subsets of One Match Training/Test of the Same Team and One Match Training/Tests of Different Teams

This experiment simulates a more realistic scenario, which is the separation of the matches given the teams: AT Humboldt, Helios and Brazil.

Figure 7 is structured according to the learning algorithms and the proposed scenario for this experiment. In this Figure the training/test combinations are represented as follows: ATH07/ATH07 (1); ATH07/Helios (2); ATH07/Brasil (3); Helios/Helios (4); Helios/ATH07 (5); Helios/Brazil (6); Brazil/Brazil (7); Brasil/ATH07 (8) and Brazil/Helios (9). The learning algorithms Multilayer Perceptron, J48 and PART are excluded from the Figure 7 because they present very high error rates relatively to the other learning algorithms.

The experiments ATH07/Brasil (3), Helios/Brazil (6) and Brazil/Helios (9) performed with the Brazil team are those with the highest error rates, possibly because the Brazil team is a weak team when compared with the others, as the Figure 7 shows. The SMO learning algorithm, in this experiment, had six times the lowest error rate and the IBK-5 learning algorithm had three times the lowest error rate.

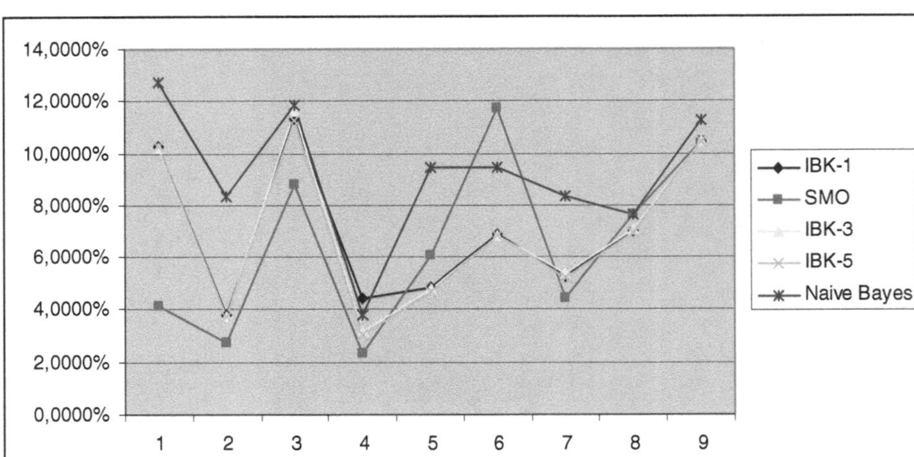

Fig. 7. Error rate of one match for training, with n matches of different teams with the most representative learning algorithms

As IBK-5 showed low error rates (Figure 7), the Shapiro-Wilk test was also made for the data distribution of SMO-IBK5. This test indicated, for a significance level of 5%, that the data distribution didn't differ from a normal distribution. The t-Student test showed that the differences were not statistically significant between the averages of these learning algorithms.

Given the results of these experiments we conclude that the SMO learning algorithm is more suitable for modeling the detection of the teams' formation.

8 Conclusions and Future Work

This work aimed to build a Data Mining methodology for the forecast of team formation in simulated robotic soccer (2D simulation league).

The experiments show that the learning algorithm that generates the most appropriate model for predicting the formation of a team in simulated robotic soccer matches is the SMO. A tool developed with the Data Mining methodology enables the coach of robotic soccer team to be assisted with a decision support system when for instance a given team changes its formation.

To continue these experiments we plan to build a forecast model during the soccer matches (on-line forecast of formations) in the robotic soccer domain. In the data preparation stage we plan to conduct more detailed studies with the aim to decrease the percentage of cases incorrectly classified, for example a situation in which a player may be out of formation with the possession of the ball. Another example which may contribute to the reduction of cases incorrectly classified would be the analysis of time spent by a team in the transition from one formation to another.

Acknowledgments

This project was partially supported by project FCT/PTDC/EIA/70695/2006: ACORD – Adaptative Coordination of Robotic Teams.

References

1. Chen, M., Foroughi, E., Heintz, S., Kapetanakis, S., Kostiadis, K., Kummeneje, J., Noda, I., Obst, O., Riley, P., Steffens, T., Wang, Y., Yin, X.: RoboCup Soccer Server manual for Soccer Server version 7.07 or Latest, `http://sourceforge.net/projects/sserver` (acessed on: October 01, 2003)
2. Reis, L.P., Lau, N.: FC portugal team description: RoboCup 2000 simulation league champion. In: Stone, P., Balch, T., Kraetzschmar, G. (eds.) RoboCup 2000. LNCS (LNAI), vol. 2019, pp. 29–40. Springer, Berlin (2001)
3. Lau, N., Reis, L.P.: FC Portugal – High Level Coordination Methodologies in Soccer Robotics. In: Lima, P. (ed.) Robotic Soccer, p. 598. Itech Education and Publishing, Vienna (2007)
4. Visser, U., Drücker, C., Hübner, S., Schmidt, E., Weland, H.-G.: Recognizing formations in opponent teams. In: Stone, P., Balch, T., Kraetzschmar, G.K. (eds.) RoboCup 2000. LNCS (LNAI), vol. 2019, pp. 391–396. Springer, Heidelberg (2001)

5. Ramos, F., Ayanegui, H.: Discovering Tactical Behavior Patterns Supported by Topological Structures in Soccer Agent Domains. In: International Conference on Autonomous Agents, Proceedings of the 7th International joint conference on Autonomous Agents and Multiagent Systems, Estoril, vol. 3, pp. 1421–1424 (2008)
6. Pro Evolution Soccer 2008. Konami Digital Entertainment GmbH, Frankfurt (2008)
7. Weka. Weka Machine Learning Project, `http://www.cs.waikato.ac.nz/~ml/index.html` (acessed: October 04, 2008)
8. Witten, I.H., Eibe, F.: Data Mining: Practical Machine Learning Tools and Techniques with Java Implementations, 2nd edn. Morgan Kaufmann, St. Louis (2005)
9. Hastie, T., Tibshirani, R., Friedman, J.: The Elements of Statistical Learning – Data Mining, Inference and Prediction. Springer, New York (2002)
10. Maroco, J.: Análise Estatística, 3rd edn. Edições Sílabo, Lisboa (2007)

A Cooperative CiberMouse@RTSS08 Team

João Azevedo[1], Miguel Oliveira[1], Pedro Pacheco[1], and Luís Paulo Reis[1,2]

[1] DEI/FEUP - Departamento de Eng. Informática, Faculdade de Engenharia da Universidade do Porto

[2] LIACC - Laboratório de Inteligência Artificial e Ciência de Computadores da Universidade do Porto

Rua Dr. Roberto Frias, s/n 4200-465 Porto Portugal

{ei05028,ei05053,ei05058,lpreis}@fe.up.pt

Abstract. This paper describes the strategy and implementation details of a cooperative agent team for the CiberMouse@RTSS08, a robotics simulation competition. The paper introduces several concepts concerning cooperative robotics, giving an overview of its applications and challenges. It also presents the CiberMouse@RTSS08 competition rules and the associated simulation system. The proposed approach is based on a deliberative architecture, thus providing an autonomous intelligent behaviour. A probabilistic mapping procedure, based on the Bayes' theorem, is used to maintain an internal world state. Quadtrees and A* are used for path planning and plan execution. A specific methodology was developed for beacon finding. The agents cooperate on exchanging world and beacon information. In order to overcome the simulator's broadcasting distance limitation, a communication network between the agents was created. The paper analyses the impact of cooperation on this particular problem, by comparing the team's performance in four different situations: communication with network and beacon exchanging, communication without network, communication without beacon exchanging and no communication at all.

1 Introduction

The interest for cooperative robotics has increased dramatically since the 1990s decade and has been the focus of attention of many research groups in recent years. The idea of using a team of robots instead of a single one to execute a task, came from the necessity of accomplishing a task that is too difficult or too complex for a single robot. In other situations, to use a group of simple robots can be more efficient, easier, less expensive, more flexible and more fault-tolerant than having a single powerful, highly specialized robot for each task [21].

This interest lead to the creation of plenty of robotics competitions, where participants have to develop a cooperative team of robotic agents. Among them are the RoboCup Leagues [17] and the CiberMouse@RTSS08 [1,7]. In the latter competition, in addition to its individual abilities for mapping the environment and to plan a path [3], each agent has to cooperate with the rest of its teammates. For this cooperation, agents are allowed to communicate with each other under certain restrictions. This poses some communication challenges [15]:

L. Seabra Lopes et al. (Eds.): EPIA 2009, LNAI 5816, pp. 251–262, 2009.

- **What to Communicate?**
  - Individual world state to improve world state accuracy
  - Useful events for coordination

- **When to Communicate?**
  - Communication utility is very high or is greater then communication utility (modeled) of teammates
  - Creation of a communicated world state

In order to present an approach for a CiberMouse@RTSS08 team, this paper is organized as follows. Section 2 introduces the competition, giving an overview of the rules and presenting its simulator. Section 3 is about the agents' individual abilities: mapping procedure, path planning, plan execution and beacon finding. Section 4 describes the general strategy applied to the collaborative team of mice.

2 The CiberMouse@RTSS08 Competition

2.1 Rules Overview

The CiberMouse@RTSS08 is a competition for virtual robots that takes place in a simulated environment. The simulation system creates a virtual arena, populated by obstacles, a starting grid, a target area signaled by a beacon and the bodies of the robots. The bodies are composed by a circular base and are equipped with sensors, actuators and command buttons.

Participants must provide the software which controls the movements of a team composed by five virtual robots. Each robot is controlled by an independent program and is allowed to communicate with the rest of the team within given restrictions. Each team has to find the target area and then position the robots near it. Score is based on the fulfilment of this goal and on suffered penalties associated with time spent and number of collisions.

2.2 The Simulator

The competition environment is based on distributed computing, using a server-client architecture. The entities involved in the simulation are: the simulator, that works as the server, the viewer and the robotic agents that are the clients. The communication between server and clients is made with sockets, therefore, robotic agents can be programmed in any language that supports the use of sockets. The simulator and viewer are available at CiberMouse@RTSS08 official page [7], as well as some mazes that were used to test the agent team.

3 The Individual Agent

The team agents are controlled by the same software. So, they share the same individual behaviour and architecture, which consists of three main modules:

- **Mapping Procedure** - used to build and maintain an internal state of the world [5,11,19];
- **Path Planning and Plan Execution** - calculates paths between points of the map and drives the agent across them;
- **Beacon Finding** - determines the beacon position, allowing the above module to drive the agent to it.

3.1 Mapping Procedure

The first problem with mapping comes from the need of the agent to know where it is [10,18]. Contrary to the original CiberRato specifications [8], on the CiberMouse@RTSS08 the agents have full access to the GPS sensor, under some limitations. The most aggravating is the fact that it is highly noisy, thus not liable for regular position updates. However, it is useful to identify the original mouse position, hence providing a reference all agents can share. To be the most precise, each agent, prior to the start of the simulation, spends its initial cycles standing on the start position, collecting values from the GPS. After 10 cycles (and 10 sensor readings), an average is computed on each parameter (x coordinate, y coordinate, and orientation). This average provides a reasonable approximation to the mouse original position, and is a reliable reference for the team of agents. One should note that the number 10 was obtained due to simple observation, and provided a good time-performance relationship, with deviations below 0.5 on this particular simulation parameters.

In order to execute a proper path planning, the CiberMouse agent must be able to obtain a map description from the readings it gets from the obstacle sensors. To register the map information, a bidimensional matrix is used, in which each position corresponds to 0.1 of the real map. This increase in granularity provides a mapping less suitable to errors. Each cell holds a probability of existence of obstacles, a value ranging from 0 to 1.

It was observable that the value of the reading varied inversely to the distance of the sensor to an obstacle. It is also known that the sensors are noisy. Knowing

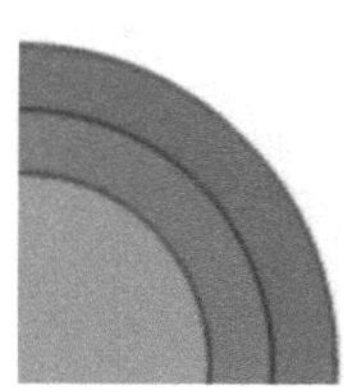

Fig. 1. Illustration of the area covered by each obstacle sensor

this, given a reading R, and a deviation D, an obstacle is between 1/(D + R) and 1/(D - R). The positions between the sensor and 1/(D + R) (light green in figure 1) can then be updated to have minimum probability of an obstacle. Another information that can be obtained from the simulation parameters is the minimum wall width (which will be referenced as W). The positions between 1/(D - R) and 1/(D + R) + W (red in figure 1) are likely to have an obstacle, thus its probability is increased. The positions between 1/(D + R) and 1/(D - R) (dark green in figure 1) have an average probability.

Taking the previous information into account, the probability matrix can be updated, on each cycle, with the information gathered from the sensors. Initially, each cell has a probability 0.5 of having an obstacle. On each cycle, for each sensor that has been requested, a circular sector with the same aperture of the sensor is drawn and the points inside it are processed. The radius of the circular sector is 1/(D + R) + W, which is the maximum distance at which the state of the world can be predicted with an acceptable precision. To avoid further errors, if this value is too big, a reference value of 20 cells is taken for the radius. The Bayes' theorem [4] is used to properly update the probability at each cell:

$$P(H|s_n) = \frac{P(s_n|H)P(H|s_{n-1})}{P(s_n|H)P(H|s_{n-1}) + P(s_n|\neg H)P(\neg H|s_{n-1})}$$

On the formula, $P(H|s_n)$ is the probability, at each cell, to have an obstacle given a certain reading at time n, and $P(s_n|H)$ is the probability, at each cell, to obtain a certain reading knowing that the cell is occupied. This last probabilities are easily deduced, as it was did on the previous paragraphs.

Another challenge is to find an effective way to process the cells the sensor covers. In order to achieve this, a circular sector is virtually drawn on the probability matrix, marking the boundary cells as visited. Then, starting at the center of the sector, all the cells marked as unvisited can be recursively visited and processed with in an algorithm known as flood-fill. To build the boundary, a rasterization algorithm known as midpoint or Bresenham algorithm is used, both for the partial circle [14,20] and the lines [6]. The algorithm is based on the sweep through a given axis, adding a proper increment/decrement to the other

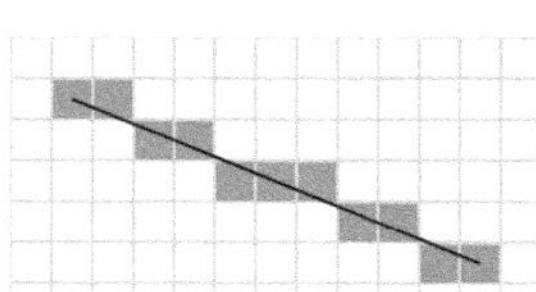

Fig. 2. Illustration of the result of Bresenham's line algorithm

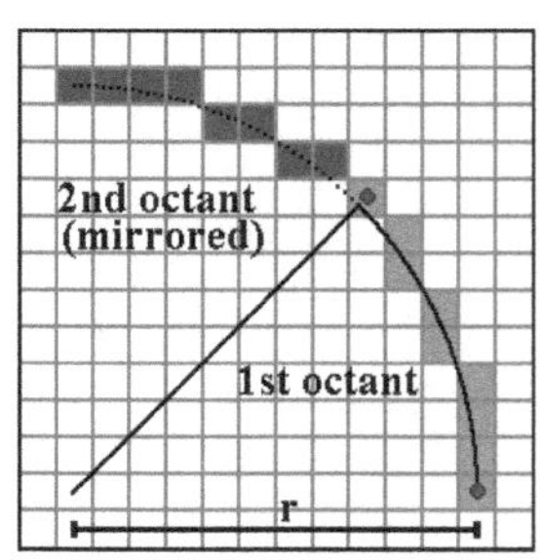

Fig. 3. Rasterization of a circle by the Bresenham algorithm

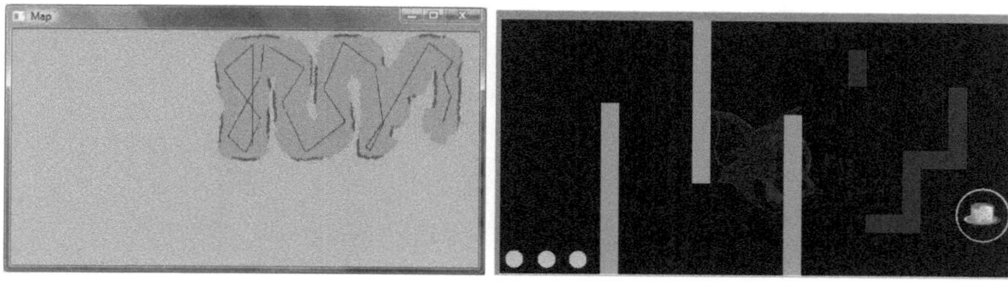

Fig. 4. Mapping of a maze obtained from sensor readings

coordinate. An example of a line and circle drawn by this algorithm can be seen in figures 2 and 3.

At this point, there's enough data to build and update a matrix of the map, as can be seen in figure 4.

3.2 Path Planning and Plan Execution

After obtaining a reasonable description of the environment, the agent must be able to plan a trip to the beacon. Since the environment is highly probabilistic and very susceptible of errors, there is the need to do some high level pre-processing before considering the cells into which the agent could move.

There are a lot of approaches to build a graph from the world definition. The one used is based on quadtrees [12,16]. The general approach is to recursively subdivide the map area into four areas until a given sector shares similar properties. In this case, the properties of interest are all the cells having a probability of existence of obstacle higher than 0.5, all the cells having a probability of existence of obstacle lower than 0.5 or all the cells having a probability of existence of obstacle equal to 0.5 (not visited yet). An efficient way to do this is by maintaining a matrix of size equal to the map matrix. In this matrix, the sum of all cells is kept with $x < x_i$ and $y < y_i$. This can be done in $\Theta(width * height)$ time, since:

$$sum[x][y] = sum[x-1][y] + sum[x][y-1] - sum[x-1][y-1] + probability[x][y]$$

Having this matrix calculated, the sum from (x_i, y_i) to (x_f, y_f) is given by:

$$\begin{aligned} sum((0,0),(x_f,y_f)) &= sum[x_f][y_f] \\ sum((x_i,y_i),(x_f,y_f)) &= sum((0,0),(x_f,y_f)) \\ &- sum((0,0),(x_i,y_f)) \\ &- sum((0,0),(x_f,y_i)) \\ &+ sum((0,0),(x_i,y_i)) \end{aligned}$$

With this function, obtaining a quadtree is quite easy. The idea is to, starting at $((0,0),(width,height))$, recursively subdivide the rectangle in four subrectangles

Fig. 5. Agent plan execution. Lines mark the path, the full circle corresponds to the next checkpoint.

until the sum of the sector is 0 or $width_i * height_i$ or the sector is still an unexplored area. On the first and last cases, the center of the polygon is used as a vertex for the high-level graph.

After obtaining a quadtree within a given map, the center of each unoccupied node is considered a node for the graph. Having this, an edge is added for each pair of points if they're visible one another (there's a clear path without obstacles between them).

With the graph built, a short path within those nodes can be computed using the A* search algorithm [9,13,16]. Having a collection of points which constitute the path, they are sequentially processed as beacons, using a strategy similar to the one used on the previous reactive agent [2], over which some additional rules were applied.

Using a path following strategy with an unknown map has some issues, because the map is constantly changing. To overcome the change that can lead to some erratic behaviour of the agent, a few additional rules to the plan execution were applied. First of all, it was observable that a path which leads to unknown areas is subject to almost constant change, which can lead to a lot of time being spent by the agent on twists and turns. It was seen that whenever a checkpoint was located behind a wall, the agent, while following it, occasionally made moves on the wall direction, wasting some time to be repositioned. The wall-following behaviour allows the agent to efficiently overcome obstacles whenever a checkpoint is situated behind them. An example run of the agent, following a path to a randomly chosen spot on the map, can be seen on figure 5.

3.3 Beacon Finding

The beacon finding strategy assumes a higher importance on this particular environment, since the beacon signal is, besides blocked from high walls, limited in its radius. The value of the radius isn't provided on the rules, but a value of 5 metric units was assumed through simple observation. Originally, if the mouse doesn't have a single clue where the beacon might be, it moves to a random unvisited position. Whenever the beacon signal is detected, a probabilistic mapping of its position starts being built. Each cell holds the number of times the beacon has been sighted. Whenever a signal from the beacon is received, the cells covered by a ray launched from the center of the mouse to the signal direction, of distance 10 (the maximum beacon coverage), are processed and their sights are incremented by 1. Having a total number of sights on the map, the probability of the beacon to be on a given cell is simply its number of sights over the total number of sights:

$$p[x][y] = \frac{sights[x][y]}{\sum_{i=0}^{width} \sum_{j=0}^{height} sights[i][j]}$$

Each agent then concludes that the beacon must be on the cell with higher probability. An example of a beacon area built with this strategy, and marked as yellow can be seen on figure 6.

Fig. 6. Probabilistic beacon area

4 Communication and Agent Interaction

Taking into account each agent's individual behaviour, there is also room for cooperation to maximize each one's utility. The first approach followed was based on each agent broadcasting the obstacle sensor readings it had on each cycle. This information, along with the sensor positions, allows for each agent to reconstruct the map with additional information. This alone increases each agent's world knowledge by a maximum factor equal to the number of agents on the simulation, providing that all are in range of each other and in different positions. The fact that the values exchanged are based on the sensor values allows each agent to use them differently, hence not forcing any world knowledge. A sample of this approach, using three mice, can be seen on figure 7.

Although this reduces the time each agent spends on finding the beacon, because the map is discovered cooperatively, it is also generally a good idea to broadcast the exact beacon position whenever one is found. This is done whenever an agent has sufficient information about it (i.e. has seen the beacon at least once) and the information passed are the cell coordinates with highest probability of beacon. Whenever an agent receives such a message, it increases the number of sights of the cell accordingly. This approach doesn't force an agent

Fig. 7. Mapping of an agent's world knowledge, using other agent's information

to fully accept another agent's information, as the number of previous beacon sights on another cell can still be superior.

The idea behind the sensor sharing was further improved, since it doesn't work well for agents who are far apart from each other. In order to partially overcome those situations, a network of agents was created, in which each agent, besides broadcasting their own sensor readings, broadcasts readings it hasn't seen before. This allows an agent to serve as a router for another one, complementing his world information. This implies that each agent keeps a record of the sensor readings it hasn't processed yet. This is easily done by sending, along with each sensor information, the time and id of the sender, thus identifying each particular message. Since each agent requests, at most, one obstacle sensor per cycle, the limit of 100 bytes is enough for each agent to broadcast, at least, 5 sensor readings.

5 Conclusions and Results

In order to test the benefits of communication on this particular problem, a team of 5 agents challenged 3 different mazes from the 2008 CiberMouse@RTSS competition. The tests were run with communication, without communication, with communication without networking and with communication and networking but without beacon position exchange. The results, in terms of number of mice to reach the beacon and percentage of map known can be seen on the following figures. All the tests were run under the rules of CiberMouse@RTSS 2008, except the elimination of GPS noise and every run had a simulation time of 5000 and key time of 2400.

Figures 8 to 10 show statistics on the number of agents to reach the target on the mazes from the 2008 competition. The first map is a rather simple one, yet surprisingly the absence of network provides better results than any other combination, allowing 5 agents to reach the target on 7 out of 10 attempts. This can be due to the increased simplicity of the map, which can lead to propagation of errors when network is in use. One other thing to note is that the absence of beacon information exchange provides a maximum of 4 agents reaching the target,

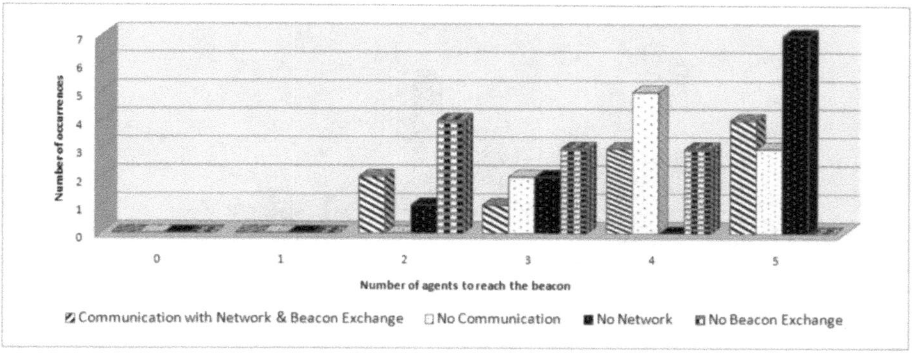

Fig. 8. Test results for the CiberMouse@RTSS08 Manga1 Lab, in terms of number of agents to reach the beacon

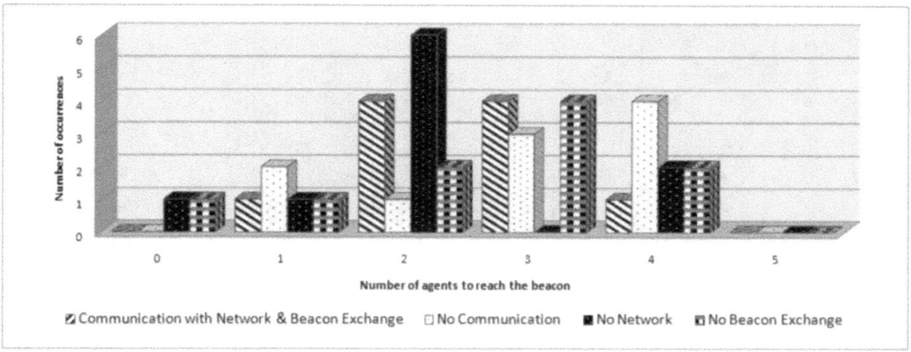

Fig. 9. Test results for the CiberMouse@RTSS08 Manga2 Lab, in terms of number of agents to reach the beacon

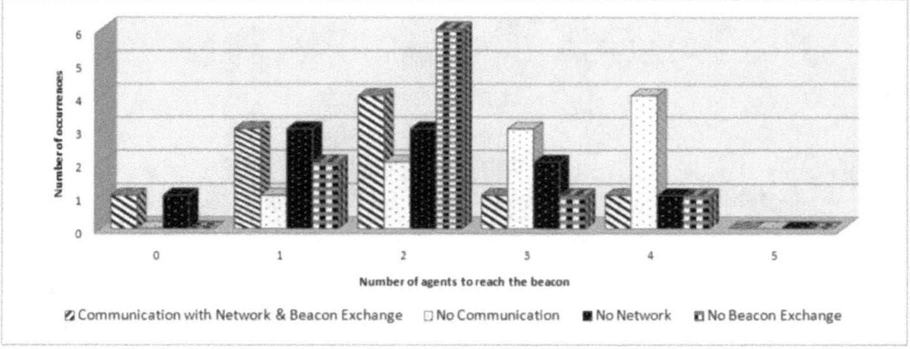

Fig. 10. Test results for the CiberMouse@RTSS08 Final Lab, in terms of number of agents to reach the beacon

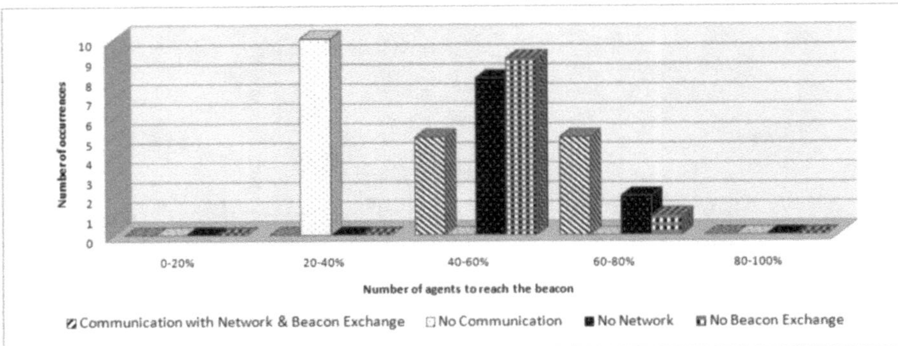

Fig. 11. Test results for the CiberMouse@RTSS08 Manga1 Lab, in terms of percentage of map known

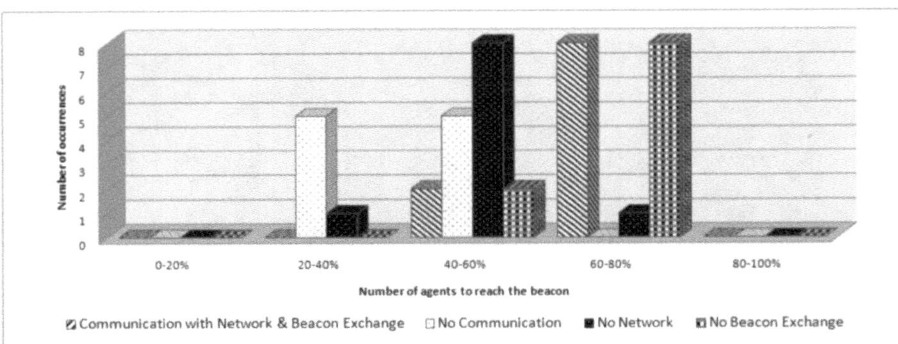

Fig. 12. Test results for the CiberMouse@RTSS08 Manga2 Lab, in terms of percentage of map known

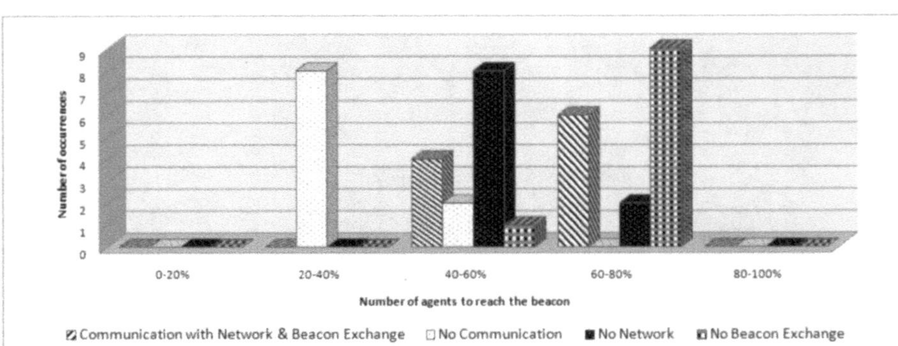

Fig. 13. Test results for the CiberMouse@RTSS08 Final Lab, in terms of percentage of map known

thus not maximizing the overall utility. On the second map, no combination is able to get 4 agents in the target, due to the map complexity. The results for this map are even more surprising, as no communication at all seems to provide better results. This might be due to errors propagating on the probabilistic mapping procedure. However, communicaton with network and beacon exchange provides the most consistent results, less subject to noise introduced by the simulator. The third and last map results build on the theory described for the second map, as no communication at all provides the best overall performance. This map has the particularity of the beacon being visible but not reachable right from the start of the run. By denying communication, the wall-following behaviour eventually leads the agents to the beacon, thus allowing for better results without communication, as this is less suitable to errors propagating from the mapping procedure.

Figures 11 to 13 show statistics on the percentage of the map known by the end of the run on the mazes from the 2008 competition. The results on this are rather similar for all 3 maps, as communication with network always leads to a better overall knowledge of the map. The second and third maps also show an increase of the map knowledge when beacon exchange is disabled. This can be easily explained due to the fact that whenever an agent has a known position for the beacon, it exits from the exploratory behaviour and proceeds through the shortest path to the target. Whenever this happens early in the run, the agents tend to lead similar paths, thus exploring the same areas of the map and reducing the overall map knowledge. One thing one should note is that the average percentage of map known increases when communication is in use, and allows a broader knowledge for the team when networking is used. Answering the questions from section 1, one can say that communicating the individual world knowledge is too costly for this particular problem, so single sensor events are much more useful. As seen from the results, one should always communicate as long as the overall utility of the group of agents increases. The sharing of the beacon position always provides better results and the broadcast of the sensor readings enables an increase on the overall map knowledge. The latter doesn't always provide better practical results due to the noise involved on the mapping procedure. This innovative approach in communication enables a group of agents to be very aware of its surroundings without the share of too much information, thus avoiding the need for encryption. In fact, by sharing and broadcasting the sensor readings, each agent performs reasonably better than on its own. The strategy implemented on communication along with the mapping, path planning and beacon finding procedures follows a complete approach on building a team of autonomous agents.

Acknowledgements

This work was partially supported by FCT Project PTDC/EIA/70695/2006 "ACORD - Adaptative Coordination of Robotic Teams".

References

1. Almeida, L., Azevedo, J.L., Cunha, B., Fonseca, P., Lau, N., Pereira, A.: Micro-Rato Robotics Contest: Technical Problems and Solutions. In: Proc. Controlo 2006: Seventh Portugese Conference on Automatic Control, Lisboa, PT (2006)
2. Azevedo, J., Oliveira, M., Pacheco, P.: Ciber-Rato - A Simple Subsumption Architecture, Intelligent Robotics, FEUP (2008/2009)
3. Azevedo, J., Oliveira, M., Pacheco, P.: Probabilistic Mapping and A* Navigation on a Ciber-Rato agent, Intelligent Robotics, FEUP (2008/2009)
4. Bayes, T.: An Essay Toward Solving a Problem in the Doctrine of Chances. Philosophical Transactions of the Royal Society of London 53, 370-418 (1764)
5. Borenstein, J., Everett, B., Feng, L.: Navigating Mobile Robots: Systems and Techniques. A. K. Peters, Ltd, Wellesley, MA (1996); ISBN 1-56881-058-X
6. Bresenham, J.E.: Algorithm for computer control of a digital plotter. IBM Systems Journal 4(1), 25–30 (1965)
7. CiberMouse@RTSS08 Official Site (January 29, 2009), `http://www.ieeta.pt/lse/ciberRTSS08/`
8. CiberRato 2008 Rules and Technical Specifications (January 29, 2009), `http://microrato.ua.pt/main/Docs/RegrasCiberRato2008_EN.pdf`
9. Dechter, R., Pearl, J.: Generalized best-first search strategies and the optimality of A*. Journal of the ACM 32(3), 505–536 (1985), doi:10.1145/3828.3830
10. Djugash, J., Singh, S., Kantor, G., Zhang, W.: Range-only slam for robots operating cooperatively with sensor networks. In: Proceedings of IEEE Int. Conference on Robotics and Automation 2006 (ICRA 2006), pp. 2078–2084 (2006)
11. Fenwick, J., Newman, P., Leonard, J.: Cooperative concurrent mapping and localization. In: IEEE International Conference on Robotics and Automation Proceedings ICRA 2002, vol. 2, pp. 1810–1817 (2002)
12. Finkel, R., Bentley, J.L.: Quad Trees: A Data Structure for Retrieval on Composite Keys. Acta Informatica 4(1), 1–9 (1974), doi:10.1007/BF00288933
13. Hart, P.E., Nilsson, N.J., Raphael, B.: A Formal Basis for the Heuristic Determination of Minimum Cost Paths. IEEE Transactions on Systems Science and Cybernetics SSC 4(2), 100–107 (1968), doi:10.1109/TSSC.1968.300136
14. Pitteway, M.L.V.: Algorithm for Drawing Ellipses or Hyperbolae with a Digital Plotter. Computer J. 10(3), 282–289 (1967)
15. Reis, L.P.: Coordination in Multi-Robot Systems: Applications in the Simulation League (January 29, 2009), `http://paginas.fe.up.pt/~lpreis/robo2008`
16. Reis, L.P., Lau, N.: Intelligent Robotics - Mapping and Navigation (January 29, 2009), `http://paginas.fe.up.pt/~lpreis/robo2008`
17. RoboCup Official Site (January 29, 2009), `http://www.robocup.org/`
18. Shenoy, S., Tan, J.: Simultaneous localization and mobile robot navigation in a hybrid sensor network. In: Proceedings of IEEE/RSJ Int. Conference on Intelligent Robots and Systems 2005 (IROS 2005), vol. 1 (2005)
19. Thrun, S.: Robotic Mapping: A Survey. In: Lakemeyer, G., Nebel, B. (eds.) Exploring Artificial Intelligence in the New Millenium (2002)
20. Van Aken, J.R.: An Efficient Ellipse Drawing Algorithm. CG&A 4(9), 24–35 (1984)
21. Wanas, N.: Research Interests (January 25, 2009), `http://pami.uwaterloo.ca/~nwanas/research.htm`

Embodied Language Acquisition: A Proof of Concept

Aneesh Chauhan[1], Amanda Nascimento[3], Bruno Werneck[4], and Luís Seabra Lopes[1,2]

[1] IEETA, Universidade de Aveiro, Aveiro, 3810-193, Portugal
[2] DETI, Universidade de Aveiro, Aveiro, 3810-193, Portugal
[3] Instituto de Computação, Universidade Estadual de Campinas, Avenida Albert Einstein, 1251 Caixa, Postal 6176, 13083-970, Campinas, SP, Brasil
[4] Grupo Olimpo, Rua T-55, nº 740, Setor Bueno, 74223-230, Goiânia, Goiás, Brasil
{aneesh.chauhan,lsl}@ua.pt,
{amanda.nascimento,brunowerneck}@gmail.com

Abstract. For robots to interact with humans at the language level, it becomes fundamental that robots and humans share a common language. In this paper, a social language grounding paradigm is adopted to teach a robotic arm basic vocabulary about objects in its environment. A human user, acting as an instructor, teaches the names of the objects present in their shared field of view. The robotic agent grounds these words by associating them to visual category descriptions. A component-based object representation is presented. An instance based approach is used for category representation. An instance is described by its components and geometric relations between them. Each component is a color blob or an aggregation of neighboring color blobs. The categorization strategy is based on graph matching. The learning/grounding capacity of the robot is assessed over a series of semi-automated experiments and the results are reported.

1 Introduction

Robotics is often described as "the intelligent connection of perception to action" [1]. Although we are far off from an all-satisfying definition of intelligence, there is a consensus amongst researchers over a set of properties any intelligent system should exhibit [11]: ability to learn, ability to reason, responsiveness to external stimuli, and ability to communicate. Sentience can be described as a mix of these components.

Motivated by the need to create user friendly robots, there is an increasing interest in the field of robotics to build sentient robots. The state of the art robots (e.g. Rhino [2], Keepon [8], Leo [18]) have shown a certain degree of sentience. This paper introduces one such robot, which was built primarily to study the process of grounding a language.

For extended adaptability, flexibility and user-friendliness, a robot will need to understand, use and share the language with its human users, requiring human users to act as teachers or mediators ([12], [16]). Here language is being considered as a cultural product [10], which is created/acquired through social transmission. Both horizontal ([15], [17]) and vertical modes ([7], [16]) of language transmission have been studied in populations of robots.

L. Seabra Lopes et al. (Eds.): EPIA 2009, LNAI 5816, pp. 263–274, 2009.

In the present paper, language acquisition follows vertical transmission, where a human instructor gradually teaches the robot the names of the objects in their shared field of view. The presented robot grounds the names of these objects by associating them with their respective concept descriptions. The instructor can also provide corrective feedback in case of misclassification.

Language processing involves manipulation of symbols. By symbol it is meant a pattern that represents some entity in the world by association, resemblance or convention [12]. These symbols have no meaning, unless they are grounded in reality [5]. The robot presented in this paper grounds the names of the categories by associating them with sensor-based concept descriptions.

Language acquisition is an open-ended process. Categories as well as their corresponding names will have to be acquired incrementally. An open-ended category learning and language acquisition system must be supported by long-term learning capabilities. Long-term learning is usually included at the core of cognitive theories [6]. Work reported in this paper was built atop a lifelong category learning platform previously described in [12]. This paper introduces a novel component-based approach to object representation, category learning and recognition. The performance of this method was analyzed over a series of experiments.

The presented robot comprises a robotic arm and a camera to help it perceive as well as operate in its surroundings. Action capabilities include linguistic response to the user and the manipulation of objects by the robotic arm.

This paper is structured as follows: Section 2 describes the robot's hardware and software architecture. Section 3 provides an overview of robotic arm control. Section 4 details the novel component-based learning and categorization methodologies. Section 5 reports the conducted experiments and Section 6 presents the conclusions.

2 Agent Architecture

Physical Architecture. The robot is physically embodied with a robotic arm and a camera, while all its cognitive functions are carried out on an attached computer. The robot's world includes a user, a scenario visually shared with the user and objects whose names the user may wish to teach.

The robotic arm is an SG6-UT[1] educational arm manufactured by Crust Crawler Robotics (Fig. 1). It is shipped with a PSC-USB board (Parallax Servo Controller with USB interface) and contains 6 servos for 5 arm joints and a gripper, comprising 6 degrees of freedom. The pay load of this arm is around 400 grams. A client interface was developed for the PSC-USB enabling to control the arm directly from the computer. The camera is an IEEE1394 compliant digital camera[2]. It is placed in a fixed position over the work area of the robotic arm. This device acts as the primary perception instrument for the robotic agent. The computer runs the human-robot communication interface, the visual perception module, learning and recognition systems and robotic arm control functions.

---

[1] SG6-UT - a 6 degree of freedom robotic arm, supplied online at: http://www.crustcrawler.com/

[2] IEEE 1394 compliant firwire camera called "fire-i", supplied online by Unibrain at: http://www.unibrain.com/Products/VisionImg/Fire_i_DC.htm

Fig. 1. The CrustCrawler SG6-UT robotic arm

Software Architecture. The robot's software includes a perception system, a learning and recognition system and an action system. The user, not visible to the robot, will act as the instructor. Fig. 2 illustrates the complete system architecture and the relations between its various parts.

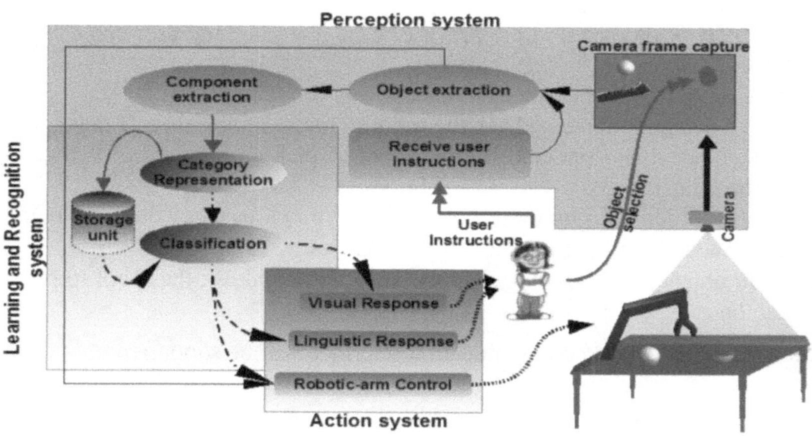

Fig. 2. System architecture

Perception System. The keyboard, the mouse and the camera are the sources of input to the perception system. The perception system extracts the image of the object selected by the user (by mouse clicking). The publicly available library for vision routines openCV[3] has been used for capturing the frames from the camera and extracting the object from the image. If the robot has been instructed to perform either learning or recognition, the extracted object is further processed to find its visual components. A novel strategy based on object's color and shape information was implemented for extracting these components (see Section 4).

Learning and Recognition System. An original approach to category learning using graph-based object and category representation is proposed. Section 4 is devoted to a thorough explanation of these modules.

[3] http://opencv.willowgarage.com/wiki/

Action System. The primary task of the action system is to provide appropriate feedback to the user. Depending on the user instructions and the information received from the previous cognition modules, the action system can perform actions of the following types:

1. Linguistic response: provide the classification results back to the user,
2. Visual response: Visually report the results of the "search and locate" tasks, and
3. Manipulation actions: the robotic arm manipulates the objects in the robot's environment (details on arm dynamics and control are discussed in Section 3).

Human-Robot Interaction. Using a simple menu-based interface, the user can select (by mouse-clicking) any object from the visible scene, thereby enabling shared attention. The user can choose the instruction she/he wants the robot to follow as well as teach new words. The following instructions are supported:

1. Teach the category name of the selected object;
2. Ask the category name of the selected object, which the agent will predict based on previously learned knowledge;
3. If the category predicted in the previous case is wrong, the user can send a correction.
4. Ask the robot to pick the selected object using the robotic arm;
5. Provide a category name and ask the robot to locate an instance of that category;
6. Provide a category name and ask the robot to pick an instance of that category using the arm;
7. If the object identified by the robot in the two previous cases does not belong to the requested category, the user can provide its true category;
8. Once an object has been picked, select a location and ask the robot to place the object there.

In the future, a speech based communication interface will be supported.

3 Robotic Arm Control

To pick an object using the robotic arm, it is necessary to know the exact placement and the orientation of that object. Since the camera is the only available sensor, the suitable picking position is found by further processing the extracted object image. A linear mapping between camera and arm coordinates is assumed.

Finding Grasp Position and Orientation. The object should be grasped such that it does not rotate or fall down. A suitable picking location (see Fig 3) is found by taking the following conditions into account:

1. The gripper should be centered at the geometric center of the object
2. The distances *A1B1*, *A2B2* and *A3B3* must be less than the maximum gripper width;
3. The areas of the triangles formed by the points *A1A2A3* and *B1B2B3* must be less than a threshold (ideally zero);
4. Angles α and β between the gripper ends and lines *A1A3* and *B1B3* respectively, should be close to zero.

Depending on the object's structure, there will be more than one possible location to pick it up. The first suitable location to pick the object is used. Once the joint angles have been obtained, these values are passed to the arm's servo controller, for it to pick up the object.

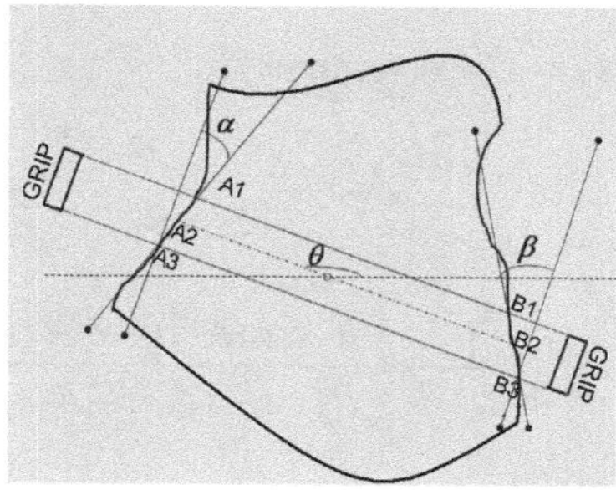

Fig. 3. A hypothetical object and one possible gripper position

Arm Kinematics. Fig. 4a shows a simplified model of the arm. R_1, R_2 *and* R_3 are the arm link lengths and α_1, α'_2, α_2, α_3 and α_4 are the joint angles to be determined. α_1 can be easily found by using basic trigonometry:

$$\alpha_1 = \tan^{-1}\left(\frac{y}{x}\right)$$

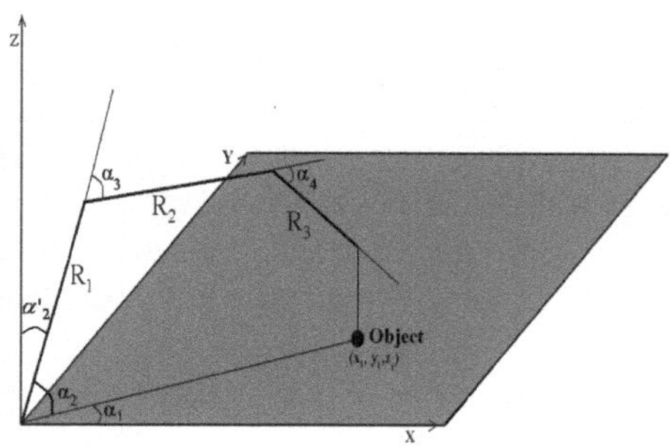

(a)

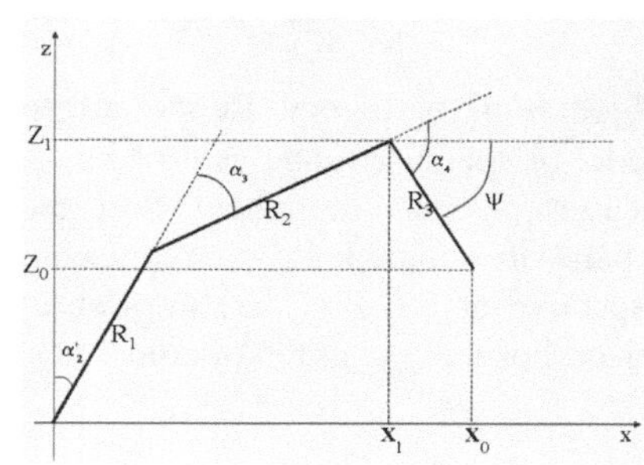

(b)

Fig. 4. (a) A simplified model showing arm joints and the object location; (b) Robotic arm plane

To calculate the rest of the angles, consider the plane of the robotic arm, as in Fig. 4b. x_0 and z_0 are given by:

$$x_0 = R_1 \cdot \sin(\alpha'_2) + R_2 \cdot \sin(\alpha'_2 + \alpha_3) + R_3 \cdot \sin(\alpha'_2 + \alpha_3 + \alpha_4)$$
$$z_0 = R_1 \cdot \cos(\alpha'_2) + R_2 \cdot \cos(\alpha'_2 + \alpha_3) + R_3 \cdot \cos(\alpha'_2 + \alpha_3 + \alpha_4) \quad (1)$$

We have two equations and three variables to determine. To solve this problem, the angle Ψ between the third link and the horizontal coordinate is forced to be $\pi/2$. This means, the wrist of the robotic arm will always be perpendicular to the base of the table. This causes no significant problem, since it is the best position for a successful grasp. Given this, Z_1 and X_1 can be determined by:

$$\begin{aligned} Z_1 &= Z_o + R_3 \\ X_1 &= X_o \end{aligned} \tag{2}$$

Using (1) and (2), α_3 and α'_2 can be determined as:

$$\alpha_3 = \pm\cos^{-1}\left[\frac{\left(Z_1^2 + X_1^2 - R_1^2 - R_2^2\right)}{\left(2R_2R_1\right)}\right]$$

$$\alpha'_2 = \pm\tan^{-1}\left[\frac{X_1(R_1 + R_2\cos(\alpha_3)) - Z_1R_2\sin(\alpha_3)}{Z_1(R_1 + R_2\cos(\alpha_3) + W_1R_2\sin(\alpha_3)}\right]$$

Now the final unknown angle can be given as:

$$\alpha_4 = \psi - \alpha'_2 - \alpha_3$$

4 Category Learning and Recognition

This paper uses a component-based approach to category learning and object categorization. An object instance is represented by its components and geometric relations between them. The relations between components are represented using non-directed labeled graphs. Taking into consideration the attributes of the nodes and edges, a novel strategy for categorization is also proposed.

Object and Category Representations. An object is represented using a graph model of spatial arrangement of its components, referred as *graph of components*. In such graph, each component is represented by a different node. The relation between a pair of components is represented by a non-directed edge connecting their respective nodes. Fig. 5c shows an example graph of components for the toy train object. Formally, a graph of components can be described as:

$$G = < C, R, A>$$

where the three items are the following:

- $C = \{c_i\}$, $i = 1,\ldots, n_C$, is the set of all components of the object, represented by nodes in the graph;
- $R = \{(c_i, c_j)\}$, $c_i \in C$, $c_j \in C$, is the set of existing contact relations between components, represented as edges in the graph; and
- $A = \{(c_i, c_j, c_k)\}$, is the set of all ternary relations between components such that $(c_i, c_j) \in R$, $(c_i, c_k) \in R$.

The properties of a graph of components are derived from the organization of the components inside the object. Each component c_i (*i.e.* each node of the graph) is characterized by the following features:

- a_i - relative area, given by the ratio of number of pixels in the component to the total number of pixels present in the object;
- r_i – relative radius, given by the ratio between the radius of a circle, with the same area as that of the component, and the radius of a circle with the same area as that of the whole object; and
- d_i - relative degree, given by the ratio between the degree of a node and the total number of nodes in the graph.

The contact relation $(c_i,c_j)\in R$ between connected components c_i and c_j is characterized by a single feature:

- d_{ij} - relative distance between two connected components c_i and c_j. This is measured as the ratio of the distance between the geometric centers of two connected components and the diameter of the object.

Finally, each ternary relation $(c_i, c_j, c_k)\in A$ is also characterized by a single feature:

- a_{ijk} - the relative angle between edges (c_i, c_j) and (c_i, c_k). The ratio of the smaller angle between the two edges with respect to π is taken into use.

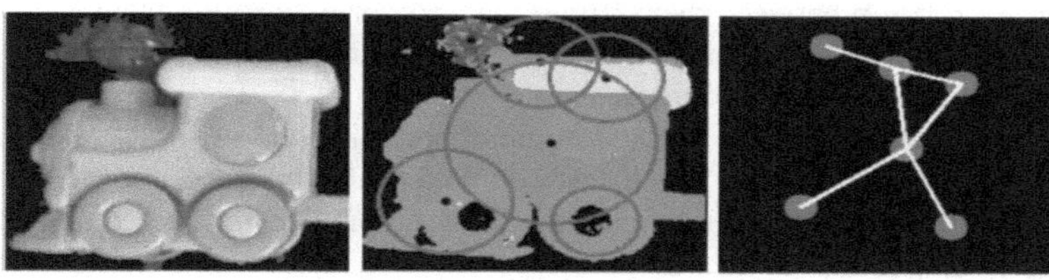

a b c

Fig. 5. a) The "toy train" object; b) Extracted components and the circles with the same area as that of the components, centered at the geometric centres of the components (the components are extracted in HSV color space, but here, for visual perception the second image is converted back into RGB); c) Graph of components of the given object

The graph features listed above give a scale, translation and rotation invariant representation of an object. An instance-based approach is adopted for category representation. The learning module stores the object instance (i.e. the graph's structural information as well as all its features) in an internal database. A category is represented by one or more instances that belong to that category.

Component Extraction. This work uses the HSV (Hue, Saturation and Value) color space for locating and extracting object components. A list of the most relevant color ranges in the given object is initially computed: $[R_1, \ldots, R_n]$. Each range R_i is represented as a tuple (a, b, m, A), where a and b are respectively the start and end values (hue) of the color range, m is the most frequent color value and A is the area of the object (number of pixels) in that color range. These ranges are found using the algorithm described in [13]. Once the color ranges have been found, the image is modified by replacing all the hue values in a range R_i by its corresponding most frequent color m.

The object image is then processed such that the neighboring pixels with same hue are aggregated to form the initial set of components. Connections are established between any two components physically in contact with each other (i.e. with adjacent pixels). These components are further merged based on the following steps:

1. Compute the geometric center and the average radius of each component and abstract the component as a circle with that radius and center;
2. If the circles of any two components overlap considerably (covering more than 90% of at least one of the components) they are merged to form a single component.
3. If the circles of any two components overlap, covering an area between 35% and 90% of at least one of the components, check for hue similarity. If the hue values present in one component are similar to the ones present in the other, merge the components;
4. Repeat these steps until no components can be merged.

Figure 5 displays the components and contact relations for the "toy train" object. A contact relation between any two components c_i and c_j is found based on the following criterion:

1. If c_i and c_j are physically connected or extremely close to each other, there is a contact relation between them. If any two border pixels, one from each component, are closer than a threshold (3 pixels in the implementation), then the components are considered connected.
2. If a component is found to have no neighbor using the previous rule, then it is considered connected to its closest component. In this case, for simplicity, the distance between (the borders of) the circles, centered in the geometric centers of the components, is measured.
3. The graph structure is derived directly from the contact relations. However, this strategy has the drawback that the graph may not always be completely connected. That is, instead of one connected graph, the graph of components may end up as a set of two or more connected subgraphs. This problem is solved by locating components, one in each subgraph, with the closest contact relation and then connecting these nodes.

Object Classification. To compute a measure of similarity between a target object O and a category instance I, the graph structure similarity of the respective graphs, G_O and G_I, is evaluated. This is based on locating the Maximum Common Subgraph (MCS) between them (Fig. 6). [3] defines MCS as "*the largest set of all linked nodes that the two have in common*". It is important to notice here that MCS is not always unique. Once $MCS(G_O, G_I)$ is obtained, the following similarity measure is computed:

$$S_{MCS}(G_O,G_I)=\frac{g(MCS(G_O,G_I))}{g(G_O)+g(G_I)-g(MCS(G_O,G_I))} \tag{3}$$

where $g(G)$ corresponds to the sum of the total number of nodes and total number of edges of a graph G.

If $MCS(G_O, G_I)$ is not null, it implies the existence of a common structure of nodes and edges between the graphs G_O and G_I. Having a common structure makes it possible to build a mapping between nodes and edges of these graphs. This mapping is found by performing breadth first search [4]. Considering Fig. 6 again, we can see that the mapping between the nodes and edges of graphs G_O and G_I can be:

- Mapping between nodes: a↔1; b↔2; c↔3
- Mapping between edges: ab↔12; bc↔23; ca↔31

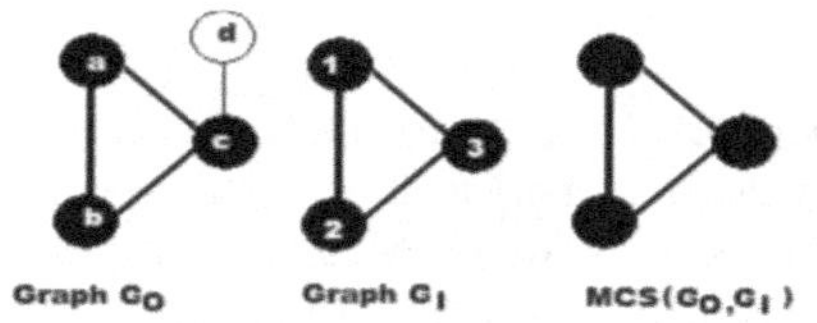

Fig. 6. An example of $MCS(G_O, G_I)$

where "↔" indicates the mapping. In a similar manner the angles can also be mapped. Once the $MCS(G_O, G_I)$ and the mappings for the two graphs G_O and G_I are known, their dissimilarity is measured using the following auxiliary function:

$$d_X(G_O, G_I) = \sqrt{\frac{\sum_{i=1}^{n}\left(\frac{\sum_{j=1}^{k}(O_X(i,j) - I_X(map(i),j))^2}{k} \times M_X(i) + (1 - M_X(i))\right)}{n}}$$

where

- X represents each of the three items of each graph of components (i.e. the set of components, C, the set of contact relations, R, and the set of ternary relations, A);
- n is the cardinality of X in G_O;
- k is the number of features of each element of X (according to previous explanations, k=3 for the components in C and k=1 for the elements in R and A);
- $O_X(i,j)$ is the value of feature j for element i of item X of G_O;
- $I_X(i,j)$ is the value of feature j for element i of item X of G_I;
- $map(i)$ is the element in G_I to which element i of G_O is mapped
- $M_X(i)$ = 1 if element i of item X of G_O is mapped to a corresponding element in G_I, otherwise $M_X(i) = 0$

Based on this, the dissimilarity between the two objects is computed as follows:

$$d(G_O, G_I) = w_C\ d_C(G_O, G_I) + w_R\ d_R(G_O, G_I) + w_A\ d_A(G_O, G_I) \quad (4)$$

where w_C, w_R, and w_A are weights, with $w_C + w_R + w_A = 1$ (in the implementation $w_C = 0.55$; $w_R = 0.35$; *and* $w_A = 0.1$).

Joining the similarity measure in (3) and the dissimilarity measure in (4), the final measure of graph similarity is given as:

$$S(G_O, G_I) = w_S\ S_{MCS}(G_O, G_I) + w_d\ (1\text{-}d(G_O, G_I))$$

where w_S and w_d are weights (0.3 and 0.7, respectively, in the implementation).

Given an object to be classified, its graph of components is compared with the graphs of all the stored instances. The category of the instance most similar to the object to be classified (*i.e.* with the highest $S(G_O, G_I)$) is identified as the category of that object.

5 Experimental Evaluation

The objective of the experiments was to evaluate the performance of the proposed component-based learning approach in a supervised, incremental, open-ended and online learning system. The system was evaluated using the *teaching protocol* proposed in [12]. In each experiment, categories are incrementally taught until the learning capacity of the agent reaches a breakpoint. Classification precision is used as the primary performance evaluation measure. It's evolution from start to breakpoint is analyzed in each experiment.

It should be noted that, because of the exhaustive nature of this protocol, a single experiment can take weeks to finish. Authors have previously conducted a long duration experiment [14] which took more than a week's time. So as to help facilitate later experiments, the images from this experiment were stored along with their respective category names as provided by the human user. Overall, a database of almost 7000 images (pertaining to 68 categories) was created [14].

The most time consuming task, with respect to experiments, was having a human user to show a new object instance every few seconds. For that purpose, a simulated user was implemented. The actions of the simulated user are limited to the teaching actions of the human user: teaching, asking and correction. When the simulated user runs out of images in a particular category, the real user is called to show additional instances. This way, semi-automated experiments can be carried out. In total, a series of 10 semi-automated experiments were conducted (see Table 1).

Figure 7 shows the evolution of classification precision in the first experiment. In general, the introduction of a new category to the agent leads to the deterioration in

Table 1. Summary of all experiments

Exp #	# categories at breakpoint	# Question /correction iterations	Classific. precision at breakpoint (%)	# instances per category (± std)
1	9	345	48	17 ± 7.42
2	9	384	56	18 ± 11.26
3	7	289	62	22 ± 10.58
4	11	559	66	23 ± 13.21
5	8	281	54	18 ± 7.34
6	5	174	60	21 ± 6.88
7	9	460	33	28 ± 11.63
8	7	206	52	13 ± 4.81
9	11	656	45	29 ± 13.74
10	6	142	61	12 ± 4.05

classification precision followed by gradual recovery. This process continues until the system starts to confuse the category descriptions to an extent that it can no longer recover. All the experiments followed similar evolution pattern. This pattern has been previously observed in [12] and [14].

In the first experiment, the agent could learn 8 categories, reaching the breakpoint after the introduction of the 9th category. For each of the introduced categories, the performance evolved in the standard way: initial instability followed by recovery. After introducing the last category, classification precision mostly fluctuates around 55% without showing any sign of recovery. This trend is noticed for around 150 question/correction iterations leading the simulated user to conclude that the breakpoint was reached.

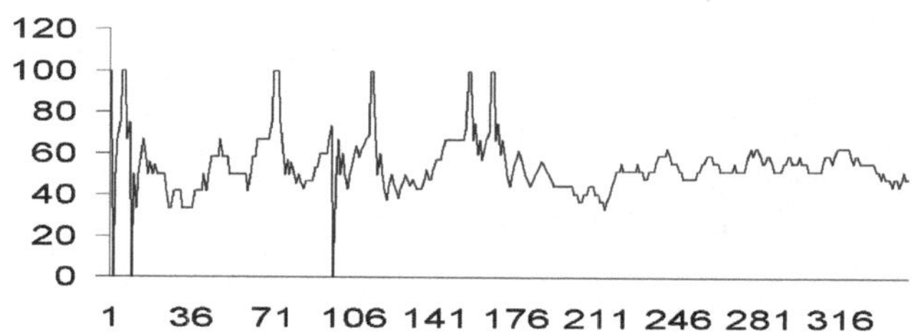

Fig. 7. Evolution of classification precision versus number of question/correction interactions in a single experiment (breakpoint at the 9th category)

6 Conclusions and Future Work

This paper presented a physically embodied robot with the abilities to learn throughout its life, respond intelligently to external stimuli and communicate with its users. The robot has both cognitive and functional abilities. It interacts with human users in a shared environment, where the human user acts as a teacher and helps the robot in acquiring the vocabulary about the objects present in their shared surroundings.

The robot's learning system incrementally grounds the names of new objects introduced by a human user. This system was built on top of a novel component based category representation strategy. The components of the object are extracted using only color information. An original graph based methodology was proposed to represent the spatial arrangement of the components inside an object. A new classification strategy based on a graph similarity measure was also implemented.

This limitation on the number of words learned implies that the discrimination capability of the presented strategy in its current state is very limited, and there is definitely room for improvement. We believe, however, that the approach is promising. It is worth mentioning that the results reported here are comparable to other works with respect to the number of learned words (12 words [12]; 5 words [9]; 12 words [19] etc.). However, certain works have reported learning considerably more words (e.g. 68 words [14].

Future work will entail refining the quality of the component extraction approach, which depends highly on the image quality. An efficient handling of this noise will be crucial in taking this method further. Improvement of similarity measures, in a way that is more robust to variations in detected components, is also expected to improve the overall performance.

Acknowledgments. The Portuguese Research Foundation (FCT) supported this work under contract POSI/SRI/48794/2002 (project "LANGG: Language Grounding for Human-Robot Communication"), which is partially funded by FEDER, and a PhD scholarship to the first author.

References

1. Brady, M.: Artificial Intelligence and Robotics. Artificial Intelligence 26(1), 79–121 (1985)
2. Burgard, W., Fox, D., Hähnel, D., Lakemeyer, G., Schulz, D., Steiner, W., Thrun, S., Cremers, A.B.: Real Robots for the Real World – The RHINO Museum Tour-Guide Project. In: Proc. of the AAAI 1998 Spring Symposium on Integrating Robotics Research, Taking the Next Leap, Stanford, CA (1998)
3. Cunningham, C., Weber, R., Proctor, J.M., Fowler, C., Murphy, M.: Investigating Graphs in Textual Case-Based Reasoning. In: ECBR 2004, pp. 573–586 (2004)
4. Diestel, R.: Graph Theory. Springer, Heidelberg (2000)
5. Harnad, S.: The symbol grounding problem. Physica D 42, 335–346 (1990)
6. Kennedy, W.G., Trafton, J.G.: Long-Term Symbolic Learning. Cognitive Systems Research 8, 237–247 (2007)
7. Kirby, S., Hurford, J.: The Emergence of Linguistic Structure: An overview of the Iterated Learning Model. In: Cangelosi, A., Parisi, D. (eds.) Simulating the Evolution of Language, pp. 121–148. Springer, Heidelberg (2002)
8. Kozima, H., Nakagawa, C.: Social robots for children: practice in communication-care. In: 9th IEEE International Workshop on Advanced Motion Control (2006)
9. Levinson, S.E., Squire, K., Lin, R.S., McClain, M.: Automatic language acquisition by an autonomous robot. In: Proceedings of the AAAI Spring Symposium on Developmental Robotics, pp. 21–23 (March 2005)
10. Love, N.: Cognition and the language myth. Language Sciences 26, 525–544 (2004)
11. Seabra Lopes, L., Connell, J.H.: Semisentient robots: Routes to integrated intelligence. IEEE Intelligent Systems 16(5), 10–14 (2001)
12. Seabra Lopes, L., Chauhan, A.: How many Words can my Robot learn? An Approach and Experiments with One-Class Learning. Interaction Studies, vol 8(1), 53–81 (2007)
13. Seabra Lopes, L., Chauhan, A., Silva, J.: Towards long-term visual learning of object categories in human-robot interaction. In: Maia Neves, J.C., Santos, M.F., Machado, J.M. (eds.) New Trends in Artificial Intelligence, APPIA, pp. 623–634 (2007)
14. Seabra Lopes, L., Chauhan, A.: Open-ended category learning for language acquisition. Connection Science 8(4) (2008)
15. Steels, L.: Language games for autonomous robots. IEEE Intelligent Systems 16(5), 16–22 (2001)
16. Steels, L., Kaplan, F.: AIBO's first words: The social learning of language and meaning. Evolution of Communication 4(1), 3–32 (2002)
17. Steels, L.: Evolving Grounded Communication for Robots. Trends in Cognitive Science 7(7), 308–312 (2003)
18. Thomaz, A.L., Breazeal, C.: Robot Learning via Socially Guided Exploration. In: Proc. of ICDL 2006, Imperial College, London (2007)
19. Yu, C.: The emergence of links between lexical acquisition and object categorization: A computational study. Connection Science 17(3), 381–397 (2005)

Predictive Control for Behavior Generation of Omni-directional Robots

João Cunha, Nuno Lau, João Rodrigues, Bernardo Cunha, and José Luis Azevedo

IEETA / Department of Electronics, Telecommunications and Informatics
University of Aveiro, Portugal
{joao.cunha,nunolau,jmr,mbc,jla}@ua.pt

Abstract. This paper describes the approach developed by the CAMBADA robotic soccer team to address physical constraints regarding omni-directional motion control, with special focus on system delay. CAMBADA robots carry inherent delays which associated with discrete time control results in non-instant, non-continuous control degrading the performance over time. Besides a natural maximum velocity, CAMBADA robots have also a maximum acceleration limit implemented at software level to provide motion stability as well as current peaks avoidance on DC motors. Considering the previous constraints, such as the cycle time and the overall sensor-action delay, compensations can be made to improve the robot control. Since CAMBADA robots are among the slowest robots in the RoboCup Medium Size League, such compensations can help to improve both several behaviours as well as a better field coverage formation.

1 Introduction

CAMBADA[1] is the University of Aveiro's robotic soccer team. The project was started in 2003 by the IEETA[2] ATRI[3] research group which involves researchers from different scientific areas such as image analysis and processing, control, artificial intelligence, multi-agent coordination, sensor fusion.

CAMBADA currently participates in RoboCup's Middle Size League. Robo Cup[4] is an international project focused on fostering innovation in robotics and related fields. In this league a team of 4 to 6 robots with maximum dimensions of $50cm \times 50cm \times 80cm$ and a maximum weight of 40kg play soccer in a $12m \times 18m$ field complying with robot-adapted official FIFA rules [1].

[1] CAMBADA is an acronym for Cooperative Autonomous Mobile roBots with Advanced Distributed Architecture.

[2] Instituto de Engenharia Electrónica e Telemática de Aveiro - Aveiro's Institute of Electronic and Telematic Engineering.

[3] Actividade Transversal em Robótica Inteligente - Transverse Activity on Intelligent Robotics.

[4] http://www.robocup.org/

L. Seabra Lopes et al. (Eds.): EPIA 2009, LNAI 5816, pp. 275–286, 2009.

Fig. 1. A CAMBADA robot

Given the dynamic environment of a soccer game, accurate robot movement plays a crucial role since most of the game duration the team's success depends on placing the robot in the desired position. This paper explains some methods applied in the CAMBADA project to effectively control an omni-directional robot. In Section 2 an overview of the CAMBADA robot's motion and various physical constraints are presented. The predictive control implementation is discussed in Section 3. Section 4 describes the methods involved in the parameters estimation of the model and the respective results are in Section 5. Finally, Section 6 presents the conclusions.

2 Omni-directional Robot Motion

As stated before, CAMBADA robots have an omni-directional motion. This is accomplished by a set of 3 swedish wheels placed at the periphery of the robot at angles that differ 120 degrees from each other. Such configuration enables a robot to move in any direction while facing any orientation. Since all degrees of freedom are controlable the robot's motion is holonomic.

Fig. 2. Detail of the wheel configuration which enables an holonomic motion

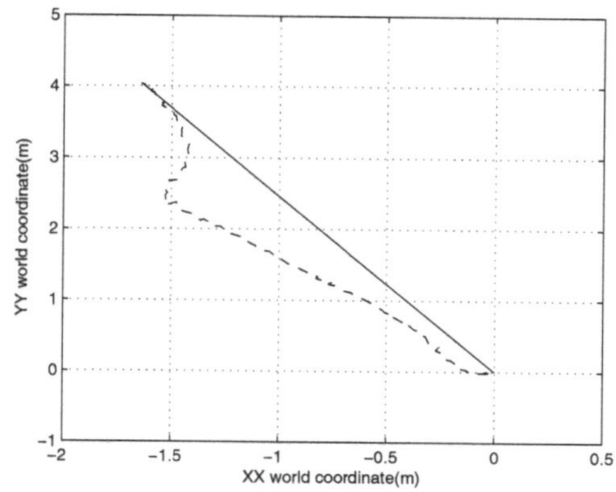

Fig. 3. Deviation in the robot movement when it rotates and moves simultaneously. The dashed line is the real robot path and the solid line would be the ideal straight path. The robot is rotating clockwise and moving towards (0,0).

To successfully move a robot to a desired pose, setpoints to each of the robot's wheels must be provided at every control cycle. This is firstly done by translating the desired pose from field coordinates to robot coordinates which gives an offset relative to the robot's current pose. From this offset, error measurements are determined that are then applied to PID controllers to determine the linear and angular velocities to be applied at the robot's frame. These are in turn mapped to setpoints, the velocities to be applied at each wheel, using the robot's kinematic model [2], to achieve the desired movement.

Ideally the robot's linear and angular velocities would be mutually independent. This means that a robot could move in a straight line while rotating over itself. In practice, such control is negatively affected by a diverse array of factors that if ignored results in an undesired robot movement.

While rotating and moving at the same time, the robot deviates considerably from the ideal straight line. This deviation is consistently to the right when rotating clockwise and to the left when rotating counter-clockwise.

An initial solution to minimize the deviation consists in rotating the robot at the initial position and then applying the linear velocity. This solution is not ideal since it doesn't take advantage of holonomic motion. Also, CAMBADA robots are among the slowest moving robot teams in the MSL [3][4][5][6], so this solution only emphasizes the speed difference.

The physical restraints affecting holonomic motion control dealt with in this paper are: discrete time control, maximum acceleration, actuator saturation, and control latency. Given the difficulty in quantification, wheel slippage and slacks are not accounted for the solution of the problem at this stage.

2.1 Discrete Time Control

Firstly, no digital computer closed loop control exists that can update its output on a continuous basis since these systems are discrete in nature. Also no real

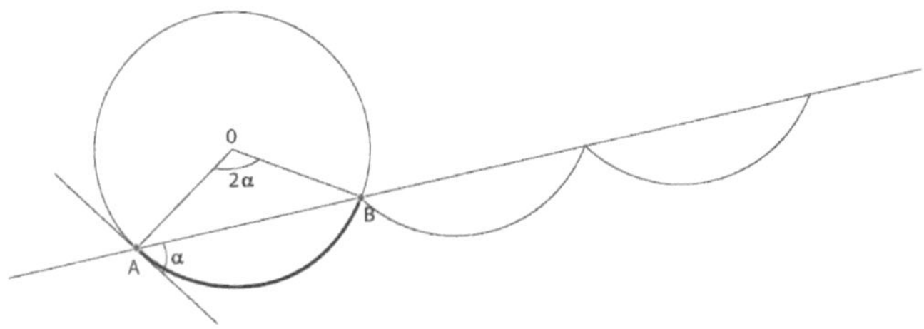

Fig. 4. While rotating and moving simultaneously the robot will describe a series of arcs along the straight line

system cannot read their sensors measurements, process and apply commands instantaneously. Therefore discrete time control usually happens sequentially over a course of time defined as control cycle. This means that a command applied at any given instant is active until the command of the following cycle is applied.

This limitation prevents some robot movements as is the case of moving in a straight line while rotating over its center, as this movement would require continuous variations of the wheels speed setup. Using constant setups during the control cycle, the robot will describe an arc instead of moving over a straight line. The solution is to make the initial and final positions of the arc described in each control cycle lie on the pretended straight line. This can be obtained applying an angle offset to the linear velocity vector. Besides this angular offset, the speed needs to be increased since the length of an arc is longer than the length of its corresponding chord.

This problem can be addressed mathematically using the circle geometry and the chord-arc relationship. The direction deviation is given by the angle between the chord and the tangent to the arc in the chord's initial position. This shall be half the integral of the angular velocity. The chord-arc relationship states that given a chord and its central angle, the length of the arc connecting the initial and final positions of the chord is given by multiplying the chord's length by,

$$\frac{ArcLength}{ChordLength} = \frac{2\alpha r}{2\sin(\alpha)r} = \frac{\alpha}{\sin(\alpha)}$$

Since the angle used for correcting the direction is an inscribed angle, the arc's central angle shall be the double, as shown by Fig 4.

So, as mentioned before, $\alpha = \frac{(RotationalVelocity \times \Delta t)}{2}$.

In the robot, at every cycle, the length of the chord or straight line is calculated by integrating desired linear velocity to be applied over a cycle time. Then if the desired rotational velocity is not zero the length of the arc is calculated as mentioned above. The final velocity to be applied is obtained by deriving the arc's length, $v_{arc} = \frac{\alpha}{\sin(\alpha)} \times v_{line}$.

2.2 Acceleration

Other restrictions affecting omni-directional motion are the allowed values for the acceleration. In the RoboCup Small Size League some teams limit their robots

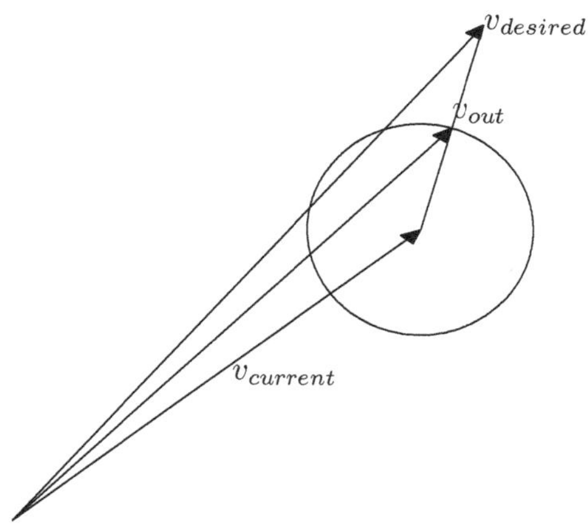

Fig. 5. Acceleration limiter. The circle represents all the velocities that can be achieved given the maximum acceleration.

acceleration by wheel traction only [7]. Given the Middle Size League robot's dimensions, this would result in a very dangerous behavior for the robot because if it is allowed to achieve, in a single cycle, a velocity with a different direction from the previous cycle there is a possibility of tipping off, severely damaging the robot's components. Given the electric nature of the used motors such unlimited acceleration can also cause large current peaks reducing the hardware lifetime and battery charge.

Therefore, the CAMBADA robots have an acceleration limiter at software level, which means that at each cycle the robot's velocity is allowed to varies only up to a certain amount around the previous cycle's velocity. The velocity then changes over time smoothly.

2.3 Actuator Saturation

A factor adversely affecting an omni-directional robot control is the saturation of its different actuators. Of all the different actuators of CAMBADA robots, this paper will focus only on the motors controlling the omni-wheels. The saturation of the motors is an indirect indication of the maximum velocity a robot can achieve. In the CAMBADA case, simulation results point to a maximum speed of 2.2 m/s. This physical factor must not be overlooked. It affects not only the proportion between linear and angular velocities but also the proportion between the linear velocities components (v_x, v_y) diverting the robot from its path in case of actuator saturation.

Assuming a saturation value C, considering the 3 omni wheels, the velocities v_x, v_y and v_a, as the velocities along the robot's axis and angular velocity, respectively, the setpoints to apply at each wheel are calculated. Assuming that all setpoints exceed C, if no measure is taken the robot would rotate at maximum speed instead of moving according v_x, v_y and v_a. The solution involves determining a correction factor to be multiplied by all the velocities to be applied [8].

This correction factor is $\frac{C}{|S|}$, where S is the highest setpoint calculated.

This ensures that one of the setpoints is applied the maximum input possible and the others are in the original proportion before the saturation limitation. The resulting movement will be slower than desired but the direction of movement will be maintained while moving as fast as possible.

2.4 Delay

The final physical restraint mentioned in this paper is the system delay. In the RoboCup Middle Size League, some teams have already addressed this issue,as is the example of the Tribots team [9]. System delay results of the sums of all small delays in the control loop and greatly affects the robot control. A delay between the sensory input and the actuator output means a command calculated based on a worldstate A will be executed on a worldstate B that may or may not be the same as A. Considering the highly dynamic nature of a robotic soccer game, the worldstates will most likely not be the same.

The problem worsens as the delay increases not only because the error between the worldstates increases but also because as the delay overcomes the cycle time, more and more commands will affect the worldstate before the current command will start to have effects. This fact explains the hard deviation while moving and rotating simultaneously shown in Fig 3. The robot is stopped, and will try to move and rotate. Since the command calculated in the initial cycle will only reach the actuator some cycles later, all the control cycles in between them will calculate the same command since the robot will not move until the first command arrives. Ideally after the robot moved from the first command, a new one should be input considering the robot's new pose.

3 Predictive Control

Reflecting other teams solutions [7], a prediction module was implemented to determine the pose of a robot when the current command will reach the actuators, given the sensed pose and a buffer storing the commands that have already been issued but have yet executed due to the system delay. Thus, all commands are calculated without delay. The commands considered in the buffer of the prediction module do not reflect the desired velocities, but the actual input commands at the motors, after the saturation and acceleration limiters are taken in to account.

Considering the CAMBADA software structure [10], the desired commands are calculated on the agent process and transmitted to the low-level communication handler process, or HWcomm, through the RTDB[5], where they are processed through the saturation and acceleration limiters before being mapped

[5] Real-Time Data Base.

to setpoints. In order to implement the prediction module in the agent process where the desired commands will be calculated accounting the predicted robot pose, the output commands of HWcomm must be sent back to the agent process, again through the RTDB. At the agent, as each command is active for an entire cycle and given the electric motors used, a purely uniform movement is assumed for each cycle. Then the predicted pose,$\hat{p}_{t_{pred}}$ for the robot is given by,

$$\hat{p}_{t_{pred}} = p_{t_{sensed}} + rem \cdot c_{t_{n-1}} + \sum_i c_{t_i} \Delta t, \; i = sensed - n..sensed - 1$$

where

- $p_{t_{sensed}}$ is the self-localization determined pose,
- c_{t_i} is the command issued in the i-th control cycle,
- $n = \lfloor \frac{t_{delay}}{t_{cycle}} \rfloor$,
- $rem = delay - n \cdot \Delta t$.

3.1 New Acceleration Limiter

Surprisingly the resulting path using predictive control was not the expected as the robot still doesn't move in a straight line. This is an undesired result from the current implementation of the acceleration limiter. As can be seen in Fig 5, if the desired velocity diverges too much from the current velocity, the output of the limiter will be a velocity that will neither be in the desired orientation nor in the desired norm. A solution to this problem is to increase the maximum acceleration of the robot, increasing the velocity variation every control cycle. However, simulation results showed that to compensate the large divergences between the velocities, the acceleration would have to be increased to values where the robot's motion stability would be compromised. These conditions when tested revealed another issue. While such high maximum acceleration allows for great velocity variations from cycle to cycle, the same high variations produce a considerable wheel slippage. Since this factor is not accounted for in the model, the resulting prediction will be very inaccurate. Therefore, the robot will not generate the anticipated path, as shown by Fig 6.

In this section, a new algorithm to update the velocity while complying with a maximum acceleration is suggested which prioritizes the velocity's direction over its norm.

The solution involves reducing the robot speed, in order to successfully rotate, similarly to what we humans do when driving. In order to reduce the speed by a minimum necessary the following situations are considered:

Firstly, the closest point from the current velocity to the desired velocity vector is calculated. Uniting this point to the current velocity always creates a perpendicular line to the desired velocity. So the distance,d , between the current velocity and the closest point will be,

$$d = sin(\Theta) \times |currentVelocity|,$$

where Θ is the angle difference between the desired and current velocities.

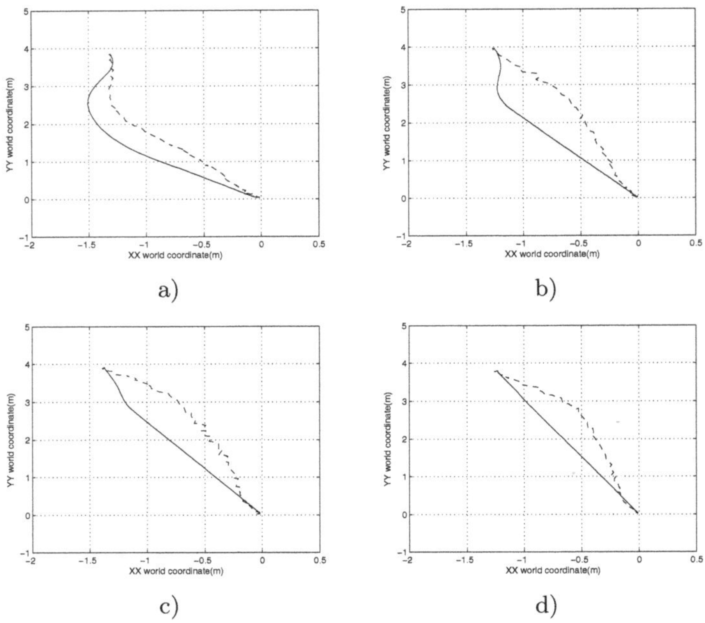

Fig. 6. Robot path with different values of maximum acceleration. The dashed line represents the real robot path while the solid line represents the simulated robot path. a) Maximum acceleration $3m/s^2$. b) Maximum acceleration $5m/s^2$. c) Maximum acceleration $7m/s^2$. d) Maximum acceleration $10m/s^2$.

Then if the distance is larger than the maximum velocity variation allowed, it means the robot doesn't have enough acceleration to reach the desired velocity direction. So to minimize the direction error, the output velocity of the acceleration limiter will be in the direction of the closest point.

If the distance is smaller, that means the robot can achieve the desired direction of the velocity even if not at the same norm. So the interception point between a circumference centered at the current velocity and with a radius of maximum velocity variation and the desired velocity vector is calculated. This point represents the maximum velocity the robot can achieve given the maximum acceleration limit while moving at the desired direction.

An exception must be made when the angle difference between the desired velocity and the current velocity is greater than 90 degrees. The resulting velocity using the perpendicular method would point in the opposite direction of the desired velocity. In this case the original implementation of the acceleration limiter is used.

4 Estimating Model Parameters

The next step is to determine the control delay. For this purpose some captures were made while the robot moved. In these captures, the robot pose determined

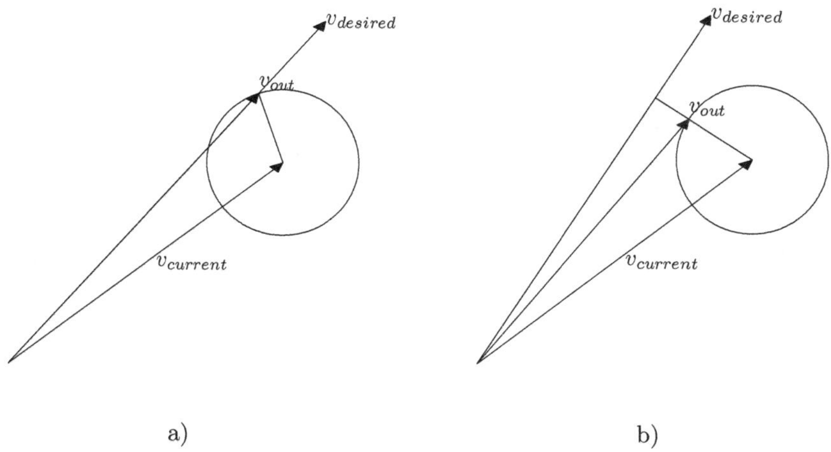

Fig. 7. New implementation of the acceleration limiter. Left a): Priority is given to the direction of the desired velocity over its norm. b): When the desired velocity can't be achieved given the maximum acceleration the output will be in the perpendicular line to the desired velocity that passes in the current velocity point.

by self-localization and the commands sent to the actuators were recorded. Since the capture produces results every cycle, the delay is determined by the difference between the cycle corresponding to the first command sent and the cycle corresponding to the robot movement. This way, it means that when the robot pose changed the first command arrived at the motors. However, since the framerate of the camera used is 25 fps, it means the delay will be in an interval of $\frac{1}{25} = 0.040$ seconds. Using this method the delay affecting the CAMBADA robots would be in $[0.160; 0.200[$ seconds. Experiments were conducted to determine the delay with more precision, which tried to minimize the error between the simulated robot path and the robot real path. However at this stage none have proven trustworthy. So, as last resort, different delay values, between 0.160 and 0.200 seconds, were tested while the robot moved between the same two points. This method showed that when delay tends to 0.200 the robot path deviates further from the straight line. The chosen value for delay was 0.165 seconds, which provided the best resulting paths.

5 Results

Using the prediction module combined with the new acceleration limiter implementation the robot successfully moved in a straight line while rotating simultaneously as shown in Fig 8.

An experience was then conducted to compare the developed solution and the original solution, where the robot rotates first and moves afterwards. The experience consisted on moving the robot between two points using the previously

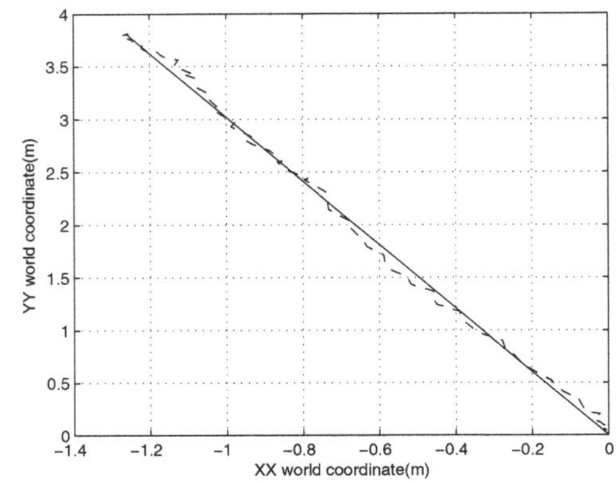

Fig. 8. The robot path using new acceleration limiter and robot pose prediction after delay. The delay value is 0.165 seconds. The robot is rotating counter-clockwise towards (0,0).

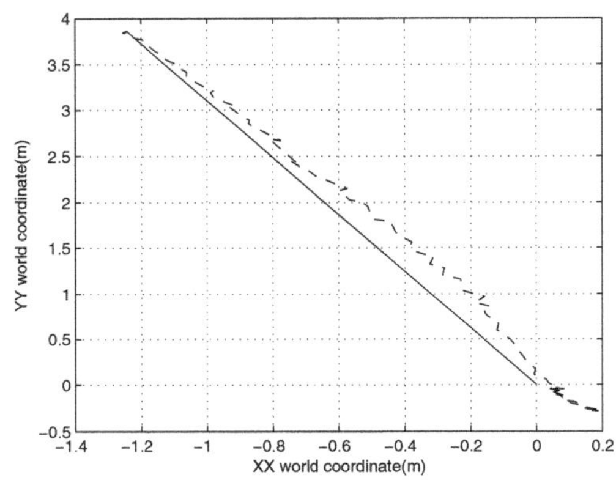

Fig. 9. The resulting robot path with constant angular velocity. The robot is rotating counter-clockwise towards (0,0).

mentioned solutions. The process was repeated ten times and the times were recorded for every run.

With the original solution, the robot took an average 3.62 seconds to move from one point to the other with a standard deviation of 0.11 seconds. With the developed solution, the robot took an average 3.28 seconds to move between the same two points with a standard deviation of 0.16 seconds.

This results in a mean time difference of 0.34 seconds. Although the improvement is not considerably large, given the fast pace of a soccer game, the increased speed might prove crucial in some game situations.

Finally an experience was conducted where the robot moved with a constant angular velocity. Even in this adverse condition the robot performance was acceptable, even despite not moving in a straight line and producing an overshoot.

6 Conclusion

An overview of different physical constraints affecting CAMBADA robots motion were presented with special focus on sensor-action delay. The various solutions developed to minimize the constraints' effects were described. A predictor module was implemented to address the delay affecting the robot along with an algorithm to update the robot velocity prioritizing the velocity direction. This initial implementation of predictive control improved robot motion and speed.

In the future the predictive control should be integrated with the existing behaviours of CAMBADA robots, enhancing ball handling, obstacle avoidance and team formation. For consistency a predictive model of the ball should also be implemented to predict its position. Since the teammate's position and velocity is shared between all robots the predictive model can be expanded predicting the teammates' positions. On the other hand since robot communication is not synchronized with the control cycle the resulting prediction might be very inaccurate. Also predicting the opponents position is impossible since at this date no opponent tracking is made being treated as stationary for obstacle avoidance purposes only.

Acknowledgments

This work was partially supported by project ACORD Adaptive Coordination of Robotic Teams, FCT/PTDC/EIA/70695/2006.

References

1. MSL Technical Committee 1997-2009: Middle Size Robot League Rules and Regulations for 2009 (2008)
2. Campion, G., Bastin, G., D'Andréa-Novel, B.: Structural Properties and Classification of Kinematic and Dynamic Models of Wheeled Mobile Robots. IEEE Transactions on Robotics and Automation 12(1) (1996)
3. Oubbati, M., Schanz, M., Buchheim, T., Levi, P.: Velocity control of an omnidirectional roboCup player with recurrent neural networks. In: Bredenfeld, A., Jacoff, A., Noda, I., Takahashi, Y. (eds.) RoboCup 2005. LNCS, vol. 4020, pp. 691–701. Springer, Heidelberg (2006)
4. Hafner, R., Lange, S., Lauer, M., Riedmiller, M.: Brainstormers Tribots Team Description, RoboCup International Symposium 2008, CD Proc., Suzhou, China (2008)
5. Sato, Y., Yamaguchi, S., et al.: Hibikino-Musashi Team Description Paper, RoboCup Int. Symposium 2008, CD Proc., Suzhou, China (2008)
6. EtherCAT Robots win German Open, Press Release, EtherCAT Technology Group (May 8, 2008)
7. Behnke, S., Egorova, A., Gloye, A., Rojas, R., Simon, M.: Predicting away Robot Control Latency. In: Proc. of 7th RoboCup Int. Symposium, Padua, Italy (2003)
8. Indiveri, G., Paulus, J.J., Plöger, P.G.: Motion control of swedish wheeled mobile robots in the presence of actuator saturation. In: Lakemeyer, G., Sklar, E., Sorrenti, D.G., Takahashi, T. (eds.) RoboCup 2006: Robot Soccer World Cup X. LNCS (LNAI), vol. 4434, pp. 35–46. Springer, Heidelberg (2007)

9. Lauer, M.: Ego-motion estimation and collision detection for omnidirectional robots. In: Lakemeyer, G., Sklar, E., Sorrenti, D.G., Takahashi, T. (eds.) RoboCup 2006: Robot Soccer World Cup X. LNCS, vol. 4434, pp. 466–473. Springer, Heidelberg (2006)
10. Neves, A.J.R., Azevedo, J.L., Cunha, M.B., Lau, N., Corrente, G., Santos, F., Pereira, A., Almeida, L., Lopes, L.S., Pedreiras, P., Vieira, J., Martins, D., Figueiredo, N., Silva, J., Filipe, N., Pinheiro, I.: CAMBADA 2009 Team Description (2009)

Towards a Spatial Model for Humanoid Social Robots*

Dario Figueira[1], Manuel Lopes[1], Rodrigo Ventura[1], and Jonas Ruesch[2]

[1] Institute for Systems and Robotics
Instituto Superior Técnico
Lisbon, Portugal
{dfigueira,macl,rodrigo.ventura}@isr.ist.utl.pt
[2] Artificial Intelligence Laboratory, Department of Informatics
University of Zurich
Switzerland
ruesch@ifi.uzh.ch

Abstract. This paper presents an approach to endow a humanoid robot with the capability of learning new objects and recognizing them in an unstructured environment. New objects are learnt, whenever an unrecognized one is found within a certain (small) distance from the robot head. Recognized objects are mapped to an ego-centric frame of reference, which together with a simple short-term memory mechanism, makes this mapping persistent. This allows the robot to be aware of their presence even if temporarily out of the field of view, thus providing a primary spatial model of the environment (as far as known objects are concerned). SIFT features are used, not only for recognizing previously learnt objects, but also to allow the robot to estimate their distance (depth perception). The humanoid platform used for the experiments was the iCub humanoid robot. This capability functions together with iCub's low-level attention system: recognized objects enact salience thus attracting the robot attention, by gazing at them, each one in turn. We claim that the presented approach is a contribution towards linking a bottom-up attention system with top-down cognitive information.

1 Introduction

Although Artificial Intelligence (AI) having accomplished notable results on many specific domains, being Kasparov's defeat to Deep Blue in 1997 one popular account of that success [1], general intelligence constitutes, still, largely an open issue [2]. This is particularly true for the case of physical agents, namely robots. Unlike symbolic environments, for which sophisticated AI techniques have been developed (reasoning, knowledge representation, and so on), physical agents operating in the real world demand several "basic" problems to be solved.

* This work was supported by the European Commission, Project IST-004370 RobotCub, and by the Portuguese Government — FCT (ISR/IST plurianual funding), and through the project BIO-LOOK, PTDC / EEA-ACR / 71032 / 2006.

L. Seabra Lopes et al. (Eds.): EPIA 2009, LNAI 5816, pp. 287–298, 2009.

One such problem is *perception*, in the sense of associating raw sensory data with internal representations.

Consider, for instance, a cup that is positioned in the field of view of the robot. The presence of this object is expected to enact some kind of internal representation. Does the robot recognize this cup in particular, or as a new, unknown object? is it graspable? However, for this level of representation, the physical nature of the robot demands the designer to deal with the problem of how to bridge the gap between the pixels that correspond to the cup (and to the background), and the concept of *object*.

A variety of cognitive architectures has been proposed with the goal of answering the problem of general artificial intelligence [3]. One aspect common to virtually all cognitive architectures is the concept of *object*. Most models assume that the system is capable of perceptually segmenting the world in objects, some of which can be grasped, while others cannot, as in the previous example of the cup.

Instead of taking one particular architecture, we address the problem of robot intelligence following a bottom-up approach, *i.e.*, constructing building blocks towards cognitive behavior. This approach, being both constructionist and minimally constrained by prior assumptions, ends up being fairly agnostic in terms of the cognitive architecture where it can be part of.

This paper addresses the problem of learning new objects and representing their presence in the environment in a spatial model. This capability builds upon an existing perceptually-driven attention system. The proposed spatial model tackles two aspects: (1) the identification of the object, and (2) its position in the environment. For the first aspect, Scale Invariant Feature Transform (SIFT) [4] features are being used to learn new objects and to recognize them in the environment.

The existing attention system provides a saliency map with respect to a robot-centric coordinate system (ego-sphere) [5]. This saliency map, together with a inhibition of return mechanism (IOR), allows the robot to saccade from salient point to salient point. However, these salient points correspond to pre-attentive features, e.g., movement, color, and shape, that do not incorporate the concept of object.

The environment is being modeled with a saliency map [6]. Objects are recognized continuously in the camera images by the SIFT algorithm. The recognized objects in the robots field of vision are inserted into the egocentric map. Each one of these objects enacts one salient point, which attracts the robot attention. Thus, with several known objects, the robot is expected to commute automatically its attention focus from recognized object to recognized object. Moreover, this saliency persists even when the robot is not directly looking at them. Instead of the short-time memory of the previous works [5,6], the system remembers where known objects are at longer time scales.

We also implemented an algorithm to automatically store to a database new objects as they get close to the robot. This draws from the idea of grasping an

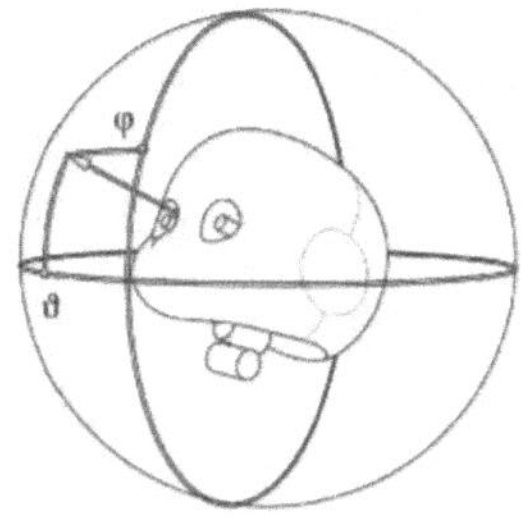

Fig. 1. Ego-sphere: a spherical map of the surroundings with a spherical coordinate system (azimuth ϑ and elevation φ)

object for inspection. As the robot has no arms (at the time of the experimental work), this was replaced by the detection of proximity.

To do so, we compute the depth of each pair of matched SIFT features by computing the disparity between them. By using this algorithm for detecting distance, we define a new object as a cluster of SIFT features in close proximity to the cameras. This approach is robust to non-convex objects as well as objects with holes, but learns two objects shown side by side as a single object.

By integrating this capability into the existing architecture, the attention module will be able to acknowledge the saliency of known objects, because they are recognized as such. Moreover, the capability of recognizing known objects by visual features paves the way for higher level cognitive modules, such as language.

We project the surrounding space and objects into a spherical coordinate system centered in the neck of the robot, an egocentric sphere or ego-sphere, as defined in [5] (Figure 1). A spatial model for the robot is here understood as a model representing the environment surrounding it, namely the known objects, together with their relative positions to the robot.

The research described here was carried out using a humanoid robotic head, composed of an anthropomorphic head with 6 degrees of freedom, and a pair of stereo cameras with individual pan and common tilt. This head is part of the iCub humanoid robot, which has been designed as a platform for research on cognition from a developmental point of view [7]. We consider a robot centered coordinate system, specifically, a torso anchored coordinate system. The software module that resulted from this research fits well into the iCub software architecture being developed in the context of the RobotCub project[1].

The problem of automatically associating sensor data with internal symbolic representations has been formulated in a domain independent way as the symbol anchoring problem [8,9]. These approaches assume however a dualistic view of perception and symbolic representations. Another approach, closer to representations of sensorimotor nature, concerns learning affordances of objects by interaction [10,11]. The identification of objects is often simplified by using colored objects and pre-wired recognition algorithms.

[1] http://www.robotcub.org/

In the next section the architecture of the proposed system is described, leaving out the implementation details to be discussed in the third section. The forth section presents the experiment in which the functioning of the system is illustrated, and experimental results are presented to validate the approach. Finally, we finish with some conclusions and future work.

2 Architecture

The architecture, displayed in Figure 2, comprises several interconnected modules, forming a sensing-deliberation-actuation chain. It is motivated on the Itti and Koch model [12] where stimuli from various sources are represented and combined into a single saliency map. Then, the point that maximizes this map is selected, as the one winning the robot attention. Finally the robot gazes towards the new selected attention point.

The ego-sphere keeps a short-memory of the previously looked upon positions, in the form of an inhibition-of-return mechanism (IOR). The IOR information reduces the salience levels of the already observed locations. The resulting behavior is the capability of the robot to fully explore its environment without being stuck on the absolute maxima of the saliency maps.

Our work adds a level of abstraction — the concept of object — to the previous architecture. To acquire this knowledge the robot has to solve two problems. *What* and *when* to learn a new object. A new object is learned when it is detected in close proximity of the robot. The object is assumed to consist in the image patch that is close to the robot. The proximity measure is defined based on the arms length distance, *i.e.,* the reachable objects. New objects are stored together with a "label", corresponding to a number (the order of appearance). When the robot has the possibility to ask humans around him for the names of

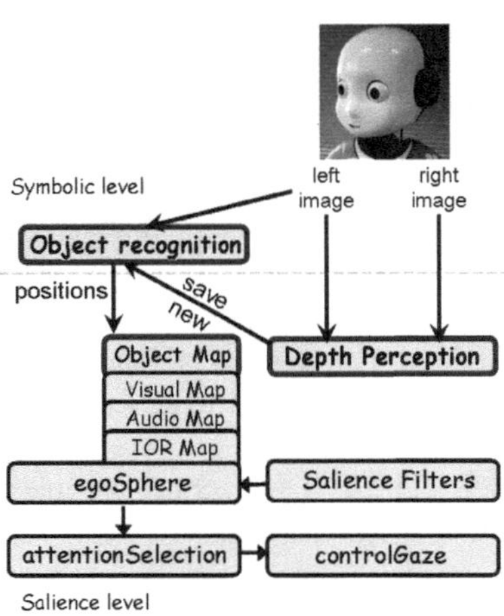

Fig. 2. System architecture, after introducing the modules presented here (dark red border): object recognition, depth perception, and a new map, the objects map

the objects it is discovering and storing, new possibilities concerning associating object representations to names arise.

3 Implementation

3.1 Object Recognition

Many different approaches have been used in computer vision to enable recognition, for instance, eigenspace matching has been used successfully by Schiele [13], others have used Speeded Up Robust Features (SURF) [14], and many have benefited from David Lowe's Scale Invariant Feature Transform (SIFT) [4]. We have followed the latter, tackling both problems of object segmentation and recognition. We chose SIFT over eigenspace matching for reasons such as invariance to scale and excelling in cluttered or occluded environments (as long as three SIFT features are detected, the object is recognized). And while the SURF algorithm is faster and performs generally well, SIFT's recognition results are still superior [15].

SIFT [4] is an algorithm that extracts, features from an image. These features are computed from histograms of the gradients around the key-points, and are not only scale invariant features, but also invariant to affine transformations (*e.g.*, rotations invariant). Furthermore, they are robust to changes in lighting, robust to non-extreme projective transformations, robust up to 90% occlusion, and are minimally affected by noise. We use the SIFT algorithm to enable the recognition in our system because of all these powerful characteristics. However, we observed two drawbacks on its use. The first one is that it is computationally expensive, as the most efficient and freely available implementations are not able to run in real time. Due to the nature of the SIFT features, its second drawback is the inability to extract features from a texture-less object, as shown in Figure 3: few or no features, in yellow dots, are found in areas with homogeneous color, such as on the table, on the ground, or on the wall.

Fig. 3. Example of SIFT feature extraction; the dots (yellow) correspond to the extracted features positions

3.2 Depth Perception

The common way to determine depth, with two stereo cameras, is by calculating disparity. Disparity is defined as the subtraction, from the left image to the right image, of the 2D coordinates of corresponding points in image space. To calculate depth we require the knowledge of the following camera parameters: focal length f, camera baseline β, and pixel dimension γ. Also, we need to correctly match a point of the environment, seen in both stereo images, with pixel coordinates (x_1, y_1) in the first image and (x_2, y_2) in the second. The point's coordinates in the camera references are (X_1, Y_1, Z) for the first camera and (X_2, Y_2, Z) for the second. Then, we can calculate how far away the matched point is (depth Z) by derivation (1), and illustrated in Figure 4.

$$\begin{cases} \gamma\, x_1 = f\, \frac{X_1}{Z} \\ \gamma\, x_2 = f\, \frac{X_2}{Z} \end{cases} \Leftrightarrow Z = \frac{f\,\beta}{\gamma\,(x_1 - x_2)} \tag{1}$$

where $\beta = X_1 - X_2$.

Usual ways of match corresponding points include pixel by pixel probabilistic matching with a Bayesian formulation [16], and histogram matching of the neighborhood of the pixel [17].

The SIFT features, with their invariance and robustness, suggest a different approach to solve the problem of matching corresponding points in stereo images. We generate a sparse disparity map by extracting the SIFT features from stereo images, and look for matches between both sets. Assuming that the robot's eyes are roughly aligned in the horizontal (*i.e.*, misalignment of under 30 pixels) we compute the disparity between matching features from the pair of stereo images. Matches that have a high horizontal disparity are assumed to be part of an object in close proximity to the robot's face and matches with low horizontal disparity belong to the "background." Matches with high vertical disparity or negative horizontal disparity are considered outliers, and thus discarded.

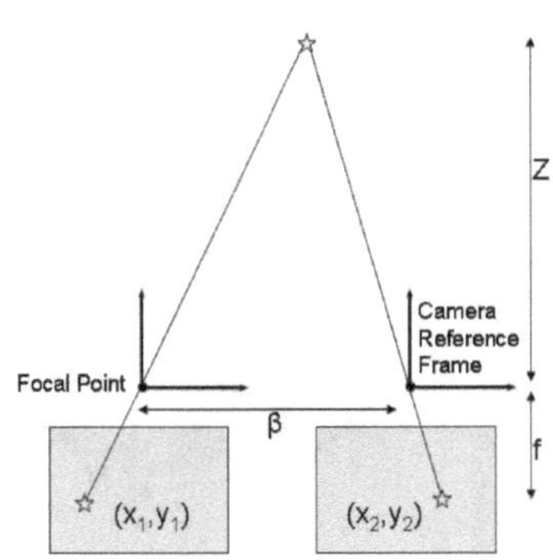

Fig. 4. Pinhole camera model used to calculate depth, f: focal distance, β: distance separating the parallel cameras, γ: pixel-to-meter ratio in the camera sensors, (x_1, y_1): pixel coordinates of point we wish to calculate depth, Z: depth

Comparing the extracted features of different images in different resolutions [18], a threshold for the horizontal disparity T_h was found empirically to be the width of the image divided by 6.4. Moreover, the vertical threshold T_v to determine outliers was also empirically found to be the height of the image divided by 16.

If the matches between detected features are close enough (each match having its horizontal disparity greater than the threshold), the group is stored in the database as a new object. Only the features that are correctly matched between the two stereo images with high horizontal disparities are stored, because only these features are believed to belong to the close object. For instance, the features from the background being seen by a hole in the object are then automatically ignored.

Figure 5(a) and Figure 5(b) exemplify in blue crosses the features that are correctly matched between the two stereo images as being the same, and therefore stored to the database as a new object (if not recognized as part of an already known object).

(a) Left image (b) Right image

Fig. 5. Matching SIFT features in a pair stereo images: features in dots (yellow); matched features in crosses (blue). Images cropped for clarity.

3.3 Recognition

To decide upon the presence of an object in the image, SIFT relies on a voting mechanism that is implemented by a Hough transform. Defining pose as the position, rotation and scale of an object, each match votes on an object-pose pair in the image. The Hough transform is computed to identify clusters of matches belonging to the same object. Finally, a verification through least-mean-squares is conducted for consistent pose parameters along all matches (verifying if the matches found have correct relative positions).

After experimenting with several objects, having the robot store them to the database and then holding them farther and farther away, the algorithm was able to recognize them until roughly two meters away, when the number of extracted

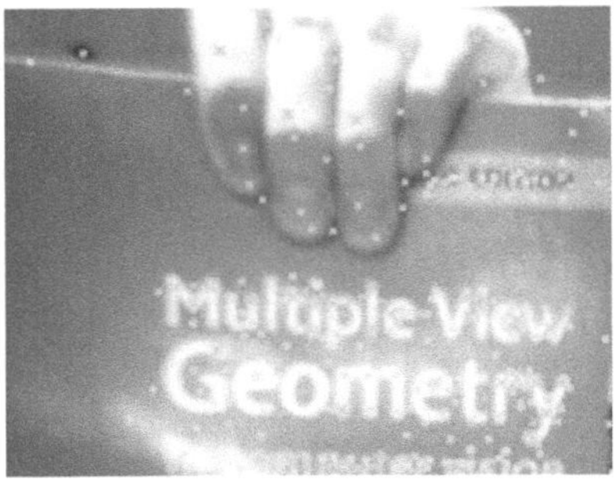

(a) Object saved to database; SIFT features in dots (yellow), and SIFT features saved to the database in crosses (blue).

(b) Marked rectangle (in red): recognized object, SIFT features in dots (yellow), and SIFT features matched with the database in squares (purple).

Fig. 6. Recognition of saved object in the environment. Images cropped for clarity.

features declines significantly. Of the many features stored in the database and shown in blue crosses in Figure 6(a), only the few extracted ones, depicted in purple filled squares, are needed to recognize the object in Figure 6(b).

3.4 Database and Mapping

New objects are stored into a database, associating object identifiers (labels) to sets of SIFT features. When an object is recognized in the environment, its position is mapped into the ego-sphere [5]. Object representations are stored in the database (long-term memory), while their positions, whenever recognized by the robot, are represented solely in the ego-sphere (short-term memory, forming the robot's spatial model).

The egocentric saliency map used for attention selection is obtained from the composition of several specialized maps: a visual map (M_{vis}), containing saliency information extracted from visual features (e.g., motion, color), and an auditory map (M_{aud}), obtained from sound stimuli captured by the robot's microphones [5]. These maps cover the entire space surrounding the robot with a spherical coordinate system (azimuth $\vartheta \in [-180\,°; 180\,°]$ and elevation $\varphi \in [-90\,°; 90\,°]$). The saliency information stored in these maps is continuously decayed ($M_{vis}(k+1) = d_{vis}\, M_{vis}(k)$, $M_{aud}(k+1) = d_{aud}\, M_{aud}(k)$), according to a forgetting factor ($d_{vis} = d_{aud} = 0.95$ in the experiments). This factor together with a maximum frame-rate of 20 FPS, yields a half-life of less than a second, 14 frames.

In order to integrate the system described in this paper with the attention selection mechanism, the recognized objects are projected onto a third map (an object map M_{obj}). This map, combined with the other two, contributes for the ego-centric saliency map: $M_{ego} = max(M_{vis}, M_{aud}, M_{obj})$. As the others, this map is also subject to a continuous decay of its information, albeit with a much longer forgetting factor ($M_{obj}(k+1) = d_{obj}\, M_{obj}(k)$, where $d_{obj} = 0.9995$ in the experiments). How long should the robot remember where objects of interest were? How long before such information is unreliable? Those are not trivial questions to answer, at least with contextual knowledge. Therefore, to fulfill the practical goal of this work, of enabling the robot to switch its attention focus from recognized object to recognized object, even when such objects are not continuously in the robots field of view, this simple decaying memory with such a forgetting factor, that gives an half-life of little over one minute, seems sufficient.

To verify the repeatability of the mapping of an object position from coordinates (x, y) of in the image frame to the corresponding coordinates (ϑ, φ) in the ego-sphere frame the following experiment were conducted: An object was left on the table in front of the robot, while the robot's head was slowly turned. We concluded that, when the object is visible, it is repeatedly mapped to the same location with an error under one degree elevation and two degrees azimuth. When on the verge of leaving the image, the error in mapping jumps up to two degrees elevation and four degrees azimuth.

The objects are mapped into the ego-sphere as gaussian peaks in salience. To account for the mapping uncertainty, the gaussian parameters used were $\sigma_\vartheta = 30$ and $\sigma_\varphi = 15$.

4 Results

To validate the approach, several experiments were conducted. In all of them, the robot operates autonomously, meaning that object learning was triggered by its proximity to the robot, and the successful recognition of objects was verified by the robot gaze. In all these experiments, saliency depends only on known objects, *i.e.,* the other saliency maps in figure 2 were disabled.

In the first experiment, two previously learnt objects were shown to the robot, both initially visible, but sufficiently apart so that one of them is not visible while the other is being gazed at. In this experiment, the robot was able to successfully switch its gaze towards each one of the objects, pausing to gaze at each object in turn [18]. Persistence of the objects positions in the spatial model is necessary for this. Figure 7 shows the objects as seen by the robot, together with the resulting saliency map.

The second experiment aimed at evaluating the behavior of the system with both unknown and known objects. First, an unknown object was shown, which did not attract the robot gaze. This object was then shown close to the robot, triggering its acquisition. Then, this object returned to its previous position, after which the robot was able to recognize it, gazing at it. The procedure was repeated for a second, and for a third object. In all of these steps, the robot ignored the new introduced object before learning it, and gazing at it afterwards. In the end, the robot shared its time among gazing at each one of the objects.

(a) First object (b) Second object (c) Saliency map

Fig. 7. Recognizing and gazing at objects in the environment: camera views of each one of the objects in (a) and (b) individually gazed at, and the saliency map (c) showing the positions of both objects in the ego-sphere frame of reference

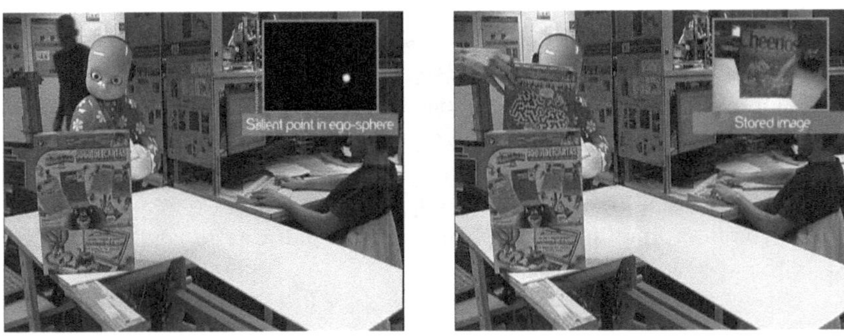

(a) Gazing at first object (b) Learning second object

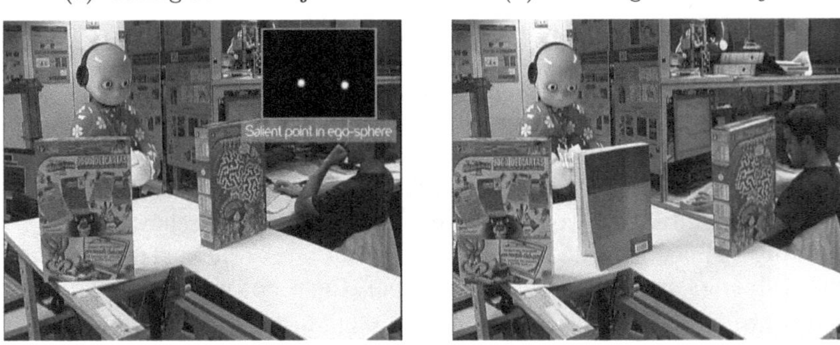

(c) Two known objects (d) Three known objects

Fig. 8. Setup for the second experiment (see text), showing (a) the robot gazing at the first object shortly after acquisition, with the saliency map also shown, (b) learning the second object, (c) two known objects, together with the saliency map, and (d) three known objects

Note that the reported experiments are robust to dynamic backgrounds and non-uniform illumination of the scene, as they were performed in a busy lab, without any special preparation. This robustness is mostly due to the choice of the SIFT features for object learning and recognition.

5 Conclusions and Future Work

The work presented here aimed at the implementation of a spatial model of the space surrounding a humanoid robot, including the salient objects which the robot encounters in its explorations. This model is used to commute the robot's attention focus automatically between objects, while not being dependent on the robot field of vision, nor on the objects visibility conditions.

To this end, we mapped recognized objects by introducing salience peaks on the ego-sphere [5]. The robot can now explore its environment based on low-level saliency but also on high-level information (objects).

With this long-term object memory implemented, the goal of making this spatial model non-dependent on the robot's field of vision was achieved. As depicted in the results, the robot returns its focus to previously observed objects that were at the moment not in its field of view.

Real-time operation of the implemented system is hindered by the fact that the computation of the SIFT features is computationally demanding. In the future, we expect to improve the object recognition by introducing other kinds of features, not only to address this performance issue, but also to be able to recognize texture-less regions in objects, as SIFT features perform poorly on regions of this nature.

At the time of writing, the iCub platform is already equipped with arms, thus opening new possibilities in terms of integrating the module here presented with grasping behaviors of the robot. Manipulation of objects by the robot also raises interesting possibilities of combining affordances with feature-based object recognition.

Acknowledgments

The authors gratefully acknowledge the contribution of Alexandre Bernardino's reviews, comments and insights in the matter of depth perception.

References

1. Hamilton, C.M., Hedberg, S.: Modern masters of an ancient game. AI magazine 18(4), 137–144 (1997)
2. Nilsson, N.J.: Human-level artificial intelligence? be serious! AI magazine 26(4), 68–75 (2005)
3. Vernon, D., Metta, G., Sandini, G.: A survey of artificial cognitive systems: Implications for the autonomous development of mental capabilities in computational agents. IEEE Transactions on Evolutionary Computation 11(2), 151–180 (2007)
4. Lowe, D.G.: Distinctive image features from scale-invariant keypoints. International Journal of Computer Vision 60(2), 91–110 (2004)
5. Ruesch, J., Lopes, M., Bernardino, A., Hornstein, J., Santos-Victor, J., Pfeifer, R.: Multimodal saliency-based bottom-up attention, a framework for the humanoid robot icub. In: IEEE International Conference on Robotics and Automation Pasadena, CA, USA (May 2008)

6. Dankers, A., Barnes, N., Zelinsky, A.: A reactive vision system: Active-dynamic saliency. In: Proc. of the 5th International Conference on Computer Vision Systems, ICVS, Bielefeld, Germany (March 2007)
7. Metta, G., Sandini, G., Vernon, D., Caldwell, D., Tsagarakis, N., Beira, R., Santos-Victor, J., Ijspeert, A., Righetti, L., Cappiello, G., Stellin, G., Becchi, F.: The RobotCub project: an open framework for research in embodied cognition. In: Proceedings of the 2005 IEEE-RAS International Conference on Humanoid Robots (2005)
8. Coradeschi, S., Saffiotti, A.: Perceptual anchoring of symbols for action. In: Proceedings of the 17th International Conference on Artificial Intelligence (IJCAI 2001), Seattle, WA, pp. 407–412 (2001)
9. Chella, A., Coradeschi, S., Frixione, M., Safotti, A.: Perceptual anchoring via conceptual spaces. In: Proceedings of the AAAI 2004 Workshop on Anchoring Symbols to Sensor Data. AAAI Press, Menlo Park (2004)
10. Stoytchev, A.: Toward learning the binding affordances of objects: A behavior-grounded approach. In: Proceedings of AAAI Symposium on Developmental Robotics, pp. 17–22. Stanford University, Menlo Park (2005)
11. Montesano, L., Lopes, M., Bernardino, A., Santos-Victor, J.: Learning object affordances: From sensory motor maps to imitation. IEEE Transactions on Robotics 24(1), 15–26 (2008)
12. Itti, L., Koch, C.: A saliency-based search mechanism for overt and covert shifts of visual attention. Vision Research 40(10-12), 1489–1506 (2000)
13. Schiele, B., Crowley, J.L.: Object recognition using multidimensional receptive field histograms. In: European Conference on Computer Vision, vol. I, pp. 610–619 (1996)
14. Bay, H., Tuytelaars, T., Van Gool, L.: SURF: Speeded up robust features. In: Leonardis, A., Bischof, H., Pinz, A. (eds.) ECCV 2006. LNCS, vol. 3951, pp. 404–417. Springer, Heidelberg (2006)
15. Bauer, J., Sunderhauf, N., Protzel, P.: Comparing several implementations of two recently published feature detectors. In: International Conference on Intelligent and Autonomous Systems (IAV), Toulouse, France (2007)
16. Bernardino, A., Santos-Victor, J.: A binocular stereo algorithm for log-polar foveated systems. In: Biological Motivated Computer Vision, Tuebingen, Germany (November 2002)
17. Prazdny, K.: Detection of binocular disparities. Biological Cybernetics 52(2), 93–99 (1985)
18. Figueira, D., Lopes, M., Ventura, R., Ruesch, J.: From pixels to objects: Enabling a spatial model for humanoid social robots. In: Proceedings of the IEEE International Conference on Robotics and Automation (ICRA 2009), Kobe, Japan (May 2009)

Control and Monitoring of a Robotic Soccer Team: The Base Station Application

Nuno M. Figueiredo, António J.R. Neves, Nuno Lau, Artur Pereira, and Gustavo Corrente

Institute of Electronics and Telematics Engineering of Aveiro
University of Aveiro, 3810-193 Aveiro, Portugal
{nuno.figueiredo,an,nunolau,artur,gustavo}@ua.pt

Abstract. In robotic soccer, teams of autonomous robots play soccer according to rules similar to the official FIFA rules. The game is refereed by a human and his orders are communicated to the teams using an application called "Referee Box". No human interference is allowed during the games except for removing malfunctioning robots and re-entering robots in the game. The base station, a software application as described in this paper, has a determinant role during the development of a robotic soccer team and also during a game. This application must control the agents interpreting and sending high level instructions, like `Start` or `Stop`, and monitor information of the robots, for example the position and velocity, allowing easily to attest the feasibility of the robots behavior. This paper discusses the importance of the control and monitoring of a robotic soccer team, presenting the main challenges and the approaches that were used by the CAMBADA team in the conception of the base station application. As far as we know, no previous work has been published about the study of these important problems and the discussion of an efficient architecture to a base station application. The results obtained by the team confirms the good performance of this software, both during the games and in the development of the team.

1 Introduction

Robotic soccer is nowadays a popular research domain in the area of multi-robot systems. RoboCup[1] is an international joint project to promote research in artificial intelligence, robotics and related fields. RoboCup chose soccer as the main problem aiming at innovations to be applied for socially relevant problems. It includes several competition leagues, each one with a specific emphasis, some only at software level, others at both hardware and software, with single or multiple agents, cooperative and competitive.

In the context of RoboCup, the Middle Size League (MSL) is one of the most challenging. In this league, each team is composed of up to 5 robots, one of whom is the goalkeeper, with a maximum size of $50cm \times 50cm$ width, $80cm$ height and a maximum weight of 40Kg, playing in a field of $18m \times 12m$. The rules of the

[1] `http://www.robocup.org/`

L. Seabra Lopes et al. (Eds.): EPIA 2009, LNAI 5816, pp. 299–309, 2009.

game are similar to the official FIFA rules, with minor changes required to adapt them for the playing robots [1].

The rules of this league establish several constraints to simplify perception and world modeling. In particular, the ball is orange, the field is green, the field lines are white and the players are black. The duration of a game is 30 minutes, not including a half-time interval of 5 minutes. The game is refereed by a human and his orders are communicated to the teams using an application called "Referee Box" operated by an assistant referee.

No human interference is allowed during the games except for removing malfunctioning robots and re-entering robots in the game. Each robot is autonomous and has its own sensorial means. They can communicate among each other and with an external computer through a wireless network. This external computer, that has no sensor of any kind, runs the base station application. The base station only "knows" what is reported by the playing robots and the orders received from the referee box. The agents should be able to evaluate the state of the world and take decisions suitable to fulfill the cooperative team objective.

CAMBADA[2], *Cooperative Autonomous Mobile roBots with Advanced Distributed Architecture*, is the Middle Size League Robotic Soccer team from the University of Aveiro. The CAMBADA research project started in 2003, coordinated by the Transverse Activity on Intelligent Robotics (ATRI)[3] group of the Institute of Electronic and Telematic Engineering of Aveiro (IEETA)[4]. Since then, it has involved people working on several areas for building the mechanical structure of the robot, its hardware architecture and controllers [2] and the software development in areas such as image analysis and processing [3,4,5,6,7], sensor and information fusion [8], reasoning and control [9].

Since its creation, the team has participated in several competitions, both national and international. Each year, new challenges are presented, and new objectives are defined, always with a better team performance in sight. After achieving the first place in the national competition Robótica 2007 and Robótica 2008, the 5th place in the world championship RoboCup 2007, in 2008 the team achieved the first place in the world championship RoboCup 2008.

This paper focuses the role of the control and monitoring activities in the development and during a game of a robotic soccer team. We start this paper clarifying the concepts of control and monitoring in the context of this paper. This step takes special importance due to the fact of these concepts are widely used in other contexts and could led to a misunderstanding about our purposes. In Section 3, we present an overview of the communication and internal architecture of the CAMBADA team, in order to explain some of the used approaches. In the Section 4 will be addressed the main challenges and requirements that these activities demands on to the development of the application. Section 5 describes the approaches used in the development specifically for each activity

[2] `http://www.ieeta.pt/atri/cambada`
[3] `http://www.ieeta.pt/atri`
[4] `http://www.ieeta.pt`

focusing the implemented features. Finally we present our main conclusions and future improvements to the project.

2 Control and Monitoring in a Robotic Soccer Team

For control and monitoring we can find multiple definitions of their meaning. In the context of this paper, to avoid some misunderstandings, we will clarify what we are meaning when we refer each one.

We can find the "Control" concept applied in many areas like engineering or management. In engineering the "Control" concept implies an ability to keep a certain observed variable (output) constrained, acting in the variable/variables (inputs) that change the state of the referred observed variable. In a robotic team the actions of the robots are decided autonomously, it is the robot that have to observe the state of the world (outputs) and act accordingly (inputs). However in the development phase, and only that, it is useful provide a certain level of manual control in order to directly observe some wanted behavior.

In this paper, when we refer control, it means the ability to instruct the robotic agent to perform a certain high level behavior, like start, stop or assign a certain role. However, it is important to refer that during the game the control of the robots are autonomous and guaranteed by individual processing of the information of the game.

The monitoring of the robots implies the ability to observe a specific behavior or characteristic, for instance the charge of the batteries is an important hardware characteristic that must be constantly monitored. In the context of this paper, performing monitoring is essentially concerned with three things:

- observe the consequences of the control actions;
- observe the internal states and hardware information of the robots;
- detect errors related with incorrect algorithm implementations.

3 Communication and Internal Architecture

In this section, the communication and internal architecture of the CAMBADA team will be explained. The description will be based on the characteristics of interest that were used in the development of the base station application. More specifically, concerning communication, we present the way as information is exchanged between the different agents, what are the used protocols and access mechanisms implemented in the team.

Concerning the internal architecture of the team, it will be explained the structures that support the information. This description will be based essentially in the description of the `WorldState` model implemented.

To exchange the information between the agents in the field, it is used a Wireless LAN [12,13] and each team has a different one. In the connection between Referee Box and base station is used a wired TCP LAN connection using a standard protocol [1] to report the events of the game. In the team network no

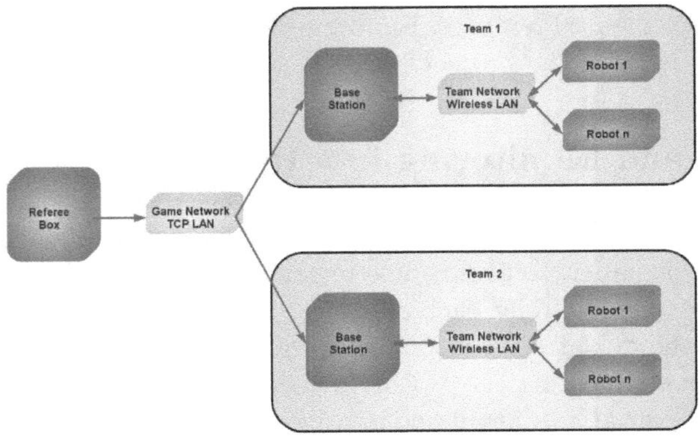

Fig. 1. The network configuration used in a soccer game

restrictions are made, each team is free to choose the connection protocol and the information exchanged between its agents. In Fig. 1 are presented a model of the connections used.

The internal communication protocol is based on the exchange of the `WorldState` information between each agent. At each communication cycle the agents report their internal state creating a virtual representation, shared by all, of the global `WorldState`. This virtual representation is named Real-Time DataBase (RTDB) [10]. This mechanism simplifies the information management and access. In the point of view of an application, one single data structure represents all the needed information of the shared `WorldState`. The base station application uses this mechanism to access the individual information of each player and also to send information to each one. Also the coach application uses this mechanism to communicate with the players. The coach is independent from the base station application. This application is responsible to solve the problems related with dynamic role assignment of the players in the field. In Fig. 2 are shown how information is exchanged between all the agents in the field.

Regarding the internal architecture, we will detail the most relevant information exchanged in this process, more specifically, what are the most relevant information that can be useful to the mentioned activities, control and monitoring.

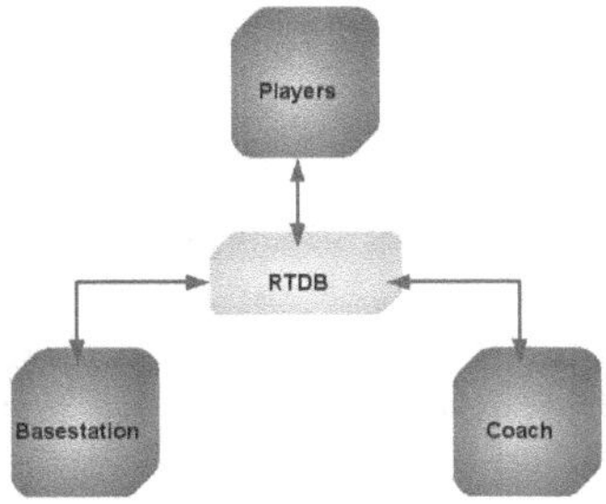

Fig. 2. The communication between all robots is accomplished through the RTDB

As it was mentioned before, each agent exchange information of their `WorldState` among all the team mates. For this purpose, we categorized the information accordingly with the mentioned activities:

- **Control Information** – this information is related with the high level orders that can be sent to the agents:
  - game signals, including `Start` and `Stop` actions;
  - team color;
  - goal side;
  - role.
- **Monitoring Information** – this kind of information is related with the internal states and the functional information that indicates the performance of the agent in a certain instant:
  - game states;
  - position of the ball and the robot;
  - angle of the robot;
  - velocity of the ball and the robot;
  - batteries information;
  - ball engaged and visible;
  - the actual Role and Behavior;
  - the actual Team color and goal side;
  - debug point.

The base station uses these information to perform the control and monitoring of the robots.

4 Main Challenges and Requirements

The base station application must provide a set of tools to perform the activities mentioned above. Regarding the control activity, this application must allow high level control of the robots sending basic commands/information in particular the `Run` and `Stop` commands, play mode, role assignment, etc.

This application must also provide a high level monitoring of the robots internal states, namely the position in the field, velocity, battery charge, among other relevant information related with the robots and the game.

Furthermore, this application should provide an easy mechanism that can be used to easily show a specific behavior of the robot, allowing debugging.

Besides that, the base station has a fundamental role during a game, while receiving the commands from the referee box, translating them to internal game states and broadcasting the results to the robots. During a game, no human interference is allowed except for removing malfunctioning robots and re-entering robots in the game.

The role of the base station during these phases, development and games, demands the fulfillment of some requirements, being the most important the following:

Reliability / Stability: during the game, the base station is not accessible for human interaction of any kind and thus, it has to be a very robust application, all team depends on that.

Usability: the information displayed in the base station should be easy to interpret, allowing, for instance, a fast detection of a problem in a robot. It should be possible to choose different levels of details in the displayed information. Moreover, the base station has to be easy to use, allowing an intuitive management of the robots.

Adaptability: a robotic soccer team is in a permanent development stage, which may lead to significant changes within a short period of time.

Specifically to each phase the base station should provide the following features:

- **Development phase**

  Manual role assignment: acting as a cooperative team, each robot has a specific role which is, during a real game, dynamically assigned. In the development phase, it should be possible to manually assign a role to a specific robot.

  Local referee box: the base station should provide an interface widget to emulate a real referee box in order to simulate events of a real game.

  Visualization Tool: the application should provide a representation of the field and the robots in that context. Moreover, some visual information should be attached in order to improve the visual perception of the internal states of each robot.

  Multi-windows solution: the application should be a multi-window environment, allowing the user to choose between different levels of information. At least, three different levels of information should be provided: a work level that presents the controls of the robots and basic status information; a visual level that presents visual information of the position of the robots and, finally a detailed level that shows all the information related to the robots.

  Adaptable windows geometry: the multi-windows system should adapt to monitors with different resolutions. According to the new MSL rules, the base stations of each team must use an external monitor provided by the organizing committee.

- **Game situation**

  Robust communication skills: the correct operation of the team during the game is fully dependent on the communication between the robots, the base station and the referee box. Hence, the base station should provide a robust communication layer.

  Automatic processing of the game states: the base station should process the commands received from the referee box allowing the robots to change their internal game states accordingly. One specific action should be the changing of the field side at half time.

In the next section it will be detailed the approaches followed in the conception of the CAMBADA base station in order to fulfill these requirements.

5 The CAMBADA Base Station Approach

Regarding the challenges and requirements mentioned in the previous section, we will detail the used approaches in the conception of the base station application. We have divided, once again, the description in the mentioned activities in order to more precisely describe the features implemented for each one.

5.1 Performing Control

Merging the available methods provided by the communication protocol of the team we were able to implement a widget that allows an high level control of the robots. In the Fig. 3 are shown the possible actions that can be used to control the robots. All the actions were grouped to each robot and are accessible in a delimited space in order to improve the usability. These actions represents the enable/disable of each robot, the team color and goal color (in spite of the current rules don't specify goal colors, we decide keep it in order to facilitate the monitoring process), the role of the player, the re-location button, the start and stop that controls remotely the software in each robot and the bottom to launch remotely the agent.

Additionally, were created two other widgets, one to control all the team and one that implements a local referee box. These two widgets are shown in Fig. 4.

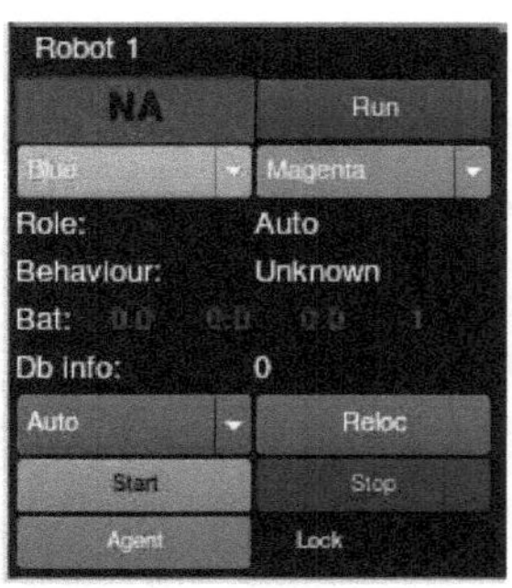

Fig. 3. Available controls and basic information of one robot

Fig. 4. Local Referee Box and team controls

5.2 Monitoring

Regarding the monitoring activity, we developed a visualization widget that makes a representation of the field and the robots. This visualization widget shows the robots number, position and orientation and the ball that each robot view. Additionally was implemented a mechanism that allows to change the orientation of the field, in order to turn possible to monitor the robots in any position of the field, increasing the usability. In Fig. 5 are shown the visualization widget and this described mechanism.

The base station has three separated windows representing three different levels of information. The main level shows the controls and relevant information about the robots state, other window only shows the visualization widget (this

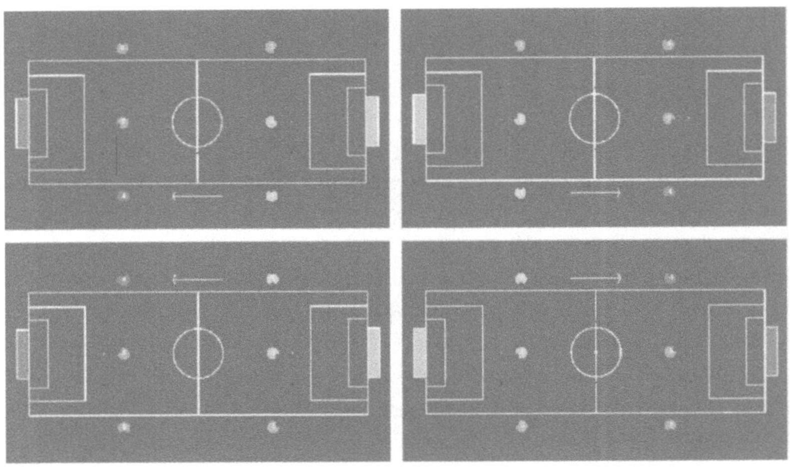

Fig. 5. Different views of the field. This mechanism allows the developers to adjust the field orientation accordingly to their point of view of the field.

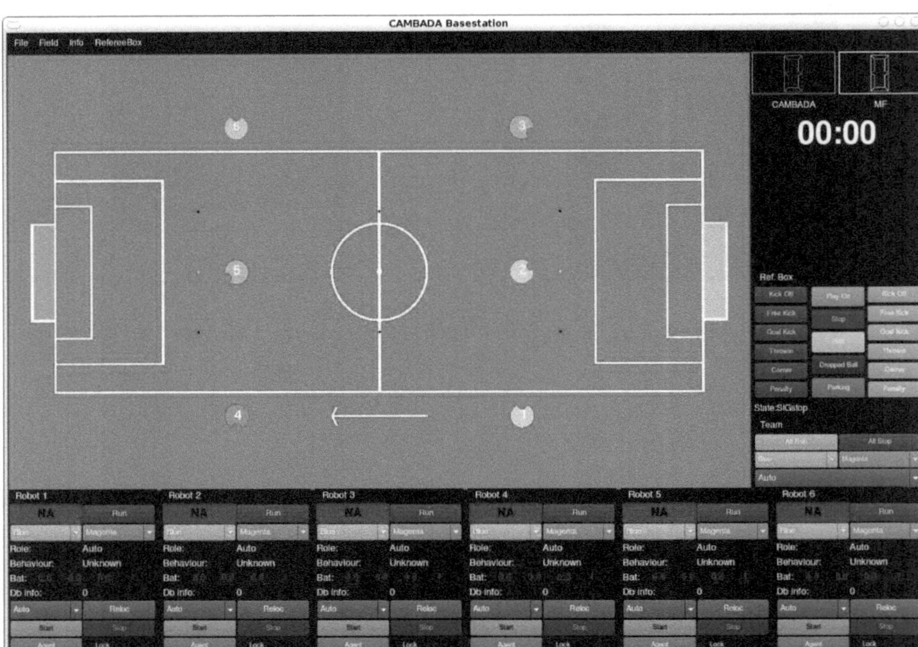

Fig. 6. The base station `Main Window`

is the window to monitor the game, according with the new rules) and finally we implemented a window with full information of the robots, all the information available in the RTDB is shown in this window. In Fig. 6, 7 and 8 are shown these three windows.

In order to perform debugging in the development phase, it was implemented, in the visualization widget, a debug mechanism. Is possible to enable this mechanism writing in a specific field of the RTDB. This field is a vector with two dimensions representing a position on the game field. There are one point of debug *per* robot and if enabled in the base station this point can be shown in the game field together with the representation of the robots. This point is free to use and can represent whatever the developer wants. For instance, this point was used to perform debug to the obstacles avoidance algorithm showing the alternative target point calculated. In Fig. 9 are shown this debug mechanism.

Additionally, the third window, considered as the full information window, allows to perform debug to the robot state, more precisely in the transition between the roles and behaviors states.

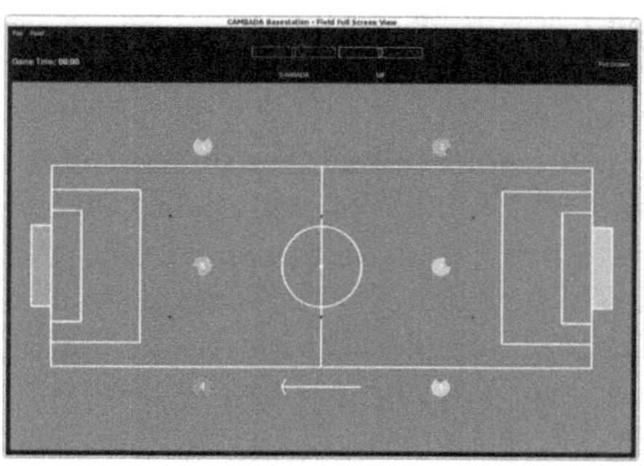

Fig. 7. The base station `Field View Window`

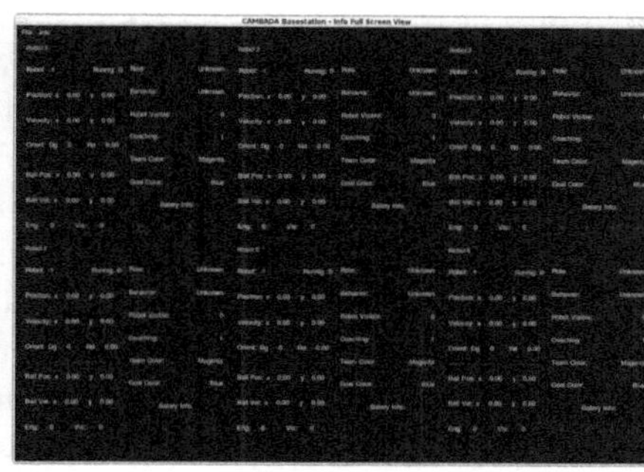

Fig. 8. The base station `Info Window`

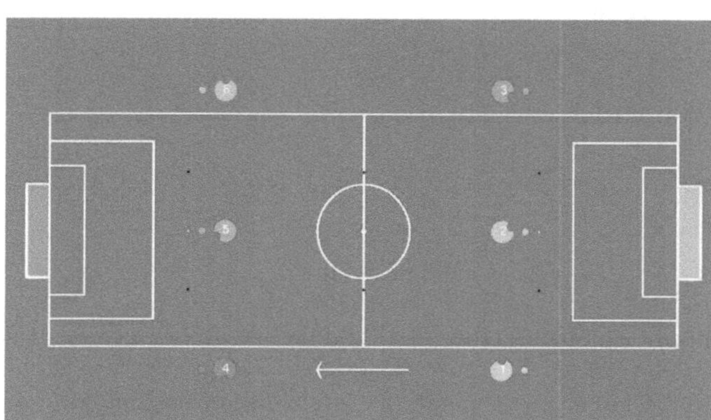

Fig. 9. The 6 robots in the field and the respective debug point

All the project were developed using the Qt [11] library using a modular architecture. This increased the reliability and stability allowing to test each module before the integration in the project.

6 Conclusion and Future Improvements

This paper presents the base station application of the CAMBADA team under the perspective of a tool that can enhance the control and monitoring capabilities of the team developers. During the paper, we reason about the importance of these activities in the phases of development and during the games, highlighting the main challenges and requirements that this application presents. Furthermore, we presented some main approaches used to solve the challenges that were identified showing some features implemented.

The current version of the base station was tested in the Portuguese championships Robótica 2008 and Robótica 2009, and in the world championships RoboCup 2008 and RoboCup 2009, showing a high level of reliability and stability helping the team to achieve the successful results in these years.

Despite of these promising results, some work still has to be done, namely future improvements in the development of new control capabilities allowing a low level control performed by this application individually to each robot. This new type of control will allow us to act directly on the main features of the robots, like motor velocity, orientation, kick power, etc. To enhance the monitoring capabilities, we are planning to implement, in a first phase, new visual debugging points, not only a numerical vector but also binary states (like semaphores). In a second phase, we are planning to implement a reliable positioning debugging based on image processing where static cameras will be used in the field with the aim to provide reference information about the objects in the field (robots, balls, obstacle, etc). This information will be used to validate the algorithms of positioning of the team.

Also in monitoring, we verified some problems with the quantity of the information displayed. It is planed in the future some improvements regarding a new way of presenting the information in order to optimize the available space.

Acknowledgment

This work was supported in part by the FCT project PTDC/EIA/70695/2006.

References

1. MSL Technical Committee 1997-2009, Middle Size Robot League Rules and Regulations for 2009 (2008)
2. Azevedo, J.L., Cunha, B., Almeida, L.: Hierarchical distributed architectures for autonomous mobile robots: a case study. In: Proc. of the 12th IEEE Conference on Emerging Technologies and Factory Automation, ETFA 2007, Greece, pp. 973–980 (2007)

3. Neves, A.J.R., Corrente, G.A., Pinho, A.J.: An omnidirectional vision system for soccer robots. In: Neves, J., Santos, M.F., Machado, J.M. (eds.) EPIA 2007. LNCS (LNAI), vol. 4874, pp. 499–507. Springer, Heidelberg (2007)
4. Neves, A.J.R., Martins, D.A., Pinho, A.J.: A hybrid vision system for soccer robots using radial search lines. In: Proc. of the 8th Conference on Autonomous Robot Systems and Competitions, Portuguese Robotics Open - ROBOTICA 2008, Aveiro, Portugal, pp. 51–55 (April 2008)
5. Martins, D.A., Neves, A.J.R., Pinho, A.J.: Real-time generic ball recognition in RoboCup domain. In: Proc. of the 11th edition of the Ibero-American Conference on Artificial Intelligence, IBERAMIA 2008, IROBOT Workshop, Lisbon, Portugal, pp. 37–48 (October 2008)
6. Caleiro, P.M.R., Neves, A.J.R., Pinho, A.J.: Color-spaces and color segmentation for real-time object recognition in robotic applications. Revista do DETUA 4(8), 940–945 (2007)
7. Cunha, B., Azevedo, J.L., Lau, N., Almeida, L.: Obtaining the inverse distance map from a non-svp hyperbolic catadioptric robotic vision system. In: Proc. of the RoboCup 2007, Atlanta, USA (2007)
8. Silva, J., Lau, N., Rodrigues, J., Azevedo, J.A.: Ball sensor fusion and ball interception behaviours for a robotic soccer team. In:Proc. of the 11th edition of the Ibero-American Conference on Artificial Intelligence, IBERAMIA 2008, IROBOT Workshop, pp. 25–36 (October 2008)
9. Lopes, L.S., Lau, N., Corrente, G.A.: CAMBADA: Information sharing and team coordination. In: Proc. of the 8th Conference on Autonomous Robot Systems and Competitions, Portuguese Robotics Open - ROBOTICA 2008, Aveiro, Portugal, pp. 27–32 (April 2008)
10. Almeida, L., Santos, F., Facchinetti, T., Pedreiras, P., Silva, V., Lopes, L.S.: Coordinating distributed autonomous agents with a real-time database: The CAMBADA project. In: Aykanat, C., Dayar, T., Körpeoğlu, İ. (eds.) ISCIS 2004. LNCS, vol. 3280, pp. 876–886. Springer, Heidelberg (2004)
11. Trolltech Co., Qt cross-platform application framework, `http://www.trolltech.com`
12. Santos, F., Almeida, L., Pedreiras, P., Lopes, L.S., Facchinetti, T.: An Adaptive TDMA Protocol for Soft Real-Time Wireless Communication among Mobile Autonomous Agents. In: Proc. of the Int. Workshop on Architecture for Cooperative Embedded Real-Time Systems, WACERTS 2004, pp. 657–665 (2004)
13. Santos, F., Corrente, G., Almeida, L., Lau, N., Lopes, L.S.: Selfconfiguration of an Adaptive TDMA wireless communication protocol for teams of mobile robots. In: Proc. of the 13th Portuguese Conference on Artificial Intelligence, EPIA 2007 (2007)

Multirobot Task Assignment in Active Surveillance

Nelson Gonçalves and João Sequeira

Instituto de Sistemas e Robótica, Instituto Superior Técnico, Lisbon, Portugal
ngoncalves@isr.ist.utl.pt, jseq@isr.ist.utl.pt

Abstract. An architecture for the assignment of tasks in a multirobot system is presented. The tasks arrival times and order are not known, and no statistical distributions are assumed. Furthermore, the execution of tasks cannot be preempted and hard deadlines are imposed on both their assignment and conclusion times. The architecture design is inspired by economic markets and a performance measure, similar to market prices, is introduced. A theoretical analysis of the architecture operation is presented and the results are applied to the dimensioning of an active surveillance system for the UPC campus at Barcelona, Spain.

1 Introduction

An architecture for the assignment of tasks in multirobot systems is presented. The target application is an active surveillance system for an urban environment. It is composed by a set of cameras, at the top of the buildings surrounding the site, and a set of mobile robots. When suspicious activities are detected by the cameras, mobile robots are dispatched to investigate the locations. The robots are also requested to periodically patrol the environment. The problem of computing optimal paths for the robots, given the current detections, can be formulated as a kinetic travelling salesman problem, [1]. This is a very hard problem to solve and often heuristic methods are employed, [2]. Although the proposed solution is sub-optimal, it is robust to hardware and communication failures and does not require the knowledge of the robots state. In addition, theoretical bounds on the architecture performance are presented.

The architecture is composed with two hierarchic levels, where at the bottom level, mobile robots are organized in distinct groups and tasks are assigned within each group in a centralized manner. Since groups may receive more tasks than others, the groups can exchange tasks among themselves at the top level, in a decentralized fashion. The tasks are assigned within a group and traded among the different groups using auction protocols. These have been used in different robotic applications, for which a survey can be found in [3]. In general assignment problems auctions have also been considered, [4,5]. The main advantages of auctions are their robustness to failures and reduced computational and communication bandwidth requirements, [6,3]. In addition, the coordination of the different system components is implicitly achieved using these protocols. For instance, a camera can request a task from the set of robots without knowing their state or the detections made by other cameras.

The concept of price is employed in market based architectures, but it is often determined *a priori* by the system designer, [3,5]. A measure denoted *task price* is presented

L. Seabra Lopes et al. (Eds.): EPIA 2009, LNAI 5816, pp. 310–322, 2009.

in this paper, with the value determined through the spontaneous and unsupervised interaction among the agents. Thus, the architecture can be identified with a catalaxy, [7]. Since prices are formed "naturally", they provide insightful information on system state. This is an important contribution because events, such as hardware failures, can be detected without the incorporation of specially designed mechanisms. Nevertheless, it must be stressed that in this paper, the economic concepts are used only as metaphors.

The paper presents theoretical bounds for the assignment delay of tasks. The relations between the assignment delays and task prices, the number of robots, and the architecture group structure are also discussed. This is another important contribution to market based architectures since few bounds or metrics are known, [8,3,6].

The remainder of the paper is as follows. The architecture is described in Section 2 and the theoretical analysis is presented in Section 3. In Section 4, an application example of the architecture is presented. Finally in Section 5 conclusions and future research directions are discussed.

2 Control Architecture

Consider a multirobot surveillance system composed by a finite, heterogeneous set of mobile robots, where each can execute a finite set of distinct tasks. The requests for the execution of tasks originate from the sensors intruder detections and pre-defined patrol route schedules. The process of generating these execution requests is exogenous to the architecture and is not considered in this paper. It is assumed that the tasks arrival order is not known, and that they can be executed in any order but cannot be interrupted. A surveillance application is considered where tasks consist in the execution of paths, but the architecture can be used in other applications if the task assumptions are verified.

A task is identified with the computer science concept of service, [9]. The execution of tasks by the robots is determined by the task specific input parameters. Also, the manner in which the task is executed is known only by the robots. These are only required to respect the execution constraints, denoted the *task contract.*

Definition 1 (Task Contract). *A contract for task τ is the tuple $\gamma_\tau = (\,\tau,\, t_a,\, t_d,\, t_e\,)$, where: t_a is the arrival instant of the contract, t_d is the assignment deadline and t_e is the maximum task execution time.*

The assignment of tasks must occur within a temporal window, the interval $[t_a,\, t_d]$, because in surveillance applications the environment is not static. The intruders, for instance, are not expected to remain idle. The maximum execution time is specified to ensure that mobile robots eventually stop and become available to execute other tasks. The task specific set of input parameters, such as the way-points in a patrol task, are also part of the respective contract. These were not included in Definition 1 because they are not relevant for the assignment of tasks.

The architecture basic unit is a group of mobile robots, denoted *local market*, composed by an arbitrary number of robots that can execute the same set of tasks. The group membership is static, limited to a single local market and defined *a priori*. The task execution requests are received by a central processor in each group, denoted

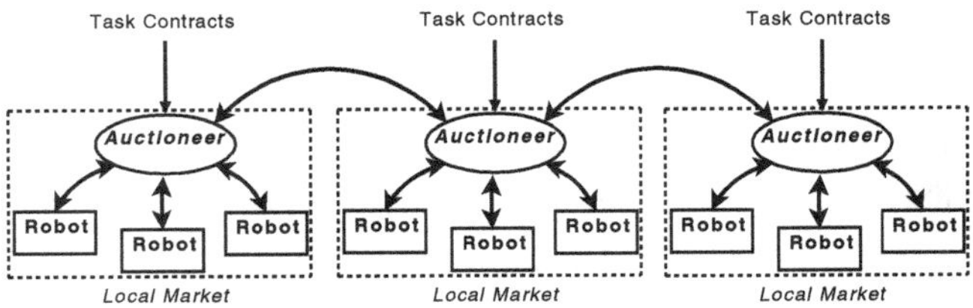

Fig. 1. Market-based task assignment architecture

the *auctioneers*. These can assign the tasks locally or trade them with other auctioneers. A general view of the architecture is represented in Fig. 1, where the arrows indicate the communication links.

2.1 Task Assignment in Local Markets

The problem is formulated as the assignment of contracts for non-preemptive tasks with hard deadlines and unknown arrival times. The available robots and their location are not known by the auctioneer. The computational complexity when the order of task arrivals and the available robots are known is in general NP-Hard, [10]. The available algorithms often require centralized coordination and computational resources. Although the solution presented is also centralized, tasks can arrive in any order and the computational complexity is polynomial, see Sub-Section 2.3. The solution is also robust to hardware and network failures in the sense that at least some contracts are assigned if there are available robots. The disadvantage is that in general, the assignment solution is not guaranteed to be optimal.

The task contracts arrive at any time instant, but are assigned periodically by the auctioneer. The assignment period is Δ, and the assignment instants are represented by the integer variable k. The auctioneers can have different assignment periods. The set of contracts received, but not yet assigned, at time k is

$$W(k) = \{\gamma_\tau : \gamma_\tau[t_a] \leq \Delta k \ < \gamma_\tau[t_d]\} \tag{1}$$

where $\gamma_\tau[.]$ is the respective tuple component. The number of unassigned contracts is $w(k)$ and these are indexed by $j = 1, \ldots, w(k)$. The number of available robots at time k is $n(k)$, indexed by $i = 1, \ldots, n(k)$. A mobile robot is considered available if it is not executing a task and can communicate with the auctioneer. The assignment of the contracts in $W(k)$ to the available robots is represented by the matrix $Y(k)$. The element y_{ij} is one if the i-th robot is assigned the j-th contract, and zero otherwise. In this paper, the assignment cost function is a linear combination of (i) the robots estimated service time for each contract and (ii) the contracts waiting time at the auctioneer, denoted their *assignment delay*. A mixed linear integer program (MLIP) is formulated to compute the optimal assignment solution Y^*:

$$\begin{aligned}
&\max \sum_i \sum_j c_{ij}(k) \cdot y_{ij}(k) \\
&s.t. \\
&\sum_i y_{ij}(k) \leq 1,\, j = 1,\, \ldots,\, w(k) \\
&\sum_j y_{ij}(k) \leq 1,\, i = 1,\, \ldots,\, n(k) \\
&y_{ij}(k) \in \{0, 1\}
\end{aligned} \tag{2}$$

where $c_{ij}(k)$ is an element of the matrix cost functional. The problem constraints state that each contract is assigned to at most one agent and vice-verse. The cost of assigning to the available i-th robot the j-th contract is

$$c_{ij}(k) = \beta(s_{ij}(k)) + (\Delta k - \gamma_j[t_a]) \tag{3}$$

where s_{ij} is the contract service time estimated by the mobile robot and $\beta(.)$ is a strictly monotonous, decreasing function with non negative output values. The term $(\Delta k - \gamma_j[t_a])$ is the assignment delay of the j-th contract. This value is known by the auctioneer, but the robots service time is not because it depends on the robot state. The number of available robots at time k is also not known by the auctioneer. The missing information is obtained using an auction protocol.

Definition 2 (Local Market Auction Protocol)

1) *At time k the contracts in $W(k)$ are announced to the robots, by the auctioneer*
2) *The robots must bid with their estimated service times until time $k + 1$*
3) *The assignment solution is computed by the auctioneer at time $k+1$ and announced to the robots that submitted bids*

Proposition 1 (Local Market Assignment Delay). *In the local market auction protocol, the assignment delay of any contract is always greater than Δ and in the worst case it is at least 2Δ.*

Proof. *Consider a contract $\gamma_j \in W(k)$, received in the interval $[k - 1, k)$. Thus $\gamma_j[t_a] = \Delta(k - 1 + \epsilon)$, with $\epsilon \in [0, 1)$. From the protocol definition it follows that the contract is assigned at instant $k_j = \Delta(k + 1 + \theta)$, with $\theta \in \mathbb{Z}_{0,+}$. The assignment delay for this contract is*

$$k_j - \gamma_j[t_a] = \Delta(k + 1 + \theta) - \Delta(k - 1 + \epsilon) = \Delta(2 + \theta - \epsilon)$$

Thus, it is always greater than Δ if $0 < \epsilon < 1$ and at least 2Δ if $\epsilon = 0$. □

The main advantage of this protocol is that the auctioneers and the system components that request the execution of tasks do not need to know the robots state or pose. Although bids must be received within a limited time period, an universal clock source is not required. Instead, a time-stamp is included by the auctioneer in the messages announcing the contracts. The time-stamp is returned in the robots bid reply messages and the auctioneer can discard bids that are received out of time.

The main disadvantage of the protocol is the delay in assigning contracts, which is always greater than the assignment period. This value cannot be made arbitrarily small because of transmission delays and the limited bandwidth of the communication network. But the greatest limitation of this approach is that the auctioneer is a single point of failure. The proposed solution to this limitation, is to create multiple local markets with a small number of robots. In this manner, the failure of an auctioneer does not completely disable the architecture.

2.2 Trading among Auctioneers

It is assumed that each auctioneer can communicate with some other auctioneers, denoted the *neighbours*. An auction protocol is used by the auctioneers to trade contracts with the purpose of balancing the local markets workload. An efficiency measure for local markets, denoted *task price*, is used by the protocol.

Definition 3 (Local Market Task Price). *The price of executing contracts for task τ in the local market with auctioneer l at instant k is*

$$p_l(k,\tau) = \frac{w_l^\tau(k-1)}{1 + y_l^\tau(k)}$$

where $w_l^\tau(k-1)$ is the number of contracts waiting to be assigned and $y_l^\tau(k)$ the number of assigned contracts. The task prices are updated after the conclusion of each local auction round.

From a perspective of economic science, task prices can be understood as resulting from the law of supply and demand. The robots at each local market constitute the supply of resources needed for the execution of contracts and the demand is formed by the contracts waiting to be assigned. The task prices are higher in local markets with fewer agents or more waiting contracts, all other things being equal. The prices can also be seen as a measure on the "difficulty" of assigning and executing contracts for a task at a local market. Thus, the auction protocol is designed such that contracts are sent to the local markets of neighbours with lower task prices.

Definition 4 (Global Market Auction Protocol)

1) *The neighbours of the auctioneer are informed of the local task prices*
2) *The neighbours must reply with their task prices, within a limited time period, Θ*
3) *The contracts to be traded are sent to the neighbours*

The global and local auctions are conducted in parallel and only the contracts that where not assigned after a local auction are traded with the neighbours. During the global auction, the neighbours do not reply to other auctioneers or initiate their own global auction. The protocol is repeated after a time interval with length σ, where $\sigma \sim Unif(\sigma_{min}, \sigma_{max})$. The value σ is denoted the *global auction assignment interval* and the values are sampled at the end of each auction. If after this time, the auctioneer is a participant in an global auction, it will wait for it to finish. The global market auction protocol described is similar to double auctions, [11], where any participant can sell or buy goods. The main differences are that (i) the global market auction is not centralized, (ii) participants can place offers asynchronously and (iii) multiple global auctions can occur simultaneously.

The number of contracts to trade with a neighbour is determined as follows. Let x be a neighbour of auctioneer l, being offered to buy contracts for task τ at price $p_l(k,\tau)$. The maximum number of contracts to send to the neighbour is $n_\tau(x)$:

$$n_\tau(x) = \max_{n \in \mathbb{Z}_{+,0}} \left\{ \frac{w_l^\tau(k-1) - n}{1 + y_l^\tau(k)} \geq \frac{w_x^\tau(k-1) + n}{1 + y_x^\tau(k)} \right\} \tag{4}$$

The value $n_\tau(x)$ is such that after the auction is concluded, the neighbours task prices are not greater than those of the auctioneer. The number of contracts for task τ sold to the neighbours are determined by the auctioneer l, solving the MLIP:

$$\begin{aligned}
&\max \sum_x r_x \cdot u_x \\
&s.t. \\
&\sum_x u_x \leq w_l^\tau(k) \\
&u_x \leq n_\tau(x), \qquad \forall x \in \mathcal{N}(l) \\
&u_x \in \mathbb{Z}_{0,+}
\end{aligned} \tag{5}$$

where u_x is the number of contracts sold to neighbour x, $\mathcal{N}(l)$ is the auctioneer set of neighbours and $n_\tau(x)$ is the maximum number of contracts requested by neighbour x. The cost values r_x represent the price difference when one contract is sold by the auctioneer to the respective neighbour.

Proposition 2 (Global Task Trading). *Consider a global auction between auctioneer l and the neighbours in $\mathcal{N}(l)$. Then for any neighbour $x \in \mathcal{N}(l)$, $n_\tau(x) \leq \frac{w_l^\tau(k-1)}{2}$. Also, the contracts of tasks such that $w_l^\tau(k-1) - y_l^\tau(k) < 2$, are not traded.*

Proof. *The first claim is a direct consequence of setting $w_x^\tau(k-1)$, $y_x^\tau(k)$ and $y_l^\tau(k)$ to zero. In this case, the task price is zero at neighbour x and it is the highest possible at the auctioneer l. The proof of the second claim is as follows. From Eq. 4, the number of contracts requested by the neighbour $x \in \mathcal{N}(l)$ is the largest, non-negative integer n_τ:*

$$n_\tau \leq \frac{y_l^\tau(1 + y_x^\tau - w_x^\tau) + m + m y_x^\tau - w_x^\tau}{2 + y_l^\tau + y_x^\tau}$$

where $m = w_l^\tau(k-1) - y_l^\tau(k)$ and the indexes k are not shown for clarity. By construction m is a non-negative integer value, because $y_l^\tau(k) \leq w_l^\tau(k-1)$. Otherwise the auctioneer would assign more contracts than those waiting to be assigned. Similarly, $y_x^\tau - w_x^\tau \leq 0$. Thus, if $m < 2$ then $n_\tau = 0$. □

Thus, no contracts are traded if auctioneers can assign locally all of their received contracts. This is an important property because the assignment delay of the traded contracts would otherwise be greater. The protocol also attempts to evenly distribute contracts through all the neighbours in order to avoid flooding them with contracts.

The coordination among the auctioneers is achieved in a decentralized and autonomous manner without an external intervention. These properties are intrinsic to the global auction protocol and the definition of task prices.

The main disadvantage of this protocol is that trading is only performed if two or more contracts are unassigned. In the event that only one contract is not assigned, then it may depart even if there where idle robots in any of the neighbouring local markets. Another disadvantage is the increased assignment delay for the contracts that are traded. This can be minimized by improving the communication infrastructure and reducing the number of local markets.

2.3 Computation and Communication Complexity

The computational complexity of the architecture is understood to be the time required by an auctioneer to solve each of the MLIPs, Eq. 2 and Eq. 5. The communication complexity is the number of exchanged messages in each of the auction protocols.

Proposition 3 (Computational Complexity). *The computational worst case complexity for the local auction is $O(\eta^3)$, with $\eta = \max\{n(k), w(k)\}$, and it is $O(2^{|\mathcal{N}(l)|})$ for the global auction, with $|\mathcal{N}(l)|$ the cardinality of set $\mathcal{N}(l)$.*

Proof. *The MLIP of the local auction is a linear assignment problem, [12], and can thus be efficiently solved with the Hungarian algorithm in $O(\eta^3)$, where η is the maximum number of available robots and waiting contracts. The Hungarian algorithm cannot be used in the global auction because a neighbour can request more than one contract. A brute-force approach is to relax the integer constraint, $u_x \geq 0$. Then solve the resulting linear program to obtain the optimal, relaxed solution u_x^*, which can be done in polynomial time using an interior-point method. The optimal solution is then obtained by evaluating all feasible solutions when rounding u_x^* to the two nearest integers, resulting in a total of $O(2^{|\mathcal{N}(l)|})$ evaluations. For the bids evaluation, in the local auction protocol, at most all robots bid for all contracts. Thus $O(n(k)\, w(k)$ evaluations are required. Similarly, in the global auction protocol, at most all neighbours bid for all tasks, and in the worst case there are $O(|\mathcal{N}(l)|)$ bids are submitted.* □

Proposition 4 (Communication Complexity). *The number of exchanged messages is $O(n(k)\, w(k)+n(k))$ for the local auction and $O(|\mathcal{N}(l)|+w(k))$ for the global auction.*

Proof. *From the auction protocol definition, Def. 2, if all agents bid for all contracts then a total of $O(n(k)\, w(k) + n(k))$ messages are exchanged between the auctioneer and the robots. Similarly, in the global auction protocol all neighbours are informed of the local task prices. If all reply with bids then $O(|N(l)| + w(k))$ messages are exchanged.* □

Since the global auction optimal solution has an exponential complexity, an heuristic procedure is instead used in practice. The first step is to organize all neighbours $x \in \mathcal{N}(l)$, in ascending order of their respective cost values r_x. The next step is to assign to the first neighbour x', the number of contracts given by: $\max\{n_\tau(x'),\, w_l^\tau(k)\}$. This step is repeated for the other neighbours, by their order, until no contracts remain.

The only difficulty in this procedure is the initial sorting of the neighbours, which can be accomplished with logarithmic complexity. Although the optimal solution is not guaranteed, the heuristic solutions verify Prop. 2.

3 Control Architecture Analysis

The auctioneers in the architecture, serve as intermediaries between the system components that request the execution of tasks and the mobile robots. Although the components and the robots do not need to know the state of each other, an assignment delay is introduced by the architecture. Thus, it is important to determine the impact of the different parameters, such as the number of robots, in the assignment delay.

Proposition 5 (Number of Assigned Contracts). *In local markets, the number of assigned contracts is always* $y(k) = \min\{w(k-1),\, n(k-1)\}$.

Proof. From the constraints of the MLIP in Eq. 2, the number of assigned contracts is always equal or less than $\min\{w(k-1),\, n(k-1)\}$. *Since all available mobile robots provide the same set of tasks, there are no negative entries in matrix* $C(k)$. *Since it is a maximization problem, the optimal solution is obtained when the number of assigned contracts is greater or equal than* $\min\{w(k-1),\, n(k-1)\}$. □

Proposition 6 (Number of Required Agents). *Consider a local market with* N *mobile robots and let their maximum service time for contracts of task* τ *be* $s_\tau \Delta$, *with* $s_\tau \in \mathbb{Z}_+$. *The maximum number of contracts arrivals for task* τ, *per assignment period* Δ, *is* $a_\tau \in \mathbb{R}_+$. *Then the assignment delay for any contract is equal or less than* 2Δ iff $N \geq \Delta \sum_\tau a_\tau(1+s_\tau)$.

Proof. Assume that for all contracts, the assignment delay is equal or less than 2Δ. *From Prop. 1 we have* $y(k) = w(k-1)$, *since all received contracts in period* $[k-2,\, k-1)$ *are assigned at instant k. Using Prop. 5 we have that* $w(k-1) \leq N - \overline{n}(k-1)$, *where* $\overline{n}(.)$ *is the number of busy agents. Let* $y_\tau(k)$ *be the number of assigned contracts for task* τ. *At instant k, the number of agents busy with contracts for task* τ *is* $\overline{n}_\tau(k)$:

$$
\begin{aligned}
&\overline{n}_\tau(k) = \overline{n}_\tau(k-1) + y_\tau(k) - y_\tau(k-s_\tau) \\
&\dots \\
&\overline{n}_\tau(k+s_\tau) = \overline{n}_\tau(k-1) + \sum_{l=0}^{s_\tau} y_\tau(k+l) - y_\tau(k-s_\tau+l)
\end{aligned}
$$

Since s_τ *is constant, we have* $\overline{n}_\tau(k-1) + y_\tau(k) = \sum_{l=0}^{s_\tau} y_\tau(k-s_\tau+l)$ *and thus* $\overline{n}_\tau(k+s_\tau) = \sum_{l=1}^{s_\tau} y_\tau(k+l)$. *Since the assignment delay is equal or less than* 2Δ, *for all k we have* $y_\tau(k) = a_\tau\Delta$ *and* $\overline{n}_\tau(k) = a_\tau s_\tau \Delta$. *Proceeding similarly for the other task types, we have* $\overline{n}(k) = \Delta\sum_\tau a_\tau s_\tau$ *and the number of agents in the local market is then* $N \geq \Delta\sum_\tau a_\tau(1+s_\tau)$. *The proof in the opposite direction is as follows. Assume that the number of agents is such that* $N < \Delta\sum_\tau a_\tau(1+s_\tau)$. *Then some contracts received up to, but excluding,* $k-1$ *are not assigned at instant k. Because otherwise* $w(k') \leq N - \overline{n}(k')$ *for all* $k' \leq k-1$ *and* $N \geq \Delta\sum_\tau a_\tau(1+s_\tau)$, *which is a contradiction. Thus, these unassigned contracts can only be assigned at* $k+1$ *or latter and their assignment delay is greater than* 2Δ. □

The lower bound presented in Prop. 6 is not tight because worst case service times and arrival rates where assumed. In practice, and depending on the distribution of these parameters, fewer agents may be used with an assignment delay almost always below 2Δ. An immediate application of Prop. 6 is to estimate the minimum required number of agents, if the arrival rates and service times are known. Another use is to compare the cost of using more expensive agents with lower service times *versus* the gain in reducing the number of agents. Finally, Prop. 6 can be used to analyze the behavior of the task prices.

Proposition 7 (Bounded Task Prices). *Consider a local market with auctioneer l, and assume that no tasks are traded with the neighbours and that the assignment deadlines are much greater than the local auction assignment period Δ. Then*

$$\forall \tau,\ p_l(k,\tau) < 1 \Leftrightarrow N \geq \Delta \sum_{\tau} a_\tau (1 + s_\tau)$$

Proof. *If Prop. 6 is verified, then all waiting contracts at $k-1$ are assigned at k and $y_l^\tau(k) = w_l^\tau(k-1)$ for all tasks. The implication follows from the definition of task prices, Definition 3. In opposite direction, the proof is as follows. If Prop. 6 is not verified, then at least for one of the tasks, not all contracts are assigned within the minimal delay. Then $w_l^\tau(k-1) > y_l^\tau(k)$ and $p(\tau,k) \geq 1$ for that task. Assume that the contract assignment deadlines are sufficiently large when compared to the auctioneer assignment period Δ. Then, from the assignment cost definition Eq. 3, the unassigned contracts are eventually assigned as soon as their delay is sufficiently large. But then contracts for the other tasks will not be assigned and will also accumulate at the auctioneer. If no contracts are traded with other auctioneers, eventually for all tasks $w_l^\tau(k-1) > y_l^\tau(k)$ and $p(\tau,k) \geq 1$.* □

The task prices at a local market can be used to signal if the surveillance system operational assumptions are not verified. From Definition 3, it is clear that prices are equal or greater than one if some contracts remain unassigned. This may occur due to hardware or network failures which reduce the number of available robots, Props. 7 and 6. Also, it can occur if the contracts arrival rate is greater than expected, Prop. 6. Although the robustness to failures is increase if multiple local markets are used, this is at a cost of an increase in the assignment delay for the traded contracts since they must also wait for the start of a global auction.

Proposition 8 (Global Auction Initiation Delay). *Consider a set of $\mathcal{N}$ auctioneers, all neighbours of each other and assume that the assignment periods Δ are equal and the global auction intervals σ are independent and identically distributed (i.i.d.). Then an auctioneer $l \in \mathcal{N}$, is expected to wait $\Theta \cdot |\mathcal{N}| \cdot \frac{\sigma_{max}+\sigma_{min}}{2}$.*

Proof. *In the worst case, all auctioneers attempt to initialize a global auction at very close time instants and an auctioneer $l \in \mathcal{N}$, must wait for those that sampled lower σ values. Since all σ are i.i.d. and sampled at the end of each global auction, the probability that auctioneer l must wait for m other auctioneers has a binomial distribution with $p = \frac{\sigma_{max}+\sigma_{min}}{2}$. Assuming that the communication delays are small enough when compared with the bid reply waiting time, then expected initialization delay is $\Theta \cdot |\mathcal{N}| \cdot \frac{\sigma_{max}+\sigma_{min}}{2}$.* □

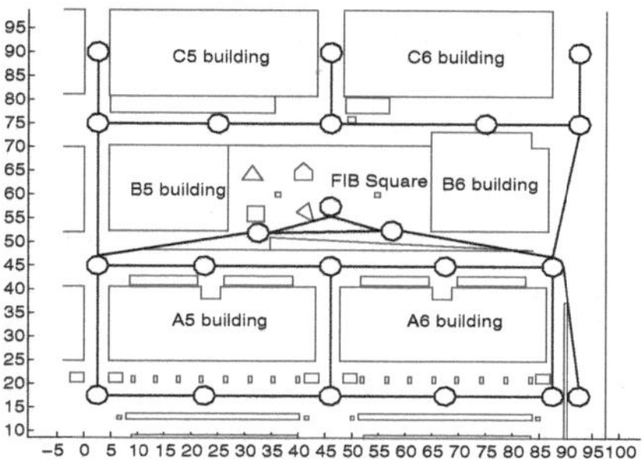

Fig. 2. URUS project urban scenario (the axes dimensions are in meters)

The organization of the mobile robots into local markets, and their neighbours, should be decided based on Prop. 6 and Prop. 8. If all robots are grouped into a single local market, then the assignment delay is minimized at the cost of introducing a critical point of failure. In the other extreme, local markets can have only one robot but the expected assignment delay is significantly increased. The trade-off between the two extremes is dependent on the communication infrastructure and number of mobile robots. Nevertheless, the use of task prices is always available to signal anomalous situations to human supervisors, Prop. 7.

4 Application Examples

The application of the architecture is exemplified to the urban environment of the URUS project, [13], with a worst case analysis. The scenario is a square in the UPC campus at Barcelona, Spain, with approximately 100 meters in each side and is represented in Fig. 2. The robots navigate in this environment using the topological map superimposed on Fig. 2, with 22 locations. The active surveillance system is composed by a set of cameras place on the top of the site buildings and has available four Pioneer P3-AT mobile robots to execute tasks. The robots maximum linear velocity is limited to $0.3m/s$ for safety reasons and also to extend the battery life.

Consider the case where all robots belong to a single local market, with an assignment period of $\Delta = 3s$, and that the only task is the inspection of the suspect locations detected by the cameras. Since the robots maximum velocity is $0.3m/s$, at least $471.4s$ are required for a robot to reach any arbitrary location if moving in a straight line. This is not always possible and some extra time is also required for collecting images. Therefore the maximum service time of the inspection task is empirically rounded up to $540s$. From Prop. 6, the assignment delay is less or equal than 2Δ if and only if the arrival rate of inspection contracts verifies

$$a_{inspection} \leq \frac{N}{\Delta(1 + s_{inspection})} = \frac{4}{\Delta(1 + 180)} = \frac{0.0221}{\Delta} \tag{6}$$

or approximately less than 26 contracts per hour. In practice much fewer detections are expected and the robots can execute other tasks, such as patrol and battery recharge. A total of three patrol task are now included, the first two are requested every hour and the other every two hours, $a_{1,2} = \frac{0.0025}{\Delta}$ and $a_3 = \frac{0.00125}{\Delta}$. In the first two patrols, the robots must travel along each of the diagonals of the square, $s_{1,2} = 158$, and in the other they must patrol the perimeter, $s_3 = 445$. The robots use sealed lead-acid batteries, which in our indoors laboratory endure approximately 4 hours but in urban environments it can be substantially less. Suppose that human operators manually swap the batteries of a robot in 5 minutes, at a central station located at southwest corner, $s_{recharge} = 158 + 100$. Two recharge tasks are also included, auctioned every two hours, $a_{recharge} = \frac{0.0025}{\Delta}$ but are assigned only if the robots battery level is below some threshold. With the additional five tasks, the system can handle inspection tasks at a maximum arrival rate of $\frac{0.011}{\Delta}$, or approximately 13 per hour.

The worst case service time of the inspection task is large because robots must cover the entire environment. Although the inclusion of more robots can reduce the average service time, it will not reduce the worst case. Thus an alternative setup is to add four more robots and divide the total in four identical groups, each responsible for the inspection tasks in a quarter of the environment. In this setup, the worst case travel time of the robots is reduced to $117.85s$. But since the other tasks are shared by all groups, their assignment delay is expected to increase, Prop. 8, and the cameras must know the local markets responsible for each quarter of the environment.

Another possible setup is to allow the robots to travel at the higher velocity of $0.5m/s$. The worst case travel time is reduced to $282.84s$ but their batteries must be replaced more often. Assume that the recharge tasks must now be auctioned at every hour, the other tasks arrival rates remain unchanged and the inspection task service time is empirically rounded up to $300s$. Then the surveillance system can handle a maximum arrival rate of inspection tasks of $\frac{0.023}{\Delta}$, or approximately 27 per hour. A higher rate is obtained because with a higher velocity, all tasks are executed in less time. But this is at the cost of greater mechanical tear and the need of more reliable collision and navigation algorithms. A similar procedure can be used to account for other tasks or different setups. For instance, if the robots must charge their own batteries and thus wait a longer period of time.

It must be stressed that the worst case was considered for all of the tasks parameters and in practice, their values can be smaller. The worst case analysis is important to surveillance systems because these are more exposed to the occurrence of unexpected events, resulting in greater damages. The behavior of the architecture for the average case can be analysed through simulation. This is not presented due to the lack of space and also because reasonable values where used in the worst case analysis.

4.1 Surveillance Patrols

The performance of the architecture, with respect to the optimal solution, is evaluated in a simple setup, where all the map locations must be visited in the shortest possible time. The mobile robots start at location $(2, 17)$, see Fig. 2, and their velocity is limited to $0.3m/s$. An inspection task contract is created for each location in the map, 22 in total and the auctioneers assignment period is 2 seconds. The optimal minimum travel distance is directly obtained by summing the distances between each neighbouring pair of nodes but some pairs, $(92, 17)$ and $(87, 17)$ for example, are summed twice. The

Table 1. Performance of the architecture, as a percentage of the optimal values

Surveillance System Setup	Max. Individual Distance (%)	Sum of Distances (%)	Completion Time (%)
One local market, one robot	103.84	103.84	107.08
One local market, four robots	62.38	214.99	65.81
Two local markets, two robots each	62.88	199.35	46.47
Four local markets, one robot each	50.45	174.64	51.29
Four local markets, with failures	78.16	144.02	79.39

completion time is obtained by dividing the travel time by the robots maximum velocity. In Table 1 is presented performance of different architecture configurations.

The last configuration in Table 1 is identical to the third, except that the robots are inoperative in two of the local markets and they must thus trade their contracts.

The percentage of total travelled distance can be understood as measure of the task planning quality. If the setup total travel time is greater than the optimal value, then the robots passed more than once at previously inspected locations. Since the robots start at the same location, the total travelled distance would always be greater than the optimal. Nevertheless in almost all configurations the total travelled distance is much greater than the optimal value. The percentage of the completion time can be understood as a measure of the assignment delay introduced by the proposed architecture. It is visible in Table 1 that the completion time is greatly reduced when multiple robots are used, even with the occurrence of failures. These performance results where expected because the auctioneers only attempt to reduce the latency time of the contracts. But because auctioneers do not plan the contracts assignment order, the architecture is not suitable for task planning purposes.

5 Conclusions and Future Work

An architecture for the assignment of tasks in an active surveillance system was presented. The architecture is organized in two hierarchy levels. At a lower level, a centralized task assignment approach is used, while at the higher level the approach is decentralized. Since auction protocols are used to compute the assignment solutions, the architecture is robust to failures, such as the breakdown of some robots. The two protocols exhibit polynomial computational and communication complexities almost always and a sub-optimal method was presented to efficiently compute the solution at the higher level. A set of theoretical bounds where presented for the architecture assignment delay. This could be further reduced if, for instance, the robots state was known by the auctioneer or the distribution of the tasks arrival times is known. Nevertheless the former would require a more reliable network with a higher bandwidth and the it would only improve the assignment solution quality for the average situation. In addition, the system performance in unusual operating conditions could be seriously degraded due to these assumptions. A measure of the architecture performance, similar to economic prices, was presented. A theoretical relation was shown between task prices and the departure of unassigned task contracts. The measure is also used by the upper hierarchy level, to trade unassigned contracts among local markets. Furthermore, tasks prices can be used to detect anomalous operating conditions, such as an unexpected high arrival rate of tasks. Future work includes (i) the design of a system supervisor using the task prices as feedback information and (ii) further analysis of the architecture top level operation.

Acknowledgments

This work was supported by the European Project FP6-2005-IST-6-045062-URUS, and ISR/IST plurianual funding through the POS_Conhecimento Program that includes FEDER funds. Nelson Gonçalves is working under grant SFRH/BD/23804/2005 from Fundação para a Ciência e a Tecnologia.

References

1. Helvig, C.S., Robins, G., Zelikovsky, A.: The moving-target traveling salesman problem. Journal of Algorithms 49(1), 153–174 (2003); 1998 European Symposium on Algorithms
2. Del Bimbo, A., Pernici, F.: Towards on-line saccade planning for high-resolution image sensing. Pattern Recogn. Lett. 27(15), 1826–1834 (2006)
3. Dias, M.B., Zlot, R., Kalra, N., Stentz, A.: Market-based multirobot coordination: a survey and analysis. Proceedings of the IEEE 94(7), 1257–1270 (2006)
4. Brydon, M.: Economic metaphors for solving intrafirm allocation problems: What does a market buy us? Decision Support Systems 42(3), 1657–1672 (2006)
5. Nisam, N., Roughgarden, T., Tardos, E., Vazirani, V.V.: Algorithmic Game Theory. Cambridge University Press, Cambridge (2007)
6. Gerkey, B.P., Mataric, M.J.: Multi-robot task allocation: analyzing the complexity and optimality of key architectures. In: Proceedings of the IEEE International Conference on Robotics and Automation 2003, vol. 3, pp. 3862–3868 (2003)
7. Hayek, F.A.: Law, Legislation and Liberty. Taylor & Francis Books Ltd., Routledge (1982)
8. Mosteo, A.R., Montano, L.: Comparative experiments on optimization criteria and algorithms for auction based multi-robot task allocation. In: IEEE International Conference on Robotics and Automation, pp. 3345–3350 (2007)
9. Specification, O.O.C.: Reference model for service oriented architecture 1.0. Technical report, OASIS (August 2006)
10. Jungwattanakit, J., Reodecha, M., Chaovalitwongse, P., Werner, F.: A comparison of scheduling algorithms for flexible flow shop problems with unrelated parallel machines, setup times, and dual criteria. Computers and Operations Research 36(2), 358–378 (2009); Scheduling for Modern Manufacturing, Logistics, and Supply Chains
11. Gjerstad, S., Dickhaut, J.: Price formation in double auctions. Games and Economic Behavior 22(1), 1–29 (1998)
12. Burkard, R.E.: Selected topics on assignment problems. Discrete Appl. Math. 123(1-3), 257–302 (2002)
13. Sanfeliu, A., Andrade-Cetto, J.: Ubiquitous networking robotics in urban settings. In: Workshop on Network Robot Systems Procs. of 2006 IEEE/RSJ International Conference on Intelligente Robots and Systems (IROS2006) (October 2006)

Roles, Positionings and Set Plays to Coordinate a RoboCup MSL Team

Nuno Lau, Luís Seabra Lopes, Nelson Filipe, and Gustavo Corrente

Transverse Activity on Intelligent Robotics,
IEETA / Universidade de Aveiro, 3810-193 Aveiro, Portugal
{nunolau,lsl,nelson.filipe,gustavo}@ua.pt

Abstract. This paper presents the team coordination methodologies of CAMBADA, a robotic soccer team designed to participate in the RoboCup middle-size league (MSL). The coordination model extends and adapts previous work in the Soccer Simulation League to the MSL environment. The approach is based on flexible positionings and priority-based dynamic role/positioning assignment. In addition, coordinated procedures for passing and setplays have been implemented. With the described design, CAMBADA reached the 1st place in the RoboCup'2008 world championship, becoming the first Portuguese real robot team to win in RoboCup. Competition results and performance measures computed from logs and videos of real competition games are presented and discussed.

Keywords: Multi-robot team coordination, strategic positioning, dynamic role assignment, coordinated procedures.

1 Introduction

As robots pervade different areas of human activity, researchers are naturally prompted to investigate how robots can cooperate in order to perform complex tasks. Moreover, progress in wireless communication technologies enables information sharing and explicit coordination between robots. These are basic capabilities needed to support sophisticated cooperation and coordination algorithms. Given this increasing availability of robots and communication technologies, multi-robot systems have, in the last two decades, been receiving increasingly attention from researchers [2][6][25].

Multi-robot systems also present advantages with respect to single robots. First, some tasks are difficult or even impossible to be carried out by a single robot. In other cases, by providing a larger work force, multi-robot systems can carry out tasks faster. Multi-robot systems also facilitate scalability, as larger problems can often be solved by adding more robots to the team. Finally, through their inherent redundancy, multi-robot systems offer robustness, as they may still work when a team member is damaged or malfunctioning.

The development of multi-robot systems raises many new research issues concerned with how robots can coordinate their actions to carry out the assigned tasks as efficiently as possible. Among other issues, the following can be mentioned: How are

L. Seabra Lopes et al. (Eds.): EPIA 2009, LNAI 5816, pp. 323–337, 2009.

different sub-tasks assigned to different robots [10]? How can different roles be assigned to different robots [19] [21][25]? If robots need to move in formation, how can it be controlled [5]? How can multi-robot plans be generated and/or executed [1]? Which information should robots exchange to enable coordination [13]? How can multi-robot systems be debugged [9]?

The authors have been addressing several of these issues in the robotic soccer domain. In particular, the authors contributed to the development of CAMBADA, a RoboCup middle-size league (MSL) team (Fig. 1). The MSL is one of the most challenging leagues in RoboCup. Robotic players must be completely autonomous and must play in a field of 12m × 18m [16]. Teams are composed of at most six robots with a maximum height of 80 cm. Human interference is allowed only for removing malfunctioning robots and re-entering robots in the game.

Fig. 1. CAMBADA robotic team

Building a team for the MSL is a very challenging task. Robots must be robust, fast and possess a comprehensive set of sensors. At the software level they must have an efficient set of low-level skills and must coordinate themselves to act as a team. Research conducted within CAMBADA has led to developments concerning hardware [4], computational and communications infrastructure [20], vision system [7], monitoring / debugging [9] and high-level deliberation and coordination [13]. This paper focuses on the last aspect, providing a detailed and up-to-date account of the currently used algorithms and their performance.

The complexity of MSL explains why most teams have implemented relatively simple coordination capabilities. The more advanced teams achieve coordination through the assignment of different roles to the robots [3][19][27]. Typically there is, at least, an attacker, a defender, a supporter and a goalie. As perception and sensori-motor capabilities become more sophisticated it will be possible to develop more sophisticated coordination algorithms. This trend is pushed further by the increase in team size (number of robots) as well as field size. A natural source of inspiration is the RoboCup Soccer Simulation League, where teams have been using coordination layers with strategy, tactics and formations [22][25], coordination graphs [12] and reinforcement learning [23][16].

CAMBADA participated in several national and international competitions, including RoboCup world championships (5th place in 2007, 1st place in 2008, 3rd place in 2009) and the Portuguese Open Robotics Festival (3rd place in 2006, 1st place in

2007, 2008 and 2009). This paper presents the coordination methodologies developed for RoboCup'2008. These methodologies largely explain the great success achieved, as the CAMBADA robots are among the slowest of the league.

This paper is organized as follows: Section 2 presents the hardware and software architectures of CAMBADA players. Sections 3 and 4 describe the adopted coordination methodologies. Section 5 presents and discusses competition results and various performance measures. Section 6 concludes the paper.

2 Hardware and Software Architecture

CAMBADA robots (Fig. 1) were designed and completely built at the University of Aveiro. Each robot fits into a cylindrical envelope with 485 mm in diameter. The mechanical structure of the players is layered and modular. The lower layer contains motors, wheels, batteries and an electromechanical kicker. The middle layer contains the control electronics. The upper layer contains a laptop computer, a catadioptric omnidirectional vision system, a frontal vision system and an electronic compass.

The robots use three Swedish wheels for holonomic motion, and move at a maximum speed of 2.0 m/s. This is less than many other MSL teams, which can currently move at speeds typically between 2.5 and 4.0 m/s (e.g. [18] [11] [24] [8]). Robots also carry encoders, battery status sensors and an IR ball presence sensor.

The computational system in each robot is a set of processing nodes (small microcontrollers plus a laptop) connected through a CAN bus. Communication within the team is based on standard wireless LAN protocol IEEE 802.11. The team receives referee instructions using a wired LAN TCP link. On the laptop, CAMBADA players run several software processes, for image acquisition and analysis, information integration, deliberation and communication with the low-level modules. The order and activation schedule of the processes is performed by a process manager [20].

The top-level processing loop starts by integrating perception information gathered locally from the vision processes, odometry, compass and ball presence sensors. All this information is stored in a shared data structure called Real-Time Data Base (RTDB). The RTDB has a local area, shared only among local processes, and a global area, shared with the other players. The global area is transparently replicated in all players in real-time. Self-localization uses a sensor fusion engine based on the publicly available engine described in [14]. Compass information is used to resolve ambiguities and detect self-localization errors. The final fusion step is to integrate local information with information shared by teammates.

Deliberation in CAMBADA considerably relies on the concepts of *role* and *behavior*. During open play, the CAMBADA agents use only four roles: *RoleGoalie*, *RoleSupporter* and *RoleStriker*. Further details about the developed roles and respective coordination mechanisms will be presented in sections 3 and 4.

Roles select the active behavior at each time step. Behaviors are the basic sensorimotor skills of the robot, like moving to a specific position or kicking the ball. The set of behaviors that are implemented in the CAMBADA agent are adapted to its catadioptric omnidirectional vision and holonomic driving systems. In brief, the current set of behaviors is the following:

- ***bMove*** uses two symbolic parameters: the target position where to move; and the position which the player should be facing in its path to the target. This behavior may avoid obstacles and avoid the ball (used during the game repositions).
- ***bMoveToAbs*** allows the movement of the player to an absolute position in the game field, and also allows the player to face any given position.
- ***bPassiveInter*** moves the player to the closest point in the ball trajectory.
- ***bDribble*** is used to dribble the ball to a given relative player direction.
- ***bCatchBall*** is used to receive a pass. The player aligns itself with the ball path and, when the ball is close, moves backwards to soften the impact.
- ***bKick*** is used to kick the ball accurately to one 3D position, either for shooting to goal or passing to a teammate. Polynomial functions, whose coefficients were determined by experimentation, are used to compute kick power.
- ***bGoalieDefend*** is the main behavior of the goalie.

3 Positionings and Roles

For open play, CAMBADA uses an implicit coordination model based on notions like *strategic positioning*, *role* and *formation*. These notions have been introduced and/or extensively explored in the RoboCup Soccer Simulation League [25][21]. In order to apply such notions in the MSL, some new algorithms had to be designed. The approach is presented in detail in this section.

3.1 Formations and Strategic Positionings

Formations are sets of positionings, where each *positioning* is a movement model for a player. The assignment of players to specific positionings is dynamic. Each positioning is specified by three elements:

- Home position, i.e. the target position when the ball is at the centre of the field
- Region of the field where the player can move, and
- Ball attraction parameters, used to compute the *target position* of the player in each moment based on the current ball position

Using different home positions and attraction parameters for the positionings allows a simple definition of defensive and attack strategic movement models. Fig. 2 shows the formation of the team used in RoboCup'2008 for several ball positions.

3.2 Roles in Open Play

CAMBADA robots use three roles in open play: *RoleGoalie*, activated for the goalkeeper, *RoleSupporter* and *RoleStriker*. *RoleStriker* is an "active player" role. It tries to catch the ball and score goals.

Only one player at a time is supposed to run RoleStriker. The striker is helped by teammates that take on *RoleSupporter* [13]. Supporters keep their target positions as determined by their positioning assignments and the current ball position. As a result, supporters accompany the striker as it plays along the field, without interfering. When the striker cannot progress with the ball towards the opponent goal and the ball remains behind the striker for more than some fixed time (e.g. 2 sec), supporters can take a more active behavior. In this case, the closest supporter to the ball also approaches the ball, acting as "backup striker".

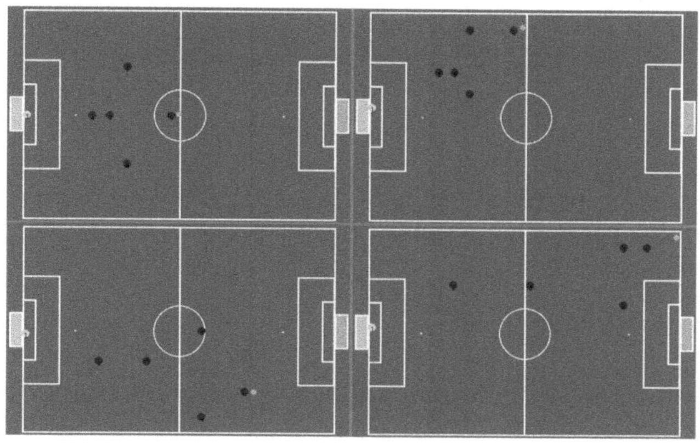

Fig. 2. Target player positions for several different ball positions

```
Algorithm: role and positioning assignment
Input: POS - array of N positioning, BallPos - ball position
Input/output: PL - array of K active players (K =< N)
Local: TP - array of N target positions
{
  clearAssigments(PL);
  TP = calcTargetPositions(POS,BallPos);
  for each POS[i], i ∈ 1..N, in descending order of priority
  {
    if there is no free player then return;
    p = the free player closest to TP[i];
    PL[p].positioning = i;
    PL[p].targetPosition = TP[i];
    if POS[i] has highest priority then PL[p].role= striker;
      else PL[p].role = supporter;
  }
}
```

Fig. 3. CAMBADA Positioning and role assignment algorithm

3.3 Role and Positioning Assignment

The play-on decision that assigns roles and positionings to the active players is performed using a new algorithm that takes into account different priorities for the different roles and positionings, so that the most important ones are always covered. This is an important feature since the number of available players varies as a result of several common situations in the MSL, namely hardware and software malfunctions and referee orders (see section 5.1 for concrete measures).

The role assignment algorithm is presented in Fig. 3. Consider a formation with N positionings and a team of $K \leq N$ available field players (goal-keeper is not counted). Firstly, the distances of robots to each of the target positions are calculated. Then the striker role is assigned to the robot that is closest to the highest priority strategic positioning, which is in turn the closest to the ball. From the remaining K-1 robots, the algorithm proceeds assigning the positionings, in priority order, to the closest unassigned robot to the associated target position. This algorithm may be performed by the coach agent in the base station, ensuring a coordinated assignment result, or locally by each robot, which may lead to some inconsistencies. In the latest competitions, positioning assignments were carried out by the coach at intervals of 1 second and the role assignments were individually carried out by each player.

4 Coordinated Procedures

Coordinated procedures are short plans executed by at least two robots. In some cases, these plans involve communication resulting in explicit coordination. In the case of CAMBADA, coordinated procedures are used for passes and set plays.

4.1 Passes

Passing is a coordinated behavior involving two players, in which one kicks the ball towards the other. Until now, MSL teams have shown limited success in implementing and demonstrating passes. In RoboCup 2004, some teams had already implemented passes, but the functionality was not robust enough to actually be useful in games [15] [26]. The CoPS and Tribots teams also support pass play [28][16].

Two player roles have recently been developed for coordinated passes in the CAMBADA team. In the general case, the player running *RoleStriker* may decide to take on *RolePasser*, choosing the player to receive the ball. After being notified, the second player takes on *RoleReceiver*. These roles were not used in real competition games in 2008, but they have been demonstrated in RoboCup'2008 MSL *Free Technical Challenge*. A similar mechanism has been used for corner kicks (see below). In the free challenge, several passes occurred until a position to score a goal was reached. The sequence of actions on both players is described in Table 1. The coordination between passer and receiver is based on passing flags, which can take the following values: READY, TRYING_TO_PASS and BALL_PASSED.

4.2 Set Plays

CAMBADA also uses coordinated procedures for set plays, in situations such as kick-off, throw-in, corner kick, free kick and goal kick. Set play procedures define a sequence of behaviors for several robots in a coordinated way. For that purpose, the involved players take on specific roles. This role-based implementation of set plays not only was easy to integrate with the previous agent architecture, but also facilitated the test and tune of different plans allowing for very efficient final implementations.

Table 1. Coordinated action in a pass

RolePasser	RoleReceiver
PassFlag ← TRYING_TO_PASS	
Align to receiver	Align to Passer PassFlag ← READY
Kick the ball	
PassFlag ← BALL_PASSED	
Move to next position	Catch ball

RoleToucher and *RoleReplacer* are used to overcome the MSL indirect rule in the case of indirect set pieces against the opponent. The purpose of *RoleToucher* is to touch the ball and leave it to the *RoleReplacer* player. This scheme allows the replacer to score a direct goal if the opportunity arises. Two toucher-replacer procedures were implemented. In the case of *corner kicks*, the toucher passes the ball to the replacer, which catches it and shoots to the goal (pseudo-code in Fig. 4). The passing algorithm is as explained above. Another toucher-replacer procedure is used for *throw-in*, *goal kick* and *free kick* situations. Here, the toucher touches the ball pushing it towards the replacer until the ball is engaged by the replacer, then withdraws leaving the ball to the replacer. The replacer also moves towards the ball, waits that the toucher moves away and then shoots to the opponent goal. Both toucher and replacer position themselves on the shoot line, so that, as soon as the toucher moves away, the replacer is ready to shoot. For the kick-off, the procedure is the same, except that robots must be in their own side of the field.

```
Algorithm: RoleReplacer // for corner kicks
{
   if I have Ball then shoot to opponent goal
   else if Ball close to me then move to Ball
     else if Toucher already passed ball then catch Ball
       else wait that Ball is passed
}
```

Fig. 4. Replacer role algorithm for corner kicks

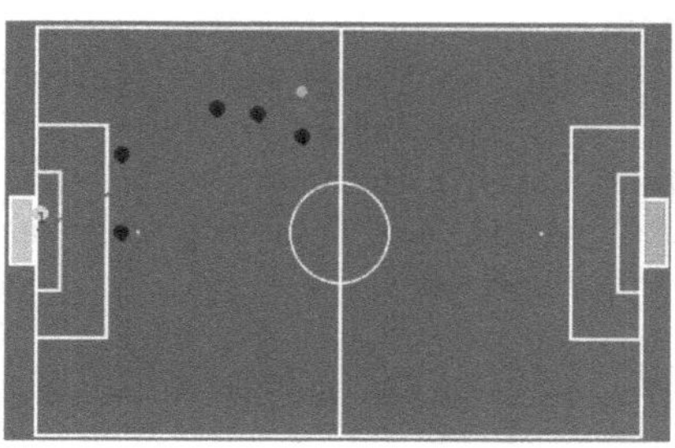

Fig. 5. Placement of RoleBarrier players

Finally, in the case of set pieces against CAMBADA, *RoleBarrier* is used to protect the goal from a direct shoot. The line connecting the ball to the own goal defines the barrier positions. One player places itself on this line, as close to the ball as it is allowed. Two players place themselves near the penalty area. One player is placed near the ball, 45º degrees from the mentioned line, so that it can observe the ball coming into play. The last player position prevents progression of the ball through the closest side of the field. The placement of players is illustrated in Fig. 5.

The assignment of the *RoleBarrier*, *RoleReplacer* and *RoleToucher* roles is executed by sorting the agents according to their perceived distances to the ball and selecting the closest ones, up to the maximum number of agents in each role. When selecting an exclusive role (ex: *RoleReplacer*) the agent looks at the other teammates role decisions and if it finds the same role in a player with a lower *id* it will not select that role. This assignment is always performed locally by each robot.

5 Performance Evaluation

The CAMBADA team participated and won the MSL world championship in RoboCup'2008 (Suzhou, China, July 2008). Most performance evaluation results presented in this section were obtained by analyzing log files and videos of games in this championship. RoboCup'2008 competition results will also be presented. The logs are created by the coach agent. At 1 second intervals, the coach takes a snapshot of relevant information retrieved from each robot, including current role, strategic positioning, behaviour, self position and ball position. A software tool was developed to analyse game logs and extract relevant evaluation measures. As the CAMBADA team made it to the final, it was scheduled to play 13 games. One of them was not played due to absence of the opponent. For two other games, the log files were lost. Thus, the results presented below are extracted from log files of the remaining 10 games.

5.1 General Game Features

Three main classes of game states are *open play*, *set piece against* CAMBADA and *set piece for* CAMBADA. Table 2 shows the respective time distribution in percentage of full game duration, computed over the 10 game logs mentioned above. The time spent in set pieces, considerably higher than what might be expected, results from the dynamics in MSL games. In fact, robots fast moving capabilities (up to 4m/s) and powerful ball kicking capabilities are not accompanied by sufficiently effective ball control capabilities, thus causing various types of set pieces. The time spent in set pieces justifies the investment in the development of the Replacer & Toucher combination in CAMBADA. A high efficiency rate in set pieces makes a real difference in the final team performance.

Table 2. Time distribution for different classes of game states

Game state	Time (%)
Open play	53.1
Set piece for	21.5
Set piece against	25.4

Another common feature in MSL teams is that, due to reliability issues, the number of playing field robots is often less than the maximum of five. Table 3 shows the average percentage of game time (in the 10 mentioned game logs) for different numbers of playing field robots in the CAMBADA team.

Table 3. Percentage of game time for different numbers of playing field robots

	#running robots					
	0	1	2	3	4	5
Time (%)	0.3	4.5	3.5	16.1	39.3	36.3

The average number of running field robots for the CAMBADA team was 3.98. This reveals the reliability problems that were experienced mostly in the beginning of the championship. These were solved to some extent during the championship and reliability improved in later games. In the final game the average number of running field robots was 4.33.

Capabilities for shooting to goal, although not directly based on coordination methodologies, are essential for a team's success. Fig. 6b shows the location from where the ball was shot to goal in the RoboCup'2008 MSL final (CAMBADA-TechUnited). CAMBADA showed good scoring abilities in the competition. Table 4 shows the results of all the shots made in the final game within 9 meters of the opponent goal (for larger distances, a shot doesn't have enough power to pose a real threat to the opponent team). A total of 15 shots were made, of which 1 was missed, 1 hit the post and another hit the bar. The remaining 12 hit the intended target within the goal. This gives an accuracy rating of 80%. From all the 15 shots made, 7 resulted in a goal being scored. This gives a goal scoring success rate (within 9 meters) of 46.7%.

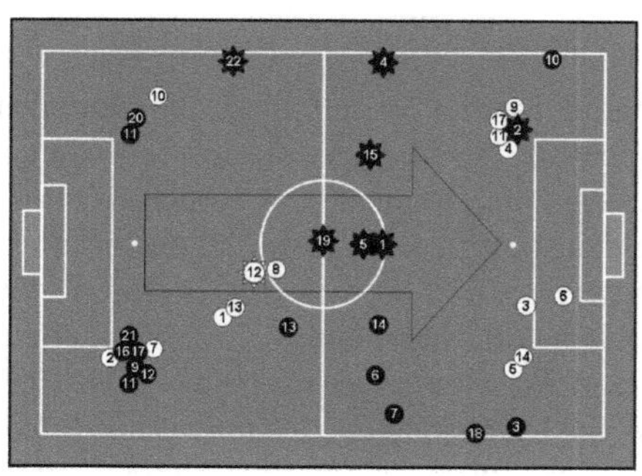

Fig. 6. Shoot locations in the final CAMBADA (black, on the left) - TechUnited (white, on the right) game in RoboCup 2008 (shoots are circles and goals are sun-like forms)

Table 4. Goal scoring performance

Result	Number
Missed	1
Post/bar	2
Defended	5
Goal	7
Total	15

This high success rate is the result of accurate ball placing when kicking. In 5 of the 7 scored goals, the goalkeeper was actually well positioned and in the path of the ball. However, the accurate calibration and power selection for each kick made the ball reach the opponent goal at an height slightly above 80 cm which effectively caused it to go over the goalkeeper, and creating a shot that is very difficult to defend.

5.2 Roles and Behaviors

Table 5 shows the average percentage of time any given player spends in each role, with respect to the total time the player is active in each game. It can be observed that players spend a considerable amount of time (45.2 %) as *RoleSupporter*. This is to be expected since there may be up to 4 players with the Supporter role in open play, while there is at most one player acting as *RoleStriker*. This largely explains why the *RoleStriker* time is approximately 1/4 of the *RoleSupporter* time. The small deviation from the exact 1/4 relation is explained by two main factors: first, *RoleSupporter* is also taken by some players during set plays for CAMBADA; and, second, the number of field robots is often less than the maximum of five, as described above.

Table 5. Average time (± standard deviation) spent by players in different roles (in %)

Role	% Time
RoleStriker	10.4 ± 5.2
RoleSupporter	45.2 ± 10.0
RoleToucher	5.9 ± 4.1
RoleReplacer	5.6 ± 4.6
RoleBarrier	28.4 ± 6.5
RoleParking	4.4 ± 6.4

It can also be seen that more time is spent in set plays against CAMBADA (28.4%, since usually four players take the Barrier role in these situations) than in set plays against the opponent (11.5% in Toucher and Replacer roles). *RoleParking* moves robots outside of the field at the end of the first half and at the end of the game

A more in-depth perspective is given by Table 6, which shows the role time distribution across the three classes of game states. It can be seen that in open play basically only *RoleStriker* and *RoleSupporter* are used. In set pieces for CAMBADA, players take the roles of *RoleReplacer*, *RoleToucher* and *RoleSupporter*. In set pieces against CAMBADA, all field robots act is *RoleBarrier*. Underlying the numbers in Table 6 is the fact, already mentioned above, that CAMBADA had an average of nearly 4 field players. That explains why the time spent as supporter in open play is approximately 3 times that of striker, and the time spent as supporter in set pieces for CAMBADA is approximately 2 times that of toucher or replacer.

Table 7 shows the average percentage of time any given player spends running each implemented behavior. The second column of the table shows such percentages irrespective of the role taken. The third column shows the percentages of time considering only the periods in which players acting as *RoleStriker*.

Table 6. Average time spent by players in different roles (in %) for different game states

Role	Open play	Set piece for	Set piece against
RoleStriker	24.3	0.3	0.4
RoleSupporter	75.3	51.5	0.3
RoleToucher	0.4	23.7	0.0
RoleReplacer	0.0	24.5	0.0
RoleBarrier	0.0	0.0	99.3

Table 7. Average time (± standard deviation) spent by players running different behaviors

Behaviour	%time (any role)	%time (Striker)
bMove	4.9 ± 3.0	43.7 ± 4.4
bMoveToAbs	74.7 ± 12.6	25.3 ± 4.7
bDribble	1.4 ± 1.2	13.4 ± 4.5
bKick	1.8 ± 1.5	14.6 ± 7.7
bCatchBall	0.2 ± 0.3	

These values highlight the specificity of *RoleStriker*: much less time moving to absolute positions, since the striker most of the time ignores its strategic positioning assignment; much more time in moving (to the ball), dribbling and kicking.

5.3 Coordination

In the final game of RoboCup'2008 (CAMBADA-TechUnited), the ball was in the opponent's side 73% of time, mainly in the centre of the field towards the opponent's side. This results from the effectiveness of the CAMBADA's coordination approach.

Some measures of coordination performance have been extracted. According to the logs, players change roles 2.02±1.02 times per minute. As role assignment is distributed (implicit coordination), it occasionally happens that two players take on *RoleStriker* at the same time. On average, all inconsistencies in the assignment of the Striker role have a combined total duration of 20.9±27.4 seconds in a game (~30 minutes). The high standard deviation results mainly from one game in which, due to magnetic interference, localization errors were higher than normal. In that game, role inconsistencies occurred 45 times for a combined total of 101 seconds.

Concerning strategic positionings, relevant mainly to supporters, the average distance of the player to its target position is 1.38±0.48 m. The strategic positioning assignment for each player is changed on average 9.83±2.23 times per minute.

As the CAMBADA players do not track the positions and actions of the opponent players, it is not possible to compute an exact measure of ball possession. However, the game logs enable to compute related measures, as shown in Table 8. The closest player to the ball is at an average distance of 1.2m from the ball (the field is 18m × 12m). The ball is perceived by at least one robot of the CAMBADA team 91.7% of the time. The ball is engaged in a robot's grabber device 9.8% of the time.

Some additional analysis was carried out based on the log of the final game. Table 9 provides information on set pieces, identifying the total number of times each set piece was executed as well as the number of times it was correctly executed.

Table 8. Measures related to ball possession (average ± standard deviation)

Measure	Value
Average minimum distance to the ball (meters)	1.246 ± 0.325
Average time with ball visible (%)	91.7 ± 3.5
Average time with ball engaged (%)	9.8 ± 4.7

Table 9. Set-piece performance in the final game

Set piece	#Occurrences	#Correct
Kick-off	2	2
Free kick	1	1
Throw-in	6	5
Goal kick	10	8
Corner kick	2	2
Total	21	18

In 21 set pieces, 18 were correctly executed (85.7%). The failed throw-in occurred due to magnetic interference in one area of the field, causing the robot to mislocalise itself. The two missed goal kicks occurred because the robot acting as *RoleToucher* movement, while pushing the ball towards the Replacer, wasn't accurately aligned and did not succeed in delivering the ball to the Replacer. This can be due to some small localisation errors experienced near the goal kick marker.

Table 10 provides information on goal scoring success in set piece situations in which the set piece procedure was correctly executed and the distance to the opponent goal was less that 9 meters. In the 6 set pieces for CAMBADA carried out under these conditions, 4 resulted in a goal being scored. This is a very good success rate. It should be noted that from the 7 goals scored in this game, 4 resulted from set pieces. This shows the importance of having accurate, reliable and swift set pieces in MSL games. These high values were observed consistently throughout the whole championship. They were crucial in the team's success, proving to be a powerful asset for achieving victories.

Table 10. Set-piece performance

Set piece	Occurrences	Success
Kick-off	2	2
Free kick	1	0
Throw-in	3	2
Total	6	4

5.4 Competition Results

Table 11 presents the competition results of CAMBADA in RoboCup'2008. The team won 11 out of 13 games, scoring a total of 73 goals and suffering only 11 goals.

Table 11. RoboCup 2008 competition results

	#games	#goals scored	#goals suffered	#points
Round-robin 1	5	41	2	15
Round-robin 2	4	16	3	9
Round-robin 3	2	5	2	3
Semi-final	1	4	3	3
Final	1	7	1	3
Total	13	73	11	33

6 Conclusion

The paper presented and evaluated the coordination methodologies of the CAMBADA team, the current world champion in RoboCup'2008 MSL.

During open play, an implicit coordination approach, based on role assignment, formations and flexible positionings, is used. The positioning of the team adapts to the external conditions and has maintained a strong defense and a good backup to striker role during the competition. In particular, although robot malfunctions decrease the number of field players, the dynamic positioning/role assignment algorithm maintains a competitive formation. This can be seen, not only from the competition results, but also from the detailed analysis of game logs and videos presented in the paper. More importantly, these results were obtained despite the fact that CAMBADA robots clearly move at low speed (2m/s), when compared to most of the main competitors.

The development of predefined role-based set plays proved to be very efficient both during the development phase, and during their execution in games. More than half of the 73 scored goals are direct result of these set plays.

One of the most significant aspects of this work is the integration of these coordination methodologies in a complex multi-robot system and their validation in the challenging RoboCup MSL competition. This contrasts with other approaches which are validated in controlled robotic environments, if not in simulation.

Acknowledgments. The CAMBADA team was funded by the Portuguese Government – FCT,POSI/ROBO/43908/2002 (CAMBADA) and currently FCT, PTDC/EIA/70695/2006 (ACORD). We would also like to thank the rest of the CAMBADA team for an excellent work environment.

References

[1] Lesser, V., et al.: Evolution of the GPGP/TAEMS Domain-Independent Coordination Framework. Autonomous Agents and Multi-Agent Systems 9(1), 87–143 (2004)

[2] Noreils, F.R.: Toward a robot architecture integrating cooperation between mobile robots: Application to indoor environment. International Journal of Robotics Research 12, 79–98 (1993)

[3] Arbatzat, M., et al.: Creating a Robot Soccer Team from Scratch: the Brainstormers Tribots. In: Proc. of Robocup 2003, Padua, Italy (2003)

[4] Azevedo, J.L., Cunha, M.B., Almeida, L.: Hierarchical Distributed Architectures for Autonomous Mobile Robots: a Case Study. In: Proc. ETFA2007- 12th IEEE Conference on Emerging Technologies and Factory Automation, Patras, Greece, pp. 973–980 (2007)
[5] Balch, T., Arkin, R.C.: Behavior-based formation control for multirobot teams. IEEE Transactions on Robotics and Automation 14(6), 926–939 (1998)
[6] Balch, T., Parker, L.E.: Robot Teams: From Diversity to Polymorphism. A.K Peters Ltd, Natick, Massachusetts (2002)
[7] Cunha, B., Azevedo, J., Lau, N., Almeida, L.: Obtaining the inverse distance map from a non-SVP hyperbolic catadioptric robotic vision system. In: Visser, U., et al. (eds.) RoboCup 2007: LNCS (LNAI), vol. 5001, pp. 417–424. Springer, Berlin (2008)
[8] EtherCAT Robots win German Open, Press Release, EtherCAT Technology Group (May 8, 2008), http://ethercat.org/pdf/english/etg_032008.pdf
[9] Figueiredo, J., Lau, N., Pereira, A.: Multi-Agent Debugging and monitoring framework. In: Proc. First IFAC Workshop on Multivehicle Systems (MVS 2006), Brasil (October 2006)
[10] Gerkey, B.P., Mataric, M.J.: A formal analysis and taxonomy of task allocation in multi-robot systems. International Journal of Robotics Research 23(9), 939–954 (2004)
[11] Hafner, R., Lange, S., Lauer, M., Riedmiller, M.: Brainstormers Tribots Team Description. In: RoboCup International Symposium, CD Proc., Suzhou, China (2008)
[12] Kok, J., Spaan, M., Vlassis, N.: Non-communicative multi-robot coordination in dynamic environments. Robotics and Autonomous Systems 50(2-3), 99–114 (2005)
[13] Lau, N., Seabra Lopes, L., Corrente, G.: CAMBADA: Information Sharing and Team Coordination. In: Proc. of the Eigth Conference on Autonomous Robot Systems and Competitions, Portugal, Universidade de Aveiro, pp. 27–32 (April 2, 2008)
[14] Lauer, M., Lange, S., Riedmiller, M.: Calculating the perfect match: An efficient and accurate approach for robot self-localization. In: Bredenfeld, A., et al. (eds.) RoboCup 2005. LNCS (LNAI), vol. 4020, pp. 142–153. Springer, Heidelberg (2006)
[15] Lima, P., et al.: RoboCup 2004 Competitions and Symposium: A Small Kick for Robots, a Giant Score for Science. AI-Magazine 6(2), 36–61 (2005)
[16] Müller, H., Lauer, M., Hafner, R., Lange, S., Merke, A., Riedmiller, M.: Making a robot learn to play soccer using reward and punishment. In: Hertzberg, J., Beetz, M., Englert, R. (eds.) KI 2007. LNCS (LNAI), vol. 4667, pp. 220–234. Springer, Heidelberg (2007)
[17] MSL Technical Committee 1997-2008, Middle Size Robot League Rules and Regulations for 2008. Draft Version - 12.2 20071109 (November 9, 2007)
[18] Oubbati, M., Schanz, M., Buchheim, T., Levi, P.: Velocity control of an omnidirectional roboCup player with recurrent neural networks. In: Bredenfeld, A., et al. (eds.) RoboCup 2005. LNCS, vol. 4020, pp. 691–701. Springer, Heidelberg (2006)
[19] Pagello, E., D'Angelo, A., Menegatti, E.: Cooperation Issues and Distributed Sensing for Multirobot Systems. Proc. of the IEEE 94(7), 1370–1383 (2006)
[20] Pedreiras, P., Almeida, L.: Task Management for Soft Real-Time Applications Based on General Purpose Operating Systems. In: Lima, P. (ed.) Robotic Soccer, pp. 598–607. Itech Education and Publishing, Vienna, Austria (2007)
[21] Reis, L.P., Lau, N., Oliveira, E.C.: Situation based strategic positioning for coordinating a team of homogeneous agents. In: Hannenbauer, M., et al. (eds.) Balancing Reactivity and Social Deliberation in Multiagent Sytems: From RoboCup to Real Word Applications. LNCS (LNAI), vol. 2103, pp. 175–197. Springer, Heidelberg (2001)
[22] Reis, L.P., Lau, N.: FC portugal team description: RoboCup 2000 simulation league champion. In: Stone, P., et al. (eds.) RoboCup 2000. LNCS, vol. 2019, pp. 29–40. Springer, Heidelberg (2001)

[23] Riedmiller, M., Gabel, T.: On Experiences in a Complex and Competitive Gaming Domain: Reinforcement Learning Meets RoboCup. In: Proc. of the 3rd IEEE Symposium on Computational Intelligence and Games (CIG 2007), pp. 17–23. IEEE Press, Los Alamitos (2007)

[24] Sato, Y., Yamaguchi, S., et al.: Hibikino-Musashi Team Description Paper. In: RoboCup Int. Symposium 2008, CD Proc.,, Suzhou, China (2008)

[25] Stone, P., Veloso, M.: Task Decomposition, Dynamic Role Assignment and Low Bandwidth Communication for Real Time Strategic Teamwork. Artif. Intelligence 110(2), 241–273 (1999)

[26] van der Vecht, B., Lima, P.: Formulation and implementation of relational behaviours for multi-robot cooperative systems. In: Nardi, D., Riedmiller, M., Sammut, C., Santos-Victor, J. (eds.) RoboCup 2004. LNCS (LNAI), vol. 3276, pp. 516–523. Springer, Heidelberg (2005)

[27] Weigel, T., Auerbach, W., Dietl, M., Dümler, B., Gutmann, J.-S., Marko, K., Müller, K., Nebel, B., Szerbakowski, B., Thiel, M.: CS freiburg: Doing the right thing in a group. In: Stone, P., Balch, T., Kraetzschmar, G.K. (eds.) RoboCup 2000. LNCS (LNAI), vol. 2019, pp. 52–63. Springer, Heidelberg (2001)

[28] Zweigle, O., Lafrenz, R., Buchheim, T., Käppeler, U.-P., Rajaie, H., Schreiber, F., Levi, P.: Cooperative agent behavior based on special interaction nets. In: Arai, T., et al. (eds.) Intelligent Autonomous Systems 9. IOS Press, Amsterdam (2006)

Semantic Image Search and Subset Selection for Classifier Training in Object Recognition

Rui Pereira[1], Luís Seabra Lopes[1,2], and Augusto Silva[1,2]

[1] IEETA, Universidade de Aveiro
[2] Departamento de Electrónica, Telecomunicações e Informática, Universidade de Aveiro
{ruipereira,lsl,augusto.silva}@ua.pt

Abstract. Robots need to ground their external vocabulary and internal symbols in observations of the world. In recent works, this problem has been approached through combinations of open-ended category learning and interaction with other agents acting as teachers. In this paper, a complementary path is explored, in which robots also resort to semantic searches in digital collections of text and images, or more generally in the Internet, to ground vocabulary about objects. Drawing on a distinction between broad and narrow (or general and specific) categories, different methods are applied, namely global shape contexts to represent broad categories, and SIFT local features to represent narrow categories. An unsupervised image clustering and ranking method is proposed that, starting from a set of images automatically fetched on the web for a given category name, selects a subset of images suitable for building a model of the category. In the case of broad categories, image segmentation and object extraction enhance the chances of finding suitable training objects. We demonstrate that the proposed approach indeed improves the quality of the training object collections.

1 Introduction

In robotics, as in human cognition, reasoning and communication are activities that involve the manipulation of symbols. Symbols must ultimately be grounded in categories learned through observation, sensorimotor experience and interaction with other agents [1][6][13].

This paper focuses on category learning and symbol grounding through visual perception. This is relevant for grounding the names of (or internal symbols used to refer to) physical objects. In the computer vision literature, this problem has been normally addressed through approaches based on gathering training examples for a pre-defined set of categories, running an algorithm to induce some knowledge about the categories and, finally, testing the induced knowledge on a set of unseen cases [5]. A recent exception is the approach of [18], in which an incremental version of Support Vector Machines is used to acquire visual categories. In the context of human-robot interaction, some recent approaches also explore the combination of incremental learning and interaction with teachers to ground vocabulary about physical objects [11][12][13][14].

L. Seabra Lopes et al. (Eds.): EPIA 2009, LNAI 5816, pp. 338–349, 2009.

In a technological world with endless information resources easily accessible, the dynamic combination of direct perception of the environment and human-robot interaction can be complemented by unsupervised semantic searches e.g. on the Internet. The present paper explores this complementary path. Specifically, the paper focuses on semantic retrieval of images (from the Internet) and unsupervised image subset selection for visual category learning.

This work was carried out in the context of the development of UA@SRVC, a software agent that participated in the Semantic Robot Vision Challenge (2nd edition, Anchorage, Alaska, July 2008, sponsored by NSF and Google). In this challenge, the competing agents are initially given a list of names of categories (e.g. 'coffee cup' or 'Coca Cola can'). Spelling of these names follows some conventions: proper names have their first letter capitalized; common names are given in lower case; titles of books, films, etc., are given between quotes. In a learning phase, agents can search for information about the categories on the Internet. In the performance phase, they will have to search for specific instances of the categories in an environment prepared by the SRVC organizers (or, in the case of software agents, in images of that environment). Other aspects of UA@SRVC are presented in a separate paper[10].

The work presented in this paper is concerned with the Internet search phase. The basic problem addressed here is the following: given the name of a category of objects, gather a set of representative instances of that category and build a model that can be used later to recognize other, previously unseen, instances.

This is a case of unsupervised learning from uncategorized images [5][4] (as opposed to learning from labeled training data[19]): we cluster the images together according to their visual similarities. Several approaches for automated subset selection (or ranking) of uncategorized images exist. In [17], a method to filter Internet image search results based exclusively on visual content is introduced. Inconsistent or strange images are iteratively removed until the k-Nearest-Neighbor strangeness measure drops below a threshold for any of the remaining images. In each iteration, the same measure is used to choose the image that should be removed. A visual model learning method, applied to images obtained via Google, was proposed by [2]. Firstly, the query is translated to multiple languages. Then, using multiple-topic *pLSA* methods, image category models are learned. The same authors [3] had previously developed a method for visual category filtering on Google images, by identifying visual consistencies in the images and using that information to rank them.

The sparse multiple-instance learning (sMIL) approach [16] divides training images into positive and negative bags. Positive bags are those that contain at least one positive instance, while negative bags contain only negative instances. The classifier can discriminate the positive from the negative instances, even if their sparsity in the positive training bags is high. To discriminate between positive and negative bags, an objective function is used to determine a decision boundary, taking into account that the positive bags can be randomly sparse. It's assumed that images retrieved from the Web contain at least one category instance, thus forming a positive bag. In [7], the authors use the first *15* images returned by a search engine as the seed of a category, to learn a Hierarchical Dirichlet Process category model. This model is then used to classify additional images. When these are positively classified they are also incorporated in the model.

Figure 1 illustrates the flow of information in the category learning module that was developed for the UA@SRVC agent. The agent takes as input a category name (or a list of category names) and starts by searching and retrieving images from the Web, using queries containing that category. In the case of broad categories, these images suffer a process of object extraction, in which images that contain more than one object are segmented into sub-images and noise is discarded as much as possible. Ideally, each sub-image should contain a single object. After this initial pre-processing step, we select a subset of images for training. The goal is to discard as many unrepresentative images as possible, while keeping a good set of category instances. The learning phase is concluded by building models for the categories that are invariant to scale, rotation and, to some extent, deformation.

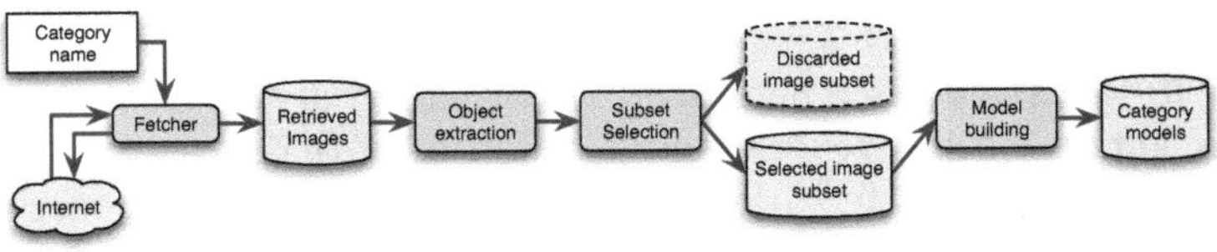

Fig. 1. System overview

The paper is organized as follows: Section 2 describes image retrieval and pre-processing. Section 3 describes the used representations. Section 4 describes the unsupervised subset selection approach that is proposed. Section 5 describes the experiments that were carried out to evaluate subset selection performance and the results obtained. Finally, section 6 concludes the paper.

2 Image Retrieval and Pre-processing

Images are initially searched and retrieved using Google. Since many of these images may contain several (possibly irrelevant) objects, these objects are extracted and separately considered.

Image search and retrieval. A *Perl* script, developed based on the *WWW::Google::Images* module, was used to retrieve a set of images from the Internet using the *Google* search engine. Only JPG images with a maximum width of *1200* pixels are retrieved. The maximum number of downloaded images is *20* for specific categories and *40* for general categories. If more images than the maximum are found, only the best images, according to the Google ranking, are used.

General categories are searched with a query beginning in *allinurl:*, meaning all query words must be found in the image URL. Since, for the most part, general categories don't have many words in their name, we maximize the chances of retrieving good images if we force the name to be in the URL. If a search for a specific category doesn't retrieve the maximum number of images and the query contains quotes, then a new search is conducted, removing the quotes from the query. Since we don't use color information, when a search for a general category doesn't return the maximum number of images and the category name has a color in it (e.g. "red apple"), a new search is conducted, removing the color information from the query. When searching for a general category, if the maximum number of images is not reached, a new search is conducted, removing *allinurl:* from the beginning of the query. Note that this can happen after the removal of the color information from the query.

Object Segmentation and Extraction. When processing a retrieved image, the agent must check if the image contains objects other than the intended. An image with several objects, for example, will produce a shape representation that can't be used for anything useful, unless the goal is to detect those objects in the same relative positions in other scenes. These problems are solved by object segmentation and extraction. Due to space limitations, only a very coarse description of the used method will be provided here.

The image is first smoothed by using a Gaussian filter to reduce noise. A Canny edge detector is used to find the edges. The result is a set of white pixels over a black background. Next, the detected edge pixels are followed, trying to isolate individual objects. After detecting a pixel at the boundary of an object, region growing is used to extract its shape. The neighboring pixels of the detected pixel are scrutinized to determine if they should be added to the object being segmented, i.e., if it's also part of the contour. If a bifurcation is reached, its localization is saved and one of the branches is followed. When this path terminates, the process backtracks to the last found bifurcation and takes the unexplored branch.

After the contour is established, its extreme coordinates (bottom, top, left and right) are determined. In a first scan, if a pixel is determined to be inside the contour window and it has white pixels below, above and at both sides, then it's also marked as white. In a second scan, pixels that are inside the same window but are black are also added to the shape if the majority of their *8* neighbors is white. This is useful because a shape is not always defined by connected edges. In fact, there are several possibilities for a contour to be a candidate object or object part, as seen in Figure 2.

If we start in a point and end up in the vicinity of the same point (Figure 2(a)), or if the edge leads to the image boundary (Figure 2(b)) or if it is not continuous but defines an area (Figure 2(c)) then it's possible that this edge defines an object or a component of one.

The next step is the aggregation of edges potentially belonging to the same object. Since an edge doesn't necessarily define an object, edges are grouped together according to the average distance of their pixels to their geometric

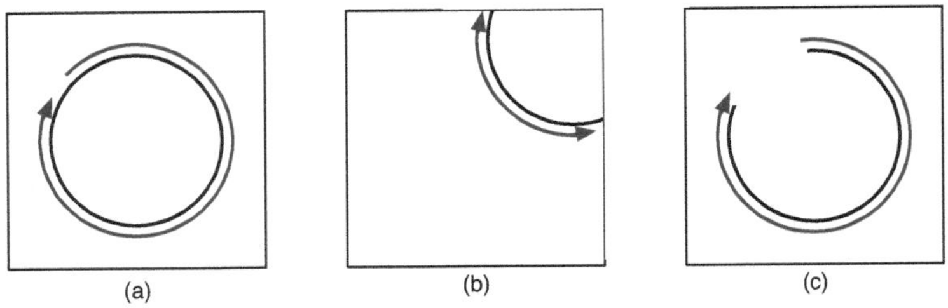

Fig. 2. Extraction cases. These are the basic cases we might encounter while extracting the objects. (a) The object has a defined an continuous contours. (b) The object contours touch the image edges and are continuous. (c) The contours are not continuous.

centers, *GC*, and the distance between geometric centers. If the distance between the GCs of the edges is smaller than the sum of the average distances of their respective pixels to their GCs multiplied by a constant factor k[1], then the edges are aggregated and count as a single object. This is an iterative process, which stops when no more edges can be aggregated.

Finally, two filtering operations are carried out. The first will identify and remove small objects, which are likely to be noise. The other filtering step consists of removing the objects with a number of edge pixels clearly above average, which most likely are cluttered images.

3 Representations and Similarity Measures

Broad and narrow categories. The UA@SRVC agent divides categories into two main groups: broad (general) categories, whose instances can exist in a wide variety of forms and narrow (specific) categories, whose characteristics are regular and well defined, therefore resulting in high intra-category similarity. Broad categories are identified by common nouns in natural language (e.g.: chair, table, etc.). Narrow categories are identified by proper nouns (frequently brand names) or quoted expressions.

The need for this distinction between broad and narrow categories arises from the fact that some methods are more suited to broad categories while others are more suited to specific categories[10]. For instance, SIFT [9] local features are highly distinctive and are, therefore, very useful for modeling narrow categories, that are rich in descriptive features and with low intra-category variation. However, they fail on more general categories, low in descriptive features and with high intra-category variation. In contrast, shape representations are good for representing the common features of objects in broad categories, but may fail to capture the distinctive details in narrow categories. In this work, we use a global shape representation for broad categories and a SIFT-based representation for narrow categories.

[1] In the current version, the multiplicative factor k has the value of 1.0.

Global shape context. The used shape representation is a polar histogram of edge pixels[10]. A frame of reference is located at the geometric center of the object. Then, the space around the centre up to the most excentric pixel of the object is divided into a slices (angle bins) and d layers (distance bins)[2]. The intersection of slices and layers results in a polar matrix (Figure 3) that will be mapped to a 2D histogram counting the number of pixels in each cell. This histogram is finally normalized by dividing the counts for each cell by the total count. The histogram is built in $O(n)$ time, where n is the number of edge pixels.

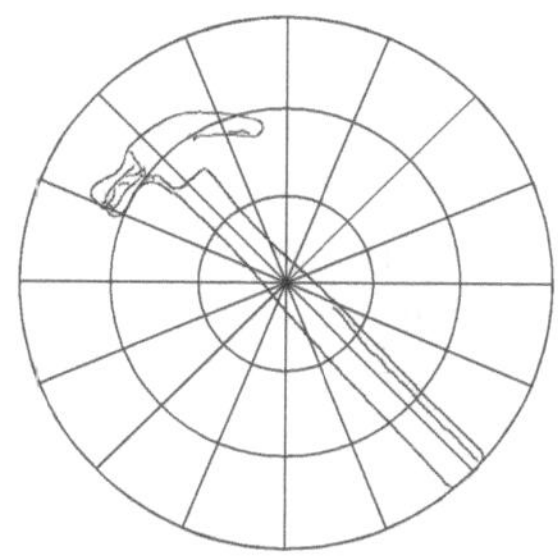

Fig. 3. Shape Context as a global descriptor

The proposed representation is translation invariant since it's computed in a frame of reference centered in the object. It is also scale invariant because the histogram is normalized by the radius of the minimal circle enclosing the object and centered in its geometric center. The histogram itself is not invariant to rotation. To make a rotation invariant matching possible, we rotate one of the histograms a times while comparing the two shapes. The lowest distance is the one used to calculate the similarity between the two shapes.

The χ^2 distance is used to represent the distance between the histograms. For further details, including comparative performance evaluation, see [10].

SIFT local features. As mentioned above, the UA@SRVC agent represents objects in "narrow" categories through sets of local features extracted by SIFT (Scale Invariant Feature Transform) [9]. SIFT produces highly distinctive image features that can be used for matching objects with different scales, positions and orientations, as well as with some variations in illumination. These features are computed in reference frames aligned with image gradients.

When matching two objects, the features in each of them are paired according to a nearest-neighbor criterion. Then, instead of using a global threshold to discard matches, the distance to the nearest neighbor and to the second nearest is compared. If the ratio between the former and the latter is greater than *0.35*, the pair of features is rejected. Finally, similarity between two objects is given by the number of accepted pairs of features.

[2] a=40 and d=10 were used.

As similarity computation does not depend on object segmentation and extraction, such pre-processing is not used in categories processed by SIFT.

Category representations. Broad (or general) categories are represented by the sets of objects that were selected, where each object is represented by its global shape context. Narrow categories are represented by the concatenation of the SIFT features of each individual object selected for that category.

4 Unsupervised Subset Selection

Image sets retrieved from the Web for a category will always have an amount of noise. This section presents an unsupervised method for selecting a subset of representative images, discarding those irrelevant or noisy. The approach is based on repeating a basic clustering algorithm a number of times and ranking images based on how often they were included in the largest cluster.

Object clustering algorithm. An unsupervised clustering process is conducted over the images obtained through the Internet search and pre-processing steps. Clustering the images according to their similarity usually results in: a large cluster with most of the good representatives of the target category (i.e. images containing true instances of the category and with little noise); several other (usually smaller) clusters with various outliers. The larger the percentage of good images in the initial set, the higher is the probability that the largest cluster actually contains good representatives of the target category.

Clustering is done using the *k-means*[15] algorithm with Lloyd's iterative refinement heuristic [8] and some additional modifications designed to solve our problem. Lloyd's heuristic starts with seeding a number k of clusters by randomly selecting k images from the initial set of N images, where $k < N$. Then, the remaining $N-k$ images will be added to the closest clusters. Since the object representations described above are not organized in vector spaces (the number of extracted SIFT features varies from object to object and the matching of shape contexts requires rotation), the used clustering algorithm does not compute centroids. Instead, the proximity of an object to a cluster is evaluated by average similarity to the members of the cluster (the similarity measures were identified in the previous section).

After setting up this initial group of clusters, the iterative refinement process starts. In each iteration, for each object, the average similarity to the remaining members of its current cluster and the average similarities to the members of the remaining clusters are computed. If the minimum value is obtained for a cluster that is different from the current cluster of the object, the object is moved to that cluster. The process terminates when a complete iteration is run without transferring objects between clusters. A post-processing step makes sure there is only one cluster with the largest number of objects. If there is a tie between two or more clusters, the cluster having the closest non-member will receive this extra object, therefore becoming the single largest cluster.

Object ranking and selection. The basic clustering algorithm just described is run for different values of the number of clusters, k. It starts with $N/4$ and incrementally gets to $N/2-1$. Since randomness leads to variations in the clusters produced in each run, the whole process described until now is repeated a certain number of times, K, to provide a reliable sampling[3]. The total number of runs is then $K \times (N/2 - N/4)$.

The number of times, X_i, each object i was included in the main cluster in these runs is updated after every run. At the end, the images are ranked according to X_i. The final selection is determined by going through the images in descending order of X_i and adding them to the selection while the following condition holds:

$$\sum_{s=1}^{S} X_{i(s)} < \eta \times \sum_{i=1}^{N} X_i \tag{1}$$

where S is the number of images included in the selection, s is a rank position, $i(s)$ identifies the image in rank position s, and $\eta \in [0, 1]$ is the reject threshold[4]. When the selection process terminates, the remaining $N - S$ images are assumed as noisy/irrelevant and therefore discarded.

5 Performance Evaluation

Images retrieved from the Web are matched among themselves and clustered, using the modified *K-means* algorithm described above, to select a subset that correctly represents the target category. Before this selection, we perform a manual, visual analysis of the retrieved images and count how many of them constitute suitable training images to build a correct model of the category. In the case of shape-based subset selection, images containing several instances of the target category, or with highly stylized objects, or with high background noise around the contours, or not containing any instance of the category are not good training images.

Building a good SIFT model for an object doesn't require such a strict selection as is necessary for a good shape model. First, since SIFT is used for specific categories, it will already start with some advantage. Furthermore, because SIFT is tolerant to occlusion, noise, etc., an image can have a partially hidden, deformed or not alone object and still be useful for building a model.

We compare the percentage of good images in the original set with the percentage of good images in the selected subset to determine if improvement exists.

Shape-based subset selection without object extraction. A total of *31* categories (some of which were used in SRVC'2007 and '2008) were selected to benchmark the subset selection based on shape analysis. For each of these categories, 37 images, on average, were retrieved from the Internet. Only 40% of the retrieved images could be considered good for training.

[3] $K = 100$ was used in the implementation.

[4] $\eta = 0.85$ was used in the implementation.

After selecting the good images in the initial set, we check to see which ones were selected. Figure 4(a) plots the percentage of good images in the selection versus the percentage of good images in the initial set. The categories are identified by numbers in Figure 4 and their names are listed on the right. The linear regression line is given by the function $f(x) = 1.33x - 0.04$. For $x > 0.15$, the regression line has the property of $f(x) > x$, meaning there's improvement. It can be concluded that subset selection improves the quality of the training set.

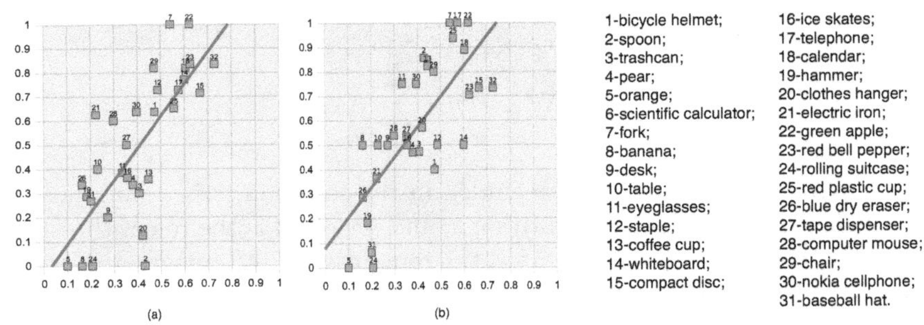

Fig. 4. Percentages of good images after shape-based subset selection (yy axis) versus the respective percentages of good images in the initial set (xx axis): (a) without object extraction. (b) with object extraction. Also shown are the linear regression lines for the plotted points.

Shape-based subset selection with object extraction. In this case, we run object extraction on the initial set, obtaining a larger set of smaller images. Figure 4(b) plots the percentage of good images after the subset selection as a function of the percentage of good images in the initial set. The linear regression line equation is $f(x) = 1.24x + 0.08$. It can be seen that for all values of x, the regression line has the property of $f(x) > x$, i.e. the values of the percentages of good images in the selected subset are superior to the initial percentages. This line, compared to the one in Figure 4(a), for the same values of x, always has higher $f(x)$ values, which means object extraction improves the final result.

SIFT-based subset selection. We selected *25* categories for this test. The categories are identified by numbers in Figure 5 and their names are listed to the right of this figure. For each category, 19 images were obtained through Internet search, on average. In the initial sets, the percentage of good images was 53% on average.

The performance of subset selection with SIFT for narrow categories is very good. After subset selection, this percentage increases to 79%. Figure 5 plots the percentage of good images in the subset (yy axis) as a function of the percentage of good images in the initial set (xx axis). The figure also shows a linear regression line $f(x) = 1.29x + 0.1$, where from the beginning ($x = 0$) the values of $f(x)$ are always higher than x, meaning there is a significant improvement of the subset with respect to the initial group. The slope is inferior to the ones of Figure 4 (shape-based subset selection), even though we have a significantly better improvement in narrow categories using SIFT-based subset selection. This fact can be explained by the number of categories located in the lower values of x, i.e., categories with poor percentages of good images. In the case of Figure 5, this quantity is smaller, a basis that also accounts for the better performance.

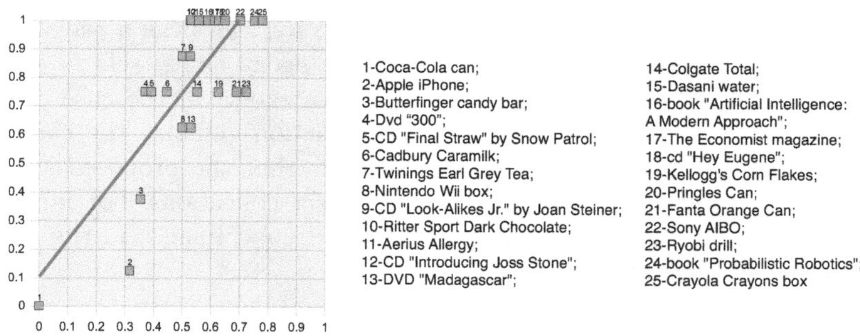

Fig. 5. Subset selection with SIFT: percentages of good images after the subset selection (yy axis) versus the respective percentages of good images in the initial set (xx axis). Also shown is the linear regression line for the plotted points.

These images, which are rich in features, provide a solid basis for the clustering algorithm to filter out the noise. Only one category - *Aerius Allergy* (category number 11) - gave worse results in the selected subset than in the initial set of images. It's also worth noting that, apart from category number *9* (*CD "Look Alikes Jr." by Joan Steiner*), which had *0* good images in the initial set, hence being impossible to improve, the category *Aerius Allergy* is the one with the lowest percentage of good images in the initial group. Searching for *Aerius Allergy* returns images with two different brand designs. In other words, this category is heterogeneous and the two retrieved sub-categories don't share enough SIFT features to build the category model. Due to this heterogeneity and to the low number of good training images, the clustering and subset selection don't perform so well. On the positive end, we can also see that many categories originated a subset where *100%* of the images are good training images.

6 Conclusions and Future Work

This paper explored semantic web searches and unsupervised subset selection for gathering images that can be used for building models of visual categories. Although there may be other applications, the described functionalities appear relevant in the context of robotics as a complementary means for enabling robots to ground the symbols they use in reasoning and communication. English expressions refering to physical objects are mapped to visual categories. SIFT local features are used for representing narrow categories while shape contexts are used as global descriptors for broad categories. The use of shape contexts as global descriptors for broad categories provides a faster and simpler method than the method in which shape contexts were originally used.

Retrieving images from the Web using only keyword-based searches results in sets of images that cannot be directly used for category representations. In fact, it was observed that between 47% and 60% of the retrieved images are irrelevant or noisy. To solve this problem, a new unsupervised image clustering, ranking and selection method was proposed that, starting from a set of images automatically fetched on the web for a given category name, selects a subset of images suitable for building a model of the category. In the case of broad categories, image segmentation and object extraction enhance the chances of finding suitable training objects. We demonstrate that the proposed approach indeed improves the quality of the training object collections. For initial sets with 50% of good images, the final percentage of good images in the selected subset varies between 63% and 75%.

Improvements on the segmentation algorithm and inquiries on the possibility of a better method to discriminate two different shapes while extracting objects, as well as a better way to remove noise, should be studied in future work. Also, since our work ignores color information, categories such as "*green apple*" or "*red pepper*" do not benefit from this distinguishing feature, a limitation that should be tackled in future iterations. The integration of the system in a hardware platform would be an interesting step in its development.

Acknowledgements

The first author is currently with a research grant funded by Aveiro University. The participation of the UA@SRVC team in SRVC'2008 was partially funded by Google. The implementation of SIFT used in our work was developed by Rob Hess and is publicly available. The implementation also used OpenCV extensively.

References

1. Belpaeme, T., Cowley, S.: Extended symbol grounding. Interaction Studies 8(1), 1–6 (2007)
2. Fergus, R., Fei-Fei, L., Perona, P., Zisserman, A.: Learning object categories from google's image search. In: ICCV 2005: Proceedings of the Tenth IEEE International Conference on Computer Vision, pp. 1816–1823. IEEE Computer Society Press, Washington (2005)
3. Fergus, R., Perona, P., Zisserman, A., Science, D.E.: A visual category filter for google images. In: Proc. ECCV, pp. 242–256 (2004)
4. Fritz, M., Schiele, B.: Towards unsupervised discovery of visual categories. In: Franke, K., Müller, K.-R., Nickolay, B., Schäfer, R. (eds.) DAGM 2006. LNCS, vol. 4174, pp. 232–241. Springer, Heidelberg (2006)

5. Grauman, K., Darrell, T.: Unsupervised learning of categories from sets of partially matching image features. In: IEEE Computer Society Conference on Computer Vision and Pattern Recognition 2006, pp. 19–25 (2006)
6. Harnad, S.: The symbol grounding problem. Physica D 42, 335–346 (1990)
7. Li, L.-J., Wang, G., Fei-Fei, L.: Optimol: automatic online picture collection via incremental model learning. In: IEEE Conference on Computer Vision and Pattern Recognition, CVPR 2007, pp. 1–8 (2007)
8. Lloyd, S.: Least squares quantization in pcm. In: IEEE Transactions on Information Theory, vol. 28, pp. 129–137 (1982)
9. Lowe, D.G.: Distinctive image features from scale-invariant keypoints. International Journal of Computer Vision 60, 91–110 (2004)
10. Pereira, R., Seabra Lopes, L.: Learning visual object categories with global descriptors and local features. In: Seabra Lopes, L., et al. (eds.) EPIA 2009. LNCS(LNAI), vol. 5816, pp. 225–236. Springer, Heidelberg (2009)
11. Roy, D., Pentland, A.: Learning words from sights and sounds: a computational model. Cognitive Science 26, 113–146 (2002)
12. Seabra Lopes, L., Chauhan, A.: How many words can my robot learn? an approach and experiments with one-class learning. Interaction Studies 8(1), 53–81 (2007)
13. Seabra Lopes, L., Chauhan, A.: Open-ended category learning for language acquisition. Connection Science 8(4), 277–298 (2008)
14. Steels, L., Kaplan, F.: Aibo's first words: the social learning of language and meaning. Evolution of Communication 4(1), 3–32 (2002)
15. Steinhaus, H.: Sur la division des corp materiels en parties. Bulletin L'Acadmie Polonaise des ScienceIV C1. III, 801–804 (1956)
16. Vijayanarasimhan, S., Grauman, K.: Keywords to visual categories: Multiple-instance learning for weakly supervised object categorization. In: Proceedings of the IEEE Conference on Computer Vision and Pattern Recognition (2008)
17. Wnuk, K., Soatto, S.: Filtering internet image search results towards keyword based category recognition. In: IEEE Conference on Computer Vision and Pattern Recognition CVPR 2008, pp. 1–8 (June 2008)
18. Yeh, T., Darrell, T.: Dynamic visual category learning. In: IEEE Conference on Computer Vision and Pattern Recognition CVPR 2008, pp. 1–8 (2008)
19. Zhou, X.S., Huang, T.S.: Relevance feedback in image retrieval: A comprehensive review. Multimedia Systems 8(6), 536–544 (2003)

Obstacle Detection, Identification and Sharing on a Robotic Soccer Team

João Silva, Nuno Lau, António J.R. Neves, João Rodrigues, and José Luís Azevedo

IEETA/Department of Electronics, Telecommunications and Informatics,
University of Aveiro, Portugal
{joao.m.silva,nunolau,an,jmr,jla}@ua.pt

Abstract. When building a representation of the environment for a robot in a multi-agent application, as is the case of robotic soccer, sensor and information fusion of several elements of the environment are an important task. To build an increasingly better world model, one of the aspects that one should consider is the treatment of obstacles. This paper gives an insight of the general steps necessary for a good obstacle representation in the robot world model. A first step is the visual detection of the obstacles in the image acquired by the robot. This is done using an algorithm based on radial search lines and colour-based blobs detection, where each obstacle is identified and delimited. After having the visually detected obstacles, a fusion with a-priori known information about the obstacles characteristics allows the obstacle separation and filtering, so that obstacles that don't fill the criteria are discarded. With the position information shared by team mates, the matching of the obstacles and the team mates positions is also possible, thus identifying each of them. Finally, and with the purpose of having a team world model as coherent as possible, the robots are able to share the obstacle information of each other. The work presented in this paper was developed for the CAMBADA robotic soccer team. After achieving the 1st place in the Portuguese robotics open Robótica2008 and in the Robocup2008 world championship, the correct treatment of obstacles was one of the new challenges proposed among the team to improve the performance for the next competitions.

1 Introduction

Nowadays, there are several research domains in the area of multi robot systems. One of the most popular is the robotic soccer. RoboCup[1] is an international joint project to promote artificial intelligence, robotics and related fields. Most of the RoboCup leagues have soccer as platform for developing technology, either at software or hardware levels, with single or multiple agents, cooperative or competitive [1].

Among RoboCup leagues, the Middle Size League (MSL) is one of the most challenging. In this league, each team is composed of up to 5 robots with maximum size of 50x50cm base, 80cm height and a maximum weight of 40Kg, playing in a field of 18x12m. The rules of the game are similar to the official FIFA rules, with required changes to adapt for the playing robots [2].

[1] http://www.robocup.org/

L. Seabra Lopes et al. (Eds.): EPIA 2009, LNAI 5816, pp. 350–360, 2009.

Each robot is autonomous and has its own sensorial means. They can communicate among them, and with an external computer acting as a coach, through a wireless network. This coach computer cannot have any sensor, it only knows what is reported by the playing robots. The agents should be able to evaluate the state of the world and make decisions suitable to fulfil the cooperative team objective.

Fig. 1. Picture of the team robots used to obtain the results presented on this paper

CAMBADA, *Cooperative Autonomous Mobile roBots with Advanced Distributed Architecture*, is the Middle Size League Robotic Soccer team from the University of Aveiro. The project started in 2003, coordinated by the IEETA[2] ATRI[3] group and involves people working on several areas for building the mechanical structure of the robot, its hardware architecture and controllers and the software development in areas such as image analysis and processing, sensor and information fusion, reasoning and control.

While playing soccer, the robots have the need to navigate around the field effectively, which means they have to reposition themselves or dribble the ball avoiding the obstacles on the field, that can be either team or opponent robots, or eventually the referee.

An increasing necessity felt by the team, to improve its performance, is the need for a better obstacle detection and sharing of obstacle information among team mates. This need is important to ensure a global idea of the field occupancy, since the team formation usually keeps the robots spread across the field. With a good cover of field obstacles, pass lines and dribbling corridors can be estimated more easily allowing improvements on team strategy and coordination.

This is essentially an information fusion problem, as the information available from the sensors of each robot and the shared information must be matched and refined. The final result of this fusion is a representation of the state of the surrounding world. In the CAMBADA team, there is an integration process responsible for that task. It is a step executed after image analysis and is responsible to take raw information from

[2] Instituto de Engenharia Electrónica e Telemática de Aveiro - Aveiro's Institute of Electronic and Telematic Engineering.

[3] Actividade Transversal em Robótica Inteligente - Transverse Activity on Intelligent Robotics.

the vision and other robot sensors and make a sensor fusion of all sources. For that, it may use the values stored in the previous representation, the current sensor measures (eventually after pre-processing) that has just arrived, the current actuator commands and also information that is available from other robots sensors or world state.

All the information available from the sensors in the current cycle is kept in specific data structures (Fig. 2), for posterior fusion and integration, based on both the current information and the previous state of the world.

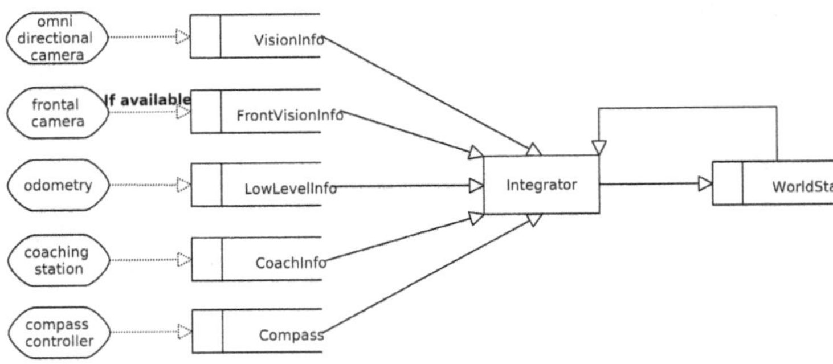

Fig. 2. Integrator functionality diagram

This paper focuses on the description of the obstacle treatment in the CAMBADA team. In Section 2 a general description of how the obstacles are detected by the vision process is presented, also describing how the raw information is passed to the integration process. Section 3 describes how the raw information is read and, based only on the local robot information, how the identification is processed. Section 4 presents how the sharing and acceptance of team mates obstacles is made. Section 5 concludes this document.

Note that most of the figures presented in this paper, after this point, are images acquired by the omni-directional camera of the robots. To ensure the comprehension of the figures, in most of them, lines were made around the areas of interest of the image. Also, the triangles and squares representing the obstacle centres and limits inside that areas of interest were increased in size and intensity, since the original image capture squares are more difficult to see in images of the presented size.

2 Visual Obstacle Detection

The first step for obstacle avoidance is its detection. The CAMBADA robots gather their information about the surroundings by means of a robotic vision system. Currently, only the omni directional camera gathers information about obstacles, as no frontal camera is being used at this time.

According to RoboCup rules, the robots are mainly black. Since in game robots play autonomously, all obstacles in the field are the robots themselves (occasionally the referee, which is recommended to have black/dark pants). The vision algorithm takes advantage of this fact and detects the obstacles by evaluating blobs of black colour inside the field of play [3]. Through the mapping of image positions to real metric positions [4], obstacles are identified by their centre (triangle on the image captures) (Fig. 3b)) and left and right limits (squares on the image captures) (Fig. 3b)). This is done by creating, from the centre of the image (the centre of the robot), radial sensors around the robot, each one representing a line with a given angle, which are then analysed for the search of black regions. These are called *scanlines* [5].

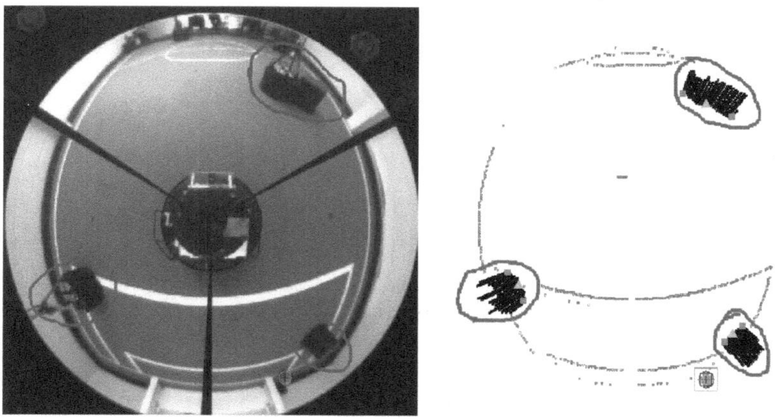

a) b)

Fig. 3. Captures of an image acquired by the robot camera and processed by the vision algorithms, areas of interest were surrounded. Left a): the image acquired by the camera; Right b): the same image after processing. It is visible how the obstacles are identified by their centre (triangle), left and right limits (squares). It is also visible that the 2 obstacles aligned are detected as a single bigger obstacle (top right of the frames).

The detection of black colour on the scanlines is analysed both in angular intervals and length intervals, to define the limits of each black blob. Since the vision system is a non-SVP hyperbolic catadioptric system [4], the sizes of objects on the image vary with the distance to the robot. Due to an inverse distance map calculation, by exploring a back-propagation ray-tracing approach and the mathematical properties of the mirror surface, the relation of distances in the image and the real world is known (Fig. 4).

Through the function represented in Fig. 4, it is possible to create a normalised relation of blobs widths and lengths with the distance. Sometimes an obstacle is separated in several blobs, mainly due to the noise in the image and problems in colour classification, which leads to fails in the detection of black regions in the scanlines. To avoid these situations, an offset is considered to decide when the angular space between blobs is considered enough to represent a real obstacle separation. The same principle is considered concerning the position of the black area in consecutive scanlines.

The separation offsets of a blob close to the robot are bigger than the ones at a high distance, to maintain coherent precision. The angular separation offset is considered for situations where robots are side-by-side, at the same distance, but there is no visual contact between each blob; the length separation offset is checked for situations where,

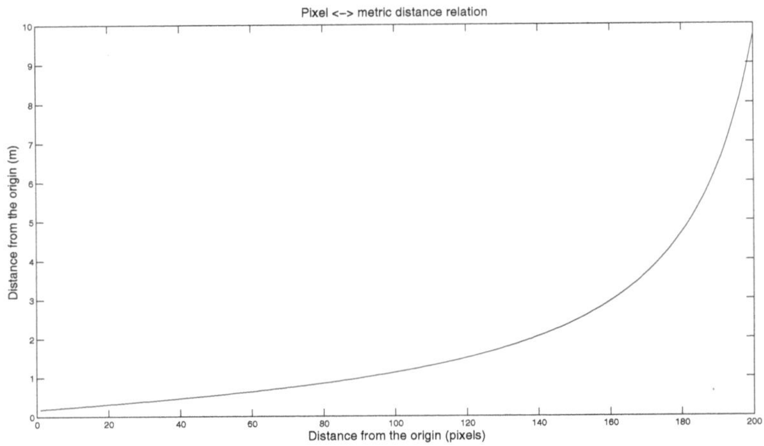

Fig. 4. Relation between pixels and metric distances. The centre of the robot is considered the origin and the metric distances are considered on the ground plane.

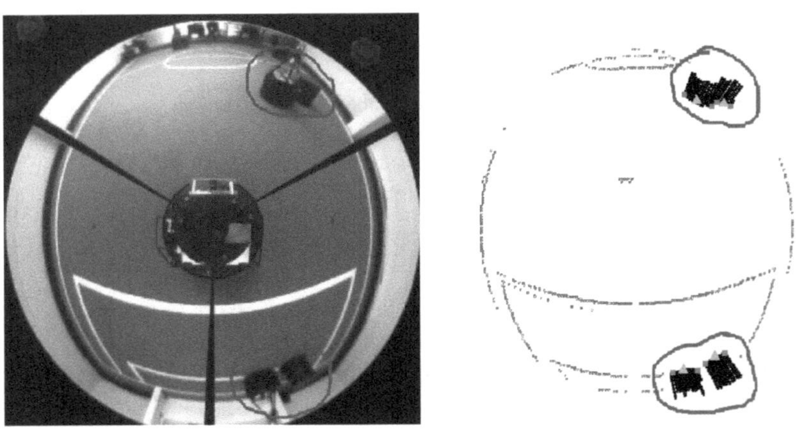

a) b)

Fig. 5. Example of an image acquired by the robot camera and processed by the vision algorithm. The areas of interest are surrounded. Left a): the image acquired by the camera; Right b): the same image after processing. It is visible the 2 possibilities of separation made: angular separation, on the bottom pair of obstacles; length separation, on the top pair of obstacles.

on sequential scanlines, there are blobs with visual contact but the robots are actually at different distances. Both situations are depicted in Fig. 5.

For each detected blob, their pixel sizes are calculated and an estimation of the obstacles left and right limits, as well as their centres, is made. This information is made available for the integration process to filter and treat.

Note that the work described in the remaining of this paper is independent of the vision algorithm, as long as the described information is available. Several approaches exist concerning obstacle identification. The work presented in [6] describes an approach for a similar application but with a non omni-directional vision system. In [7,8], visual colour and edge based detection algorithms are described, but both with times too high for use in the MSL environment. Other applications use several other sensors like laser range, stereo cameras or offline setup, but the financial and space costs of such solutions is much higher [9,10].

3 Obstacle Selection and Identification

With the objective of refining the information of the obstacles, and have more meaningful and human readable information, the obstacles are selected and a matching is attempted, in order to try to identify them as team mates or opponents.

Due to the weak precision at long distances, a first selection of the obstacles is made by selecting only the obstacles closer than a given distance as available for identification (currently 5 metres). Also, obstacles that are smaller than 10 centimetres wide or outside the field of play margin are ignored. This is done because the MSL robots are rather big, and in game situations small obstacles are not present inside the field. Also, it would be pointless to pay attention to obstacles that are outside the field of play, since the surrounding environment is completely ignorable for the game development.

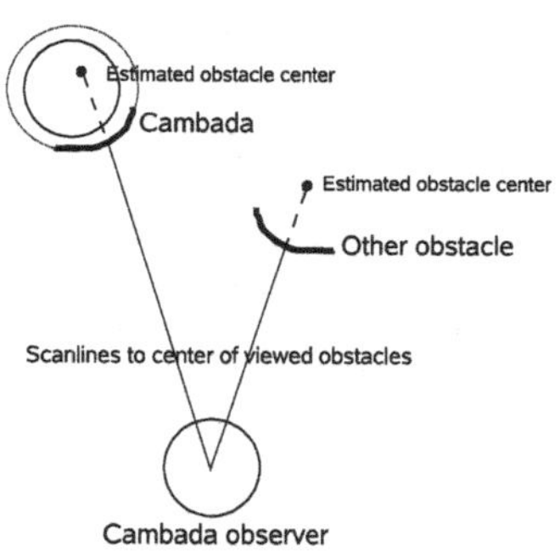

Fig. 6. When a CAMBADA robot is on, the estimated centres of the detected obstacles are compared with the known position of the team mates and tested if they are within the robot radius; the left obstacle is within the CAMBADA radius, the right one is not

To be able to distinguish obstacles, to identify which of them are team mates and which are opponent robots, a fusion between the own visual information of the obstacles and the shared team mates positions is made. By creating a circle around the team mate positions with the robot radius plus an error margin, varying with the distance, a matching of the estimated centre of visible obstacle within the team mate area is made (Fig. 6), and the obstacle is identified as the corresponding team mate in case of a positive matching (Figs. 7c), 8c)).

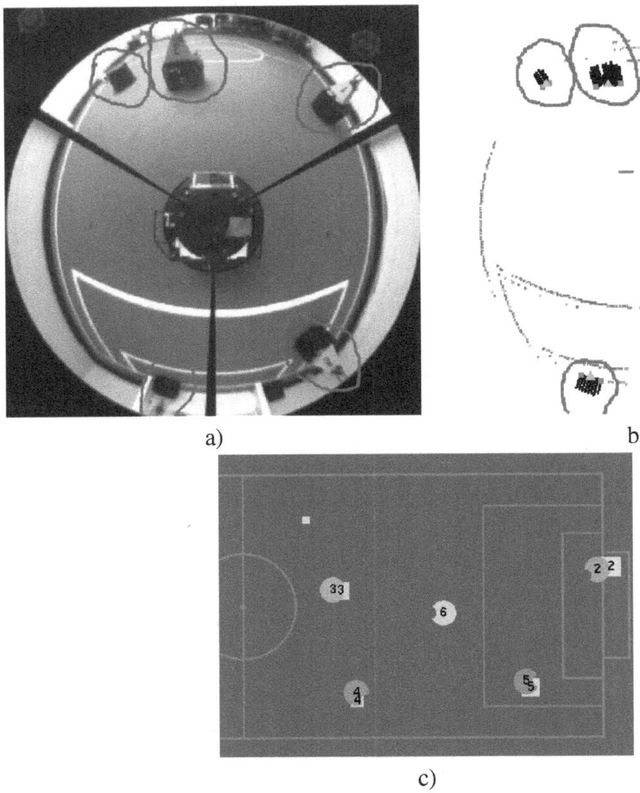

Fig. 7. Illustration of single obstacles identification. Top Left a): image acquired from the robot camera, denoting the single obstacles selected for identification (with lines surrounding them); Top Right b): the same image after processing. The visual detection of the same obstacles are also denoted; Bottom c): image of the control station, where each robot represents itself and robot 6 (the lighter grey) draws all the 5 obstacles in evaluation conditions (represented by squares with the same grey scale as itself). All the obstacles correspondent to team mates were correctly identified (marked by its corresponding number over the obstacle square) and the opponent is also represented with no number. Note that the positions of the robots visible in the image (each has its number on the body) is inverted due to the mirrored vision system.

Since the obstacles detected can be large blobs, the above described identification algorithm cannot be applied directly to the visually detected obstacles. If the detected obstacle fullfills the minimum size requisites already described, it is selected as candidate for being a robot obstacle. Its size is evaluated and classified as robot if it does not exceed the maximum size allowed for MSL robots [2] (Fig. 7a) and 7b)).

If the obstacle exceeds the maximum size of an MSL robot, a division of the obstacle is made, by analysing its total size and verifying how many robots are in that obstacle. This is a common situation, robots clashing together and thus creating a compact black blob, originating a big obstacle (Fig. 8a) and 8b)).

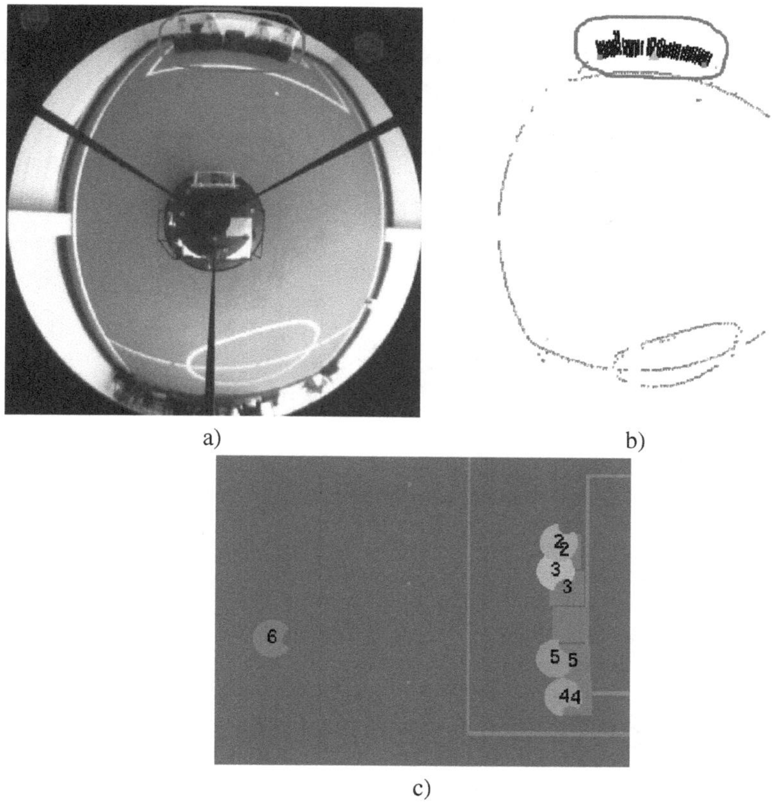

Fig. 8. Illustration of multiple obstacles identification. Top Left a): image acquired from the robot camera, denoting the obstacles aligned (with a line surrounding it); Top Right b): the same image after processing. Visually, the aligned robots are only one large obstacle (marked with its centre with a triangle and side limits with squares); Bottom **c)**: image of the control station, where each robot represents itself and robot 6 (the darker grey) draws all the 5 obstacles (represented by squares with the same grey scale as itself). The visual obstacle was successfully separated into the several composing obstacles, and all of them were correctly identified as the correspondent team mate (marked by its corresponding number over the obstacle square) and the opponent is also represented with no number.

4 Obstacle Sharing

With the purpose of improving the global perception of the team robots, the sharing of locally known information is an important feature. Obstacle sharing allows the team robots to have a more global perception of the field occupancy, allowing them to estimate, for instance, passing and dribbling corridors more effectively.

However, one have to keep in mind that, mainly due to illumination conditions and eventual reflexive materials, some of the detected obstacles may not be exactly robots, but dark shadowy areas. If that is the case, the simple sharing of obstacles would propagate an eventually false obstacle among the team. Thus the algorithm for sharing the obstacles makes a fusion of the several team mates information.

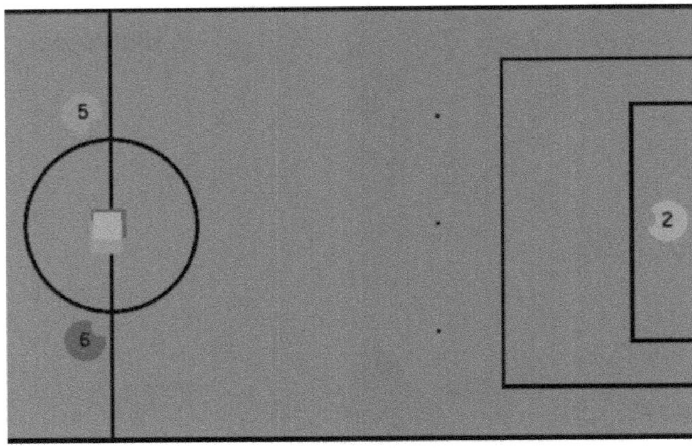

Fig. 9. Image of the control station showing an obstacle of robot 2 that was not seen by itself (on the centre of the field). In this case it assumes the obstacle by confirmation of both robots 5 and 6.

The fusion of the information is done mate by mate. After building the worldstate by its own means, the agent checks all the team mates available, one by one. Their obstacles are matched with the own ones. If the agent does not know an obstacle shared by the team mate, it keeps that obstacle in a temporary list of unconfirmed obstacles. This is done to all the team mates obstacles. When another team mate shares a common obstacle, that same obstacle is confirmed and it is transferred to the local list of obstacles. In the current cycle, the temporary obstacles that were not confirmed are not considered. An outline of the algorithm is presented next.

```
for c := 1 to total_number_of_team_mates
  for o := 1 to total_obstacles_of_team_mate
    for m := 1 to total_own_obstacles
      if m matches o
        I already know this obstacle, do nothing
      else
        if previously known by another team mate
          obstacle confirmed and added
        else
          obstacle considered temporarily
          waits for confirmation by another team mate
        end
      end
    end
  end
end
```

The matching of the team mate obstacles with the own obstacles is done in a way similar to the matching of the obstacle identification with the team mate position described in

Section 3. The cambada pivot in Fig. 6 is replaced by the current team mate obstacle for the matching test.

Figure 9 shows a situation where robot 2, in the goal area, was too far to see the obstacle on the middle of the field. Thus, it considered the obstacle in question, only because it is identified by both robots 5 and 6, as visible in the figure.

5 Conclusion

The integration of obstacles in the robot representation of the world is an important issue for it to be able to play the game. Even though the performance of the described work is yet to be tested in competition, the intensive tests of the detection and identification have shown a good effectiveness of the process so far.

The improvement on obstacle treatment allows modifications on the overall team strategy, particularly regarding passing possibilities. It also allows the improvement of the robots movement, since team mate obstacles can have a different treatment than the opponents, because team mates have velocities and other information available.

Having achieved the 1st place in the Portuguese robotics open Robótica2008 and in the Robocup2008 world championship, one of the ways to try to improve the CAMBADA team performance was to increase the world model accuracy. This new obstacle treatment, although not yet tested in competition environment, is expected to open new opportunities for the game effectiveness in the next competitions.

Acknowledgements

This work was partially supported by project ACORD Adaptive Coordination of Robotic Teams, FCT/PTDC/EIA/70695/2006.

References

1. Kitano, H., Asada, M., Kuniyoshi, Y., Noda, I., Osawa, E.: RoboCup: The Robot World Cup Initiative. In: Proceedings of the first international conference on Autonomous agents, pp. 340–347 (1997)
2. MSL Technical Committee 1997-2008: Middle Size Robot League Rules and Regulations for 2008 (2007)
3. Neves, A.J.R., Corrente, G.A., Pinho, A.J.: An omnidirectional vision system for soccer robots. In: Neves, J., Santos, M.F., Machado, J.M. (eds.) EPIA 2007. LNCS (LNAI), vol. 4874, pp. 499–507. Springer, Heidelberg (2007)
4. Cunha, B., Azevedo, J.L., Lau, N., Almeida, L.: Obtaining the inverse distance map from a non-svp hyperbolic catadioptric robotic vision system. In: Visser, U., Ribeiro, F., Ohashi, T., Dellaert, F. (eds.) RoboCup 2007. LNCS (LNAI), vol. 5001, pp. 417–424. Springer, Heidelberg (2008)
5. Neves, A.J.R., Martins, D.A., Pinho, A.J.: A hybrid vision system for soccer robots using radial search lines. In: Proc. of the 8th Conference on Autonomous Robot Systems and Competitions, Portuguese Robotics Open - ROBOTICA 2008, Aveiro, Portugal, pp. 51–55 (2008)

6. Lenser, S., Veloso, M.: Visual sonar: Fast obstacle avoidance using monocular vision. In: Proceedings of the 2003 IEEE/RSJ International Conference on Intelligent Robots and Systems, pp. 886–891 (2003)
7. Das, A.K., Fierro, R., Kumar, V., Southall, B., Spletzer, J., Taylor, C.J.: Real-time vision-based control of a nonholonomic mobile robot. In: Proceedings of the 2001 IEEE International Conference on Robotics and Automation, pp. 1714–1719 (2001)
8. Koyasu, H., Miura, J., Shirai, Y.: Realtime omnidirectional stereo for obstacle detection and tracking in dynamic environments. In: Proceedings of the 2001 IEEE/RSJ International Conference on Intelligent Robots and Systems, pp. 31–36 (2001)
9. Manduchi, R., Castano, A., Talukder, A., Matthies, L.: Obstacle detection and terrain classification for autonomous off-road navigation. Autonomous Robots, 81–102 (2005)
10. Michels, J., Saxena, A., Ng, A.Y.: High speed obstacle avoidance using monocular vision and reinforcement learning. In: Proceedings of the 22nd International Conference on Machine Learning (2005)

Chapter 8

KDBI – Knowledge Discovery and Business Intelligence

An Algorithm to Discover the k-Clique Cover in Networks

Luís Cavique[1], Armando B. Mendes[2], and Jorge M.A. Santos[3]

[1] University Aberta, R. Escola Politécnica 147, 1269-001 Lisboa, Portugal
lcavique@univ-ab.pt
[2] University of Azores, R. Mãe de Deus, 9501-801 Ponta Delgada, Portugal
amendes@uac.pt
[3] University of Evora, Largo dos Colegiais 2, 7000 Evora, Portugal
jmas@uevora.pt

Abstract. In social network analysis, a k-clique is a relaxed clique, i.e., a k-clique is a quasi-complete sub-graph. A k-clique in a graph is a sub-graph where the distance between any two vertices is no greater than k. The visualization of a small number of vertices can be easily performed in a graph. However, when the number of vertices and edges increases the visualization becomes incomprehensible. In this paper, we propose a new graph mining approach based on k-cliques. The concept of relaxed clique is extended to the whole graph, to achieve a general view, by covering the network with k-cliques. The sequence of k-clique covers is presented, combining small world concepts with community structure components. Computational results and examples are presented.

Keywords: Data mining, graph mining, social networks.

1 Introduction

After the Tim Berners-Lee [2] communication in the International World Wide Web Conference WWW2006 about the three ages of the Web, there has been an explosion of interest in the social networks associated with Web 2.0 in an attempt to improve socializing and come up with a new model for knowledge management.

The term social network was coined by Barnes in 1954. However, the visualization using a graph, called sociogram, was presented by Moreno [18]. This scientific area of sociology tries to explain how diffusion of innovation works, why alliances and conflicts are generated in groups, how the leadership emerges and how the group structure affects the group efficacy.

A major development on the structure of social networks came from a remarkable experiment by the American psychologist Stanley Milgram [16]. Milgram's experiment consisted in sending letters from people in Nebraska, in the Midwest, to de received in Boston, on the East Coast, where people were instructed to pass on the letters, by hand, to someone else they knew. The letters that reached the destination were passed by around six people. Milgram concluded that the experiment showed that, on average, Americans are no more than six steps away from each other. This experiment led to the concepts of the six degrees of separation and the notion of small-world.

L. Seabra Lopes et al. (Eds.): EPIA 2009, LNAI 5816, pp. 363–373, 2009.

An interesting example of a small-world is the "Erdos Number" [12]. Erdos is the most prolific mathematician, being author of more than 1500 papers with more than 500 co-authors. Erdos is the number zero and the researchers who worked with him are called Erdos number of 1. The co-authors of Erdos number of 1 are the Erdos number of 2, and so on, building one of the oldest small-world known. The work of Erdos and Renyi [8] presents interesting properties of random graphs. A brand new interest was revived with the Watts and Strogatz model, published in the Nature journal [22], that studies graphs with small-world properties and power-law degree distribution.

The analysts of social networks need to survey each person about their friends, ask for their approval to publish the data and keep the trace of the population for years. On the other hand, the social networks like MySpace or LinkedIn provide the required data.

The visualization of a small number of vertices can be completely mapped. However, when the number of vertices and edges increases the visualization becomes incomprehensible. The large amount of data extracted from the Internet is not compatible with the complete drawing. There is a pressing need for new patterns recognition tools and statistical methods to quantify large graphs and predict the behavior of network systems.

Graph mining can be defined as the science and the art of extracting useful knowledge like patterns and outliers provided respectively by repeated and sporadic data, from large graphs or complex networks [9], [6]. There are many differences between graphs; however, some patterns show up regularly and the main ones appear to be: the small worlds, the degree distribution and the connected components. The connected components have essentially been studied in two contexts: (a) the local neighborhoods, such as the clustering coefficient and (b) the node groups, such as the graph partitions and bipartite cores [6]. In this work the connected components are studied using the graph partition approach. The proposed Socratic query is the following: How many small world components (or k-cliques) are needed to cover (or to create partitions of) the whole graph?

In this paper, we propose new graph mining measures based on k-clique covering, to obtain a general view of the graph. In section 2 we review the social network concepts, detailing the cohesive subgroup structures. In section 3 we present the two-phase algorithm that looks first for cohesive subgroups and second to the minimum set of cohesive subgroups that cover all the vertices. In section 4 computational results and examples are presented. Finally, in section 5 we draw some conclusions.

2 Network Concepts

Social Network Analysis is a very relevant technique, which has emerged in modern sociology and studies the interaction between individuals, organizations and other kinds of entities. See [19] and [21] for the theoretical basis and key techniques in social networks.

The representation of a social network was quite influenced by graph theory. In the social networks the set of vertices (or nodes) correspond to the "actors" (i.e. people, companies, social actors) and the set of edges corresponds to the "ties" (i.e. relationships, associations, links).

The sociologic applications of cohesive subgroups can include groups such as work groups, sport teams, political party, religious cults, or hidden structures like criminal gangs and terrorist cells. In this section we will detail some techniques for cohesive subgroups like the cliques and relaxed cliques, such as k-clique, k-club/k-clan and k-plex.

2.1 Clique

Given an undirected graph G= (V, E) where V denotes the set of vertices and E the set of edges, the graph G1= (V1, E1) is called a sub-graph of G if V1⊆V, E1⊆E and for every edge (vi, vj)∈ E1 the vertices vi,vj∈ V1. A sub-graph G1 is said to be complete if there is an edge for each pair of vertices. A complete sub-graph is also called a clique, see figure 1. A clique is maximal, if it is not contained in any other clique. The clique number of a graph is equal to the cardinality of the largest clique of G and it is obtained by solving the maximum clique NP-hard problem.

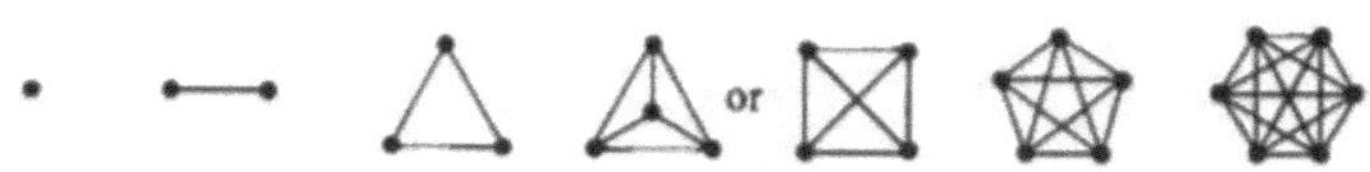

Fig. 1. Cliques with 1, 2, 3, 4, 5 and 6 vertices

The clique structure, where there must be an edge for each pair of vertices, shows many restrictions in real life modeling. So, alternative approaches were suggested in order to relax the clique concept, such as k-clique, k-clan/k-club and k-plex.

2.2 k-Clique

Luce [15] introduced the distance base model called k-clique, where k is the maximum path length between each pair of vertices. A k-clique is a subset of vertices C such that, for every i, j∈ C, the distance d(i, j)≤ k. The 1-clique is identical to a clique, because the distance between the vertices is one edge. The 2-clique is the maximal complete sub-graph with a path length of one or two edges. The path distance two can be exemplified by the "friend of a friend" connection in social relationships. In social websites like the LinkedIn, each member can reach his own connections and also the two and three degrees away. The increase of the value k corresponds to a gradual relaxation of the criterion of clique membership. See figure 2.

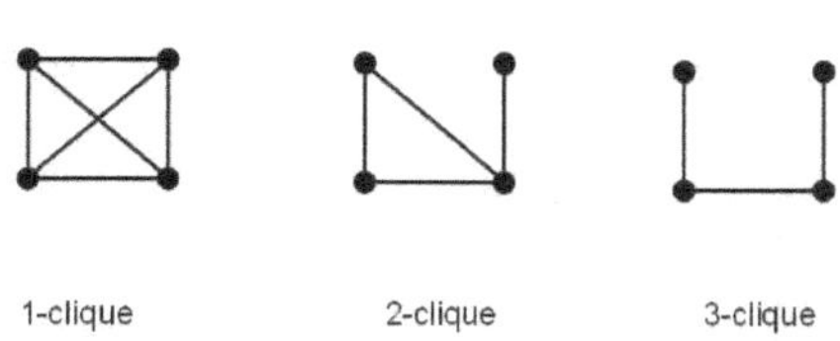

Fig. 2. k-cliques examples

2.3 k-Clan and k-Club

A limitation of the k-clique model is that some vertices may be distant from the group, i.e. the distance, between two nodes, may correspond to a path involving nodes that do not belong to the k-clique. To overcome this handicap Alba [1] and Mokken [17] introduced the diameter based models called k-club and k-clan. The length of the shortest path between vertices u and v in G is denoted by the distance d(u,v). The diameter of G is given by diam(G)= max d(u, v) for all u,v∈ V. To find all k-clan, firstly all the k-cliques S^i must be found and then the restriction diam(G[S])≤ k applied to remove the undesired k-cliques. In figure 3, on the left, the 2-clique {1,2,3,4,5} was removed because the d(4,5)=3. Another approach to the diameter models is the k-club which is defined as a subset of vertices S such that diam(G[S])≤ k. In the following figure two 2-cliques: {1,2,3,4,5} and {2,3,4,5,6}, one 2-clan: {2,3,4,5,6} and three 2-clubs: {1,2,3,4}, {1,2,3,5} and {2,3,4,5,6} can be found.

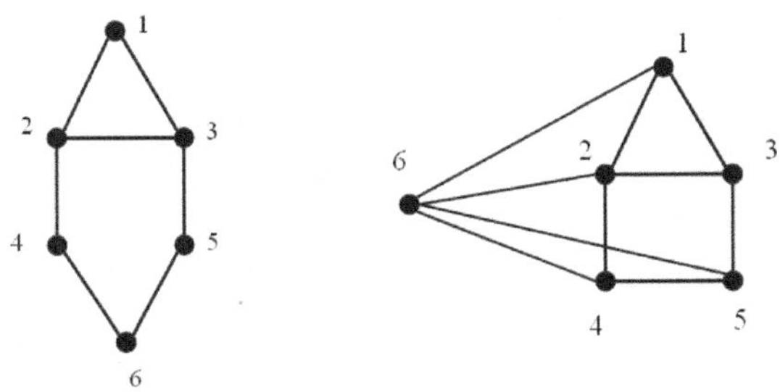

Fig. 3. 2-clans, 2-clubs (left) and 3-plex (right)

2.4 k-Plex

An alternative way of relaxing a clique is the k-plex concept which takes into account the vertices degree. The degree of a vertex of a graph is the number of edges incident on the vertex, and is denoted deg(v). The maximum degree of a graph G is the maximum degree of its vertices and is denoted by Δ(G). On the other hand, the minimum degree is the minimum degree of its vertices and is denoted by δ(G). A subset of vertices S is said to be a k-plex if the minimum degree in the induced sub-graph δ(G[S])≥ |S|– k. In figure 3, on the right, the graph with 6 vertices, |S|=6, and the degree of vertices 1, 3, 4 and 5 does not exceed the value 3. So, the minimum degree in the induced sub-graph δ(G[S]) is 3. For |S|=6, k=3 is obtained.

3 The Two Phase Algorithm

Complex network and graph mining measures are essentially based on low complexity computational procedures like the diameter of the graph, the degree distribution of the nodes and connectivity checking, underestimating the knowledge of the graph structure components. In this paper we propose a graph mining measure based on k-clique cover, to understand the structure of the graph better, by combining small worlds with the cohesive subgroup analysis.

In order to find the k-cliques minimum cover a two-phase algorithm is proposed. First, all the maximal k-cliques in the graph are found. Second, the minimum subset of the k-cliques is chosen to cover all the vertices of the graph.

To find all the maximal k-cliques in the graph, we use a simple transformation of the graph, in such a way that we can reuse an already studied algorithm, the maximum clique algorithm.

Procedure 1. A two-phase algorithm to find the k-clique cover
Input: distance k and graph G
Output: k-clique cover
1. Find all maximal k-cliques in graph G
1.1. Graph transformation into a k-G (Proc. 2)
1.2. Apply maximum clique algorithm (Proc. 3)
2. Find the minimum cover of G with k-cliques
2.1. Apply set covering algorithm (Proc. 4)

3.1 Maximal k-Cliques in Graph G

This section details in graph transformation procedure and the generation of the maximal k-cliques.

3.1.1 Graph Transformation

The transformation of a graph G(V,E) into a graph such that for every $i,j \in V$, the distance $d(i, j) \leq k$, we denote graph k-G(V,E).

To create a graph k-G(V,E), the Floyd Algorithm [10] that finds all the shortest paths in a graph is reused; and then for each edge less or equal to k, an edge is created in the new graph.

Procedure 2. Graph transformation
Input: k, M[n,n] the adjacent matrix of graph G
Output: D[n,n] the k-distance matrix of graph G (or k-Graph)
1. D=M
2. For each (h,i,j) D[i,j] = min(D[i,j], D[i,h]+D[h,j])
3. For each (i,j) if (D[i,j] <=k) D[i,j]=1 else D[i,j]=0
4. Return D;

3.1.2 Maximum Clique Algorithm

The Maximum Clique is a NP-hard problem that aims to find the largest complete sub-graph in a given graph. In this approach we intend to find a lower bound for the maximization problem, based in the heuristics proposed by Johnson [13] and in the meta-heuristic that uses Tabu Search developed by Soriano and Gendreau [20]. Part of the described work in this section can also be found in [4] and [3].

We define A(S) as the set of vertices which are adjacent to vertices of a current solution S. Let $n=|S|$ be the cardinality of a clique S and $A^k(S)$ the subset of vertices with k arcs incident in S. A(S) can be divided into subgroups $A(S) = \cup A^k(S)$, $k=1,..,n$. The cardinality of the vertex set $|V|$ is equal to the sum of the adjacent vertices A(S) and the non-adjacent ones $A^0(S)$, plus $|S|$, resulting in $|V|= \Sigma|A^k(S)|+n$, $k= 0,.., n$. For a given solution S, we define a neighborhood N(S) if it generates a feasible solution S'. In this work we are going to use three neighborhood structures.

We consider the following notation:

$N^+(S) = \{S': S' = S \cup \{v^i\}, v^i \in A^n(S)\}$
$N^-(S) = \{S': S' = S \setminus \{v^i\}, v^i \in S\}$

$N^0(S) = \{S': S' = S \cup \{v^i\} \setminus \{v^k\},\ v^i \in A^{n-1}(S),\ v^k \in S\}$
S – the current solution
S*– the highest cardinality maximal clique found so far
T– the tabu list
N(S) – neighborhood structures

Procedure 3. Tabu Heuristic for the Maximum Clique Problem
Input: k-Graph, complete sub-graph S
Output: clique S*
1. T=∅; S*=S;
2. while not end condition
2.1. if ($N^+(S)\setminus T \neq$ null) choose the maximum S'
2.2. else if ($N^0(S)\setminus T \neq$ null) choose the maximum S'; update T
2.2.1. else choose the maximum S' in $N^-(S)$; update T
2.3. update S=S'
2.4. if (|S|>|S*|) S*=S;
3. end while;
4. return S*;

Finding a maximal clique in a k-graph is the same as finding a maximal k-clique in a graph. To generate a large set of maximal k-cliques, a multi-start algorithm is used, which calls the Tabu Heuristic for Maximum Clique Problem.

3.2 Minimum k-Cliques Cover

The input for the k-clique cover is a matrix where the lines correspond to the vertices of the graph and each column is a k-clique that covers a certain number of vertices. The Clique Cover heuristic proposed by Kellerman [14] and improved by Chvatal [5] is described in the following pseudo-code.

We consider the following notation:

M[line, column] or M[vertex, k-clique] – input matrix
C – vector of the cost of each column
V – vertex set of G(V,E)
S – the set covering solution

Procedure 4. Heuristic for the k-clique covering
Input: M [line, column], C, V
Output: the cover S
1. Initialize R=M, S=∅,
2. While R ≠ ∅ do
2.1. Choose the best line i*∈ R such as $|M(i^*,j)|=\min |M(i,j)|\ \forall j$
2.2. Choose the best column j* that covers line i*
2.3. Update R and S, $R=R\setminus M(i,j^*)\ \forall i$, $S=S\cup\{j^*\}$
3. End while
4. Sort the cover S by descending order of costs
5. For each Si do if (S\Si is still a cover) then S=S\Si
6. Return S

In the constructive heuristic, for each iteration, choose a line to be covered, the best column that covers the line and update the solution S and the remaining vertex R. The chosen line is usually the line that is more difficult to cover, i.e. the line which corresponds to fewer columns. After reaching the cover set, the second step is to remove redundancy, by sorting the cover in descending order of cost and checking if each k-clique is really essential.

This constructive heuristic can be improved using a Tabu Search heuristic that removes the most expensive columns and re-builds a new solution as presented in [11].

The set partition problem is very similar to the set covering one. The partition of a set is a division into non-overlapping parts that cover all the set. On the other hand, the set covering problem allows overlapping called over-covered elements. In both problems less-covered elements are not allowed.

3.3 Numeric Example

Given a graph with 5 vertices and 4 edges with E={(1,2), (2,3), (3,4) ,(4,5)} in figure 4, applying the graph transformation, Procedure 2, with k=2, a new graph with 5 vertices and 7 edges is obtained with k-E={(1,2), (1,3), (2,3), (2,4), (3,4) ,(3,5),(4,5)}.

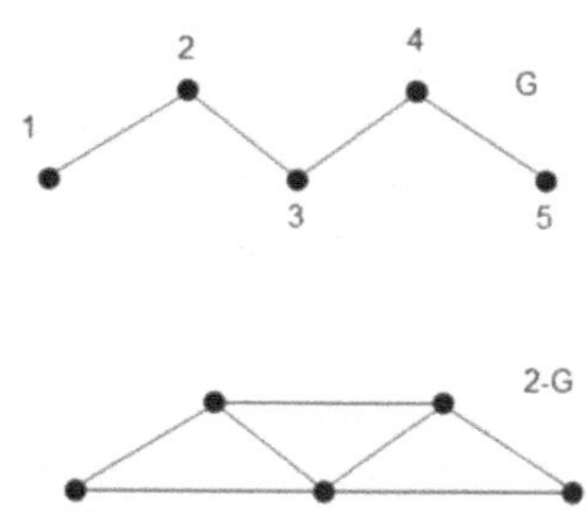

Fig. 4. Example of a graph G and its transformation into a 2-G (Proc. 2)

Running a multi-start algorithm, Procedure 3, with the maximum clique problem, three maximal cliques of size 3 can be easily identified: (1,2,3), (2,3,4) and (3,4,5).

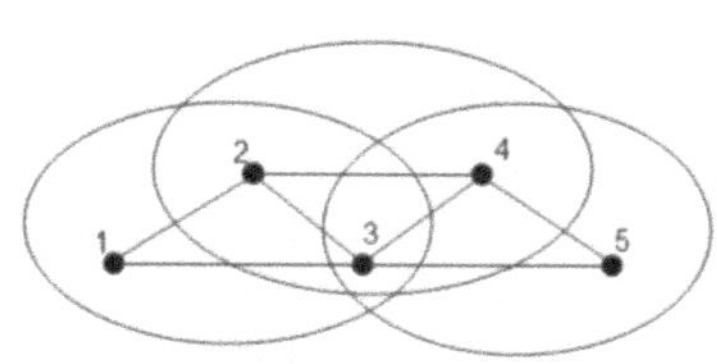

Fig. 5. k-clique generation (Proc. 3)

Finally, running the k-cliques cover, Procedure 4, two subgroups are found that cover all the vertices. The 2-clique cover is equal to two. Notice that the vertex number 3 appears in the two sets. In social network analysis this is called a "bridge". Indeed, vertex 3, with distance 2 can reach any other vertex.

nodes	C1	C2	C3	over covered
active columns	1	0	1	
1	1			
2	1	1		
3	1	1	1	1
4		1	1	
5			1	

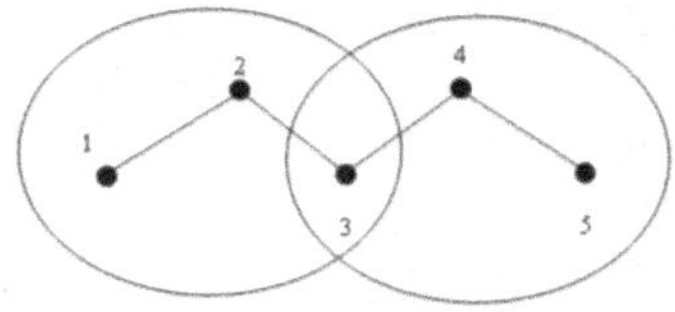

Fig. 6. Two 2-cliques cover the whole graph (Proc. 4)

Figure 6 presents the two subsets solution using a matrix representation and a graph. For large graphs and a large number of subsets the visualization gets worse. To get a better general view of the data we suggest the matrix representation, which is the output of the set covering heuristic.

4 Computational Results

To implement the computational results of this algorithm some choices must be made such as the computational environment, the datasets and the graph mining measures.

The computer programs were written in C language and the Dev-C++ compiler was used. The computational results were obtained from a 2.53GHz Intel Core-2Duo processor with 4.00 GB of main memory running under the Windows Vista operating system.

To validate the two-phase algorithm two groups of datasets were used, the Erdos graphs and some clique DIMACS [7] benchmark instances. In Erdos graphs each node corresponds to a researcher, and two nodes are adjacent if the researchers published together. The graphs are named "ERDOS-x-y", where "x" represents the last

Table 1. Sequence of k-clique cover

graph	nr nodes	longest path	cardinality of the k-clique cover									
			k=1	k=2	k=3	k=4	k=5	k=6	k=7	k=9	k=18	k=40
Test	18	6	7	4	3	2	2	1	--	--	--	--
Erdos-97-1	472	6	9	8	7	7	4	1	--	--	--	--
Erdos-98-1	485	7	8	8	7	5	1	1	1	--	--	--
Erdos-99-1	492	7	8	8	7	7	1	1	1	--	--	--
brock200_1	200	2	24	1	--	--	--	--	--	--	--	--
brock200_2	200	2	26	1	--	--	--	--	--	--	--	--
brock400_1	400	2	26	1	--	--	--	--	--	--	--	--
brock400_2	400	2	23	1	--	--	--	--	--	--	--	--
c-fat200-1	200	18	16	11	9	8	7	7	6	5	1	--
c-fat200-2	200	9	9	7	5	4	3	3	3	1	--	--
c-fat500-1	500	40	16	12	9	7	7	6	6	4	3	1

two digits of the year that the graphs was create, and "y" the maximum distance from Erdos to each vertex in the graph. The second group of graphs contains some clique instances from the second DIMACS challenge. These include the "brock" graphs, which contain cliques "hidden" within much smaller cliques, getting hard to discover cliques in these graphs. The "c-fat" graphs are a result of fault diagnosis data.

In this paper we propose a graph mining measure based on k-cliques, to understand the structure of the graph better, by combining small worlds with the cohesive subgroup analysis. The measure for small worlds can be obtained using the diameter of the graph, i.e. the longest shortest path in the graph, as already stated. For the cohesive subgroups study, we use the concept of k-clique.

For the analysis of each graph, we consider the number of nodes, the longest path, the average path and the cardinality of the set of k-cliques that cover all the nodes, varying k from 1 to the longest path.

The "test" graph with 18 nodes, has the longest path equal to 6. To cover the graph seven 1-clique are needed, or four 2-cliques are needed, and so on, until one 6-clique is needed. Figure 7 shows the 3-clique cover.

For the Erdos-98-1 and Erdos-99-1, with the longest path of 7, the graphs are covered with only one 5-clique. These values exemplify the difference between k-cliques and k-clans, these graphs are 5-cliques but not 5-clans because the diameter is equal to seven.

The "brock" graphs, known as hiding cliques, have a short longest path, equal to 2, and to cover the graph one 2-clique is enough. Most of the DIMACS instances present this profile. On the other hand, the "c-fat" graphs, have the shortest path larger than 7, generating long sequences of k-clique cover.

In the proposed measure, the sequence of k-clique covers, identifies families of graphs, and seems to be very promising.

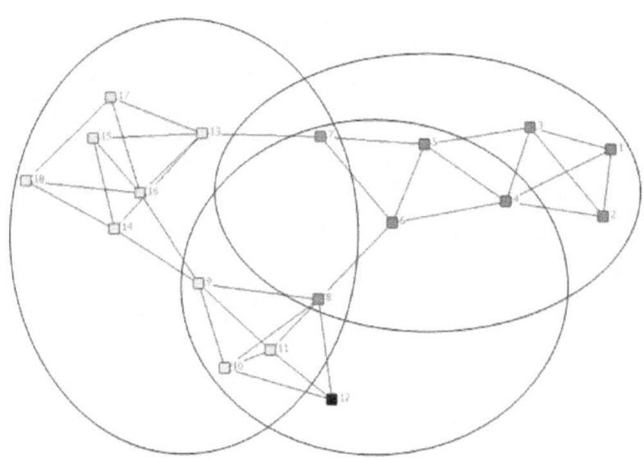

Fig. 7. Three 3-clique are needed to cover the Test graph

5 Conclusions

The popular saying that establishes that "to be right is not enough, someone needs to say you are right" agrees with the relevance of social networks in the area of artificial intelligence. The model of artificial intelligence focused on a single entity tends to soon become soon outdated. On the other hand, models based on the agents' interaction are emerging, strengthening the concept of social networks.

Given the large amount of data, provided by the Web 2.0, there is a pressing need to obtain new measures to better understand the networks' structure; how their components are organized and the way they evolve over time.

Complex network measures are essentially based on low complexity computational procedures like the diameter of the graph, the degree distribution of the nodes and connectivity checking, while underestimating the knowledge of the graph structure components.

In this paper the concept of relaxed clique is extended to the whole the graph, to achieve a general view, by covering the network with k-cliques. The sequence of k-clique covers is presented, combining small world concept with community structure components. The analysis of the sequences shows that different graph families have different structures.

Additional, non-mentioned features in this paper, like the over-covered nodes, the k-cliques cardinality and the k-clique composition can be obtained.

Social networks do not exceed a hundred nodes. In this work the proposed two-phase algorithm deals with graphs with hundreds of nodes, with a running time performance of a few seconds. In future work, we would like to extend this approach to larger datasets, with thousands of nodes.

References

1. Alba, R.D.: A graph-theoretic definition of a sociometric clique. Journal of Mathematical Sociology 3, 113–126 (1973)
2. Berners-Lee, T.: The Next Wave of the Web: Plenary Panel. In: 15th International World Wide Web Conference, WWW2006, Edinburgh, Scotland (2006)
3. Cavique, L., Luz, C.: A Heuristic for the Stability Number of a Graph based on Convex Quadratic Programming and Tabu Search, special issue of the Journal of Mathematical Sciences, Aveiro Seminar on Control Optimization and Graph Theory, Second Series (to appear, 2009)
4. Cavique, L., Rego, C., Themido, I.: A Scatter Search Algorithm for the Maximum Clique Problem. In: Ribeiro, C., Hansen, P. (eds.) Essays and Surveys in Metaheuristics, pp. 227–244. Kluwer Academic Publishers, Dordrecht (2002)
5. Chvatal, V.: A greedy heuristic for the set-covering problem. Math. Oper. Res. 4, 233–235 (1979)
6. Cook, D.J., Holder, L.B. (eds.): Mining Graph Data. John Wiley & Sons, New Jersey (2007)
7. DIMACS: Maximum clique, graph coloring, and satisfiability, Second DIMACS implementation challenge (1995), `http://dimacs.rutgers.edu/Challenges/` (accessed April 2009)
8. Erdos, P., Renyi, A.: On Random Graphs. I. Publicationes Mathematicae 6, 290–297 (1959)
9. Faloutsos, M., Faloutsos, P., Faloutsos, C.: On power-law relationships of the Internet topology. In: SIGCOMM, pp. 251–262 (1999)
10. Floyd, R.W.: Algorithm 97: Shortest Path. Communications of the ACM 5(6), 345 (1962)

11. Gomes, M., Cavique, L., Themido, I.: The Crew Time Tabling Problem: an extension of the Crew Scheduling Problem. Annals of Operations Research, volume Optimization in transportation 144(1), 111–132 (2006)
12. Grossman, J., Ion, P., Castro, R.D.: The Erdos number Project (2007), http://www.oakland.edu/enp/ (accessed April 2009)
13. Johnson, D.S.: Approximation algorithms for combinatorial problems. Journal of Computer and System Science 9, 256–278 (1974)
14. Kellerman, E.: Determination of keyword conflict. IBM Technical Disclosure Bulletin 16(2), 544–546 (1973)
15. Luce, R.D.: Connectivity and generalized cliques in sociometric group structure. Psychometrika 15, 159–190 (1950)
16. Milgram, S.: The Small World Problem. Psychology Today 1(1), 60–67 (1967)
17. Mokken, R.J.: Cliques, clubs and clans. Quality and Quantity 13, 161–173 (1979)
18. Moreno, J.L.: Who Shall Survive? Nervous and Mental Disease Publishing Company, Washington DC (1934)
19. Scott, J.: Social Network Analysis - A Handbook. Sage Publications, London (2000)
20. Soriano, P., Gendreau, M.: Tabu search algorithms for the maximum clique. In: Johnson, D.S., Trick, M.A. (eds.) Clique, Coloring and Satisfiability, Second Implementation Challenge DIMACS, pp. 221–242 (1996)
21. Wasserman, S., Faust, K.: Social Network Analysis: Methods and Applications. Cambridge University Press, Cambridge (1994)
22. Watts, D.J., Strogatz, S.H.: Collective dynamics of small-world networks. Nature 393(6684), 409–410 (1998)

Cost-Sensitive Learning Vector Quantization for Financial Distress Prediction

Ning Chen[1], Armando S. Vieira[1], João Duarte[1],
Bernardete Ribeiro[2], and João C. Neves[3]

[1] GECAD, Instituto Superior de Engenharia do Porto, Instituto Politecnico do Porto
[2] CISUC, Department of Informatics Engineering, University of Coimbra, Portugal
[3] ISEG-School of Economics, Technical University of Lisbon, Portugal
{cng,asv,jmmd}@isep.ipp.pt, bribeiro@dei.uc.pt, jcneves@iseg.utl.pt

Abstract. Financial distress prediction is of crucial importance in credit risk analysis with the increasing competition and complexity of credit industry. Although a variety of methods have been applied in this field, there are still some problems remained. The accurate and sensitive prediction in presence of unequal misclassification costs is an important one. Learning vector quantization (LVQ) is a powerful tool to solve financial distress prediction problem as a classification task. In this paper, a cost-sensitive version of LVQ is proposed which incorporates the cost information in the model. Experiments on two real data sets show the proposed approach is effective to improve the predictive capability in cost-sensitive situation.

Keywords: Distress prediction, neural network, learning vector quantization, classification, cost-sensitive learning.

1 Introduction

Financial distress prediction is a research issue of credit risk analysis in a considerably wide range of financial areas to reduce the risk of credit process, lessen the negative impact of inappropriate credit decisions, and shorten the time of credit evaluation [1]. The main concern of financial distress prediction is to predict the bankruptcy of a firm or person regarding the financial ratios and historical distress events. Within the data mining literature, it can be solved as a classification problem to differentiate between good and bad credits based on the analysis of financial characteristics. Currently, the importance of distress prediction becomes more serious due to the rapid growth of credit industry and the increasing complexity of credit decisions. Despite numerous methods proposed so far, researchers in different disciplines continuously study new methods to effectively support the credit decision. The related literature is reviewed in a recent paper [2].

Cost-sensitive learning is very important since the misclassification cost becomes critical in diverse applications such as credit risk analysis, medical diagnostics and fraud detection. Furthermore as indicated in [3], the pervasive

L. Seabra Lopes et al. (Eds.): EPIA 2009, LNAI 5816, pp. 374–385, 2009.

class imbalance problem could be solved in a similar manner as unequal cost setup. That is the reason cost-sensitive learning becomes a hot topic in machine learning. Cost-sensitive classification algorithms that enable effective prediction, where the costs of misclassification can be very different, are crucial to creditors and auditors in credit risk analysis. Many cost-sensitive learning approaches have been presented. However, to the best of our knowledge no work is reported on learning vector quantization (LVQ) that takes the misclassification costs into account.

In this paper, a cost-sensitive version of LVQ is proposed to classify data when the misclassification costs of different classes are unequal and known. The cost information is taken into consideration when performing the update of map neurons. Additionally, this approach is adapted to a variant of LVQ that is able to handle both numerical and categorical variables. To illustrate the effectiveness of the proposed methods, experiments are undertaken on two real data sets, one is for bankruptcy prediction of French private firms and the other is for credit approval forecast of Australian applicants. The empirical results indicate that when compared to traditional LVQ that does not incorporate cost information, the proposed algorithm can lead to lower overall misclassification cost.

The remaining of this paper is organized as follows. Section 2 reviews the related work about financial distress prediction and cost-sensitive learning. Section 3 presents the methodology of cost-sensitive LVQ. In section 4, the validity of proposed method is explored through empirical study on two different data sets of finance domain. Lastly, the contributions and future remarks are addressed in section 5.

2 Related Work

Generally, the existing methods of distress prediction fall into two groups: statistical methods and intelligent methods [4]. The statistical methods include Linear Discriminant Analysis (LDA), Multivariate Discriminant Analysis (MDA), Probit Analysis and Logistic Regression, etc. The intelligent methods comprise Artificial Neural Networks, Decision Trees, Genetic Algorithms, Case-based Reasoning, Support Vector Machines, Rough Sets, etc. Artificial Neural Network (ANN) is a powerful machine learning method with several useful properties such as nonlinear modelisation, computational simplicity, generalization capability and noise insensitivity.

Considerable efforts have been invested into the comparison of ANN with various linear or nonlinear methods for distress prediction. For example, back-propagation neural network is superior to discriminant analysis and logistic regression on bankruptcy prediction of Korean firms [5]. In [6], the capability of self-organizing map (SOM) in determining the credit class is investigated through a visual exploration. Neves & Vieira shows that an enhanced version of Hidden Layer Learning Vector Quantization can boost the performance of ANN [7].

LVQ is employed to detect the distressed French companies with satisfactory performance [8]. Based on the study of financial failure prediction of Turkey banks, LVQ is reported as one of the most successful models with comparison to other neural networks, support vector machines and multivariate statistical methods [9]. A hybrid model of SOM, k-means and LVQ is developed to solve municipal creditworthiness problem [10].

Most of the studies address the credit trustfulness considering an equal cost situation, i.e., the risk of a bad classification has an equal cost. However, it is well known that misclassifying a bad credit (default) as a good (non-default) will cost much more than the reverse [11]. Due to the presence of unequal misclassification costs in reality, it is important to include the cost information in classification. Although the misclassification costs are considered in the evaluation of prediction models in [1,12], the models are not cost-sensitive in the sense that the cost information has no impact on classification results.

Regarding the phase of manipulation, the cost-sensitive learning methods can be divided into three categories. In pre-learning approaches, the distribution of original data is modified using different forms of sampling techniques so that the cost information is conveyed by the occurrence of examples. Over-sampling increases the amount of expensive examples, on the contrary, under-sampling decreases the amount of inexpensive examples. However, the sampling techniques have been criticized since they artificially increase the number of data for over-sampling, or discard useful examples for under-sampling [13].

The in-learning approaches make a specific classification method cost-sensitive by changing the learning methodology in the algorithm level. The cost information is considered in the splitting criterion for attribute selection to build a cost-sensitive decision tree [14]. The instance-weighting C4.5 decision tree assigns the samples of different classes with different weights proportional to the corresponding costs [15]. Similarly, a cost-sensitive extension of regularized least square algorithm uses different weights to penalize different fractions of classes in medical diagnosis [16]. Three weighting strategies are presented to introduce cost items into the boosting learning framework [17]. The cost matrix is incorporated into back-propagation neural network [18], mathematical programming and genetic algorithm based neural network [19] by modifying the objective functions. In this article, the cost-sensitive LVQ variant is presented based on the modification of basic LVQ algorithm by incorporating the cost information into the model.

Finally, the post-learning solutions rely on the manipulation of the output of classifiers. For the decision tree, the class label is assigned to the leaf nodes to minimize the cost [20]. A threshold-moving technique is applied to the real-valued output of the neural network [21]. In order to detect the optimal threshold, a bisection method is developed that minimizes the overall misclassification cost. In the support vector machine and maximum entropy method, over-sampling and threshold-moving techniques are incorporated to obtain sensitive and accurate classifiers on highly unbalanced drug data [22].

3 Methodology of Cost-Sensitive Learning Vector Quantization

Based on the neurons representing prototype vectors and the nearest neighbor approach for classifying data, LVQ is a neural network approach useful for complicated non-linear separation problems. The neurons are arranged on a regular low-dimensional grid and associated with the input vectors by prototypes. LVQ starts from a trained map with class label assignment to neurons and attempts to adjust the boundary of class regions in a supervised way. LVQ can be trained either in sequential way or in batch way. In the former the prototypes are updated at each training step, and in the latter the prototypes are updated at the end of an iteration of all input data. The cost-sensitive LVQ resembles the basic batch LVQ except that the misclassification costs are utilized as weights guiding the prototype learning so that more attention is paid to the class associated with higher cost.

During the training process, an input vector x is projected to the best-matching unit (BMU), i.e., the winner with the closest prototype according to the distance measurement d.

$$BMU(x) = \underset{1 \leq i \leq m}{\operatorname{argmin}}\ d(x, m_i) \tag{1}$$

The projection of input x_i $(1 \leq i \leq n)$ is defined by an indicative function h_{ip} whose value is 1 if m_p is the BMU of x_i, and 0 otherwise.

$$h_{ip} = \begin{cases} 1 \text{ if } m_p = BMU(x_i) \\ 0 \text{ otherwise} \end{cases} \tag{2}$$

Regarding the BMU, a Voronoi set V_i is generated for each neuron and composed of the observations projected to the neuron. In the Voronoi set, an element is positive if its class label agrees with the map neuron, and negative otherwise. Positive examples move the prototype towards the input while negative examples move the prototype away from them. Intuitively, the positive examples of relatively higher cost should impose more impact on the prototypes so that they are harder to be misclassified. The denotative function s_{ip} takes $C_{label(x_i)}$, which is the misclassification cost associated with the class of observation x_i, as the value in case of positive example, and -1 otherwise.

$$s_{ip} = \begin{cases} C_{label(x_i)} & \text{if } label(m_p) = label(x_i) \\ -1 & \text{otherwise} \end{cases} \tag{3}$$

The indicative and denotative functions are then used in the prototype update, which combines the contribution of positive examples and suppression of negative examples to each neuron in a batch round. Let $m_p(t)$ be the prototype vector of the pth unit at epoch t. The update rule of cost-sensitive LVQ is formulated as follows (If the denominator is 0 or negative for some m_p, no updating is done.):

$$m_p(t+1) = \frac{\sum_{i=1}^{n} h_{ip} s_{ip} x_i}{\sum_{i=1}^{n} h_{ip} s_{ip}} \tag{4}$$

Additionally, the cost-sensitive method can be used in other batch LVQ algorithms, such as BNCLVQ (batch numeric and categorical learning vector quantization algorithm) [23] in a similar way. In this algorithm[1], the indicative and denotative functions are used to update the categorical features for the next epoch. For lack of space the detailed description is not included in the paper.

As a special case of SOM, the LVQ algorithms benefit from a trained map by a preceding SOM in the initialization [24]. In one round, one instance x_i is input and the distance between x_i and prototypes is calculated, consequently the input is projected to the BMU according to Equation (1). After all the inputs are processed, the neurons are assigned by the majority of class labels in Voronoi set for acquiring the labeled map. In other words, if there are more 'good' examples than 'bad' examples, the unit is labeled as 'good' and conversely. Then the values of indicative and denotative functions are calculated for each pair of input and neuron regarding Equation (2) and (3). Afterwards, the prototypes are updated according to Equation (4). This training process is repeated iteratively until the maximum number of iteration is reached or the amount of variation of prototypes between two consecutive iterations is less than a specified threshold. In summary, the algorithm is performed as follows:

1. For $p = 1, ..., m$, initialize the map with prototypes m_p;
2. For $i = 1, ..., n$, input instance x_i to the map and project it to the BMU;
3. For $p = 1, ..., m$, assign the class to $m_p(t)$ by majority labeling principle;
4. For $i = 1, ..., n, p = 1, ..., m$, calculate h_{ip} and s_{ip};
5. For $p = 1, ..., m$, calculate the new prototype $m_p(t + 1)$ for the next epoch;
6. Repeat from Step 2 a few iterations until the termination condition is satisfied.

4 Empirical Analysis

The proposed cost-sensitive LVQ algorithms are implemented based on *somtoolbox* [25] in *Matlab*. We mainly concern about the effectiveness of the proposed algorithms on the tradeoff between two kinds of errors and the improvement on the total misclassification error rather than on the comparison with competing classification models.

4.1 Data Sets

In this paper, the capability of cost-sensitive LVQ is validated by two data sets, one is for bankruptcy prediction and the other is for personal credit approval.

The Diane data set contains financial statements of 1200 private-owned French firms of small or medium size in which 600 examples are 'good' and the rest is 'bad' (distress in 2007). As described in Table 1, each firm is characterized by a set of 29 financial ratios besides the independent class. The problem is to predict whether a firm may become bankruptcy according to the financial ratios

[1] We call it cost-sensitive BNCLVQ.

Table 1. Financial ratios of Diane companies

Var.	Description	Var.	Description
x1	Number of Employees	x16	Cashflow / Turnover
x2	Capital Employed / Fixed Assets	x17	Working Capital / Turnover days
x3	Financial Debt / Capital Employed	x18	Net Current Assets/Turnover days
x4	Depreciation of Tangible Assets	x19	Working Capital Needs / Turnover
x5	Working Capital / Current Assets	x20	Added Value per Employee
x6	Current ratio	x21	Total Assets Turnover
x7	Liquidity Ratio	x22	Operating Profit Margin
x8	Stock Turnover days	x23	Net Profit Margin
x9	Collection Period days	x24	Added Value Margin
x10	Credit Period days	x25	Part of Employees
x11	Turnover per Employee	x26	Return on Capital Employed
x12	Interest / Turnover	x27	Return on Total Assets
x13	Debt Period days	x28	EBIT Margin
x14	Financial Debt / Equity	x29	EBITDA Margin
x15	Financial Debt / Cashflow	x30	Class (healthy, distress)

describing the situation of the firm over a given period (We consider one year proceeding the default in the paper).

To mitigate the scatter distribution of the data, the ratios are preprocessed by logarithmized operation.

$$y = \begin{cases} log(x+1) & \text{if } x > 0 \\ -log(1-x) & \text{otherwise} \end{cases} \tag{5}$$

The features are then normalized for the purpose of equal influence on classification. We use the linear normalization which transforms the maximum value to 1 and the minimum value to 0.

$$y = \frac{x - min(x)}{max(x) - min(x)} \tag{6}$$

Australian credit approval data from UCI Machine Learning Repository [26] has a total of 690 applicants which includes 307 'bad' credits and 383 'good' credits. It concerns the credit approval prediction with respect to 6 continuous and 8 categorical attributes to prevent bad loan and sustain profitability. The continuous features are standardized in the same way as that for *Diane* data. Due to the categorical values contained in credit data, the cost-sensitive BNCLVQ algorithm is used [23].

4.2 Evaluation Criteria

The classification result is usually represented by a confusion matrix which contains the distribution of instances in the real class and predicted class. Given the confusion matrix outlined in Table 2, several criteria for predictive capability

Table 2. Confusion matrix

real	predicted class		
class	bad	good	total
bad	B_b	B_g	B
good	G_b	G_g	G
total	b	g	T

assessment could be defined. Type I error rate is the fraction of 'good' instances classified incorrectly to 'bad', i.e., $\frac{G_b}{G}$. Type II error rate is the fraction of 'bad' instances classified incorrectly to 'good', i.e., $\frac{B_g}{B}$. Overall error rate is the percent of instances classified incorrectly, i.e., $\frac{B_g+G_b}{T}$. Accordingly, the complementary rates denote the percent of observations classified correctly.

The overall error treats two kinds of errors, namely type I error and type II error equivalently. However, as claimed in [11], the cost associated with type II error is significantly higher. Expected misclassified cost (EMC) is a criterion used in credit risk analysis [12]. As shown in Equation (7), it combines type I error rate with type II error rate weighted by the prior possibility and corresponding cost. In the formulation, C_b is the misclassification cost associated with class 'bad', and C_g is the misclassification cost associated with class 'good', P_b is the prior probability of class 'bad', and P_g is the prior probability of class 'good'.

$$\begin{aligned} EMC &= C_b * P_b * \tfrac{B_g}{B} + C_g * P_g * \tfrac{G_b}{G} \\ &= C_b * \tfrac{B}{T} * \tfrac{B_g}{B} + C_g * \tfrac{G}{T} * \tfrac{G_b}{G} \\ &= C_b * \tfrac{B_g}{T} + C_g * \tfrac{G_b}{T} \end{aligned} \tag{7}$$

4.3 Experimental Results

The experiments are performed in the following steps:

1. The entire data set is divided randomly into ten folds for cross-validation, in which 9 folds are used for model training, and the remaining is used for testing the generalization capability of the built model.
2. In each trial, the cost-sensitive LVQ algorithm is applied to the training data set.
3. For validation, each sample of the test data set is input to the resultant map and the predicted class is the label of the BMU.
4. After the experiment is repeated 10 times, the confusion matrix is calculated by comparing the real class to the predicted class for the entire data. Then the evaluation criteria are obtained from the confusion matrix.

In the experiment of *Diane* data, a map of [9 x 5] grid is used to build the predictive model. For simplicity, the misclassification cost C_g is set as 1, and C_b a real value. The relative cost ratio (C_b/C_g) steps from 1 to 30. The confusion matrix is summarized in Table 3. At the equal cost setup, 102 misclassifications occur on 'bad' class and 43 on 'good' class. Increasing the cost ratio to 2, the

Table 3. Classification results on Diane data

	predicted class							
real class	bad	good	bad	good	bad	good	bad	good
	(1:1)		**(2:1)**		**(7:1)**		**(20:1)**	
bad	498	102	512	88	518	82	512	88
good	43	557	54	546	72	528	74	526
total	541	659	566	634	590	610	586	614
	(1.2:1)		**(3:1)**		**(10:1)**		**(25:1)**	
bad	506	94	515	85	515	84	517	83
good	45	555	63	537	74	526	74	526
total	551	649	578	622	590	610	591	609
	(1.5:1)		**(5:1)**		**(15:1)**		**(30:1)**	
bad	511	89	513	87	516	84	520	80
good	54	546	70	530	74	526	74	526
total	565	635	583	617	590	610	594	606

former decreases to 88 while the latter steps up to 54. At a cost ratio of 30, type II error shrinks to 80 and type I error becomes 74. It can be concluded that the cost-sensitive LVQ is able to improve the predictive capability on the class with higher cost without great degradation on the other class. Since the misclassification cost on 'bad' category is higher, the classifier achieving lower type II error is preferred in practice.

We compare the performance of cost-sensitive LVQ against the sole LVQ without incorporating costs. The performance tendency can be detected in Figure 1, in which the top graph shows the error rates with respect to the varying cost ratios, and the bottom graph shows the EMC values. It is observed that the proposed method has a robust tradeoff between two kinds of errors while basically remaining the overall capability. Particularly, Type II error goes down with the increase of the cost ratio. Although the tendency is not significant when the cost ratio is greater than 10, the improvement is exhibited explicitly for a relatively lower cost ratio than 5 as recommended in [11]. As expected, the cost-sensitive LVQ outperforms the sole LVQ in terms of expected misclassification cost criterion. This gives the evidence in favor of the validity of the proposed approach for distress prediction in cost-sensitive situation.

To test the difference significance of cost-sensitive algorithms at various cost ratios, the cross-validation process is repeated for 10 times using random split. A t-test is employed to the observed difference at the 1% level and the results are shown in Table 4. If a test of significance gives a p-value lower than the 0.01-level, the null hypothesis is rejected at the significance of 1%. We may then conclude the performance differences found are significant. For Diane data, the cost-sensitive LVQ produces significant improvement on type II error especially when the cost ratio is smaller than 5. Although the type I error significantly increases, the overall error seems to keep relatively stable. The results on Credit data set are similar to those of Diane data set. In this case the gain is not so evident as in *Diane* data set: increasing the cost ratio, the decrease of type II

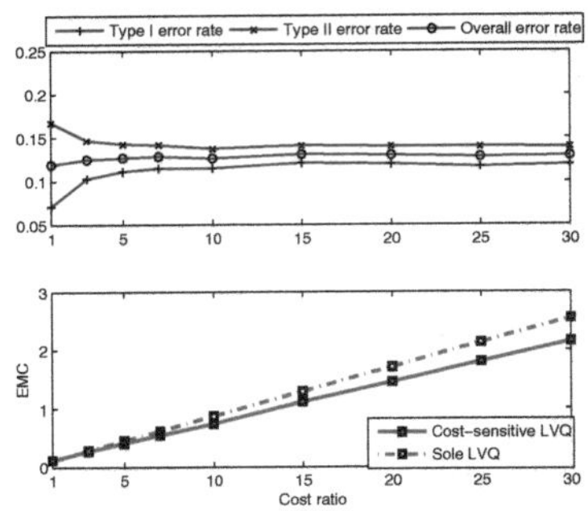

Fig. 1. Prediction capability vs. cost ratio on Diane data

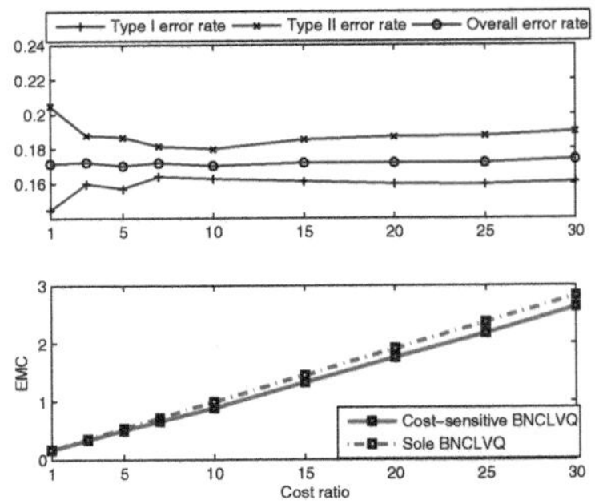

Fig. 2. Prediction capability vs. cost ratio on Credit data

Table 4. Comparison test (*significant at the 1% level)

Error	1	5	10	t-value	p-value	1	5	10	t-value	p-value
			Diane					Credit		
	7.12	11.15		-12.35	0.000*	14.46	15.69		-2.24	0.052
Type I		11.15	11.52	-1.36	0.206		15.69	16.27	-2.4	0.040
	7.12		11.52	-11.52	0.000*	14.46		16.27	-3.59	0.006*
	16.75	14.25		7.5	0.000*	20.49	18.67		2.66	0.026
Type II		14.25	13.73	2.08	0.067		18.67	17.98	1.89	0.091
	16.75		13.73	6.99	0.000*	20.49		17.98	4.55	0.001*
	11.93	12.7		-3.94	0.003*	17.14	17.02		0.30	0.774
		12.7	12.6	0.67	0.518		17.02	17.03	-0.08	0.939
Overall	11.93		12.6	-2.38	0.05	17.14		17.03	0.33	0.749

error does not appear significant until the cost ratio is 10. Nevertheless, it confirms that the algorithm is effective in cost-sensitive learning because it produces significantly lower (at the 1% level) EMC than sole LVQ as shown in Figure 2.

As claimed in [27], cost-sensitive learning is a good solution to the class imbalance problem by assigning different costs to different classes. Hence the proposed algorithm can be employed for distress prediction in the case of imbalance class distribution. In order to test the capability of cost-sensitive LVQ in handling the imbalance problem, we changed the imbalance level by discarding some 'bad' data from the original Diane data and generated a series of data sets of varying imbalance levels (In practice the 'bad' class is much less than the 'good' class.). For each data set, the value of cost ratio is set as G/B (the ratio of the number of majority class to the number of minority class). The performance tendency is shown in Figure 3. As the fraction of 'bad' samples decreases, the data set turns out to be more skewed. Consequently, the 'bad' samples become harder to be classified correctly and the type II error increases. Particularly, when the 'bad' samples are seriously rare ($B/G < 8\%$), cost-sensitive LVQ performs much better than sole LVQ which fails to distinguish them from the other class at all.

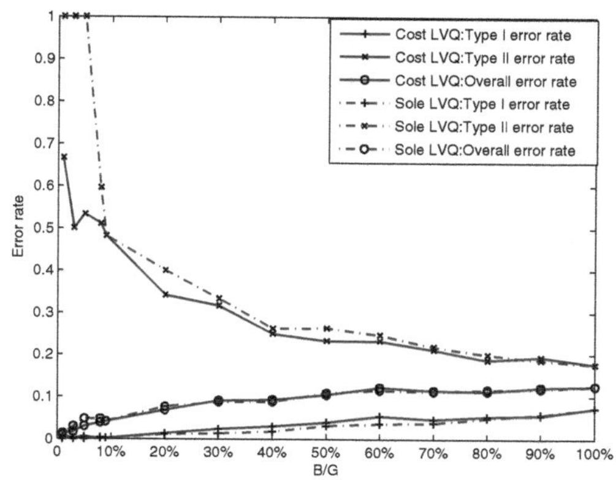

Fig. 3. Classification results on imbalanced Diane data

Although it produces a slightly higher Type I error than the sole LVQ, the overall accuracy is not degraded greatly. We can conclude that cost-sensitive LVQ algorithm is capable of improving the misclassification on the minority class samples which is a relatively difficult task for the sole LVQ.

5 Conclusions and Future Remarks

Financial distress prediction has been considered an important topic in many financial domains to evaluate the risk associated in credit decisions concerning a company or an individual. Due to the presence of unequal misclassification costs in practical applications, the cost-sensitive classification is of particular importance to distress prediction. This paper presents a simple, yet reasonably effective modification of LVQ by integrating the cost information into the model. The prediction tasks performed on two different financial data sets by cross-validation illustrate the benefit of cost-sensitive LVQ on the tradeoff between two kinds of prediction errors. The results reveal the proposed algorithm is a good supporting tool in improving classification performance when the misclassification costs are unequal or the class distribution is imbalanced.

In the future plan, the presented algorithm will be compared with state-of-the-art cost-sensitive classification methods using more data sets in financial domain as well as other domains where the unequal cost problem is critical. Comparative studies between multiple classifiers and data sets are expected to examine the significance of improved performance through statistical testing procedures [28]. As indicated in [13], the cost-sensitive for multi-class classification is more difficult than the binary classification due to various types of cost function. How to adapt the proposed algorithm to multi-class data is an interesting issue. Additionally, this paper uses a simple approach to tune the cost ratio when coping with data of different skew levels. However, it is not necessarily optimal. Finding an appropriate value of cost ratio is a challenging problem. Experiments will be performed on the selection of cost-sensitivity through cross-validation in future work. When the imbalance becomes a serious problem, the novel detection algorithms [29] might be favorable and of interest for future research.

Acknowledgements

This work was supported by project C2007-FCT/442/2006-GECAD/ISEP (Knowledge Based, Cognitive and Learning Systems).

References

1. Abdou, H.A.: Genetic Programming for Credit Scoring: The Case of Egyptian Public Sector Banks. Expert Systems with Applications (2009), doi:10.1016/j.eswa.2009.01.076
2. RaviKumar, P., Ravi, V.: Bankruptcy Prediction in Banks and Firms via Statistical and Intelligent Techniques–A Review. European Journal of Operational Research 180(1), 1–28 (2007)
3. Maloof, M.A.: Learning When Data Sets are Imbalanced and When Costs are Unequal and Unknown. In: 20th International Conference on Machine Learning (ICML 2003), Washing D.C., USA, pp. 154–160 (2003)
4. Min, J.H., Jeong, C.: A Binary Classification Method for Bankruptcy Prediction. Expert Systems with Applications 36, 5256–5263 (2009)
5. Lee, K., Booth, D., Alam, P.: A Comparison of Supervised and Unsupervised Neural Networks in Predicting Bankruptcy of Korean Firms. Expert Systems with Applications 29, 1–6 (2005)
6. Merkevicius, E., Garsva, G., Simutis, R.: Forecasting of Credit Classes with the Self-Organizing Maps. Informaciens Technologijos Ir Valsymas Nr.4(33), 61–66 (2004)
7. Neves, J.C., Vieira, A.: Improving Bankruptcy Prediction with Hidden Layer Learning Vector Quantization. European Accounting Review 15(2), 253–271 (2006)
8. Chen, N., Vieira, A.: Bankruptcy Prediction based on Independent Component Analysis. In: 1st International Conference on Agents and Artificial Intelligence (ICAART 2009), Porto, Portugal, pp. 150–155 (2009)
9. Boyacioglu, M.A., Kara, Y., Baykan, O.K.: Predicting Bank Financial Failures using Neural Networks, Support Vector Machines and Multivariate Statistical Methods: A Comparative Analysis in the Sample of Savings Deposit Insurance Fund (SDIF) Transferred Banks in Turkey. Expert Systems with Applications 36, 3355–3366 (2009)
10. Hájek, P., Olej, V.: Municipal creditworthiness modelling by kohonen's self-organizing feature maps and LVQ neural networks. In: Rutkowski, L., Tadeusiewicz, R., Zadeh, L.A., Zurada, J.M. (eds.) ICAISC 2008. LNCS (LNAI), vol. 5097, pp. 52–61. Springer, Heidelberg (2008)
11. West, D.: Neural Network Credit Scoring Models. Computers and Operations Research 27, 1131–1152 (2000)
12. Lee, T., Chen, I.: A Two-Stage Hybrid Credit Scoring Model using Artificial Neural Networks and Multivariate Adaptive Regression Splines. Expert Systems with Applications 28(4), 743–752 (2005)

13. Zhou, Z.H., Liu, X.Y.: Training Cost-Sensitive Neural Networks with Methods Addressing the Class Imbalance Problem. IEEE Transactions On Knowledge and Data Engineering 18(1), 63–77 (2006)
14. Ling, C.X., Yang, Q., Wang, J., Zhang, S.: Decision Trees with Minimal Costs. In: Brodley, C.E. (ed.) 21st International Conference on Machine Learning (ICML), Banff, Canada. ACM International Conference Proceeding Series, vol. 69 (2004)
15. Ting, K.M.: An Instance-Weighting Method to Induce Costsensitive Trees. IEEE Transactions on Knowledge and Data Engineering 14(3), 659–665 (2002)
16. Vo, N.H., Won, Y.: Classification of Unbalanced Medical Data with Weighted Regularized Least Squares. In: Frontiers in the Convergence of Bioscience and Information Technologies, pp. 347–352 (2007)
17. Sun, Y.M., Kamela, M.S., Wong, A.K.C., Wang, Y.: Cost-Sensitive Boosting for Classification of Imbalanced Data. Pattern Recognition 40, 3358–3378 (2007)
18. Nanda, S., Pendharkar, P.: Linear Models for Minimizing Misclassification Costs in Bankruptcy Prediction. Int. J. Intell. Syst. Account Finance Manage 10, 155–168 (2001)
19. Pendharkar, P., Nanda, S.: A Misclassification Cost-Minimizing Evolutionary–Neural Classification Approach. Naval Research Logistics 53(5), 432–447 (2006)
20. Zadrozny, B., Elkan, C.: Learning and Making Decisions When Costs and Probabilities are Both Unknown. In: 7th International Conference on Knowledge Discovery and Data Mining, San Francisco, CA, pp. 204–213 (2001)
21. Pendharkar, P.C.: A Threshold Varying Bisection Method for Cost Sensitive Learning in Neural Networks. Expert Systems with Applications 34, 1456–1464 (2008)
22. Eitrich, T., Kless, A., Druska, C., Meyer, W., Grotendorst, J.: Classification of Highly Unbalanced CYP450 Data of Drugs Using Cost Sensitive Machine Learning Techniques. J. Chem. Inf. Model. 47, 92–103 (2007)
23. Chen, N., Marques, N.C.: A Batch Learning Vector Quantization Algorithm for Categorical Data. In: 1st International Conference on Agents and Artificial Intelligence (ICAART 2009), Porto, Portugal, pp. 77–84 (2009)
24. Kohonen, T.: Self-Organizing Maps, 3rd edn. Springer, Heidelberg (2001)
25. Laboratory of Computer and Information Sciences & Neural Networks Research Center, Helsinki University of Technology: SOM Toolbox 2.0
26. Asuncion, A., Newman, D.J.: UCI Machine Learning Repository. University of California, Department of Information and Computer Science, Irvine, CA, `http://www.ics.uci.edu/~mlearn/MLRepository.html`
27. Liu, X.Y., Zhou, Z.H.: The Influence of Class Imbalance on Cost-Sensitive Learning: An Empirical Study. In: 6th IEEE International Conference on Data Mining (ICDM), Hong Kong, pp. 970–974 (2006)
28. Demsar, J.: Statistical Comparisons of Classifiers over Multiple Data Sets. Journal of Machine Learning Research 7, 1–30 (2006)
29. Lee, H.J., Cho, S.: Application of LVQ to Novelty Detection using Outlier Training Data. Pattern Recognition Letters 27, 1572–1579 (2006)

An Intelligent Alarm Management System for Large-Scale Telecommunication Companies

Raúl Costa[1,2], Nuno Cachulo[2], and Paulo Cortez[1]

[1] Department of Information Systems/Algoritmi R&D Centre, University of Minho, 4800-058 Guimarães, Portugal
[2] PT Inovação, Rua Eng. José Ferreira Pinto Basto, 3810-106 Aveiro, Portugal
{raul-s-costa,est-n-cachulo}@ptinovacao.pt, pcortez@dsi.uminho.pt

Abstract. This paper introduces an intelligent system that performs alarm correlation and root cause analysis. The system is designed to operate in large-scale heterogeneous networks from telecommunications operators. The proposed architecture includes a rules management module that is based in data mining (to generate the rules) and reinforcement learning (to improve rule selection) algorithms. In this work, we focus on the design and development of the rule generation part and test it using a large real-world dataset containing alarms from a Portuguese telecommunications company. The correlation engine achieved promising results, measured by a compression rate of 70% and assessed in real-time by experienced network administrator staff.

Keywords: Network Management, Association Rules, Event Correlation.

1 Introduction

During the last decades, with the growth of the Internet and cellular phones, there has been an increase in telecommunications demand. To support this growth, telecommunication companies are investing in new technologies to improve their services. In particular, real-time monitoring of infrastructures and services is a key issue within any telecommunication operator. On one hand, the quality of service has to be assured by a timely fault diagnosis with evaluation of service impact and recovery. This is particularly needed to fulfill the Service Level Agreements (SLAs) that are set between the service provider and customers. On the other hand, operational tasks must be simplified to guarantee reduced OPerating EXpenses (OPEX). Hence, there are a wide variety of software tools and applications that were developed to address this issue [5][19] and most of these tools require a human intervention for corrective action. In particular, several of these solutions incorporate correlation engines, which is the "smart" part of the management platform. The goal is to exploit data collected by monitoring subsystems, as well as notifications sent spontaneously by managed entities. However, as networks become larger, with more intricate dependencies and dynamics, new challenges are posed to these correlation engines, such as [11]:

L. Seabra Lopes et al. (Eds.): EPIA 2009, LNAI 5816, pp. 386–399, 2009.

(i) Large telecommunication companies' networks are very heterogeneous and event correlation rules rely heavily on information provided by the vendor, which may not be always available. Hence, the effectiveness of these solutions depends heavily on the business relation with the device vendor.
(ii) Most paradigms for rule correlation, including rule-based reasoning, probabilistic reasoning, model-based reasoning and case-based, are configured out of the box (i.e. predefined) and they do not learn with experience, thus they cannot respond properly to new situations.
(iii) "Keeping users in the loop", i.e., maintaining users informed of changes in service availability is not always done properly. Therefore, it is difficult to assess effectiveness of the results on problem reporting. What if trouble ticketing does not point the correct root cause for a certain situation or what if the problem description is incomplete and misses important event details?

Ideally, an intelligent alarm management system should be capable of parsing the massive amount of received alarm events while reducing human intervention. Yet, designing and maintaining such an ideal system is not a trivial process. Traditional event correlation paradigms do not work well when the managed domains that they cover are large-scale and dynamic (i.e. change through time) [18].

Advances in information technologies have made it possible to collect, store and process massive, often highly complex datasets. All this data hold valuable information such as trends and patterns, which can be used to improve decision making and optimize chances of success. Data mining techniques, such as association rules [4], aim at extracting high-level knowledge from raw data [22]. The goal of this paper is to study the feasibility of building a decision support tool for large telecommunications operators using data mining algorithms. Similar to market-basket data sequences [7], we will assume that a network generates sets of events that are related to the same situation. For example, in the access network of GSM systems, the Base Station Subsystem (BSS) contains Base Stations (BS) that are connected via a multiplexing transmission system to the Base Station Controller (BSC). These connections are very often realized with microwave line-of-sight radio transmission equipment. Heavy rain or snow can temporarily disturb the connections between the antennas. The temporary loss of sight of a microwave disconnects all chained BS from the BSC and results in an alarm burst. Our goal is to automatically discover these patterns. When this information is combined with other features (e.g. trouble-ticket data) it is possible to generate rules that lead to alarm correlation and root cause analysis. The data mining algorithms can generate these rules automatically, from the collected data, in opposition to traditional systems where the rules are pre-coded or manually configured. Thus, our approach may have a large impact in the business, since it can potentially save the company a considerable amount of lost revenue. A timely and correctly identification of the root cause will aid in the anomaly correction, reducing the maintenance costs. Furthermore, by providing a better service, it is expected that the costumer complaints will be reduced, diminishing the costumer risk of leaving the operator.

In this paper, we propose an architecture that is targeted to address an adaptive and self-maintained alarm correlation system. In particular, we are working on an automatic rule discovery approach applied to a large telecommunications operator. Our approach adapts an association rule algorithm (i.e. Generalized Sequential Patterns) to the telecommunication domain. It has the advantage of being independent of the network topology and uses trouble-ticket information to get feedback from the event correlation results. The final aim of this line of research is to incorporate a reinforcement learning system that will guide the association rule generation and selection. As such, this is a milestone where implementation results are assessed and overall architecture presented for the first time.

2 Related Work

The concept of sequential pattern was introduced by Agrawal and Srikant [3] from a set of market-basket data sequences, where each sequence element is a set of items purchased in the same transaction. The same researchers also proposed in [2] the Generalized Sequential Patterns (GSP) algorithm, which allows a time-gape constraint, where an item from a given sequence can span a set of transactions within a user-specified window. In addition, the algorithm allows that the item can cover different taxonomies.

Mannila et al. [16][17] presented the WINEPI framework for discovering frequent episodes from alarm databases, allowing the discrimination of serial and parallel episodes. Later, this framework was adopted to analyze Synchronous Digital Hierarchy (SDH) [9] and GSM [21] network alarms. In [24][26], Wang et al. studied the data mining of asynchronous periodic patterns in time series data with noise, proposing a flexible model, based on a two-phase algorithm, for dealing with asynchronous periodic patterns. They only considered the model in the time series domain and did not consider other periodic patterns in the data.

Sequential algorithms are helpful for mining alarm databases in order to support the creation of rule-based expert systems. Rules like "'If A and B then C'' are the main approach for solving the alarm correlation problem and root cause analysis. An advanced event correlation system is the EMC Smarts Network Protocol Manager [8], which uses the patented "Code Book". It works as a black box, retrieving a problem from a set of symptoms. The drawback of this solution is that the rules are pre-coded (i.e. static) and rely heavily on information provided by the vendor.

A problem that often comes from the usage of unsupervised learning processes, such as the popular Apriori algorithm, is the large quantity of rules generated. In order to select only the most interesting rules it is necessary to select proper criteria to filter and order them. Several measures of interestingness have been proposed within the context of association rules (e.g. confidence, support and lift). Choosing an adequate metric is a key issue for the success of generating useful rules.

There are also other techniques that have been applied by several commercial network management solutions. Smart-Plugins (SPIs) are being utilized for managing new devices and protocols. These plugins extend the base management capabilities with specific vendor/technology functionalities. HP OpenView's Network Node Manager (NNM) [13] offers a broad multi-vendor device coverage by allowing deployment of several SPIs. However, often the required information to develop SPIs is difficult to get due to the existence of proprietary protocols and technology.

In an attempt to resume the state-of-the-art in network management and present future perspectives, Gupta [11] listed several innovative frameworks, such as EMC

SMARTS and SPIs that are being used for advanced root cause analysis. As a future direction, Gupta suggests the implementation of environment aware network management solutions. The concept is to use historical data collected from the network to help identify anomalous situations from the deviation of the traditional patterns. Expert systems are also pointed as a way to reduce human intervention. Such a system would learn from human experience and assist the proposal for repair actions. It could also be used to teach standard procedures to new team members.

Martin et al. [18] explain why event correlation is still an open issue. The complexity of event correlation has increased over the last few years. Current algorithms make inappropriate simplifying assumptions and new models, algorithms and systems are required to deal with such complex and dynamic networks. To overcome current limitations, it is necessary to improve network information in order to build learning models to assist infrastructure managers. Such models are required to deal with uncertain knowledge and learn from past experience.

Often, equipment vendors are responsible for specifying alarm's parameters, and telecommunication companies do not have the flexibility to adapt them to their specific necessities. For example, alarm severity is defined in the X.733 standard (ITU-T, 1992). It would be expected that severity level is closely related to the malfunction priority, but this is not always true. Assigning a malfunction's priority relies heavily on network's administrator's experience, depending on a dynamic evaluation of redundancy, network topology and eventual SLAs. Wallin and Landén [23] proposed a solution that uses neural networks to automatically assign alarm priorities. The authors point that the advantages of using neural networks come from their good noise tolerance capabilities and the ability to learn from network administrator staff by using the manually assigned priorities in trouble ticket reports.

3 Proposed Architecture

A common fragility of most paradigms for event correlation is the lack of ability to learn with experience or adapt to situations that have not been pre-coded. In contrast, we propose an alarm management system that automatically extracts correlation rules from historical alarm data. Changes in the network will not affect the correlation performance, since the extraction process will run periodically. The information is provided to network administrators for supporting the associated trouble tickets management. By supervising the trouble ticket lifecycle we gain feedback on the rules' performance and this information can be used to adjust selection from the pool of available rules.

Within the considered telecommunications operator (PT Inovação), the Fault Management and Fault Reporting modules work independently. Some interface features are used to enhance trouble ticket generation, but users still have to manually select related alarms and indicate one that is pointed to be the cause the problem. This type of system is quite similar to what can be found in the majority of the network operating centers.

The following steps can describe the telecommunication alarm management tasks:

- parse the received alarms and group the ones related to the same problem;
- associate alarms with a trouble ticket to manage the problem resolution process and indicate the cause (i.e. to identify the root cause);

- assign a priority to the trouble ticket; and
- analyze and fix the problem.

To achieve the above goals, we proposed an integrated intelligent management architecture that is illustrated in Fig. 1. The main components of the system are:

- **Fault Management Platform** – collects, processes and displays alarm events via a Web GUI integrated in the portal Server.
- **Fault Reporting Platform** – records and forwards fault reports, also known as TTKs (Trouble Tickets), to suppliers.
- **Preprocessing** – is responsible for the correct linking of all the values in order to create valid records. It proceeds with the copy of the values entered by network administrators during fault reporting activity and also alarm events.
- **Assurance Warehouse** – stores information about alarms (events plus user operation logs) and TTKs creation and management, with information on intervention or unavailability.
- **Rules Generator** – generates rules for alarm correlation and root cause analysis from off-line training using the data from the warehouse. Rules can also be created by a human editor. It runs with a predefined periodicity (a configuration parameter) in order to allow the replacement of poor performing rules. Possible algorithms are Case-Based Reasoning [9], a solving paradigm that relies on previously experienced cases, and association rules (addressed in this paper).
- **CORC Rule Database** – stores the correlation and root cause analysis rules along with several evaluation metrics. The evaluation metrics include support, lift, support and information on reception order. These statistics are updated every time new information is collected.
- **Reinforcement Learning Module** – refines the rules database based on feedback obtained from the Portal Server. This process receives feedback from two distinct ways: after the resolution of the network malfunction reported in TTK, it is possible to evaluate if proposed correlation and root cause were correct, by means of text mining [6]; also, it is expected that all alarms related to one malfunction cease nearly at the same time and immediately after its root cause resolution.
- **Alarm Prioritization** – it uses a supervised learning algorithm (e.g. neural networks) to learn from alarm priorities assigned by network administrators in TTK. This module has been already been proposed in [23] with a 71% success rate. This information is passed to users and is also used so that in overflow situations the most important alarms are processed first by the management mechanism.
- **Management** – receives real-time alarms from the fault management and processes them. A business rules engine is included to support output from the Rules Management System and from Alarm Prioritization and returns decision-making logic. The enriched result is then passed to the Fault Management platform that has a dedicated web-based GUI to present correlated alarms with visual indication of root cause and assigned priority.

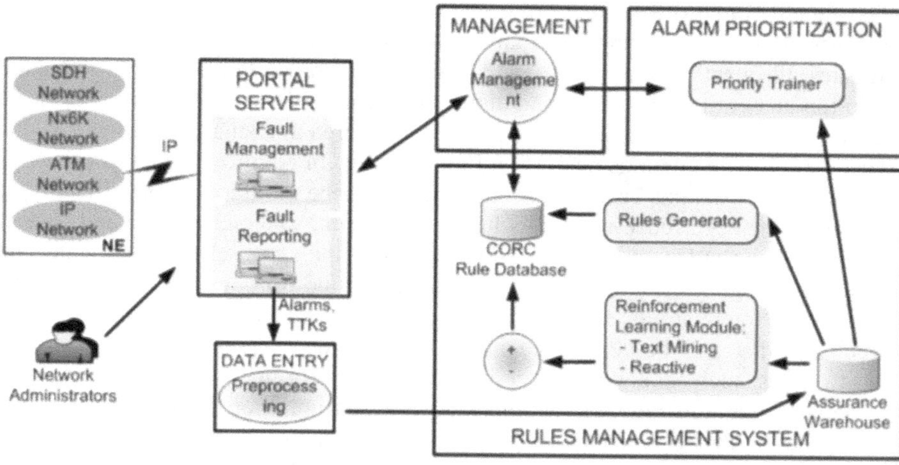

Fig. 1. The proposed intelligent alarm management architecture

As indicated in the figure, we propose feedback loops for making correlation and root cause analysis. The first loop is periodically executed and involves calculating candidate rules by several specialized association rules algorithms utilizing more static information on the alarm history. The output of the algorithms is combined in one rule database which is used to dynamically associate related alarms and select root cause. In the second loop we continuously gather and evaluate user reaction to the presented suggestions. The learning module uses this information to refine the associations and root causes in the database and thus to immediately affect the selection of future results. In the present paper, we will focus only in the automatic correlation rule discovery part of the proposed architecture (module Rules Generator from Figure 1).

4 Materials and Methods

4.1 Alarm Data

This study will consider an alarm database from a major Portuguese telecommunication company. The data was collected from PT Inovação's alarm management system, called Alarm Manager. This platform's architecture follows the most recent guidelines for the implementation of next generation Operations Support Systems (OSS), as laid down in TM Forum's NGOSS [20]. It was developed in Java and contains J2EE middleware. This system is operating stably for more than 2 years, dealing daily with huge amounts of data collected from heterogeneous networks including access, aggregation/metro and core segments of transport and technologies, such as IP/MPLS, CET, ATM, SDH, PDH, DSL or GPON.

The dataset contains the history of alarm events that occurred from March 2007 to November 2008. Each alarm record already includes a basic type of correlation that aggregates all events if they represent repetitions of an active alarm with the same description and entity. The beginning and termination of the alarm occurrence, along with other events that occurred in between, are registered as a single record.

The overall table contains near 15 million of rows. In addition to identification of related fields, it contains several attributes that describe an alarm event. Thereby, it has several time occurrence values, including the starting and ending time and date of an alarm. Other time stamps are the moment where the alarm changed its state, the time it was recognized by a network supervisor and the time it was archived in the history table. Note that only the alarms terminated have this last time stamp and these are the ones that will be considered in this work. Moreover, the database contains other attributes, such as: ending type (an alarm can be terminated normally, manually by a network administrator or automatically by configuration on the management system); the number of events that each alarm aggregates; network domain and, finally, a description of the specific problem that the alarm reports.

Before applying the data mining algorithms, we first performed a cleaning and data selection stage. Experts from PT Inovação were consulted in order to discard irrelevant variables. Some statistical tests were additionally performed (e.g. Pearson correlation [1]) to check each attribute independency. Furthermore, we noticed that certain attributes had a very limited range of values and were not strictly related to the alarm occurrence, thus these were also discarded. Finally, we discard all topological attributes, as our approach does not require such data and we do not want to constrain the data mining process. Table 1 resumes the selected attributes that will be used in the analysis.

We performed additional preprocessing operations, after a feedback that was obtained from the network management people. For instance, we removed alarms terminated manually by network managers or automatically by system configuration, since these suffered from an abnormal ending. In addition, the **Specific Problem** records were reported in two different languages (i.e. English or Portuguese). Thus, we standardized these records by using auxiliary information that was available in supplied catalogs.

Table 1. Summary of the selected alarm data attributes

Attribute	Description
Alarm ID	Alarm identification, an information that can be used to obtain the order of the alarms arrival into the Alarm Manager.
Event Counter	The number of alarm events aggregated into a single alarm.
Starting Time	The initial time of the alarm.
Ending Time	The ending time of the alarm.
Specific Problem	The specific problem occurred in the network that the alarm carries with it.
End Type	Information on how the alarm was terminated.

4.2 Methods

We will base the alarm correlation and root cause detection on the events' time and its characteristics. This approach is closely related to the problem of finding sequential patterns in large amounts of data. Therefore, we adopted the GSP algorithm, which already has an implementation in the open source data mining tool Weka [25]. The GSP algorithm uses the concept of a sliding window to group raw data into candidate sequences of alarms that regular association algorithms, such as the well-known Apriori, are capable to use. Apriori based algorithms are then able to find the sequential patterns that we aim. However, the GSP was not specialized enough. More context orientation was required for pre-processing and candidate sequence extraction stages. Not to mention that the issue of root cause is obviously not covered by this algorithm and needs to be addressed here.

The first obstacle in applying our approach came from the high number of consecutive alarms, or very close in, having the same specific problem. This happens because a single problem might generate errors in several dependent entities. For example, the same Alarm Indication Signal is sent for all the ports in a SDH slot when the connected STM is down with a Loss of Signal. Thus, we decided to aggregate similar alarms to obtain rules containing only different ones, updating the event counter for the resulting alarm to be used in candidate extraction. The sliding window is used to modulate data and the time window for this aggregation should be equal to the maximum interval defined for timely windows. An example of the data to sequence extraction is represented in Tables 2 and 3.

At this point it is possible to extract candidate sequences. To achieve this, sliding windows were adopted for the starting time and ending times. This way, two or more alarms are only aggregated in the same sequence if both the starting and ending times fit the sliding window. This should highly improve the confidence of candidate extraction. Also, a degree of flexibility is considered so that sliding windows can adapt to particular situations. Based on preliminary experiments, we set heuristically a minimum interval of three seconds. This interval was corroborated by a network expert as a recommended value. Nevertheless, if a sequence is being constructed and this time is reached, the sliding window is extended to a maximum value in which the found alarms are joined into the sequence. Again, for the same reasons, this value was set to five seconds. This process is done over the preprocessed data ordered by the alarms starting date. Result sequences, after applying the described methods to the previous example dataset, would be:

- Sequence 1: B / A / C;
- Sequence 2: D / E;

Before candidate sequences proceed to the rule finding phase, they are sorted to ensure that the order of constituting elements is always the same. For instance, we want that the sequence B / A / C is considered equally as the sequence A / B / C, because the relation between the constituting events is the same.

Table 2. Example of the original dataset

Specific Problem	Starting Time	Ending Time	Event Counter	Alarm ID
B	00:00:01	00:00:06	1	2
A	00:00:01	00:00:06	1	1
B	00:00:01	00:00:06	1	4
B	00:00:01	00:00:06	1	3
C	00:00:03	00:00:07	1	5
D	00:00:10	00:00:15	2	6
E	00:00:13	00:00:15	2	7
B	00:00:01	00:00:06	1	2

Table 3. Example of the dataset result after event aggregation

Specific Problem	Starting Time	Ending Time	Event Counter	Alarm ID
B	00:00:01	00:00:06	3	2
A	00:00:01	00:00:06	1	1
C	00:00:03	00:00:07	1	5
D	00:00:10	00:00:15	2	6
E	00:00:13	00:00:15	2	7

By now, the information on probable root cause for each built candidate sequence must be considered. In our analysis, root cause calculation is based in two factors: the first alarm of a sequence found in time and the number of events aggregated by each alarm. It is frequent to have several events with the same generation time stamp, because time precision is measured in milliseconds. For these situations, first event received in Alarm Collection Gateway is considered. This solution has some risks that might mislead root cause analysis due to different event propagation times in the network (the protocol most used is SNMP). However, considering the vast dataset used for modeling, there are some guaranties of attribute relevance. Moreover, in particular analysis scenario, there is an acknowledge (ACK) mechanism between monitoring agents and alarm collection which guaranties delivering and correction of order over SNMP's connectionless protocol. On other hand, the usage of event counters is based on the observation that typically the root cause is a single alarm event that can cause a wide number of alarm events. These two aspects are combined in an editable rule system, which is used to classify the probability of the root cause for each sequence. For example, if we have a rule where the percentage of an alarm being the first to appear is very high, then it is highly probable that this is the root cause. Also, if the percentage of occurrences is low, when compared to the remaining events of the sequence, then this increases the probability of being the root cause. If none of these situations occur, the confidence of the suggestion is set to a negligible value. Going back to our example dataset, we had the following root cause information for our sequences:

- Sequence 1: First Alarm – A, Event Counter – A:1,B:3,C:2;
- Sequence 2: First Alarm – D, Event Counter – D:2,B:2;

After founding a frequent rule, all the information related to managing root cause selection must be updated. We have now candidate sequences and the last step is to call the Apriori algorithm to build and classify the resulting association rules. Apriori bases its behavior on the support of candidate sequences, by removing candidates that are below a given threshold. The use of Apriori instead of a simple counting of candidates is justified by its main principle that increases the rule finding scalability: if a sequence is frequent then all of its subsets should also be frequent. In other words, if a sequence is infrequent then all the sequences that contain that sequence can be pruned and not taken into process. The Apriori algorithm implemented also computed additional metrics, such as the confidence and lift, for a more detailed rule evaluation, as we are going to describe in next section.

4.3 Evaluation

As said before, the classic Apriori algorithm only classifies a sequence for its support, which is clearly insufficient for our purpose. We do not only want to know high frequent sequences present in data, but also less frequent ones that also apply as good modeling rules. In fact, these rules are also very interesting in terms of business value because as rare as rules become, the more difficult is for network administrators to discover their underlying behavior. The inheriting risk is a possible overflow of rules, so it is mandatory to define a minimum support threshold.

In order to classify the discovered rules, we will adopt two additional measures, well known within the association rules context, confidence and lift, and try to adequate their meaning to the present problem of discovering sequential alarm patterns. Lift provides information about the change in probability of the consequent in presence of the antecedent. The 'IF' component of an association rule is known as the antecedent. The THEN component is known as the consequent. The antecedent and the consequent are disjoint; they have no items in common. Both metrics depend on the division of the association rule in two parts (the antecedent and the consequent) but this is not really consistent with the rules we want to obtain, where there is only an unordered sequence of alarms that are somehow correlated. To make possible the use of this metric, we assume that the rule's lift is the maximum possible for that sequence. In other words, we find the antecedent that maximizes the confidence rule metric, because its formula depends on the antecedent support. This is done because it is more harmful to lose a good rule than to over classify one. We have to keep in mind that the rules will suffer posterior evaluation from feedback results and even might get eliminated by the reinforcement learning system (not presented in this work but to be addressed in the future). The confidence of a rule indicates the probability of both the antecedent and the consequent appear in the same transaction. Confidence is the conditional probability of the consequent given the antecedent. This gives us a better classification for the items within a rule than the simple support of the occurrence of all of them together. Confidence can be expressed in probability notation as the support of A and B together dividing by the support of A:

$$\textbf{Confidence}\text{ (A implies B)} = P(B/A), \text{ or} \\ \textbf{Confidence}\text{ (A implies B)} = P(A, B) / P(A)\,. \tag{1}$$

Regular confidence implementation cannot be used for Apriori because we are not interested in finding rules with antecedents and consequents. These are more appropriate, for instance, within the retail industry, where it is relevant knowing the difference between rules such as "buying milk implies buying cereal" or vice-versa. In our case, we calculate the highest confidence of a rule, selecting the possible antecedent for a rule with least support.

Both support and confidence will be used to determine if a rule is valid. However, there are times when both of these measures may be high, and yet still produce a rule that is not useful. If in our case the support of the rule consequent, not used in calculation of confidence, is very high then we are producing a rule that, even with high confidence, is not very interesting because it is normal that the antecedent is commonly seen with the consequent, given the fact that the consequent is very frequent. Thus, a third measure is needed to evaluate the quality of the rule. Lift indicates the strength of a rule over the random co-occurrence of the antecedent and the consequent, given their individual support. It provides information about the improvement, the increase in probability of the consequent given the antecedent. Lift is defined as [12]:

Lift (A implies B) = (Rule Support) / (Support(A) * Support(B)) (2)

Any rule with an improvement (lift) of less than 1 does not indicate an interesting rule, no matter how high its support and confidence are. Lift will be used as another parameter that classifies a rule and gives it more reliability. For example, a rule with low confidence but high lift has a higher degree of reliability than if we are just looking for the confidence metric. The computation of lift in our work is based in the same purpose used to calculate confidence, using the earlier defined antecedent and consequent of a rule to get the needed values for lift formula.

5 Current Results

To test our approach, we considered a recent sample of the alarm database, from 1st of March 2009 until the 15th of the same month, with a total of approximately 2.4 million of alarm events. The dataset was further divided into two subsets: the first 2/3 of the data was used to extract the candidate sequences, while the remaining 1/3 was used for testing. In the training stage, minimum thresholds considered were: for support 1%, confidence 40% and lift 1. The minimum sliding window time interval was restricted to 3 seconds. Under this setup, the rule that aggregated a maximum number of alarm types contained 7 elements and 268 rules were discovered. The rules with maximum support and lift are presented in Fig. 2. The first result shows a sequence of two alarms IMALINK (IMA Link Error) and LOC (Loss of Cell Delineation). Due to monitored network's characteristics, this sequence occurs very frequently, with a support of 1057 and a lift above 2. This sequence represents the situation when a group of virtual ports have an ATM layer above them working as a single communication channel. One problem in a single port is sufficient to affect all others in the same group and also the ATM layer. So, in some error situations, virtual ports send IMALNK alarms and the LOC is related to the ATM layer.

2 Alarm Types		SUPPORT	LIFT					
IMALNK	LOC	1057	2,02					
LP-PLM	LP-UNEQ	81	67,89					
3 Alarm Types			SUPPORT	LIFT				
SD	IMALNK	LOM	1190	2,01				
OOF	HP-RDI	MS-RDI	40	106,54				
4 Alarm Types				SUPPORT	LIFT			
OOM2	IMALNK	SD	LOM	617	1,74			
OOM2	TU-AIS	AU-AIS	DNU	7	108,37			
5 Alarm Types					SUPPORT	LIFT		
OOM2	IMALNK	SD	LOM	LOF	87	1,71		
HP-RDI	LOS	DNU	MS-RDI	TU-AIS	4	41,55		
6 Alarm Types						SUPPORT	LIFT	
OOM2	OOM1	IMALNK	SD	LOM	LOF	14	1,99	
OOM2	AIS	IMALNK	LP-PLM	LP-UNEQ	TU-AIS	4	2,54	
7 Alarm Types							SUPPORT	LIFT
OOM2	AIS	LP-RDI	IMALNK	LP-PLM	LP-UNEQ	TU-AIS	4	1,53
RAI	OOM2	LP-RDI	IMALNK	SD	LOM	LOF	3	4,63

Fig. 2. Examples of discovered association rules (with highest support and lift values)

A prototype was implemented using JRules, an open source and standards-based business rules engine [14]. The previous discovered rules were adapted to fit JRules requirements and then events from the testing set were injected into the rules engine, simulating a real-time alarm collection scenario. This was performed for a total of 501.218 events. The objective was to measure the degree of compression of the alarms that would be presented to end users, if using our correlation method, and to validate the real significance of discovered sequences.

In result of compression using the discovered correlation rules, the number of correlated alarms was 158.191, achieving a compression rate of near 70%. This rate is similar to the results achieved by the currently used systems [27]. In correlation by compression, alarm events from the same alarm type and regarding the same entity are grouped, as well as end notifications of respective alarms.

We asked a very skilled network administrator to validate the discovered rules with higher support and lift values (from Figure 2). In this expert's opinion, this approach is very interesting, "as it reveals certain patterns not strongly presented in network protocols, but discovered with experience". Also, this solution enables a service oriented monitoring which is clearly more effective than the current single network entity approach. Regarding the previous described example (rule for IMALINK and LOC), during the performed runtime experiments our correlation engine grouped sequences of 4 to 8 alarms of type IMALNK associated with 1 LOC alarm. In this way, an immediate action can be set in order to create the respective trouble ticket, which launches the reporting of this malfunction to the operational staff. While reducing the supervisor's parsing work, the process of reparation is also speeded up, contributing to better service levels.

6 Conclusions

Fault management is a critical but difficult task in network management. The flow of alarms received by a management center should be correlated automatically to a more intelligible form, in order to facilitate identification and correction of faults. Unfortunately, the construction of an alarm correlation system requires high expertise and developing time. In opposition to current adopted solutions, with static pre-coded rules, we propose a smarter system that is able to learn from raw data and based in data mining techniques (for rule generation) and reinforcement learning (for rule selection). In particular, we focus on one component of the proposed architecture, the rule generator. A prototype was implemented to test it in a J2EE environment with real-world data from a large Portuguese telecommunications operator. A total of 15 millions of alarm records were used for training and testing, resulting in 268 association rules. The employment of correlation methods compressed the total amount of events with a 70% rate and the network administrator feedback was that there is a great potential to reduce operational costs, fault identification and reparation times. In future work, we intend to explore additional measures of interest for rule selection (e.g. Loevinger rank) [15]. We also expect to develop the remaining components, until the final architecture is implemented and tested in a real-world environment.

References

1. Aczel, A.: Statistics - Concepts and Applications. IRVIN (1996)
2. Agrawal, R., Srikant, R.: Fast Algorithms for Mining Association Rules. In: Proceedings of 2nd Int. Conference on Very Large Databases, pp. 487–499 (1994)
3. Agrawal, R., Srikant, R.: Mining Sequential Patterns. In: Proceedings of Eleventh International Conference on Data Engineering, pp. 3–14 (1995)
4. Agrawal, R., Srikant, R.: Mining Sequential Patterns: Generalizations and Performance Improvements. In: Apers, P.M.G., Bouzeghoub, M., Gardarin, G. (eds.) EDBT 1996. LNCS, vol. 1057, Springer, Heidelberg (1996)
5. Bernstein, L., Yuhas, C.M.: Basic Concepts for Managing Telecommunications Networks: Copper to Sand to Glass to Air. Academic/Plenum Publishers (1999)
6. Berry, M.W.: Survey of text mining: clustering, classification, and retrieval. Springer, Heidelberg (2003)
7. Brin, S., Motwani, R., Silverstein, C.: Beyond market basket: Generalizing association rules to correlations. In: Proceedings of ACM SIGMOD International Conference Management of Data, pp. 265–276 (1997)
8. EMC Corporation, EMC Smarts Network Protocol Manager, `http://www.emc.com/products/detail/software/network-protocol-manager.htm` (accessed April 2009)
9. Gardner, R.D., Harle, D.A.: Methods and systems for alarm correlation. In: Proceedings of GLOBECOM 1996, vol. 1, pp. 136–140 (1996)
10. Gardner, R.D., Harle, D.A.: Fault Resolution and Alarm Correlation in High-Speed Networks using Database Mining Techniques. In: Proceedings of Int. Conference on Information, Communications and Signal Processing, vol. 3 (1997)
11. Gupta, A.: Network Management: Current Trends and Future Perspectives. Journal of Network and Systems Management 14, 483–491 (2006)
12. Hahsler, M., Grün, B., Hornik, K.: arules – A Computational Environment for Mining Association Rules and Frequent Item Sets. Journal of Statistical Software 14(15), 1–25 (2005)
13. HP Corporate, HP Network Node Manager (NNM) Advanced Edition software, `http://www.openview.hp.com/products/nnm` (accessed April 2009)

14. JBoss devision of Red Hat, JBoss Rules, `http://www.jboss.com/products/rules/` (accessed April 2009)
15. Lenca, P., Meyer, P., Vaillant, B., Lallich, S.: On selecting interestingness measures for association rules: User oriented description and multiple criteria decision aid. European Journal of Operational Research 184(2), 610–626 (2008)
16. Mannila, H., Toivonen, H., Verkamo, A.: Discovering frequent episodes in sequences. In: Proceedings of 1st Conference on Knowledge Discovery and Data Mining (KDD 1995), pp. 210–215 (1995)
17. Mannila, H., Toivonen, H.: Discovering Generalized Episodes Using Minimal Occurrences. In: Proceedings of Second International Conference on Knowledge Discovery and Data Mining, pp. 146–151 (1996)
18. Martin, J.P., Flatin, M., Jakobson, G., Lewis, L.: Event Correlation in Integrated Management: Lessons Learned and Outlook. Journal of Network and Systems Management 15(4), 481–502 (2007)
19. Raman, L.: OSI Systems and Network management. IEEE Communications Magazine 36(3), 46–53 (1998)
20. TM Forum Association, TM Forum Solution Frameworks (NGOSS) Overview, `http://www.tmforum.org/Overview/1912/home.html` (accessed April 2009)
21. Tuchs, K., Jobman, K.: Intelligent Search for Correlated Alarm Events in Database. In: Proceedings of IFIP IEEE International Symposium on Integrated Network Management, pp. 405–419 (2001)
22. Turban, E., Sharda, R., Aronson, J., King, D.: Business Intelligence: A Managerial Approach. Prentice-Hall, Englewood Cliffs (2007)
23. Wallin, S., Landén, L.: Telecom Alarm Prioritization using Neural Networks. In: Proceedings of 22nd International Conference on Advanced Information Networking and Applications, pp. 1468–1473 (2008)
24. Wang, W., Yang, J., Yu, P.: Mining Patterns in Long Sequential Data with Noise. ACM SIGKDD Explorations Newsletter 2(2), 28–33 (2000)
25. Witten, I.H., Frank, E.: Data Mining: Practical Machine Learning Tools and Techniques, 2nd edn. Morgan Kaufmann, San Francisco (2005)
26. Yang, J., Wang, P., Yu, P.: Mining asynchronous periodic patterns in time series data. In: Proceedings of ACM SIGKDD, pp. 275–279 (2000)
27. Yemini, Y., Yemini, S., Kliger, S.: Apparatus and Method for Event Correlation and Problem Reporting, United States Patents and Trademarks Office, Patent Nos. 7003433, 6868367, 6249755 and 5528516 (2008)

Construction of a Local Domain Ontology from News Stories

Brett Drury[1] and J.J. Almeida[2]

[1] LIAAD-INESC
[2] University of Minho

Abstract. The identification of "actionable" information in news stories has become a popular area for investigation. News presents some unique challenges for the researcher. The size constraints of a news story often require that full background information is omitted. Although this is acceptable for a human reader, it makes any form of automatic analysis difficult. Computational analysis may require some background information to provide context to news stories. There have been some attempts to identify and store background information. These approaches have tended to use an ontology to represent relationships and concepts present in the background information. The current methods of creating and populating ontologies with background information for news analysis were unsuitable for our future needs.

In this paper we present an automatic construction and population method of a domain ontology. This method produces an ontology which has the coverage of a manually created ontology and the ease of construction of the semi-automatic method. The proposed method uses a recursive algorithm which identifies relevant news stories from a corpus. For each story the algorithm tries to locate further related stories and background information. The proposed method also describes a pruning procedure which removes extraneous information from the ontology. Finally, the proposed method describes a procedure for adapting the ontology over time in response to changes in the monitored domain.

Keywords: Ontology Construction and Population, News, Linked Data.

1 Introduction

The news has become an increasingly popular area for research. News can contain timely information which may be useful in a variety of tasks which rely upon accurate current affairs information. News provides some unique problems because it implicitly relies upon the accumulated knowledge of the reader. This knowledge is not static because over time new information is absorbed and outdated information is expelled. The computational analysis of news may require this information to be represented in a formal manner.

There have been a number of attempts to model information gathered from the news[9][14] [6], but the knowledge captured was more for the demonstration of a technique, rather than to produce a rich representation of background knowledge.

L. Seabra Lopes et al. (Eds.): EPIA 2009, LNAI 5816, pp. 400–410, 2009.

Research conducted in the area of news recommender systems has attempted to provide techniques where background information is modelled in an ontology. [5] The capture of background information has been used to improve categorization of news [2]. These approaches relied heavily upon manual intervention either from a user or a knowledge engineer. These approaches did not attempt to model a domain extensively, however they did provide descriptions of constructing formal knowledge representations of news.

The most frequently cited knowledge representation method for modelling background information for news are ontologies. The rest of the paper will refer to the construction of ontologies. The aforementioned construction methods can be categorized as the following: manual, semi-automatic / automatic. The current methods have their flaws which make them unsuitable for our needs. The manual methods produced rich and detailed ontologies, however it is normally a slow process and the updating of the ontology is irregular and sluggish. This is due to the method's reliance upon human experts. [10]. The semi-automatic / automatic approaches may be faster than the manual method, however some manual intervention is required.[5] The user may be required to select a number of seed stories from which the ontology is constructed. It is likely that a human will be poor in analysing a large number of stories and consequently may not select a sufficiently large sample of stories. This will produce a less than optimum ontology. It is possible that a human will be inconsistent in the seed story selection, this will produce errors in the ontology.

This paper will present an automatic method of ontology construction and population. The paper will present the following: 1. Corpus Construction 2. A method which will use the unique structure of news to select stories and further information sources for inclusion in the ontology. 3. An enrichment process where the initial seed stories will be supplemented by further information and stories. 4. Methods for eliminating errors. 5. the paper will discuss methods for maintaining the ontology over time and some proposals for further work.

2 Corpus Construction

The corpus was constructed from news stories which were culled from free sources on the Internet. A crawler harvested these stories at the same time each day. The stories were published by the content providers in Really Simple Syndication (RSS) format. The crawler recorded Headline, Description, Story Text, HTML, Published Date and Harvested Date information. The content providers embedded links in the stories between related stories and background information. This information was also recorded.

It was important that the corpus was of a significant size and had some rudimentary structure. The intention was not to demonstrate a technique, but to generate an ontology which had sufficient detail to provide reasonable coverage of the studied area. The structure of the corpus was a significant factor in the development of the proposed method for the following reasons: 1. A series of connections could be made between stories as well as between stories and background information, 2. The structure allowed the identification of the story at an increasing level of granularity with headlines being the most narrow and the story text being the widest. The corpus size and the number of links to background information had a significant bearing on the results as it was assumed that large volumes of structured data may generate detailed ontologies with less sophisticated methods. [4]

2.1 Corpus Characterization

The news sources chosen for the corpus were selected for the quality of reporting and their varying political associations. The corpus contained 5 "broadsheet" newspaper sources, 1 national broadcaster and 1 specific financial newspaper. The corpus had more than 23,000 news stories and 9148K words.

3 Local Ontology Construction

3.1 Opposing Ontology Construction Methods

Two competing approaches were considered: 1. Generate an ontology from the whole of the corpus and select the neighbourhood of the entities that are of interest. 2. Generate a domain specific ontology from a selection of highly relevant selection of stories and resources. The first approach was considered, and consequently dismissed. It was thought that this method would increase the likelihood of ambiguity and error, for example there is more than one political party with the title of The Labour Party. The inclusion of all stories which concern "The Labour Party" may cause some "contamination" due to the mixing of assertions. The number of errors will increase because stories which are deliberately misleading or satirical would be included [1]. The restriction of stories to a specific domain would exclude a number of stories with irrelevant information. This approach would reduce the number of errors and instances of ambiguity.

3.2 Local Domain Ontology Construction

The ontology structure was flat, i.e all classes were a subclass of OWL:Thing. The Open Calais web service [11] was used to provide meta data. This meta data included named entity extraction. The classes were defined by the entity type. For example, if an entity had the type Person and the person class did not exist then the class person will be created and the value added as an individual. Open Calais provided nominal relationship information. [11] Normalization tables were used to provide a more understandable and descriptive relationship.

As an illustration of the proposed method, a case study of the domain of Microsoft will be presented. It should be possible to validate the assertions because the domain is widely known.

[1] In Anglo Saxon cultures on the 1st of April newspapers publish misleading stores as part of April fools day, for example: `http://www.telegraph.co.uk/news/uknews/1583456/April-Fools-Day-story-round-up.html`

3.3 "Bootstrapping" the Construction Process

To "bootstrap" the ontology construction process a number of highly relevant seed stories were required. A seed set of stories was selected by searching the headlines for the keyword, "Microsoft". These stories were relevant because headlines are good indicators of the following story text[1]. This seed set was expanded with stories and background information which were linked to by the initially selected stories. The depth of linking was kept to the immediate stories because of the rapid decrease in relevance at linking depth of 2 or more.[2]

The Open Calais meta data consisted of a list of entities and nominal relationship information. The entity data was in some circumstances supplemented with background information from external sources, for example DBPedia and Reuters. Open Calais labels this information as Linked Data. The keyword for document selection referred to an entity, consequently it was possible to expand the search terms. The Open Calais Linked Data contained the OWL predicate "SameAS" [7]. This predicate referred to keywords which were the same as the initial keyword. In the case study the SameAs predicate referred to companies which were owned by Microsoft or names by which Microsoft is also known as. There is a publicly available example of Linked Data for IBM, in this example "SameAS" referred to the following: International Business Machines, Sequent Computer Systems, Holosofx, and Taligent. [12] The example page also had links to further information which in this example was Wikipedia and Reuters.

The expanded set of stories for the construction of the ontology can be described as:

```
K =Stories returned using keywords, L= Linked Stories to K,
E=Stories returned using expanded key words,
LE=Linked Stories to E, S = Seed Stories,
LD = Open Calais Linked Data
LDE = Extra Information Sources Pointed to by LD
```

$S = K \cup L \cup E \cup LE \cup LD \cup LDE$

3.4 Normalization of Relations

The story metadata was parsed with the CalaisDotNet [3] library. The library returned the meta data in the form of objects. The objects contained an array of named entities (person,company etc) and an array of properties for each named entity. Each entity may have a relation with one or more entities and the relation may have more than one property. The relations were transformed to binary relations, therefore a relation could only be between two entities and could contain only one property. The binary relation format was chosen because binary relations may be repeated which assisted in conflict resolution, they were more robust than the previous format and were easier to manipulate.

[2] This was confirmed initially through a manual inspection and subsequently through the use of a relevance score.

The transformation of the data was made via normalization tables. The normalization tables used the relationship type information and the entity type values from item pairs in the array to provide a binary relation and a description of the relation.

The function *normRel* is the function that normalizes Relationship objects and can be described as:

$$
\begin{aligned}
&normRel(r) \stackrel{\text{def}}{=} \\
&\quad \textbf{let}\ (relname, args) = r \\
&\qquad (fst : oths) = args \\
&\quad \textbf{in}\ \textbf{foreach}\ (a \in oths) \\
&\qquad \begin{cases} newname = norm(relname, type(fst), type(a)) \\ add(newname, fst, a) \end{cases}
\end{aligned}
$$

The function *norm* generates a normalization of relation names.

The norm function returned the description of the relationship. This was to allow for a manual inspection of the ontology and the description needed to convey the nature of the relationship. Further tables held pairs of incompatible assertions which allowed the identification of incompatible relationships. An example of the output of the normalization table can be found in table 1.

3.5 Identification of Implicit Relationships

The Relationship object provided an opportunity to infer further information about an entity. If the array contained information concerning two or more entities than it was possible to reverse the relationship. In the example of Microsoft it was asserted that "Steve Ballmer is an employee of Microsoft". It was consequently possible to reverse the relationship to assert that "Microsoft employs Steve Ballmer".

3.6 Initial Results

The ontology generated from the seed information had a level of detail which was broad and detailed, for example a person class was created with 60 individuals each of which had at least 2 assertions and the industry term class had a further 146 individuals. A manual inspection of the ontology revealed that it had a large number of assertions which could be described as "commonly known information". This information was complemented with assertions about less well known entities. Table 1 provides some example assertions from the Microsoft entity. The Microsoft entity was the central entity in our case study, and as the table indicates that after the headline pass it contained in excess of 200 assertions.

3.7 Enriching the Ontology

The initial seed sources were directly related to the chosen domain. It was possible to increase the richness of the domain by adding further stories which have

Table 1. Selection of assertions which concern Microsoft

Microsoft	CompetitorOf	Google
Microsoft	CompetitorOf	SalesForce.Com
Microsoft	Employs	Ray Ozzie
Microsoft	Employs	Sean Poulley
Microsoft	Produces	Windows
Microsoft	Produces	Silverlight
Microsoft	HasRelationship	Dell
Microsoft	HasRelationship	Verizon
Microsoft	ParentOf	Aquantive
Microsoft	PlannedPurchaseOf	Yahoo
Microsoft	LocatedIn	Seattle
... and more than 200 further assertions		

a less obvious or indirect relationship with the domain. The expanded keywords which were present in the story or description text of a number of stories may have provided an indication that the story might have a degree of relevance to the domain, but there was no guarantee that the stories had a sufficient relationship to be included. The ontology constructed from the seed stories was sufficiently detailed to provide a similarity measure to evaluate the expanded set of stories. The similarity measure was a simply a measure of the percentage of intersecting terms from the news story when compared to the constructed ontology.

Selecting Story Relevancy Boundary. There was an assumption that there existed a set of relevant stories in the corpus and these stories were identifiable. The aforementioned similarity measure provided a measure of relevance to each story and the author's experiments were designed to identify a general boundary at which stories contained sufficient information to be relevant to a chosen domain. It was not possible to annotate all the news stories, consequently a statistically representative sample of documents were selected. These documents contained at least one keyword to ensure there were sufficient documents with relevancy greater than 0. The selection of a hard border is a subjective process and it was necessary to use a human judge to separate the selected documents into categories which adhered to a pre-set relevance score. The categories were: Category 1 $\in$ [0..0.20], Category 2 $\in$ [0.21..0.40] Category 3 $\in$ [0.41..0.60] , Category 4 $\in$ [0.61..0.80] and Category 5 $\in$ [0.81..1]. The authors accept that this is a manually intensive task, but it is a "one-off task" because the derived boundary score may be used in new domains.

In Figure 1 some points were obscured because there are multiple data points which had the same category and similarity score. There were the expected overlaps between the categories. It was necessary to eliminate all of the documents which have no relevance to the domain (category 1) and keep all the documents which have some relevancy to the domain. A similarity score of 0.23 was chosen as this was the lowest score which had no category 1 documents.

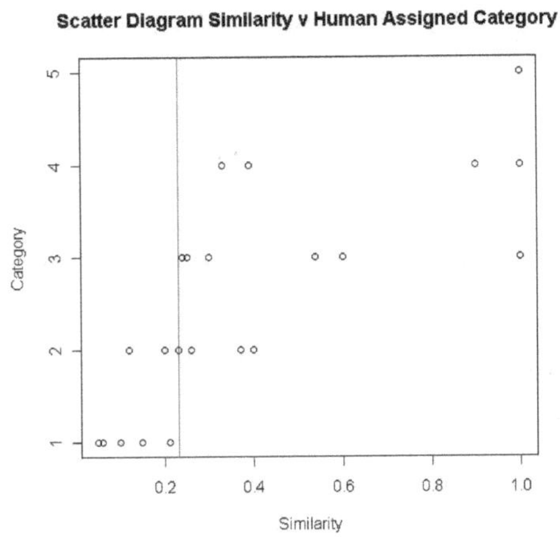

Fig. 1. Scatter Diagram For Border Data

Continuation of Enrichment Process. The enrichment process can be described as the following process:

- Extract stories from the corpus which contain the target word in the description, but not in the headline
- Calculate the similarity between the stories and the existing ontology
- If similarity is more than 0.23 accept story and add to the ontology
- Extract stories from the corpus which contain the target word in the body text, but not in the description or headline
- Repeat step 3
- Extract all stories which were not present in the previous steps
- Repeat step 3

After each enrichment stage the ontology had an increasing level of detail. The person class contained 60 individuals after the 1st pass and 109 at the end of the enrichment process. The increasing level of detail of the Person class was reflected through out the ontology.

4 Pruning the Ontology

4.1 Pruning of Entities

There were a number of entities which were common to a large number of stories in the corpus. These entities did not reveal any relevant information and were the equivalent of "stop words" in information retrieval and needed to be removed. These "stop-entities" were identified through the application of a TF-IDF score for each entity in the corpus. [15].

4.2 Pruning Conflicting Information

The ontology contained obvious errors. This was due to mistakes made in either the information sources or errors made by OpenCalais. These errors were identified by the aforementioned list of incompatible assertions. An example of an error which was flagged as a conflict was the assertion that Yahoo was both the owner and competitor of Microsoft. The assertion that Yahoo owned Microsoft was made once and the contrary assertion was made multiple times. A simple voting procedure identified the correct assertion. This technique may only be used when an assertion is made once and the contrary assertion is asserted more than once. In the experiments for this paper mistakes were never asserted more than once.

4.3 Pruning of Outdated Information

Temporal errors were caused through the inclusion of outdated information. Information in news can have a time limit. This paper proposes two methods for identifying and correcting "stale" information. The two proposed methods are: state changes and contrary information.

For the purpose of this paper a state change is determined to be a process where an entity's relationship with another entity or property changes. A state change was reported in a news story if the news of the state change had sufficient utility [8] to be published. Open Calais indicated a state change by the linguistic cue word "Change". An example of a Open Calais state change was a relationship object having the type "EmploymentChange". The metadata provided sufficient information about the entity's new relationship to update the ontology.

If a state change does not merit enough utility [8] to be published or the story was published between crawler runs, it was possible in certain circumstances to infer a state change from contrary information published at a later date. There was an example in the Microsoft case study. There was a state change for a major competitor (Yahoo) when Jerry Yang left his post as CEO. This story was not in the corpus. The corpus did have a number of stories where Carol Bartz was identified as the CEO of Yahoo. All of the stories concerning Carol Bartz had a later published date than the stories which assert that Jerry Yang was the CEO. It is reasonable to assume a state change for both Jerry Yang and Carol Bartz.

4.4 Monitoring the Domain

In the case study the domain was monitored by applying the aforementioned enrichment and pruning techniques to news stories gathered from The New York Times NewsService[13]. The enrichment and pruning techniques allowed new information to be gathered from relevant stories while the pruning techniques attempted to remove outdated information.

5 Results

The initial results were encouraging. The keyword searching of the headline, description and text returned documents which had an increasing large variance in relevance to the target domain. This variance in quality was counter balanced by the increasing richness of the ontology at each stage of enrichment. This characteristic allowed the identification of stories which had a strong, but not an easily identifiable relationship with the domain. The ontology was not error free. The pruning and conflict resolution rules removed some erroneous information, however over time the number of errors increased. It was necessary to provide a time limit to exclude stories which had out dated information from the construction process.

The ontology did not function well on short stories with few entities (1-2) which did not provide any other cues to their relevance. A rule was introduced to ensure that a news story had to have a minimum number of entities before being assigned a relevance score.

A comparison between other methods was attempted. The manual method was partially abandoned as it was very time consuming. The semi-automatic method of the user choosing the stories had the problem that the volume of news prohibited the selection of a complete set of relevant stories. Keywords were used to limit the choice, however the selection of the stories was still a time consuming task. The semi-automatic method had the drawback that the concepts in the ontology would have to defined by hand and the method did not provide a method of updating over time.

6 Conclusion

The proposed method allows for the quick generation of a rich and detailed domain ontology. This will be a very useful tool as the information it generates will assist in further analysis of news as it allows the researcher to change domains quickly.

The process was not perfect. Although there were rules for pruning and eliminating errors they did not remove all erroneous information. A significant number of the errors are on the extremity of the ontology, however these errors should not be ignored and further work on pruning rules is required. A major source of these errors were temporal, e.g. outdated information. In volatile domains it is likely that the regular regeneration of domains with time limits of the accepted information for ontology construction will remove these errors. In general the proposed method provides a solid foundation for further investigation into news and its related components.

7 Further Work

The subsequent work in this area will concentrate on developing a framework of decaying relationships over time. The relationships may be refreshed, however if the assertion is not refreshed it will be eventually expelled from the ontology. This method may improve the identification of "stale" information. A further area of improvement may be in identifying an entity's importance, this may include using coverage (i.e how many times an entity is mentioned) and alignment with external events such as financial markets.

References

1. Andrew, B.C.: Media-generated shortcuts: Do newspaper headlines present another roadblock for low-information rationality? The Harvard International Journal of Press/Politics 12(2), 24–43 (2007)
2. Borsje, J., Levering, L., Frasincar, F.: Hermes: a semantic web-based news decision support system. In: The 23rd ACM Symposium on Applied Computing (SAC 2008), Special Track on Web Technologies (2008)
3. Emargee, E.: A .net 3.5 class library wrapper for the calais web service, `http://www.codeplex.com/CalaisDotNet` (consulted in 2009)
4. Halevy, A., Norvig, P., Pereira, F.: The unreasonable effectiveness of data. Intelligent Systems, IEEE 24(2), 8–12 (2009)
5. Levering, L., Frasincar, F., Borsje, J.: A semantic web-based approach for building personalized news services. International Journal of E-Business Research (2009)
6. Lloyd, L., Kechagias, D., Skiena, S.: News and blog analysis with lydia. In: 12 Internation Conference Spire, pp. 161–166 (2005)
7. McGuinness, D.L., van Harmelen, F., et al.: OWL Web Ontology Language Overview. W3C Recommendation 10, 2004–3 (2004)
8. McManus, J.: An economic theory of news selection. In: Annual Meeting for Education in Mass Media and Journalism (1988)
9. Newman, D., Chemudugunta, C., Smyth, P., Steyvers, M.: Analyzing entities and topics in news articles using statistical topic models. In: IEEE International Conference on Intelligence and Security Informatics (2006)
10. Castells, P., Perdrix, F., Pulido, E., et al.: Newspaper archives on the semantic web. In: HCI related papers of Interaccion 2004, pp. 267–276 (2004)
11. Reuters. Calais web service, `http://opencalais.com/` (consulted in 2009)
12. Reuters. Calais web service linked data, `http://d.opencalais.com/er/company/ralg-tr1r/9e3f6c34-aa6b-3a3b-b221-a07aa7933633.html` (consulted in 2009)
13. The New York Times. New york times news service, `http://developer.nytimes.com/docs/` (consulted in 2009)
14. Vargas-Vera, M., Celjuska, D.: Event recognition on news stories and semi-automatic population of an ontology. In: Proceedings of the 2004 IEEE/WIC/ACM International Conference on Web Intelligence, pp. 615–618 (2004)
15. Weiss, S.M., Indurkhya, N., Zhang, T., Damerau, F.: Text Mining - Predictive Methods for Analyzing Unstructured Information. Springer, Heidelberg (2005)

A Ontology Browsing with Growl

The extracted ontology is described in RDF and consequently it can be analysed with standard ontology in tools. The diagram Figure 2 was produced with GrowlView in Protege. The diagram is intended to show the richness and scale of the ontology and not individual details.

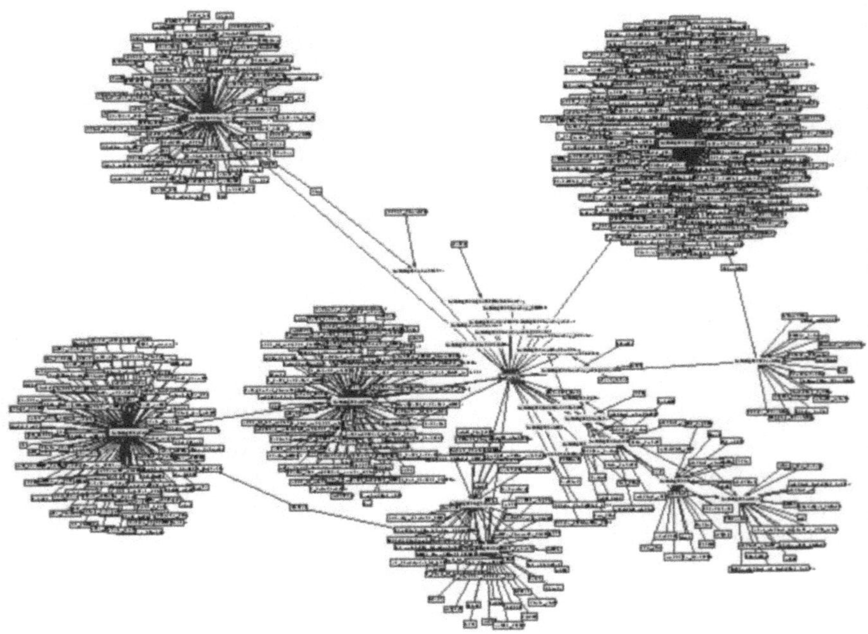

Fig. 2. Ontology After Final Enrichment Pass

Efficient Coverage of Case Space with Active Learning

Nuno Filipe Escudeiro[1,3] and Alípio Mário Jorge[2,3]

[1] Instituto Superior de Engenharia do Porto, Portugal
[2] Faculdade de Ciencias, Universidade do Porto, Portugal
[3] LIAAD INESC Porto L.A., Portugal

Abstract. Collecting and annotating exemplary cases is a costly and critical task that is required in early stages of any classification process. Reducing labeling cost without degrading accuracy calls for a compromise solution which may be achieved with active learning. Common active learning approaches focus on accuracy and assume the availability of a pre-labeled set of exemplary cases covering all classes to learn. This assumption does not necessarily hold. In this paper we study the capabilities of a new active learning approach, d-Confidence, in rapidly covering the case space when compared to the traditional active learning confidence criterion, when the representativeness assumption is not met. Experimental results also show that d-Confidence reduces the number of queries required to achieve complete class coverage and tends to improve or maintain classification error.

1 Introduction

Collecting and annotating cases is a critical and demanding stage in classification tasks [14]. It is critical because it is one of the first stages of the whole process and limits the performance of all the following stages. It is demanding because it requires domain specialists to retrieve and label exemplary cases for all classes to learn.

The effort required to retrieve and label these representative cases is not only related to the number of target classes [2]; it is also related to class distribution in the available pool of examples. On a highly imbalanced class distribution, it is particularly demanding to identify examples from minority classes. These, however, may be important in terms of representativeness. It is the case of a document collection on the Web. Minority classes may correspond to specific information needs which are relevant for specific subgroups of users. If this specificity is not taken into account, many queries will be required before these special cases are retrieved. In many situations, such as fraud detection, clinical diagnosis, news [17] and Web resources [9], we face the problem of imbalanced class distributions. Failing to identify cases from under-represented classes may have costs.

The main goal of our current work is to identify representative examples for a set of classes from a pool of unlabeled cases, in the absence of any prior

L. Seabra Lopes et al. (Eds.): EPIA 2009, LNAI 5816, pp. 411–422, 2009.

description of the classes to learn. Furthermore, this must be achieved with a reduced number of labeled examples in order to reduce labeling effort.

Active learning may reduce the number of labels that are required, when compared to expensive supervised solutions, without compromising the performance of the following stages, i.e., while keeping similar accuracy. In this setting, the learner is allowed to ask an oracle (typically a human) to label examples – these requests are called *queries*. The most informative queries are selected by the learning algorithm instead of being randomly selected. It is expected that criterious selection avoids redundant queries that do not improve the current classifier.

Active learning is frequently focused on reducing version space assuming that we already have a pre-labeled set covering all classes. This representativeness assumption does not necessarily hold in the initial stage of collecting and annotating training cases. In general, uncovered regions of the case space may contain cases of unknown classes. On the other hand, even known classes may have distinct subgroups with specific characteristics in unknown regions of the case space. In such a setting it is important to achieve an effective coverage of case space which rapidly increases the knowledge about relevant classes.

In this paper we propose a new active learning approach, *d-Confidence*, that tends to explore unseen regions in case space, thus selecting cases from unseen classes faster – with fewer queries – than traditional active learning approaches. D-Confidence selects queries based on a criterion that aggregates the posterior classifier confidence – a traditional active learning criterion – and the distance between queries and known classes. This criterion is biased towards cases that do not belong to known classes (low confidence). Simultaneously, it explores unseen areas in case space (high distance to known classes).

D-confidence is more effective than confidence alone in achieving an homogeneous coverage of the classes of interest. Our aim is to identify exemplary cases from all classes as early as possible, with a reduced number of queries. To our knowledge, this problem has not yet been addressed.

In the rest of this paper we start by describing active learning, in section 2. Section 3 describes d-Confidence. Section 4 describes the evaluation process, including the experimental plan and the presentation and discussion of results. In section 5 we state our conclusions and expectations for future work.

2 Active Learning

Active learning approaches [3, 5, 18, 16] reduce label complexity – the number of queries that are necessary and sufficient to learn a concept – by analyzing unlabeled cases and selecting the most useful ones once labeled.

The general idea is to estimate the value of labeling one unlabeled case. Query-By-Committee [20], for example, uses a set of classifiers (the committee) to identify the case with the highest disagreement. Schohn et al. [19] worked on active learning for Support Vector Machines (SVM) selecting queries by their proximity to the dividing hyperplane. Their results are, in some cases, better than if all available data are used for training. Cohn et al. [6] describe an optimal solution that selects the case that, once labeled and added to the training set, produces the minimum expected error. This approach, however, requires high computational effort. Common active learning heuristics aim at reducing uncertainty by selecting the next query as the unlabeled example on which the classifier is less confident [13].

Dasgupta [7] defines theoretical bounds showing that active learning has exponentially smaller label complexity than supervised learning under some particular and restrictive constraints. This work is extended by relaxing some of these constraints [12]. An important conclusion of this last work is that the gains of active learning are much more evident in the initial phase of the learning process, after which they degrade and the speed of learning drops to that of passive learning. Agnostic Active learning [4] achieves an exponential improvement over the usual sample complexity of supervised learning in the presence of arbitrary forms of noise. This model is further studied by Hanneke [11] setting general bounds on label complexity.

All these approaches assume that we have an initial labeled set covering all the classes of interest.

Recent work explores clustering to provide an initial structure to data or to suggest valuable queries. Adami et al. [2] merge clustering and oracle labeling to bootstrap a predefined hierarchy of classes. This approach demands for a high validation effort, especially when these clusters are not aligned with class labels. Dasgupta et al. [8] propose a cluster-based method that consistently improves label complexity over supervised learning. Their method detects and exploits clusters that are loosely aligned with class labels. The method has been applied to the detection of rare categories achieving significant gains in the number of queries that are required to discover at least one example from each class. This latter work is in line with our own efforts for devising a method capable to swiftly identify cases from unknown classes [10].

As described, common active learning methods focus on improving the decision functions for previously labeled classes, assuming the representativeness of the known cases. In this paper we study how diverging classifier attention to unkown regions of the case space improves the chances of finding new labels. This idea is marginally suggested by Dasgupta et al. [8] – avoid sampling from clusters confidently identified as pure, focusing on other. Like us, they also report significant gains in the number of queries required to detect unknown classes. Our approach, though, is distance based, rather than cluster based.

3 D-Confidence Active Learning

Given a target concept with an arbitrary number of classes together with a sample of unlabeled examples from the target space (the working set), our purpose is to identify representative cases covering all classes while posing as few queries as possible, where a query consists of requesting a label to a specific case. The working set is assumed to be representative of the class space – the representativeness assumption [15].

Active learners commonly search for queries in the neighborhood of the decision boundary (Figure 1a), where class uncertainty is higher. Limiting case selection to the uncertainty region seems adequate when we have at least one labeled case from each class. This class representativeness is assumed by all active learning methods. In such a scenario, selecting queries from the uncertainty region is very effective in reducing version space.

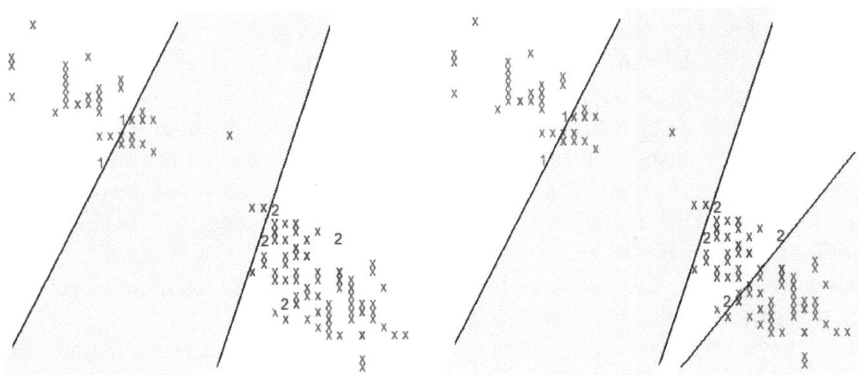

(a) Perceived uncertainty region (b) Real uncertainty region

Fig. 1. Uncertainty region (shaded). n represents labeled cases from class n and $\times$ represents unlabeled cases. We assume that the concept to learn has three distinct classes and one has not yet been identified.

3.1 D-Confidence

The most common active learning approaches rely on classifier confidence to select queries [3] and assume that the pre-labeled set covers all the labels to learn. Our scenario is somehow different: we do not assume that we have labeled cases for all classes and, besides error, we are mainly concerned with the fast identification of representative cases from all classes. To achieve our goals we propose a new selection criterion, *d-Confidence*, which is effective in the early detection of exemplary cases from unseen classes. Instead of relying exclusively on classifier confidence we propose to select queries based on the ratio between classifier confidence and the distance to known classes. D-Confidence, weighs the confidence of the classifier with the inverse of the distance between the case at hand and previously known classes.

D-Confidence is expected to favor a faster coverage of case space, exhibiting a tendency to explore unseen regions in case space. As a consequence, it provides faster convergence than confidence alone. This drift towards unexplored regions and unknown classes is achieved by selecting the case with the lowest d-Confidence as the next query. Lowest d-Confidence is achieved by combining low confidence – probably indicating cases from unknown classes – with high distance to known classes – pointing to unseen regions in the case space. This effect produces significant differences in the behavior of the learning process. Common active learners focus on the uncertainty region asking queries that are expected to narrow it down. The issue is that the uncertainty region is determined by the labels we known at a given iteration. Focusing our search for queries exclusively on this region, while we are still looking for exemplary cases on some labels that are not yet known, is not effective. Unknown classes hardly come by unless, by chance, they are represented in the current uncertainty region.

On Table 1 we present the d-Confidence algorithm – an active learning proposal specially tailored to achieve a fast class representative coverage.

Table 1. d-Confidence algorithm

(1) given W and L_1
(2) compute pairwise distance between all cases in W
(3) $i = 1$
(4) while (not stopping criteria) {
(5) $U_i = W - L_i$
(6)   learn h_i from L_i
(7)   apply h_i to U_i generating $conf_i(c_k \mid u_j)$
(8)   foreach($u_j \in U_i$){
(9)   foreach($c_k \subset \{label(l) \mid l \in L_i\}$){
(10) $dist_i(u_j, c_k) = median\left(dist\left(u_j, \{u \in L_i \mid label\left(u\right) = c_k\}\right)\right)$
(11) $dconf_i(u_j, c_k) = \frac{conf_i(c_k \mid u_j)}{dist_i(u_j, c_k)}$
(12)   }
(13) $dConf_i(u_j) = max_{c_k}\left(dconf_i(u_j, c_k)\right)$
(14)   }
(15) $q_i = \underset{u_j}{\text{argmin}}(dConf_i(u_j))$
(16) $L_{i+1} = L_i \cup < q_i, label(q_i) >$
(17) $i{+}{+}$
(18) }

W is the working set, a representative sample of cases from the problem space. L_i is a subset of W. Members of L_i are the cases in W whose labels are known at iteration i. U, a subset of W, is the set of unlabeled examples. At iteration i, U_i is the (set) difference between W and L_i; c_k is a target class; h_i represents the classifier learned at iteration i; q_i is the query at iteration i; $conf_i(c_k \mid u_j)$ is the posterior confidence on class c_k given case u_j, at iteration i.

Computing d-Confidence for unlabeled cases is accomplished at steps (8) to (14) in Table 1 as explained below. In (15) we select the next query – the unlabeled case with the minimum d-Confidence – which is added to the labeled set (16).

Computing d-Confidence. d-Confidence is based on the ratio between confidence and distance among cases and known classes (Equation 1).

$$dConf(u) = max_{c_k}\left(\frac{conf(c_k \mid u)}{median_j(dist(u, \{u \in L_i \mid label\,(u) = c_k\}))}\right) \quad (1)$$

For a given unlabeled case, u, the classifier generates the posterior confidence w.r.t. known classes (7). Confidence is then divided by an indicator of the distance, $dist()$, between unlabeled case u and all labeled cases belonging to class c_k, $\{u \in L_i \mid label\,(u) = c_k\}$ (10). This distance indicator is the *median* of the distances between case u and all cases in $\{u \in L_i \mid label\,(u) = c_k\}$. We expect the median to soften the effect of outliers. At step (11) we compute $dconf_i(u, c_k)$ – the d-Confidence for each known class, c_k, given the case u – by dividing class confidence for a given case by aggregated distance to that class.

Finally, we compute d-Confidence of the case, $dConf_i(u)$, as the maximum d-Confidence on individual classes, at step (13).

4 Measuring Case Space Coverage

Our aim is to assess the ability of d-Confidence in achieving fast coverage of case space and in identifying cases from under-represented classes. We also want to measure the impact of d-Confidence on the overall generalization error. Are we trading accuracy for coverage? Another aim of these experiments is to get an insight into how the features of the datasets influence the results of d-Confidence.

We have evaluated d-Confidence on artificial datasets using a SVM classifier. These datasets were designed according to certain global properties (meta-attributes) allowing us to study how the performance of d-Confidence depends on global dataset attributes. We have complemented these results repeating the experiments on a real dataset, Iris, with the aim of further illustrating the robustness of d-Confidence.

In all these experiments we have compared the common confidence active learning setting – where query selection is based on low posterior confidence of the current classifier – with our d-Confidence proposal.

4.1 Experimental Setting

Artificial datasets have been generated to hold a set of properties describing global dataset characteristics: cluster alignment, label distribution, cluster morphism and cluster separability. All these properties are defined as binary. Cluster alignment may refer to non-collinear centroids (0) or collinear centroids (1), collinear centroids means that data clusters gravitational centers lie in or close to a straight line in feature space; label distribution may be balanced (0) or imbalanced (1), balanced datasets have a uniform label distribution in the working set; cluster morphism may be polymorphic (0) or isomorphic (1), polymorphic datasets have distinct clusters of cases belonging to the same class in distinct regions of feature space; cluster separability may be overlapping (0) or separable (1), this separability refers to feature space – on separable clusters it is possible to define linear decision boundaries between all clusters. We have generated 16 artificial datasets to get all the possible combinations of these four binary meta-descriptors. We expect that a group of artificial datasets covering the possible combinations of these properties may simulate a wide range of real datasets arising in classification tasks. These datasets have been named with a four digit key where each digit refers to a given property as previously defined. For instance, the *ds0010* dataset has non-collinear centroids, balanced – uniform – label distribution, isomorphic and overlapping clusters.

Artificial cases are described by two numeric attributes and one class attribute. Numeric attributes are random variables with uniform distribution with range $2R$. R is a parameter of our artificial dataset generator used to specify attribute limits ($-R$ and R) which are set according to the pattern we want to simulate. Random values that do not conform to the patterns we seek are filtered out. After that, white noise, with amplitude of 20% of R, is added to both attribute values. The class attribute has three distinct values. Regular classes have 100 cases and under-represented classes have 10 cases.

4.2 Results

We have performed 10-fold cross validation on all datasets – test sets are stratified random samples. Labels in the training set are hidden from the classifier. For each fold, we start with two labeled cases, and perform train-select iterations until all cases are selected. For the initial iteration in each fold we give two labeled cases – from two distinct classes – to the classifier. Given the dataset and the fold, the same initial labeled cases are provided at the first iteration for both confidence and d-Confidence. In each iteration, each algorithm asks a single query (i.e., asks the label of a case), selected by its own criteria, which is then added to the labeled pool for the next iteration. On all the datasets, including Iris, the concept to learn has three distinct classes. We provide labeled examples on two of these classes keeping the third one hidden from the classifier.

We have recorded, on every iteration, the newly added query, the number of distinct labels known to the classifier and generalization error for both selection criteria under evaluation – confidence and d-Confidence. From these, we have computed, on each dataset, mean coverage, mean number of queries required to identify the hidden class and mean generalization error in each iteration over all cross validation folds (Table 2).

Case space coverage is the percentage of cases in the working set that lie on a given neighborhood of labeled cases. We assume that cases yielding a distance to any of the labeled cases lower than $\frac{1}{10}$ of the maximum distance between cases in the working set are covered. The progression of case space coverage is depicted in Figure 2 where we can see the percentage of covered cases, for each dataset and for each selection criterion – confidence or d-Confidence, after querying one, four, 16 and 64 cases. On every dataset we have computed mean coverage and mean error over all iterations and over the 10 folds for confidence and for d-Confidence. This process generated two paired samples – one for confidence and one for d-Confidence – with the size equal to the number of iterations for case space coverage. Two more paired samples are recorded to evaluate error. With these samples we have tested the significance of the difference of the means using paired

Table 2. Coverage, mean number of queries to identify one case from the unknown class and error with an SVM classifier on artificial data. Mean coverage and error are computed over all iterations in all cross validation folds for every artificial dataset. *c* stands for confidence and *dc* stands for d-Confidence.

Dataset	Coverage (c)	Coverage (dc)	Queries (c)	Queries (dc)	Error (c)	Error (dc)
ds0000	0.967	**0.979**	20	**6**	0.038	**0.023**
ds0001	0.922	**0.937**	19	22	0.192	**0.174**
ds0010	**0.920**	0.908	19	**2**	0.032	**0.014**
ds0011	0.893	0.886	27	**3**	0.137	**0.104**
ds0100	0.897	**0.945**	9	10	**0.032**	0.046
ds0101	0.914	**0.933**	35	**13**	0.112	0.106
ds0110	0.877	**0.894**	28	**2**	0.052	**0.019**
ds0111	0.875	0.870	34	**11**	0.111	**0.086**
ds1000	0.908	**0.974**	29	**3**	**0.077**	0.088
ds1001	0.953	**0.976**	11	**7**	**0.240**	0.255
ds1010	0.893	**0.958**	24	**2**	0.039	**0.016**
ds1011	0.911	**0.933**	25	**6**	0.174	**0.144**
ds1100	**0.883**	0.819	55	**13**	**0.183**	0.198
ds1101	**0.852**	0.835	22	**11**	0.188	**0.178**
ds1110	0.862	**0.877**	29	**2**	0.052	**0.028**
ds1111	0.803	**0.827**	32	**3**	0.128	0.120
Iris	0.918	**0.947**	18	**5**	0.134	**0.082**

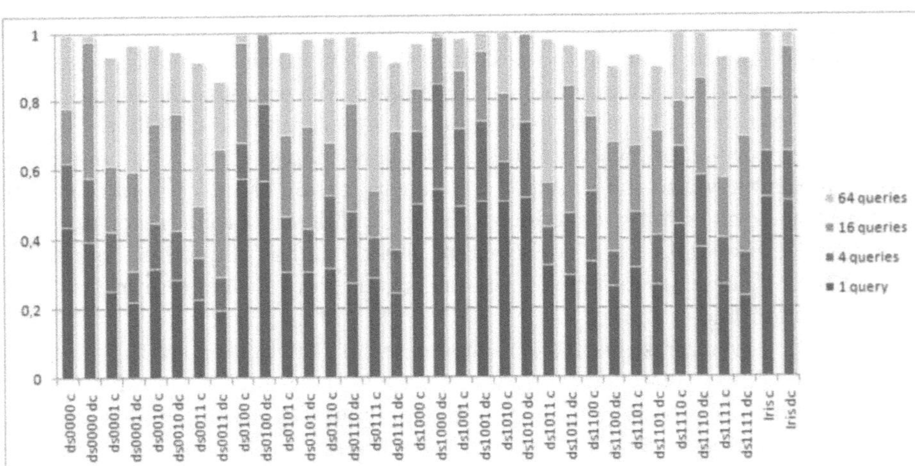

Fig. 2. Progression of case space coverage as new queries are added. *c* stands for confidence; *dc* satnds for d-Confidence.

t-tests. The number of queries required to identify one case from the unseen class is the average over the 10 folds for confidence and for d-Confidence. These means have also been tested for each dataset with paired t-tests. Statistically different means, at a significance level of 5%, are bold faced on Table 2.

4.3 Discussion

D-Confidence consistently improves case space coverage over confidence. This behavior is observed irrespectively of dataset properties. D-Confidence performs better than confidence on six out of eight collinear datasets – collinear datasets have the first numerical digit on their name set to *1*, *ds1???*, see Section 4.1. This same figure is observed on balanced datasets (*ds?0??*), on polymorphic (*ds??0?*) and also on overlapping (*ds???0*) datasets. On all the other groups of datasets – non-collinear (*ds0???*), imbalanced (*ds?1??*), isomorphic (*ds??1?*) and separable (*ds???1*) – d-Confidence outperforms confidence on five out of eight datasets. These conclusions are based on the observed differences between case space coverage, when using confidence and d-Confidence, which are significant at a 5% significance level. The results on polymorphic datasets are particularly interesting since these contain classes with distinct subgroups. Although the coverage efficiency of d-Confidence is not as clear as in isomorphic datasets, it is better than confidence. From Figure 2 we observe that confidence generally achieves a better coverage than d-Confidence on the initial queries. After these few initial queries d-Confidence exceeds confidence on case space coverage.

When analyzing the number of queries that are required to hit an example of the hidden class (class coverage), d-Confidence always performs better than confidence with 5% confidence, except for *ds0001* and *ds0100*. The overall mean number of queries required to identify the third class is one order of magnitude lower when using d-Confidence (26 with confidence against 7 with d-confidence).

Finally, we observe that d-confidence most of the times does not degrade accuracy, and sometimes even improves it. In other words, improved class coverage is not done at the cost of increasing error. Cluster morphism seems to have a strong impact on the error rate. From all the isomorphic datasets, d-Confidence has a significatively lower mean error than that of confidence on seven out of eight datasets. However, on polymorphic datasets, confidence and d-confidence have similar results. Confidence outperforms d-Confidence on four out of eight datasets, while the inverse occurs on three out of eight datasets.

These observations lead us to conclude that d-Confidence active learning outperforms the traditional confidence approach. D-Confidence improves case space coverage and reduces the number of queries required to identify cases from unknown classes without degrading acuracy – in fact, improving it on average – when compared to confidence.

Such results on simulated data have been checked on a real dataset (Figure 3). We have applied a similar experimental plan to the Iris dataset [1] to evaluate the features under analysis – case space coverage, number of queries required to identify cases from unseen classes and generalization error. The results we have achieved on Iris confirm the previous results on artificial data. Case space coverage is more efficient when using d-Confidence.

On the Iris dataset we have also recorded the number of queries required to get a full coverage of case space. Case space is assumed to be fully covered when all cases in the working set lie closer than a certain predefined distance from at least one labeled case. This predefined distance has been set to $\frac{1}{10}$ – the

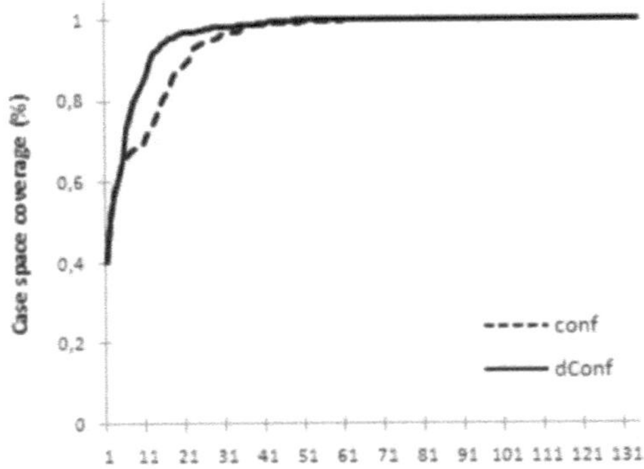

Fig. 3. Case space coverage on the Iris dataset as new queries are added

initial setting – and then to $\frac{1}{8}$, $\frac{1}{6}$ and $\frac{1}{4}$ of the maximum distance between cases. It is expected that the number of queries required to achieve a full coverage decreases as the radius of the assumed covered neighborhood increases. This should be more evident when newly added queries belong to remote regions in case space thus having reduced intersection with previously covered cases. Our purpose is to evaluate if d-Confidence is in fact exploring unseen regions in case space more efficiently than confidence. We have observed that the number of queries required to get a 100% coverage of case space decreases from 84 to 35 – a reduction of 58% in the labeling effort – with confidence, when the neighborhood radius goes from $\frac{1}{10}$ to $\frac{1}{4}$. On this same scenario, d-Confidence labeling effort to get a full coverage is reduced from 51 to 8 queries – a reduction of 84%. These results confirm that d-Confidence selects queries from remote regions – where the density of known (labeled) cases is sparse – more efficiently than confidence.

The mean number of queries required to identify cases from the unseen class is 18 for confidence against 5 for d-Confidence. The mean error on the Iris dataset is 13.4% when using confidence, which is reduced to 8.2% when using d-Confidence.

5 Conclusions and Future Work

We have collected empirical evidence on artificial datasets, and on Iris, confirming our hypothesis that d-Confidence reduces the labeling effort, without compromising error, when compared to confidence.

Case space is covered more efficiently when using d-Confidence, creating conditions to identify representative cases from unknown classes earlier. On average, d-Confidence requires almost four times less queries to identify cases from unknown classes than confidence.

Regarding the global properties of the datasets, d-confidence is clearly better than confidence on "well behaved" datasets (balanced, collinear, isomorphic and separable). On not so well behaved datasets, d-confidence is also better, but not as clearly, especially with respect to classification error. In fact, although marginally, d-Confidence improves the accuracy of the classification process while looking for representative cases for unknown classes.

We are working on the evaluation of d-Confidence applied to text, expecting it to be useful for information retrieval and corpus organization, as well as other tasks where costly human labeling is required, many classes exist, and new classes may pop up all the time. We will also study the problem of how to retrieve exemplary cases when the representativeness assumption does not hold.

References

[1] Uc irvine machine learning repository (2009), `http://archive.ics.uci.edu/ml/`

[2] Adami, G., Avesani, P., Sona, D.: Clustering documents into a web directory for bootstrapping a supervised classification. Data & Knowledge Engineering 54, 301–325 (2005)

[3] Angluin, D.: Queries and concept learning. Machine Learning 2, 319–342 (1988)

[4] Balcan, M.-F., Beygelzimer, A., Langford, J.: Agnostic active learning. In: ICML, pp. 65–72. ICML (2006)

[5] Cohn, D., Atlas, L., Ladner, R.: Improving generalization with active learning. Machine Learning (15), 201–221 (1994)

[6] Cohn, D., Ghahramani, Z., Jordan, M.: Active learning with statistical models. Journal of Artificial Intelligence Research 4, 129–145 (1996)

[7] Dasgupta, S.: Coarse sample complexity bonds for active learning. In: Advances in Neural Information Processing Systems, vol. 18 (2005)

[8] Dasgupta, S., Hsu, D.: Hierarchical sampling for active learning. In: Proceedings of the 25th International Conference on Machine Learning (2008)

[9] Escudeiro, N.F., Jorge, A.M.: Semi-automatic Creation and Maintenance of Web Resources with webTopic. In: Ackermann, M., Berendt, B., Grobelnik, M., Hotho, A., Mladenič, D., Semeraro, G., Spiliopoulou, M., Stumme, G., Svátek, V., van Someren, M. (eds.) Semantics, Web and Mining. LNCS (LNAI), vol. 4289, pp. 82–102. Springer, Heidelberg (2006)

[10] Escudeiro, N., Jorge, A.: Learning partially specified concepts with d-confidence. In: Brazilian Simposium on Artificial Intelligence, Web and Text Intelligence Workshop (2008)

[11] Hanneke, S.: A bound on the label complexity of agnostic active learning. In: Proceedings of the 24th International Conference on Machine Learning (2007)

[12] Kääriäinen, M.: Active learning in the non-realizable case. In: Algorithmic Learning Theory, pp. 63–77. Springer, Heidelberg (2006)

[13] Lewis, D.D., Gale, W.A.: A sequential algorithm for training text classifiers. In: SIGIR 1994: Proceedings of the 17th annual international ACM SIGIR conference on Research and development in information retrieval, pp. 3–12. Springer, New York (1994)

[14] Li, M., Sethi, I.: Confidence-based active learning. IEEE Transactions on Pattern Analysis and Machine Intelligence 28, 1251–1261 (2006)

[15] Liu, H., Motoda, H.: Instance Selection and Construction for Data Mining. Kluwer Academic Publishers, Dordrecht (2001)

[16] Muslea, I., Minton, S., Knoblock, C.A.: Active learning with multiple views. Journal of Artificial Intelligence Research 27, 203–233 (2006)

[17] Ribeiro, P., Escudeiro, N.: On-line news "à la carte". In: Proceedings of the European Conference on the Use of Modern Information and Communication Technologies (2008)
[18] Roy, N., McCallum, A.: Toward optimal active learning through sampling estimation of error reduction. In: Proceedings of the International Conference on Machine Learning (2001)
[19] Schohn, G., Cohn, D.: Less is more: Active learning with support vector machines. In: Proceedings of the International Conference on Machine Learning (2000)
[20] Seung, H., Opper, M., Sompolinsky, H.: Query by committee. In: Proceedings of the 5th Annual Workshop on Computational Learning Theory (1992)

Tracking Recurring Concepts with Meta-learners

João Gama[1] and Petr Kosina[2]

[1] LIAAD-INESC Porto, FEP-University of Porto
jgama@fep.up.pt
[2] Fac. of Informatics, Masaryk University, Brno
soso@mail.muni.cz

Abstract. This work address data stream mining from dynamic environments where the distribution underlying the observations may change over time. In these contexts, learning algorithms must be equipped with change detection mechanisms. Several methods have been proposed able to detect and react to concept drift. When a drift is signaled, most of the approaches use a forgetting mechanism, by releasing the current model, and start learning a new decision model, Nevertheless, it is not rare for the concepts from history to reappear, for example seasonal changes. In this work we present method that memorizes learnt decision models whenever a concept drift is signaled. The system uses meta-learning techniques that characterize the domain of applicability of previous learnt models. The meta-learner can detect re-occurrence of contexts and take pro-active actions by activating previous learnt models. The main benefit of this approach is that the proposed meta-learner is capable of selecting similar historical concept, if there is one, without the knowledge of true classes of examples.

Keywords: Data Streams, Concept Drift, Recurring Concepts.

1 Motivation

We are living in time of information. Information becomes more and more valuable for any kind of business. It can help to make strategic decisions, save lives when used in medicine, produce better products, find new customers etc. Therefore the increasing computational power and storage space, vast amounts of data are produced and gathered every moment. It is not possible for human to manually study all the data and look for interesting or valuable piece of information. Computers can aid us to automatically process data, search for and retrieve relevant answers. Some of the sources can produce more or less static data, but more often we are faced to evolving dynamics. For example there can be many measurements how some antibiotic works against certain types of organisms. But they can become resistant and previous measurements do not describe the current state anymore. Therefore also methods, intended for data analysis, should not be static but be able to adapt. Observing the behavior of nature can give us more than just the idea of evolution of concepts. There is also the tendency of its reappearance. The most obvious example could be seasonal changes and the

L. Seabra Lopes et al. (Eds.): EPIA 2009, LNAI 5816, pp. 423–434, 2009.

reactions of animals or people to those changes. Even long time ago people knew that after summer comes autumn and then winter etc. and prepared reserves for worse conditions. That is why even computer decisions should consider using historical information and try to predict its recurrence. In this work we present an approach that posse both qualities: adaptation and using historical information. The paper is organized as follows. The next section review related work on change detection and recurrent concepts. The section 3 describes the two layer learning architecture. The Section 4 presents the experimental validation of the proposed system, and last section concludes the paper.

2 Related Work

Existing works in mining data streams usually deal with concept drift by detecting them and learning new classifier that is used either alone as in [2] or as a part of ensemble like in [12,14]. But there are not many of them taking into consideration the recurrence of concepts in the streams. An ensemble classifier with recurrence taken into account is presented in [8]. In their work, classifiers of new concepts are stored in global set. Only the models with performance on preceding data points better than threshold are part of ensemble for labeling the examples. The threshold is set as selected fraction of error of classifier that predicts randomly (e.g. probability of classification to class c is equal to c's class distribution). This ensures that relevant classifiers, with weight assigned, are in the ensemble. If none of the classifiers in global set or the ensemble of them perform better than permitted error, a new classifier is built. Classifiers are tested, selected to ensemble or new one is created with every labeled chunk of examples. Also in [16] a method reusing historical concepts is proposed. It uses proactive approach, e.g. to select concept from history that will most likely follow after the current concept according to transition matrix. History of concepts is treated like a Markov chain with concepts as states. If this approach does not have enough information to distinguish among some historical concepts, it makes decision based on historical-reactive scheme, which means it tests the historical concepts with recent examples and the one with the best accuracy is chosen. In case none of these approaches has satisfying accuracy, a new concept is learnt. Building a concept history can be boosted measuring conceptual equivalence (CE). CE compares classifications of classifier from new concept to results of each of the historical ones and computes score for each pair. If the score for one of the historical concepts is above defined threshold, new concept replaces old one in concept history. In [4] Conceptual Clustering and Prediction (CPP) is presented to handle streaming data with recurrent concepts. Short batches of examples are transformed into conceptual vectors describing them (e.g. mean and standard deviation for numeric attributes, probability of attribute given the class for nominal). Conceptual vectors are clustered by their distance and for each cluster a classifier is learnt. Recurrent concepts are also considered in [6], where multiple windows are used for tracking the concept drift. By predicting the rate of change, size of window could be adapted and when drift is estimated, repository of stored historical concepts is checked for recurrence. Concepts are described by averages of attributes (numeric) and similarity is measured by any feature distance metric. In this work we present another approach to select older models learnt on data with similar underlying concept. Single classifier is used for predicting class labels and meta-learner is used to choose the most appropriate model from history. Every time new classifier is not sufficient and warning is signaled, referees are asked for predictions. Whenever there is drift detected the classifier and its referee are stored in a pool for further use. Model is re-used when the percentage of votes of its referee exceeds some given threshold, otherwise new classifier is learnt. The idea of using such referees is taken from [9] where meta-learning scheme was used in off-line learning to select predictions from ensemble of classifiers. We tried to apply the scheme in on-line learning with single classifier for simplicity.

3 The Two-Layers Learning System

The system we propose uses a two layer learning scheme. Each layer trains its own classifier and receives its own data. The first layer receives the data stream and trains a classifier using the labeled examples. For each incoming example $\boldsymbol{x}, y$, the current classifier predicts a class label. If the example is not classified, i.e. $y = ?$, the current model classifies the example, and reads the next example. Otherwise, e.g. the example is classified; we can compute the loss, and update the current decision model with the example. Assuming the 0-1 loss function, the prediction is either correct or incorrect, and an example is generated to train the second layer classifier. This example has the same attribute values as in the layer 0, but the class value is $+$ if the example was correctly classified or $--$ if the example was misclassified. Doing so, the meta-learner learns the regions of the instance space where the base classifier performs well.

3.1 Base Model: Naive Bayes

Our approach does not dependent of a specific learning algorithm. Any classifiers could be used for either level 0 or level 1 classifier with probably different results. We choose a Naive Bayes [15] classifier to be used in our experiments for good reasons. It is easy to implement and it is incremental. It has clear semantics, it's simple in representing, using and learning probabilistic knowledge, works well with continuous attributes and finally in [9] it is reported good results as meta-learner. Prior probabilities, used in computation, are usually small numbers and the product of such numbers gives us even smaller numbers, which can easily lead to underflow while using computers. It is better to use the sum of logarithms and receive a score that is proportional to its probability. The formula is $\log P(c_i|\boldsymbol{x}) \propto \log P(c_i) + \sum_{k=1}^{n} \log P(x_k|c_i)$.

For a two class problem we can also use the expression in the form:

$$\log \frac{P(c_+|\boldsymbol{x})}{P(c_-|\boldsymbol{x})} \propto \log \frac{P(c_+)}{P(c_-)} + \sum_{k=1}^{n} \log \frac{P(x_k|c_+)}{P(x_k|c_-)} \quad (1)$$

The class of the example is then assigned: if $\log \frac{P(c_+|\boldsymbol{x})}{P(c_-|\boldsymbol{x})} > 0$ class is $+$, - otherwise.

Since we are dealing with data streams, it was necessary to use the incremental version of Naive Bayes, which needs to process each example just once. To compute incremental version of Naive Bayes described in [3].

For handling the continuous attributes, the classical method that approximates some distribution was chosen. In this case it was the normal or Gaussian distribution. We assume that $P(x_k|c_i) = \frac{1}{\sigma_{ki}\sqrt{2\pi}} exp\left(\frac{-(x-\mu_{ki})^2}{2\sigma_{ki}}\right)$, where μ_{ki} is mean and σ_{ki} is standard deviation.

3.2 Drift Detection

In many real-world situations we can see that behavior of subject is changing over time (for example new factory raises the power demand). Such changes in class distributions are called drifts and there are many known methods how to detect them. In this work we used approach from [2] which assumes that if the distribution of the examples is stationary, the error-rate of the learning algorithm will decrease when the number of examples increases. The drift detection method manages two registers during the training of the learning algorithm, p_{min} and s_{min}, where p is error-rate and s is standard deviation. Every time a new example i is processed those values are updated when $p_i + s_i$ is lower than $p_{min} + s_{min}$. We use a warning level to define the optimal size of the context window. The context window will contain the old examples that are on the new context and a minimal number of examples on the old context. In the experiments the warning level is reached if $p_i + s_i \geq p_{min} + 2 * s_{min}$ and the drift level is reached if $p_i + s_i \geq p_{min} + 3 * s_{min}$. Suppose a sequence of examples where the error of the actual model increases reaching the warning level at example k_w, and the drift level at example k_d. A new decision model is induced using the examples starting in k_w till k_d. It is possible to observe an increase of the error reaching the warning level, followed by a decrease. We assume that such situations correspond to a false alarm, without changing the context.

3.3 Learning with Model Applicability Induction

When dealing with possibly infinite data streams one can expect there would be concept changes in data and the concepts could re-appear. We need to have some tool for recognizing if older model is appropriate for new data. Such a tool can be a referee which is a meta-learner working in similar fashion as in [9]. There are two layers in our suggested approach. The first layer is the primary model that serves as normal classifier (or level 0 classifier). Then the second layer denoted as referee (or level 1 classifier).

As in real situations there is delay between obtaining example and observing true label. Level 0 classifier makes the prediction when the example arrives. Once the true value of example's class is observed new prediction for the example is made so that the evaluation would reflect current state of the model. Then the classifier is updated and the example is passed, if defined conditions for learning are met, to the referee with new class attribute, which reflects whether or not the prediction was correct. The data set for referee is therefore created from all the example attributes, apart from the class attribute, which is replaced by 0 (or false) when the prediction was wrong or 1 (or true) when the prediction was correct. The process can be illustrated by figure 1 (left).

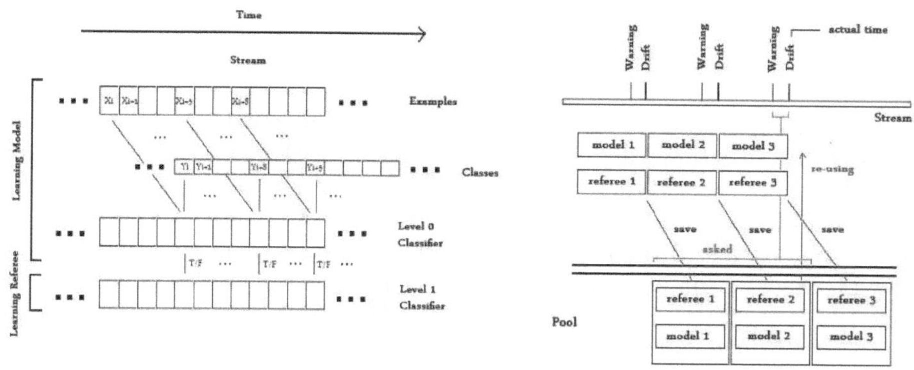

Fig. 1. (Left) Learning process. Once obtained the true label is passed along with the example attributes to level 0 classifier. Then example with true/false label is used for training level 1 classifier. (Right) Referee strategy is shown in the time of third drift. After warning, the referees in the pool were asked, model 2 was selected for re-using while model 3 and its referee were stored in the pool.

Referee is built in the same time when primary model is built. First examples are not used in referee learning, because the misclassifications of the model are mainly due to the lack of information (in our case it was 50 examples). In fact, we have two parallel classifiers on one data stream. When there is a warning we store the incoming examples in a short term memory. This has two reasons. First, if the warning was a false alarm then we use those examples for learning like there was no warning at all. Second, if there is a drift, we use these recent examples, potentially examples from new concept, for building a new model. At this time, new referee is not learning for the same reason like in the beginning. Part of the reaction on warning is that we stop learning primary model and we start asking the referees about the performance of their models. If model is still in the warning phase after defined number of examples, the probability of false alarm is much smaller and the examples in memory that still did not receive their labels are also used to ask referees. If referee's prediction about the applicability of its model is greater than selected threshold, the correspondent model is chosen to be used for evaluating next examples. Otherwise process continues till drift level defined by drift detection is reached or referee's threshold value is exceeded, which is checked every 100 examples. This is the main advantage of using referees. Many examples that do not have their labels are stored in the memory and we could exploit them to predict the change sooner with reusing old classifiers. That way it is not necessary to passively wait till drift is reached, but pro-actively select recurrent model. All new models and their referees are stored in a pool, like on the figure 1 (right). When model is to be re-used, it is taken from the pool together with its referee and updated version is put back after drift occurred. For similar concepts there is one classifier with one referee that is continuously updated.

3.4 Loading Data

Data for stream mining can come and be processed either one by one or in batches. Both situations can be seen in applications. Although waiting for certain amount of examples and then processing the whole batch could be more efficient, data points in this work are taken one by one. Every time a new example is loaded, it is passed to the primary classifier to make a prediction. To simulate behavior in real world, the true value of the class attribute needed for evaluation of model is not observed immediately, but after some delay (500 examples in this situation). Meanwhile the examples and predictions are stored in the memory.

3.5 Optimizing Performance

While making experiments with our referee-advised recurrence tracking method we encountered several problems closely connected to skewness of data. The distribution of examples for referees reflects the error-rate of level 0 classifier. Good performance of the primary classifier means that there will be a lot of positive examples and much less negative examples. This implies the need for some method to deal with this skewed data. A technique without parameters is used to eliminate skewness. The referee makes decision about classifier's prediction and learn it just when it's decision is wrong e.g. referee predicted the classifier to be correct on incoming example and classifier made a mistake or vice versa. In order to be able to make decisions the referee learns from some examples in the beginning, it was 100 examples in our experiments. In our case, we chose Naive Bayes classifier to be the referee. Since this meta-learning is a two class problem, we implemented the classifier as log-odds version of Naive Bayes defined by equation 1. The decision of classifier is chosen to be in favor for *true* only if the log-odds score is above 0.1 not 0 like in usual cases. This scenario is more pessimistic one because it's better to start building a new model than using an old inappropriate one. Another constraint was introduced in the process of saving referees. Since referees with practically the same means and standard deviations for both classes (*true* and *false*) were obtained, we decided to save them only in certain conditions (reaching minimum quality): $if\ \left(\sum |\mu_i^1 - \mu_i^2|\right) > \phi$, where ϕ is selected threshold (in this case 0.002) and μ_i^1, μ_i^2 are means of attributes of *true* and *false* class respectively. Bad quality and skewness of data, could lead to a situation, where referee predicts model to be correct in 100 % cases because of higher prior probability of positive class, even though above mentioned precautions were taken. Therefore results with 100% are not taken into account.

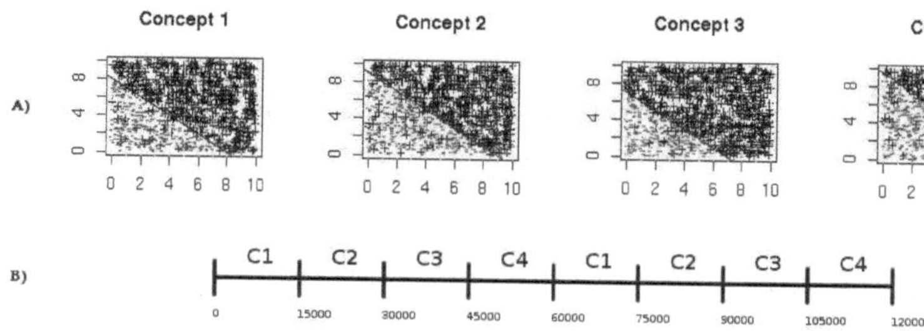

Fig. 2. A) samples of data concepts with 1000 examples each and B) layout of concepts in experimental data

4 Experimental Work

4.1 Data Sets

SEA Concepts. In order to test the method we proposed, we needed data that changes over time e.g. concept drifts are present. We used artificial data described in [12]. Samples of data concepts with the relevant features are plotted in the figure 2(A). Each concept had 15,000 examples with about 10 % of class noise.

Description in [12] holds for our data set with one improvement. Since we wanted to re-use the old models and to study how our method works, we doubled the size by concatenating original set with another copy of it. We obtained data set with 120,000 examples and eight concepts such that concept 1 is the same like concept 5, concept 2 equals concept 6 etc. Figure 2(B) illustrates the data layout. This way the recurrence is present and concepts are not just similar, but exactly the same. Normally we would probably never encounter such strong recurrence, but it serves well for studying the problem.

LED Data. Drift data stream generator from [5] with default settings was used to create another data set. Every 10,000 we change the number of attributes with drift. We generated 120,000 examples with the following randomly chosen numbers of attributes with drift: $2, 4, 3, 1, 4, 3, 2, 5, 1, 4, 3, 5$.

Intrusion. This data set was used in KDD Cup 1999 Competition described in [17]. The full dataset had about five million connection records, but we also used data set with only 10 % of the size finding it more illustrative. The original task had 24 training attack types. The original labels of attack types were changed to label *abnormal* keeping the label *normal* for normal connection. This way we simplified the set to 2 class problem.

4.2 Using the Referee vs. Simple Drift Detection

Handling concept drifts is well-studied problem in data stream mining and many solutions could be found and used. For example by detecting the drift and building a new model while forgetting the old one, we can achieve better results.

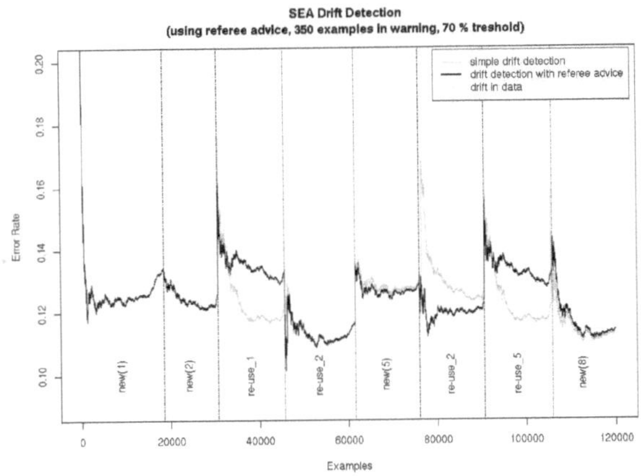

Fig. 3. Comparison of error-rates with re-using models (70 % threshold) and without re-using on SEA Concepts

Furthermore, we can store examples in short-term memory during the warning phase and use these recent examples that are potentially representative of a new concept, for learning a new model. In this paper we introduced a new way to improve these techniques. The idea is to store the old models instead of forgetting them and try to re-use them when there is similar underlying concept in new data. The threshold for re-using old model was set to 70 % in all data sets. Different settings for different sets could improve the performance, but we would like to use more universal threshold. To avoid unnecessary testing when there's false alarm the method waits and if it's still in warning phase after 350 examples all unlabeled examples from the memory are tested by referees.

On the figures 3,4 (left) there are results for SEA Concept data set. As we can see re-using model from concept 1 for concept 3 lead to slightly worse results, because those two are not that similar as concept 2 and concept 4 (see figure 2), where re-using performed the same as building a new model. Moreover, re-using model from concept 2, learnt also on concept 4, on data from the sixth one lead to better results than in the case of learning new classifier. In concept 7 we can see the same situation as in concept 3.

The goal of predicting drift and recurrence was quite successful, three out of four cases of re-using reported drift sooner. 183.5 points improvement on average considering times when drift occurred. The average number of examples in warning, considering all the warning phases, decreased by 80 examples, which was improvement of 9.25%. When model was re-used, it was immediately after those 350 examples. It would suggest lowering the number and drift could be reported even sooner, but with fewer examples in warning referees tended to report drift and change the model when there were false alarms.

We were interested what would be the performance if, in the case of SEA Concepts data, the referee would choose exactly the models that were learnt on

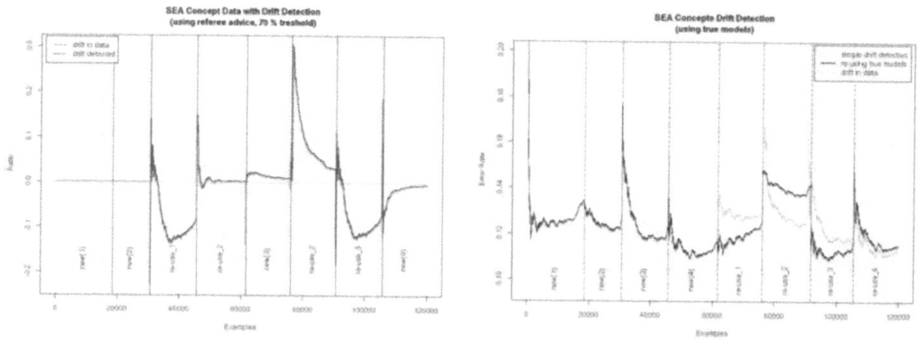

Fig. 4. (left) Logarithm of ratio between error-rates without and with re-using models on SEA Concepts. Curve above 0 is in favor of method with referees. (right) Comparison of error-rates with re-using true models and without re-using on SEA Concepts.

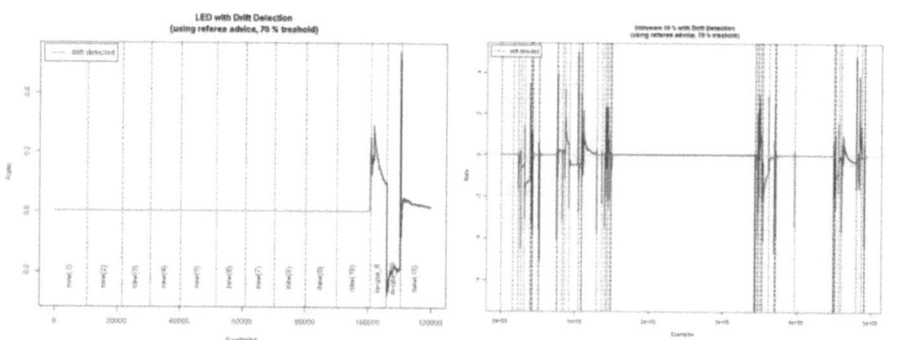

Fig. 5. Ratio between error-rates without and with re-using models on LED data set (left) and Intrusion (right). Above 0 is in favor of referees.

the same concepts in history. It should be mentioned that this experiment was conducted just because the set was artificial and the concepts and recurrence was known. In real data sets this kind of learning is impossible to do so. We manually re-used the historical concepts e.g. first model for fifth concept etc. On figure 4 (right) we can see that the performance also was not ideal. Slow continual increase in error-rate caused the warning to be reported much sooner and second model learnt from examples of fifth concept that were stored in short memory during the warning phase.

The figure 5 (left) shows the results of using proposed method on LED data. Both approaches (referee-advice and without re-using models) are same till the concept 11, where referee chooses model 6. As can be seen in data description, both concepts were generated with same number of attributes with drift; therefore the performance was better than without re-using any model. However, the model had increasing tendency in error rate and warning was reported very soon. The situation was similar to the one in experiment with true models in SEA Concepts. In this case new incorrect drift was detected, model 10 was re-used which caused decrease in accuracy. The actual drift after concept 10 was detected 1022 examples sooner, but the other true drift was then delayed 301 examples.

Running our method on data from KDD Cup gave us results captured on figure 5 (right). The set tend to have structure of many different-length groups of consecutive instances of the same class. Drifts occurred in the data because different types of attack, and therefore different protocols etc. used for the connection, were labeled with the same class, but also because normal connections had different properties. Those concepts were re-appearing in the data set making it suitable for the tests. Even though in most of the cases drifts were abrupt and quickly detected, some minor improvements were to be found.

4.3 Using Model Advice vs. Referee Advice

In this section we compare results obtained by our approach and those obtained by testing the accuracy of models during warning phase instead of asking referees. For re-using selection was the threshold set to approximately average performance of the models. We have to say it was not expected that referees would have better results. It is obvious that with the information about true label it is much easier to select proper model, but labels in real situations are obtained after delay while attributes of examples are available. Therefore this section shows how close or far is referee's results. As in re-using true models in concept 5 there was warning reported too early. But this time re-using of second model was not forced so new model was learnt from warning examples combining examples from fifth and sixth concept and therefore drifted very soon. Too

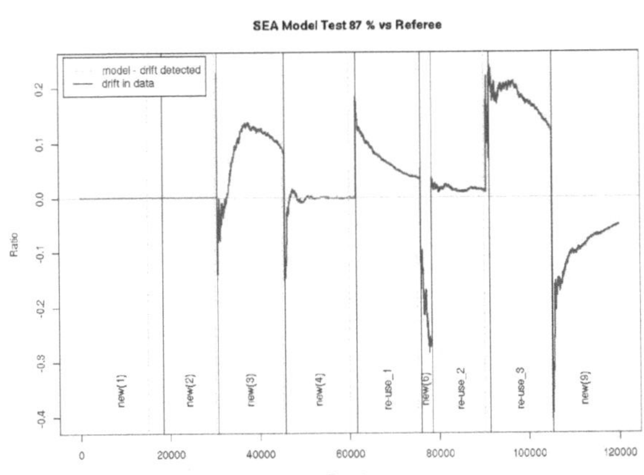

Fig. 6. Ratio between error-rates with model-advised and referee-advised re-using on SEA Concepts - above 0 is in favor of model-advised approach

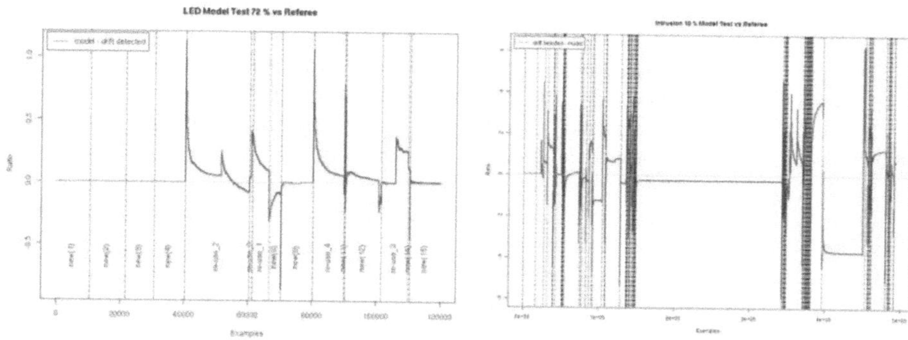

Fig. 7. Ratio between error-rates with model-advised and referee-advised re-using on LED data (left) and on Intrusion (right) - above 0 is in favor of model-advised approach

early warning occurred also at the end of concept 7. Otherwise model-advised approach was prevailing as expected. Comparison of these two approaches is illustrated on the figure 6.

Model-advised classifier also performed better on LED data (figure 7 on the left), as expected, with the exception in seventh concept, where there was data generated with same settings as in re-used concept 1. Nevertheless, re-using caused that non-existing drift was reported and new classifier was learnt in the middle of actual concept in data. Model-advised approach on Intrusion data set 7 (right) was not very successful. Despite of setting the threshold to 99.5 % drifts were reported too often. It resulted in needless changes of context and therefore downgrading the overall performance. Compare 64 drifts of simple drift detection to 372 of model-advised approach.

5 Conclusions

In this work, we introduce a new method for tracking recurrent concepts. The proposed method simultaneously learns two decision models, where the meta-learner characterizes the domain of applicability of the base model. This is the first work that explores a learning to learn technique to learn decision models able to self-improve, self-adapt, and able of predictive self-diagnosis. The system works online, processing each example once, relevant properties in the context of high-speed data streams.

Even though there was not great improvement on overall accuracy, the method can detect drift sooner when re-using previous learnt models. Nevertheless, there are still space for improvement and future work. Other types of classifiers or ensemble of classifiers could be used either as primary classifier or as meta-learners. We believe that future further study of the method could bring interesting results.

References

1. Gama, J., Fernandes, R., Rocha, R.: Decision Trees for Mining Data Streams. In: Intelligent Data Analysis, pp. 23–45. IOS Press, Amsterdam (2006)
2. Gama, J., Medas, P., Castillo, G., Rodrigues, P.: Learning with drift detection. In: Bazzan, A.L.C., Labidi, S. (eds.) SBIA 2004. LNCS (LNAI), vol. 3171, pp. 286–295. Springer, Heidelberg (2004)
3. Gama, J., Gaber, M.M. (eds.): Learning from Data Streams: Processing Techniques in Sensor Networks. Springer, Heidelberg (2007)
4. Katakis, I., Tsoumakas, G., Vlahavas, I.: An Ensemble of Classifiers for coping with Reurring Contexts in Data Streams. In: 18th European Conference on Artificial Intelligence. IOS Press, Patras (2008)
5. Kirkby, R.: Massive Online Analysis. University of Waikato, Hamilton, New Zealand (2007), `http://sourceforge.net/projects/moa-datastream/`
6. Lazarescu, M.: A Multi-resolution Learning Approach to Tracking Concept Drift and Recurrent Concepts. PRIS (2005)
7. Gaber, M., Gama, J., Ganguly, A., Omitaomu, O., Vatsavai, R.: Knowledge Discovery from Sensor Data. Taylor & Francis, Abington (2008)
8. Ramamurthy, S., Bhatnagar, R.: Tracking Recurrent Concept Drift in Streaming Data Using Ensemble Classifiers. In: Proc. of the Sixth International Conference on Machine Learning and Applications, pp. 404–409 (2007)
9. Seewald, A.K., Fürnkranz, J.: Grading Classifiers. Austrian Research Institute for Artificial Intelligence, OEFAI-TR-2001-01, Wien, Austria (2001)
10. Schlimmer, J.C., Granger Jr., R.H.: Incremental Learning from Noisy Data. Machine Learning 1, 317–354 (1986)
11. Stanley, K.O.: Learning concept drift with a committee of decision trees. Tech. Report UT-AI-TR-03-302, Department of Computer Sciences, University of Texas at Austin, USA (2003)
12. Nick Street, W., Kim, Y.: A streaming ensemble algorithm SEA for large-scale classification. In: Proc. seventh ACM SIGKDD international conference on Knowledge discovery and data mining, pp. 377–382. ACM Press, New York (2001)
13. Tsymbal, A.: The Problem of Concept Drift: Definitions and Related Work, `http://citeseer.ist.psu.edu/tsymbal04problem.html`
14. Wang, H., Fan, W., Yu, P., Han, J.: Mining concept-drifting data streams using ensemble classifiers. In: Proc. KDD (2003)
15. Witten, I.H., Frank, E.: Data Mining: Practical Machine Learning Tools and Techniques With Java Implementations. Morgan Kaufmann Publishers, San Francisco (1999)
16. Yang, Y., Wu, X., Zhu, X.: Mining in Anticipation for Concept Change: Proactive-Reactive Prediction in Data Streams. In: Proc. 11th ACM SIGKDD International Conference on Knowledge Discovery and Data Mining, pp. 710–715 (2005)
17. Stolfo, S., Fan, W., Lee, W., Prodromidis, A., Chan, P.: Cost-based Modeling for Fraud and Intrusion Detection, DARPA Information Survivability Conference, pp. 130–144. IEEE Computer Society Press, Los Alamitos (2000)

Detecting Errors in Foreign Trade Transactions: Dealing with Insufficient Data

Luis Torgo[1,2], Welma Pereira[1], and Carlos Soares[1,3]

[1] LIAAD-INESC Porto, Univ. of Porto, R. Ceuta, 118, 6., 4050-190 Porto, Portugal
[2] Faculdade de Ciências, University of Porto
[3] Faculdade de Economia, University of Porto
ltorgo@liaad.up.pt, welma.pereira@gmail.com, csoares@fep.up.pt
http://www.liaad.up.pt/{~ltorgo,~csoares}

Abstract. This paper describes a data mining approach to the problem of detecting erroneous foreign trade transactions in data collected by the Portuguese Institute of Statistics (INE). Erroneous transactions are a minority, but still they have an important impact on the official statistics produced by INE. Detecting these rare errors is a manual, time-consuming task, which is constrained by a limited amount of available resources (e.g. financial, human). These constraints are common to many other data analysis problems (e.g. fraud detection). Our previous work addresses this issue by producing a ranking of outlyingness that allows a better management of the available resources by allocating them to the most relevant cases. It is based on an adaptation of hierarchical clustering methods for outlier detection. However, the method cannot be applied to articles with a small number of transactions. In this paper, we complement the previous approach with some standard statistical methods for outlier detection for handling articles with few transactions. Our experiments clearly show its advantages in terms of the criteria outlined by INE for considering any method applicable to this business problem. The generality of the approach remains to be tested in other problems which share the same constraints (e.g. fraud detection).

1 Introduction

Portuguese companies have to declare their transactions with other EU countries on a monthly basis. The Portuguese Institute of Statistics (INE) collects data about the transactions of Portuguese companies with other EU countries on a monthly basis. These data typically contain errors, with various causes (e.g. typing errors). Due to the impact of these errors on official statistics, the data has to be manually inspected with the goal of trying to detect and correct them. This paper describes a data mining approach to help in this detection task. The objective is to identify the transactions that are most likely to contain errors. The selected transactions will then be manually analyzed by specialized staff and corrected if an error really exists.

Informally, the task is to detect transactions whose values are abnormal when compared to the other transactions of the same type of articles (products). This

L. Seabra Lopes et al. (Eds.): EPIA 2009, LNAI 5816, pp. 435–446, 2009.

task can be cast as an outlier detection problem. However, it has an important characteristic which significantly differentiates it from basic outlier detection problems: it is constrained by a limited amount of expensive human resources, whose availability varies at different moments.

Outlier detection is a well studied topic (e.g. [1]). Different approaches have been followed for this task. Distribution-based approaches (e.g. [2]) assume a certain parametric distribution of the data and signal outliers as observations that deviate from this distribution. The effectiveness of these approaches is highly dependent on how closely the distribution of the data follows the one assumed by the method (e.g. Gaussian). Knorr and Ng [3] introduced distance-based outlier detection methods. These approaches generalize several notions of distribution-based methods but still suffer from several problems, namely when the density of the data points varies (e.g. [4]). Breunig and colleagues [5,4] defined density-based local outliers that handle this type of outliers. They are typically more appropriate than the previous ones for data with a complex distribution structure. The key idea of their work is that the notion of outlier should be "local" in the sense that the outlier status of any observation should be determined by the clustering structure in a bounded neighborhood of the observation.

Many of the existent outlier detection methods provide yes/no answers. For our application, this type of answers leads to sub-optimal decisions when it comes to manually inspecting the signaled cases. In effect, if the resources are limited we may well get more signals than what we can inspect and then we have to arbitrarily decide which cases to handle. In the work mentioned above [5,4], the authors defined the notion of Local Outlier Factor (LOF) for each observation, which assigns a level of outlierness to each observation. This naturally leads to the notion of outlier ranking, which, in our problem, allows the resources to be used on the top rank cases. This type of constraints is not particular of this application. Similar setups can be found in many other application areas, namely on fraud detection. Previous work on this problem has compared outlier detection methods, a decision tree induction algorithm and a clustering method [6]. The results obtained with the latter did not satisfy the minimum goals, and, thus, the approach was dropped. Loureiro *et. al.* [7] have investigated more thoroughly the use of clustering methods to address this problem, achieving a significant boost of the results. Torgo [8] has proposed an improvement of the method described in [7] to obtain degrees of outlyingness. Torgo and Soares [9] have recently applied this later methodology to the INE problem with good results. However, all the methods proposed earlier cannot be applied to articles with a small number of transactions. In this paper we extend this work by proposing a new form of handling the articles with a small number of transactions.

2 Background

2.1 The INTRASTAT Application

Transactions made by Portuguese companies with organizations from other EU countries are declared monthly to INE using the INTRASTAT form. Using this form, companies provide information about each transaction, like the article (item or product) ID, weight of the traded goods, total cost, etc.. At INE, these data are inserted into a database.

A problem with this process is that errors often occur in the process of filling forms. For instance, an incorrectly introduced item ID will associate a transaction with the wrong item. Therefore, when all of the transactions relative to a month have been entered into the database, they are manually verified with the aim of detecting and correcting as many errors as possible. In this search, the experts try to detect unusual values in the values that describe the transactions. Given that the number of transactions declared monthly is in the order of tens of thousands, this is a very costly process.

Besides kindly giving us 8 months of data, INE domain experts provided a few guidelines based on their experience with the problem. Namely,

- Among the different information provided by companies the cost per weight (Cost/Weight) item is the key attribute that they use to detect errors.
- Transactions should be analyzed by article, as different articles have significantly diverse ranges of acceptable values for Cost/Weight.
- If an article has less than 10 transactions all transactions are manually inspected.[1]

The general goal of this application is to use data mining for a better management of the resources involved in the inspection task. The system developed should be used monthly to automatically select a subset of the transactions for manual inspection. According to INE experts, to be acceptable such a system should select less than 50% of the transactions containing at least 90% of the errors. However, given that the available human resources are quite expensive and vary across different months, the smaller the number of selected transactions, the better, assuming that 90% of the errors are still detected. We will refer to the percentage of selected transactions by any method as %S, and the corresponding percentage of detected errors as the recall (%R) of the method. As we have 8 months of available data, this means that all candidate methods will be characterized by 8 pairs of %S and %R values. All values of %S should be below 50% and the corresponding values of %R above 90% to meet the operational requirements of INE.

One important issue concerning the evaluation of the results is that only a proportion of the transactions in the data provided have been manually inspected by INE experts. This means that if a transaction is flagged as an error, it is definitely an error. However, if the transaction is not flagged as an error it may have been inspected and found correct or it was simply not inspected and thus can actually be an error or not. In spite of this limitation of the available data, we can use this error information to evaluate the recall (%R) of any method. In effect, given a set of transactions that are selected by any method for manual inspection in a given month, we can calculate the recall as the percentage of the total number of flagged errors for that month that are contained on this set.

[1] Throughout the rest of the paper we will refer to these as the infrequent articles.

2.2 Previous Results

In [6] a first approach to this problem was described. The data used in that study contained transactions of five months in 1998. Four very different methods were applied. Two come from statistics and are univariate techniques: box plot [10] and Fisher's clustering algorithm [11]. The third one, Knorr & Ng's cell-based algorithm [3], is an outlier detection algorithm which, despite being a multivariate method, was used only on the Cost/Weight attribute. The last is C5.0 [12], a multivariate technique for the induction of decision trees. In this study, C5.0 obtained the best results, namely detecting 90% of the errors by inspecting 40% of the transactions. The latest approach was the only that provided a ranking of the transactions, and, thus, enabled the selection of the most suspicious transactions to be manually inspected depending on the available resources.

Loureiro *et. al* [7] have proposed a new outlier detection method based on the outcome of agglomerative hierarchical clustering methods and applied it to this problem. This approach used the size of the resulting clusters as indicators of the presence of outliers. The basic assumption was that outlier observations, being observations with unusual values, would be distant (in terms of the metric used for clustering) from the "normal" and more frequent observations, and therefore would be isolated in smaller clusters. These authors have explored several settings concerning the clustering process and experimentally evaluated them on the INTRASTAT problem. The best setup met the operational requirements of INE by detecting 94.1% of the errors on 32.7% of the transactions. In spite of this excellent result, the main drawback of this approach is that it simpy classifies each transaction as suspect or not. Thus, the set of selected transactions cannot be adapted to the inspection resources available. For instance, it may be the case that in a given month, there are not enough resources to inspect 32.7% of the transactions. In this case, we face the un-guided task of deciding which of these transactions will be inspected.

Torgo and Soares [9] have recently described a first approach to this resources constraint by applying an outlier ranking method [8], OF_H, to this problem. This method achieved competitive results when compared to a state of the art outlier ranking method like LOF ([4]), and satisfied the criteria established by INE. In this paper we try to improve these results even further.

3 Our Proposal

All previous approaches to this application have followed the guidelines given by the INE experts, in particular, that transactions of infrequent articles (i.e. with less than 10 transactions) are all manually inspected (Section 2.1). The reason for this recommendation is that it is difficult to automatically determine what is the acceptable range of values and, thus, what is an abnormal value.

However, the cost incurred by this strategy is very high. Table 1 presents the percentage of selected transactions (%S) in each of the 8 available months, by simply using this INE policy. Row %R reports the correspondent percentage of errors detected by this strategy, while in row N_R we indicate the concrete

Table 1. The effort associated with selecting all transaction of infrequent articles

	Jan/1998	Feb/1998	Mar/1998	May/1998	Jun/1998	Aug/1998	Sep/1998	Oct/1998
%S	35.7	30.8	27.7	24.5	32	21.0	17.0	22.5
%R	35.4	40.4	38.7	29.7	37	30.8	25.4	27.9
N_R	28	44	58	47	64	40	48	72

number of errors that are found. Table 1 shows that this automatic selection strategy immediately imposes a large cost in terms of %S with results in terms of recall that are far from the target 90%. In effect, given that INE requires that the inspection effort should be less than 50% for a method to be acceptable, we see that in several months we already spend around 30% of this effort by simply including all transactions of infrequent articles. This means that there are lots of articles on these conditions, i.e. with less than 10 transactions per month. This motivates our decision to investigate approaches to replace this INE policy. Here, we propose methods to automatically process these infrequent articles and show that, in combination with our previous approach, they produce better results.

The main hypothesis is that it is possible to eliminate a significant amount of transactions of infrequent articles in an automatic and statistically grounded way. The resources that are saved in this way, can be used to inspect suspicious transactions that are detected in the remaining articles, which would, otherwise, not be inspected. The main difficulty we face is the fact that we have to make decisions based on very small amount of information. In effect, for these infrequent articles we have to decide whether a value is or not "suspicious" based on a sample of 10 or less values. Still, we claim that it must be possible to do better than just inspecting all of them.

We maintain the approach of handling the transactions of each article differently, depending on their number. If it is an infrequent article (less than 10 transactions) instead of automatically sending the transactions for manual inspection we propose some methods described in Section 3.1; if it is not an infrequent article we apply the outlier ranking method used in [9] that we describe in Section 3.2.

3.1 Handling Infrequent Articles

Methods for handling infrequent articles are constrained by the lack of data for these articles, which means that they must be simple. Therefore, we resort to simple univariate statistics heuristics. In this work, we used the box-plot rule that can be used to detect outliers in a continuous variable with a normal distribution.[2] This rule declares a value as an outlier if it is outside the interval

$$[Q_1 - k \times IQR \cdots Q_3 + k \times IQR] \tag{1}$$

[2] This is a reasonable assumption for the cost per weight of the same article.

where Q_1 (Q_3) is the first (third) quartile of the variable, IQR is the interquartile range ($= Q_3 - Q_1$), and k is a constant (typically 1.5). The variable that we focus on is the Cost/Weight, which is the most informative according to the experts.

The small amounts of data reduces the power of the test (i.e., its ability to detect outliers).[3] This means that there is a compromise between finding errors in infrequent articles and reallocating resources to the remaining articles. Therefore, we have only applied the boxplot rule to infrequent articles with at least 5 transactions (i.e. values). If there are less than 5 transactions, they are all sent for inspection. Secondly, in order to try to avoid missing too many errors we have used a rather strict value of k, namely 0.0625 ($= 1.5/24$). This threshold will lead to selecting as potential outliers many of the values that would be ignored with more typical thresholds (e.g. 1.5), thus incurring a smaller risk of missing some of the flagged errors. In spite of these cautious settings we will see that this strategy has a strong impact on the number of transactions that are automatically selected for inspection. In our experiments we will call this the box plot (BP) method.

Additionally, we have created a variant of the BP method that decreases the number of infrequent articles. In the first month, it is equal to the BP method. In subsequent months, the data of infrequent articles is extended with data from previous months, referred to as *incremental dataset*. Our approach is then applied to the incremental dataset of each of those articles. This means that, if the number of transactions in the incremental dataset of a given infrequent article is 10 or more, it is handled as a frequent article. Otherwise, it continues to be handled as an infrequent article, as explained earlier.

This variant takes advantage of older data to generate more robust statistics, if the incremental dataset has less than 10 transactions. If the incremental dataset has 10 or more transactions, then it is possible to apply the more complex method for frequent articles.

We will call this the incremental box plot method (BP_{inc}). We should remark that in a real world application of this method we should limit the use of this past information. In effect, its justification lies on the assumption that the distribution of the "normal" values for the Cost/Weight attribute remains constant over time. While this is a reasonable assumption for most articles and for a period of 8 months, it may be inadequate for larger periods of time or for particular articles with temporary or permanent price volatility. In these cases a sliding window approach should probably be used instead.

3.2 Handling Frequent Articles

For articles with more data available we may use a more data-intensive approach to outlier detection. Clustering algorithms can be used to identify outliers as a side effect of the clustering process. In this paper we use an approach that takes advantage of the dendrogram generated by hierarchical clustering methods to produce a ranking of outlyingness. This approach was first described in [8].

---

[3] If the number of values is less than 3, the method is not even applicable.

Agglomerative hierarchical clustering methods proceed in an iterative fashion by merging two of the current groups (which initially are formed by single observations) based on some criterion that is related to their proximity. This decision is taken locally, that is for each pair of groups, and takes into account the density of these two groups only. This merging process results in a tree-based structure usually known as a dendrogram. The merging step is guided by the information contained in the distance matrix of all available data. Several methods can be used to select the two groups to be merged at each stage. Contrary to other clustering approaches, hierarchical methods do not require a cluster initialization process that would inevitably spread the outliers across many different clusters thus probably leading to a rather unstable approach.

Informally, the idea behind this outlier detection approach is to use the height (in the dendrogram) at which any observation is merged into a group of observations as an indicator of its outlyingness. If an observation is really an outlier this should only occur at later stages of the merging process, that is the observation should be merged at a higher level than "normal" observations because it is very different from them and thus there is a "strong resistance" to joining their group. Formally, whenever the clustering algorithm decides to merge a group of observations g_s with another group g_l at iteration i of the merging process, where $|g_s| < |g_l|$, we set the outlier factor of the members of these groups as,

$$of_i(x) = \begin{cases} \left(1 - \frac{|g_s|}{N}\right) \times \frac{i}{N} & \text{if } x \in g_s \wedge |g_s| < t \\ 0 & \text{otherwise} \end{cases} \tag{2}$$

where $|g_s|$ is the cardinality of the smallest group, g_s, t is a threshold that indicates the number of observations above which a group can not be regarded as a set of outliers for the data set, i is the step where the merge occurs, and N is the data set size.

Any observation can belong to several groups along its upward path through the dendrogram. As such, it will probably get several of these scores at different levels. These different values are in effect related to the issue of local and global outliers [8]. An observation that at a certain step gets a high score, may well have much smaller values up in the hierarchy. This happens frequently with local outliers. Until they are merged with their larger neighborhood they are regarded as outliers. After the merge, i.e. at a more global perspective, their diversity is diluted in the large cluster to which they now belong and thus they stop getting large scores. Still, these cases are outliers (local outliers), and thus they should get an overall large outlyingness score. In order to cope with these different types of outliers we set the outlyingness factor of any observation as the maximum $of_i()$ score it got along its path through the dendrogram. This means that the outlyingness factor of an observation is given by,

$$OF_H(x) = \max_i \; of_i(x) \tag{3}$$

One of the main advantages of this method is that we can use a standard hierarchical clustering algorithm to obtain the OF_H values without any additional computational cost. Here, we use a standard algorithm, with a time complexity of $O(N^2)$ and a space complexity of $O(N)$ [13]. We use the *hclust()* function of the statistical software environment R [14]. This function includes in its output a matrix (called **merge**) that can be used to easily obtain the necessary values for calculating directly the value of OF_H according to Equations 2 and 3.

4 Experimental Evaluation

In our experimental evaluation we address 3 main questions: i) the impact of our proposal to handle infrequent articles; ii) the overall performance of our error detection methodology when compared to state of the art competitors; and iii) the minimal effort that is required by our methods to attain the operational criteria required by INE (i.e. 90% recall).

We use the same experimental methodology as in previous studies with this data: we handle each month and article in turn, and we assess performance (i.e., the recall, %R, achieved for a certain inspection effort, %S, for each month), based on the errors identified by INE experts, as discussed earlier.

4.1 Different Approaches to Infrequent Articles

Our first experiments were designed to evaluate the impact of the different alternative approaches to handle infrequent articles that were described in Section 3.1.

Table 2 compares the default INE policy with the BP method. As you may confirm, this method achieves practically the same recall level, using considerably less inspection resources. This clearly indicates its advantage over the default INE policy and, moreover, it reduces the inspection effort dedicated to infrequent articles, thus enabling the inspection of more suspicious transactions from frequent articles.

Next, we evaluate the BP_{inc} method, which uses transactions from previous months to increase the amount of data available, as described earlier. For fairness, we compare BP_{INC} with the default policy of INE only on those articles that remain infrequent after being extended with data from previous months. Table 3 shows the results of this comparison. Again we observe a considerable decrease in the inspection effort with a small impact in terms of recall.

Table 2. The results of the BP method

		Jan/1998	Feb/1998	Mar/1998	May/1998	Jun/1998	Aug/1998	Sep/1998	Oct/1998
%S	*INE*	35.7	30.8	27.7	24.5	32	21.0	17.0	22.5
	BP	25.3	21.5	19.3	16.8	22.4	13.8	10.9	15.2
%R	*INE*	35.4	40.4	38.7	29.7	37	30.8	25.4	27.9
	BP	35.4	39.4	36.7	28.5	35.8	30.0	24.9	27.5
N_R	*INE*	28	44	58	47	64	40	48	72
	BP	28	43	55	45	62	39	47	71

Table 3. The results of the BP_{inc} method

		Jan/1998	Feb/1998	Mar/1998	May/1998	Jun/1998	Aug/1998	Sep/1998	Oct/1998
%S	INE_{inc}	35.7	18.0	11.1	7.6	6.3	4.1	2.6	2.5
	BP_{inc}	25.3	11.8	6.8	4.8	3.9	2.2	1.3	1.5
%R	INE_{inc}	35.4	26.6	21.3	12.7	9.2	6.9	5.3	4.7
	BP_{inc}	35.4	22.9	18.7	11.4	8.1	6.9	5.3	3.9
N_R	INE_{inc}	28	29	32	20	16	9	10	12
	BP_{inc}	28	25	28	18	14	9	10	10

In summary, both our proposals show a clear advantage over the default INE policy of handling infrequent articles, by providing a similar recall with a significantly lower inspection effort.

4.2 Overall Comparison of Outlier Ranking Methods

In this section, we compare two outlier ranking (OR) methods to detect errors in frequent articles, in combination with the BP method on infrequent articles. The first method is the clustering-based method described earlier and the second is a state of the art competitor that was also used in the work by Torgo and Soares [9], LOF [4]. Namely, we have used the implementation of LOF that is available in R on package **dprep** [15].

Both OR methods were only applied on articles with more than 10 transactions. As they both produce rankings of the transactions, we can select the amount of inspection effort to use in accordance to our current resources constraints. Given INE requirements that this should not be above 50% of the transactions in each month, we have arbitrarily selected selected 4 effort levels to present our results: 35%, 40%, 45% and 50% of the transactions. For each of these %S levels we have calculated the corresponding recall scores (%R) achieved by each competitor. We have tried out 14 variants of their parameters and the results represent the best score obtained by each competitor. For infrequent articles we have used our BP method.

The results of this comparative experiments are shown in Figure 1. The two variants are denoted by OF_H and LOF, respectively. The four points for both alternatives represent the four previously mentioned working points in terms of $\%S$. Still, we should recall that both methods would be better represented by lines as any other working points could have been selected. Some of the points are not shown on some graphs because the respective method achieved a very poor score that is outside of the used axes limits.

In the graphs of results for each month we also plot the $\%S$ and $\%R$ values of the method described in [7], which is denoted in the graphs as "LTS04". This method is not an outlier ranking algorithm. It simply outputs the transactions it judges as being outliers, which leads to a pair of $\%S$ and $\%R$ values. In this case the user is not able to adjust the $\%S$ value to the available resources. Fortunately, in none of the testing months the 50% limit of selected transactions was surpassed but with this type of methods there is no such guarantee in general. Additionally,

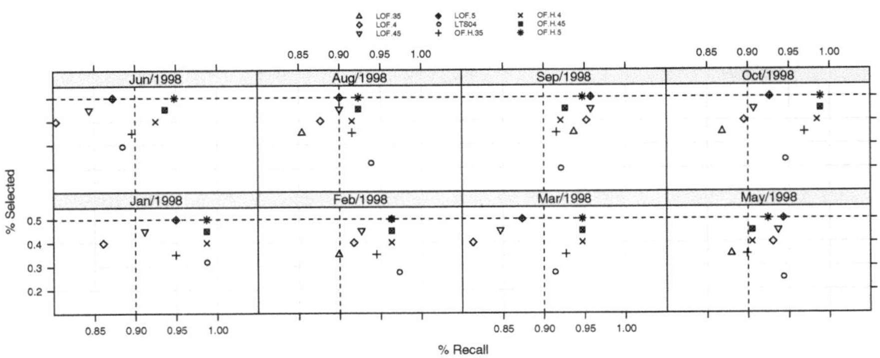

Fig. 1. The results of the comparative experiments on the INTRASTAT data

in those months where the available resources are not sufficient to analyze all the transactions selected, the experts must decide which ones to let aside. All graphs have two dotted lines indicating the experts requirements (at least 90% recall and at most 50% selected transactions).

The results of these experiments confirm that the clustering-based outlier ranking method is quite competitive with the state of the art. With the exception of two months (May and September) it consistently outperforms LOF. Moreover, it is the only method that always complies with INE operational criteria. Compared to the "LTS04" method [7], both OF_H and LOF loose a few times in terms of achieving the same $\%R$ for the same level of $\%S$. Still, we should recall that "LTS04" provides no flexibility in terms of available human resources and thus it can happen (as for instance in Jun/1998) that the solution provided by this method does not satisfy the objectives of the experts or even that it is not feasible because it requires too many resources.

4.3 Minimum Required Effort for Satisfying the Recall Goal

In this section we address the issue of which is the minimum inspection effort that is required to achieve a value of 90% of recall. This score should always be below 50%, for any method to be applicable.

In these experiments we have considered both LOF and the OF_H method, in conjunction with the 3 alternative ways of handling the infrequent articles.

The results concerning this minimum effort levels are given in Figure 2. As we may confirm, independently of the infrequent articles method, the OF_H variants always achieve 90% of recall with less than 50% of effort. The same is not true for the LOF variants in March and June. This experiment also reveals the advantages of our methods for handling infrequent articles, which generally lead to better overall results. Namely, it is worth noting that with our methods in conjunction with OF_H, we achieve a recall of 90% with an effort around 30%,

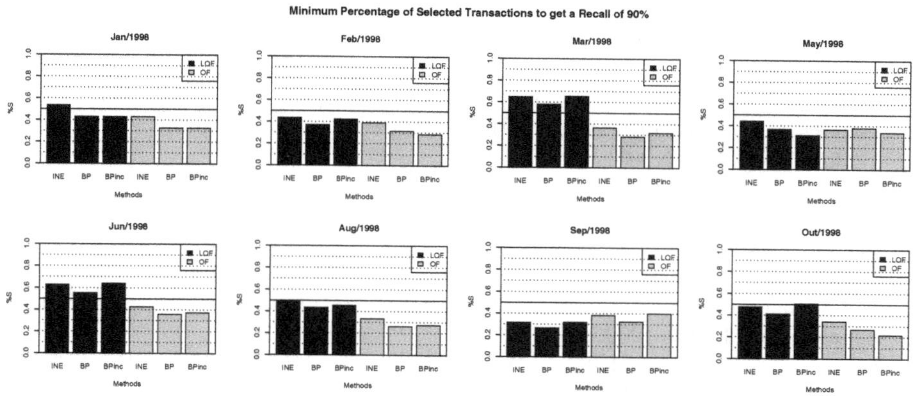

Fig. 2. Comparison between our method and *LOF*

in general. With respect to the two alternative proposals (BP and BP_{inc}) the results are quite similar with no clear winner.

5 Conclusions

In many outlier and fraud detection problems there are situations in which there is plenty of data, but there are others where it is scarse (e.g., the number of credit card transactions of a new customer of a bank). In this paper, we extend previous work by proposing an approach that addresses the issue of outlier detection with scarse data. It involves the integration of simple statistical tests, used on small amounts of data, and a more complex outlier ranking method, used when sufficient data are available. The result is a method that can cope with variable resources for the necessary inspection phases. A few variations of the new approach were tested on the problem of detecting errors in foreign trade transaction forms of Portuguese companies. However, the approach is general and can be applied in different problems.

Compared to previous approaches to this problem, this work has introduced new forms of handling articles with few transactions. Our experiments have clearly shown their advantage when compared to the previous methods. The latter are based on domain knowledge provided by experts that all transactions of infrequent articles should be analyzed. Our results contradict this, showing that it is possible to automate, at least partially, the processing of these articles.

Additionally, our experiments have shown the competitiveness of our clustering-based outlier ranking methodology when compared to other state of the art methods. Moreover, the proposal always complies with the operational requirements of INE and provides the desirable flexibility in terms of management of the available human inspection resources.

Acknowledgements. This work was partially supported by FCT projects oRANKI (PTDC/EIA/68322/2006) and Rank! (PTDC/EIA/81178/2006).

References

1. Hodge, V., Austin, J.: A survey of outlier detection methodologies. Artificial Intelligence Review 22, 85–126 (2004)
2. Hawkins, D.M.: Identification of Outliers. Chapman and Hall, 11 New Fetter Lane, London EC4P 4EE (1980)
3. Knorr, E.M., Ng, R.T.: Algorithms for mining distance-based outliers in large datasets. In: Proceedings of 24rd International Conference on Very Large Data Bases (VLDB 1998), pp. 392–403. Morgan Kaufmann, San Francisco (1998)
4. Breunig, M.M., Kriegel, H.P., Ng, R., Sander, J.: Lof: Identifying density-based local outliers. In: Proceedings of ACM SIGMOD 2000 International Conference on Management of Data (2000)
5. Breunig, M.M., Kriegel, H.-P., Ng, R.T., Sander, J.: OPTICS-OF: Identifying local outliers. In: Żytkow, J.M., Rauch, J. (eds.) PKDD 1999. LNCS (LNAI), vol. 1704, pp. 262–270. Springer, Heidelberg (1999)
6. Soares, C., Brazdil, P., Costa, J., Cortez, V., Carvalho, A.: Error detection in foreign trade data using statistical and machine learning methods. In: Mackin, N. (ed.) Proc. of the 3rd International Conference on the Practical Applications of Knowledge Discovery and Data Mining, pp. 183–188 (1999)
7. Loureiro, A., Torgo, L., Soares, C.: Outlier detection using clustering methods: a data cleaning application. In: Malerba, D., May, M. (eds.) Proceedings of KDNet Symposium on Knowledge-based Systems for the Public Sector (2004)
8. Torgo, L.: Resource-bounded fraud detection. In: Neves, J., Santos, M.F., Machado, J.M. (eds.) EPIA 2007. LNCS (LNAI), vol. 4874, pp. 449–460. Springer, Heidelberg (2007)
9. Torgo, L., Soares, C.: Resource-bounded outlier detection using clustering methods. In: Data Mining for Business Applications. IOS Press, Amsterdam (to appear 2009)
10. Milton, J.S., McTeer, P.M., Corbet, J.J.: Introduction to Statistics. McGraw-Hill, New York (1997)
11. Fisher, W.D.: On grouping for maximum homogeneity. Journal of the American Statistical Association 53, 789–798 (1958)
12. Quinlan, R.: C5.0: An Informal Tutorial. RuleQuest (1998), `http://www.rulequest.com/see5-unix.html`
13. Murtagh, F.: Complexities of hierarchic clustering algorithms: state of the art. Computational Statistics Quarterly 1, 101–113 (1984)
14. R Development Core Team. R: A Language and Environment for Statistical Computing. R Foundation for Statistical Computing (2008) ISBN 3-900051-07-0
15. Acuna, E., members of the CASTLE group: dprep: Data preprocessing and visualization functions for classification, R package version 2.0 (2008)

Chapter 9

MASTA – Multi-Agent Systems: Theory and Applications

Modeling Autonomous Adaptive Agents with Functional Language for Simulations

Richárd Legéndi, László Gulyás, Rajmund Bocsi, and Tamás Máhr

AITIA International Inc.,
Czetz János utca 48–50 1039 Budapest, Hungary
`{rlegendi,lgulyas,rbocsi,tmahr}@aitia.ai`
`http://mass.aitia.ai`

Abstract. The basic concept of agent-based modeling is to create adaptive agents to operate in a changing environment. Agents make autonomous decisions and modify their environment through continuous interactions. The Functional Agent-Based Language for Simulations (FABLES) is a special purpose language for ABM that is intended to reduce programming skills required to create simulations. The aim of FABLES is to allow modelers to focus on modeling, and not on programming. This paper provides an overview of FABLES, explaining the traits and the design concepts of this hybrid language that merges features of object-oriented, functional and procedural languages to provide flexibility in model design. To demonstrate some of these issues, we describe modeling with FABLES via the popular El Farol Bar problem from a user perspective, by means of example.

Keywords: Functional programming, agent-based simulations, multi-formalism, El Farol Bar problem.

1 Introduction

Creating agent-based models is quite a challenging task. It requires considerable knowledge in the abstraction of the analyzed real-world phenomena (*modeling*), and expert skills in at least one programming language as well. Without a deep insight in a proper programming language, the modeler is not capable to implement the model as desired, and it may not behave as expected. Solving these issues usually consumes a lot of resources and requires a great effort.

ABM is an interesting field for social scientists, economists and sociologists as well [1,2]. It is a great computational model to find emergent behaviour that propagates from lower (micro) level interactions to higher (macro) level regularities in the formalized phenomena. The method simulates individuals (connected autonomous adaptive agents) in the examined system [3,4]. Accordingly, the model of the El Farol Bar Problem [5], as we discuss in this paper, was also created to investigate autonomous individuals with bounded rationality in economics.

Researchers interested in such problems usually do not possess the necessary programming skills. As an alternative way, they may use the help of a technical

L. Seabra Lopes et al. (Eds.): EPIA 2009, LNAI 5816, pp. 449–460, 2009.

expert, but since the scientist's cognitive model of the simulation is very likely to differ from the programmer's cognitive model, it could lead to several pitfalls – and the communication between the partners requires exceptional care.

FABLES was specially designed to require minimal programming skills, as its formalism is similar to the mathematical formalism used in publications in the subject. It is intended to facilitate the concise and efficient definition of agent-based models. It combines the strengths of functional and imperative programming with object-oriented paradigms, providing unique means to implement agent-based simulations.

1.1 Motivation

The main motivation behind FABLES was that the recent tools for agent-based simulations are mostly too complex for social scientists. Various software tools and modeling environments already exist to support modelers. However, some of these tools are only application programming libraries and the users are forced to learn the corresponding programming languages before they could be used effectively (e.g. Java in the case of Repast J [6], Objective-C for Swarm [7]).

On the other hand, there are several agent-based modeling environments (like NetLogo [8] and AnyLogic [9]). These tools offer easy-to-use interface commonly allowing graphical model building, however, without extending the functionalities of the environment (i.e. writing some parts of the simulation outside of the simulation environment and import them as external resources) their usage may limit the 'space' of possible simulations.

Most recent tools allow full control over the simulation with visual model building (Repast Simphony [10], metaABM [11]), eliminating the dependency on a programming language. They provide a natural way to construct simulations by exploiting the opportunities of graphical model building.

With FABLES, we have chosen a different approach. We didn't want to eliminate the process of model implementation – we believe the description of the model should have a precise semantic to reflect the cognitive model of the researcher. The formalism used for model description should be close to the mathematical formalism because it is natural for the scientists. However, we tried to reduce the efforts required to perform any other side tasks with automatised components (like several wizard dialogs to create visualization for the model).

Our primary goal with FABLES was to create a language that:

- requires minimal programming skills,
- is able to describe the model focusing on the nature of the model, and leaves the implementation to the compiler,
- is general enough to accommodate possibly any agent-based model, but should focus on the common techniques and methods,
- supports the creation, observation and control of simulations with the help of interactive wizards,
- has a formalism similar to the mathematical formalism used in publications related to agent-based modeling. In these papers there's no space to publish algorithms and thus models are described by formulas and quantors.

We have chosen a basically functional language, because the syntax is close to the formalism of mathematical functions. To be able to control the simulation flow we allow sequential execution in specific parts of the model. The user can create special structures, *schedules*, that are used to define the events and their dispatched order. In addition, to describe agents in the model we introduced *classes*. With classes one can specify both the attributes and behaviour of the agents.

2 The El Farol Bar Problem

In this section we introduce the El Farol Bar problem [5] that is used in the article to discuss language concepts of FABLES. We created the implementation of the model based on the NetLogo version [14], which may give a good opportunity to compare the results[1]. This model is basically simple, but it is complex enough to demonstrate the work-flow with FABLES, and it provides a good possibility to show how the user may create agent-based simulations within this environment.

In the center of the problem is a popular bar in Santa Fé that is regularly visited by the workers of the Santa Fé Institute. There is a fixed population ($N = 100$), and at every Thursday each worker decides independently to either visit the bar with Irish music or stay at home.

Unfortunately, the bar is a too small and the atmosphere is relaxing only if not too many people shows up. In the original problem, if less than the 60% of the population goes to the bar, they will enjoy their stay there. If more than 60% of the population visits the bar, they will have a worse time due to overcrowdedness than if they stayed home. Agents have to decide about their actions at the same time simultaneously, and they do not know anything about the other agents' opinions. Hence they cannot wait and see if it is worth visiting the bar.

One of the aspects of the problem is that there is no deterministic pure strategy for the agents: they have to use mixed strategies. If each agent use the same deterministic strategy pattern and decide in the same way, it would certainly mean they do the same actions as the others and come to the same bad decision. For instance, if a strategy implies that the bar will not be crowded, everyone (following the same strategy) goes to the bar thus it becomes crowded. Otherwise, if the strategy implies that the bar will be crowded, nobody visits the bar thus it remains empty.

To solve this problem, we can supply agents with a limited personal memory to store the results of the used strategy of the past few weeks. Using this memory agents can develop different strategy patterns and adapt to each other, giving the possibility to maximize the results of their efforts.

The fact that Yi-Cheng Zhang and Damien Challet conceived Minority Games[2] (players who decide to be on the side that is in minority win) from this

[1] The full source code of the implemented FABLES model can be downloaded from the MASS Model Library at `http://mass.aitia.ai/downloads/model-lib`

[2] See `http://www.unifr.ch/econophysics/minority` for detailed information about research on minority games.

model, and that there are mathematical versions available in [12] and [13] makes this small model even more interesting. Fogel et al. also built a version of this model using a genetic algorithm [15], and Duncan describes the model in the context of reinforcement learning [16]. The reference implementation of the model was used to investigate if there is a connection between the agents' computational efforts and the bar attendance level [17].

3 Modeling with FABLES

There are several different implementation strategies for ABM [18]. In the following sections we are going to build up the model as follows:

1. The modeler specifies global properties of the model. These may be parameters, variables, global relations (facts), etc. specified in a declarative way.
2. The modeler specifies the basic structure of the agents used in the simulation, including their own local properties (variables, behavioral functions, etc.). Agents are considered independent objects, hence they can be defined with the use of classes.
3. The model dynamics and agent interactions may be specified with the use of schedules. FABLES uses the discrete time, discrete event paradigm for its scheduler, and to allow the user to implement action sequences.
4. The creation of visual components and charting is performed with automated tools. The initialization and execution of the model is performed in an enhanced version of the Repast J interface, featuring:
   - easy to use interface allowing simple initialization and customization of the model,
   - direct point and click activation of functions for observation and debugging reasons,
   - automated integration of charts, and
   - video recording capabilities and direct export of chart data to CSV files.

3.1 Basic Structure of the Model

Parameters. The first step is to create a FABLES model. The syntax is similar to the class definitions of other programming languages: it may contain constants, variables, functions, agent definitions (other classes), etc. We define our model *ElFarol* with the **model** keyword and with some global parameters:

Listing 1. Basic Components

```
model ElFarol {
  param numberOfAgents = 100, overcrowdingThreshold = 60
           memorySize = 5, numberOfStrategies = 10 ;
};
```

Parameters are defined with the **param** keyword. They are constant expressions, but their value may be altered before model initialization. In this case, we have defined *numberOfAgents* to specify the number of agent instances during the simulation run. The parameter *overcrowdingThreshold* declares the threshold value for the occupancy in the bar. Moreover, we define *memorySize* to denote how many preceding weeks agents can remember, and *numberOfStrategies* to specify how many strategies they can use.

Variables. In FABLES, we consider simulations as state-transitions. The state of the simulation is the state of the model and the state of its components (agents). We have introduced variables into the language to make it convenient to handle these states.

In the El Farol model, we keep track of the last few weeks' history of occupancy, to allow agents to determine their best strategy. To specify this history, we introduce a new variable with the **var** keyword:

Listing 2. Variable definition

```
var history ;
```

The modeler is not required to declare types since they can be inferred from assignments. By sorting out redundant type definitions, we believe the syntax of the language becomes extremely clear and simple for a beginner user.

Set and Sequence Expressions. In FABLES, both set and sequence types are native components of the language, and there is a huge set of built-in functions to give the opportunity to use them effectively. Basically, there are two kinds of sequences in FABLES: intervals and composite sequences.

Intervals may be defined with the [and] characters. The definition $[a..b]$ denotes a closed interval from a to b containing the elements $a, a+1, a+2, \ldots, b$. Composite sequences have a more general construction. We tried to make the syntax of the language as close to the formalism used in publications in the subject of ABM as possible. Composite sequences may be created with generators and a filter in the form of $[< element >:< iteration_1 >, < iteration_2 >, \ldots$ *when* $< condition >]$. For example, the expression of $[\ n^2 : n\ is\ [1..10]\ ]$ means a sequence of numbers in the form of n^2, where n denotes the numbers of $1, 2, \ldots, 10$.

Listing 3. Variable definition

```
var history := [ discreteUniformFromTo(1, numberOfAgents)
                 : i is [ 1 .. 2 * memorySize ] ] ;
```

In Listing 3 we defined a variable with a default value (its value is assigned to the variable at model initialization). Function *discreteUniformFromTo()* creates random numbers between 1 and *numberOfAgents*, consequently, the value of *history* is a sequence containing exactly *2*memorySize* random elements[3].

3.2 Defining Agents

In the FABLES code we can define a new agent structure with the **class** keyword. Just as the model, a class is also considered as an aggregate object: it may contain other constants, variables, functions, etc.

In the current implementation of the El Farol Bar model, each agent has a set of randomly initialized autoregressive models (sequences of AR coefficients) that are not fitted. We declare three variables for the agents: the sequence of *strategies*, the *best strategy* found so far, and a boolean flag that indicates its decision about *attendance*.

Listing 4. Agent definition

```
class Agent {
    var strategies ;
    var bestStrategy ;
    var attend := false ;
};
```

Agents are initialized with a random strategy pattern. A convenient way to handle this is to declare a global method that creates a series of random strategies:

Listing 5. Sequence construction

```
randomStrategies() =
[ [ uniform(-1, 1)  : j is [1..memorySize+1] ]
: i is [1..numberOfStrategies] ] ;
```

Listing 5 specifies a function that returns a sequence of strategies (a strategy is another sequence filled with random numbers created by the *uniform*() built-in function from the interval $(-1, 1)$, having a size of *memorySize*), containing *numberOfStrategies* elements. Therefore we can assign the following default values to the agent variables:

Listing 6. Default Values for Agent Variables

```
var strategies   := randomStrategies() ;
var bestStrategy := strategies(0) ;
```

This means that each agent is going to have a set of random strategies by default, and they declare the first strategy as their best strategy in the beginning

[3] In this sequence construction, i is a new loop variable that even might have been used to create the elements of the collection. In the current definition it was required only to specify the number of elements in the sequence.

(sequence constructions could be indexed from 0 to acquire the element at the specified position). To get the current attendance level of the bar, we define the following global *attendance()* function:

Listing 7. Attendance Level

```
attendance() = count( [ a.attend : a is Agent ] );
```

The function *count* returns the number of *true* elements in the specified collection (which contains the *attend* logical variable of all of the agents). Therefore its value equals to the current attendance of the bar.

Defining Agent Behavior. We have finished declaring the basic structure of the model, hence we can start implementing the behavioral definitions. In each simulation step agents have to rethink their beliefs by evaluating their best strategy depending on their current predictions. Therefore we declare function *updateStrategies*() for the agents.

In general, functional languages do not contain block structures, however, they offer the possibility to declare local definitions. In FABLES, local definitions may be declared for a given function with the use of the **where** keyword. Local definitions are constants that are visible only in the scope of the corresponding function and may be used to shorten the definition of the function.

In the following definition of *updateStrategies()* we define three local constants: *threshold*, *predictions* and *strategyPos*. The *threshold* local constant is used to make agents keep their actual strategy if the overall rating of the currently evaluated best one is lower than a specified value. The sequence *predictions* contains the sum of differences between the actual and the predicted attendance level (evaluated by the function *evaluateStrategy()* which is described soon) for each of the preceding weeks (as far as the agents' memory allows to determine it) for each of the agents' strategies. We consider the strategy with the minimal difference from its prediction as the best one, and *strategyPos* denotes its index in the strategies sequence.

Listing 8. Updating Agent Strategies

```
updateStrategies() =
  ( predictions( strategyPos ) < threshold ) =>
    bestStrategy := strategies( strategyPos )
  where (
    threshold = memorySize * numberOfAgents + 1 ,
    predictions = [ sum( [ evaluateStrategy( week, str )
                          : week is [1..memorySize] ] )
                  : str is strategies ],
    strategyPos = minPlace( predictions )
  ) ;
```

The body of the function is a conditional expression. In FABLES, the general form of creating conditional functions is $(< condition_1 >) => statement_1 \mid (< condition_2 >) => statement_2 \mid ... \mid otherwise => statement_N$ where some of the branches may be omitted, and it means *"If* $condition_1$ *is true then perform* $statement_1$. *Otherwise, if* $condition_2$ *is true then perform* $statement_2$, ... *If none of the above conditions were true then perform* $statement_N$*"*. The function *updateStrategies()* assigns a new value to *bestStrategy* if the prediction of the currently found best strategy is better than the specified threshold value (which is $memorySize * numberOfAgents + 1$).

We also have to define how the function *evaluateStrategy()* works. It determines the current prediction for the specified week and strategy:

Listing 9. Agent Strategy Evaluation

```
evaluateStrategy( week, str ) =
    abs( currentAttendance - prediction )
  where (
    currentAttendance = history( week - 1 ) ,
    prediction = predictAttendance( str ,
      [ history(j): j is [week..(week+memorySize-1)] ] )
  ) ;
```

The value returned by the function is the difference between the current attendance level and the prediction with the given strategy for the given week, as the *abs* function returns the absolute value of the difference. The value of *currentAttendance* is the weekth element in the history, and prediction is determined by the *predictAttendance* function that requires the current strategy and the list of attendance values preceding the weekth element of history. Formally, the function should return the following $p(t)$ prediction described in the original model:

$$p(t) = w(t) + \sum_{i=t-1}^{t-M} w(i) * a(i-1)$$

where t is the current time, $w(i)$ is the weight, $a(i)$ is the attendance level and M is the memory size. In the FABLES implementation of the model, strategies represent weights, so for a specified strategy and subsequence of history the implementation of the function is as follows:

Listing 10. Predicting Attendace

```
predictAttendance( strategy , subhistory ) =
    strategy(0) + sum( [ strategy(i) * subhistory(i-1)
                   : i is [1..memorySize] ] ) ;
```

3.3 Defining Simulation Events and Agent Actions

The final step to implement the simulation is to define the dynamics of the model. Describing the dynamics of a complex system often causes the modelers several problems. The situation is getting worse when it comes to agent interactions. In FABLES, there are basically two ways to describe simulation actions. One group of the actions have to be performed for proper initialization of the model, and the other group is used to describe the runtime dynamics of the simulation.

For initialization, we have *startUp* blocks both for agent classes and the model. The *startUp* block of the model is executed when the simulation is started; the *startUp* block of an agent is executed when the agent is created.

When the simulation is started, we have to instantiate the specified number of agents:

Listing 11. Model Initialization

```
startUp() {
    for each i in [1..numberOfAgents] do create Agent ;
};
```

When an agent is created, we have to call its *updateStrategies()* function to allow it to initialize its *bestStrategy* attribute.

Listing 12. Agent Initialization

```
class Agent {
    ...
    startUp() {
        updateStrategies() ;
    };
}
```

To describe the simulation dynamics, FABLES uses *schedules*. In general, schedules may be cyclic or acyclic, named or anonymous ones, and both the agents and models may have separate and multiple schedules. Acyclic schedules are executed only once, while the events of a cyclic one is executed succesively with a specified cycle rate. The difference between named and anonymous schedules is that named ones can be dynamically manipulated during runtime: they may be stopped, restarted, their events may be altered, etc.

Inter-agent communication may be implemented in schedules as well. FABLES does not have a fixed communication scheme, agents can interact through function calls in schedules. In the El Farol Bar model, there is no direct communication, thus the common variable *history* is the only way they interact with each other using a blackboard like approach.

For the El Farol simulation, we need two schedules: one for the agents to make them determine if they would like to attend the bar; the other one is a global one to update the *history* variable that the agents use to predict their optimal strategy.

Listing 13. Defining Agent Actions

```
class Agent {
  ...
  updateAttendance() =
      attend := prediction <= overcrowdingThreshold
    where (
        prediction = predictAttendance( bestStrategy,
          [ history(i) : i is [0..memorySize-1]])
    ) ;

  schedule cyclic 1 {
    1 : updateAttendance() ;
    2 : updateStrategies() ;
  };
};
```

Listing 14. Defining Global Events

```
schedule cyclic 1 {
  1.1 : history := [ attendance ] ++
           [ history(i) : i is [0..size(history)-2] ] ;
};
```

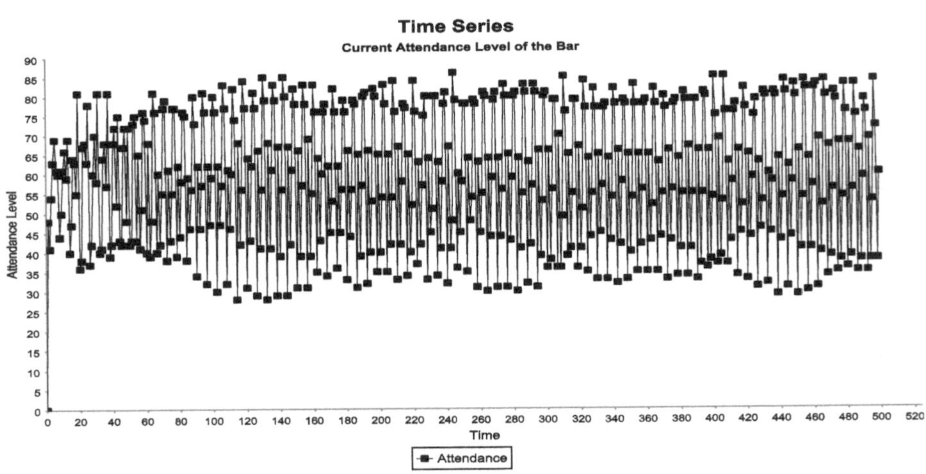

Fig. 1. The results of the implemented simulation where $N = 100$ with an attendance level of 60. The figure shows this simple model has the fluctuation of the original model.

3.4 Visualization

The FABLES Integrated Modeling environment has a powerful component called the Charting Wizard. This tool allows the modeler to create visualization for a simulation via a point and click interface. The wizard offers a selection of charts, capable of displaying derived simulation data, and contains several built-in statistics for data processing.

For the discussed El Farol model, we create a simple Time Series chart from the agents' attendance variables. The usage of the Charting Wizard is self-explanatory, we have to select the *attendance* variable in the drop-down list and add it to a Time Series chart (the wizard is not discussed here in detail due to limitations of space). The results can be seen in Figure 1.

4 Conclusion and Future Works

We have developed the above described language for agent-based simulation, its integrated development environment and a built-in observation wizard. During the development we have tried to automate as many tasks as possible, allowing the user to concentrate on models instead of the coding details and the implementation of visualisations.

We discussed the development of FABLES models as a four step process: defining global variables, defining agents, adding interactions and dynamics, and creating charts to visualize the simulations. A working reproduction of the original El Farol Bar model was described that may be compared with the original version [14]. Slight runtime differences may occur because the generated random values. The model consists of pure mathematical definitions, and no additional coding was required. Besides, visualization for the model was created with a few clicks. In addition, there are several extensions to the original model. For instance, in some versions agents are permitted to communicate with a set of other agents to discuss their opinions. This could be easily implemented in FABLES as well.

We are in the process organizing and evaluating user tests, hence we hope to have the necessary feed-back to further improve FABLES' built-in functions. Optimizing the generated code is also an important ongoing task.

Acknowledgements. The work reported here benefited from a grant of the Hungarian Government (grant #GVOP-3.2.2-2004.07-005/3.0). The partial support of the European Commission via the FP6 STREP projects QosCosGrid (contract #033883) and EMIL (contract #033841) is also gratefully acknowledged.

References

1. Epstein, J.M., Axtell, R.L.: Growing Artificial Societies: Social Science from the Bottom Up, January 1996. MIT Press Books, vol. 1. The MIT Press, Cambridge (1996)

2. Samuelson, D.A., Macal, C.M.: Agent-based Simulation Comes of Age (August 2006)
3. Axelrod, R., Tesfatsion, L.S.: A guide for newcomers to agent-based modeling in the social sciences. Staff General Research Papers 12515, Iowa State University, Department of Economics (March 2006)
4. Tesfatsion, L.S.: Agent-based computational economics: Modeling economies as complex adaptive systems. Staff General Research Papers 12974, Iowa State University, Department of Economics (August 2008)
5. Arthur, W.B.: Inductive Reasoning, Bounded Rationality and the Bar Problem. Working Papers 94-03-014. Santa Fe Institute, New Mexico, USA (1994)
6. North, M.J., Collier, N.T., Vos, J.R.: Experiences Creating Three Implementations of the Repast Agent Modeling Toolkit. ACM Transactions on Modeling and Computer Simulation 16(1), 1–25 (2006)
7. Minar, N., Burkhart, R., Langton, C., Askenazi, M.: The Swarm simulation system: A toolkit for building multi-agent simulations. Working Paper 96-06-042, Santa Fe Institute, Santa Fe (1996)
8. Wilensky, U.: NetLogo. Center for Connected Learning and Computer-Based Modeling, Northwestern University. Evanston, IL (1999), `http://ccl.northwestern.edu/netlogo/`
9. Borshchev, A., Karpov, Y., Kharitonov, V.: Distributed simulation of hybrid systems with AnyLogic and HLA. Future Gener. Comput. Syst. 18(6), 829–839 (2002)
10. North, M.J., Tatara, E., Collier, N.T., Ozik, J.: Visual Agent-based Model Development with Repast Simphony. In: Proceedings of the Agent 2007 Conference on Complex Interaction and Social Emergence, November 2007, Argonne National Laboratory, Argonne, IL, USA (2007)
11. Parker, M.: MetaABM Agent-based Modeling Software (2009), `http://metaabm.org`
12. Challet, D., et al.: Shedding light on El Farol. Game Theory and Information 0406002, EconWPA (2004)
13. Challet, D., et al.: Minority Games: Interacting Agents in Financial Markets. Oxford University Press, USA (2005)
14. Rand, W., Wilensky, U.: NetLogo El Farol model. Center for Connected Learning and Computer-Based Modeling, Northwestern University, Evanston, IL. (2007), `http://ccl.northwestern.edu/netlogo/models/ElFarol`
15. Fogel, D.B., Chellapilla, K., Angeline, P.J.: Inductive reasoning and bounded rationality reconsidered. IEEE Transactions on Evolutionary Computation 3(2), 142–146 (1999)
16. Whitehead, D.: The El Farol Bar Problem Revisited: Reinforcement Learning in a Potential Game. ESE Discussion Papers 186. Edinburgh School of Economics, University of Edinburgh (2008)
17. Rand, W., Sondahl, F.: The El Farol Bar Problem and Computational Effort: Why People Fail to Use Bars Efficiently. In: Agent 2007, November 15-17, Evanston, IL, USA (2007)
18. Gulyás, L.: On the transition to agent-based modeling: Implementation strategies from variables to agents. Social Science Computer Review 20(4), 389–399 (2002)

Recovering from Airline Operational Problems with a Multi-Agent System: A Case Study

António Mota, António J.M. Castro, and Luís Paulo Reis

LIACC-NIAD&R, FEUP, Department of Informatics Engineering, University of Porto, 4200-465 Porto, Portugal
{amota,ajmc,lpreis}@fe.up.pt

Abstract. The Airline Operations Control Centre (AOCC) tries to solve unexpected problems during the airline operation. Problems with aircraft, crewmembers and passengers are common and very hard to solve due to the several variables involved. This paper presents the implementation of a real-world multi-agent system for operations recovery in an airline company. The analysis and design of the system was done following a GAIA based methodology. We present the system specification as well as the implementation using JADE. A case study is included, where we present how the system solved a real problem.

Keywords: Disruption management, operations recovery, multi-agent system.

1 Introduction

The disruption management of an airline operation is a process by which problems that might affect the proper implementation of the operational scheduling of the company (problems related with crewmembers, aircraft, and/or passengers of a flight), are solved. This process is based on three key components: monitoring (supervising the airline operation in a particular base), event detection (identification of situations that could put at risk the operational planning), and resolution of problems (identify solutions that can mitigate the problems encountered). Since this is a very important process for the airline, it usually has a department responsible for its implementation: the Operational Control Centre (OCC). In this centre, operating 24 hours a day, working groups of people are responsible for monitoring the operation, detecting events, and proposing solutions to the Supervisor of the OCC, an entity that decides whether the solution will be implemented or not. Those solutions are achieved based mostly on the tacit knowledge of the people and there is no automated manner of how to address the resolution of the problems. Although there are software tools that help the elements of the OCC throughout the process (especially at the stage of monitoring and when obtaining information useful to solve the various problems), they are often obsolete, do not cover the whole process, and are not integrated. The work we presented here consists on the development of a Multi-Agent System (MAS) representing the OCC and the various elements existing there. The resolution of the problems will be made by a group of agents, a process known as disruption management. These agents use meta-heuristics, although the system is designed to permit the inclusion of an

L. Seabra Lopes et al. (Eds.): EPIA 2009, LNAI 5816, pp. 461–472, 2009.

unlimited number of agents that can use any method of problem resolution. This system was developed in an airline company and the motivation to develop it came from the observation of the needs of that company OCC. It was thus clear that there was a good opportunity to develop a system that, in some way, could catch and use the knowledge of the elements of the OCC, to make the process automatic, or at least to automate some of its more repetitive tasks.

Although there is extensive research applied to problems of scheduling on airlines (see, for example, [1], [3], [5] and [11]), there are very few works of really functional MAS on real airlines, capable of an integrated resolution of the type of problems that are found on the OCC. Therefore, our system would be innovative, useful not only for the company in question, but potentially also for others. Additionally, it is important to highlight the economic value that comes from the use of a system like this. First, by automating part of, or even all, the process, it is no longer required the presence of so many elements in the OCC, which lets the company reduce costs with staff; this reduction is even more evident because the OCC is a department that operates 24 hours a day. Furthermore, the use of Artificial Intelligence methods to resolve the various problems (flight delays, missing crewmembers, etc.) can contribute to the improvement of the quality of the solutions implemented, which translates into a decrease in costs associated with the modification of the operation of the airline company.

The MAS should monitor the operation that is being conducted on each operational base of the company (that is, the flights, the crewmembers who have reported for duty, etc.) detecting events that may correspond to problems that need to be resolved (some minor events can be skipped). Some of the possible events are: aircraft failures, flight delayed due to bad weather and / or congestion of air traffic, shortages of crewmembers, etc. The system should permit the definition of what is an event (a ten minutes delay of a crewmember can be a problem for one airline, but not for another). The system must have a set of agents, cooperating with each other, that are specialists in the resolution of the various types of problems. According to [6] the presence of agents that implement different methods for solving the same problem will increase the robustness of the system because of this redundancy. Finally, the system should have a visual interface that allows the supervisor to monitor the operation, to detect the events and to observe the solution proposed for the specific problem at hand.

It is important to point out that the analysis and design of this system followed a GAIA [13], [4] based methodology. For the interested reader, please see [7] for a comparison of several agent-oriented methodologies available. The rest of the paper is organized as follows. Section 2 presents some related work. Section 3 details the system specification and implementation, including the architecture, use cases and details about the specialist agents' implementation. Section 4 shows a case study and, in section 5, we conclude by discussing our work and presenting future implementations.

2 Related Work

Aircraft Recovery: Liu et al. [9] proposes a "multi-objective genetic algorithm to generate an efficient time-effective multi-fleet aircraft routing algorithm" in response to disruption of flights. It uses a combination of a traditional genetic algorithm with a multi-objective optimization method, attempting to optimize objective functions involving flight connections, flight swaps, total flight delay time and ground turn-around times. According to the authors "(...) the proposed method has demonstrated the ability to solve the dynamic and complex problem of airline disruption management".

Crew Recovery: In Abdelgahny et al. [1] the flight crew recovery problem for an airline with a hub-and-spoke network structure is addressed. The paper details and sub-divides the recovery problem into four categories: misplacement problems, rest problems, duty problems, and unassigned problems. Due to the stepwise approach, the proposed solution is sub-optimal. According to the authors the tool is able to "solve for the most efficient crew recovery plan with least deviation from originally planned schedule".

Integrated Recovery: Bratu et al. [3] presents two models that considers aircraft and crew recovery and through the objective function focuses on passenger recovery. They include delay costs that capture relevant hotel costs and ticket costs if passengers are recovered by other airlines. The objective is to minimize jointly airline operating costs and estimated passenger delay and disruption costs. According to the authors, "(...) decisions from our models can potentially reduce passenger arrival delays (...) without increasing operating costs".

Other Application Domains: Agents and multi-agent systems have been applied both to other problems in air transportation domain and in other application domains. A brief and incomplete list of such applications follows. Tumer and Agogino [12] developed a multi-agent algorithm for traffic flow management. For ATC Tower operations, Jonker et al. [8] have also proposed the use of multi-agent systems. As a last example, a multi-agent system for the integrated dynamic scheduling of steel production has been proposed by Ouelhadj [10].

3 System Specification and Implementation

System overview: Figure 1 shows the overall architecture of the multi-agent system. There are four types of agents:

- *Monitor*, which monitors the operation of the airline company.
- *Event Detector*, which defines the type of events that must be detected.
- *Resolution Manager*, which receives a problem and manages the resolution in cooperation with the specialist agents.
- *Specialist*, which is responsible for the resolution of a problem using a specific method.

The communication between the agents is done through the JADE system [2]. Additionally, Figure 1 shows the existence of a data store, that has information about the airline company operations. That data store is accessed by the *monitor* and by the *specialist* agents. Figure 1 also shows the presence of a human: the OCC supervisor.

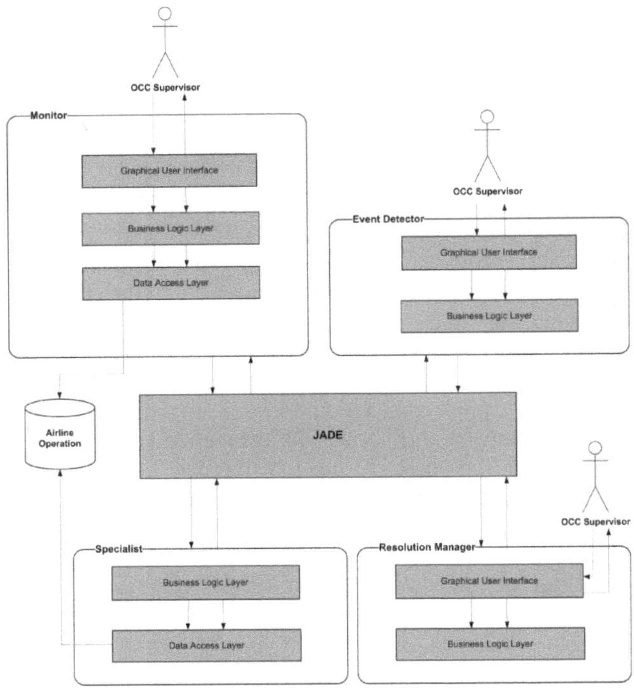

Fig. 1. Overall architecture of the Multi-Agent System

The OCC supervisor starts the monitoring process and defines the type of events that are to be considered warnings and problems. Then, the event detector agent communicates those types of events to the monitor, which shows the warnings and/or the problems to the OCC supervisor. This entity establishes the parameters of the resolution process and decides to solve a specific problem. The problem is communicated by the monitor to the resolution manager, which in turn communicates it to all the specialist agents. After arriving at a solution, each agent sends it to the resolution manager, which picks the best, i.e., the one with less cost and shows it to the OCC supervisor.

Figure 2 shows all the use cases of the system. The JADE actor is represented because the reception of messages from other agents is periodically checked by using a type of JADE behaviour (so, the JADE actor periodically asks the system to check for new messages, acting as an actor).

In the *monitoring* subsystem, the OCC supervisor can check the details of a particular flight that is being monitored, as well as order the resolution of a specific problem. The JADE system periodically asks the system to monitor the operation and to check the arrival of *MetaEvent* messages. In the *event detection* subsystem, the OCC supervisor can manage *MetaEvents*, that is, add, remove, or modify a type of event. Each time the set of *MetaEvent* is changed, a message is sent to the monitor. Finally, in the *resolution* subsystem, the OCC supervisor can manage the solving parameters and check the solution. The JADE system periodically asks the system to check the arrival of problem messages (which triggers the resolution of that problem), and solution messages (which triggers its presentation to the OCC supervisor).

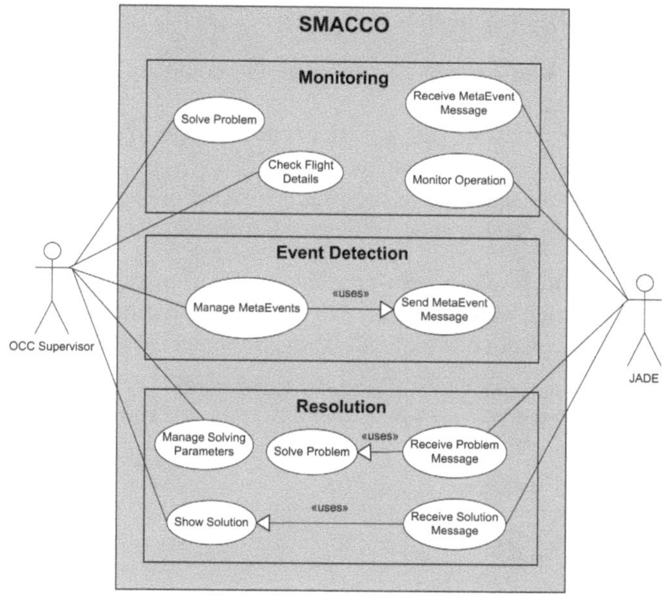

Fig. 2. System use cases

Monitoring subsystem specification: In the MAS there are three different subsystems as stated previously. Due to the lack of space we are going to present the specification for two of them: *Monitoring* and *Resolution* subsystem. Table 1 describes the use case "*Monitor Operation*".

Table 1. Use case "Monitor Operation"

UC ID:	SMACCO-BUC001.00
Name:	**Monitor Operation**
Date:	10/12/2007
Actors:	JADE
Trigger:	This use case is initiated when the JADE cyclic behaviour triggers its action (the operation monitoring).
Desc:	1. Obtain flights that are going to arrive within a specific amount of time. 2. Obtain flights that arrived within a specific amount of time ago. 3. Obtain flights that are going to depart within a specific amount of time. 4. Obtain flights that departed within a specific amount of time ago. 5. Signal the flights on the interface, separating the NB and WB flights. 6. Check if there are types of events to monitor 7. If there are types of events to monitor, check what flights (if any) match the conditions of the type of event. 8. If there are flights that correspond to the type of event conditions, signal the type of event in the interface.

The monitor agent implements five behaviours:

- A *TickerBehaviour* that periodically accesses the company's operational database to monitor the operation.
- A *CyclicBehaviour* that waits for a meta event message to arrive, using a *ReceiverBehaviour* to filter the appropriate messages.
- An *OneShotBehaviour* that sends a message with a set of events to be solved.
- A *ParallelBehaviour* that execute the former behaviours concurrently.

Monitoring subsystem implementation: The JADE implementation of the *BehaviourMonitor* class, which extends *TicketBehaviour*, is presented below. The method *onTick* contains the piece of code that will be executed periodically.

```
Class BehaviourMonitor extends TickerBehaviour {
  public BehaviourMonitor(Agent agent, long period)
  { super(agent, period); }
  @Override
  protected void onTick() {
     try {
        Monitor('NB');
        Monitor('WB');
        if(eventsDefinition.size() > 0)
          markEvents();
     }
     Catch (SQLException ex) {
        ex.printStackTrace(); }
  }}
```

The agent periodically monitors the narrow body (an aircraft with a single aisle) and wide body (an aircraft with two aisles) airline operation and, if there are any type of events to be detected, checks if any flight is under the conditions necessary to consider itself a warning or a problem. The *BehaviourProblemResolution* class, which extends *OneShotBehaviour*, is presented below. The piece of code inside the *action()* method will be executed only once.

```
class BehaviourProblemResolution extends OneShotBehaviour {
  public BehaviourProblemResolution(Agent agent)
  { super(agent); }
  @Override
  protected void action() {
     ACLMessage msgToSend = prepEventsMsg(events,
Shared.getAgents(super.myAgent, 'AgentManager'));
     send(msgToSend);
  }}
```

In this behaviour, a message is sent from the monitor agent to the resolution manager containing the list of events that triggered the problem.

Resolution subsystem specification: This subsystem receives a problem and manages the resolution in cooperation with the specialist agents. The resolution manager agent implements five behaviours:

- A *CyclicBehaviour* that waits for a problem message to arrive, using a *ReceiverBehaviour* to filter the appropriate messages.

- A *CyclicBehaviour* that waits for a solution message to arrive, using a *ReceiverBehaviour* to filter the appropriate messages.
- A *ParallelBehaviour* that executes the former behaviours concurrently.
- A *SimpleBehaviour* that sends a message with the problem to be solved to the specialist agents.

Each specialist agent implements

- A *CyclicBehaviour* that waits for a problem message to arrive, using a *ReceiverBehaviour* to filter the appropriate messages.
- A *ParallelBehaviour* that executes the former behaviours concurrently.

Two specialist's agents were implemented, each one solving the problem via different meta-heuristics: *hill-climbing* and *simulated annealing*. The *hill climbing agent* solves the problem iteratively by following the steps:

1. Obtains the flights that are in the time window of the problem. This time window starts at the flight date and ends at a customizable period in the future. This will be the initial solution of the problem. The crewmembers and aircraft exchanges are made between flights that are inside the time window of the problem.
2. While some specific and customizable time has not yet passed or a solution below a specific and customizable cost has not been found, repeats steps 3 and 4.
3. Generates the successor of the initial or previous solution.
4. Evaluates the cost of the solution according to Equation 3. If it is smaller than the cost of the current solution, accepts the generated solution as the new current solution. Otherwise, discards the generated solution. The way a solution is evaluated is described below.
5. Send the current solution to the agent that manages the resolution process.

The *simulated annealing agent* solves the problem iteratively by following the steps:

1. Obtains the flights that are in the time window of the problem.
2. While some specific and customizable time has not yet passed or a solution below a specific and customizable cost has not been found, repeats steps 3 and 4.
3. Generates the successor of the initial or previous solution.
4. Evaluates the cost of the solution according to Equation 3. If it is smaller than the cost of the current solution, accepts the generated solution as the new current solution. Otherwise, it accepts the generated solution with a probability that is given by Equation 1.

$$P = \exp\left(-\Delta E/T\right) \tag{1}$$

   Where ΔE is the difference between the cost of the generated solution and the cost of the current one, and T is given by

$$T_{t+1} = \alpha T_t \tag{2}$$

   Where α lies between 0 and 1. α was given a value of 0.8, and T was given an initial value of 10. T is updated every N iterations. N was given a value of 2.
5. Send the current solution to the agent that manages the resolution process.

Resolution subsystem implementation: The implementation of the hill-climbing algorithm on one of the specialist agents, using JADE, follows:

```
while (!Shared.para(problem.getNumSeconds(), secondsExecution,
problem.getMaximumCost(), costActualSolution)) {
  // get sucessor
  successor.Shared.newSucessor(Shared.copyArrayList(currentSolution);
  costSucessor=Shared.calcCost(sucessor, plainInitialSolution);
  if (costSucessor < costActualSolution) {
  currentSolution = sucessor;
  costActualSolution = costSucessor;
  }}
```

Solution generation and evaluation: The generation of a new solution is made by finding a successor that distances itself to the current solution by one unit, that is, the successor is obtained by one, and only one, of the following operations:

- Swap two aircrafts between flights that belong to the flights that are in the time window of the problem.
- Swap two crewmembers between flights that belong to the flights that are in the time window of the problem.
- Swap an aircraft that belongs to the flights that are in the time window of the problem with an aircraft that is not being used.
- Swap a crewmember of a flight that belongs to the flights that are in the time window of the problem with a crewmember that isn't on duty, but is on standby.

When choosing the first element (crewmember or aircraft) to swap, there are two possibilities:

- Choose randomly.
- Choose an element that is delayed.

This choice is made based on the probability of choosing an element that is late, which was given a value of 0.9, so that the algorithms can proceed faster to good solutions (exchanges are highly penalized, so choosing an element that is not late probably won't reduce the cost, as a possible saving by choosing a less costly element probably won't compensate the penalization associated with the exchange). If the decision is to exchange an element that is delayed, the list of flights will be examined and the first delayed element is chosen. If the decision is to choose randomly, then a random flight is picked, and a crewmember or the aircraft is chosen, depending on the probability of choosing a crewmember, which was given a value of 0.85. When choosing the second element that is going to swap with the first, there are two possibilities:

- Swap between elements of flights
- Swap between an element of a flight and an element that isn't on duty.

This choice is made based on the probability of choosing a swap between elements of flights, which was given a value of 0.5. The evaluation of the solution is done by an objective function that measures four types of costs:

- The costs with crewmembers. Those costs take into consideration the amount that has to be paid to the crewmember (depends on the duration of the flight), and the base of the crewmember (for instance, assigning a crewmember from Oporto to a flight departing from Lisbon has an associated cost that would not be present if the crewmember's base was Lisbon).

- The costs with aircrafts. Those costs take into consideration the amount that has to be spent on the aircraft (depends on the duration of the flight), and the base where the flight actually is.
- The penalization for exchanging elements.
- The penalization for delayed elements. The cost associated with this aspect is the highest, because the goal is to have no delayed elements.

These types of costs are taken into account in Equation 3:

$$tc = cmc + amc + exW * numE + dlW + numD \tag{3}$$

Where

$$cmc = \sum_{i=1}^{|CM|} (c_i * bcf)/numCm$$
$$\begin{aligned}&where\\&i \in CM; CM = \{all\ crewmembers\ in\ flight\}\\&1 < bcf \leq 2 : base\ crew\ factor\\&numCm : number\ of\ crew\ members\ in\ CM\end{aligned} \tag{4}$$

$$amc = \sum_{j=1}^{|AC|} (ac_j * baf)/numAc$$
$$\begin{aligned}&where\\&j \in AC; AC = \{aircraft\ same\ fleet\}\\&1 < baf \leq 2 : base\ aircraft\ factor\\&numAc : number\ of\ aircrafts\ in\ AC\end{aligned} \tag{5}$$

ExW was given a value of 1000, and *DlW* a value of 20000.

4 Case Study

This scenario is based on the delay of flight TP935 at 08/04/2008 17:20, from Lisbon (LIS) to Paris (CDG) with a schedule departure time of 17:05 and expected arrival time of 18:41. There were 15 business class passengers and 113 economy class passengers. Figure 3 shows the graphical user interface of the monitoring and event detection system. At the upper half of the interface: the flights that are arriving (in this case, is the next 80 minutes), that already arrived (in this case, in the next 15 minutes), that are departing (in this case, in the next 45 minutes), and that already have departed (in this case, until 40 minutes ago) are shown. The flight TP935 is, as expected, in the group of the flights that will depart. At the bottom half of the interface, details are shown about the flight, its crewmembers, and the aircraft used. The monitoring system is constantly monitoring the operation, so that the information presented in the interface is maintained actual. As can be seen at the figure, the system shows seven warnings and five problems. The flight TP2676 shows a warning because the flight should have arrived more than 15 minutes ago and, as a consequence, all the passengers are more than 15 minutes late. The same happens with flight TP432, that should have departed more than 10 minutes ago, which again makes all the passengers in it behind schedule.

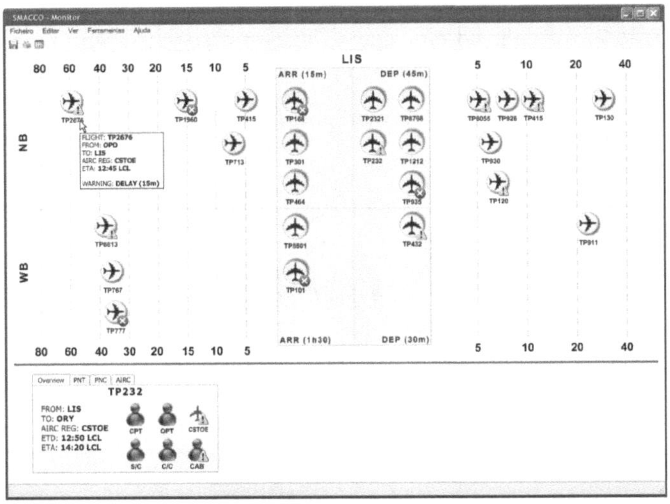

Fig. 3. Monitoring and Event Detection System

Finally, according to the system, the operation of the airline company has one warning and four problems on flight TP935:

- The flight is 20 minutes late and, therefore, that triggers a warning.
- Two crewmembers are more than 15 minutes late and that triggers two problems. Those crewmembers are late because they are on flight TP2676, which is late.
- Another crewmember is more than 10 minutes late and that triggers a problem. That crewmember did not report for duty.
- Aircraft CSTOE is more than 15 minutes late and that triggers a problem. The aircraft is late because it is the aircraft of flight TP2676, which is late.

The OCC personnel are now able to solve the problem of flight TP935 in cooperation with the problem resolution system.

Problem resolution: The system shows the description of the problem and some of the parameters that can be adjusted by the OCC personnel. For example, available time to find a solution and maximum allowed cost of the solution. Those parameters will be used when finding a solution.

The resolution process is transparent to the OCC personnel, as they don't know how many agents participated on the process and what methods did they use. The management of the process is the responsibility of an agent, which chooses the best solution among the ones given (the one with less cost according to Equation 3), and presents that solution to the OCC personnel. In this case, the solution was:

- Switch aircrafts CSTOE and CSTNJ between flight number TP935 and flight number TP1212. Because TP1212 will depart later than TP935, the aircraft CSTOE has good chances of arriving before the flight's schedule departure date.
- Switch three crewmembers between flight number TP935 and flight number TP1212.

The solution to the problem has a lower cost than to do nothing, especially because of the high penalizations associated with crew and aircraft delays. In this case, the initial solution has a cost of 98340 and the proposed by the system has a cost of 26218.

5 Conclusions and Future Work

We conclude that the goals established for this project have been achieved and that the basis for its possible near future use in the airline company was gotten underway. Indeed, it is an integrated system that automates much of the disruption management process, from the monitoring of the operation of the company in its several bases, to the detection of events and the resolution of the problems encountered. Additionally, our MAS is oriented to the future: its distributed nature and the fact that it is based on agents that are specialists in solving problems easily allows the insertion into the system of new agents that solve new kinds of problems that were identified in the meantime, or that resolve the current types of problems using different methods. It is thus a truly scalable solution, prepared to sustain the growth of the airline company.

Of course, some difficulties arose during the development of the project. Obtaining a graphical interface that would allow the OCC personnel to view, in an easy and efficient way, the operation of the company at a particular base was a task that involved a lot of effort, with the need to refine it over time. Cooperation with some elements of the airline company was crucial in this process. With regard to the obtaining of the information, the analysis of the database that contains information on the operation of the airline was an arduous task, given its complexity and the strong presence of specific language to the domain of aviation. Finally, some difficulties have arisen in the fine-tuning of the objective function of the various meta-heuristics used, particularly in the choice of the weights to be given to each factor. Nonetheless, the number of experiments performed enabled reaching values that generated quite acceptable solutions.

From the case study presented we cannot assume that our system will always have this behaviour in all situations. For that, we need to perform several tests using simulated and/or real events or, if possible, running our system in parallel with the current system at the airline company. Due to the probabilistic nature of the simulated annealing algorithm and without performing more tests, we cannot generalize the results presented here.

Although the goals have been achieved, it is important to consider a number of improvements that could be made on future developments and that could enrich it. In terms of the algorithms used to solve the problems, other meta-heuristics can be implemented, as well as methods based in the area of operational research

Another useful improvement for the system would be to provide it with the ability to implement the solution, which currently is made by the supervisor of the OCC.

Despite being somewhat technologically accessible, this add-on to the system should be the subject of special care because of the critical nature of the operation.

Acknowledgments. The second author is supported by FCT (Fundação para a Ciência e Tecnologia) under research grant SFRH/BD/44109/2008. The authors are grateful to TAP Portugal for allowing the use of real data from the company.

References

1. Abdelgahny, A., Ekollu, G., Narisimhan, R., Abdelgahny, K.: A Proactive Crew Recovery Decision Support Tool for Commercial Airlines during Irregular Operations. Annals of Operations Research 127, 309–331 (2004)
2. Bellifemine, F., Caire, G., Trucco, T., Rimassa, G.: JADE Programmer's Guide. JADE 3.3 TILab S.p.A (2004)
3. Bratu, S., Barhhart, C.: Flight Operations Recovery: New Approaches Considering Passenger Recovery. Journal of Scheduling 9(3), 279–298 (2006)
4. Castro, A., Oliveira, E.: The rationale behind the development of an airline operations control centre using Gaia-based methodology. In: Int. J. Agent-Oriented Software Engineering, vol. 2(3), pp. 350–377 (2008)
5. Clausen, J., Larsen, A., Larsen, J.: Disruption Management in the Airline Industry – Concepts, Models and Methods. Technical Report, 2005-01, Informatics and Mathematical Modeling, Technical University of Denmark, DTU (2005)
6. Castro, A.J.M., Oliveira, E.: Using Specialized Agents in a Distributed MAS to Solve Airline Operations Problems: a Case Study. In: Proceedings of IAT 2007, Intelligent Agent Technology Conference, Silicon Valley, California, USA, November 2-5, pp. 473–476. IEEE Computer Society, Los Alamitos (2007)
7. Henderson-Sellers, B., Giorgini, P. (eds.): Agent-Oriented Methodologies. Idea Group Publishing (2005) ISBN: 159140586-6
8. Jonker, G., Meyer, J.-J., Dignum, F.P.M.: Towards a market mechanism for airport traffic control. In: Bento, C., Cardoso, A., Dias, G. (eds.) EPIA 2005. LNCS (LNAI), vol. 3808, pp. 500–511. Springer, Heidelberg (2005)
9. Liu, T., Jeng, C., Chang, Y.: Disruption Management of an Inequality-Based Multi-Fleet Airline Schedule by a Multi-Objective Genetic Algorithm. Transportation Planning and Technology 31(6), 613–639 (2008)
10. Ouelhadj, D.: A Multi-Agent System for the Integrated Dynamic Scheduling of Steel Production, Ph.D. dissertation, The University of Nottingham, School of Computer Science and Information Technology, England (2003)
11. Rosenberger, J., Johnson, E., Nemhauser, G.: Rerouting aircraft for airline recovery. Technical Report, TLI-LEC 01-04, Georgia Institute of Technology (2001)
12. Tumer, K., Agogino, A.: Distributed Agent-Based Air Traffic Flow Management, In:6th International Joint Conference on Autonomous Agents and Multiagent Systems (AAMAS 2007), Honolulu, Hawaii (2007)
13. Zambonelli, F., Jennings, N., Wooldridge, M.: Developing multi-agent systems: the Gaia methodology. ACM Transactions on Software Engineering and Methodology 12(3), 317–370 (2003)

EcoSimNet: A Multi-Agent System for Ecological Simulation and Optimization

António Pereira[1], Luís Paulo Reis[1], and Pedro Duarte[2]

[1] NIAD&R-LIACC / DEI-FEUP – Faculty of Engineering, University of Porto
Rua Dr. Roberto Frias s/n, 4200-465 Porto, Portugal
Tel.: +351 22 508 14 00
[2] CIAGEG-UFP – University Fernando Pessoa
Praça 9 de Abril, 349, 4249-004 Porto, Portugal
Tel.: +351 22 507 13 00
{amcp,lpreis}@fe.up.pt, pduarte@ufp.edu.pt

Abstract. Ecological models may be very complex due to the large number of physical, chemical, biological processes and variables and their interactions, leading to long simulation times. These models may be used to analyse different management scenarios providing support to decision-makers. Thus, the simultaneous simulation of different scenarios can make the process of analysis and decision quicker, provided that there are mechanisms to accelerate the generation of new scenarios and optimization of the choices between the results presented. This paper presents a new simulation platform – EcoSimNet – specially designed for environmental simulations, which allows the inclusion of intelligent agents and the introduction of parallel simulators to speed up and optimize the decision-making processes. Experiments were performed using EcoSimNet computational platform with an agent controlling several simulators and implementing a parallel version of the simulated annealing algorithm for optimizing aquaculture production. These experiments showed the capabilities of the framework, enabling a fast optimization process and making this work a step forward towards an agent based decision support system to optimize complex environmental problems.

Keywords: Ecological Simulations, Agent-Based Applications, Multi-Agent Simulation and Modelling, Optimization, Parallel Simulated Annealing.

1 Introduction

The simulation of aquatic ecosystems is an emerging area of research allowing an interdisciplinary approach necessary to understand the complexity of these environments. The need of environmental impact studies when planning interventions in estuaries, lagoons or other coastal areas, has increased the interest in this type of simulations, especially when these ecosystems are used for aquaculture and other economic activities (recreation or tourism) that contribute to the local economy and the dynamics of employment in the region.

In most cases, ecological models are used to test and/or validate hypothetical scenarios of operation or configuration of specific regions or environments. Often, the

L. Seabra Lopes et al. (Eds.): EPIA 2009, LNAI 5816, pp. 473–484, 2009.

goal is optimizing the management of a natural resource capable of producing goods and services of interest to humans. As models try to reflect reality, they tend to incorporate more processes, increasing their complexity and making simulations, necessarily, slower.

The case of coastal environments is paradigmatic because these ecosystems always played an important role in the life of human beings, are very complex from a biological, a chemical and a physical point of view and are very sensitive to environmental and management decisions. They allow an enormous amount of possible activities (such as fishing, aquaculture, harbour activities, tourism, etc.), and guarantee several basic services to humanity, but they are also the final destination of many pollutants generated by agriculture and other human activities [1]. In the last century, human population migrated intensively from inland to coastal boundaries and, nowadays, the World Bank estimates that 50% of the world's population lives within 60km from the sea [2]. These numbers are more relevant in Portugal where almost 89% of the population lives within 50km from the sea in about 39% of the territory [3]. Usually, there are many conflicting human interests on these ecosystems and, unfortunately, there are examples of some recent environmental disasters in coastal areas that could have been minimized, or even avoided, if proper management options had been followed at appropriate times with the commitment of the authorities and the stakeholders.

When coastal ecosystems are exploited for shellfish aquaculture one of the issues that always arises is how far the holders can increase the production in their assets without exceeding ecosystem carrying capacity [4]. Usually, the balance is maintained by legislation, which limits the areas of exploitation and thus the number of licenses in each area. Stakeholder's experience, usually acquired by trial and error, successes and failures, leads them to have an empirical perception of what is the optimal exploitation density of each species per unit area, without much consideration for potential environmental impacts, except those that may hinder their production and profit.

The results of the development of an intelligent bivalve farmer agent to find out the best combination of bivalve seeding areas, within an allowed area of exploitation, without exceeding the carrying capacity of the system, were reported by Cruz et al. [5] and showed promising guidelines. One of the constraints pointed out in the conclusions of that study was the time consumed by the large number of simulations necessary to find the best combinations mentioned above. Therefore, the usage of a network of simulators to speed up the decision process was the natural follow up of that study.

This paper presents an outline of a multi-agent simulation system of ecological models capable of integrating the human interests, accelerating the generation of results taking advantage from parallel simulation of various scenarios of operation and their analysis in real time.

The architecture presented (EcoSimNet) exploits the concept of computing clusters and parallel computation, creating simulation islands where an agent monitors a set of simulators, simultaneously simulating independent scenarios. One of the agents took the lead role, taking the initiative to encourage other agents to obtain the desired results as quickly as possible.

Coordination is ensured by the existence of points of synchronization during the course of the experiments, allowing the exchange of results between the various agents and the adoption of the best result as a starting point for a new round of independent simulations until the next point of synchronization. The stop order is given by the coordinator agent when a maximum number of rounds of simulation or a time limit are exceeded or when a criterion of optimization is reached.

This approach was tested with farmer agents trying to get the best combination of areas for cultivation of shellfish in a wider area, maximizing the production without exceeding the permitted area of cultivation.

The remaining of this paper is structured as follows: (i) The next section describes the problem in analysis, followed by the presentation of the architecture for ecological simulations (EcoSimNet) and the solution adopted to do this study; (ii) Section 3 presents the experimental approach pursued and the results obtained; (iii) The paper ends with an analysis of the results, the conclusions and a description of future work to be done.

2 Problem in Analysis

The study and experiences were done with one validated ecosystem model for Sungo Bay, People's Republic of China [4], already implemented in the EcoDynamo simulator [6]. The lagoon is modelled with a two-dimensional vertically integrated, coupled hydrodynamic-biogeochemical model, based on a finite difference bathymetric staggered grid with 1120 cells (32 columns x 35 lines) and a spatial resolution of 500m – Figure 1. The model has a land and an ocean boundary and the time step used was 30 seconds.

A previous bivalve farmer agent was developed by Cruz et al. [5] with the objective of maximize bivalve production, finding the best combinations of locations to seed and harvest bivalve species within a delimited area of exploitation, using the previous model. In that work, the farmer agent had to choose the best five cells (corresponding each one to a 500m x 500m area) within an area of 88 admissible cells to explore oysters – corresponding to more than 39 millions of possible combinations. One realistic simulation for the complete bivalve culture cycle should cover approximately 1.5 years, equivalent to more than 1,576,800 simulation steps; in a computer with an Intel® Core™ 2 CPU 6300 @ 1.86GHz and 2.00GB of RAM, the time to run the complete simulation is 10 hours. The long time and the heavy processor power required for one complete simulation, limited the previous experiments to use only 1000 simulation steps in each cycle, extrapolating the results for the complete growth cycle – the computer used ran 1000 steps in about 22 seconds and one experimental round (341 simulations) was completed in approximately two hours.

The usage of a computer network allows decreasing the time needed to generate results and performing longer simulations to obtain more realistic results. The approach idealized was:

- Confirm the results achieved by the experiments made by Cruz et al. [5] using one and four simulators, and more powerful computers;
- Extend the number of simulation steps and compare the results obtained in terms of temporal savings and quality of the final solutions achieved – e.g. confirm if the extrapolation assumed by previous experiments remains valid;
- Repeat the experiments with more cells to further explore, and analyse the results.

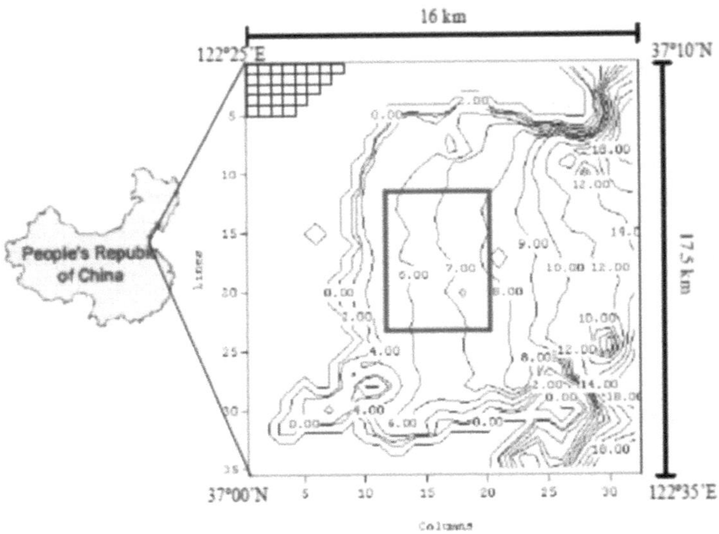

Fig. 1. Location of Sungo Bay, including model domain and bathymetry [4] with delimited area of exploitation marked

The experiments used the base algorithms implemented by Cruz et al. [5], controlled by a simulated annealing algorithm [7] modified to support parallelisation and with more flexibility to control the number of simulations in each experimental round.

The new experiments were performed in computers with processors Intel® Core™ 2 Quad CPU Q9300 @ 2.50GHz, with 8.00 GB of RAM. In these computers, the complete bivalve culture cycle is simulated in about six hours and three quarters.

3 Implementation

3.1 System Architecture

The system architecture was designed to perform complex simulations of aquatic ecosystems, to integrate easily new applications in the system, like plug-and-play hardware in computers, and enabling communications between different applications.

The Ecological Simulation Network (EcoSimNet) follows the general architectures for intelligent agents [8] and multi-agent systems [9] where all the applications communicate via TCP/IP with messages formatted according to the specification of the ECOLANG language [10]. The framework can support several EcoDynamo simulators [6], to allow parallel or concurrent simulations, and different agents representing the human interests over the simulated ecosystem (Figure 2).

The ECOLANG language specification forces messages to be simple, expansible, independent from any computational platform or operating system, and readable by the humans, allowing easy traceability.

This architecture permits the exploitation of machine learning algorithms with the inclusion of agents in the network [11][12][13].

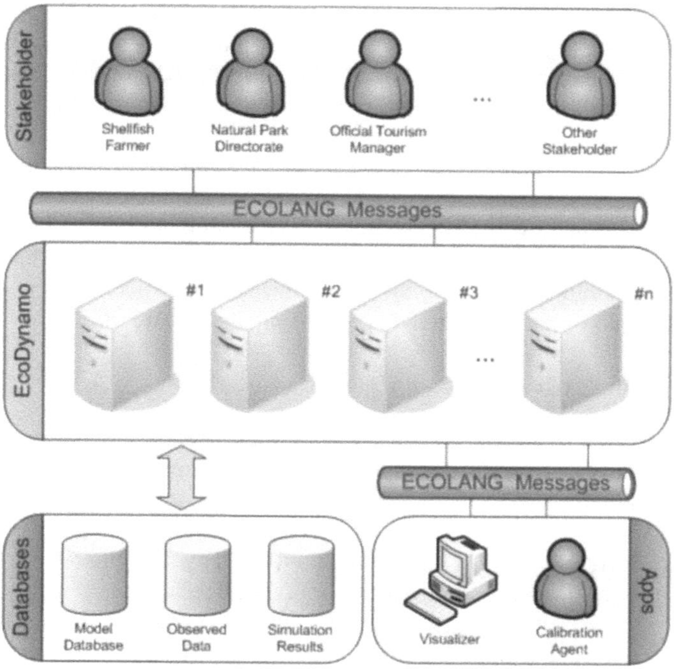

Fig. 2. EcoSimNet architecture

The simulator has a simple graphical user interface where users can interact with most of the ecological model properties: select the model to use, the processes to simulate, the period of time simulated, the variables for output, and the output formats. Definitions such as system morphology, geometric representation, dimensions and number of model grid cells, and initial values of variables and parameters are fixed when the model is created. One script file is provided to each simulator for the start up, indicating its identification in the network and the model to run.

Only the simulators have direct access to the models' databases. The agents acquire information about the model through the ECOLANG messages exchanged with the simulators. This approach ensures true independence between the simulator and the agents.

3.2 Farmer Agent Implemented Algorithms

The original agent developed a system of customizable tactics [5] to implement the sense of intelligence which may, in some sense, simulate the reasoning of the human farmer. The base algorithm developed for this agent was a simple hill-climbing optimization algorithm, based on simulated annealing with Monte Carlo probability [7] [14] – the agent seeks iteratively a new solution and saves the one with higher quality as the best. Several configurable optimizations can be activated to influence the selection logic of the new solutions [5]. The generation of the new solutions was facilitated and improved by the inclusion of known algorithms, like tabu search [15], genetic algorithms [16] and reinforcement learning [17], that can be triggered at any stage of the optimization process. The novelty of this approach is centred in the system of customizable tactics that enables the activation (automatic or configurable) of any one of the implemented algorithms during the experiment, and the possibility of having, simultaneously, the various algorithms involved in choosing the best solution.

The original agent communicated only with one simulator. To manipulate the information of several simulators, it was necessary to create a different agent, extending the former one and making it able to communicate simultaneously with several simulators, with a decision-making process that should integrate, in real time, the results from the various simulators as they were generated. The choice made was the implementation of a kind of parallel simulated annealing algorithm [18].

3.3 Parallel Simulated Annealing Algorithm

Simulated annealing (SA) is considered a good tool for complex nonlinear optimization problems [7] but one of its major drawbacks is its slow convergence. One way to improve its efficiency it's parallelisation (the development of a parallel version of the algorithm).

Many implementations of this algorithm exist but they are, inherently, problem dependent. Ram et al. [18] proposed two distributed algorithms for parallel simulated annealing – the clustering algorithm (CA) and the genetic clustering algorithm (GCA). Both explore the evidence that a good initial solution results in a faster convergence.

The CA technique starts n nodes of the network to run SA algorithm using different n initial solutions. After a fixed number of iterations, the nodes exchange their partial results to get the best one. All the nodes accept that solution and restart new SA round based on that solution. This process is repeated a predefined number of times. There must be a coordinator node to choose the best solution and to determine the time to stop the rounds and finishing the process.

The process implemented in the experimental agent can be viewed as integrating the CA technique described: all the agents can have the function of generating solutions (worker node) and one agent has to perform the functions of coordination (coordinator node); the generation of the new solutions is driven by the tactics chosen in each agent taking advantage of their autonomy. The flexibility of the framework allows each agent to control only a part of the network simulators. It can be seen as a collection of simulation islands or clusters. The basic algorithm for the coordinator node is presented in Figure 3.

The number of synchronization points determines the number of times the worker nodes exchange partial results with the coordinator node, and this is important to speed up the optimization process. With this process, the number of iterations is distributed uniformly by the agents (worker nodes) but not necessarily by the simulators: while the coordinator node waits for agents synchronization to exchange the partial results (Figure 3, line 3.2), each worker node controls the number of iterations with all simulators monitored by it, which means that if there is one very fast simulator and another one very slow, it is expectable that the faster one runs more simulations than the slower.

As simulators run in different computers, each one finalizes its simulation independently and the agent compares the result against all results accumulated so far; there is no need to synchronize the simulators.

```
Parallel SA – coordinator node

Parameters:
initialTemperature – initial temperature
temperatureModifier – decrease temperature factor
N – maximum number of iterations
W – number of worker agents
P – number of synchronization points

Global Variables:
counterMS – number of missing synchronizations
bestResult – best production value returned by the agents
bestSolution – solution that generates the best result

Algorithm:
  1:  for each agent w
          initSA (initialTemperature, temperatureModifier,
                  N / (W * P), 0, <empty>)
  2:  bestResult = 0;
  3:  bestSolution = <empty>;
  4:  counterMS = P;
  3:  while (counterMS > 0)
      {
3.1:      for each agent w
              runSA ( );
3.2:      for each agent w
              results[w] = collectResults (w);
3.3:      choose (results[ ], bestResult, bestSolution);
3.4:      for each agent w
              prepareSA (bestResult, bestSolution);
3.5:      decrement (counterMS);
      }
  4:  publish (bestResult, bestSolution);
```

Fig. 3. Parallel Simulated Annealing Algorithm – coordinator node

Taking into account the time needed for each simulation and the time required to choose the best solution, often there are benefits if one agent accumulates the coordinator and worker tasks.

4 Experiments and Results

The experiments were carried out with only one agent that implements the algorithms previously used by Cruz et al. [5] with the inclusion of the presented parallel SA algorithm and a new user-friendly interface to configure and parameterize the implemented algorithms and tactics. The agent accumulates the coordinator and worker roles.

Two training experiments were conducted to validate the framework and see if the results reported by Cruz et al. were reproducible. The first training experiment runs with one simulator and the second with four simulators; in each experimental round the agent controlled the same number of simulations with 1000 steps (341 iterations, each one simulating eight hours and 20 minutes of real time). The oysters were seeded with a fixed density of 55.15 units per square meter, and each oyster had 0.0005g of shell weight and 0.00002g of meat weight.

In terms of results quality and time savings, it seems that the new approach is working as expected – the results maintain the tendency observed previously by Cruz et al. [5] occupying the northeast side of the region - and the time savings are directly related to the number of simulators in the network – the first training experiment rounds spent about one hour and 27 minutes and the second ones about 23 minutes, a save of 75%, as expected. In these experiments, the difference between the maximum and the minimum production value indicators was irrelevant due to the low simulated time.

Due to the memorization by the agent of all the solutions tested previously, the log of the last experiment revealed that 1598 solutions were tested but only 341 new combinations were explored and simulated, those that the outcome of the simulation was unknown. The randomness of the initial solution guarantees the necessary diversity required for this type of optimization algorithms.

The production value indicator is calculated based on the quantity of shellfish harvested, in tonnes, and its economical weight.

First Experiment. To take advantage of the new computing platform, in the first experiment the number of simulation steps was increased to cover one month of real time oysters growth (from 1000 to 86 400 steps) to verify if the extrapolation assumed in the training experiments remains valid. Each experimental set took about 1 day and 6 hours to finish. The difference between the maximum and the minimum production value indicators was now 15.2% of the minimum and partial results are presented in Table 1 and Figure 4.

Table 1. Five best results and worse result of the first experimental set

Rank	Production Value (Indicator)	Seeded Cells
1	19 922.9	31, 45, 47, 70, 78
2	19 908.8	37, 38 45, 69, 78
3	19 879.6	38, 53, 54, 61, 87
4	19 876.9	30, 46, 53, 63, 87
5	19 813.0	22, 27, 30, 52, 60
worse	17 298.4	2, 7, 16, 41, 74

The results of this experiment show a spread of best solutions that smoothly reveals a trend to seed in the east side of the delimited region, near the open sea. It is important to note that the ecosystem in question is subjected to tides, which influence how organic substances and phytoplankton are transported along the bay. The availability of these two items – the main bivalve food sources – determines oyster growth and production.

It is no surprise that the trends revealed in the initial experiments were only partially confirmed, due to their very short simulation time. The simulated eight hours is insignificant when compared to water residence time in the bay – between one and 19 days [4]. Therefore, eight hours is not enough to simulate properly the mixing processes and the food variability affecting oyster growth. Furthermore, when oyster biomass increases, important feedbacks to available food become apparent where local depletion of food items may limit bivalve growth [19].

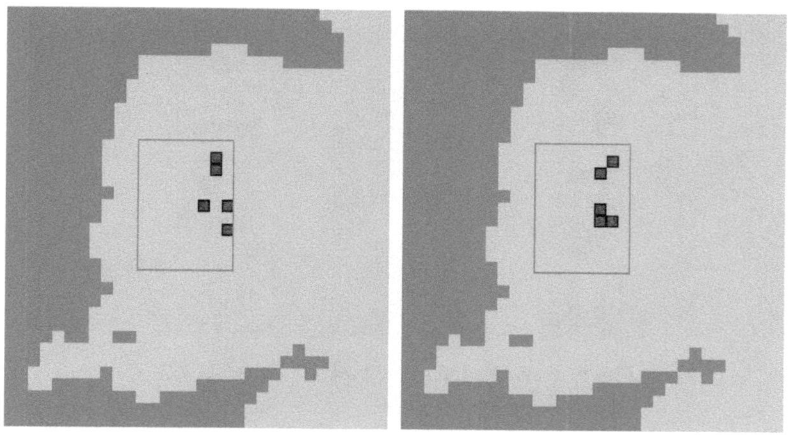

Fig. 4. Visualization of the best solutions (set #1)

Second Experiment. The second set of experiments extended the first one increasing the number of cells to seed to 30. Even without an obvious tendency in the area occupation, this experimental set was realized to verify if the results were more reliable when the ratio between occupied area vs. exploitation area increases – from 5.7% in the previous experiments to 34.1% in this one (from five to 30 cells to seed within the same area of 88 cells to explore). With no surprise the time required for each experiment is equal to that of previous experience, since it is dependent on the number of simulation steps and not on the number of areas occupied by aquaculture. The results are presented in Table 2 and Figure 5.

Table 2. Five best results and worse result of the second experimental set

Rank	Production Value (Indicator)	Seeded Cells
1	57 756.5	Different sets of 30 cells
2	57 720.9	
3	57 659.5	
4	57 639.2	
5	57 538.1	
worse	55 026.6	

The solutions present different patterns but with a tendency to concentrate oysters in the north and east sides of the exploitation area. The patterns strengthen the tendency to fill the areas near the open sea, where sea water exchanges are more intense and food tends to be more abundant.

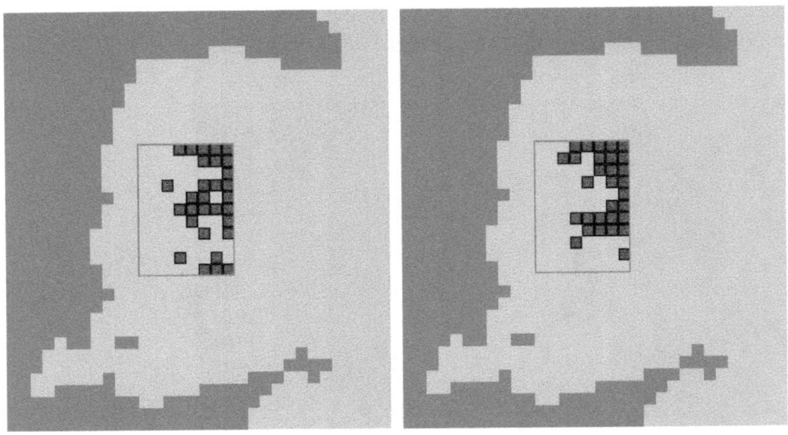

Fig. 5. Visualization of the best solutions (set #2)

Another interesting result is the coincidence in the occupied areas – the 2 best solutions share 18 cells out of 30 (60%) and in the five best solutions 12 cells remain selected (40%). The difference between the maximum and the minimum production value indicator decreases to 5.0% of the minimum.

The expected production value indicators (approximately six times larger than those of previous experience) were not confirmed; in fact it is a little bit less than three times more. The most likely explanation is local food depletion leading to slower bivalve growth as cultivated area increases. Experiments with this population density showed that the relationship between bivalve's production and cultivated area is linear if the number of cells to seed is less than 10; for greater values of seeded cells the production per cultivated grid cell decreases. More experiments should be performed with lower densities to find the value at which growth ceases to be linear.

5 Conclusions and Future Work

This paper presented a new framework for complex ecological simulations and optimization - EcoSimNet. This framework allows the coexistence of multiple simulators in the network, controlled by different agents, enabling the parallel simulation of different scenarios, increasing the number of simulations and the real time simulated, without compromising the quality of results and ensuring a more complete analysis of scenarios. As the number of parallel simulators on the network increases, the time needed to find a "near" optimal solution decreases proportionally.

The strategy followed in the implementation of the parallel simulated annealing algorithm, separating the roles of the coordinator and the worker nodes, allowed the independence of each agent tactics for optimization; the experiments showed that the inclusion of the two roles in the same agent didn't compromise the agent's rationality.

In this kind of ecological models the main advantage of using parallel simulations is the computational performance achieved, because issues like conceptual distribution of different aspects of the reality simulated are very difficult to separate in different simulators – the mixing processes and the food variability affecting oyster growth, the feedbacks to available food and the local depletion of food items that limit bivalve growth must be integrated in each simulation step by all entities, and the synchronization effort required for synchronization between the simulators would make the system much slower.

This work is a step forward towards an agent based decision support system to optimize complex environmental problems. At the moment the architecture presented is exploiting the concept of simulation islands or clusters, each one composed by one agent controlling several simulators, simultaneously simulating independent scenarios. One of the agents took the lead role, taking the initiative to encourage other agents to obtain the desired results as quickly as possible.

More experiments need to be done, increasing the number of simulators and agents in the network, in order to have a clear idea of what reasonable limits should be imposed on the size of the EcoSimNet framework.

The next steps in this platform will incorporate automatic decision in the coordinator agent, to decide how many simulators and worker agents will be necessary to consider new scenarios, and to determine degrees of similarity with scenarios already exploited. Furthermore, multi-criteria optimization simulations will be tested, where agents will evaluate different scenarios according to environmental and economical objectives.

The results were encouraging, and the researchers plan to use this approach for testing variations of the optimization criteria: considering a fixed exploitation area and different bivalve densities, considering the joint exploitation of several species of bivalves in the same area, and considering the commercial market value of each bivalve species and optimizing the production ensuring the largest economic return on investment.

Acknowledgements. This work was started during the ABSES project – "Agent-Based Simulation of Ecological Systems" (FCT/POSC/EIA/57671/2004) and António Pereira was supported by the FCT scholarship SFRH/BD/1633/2004 during part of its execution.

References

1. Duarte, P., Azevedo, B., Ribeiro, C., Pereira, A., Falcão, M., Serpa, D., Bandeira, R., Reia, J.: Management oriented mathematical modelling of Ria Formosa (South Portugal). Transitional Water Monographs 1(1), 13–51 (2007)
2. Watson, R.T., Zinyowera, M.C., Moss, R.H.: Climate Change 1995 - Impacts, adaptations and mitigation of climate change. In: I.-I.P.o.C Change (ed.) Scientific-Technical Analyses, vol. 1. Cambridge University Press, Cambridge (1996)
3. INE, Instituto Nacional de Estataistica. Statistical Yearbook of Portugal 2007. 1st edn., vol. 1. Instituto Nacional de Estatística, IP, Lisboa (2008)

4. Duarte, P., Meneses, R., Hawkins, A.J.S., Zhu, M., Fang, J., Grant, J.: Mathematical modelling to assess the carrying capacity for multi-species culture within coastal waters. Ecological Modelling 168(1-2), 109–143 (2003)
5. Cruz, F., Pereira, A., Valente, P., Duarte, P., Reis, L.P.: Intelligent Farmer Agent for Multi-agent Ecological Simulations Optimization. In: Proceedings of the 13th Portuguese Conference on Artificial Intelligence, Guimaraes, Portugal, pp. 593–604 (2007)
6. Pereira, A., Duarte, P., Norro, A.: Different modelling tools of aquatic ecosystems: A proposal for a unified approach. Ecological Informatics 1(4), 407–421 (2006)
7. Kirkpatrick, S., Gelatt, C.D., Vecchi, M.P.: Optimization by Simulated Annealing. Science 220(4598), 671–680 (1983)
8. Wooldridge, M.: Intelligent Agents. In: Weiss, G. (ed.) Multiagent Systems: A Modern Approach to Distributed Artificial Intelligence, pp. 27–77. The MIT Press, Cambridge (1999)
9. Huhns, M.N., Stephens, L.M.: Multiagent Systems and Societies of Agents. In: Weiss, G. (ed.) Multiagent Systems: A Modern Approach to Distributed Artificial Intelligence, pp. 79–120. The MIT Press, Cambridge (1999)
10. Pereira, A., Duarte, P., Reis, L.P.: ECOLANG - A communication language for simulations of complex ecological systems. In: Proceedings of the 19th European Conference on Modelling and Simulation ECMS 2005, Riga, Latvia, pp. 493–500 (2005)
11. Dzeroski, S.: Applications of symbolic machine learning to ecological modelling. Ecological Modelling 146(1-3), 263–273 (2001)
12. Russel, S.J., Norvig, P.: Artificial Intelligence: A Modern Approach, 2nd edn. Prentice Hall, New Jersey (2002)
13. Pereira, A., Duarte, P., Reis, L.P.: Agent-Based Simulation of Ecological Models. In: Proceedings of the 5th Workshop on Agent-Based Simulation, Lisbon, Portugal, pp. 135–140. SCS Publishing House (2004)
14. Mishra, N., Prakash, M., Tiwari, K., Shankar, R., Chan, F.T.S.: Hybrid tabu-simulated annealing based approach to solve multi-constraint product mix decision problem. Expert systems with applications 29(2), 446–454 (2005)
15. Glover, F.: Future paths for integer programming and links to artificial intelligence. Computers & Operations Research 13(5), 533–549 (1986)
16. Holland, J.H.: Adaptation in natural and artificial systems. The University of Michigan Press, Ann Arbor (1975)
17. Sutton, R.S., Barto, A.G.: Reinforcement Learning: An Introduction, vol. 1. MIT Press, Cambridge (1998)
18. Ram, D.J., Sreenivas, T.H., Subramaniam, K.G.: Parallel Simulated Annealing Algorithms. Journal of Parallel and Distributed Computing 37(2), 207–212 (1996)
19. Duarte, P., Hawkins, A.J.S., Pereira, A.: How does estimation of environmental carrying capacity for bivalve culture depend upon spatial and temporal scales. In: Dame, R.F., Olenin, S. (eds.) Comparative Roles of Suspension-Feeders in Ecosystems, Nida, Lithuania, pp. 121–135 (2005)

DarkBlade: A Program That Plays Diplomacy

João Ribeiro[1], Pedro Mariano[2], and Luís Seabra Lopes[2]

[1] XLM – Serviços de Informática, Lda
jbsr@ua.pt
[2] Transverse Activity on Intelligent Robotics – IEETA – DETI,
Universidade de Aveiro, Portugal
plsm@ua.pt, lsl@ua.pt

Abstract. Diplomacy is a 7-player game that requires coordination between players in order to achieve victory. Its huge search space makes existing search algorithms useless. In this paper we present Darkblade, a player designed as a Multi-Agent System that uses potential fields to calculate moves and evaluate board positions. We tested our player against other recent players. Although there are some limitations, the results are promising.

1 Introduction

Two-player games have been the subject of intense research in order to come up with an agent capable of beating the human champion. Checkers and Chess have already seen the appearance of such agents. Moreover, in the game of Checkers a partial proof of being a draw has been established [1]. Research has been focusing on building databases of end-positions, which can be used to classify the position as a win for one of the players or as a draw. Search algorithms and specialised hardware have been the tools to achieve this goal. However, research in games with more than two players where alliances between players are crucial in order to reach the winning position has been neglected. The relation between any two players will affect the strategy of a player [2]. If relations may shift during the course of a game, agents must take into account backstabbing behaviour if there is no entity to enforce agreements [3].

Work by Krauss [4], Loeb [5] and others on multi-player games used Diplomacy and show its potential for serving as a test-bed to new theories and practical approaches for solving such highly complex games. The game's rules are simple but the sheer number of possible plays for each turn is staggering. The number of possible openings is determined to be over 4×10^{15} which is far superior to the 20 different opening moves in chess [5]. As for the number of possible movements per turn it is roughly estimated to be around 34^{16} (see [4]). This presents a new problem that requires a different approach, even if Diplomacy and Chess have similar mechanics, the size of the search space makes a purely search space based solution unfeasible due to its computational requirements.

L. Seabra Lopes et al. (Eds.): EPIA 2009, LNAI 5816, pp. 485–496, 2009.

2 Diplomacy

2.1 Rules

The game of Diplomacy is played on a board that depicts nations and regions in Europe in the beginning of the 20th century [6]. The map is divided in provinces which can be inland, water and coastal. Some inland and coastal provinces have supply centres which may be owned by a player. There are a total of 34 supply centres and victory is achieved when a player owns 18 supply centres.

Each player controls units. These may be either armies or fleets. Only one unit may be located in a province. Common sense dictates what province type may hold some unit type. An exception occurs with fleets in that they do not occupy a coastal province, but rather its coast or one of its coasts. In the case of coastal provinces with two provinces, fleets can only travel to some coasts in adjacent coastal provinces.

At the start of a game each player is randomly assigned a nation, which corresponds to 3 supply centres and 3 units, with the exception of Russia that has 4 of each. The initial supply centres are termed *home supply centres*. They are the only places where a player can put new units. Figure 1 shows the map in the beginning of a game.

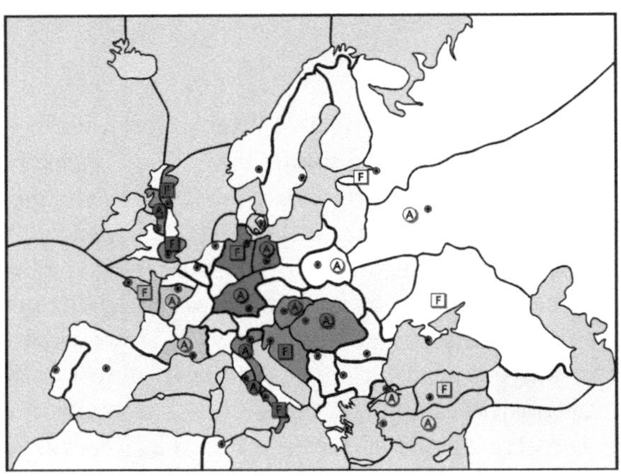

Fig. 1. Map game and initial state at *Spring* of 1900

Normal play is divided in two types of turns called *Spring* and *Fall*. Both have the following phases: 1) diplomatic; 2) order writing; 3) order resolution; 4) retreat and disband. Fall turns have a fifth phase: gain or lose units. A game starts at turn Spring of year 1900.

Each player assigns to its unit one of the following orders: *hold* its position, *move* to a reachable province, *convoy* a land unit, or *support* another unit. Only fleets can convoy. A unit may give support to a unit to: 1) hold its position if the supported unit is in a reachable province; 2) move to a reachable province.

This province must be reachable by the supporting unit. Support orders are an important aspect of this game, since if two units try to move to the same province without any support, they will fail. If they are supported, the unit with highest support wins.

The game focuses on negotiation, alliances, defection and treason (agreements are not enforceable).

2.2 DAIDE Application

DAIDE (Diplomacy AI Development Environment) is a client/server application which was developed in order to foster the development of artificial agents to play Diplomacy. Clients are players and they send orders and diplomatic messages to the server. The server is responsible for managing a game, processing orders, and dispatch diplomatic messages to players. Diplomatic messages are organised in levels, ranging from alliance proposals (level 10) to explanations (level 130). Currently few agents use level 10 messages. DAIDE can also be used to play no-press games, i.e., no diplomatic messages are allowed. From this point we will use the word bot to refer to an artificial player designed to play Diplomacy through DAIDE.

3 Previous Work

3.1 Israeli Diplomat

The Israeli Diplomat [4], by Kraus and Lehmann, was a continued effort in developing a Diplomacy agent first published in 1988 [7] with impressive results and providing an obvious inspiration to some of the most recent agents, like HaAI [8]. It remains one of the most complete implementations of a Diplomacy agent with reasonable performance in both strategic analysis and negotiation and capable of winning games with press against human competition. It uses a dynamic multi-process layer-based architecture. Each process is responsible for a part in a specific aspect of the game (negotiations, movements, etc). It supports a decent protocol of communication that allows for basic alliance/peace negotiations as well as more detailed order negotiations. The strategy plan includes a one-season movement analysis that considers the gain of a set of moves and current or future alliances or agreements with other powers. Some emphasis on variable personality was included to prevent a deterministic form of play.

The use of personality traits that influence decisions on how the agent system acted when facing the same problems is also mentioned but the details about this method are not specified.

3.2 The Bordeaux Diplomat

Bordeaux Diplomat [5], by Loeb, like the Israeli Diplomat also makes use of modules to divide the game's complexity. It has a negotiation module and a strategy planning module. The negotiation module deals only with communication with other powers and the strategic core tries to find the best moves for each power ignoring the power it represents. The strategic module uses an improved best-first search algorithm, Refined Evolutionary Search, to find the best moves for one season starting with a seed of movements and them mutating it until it contains the best set of moves for each power or alliance of powers. In this search, Nash Equilibria, when found, are not lost since each alliance (be it one single power or a group of allied powers) has no profit in mutating its moves. For modelling the loyalty of each ally it uses a Friendliness Matrix. This matrix holds a minimum gain value for each power that represents the likeliness of a certain power to back-stab another if at any given time it can achieve that gain in the field. For builds and retreats it uses a complete search space algorithm since the number of combinations is not overwhelming in terms of computational effort.

3.3 LA Diplomat

Shapiro, Fuchs and Leginson's LA Diplomat [9], works by learning new moves in consecutive plays with itself. It uses a hierarchy of pattern-weights to represent partial positions on the world map or specific moves. It then uses time difference learning for the evaluation of each pattern, thus giving certain powers more value than others. This approach has some interesting results, with the agent actually learning some book openings by itself. However some unrealistic move patterns end up with high value.

3.4 HaAI Bot

HaAI [8], by F. Haard and S. Johansson, is a multi-agent approach where each unit is modelled by a sub-agent. HaAI proposes what it believes is the best movement and the needed supports to a common pool of orders. To select the season orders it uses an adapted Contract Net to coordinate sub-agents, where each sub-agent is both a manager and a contractor. The supports being the contracts that can be bid on by other agents.

The game board is modelled using a weighted world map where only supply center provinces have values. A province's total value, however, is derived from its base value (in case it is a supply center) and a fraction of the value of the adjacent provinces. This is then used by unit sub-agents to determine the best movement considering the closest maximum profit. Unit building is handled by a new unit sub-agent and uses an army/fleet ratio. This bot has proven rather successful against other DAIDE projects prior to 2005.

3.5 Diplominator Bot

Diplominator [10] is a recent bot and produces interesting results. It is capable of basic peace negotiations, partially supporting Level 10 of the DAIDE Diplomacy

Protocol, and shows, to some extent, how negotiation, even in its basic level, influences an agent's results. It was tested only against DumbBot. When not using negotiation it falls slightly behind DumbBot, but when negotiation is active it performs slightly better.

In terms of strategic analysis, Diplominator attempts to maximise a unit profit one at a time, thus using a monolithic system. For profit evaluation it uses province values and value propagation to determine the most profitable destination. To avoid deterministic factor it uses a random selection of the most profitable provinces.

3.6 DumbBot

This is a bot developed by David Norman that belongs to DAIDE Community bots [11]. Despite being a simple agent, as described by the author, it performs well and some times is able to beat other more sophisticated bots as well as un-experienced human players in no-press diplomacy. Movement is determined by calculating weights for each province and moving the units to more valuable provinces. It is a widely used agent for comparison and almost all bots use it in their tests.

4 Nomenclature

Before describing our model, we must formalise the description of the map. The map is composed of provinces that are represented by set $\mathcal{P}$. The ones that are supply centers are represented by set $\mathcal{P}_c$, and the ones that are home supply centers by set $\mathcal{P}_h$, that is to say, $\mathcal{P}_h \subset \mathcal{P}_c \subset \mathcal{P}$. These symbols are used to refer to supply centres owned by a power. Regarding province connectivity, we define $\mathcal{V}_p$ as the set of neighbouring provinces of province p that a unit of some type can move to.

5 Agent Description

5.1 Architecture

Darkblade is a multi-agent system with agents organised in a 2-layer hierarchy. Each owned unit is assigned an agent, named *General*, that is responsible for proposing orders for its unit. These orders are submitted to the agent at the top layer, named *President*, that is responsible for calculating the most profitable order combination. The architecture is organised in three modules. The Strategic module contains the President, the Generals and the data structure where generals put their orders and the president fetches them. The Knowledge and Belief Base module only contains data about board state, personality parameters and diplomatic relations. This data is used by both types of agents. A third module is responsible for communication with the DAIDE server.

Figure 2 shows the architecture of our agent with threads pictured as ovals and data structures as rectangles with round corners and solid lines. Arrows indicate information flow.

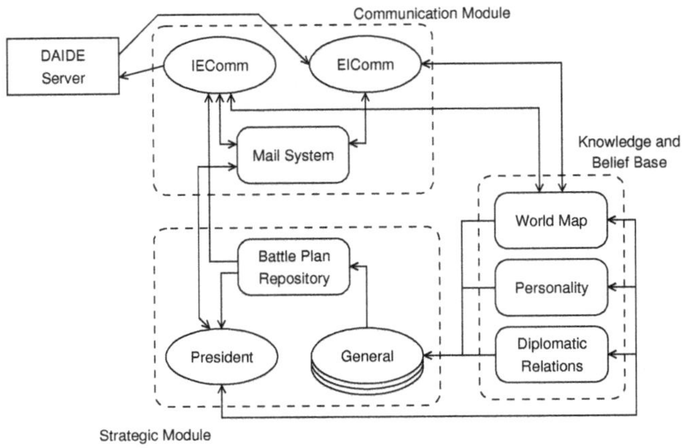

Fig. 2. Darkblade architecture

5.2 Personality Traits

Personality traits applied to a Diplomat were first suggested by Kraus in [4] and later [12]. The idea behind using personality traits is to implement a set of parameters that condition the agent's behaviour, i.e., how the agent feels and acts about what it perceives. These parameters can be used to assess the threat of an unit moving towards us, to decide whom to attack or ally with, etc.

The model chosen for personality traits is Norman's Five Factor Model [13]. Norman's model is simple and efficient. It has also been used as an Artificial Intelligence personality model [14]. Application of Norman's taxonomy of personality attributes to Darkblade yields the following traits:

Aggressiveness:[1] The desire to conquer new territory. A personality with low aggressiveness tends to be more defensive and conquer only when it is sure of success and never at the expense of a possible defensive loss.

Conscientiousness: Methodical and reliable behaviour. A conscientious agent follows a defined plan and doesn't change its plan at the first obstacle. After choosing a target it tends to focus on it instead of constantly changing its goals.

Agreeableness: Capacity for cooperation with others, trusting. A disagreeable agent tends to trust only himself and be suspicious of others.

Extroversion: Capacity to create friends and enemies faster. A high extrovert agent quickly makes a friend of someone that has moved away from their common front, but just as quickly will be viewed as an enemy if he gets closer. On the other hand, an introvert agent is slower at making both friends and enemies.

Neuroticism: Associated with uneasiness, neurotic and paranoid behavior. A neurotic personality will try to react to the simplest sign of threat from an opponent.

[1] In the original proposal this factor is called openness.

5.3 Strategic Evaluation

In order to tackle the problem of searching a good set of orders for a turn, two types of values are used: province value and unit threat. Province values are represented in two dimensions: one that distinguishes land provinces from sea provinces, and another that distinguishes between owned provinces from not-owned provinces. Unit threat history keeps track of unit movement. Province values of $\{p\} \cup \mathcal{V}_p$ influence the probability of a unit in p to move or to hold. These probabilities add up to form the opposing strength, S_p, of a power in province p.

This approach is similar to swarm systems that are based on the collective behaviour exhibited by social insects [15]. Not-owned provinces emanate a pheromone that attracts an agent units, while owned provinces emanate a pheromone that attracts units of a defensive agent. Likewise, the threat of adversary units, also attracts units of an attacking agent. The propensity to either attack or defend is a function of Darkblade personality.

Province Value. Province values, v_p, are calculated using the following equation:

$$v_{p_i} = \sum_{\{p_j : d(p_i,p_j) \leq 2\}} \frac{b_{p_j}}{a^{d(p_i,p_j)}} \tag{1}$$

where $d(p_i, p_j)$ is a function that returns the length of the shortest path between provinces p_i and p_j. Parameter a influences the maximum value of v_p. Constant b_p represents the base value of a province. Since home supply centres have a strategic value superior to normal supply center (recall that they are the ones where the agent may build new units), their base value is the highest. We limit propagation to provinces that are at most 2 nodes from the origin, otherwise, province values would be homogeneous. A province base value is defined as follows:

$$b_p = \begin{cases} 2 & \text{if} \quad p \in \mathcal{P}_h \\ 1.5 & \text{if} \quad p \in \mathcal{P}_c \setminus \mathcal{P}_h \\ 0 & \text{otherwise.} \end{cases} \tag{2}$$

Province values depend on two parameters: 1) ownership; 2) unit type. Owned provinces inside the territory should have a lower value than borderline provinces. On the other hand, not-owned provinces should be valued higher and Darkblade must calculate a set of orders to gain them. Recall that armies can only be located in inland or coastal provinces, while fleets can be located in coastal and sea provinces. Therefore some provinces have no value for some units. The bottom line is we have four distinct v_p values for each p.

Each v_p corresponds to a potential field and higher potentials attract Darkblade units. This field decays with the distance other provinces are from province p. Therefore, parameter a must be greater than 1. This parameter also represents the fact that units that are far away have more provinces to move to. In the present case we used $a = 4$.

Unit Threat. Unit threat in a province is also calculated through a similar equation to (1) in that the base value of a unit is propagated to adjacent provinces. However a threat of a fleet does not propagate to inland provinces and, likewise, the threat of an army does not propagate to sea provinces. Propagation is done only to provinces a unit can move to. Since units have the same strength, 1 is used as the base value. Unit threat represents the strength a power has in moving towards or holding a certain province.

Hold or Move Probability. The probability of a unit u holding or moving to province p is linearly proportional to the province value as seen in the following equation:

$$S_{u,p} = \frac{v_p - \underline{v_p}}{\overline{v_p} - \underline{v_p}} 0.5 + 0.3 \tag{3}$$

where $\underline{v_p}$ and $\overline{v_p}$ are, respectively, the lowest and highest province value of $\{p\} \cup \mathcal{V}_p$.

Opposing Strength in a Province. This value is calculated by adding the probability of each unit of a power[2]:

$$S_p = \sum_u S_{u,p}. \tag{4}$$

This sum represents the most probable attack or defensive strength of a certain power over a certain province. Note that support to hold or to move requires the supporting unit being able to move to, respectively, the unit's province or the unit's destination. Therefore this equation allows us to consider *support* orders. Units that, despite being adjacent to the province, are unable to reach it (e.g. a fleet in a coastal province can not reach an inland province) are not considered when determining a power's opposing strength.

This method has some disadvantages and obviously doesn't take into account all information acquired by the agent's perception. For example, threat variation could be used to better assess the probability of a power moving its units towards a certain province. Despite this, the function itself produced satisfactory results guessing some moves not only by other Darkblade instances but also from other agents.

Province Profit. Province profit is made of two values: defensive, π_d, and offensive, π_o. The first represents how valuable an owned province is, and thus how much effort should be spent in order to keep it. The second represents the value of gaining one more province. These values are a function of unit threat, opposing strength (see (4)), and personality parameters. Due to its complexity we refer to [16] for more details.

---

[2] Recall that all units have the same strategic value in the game.

Success Rate. When a *General* proposes a set of orders for its unit (either to hold or to move combined with support orders for adjacent units) it calculates a success rate. This is based on the number of units, n, supporting its unit and S_p:

$$\begin{cases} \dfrac{n}{S_p} & \text{if holding} \\ \dfrac{n}{1+S_p} & \text{if moving.} \end{cases} \tag{5}$$

Recall that whenever two units are ordered to move to the same province, the unit with the highest support wins.

Hold and Move Orders. Whenever a *General* submits a set of orders, it assigns it a value that is based on defensive and offensive profit and the aggressiveness personality trait, O:

$$\pi_d(1-O)+\pi_o(1+O). \tag{6}$$

In order to decrease computational requirement of finding the best combination of orders, there is a threshold on the success rate of the submitted set of orders. This threshold increases as the agent gains more units. The *President* selects the combination of set orders that maximises the profit.

Retreat Orders. When considering where to retreat to, we consider the province with the highest value, v_p.

Build Orders. In *Fall* phase, when it is time to build or to remove units, we choose the type of unit to build or to remove based on two ratios: 1) number of army units versus number of fleets; 2) land versus sea provinces adjacent to home supply centres. The type of unit is chosen in order to keep the two ratios equal. This tries to model the fact that some powers are more prone to sea expansion while others by land.

6 Experiments

6.1 Setup

We ran different experiments with Darkblade against itself and other agents designed to work with DAIDE Server. When running the experiments a few problems arose so most tests had to be launched one at a time to make sure all were executed properly. Some of these problems include random disconnects, messages getting lost or, less frequently, clients failing to establish a session with the server, usually when more than one client started a connection at the same time. Game duration was a factor that limited the amount of tests performed. Some games, due to Darkblade's nature of play, lasted past year 1950 (100 game turns) and, on later stages of the game, the amount of units in the board resulted in a bot taking as long as 15 minutes to issue its orders. These issues limited the number of tests done.

We chose two of the agents introduced in Sec. 3: Diplominator and DumbBot. Diplominator for being one of the latest agents and using similar evaluation processes as Darkblade. DumbBot was chosen since it is used by other agents developed for DAIDE, such as HaAI [8] and Shaheed's Diplomat [17], and thus allows us to indirectly evaluate Darkblade's performance against other agents which were unavailable for tests. Another factor that made us choose these two agents is the fact that neither of them supports Convoys, just like Darkblade. Despite the use of Convoys being sporadic, for some powers it is one of the most profitable moves in the long term. For example, England, when it establishes itself in the north of Europe, convoying armies into the main land will allow it a faster win than relying exclusively on conquering coastal supply centres. This is the reason why England is one of the powers that produces most wins in Human vs Human matches [18].

Bot fitness was measured using a point system defined as:

- **10** Won the game
- **7** Survived with 10 or more supply centres
- **4** Survived with more than its initial supply centres
- **1** Survived with the same or less than its initial supply centres
- **0** Was eliminated before the end of the game

For each group of bots being evaluated, a certain number of games were performed assuring that each bot played with all powers at least once.

Table 1. Personality parameters of Darkblade instances

	DB42	DB44
Aggr	0.70	0.80
Cons	0.70	0.80
Agre	0.60	0.80
Extr	0.50	0.80
Neur	0.30	0.80

Table 2. Results from games between Darkblade and selected bots. Average points per power for each bot.

	DB42	DB44	DumbBot	Diplominator
AUS	1.13	3.67	0.17	0.00
ENG	4.50	5.50	4.71	2.57
FRA	6.14	7.70	1.71	3.43
GER	2.43	3.50	0.00	0.20
ITA	3.00	3.00	1.43	0.57
RUS	5.86	3.50	3.33	3.00
TUR	4.50	4.00	1.67	3.14
Average	3.89	4.17	1.87	1.96

Table 3. Bot win ratio comparison

Agent	**Ratio**
DB44	1.53
HaAI Berserk	1.25
DB42	1.00
HaAI Vanilla	0.93
Diplominator	0.85

6.2 Results

The first set of experiments consisted in searching the set of personality parameters that maximised Darkblade fitness. In these experiments only Darkblade bots where involved. After this phase, the two best Darkblade configurations played with DumbBot and Diplominator. Bot instances were 1 DB44, 2 DB42, 2 DumbBot and 2 Diplominator. A total of 23 games were performed with this bot setting. Selected Darkblade personality parameters are presented in Tab. 1. Average points per game obtained and power played by each bot are shown in Tab. 2.

From these results it is clear that Darkblade outperforms some recent bots. As for bots that were not available, but results against DumbBot are available, Tab. 3 shows the win ratio between these bots using DumbBot as benchmark. A value of x means that the corresponding bot has x times more victories compared to DumbBot. For instance BD42 has many victories as DumbBot, while the number of victories BD44 has is 50% superior to the victories achieved by DumbBot.

7 Conclusions and Future Work

We have presented a multi-agent system capable of playing the game of Diplomacy, through the DAIDE environment. Strategic evaluation was based not only on province value, but also on unit threat and threat history, an innovation compared to previous approaches. There are already some results using unit threat but not with threat history which has been also used to detect who are the most attacking or defending adversaries. Games with available bots [10] and comparative results with other bots [8] showed the merits of our approach. Still, there are some shortcomings, as *convoy* orders were not considered. Diplomatic relations lack in our work. As such, future work must include all types of orders and tackle the different diplomatic message levels that DAIDE provides. These should be thoroughly tested instead of the few tests reported in [12].

Regarding the applicability to other games, the potential field, that we have designed for each province, can be used in games where territory is an important factor. As an example we have the game of Risk which is also a n-player game.

References

1. Schaeffer, J., Burch, N., Björnsson, Y., Kishimoto, A., Müller, M., Lake, R., Lu, P., Sutphen, S.: Checkers is solved. Science 317(5844), 1518–1522 (2007)
2. Loeb, D.E.: Stable winning coalitions. In: Nowakowski, R.J. (ed.) Games of No Chance, Cambridge, pp. 451–471 (1996)
3. Duffy, J., Feltovich, N.: Do actions speak louder than words? An experimental comparison of observation and cheap talk. Games and Economic Behaviour 39, 1–27 (2002)
4. Kraus, S., Lehmann, D.: Designing and building a negotiating automated agent. Computational Intelligence 11(1), 132–171 (1995)

5. Loeb, D.E.: Challenges in multi-player gaming by computers: A treatise on the diplomacy programming project (1995), `http://www.diplom.org/Zine/S1995M/Loeb/Project.html`
6. Hill, A.: The rules of diplomacy, `http://www.wizards.com/default.asp?x=ah/prod/diplomacy`
7. Kraus, S., Lehmann, D.: Diplomat, an agent in a multi agent environment: An overview. In: Proceedings of Seventh Annual International Phoenix Conference on Computers and Communications, 1988, pp. 434–438 (1988)
8. Håård, F.: Multi-agent diplomacy: Tactical planning using cooperative distributed problem solving. Master's thesis, Blekinge Institute of Technology (2004)
9. Shapiro, A., Fuchs, G., Levinson, R.: Learning a game strategy using pattern-weights and self-play. In: Schaeffer, J., Müller, M., Björnsson, Y. (eds.) CG 2002. LNCS, vol. 2883, pp. 42–60. Springer, Heidelberg (2003)
10. Webb, A., Chin, J., Wilkins, T., Payce, J., Dedoyard, V.: Automated negotiation in the game of diplomacy (2008), `http://www.doc.ic.ac.uk/project/2007/362/g0736203/TheDiplominator/`
11. Norman, D.: David's diplomacy ai page, `http://www.ellought.demon.co.uk/dipai/` (last checked, March 2008)
12. Kraus, S.: Negotiation and cooperation in multi-agent environments. Artificial Intelligence 94(1-2), 79–97 (1997)
13. McCrae, R.R., John, O.P.: An introduction to the five-factor model and its applications. Journal of Personality 60(2), 175–215 (1992)
14. Talman, S.: The adaptive multi-personality agent. Master's thesis, Bar Ilan University, Ramat Gan, Israel (2004)
15. Bonabeau, E., Dorigo, M., Theraulaz, G.: Swarm Intelligence: From Natural to Artificial Systems. Santa Fe Institute Studies in the Sciences of Complexity. Oxford University Press, Oxford (1999)
16. Ribeiro, J.: Darkblade - an artificial inteligent agent for diplomacy. Master's thesis, University of Aveiro (2008)
17. Shaheed, J.: Creating a diplomat. Master's thesis, Imperial College, UK (2004)
18. Windsor, P.D.: Geography is destiny, how the standard map dictates fortunes and strategies (1999), `http://devel.diplom.org/Zine/F1999R/Windsor/dipmap.html`

Agent Inferencing Meets the Semantic Web

Paulo Trigo[1] and Helder Coelho[2]

[1] Departamento de Eng. de Electrónica e Telecomunicações e de Computadores
Instituto Superior de Engenharia de Lisboa, Portugal
ptrigo@deetc.isel.ipl.pt
[2] Departamento de Informática
Faculdade de Ciências da Universidade de Lisboa, Portugal
hcoelho@di.fc.ul.pt

Abstract. We provide an agent the capability to infer the relations (assertions) entailed by the rules that describe the formal semantics of an RDFS knowledge-base. The proposed inferencing process formulates each semantic restriction as a rule implemented within a SPARQL query statement. The process expands the original RDF graph into a fuller graph that explicitly captures the rule's described semantics. The approach is currently being explored in order to support descriptions that follow the generic Semantic Web Rule Language. An experiment, using the Fire-Brigade domain, a small-scale knowledge-base, is adopted to illustrate the agent modeling method and the inferencing process.

1 Introduction

The content of the Web is growing in a way that is mainly oriented to human consumption. The Semantic Web (SW) vision aims to overcome such human-oriented tendency in order to better explore the full power of the Web [2]. The SW is taking place and one of the goals is to utilize artificial agents as full participants and helpers in the process of querying and extracting knowledge from the Web contents.

We explore the foundational SW description language, named "Resource Description Language" (RDF), together with one of its most recent query languages, "SPARQL Protocol and RDF Query Language" (SPARQL), in order to build an inferencing process to be incorporated within an agent. The goal is to design an agent capable of obtaining the implicit knowledge by reasoning over the explicitly stored Web information.

Agent inferencing over SW descriptions gives organizations the opportunity to use the Internet as a "huge" collective-knowledge-representation platform. The SW tools provide greater collaboration among users, content suppliers and enterprises [7]. Hence, organizational decision-making is now under pressure as different views, prospects, contributions and collaborations are required in order to improve decision-taking at the different levels of an organization. Two consequences, already visible, are the arrival of Business Intelligence (BI) 2.0 and the Mobile BI. The meaning of this is clear: "there is an extended spectrum of

L. Seabra Lopes et al. (Eds.): EPIA 2009, LNAI 5816, pp. 497–507, 2009.

applications and technologies for storing, searching and retrieving, data, information and knowledge"; also, management is given the means to achieve a more interactive, collaborative and decentralized profile.

Against this background, the progress towards the SW is unequivocal and appears in the form of the standardization of languages and in the increasing maturity of related models, tools and technologies. The SPARQL enables to extract the RDF explicitly stored information while the SW rules (or semantic constraints) claim for ways of extracting the implicitly represented information. Therefore, we propose a simple way of combining the SPARQL expressiveness with the RDF homogeneous way of representing information (e.g., the unified description of data and meta-data) in order to transform implicit knowledge into explicitly stored information. The approach's motivation is to provide users (e.g., institutions) tools to foster the early adoption of the SW concepts and the already available knowledge; the ideia is to "start taking advantage of SW with the existing explicitly stored information".

Previous work that explores similar approaches discuss the formal semantics of SPARQL and its extensions as well as the links from SPARQL to deductive systems [15,14]; others discuss the logical foundation of "RDF Schema" (RDFS) [6] and the construction of complete and sound deductive systems for RDFS fragments [13] and also the complexity of SPARQL [14] along with the formulation of theoretical algebraic operators [5]. Our work takes a practical stance and assumes that the currently available SPARQL specifications [1,16] do not support RDFS entailment. Therefore, we combine the SPARQL and RDF specifications [11] (also resorting to RDFS semantic constraints) to build an inferencing scenario driven by the ongoing SW appeal.

The next section briefly presents the RDF, RDFS and SPARQL languages (W3C recommendations), followed by the description of the proposed inference process and the agent modeling within an illustrative domain; the last section outlines some conclusions and future goals.

2 RDF, RDFS and SPARQL

The RDF [11] has emerged as the main data model for representing information about the resources available in the Web. The companion specification of RDF is the RDFS [3] which provides the basic mechanisms for describing the semantic relations among Web resources. The SPARQL [1,16] is a language specially designed to query RDF-based repositories. Thus, RDFS is the foundation block of the Semantic Web concept and the SPARQL language is its most recent query approach. The next sections briefly describe RDF, RDFS and SPARQL.

2.1 The RDF Model

Usually an RDF expression is simply described as "a *statement* about *resources*" where a *resource* is anything that owns an Universal Resource Identifier (URI).

Each *statement* is composed of three *resources*: i) the *subject*, ii) the *predicate*, and iii) the *object*. A RDF graph, $\mathcal{G}$, is a set of *statements* where each *subject* and *object* are represented by nodes being connected by a *predicate* edge.

Formally, let the sets $\mathcal{U}$, $\mathcal{B}$ and $\mathcal{L}$ represent, respectively, URI references, blank nodes (i.e., anonymous *resources*) and literals. A tuple $(s, p, o) \in \mathcal{UBL} \times \mathcal{U} \times \mathcal{UBL}$, where $\mathcal{UBL} = \mathcal{U} \cup \mathcal{B} \cup \mathcal{L}$, is called an RDF triple, where s is the *subject*, p is the *predicate* and o is the *object*; we follow current formulation approaches that permit literals to occur as a *subject* component [13,4].

An RDF graph is a set of RDF triples and a subgraph is a subset of a graph. The $universe(\mathcal{G})$ denotes the elements in $\mathcal{UBL}$ that occur in the triples of $\mathcal{G}$ and the $vocabulary(\mathcal{G}) = universe(\mathcal{G}) \cap (\mathcal{U} \cup \mathcal{L})$, i.e., the $\mathcal{G}$ vocabulary excludes anonymous *resources*.

RDF semantics. The normative semantics for RDF graphs [9] follows classical treatment in logic with the notions of interpretation and entailment. Intuitively, an interpretation represents a possible configuration of the world, such that we can verify whether, or not, what is said in a graph $\mathcal{G}$ is true on that world configuration [12]. For example, the triple (s, p, o) states that the binary *predicate*, p, holds for the (s, o) *subject* and *object* pair. An interpretation provides such an association and any given graph will be true if none of its triples state something false. Thus, the graph $\mathcal{G}$ restricts the space of possible world configurations to those in which $\mathcal{G}$ is true; and such restriction represents the information provided by the graph.

RDF interpretation. Formally, an interpretation, over a specific vocabulary V, is described by the tuple $I = (I_{\mathcal{R}}, I_{\mathcal{P}}, I_{MAP}, I_{EXT})$, where $I_{\mathcal{R}}$ is a nonempty set of *resources* called the domain or universe of I, the $I_{\mathcal{P}} \subseteq I_{\mathcal{R}}$ is a set of *property* names, $I_{MAP} : V \rightarrow I_{\mathcal{R}}$ is the interpretation mapping, i.e., a mapping that assigns a *resource* to each vocabulary element, and $I_{EXT} \rightarrow 2^{I_{\mathcal{R}} \times I_{\mathcal{R}}}$ is a mapping that assigns an extension to each *property* name [13,9].

RDF entailment. The entailment concept follows from the idea of satisfaction of a graph under a certain interpretation. An RDF triple (s, p, o) is true under the interpretation I iff $s, p, o \in V$ and $I_{MAP}(p) \in I_{\mathcal{P}}$ and $(I_{MAP}(s), I_{MAP}(o)) \in I_{EXT}(I_{MAP}(p))$ [12,9].

Intuitively it means that a triple is true (under I) whenever its *subject*, *predicate* and *object* belong to the vocabulary, the *predicate* is interpreted as a *property* name, the *subject* and *object* are both interpreted as *resources* whereas the whole couple belongs to the extension of the *property* assigned to *predicate*.

A given graph $\mathcal{G}$ entails another $\mathcal{G}'$, $\mathcal{G} \models \mathcal{G}'$, iff every interpretation that satisfies $\mathcal{G}$ also satisfies $\mathcal{G}'$. Broadly, the notion of entailment captures information inferencing, in that if $\mathcal{G} \models \mathcal{G}'$, the information in $\mathcal{G}'$ is also, explicitly or implicitly, present in $\mathcal{G}$.

2.2 The RDF to RDFS Extension

The RDFS incorporates semantics into the RDF vocabulary by formally describing the (sub)class and (sub)property concepts, along with the notion of domain and range of (sub)properties. Thus, with RDFS the world is described using a vocabulary that is semantically framed by the concepts of typing and inheritance of classes and properties.

An RDFS interpretation is an RDF interpretation plus: i) a set $I_{\mathcal{C}} \subseteq I_{\mathcal{R}}$, representing the RDFS classes, and ii) a mapping, $I_{CEXT} : I_{\mathcal{C}} \rightarrow 2^{I_{\mathcal{R}}}$, that represents the *resources* being related by the RDF `rdf:type` predefined *property.* Thus, RDFS extends RDF starting from the set $I_{CEXT}(C) = \{x \in I_{\mathcal{R}} : (x, C) \in I_{EXT}(I_{MAP}(\texttt{rdf:type}))\}$ and adding the conditions fully enumerated by Hayes [9]. The same conditions are also described by Chen et al. [5] using the following simpler to read and rule-like formulation (we consider $x, y, z, a, b, p \in \mathcal{UBL}$, `rdf` and `rdfs` as prefixes, respectively, of RDF and RDFS vocabulary elements):

$$\begin{aligned}&\text{Class:}\\ &\quad(x, \texttt{rdf:type}, y)\\ &\Rightarrow (y, \texttt{rdf:type}, \texttt{rdfs:Class}) \qquad (1)\end{aligned}$$

The rule (1) defines the concept of class as a *resource* that is specified as the type for any other *resource.* For example, given that we have the triple $(\mathit{Lisbon}, \texttt{rdf:type}, \mathit{Place})$ we conclude that *Place* is a class, i.e., we also have the valid triple $(\mathit{Place}, \texttt{rdf:type}, \texttt{rdfs:Class})$.

$$\begin{aligned}&\text{Sub Class:}\\ &\quad(x, \texttt{rdf:type}, \texttt{rdfs:Class})\\ &\Rightarrow (x, \texttt{rdfs:subClassOf}, x) \qquad (2)\\ &\quad(x, \texttt{rdfs:subClassOf}, y) \wedge (y, \texttt{rdfs:subClassOf}, z)\\ &\Rightarrow (x, \texttt{rdfs:subClassOf}, z) \qquad (3)\\ &\quad(x, \texttt{rdfs:subClassOf}, y) \wedge (a, \texttt{rdf:type}, x)\\ &\Rightarrow (a, \texttt{rdf:type}, y) \qquad (4)\end{aligned}$$

The rules (2) and (3) describe, respectively, the reflexive and transitive properties of (sub)class statements. The rule (4) formulates the typing inheritance mechanism.

$$\begin{aligned}&\text{Property:}\\ &\quad(x, p, y)\\ &\Rightarrow (p, \texttt{rdf:type}, \texttt{rdfs:Property}) \qquad (5)\end{aligned}$$

The rule (5) defines the notion of property as a *resource* that plays the role of *predicate* within a triple.

Sub Property:

$$(x, \texttt{rdf:type}, \texttt{rdfs:Property}) \Rightarrow (x, \texttt{rdfs:subPropertyOf}, x) \tag{6}$$

$$(x, \texttt{rdfs:subPropertyOf}, y) \wedge (y, \texttt{rdfs:subPropertyOf}, z) \Rightarrow (x, \texttt{rdfs:subPropertyOf}, z) \tag{7}$$

$$(x, \texttt{rdfs:subPropertyOf}, y) \wedge (a, x, b) \Rightarrow (a, y, b) \tag{8}$$

The rules (6) and (7) describe, respectively, the notion of reflexive and transitive (sub)property statements; rule (8) formulates the *property* inheritance mechanism.

Domain and Range:

$$(p, \texttt{rdfs:domain}, d) \wedge (x, p, y) \Rightarrow (x, \texttt{rdf:type}, d) \tag{9}$$

$$(p, \texttt{rdfs:range}, d) \wedge (x, p, y) \Rightarrow (y, \texttt{rdf:type}, d) \tag{10}$$

The rules (9) and (10) define the notion, respectively, of domain and range of a *resource* in terms of the underlying typing relations.

2.3 The SPARQL Query Language

The SPARQL is a language for querying graphs designed as sets of RDF triples. A query is a specification of conjunctions and disjunctions of triple patterns and the answer consists on the values, of the variables, that match the specified triples' patterns.

A SPARQL graph pattern expression, P, is defined recursively, by Perez et al. [14], given a set, $\mathcal{V}$, of variables and $\mathcal{ULV} = \mathcal{U} \cup \mathcal{L} \cup \mathcal{V}$, as: i) a tuple from $\mathcal{ULV} \times \mathcal{ULV} \times \mathcal{ULV}$ is a graph pattern, ii) if P_1 and P_2 are graph patterns, then the expressions $\{ P_1 \texttt{ AND } P_2 \}$, $\{ P_1 \texttt{ OPTIONAL } P_2 \}$ and $\{ P_1 \texttt{ UNION } P_2 \}$ are graph patterns, and iii) if P is a graph pattern and R is a filter expression, then $\{ P \texttt{ FILTER } R \}$ is a graph pattern.

The SPARQL expressions are very intuitive and almost self explanatory. The SPARQL formal semantics is described, cf. [16], by the $eval(\mathcal{G}, P)$ definition, for any RDF graph $\mathcal{G}$ and SPARQL query graph pattern expression P.

For our purposes the most relevant aspect is that SPAQRL is a query language that operates as a graph pattern matching for RDF statements. Therefore, although SPARQL does not provide entailment capabilities it is a very convenient way of formulating RDF queries.

3 The Inference Process

The SPARQL language queries the information explicitly represented within an RDF graph. The implicit RDF triples are the ones that may be inferred from the rules that characterize each domain interpretation, e.g., the RDFS domain is characterized by the previously enumerated rules (cf. section 2.2).

The inference process considers the following typical representative of the rule format:

$$(\alpha \Rightarrow \beta)$$

where α is the rule antecedent formulated as a conjunction of several triples where each triple component belongs to the $\mathcal{ULV}$ set (i.e., it is possibly a variable), and β is the rule consequent formulated as a single triple where each component also belongs to the $\mathcal{ULV}$; their are no free variables in β, i.e., let $vars(x)$ be the set of variables in expression x, then we always have: $vars(\beta) = (vars(\beta) \cap vars(\alpha))$.

The inference process expands a graph $\mathcal{G}$ into a graph $\mathcal{G}'$ which explicitly includes the triples that, given rule $(\alpha \Rightarrow \beta)$, only existed implicitly in $\mathcal{G}$.

Operationally, the semantics of a finite rule set, $\mathcal{RS}$, can be described by a forward reasoning process. Starting with an initial graph $\mathcal{G}$ (knowledge-base) a series of graphs, $\mathcal{G}^{(0)}, \mathcal{G}^{(1)}, \ldots$ is constructed, where $\mathcal{G}^{(0)} = \mathcal{G}$ and $\mathcal{G}^{(i+1)}$ is obtained from $\mathcal{G}^{(i)}$ by adding the assertions in β whenever $\mathcal{RS}$ contains a rule $(\alpha \Rightarrow \beta)$ such that the assertions in α are satisfied by $\mathcal{G}^{(i)}$ (i.e., $\mathcal{G}^{(i)} \models \alpha$) and $\mathcal{G}^{(i)}$ does not contain β. This procedure eventually halts because the initial graph $\mathcal{G}$ (knowledge-base) contains only finitely many assertions and there are only finitely many rules; hence, there are only finitely many assertions that can possibly be added to $\mathcal{G}$.

The algorithm 1 implements the construction of $\mathcal{G}'$ such that $\mathcal{G} \models_{(\alpha \Rightarrow \beta)} \mathcal{G}'$, i.e., the new graph that may be inferred from $\mathcal{G}$ given the rule $(\alpha \Rightarrow \beta)$. The first step is to translate α into a SPARQL statement (cf. line 2); the next step applies the SPARQL statement to the graph and the result is used to build the triple set according to the information given by the β part of the rule; finally the graph is expanded with the new triples. The α to SPARQL translation is a direct mapping that may be implemented with any common-purpose programming language, e.g. Python [17], or a transformation oriented tool, e.g. the Extensible Stylesheet Language Transformation (XSLT) [21]. Within our implementation the SPARQL query execution resorts to the RDFLib implementation [18] (a Python API for the Semantic Web approaches).

The algorithm 2 illustrates the inferencing process with the computation of the closure of RDFS rules given an RDF graph $\mathcal{G}$.

As a very simple illustrative example consider:

$$\mathcal{G} = \{ (\mathit{Lisbon}, \texttt{rdf:type}, \mathit{Place}) \}$$

Algorithm 1. Expand graph $\mathcal{G}$ with rule $(\alpha \Rightarrow \beta)$

function EXPAND($\mathcal{G}$, $(\alpha \Rightarrow \beta)$, N)
 $SPARQL \leftarrow buildQuery(\alpha)$
 repeat ▷ apply $(\alpha \Rightarrow \beta)$ rule
  $N' \leftarrow N$
  $result \leftarrow getAnswer(SPARQL, \mathcal{G})$
  $tripleSet \leftarrow buildTripleSet(\beta, result)$
  for each $(s, p, o) \in tripleSet$ **do**
   if $(s, p, o) \notin \mathcal{G}$ **then** ▷ expand $\mathcal{G}$
    $add((s, p, o), \mathcal{G})$
    $N \leftarrow N + 1$
   end if
  end for
 until $N == N'$
 return $(\mathcal{G}, N)$
end function

Algorithm 2. Closure of graph $\mathcal{G}$ with RDFS rule set

1 **function** RDFS-CLOSURE($\mathcal{G}$)
2 $\mathcal{RS} \leftarrow \{ \mathrm{r}(1), \ldots, \mathrm{r}(10) \}$ ▷ cf. section 2.2
3 $N \leftarrow 0$
4 **repeat**
5   $N' \leftarrow N$
6   **for each** $(\alpha \Rightarrow \beta) \in \mathcal{RS}$ **do**
7    $(\mathcal{G}, N) \leftarrow$ `EXPAND`$(\mathcal{G}, (\alpha \Rightarrow \beta), N)$
8   **end for**
9 **until** $N == N'$
10 **return** $\mathcal{G}$
11 **end function**

The execution of algorithm 2 entails:

$$\begin{aligned}\mathcal{G}' = \{\ & (\ Lisbon, \texttt{rdf:type}, Place\ ),\\ & (\ Place, \texttt{rdf:type}, \texttt{rdfs:Class}\ ),\\ & (\ \texttt{rdfs:Class}, \texttt{rdf:type}, \texttt{rdfs:Class}\ ),\\ & (\ \texttt{rdf:type}, \texttt{rdf:type}, \texttt{rdfs:Property}\ ),\\ & (\ \texttt{rdf:Property}, \texttt{rdf:type}, \texttt{rdfs:Class}\ )\\ \}\ & \end{aligned}$$

The rule set (cf. $\mathcal{RS}$ in algorithm 2, line 2) only contains the semantic rules that describe the RDFS language. In order to incorporate the domain-dependent knowledge we define,

$$\mathcal{RS} \ = \ \mathcal{RS}' \ \cup \ \mathcal{RS}oD \tag{11}$$

where $\mathcal{RS}'$ contains the predefined RDFS rules (i.e., $\mathcal{RS}' = \{\, \mathrm{r}(1),\ \ldots,\ \mathrm{r}(10)\, \}$; $\mathrm{r}(\,i\,)$ is a rule as defined in section 2.2) and the set $\mathcal{RS}oD$ contains the semantic rules that a (human) designer uses to describe a specific target domain.

The $\mathcal{RS}$ used in algorithm 2 (line 2) represents the general scenario where $\mathcal{RS}oD = \emptyset$, i.e., without any specific domain being described.

We now use $\mathcal{RS}oD$ (cf., expression 11) to describe the semantics of a specific domain so that agents can use such a description to support their automatic reasoning processes.

4 The Fire-Brigade (Agent Inferencing) Target Domain

Why is the inference process an interesting topic for agents applications? Let us pick a simplified scenario, taken from the fire-brigade domain, which is motivated by the search-and-rescue problem (e.g. as proposed by the RoboCup Rescue [10] simulation project). The real-world institutions related with fire-brigade domain can clearly take advantage of SW early adoption. Those institutions rely on diverse sources of information thus depending on (automated) mechanisms for concepts' interpretation, classification and integration. For example, the Portuguese SNBPC (Serviço Nacional de Bombeiros e Protecção Civil – "National Fire Service and Civil Defense") must interpret (and integrate) the information provided by the set of fire-brigade command centers in order to plan and coordinate the huge amount of (annual) florestal fires; automated knowledge-handling would certainly be a helper "to follow the ambition on reducing" the (typical) Portuguese post-summer annual landscape of grievously huge burnt areas.

The fire-brigade domain contains several fire-brigade centers each being responsible for a certain physical region that holds a set of smaller places (e.g., house blocks within a town). There is also information regarding the distance between the representative points of adjacent places. Each fire-brigade center receives information regarding fires and always acts whenever a fire occurs in a region under their responsibility.

The fires are classified according to their priority and several strategies have been devised for scenarios with several simultaneous fires. For example, simultaneous fires in different buildings may be prioritized according to additional information (apart from the fire intensity) such as each building's neighborhood density, the total construction area and the construction type [19] while the decision-making process follows the hierarchical relations among agents [20].

Figure 1 shows the basic RDF constituents used to describe the fire-brigade domain. Each arc represents a *property* and each oval shaped node represents a *resource*, the node `b` represents an anonymous *resource* (i.e., a blank node), the rectangle shaped node `v` represents a literal and the qualifier `D` represents the domain namespace. The graph (cf. figure 1) is informally interpreted as follows:

- a fire-brigade (`D:FBC`) is responsible (`D:responsible`) for a region (`D:Region`),
- a region contains a collection of place instances (`D:Place`), and
- two adjacent places are linked (`b`) under a certain traveling cost (`v`),
- each fire (`D:Fire`) contains the collection of places where a fire occurs.

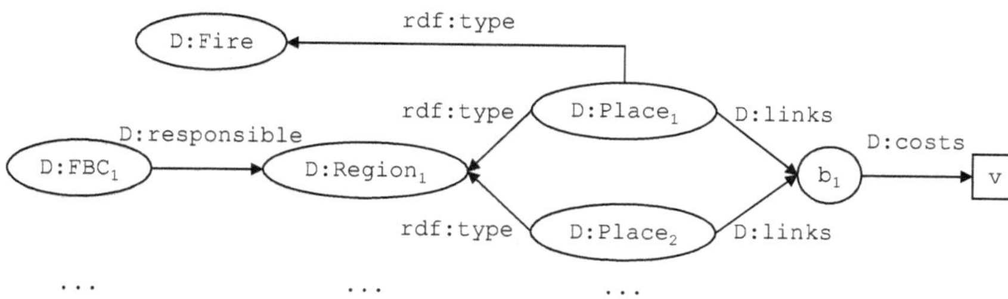

Fig. 1. The RDF basic graph structure of the fire-brigade domain

This simplified model only describes the basic properties; additional information includes, e.g. fire intensity and geographical data.

Before constructing the $\mathcal{RSoD}$ we introduce the following two ideas:

i. the **D:links** transitive property formulation may account for the cost value,
ii. a region is in fire whenever one, or more, of its places is in fire.

We formulate item i (above) using a "constructor" and an "updater" rule.

The "constructor" describes the cost of a newly inferred **D:links** property; it is formulated, by rule (12), as follows:

$$\begin{aligned}&\text{“Constructor” of } \mathtt{D{:}links} \text{ Transitivity Property:}\\ &\quad (Pa,\ \mathtt{D{:}links},\ b1) \wedge (Pb,\ \mathtt{D{:}links},\ b1) \wedge (b1,\ \mathtt{D{:}costs},\ v1) \wedge\\ &\quad (Pb,\ \mathtt{D{:}links},\ b2) \wedge (Pc,\ \mathtt{D{:}links},\ b2) \wedge (b2,\ \mathtt{D{:}costs},\ v2) \wedge\\ &\quad \neg(Pa,\ \mathtt{D{:}links},\ b3) \wedge \neg(Pc,\ \mathtt{D{:}links},\ b3)\\ &\Rightarrow\\ &\quad (Pa,\ \mathtt{D{:}links},\ b3) \wedge (Pc,\ \mathtt{D{:}links},\ b3) \wedge\\ &\quad (b1,\ \mathtt{D{:}costs},\ v1 + v2)\end{aligned} \tag{12}$$

The "updater" computes the minimum **D:costs** value of a previously inferred **D:links** property; it is formulated, by rule (13), as follows:

$$\begin{aligned}&\text{“Updater” of } \mathtt{D{:}links} \text{ Transitivity Property:}\\ &\quad (Pa,\ \mathtt{D{:}links},\ b1) \wedge (Pb,\ \mathtt{D{:}links},\ b1) \wedge (b1,\ \mathtt{D{:}costs},\ v1) \wedge\\ &\quad (Pb,\ \mathtt{D{:}links},\ b2) \wedge (Pc,\ \mathtt{D{:}links},\ b2) \wedge (b2,\ \mathtt{D{:}costs},\ v2) \wedge\\ &\quad (Pa,\ \mathtt{D{:}links},\ b3) \wedge (Pc,\ \mathtt{D{:}links},\ b3) \wedge (b3,\ \mathtt{D{:}costs},\ v3)\\ &\Rightarrow\\ &\quad (Pa,\ \mathtt{D{:}links},\ b3) \wedge (Pc,\ \mathtt{D{:}links},\ b3) \wedge\\ &\quad (b1,\ \mathtt{D{:}costs},\ \min(v1 + v2,\ v3))\end{aligned} \tag{13}$$

The formulation of item ii (above) follows the RDF structure (cf. figure 1) to find an instance relation between a **D:Region** and a **D:Fire**; it is formulated, by rule (14), as follows:

$$
\begin{aligned}
&\text{Region in Fire} \\
&\quad (\,Pa,\ \texttt{rdf:type},\ \texttt{D:Fire}\,) \wedge (\,Pa,\ \texttt{rdf:type},\ R\,) \wedge \\
&\quad (\,FB,\ \texttt{D:responsible},\ R\,) \\
&\Rightarrow \\
&\quad (\,R,\ \texttt{rdf:type},\ \texttt{D:Fire}\,)
\end{aligned}
\tag{14}
$$

Therefore, we define $\mathcal{RS}o\mathcal{D} = \{\, \mathrm{r}(12),\ \mathrm{r}(13),\ \mathrm{r}(14)\,\}$ (cf., expression 11), where $\mathrm{r}(\,i\,)$ represents the ith (above) described rule).

Modeling the fire-brigade agent. The agent designer uses the RDF framework to describe the domain *resources* and *properties* and then he defines the $\mathcal{RS}o\mathcal{D}$. The agent executes the inference process using the $\mathrm{r}(12)$ and $\mathrm{r}(13)$ rules, thus expanding the original $\mathcal{G}$ into a $\mathcal{G}'$ (inferred RDF representation) that contains the minimum cost value between any two places; the $\mathcal{G}'$ supports the path planning processes. Whenever the agent receives a fire report the corresponding assertion is added to $\mathcal{G}'$ and the $\mathrm{r}(14)$ rule enables to determine the region of the fire and thus the fire-brigade center that has the responsibility of attacking the fire.

5 Conclusions

The Web is moving towards the semantic formalization of its contents to provide higher forms of querying. Our work picks the most recent Web-based query approach (SPARQL) and describes a way of exploring the homogenous RDF representation in order to automatically extend a given Web (RDF) repository with the new statements inferred from a given formally specified interpretation.

The approach supports the design of a reasoning agent that adopts the RDF graph structure as its knowledge representation model. The graph querying capabilities of the SPARQL language are exploited as a means to provide, the agent, a reasoning mechanism. Institutional agents (e.g., fire-brigade) can be designed to take advantage of the collective-knowledge-representation perspective of the Internet space and to foster the early adoption, by the institutions, of the SW concepts and technologies.

This is a preliminary work that is currently being developed in order to exploit the crosscutting between the agent-based system modeling and the Web-based methodologies given the emphasis on the emerging ideas (and tools) that populate the Web Semantic area.

Future goals include incorporating typical rule engine techniques, e.g., the RETE algorithm [8] in order to optimize the rule evaluation process, and extending the approach to provide some characteristics of a truth maintenance system.

References

1. Beckett, D., Broekstra, J.: SPARQL query results XML format. W3C Recommendation (January 2008)
2. Berners-Lee, T., Hendler, J., Lassila, O.: The Semantic Web - a new form of Web content that is meaningful to computers will unleash a revolution of new possibilities. Scientific American Magazine (May 2001)

3. Brickley, D., Guha, R.: RDF vocabulary description language 1.0: RDF Schema. W3C Recommendation (Febuary 2004)
4. Carroll, J.J., Bizer, C., Hayes, P., Stickler, P.: Named graphs, provenance and trust. In: Proceedings of the 14th International Conference on World Wide Web (WWW 2005), Chiba, Japan, pp. 613–622. ACM Press, New York (2005)
5. Chen, L., Gupta, A., Kurul, E.: A semantic-aware RDF query algebra. In: Proceedings of the International Conference on Management of Data (COMAD 2005), Hyderabad, India (2005)
6. de Bruijn, J., Heymans, S.: Logical foundations of (e)RDF(S): Complexity and reasoning. In: Aberer, K., Choi, K.-S., Noy, N., Allemang, D., Lee, K.-I., Nixon, L.J.B., Golbeck, J., Mika, P., Maynard, D., Mizoguchi, R., Schreiber, G., Cudré-Mauroux, P. (eds.) ISWC 2007. LNCS, vol. 4825, pp. 86–99. Springer, Heidelberg (2007)
7. Ferreira, J., Trigo, P., Coelho, H.: Evaluation of collaborative annotation systems and simulation of user behavior on social network. In: Proceedings of the 1st Brazilian Workshop on Social Simulation within the 19th Brazilian Symposium on Artificial Intelligence (SBIA 2008), Bahia, Brazil, October 26-30 (2008)
8. Forgy, C.: Rete: A fast algorithm for the many pattern/many object pattern match problem. Artificial Intelligence 19(1), 17–37 (1982)
9. Hayes, P.: RDF semantics. W3C Recommendation (Febuary 2004)
10. Kitano, H., Tadokoro, S.: RoboCup Rescue: A grand challenge for multi-agent systems. Artificial Intelligence Magazine 22(1), 39–52 (2001)
11. Manola, F., Miller, E.: RDF primer. W3C Recommendation (Febuary 2004)
12. Marin, D.: A formalization of RDF (applications de la logique á la sémantique du Web). Technical report, Dept. Computer Science, Ecole Polytechnique, Universidad de Chile, TR/DCC-2006-8 (2006)
13. Muñoz, S., Pérez, J., Gutierrez, C.: Minimal deductive systems for RDF. In: Franconi, E., Kifer, M., May, W. (eds.) ESWC 2007. LNCS, vol. 4519, pp. 53–67. Springer, Heidelberg (2007)
14. Pérez, J., Arenas, M., Gutierrez, C.: Semantics and complexity of SPARQL. In: Cruz, I., Decker, S., Allemang, D., Preist, C., Schwabe, D., Mika, P., Uschold, M., Aroyo, L.M. (eds.) ISWC 2006. LNCS, vol. 4273, pp. 30–43. Springer, Heidelberg (2006)
15. Polleres, A.: From SPARQL to rules (and back). In: Proceedings of the 16th International World Wide Web Conference (WWW 2007), Alberta, Canada, May 2007, pp. 787–796 (2007)
16. Prud'hommeaux, E., Seaborne, A.: SPARQL query language for RDF. W3C Recommendation (January 2008)
17. Python2.5.2. Python programming language (Febuary 2008), `http://www.python.org/`
18. RDFLib2.4.0. Python library for RDF (April 2007), `http://rdflib.net/`
19. Trigo, P., Coelho, H.: Decisions with multiple simultaneous goals and uncertain causal effects. In: Artificial Intelligence in Theory and Practice II. IFIP International Federation for Information Processing, vol. 276, pp. 13–22. Springer, Heidelberg (2008)
20. Trigo, P., Coelho, H.: Decision making with hybrid models: the case of collective and individual motivations. International Journal of Reasoning-based Intelligent Systems (IJRIS) 1(2) (2009)
21. XSLT. XSL transformations (XSLT) (November 1999), `http://www.w3.org/TR/xslt`

How Much Should Agents Remember? The Role of Memory Size on Convention Emergence Efficiency

Paulo Urbano[1], João Balsa[1], Paulo Ferreira Jr.[2], and Luis Antunes[3]

[1] LabMAg, DI/FCUL, Portugal
[2] Univ. Federal de Pelotas, Brasil
[3] GUESS, LabMAG, Univ. Lisboa

{pub,jbalsa}@di.fc.ul.pt, paulo.ferreira.jr@gmail.com, xarax@di.fc.ul.pt

Abstract. One way of coordinating actions is by the adoption of norms: social conventions and lexicons are good examples of coordinating systems. This paper deals with the efficiency of the emergence of norms (adopted from a given initial set), inside a population of artificial agents that interact in pairs. Agents interact according to some well defined behavior each one implements. In order to conduct our work, we used a bench-mark agent behavior: the external majority, where agents keep a memory of its latest interactions, adopting the most observed choice occurring in the last m interactions, where m (memory size) is a given parameter. We present an empirical study in which we determine the best choices regarding the memory size that should be made in order to guarantee an efficient uniform decision emergence. In this context, a more efficient choice is one that leads to a smaller number of needed pair wise interactions. We performed a series of experiments with population sizes ranging from 50 to 5,000, memory ranging from 2 to 10, and for five network topologies (fully connected, regular, random, scale-free and small-world). Besides we also analyzed the impact on consensus emergence efficiency of the number of available initial choices (from 2, to the number of agents) together with different memory sizes.

1 Introduction

The achievement of global conventions in multi-agent systems was first addressed by Shoham and Tennenholtz [8] in the beginning of the 90s but it is still the subject of more recent research [3,4,7,12]. Conventions specify a choice common to all agents in a population, and are a straightforward means for achieving coordination in a multi-agent system. The issue at stake here relates to collective choice and coordination mechanisms: a homogeneous group is in presence of several strategies and has to select one of them. As strategies are considered equally good, what is important is that the choice is consensual (the particular chosen strategy is irrelevant). An example of such norm is the lane of traffic on a given country. It is irrelevant whether right lane or left lane is chosen, as long as everybody uses the same.

L. Seabra Lopes et al. (Eds.): EPIA 2009, LNAI 5816, pp. 508–519, 2009.

Legislating conventions before hand (off-line), or developing a central control mechanism for generating them can be a problematic and intractable task in dynamic situations [10]. This explains the interest on the design of emergent conventions through a co-learning process [9]: individual agents occasionally meet and observe each other, and they may adapt their behavior, based on local information, synchronizing their behavior with those of the group.

The guarantee of achieving a global consensus and the efficiency of convergence towards it, have been natural concerns in the design of local interaction behaviors. Shoham and Tennenholtz compared several strategy update rules, including the Highest Cumulative Reward (HCR) and the External Majority (EM) with full and limited memory for registering the interaction history.

In the initial research on convention emergence, there were no restrictions on interactions; any agent could interact by chance with any other individual. Kittock [6] introduced interaction graphs in order to specify restrictions on interactions and made experiments with the HCR update rule along different interaction graphs. Kittock also made experiments with regular graphs that showed that interaction topology is important in the efficiency of convention emergence — he conjectured that efficiency depends on the diameter of the graph. Other graph properties like clustering coefficient and average path length are also important. Delgado et al [3,4] have made experiments with HCR update rule for fully connected, regular, scale-free and small-world graphs [2], and their results were consistent with Kittock's, confirming the relation between efficiency and graph diameter. Delgado observed also that scale-free and small-world networks were as efficient as fully connected ones, but small-world networks were slower to converge to a unique choice. Both Kittock and Delgado used a memory size of 2 without presenting any empirical or analytical evidence for their choice. Shoham and Tenneholtz [10] showed that EM and HCR are equivalent strategy update rules in the case there is a repertoire of two strategies to select. That's not the case if there are more than 2 strategies in competition: in this case HCR is much less efficient than EM regarding the average number of interactions necessary for convergence. This is the reason we adopted EM for an empirical analysis on the role of memory size.

In general, researchers on convention emergence study strategy update rules in cases where there are only 2 options competing to be adopted, like driving on the left or right side, or the priority rule (right or left) — we name it the *2-strategies* scenario. We are going to experiment with cases where there are more than only two strategies in the competition for consensual choice. In fact, we will deal with the extreme case where each agent adopts initially its own strategy: there will be N strategies for N agents — the *N-strategies* scenario.

In the following section we will describe the External Majority strategy update rule (EM); in section 3 we present the different network topologies (fully connected, regular, random, scale-free and small world) that we experimented with. In section 4 we present the result of the experiments where we tested convention emergence efficiency varying memory size for different population sizes. We conclude with the presentation of some conclusions.

2 Strategy Update Rule: *External Majority*

The External Majority strategy update rule (EM) was introduced by Shoham and Tennenholtz [8] and is the following: *adopt the strategy that was observed more often in other agents in the last* m *interactions, and remain with your current strategy otherwise — in case of a draw do not change.* In EM, memory is used to register the strategies observed during the last interactions. Agents participate in a sequence of encounters where they observe their partners' strategies. An agent updates its memory after observing its partner strategy and then decides to change to a new strategy only in case it was more frequently observed than the current one. If, after an interaction, the current strategy stops being the most frequent and more than one of the others have the same (highest) frequency, the agent will adopt the most recently observed of the tied strategies.

In the context of lexical emergence, Kaplan [5] introduced a strategy update rule called *Positive Feedback with Score*, which is pretty much the same as EM. The most referred strategy update rule is the Highest Cumulative Reward update rule (HCR), which was developed in the context of game theory by Shoham and Tennenholtz [9].

3 Interaction Graph Topologies

An interaction graph is a general way of modeling restrictions on interactions. Restrictions could be due to spatial barriers, communicating links, different castes, social groups, etc. We have experimented with five network topologies: fully connected, regular, scale-free, small-world and random. These topologies cover a wide spectrum of values regarding three important network properties: average path length, network diameter and clustering coefficient.

The average path length is calculated by finding the shortest path between all pairs of nodes, adding them up, and then dividing by the total number of pairs. This indicates, on average, the number of steps it takes to get from one member of the network to another. The diameter of a graph is the longest shortest-path between nodes. The clustering coefficient is a measure of "all-my-friends-know-each-other" property. When it is high, we may say: "the friends of my friends are my friends." The clustering coefficient of a node is the ratio of existing links connecting a node's neighbors to each other to the maximum possible number of such links. The clustering coefficient for the entire network is the average of the clustering coefficients of all the nodes.

3.1 Regular Graphs

By definition, a graph is considered regular when every node has the same number of neighbors. We are going to use a special kind of regular graph, explored in [6] and named Contract Net with Communication Radius K in [11]. $C_{N,K}$ is the graph (regular ring lattice) on N nodes such that node i is adjacent to nodes $(i + j)$ *mod* N and $(i - j)$ *mod* N for $1 \leq j \leq K$. In a $C_{N,K}$ graph, every node has connectivity $2 * K$. These are highly clustered graphs but have very long path lengths (average path length and diameter grow linearly with the number of nodes).

3.2 Fully Connected Graphs

In this type of graph topology, named K_N, there are no restrictions on the pattern of interactions: each agent is connected to every other agent in the society. This means that an agent can potentially interact with any other agent. K_N is a special case of a regular graph where each agent has $N - 1$ neighbors, in a group of N agents.

3.3 Random Graphs

$R_{N,K}$ are random graphs with N nodes and average connectivity of K. Every node, has on average, K neighbors chosen randomly. The clustering coefficient of $R_{N,K}$ tends to 0 and the average path length is small and grows logarithmically with N.

3.4 Scale-Free Graphs

This network type, $S_{N,\gamma}$ has a large number of nodes connected only to a few nodes and a small number of well-connected nodes called hubs. The power law distribution highly influences the network topology. It turns out that major hubs are closely followed by smaller ones. These ones, in turn, are followed by other nodes with an even smaller degree, and so on. As the network changes in size, the ratio of hubs to the number of nodes in the rest of network remains constant — this is why it is named scale-free. The connectivity of a scale-free network follows a power law $P(k) \sim k^{-\gamma}$. Such networks can be found in a surprisingly large range of real world situations, ranging from the connections between websites to the collaborations between actors.

To generate the scale-free graphs we have used the Albert and Barabsi extended model [1], since Delgado argues that it allows some control over the exponent (γ) of the graph [3]. The inspiration of this algorithm is that of "preferential attachment", meaning that the most "popular" nodes get most of the links. The construction algorithm relies on four parameters: m_0 (initial number of nodes), m (number of links added and/or rewired at every step), p (probability of adding links), and q (probability of edge rewiring). The algorithm starts with m_0 isolated nodes and at each step performs one of these three actions until the desired number N of nodes is obtained:

1. With probability p, add m ($\leq m_0$) new links. Pick two nodes randomly. The starting point of the link is chosen uniformly and the end point of the link is chosen according to the probability distribution:

$$\Pi_i = \frac{(k_i + 1)}{\sum_j (k_j + 1)}$$

where Π_i is the probability of selecting the ith node and k_i is the number of edges of node i. This process is repeated m times.
2. With probability q, m edges are rewired. That is, repeat m times: choose uniformly at random one node i and one link l_{ij}. Delete this link and choose a different node k with probability $\{\Pi_l\}_{l=1,\dots,N}$ and add the new link l_{ik}.
3. With probability $1-p-q$ add a new node with m links. These new links will connect the new node to m other nodes chosen according to $\{\Pi_l\}_{l=1,\dots,N}$. Using this algorithm, the parameter γ is a function of m and p:

$$\gamma = \frac{(2m(1-p)+1)}{m+1}$$

3.5 Small-World Graphs

The Small World graphs are highly clustered graphs (like regular graphs) with small average path lengths (like random graphs, described above). To generate small world graphs we use the Watts-Strogatz model [13,14]. It depends on two parameters, connectivity (K) and randomness (P), given the size of the graph (N).

This model starts with a $C_{N,K}$ graph and then every link is rewired at random with probability P, that is, for every link l_{ij} we decide whether we change the "destination" node with probability P; if this is the case, we choose a new node k uniformly at random (no self-links allowed) and add the link l_{ik} while erasing link l_{ij}. In fact, for $P=0$ we have $W_N = C_{N,K}$ and for $P=1$ we have a completely random graph (but not scale-free). For intermediate values of P there is the "small-world" region, where the graph is highly clustered (which means it is not random) but with a small characteristic path length (a property shared with random graphs).

Albert-Barabsi model graphs do not have the small-world property and reciprocally the Watts-Strogatz model does not generate scale-free graphs (it generates an exponential connectivity distribution, not a power law).

4 Comparing the Best Memory Size for Different Scenarios

We are going to consider two scenarios: the case where there are only two strategies to choose from, and a second scenario where there are N different strategies for N agents. We could, of course, study cases where there are 3, 4, ... strategies to choose from but in order to be pragmatic we analyze only these two scenarios as they represent extreme situations. When agents have only two choices (*2-strategies* scenario), the system starts with half of the agents adopting randomly one of the strategies (50% possibilities for each). In the *N-strategy* scenario each agent starts with its own unique strategy.

Note that all agents start with empty memories. According to the external majority rule, this implies that each agent will adopt the strategy of its first meeting partner, since after the first meeting that strategy will be the only one memorized (thus the one in majority).

In each step, every agent, in an asynchronous way, is selected and chosen for asymmetric strategy updating. The order of selected agents is completely random and changes in each iteration (although we think that the order of agents for strategy update is not an issue, because strategies are randomly adopted initially).

We use in this paper the same measure of performance as in [6][3]: *the average number of interactions to a fixed convergence*, where convergence means the fraction of agents using the majority strategy. For each experiment (a different parameter setting) we made a sequence of 500 runs and calculated the average performance (measured by the number of encounters until 90% convergence).

In all of the described experiments we will vary memory size from 2 to 10. We discard the $m = 1$ case since we know from the work of Kaplan [5] that with pure imitators nothing directs the group towards convergence, as every option can increase its influence with equal probability. During an interaction where agents have memory size equal to 1 (only the strategy of the current partner is registered), agents are pure imitators: they adopt immediately the strategies of their partners. In general, convergence is assured after an important series of oscillations in a time quadratic with the number of agents [5].

We present in the subsequent sections the results obtained for different network topologies.

4.1 Fully Connected Networks

Others authors [6][3][8] have made experiments regarding the role of memory forgetting in consensus efficiency in fully connected network, in the *2-strategies* scenario. They concluded that it is more effective to partially forget than to memorize the full history of meetings. They concluded that the best memory size should be 2 or 3. Nevertheless we decided to repeat these experiments and extend them to the *n-strategies* scenario (for which there are no previous results).

In the experiments we made, we varied the number of agents (N) from 100 to 5000, and tested for both scenarios. In table 1 we show the results for the 2-strategies scenario and in table 2 for the *N-strategies* one. In both cases we present the average number of meetings needed to achieve a 90% consensus. The best values for each column are emphasized in these tables. Due to space limitations, we only show the values for some of the population sizes.

Regarding the 2-strategies scenario we confirmed the above mentioned results, being $M = 3$ clearly the best case. The cases of $M = 2$ and $M = 5$ always present values close to the best. It is interesting to note that for consecutive values of M, the value for the odd M is always better than the value for the even one.

For the *N-strategies* scenario the pattern of results is different. We observe that for population sizes between 100 and 1000 the best case is always $M = 4$ (except for N=100), but for higher values, like N=5000, the performance for $M = 4$ degrades and $M = 8$ becomes the best option. We can also observe that for smaller values of M, performance gets worse with the increase of the population size (this is clear in the table for $M = 2$ and $M = 3$).

Table 1. Average number of meetings for different setups (number of agents and memory sizes) with fully connected networks for the $2 - strategies$ scenario

M / N	100	500	1000	5000
2	901	6.275	13.639	82.812
3	**860**	**5.942**	**12.812**	**77.620**
4	1.008	6.691	14.789	90.521
5	940	6.161	13.949	82.894
6	1.050	7.341	15.692	95.132
7	999	6.763	14.752	84.837
8	1.107	7.652	17.019	103.547
9	1.045	7.097	15.821	96.030
10	1.138	7.972	16.271	108.970

Table 2. Average number of meetings for different setups (number of agents and memory sizes) with fully connected networks for the $N - strategies$ scenario

M / N	100	500	1000	5000
2	2.120	19.540	50.998	510.128
3	1.715	12.098	27.356	319.507
4	1.691	**11.565**	**25.681**	276.244
5	**1.684**	11.737	25.897	257.609
6	1.725	12.055	26.798	251.692
7	1.744	12.360	27.258	245.744
8	1.792	12.957	28.820	**242.724**
9	1.811	13.139	29.274	243.619
10	1.842	13.510	30.218	245.733

These results seem to indicate that the role of memory size on convergence efficiency depends both on the population size and on the number of initial strategies.

One possible explanation for these results is that when the memory size is very small, during the preliminary stages of the simulation agents behave like pure imitators, as if they have memory size equal to 1. With a greater number of strategies and a small memory it will be less likely that an agent meets two agents with the same strategy (in a sequence of encounters that can be preserved in memory). As soon as the agent looses track of the event that lead to its current strategy, it will be ready to imitate the next agent he meets. This is more critical with smaller memory sizes and greater populations (number of different initial strategies).

This is not a problem in the 2-strategies scenario, even for smaller memory sizes and greater populations, since it is easy to have two registered encounters with the same strategy.

We are still working in experiments with more than 5000 agents, in order to clearly confirm these results.

Considering the explanation of results, in the n-strategy scenario, when the memory is very short, agent behaviour resembles more an imitation behaviour (memory=1). As memory increases, agents will only change when they in fact observe a majority of other strategies. Note that, in this scenario, the probability of interacting with two agents with the same strategy is very low. This does not happen in the 2-strategy scenario.

4.2 Random Networks

We made two kinds of experiments with random networks. Firstly, we analyzed the variation of results with an initial fixed communication radius K $(= 10)$. Secondly, we analyzed, for a fixed size population, the influence of different connectivity values (a random network $R_{N,K}$ has average connectivity $2 * K$).

Using a fixed K. In tables 3 and 4 we can see the average number of meetings in random networks $R_{N,10}$, varying the number of agents and memory sizes. For the 2-strategies scenario, M=3 is again the winner, being M=2 and M=5 also close to the best, like it happened in the fully-connected case.

Table 3. Average number of meetings for different setups (number of agents and memory sizes) with random networks ($R_{N,10}$) for the $2 - strategies$ scenario

M / N	100	300	500	800	1000
2	988	3.953	6.932	12.058	15.117
3	**936**	**3.494**	**6.544**	**11.151**	**14.550**
4	1.130	4.157	7.768	13.464	17.757
5	1.012	3.868	6.974	12.172	15.775
6	1.223	4.709	8.782	15.116	19.006
7	1.137	4.399	7.741	13.948	17.365
8	1.267	5.218	9.351	16.341	20.805
9	1.166	4.764	9.092	15.021	19.578
10	1.339	5.311	10.033	16.031	22.702

Table 4. Average number of meetings for different setups (number of agents and memory sizes) with random networks ($R_{N,10}$) for the $N - strategies$ scenario

M / N	100	300	500	800	1000
2	2.213	10.061	20.119	39.467	53.120
3	**1.851**	7.340	**13.517**	23.633	30.904
4	1.922	**7.325**	13.555	**23.574**	**30.718**
5	1.967	7.755	14.333	24.982	32.194
6	2.032	8.378	15.478	27.478	35.156
7	2.101	8.808	16.438	29.792	37.955
8	2.238	9.330	17.413	32.033	41.856
9	2.290	9.695	18.454	34.294	44.046
10	2.384	9.807	19.653	35.249	46.740

In the N-strategies scenario, M=2 is clearly a bad option, and there is a shift to M=4, in some of the cases, being M=3 always close to M=4, what did not happened in the fully-connected case.

Evaluating the impact of connectivity. The results are depicted in tables 5 and 6. Again, M=3 provided the best performance in the *2-strategies* scenario. In the $N - strategies$ scenario we observe again an increase of the best memory size with the increase on connectivity converging to the fully-connected case.

Table 5. Average number of meetings for different setups (connectivity values and memory sizes) with random networks ($R_{100,K}$) for the $2 - strategies$ scenario

M / %Con.	10	30	50	70	90
2	1.158	983	899	890	913
3	**1.071**	**899**	**864**	**860**	**865**
4	1.342	1.048	1.007	979	996
5	1.250	991	921	919	906
6	1.538	1.142	1.115	1.069	1.090
7	1.370	1.089	1.014	997	1.005
8	1.651	1.192	1.204	1.083	1.106
9	1.554	1.152	1.084	1.073	1.055
10	1.929	1.263	1.194	1.147	1.136

Table 6. Average number of meetings for different setups (connectivity values and memory sizes) with random networks ($R_{100,K}$) for the $N - strategies$ scenario

M / %Con.	10	30	50	70	90
2	2.516	2.208	2.156	2.163	2.189
3	**2.165**	1.771	1.735	1.728	1.675
4	2.290	**1.760**	**1.690**	1.678	1.663
5	2.416	1.806	1.695	**1.677**	**1.648**
6	2.640	1.873	1.847	1.752	1.689
7	2.744	1.893	1.846	1.783	1.708
8	2.959	2.016	1.907	1.833	1.771
9	3.055	2.025	1.912	1.866	1.843
10	3.269	2.132	1.967	1.907	1.853

Nevertheless, higher memories perform much better than in the regular case for lower values of connectivity.

4.3 Regular Networks

We made a set of experiments similar to the ones described in the previous section for random networks. Firstly, we analyzed the variation of results with a fixed communication radius K (= 40). Secondly, we analyzed, for a fixed size population, the influence of different connectivity values (a regular network $C_{N,K}$ has connectivity $2 * K$).

Using a fixed K. In table 7 we can compare the average number of meetings in regular networks $C_{N,40}$, varying the number of agents and memory sizes. For the 2-strategies scenario, M=3 is again the best alternative. For the N-strategies scenario, the results are more irregular (see the end of this section for more detailed comments).

Table 7. Average number of meetings for different setups (number of agents and memory sizes) with regular networks ($C_{N,40}$) for the $2 - strategies$ (left) and N-strategies (right) scenarios

	2-strat			n-strat		
M / N	100	300	500	100	300	500
2	909	22.738	198.296	2.160	**27.454**	554.003
3	**872**	**12.617**	**175.724**	1.720	31.677	**466.432**
4	1.021	56.525	242.244	1.725	140.339	1.640.021
5	936	53.919	227.323	**1.645**	123.611	1.418.211
6	1.082	82.108	240.133	1.738	302.986	3.025.607
7	982	85.750	270.996	1.736	251.393	2.587.562
8	1.102	91.744	225.578	1.785	492.313	4.682.981
9	1.092	76.718	266.662	1.813	391.296	4.270.896
10	1.186	93.237	209.686	1.909	656.384	6.262.580

Studying the impact of connectivity. In these experiments we used a fixed size population of 100 agents and varied the connectivity in terms of a percentage of the population size. A connectivity value of 10% (10% Con.) means that each agent has 10 neighbors ($K = 5$).

For the $2 - strategies$ scenario (table 8), regardless of the percentage value, the best results are always obtained with $M = 3$. Besides, as the connectivity increases the performance of higher values for M have a better improvement ratio. Compare, for instance, the relative performances of M=10 with M=3, for connectivity values of 10% and 90%.

Table 8. Average number of meetings for different setups (connectivity values and memory sizes) with regular networks ($C_{100,K}$) for the $2 - strategies$ scenario

M / %Con.	10	30	50	70	90
2	38.471	2.917	1.037	927	893
3	**26.159**	**2.450**	**981**	**836**	**877**
4	73.456	6.386	1.241	1.016	1.005
5	63.678	5.589	1.070	936	939
6	132.453	13.341	1.387	1.084	1.081
7	100.787	11.429	1.265	1.016	991
8	176.152	16.005	1.795	1.155	1.110
9	159.629	19.328	1.551	1.043	1.066
10	218.900	24.208	2.048	1.153	1.126

In the N-strategies scenario (table 9), M=3 is not the obvious choice anymore. The values observed converge to the fully-connected case (that corresponds to 100%, as illustrated in table 2), where M=5 was the best result. Note also, that the best memory value increases with the increase of the connectivity.

Table 9. Average number of meetings for different setups (connectivity values and memory sizes) with regular networks ($C_{100,K}$) for the $N-strategies$ scenario

M / %Con.	10	30	50	70	90
2	67.881	**4.999**	2.208	2.170	2.157
3	**55.886**	5.056	**1.891**	1.735	1.720
4	104.299	15.644	2.069	1.730	**1.656**
5	100.687	13.171	2.095	**1.720**	**1.656**
6	129.208	25.016	2.632	1.794	1.722
7	124.743	25.434	2.579	1.832	1.760
8	139.873	46.847	3.122	1.856	1.816
9	145.540	39.463	3.443	1.907	1.824
10	153.484	58.325	4.042	1.933	1.870

For the 2-strategies scenario M=3 is always the memory size that performs better. As we increase the number os initial strategies both population size and connectivity play an important role in the choice of the memory size that leads to more efficient convergence.

As with fully-connected networks the best memory size increases with population size but that increment is very sensible to connectivity, i.e., in a less connected network M=3 is still a good option. Note that a connectivity of 80 represents 80% of a population of 100, but only 16% of a population of 500.

4.4 Small-World and Scale-Free Networks

We also performed some experiments with small-world and scale-free network topologies, but as we didn't explore alternate network parameters, we only have preliminary results for population sizes between 100 and 400. Nevertheless we could observe again for the 2-strategies scenario that, for both network topologies ($S_{N,2.15}$ and W_N, with $p = 0.1$), M=3 shows the best results.

For the N-strategies scenario, with a small-world topology M=2 seems to be the best memory size, while in the scale-free case, M=3 is again the winner.

Another clear difference between these two types of networks is that for the small-world ones, efficiency is greatly affected by the increase in memory size, presenting a clear degradation.

5 Conclusions

We have studied the efficiency of the convention emergence in multi-agent systems, in particular through the empirical study on the role that memory size plays in the performance of the well known external majority rule for strategy update. We have tested different memory sizes along different population sizes where social relationships are represented by different types of graphs, namely fully-connected, regular, random, and complex networks (small-world and scale-free). We have considered two extreme scenarios: one where there are only two initial strategies that can be adopted and the other where there is one different possible strategy per agent (N agents = N initial strategies).

The results of our experiments showed that in the 2-strategies scenario, a memory size of 3 is consistently the best option for all type of networks and population sizes. This is not the case for the N-strategies scenario, where the number of initial strategies, the network topology, and its average connectivity, together with the population size, are critical factors to guide the choice of the best memory size. This results can be very useful in situations where external majority behavior can be adopted for agent coordination, since we concluded that memory size is determinant for the efficiency of the process. In the near future we will progress this research in two main directions. Firstly, by increasing the population size to higher values (tens and hundreds of thousands of agents). Secondly, by experimenting further with the complex network topologies.

References

1. Albert, R., Barabási, A.: Topology of evolving networks: local events and universality. Physical Review Letters 85, 5234–5237 (2000)
2. Barabási, A.L.: Linked: The New Science of Networks. Perseus Publishing, Cambridge (2002)
3. Delgado, J.: Emergence of social conventions in complex networks. Artificial Intelligence 141(1/2), 171–185 (2002)
4. Delgado, J., Pujol, J.M., Sangüesa, R.: Emergence of coordination in scale-free networks. Web Intelligence and Agent Systems 1(2), 131–138 (2003)
5. Kaplan, F.: L'Emergence D'un Lexique Dans Une Population d'Agents Autonomes. PhD thesis, Université de Paris 6 (2000)
6. Kittock, J.E.: Emergent conventions and the structure of multi-agent systems. In: Nadel, L., Stein, D. (eds.) 1993 Lectures in Complex Systems. SFI Studies in the Sciences of Complexity, Addison-Wesley, Reading (1995)
7. Sen, S., Airiau, S.: Emergence of norms through social learning. In: Veloso, M.M. (ed.) IJCAI, pp. 1507–1512 (2007)
8. Shoham, Y., Tennenholtz, M.: Emergent conventions in multi-agent systems. In: Rich, C., Swartout, W., Nebel, B. (eds.) Proceedings of Knowledge Representation and Reasoning (KR&R 1992), pp. 225–231 (1992)
9. Shoham, Y., Tennenholtz, M.: Co-learning and the evolution of social acitivity. Technical Report CS-TR-94-1511, Stanford University, Department of Computer Science (1994)
10. Shoham, Y., Tennenholtz, M.: On the emergence of social conventions: Modeling, analysis and simulations. Artificial Intelligence 94(1–2), 139–166 (1997)
11. Tennenholtz, M.: Convention evolution in organizations and markets. Computational & Mathematical Organization Theory 2(4), 261–283 (1996)
12. Urbano, P., Balsa, J., Antunes, L., Moniz, L.: Force versus majority: A comparison in convention emergence efficiency. In: Dignum, V., Matson, E. (eds.) Proceedings of the AAAI/COIN Workshop on Coordination, Organization, Institutions and Norms in Agent Systems (2008)
13. Watts, D.J.: Small Worlds: The Dynamics of Networks Between Order and Randomness. Princeton University Press, Princeton (1999)
14. Watts, D.J., Strogatz, S.H.: Collective dynamics of 'small-world' networks. Nature 393, 440–442 (1998)

Computing Confidence Values: Does Trust Dynamics Matter?

Joana Urbano, Ana Paula Rocha, and Eugénio Oliveira

Faculdade de Engenharia da Universidade do Porto
Rua Dr. Roberto Frias, 4200-465 Porto, Portugal
{joana.urbano,arocha,eco}@fe.up.pt

Abstract. Computational Trust and Reputation (CTR) systems are platforms capable of collecting trust information about candidate partners and of computing confidence scores for each one of these partners. These systems start to be viewed as vital elements in environments of electronic institutions, as they support fundamental decision making processes, such as the selection of business partners and the automatic and adaptive creation of contractual terms and associated enforcement methodologies. In this article, we propose a model for the aggregation of trust evidences that computes confidence scores taking into account dynamic properties of trust. We compare our model with a traditional statistical model that uses weighted means to compute trust, and show experimental results that show that in certain scenarios the consideration of the trust dynamics allows for a better estimation of confidence scores.

1 Introduction

Computational Trust and Reputation (CTR) systems are systems capable of collecting trust information about candidate partners and of computing confidence scores for each one of these partners. In this document, we envision trust as the confidence that the *trustier* agent has on the capabilities and the willingness of a candidate partner (*trustee*) in fulfilling its assigned tasks, in conformance to a given associated Service Level Agreement (SLA). CTR systems can be centralized, as adequate to electronic institutions and virtual organizations (VO), or decentralized, as adequate to extremely open environments where agents can enter and leave the society at any time.

Although practical examples of CTR systems do already exist (e.g. in e-commerce sites of eBay.com, Amazon.com, and Epinions.com[1]), there are still many open questions in this research area. In fact, current work on trust and reputation has diversified in multiple subfields. In the theoretical domain, there is important work on trust and reputation as elements of social intelligence. Conte (2002) addresses the theoretical issues related to reputation and image in artificial societies and social simulation [1], and this cognitive model of reputation was recently extended in order to more thoroughly address the transmission of reputation [2]. In a more practical sense, a great deal of research effort is being put in the representation and aggregation of social

[1] http://ebay.com; http://www.amazon.com; http://www.epinions.com

L. Seabra Lopes et al. (Eds.): EPIA 2009, LNAI 5816, pp. 520–531, 2009.

evaluations into trust and/or reputation scores, which would serve as input to partner selection in electronic business scenarios. These models range from arithmetic means and weighted means ([3] [4] [5]), to Beta ([6]) and Dirichlet distributions ([7]), Bayesian approaches ([8] [9]), and trust learning approaches ([10] [11] [12]). Some of these models are implemented using cognitive based beliefs, desires and intentions (BDI) architectures ([5] [13]). A new trend of investigation in this area is the exploration of the business context to improve the decision making, raising significantly the number and type of information that the evaluator has in order to compute trust. However, few proposals have been made in this specific area ([14]).

Another area of little research work is the consideration of the *dynamics of trust* in the computation of confidence scores. Our hypothesis is that the use of an aggregation engine that encompasses the past experiences of the trustee agent and that accounts for fundamental dynamics of trust could allow for a better estimation of the trustee trustworthiness than probabilistic and statistical approaches that exist in the literature. Due to the relevance of this issue on our work, we dedicate the next section to the presentation of relevant dynamics of trust.

The remaining of this paper is structured as follows. In section 2, we present SinAlpha, a non-statistical aggregation engine that uses an S-shape curve to compute trust scores, taking into account three properties of trust dynamics: the asymmetry, the distinguishability of past evidences and the consideration of distinct maturity phases on the behaviour of target agents. Section 3 presents the experimental phase of our work. It introduces STexVM, a simulated virtual textile marketplace that we have developed in agent technology in order to evaluate the SinAlpha model and to compare it with other strategies. Then it proceeds with the presentation of the results of our experiments and with the analysis of these results. Section 4 presents the concluding remarks and future work.

1.1 The Dynamics of Trust

The evolution of trust over time was baptized by Elofson in 1997 [15] as the *dynamics of trust*, and was addressed one year later by Castelfranchi and Falcone [16]. An interesting formalization of the dynamics of trust is presented by Jonker and Treur in 1999 [17], who defend the need for a continuous verification and validation in the trust building process, and define six different types of trust dynamics:

- *Blindly positive*: the agent is unconditionally trusted or after a certain number or sequence of positive trust experiences (i.e. evaluated events) the agent reaches the state of unconditional trust and stays there for good;
- *Blindly negative*: the agent is unconditionally distrusted or after a certain number or sequence of negative trust experiences the agent reaches the state of unconditional distrust and stays there for good;
- *Slow positive, fast negative*: it takes a lot of trust-positive experiences to gain trust and it takes only a few trust-negative experiences to lose trust;
- *Balanced slow*: trust moves in slow dynamics in both positive and negative sense;
- *Balanced fast*: trust moves in fast dynamics in both positive and negative sense;
- *Slow negative, fast positive*: it takes a lot of trust-negative experiences to lose trust and it takes only a few trust-positive experiences to gain trust.

The authors also suggest that the dynamics of trust can be formalized through *trust evolution functions* (mathematical functions that relate sequences of experiences to trust representation) or through *trust update functions* (mathematical functions that relate a current trust representation and a current experience to the next trust representation). They formally define both functions and provide a set of interesting properties that can be associated to each one of the functions. Although this work is based on simple assumptions such as past direct experiences and binary evaluated events, it provides important considerations that shall be taken into account when designing an aggregation engine. Also, the slow positive, fast negative type of trust dynamics responds to the common sense idea that trust shall grow slower and decline faster, as interestingly put in the famous words of the English poet Alexander Pope: '*At every word a reputation dies*'. At this respect, Marsh [18] also strongly suggested to penalize deceit behaviour stronger than to award the cooperative ones, as in the real world it is easier to loose, than to gain trust.

Melaye and Demazeau (2005) [19] further explore the dynamics of trust, proposing a Bayesian trust formalism based on Castelfranchi and Falcone's cognitive model. They use a Kalman filter to address two dimensions of the trust dynamics: the asymmetric increase/decrease of trust and the inherent speed of switching from trust to distrust and *vice versa*, which they name *inertia*; and the *erosion* of trust that happens due to the absence of new observations. In their model, the outcome of an execution is statistically dependent of previous executions, supporting, therefore, the mentioned trust dynamics. The introduction of the erosion dimension is of particular interest, as current trust and reputation systems tend to omit this characteristic, particularly those whose aggregation engine is based on statistical operations. However, the proposed Bayesian presents some drawbacks. In one hand, the model seems not to be scalable in the case of several beliefs and several source beliefs, and the authors assume statistical independence between each one of the belief and source beliefs' levels. Also, as the authors indicate, the inertia of trust and distrust is fixed *a priori* by a specialist, requiring one instance of the model per context. Finally, the proposed model seems to be *too sensitive* in relation to single occurrences of deceptive behaviour. In fact, in one experiment described in [19], a single negative observation that happens after a high number of previously observed positive experiences makes the trust level to decrease sharply, after which it takes a long sequence of positive observations to getting back to the previously trust value. In our opinion, this strong penalization does not reflect the real world response to one exceptional bad result of a previously trustable partner.

2 The SinAlpha Aggregation Engine

As already mentioned, we are interested in designing and implementing mechanisms that allow for an expressive representation of the dynamics of trust, when aggregating trust evidences. Particularly, we are interested in the *asymmetry* property, that stipulates that trust is hard to gain and easy to lose; in the *maturity phase* of targets property, where the slope of growth can be different in different stages of the partner trustworthiness; and in the *distinguishability* property of past behaviour. The sigmoid curve represented in Figure 1 presents interesting characteristics that seem to fit the desideratum well. For simplicity, we assume that the available information about a candidate partner is given by a central trust authority (e.g. a CTR service that serves the VO), and that it takes the form of binary values, either representing past successful (1) or violated (0) contracts by the partner.[2]

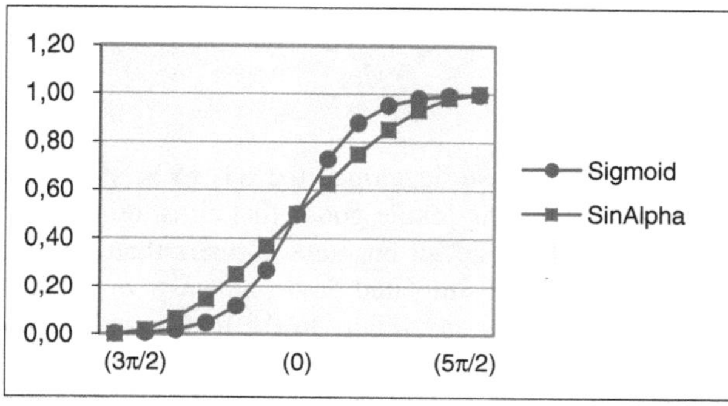

Fig. 1. Two S-shape curves, one exponential (Sigmoid) and one trigonometric (SinAlpha)

The constructing of trust for this partner using the sigmoid curve implies a slow growth upon positive results when the partner is not yet trustable, it accelerates when it is acquiring confidence, and finally slows down when the partner is considered trustable (i.e., in the top right third of the curve). The decrease movement upon negative results follows the same logic. However, we intuitively feel by graphically analysing the curve that it permits a probably too soft penalisation of partners that proved to be trustable but that failed the last *n* contracts. Therefore, we lightly soften the slope of the sigmoid shape at the top and bottom thirds of the curve, by using instead the trigonometric formula presented in (1) and depicted in Figure 1, with the name of SinAlpha.

$$y(\alpha) = \delta.\sin\alpha + \delta, \quad \alpha_0 = 3\pi/2\,, \qquad \alpha = \alpha + \lambda.\omega\,. \tag{1}$$

In the formula above, δ is a constant value of 0.5, and α ranges from $3\pi/2$ to $5\pi/2$, allowing for aggregated trust scores within the range [0, 1]. The incremental step of α is also shown in (1); ω represents the pace of trust growth (we assume the value of $\pi/2$ in our experiments), and λ is the parameter of the incremental step that allows to differentiate between positive and negative results (in our experiments, λ equals +1 for each positive result to be aggregated, and -1.5 for each violated contract). This way, in each one of the three stages of trust construction, trust grows slower and decreases faster. At this point, we must remind our interest in studying how a curve like the one we propose, which, in a certain way, 'encompasses' the historical behaviour

[2] We use these two assumptions in our experiments, although our proposed aggregation engine might be extended in the future to more complex and diversified representation of trust information. In the same way, the aggregation engine might be used in decentralized systems, to aggregate information from distinct sources of information (e.g. reputation and image).

of the partner under evaluation, is able to catch the dynamics of trust in the presence of certain partners' patterns of behaviour. We are also willing to know how this model can be compared with the common statistical approach that aggregates trust information using weighted means.

3 Experiments

3.1 The STexVM System

In order to run our experiments, we developed the STexVM system. This is a simulated virtual marketplace for trading textile goods that aims to ensure reliable transactions, in a sense that it is able to detect business partners that in some moment start behaving in a defective way. The simulated environment is based on existent online virtual marketplaces where buyers and sellers in the textile and fashion industry can post buying and selling leads (e.g. the Fibre2Fashion marketplace[3]). It follows the multi-agent paradigm, and is implemented over Jade platform, using the standard behaviours of Jade and FIPA performatives and interaction protocols[4]. The key agents in this environment have the roles either of buyers or suppliers (Figure 2).

At each round, a buyer issues a call for proposal (cfp) stipulating a specific good and associated quantity that needs to be provided, and each candidate partner responds indicating the quantity it is able to provide in the present business opportunity, or refusing the offer. A contract-net like negotiation occurs, and the buyer selects a number $n > 0$ of partners that optimizes the expected utility $E(u)$, using equation (2).

$$E(u) = \arg\max_i \text{ for each } i \ \Sigma_j \ util_j * trust_j \ . \tag{2}$$

In the equation above, i stands for the possible combinations of suppliers' proposals that fit the quantity specified in the current cfp, not exceeding it; j represents the suppliers considered in each of these combinations, and $trust_j$ is the confidence score computed for supplier j at selection time. Finally, $util_j$ is the quantity proposed by each supplier j in the round, normalized by the quantity specified in the cfp, i.e., $quant_j/Quant$. In our system, a buyer can accept less quantity than the maximum quantity (*Quant*) defined in the cfp, but it cannot exceed *Quant*. Also, a buyer cannot accept partial quantities of the received bids.

Each supplier that enters the simulated virtual marketplace sells two different types of fabric (e.g. cotton and chiffon). These and their associated quantities (e.g. 180,000 meters) are randomly assigned at creation time. Buyers are characterized by the good and quantity they need to purchase, also randomly picked up at creation time. The remaining agents of the STexVM system are the Agent Simulation Manager, who manages the configuration parameters related with buyers and suppliers; the Agent DF, which registers competences of buyers and suppliers; and the Agent CTR, which gathers information about the performance of suppliers and computes their confidence scores on-demand, when requested by the buyers. Figure 2 illustrates the relation between these agents.

---

[3] http://fibre2fashion.com/

[4] Jade: http://jade.tilab.com/; FIPA: http://www.fipa.org/

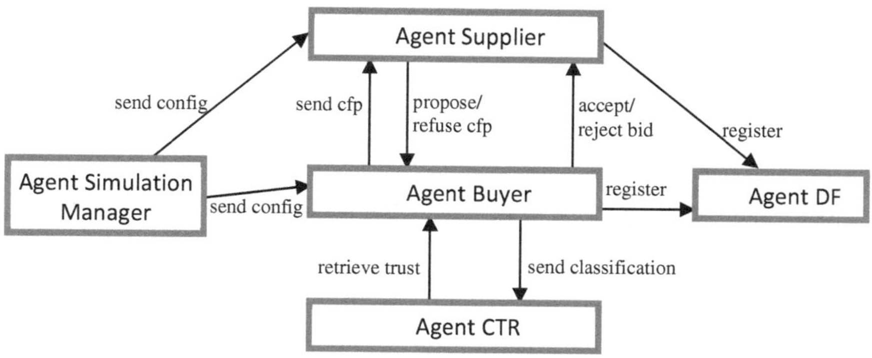

Fig. 2. Interactions between agents in the STexVM system

3.2 Approaches in Evaluation

In the following experiments, a buyer agent can be assigned one of four different approaches for selecting partners. The SINALPHA approach uses equation (1) to estimate a truth score for each candidate partner and weights the resulting score with a recency factor. The ASYM+ approach is a similar, former model that we proposed in [20] that also accounts for the dynamics of trust. The WMEAN approach uses an aggregation engine that computes the mean of the last 10 results weighted by the recency of these results (cf. Huynh, 2006 [21]). As mentioned earlier, there are several CTR models that use weighted means to aggregate social evaluations, therefore the WMEAN approach will allow us to compare SINALPHA with one model that is disseminated in the trust and reputation community. Finally, the QUANT model selects partners by the quantity they are able to provide, and does not take into consideration the trust values of the suppliers.

For all the models, in the first rounds of each experiment the buyers start to explore the space of available candidate partners, by randomly selecting the partners, and after some rounds they progressively increase the exploitation by selecting partners based on the selected model. In the current experiments (Table 2) the exploration phase ends up at round 39 (of 60), for all buyers, meaning that their selection decision relies exclusively on the adopted model after round 40.[5]

3.3 Experimental Methodology

In order to evaluate the approaches described above, we consider that the candidate partners have different behaviours and are divided accordingly into categories "S_A", "S_B", and "S_C". The behaviour of a supplier is related to the results of the contracts it makes, during its lifecycle, with buyer agents. A behaviour is assigned to each supplier at its creation time, following a uniform distribution over the three possible categories. We consider that the capacity of each type of suppliers in fulfilling the contract is modelled by a Markovian process with two states (1 and 0, standing for contract

[5] In future versions of STexVM, we will allow for the system to keep results between experiments, avoiding the need to bootstrap the system every time an experiment is run.

fulfilment and contract violation, respectively) and transition probabilities P11 (Fulfilment-to-Fulfilment) and P01 (Violation-to-Fulfilment). In these experiments, we consider two distinct populations, A and B, as defined at Table 1.

Table 1. Transition probabilities. Initial probabilities $P_0 = P_1 = 0.50$ for both populations

	Type "S_A"		Type "S_B"		Type "S_C"	
	P11	P01	P11	P01	P11	P01
Pop A	0.90	1.00	0.80	0.75	0.50	0.50
Pop B	0.90	0.20	0.90	0.20	0.80	0.60

As can be seen from the table above, in population A, suppliers of type S_A have high probability of success and never fail two contracts in a row (once P00 is zero). Types S_B and S_C correspond to progressively worse behaviours. With this population, we want to evaluate the capacity of each strategy in choosing the best partners, i.e., partners of type S_A. Population B, on the other hand, presents a bursty-like pattern of behaviour, where candidate partners of types S_A and S_B generally fulfil several contracts in a row, but when they fail a contract they generally enter in a long burst of violated contracts. Type S_C presents smaller bursts of both positive and negative behaviour. With this population, we pretend to evaluate the performance of each strategy in avoiding long sequences of negative results and in abandoning a good provider when it starts to behave in a deceptive way.

In every experiment, we instantiated 16 suppliers and 8 buyers: two of type SINALPHA, two of type ASYM+, two of type WMEAN and the remaining two of type QUANT. Every buyer was allowed to run 60 rounds, corresponding to the launching of 60 different cfps. Every experience was run 12 times. Finally, the utility gained by each buyer at each negotiation round was recorded, and at the end of the experiments the average utility of a buyer and the corresponding standard deviation were evaluated for each one of the considered approaches. The average utility captures the capacity of the buyer in selecting good partners, and, this way, allows for the evaluation of the performance of each one of the three approaches. Table 2 presents compact data about the experiments.

Table 2. Values and parameters used in the experiments

Fabrics and Quantity	Chiffon, Cotton; 180000
# buyers	2 SINALPHA, 2 ASYM+, 2 WMEAN, 2 QUANT
# of sellers	16
Types of sellers	Chosen upon a uniform distribution over the types {"S_A", "S_B", "S_C"}
# issued CFP per buyer, per run	60
# runs per experiment	12
Exploit/Exploration formula	Uniform distribution over f(x), where $f(x) = 100 - round_i * 7$, $f(x) = 5$, if $(100 - round_i * 7 < 10)$, $f(x) = 0$ if $round_i > 40$; $0 < i < 60$
SinAlpha parameters	$\delta = 0.5$; $\omega = \pi/2$; $\lambda = +1$ for successful contracts, and $\lambda = -1.5$ for violations

3.4 Results

We used three different metrics to evaluate the performance of the three approaches in evaluation in the experiments with population A. First, we measured the utility gained by each buyer in the last 20 rounds in each experiment, and averaged the results obtained for each approach over the 12 experiments. The results concerning the average utility showed that the both models that accounts for the described dynamics of trust outperformed the other two models (SINALPHA: 92.1%; ASYM+: 93.3%; WMEAN: 87.1%; QUANT: 79.8%). Then, we counted the number of violated contracts per buyer in its last 10 transactions, and averaged this number per approach and over the 12 runs of the experiment. The results show a clear advantage of SINALPHA in avoiding partners with past bad experience: 11.7% of violated contracts (vc), with standard deviation (sd) of 0.78, when compared to ASYM+ (12.1% vc, 1.38 sd), WMEAN (18.3% vc, 1.37 sd) and QUANT (22.1% vc, 3.20 sd).

Finally, we counted the number of suppliers of types S_A, S_B and S_C that were chosen by each buyer in its last 20 transactions, and averaged this number per approach, over the 12 runs. In this step, we intend to further understand the differences between the proposed SinAlpha curve and the weighted mean approach, and, this way, we only present the results obtained for SINALPHA and WMEAN. The results showed that with the SINALPHA approach the buyers were able to choose the best suppliers (of type S_A) 91% of the times, and suppliers of type S_B the remaining 9%. On the other hand, buyers that used the WMEAN approach were less effective in choosing suppliers of type S_A (they did it 75% of the times) and they even choose bad suppliers of type S_C 5% of the times. Suppliers of type S_B were chosen 20% of the times.

We repeated the first two procedures described above with population B, and the results are as follows. SINALPHA got an average utility of 79.8%, outperforming ASYM+ (78.8%) and QUANT (62.3%), but underperforming the WMEAN approach, that achieved an average utility in the last 20 rounds of 83.3%. Concerning the average of violated contracts in the last 10 transactions of each buyer, SINALPHA performed a little better than the remaining approaches, getting 22.9% of violated contracts (vc) and standard deviation (sd) of 2.11, against the results of ASYM+ (25% vc, 1.91 sd), WMEAN (24.6% vc, 2.75 sd) and QUANT (38.3% vc, 3.31 sd).

3.5 Interpretation of the Results

Starting with Population A, we verified that the QUANT approach gets the worse results as expected, as it is not able to differentiate between partners of types S_A, S_B, and S_C. We also verified that SINALPHA and ASYM+ tend to perform in a similar way, with SINALPHA slightly outperforming ASYM+. This is because both models use sigmoid like curves and accounts for the same described trust dynamics. Because of space concerns, we relegate a further comparison of these two our models to a future paper. Finally, we observed that the SINALPHA approach outperforms the WMEAN approach, particularly when we attend to the figures related to the violated contracts in the last 10 interactions and to the capacity of each approach in selecting good (S_A) partners. By analyzing the traces of the experiments, we realize that the SINALPHA strategy selects primarily partners of type S_A, while the WMEAN equally selects partners of types S_A and S_B. The difference between both approaches is that in

SINALPHA all the historical path is taken into account in the process of trust construction, and partners have to accumulate several good experiences in the past until they are able to get an average to high trust score. In opposition, by aggregating up to the last N results, the WMEAN approach allows the selection of partners with fewer past events. In reality, we verified that the bad choices of WMEAN on population A were related to the selection of S_B and S_C partners in two distinct situations: i) when they were selected with less than 10 past results (e.g. the pattern of the previous evidences to the time of selection where *V-F-F-V-F-F*, where *V* means a violated contract and *F* a fulfilled contract); and ii) when they showed an intermittent pattern followed by a short number of positive evidences (e.g. *F-V-V-F-V-F-V-V-F-F-F-F-F*). This last pattern of behaviour is indeed severely punished by the SINALPHA approach, where violations weight more than fulfilments (therefore penalizing undesirable intermittent patterns), and where the last five positive evidences are not sufficient to 'push' the confidence level of the partner to the second third of the SinAlpha curve.

In the experiments with population B, we intended to study the performance of the SINALPHA and the WMEAN strategies in the presence of extreme partners' behaviour, particularly the cases where good partners, which have been successfully in fulfilling their obligations, suddenly start having systematic deceptive behaviour. By analysis of the traces of the experiments, we realized that both strategies act quite differently as they tend to select different partners in similar conditions. In fact, the WMEAN strategy privileges recency and puts a limit to the historical analyses (in our experiments, it aggregates the last 10 contract results). In one hand, this permits that a candidate partner with few past results (let us say 6 past results, while majority positives), is chosen in detriment of a partner that has been reliable for a long time but that violated the last 2 to 4 contracts. As we are selecting partners using too few results, a considerable risk is associated to the partner's selection using WMEAN.[6] On the other hand, in similar conditions, the SINALPHA approach does not select the described partners, as the SinAlpha curve encompasses a "growing path" that partners shall run until they acquire middle to high trust (i.e., until they reach the last two thirds of the curve). This means that in the scenario of population B, the SINALPHA approach has bigger tendency to enter a burst of deceptive behaviour and is somewhat slower in penalizing good partners that inverted their behaviour. However, we detected another problem associated to the WMEAN approach, which helps to explain the results in terms of violated contracts: as this strategy privileges recency, it actually assigns high trust levels to candidate partners that systematically behaved deceptively in the past, had no classification for a long time, and then got one positive classification in the present. Using common sense, we can deduce that this kind of behaviour encompasses a high degree of risk; however, we realized that in the described cases the WMEAN approach chooses these partners in detriment of more stable partners that happened to fail the last couple of contracts.

Although not mentioned in section 3.3, we run a different type of experiment using population A and the Repast agent simulator[7]. In this experiment, we run the SINALPHA and the WMEAN approaches separately; i.e., we maintained the number of

[6] A confidence value could be used along with the computed trust score. However, these experiments aim to evaluate the aggregating processes by themselves.

[7] http://repast.sourceforge.net/

suppliers (16), but all the 8 buyers were either using SINALPHA or WMEAN. Each run took 100 rounds. In the first 40 rounds, the selection of suppliers was done randomly, and in the last 60 rounds the selection was done taking into account the approach used by the buyers. At round 70, for both approaches, all suppliers of type S_A abruptly changed their behaviour and assumed the characteristics of type S_C, and the remaining suppliers kept their initial behaviour. With this experiment, we intended to study the *abuse of prior information* scenario defined in [8]. The results that we obtained showed a similar capacity of SINALPHA and WMEAN in detecting and penalizing the change of behaviour of suppliers that were originally of type S_A. However, the most interesting result of this experiment was the capacity of SINALPHA buyers in adapting to the situation by massively choosing suppliers of type S_B after round 70. Concerning WMEAN buyers, although they also increased the number of selected S_B partners after round 70, they show an undesirable side effect of also considerably increasing the selection of partners that were originally of type S_C. This behaviour shall be analysed with further detail in future work.

4 Concluding Remarks and Future Work

The work presented in this paper started by empirically searching a mathematical function that would allow to aggregate evaluations on a given partner that encompasses the evolutionary performance of the target. This search was driven by economical common sense. For example, and simply putting, a business player would certainly distinguish between the following patterns of behaviour: *good-good-good-good-bad-bad-bad-bad*, *good-bad-good-bad-good-bad-good-bad* and *bad-bad-good-bad-good-good-good-bad*. We have put thorough attention in the sequences of possible results, always taking into consideration common sense about business notions. For instance, a partner that ever succeed with its obligations and achieved a high degree of trustworthiness should not be severely punished if he accidentally is not successful in the last actual transaction; a partner that succeed the first two obligations but does not entered any other transaction after that cannot be considered highly reputed, as there is not enough information on the past he had carried out until be considered reputable. Also, a partner that achieved a given trust level should not maintain this level if he starts behaving in an intermittent way. Following this reasoning process, we came across the SinAlpha function.

The experiences we run on two different populations allow us to conclude that the SinAlpha function actually gets better results than a weighted mean by recency approach, because it takes into account the dynamics of trust. Also, the results obtained seem to show that there is still margin to improve the performance of the proposed mechanism by adapting/learning the values of parameters λ and ω to the perceived patterns of the current populations. In fact, the next phase of our work would be dedicated to this topic, and to the inclusion of the erosion property of trust in our approach. Different type of behaviour patterns shall be defined, as well as experimental procedures (e.g. the use of the metric *converge speed* defined in [8]).

In the same way, we will continue progressively improving our approach, and several research challenges would certainly be presented. Namely, we propose as future work to identify and to categorize patterns of behaviour as new target evidences appear, through the usage of clustering techniques; and to consider multi-attribute evaluations (e.g. price, delivery time, and quality).

Acknowledgements. The first author enjoys a PhD grant with reference SFRH/BD/39070/2007 from the Portuguese Fundação para a Ciência e a Tecnologia.

References

1. Conte, R., Paolucci, M.: Reputation in Artificial Societies: Social Beliefs for Social Order. Kluwer Academic Publishers, Dordrecht (2002)
2. Salvatore, A., Pinyol, I., Paolucci, M., Sabater-Mir, J.: Grounding Reputation Experiments. A Replication of a Simple Market with Image Exchange. In: Proceedings of the Third International Model-to-Model Workshop, France, pp. 32–45 (2007)
3. Ramchurn, S., Sierra, C., Godo, L., Jennings, N.R.: Devising a trust model for multi-agent interactions using confidence and reputation. Int. J. Applied Artificial Intelligence 18, 833–852 (2004)
4. Sabater, J.: Trust and Reputation for Agent Societies. Number 20 in Monografies de l'institut d'investigacio en intelligència artificial. IIIA-CSIC (2003)
5. Carbo, J., Molina, J., Davila, J.: A BDI Agent Architecture for Reasoning about Reputation. In: IEEE International Conference on Systems, Man, and Cybernetics (2001)
6. Jøsang, A., Ismail, R.: The Beta Reputation System. In: Proceedings of the 15th Bled Electronic Commerce Conference, Sloven (2002)
7. Reece, S., Rogers, A., Roberts, S., Jennings, N.R.: A Multi-Dimensional Trust Model for Heterogeneous Contract Observations. In: 22nd AAAI Conf. on Artificial Intelligence (2007)
8. Zacharia, G., Maes, P.: Trust management through reputation mechanisms. Applied Artificial Intelligence 14(9), 881–908 (2000)
9. Haller, J.: A Bayesian Reputation System for Virtual Organizations. In: Dagstuhl Seminar Proceedings 06461, Negotiation and Market Engineering (2006)
10. Hang, C., Wang, Y., Singh, M.P.: An adaptive probabilistic trust model and its evaluation. In: Proceedings of the 7th international Joint Conference on Autonomous Agents and Multiagent Systems, Estoril, Portugal, May 12 – 16, 2008, vol. 3 (2008)
11. Erete, I., Ferguson, E., Sen, S.: Learning task-specific trust decisions. In: Procs. 7th Int. J. Conf. on Autonomous Agents and Multiagent Systems, Portugal, vol. 3 (2008)
12. Smith, M., desJardins, M.: Learning to trust in the Competece and Commitment of Agents. Autonomous Agent Multi-Agent Systems 18, 36–82 (2009)
13. Sabater, J., Paolucci, M.: On Representation and Aggregation of Social Evaluations. Computational Trust and Reputation Models, Int. J. Approx. Reasoning (2007)
14. Rettinger, A., Nickles, M., Tresp, V.: A statistical relational model for trust learning. Procs. 7th Int. J. Conf. on Autonomous Agents and Multiagent Systems 2 (2008)
15. Elofson, G.: Developing Trust with Intelligent Agents: An Exploratory Study. In: Proceedings of the First International Workshop on Trust, pp. 125–139 (1998)
16. Falcone, R., Castelfranchi, C.: Principles of trust for MAS: cognitive anatomy, social importance, and quantification. In: Procs. Int. Conference on Multi-Agent Systems (1998)
17. Jonker, C.M., Treur, J.: Formal Analysis of Models for the Dynamics of Trust Based on Experiences. In: Garijo, F.J., Boman, M. (eds.) MAAMAW 1999. LNCS, vol. 1647, pp. 221–231. Springer, Heidelberg (1999)

18. Marsh, S.P.: Formalising Trust as a Computational Concept, PhD Thesis, University of Stirling (1994)
19. Melaye, D., Demazeau, Y.: Bayesian Dynamic Trust Model. In: Pěchouček, M., Petta, P., Varga, L.Z. (eds.) CEEMAS 2005. LNCS (LNAI), vol. 3690, pp. 480–489. Springer, Heidelberg (2005)
20. Urbano, J., Rocha, A.P., Oliveira, E.: Trust Evaluation for Reliable Electronic Transactions between Business Partners. In: Fischer, K., Muller, J.P., Odell, J. (eds.) Procs. The AAMAS 2009 Workshop on Agent-based Technologies and applications for enterprise interOPerability (ATOP), Budapest, pp. 85–96 (2009)
21. Huynh, T.D., Jennings, N.R., Shadbolt, N.R.: An integrated trust and reputation model for open multi-agent systems. Autonomous Agents and Multi-Agent Systems 13(2), 119–154 (2006)

Chapter 10

SSM – Social Simulation and Modelling

Games on Cellular Spaces: An Evolutionary Approach

Pedro Ribeiro de Andrade, Antonio Miguel Vieira Monteiro, and Gilberto Câmara

INPE – National Institute for Space Research,
Av. dos Astronautas 1758, CEP 12227-001, São José dos Campos, Brazil
{pedro,miguel,gilberto}@dpi.inpe.br

Abstract. By using differential equations, evolutionary game theory shows that most of the games of competition for resources have equilibrium strategies named Evolutionary Stable. Although this approach can deduce these points, it is not possible to say how or whether a population will reach such equilibrium. We present an evolutionary agent-based model where individuals compete for space using mixed strategies. Agents belong to spatial locations that settle with whom they can interact, but they can freely move to contiguous partitions according to a definition of satisfiability. The simulation results show that, although the agents do not have any knowledge about equilibrium points, the population's mean strategy always converges to a stable state, close and above to the analytic equilibrium. Moreover, it is reached independently of the initial population.

Keywords: Spatial Games, Agent-Based Modelling, Chicken Game, ESS.

1 Introduction

Since the works of Maynard Smith on evolution and the theory of games [1], it has been shown that Game Theory can be used for studying species competing for resources. By using replicator equations, evolutionary game theory shows that there exist equilibrium points named Evolutionary Stable Strategy (ESS). It means that, if all members of a population adopt this strategy then no mutant strategy could spread under the influence of natural selection.

Although this approach can deduce equilibrium points, it does not say how or whether the population will reach such equilibrium. Computer models are the way to show how this happens by growing the patterns observed in real world, because finding equilibrium points is not enough to show that a population will reach such equilibrium: it is necessary to build these patterns in a generative way [2].

Authors that propose simulation models try to flexibilize some assumptions of the mathematical model, criticizing the fact that some of its assumptions are not applicable to the real world. The critics rely mainly in the use of infinite populations. An example is the work of Orzack and Hines, showing that the probability an ESS will evolve is proportional to the population size [3]. Another example is the work of Fogel and others, which describes models with a population starting at ESS but,

L. Seabra Lopes et al. (Eds.): EPIA 2009, LNAI 5816, pp. 535–546, 2009.

instead of staying stable, the models evolve to other strategies [4]. In both cases, each agent competes with all other agents of the model in order to calculate its fitness. These models have two main disadvantages. First, they rarely converge to a stable state, be it an ESS or not. Second, they are strongly dependant on the composition of their initial population.

By adding space as a new dimension for studying these competitions, we can relax the assumptions of agents having to compete with each other and working with infinite populations. There are some experiments in the literature showing that members of populations compete for space because they need to guarantee food, which can decide their fate. An experimental evidence that owning space may lead to survivor is presented by [5]. The author describes the percentage of diary corporal weight change of spiders. There are two groups of spiders: one that owns some territory and another that does not. Most of spiders that do not own a territory lose weight, while almost all owners increase their weight, which leads to a greater chance to survive.

However, much of the simulation studies that add space as a fundamental component of the model are interested in the evolution of cooperation using only pure strategies or meta-strategies that use the last results to choose the next action [6]. In these works, only the strategy spreads over the space, or, in some other cases, the agents have little mobility, mainly waiting for an empty cell to move [7]. In this work, we study the evolution of a population that compete for space using *mixed* strategies, and whose members can freely move according to a definition of satisfiability.

The main objective of this work is to investigate whether a population evolves to a stable equilibrium within this environment, and how the reached equilibrium is related to the theoretical equilibrium. We present initial results of the proposed model, analysing the effects of mutation and initial population on the evolutive process.

2 Non-cooperative Games, Nash Equilibrium, and ESS

A game with n players is said to be non-cooperative when we have, for each player:

1. a finite set of pure strategies (actions);
2. a payoff function, mapping all n-tuples with pure strategies to real numbers.

One mixed strategy is a collection of non-negative numbers adding up to 1, corresponding to probabilities of using each of the pure strategies. The mixed strategy defines the tendencies of a player. Each time it plays, it will choose randomly one of its pure strategies, based on the probabilities defined by the mixed strategy.

For example, let us take the chicken game. Two players have the choice to escalate (E) or not to escalate (~E) a brawl. If none of them escalates, nothing happens. If only one escalates, the other player runs away, and the winner receives 1 from the coward player. But, if both decide to escalate, each player pays 10 due to medical care. This game is said to be symmetric, because both players employ the same pure strategies and payoffs, as shown in Table 1. Given that this game has only two pure strategies, we say that s_x, $0 \le x \le 1$, is the mixed strategy of escalating with probability x.

Table 1. Chicken game payoffs, in pairs (A, B)

	B escalates	*B* does not escalate
A escalates	(–10, –10)	(+1, –1)
A does not escalate	(–1, +1)	(0, 0)

Nash proved that, given any non-cooperative game of n players, there is always an equilibrium point, a set of mixed strategies for each player that, if a player changes its mixed strategy, the best result it may get will be the same as in the equilibrium [8]. No player has incentive to deviate one-sidedly from its strategy as long as the other players remain in the equilibrium. This is known as the Nash equilibrium.

But this concept of equilibrium may cause controversy. Let the chicken game and two players, A and B, following strategies s_a and s_b, respectively. The expected payoff of A is $-10s_a s_b + s_a - s_b$. If A would know exactly the value of s_b, it would be possible to calculate the best action for A. If s_b is greater than 10%, the best choice for A is never to shoot ($s_a = 0$), implying in a payoff of $-s_b$. If s_b is less than 10%, A should always shoot ($s_a = 1$), because its payoff would be $1-11s_b$. But, if s_b is exactly 10%, all strategies for A lead to the same payoff (–0.1). Thus, if s_a is also fixed at 10%, no other strategy could increase its payoff against A by changing its own mixed strategy. Applying the same reasoning for B, we arrive to the conclusion that when both players follow $s_{0.1}$ the game is in a Nash equilibrium. Most game theorists agree on $s_{0.1}$ as the rational solution for this game, but the argument is weak [9]. Although deviating from the equilibrium does not increase the utility of a player, it does not decrease as well, as long as the opponent follows equilibrium. Thus, this equilibrium it is not *strict*.

A clearer explanation can be found when it is played not by only two players, but within a population. Maynard Smith viewed this game in a population-dynamical setting. In his model, an infinite number of players meet randomly in contests where they have to decide whether to escalate or not. If the estimated overall probability is greater than 0.1, it is better not to escalate. If it is less than 0.1, it is better to escalate. But if it is exactly 0.1, then there is no better strategy than $s_{0.1}$. In this sense, self-regulation leads to $s_{0.1}$ – self-regulation, not between two players, but within a population. Nash has also proposed a similar interpretation for the equilibrium points, the *mass-action* [8], forgotten for decades in his unpublished thesis.

Maynard Smith pointed out two possible interpretations for the ESS. The first interpretation refers mixed strategies, meaning that each member of the population follows the same equilibrium mixed strategy. In the case of the chicken game, the whole population would follow $s_{0.1}$. The second solution works with pure strategies. We have players following different pure strategies in such a way that the mean strategy of the overall population is at equilibrium. Again with the chicken, the stable state has 90% of the population following $s_{0.0}$ and 10% following $s_{1.0}$.

In this work, we will study how this non-strict equilibrium behaves in a spatial context where the agents' mobility is based on the results of the games. We relax the assumptions of finite population and matches among all members of the population, and add new parameters such as fitness, satisfiability, and mutation.

3 The Basic Model

The approach of this work is based on a non-evolutive model proposed Andrade and others [10]. The model takes place in a cellular space. A cellular space is a network of cells connected by neighbourhood relations. The simplest example of a cellular space is a grid, with square cells having four touching neighbours. The cellular space is populated with agents. Each agent belongs to a cell, which has enough space for it to live. Initially, a cell contains a set of agents, which have to compete for it through a non-cooperative game. Whenever an agent is playing a non-cooperative game, we call it *player*.

The basic assumption of this model is that whenever an agent arrives at a cell it is satisfied with it, and it will not move until it becomes dissatisfied. Two agents within the same cell may play a game competing for it, and the result of the game affects the satisfaction of both agents. This is the only memory an agent has, and it is called the local satisfaction. It starts with a positive value when an agent arrives at a cell, and when this value reaches zero or less, the agent randomly picks a neighbour cell and moves to it, looking for a better cell to compete for. Therefore, this movement is a random walk.

Each agent also has a global satisfaction, starting with a positive value significantly greater than the local satisfaction, but also affected by the payoffs of the games. All agents have the same global satisfaction at the beginning of the model. An agent that got dissatisfied many times and its global satisfaction reaches zero or less leaves the model. As we need local and global satisfaction decreasing along the simulation, the expected payoff of the game used in the model has to be almost always negative.

To create a metric for satisfaction, we say the satisfaction of an agent is measured by its fitness. Local satisfaction represents the maximum effort one can dispend when competing for a cell and global satisfaction is the initial fitness. Agents are identical if we consider satisfaction, but they differ in their mixed strategies, which cannot be identified by any other agent.

The basic model has a finite number of turns, each one with two steps. The first step establishes the games, randomly choosing pairs of agents in each cell, and then carries out the games with each pair. Cells with an odd number of agents have one random idle agent. No agent will play more than once in each turn.

The second step defines the dynamical part of the model. Once each agent already knows its own payoff, it updates its local and global satisfactions with the earned payoff. Then, it checks if any satisfaction has reached zero or less to perform a movement or to leave the model. The model executes until it reaches a stable state, which can be when there is at most one agent in each cell, or when the overall satisfaction stops to decrease.

The model of games on cellular space can be formalized as a 9-tuple:

$$M = (C, n, S, p, A, s, k, g, l), \text{ where}$$

- C is the cellular space in which the games take place,
- n is the number of players involved in the non-cooperative game,
- S is the set of actions (pure strategies) each player can take,
- p: $X \rightarrow \Re$, X=, is the payoff function,
- A is the set of sorts of agents,

- $s: A \times S \rightarrow [0,1]$, $\forall a \in A$, $\Sigma_{b \in S}\, s(a, b) = 1$, represents the mixed strategies,
- $k \in$ N, is initial number of agents of each given sort,
- $g \in \Re$, is the global satisfaction threshold,
- $l \in \Re$, is the local satisfaction threshold.

Therefore, given s_x, we have that $s(s_x, E)=x$ and $s(s_x, \sim E)=1-x$. An agent using a mixed strategy commits to a randomization device. Each time the agent plays, it chooses one of its pure strategies, based on the probabilities specified by its mixed strategy. As an example of model, the following describes the traditional chicken game:

$$M_c = (Cc, 2, , u, \{s_a, s_b\}, s, 1, \infty, \infty).$$

The cellular space *Cc* has one cell with two agents, one following s_a and the other s_b. They have the same set of possible actions, "escalate" and "not escalate," and the same payoff matrix u (shown in Table 1), but they do not have to follow the same mixed strategy. Both agents always stay in the cell, and never leave the model.

In this work, we apply the chicken within this basic framework. The expected payoff of chicken is almost always negative, only in the case where both players never escalate it is zero. Thus, this game fits in with the need of reducing satisfaction to make the agents move. C is a squared grid with 20x20 cells, such that the possible movements are at most to four neighbours (up, down, left, and right). Cells on the edges have three choices, and cells on the corners have only two.

4 The Evolutionary Model

The evolutive model is based on the idea that agents that own cells at the end of the basic model deserve to pass their strategies to the next generation. Therefore, the model considers a competition of the basic model as one evolutive step, a survival of the fittest. Once a competition finishes, each agent that has conquered a partition of space produces descendants within the cell it has conquered. The agent tries to transfer its own strategy to its offsprings, but their learning ability is limited, and then they may have a strategy slightly different from the father, according to a predefined mutation probability. Whenever this mutation is activated, the offspring has the strategy of its father with some random change; otherwise it takes exactly the same strategy. Therefore, there are three additional parameters if compared with the basic model: number of descendants, mutation probability, and the mutation itself.

The father leaves the model right after it generates its descendants. This leads to non-overlapping generations, which is a common approach in the literature. This evolutive process can be repeated indefinetly, and it depends only on the initial population of the basic model.

The model has five stochastic ingredients, three of them coming from the original model, and the other two added by the evolutive part. They are:

1. selecting pairs of agents within the same cell to play,
2. choosing the agent's pure strategy based on its mixed strategy,
3. relocating, once one agent is unsatisfied,
4. mutating or not a given strategy to a descendant, and
5. choosing the mutation change, once it is activated.

5 Experiments

In this work, we present early results that examine the convergence of a population and the effect of mutation on evolution. The parameters chosen were: 3 as the number of descendants, 0.1% as chance of mutation, and ±0.1 as the change in the inherited strategy, with 50% of probability of each, once the mutation is activated. Agents following $s_{0.0}$ and $s_{1.0}$ can only produce mutants of $s_{0.1}$ and $s_{0.9}$, respectively.

The model was implemented using TerraME framework [11]. Although the model has five random ingredients, the simulations had similar development. Thus, the results presented in this section are single runs of the model.

5.1 Evolutionary Equilibrium

As initial test for studying the evolutionary capabilities of the model, we examine a model whose population is initially composed by $s_{1.0}$ agents. The model has the following arrangement:

$$M_0 = (Cc, 2, \{E, \sim E\}, u, \{s_{1.0}\}, s, 1200, 200, 20).$$

Figure 1 shows the results, with the left side showing a zoom in the first generations of the simulation. We can see that $s_{1.0}$ starts filling the whole cellular space, but it cannot maintain this situation, stabilizing with agents in 75% of the cellular space. This happens because two agents within a cell may shoot, reach the threshold, and leave the cell.

When the first mutation to $s_{0.9}$ arises in the population, this new strategy rapidly spreads, crushing $s_{1.0}$ and dominating the whole cellular space. This strategy can then produce agents following $s_{0.8}$, then $s_{0.7}$, and so on, each one surpassing the previous strategy, until $s_{0.1}$ appears, as shown in the left part of Figure 1. But $s_{0.1}$ cannot get rid of $s_{0.2}$ and both compete undefinetly. The results agree with [10], that state that as more frequently an agent escalates, greater is its ability to realize cells with a higher

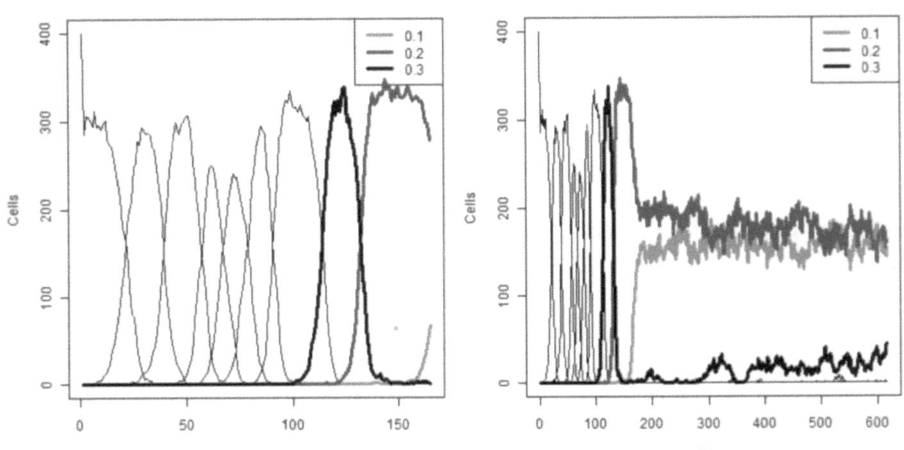

Fig. 1. Development of strategies in a simulation with population of $s_{1.0}$

number of agents that also escalate frequently, as it will reach its threshold for moving faster than the ones that escalate less. Moreover, it gets even more important because the agents have limited fitness and need to stay alive. This leads to an increase in the surviving chance of sub-optimal strategies such as $s_{0.2}$ and $s_{0.3}$. Therefore, although there is a single theoretical equilibrium, there is no single best strategy in this competition for space.

Although neither strategy can surpass all other strategies and dominate the overall population, an evolutive process indeed occurs. If we calculate the average strategy of the population by summing the mixed strategies of every owner at the end of a generation and divide by the total number of agents, we can verify that the population indeed converges to a stable state. In Figure 2, we have the average strategy of the population, with a dashed line showing the theoretical equilibrium point. The average strategy converges to a stable state before the 200th generation and stays close and above the equilibrium point until the end of the simulation.

The generative result of this model is a mixing of the two definitions of equilibrium pointed by Maynard Smith. In the results, we do not have the overall population following the same equilibrium strategy, nor agents following only pure strategies, but what really happens is a combination of mixed strategies whose average is a stable equilibruim point.

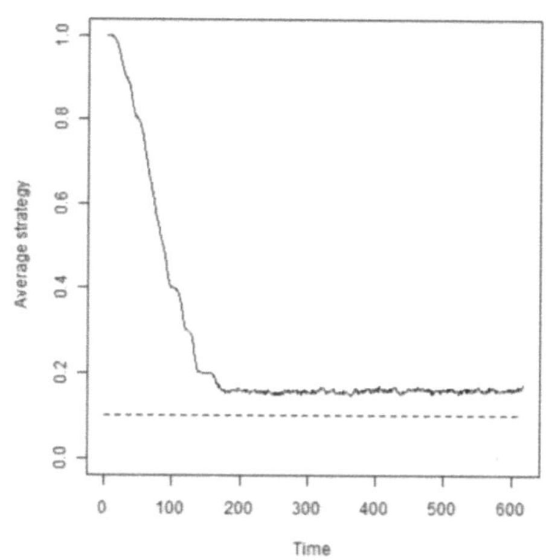

Fig. 2. Convergence of the mean strategy using different initial populations

5.2 Mutation Effects

A question that arises from the result of the initial model is how the mutation rate can affect the model development. Eight simulations were carried out, each one with a single mutation rate, varying from 0.1% (the previous experiment) to 50%. It is not feasible to have the mutation rate greater than 50% because, in this case, most of the descendants would follow a strategy different from their predecessors.

It is straightforward that increasing mutation leads to a faster convergence to a stable state, as shown in Figure 3. With mutation of 0.1%, it takes more than 150 generations to converge, while with 50% it converges in less than 25 generations. But note

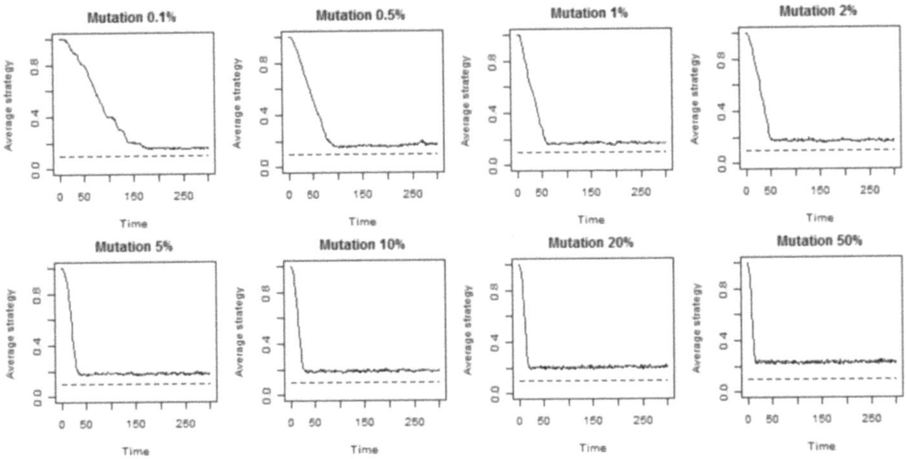

Fig. 3. Effects of changing the mutation rate in the convergence of the model

that the distance between the average strategy and the theoretical equilibrium is proportional to the mutation rate. It is difficult to see comparing two consecultive mutation rates, but we can see clearly comparing the results of 0.1% and 50%.

Mutation induces other impacts in the development of the model. Increasing it leads to a greater diversity of strategies, and then to a higher probability of generating far from equilibrium strategies. However, there is a consequence of increasing the mutation rate that is not straightforward. Figure 4 shows the number of agents following each strategy at the end of each generation, in the same simulations of Figure 3. After the model converges to a stable mean strategy, each individual strategy reduces its oscillation as the mutation increases, stabilizing in a well-defined small interval.

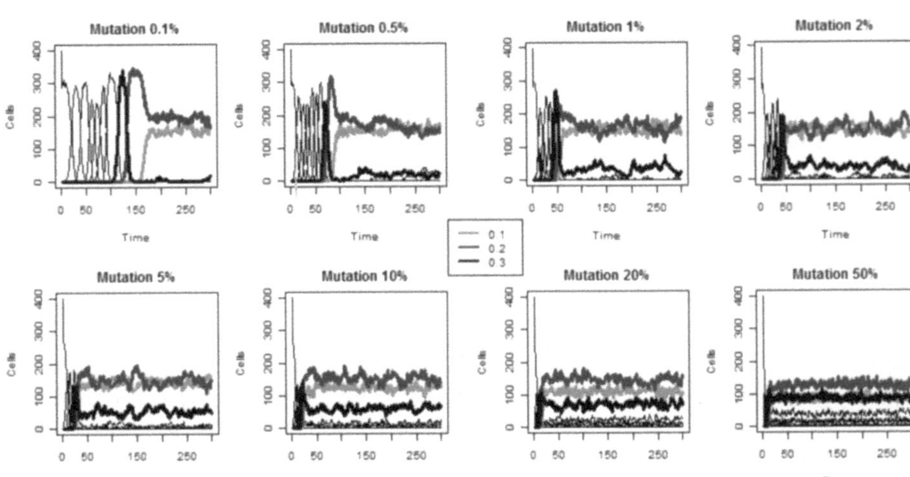

Fig. 4. Effects of mutation on the stability of the final distribution of individual strategies

That happens because, with higher mutation, the model has a more homogeneous distribution of strategies in space, being difficult for a strategy to conquer many cells, and easy for it to maintain a minimum number of cells.

The increase in the mutation rate makes possible the appearance of agents following almost each possible strategy. Strategies with a higher chance of escalating have a major disadvantage when they interact with other agents following a similar strategy. But, as they can avoid themselves moving to other cells, it is possible to keep a few of them in the model. Consequently, these few agents away from equilibrium increase the average strategy significantly, as shown in Figure 3.

The increase in the mutation rate also makes the distribution of individual strategies converge towards a discretized gamma distribution. This result can be seen in Figure 5, where $s_{0.1}$ decreases and $s_{0.3}$ increases as mutation increases, until they almost draw when we have mutation of 50%. Note that increasing mutation allows the development of strategies away from the theoretical equilibrium, making the overall distribution smoother.

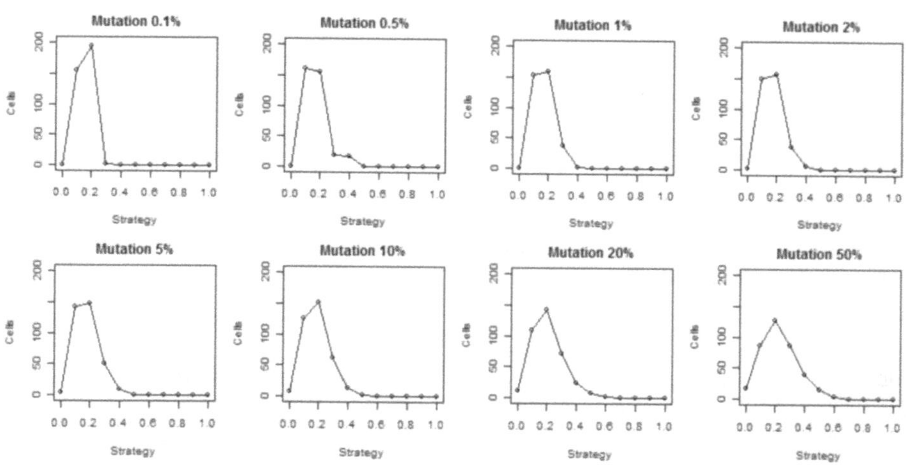

Fig. 5. Mean number of agents of each strategy after convergence, with eight mutation rates

Another result of changing the mutation rate is the number of agents that survive at the end of each simulation. There can exist some empty cells at the end of the simulation because, when there are only two agents within a cell, both might escalate, reach the threshold, and decide to leave the cell. Figure 6 shows the number of agents that give rise to descendants in each generation. The eight simulations have a minimum around 70% of the cellular space in the early generations. After that, the number of agents grows and stabilizes. In each graphic, there is a dashed line pointing out 90% of occupation of the space. In mutation 0.1%, the population stabilizes below this line, while in mutation 10% or more, the mean number of cells surpasses the line. A greater diversity in the number of strategies allows a better occupation of the cellular space at the end of each generation. As there are more agents with different strategies with the increase in the mutation, the fitness of the agents is reduced more heterogeneously, which leads to a lower probability of two agents remove themselves from the model simultaneously.

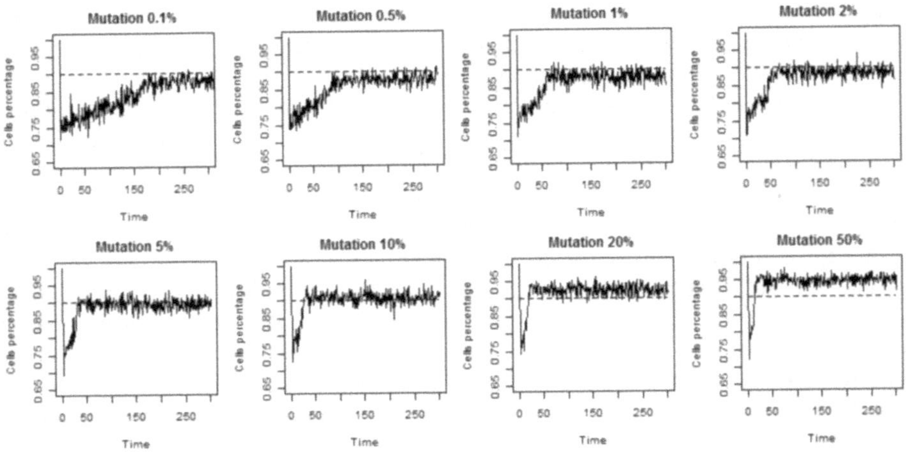

Fig. 6. Effects of mutation on the number of occupied cells at the end of each generation. Note that it also means the number of agents, once we have one agent in each occupied cell.

5.3 Different Initial Populations

The previous results show the impact of mutation over the evolution of the population, but they cannot enlighten whether the evolutive process always happens. To test the evolutionary capability of the model, we need to examine different initial populations. This section presents four models, each one with a single initial population, with the following arrangements:

$$M_k = (Cc, 2, \{E, \sim E\}, u, \{s_k\}, s, 1200, 200, 20),$$

where $k \in \{0.0, 0.1, 0.5, 1.0\}$. That is, the first population of each model has a single strategy. They are: never escalate, equilibrium, random, and always escalate.

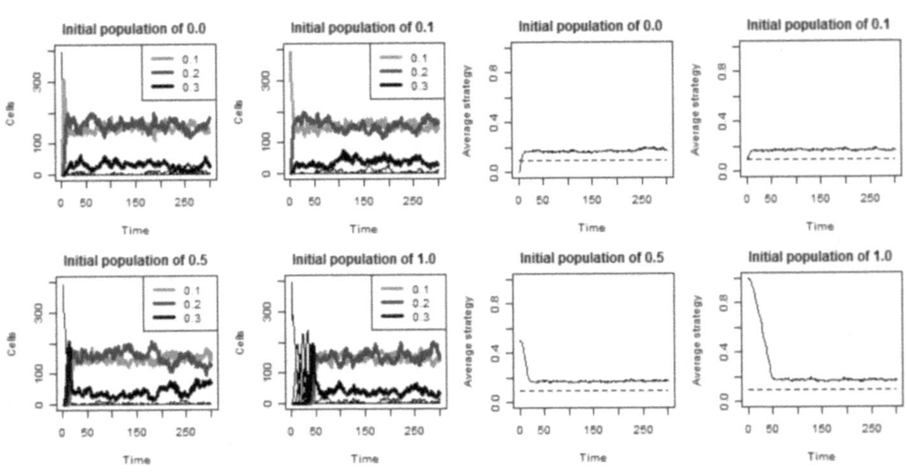

Fig. 7. Individual strategies using different initial populations

Figure 7 shows the results of the four models. In the left, it contains the number of agents following each strategy at the end of each generation, with the three most successful strategies ($s_{0.1}$, $s_{0.2}$, and $s_{0.3}$) as coloured lines. These strategies have similar development in the four cases, with none of them surpassing the other two and dominating the whole population, similarly to the previous results. In the right side, the figure shows the mean strategy of the overall population in each simulation. The four simulations converge to the same stable state, despite the initial arrangement of the models. Both results show that the model is capable to converge to a stable state independently of the initial population. It makes the model stronger, and shows that, although there are five random ingredients in the model, their effects do not make the model chaotic.

6 Concluding Remarks

In this work, the evolution of a population is defined by adding simple rules of reproduction and mutation over a previous work in the literature. The selective step, proposed by Andrade and others, selects the best strategies in a given population, whatever average strategy it follows. The mutation allows some change in the strategy when creating a new generation, which can represent an error when passing the strategy to the descendants. This error leads to the diversity on the population and allows the evolutive process to take place.

The results of our experiments show that, although the agents do not have any knowledge about equilibrium points and cannot even change their individual strategies along their lifetime, the average strategy of the population always converges to a stable state, close and above to the analytic equilibrium. Moreover, this equilibrium is reached independently of the initial population. These two points corroborate the hypothesis that populations evolve to a stable state even if we use a finite population. The results also agree with the statements of Nash, who said that "we can only expect some sort of approximate equilibrium, since [...] the stability of the average frequencies will be imperfect" [8]. As it is almost impossible to validate this kind of model with real world data, showing that the model is independent of the initial population is a reasonable way to make it trustworthy.

A coupple of questions are still not solved within the context of the proposed model. As changing the chance of mutation produce effects on the evolutive process, other parameters may also lead to different results. We can cite:

- Reduce the interval of mutation, for example from ±0.1 to ±0.01, or even allow the complete [0,1] range,
- Change parameters such as initial population size and fitness, number of descendants, and mobility threshold, and
- Use games with other equilibrium points.

If we change these parameters, will the model converge to closer and above to the theoretical equilibrium point? Another point that worth some investigation is, can these results be inferred from mathematical equations, or only simulation models can produce that?

References

1. Maynard Smith, J.: Evolution and the Theory of Games. Cambridge University Press, Cambridge (1982)
2. Epstein, J.M., Hammond, R.A.: Non-Explanatory Equilibria: An Extremely Simple Game With (Mostly) Unattainable Fixed Points. Complexity 7(4), 18–22 (2002)
3. Orzack, S.H., Hines, W.G.S.: The Evolution of Strategy Variation: Will an ESS Evolve? Evolution 59(6), 1183–1193 (2005)
4. Fogel, G.B., Andrews, P.C., Fogel, D.B.: On the instability of evolutionary stable strategies in small populations. Ecological Modelling 109, 283–294 (1998)
5. Riechert, S.E.: The consequences of being territorial: spiders, a case of study. American Naturalist 117, 871–892 (1981)
6. Nowak, M.A., Sigmund, K.: Games on Grids. In: Dieckmann, U., Law, R., Metz, J.A.J. (eds.) The Geometry of Ecological Interactions: Simplifying Spatial Complexity, pp. 135–150. Cambridge University Press, Cambridge (2000)
7. Epstein, J.M.: Zones of Cooperation in Demographic Prisoner's Dilemma. Complexity 4(2), 36–48 (1997)
8. Nash, J.: Non-cooperative games. In: Mathematics Department, Princeton University Press, Princeton (1950)
9. Sigmund, K.: Games of Life. Oxford University Press, Oxford (1993)
10. Andrade, P.R., et al.: Games on Cellular Spaces: How Mobility Affects Equilibrium. Journal of Artificial Societies and Social Simulation 12(1), 5 (2009)
11. Carneiro, T.G.S.: Nested-CA: a foundation for multiscale modeling of land use and land change. In: Image Processing Division. INPE, São José dos Campos (2006)

Context Switching versus Context Permeability in Multiple Social Networks

Luis Antunes, Davide Nunes, Helder Coelho, João Balsa, and Paulo Urbano

GUESS/LabMAg/Universidade de Lisboa, Portugal
{xarax,davide.nunes,hcoelho,jbalsa,pub}@di.fc.ul.pt

Abstract. In social life, actors engage simultaneously in several relations with each other. The complex network of social links in which agents are engaged is fundamental for any realistic simulation of social life. Moreover, not only the existence of multiple-modality paths between agents in a simulation, but also the knowledge that those agents have about the quality and specificity of those links are relevant for the decisions the agents make and the consequences they have both at an individual and at a collective level. Each actor has a context in each of the relations that are represented as support of a simulation. We build on previous work about permeability between those contexts to study the novel notion of context switching. By switching contexts, individuals carry with them their whole set of personal characteristics to a different relation, while abandoning the previous one. When returning to the original context, all previous links are resumed. We apply these notions to a simple game: the consensus game, in which agents try to collectively achieve an arbitrary consensus through simple locally informed peer-to-peer interactions. We compare the results for context switching with results from simulating the simple game and the game with context permeability.

1 Introduction

In social science research, the context in which actors are immersed is very important. It determines their interacting partners, the social and geographical settings in which action takes place, the scope of collaboration, and, through the notion of role [12], it constrains the kinds of interactions that can occur in each moment and with each partner. Usually, in social simulations, the actors are connected together through relations that are explicitly stated. In most cases, there will be several such relations linking actors, hence forming a web of connections with several characteristics: rich in general and specific knowledge, structured and providing structure to the social life, each relation can be differently endowed with specific attributes that may have relevance to the research questions at hand.

Sometimes, the intricacy of these social relations is hindered behind one such single relation, with the goal of representing the whole complexity of social connections, some kind of "social distance." There are good reasons to do so, like

L. Seabra Lopes et al. (Eds.): EPIA 2009, LNAI 5816, pp. 547–559, 2009.

keeping the ability to detect visual patterns in simulations, and especially managing complexity along the research simulations. In some sense, to abstract away from social structure and freeze that component while others are focused. Later, social structure can become the main focus and more complex and realistic connections might be explored, in a progressive deepening manner [8].

Antunes and colleagues [4] have investigated some consequences of keeping separate relations linking agents in a setting where a very simple game (the consensus game) was played to achieve a global result for the society. They have experimented with homogeneous agents following the same interaction rule in up to five different concomitant relations of several kinds: regular random networks in which the number of links each agent maintains ranged from 4 to 50, and also scale-free networks generated with the Albert and Barabási algorithm [1].

Nevertheless, [4] only considers what they call "context permeability:" agents are immersed in several relations simultaneously and any link in any of those relations may be selected to produce an interaction. The authors did not consider the case of an agent moving from one relation to another: this transference of an agent from its context in a relation to a different context in another *while leaving the original relation*, is what we call "context switching," and is the theme of these paper. A possible application of these concepts might be found in the management of highly-protected clustered computer networks.

The paper is organised as follows. In the next section we describe the overall context of this research, and place it along the lines of previous research on context permeability, our comparison reference. Section 3 describes the overall idea of context in a multiple social relations setting, and the consensus game as an abstract noncommital collective endeavour. Section 4 introduces context switching, and motivates its usefulness for social simulation. Section 5 describes the models we use for the present series of experiments. Finally, we analyse and discuss the results and compare them to previous results of context permeability.

2 Context of Research

We are interested in discovering how the structure of social relations influences the dissemination of phenomena (e.g. Obama's internet campaign) in a society. In this line of research, we have focused on the idea of keeping separate explicit descriptions of the several social relations in which agents are immersed. Following the work of Antunes and colleagues [3,4], we are interested in freezing everything in the society description except for the number of such relations, and structure they possess. Given a social relation, we call context to a neighbourhood around a given agent, that is, the set of agents that are directly connected to that agent.

Of course, relations and contexts should be seen as highly dynamic and information-rich. However, since we want to focus on the mathematical properties of these relations, in particular in what concerns context permeability and switching, we use statical versions of those relations, and the dynamics is only possible as controlled spanning over our set of experimental design options. This is surely a simplified and simplistic view of the problem, and we see it as a preliminary exploration of the huge design space at stake. Moreover, Information-rich settings are usually highly domain-dependent, and before moving into specialised application domains we want to have a look at the problem and its implications from a more abstract, uncommitted standpoint. In some sense, we are still dwelling on the problem, not yet looking for solutions.

For all these reasons, and to be able to compare our results with others from the literature, we have picked a very abstract game: the consensus game [10,16,3]. Each agent has a current choice towards one of two possible options which are for basically arbitrary (say, red and green). Hence, there is no rationality of strategic reasoning involved. The particular options that gets collectively selected is irrelevant, what is important is that overall agreement is achieved. For instance, you can think of the side of the street in which you drive: it is irrelevant whether it is left or right as long as everyone respects the standing consensus. Agents can change their option. In our present approach, agents have the chance of changing the option when they have an interaction with another agent in its neighbourhood (context), by playing the majority game: agents keep track of their previous interactions and choose the colour that they have seen most often in the past. Note that other interaction rules are possible and being investigated [17]. We say that consensus is achieved when all the agents share the same option. In the literature [10], and to avoid awkward cases, it is often demanded only that 90% of agents share the same options. We are planning to redo our experiments with this stopping criterion to check whether our findings still hold.

3 Contexts in Multiple Relations

In most target phenomena, agents will be involved in several relations simultaneously. When individuals are embedded in networks that are embedded in networks we have a "multi-modal" structure, such as students who together with a teacher form a classroom, of which in turn a school is composed of [7]. Surely the panorama can get more complicated, as these several networks of relations do not necessarily have such a "regular" meta-structure.

While we keep parallel building of agents closely related to real actors, it is possible that the multi-agent system is designed in different ways. This is the case of the the study of decision change in agricultural networks conducted by Amblard and Ferrand [2]. They propose a multi-agent system whose agents represent the model actors, the relations between them and the cliques formed by those actors. Actors are characterised by general, relational and decisional attributes. This model possesses some self-reflective characteristics that render it quite general. The behavioural dynamics is based on relations, which allows for self-motivated agent re-structuring. This offers an alternative to data driven models [9], although possibly empirically less reliable.

At this point in our research, we attempt to control complexity and focus on the study of dynamic consequences of the topological structures underlying social simulations, so opting for a "first order" approach. We will take actors and relations between them as givens of the problem, in a similar way as what is done in [13]. Here the authors select relations among scholars in a series of scientific conferences, namely *meets*, *knows*, and *collaborates*. Our agents will be the atomic individuals of the simulations, but our relations will be kept abstract, so that we can concentrate on the dynamics they induce. We can think of the relations in our simulation as reasonably stable, such as family ties, or work colleagues, while we study the consequences of their mutual connectedness.

Most graph representations of real world social networks follow patterns that have only recently being revealed. Such is the case of scale-free networks [5]. Scale-free networks can be defined as a connected graph in which the number of links (k) connected to a given node follows a power law distribution, $P(k) \sim k^{-\gamma}$. Scale-free networks are to be found in a great variety of real situations, and display the property that most of the nodes have little connections, whereas some network nodes (usually called "hubs") are highly connected. This is depicted by a right-skewed, of "fat tail" distribution. Barabási and colleagues proposed a simple generative mechanism called "preferential attachment" (cf. [1]). Although these mechanisms only generate a subset of the universe of scale-free networks, this is what we used for our experiments, and with γ fixed to 3 (most real data exhibit γ on the range [2, 3], although sometimes, smaller exponents can arise [15]. Scale-free networks have interesting properties, such as a close to constant diameter as the number of nodes grow ($d \sim \ln \ln n$), or a certain "fault-tolerant" behaviour (problems affecting random nodes will hardly fall on the critical hub nodes).

Most of the analysis of social networks is done in quite statical terms. Mathematics and statistics tools only start to provide the possibility of dynamical analysis [6]. Given the purpose of multi-agent-based social simulation, it is fundamental that useful dynamical properties, even some ones linking individual behaviours to global behaviours, can be derived from the network analysis. With our approach, we aim to contribute to such research endeavour, by bringing the fields closer together and feeding on each other. Our approach is to use simulation to explore the design space, not only of agents, but also of societies and even experiments. The key point in these simulations is to understand to what extent the structure of connections the agents engage in simultaneously can have a role in the shape of convergence towards a simple collective common goal, an arbitrary consensus.

4 Context Switching

In this study, we introduce the notion of context switching. Whereas in previous studies agents would keep several concomitant relations, here each agent in each moment is present in one relation only. Whenever it decides to move away from that relation, it leaves it space empty, and "phisically" moves to the other relation, hence switching to a new context and abandoning the other.

A good example of Context Switching is the Internet (Viral Marketing) Campaign, namely Obama's, which changed politics because a new medium (Internet and social networking tools) was explored to the fullest. The intersection of politics and Web 2.0 implied other interactive tools in order to move supporters to organise, to listen to the candidates's own words in face of attacks, to use free advertising and adaptive (word-of-mouth) marketing, to raise other sources of funds, to incorporate friends (close relations) in a campaign, and to make connection with causes they care about. The interesting thing in a campaign is finding new and creative ways to fuel, scale up, and adapt to a world in which the concept of community has grown recently due to such systems as MySpace and Facebook.

Damasio's social space covers two main ideas: 1) agents in relation to other ones, instead of lone supporters, and 2) social functions (choices, behaviours, decision-taking and beliefs) [11].

With context switching we can talk about landscapes and scenarios and to the access to neighbours. Tag annotation is good for context switching because context profiles, scenarios need to be marked.

With this new idea of swapping contexts, we are covering some space left undeveloped in Antunes and colleagues original work [3]. The basic mechanism is the following: 300 agents are created, and then p different relations are created according to the previously decided designs (including regular with $2k$ random connections for each agent and scale-free with $\gamma = 3$). Then, whenever an agent is given the opportunity to interact, it plays the majority game to choose whether to keep or change its colour, and finally randomly decides (with probability ζ) whether to change to a different relation.

This mechanism corresponds to a complete change (switching) from a context in a relation to another context in another relation. But the exact context the agent is transported to in the different relation is fixed from the start. In some sense this corresponds to immigrating to Australia, having neighbours and colleagues there, and then returning home to the previous neighbours and colleagues. The idea is to depict some stability in contexts even when the agent is not actively engaged in interactions in that relation.

To some extent, if we relate these context switching to some kind of dynamics, this switching mechanism is very close to the concept of role. Agents engage into different roles during their time, and each role has its own specificity, including possible interacting agents. And in this representation, each context switching would carry along new constraints. For instance, I can be a subservient agent in a work context, and an authoritarian agent in a family context. For the time being, our agents are homogeneous across all society and across their life span. But in future work, we may undertake and study different consequences of context switching, including character traits, mental concepts, strategic reasoning, etc. The several lines of research being considered in Antunes work and here might provide a new stance towards the design and study of such complex and intertwined concepts such as contexts and roles [12,14], allowing to overcome known problems as the lack of grounding with essential (corporeal/bodily/motivational) features of the agent, which carries through several modalities, including time, which is fundamental to simulation.

5 Model of the Experiments

The experiments were developed in NetLogo [18], using different heights in a 3D cube to depict the p planes. Each experiment consists of 80 runs in which 100 agents interact until 3000 cycles (with 100 interactions per cycle) pass, or total (100%) consensus is reached.

In a first series of experiments we explored the space to find the appropriate ζ to consider. In these preliminary experiments we considered two relations and spanned ζ from 0.05 to 1 in intervals of 0,05. Apparently, the interesting points to consider were centred wound 0.25, 0.5 and 0.75, so we used these values of $zeta$ for the subsequent experiments. In these latter, we kept homogenous values of ζ for all the relations involved.

In a second series of experiments, for each $\zeta \in \{0.25, 0.5, 0.75\}$ we run experiments with $p = 1, 2, 3, 4$ relations. Experiments with $p = 1$ confirmed previous results and are not reported here. For higher values of p, each experiment proceeded with the mechanisms described above: agents play the interaction game with majority (full memory) and then decide to switch plane according to ζ. Next section focuses on the details of the results.

The other source of variability in the experiments was the network topology. We considered all combinations of p networks, whose type was regular with k spanning $\{1, 2, 3, 4, 5, 10, 20, 30, 40, 50\}$, and also scale-free. Note that for $k = 50$ the network is fully connected. note also that whenever 2 or more regular networks are involved in the simulations, we keep k the same for all of them (this constraint will be relaxed in future work, but here we wanted to grant full comparability with previous literature results).

6 Discussion of Experimental Results

Since the major difference between context switching and context permeability is in the change from one relation to the other, we started off by trying to understand the influence of the frequency of change, represented by probability ζ. We assessed the importance of ζ for the simulations through a series of exploratory simulations in which we take two relations and make ζ span over $[0, 1]$ in steps of 0.05. Figure 1 shows the landscape for two networks: regular with $k = 10$ and scale-free, while ζ varies.

Figure 2 shows the landscape of the average number of meetings to achieve consensus for two scale-free networks when we make ζ span $[0, 1]$.

In figure 3 we show the average number of meetings to achieve for two regular networks with $k = 10$ when we make ζ span $[0, 1]$.

Our decision was to take homogeneous values of $\zeta = 0.25, 0.5, 0.75$. Apparently those values are close to the "interesting" outcomes in all of the cases.

The first notable result we obtained was that for $p > 1$ we achieved consensus 100% of the times for a vast majority of the cases. For $p = 1$ of course o switching occurs, and our results replicate closely the results of [4]. However, as soon as we include more relations, convergence is achieved in 100% in all but the cases

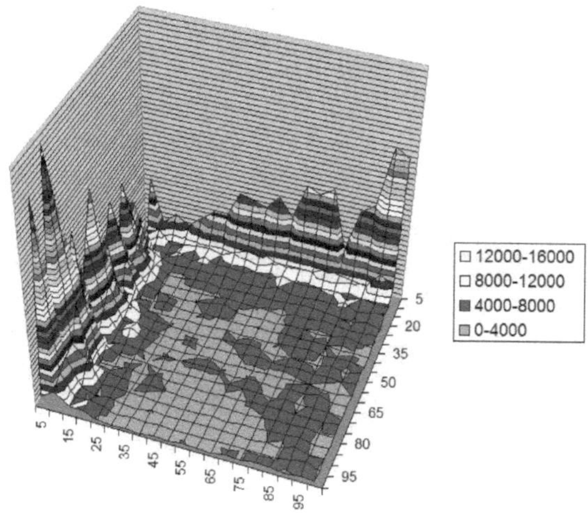

Fig. 1. Meetings to achieve consensus for a scale-free and a 10-regular network with $\zeta \in [0, 1]$

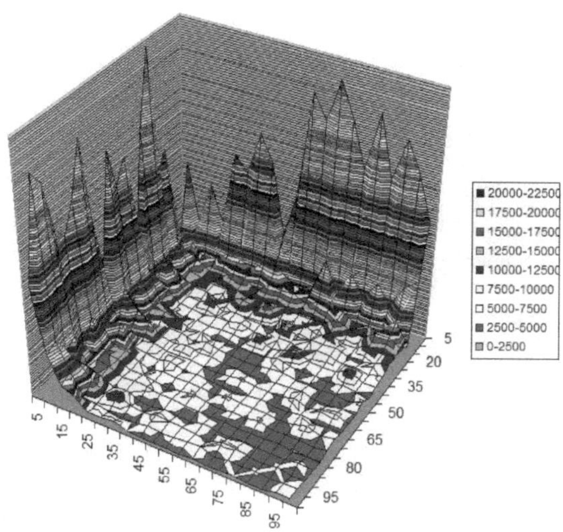

Fig. 2. Meetings to achieve consensus for two scale-free networks with $\zeta \in [0, 1]$

where $k = 1$ and $\zeta = 0.25$ for $p = 3$ (99%) and $p = 4$ (93%). Consensus is always achieved for combinations of several scale-free networks.

We will see later that the degradation of results for higher p can occur. Nevertheless, for the moment just considering percentage of consensus achievement, we conclude that context switching is far better than context permeability, since in the latter consensus was not achieved to the fullest in several cases, as shown in table 1 of [4]. In this table, we had seen that for scale-free networks the percentage of success as 34% for $p = 2$, 82% for $p = 3$, and 94% for $p = 4$. Now with context switching we have 100% for all p.

Table 1. Context switching: average number of meetings to achieve consensus with all planes equal in kind

$k =$	1	2	3	4	5	10	20	30	40	50	s-f
1 pl						3229	1700	1805	1675	1546	
2 pl $\zeta = .25$	34059	15246	16484	13828	8406	4710	2006	1714	1691	1615	10341
2 pl $\zeta = .5$	15618	7925	5855	4681	3586	2646	2283	2288	2026	2221	5600
2 pl $\zeta = .75$	11731	6870	5470	4213	4391	4265	3291	3809	3100	3943	4660
3 pl $\zeta = .25$	75246	31467	25893	18684	12991	4785	2169	1991	1766	1937	15163
3 pl $\zeta = .5$	37726	14869	9943	7524	5324	3198	2515	2216	2271	1959	8805
3 pl $\zeta = .75$	22360	10306	7721	6044	5023	3748	3318	3339	3448	3008	7729
4 pl $\zeta = .25$	85449	51340	31415	25494	19229	6398	3014	2336	2203	2071	18775
4 pl $\zeta = .5$	58314	25559	17261	11280	8241	3576	2631	2501	2213	2234	13224
4 pl $\zeta = .75$	39279	14740	12553	7795	7045	4673	3704	3426	3740	3200	14309

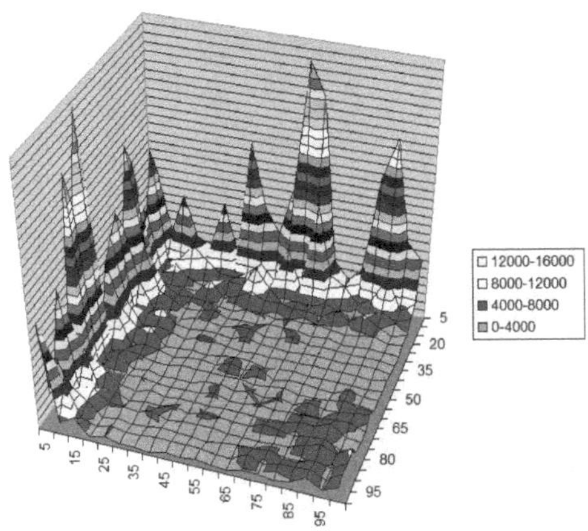

Fig. 3. Meetings to achieve consensus for two 10-regular networks with $\zeta \in [0, 1]$

Table 2. Context permeability: average number of meetings to achieve consensus with all planes equal in kind (from [4])

$k =$	1	2	3	4	5	10	20	30	40	50	s-f
1 pl						3073	2314	2584	1700	1475	
2 pl	96050	58485	43481	14286	9997	4718	2505	2125	1895	1950	58196
3 pl	50746	6839	3845	3640	3210	2530	2317	1861	1950	1911	22035
4 pl	21070	9711	5025	2895	3230	1960	1812	2166	2054	2044	13353

Now focusing on the average number of meetings needed to achieve full consensus, we will compare the results of context switching (see table 1) with the previous results of context permeability (for ease of comparison we replicate here table 2 of [4], see table 2). See also figure 4 for a visual comparison of the convergence results.

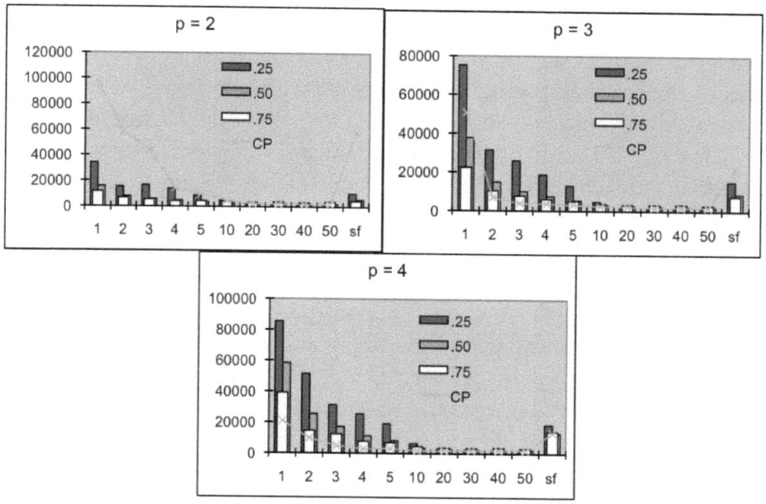

Fig. 4. Comparison of the average convergence numbers for context switching with $\zeta \in \{0.25, 0.5, 0.75\}$ and context permeability

It is obvious right away that the figures for scale-free networks are quite better: as we seen before total convergence is possible 100% of the times with context-switching, whereas in context-permeability it was possible only part of the times (and more often as the number of concomitant relations grew). The average number of meetings needed for full consensus is also quite lower most of the times in context switching.

For concomitant scale-free networks, we notice slightly different behaviours for context switching and context permeability. Whereas with context permeability the number of meetings needed for consensus decreases significantly with the number of relations, with context switching the effect is the opposite. The best results occur for 2 relations only. What does make a difference in this case (see the last column of table 1) is the probability ζ of switching context: for a given number p of relations results are better as ζ grows. Consequently, the overall best results for scale-free networks are obtained with 2 relations and $\zeta = 0.75$. Seeing that for one relation only the consensus is never achieved, we conclude that including a secondary concomitant scale-free relation provides the necessary links to ensure the consensus, and faster when agents switch relation frequently.

The results for regular networks are also very interesting. The global behaviour for context switching can be described like this: for a small amount of neighbours (small k, sometimes $k \leq 10$, other times $k \leq 5$) convergence is faster when ζ grows. Then for bigger k, the increase of ζ yields slower convergence. We could explain this phenomenon by saying that when an agent has a small number of friends, it pays off to switch context frequently, whereas when an agent is surrounded by a high number of friends, and perhaps in a situation when in this neighbourhood has already locally converged, moving context frequently slows down convergence.

Comparing context switching with context permeability for regular networks, results are a bit intriguing. For $p = 2$ and a small number of neighbours ($k \leq 10$) the results of context switching are much better than those of context permeability. However, as k grows, the effect of increasing ζ is to worsen the average, and indeed for $k \geq 20$ and $\zeta \geq 0.5$ context switching yields slower convergence, although not dramatically (comparable order of magnitude). Again, the explanation might be that for agents with higher number of neighbours, local convergence may be achieved earlier, and switching context introduces an element of disturbance in this otherwise settled neighbourhood.

Context switching is never better than context permeability for $p = 4$, whereas for $p = 3$ they are only comparable for big k and small ζ. Nevertheless, looking at context switching only, the pattern for $p = 3$ and $p = 4$, resembles that of $p = 2$, but with the effect is even more marked. Context switching seems to work best for $p = 2$, for both regular and scale-free networks.

A possible explanation for the more frequent convergence is that context switching allows for more isolated nodes to be reached in sparsely connected networks (of which scale-free are a paradigmatic example). We should notice something overlooked in [4]: for $p = 4$ even the context permeability results for higher k were already worse than for smaller p. This could mean that the introduction of new relations is providing an excessive number of (somewhat orthogonal) links, and so, opportunities for agents to change when perhaps their situations had been previously settled (e.g. towards the overall majority). This phenomenon seems to have been amplified by context switching in much the same way as the faster convergence was an amplified effect for lower p and k.

Our more abstract explanation for the good to very good results of context switching goes towards considering that it emphasises locally what is already a known global effect even for one relation only: as soon as a significant amount of agents opts for one of the strategies, say above a threshold that emerges after an initial instability phase, there is only a very small possibility that this strategy is not the winner. The balance between local stability and the possibility of contacts outside the current context yielded by context switching seems to have a local effect similar to this one, and this vastly accelerates convergence in some cases (and is comparable to permeability in the rest). Basically, we could see this as: once I and my friends in Portugal have settled for green, an occasional visit to Spain will not change the my Portuguese neighbourhood but helps foster green in my neighbourhood in Spain.

As done in [4], to observe results of heterogeneous networks we concentrate on three relations only, and reduce the spanning of k to $\{1, 2, 3, 4, 5, 10\}$. Table 3 shows the average and standard deviation of the number of meetings for heterogeneous combinations of networks. We suppress percentage of times consensus was achieved, since it was 100% or close every time. the As before, we show results for $\zeta \in \{0.25, 0.5, 0.75\}$. In table 4 we replicate part of table 3 from [4] for ease of comparison.

First, we must note that context switching yielded convergence in 100% of the experiments we carried out. Looking at average number of meetings needed for

Table 3. Context switching: average and standard deviation of the number of meetings for heterogeneous combinations of networks

$k=$	1	2	3	4	5	10
	reg/reg/s-f $\zeta = 0.25$					
avg	24209	17752	12370	11031	8684	5232
st dev	16725	11516	7587	6846	5949	3077
	reg/reg/s-f $\zeta = 0.5$					
avg	13087	11006	7079	6228	5243	3814
st dev	8961	7889	4071	3563	2541	2125
	reg/reg/s-f $\zeta = 0.75$					
avg	11927	7797	7107	6810	5560	4277
st dev	10200	4058	5347	4849	3466	2596
	reg/s-f/s-f $\zeta = 0.25$					
avg	9154	15095	12267	11105	9424	6338
st dev	8828	10346	8648	6973	5199	3071
	reg/s-f/s-f $\zeta = 0.5$					
avg	12439	7984	7734	6904	6335	5164
st dev	8342	4733	4319	3931	3165	2614
	reg/s-f/s-f $\zeta = 0.75$					
avg	11927	7797	7107	6810	5560	4277
st dev	10200	4058	5347	4849	3466	2596

Table 4. Context permeability: percentage of consensus achievement, average and standard deviation of the number of meetings for heterogeneous combinations of networks (adapted from [4])

$k=$	1	2	3	4	5	10
	reg/reg/s-f					
%cong	72%	88%	98%	98%	95%	98%
avg	32688	26677	11817	14858	10839	4946
st dev	56992	60585	25437	31245	32514	7148
	reg/s-f/s-f					
%conv	77%	88%	92%	87%	95%	98%
avg	26293	23798	18082	20348	22354	25408
st dev	26451	44289	26630	42599	46392	54061

convergence in both tables 3 and 4 we notice that results for context switching are almost always better than those of context permeability when we have two regular networks and one scale-free network. Moreover, results are always better for context switching when we have two scale-free networks and one regular network. In this latter case, the improvement in velocity of convergence is quite significant. Another impressive point to make is that whereas with context permeability the standard deviations were quite high, with context switching the standard deviations are of magnitude smaller than the average. This means that not only the aggregate results for convergence are better or much better, but also the worst case scenario is probably significantly better with context switching.

7 Conclusion

These results with heterogeneous social relations show that context plays a significant role in the dissemination of social concepts in structured societies. If we consider that scale-free networks seem to be present in a significant amount of real social relations, the mechanisms of context permeability and especially of context switching with several concomitant networks can have a decisive role in enhancing the conditions for achieving overall dissemination of a given phenomenon, as well as significantly increasing the speed of such convergence. On top of that, context switching seems to have the additional advantage of significantly stabilising the conditions for convergence, so rendering the outcome of dissemination mechanisms more predictable. Redundancy with a regular network, which can be ensured by a number of ways, can be a decisive means to ensure dissemination. An example we would like to explore would be the propagate software such as anti-virus through gossip mechanisms in highly protected network clusters. The redundant regular network is readily available, for instance, the electric power lines.

Acknowledgement

We would like to thank the anonymous reviewers for their valuable comments.

References

1. Albert, R., Barabási, A.-L.: Statistical mechanics of complex networks. Reviews of Modern Physics 74(1), 47 (2002)
2. Amblard, F., Ferrand, N.: Modélisation multi-agents de l'évolution de réseaux sociaux. In: Ferrand, N. (ed.) Actes du Colloque Modèles et Systèmes Multi-agents pour la gestion de l'environment et des territoires, pp. 153–168 (1998)
3. Antunes, L., Balsa, J., Urbano, P., Coelho, H.: The Challenge of Context Permeability in Social Simulation. In: Proceedings of Fourth European Social Simulation Association Conference, Toulouse, France (September 2007)
4. Antunes, L., Balsa, J., Urbano, P., Coelho, H.: Exploring context permeability in multiple social networks. In: Deffuant, G., Cioffi-Revilla, C. (eds.) Proceedings of the World Congress on Social Simulation (2008)
5. Barabási, A.-L., Albert, R.: Emergence of scaling in random networks. Science 286(5439), 509–512 (1999)
6. Brelger, R., Carley, K., Pattison, P.: Dynamic Social Network Modeling and Analysis: Workshop Summary and Papers. National Academy Press, Washington (2004)
7. Hanneman, R.A., Riddle, M.: Introduction to Social Network Methods. University of California, Riverside (2005), `faculty.ucr.edu/hanneman`
8. Hassan, S., Antunes, L., Arroyo, M.: Deepening the demographic mechanisms in a data-driven social simulation of moral values evolution. In: MABS 2008: Multi-Agent-Based Simulation (2008)
9. Hassan, S., Antunes, L., Pavon, J., Gilbert, N.: Stepping on Earth: A Roadmap for Data-driven Agent-Based Modelling. In: Squazzoni, F. (ed.) Proceeedings of the Fifth Conference of the European Social Simulation Association (ESSA) (2008)

10. Kaplan, F.: The emergence of a lexicon in a population of autonomous agents (in French). PhD thesis, Université de Paris 6 (2000)
11. Koenigs, M., Young, L., Adolphs, R., Tranel, D., Cushman, F., Hauser, M., Damasio, A.: Damage to the prefrontal cortex increases utilitarian moral judgements. Nature (March 21, 2007)
12. Masolo, C., Vieu, L., Bottazzi, E., Catenacci, C., Ferrario, R., Gangemi, A., Guarino, N.: Social roles and their descriptions. In: Dubois, D., Welty, C.A., Williams, M.-A. (eds.) Principles of Knowledge Representation and Reasoning: Proceedings of the Ninth International Conference (KR 2004), pp. 267–277. AAAI Press, Menlo Park (2004)
13. Matsuo, Y., Hamasaki, M., Nakamura, Y., Nishimura, T., Hasida, K., Takeda, H., Mori, J., Bollegala, D., Ishizuka, M.: Spinning multiple social networks for semantic web. In: Proceedings, The Twenty-First National Conference on Artificial Intelligence and the Eighteenth Innovative Applications of Artificial Intelligence Conference, Boston, Massachusetts, July 16-20, 2006. AAAI Press, Menlo Park (2006)
14. McCarthy, J.: Notes on formalizing context. In: Proceedings of IJCAI, pp. 555–562 (1993)
15. Seyed-allaei, H., Bianconi, G., Marsili, M.: Scale-free networks with an exponent less than two. Physical Review E 73(046113) (2006)
16. Urbano, P.: Decentralised Consensus Games (in Portuguese). PhD thesis, Faculdade de Ciências da Universidade de Lisboa (2004)
17. Urbano, P., Balsa, J., Antunes, L., Moniz, L.: Force versus majority: A comparison in convention emergence efficiency. In: Dignum, V., Matson, E. (eds.) AAAI/COIN 2009. LNCS (LNAI), Springer, Heidelberg (2009)
18. Wilensky, U.: NetLogo, Center for Connected Learning and Computer-Based Modeling, Northwestern University. Evanston, IL (1999), `http://ccl.northwestern.edu/netlogo/`

Risk Tolerance and Social Awareness: Adapting Deterrence Sanctions to Agent Populations

Henrique Lopes Cardoso and Eugénio Oliveira

LIACC, DEI / Faculdade de Engenharia, Universidade do Porto
R. Dr. Roberto Frias, 4200-465 Porto, Portugal
hlc@fe.up.pt, eco@fe.up.pt

Abstract. Normative environments for multi-agent systems provide means to monitor and enforce agents' compliance to their commitments. However, when the normative space is imperfect, contracts to which norms apply may be unbalanced, and agents may exploit potential flaws to their own advantage. In this paper we analyze how a normative framework endowed with a simple adaptive deterrence sanctioning model responds to different agent populations. Agents are characterized by their risk tolerance and by their social attitude. We show that risk-averse or socially concerned populations cause lesser deterrence sanctions to be imposed by the normative system.

1 Introduction

Interaction infrastructures for multi-agent systems have been extensively studied. Within such efforts, some attention has been given to normative environments (e.g. [1-3]), consisting of middleware that provides support for explicitly handling normative relations among agents (such as contracts specified through normative operators, e.g. obligations). Fewer efforts have been put on the development of dynamic capabilities in normative environments, where the infrastructure itself seeks to adapt its enforcement policies to the actual interaction scenario that is taking place.

In fact, when embedded in some notion of "institution", normative environments take an active role in checking agents' compliance with their commitments, and furthermore in enforcing such compliance. The goal is to establish trust among participants in a norm-regulated relationship – this gives contracts a binding force.

An important feature of interaction infrastructures with a contracting emphasis is the assistance of contract formation, namely by providing a normative framework that specifies norms applicable to different contractual settings. Given that complete contract negotiation automation is not likely to be possible (both in terms of technological limitations and real-world acceptance), software agents may rely on background normative frameworks that fill-in the normative body of contracts. This feature is particularly important when considering contrary-to-duty situations, which should describe a normative response in case of non-compliance to contractual terms. In certain cases, however, there will be no specified response. This is where other coercive approaches may be relevant, in situations where agents try to take advantage of their potential gain when violating norms (because they might be more self-interested than socially concerned).

L. Seabra Lopes et al. (Eds.): EPIA 2009, LNAI 5816, pp. 560–571, 2009.

In the literature (e.g. [4, 5]) we find two basic kinds of sanctions that an institution may apply in order to incentive norm compliance (or, to put it another way, to discourage deviations). *Direct material sanctions* have an immediate effect, and consist of affecting the resources an agent has (e.g. by applying fines). *Indirect social sanctions*, such as changing an agent's reputation, may have an effect that extends through time. Depending on the domain and on the set of agents that inhabit the institutional environment, the effectiveness of such sanctions may be different: if agents are not able to take advantage of other agents' reputation information, material sanctions should be used instead.

There are two general policies used when applying (direct) sanctions, which concern their intended effects: (i) *deterrence* aims at punishing the violator so as to discourage future violations; (ii) *retribution* aims at compensating the addressee of the violation. Bringing these policies to an electronic institution realm, we consider that retribution sanctions are those specified in contractual norms, be they negotiated or inherited from a preexistent normative framework. In this case the institution, while monitoring norm compliance, acts as a mediator. As for deterrence sanctions, they will be applied by the institution itself, and may be used so as to maintain order (by motivating agents to comply) and consequently trust in the system.

Deterrence has been studied in political science [6] with a different perspective, where theories are proposed for explaining international relations in tense periods such as the Cold War. Deterrence is based on threats between different nations.

Economic approaches to law enforcement have suggested analyzing sanctions and their amplitude by taking into account their effects on parties' activities. Agents committing to norms that have associated deterrence sanctions enter risky activities, because they may unintentionally violate them. It has been argued [7] that under strict liability (where violators are always sanctioned) sanctions should equal harm done. An increase in the level of activity brings an increase in the expected harm; if damages imposed by sanctions equal harm, parties will have socially correct incentives to engage in risky activities (that is, to establish commitments). However, this conclusion relies on the additional assumption that parties are risk-neutral. According to [7], if agents are risk-averse the optimal level of damages tends to be lower than harm. With risk-aversion, a sanction imposes a cost which does not exist under risk neutrality: risk-aversion introduces costless deterrence [8] and the policy-maker should take that into account when choosing the optimal sanction.

Our normative environment model makes two simplifying assumptions: 1) strict liability (norm violations are always detected); 2) costless enforcement (monitoring and sanctioning have a negligible cost to the institution).

With these assumptions in place, we will describe an adaptive model for a normative framework. The model tries to avoid over-constraining the environment while ensuring a certain level of norm compliance, by adjusting deterrence sanctions.

In this paper we analyze how the adaptive model responds to different agent populations, where each agent is characterized by a risk tolerance parameter and a social awareness parameter. The former represents an agent's willingness to contract in the presence of violation fines. The latter allows us to embed in our agents some notion of social welfare; that is, although we will take agents as utility maximizers, agents are not all equally self-interested.

The rest of the paper is organized as follows. Section 2 introduces the reader with the adaptive model for deterrence sanctions, and Section 3 provides a feeling of how the model works with a simple scenario. Section 4 presents several experiments conducted with various agent populations, with different risk tolerance and social awareness distributions. Finally, Section 5 concludes.

2 A Normative Framework with Deterrence Sanctions

In our approach we take the stance that agents are truly autonomous, and thus cannot be forced to fulfill their obligations. The institution may, however, impose certain fines as deterrence sanctions: such fines are assumed to be fully regimented (that is, agents cannot escape them, e.g. because they were required, upon entering the institution, to make a deposit that is in control of the institution).

We are mainly concerned with contracting scenarios, in which agents make mutual commitments and create business expectations. Violations, even when handled by contractual norms, are seen as abnormal situations. Thus, if a certain kind of violation becomes frequent, response should be taken through an increase of sanctions.

2.1 Commitment Trees

In order to obtain a tractable model for handling contractual commitments, we use a tree-based representation for interdependent obligations. This representation is useful for understanding the simulation model that we use.

When establishing contracts, agents create a network of directed obligations, some of which are dependent on the fulfillment or violation of other obligations. Consider the following two-party contract: agent a will pay p units to agent b, after which b will deliver x to a. In case b fails to deliver, he must return $p'=p+\delta$ to a. This sequence of commitments is illustrated in Figure 1, in a tree-like structure – a *commitment tree*[1]. Each node represents an obligation, and each labeled directed edge indicates, in the child node pointed to, what follows when the obligation contained in the parent node is fulfilled (*Fulf*) or violated (*Viol*). Note that in this simple example nothing is specified yet if agent a violates his commitment to pay p, nor if agent b violates his commitment to return p'.

The violation of an obligation with a prescribed sanction may simply denote a case where an agent preferred to incur the sanctions for matters of conflicting goals (e.g. he had another contract which was more important than this one, and could not stand for both). If such violation becomes frequent, however, this may denote a flaw in the normative system that agents are being able to exploit to their own advantage.

The importance of adaptation in a normative framework resides in the fact that contracts may be unfair in certain execution outcomes. If self-interested agents try to explore such flaws to their own profit, action should be taken so as to discourage such behaviors. Aiming at a model that adapts the normative framework in a domain-independent way, we focus on adding deterrence fines to the system (which are not violable), instead of adjusting prescribed obligations in each violation situation.

[1] Although the commitment structure may be more complex, we simplify it to a binary tree; while not limiting the applicability of our adaptation approach, this choice makes the model easier to follow.

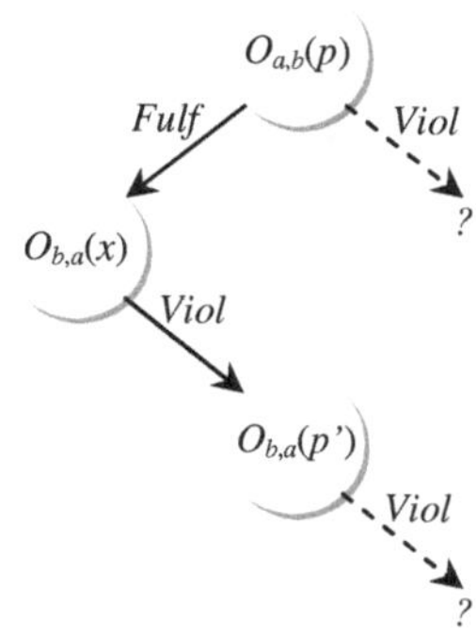

Fig. 1. Sample commitment tree

The normative framework's adaptation is based on associating, with each obligation, a *fine* that can be strengthened or weakened. With this approach, every obligation will have a (potentially null) fine to be imposed on the bearer in case of violation; this fine is added up to the violation consequence in the child node already in the tree, if there is one. The fine-update function is based on fine application frequency. Fines will increase when they are applied often, and decrease when they are not used. A low level of fine usage indicates that obligations are being fulfilled or they are not being used as often as desired: in both cases fines should be decreased, since they either are not needed or are inhibiting activity. On the other hand, a high level of fine usage means that agents still prefer to go through the sanction, and as such it should be increased as a deterrence mechanism. In sum, this approach tries to make fines (a) strong enough to discourage deviation and (b) weak enough to avoid unnecessary institutional control.

2.2 Contract Enactment

We developed a simulation prototype that allows us to experiment with the adaptation model briefly introduced above. In our system we shall have a number of agents that will each be given an opportunity to sign a contract. The contract structure is defined by a number of enacting roles and by an underlying binary commitment tree (BCT from now on). Roles are used as bearers or counterparties of the obligations in the tree. Furthermore, each obligation has an associated cost (to be supported by a fulfilling bearer) and benefit (to be collected by the counterparty of a fulfilled obligation). Figure 2 more clearly depicts the characterization of each node in a BCT.

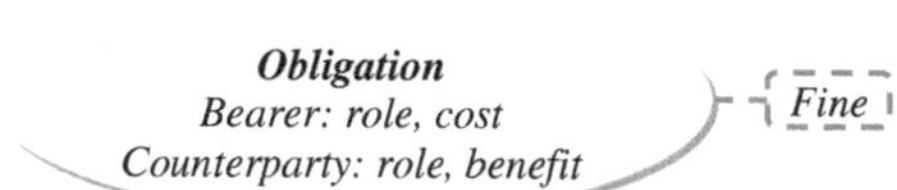

Fig. 2. A BCT node and its configuration

When an agent decides to sign a contract, he will enact the corresponding commitment tree with a role assigned to him before contracting. We say that the *state* of a contract enactment is the commitment currently under appreciation. If the bearer of such a commitment is the agent that decided to contract, he will be asked for a play: either to fulfill or to violate such a commitment. If the commitment's bearer is not the agent, the system will decide whether the commitment will be fulfilled or not, according to a uniform strategy. The current state will be updated according to the decision taken: if the choice is to fulfill, the state will become the root commitment of the fulfillment sub-tree; if the choice is to violate, the state will become the root commitment of the violation sub-tree. The contract terminates when the state reaches a null value (no fulfillment/violation sub-tree exists upon a fulfill/violate decision).

2.3 Agent Decision-Making

Each agent has two distinct kinds of decisions to make. If he does not have an ongoing contract, he is given the opportunity to sign one. For that, a random role from the contract structure is selected and the agent is asked if he wants to contract with that role. Each agent is configured with a *risk tolerance* parameter $Rt \in [0; 1[$, which denotes his willingness to contract in the presence of violation fines. If $Rt = 0$, the agent decides to contract only if he will be subject to no fines at all. If $Rt \approx 1$, the agent will always risk to contract, regardless of any fines. An agent will decide to contract depending on the highest fine that is associated with commitments for the assigned role. In order to contract, the following relation should be true:

$$highestFine(role) \leq b * Rt / (1 - Rt) \tag{1}$$

where b is a slope parameter associated with the agent's budget. We assume that agents always prefer to contract, regardless of commitment costs or benefits. The contract is presumably beneficial to all partners should they fulfill their commitments.

When an agent has an ongoing contract, if the current state is a commitment with him as the bearer he will decide whether to fulfill or to violate. Depending on a so-called *in-contract strategy*, the agent will explore the contract's BCT in order to decide which option is best for him. Such strategies may vary from simply comparing the cost of fulfillment with the applicable fine in case of violation, to computing the path with the best outcome from the whole BCT (more on this in Section 3.2).

Agents are essentially expected utility maximizers. This means that, in principle, they will fulfill obligations only when the expected outcome from this choice is better than the expected outcome from violating (according to the employed in-contract strategy). We do however embed in our agents some notion of social welfare, which impels them to fulfill even when they do not have a strict advantage in doing so. While for now we do not consider the effect of reputation in future contracts, we allow in our model that agents are not all equally self-interested. For that we introduce a *social awareness* parameter $Sa \in [0; 1[$. If $Sa = 0$, the agent will violate whenever the outcome from this choice is better than the outcome from fulfilling. On the other extreme, if $Sa \approx 1$ the agent will always choose to fulfill. The agent will decide to fulfill an obligation o whenever the following relation is true:

$$violationOutcome(o) - fulfillmentOutcome(o) \leq b * Sa / (1 - Sa) \tag{2}$$

where b is a slope parameter associated with the agent's budget. The violation and fulfillment outcomes are calculated by the in-contract strategy.

2.4 Fine-Update Policy

After all agents running in the simulation have a chance to play, the contract structure will adapt, that is, fines associated to the BCT will be updated. Each fine is updated independently of all other fines.

In order to delineate a fine update policy, we first need to define the goal function that will be pursuit. As mentioned before, fine updates should take into account how often they are applied. We define a threshold parameter $Th \in [0; 1]$ that indicates the highest percentage of fines that the system should accept as normal. For instance, with a value $Th = 0.1$ we are saying that if more than 10% of the agents running in the simulation violate a given obligation, the normative system will raise the fine in the next step – we say that 10% of the total number of agents is the number of *tolerated* violations. Furthermore, since not all agents will be in the same state at a given time point, we adjust the threshold according to the number of agents that did in fact make a decision concerning the fulfillment or violation of a specific obligation (because they were in that state). A state's fine will be increased if the number of violations exceeds the following tolerated violations function:

$$toleratedViolations = 2*Th*Nag \,/\, (1 + e^{-(5/Nag)*x}) - Th*Nag \qquad (3)$$

where Nag is the number of agents running in the simulation and x is the number of agents that were in this state. This is a sigmoid function with an upper bound set at $Th*Nag$ (a percentage of the total number of agents).

The system should keep fines as low as possible, while still conforming to the goal function outlined above. This is because the overall goal of the system is to maximize contract activity, which should be obtained with less risk exposure in an agent population with unknown risk tolerance. Therefore, whenever the number of violations does not exceed the number of tolerated violations, the fine will be decreased. Fines are increased heavier than they are decreased. We have set an increase step of 0.1 and a decrease step of 0.01. Fines will be applied rounded to the first decimal place, which gives a sense that it takes ten simulation steps (without exceeding the tolerated violations function) to decrease the fine value.

3 Scenario

In this section we present a scenario on which experiences reported in Section 4 are based. We show the deterrence sanction adaptation in a uniform distribution setting.

3.1 Contract Structure

Since we are not concerned with the correctness of the contract to be signed, we may experiment with a large number of different BCTs (some arbitrary examples can be found in [9]). However, for space limitations we will concentrate on a simple contract structure with two roles, whose BCT is illustrated in Figure 3. This BCT includes two complementary obligations 0 and 1, and their respective *contrary-to-duties* 3 and 2. We shall call obligation 1 the *to-duty* obligation of obligation 0.

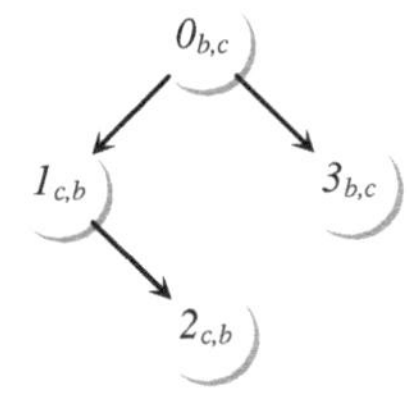

Fig. 3. Binary commitment tree for a contract structure with two roles: each node $Id_{i,j}$ is an obligation where i is the bearer and j is the counterparty. This BCT includes two complementary obligations (0 and 1) and their contrary-to-duties (3 and 2).

For all experiments reported in this paper, obligation costs are set at 10.0 and benefits at 12.0 (setting benefits higher than costs tries to give all partners some gain when the contract is well-balanced). Also, fines are initialized at 0.0.

3.2 Agent In-Contract Strategy

As explained in Section 2.3, when deciding whether to comply with commitments agents use an in-contract strategy in order to compute the violation/fulfillment outcomes. Several in-contract strategies can be devised (see [9] for some examples), representing the reasoning abilities of agents when deciding whether to fulfill or violate an obligation.

In this paper we will assume that agents are capable of analyzing the whole BCT, in order to compute the path that will bring them the best possible outcome when assuming that the contract partner will use the same strategy. This is a *minimax* strategy: the agent will maximize his own expected utility while assuming that the other agent will do the same. For instance, considering the BCT at Figure 3 with no fines, the agent will choose to violate on every obligation. While this seems obvious for obligations 1, 2 and 3 (there is no personal benefit in fulfilling), in obligation 0 the agent chooses to violate because he assumes that the counterparty will violate on 1 and 2, bringing him no benefit that can compensate the cost of fulfilling on 0.

This strategy seems counterintuitive with the very decision of establishing a contract. However, for the sake of testing the adaptation capabilities of the normative framework, this agent decision practice is bearable.

For all experiments reported in this paper, a uniform strategy "always fulfill" is used by the system for commitments whose bearer is not a simulation agent.

3.3 Adaptation to Population with Uniform Distribution

When addressing an agent population with uniform distributions over risk tolerance (*Rt*) and social awareness (*Sa*) parameters, the adaptation of fines proceeds as illustrated in Figure 4. Every agent will start violating every obligation, which causes an increase of every fine. However, when fines 3 and 2 are high enough, fines 0 and 1 are no longer necessary to persuade agents to fulfill the respective obligations.

We should emphasize that the system tries continuously to lower fines, which is observable by the slight fluctuations of fines towards the end of the curves in figure 4. Therefore, system imposed fine levels are the lowest that keep violations below the tolerated violations function.

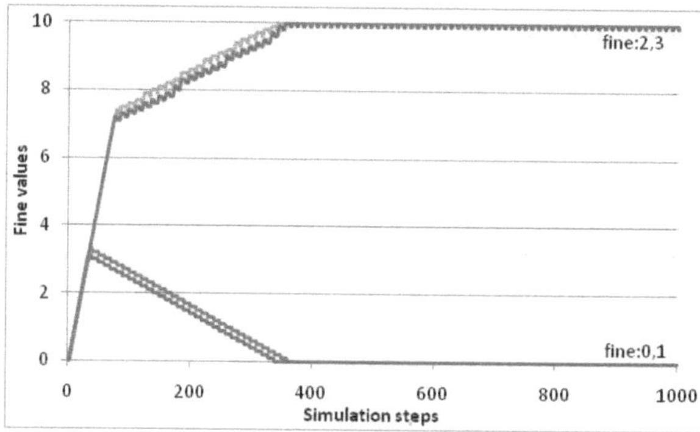

Fig. 4. Fine evolution (*Th*=0.1, *Nag*=10000) for 1000 simulation steps with uniform distributions of risk tolerance and social awareness

4 Adaptation to Different Agent Populations

In this section we analyze the adaptation of the system when handling different agent populations, in which risk tolerance and social awareness distributions are concerned.

4.1 Risk Tolerance

With this first group of experiments we aimed at observing the behavior of the deterrence sanction adaptation model when facing agent populations with different risk

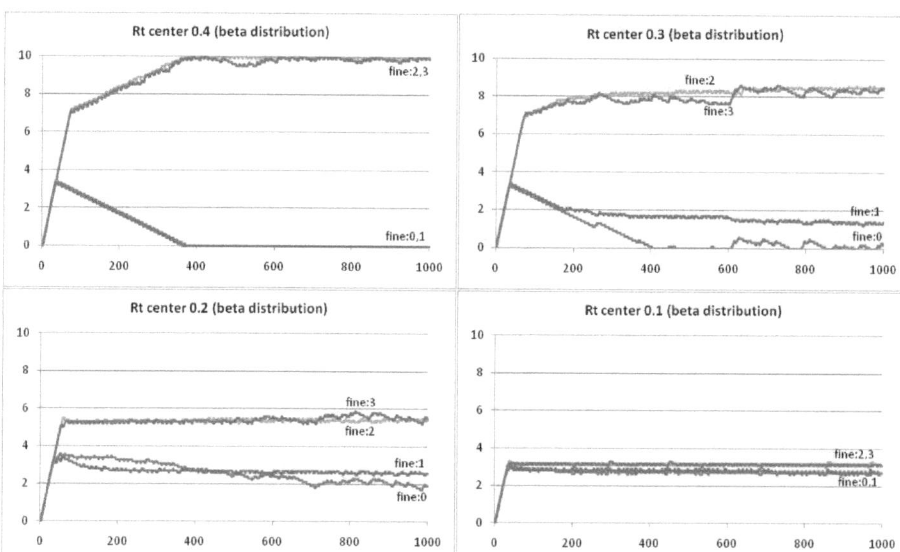

Fig. 5. Fine evolution (*Th*=0.1, *Nag*=10000) for 1000 simulation steps with different beta distributions of risk tolerance and uniform distributions of social awareness

tolerance distributions. In a population that tends to be more risk-averse, higher fines should tend to decrease. In these experiments we used beta distributions centered at different risk tolerance values, in order to represent populations having a predominance of agents with specific risk tolerances. For each beta distribution, we set $\alpha=1+(c*p-c)$ and $\beta=p-(c*p-c)$, where c is the center value and p is a peak factor that we have set to 100.

Figure 5 shows fine evolutions for different risk tolerance center values. As expected, higher fines tend to decrease with lower risk tolerance values. This is due to the fact that, when deciding whether to contract or not, agents compare risk tolerance with the highest applicable fine.

Another interesting observation is that while the highest fines tend to decrease, the system tries to compensate this potentially lower ability to ascertain the desired level of compliance by increasing other sanctions. More specifically, since fines 3 and 2 are lowered, they lose their effect on decisions taken in states 0 and 1, respectively. As a consequence, fines in these states are raised.

This outcome turns out to be an important emergent property of the normative system: the ability to grasp interdependencies between fines applied to different nodes in the BCT, without being preprogrammed to do so (the fine update policy adapts fines in an independent way). Furthermore, such interdependencies are caused by the in-contract strategy used by agents; if agents do not take into account possible "future" fines when making a decision (see [9]), then the system behavior will not pointlessly make a connection between fines.

4.2 Social Awareness

With this second group of experiments we aimed at observing the behavior of the deterrence sanction adaptation model when facing agent populations with different social awareness distributions. In a population that tends to be more socially concerned, fines should tend to decrease. Selfish agents will only fulfill if it is in their own interest, while higher social awareness impels agents to fulfill even when they do not benefit directly from that option.

Figure 6 shows fine evolutions for different social awareness center values (using beta distributions as before). As expected, fines tend to increase with lower social awareness values. By doing so, the system tries to discourage commitment violations.

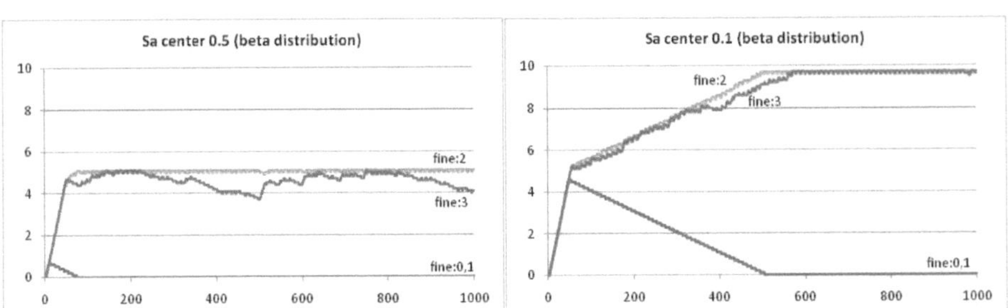

Fig. 6. Fine evolution (*Th*=0.1, *Nag*=10000) for 1000 simulation steps with uniform distributions of risk tolerance and different beta distributions of social awareness

The dependency mentioned before between fines is also visible here: fines 3 and 2 tend to absorb the effects of fines 0 and 1 sooner for higher social awareness values, and the system is able to find these intricacies.

4.3 Combining Risk Tolerance and Social Awareness

By adjusting both parameters when setting up an agent population, we get a combination of the effects identified above. Figure 7 shows what happens when we set both risk tolerance and social awareness to beta distributions centered at 0.1. In this case, since highest fines are limited by a low risk tolerance, the system raises fines 0 and 1 as much as it can, in order to try to force a population of mostly self-interested and risk-averse agents to contract and also comply with contractual commitments. We should add that in these extreme and unlikely conditions the normative system is not successful: the obtained fine levels are insufficient to force compliance, and at the same time too demanding to motivate contractual activity. This means that the few agents that do contract (which nevertheless are in essence risk-averse) will violate their commitments (because they are also too self-interested).

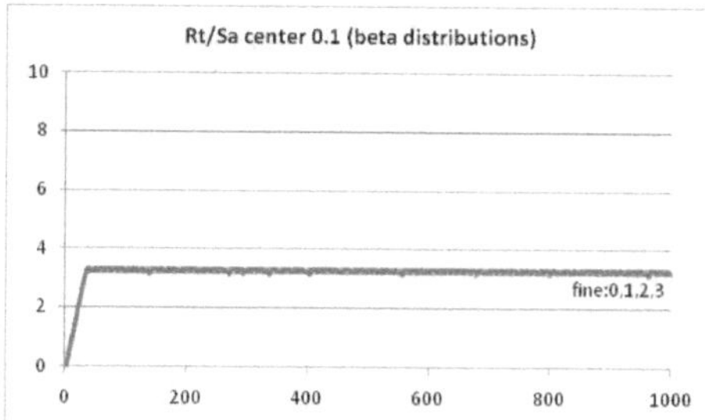

Fig. 7. Fine evolution (*Th*=0.1, *Nag*=10000) for 1000 simulation steps with beta distributions of risk tolerance and social awareness centered at 0.1

5 Conclusions

Embedding adaptive enforcement mechanisms in normative frameworks is important in open environments. Adapting deterrence levels to the behavior of an agent population is important when the normative space has imperfections that make the contracts to which norms apply unfair, opening the possibility for self-interested agents to exploit their potential advantage.

In this paper we have studied how an adaptive deterrence sanction model that tries to "maintain order" responds when facing different agent populations. Such populations were characterized by a predominant level of risk tolerance and social awareness. The former is inspired on economic theory on deterrence sanctions [7], stating that agents incur a risk when making contracts that are subject to deterrence sanctions. The latter is comparable to other approaches in MAS research that try to model different social attitudes (e.g. [2, 10]).

With the adaptive model described in this paper, imposed fines tend to be lower when agents are more risk-averse or when agents are more socially concerned. Also, we observed that when a combination of sanctions is able to drive agents to comply with their commitments, the adaptive mechanism is able to pursue such a combination when constraints limit some options – such constraints are rooted in the agent population (namely the predominant risk tolerance), and are implicitly captured in the fine update policy. This ability is an interesting emergent property of the system.

Dynamic properties of normative systems have been studied from different perspectives. In [11] norms are seen as patterns of behavior that may emerge from agent interactions. In our case, the normative system is external to the agents; we seek to adapt it to a specific agent population in order to pursue an overall system goal.

Sanction-based self-adaptation of institutional normative environments is also studied in [12]. However, their adaptation model is based on the definition of domain-dependent transition functions, stating what specific change should be made in a specific norm when some goal specification is not met. Also, their model does not assume strict liability: agents are able to violate norms while not being detected.

In this paper we have not considered the influence of reputation on agent's contractual behavior. It has been argued [13] that in the presence of reputation mechanisms there is a lesser need for deterrence policies. We leave for future work such analysis.

Acknowledgments. The first author is supported by FCT (Fundação para a Ciência e a Tecnologia) under grant SFRH/BD/29773/2006.

References

1. Arcos, J.L., et al.: Environment engineering for multiagent systems. Engineering Applications of Artificial Intelligence 18(2), 191–204 (2005)
2. Boella, G., van der Torre, L.: A Game-Theoretic Approach to Normative Multi-Agent Systems. In: Normative Multi-agent Systems, Schloss Dagstuhl (2007)
3. Lopes Cardoso, H., Oliveira, E.: A Context-based Institutional Normative Environment. In: Hubner, J., et al. (eds.) Coordination, Organizations, Institutions, and Norms in Agent Systems IV, pp. 140–155. Springer, Heidelberg (2009)
4. Pasquier, P., Flores, R.A., Chaib-Draa, B.: Modelling Flexible Social Commitments and their Enforcement. In: Gleizes, M.-P., Omicini, A., Zambonelli, F. (eds.) Engineering Societies in the Agents World V, pp. 139–151. Springer, Toulouse (2005)
5. Grossi, D., Aldewereld, H., Dignum, F.: Ubi lex, ibi poena: Designing norm enforcement in e-institutions. In: Noriega, P., et al. (eds.) Coordination, Organizations, Institutions, and Norms in Agent Systems II, pp. 101–114. Springer, Heidelberg (2007)
6. Zagare, F.C., Kilgour, D.M.: Perfect Deterrence. Cambridge University Press, Cambridge (2000)
7. Polinsky, A.M., Shavell, S.: Punitive Damages. In: Newman, P. (ed.) The New Palgrave Dictionary of Economics and the Law, pp. 192–198. Stockton Press, New York (1998)
8. Garoupa, N.: The Theory of Optimal Law Enforcement. Journal of Economic Surveys 11(3), 267–295 (1997)
9. Lopes Cardoso, H., Oliveira, E.: Adaptive Deterrence Sanctions in a Normative Framework. In: The 2009 IEEE/WIC/ACM International Conference on Intelligent Agent Technology (IAT 2009). IEEE Computer Society Press, Milan (to appear, 2009)

10. Castelfranchi, C.: Engineering Social Order. In: Omicini, A., Tolksdorf, R., Zambonelli, F. (eds.) Engineering Societies in the Agents World, pp. 1–18. Springer, Berlin (2000)
11. Sen, S., Airiau, S.: Emergence of norms through social learning. In: 20th Int. J. Conf. on Artificial Intelligence, Hyderabad, India, pp. 1507–1512 (2007)
12. Campos, J., et al.: Formalising Situatedness and Adaptation in Electronic Institutions. In: Hubner, J., et al. (eds.) Coordination, Organizations, Institutions, and Norms in Agent Systems IV, pp. 126–139. Springer, Heidelberg (2009)
13. Luck, M., et al.: Trust and Norms for Interaction. In: Proceedings of the IEEE SMC 2004 International Conference on Systems, Man & Cybernetics, pp. 1944–1949. IEEE, The Hague (2004)

Sensitivity Analysis of a Tax Evasion Model Applying Automated Design of Experiments

Attila Szabó[1], László Gulyás[1,2], and István János Tóth[3]

[1] Loránd Eötvös University, Pázmány Péter sétány 1/c
1117 Budapest, Hungary
[2] AITIA International Inc, Czetz János utca 48-50
1039 Budapest, Hungary
[3] Research Institute of Economics and Enterprises,
Hungarian Chamber of Commerce and Industry, Bécsi út 126-128
1034 Budapest, Hungary
{aszabo,lgulyas}@aitia.ai, tothij@gvi.hu

Abstract. Risk, audit frequency, expected utility, decision on the rate of tax evasion: probably these words occur to the reader first about tax evasion modeling. However, it can easily turn out in the real world that the 'everyday evader' hasn't got reliable information about the risks of evasion, about the possible amount of fine, or about the efficiency of the tax authorities. The TAXSIM agent-based tax evasion model was developed to understand the macro-level taxpayer behavior better with its help. The model and first simulation results were presented on the ESSA 2008 conference. The aim of this article is to present a sensitivity analysis of the model. We applied Design of Experiments method to reveal the main parameter-response correlations on a selected parameter domain and used two extreme parameter sets to examine on what level the contradictory factors can compensate each other.

Keywords: Agent-based computational economics, agent-based simulation, tax modeling, tax evasion.

1 Introduction

In our paper at ESSA 2008 [14] we introduced the tax evasion model in its complexity. We also presented simulation results of taxpayer behavior in life inspired scenarios in which i) the quality of governmental services increases permanently, ii) a market leader unilaterally adopts the legal position, and iii) multi-national companies with tax allowances enter the market. The first experimental results showed that TAXSIM might be a useful tool to understand the tax evasion phenomena better. However many questions remained about the system behavior. Two type of model 'investigations' were planned to test the model usability: one was to reveal the parameter-response correlations and the other was to reproduce statistical data collected on actual tax evasion. This article discusses the parameter-response correlations of the TAXSIM model. We also publish results on compensating the tax authority activities.

L. Seabra Lopes et al. (Eds.): EPIA 2009, LNAI 5816, pp. 572–583, 2009.

Agent-based models brought important new results on tax evasion. Altering the compliance strategy of the inhomogeneous agents' periodically (honest, 'imitative', 'free rider' [11] or honest, 'susceptible' and 'evader' [7] strategies) as environment changes can better explain how low number of audits can result a compliant population [5]. Balsa et al. created a generative set of models those demonstrate how can some extensions raise the predictive power of the standard theory [1][3] of tax evasion [2]. These extensions were: agent individuality and adaptivity, social perceptions and social interactions. Korobow et al. found that even in case of almost chaotic dynamics on the agent-level a predominantly compliant equilibrium can emerge. They also demonstrated that when agents weight neighbors' compliance strategy payoffs more heavily in their decisions, noncompliance tends to increase [9].

In these models the urge for evasion is a built-in part of taxpayer strategies. On the contrary law enforcement (i.e. tax audits) is the direct and – because of agents' awareness to their environment - indirect motivation for compliance (that is affected by other factors: e.g. the weight of neighbors' behavior affects the taxpayer strategy). These models help to understand how agents react to different enforcement techniques applied on various levels assuming realistic taxpaying strategies and inhomogeneous agents. Still, some assumptions might be useful to take in account too.

All regulation is more than a collection of arbitrary rules. For example a driver may respect a stop sign not because she wants to avoid being prosecuted committing a crime, but because of her own interest in avoiding a car accident. On the other hand even those who want to exceed the speed limit can be prevented from speeding easily by a traffic jam. Analogue ideas motivated the development of the TAXSIM model: we made an effort to take the taxpayer's reasonability (or her interests beyond maximizing the wage) and opportunities into account. This approach has the promise to gain information about how can be the taxpayers motivated to comply when the aggravation of enforcement is not viable.

In the following we will discuss some experimental results of the TAXSIM model that aggregates taxpayer motivations, market labor characteristics and authority activities. In the previous paper at ESSA [14] we presented the TAXSIM's architecture in details. It [14] also includes simulation results of some realistic scenarios. After testing the model as a whole we decided to run a sensitivity analysis.

This paper is structured as follows. Section 2 overviews the model. Section 3 describes the sensitivity analysis: subsection 3.1 presents the method of the experiment, while the experimental results are demonstrated in the following subsection. Section 4. The last section concludes the paper.

2 Short Overview of the Model

The TAXSIM model is a complex agent-based approach for tax evasion (and tax compliance) simulations. The novelty of TAXSIM is that taxpayer compliance is strongly affected by the environment of the agent. An agent who decides to evade tax on a certain level has to find a job offer that meets her preferences: if she was unable to find one, she will make a compromise and accept an available offer that closest to her decision. The other novelty is that agents accept the need for taxes in TAXSIM. That is, taxpayers experience taxes as the price of services they resort (e.g. courts, education, etc.).

The model is concerned with the operations of a single market sector, where there are four kinds of agents involved: employee, employer, (tax) authority and government. The economic well-being of employees depend on their net wages, while that of the employers' is a function of the market demand and the level of gross wages they are forced to pay. The rate of tax evasion is an agreement between an employer and an employee that is made when the employee occupies a new job. As the agreed employment type determines the income of the employee and the (producing) costs of the employer, both participating agents have a motivation to evade.

The government and the tax authority have service providing and regulatory roles, respectively. Since the market demand is modeled as an exogenous component and employers and employees are assumed to be homogeneous in technological and productive ability, competitiveness is determined by the agents' approach to taxes.

In this model tax evasion is a technique to reduce costs (and to raise wages). Therefore a more refined measure of level of the evasion fits better our purposes than the classical binary or ternary choice (e.g., complier/evader, or complier/evader/skeptic). Thus, we used the five types of income (those found empirically most common in Hungary – both legal and illegal ones) to create employment types. An employment type is the combination of reported wage, fringe benefits, ad hoc engagement agreement, unreported wage and payment in kind. The employment types are grouped so that when there's no reported wage it is termed *illegal* (or *hidden*) and it is called *legal* when there's only reported wage and fringe benefits. The remaining combinations belong to the group of *mixed* employment.

The agents have no perfect information about the policies of the government and of the accuracy of the tax authority. They learn from these previous experiences and from interactions within their social network. Thus, in addition to the agents, the last major component of the model is the social network of both the employees and the firms. The employees and employers use their knowledge during the so called negotiation process that takes place when an employee occupies a new job. During the negotiation procedure both the employer's and the employee's expectations depend on their respective satisfaction with the government and on the estimated costs and benefits of evasion. Previous interactions with the authority agent (audits) and information derived from the social network determine cost and benefit estimations. It is also assumed that all agents utilize some services provided by the government (e.g. a company wants to register a trademark, or a person wants to get a passport). These interactions (the experienced effectiveness, corruption, etc.) determine the contentment of the agent.

The model of the market sector is kept as simple as possible. Companies (employers) producing the cheapest goods sell first. When demand is less than the actual productivity, companies producing most expensive goods will meet losses that may force them towards evasion. A similar force is faced by the employees: after a period of unemployment (the length depending on the agents reserves that in turn, depend on the length of previous employment) an employee decreases its expectations and will eventually accept any job offer. An employee becomes unemploymed when its employer fires her due to financial reasons.

Employer agents start to operate by hiring employees and selling products. Costs are the wages, while income is the price of the sold products (the price of a single product depends on the employer's average wage cost and the profit margin, the latter being a model parameter). Employers operate until becoming bankrupt.

As discussed above, employers have an implicit strategy to produce as cheap as possible, which is realized by making tax evasion deals with employees. The key this is the negotiation process, in which employers make job offers. (A job offer is a pair of a wage and an employment type.) The agents try to optimize the following function:

$$V(B, a_2) = B\cdot(a_1 - a_2) - p\cdot q\cdot f\cdot B\cdot(a_1 - a_2) \rightarrow \max(a_2)\ . \quad (1)$$

Where B is the gross salary (constant within a simulation), a_1 is the tax rate (constant within a simulation), a_2 is the actual tax rate paid, p is the chance of audit, q is the chance of being caught during an audit in case of evasion (accuracy of the authority) and f is the fine rate (constant within a simulation). The agent learns the value of p and q.

However this function is constrained by the employer's contentment level, derived from governmental interactions that determine the minimum level of compliance (that can be zero). Moreover, the produced new offer needs to match the employee's preferences. Feedback from employees modifies the employer's strategy when no one accepts the offer for a period of time.

TAXSIM employees attempt to get a job of their preferences, or any job possible if they are unemployed for a given amount of time. Employees try to maximize their income by avoiding taxes, counting in the potential drawbacks of evasion (e.g. lower expected pension). Note that a greater take-home wage doesn't necessarily imply a greater expected income automatically due to additional estimated costs. Expected income is calculated by the following function:

$$v(N, \Delta_1, \Delta_2) = N - p_1\cdot N\cdot\Delta_1\cdot f - p_2\cdot\Delta_2\cdot k\ . \quad (2)$$

Where N is the take-home wage, Δ_1 is the evaded tax percent, Δ_2 is the evaded medical insurance (in percent), p_1 is the chance of being caught, p_2 is the chance of illness, f is the fine rate, and k is the medical cost. The agent learns the value of p_1 and p_2. When an employee looks for a job she will evaluate more than one offers using (2). If all of the offers are too illegal (compared to the agent's minimum level of compliance) and the employee has savings (practically, she has not been unemployed for a long period) then she won't accept any of the offers but keep searching. She will accept the best offer otherwise. (Unemployed agents do not pay any taxes.)

Employees live forever: there is no ageing or any fluctuation in the population of the employees. The financial status of the employee has no effect on her work abilities, but it shortens the period she looks for a desirable job.

An employee (or an employer) evaluates (1) (or (2)) only when a decision is to be made: e.g. when looking for a new job (or wants to hire a new employee). That means agents don't change their compliance level periodically. Employers apply no radical changes on their compliance as they alter their offers by shifting the current compliance level (that is between 0 and the tax rate) one step towards the profitable direction.

TAXSIM includes two distinct social networks of agents transmitting information between neighbors: one connects the employers and the other connects the employees. For simplicity, these are modeled by Erdős-Rényi random graphs [8] in the current version. Erdős-Rényi graphs have small agent-agent distances, an important property of real-world social networks. (On the other hand, they don't match other social network attributes like the clustering coefficient or degree distribution). Both employers and employees transmit information to their neighbors about the experienced accuracy of the authorities and their level of satisfaction. The average of the data received from neighbors affects the estimated accuracy of the authorities and the level of satisfaction respectively.

The tax authority audits employees via employers: employers are picked randomly for audit in each round depending on the audit frequency parameter. During a particular audit the authority checks the employer's employees randomly (the probability is equal to the 'authority accuracy' parameter). If the authority finds mixed or illegal employment both the employer and the employee is fined, proportionally to the tax evaded, and the employee is forced to quit the illegal job.

In return of taxes paid, agents expect advantages from the government agent (e.g. health care for employees, legal certainty for employers, etc.) by 'requesting' services. The levels of quality (for employees and for employers, respectively) are parameters of the model. The services are requested in every round by the agents according to probabilities set in parameters. The response is drawn form a distribution determined by the quality of service variable. Agents update their minimum level of compliance by calculating the weighted average of current and past experiences.

Table 1. Factors of the experiment

Parameter name	**Low value**	**High value**	**Code**
Authority accuracy	20%	40%	A
Chance of a new employer	5%	25%	B
Chance of illness (employees)	10%	30%	C
Cost of health care	5	10	D
Employee network density	5%	25%	E
Employee service quality	5%	25%	F
Employer network density	5%	25%	G
Employer service quality	20%	40%	H
Need supply (employers)	5%	25%	I
Number of requested goods	380	450	J
Probability of audit (each time step)	5%	25%	K
Income (percentage of investment)	105%	125%	L
Rate of fine (percentage of evaded tax)	140%	160%	M
Search for a new job (probability)	5%	25%	N
Tax rate	35%	55%	O

3 Sensitivity Analysis

3.1 Applying Design of Experiments

We decided to use designed experiments to analyze the model: a strong motivation for applying designed experiments instead of the one-factor-at-a-time (OFAT) method is in [6]. Amongst others the application of Design of Experiments (DoE) ensures a more exhaustive investigation and therefore more relevant results. A large body of literature is available on DoE: a good summary can be found in [12]; wide range of applications is in [5].

A *screening method* seemed to be appropriate for our purposes. The *two-level fractional factorial* method is able to calculate the effect of model parameters (or *factors* in DoE terminology) on the simulation results by running simulations with a *high* and a *low* value (*levels*) of the factors [12]. See Table 1. for the examined 15 factors and their levels. In the experiment we studied the model behavior in a small environment of an illegal market equilibrium that was used previously for simulating three scenarios [14]. A small subspace was selected as not all possible parameter values can be addressed to any real world phenomena. For example having the maximum value of the audit probability (which is 1 that means every employer is being audited in each time step) is an unrealistic option for the tax authorities.

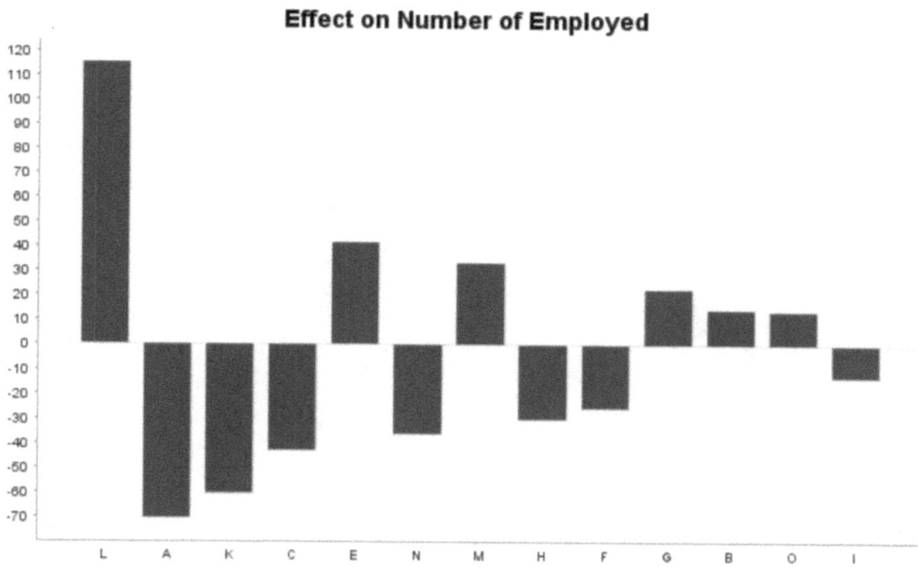

Fig. 1. Factor effects on number of employed. Category codes are in Table 1. The vertical axis shows the factor effect in the number of affected employments.

To perform a two-level fractional factorial design two levels (or "versions") of each of a number of factors (here model parameters) have to be selected and then the experiment is run in carefully chosen combinations defined by the design. In this experiment we used quantitative factors only.

To calculate the effect of a particular factor the measured response values are divided to two sets: the first set contains the response values measured at the low value of the factor; the other set contains the rest. The difference between the averages of the members of the first and the second sets is the factor effect.

DoE methods are usually applied in experiments using 2-6 parameters (in physics, chemistry, etc.), but bigger designs exist too. We applied a factorial method that reduced the number of 2^{15} runs of the full factorial method to 2^4 runs (the design specification is 2^{15-11}, resolution III: see [12] for details). The design was randomized so the experiment had a total of 240 simulation runs.

The experiments with the Repast J [13] model were run using the Model Exploration Module (MEME) [10] software tool. We also used MEME design the experiment and to process simulation data automatically.

There were initially 50 employers and 500 employees in the modeled sector (while the number of employers may change the number of employees is constant during each run). The employers' initial offers are drawn from uniform distribution. Market demand was 450 units.

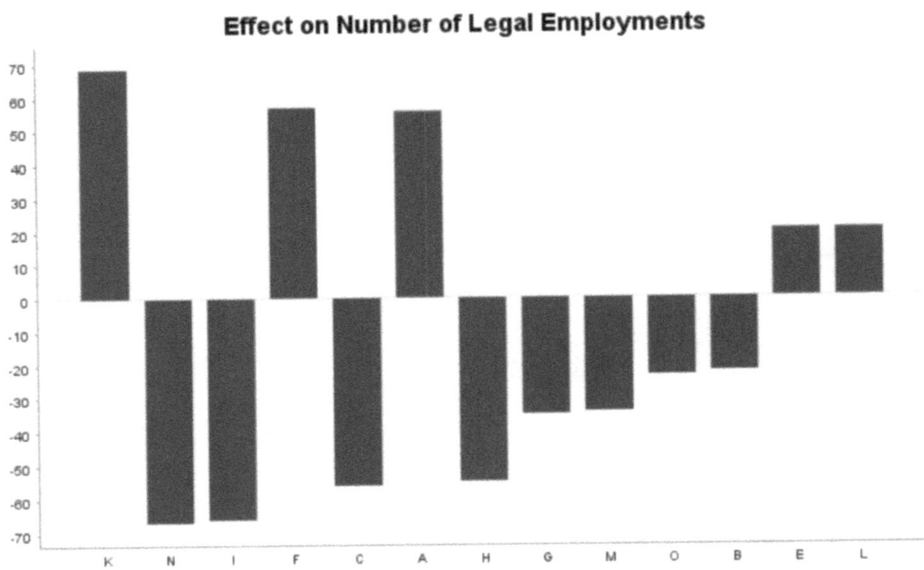

Fig. 2. Factor effects on the number of legal employments. Category codes are in Table 1. The vertical axis shows the factor effect in the number of affected employments.

3.2 Simulation Results

The following responses were considered during the experiment: number of employed, number of legal employments, number of mixed type employments and number of hidden employments. It could also be useful to focus on the aggregated tax income instead. However the selected values characterize the modeled system in a more detailed way and therefore those are more informative on the details of the results.

The two-level fractional factorial method indicates the effects of raising the factor values from the defined low values to high values (see Figures 1-4 for results). Table 1 shows the high and low values of the design factors: these factor value pairs define a parameter subspace examined during the experiments. The exact number of employments per types is unknown – only the changes are measured.

We found that income has the most powerful effect on the number of employed agents. Increasing the profit rate accelerates the simulated economy: employment rate increases in all employment types. The biggest increase is on the number of illegal employments (see factor 'L' on Figure 1-4).

An opposite effect can be observed as the accuracy and frequency of audits increase (accuracy of audits: factor 'A' and frequency of audits: factor 'K' on Figure 1-4). When the tax authority reveals an offense, the employee loses her job. Because of the high rate of illegal employments the bigger accuracy of the authority and the more frequent audits cause that the number of employed agents decreases significantly. It can be the case that the authority is too strict according to the economical environment, where the competition is very strong. Still, an accurate authority decreases the number of illegal employments significantly and legalizes the sector that can be tracked on the increasing number of legal and mixed type employments (see Figure 2-3).

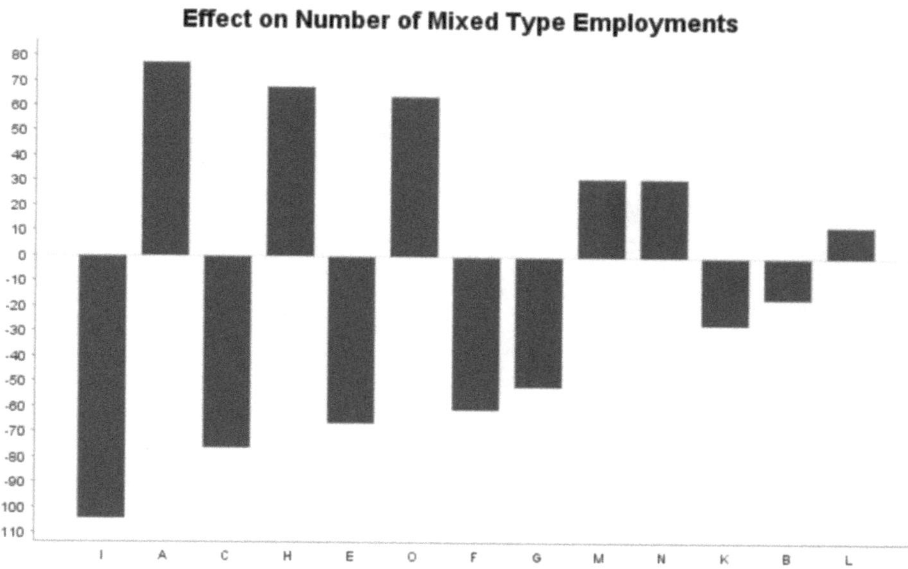

Fig. 3. Factor effects on the number of mixed type employments. Category codes are in Table 1. The vertical axis shows the factor effect in the number of affected employments.

When the social networks' density (see factor 'E' for employees and factor 'G' for employers on Figures 1-4) is higher, the unemployment rate is lower by the increasing number of illegal employments. In an environment where evasion is the 'rational' option, the more information agents have on the expected drawback on evasion, the better picture they have on the costs of having an illegal job. This result in less payment by agents caught by authorities and therefore less bankruptcy happens, and more agents can be employed (illegally). It's a very important result: well-informed agents are able to adapt a more optimal taxpaying behavior. It also accords to the phenomena Korobow et. al. found: when agents weight neighbors' compliance strategy payoffs more heavily in their decisions, noncompliance tends to increase [9]. It is common that the aggregated knowledge of agents affects the population-level compliance negatively.

The 'search probability' parameter (factor 'N' on Figures 1-4) makes employee agents to search a better job when employed so thus apply new jobs more frequently. When employed agents search for better jobs at a higher probability, the number of agents searching jobs increases. This results in an increased competition for available jobs, and decreased chance of a successful application. This influences unemployed agents more painfully as run out savings and forced to take any (in the examined case illegal) jobs. As an additional effect the agents have to decide more frequently on available jobs, they follow the changes in environment more closely and react more aptly.

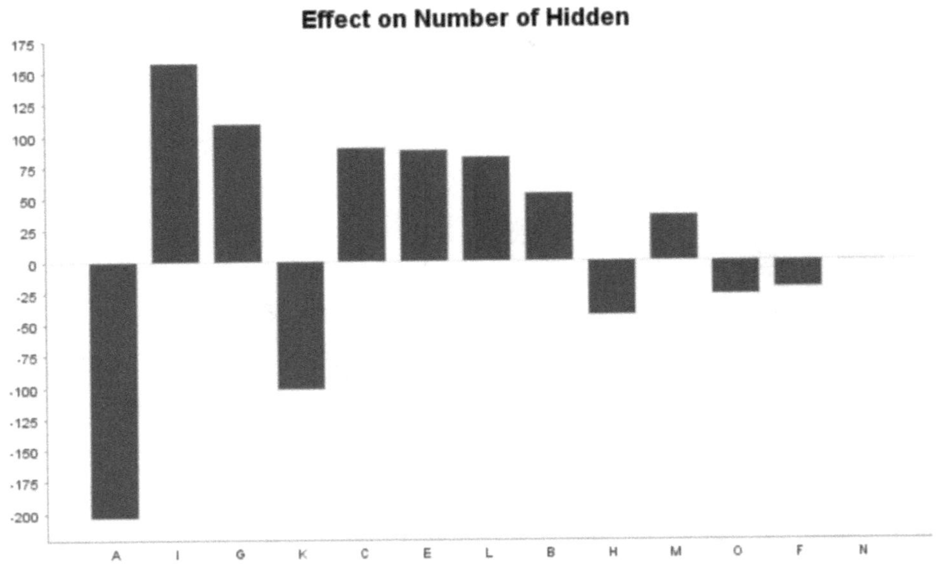

Fig. 4. Factor effects on the number of hidden employments. Category codes are in Table 1. The vertical axis shows the factor effect in the number of affected employments.

It is remarkable that a greater rate of fine alone (factor 'M') has a negative effect on the number of legal employments (see Figure 2): it requires further experiments to determine exactly what fine rate has a motivation for compliance.

On the one hand the better governmental services decrease the illegal employment rate. On the other hand the unemployment rate increases: in this case the legalization decreases the competitiveness of firms.

At a higher tax rate (factor 'O') the number of mixed type employments increases, while the other two decrease. Higher taxes result less income for employed agents that motivate them towards evasion. This moves legal agents (employees and employers) towards mixed employment types. On the other hand agent caught on not paying tax face an increased fine (due to increased amount of tax not paid). Agents anticipating on that move towards mixed type employments to reduce the cost.

4 Two Experiments in Extreme Environments

The taxpayer agents estimate the activity of the tax authority that affects their decisions strongly in an explicit way. However we wanted to demonstrate and verify that authority accuracy, the frequency of audits and the fine rate are far from being the only dominant parameters of TAXSIM on the entire parameter space. For simplicity it was examined whether taxpayer contentment (with governmental services) can compensate the abovementioned factors. No correlations between frequency of audits and taxpayer contentment were assumed; therefore agents didn't change their strategies because they experienced no punishment for evasion.

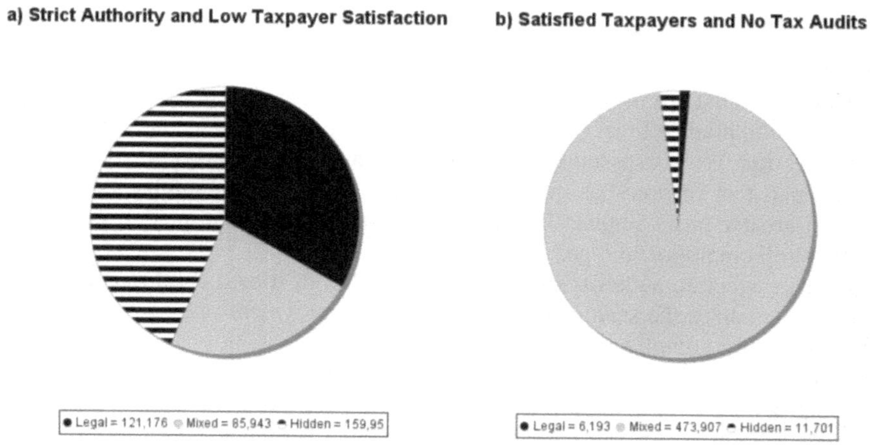

Fig. 5. Pie charts of the employment type distributions in case of a) high enforcement level and low taxpayer satisfaction and b) satisfied employers and no tax audits. Each chart depicts the time-averaged values of converged trajectories of 6000 time steps, averaged over the 216 simulation runs performed with different random number sequences.

We ran experiments to explore the taxpaying behavior in extreme environments. It was to be tested, how contradictory model factors affect the model output (the distribution of legal, mixed type and illegal employments). 500 employee agents and an initial group of 50 employers (those have dynamic lifecycles) operated in a single run. The charts below depict the time-averaged values of converged trajectories of 6000 time steps, averaged over the 216 simulation runs performed with different random number sequences.

In the first scenario a strong activity of tax authorities were present (27,5 percent of employers were audited in each turn, and discovered offenses were fined by the 250 percent of the evaded tax). On the other hand both employers' and employees' satisfaction level was extremely low (30 percent of them requested services in each turn, and only 10 percent of the responds were satisfactory). Market demand was lowered too: it was 76 percent of the modeled sector's productivity.

In the second scenario employer agents were highly compliant (90 percent of them requested services from the government in each turn, and 90 percent of the responds were satisfactory) and market demand was relatively high (only 10 percent less than the modeled sector's maximum productivity). On the other hand the agents faced no tax audits at all, and the employees' satisfaction level was relatively low (30 percent of them requested services in each turn, and only 30 percent of the responds were satisfactory).

It was trivial, that this scenario won't result a totally illegal sector, due to the parameters. The interesting result is that not just the rate of illegal, but the rate of legal employments stays marginal too (see Figure 5). This means that the low satisfaction level of employees can compensate employers' high compliance level at a certain rate.

5 Conclusions

This paper summarized the results of a sensitivity analysis of the TAXSIM model. We examined what are the most powerful motivation factors when an agent selects a certain tax compliance level in case the decision is bounded to agents' opportunities in job selection. We also assumed that agents accept the need for taxes.

We found that income has the most powerful effect on the number of employed agents: a greater profit implies lower unemployment rate in the model: it raises the number of all employment types.

Albeit an accurate authority decreases the number of illegal employments significantly and legalizes the sector, it also increase unemployment rate, if the other motivation factors for compliance are low.

We found that the more accurate information agents have on their environment the less compliant they are going to be in TAXSIM that accords to the results of Korobow et. al. [9]. They experienced that when agents weight neighbors' compliance strategy payoffs more heavily in their decisions, noncompliance tends to increase. It is common that the aggregated knowledge of agents affects the population-level compliance in a negative way.

It was also demonstrated that in the taxpayer decision mechanism of TAXSIM fine and audits are not the only dominant factors. We found that that when the taxpayer contentment is low with governmental services, the rate of illegal employment is high even in case of frequent authority audits. On the contrary a high contentment can prevent the society from total illegalization even in the lack of tax audits. It means the model has a rather complex response surface, perhaps a more complex one than to be expected from the results of initial experiments.

Acknowledgements

The work reported in this chapter was made possible by a grant from the Hungarian Government (grant #GVOP-3.2.2-2004.07-005/3.0). The partial support of the European Commission via the FP6 STREP projects QosCosGrid (contract #033883) and EMIL (contract #033841) is also gratefully acknowledged. László Gulyás also acknowledges the support of the Hungarian Government (OTKA T62455).

References

1. Allingham, M.G., Sandmo, A.: Income tax evasion: A theoretical analysis. Journal of Public Economics 1(3/4), 323–338 (1972)
2. Balsa, J.,Antunes, L., Respício, A., Coelho, H.: Tactical exploration of tax compliance decisions in multi-agent based simulation. In: Antunes, L., Takadama, K. (eds.) MABS 2006. LNCS (LNAI), vol. 4442, pp. 80–95. Springer, Heidelberg (2007)

3. Becker, G.S.: quotedblbaseCrime and punishment: an economic approach. Journal of Political Economy 76(2), 169–217 (1968)
4. Bloomquist, K.M.: A Comparison of Agent-Based Models of Income Tax Evasion. Social Science Computer Review 24(4), 411–425 (2006)
5. Box, G.E., Hunter, W.G., Hunter, J.S.: Statistics for Experimenters: Design, Innovation, and Discovery, 2nd edn. Wiley, Chichester (2005)
6. Czitrom, V.: One-Factor-at-a-Time Versus Designed Experiments. The American Statistician 53 (1999)
7. Davis, J.S., Hecht, G., Perkins, J.D.: Social Behaviors,Enforcement and Tax compliance Dynamics. Accounting Rev. 78, 39–69 (2003)
8. Erdős, P., Rényi, A.: On Random Graphs. I. Publicationes Mathematicae 6, 290–297 (1959)
9. Korobow, A., Johnson, C., Axtell, R.: An Agent-Based Model of Tax Compliance with Social Networks. National Taxc Journal (2007)
10. Ivanyi, M., Bocsi, R., Gulyas, L., Kozma, V., Legendi, R.: The Multi-Agent Simulation Suite. Emergent Agents and Socialities:Social and Organizational Aspects of Intelligence. Papers from the 2007 AAAI Fall Symposium, pp. 57–64 (2007)
11. Mittone, L., Petelli, P.: Imitative Behaviour in Tax Evasion. In: Stefansson, B., Luna, F. (eds.) Economic Modeling with Swarm. Kluwer, Amsterdam (2000)
12. NIST/SEMATECH e-Handbook of Statistical Methods (2009), `http://www.itl.nist.gov/div898/handbook/`
13. North, M.J., Collier, N.T., Vos, J.R.: Experiences Creating Three Implementations of the Repast Agent Modeling Toolkit. ACM Transactions on Modeling and Computer Simulation 16(1), 1–25 (2006)
14. Szabo, A., Gulyas, L., Toth, I.J.: TAXSIM Agent Based Tax Evasion Simulator. In: Proceedings ESSA 2008 Conference, Brescia, Italy (2008)

Chapter 11

TEMA – Text Mining and Applications

Phrase Translation Extraction from Aligned Parallel Corpora Using Suffix Arrays and Related Structures*

José Aires, Gabriel Pereira Lopes, and Luis Gomes

CITI, Departamento de Informática,
Faculdade de Ciências e Tecnologia,
Universidade Nova de Lisboa,
2829-516 Caparica, Portugal
{aires,gpl}@di.fct.unl.pt, luismsgomes@gmail.com

Abstract. In this paper, we will address term translation extraction from indexed aligned parallel corpora, by using a couple of association measures combined by a voting scheme, for scaling down translation pairs according to the degree of internal cohesiveness, and evaluate results obtained. Precision obtained is clearly much better than results obtained in related work for the very low range of occurrences we have dealt with, and compares with the best results obtained in word translation.

Keywords: Translation Equivalents, Extraction, Suffix Arrays, Parallel Corpus Alignment, Language Independent, Large Corpus.

1 Introduction

Most part of work on parallel text or alignment assumes that sentence alignment granularity is the most adequate granularity measure, mainly because automatic alignment precision obtained is close to 100% [3]. However, applications such as Statistical Machine Translation (SMT) then require a finer alignment granularity (word alignment) for enabling the extraction of statistical translation models [9, 10], including word translation and estimation of other parameters. According to our perspective on alignment, phrase-based alignment is more adequate for SMT and Example-Based Machine Translation (EBMT) [7]. In this vein, we have built an aligner [4] that rapidly aligns any parallel text collection using a translation lexicon of single and multi-word terms and expressions, that have been previously extracted, evaluated and accepted, rejected or left unverified, using accepted term or expression translation pairs as alignment correspondence segments. This aligner adapts the alignment algorithm used by [11]. As a consequence, the cycle, composed of alignment, extraction of unknown term translations, validation of extracted term translations, will be repeated until a stage where no new gains will be obtained. In this paper, we will address term translation extraction, by using a couple of association measures combined by a voting scheme, for scaling down translation pairs according to the degree of

* Research supported by FCT/MCTES, through Ph.D. scholarship, ref. SFRH/BD/48839/2008, and project VIP-Access, ref. PTDC/PLP/72142/2006.

L. Seabra Lopes et al. (Eds.): EPIA 2009, LNAI 5816, pp. 587–597, 2009.

internal cohesiveness, and evaluate results obtained. Precision obtained is clearly much better than results obtained in related work [6] for the very low range of occurrences we have dealt with, and compares with the best results obtained in word translation extraction [12, 9]. Suffix arrays [8, 17] were selected as they are a data structure allowing for efficient string frequency counting, full text indexing, efficient string matching and retrieval.

2 Background and Motivation

Extraction of single- and multi-word translations is extremely important for Machine Translation (SMT and EBMT) [9, 10, 12, 15], for Cross Language Information Retrieval [2], for bilingual lexica and terminology [14, 9], for enabling increasingly precise sub-sentence alignment, as argued in this paper. Translation extraction is mainly made by using three different approaches: based on different co-occurrence approaches [6, 14, 12], on SMT models [9, 10], and on co-occurrence and random indexing [13]. Co-occurrence approaches use different similarity measures (see an extended comparison in [12] and [5]). In this paper we present an efficient solution using the alignment of parallel texts as guidance and using Suffix Arrays and related structures to make all the terms conveniently accessible. It should be noted that even though the base of our methodology is language independent, the results analyzed in this paper were obtained from an English/Portuguese language pair subset of a European Constitution corpus, using an implementation tuned for Western languages.

3 Using the Alignment

Two texts, each in a different language, are considered parallel if one is a translation of the other. To be able to set them apart, one of those texts will be called the source and the other the target. A translation equivalent consists of a source term and a target term in which one is a translation of the other. The aligned parallel text used is obtained from a parallel text aligner developed in our research group [4], establishing language correspondences at a sub-sentence level and capable of using previously acquired knowledge for improving the alignment precision. Table 1 shows part of an alignment of two parallel texts, where the '*'s mark a known translation pair existing in the bilingual lexicon used for the alignment. Swaps and omissions between those texts prevent the monotonic aligner from doing a better job. Yet, this alignment constitutes a very good starting point for the translation equivalents extraction process, as it clearly enables the identification of possible translations such as «Eurojust's mission shall be to support and strengthen» <=> «A Eurojust tem por missão apoiar e reforçar», «strengthen» <=> «reforçar», «national investigating and prosecuting authorities» <=> «as autoridades nacionais competentes para a investigação e o exercício de a acção penal», and «serious crime» <=> «criminalidade grave», which are obtained by composing whole segments[1].

[1] The problem of extracting translation equivalents like «support» <=> «apoiar» from this kind of alignment, requiring the fragmentation of a segment (in this case, the segment «shall be to support»), will be addressed in future work.

Table 1. An alignment example

	Source segment	Known	Target segment
1	Eurojust's		A Eurojust tem por
2	mission	*	missão
3	shall be to support		apoiar
4	and	*	e
5	strengthen		reforçar
6	coordination and cooperation	*	a coordenação e a cooperação
7	between	*	entre
8	national investigating and prosecuting		
9	authorities	*	as autoridades
10			nacionais competentes para a investigação e o exercício de a acção penal
11	in relation to	*	em matéria de
12			criminalidade
13	serious	*	grave
14	crime		
15	affecting	*	que afecte

The translation equivalent «shall be to support» <=> «apoiar» is not a correct one and it can be rejected if it does not occur in the parallel texts as often as the right entries «shall be to support» <=> «será apoiar» or « support» <=> «apoiar». This shows it is not enough to simply associate terms with each other. The alignments allow a very significant narrowing of the search space, but the problems caused by the misalignments resulting from term translation ignorance, errors, language specific characteristics or even dubious translations, must also be analyzed to reduce their negative effects on final results.

With the parallel texts aligned it becomes much simpler to associate source and target terms as long as access to such terms is efficient. The idea is to take every source term of the source text, get the set of adjacent source segments that fit exactly the source term and then get the target terms from the corresponding adjacent target segments on the target text. Since we are only interested in obtaining new information, translation equivalents composed only by known segments are discarded. The number of times a target term is associated to a source term will be the matching frequency. In the end, a translation equivalent will have three basic properties: the mentioned matching frequency, the source term frequency and the target term frequency. These properties will be used to calculate the scoring measures described ahead, which will in turn be used to improve the results.

4 Implementation

Considering the need for an easy access to terms and the availability of their frequencies, our solution is based on Suffix Arrays, since these structures make the terms easily accessible and provide an efficient calculation of the frequency of every term, convenient for the scores described ahead. We had no interest in terms of every size, so a limit has been introduced, which also improved the performance. While working with Western languages, a word based solution has been developed. The following sub-sections will briefly describe the data structures used, using *T* = "to be or not to be" to help in such description, and explain their contribution.

4.1 Suffix Array

A text with *N* words will have *N* suffixes, each of them starting at the beginning of a word and spanning themselves until the end of the text. The Suffix Array keeps the offsets of those suffixes in lexicographic order, enabling an efficient binary search of a term [8]. Table 2 shows the Suffix Array of text *T*.

Table 2. Suffix Array

i	*SA*[*i*]	*T*[*SA*[*i*]]
0	16	be
1	3	be or not to be
2	9	not to be
3	6	or not to be
4	13	to be
5	0	to be or not to be

4.2 LCP Array

This structure keeps the longest common prefix (lcp) between two adjacent entries of the Suffix Array [8]. Since we are working with complete words, these lcp's must also correspond to complete words, which means that the lcp between «Europe» and «European» will be 0, even though they share a common prefix. The purpose of this structure is to aid in the construction of the Suffix Class Array, described in the following sub-section. Table 3 shows the LCP Array of text *T*.

Table 3. LCP Array

i	*LCP*[*i*]	*T*[*SA*[*i*]]	*T*[*SA*[*i*–1]]
0	0	be	(out of bounds)
1	2	be or not to be	be
2	0	not to be	be or not to be
3	0	or not to be	not to be
4	0	to be	or not to be
5	5	to be or not to be	to be
6	0	(out of bounds)	to be or not to be

4.3 Suffix Class Array

This structure holds information about every unique term present in the corpus, namely their location (through the Suffix Array) and their frequency [17]. So, every term and its prefixes (once again, whole word prefixes), sharing the same frequency will be represented by the same Suffix Class. For instance, if "European" and "European Community" both occur five times, those five instances of each of them will be represented by the same Suffix Class. However, if "Europe" also occurs five times in the text, it will not be included in the same Suffix Class because the prefix shared does not correspond to a full word match. This means each Suffix Class condensates in it all instances of a set of terms sharing the same word prefix and the same frequency. Table 4 shows the Suffix Class Array of text *T*.

Table 4. Suffix Class Array

i	LBL	SIL	*SA* range	tf	text
0	0	2	[0, 1]	2	be
1	2	15	[1, 1]	1	be or not to be
2	0	9	[2, 2]	1	not to be
3	0	12	[3, 3]	1	or not to be
4	0	5	[4, 5]	2	to be
5	5	18	[5, 5]	1	to be or not to be

Now, the fact that common word prefixes, with a common frequency, share the same Suffix Class, poses a problem and that is why the Term Array was designed, as described in the following sub-section.

4.4 Term Array

As noted above, two different terms, in which one is a word prefix of the other, can be represented by the same Suffix Class. However, we might still be interested in finding translations for both terms, individually. This is where the Term Array comes into play, by "expanding" every Suffix Class to show all their word prefixes that are not already represented by another Suffix Class. Now, all the instances of a given term[2] will be represented by one Term[3] [1]. In the end, the source Terms will be associated to the target Terms that correspond to translations of the first. Table 5 shows the Term Array of text *T*.

Since each Term structure represents all the instances of a given term, the Term Array will contain all the terms to be processed, with no repetitions. Considering L as the word limit and N as the number of words in a text, and knowing that there will be at most $2N-1$ Suffix Classes [17], each Suffix Class would generate L Terms in the worst case, so the number of elements of this structure would be $(2N-1)L$. Knowing that L rarely takes a value larger than a constant, the resulting size is $O(N)$.

[2] Term (not capitalized) is the multi-word expressions being analyzed.
[3] Term (capitalized) is the structure holding information for the multi-word.

Table 5. Term Array

i	*SC* index	term
0	0	be
1	1	be or
2	1	be or not
3	1	be or not to
4	1	be or not to be
5	2	not
6	2	not to
7	2	not to be
8	3	or
9	3	or not
10	3	or not to
11	3	or not to be
12	4	to
13	4	to be
14	5	to be or
15	5	to be or not
16	5	to be or not to
17	5	to be or not to be

4.5 Combining the Structures

All previous structures are calculated for the texts of each language and, combined with the alignment information, a series of steps are taken (also for each language) in order to extract the translation equivalents. Using Table 5 to help explaining the process, the steps are the following:

- All source terms («be», «be or», «be or not», ...) will be processed by traversing the source Term Array;
- Each source Term will have all its occurrences identified, with the aid of the corresponding Suffix Class, so that they can be used to find the corresponding alignment segments, through binary searches (the term could be composed by more than one segment) and we only keep the segment or segments when they only contain the term (when looking for «to be», we discard the segments «not to be» and «to be or»: we only want the term, nothing more and nothing less);
- Once the alignment segments are found, we can retrieve the corresponding target terms (remember that we are only interested in new information so, when the set of segments is all known, the candidate is discarded);
- The target terms are then used to find the corresponding target Terms (through binary searches) so they can be used to check if the target term has been associated with the source term (through the source Term).

So, this solution sequentially accesses all source Term structures and then accesses all target Term structures through binary searches. This procedure, combined with the structures, the alignment guidance, and the limitation on the number of words for the terms, enables us to efficiently process all translation equivalents of the candidate terms. The complexity of our solution is then $O(N\times(log_2(N))^2)$, far better than the initial N^4 (if all possible $N^2\times N^2$ were considered, with no guidance), thanks to the alignment and the structures that allow efficient storage and retrieval of terms.

5 Exploring Alignment Patterns

As noted before, the alignment has a few limitations. In Table 1, segments 12, 13 and 14 show a misalignment due to word order differences between English and Portuguese which prevent a complete word-to-word alignment. In a situation in which we have no knowledge about the languages involved, we could try every possible combination of translation equivalents from the shown alignment configuration («serious» <=> «criminalidade grave», «serious crime» <=> «criminalidade grave» and «serious crime» <=> «grave»), and expect for statistics to work in our behalf. This approach means that in order to make evident that some equivalent combinations are more "probable" than others, the larger the corpus used, the better.

However, since we know something about the languages involved, we decided to explore that. So, in this case we can see that this equivalent is "surrounded" by empty segments, and this is a common pattern found in aligned parallel texts for the English/Portuguese language pair, allowing us, in this situation, to keep just the translation equivalent «serious crime» <=> «criminalidade grave» and discard the others. An observation that could somehow justify this is the fact that any other combination would leave an alternative aligning with an empty segment while "consuming" another. For instance, admitting «serious crime» <=> «grave <empty>» would, in a way, imply «<empty>» <=> «criminalidade» which, in this case, is something that does not make sense[4] and should be merged with the previous.

6 Defining Scores to Filter Entries

As it has already been mentioned, some extracted translation equivalents are simply wrong because they result from a bad alignment, a frequent error or even a bad translation. While paying attention to the translation equivalents' properties (source, target and matching frequencies), we were able to observe that most of the wrong translations revealed significant differences between those properties. It is known that many terms can have a few different translations, so it is expectable that both terms of a translation equivalent will not have the same frequency. However, when this difference is considerable, we can conclude with some degree of certainty that the equivalent is wrong. The problem here is to define a score and a reasonable threshold that would allow us to discard all the entries bellow (or above, for that matter) that threshold value.

Usually, having two terms associated many times with each other is a good sign of correctness (it could also be a frequent error), but we should also consider their individual frequencies to detect some abnormal deviation of only one term or both. In other words, this means that the terms can have been matched many times but the

[4] There could be some word suppression, but this is not the case.

frequency of one or both of them is so much higher that we could be suspicious about the equivalent's quality.

All this considered, the following functions have been developed and evaluated for several thresholds. They use the translation equivalents' base properties, where X represents the source term frequency, Y the target term frequency and XY the matching (or co-occurrence) frequency, and return a value between 0 and 1.

6.1 Score Function 1

$$\frac{1}{3} \times \left(\frac{XY}{X} + \frac{XY}{Y} + \frac{\min(X,Y)}{\max(X,Y)}\right)$$

This measure takes into account the occurrence conditional probability of the source (target) term given that the target (source) term occurs, giving rise to sub-formula XY/X (or XY/X), and the ratio min(X,Y)/max(X,Y), where only source and target term frequencies are considered. These three individual measures are then given the same weight for obtaining the final score. The closer the frequencies X, Y and XY are, the higher will be the score.

6.2 Score Function 2

$$\frac{1}{2} \times \left(\frac{\min(X,Y)}{\max(X,Y)} + \left(1 - \frac{1}{XY}\right)\right)$$

This function only has two terms, with equal weight. One just takes separate frequencies, as above. The other just takes matching frequency, XY. The higher the value of XY, the closest this term will be to 1, thus benefiting translation equivalents with high matching frequencies. This function has shown a slight results improvement when compared to the previous one.

7 Results Analysis

In order to evaluate the scores, we randomly selected 1000 translation equivalents to be evaluated from a set of more than 250000, measuring the precision and recall for the correct and incorrect entries for a set of thresholds, as shown in Figures 1 and 2.

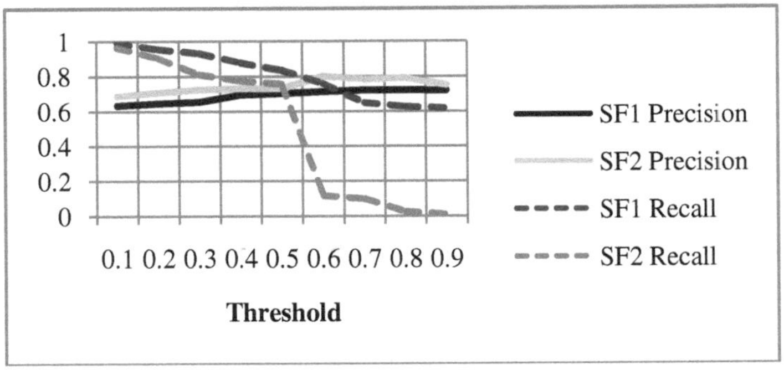

Fig. 1. Precision and recall of correct entries

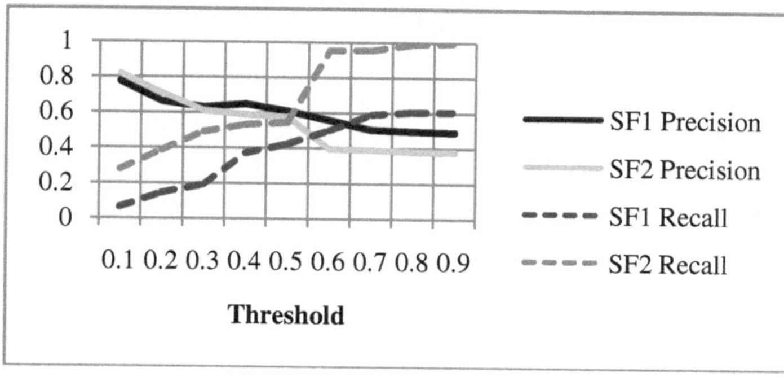

Fig. 2. Precision and recall of incorrect entries

In Table 6 we can see a few examples. These show that Score Function 1 correctly accepts the first equivalent and correctly rejects the second, while Score Function 2 correctly accepts the third term and correctly rejects the fourth.

Table 6. Some examples of translation equivalents using a 0.5 threshold

X	Y	XY	Source term	Target term	F1	F2	Correct selection
2	6	2	all information	todas as informações	0.56	0.42	Accepted by F1
5	14	3	compulsory education	obrigatório	0.39	0.51	Rejected by F1
8	9	2	em consequência de	as a result of	0.45	0.69	Accepted by F2
2	1	1	administer	administram em as zonas de soberania	0.67	0.25	Rejected by F2

8 Conclusions and Future Work

We have developed an efficient process to extract good quality single and multi-word translations on top of aligned parallel texts, whose alignment precision, recall and F-measure are close to 79%, when using evaluation metric in [16]. Suffix Arrays and their related structures were used to index a corpus with approximately 1MB of size and 200000 words for each language. We have also shown that it is possible to improve the precision of the results by developing a scoring formula using the translation equivalents' base properties (frequencies). According to the results evaluation, we can use several thresholds depending on specific demands. We might be interested in a balanced precision and recall for both the correct and incorrect entries, in which case 0.2 might be a good threshold, with a precision of 71% for both correct and incorrect entries; we might be interested in a high precision of correct entries, so 0.6 might be a good threshold choice, with at least 10% recall (considering that around 60% of the randomly chosen entries were correct, we could expect around 18000 entries with 80% precision); or we might be interested in a high precision of incorrect entries, for which 0.1 is a good threshold with almost 30% recall. These suggestions consider Score Function 2. Results obtained are far better than those obtained in [6], where precisions above 60% require frequencies well above 10 (in [13] more than 1000 is needed to reach such precision) while our results take into account frequencies equal to 1 and larger. In [9] only word translation pairs extraction is considered, with lower precision. Moreover, complexity of our extraction algorithm allows fast term translation extraction and faster evaluation due to higher precision.

The extraction does not partition segments in order to obtain equivalents for terms inside such segments. Let us take, for instance, the alignment «A B C» <=> «D», where any of the terms «A», «B» or «C» (or even «A B» or «B C») could be the equivalent of «D». This shows the need to find more alignment segments to be able to accept equivalents as being more likely, or to reject them as being less likely, and the way all such information should be used to do so still needs to be studied. Also, we shall address the benefits from using the alignment, extraction and validation cycle in terms of productivity and enhancement of alignment and translation quality.

References

1. Aires, J., Lopes, G., Silva, J.: Efficient Multi-Word Expressions Extractor Using Suffix Arrays and Related Structures. In: ACM iNEWS 2008, Napa Valley, California, USA (2008)
2. Ballesteros, L., Croft, W.B.: Phrasal translation and query expansion techniques for cross language information retrieval. In: ACM-SIGIR Conference on Research and Development in Information Retrieval, pp. 84–91 (1997)
3. Gale, W.A., Church, K.W.: A Programme for aligning sentences in bilingual Corpora. Computational Linguistics 19(1), 75–102 (1993)
4. Gomes, L.: Parallel Texts Alignment, M.Sc. Thesis, FCT/UNL (2009)
5. Henderson, J.: Word Alignment Baselines. In: HLT-NAACL Workshop on Building and Using Parallel Texts Data Driven Machine Translation and Beyond, pp. 27–30 (2003)
6. Hjelm, H.: Identifying Cross Language Term Equivalents Using Statistical Machine Translation and Distributional Association Measures. In: Proceedings of Nodalida 2007, the 16th Nordic Conference of Computational Linguistics, Tartu, Estonia (2007)
7. Langlais, P., Simard, M.: Merging example-based and statistical machine translation: An experiment. In: Richardson, S.D. (ed.) AMTA 2002. LNCS (LNAI), vol. 2499, pp. 104–113. Springer, Heidelberg (2002)
8. Manber, U., Myers, G.: Suffix arrays: A new method for on-line string searches. In: Proceedings of The First Annual ACM-SIAM Symposium on Discrete Algorithms, pp. 319–327 (1990)
9. Melamed, D.: Models of translational equivalence among words. Computational Linguistics 26(2), 221–249 (2000)
10. Och, F.J., Ney, H.: Asystematic comparison of various statistical alignment models. Computational Linguistics 29(1), 19–51 (2003)
11. Ribeiro, A., Dias, G., Lopes, G., Mexia, J.: Cognates Alignment. In: Maegaard, B. (ed.) Proceedings of the Machine Translation Summit VIII (MT Summit VIII), Santiago de Compostela, Spain, September 18-22, 2001. European Association of Machine Translation, pp. 287–292 (2001)

12. Ribeiro, A., Lopes, G., Mexia, J.: Extracting Translation Equivalents from aligned parallel texts: comparison of measures of similarity. In: Monard, M.C., Sichman, J.S. (eds.) SBIA 2000 and IBERAMIA 2000. LNCS, vol. 1952, pp. 339–349. Springer, Heidelberg (2000)
13. Sahlgren, M., Karlgren, J.: Automatic bilingual lexicon acquisition using random indexing of parallel corpora. Natural Language Engineering 11(3), 1–38 (2005)
14. Smadja, F., McKeeown, K.R., Hatzivassiloglou, V.: Translating collocations for bilingual lexicons: A statistical approach. Computational Linguistics 22(1), 1–38 (1996)
15. Venugopal, A., Vogel, S., Waibel, A.: Effective phrase translation extraction from alignment models. In: Proc. of the 41st Annual Meeting of ACL, July 2003, pp. 319–326 (2003)
16. Veronis, J., Langlais, P.: Evaluation of parallel text alignment systems: he ARCADE project. In: Veronis, J. (ed.) 'Parallel Text Processing", Text, Speech and Language Technology Series. Speech and Language Technology Series, vol. 13, pp. 369–388. Kluwer Academic Publishers, Dordrecht (2001)
17. Yamamoto, M., Church, K.: Using suffix arrays to compute term frequency and document frequency for all sub-strings in a corpus. Computational Linguistics 27(1), 1–30 (2001)

Classifying Documents According to Locational Relevance*

Ivo Anastácio, Bruno Martins, and Pável Calado

Instituto Superior Técnico, INESC-ID,
Av. Professor Cavaco Silva, 2744-016 Porto Salvo, Portugal
{ivo.anastacio,bruno.g.martins,pavel.calado}@ist.utl.pt

Abstract. This paper presents an approach for categorizing documents according to their implicit locational relevance. We report a thorough evaluation of several classifiers designed for this task, built by using support vector machines with multiple alternatives for feature vectors. Experimental results show that using feature vectors that combine document terms and URL n-grams, with simple features related to the locality of the document (e.g. total count of place references) leads to high accuracy values. The paper also discusses how the proposed categorization approach can be used to help improve tasks such as document retrieval or online contextual advertisement.

Keywords: Document Classification, Geographic Text Mining.

1 Introduction

Automated document classification is a well studied problem, with many applications in text mining and information retrieval [11]. A recent trend in text mining applications relates to extracting geographic context information from documents. It has been noted that the combination of techniques from text mining and geographic information systems can provide the means to integrate geographic data and services, such as topographic maps and street directories, with the implicit geographic information available in Web documents [2,6,9].

In this work, we propose that textual documents can be characterized according to their implicit *locational relevance*. For example, a document on the subject of computer programing can be considered *global*, as it is likely to be of interest to a geographically broad audience. In contrast, a document listing pharmacies or take-away restaurants in a specific city can be regarded as a *local*, i.e., likely to be of interest only to an audience in a relatively narrow region. Somewhere in between is a document describing touristic attractions in a specific city, likely to be of interest to both the inhabitants of that city and to potential visitors from other parts of the world. In the context of this work, locational relevance is, therefore, a score that reflects the probability of a given document being either

* This work was partially supported by the FCT (Portugal), through project grant PTDC/EIA/73614/2006 (GREASE-II).

L. Seabra Lopes et al. (Eds.): EPIA 2009, LNAI 5816, pp. 598–609, 2009.

global (i.e., users interested in the document are likely to have broad geographic interests) or local (i.e., users interested in the document are likely to have a single narrow geographic interest). This score can be produced from the confidence estimates assigned by a binary classifier such as a Support Vector Machine [12].

Previous research has addressed the problem of automatically computing geographic scopes of Web documents [1,2]. Techniques have also been proposed for detecting locationaly relevant search engine queries [3,4]. However, to the best of our knowledge, no description has ever been published on techniques for classifying documents according to locational relevance (i.e., classifying documents as either local or global). This is a significantly different problem from that of assigning documents to geographic scopes, since two documents can have the same scope but different locational relevances. For instance, the Web page of a research group in Lisbon and the Web page of a local restaurant in Lisbon have the same geographic scope, nonetheless, people visiting the restaurant's page are most probably taking into consideration the location, while people visiting the researcher's page are most probably interested in their studies, regardless from where the group is physically located.

To solve this problem, we propose an approach for categorizing documents according to their implicit locational relevance, using state-of-the-art machine learning techniques. We report a thorough evaluation of several classifiers, built using support vector machines, and explore many alternative features for representing documents. In addition, we also discuss how our classifier can be used to help improve tasks such as document retrieval or online advertisement.

The rest of the paper is organized as follows: Section 2 presents related work. Section 3 describes our classification approach, detailing the proposed features. Section 4 presents and discusses the experimental validation, also describing applications for locational relevance classifiers. Finally, Section 5 presents our conclusions and directions for future work.

2 Related Work

Traditional Information Retrieval and Machine Learning research has studied how to classify documents according to predefined categories [10,11]. The subarea of Geographic Information Retrieval has addressed issues related to the exploitation of geographic context information mined from textual documents. In this section, we survey relevant past research on these topics.

2.1 Document Classification

Document classification is the task of assigning documents to topic classes, on the basis of whether or not they share some features. This is one of the main problems studied in fields such as text mining, information retrieval, or machine learning, with many approaches described in the literature [10,11]. Some methods suitable for learning document classifiers include decision trees [14], logistic regression [15] and support vector machines [7,12]. SVMs can be considered a state-of-the-art method in binary classification, returning a confidence score in the assigned class.

Previous works have also suggested that in text domains, due to the high-dimensionality of the feature space, effective feature selection can be used to make the learning task more efficient and accurate. Empirical comparisons of different feature selection methods have been made in the past [13,16], with the results suggesting that either Chi-square or information gain statistics can provide good results. In this work, we use feature selection methods in order to examine the most discriminative features.

2.2 Mining Geographical Information from Text Documents

Previous research in the area of geographic information retrieval has addressed problems such as the recognition and disambiguation of place references present in text, and the assignment of documents to encompassing geographic scopes.

Leidner presented a variety of approaches for handling place references on textual documents [9]. The problem is usually seen as an extension of the named entity recognition (NER) task, as proposed by the natural language processing community [17,18]. More than recognizing mentions to places in text, which is the subject of NER, the task also requires for the place references to be disambiguated into the corresponding locations on the surface of the Earth, i.e., assigning geospatial coordinates to the place references [9]. Place reference disambiguation usually relies on gazetteer matching, together with heuristics such as default senses (i.e., disambiguation should be made to the most important referent, based on population counts) or spatial minimality (i.e., disambiguation should minimize the convex hull that contains all candidate referents) [9,19]. Metacarta[1] is a commercial company that sells state-of-the-art geographic information retrieval technology. The company also provides a freely-available *geotagger* Web service that can be used to recognize and disambiguate place references in text. An early version of the Metacarta *geotagger* has been described by Rauch et al. [20]. Yahoo! Placemaker[2] is another free Web service which provides recognition and disambiguation of place references in text. The complementar Yahoo! GeoPlanet[3] Web service is an example of an online gazetteer, returning descriptions of places based on their name.

Anastácio et al. surveyed different approaches for assigning documents to geographic scopes [28]. In one of the pioneering works in the area of geographic information retrieval, Woodruff and Plaunt proposed a technique with basis on the place references discovered in the text [6]. Their method was based on disambiguating the place references into the bounding polygons that correspond to the geographic area of the referents. The geographic scope of the document is afterward computed by overlapping the areas of all the polygons. More recently, Ding et al. proposed specific techniques for extracting the geographical scope of web pages [1]. For example, the *Diário de Coimbra* online newspaper has a geographical scope

[1] `http://ondemand.metacarta.com`
[2] `http://developer.yahoo.com/geo/placemaker`
[3] `http://developer.yahoo.com/geo/geoplanet`

that consists of the city of Coimbra, while the *Publico* newspaper has a geographical scope that includes the entire territory of Portugal. To compute the geographical scope of a web document, Ding et al. propose two complementary strategies: (1) a technique based on the geographical distribution of HTML links to the page, and (2) a technique based on the distribution of geographical references in the text of the page. Amitay et al. also proposed a technique for assigning Web documents to the corresponding geographic scope [2], leveraging on *part-of* relations among the recognized place references (i.e. *Lisbon* and *Porto* are both part of *Portugal*, and documents referring to both these places should have *Portugal* as the scope). Looping over the disambiguated references, this approach aggregates, for each document, the importance of the various levels in a location hierarchy. The hierarchy levels are then sorted by importance and results above a given threshold are returned as the geographic scope.

Gravano et al. proposed a technique for classifying search engine queries as either local or global, using the distributional characteristics of location names occurring in the results produced by a search engine to the query [3]. There are many similarities between the work by Gravano et al. and the proposal of this paper, but here we are instead concerned with classifying documents as global or local, instead of classifying user queries.

3 Classifying Documents According to Locational Relevance

Assigning documents to global and local classes, according to their implicit locational relevance, is a hard document classification problem. Instead of just applying a standard classification approach, based on a bag-of-words representation of the documents, we argue that specific geographic features are also well suited to reflect the locational characteristics of the documents.

Global documents often do not include any mentions to place names. Consider the home page of the Weka software package[4]. Users reading this document are probably looking for tutorials about machine learning, and they are not restricted in their interests to a specific geographic scope. Nevertheless, it is interesting to note that global documents can sometimes include mentions to place names. Consider a document describing a review of U2's latest concert in Lisbon. The location name is clearly distinguishable in the document, but the readers may have completely different geographic interests.

Local documents are, on the other hand, more likely to contain mentions to place names, particularly place names associated to small regions. Local documents are also more likely to contain references to places that are restricted to a somewhat confined area, whereas global documents can contain place references to distinct places around the world. Examples of local documents include local business listings or descriptions of local events.

[4] `http://www.cs.waikato.ac.nz/ml/weka`

3.1 Classification Features

The feature vectors used in the proposed classification scheme combine information directly extracted from the full text of the documents, or from the document URL, with higher level geographic information, mined from the documents using techniques from the area of geographic information retrieval. We group the considered features in four classes, namely (1) textual features, (2) URL features, (3) simple locative features, and (4) high level locative features. Textual and URL features are directly extracted from either the text or the URL for the document, whereas the remaining require geographic text mining.

In the case of the textual features, the idea was to capture the thematic aspects, encoded in the document's terminology, that can influence the decision of assigning a document to either a global or local class. For instance documents about restaurants or pharmacies are more likely to be local than documents about programming languages or music downloads.

The Yahoo! Term Extraction[5] Web service, a state-of-the-art industrial tool for key term extraction, was used to discover important words in the documents. Its implementation is available via an open Web service, which takes a text document as input and returns a list of significant words or phrases extracted from the document.

The full set of textual features is shown below:

– Word stems occurring in the lowercased document text, weighted according to the term frequency vs. inverse document frequency scheme (TF/IDF). Stopwords were removed according to the list provided by the Weka package.
– Lowercased words selected by the Yahoo! Term Extraction service as the most important in the document, weighted through the TF/IDF scheme.

When classifying Web documents, another source of information that can be used for classification is their Uniform Resource Locator (URL). Previous research has shown that classifiers built from features based solely on document URLs can achieve surprisingly good results on tasks such as language identification [24] or topic attribution [23]. Intuitively, URLs contain information that can be used to discriminate between local and global pages, such as top level domains or words such as *local* or *regional*. For instance, a document whose URL has a top level domain `.uk` is more likely to be local than a document with a top level domain such as `.com`. Taking inspiration on the experiments reported by Baykan et al. [23], the following features were considered:

– Character n-grams, with n varying between 4 and 8, extracted from the lower-cased document URLs and weighted according to the TF/IDF scheme.

Simple locative features essentially correspond to counts for locations recognized in the documents, through the use of the geographic text mining services provided by Yahoo!. The Placemaker text mining service provides functionalities

[5] `http://developer.yahoo.com/search/content`

for recognizing and disambiguating place references in text, returning the latitude and longitude coordinates for each place recognized. Using the GeoPlanet gazetteer service, we can expand the information returned by Placemaker with elements such as the county, state, country, continent and bounding polygon corresponding to each of the recognized place references. The combined functionalities of these two services allow us to experiment with a wide variety of locative document features.

It is important to notice that using the Yahoo! Placemaker for recognizing the place references over text has some advantages compared to the usage of a simpler dictionary-based approach. Since Placemaker uses natural language contextual clues, it helps to disambiguate whether a word like *reading* refers to the location in England or to the verb sense of *to read.* Placemaker's *geotagger* also covers many colloquial place names (e.g. *nyc* for *New York City*), as well as interest points (e.g. *Eiffel Tower*) that may appear in the text.

Having locations referenced in the document can indicate a tendency towards a higher locality, particularly if these locations are all related to a single relatively narrow region. On the other hand, having no locations whatsoever, or having many locations from different parts of the World, can indicate that the document has a global scope. We combine the location counts in various ways, aggregating the places according to containment relationships in order to group together the information for places in the same administrative divisions. We count the frequency of place references at different levels of detail (i.e., continent, country, state, city), as well as the aggregate total for all different unambiguous place references. The complete set of considered features is as follows:

- Total number of locations referenced in the text.
- Total number of unique locations referenced in the text.
- Number of unique locations, grouped by city, county, state, country and continent.
- Number of locations, grouped by city, county, state, country and continent.
- Number of unique locations, grouped by city, county, state, country and continent, considering the aggregated sub-locations that are hierarchically below (i.e., the number of counties includes the number of cities referenced in the text, the number of states includes the number of counties plus the number of cities, and so on).
- Total number of locations, grouped by city, county, state, country and continent, considering the aggregated sub-locations that are hierarchically below.

High level locative features correspond to the encompassing geographic areas computed with basis on the place references that were recognized in the text. The idea is that documents having broad geographic areas are more likely to correspond to global pages. Yu and Cai presented similar ideas for measuring the importance of geographic references in search engine queries [26]. The considered features are as follows:

- Area for the geospatial region corresponding to the geographic scope of the document, computed with the method proposed by Amitay et al. in the context of the Web-a-Where system [2].

- Area for the geospatial region corresponding to the geographic scope of the document, computed with the method proposed by Woodruff and Plaunt in the context of the GIPSY system [6].
- Area for the geospatial region that covers all the place references extracted from the document.
- Confidence score assigned by the Web-a-Where algorithm to the geographic scope that was computed for the document.
- Confidence score assigned by the GIPSY algorithm to the geographic scope that was computed for the document.

As stated in the description of the high level locative features, we implemented the scope assignment approaches proposed by Amitay et al. and by Woodruff and Plaunt [2,6]. The required geospatial computations were implemented through the use of the Java Topology Suite, an API of 2D spatial functions that supports the computation of area aggregates and intersections [8].

3.2 The Classification Method

In this work, we use Support Vector Machines (SVMs) for document classification. SVMs have been found quite effective for this task, which is characterized by having a high dimensionality in terms of the feature vectors [12]. SVM classifiers conceptually convert the original measurements of the features in the data to points in a higher-dimensional space that facilitates the separation between two classes. While the transformation between the original and the high-dimensional space may be complex, they need not to be carried out explicitly. Instead, it is sufficient to calculate a kernel function that only involves dot products between the data points, transformed from the original feature space. Commonly used functions include linear or Gaussian (radial basis) kernels, with the latter being recommended for document classification problems [12]. Determining the optimal classifier is equivalent to determining the hyper-plane that maximizes the total distance between itself and representative transformed data points (i.e., the support vectors). In our experiments, we used the Weka SVM implementation [5] with a Gaussian kernel function.

4 Experimental Evaluation

To evaluate our proposal, a large set of experiments was performed. This section describes the reference datasets, the metrics, the experimental settings, and the obtained results.

4.1 Document Collections

We used two different sets of documents containing both local and global examples. These document collections were:

- **Topix news articles collection:** We crawled a set of 100 news articles from the Topix website[6], which includes many regional news. Each document was then manually classified using the location relevance criteria that was previously introduced, resulting in a collection containing 50 local documents and 50 global documents.
- **ODP Web pages collection:** We experimented with a collection of 8000 Web pages containing at least one geographic reference, 4000 classified as *local* and 4000 classified as *global*, randomly crawled from the Open Directory Project[7] (ODP). Pages under small locations in the "Regional" portion of the directory were regarded as local (i.e., US cities and US states), while pages outside the "Regional" category or under a large region (i.e., USA) were regarded as global.

4.2 Evaluation Metrics

We considered standard information retrieval evaluation metrics to assess the performance of the various classifier configurations. Thus, precision and recall, were computed for both the local and global document classes. Precision (P) is the ratio of the number of items correctly assigned to the class divided by the total number of items assigned to the class. Recall (R) is the ratio of the number of items correctly assigned to a class as compared with the total number of items in the class. Since precision can be increased at the expense of recall, we also compute the F1 measure, which combines precision and recall into a single number using the formula $F1 = 2PR/(P + R)$.

Given the binary nature of our classification problem, we also measured results in terms of accuracy and error. Accuracy is the proportion of correct results (both true positives and true negatives) given by the classifier. Error, on the other hand, measures the proportion of instances incorrectly classified, considering false positives plus false negatives.

4.3 Results and Discussion

For both the news and the ODP document collections, we trained SVM classifiers using different combinations of the proposed features. For each case, a 10-fold cross validation was performed. The considered feature combination experiments are presented in Table 1. Tables 2 and 3 overview the results.

By looking at the results, we can see that, in both collections, the textual features, as well as the locative features, are by themselves able to provide relatively high accuracies. Nonetheless, by combining them we can improve the accuracy by more than 8% on the ODP collection and 3% on the Topix collection. High level locative features had worse results than we had anticipated. We think this might be related with a relatively poor effectiveness of both Web-a-Where and GIPSY in detecting the correct geographic scope. In a seperate study we showed that

[6] `http://www.topix.com`
[7] `http://www.dmoz.org`

Table 1. The feature combinations considered in our experimental setup

TW	Word stems derived from the entire document.
TK	Word stems generated from the key words.
TWK	Combination of the features from cases TW and TK.
U	URL n-grams.
LS	Simple locative features.
LH	High level locative features.
LSH	All the locative features.
T+L	The best textual feature, plus the best locative feature.
T+L+U	The best textual and locative features, plus the URL n-grams.

Table 2. Results obtained for the classification algorithm, over the ODP collection

	Precision		Recall		F-Measure			
Experiment	Local	Global	Local	Global	Local	Global	Error	Accuracy
TW	0.81	0.79	0.79	0.81	0.8	0.8	19.86	80.14
TK	0.74	0.74	0.74	0.74	0.74	0.74	25.86	74.14
TWK	0.82	0.8	0.8	0.82	0.81	0.81	19.09	80.92
U	0.66	0.69	0.72	0.63	0.69	0.66	32.47	67.53
LS	0.78	0.86	0.88	0.74	0.82	0.8	18.85	81.15
LH	0.56	0.69	0.87	0.3	0.68	0.42	41.31	58.69
LSH	0.58	0.82	0.93	0.31	0.71	0.45	37.58	62.42
T+L	0.89	0.91	0.91	0.88	0.9	0.89	10.43	89.57
T+L+U	0.89	0.91	0.91	0.89	0.9	0.9	10.15	**89.85**

Table 3. Results obtained for the classification algorithm, over the Topix collection

	Precision		Recall		F-Measure			
Experiment	Local	Global	Local	Global	Local	Global	Error	Accuracy
TW	0.53	1	1	0.1	0.69	0.18	45	55
TK	0.71	0.61	0.48	0.8	0.57	0.69	36	64
TWK	0.54	1	1	0.16	0.7	0.28	42	58
U	0.45	0.39	0.6	0.26	0.51	0.31	57	43
LS	0.63	0.6	0.54	0.68	0.58	0.64	39	61
LH	0.54	0.51	0.24	0.8	0.33	0.62	48	52
LSH	0.67	0.62	0.56	0.72	0.61	0.67	36	64
T+L	0.71	0.64	0.58	0.76	0.64	0.7	33	**67**
T+L+U	0.54	0.65	0.86	0.26	0.66	0.37	44	56

Web-a-Where and GIPSY assign documents to the correct scopes approximately 50% and 21% of the times, respectively [28].

Using the URL n-grams slightly improves the ODP results. The same did not happen with Topix, but it is understandable, since an information gain analysis of the features showed us that the most significative n-grams were the top level domains like *.gov* and *.us*, which are hardly found in the Topix news.

An information gain analysis of the features used in the classifiers also showed that the simple locative features are the most important, specially the ones that consider the aggregated count of sub-locations. Regarding the textual features, the same analysis pointed words like *hotel*, *restaurant*, *park*, or *hike*, as highly discriminative.

Although not exploited in this work, we believe that the proposed document classification scheme can be used to improve the quality of the results in tasks such as document retrieval or online contextual advertisement. For document retrieval applications, the locality classification can be pre-computed off-line, since it is query-independent. At query time, given that we can also classify queries as either local or global (for instance using the technique proposed by Gravano et al. [3]), we can re-rank the results so that more global or local documents are ranked higher in the results list shown to the user. The paper by Gravano et al. already provided a thorough discussion on similar ideas. For contextual advertisement, at run-time, we can attempt to localize the advertisements to either the geographical area discussed in the document (particularly interesting to pages where we have a high confidence in that they are local), or to the area of the user that is accessing the document, estimated for instance through the user's IP address (more interesting for less local pages, or for global pages).

In the context of Geographic Information Retrieval, Cai extended the vector space model in order to seperately consider a thematic similarity and a geographic similarity [27]. The confidence score produced by our SVM classifier might be a valid option for weighting these similarities in an overall formula.

5 Conclusions and Future Work

This paper presented a locational relevance categorization scheme for textual documents. We discussed how documents can be represented through features based on textual terms, URL n-grams and place references, extracted through text mining, for the purposes of determining their locational relevance. Using these features, a Support Vector Machine classifier for automatically determining the locational relevance was tested. Empirical results indicate that, for many documents, locational relevance can be determined effectively. We also compared different combinations of features to determine their impact on classification effectiveness. Results showed that using feature vectors that combine weighted text terms with features related to the locality of the document (e.g. place names extracted through text mining) results in increased performance.

Several challenges remain for future work. Assuming three document classes (i.e., global G, local L, and somewhat local SL), instead of our binary classification, we could design up to four separate classification tasks, depending on application needs: (1) to discriminate between classes L,SL and G; (2) to discriminate between classes L and SL,G; (3) to discriminate between classes L and G, ignoring the SL classes; (4) to simultaneously discriminate between all the three classes. This may help in dealing with the difficult classification cases.

We also plan to experiment with additional features in the classifier. In the context of search engine queries, Jones et al. studied the relationship between the non-location part of an explicit geographic query and the distance of the query's location part from the issuer's IP location [25]. They found that geographic queries have a varied distance distribution and, therefore, different localization capabilities. In the context of Web documents, we can also use the distance or the area of overlap between the area corresponding to the Internet address of the server hosting the document and the geographic scope of the document, as an additional feature for classifying documents as either *local* or *global*.

Moreover, some of the characteristics that make a document either local or global may not be directly observable in the document itself, but rather in other contextual information related to the document. Previous research on Web document classification has shown that better performance can be achieved trough combinations of content-based features with additional features derived from the neighboring documents in the link structure of the web graph [21,22]. Previous experiments dealing with geographic context information have already accounted with similar ideas, as for instance Gravano et al. [3], in classifying search engine queries as either local or global, used a sample of the search results returned for a given query rather than the words of the query itself. For assigning geographic scopes to Web documents, Ding et. al proposed to use the distributional characteristics of the locations associated with HTML in-links [1]. It would be interesting to integrate, into our feature vectors, information about the distributional characteristics of locations in related documents, having this notion of relatedness coming from either textual similarity or from linkage information. Our currently ongoing work is addressing these ideas, aiming at the application of locational relevance classifiers in geographical IR and contextual advertising.

References

1. Ding, J., Gravano, L., Shivakumar, N.: Computing Geographical Scopes of Web Resources. In: Proceedings of the 26th international Conference on Very Large Data Bases, pp. 545–556 (2000)
2. Amitay, E., Har'El, N., Sivan, R., Soffer, A.: Web-a-where: geotagging web content. In: Proceedings of the 27th international ACM SIGIR Conference on Research and Development in information Retrieval, pp. 273–280 (2004)
3. Gravano, L., Hatzivassiloglou, V., Lichtenstein, R.: Categorizing web queries according to geographical locality. In: Proceedings of the 12th international Conference on information and Knowledge Management, pp. 325–333 (2003)
4. Zhuang, Z., Brunk, C., Giles, C.L.: Modeling and visualizing geo-sensitive queries based on user clicks. In: Proceedings of the 1st international Workshop on Location and the Web, pp. 73–76 (2008)
5. Witten, I.H., Frank, E.: Data Mining: Practical Machine Learning Tools and Techniques with Java Implementations. Morgan Kaufmann, San Francisco (2000)
6. Woodruff, A.G., Plaunt, C.: GIPSY: Automated geographic indexing of text documents. Journal of the American Society for Information Science 45(9), 645–655 (1994)
7. Cristianini, N., Shawe-Taylor, J.: An Introduction to Support Vector Machines and other kernel-based learning methods. Cambridge University Press, Cambridge (2000)
8. Johansson, M., Harrie, L.: Using Java Topology Suite for real-time data generalisation and integration. In: Proceedings of the 2002 workshop of the International Society for Photogrammetry and Remote Sensing (2002)
9. Leidner, J.L.: Toponym Resolution: a Comparison and Taxonomy of Heuristics and Methods. PhD Thesis, University of Edinburgh (2007)

10. Yang, Y.: An Evaluation of Statistical Approaches to Text Categorization. Information Retrieval 1(1-2), 69–90 (1999)
11. Sebastiani, F.: Machine learning in automated text categorization. ACM Computer Surveys 34(1), 1–47 (2002)
12. Joachims, T.: Text Categorization with Suport Vector Machines: Learning with Many Relevant Features. In: Proceedings of the 10th European Conference on Machine Learning, pp. 137–142 (1998)
13. Forman, G.: An extensive empirical study of feature selection metrics for text classification. Journal of Machine Learning Research 3, 1289–1305 (2003)
14. Apté, C., Damerau, F., Weiss, S.M.: Automated learning of decision rules for text categorization. ACM Transactions on Information Systems 12(3), 233–251 (1994)
15. Genkin, A., Lewis, D.D., Madigan, D.: Large-Scale Bayesian Logistic Regression for Text Categorization. Rutgers University Technical Report (2004)
16. Dasgupta, A., Drineas, P., Harb, B., Josifovski, V., Mahoney, M.W.: Feature selection methods for text classification. In: Proceedings of the 13th ACM SIGKDD Conference on Knowledge Discovery and Data Mining, pp. 230–239 (2007)
17. Sang, E.T.K., De Meulder, F.: Introduction to the CoNLL-2003 shared task: Language-Independent Named Entity Recognition. In: Proceedings of the 7th Conference on Natural Language Learning, pp. 142–147 (2003)
18. Kornai, A.: Proceedings of the HLT-NAACL 2003 workshop on the analysis of geographic references (2003)
19. Garbin, E., Mani, I.: Disambiguating toponyms in news. In: Proceedings of the Conference on Human Language Technology and Empirical Methods in Natural Language Processing, pp. 363–370 (2005)
20. Rauch, E., Bukatin, M., Baker, K.: A confidence-based framework for disambiguating geographic terms. In: Proceedings of the HLT-NAACL 2003 Workshop on Analysis of Geographic References, pp. 50–54 (2003)
21. Chakrabarti, S., Dom, B., Indyk, P.: Enhanced hypertext categorization using hyperlinks. In: Proceedings of the 1998 ACM SIGMOD international Conference on Management of Data, pp. 307–318 (1998)
22. Qi, X., Davison, B.D.: Knowing a web page by the company it keeps. In: Proceedings of the 15th ACM international Conference on information and Knowledge Management, pp. 228–237 (2006)
23. Baykan, E., Henzinger, M., Marian, L., Weber, I.: Purely URL-based Topic Classification. In: Proceedings of the 18th international World Wide Web Conference, Alternate Track Papers and Posters, p. 1109 (2009)
24. Baykan, E., Henzinger, M., Weber, I.: Web page language identification based on URLs. Proceedings of the VLDB Endowment 1(1), 176–187 (2008)
25. Jones, R., Zhang, W.V., Rey, B., Jhala, P., Stipp, E.: Geographic intention and modification in web search. International Journal of Geographical Information Science 22(3), 229–246 (2009)
26. Yu, B., Cai, G.: A query-aware document ranking method for geographic information retrieval. In: Proceedings of the 4th ACM workshop on Geographical information retrieval, pp. 49–54 (2007)
27. Cai, G.: GeoVSM: An Integrated Retrieval Model for Geographic Information. GIScience, 65–79 (2002)
28. Anastáio, I., Martins, B., Calado, P.: A Comparison of Different Approaches for Assigning Geographic Scopes to Documents. In: Proceedings of the 1st INForum - Simpósio de Informática (2009)

Relieving Polysemy Problem for Synonymy Detection

Gaël Dias and Rumen Moraliyski

University of Beira Interior, Covilhã 6201-001, Portugal
ddg@di.ubi.pt, rumen@hultig.di.ubi.pt

Abstract. In order to automatically identify noun synonyms, we propose a new idea which opposes classical polysemous representations of words to monosemous representations based on the "*one sense per discourse*" hypothesis. For that purpose, we apply the attributional similarity paradigm on two levels: corpus and document. We evaluate our methodology on well-known standard multiple choice synonymy question tests and evidence that it steadily outperforms the baseline.

1 Introduction

Identifying and extracting synonyms is a crucial issue for NLP systems. Indeed, synonyms are widely used, even in narrow domains, to refer to the same concept thus avoiding repetition.

Discovering close synonyms is a difficult task. Some methods detect broad range of semantic relatedness including but not limited to synonymy such as in [1]. Other methods make use of syntactic contexts which tighten the set of detected relations but they tend to correctly solve less polysemous cases as shown in [2]. Due to the fact that only about 25% of the words are polysemous, this kind of methods solve the problem for the most part of the vocabulary. Nevertheless, most frequent words are usually highly polysemous and represent a large proportion of the texts [3]. As a consequence, there is a critical need for methods capable of separating the different meanings of a polysemous word in distinct representations.

In this paper, we propose a methodology to measure syntactic oriented attributional similarity based on the "*one sense per discourse*" hypothesis [4]. Instead of relying exclusively on corpus distributions, we build noun representations and compare them within document limits. This paper presents extended evaluation and analysis of our previous work [5].

In order to test this assumption, we implement the vector space model based on the cosine similarity measure over Term Frequency weighted by Inverse Document Frequency, Pointwise Mutual Information [6] and Conditional Probability [7]. We also implement two probabilistic similarity measures: the Ehlert model [8] and the Lin model [9]. Finally, we evaluate our methodology on a *noun subset* of well-known standard multiple choice synonymy question tests and evidence that it steadily outperforms the baseline.

2 Related Work

Most related research works use multiple choice synonymy questions for evaluation. Each question consists of five words: the target word and four response words, one of

L. Seabra Lopes et al. (Eds.): EPIA 2009, LNAI 5816, pp. 610–621, 2009.

which is the correct answer and the other ones are called decoys. In this context, the problem aims at defining a function that highlights the best synonym candidate.

One of the most famous works is proposed in [1] where document distribution is used to measure word similarity. They show that the accuracy of Latent Semantic Analysis (LSA) is statistically indistinguishable from that of a population of non-native English speakers on the same questions.

More recent works have focused on the window based vector space model (VSM). A context vector built on co-occurrence basis within the entire corpus is associated to each word from the multiple choice test. For instance, in [6], a variety of similarity metrics and weighting schemes of contexts are studied and their DR-PMI achieves a statistical tie compared to the PMI-IR proposed by [10].

The PMI-IR is one of the first works to propose a hybrid approach to deal with synonym detection. Indeed, it uses a combination of evidences such as the Pointwise Mutual Information (PMI) and Information Retrieval (IR) features like the "NEAR" and "NOT" operators of a search engine to measure similarity between pairs of words. At this point, it is important to notice that this work does not follow the attributional similarity paradigm but rather proposes a heuristic to measure semantic distances. Later, [11] refined the PMI-IR algorithm and proposed a module combination to include new features such as LSA and thesaurus evidences. However, the introduction of thesaurus features biases radically the test of synonym detection.

In parallel, some works have used linguistic resources to measure similarity. Results for a number of relatively sophisticated thesaurus-based methods which look at path lengths between words in the heading classifications of Roget's Thesaurus are given in [12]. However, this methodology does not follow the attributional similarity paradigm.

In the syntactic attributional similarity paradigm, word context vectors associated to all target words of the test are indexed by the words they co-occur with within a given corpus for a given syntactic relation. For example, *(good, adjective)* and *(have, direct-obj)* are attributes of the noun "*idea*" as illustrated in [13]. Unfortunately, to our knowledge, unlike window based approaches, syntactic based methodologies have not been evaluated against synonymy test. Rather, they have been used to build linguistic resources.

All the systems reviewed so far share the difficulty to deal with the polysemous words since they merge all the senses of a word in a single statistical representation. The importance of sense information for the purpose of semantic relation discovery is illustrated by the attempt of [14] at word sense induction (WSI). For a word w he looks for pairs of strongly associated to w words such that their context vectors sum up to the one of w and at the same time are as different as possible. This pair of words and their context vectors describe two distinct senses of w. Thus on the TOEFL task vectors pertaining to specific senses are compared and the method achieves 92.5% accuracy.

In order to summarize the most significant works proposed so far, in Table 1 we present the different results over the TOEFL question set.

3 Attributional Similarity

Theoretically, an attributional similarity measure can be defined as follows. Suppose that $X_i = (X_{i1}, X_{i2}, X_{i3}, \ldots, X_{ip})$ is a row vector of observations on p variables

Table 1. Accuracy on TOEFL question set

Work	Best result
Landauer and Dumais 1997	64.40%
Sahlgren 2001	72.00%
Turney 2001	73.75%
Jarmasz and Szpakowicz 2003	78.75%
Terra and Clarke 2003	81.25%
Elhert 2003	82.00%
Freitag et al. 2005	84.20%
Rapp 2003	92.5%
Turney et al. 2003	97.50%

(or attributes) associated with a label i, the similarity between two units i and j is defined as $S_{ij} = f(X_i, X_j)$ where f is some function of the observed values. In our context, we must evaluate the similarity between two nouns which are represented by their respective word context vectors.

For our purpose, the attributional representation of a noun consists of tuples $\langle v, r\rangle$ where r is an object or subject relation and v is a given verb appearing within this relation with the target noun. For example, if the noun "*brass*" appears with the verb "*cast*" within a object relation, we will have the following triple ⟨*brass, cast, object*⟩ and the tuple ⟨*cast, object*⟩ will be an attribute of the word context[1] vector associated to the noun "*brass*".

As similarity measures are based on real-value attributes, our task is two-fold. First, we must define a function which will evaluate the importance of a given attribute $\langle v,\ r\rangle$ for a given noun. Our second goal is to find the appropriate function f that will accurately evaluate the similarity between two verb context vectors.

3.1 Weighting Attributes

In order to construct more precise representations of word meanings, numerous weighting schemas have been proposed. In this section, we will point at the most common ones although many others could be used.

Word Frequency and IDF. The simplest form of the vector space model treats a noun n as a vector which attribute values are the number of occurrences of each tuple $\langle v, r\rangle$ associated to n i.e. $tf(n, \langle v, r\rangle)$. However, the usual form of the vector space model introduces the inverse document frequency defined in the context of syntactic attribute similarity paradigm in Equation 1 where n is the target noun, $\langle v, r\rangle$ a given attribute, N is the set of all the nouns and $|.|$ the cardinal function.

$$tf.idf(n,\langle v,r\rangle)=tf(n,\langle v,r\rangle)\times\log_2\frac{|N|}{|\{n_i\in N|\exists(n_i,v,r)\}|} \quad (1)$$

[1] From now on, we will talk about verb context vectors instead of word context vectors.

Pointwise Mutual Information. The value of each attribute $\langle v, r\rangle$ can also be seen as a measure of association with the noun being characterized. For that purpose, [6,10] have proposed to use the Pointwise Mutual Information (PMI) as defined in Equation 2 where n is the target noun and $\langle v, r\rangle$ a given attribute.

$$PMI(\langle n|r\rangle,\langle v|r\rangle)=\log_2 \frac{P(n,v|r)}{P(n|r)P(v|r)} \quad (2)$$

Conditional Probability. Another way to look at the relation between a noun n and a tuple $\langle v, r\rangle$ is to estimate their conditional probability of co-occurrence as in Equation 3. In our case, we are interested in knowing how strongly a given attribute $\langle v, r\rangle$ may evoke the noun n.

$$P(n|v,r)=\frac{P(n,v,r)}{P(v,r)} \quad (3)$$

3.2 Similarity Measures

There exist many similarity measures in the context of the attributional similarity paradigm [7]. They can be divided into two main groups: (1) metrics in a multi-dimensional space also called vector space model, (2) measures which calculate the correlations between probability distributions.

Vector Space Model. To quantify similarity between two words, the Cosine similarity measure is usually applied and estimates to what extent two vectors point along the same direction. It is defined in Equation 4.

$$cos(n_1,n_2)=\frac{\sum_{k=1}^{p} n_{1k}n_{2k}}{\sqrt{\sum_{k=1}^{p} n_{1k}^2}\sqrt{\sum_{k=1}^{p} n_{2k}^2}} \quad (4)$$

Probabilistic Models. Probabilistic measures can be applied to evaluate the similarity between words when they are represented by a probabilistic distribution. In this paper, we present two different measures i.e. the Ehlert and the Lin models.

Ehlert model: Equation5 proposed in [8] evaluates the probability to interchange two word context vectors (i.e. what is the probability that the first word is changed for the second one).

$$Ehl(n_1|n_2)=\sum_{\langle v,r\rangle\in A} \frac{P(n_1|v,r)P(n_2|v,r)P(v,r)}{P(n_2)} \quad (5)$$

with $A=\{\langle v,r\rangle|\exists(n_1,v,r)\wedge\langle v,r\rangle|\exists(n_2,v,r)\}$.

Lin model: [9] defines similarity as the ratio between the amount of information needed to state the commonality of two words and the total information available about them and is defined in Equation 6.

$$Lin(n_1,n_2)= \frac{2\times\sum_{\langle v,r\rangle\in A}\log_2 P(v,r)}{\sum_{\langle v,r\rangle\in B}\log_2 P(v,r)+\sum_{\langle v,r\rangle\in C}\log_2 P(v,r)} \quad (6)$$

with

$A=\{\langle v,r\rangle|\exists(n_1,v,r)\wedge\langle v,r\rangle|\exists(n_2,v,r)\}$,

$B=\{\langle v,r\rangle|\exists(n_1,v,r)\}$,

$C=\{\langle v,r\rangle|\exists(n_2,v,r)\}$.

3.3 Global and Local Attributional Similarity

The approaches reviewed earlier which build context attributional representations of words do so from a corpus as one huge text and do not respect the document limits. We call *Global similarities* ($Gsim$), the similarity estimations obtained in this manner.

However, this approach poses many problems for polysemous nouns as contexts which are pertinent to different meanings are gathered into a single global representation when they should be differentiated. In this context, [2] attempt to introduce a measure of difficulty of tests based on polysemy. They automatically build a number of test cases by taking two words from a synset of WordNet [15] and three randomly other words for decoys. As a result, they find strong positive correlation between polysemy and error level. However, they do not take into account the decoys. They divide their tests with respect to the sum of polysemy of the target word and the correct answer and observe that the more polysemous the test is, the more difficult it is to be solved. The conclusion is that polysemy level is characteristic of the difficulty of the test.

According to [4] "*... if a polysemous word such as 'sentence' appears two or more times in a well-written discourse, it is extremely likely that they will all share the same sense*". From this assumption follows that if a word representation is built out of single discourse evidences it probably describes just one sense of the word. Hence if we obey document borders we can avoid mixing all word senses together.

On the other hand Turney [10] demonstrates that synonyms tend to co-occur in texts more often than by chance. On a similar supposition is grounded [1] which seek for synonyms among words that co-occur in the same set of documents.

Thus, our proposal to apply the "*one sense per discourse*" paradigm takes advantage of the fact that people do not tend to repeat words; yet they repeat ideas. As a consequence, we compare attributional representations of nouns only within document's limits. Apparently, statistics gathered from a unique short text may not be reliable. In order to obtain more stable results, we average attributional similarity values over the set of documents in which both nouns occur and introduce the $Lsim(.,.)$ function in Equation 7, where $sim(.,.)$ is any function from Section 3.2. We call this value *Local similarity* ($Lsim$).

$$Lsim(n_1,n_2)=\frac{\sum_{d\in D} sim(n_1,n_2)}{|D|} \quad (7)$$

As a result, nouns that co-occur in a document but with different meanings will rarely share contexts and will end with low similarity. On the other hand, nouns that co-occur as synonyms will share contexts with greater probability hence will receive higher similarity estimations.

Rapp [14] observed that when multiple first order associates taken as a vector are used as a sense descriptor only the most frequent sense of the word tends to be reflected. Therefor he uses as sense descriptors the context vectors of set of strong first order associate words and ensures they specify as narrow as possible senses. On the other hand Local similarity relies on association vector that is monosemous and directly related to the meaning described. It can be seen as extension to the method of Rapp as he found that the multidimensional descriptor is more stable with respect to sampling errors.

In this paper, we also propose that Global and Local approaches may have properties that complement each other. In order to take advantage of both heuristics, we propose the *Product similarity* ($Psim$) measure, a multiplicative combination of both Local and Global similarities as defined in Equation 8.

$$Psim(n_1,n_2)=Gsim(n_1,n_2)^{\alpha}\times Lsim(n_1,n_2)^{(1-\alpha)} \quad (8)$$

In fact, Equation 8 is a generalization of all similarity measures. When $\alpha = 0$ only the Local similarity is taken into account, while for $\alpha = 1$ only the Global similarity is applied. We will see in section 5 that the combination of both similarity measures provides improved results in particular situations.

4 Corpus

Any work based on the attributional similarity paradigm depends on the corpus used to determine the attributes and to calculate their values. [6] use a terabyte of web data that contains 53 billion words and 77 million documents, [16] - a 10 million words balanced corpus with a vocabulary of 94 thousand words and [2,8] - the 256 million words North American News Corpus (NANC). For our experiments, we used the Reuters Corpus Volume I (RCV1) [17]. However, our proposal needs co-occurrences of both synonym candidates to appear a few times each within a single document and we observed that substantial proportion of word pairs have zero occurrence in RCV1. As we did not want to reduce our test set, we decided to build a corpus suitable to the problem at hand.

To build the Web Corpus for Synonym Detection (WCSD), we used the Google API and queried the search engine with set of different pairs of words. For each test case, we built 4 queries i.e. the target word and one of the candidate-synonyms. Subsequently, we collected all of the seed results and followed a set of selected links to gather more textual information about the queried pairs. The overall collection of web pages was then shallow parsed using the MontyLingua software [18]. Thus, the WCSD consists of 500M words in 110K documents in which each sentence is a predicate structure. The benefit of thus gathered corpus is to maximize the ratio of the observed instances to the volume of the text processed.

5 Results and Discussion

To illustrate the results of our methodology, we use 145 noun test cases i.e. all 23 noun questions taken from the ESL (English as a Second Language) multiple choice test, all 19 noun cases from the TOEFL (Test of English as Foreign Language) [1]. We also add the subset of all 103 noun questions out of the 301 manually collected test cases provided by Peter Turney [11] and referred as RD (Reader's Digest). The success over synonymy tests does not guarantee success in real-world applications and the tests also show problematic issues as shown in [2]. However, the scores have an intuitive appeal, they are easily interpretable, and the expected performance of a random guesser (25%) and of a typical non-native speaker are both known (64.5%), thus making TOEFL-like tests a good basis for evaluation.

The Table 2 shows the differences in terms of accuracy obtained by comparing the RCV1 with the WCSD. As expected, the WCSD allows significant improvement in terms of accuracy. These results clearly show that the corpus used to compute the measures influences drastically the performance of any experiment and comparisons of different methodologies should always be made based on the same statistical evidences. As a consequence, the results given in Table 1 are only indicative as better or worse results may be obtained on different experimental frameworks.

In Table 2, we present the overall results of our experiments. All the models proposed in this paper were tested on set of 145 noun questions. The figures in the table show the accuracy level by test set and measure. The Cos TfIdf as a Local similarity evidences the overall best result with an accuracy of 74% and 108 correct answers. The table shows that the Local similarity approach improves over the Global similarity for all measures. In parallel, the worst results were obtained by the Lin model and the Cos Prob for the Global approach reaching 54%. However, those are the measures that benefit most from the introduction of the Local approach respectively improving by 14% (20 additional correct guesses) and 8% (12). This situation is in accord with the finding of [19] that the performance of Lin's distributional similarity score decreases more significantly than other measures for low frequency nouns [20]. Thus Global similarity fails to realize its advantage for the less polysemous yet less frequent cases and leaves more room for improvement by Local similarity.

In order to have a better understanding of the results, we applied the measures to all tests individually, i.e. RD, TOEFL and ESL. The results are shown in Table 3. The best results are obtained by (1) the Cos TfIdf as Local similarity with 69% for the RD

Table 2. Comparison between RCV1 and WCSD

	Global		Local		Product	
	RCV1	WCSD	RCV1	WCSD	RCV1	WCSD
Cos TfIdf	38%	68%	42%	74%	42%	72%
Cos PMI	40%	63%	42%	66%	42%	63%
Cos Prob	36%	54%	40%	68%	39%	68%
Ehlert	41%	61%	44%	68%	44%	68%
Lin	38%	54%	41%	62%	42%	61%

Table 3. Accuracy by test

	Cos				
All 145	TfIdf	PMI	Prob	Ehlert	Lin
Global	68%	63%	54%	61%	54%
Local	**74%**	66%	68%	68%	62%
Product	72%	63%	68%	68%	61%
L - G	6%	3%	**14%**	7%	**8%**
RD 103	TfIdf	PMI	Prob	Ehlert	Lin
Global	64%	62%	52%	60%	50%
Local	**69%**	61%	65%	65%	56%
Product	69%	61%	60%	65%	56%
L - G	5%	-1%	13%	5%	6%

	Cos				
TOEFL 19	TfIdf	PMI	Prob	Ehlert	Lin
Global	74%	68%	47%	53%	74%
Local	79%	74%	68%	74%	74%
Product	74%	68%	**84%**	68%	68%
L - G	5%	6%	21%	21%	0%
ESL 23	TfIdf	PMI	Prob	Ehlert	Lin
Global	78%	61%	70%	74%	52%
Local	**96%**	83%	83%	74%	78%
Product	83%	70%	83%	78%	74%
L - G	18%	22%	13%	0%	26%

Table 4. Correct answers by polysemy rank

	Most	Second	Third	Least	Avg
All	6.9(38)	4.3(28)	2.8(31)	1.6(48)	3.8(145)
RD	6.5(29)	4.0(19)	2.6(20)	1.5(35)	3.6(103)
TOEFL	6.2(6)	4.0(6)	2.8(4)	1.6(3)	4.0(19)
ESL	9.6(3)	5.9(3)	3.8(7)	1.9(10)	4.0(23)

multiple choice test, (2) the Cos Prob as Product similarity[2] with 84% for the TOEFL test and (3) the Cos TfIdf as Local similarity with 96% for the ESL. These results clearly show that the type of the test influences the overall performance and also point out the fact that different measures can be tuned for different tests. As a consequence, it is important to understand the behavior of each measure as well as the characteristics of each test set.

Freitag and colleagues [2] were the first to introduce a measure to evaluate the difficulty of a test based on its polysemy. In this paper, we go further in this analysis by taking into account the level of polysemy of the correct answer compared to the decoys. The first column of Table 4 shows the level of polysemy[3] when the correct answer is the most polysemous noun among all the alternatives. Similarly, the second column shows the level of polysemy when the correct answer is the second most polysemous noun from all the decoys, and so on. The results show that on average all test sets have similar polysemy level. However, the distribution of the correct answers over the polysemy categories (i.e. Most, Second, Third and Least) is different especially for the TOEFL. This situation is crucial to understand why the Cos Prob, applied as a Product, gives better results for the TOEFL compared to other measures and test sets. In fact, the biggest proportion of correct answers is highly polysemous in TOEFL compared to RD and ESL. As a consequence, this similarity measure seems to benefit the extraction of most polysemous answers. This is indeed an important observation as most complicated cases to solve are the polysemous ones. However, we can not draw definitive conclusions from this first evidence. Indeed, we also need to understand better the behavior of each measure with respect to polysemy and frequency. In each column of Table 5, we can find the accuracy level, the number of correct answers in brackets and the type of similarity approach which gives the best result (g for global, l for local and p for product). Similarly to what we observed from the results and from the analysis of the test sets, Table 5 shows that the Product similarity only appears as the best result when the correct answer is frequent word or polysemous one. In this case, the Cos Prob and the Cos TfIdf are the only measures to show this behavior. In parallel, the Global similarity provides best results when the correct answer is the least frequent or the least polysemous alternative. In this case, the Ehlert model and the Cos PMI are the only two elected measures.

[2] The parameter $\alpha = 0.46$ from Equation 8 is tuned through ten-fold cross validation.

[3] The level of polysemy is calculated as in [2] and is the sum of the polysemy of the target noun and the correct answer given by WordNet.

Table 5. Accuracy by test characteristics

By Frequency	Most	Second	Third	Least	By Polysemy	Most	Second	Third	Least
Cos TfIdf	80% l	72% l	78% l	66% l	Cos TfIdf	76% l	**68% p**	77% l	77% l
Cos PMI	66% l	65% l	74% l	**69% g**	Cos PMI	66% l	50% l	74% l	**81% g**
Cos Prob	**81% p**	**77% p**	61% l	59% l	Cos Prob	74% l	**71% p**	71% l	63% l
Ehlert	73% l	66% l	61% l	**72% g**	Ehlert	66% l	61% l	74% l	**79% g**
Lin	59% l	51% l	78% l	59% l	Lin	55% l	57% l	71% l	65% l

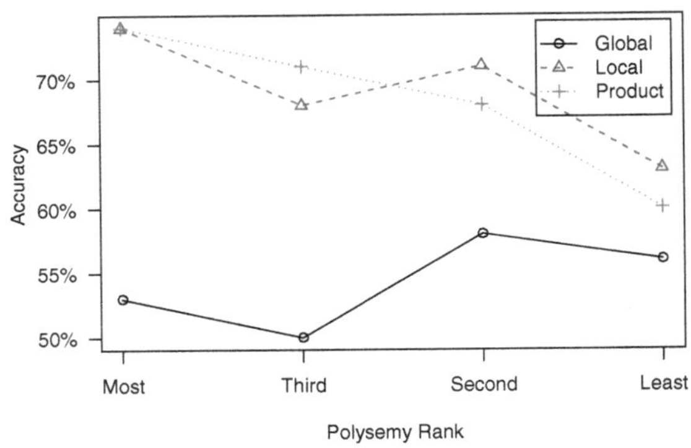

Fig. 1. Performance by polysemy rank

Finally, in order to understand better the differences between the Product, the Local and the Global similarity, we illustrate their behaviors by polysemy rank for the Cos Prob in Figure 1. The reason why Local similarity performs better than the Global similarity for more polysemous cases is that it always compares monosemous representations and is not influenced by polysemous nouns. With the decreasing of the polysemy, Global similarity becomes enough informed to solve the test correctly while Local similarity looses because less polysemous nouns are less frequent and thus become less probable to be encounter both nouns in the same documents. This is illustrated by the convergence of the Local and Global lines in Figure 1. In terms of Product similarity, its value depends on the rate of the polysemy of the test case. As we have seen before, the Product similarity is more tuned to solve more polysemous cases. Subsequently, in Figure 1, we see that the Product similarity overtakes the similarity values of both the Global and the Local similarities for most polysemous cases. However, when polysemy decreases Local similarity performs better than all other measures. At the same time, the more meanings in the test set, the more the ability of the Local similarity to implicitly disambiguate is valued and the lower the value of α is. On the other hand more weight to Global similarity should be given when the test set contains rare words and there is no enough statistics for the Local similarity.

All the observations made so far show that does not exist any single methodology to accomplish synonymy detection alone. Depending on the type of the multiple choice question set, different measures and weighting schemas may be applied to improve overall performance. However, we already saw that some measures seem highly corre-

Table 6. Inter-measure correlation

	Pearson	**Overlap**	**Optimal**
Cos Prob & Ehlert	**0.132**	**0.572**	**86% (124)**
Cos Prob & Cos PMI	0.153	0.565	84% (122)
Cos Prob & Cos TfIdf	0.334	0.677	83% (121)
Cos Prob & Lin	0.245	0.581	81% (117)
Cos PMI & Cos TfIdf	0.507	0.739	79% (115)
Ehlert & Cos TfIdf	0.555	0.773	79% (115)
Ehlert & Lin	0.448	0.675	77% (111)
Ehlert & Cos PMI	0.551	0.745	76% (110)
Lin & Cos TfIdf	0.610	0.763	76% (110)
Lin & Cos PMI	0.606	0.750	72% (104)

lated such as the Ehlert model and the Cos PMI for the Global similarity. In this case, the combination of these measures will not benefit the overall performance. For that purpose, we propose to measure the correlation between pairs of similarity measures with the Pearson Product-Moment Correlation test [21] (See Table 6). Additionally, we compute the overlap of correct answers in the second column and finally calculate the possible optimal performance that could be obtained by combining two measures both in percentage and number of possible correct answers.

The results clearly show that all similarity measures would benefit the most from their association with the Cos Prob. In particular, the optimal case could achieve 86% accuracy by combining the Cos Prob and the Ehlert model. Indeed, both measures share the second smallest proportion of correct test cases i.e. 57.2% and the smallest correlation i.e. 0.132. Moreover, by looking at Table 5, both measures individually show three of the best four results for the frequency distribution i.e. Cos Prob = 81% for the most frequent, Cos Prob = 77% for the second most frequent and Ehlert = 72% for the least frequent.

To conclude, this exhaustive evaluation allows us to say that (1) the corpus size matters, (2) the "*one sense per discourse*" paradigm improves steadily over the baseline i.e. the Global similarity, (3) different measures provide uncorrelated results and (4) the combination of similarity measures would lead to improved results.

6 Conclusion

In this paper, we presented a new heuristic based on the attributional similarity paradigm in attempt to alleviate word polysemy problem in synonymy discovery without performing explicit word sense disambiguation. Our method proved to gain greatest advantage over Global similarity namely in most polysemous cases.

In particular, we obtain 96% accuracy on ESL, 84% on TOEFL, 69% on RD and 74% over the all joined test cases.

Further experiments have also been conducted to evidence result differences between web corpora over standard collections of texts motivated by recent discussions in the NLP area and show that optimal performance is obtained with web text collections tailored for our specific task.

The main contribution is certainly the exhaustive evaluation and categorization of the different similarity measures that were tested. Indeed, as previously shown by [2], the tests show problematic issues that can influence the results of different similarity measures. For that purpose, we have first shown the differences in terms of polysemy between the RD, the TOEFL and the ESL. Then, based on these results, we have conducted further experiments that showed that some similarity metrics are more tailored to solve polysemous cases than others (e.g. the Cos Prob). Finally, by looking at the Pearson Product-Moment Correlation coefficient between pairs of measures, we clearly evidence that multiple choice question tests for synonymy detection should be solved by the optimization of a learning function based on the combination of similarity measures.

Acknowledgment

We would like to thank P. Turney, T. Landauer and D. Freitag for providing us with their collections of tests.

This work is supported by the VIPACCESS project funded by the Portuguese Agency for Research (Fundasoção para a Ciência e a Tecnologia) with the reference PTDC/PLP/72142/2006.

References

1. Landauer, T., Dumais, S.: A solution to plato's problem: The latent semantic analysis theory of acquisition, induction and representation of knowledge. Psychological Review 104(2), 211–240 (1997)
2. Freitag, D., Blume, M., Byrnes, J., Chow, E., Kapadia, S., Rohwer, R., Wang, Z.: New experiments in distributional representations of synonymy. In: Proceedings of the Ninth Conference on Computational Natural Language Learning (CoNLL), Ann Arbor, Michigan, pp. 25–32 (2005)
3. Miller, G.A., Chodorow, M., Landes, S., Leacock, C., Thomas, R.G.: Using a semantic concordance for sense identification. In: HLT 1994: Proceedings of the workshop on Human Language Technology, Morristown, NJ, USA, pp. 240–243. Association for Computational Linguistics (1994)
4. Gale, W., Church, K.W., Yarowsky, D.: One sense per discourse. In: HLT 1991: Proceedings of the workshop on Speech and Natural Language, Morristown, NJ, USA, pp. 233–237 (1992)
5. Moraliyski, R., Dias, G.: One sense per discourse for synonymy extraction (2006)
6. Terra, E., Clarke, C.: Frequency estimates for statistical word similarity measures. In: Proceedings of HTL/NAACL 2003, Edmonton, Canada, pp. 165–172 (2003)
7. Weeds, J., Weir, D., McCarthy, D.: Characterising measures of lexical distributional similarity. In: Proceedings of COLING 2004, Geneva, Switzerland (2004)
8. Ehlert, B.: Making accurate lexical semantic similarity judgments using word-context co-occurrence statistics. Master's thesis, University of California, San Diego (2003)
9. Lin, D.: An information-theoretic definition of similarity. In: Proceedings of the 15th International Conference on Machine Learning, pp. 296–304. Morgan Kaufmann, San Francisco (1998)
10. Turney, P.D.: Mining the web for synonyms: PMI-IR versus LSA on TOEFL. In: Flach, P.A., De Raedt, L. (eds.) ECML 2001. LNCS (LNAI), vol. 2167, pp. 491–502. Springer, Heidelberg (2001)

11. Turney, P.D., Littman, M.L., Bigham, J., Shnayder, V.: Combining independent modules in lexical multiple-choice problems. In: Recent Advances in Natural Language Processing III: Selected Papers from RANLP 2003, pp. 101–110 (2003)
12. Jarmasz, M., Szpakowicz, S.: Roget's thesaurus and semantic similarity. In: Proceedings of Conference on Recent Advances in Natural Language Processing (RANLP), Borovets, Bulgaria, pp. 212–219 (2004)
13. Curran, J.R., Moens, M.: Improvements in automatic thesaurus extraction. In: Proceedings of the Workshop of the ACL Special Interest Group on the Lexicon (SIGLEX), Philadelphia, USA, pp. 59–66 (2002)
14. Rapp, R.: Word sense discovery based on sense descriptor dissimilarity. In: Proceedings of the Ninth Machine Translation Summit, pp. 315–322 (2003)
15. Fellbaum, C. (ed.): WordNet: an electronic lexical database. The MIT Press, Cambridge (1998)
16. Sahlgren, M., Karlgren, J.: Vector-based semantic analysis using random indexing for cross-lingual query expansion. In: Peters, C., Braschler, M., Gonzalo, J., Kluck, M. (eds.) CLEF 2001. LNCS, vol. 2406, pp. 169–176. Springer, Heidelberg (2002)
17. Lewis, D.D., Yang, Y., Rose, T.G., Li, F.: Rcv1: A new benchmark collection for text categorization research. Journal of Machine Learning Research 5, 361–397 (2004)
18. Liu, H.: Montylingua: An end-to-end natural language processor with common sense (2004), `http://web.media.mit.edu/~hugo/montylingua`
19. Weeds, J., Weir, D.: Co-occurrence retrieval: A flexible framework for lexical distributional similarity. Computational Linguistic 31(4), 439–475 (2005)
20. McCarthy, D., Koeling, R., Weeds, J., Carroll, J.: Unsupervised acquisition of predominant word senses. Comput. Linguist. 33(4), 553–590 (2007)
21. Fisher, R.A.: Frequency distribution of the values of the correlation coefficient in samples from an indefinitely large population. Biometrika 10, 507–521 (1915)

Sentiment Classification across Domains

Dinko Lambov[1], Gaël Dias[1], and Veska Noncheva[2]

[1] Centre of Human Language Technology and Bioinformatics,
University of Beira Interior, Covilhã, Portugal
[2] Plovdiv University Paisii Hilendarski, Plovdiv, Bulgaria
d_lambov@mail.bg, ddg@di.ubi.pt, wesnon@uni-plovdiv.bg

Abstract. In this paper we consider the problem of building models that have high sentiment classification accuracy without the aid of a labeled dataset from the target domain. For that purpose, we present and evaluate a novel method based on level of abstraction of nouns. By comparing high-level features (e.g. level of affective words, level of abstraction of nouns) and low-level features (e.g. unigrams, bigrams), we show that, high-level features are better to learn subjective language across domains. Our experimental results present accuracy levels across domains of 71.2% using SVMs learning models.

1 Introduction

Over the past years, there have been an increasing number of publications focused on the detection and classification of sentiment and subjectivity in texts. Detection of sentiment in text offers enormous opportunities for various applications. It is likely to provide powerful functionality for competitive analysis and marketing analysis through topic tracking and detection of unfavorable rumors.

However, as stated in [1][2][3][4], most research have focused on the construction of models within particular domains and have shown difficulties in crossing domains. But, if sentiment is orthogonal to topic, we should be able to build classifiers that perform well on topics other than the one used to build classifier. As a consequence, our aim in constructing a classifier is to maximize accuracy across topics. For that purpose, we propose to use high-level features (e.g. level of affective words, level of abstraction of nouns) rather than low-level features (e.g. unigrams, bigrams) to learn a model of subjectivity which may apply to different domains: movie reviews, newspaper articles and automatically annotated texts downloaded from Wikipedia and Web Blogs. Since sentiment in different domains can be expressed in different ways [1][5][6], supervised classification techniques require large amount of labeled training data. However, the acquisition of these labeled data can be time-consuming and expensive. Moreover, most training sets are built for English and little has been done for other languages. From that assumption, we propose to automatically produce learning data from web resources. To do so, we propose to compare Wikipedia and Web Blogs texts to reference objective and subjective corpora and show that Wikipedia texts are representative of objectivity and Web Blogs are representative of subjectivity. As a consequence, learning data will be easy to build for many languages without manual annotation alleviating intensive and time-consuming labor. Our methodology uses

L. Seabra Lopes et al. (Eds.): EPIA 2009, LNAI 5816, pp. 622–633, 2009.

state-of-the-art characteristics that have been used to classify opinionated texts and proposes a new feature to classify sentiment texts, based on the level of abstraction of nouns. Before classification is performed, feature selection and visualization are performed to evaluate how well the datasets can be represented in the given space of characteristics. Finally, an exhaustive evaluation shows that (1) the level of abstraction of nouns is a strong clue to identify subjective texts which crosses domains, (2) high-level features allow cross-domain learning models and (3) automatically labeled dataset extracted from Wikipedia and Web Blogs get near, on average, to the best cross-domains classifiers reaching accuracy levels of 69.3% compared to 71.2% for manually annotated texts.

2 Related Work

The subjectivity and polarity[1] of language has been investigated at some length. Many features have been used to characterize opinionated texts at different levels (e.g. words [6], sentences [7] and texts [7][8][9][10]). In this section, we propose to enumerate works which focus on document.

At document level, [8] show that the unigram model with Support Vector Machines (SVM) reaches best results compared to more complex models in the domain of movie reviews. [7] propose a similar experiment based on Multiple Naïve Bayes classifiers. [8] propose a unigram SVM classifier which is applied to just subjective portions of a document. A sentence cut-based classifier is used to identify subjective parts in texts which are then used for text classification. [9] derive a variety of subjectivity cues (frequencies of unique words in subjective-element data; collocations with one or more positions filled by a unique word; distributional similarity of adjectives and verbs) from corpora and demonstrate their effectiveness on classification tasks. They determine a relationship between low frequency terms and subjectivity and find that their method for extracting subjective n-grams is enhanced by examining those that occur with unique terms. Finally, [10] present a method using verb class information, and an online resources, the Wikipedia dictionary, for determining the polarity of adjectives. They use verb-class information in the sentiment classification task, since exploiting lexical information contained in verbs has shown to be a successful technique for classifying documents.

Other research in the sentiment classification field regards cross-domain classification. How can we learn classifiers on one domain and use them on another domain? Tests have been done by [1][2][3][4]. Overall, they show that sentiment analysis is a domain-specific problem, and it is hard to create a domain independent classifier. One possible approach is to train the classifier on a domain-mixed set of data instead of training it on one specific domain [2][3][4]. Another possibility is to propose high-level features which do not depend so much on topics such as part-of-speech statistics as in [2]. In this case, the part-of-speech representation does not reflect the topic of the document, but rather the type of text used in the document. Just by looking at part-of-speech statistics, improved results can be obtained comparatively to unigram models

[1] Most papers deal with polarity as the essence of subjectivity. Although, we will see that subjectivity can be expressed in different ways.

(low-level models) when trying to cross domains. [1] use pivot features based on domain mutual information to relate training and target domains. They also measure domain adaptability by estimating the classification accuracy loss by adapting one domain to another without the use of a labeled target dataset.

3 Characterizing Subjectivity

Subjectivity can be expressed in different ways as summarized in [4] who identify the following dimensions: evaluation (positive or negative), potency (powerful or unpowerful), proximity (near or far), specificity (clear or vague), certainty (confident or doubtful) and identifiers (more or less), direct expressions, elements of actions and remarks. Based on these assumptions, our methodology aims at classifying texts at the subjectivity level (i.e. subjective vs. objective and not (positive, negative) vs. objective nor positive vs. negative) based on high-level features which can apply to different domains.

3.1 High-Level Features

Intensity of Affective Words. In most of previous works, sentiment expressions mainly depend on some words which can express subjective sentiment orientation. [11] have used a set of words extracted from WordNet Affect [12] to annotate the emotions in a text simply based on the presence of words from the WordNet Affect lexicon. WordNet Affect contains all information about the affective domain labels and the kind of mapping between Princeton WordNet 1.6 synsets and their corresponding affective domains. For example "*horror*" and "*hysteria*" express negative fear, "*enthusiastic*" expresses positive emotion, "*glad*" expresses joy. So, we propose to evaluate the level of affective words in texts as shown in Equation 1.

$$K_1 = \frac{\text{total affective words in text}}{\text{total words in text}}. \qquad (1)$$

Dynamic Adjectives and Semantically Oriented Adjectives. [13] consider two features for the identification of opinionated sentences: (1) semantic orientation, which represents an evaluative characterization of a word's deviation from the norm for its semantic group and (2) dynamic adjectives which characterizes a word's ability to express a property in varying degrees. They noted that all sets involving dynamic adjectives and adjectives with positive or negative polarity are better predictors of subjective sentences than the class of adjectives as a whole. Here, we use the set of all adjectives identified in a reference corpus i.e. the set of dynamic adjectives, manually identified by [13] and the set of semantic orientation labels assigned as in [6]. So, we propose to evaluate the level of these adjectives in texts as shown in Equation 2.

$$K_2 = \frac{\text{total specific adjectives in text}}{\text{total adjectives in text}}. \qquad (2)$$

Classes of Verbs. [10] present a method using verb class information. Their verb classes express objectivity and polarity. To obtain relevant verb classes, they use InfoXtract [14], an automatic text analyzer which groups verbs according to classes that often correspond to their polarity. As InfoExtract is not freely available, we reproduce their methodology by using the classification of verbs available in Levin's English Verb Classes and Alternations [15]. So, we propose to evaluate the level of each class of verbs (i.e. conjecture, marvel, see and positive) in texts as in Equation 3.

$$K_3 = \frac{\text{total specific verbs in text}}{\text{total verbs in text}}. \tag{3}$$

Level of Abstraction of Nouns. There is linguistic evidence that level of generality is a characteristic of opinionated texts, i.e. subjectivity is usually expressed in more abstract terms than objectivity [4][16]. Indeed, descriptive texts tend to be more precise and more objective and as a consequence more specific. [4] define specificity as "[…] the extent to which a conceptualized object is referred to by name in a direct and clear way; or is only implied, suggested, alluded to, generalized, or otherwise hinted at". In other words, a word is abstract when it has few distinctive features and few attributes that can be pictured in the mind. One way of measuring the abstractness of a word is by the hypernym relation in WordNet [17]. In particular, a hypernym metric can be the number of levels in a conceptual taxonomic hierarchy above a word (i.e. superordinate to). For example, "chair" (as a seat) has 7 hypernym levels: chair => furniture => furnishings => instrumentality => artifact => object => entity. So, a word having more hypernym levels is more concrete than one with fewer levels. So, we propose to evaluate the hypernym levels of all the nouns in texts as in Equation 4[2].

$$K_4 = \frac{\text{total hypernym levels for all nouns in text}}{\text{total nouns in text}}. \tag{4}$$

3.2 Low-Level Features

Perhaps the most common set of features used for text classification tasks is information regarding the occurrence of words or word ngrams, in the text. A vast majority of text classification systems treat documents as simple "bags-of-words" and use the word counts or presence as features. In this paper, the surface features we use are lemma unigrams and lemma bigrams associated to their TFIDF weights where w_{ij} is weight of term t_j in document d_i, N is the total number of documents in collection, and n is number of documents where term t_j occurs at least once (See Equation 5).

$$w_{ij} = tf_{ij} * \log_2 \frac{N}{n}. \tag{5}$$

---

[2] Calculating the level of abstraction of nouns should be preceded by word sense disambiguation. Indeed, it is important that the correct sense is taken as a seed for the calculation of the hypernym level in WordNet. However, in practice, taking the most common sense of each word gave similar results as taking all the senses on average. As a consequence, we believe that word sense disambiguation can be avoided for this task.

4 Feature Selection and Visualization

Before performing any classification task, it is useful to evaluate to what extent the given high-level features are discriminative and allow representing distinctively the datasets in the given space of characteristics. For that purpose, we propose to do feature selection by applying the Wilcoxon rank-sum test and to visualize the datasets using multidimensional scaling.

4.1 Corpora

To perform these experiments, we used three manually annotated standard corpora and built one corpus based on Web resources and automatically annotated.

The Multi-Perspective Question Answering (Mpqa) Opinion Corpus[3] contains 10,657 sentences in 535 documents from the world press on a variety of topics. All documents in the collection are marked with expression-level opinion annotations. The documents are from 187 different news sources in a variety of countries and date from June 2001 to May 2002. The corpus has been collected and manually annotated with respect to subjectivity as part of the summer 2002 NRRC Workshop on Multi-Perspective Question Answering. Based on the work done by [8] who propose to classify texts based only on their subjective/objective parts, we built a corpus of 100 objective texts and 100 subjective texts by randomly selecting sentences containing only subjective or objective phrases. This case represents the "ideal" case where all the sentences in texts are either subjective or objective.

The second corpus (Rotten/Imdb) is the subjectivity dataset v1.0[4] which contains 5000 subjective and 5000 objective sentences collected from movie reviews data [8]. To gather subjective sentences, [8] collected 5000 movie review snippets from www.rottentomatoes.com. To obtain (mostly) objective data, they took 5000 sentences from plot summaries available from the Internet Movie Database www.imdb.com. Similarly to what we did for the MPQA corpus, we built a corpus of 100 objective texts and 100 subjective texts by randomly selecting 50 sentences containing only subjective or objective phrases.

The third corpus (Chesley) has been developed by [10] who manually annotated a dataset of objective and subjective documents[5]. It contains 496 subjective and 580 objective documents. Objective feeds are from sites providing content such as world and national news (CNN, NPR, etc.), local news (Atlanta Journal and Constitution, Seattle Post-Intelligencer, etc.), and various sites focused on topics such as health, science, business, and technology. Subjective feeds include content from newspaper columns (Charles Krauthammer, E. J. Dionne, etc.), letters to the editor (Washington Post, Boston Globe, etc.), reviews (dvdverdict.com, rottentomatoes.com, etc.), and political blogs (Powerline, Huffington Post, etc.).

The fourth corpus is the Wiki/Blog. We downloaded part of the static Wikipedia dump archive[6] and automatically spidered Web Blogs from different domains. The final corpus contains 200 Mb of downloaded articles from Wikipedia and 100 Mb of

[3] http://www.cs.pitt.edu/mpqa/
[4] http://www.cs.cornell.edu/People/pabo/movie-review-data/
[5] http://www.tc.umn.edu/~ches0045/data/
[6] http://download.wikimedia.org/enwiki/

downloaded texts from different Web Blogs. These texts are in English and cover many different topics. As we propose to compare Wikipedia and Web Blogs texts to reference objective and subjective corpora and show that Wikipedia texts are representative of objectivity and Web Blogs are representative of subjectivity, we automatically label texts as objectives if they come from Wikipedia and subjective if they come from Web Blogs.

4.2 Wilcoxon Rank-Sum Test

We use the Wilcoxon test to show that the comparative results are statistically significant. The Wilcoxon rank-sum test is a nonparametric alternative to the two sample t-test used to compare the locations of two populations i.e. to determine if one population is shifted with respect to another. The two sample Wilcoxon test with one-sided alternative is carried out for all experiments. The samples contain 200 values for each of the sets (100 objective texts and 100 subjective) and the exact p-value is computed. If the result of the test shows that the values of subjective (resp. objective) data are shifted to the right of the values of objective (resp. subjective) for all of the sets, we can say that the distributions of subjective and objective differ by a positive shift. The estimations for the differences of the location parameters are also computed for each of the sets. The exact 95% confidence interval for the difference of the location parameters of each of the sets is obtained by the algorithm described in [18] for which the Hodges-Lehmann estimator is employed. As a consequence, for each of the sets, we are 95% confident that the interval contains the actual difference between the features values of subjective and objective texts. The observed results are consistent with the hypothesis that most of the high-level features exposed in section 3 (intensity of affective words, dynamic and semantically oriented adjectives, classes of verbs and level of abstraction of nouns) have good discriminative properties for subjectivity/objectivity identification. As illustrated in Table 1, we can see that only the level of positive verbs does not significantly separate the objective sample from the subjective one over training corpora. This is mainly due to the fact that positive verbs do not occur frequently in texts thus biasing the statistical test. As a consequence, we discarded this feature from our classification task. We can also see that Chesley's dataset shows an uncharacteristic behavior. This is mainly due to the fact that Chesley's texts are either objective or, positive or negative. Unlike the other corpora, Chesley's corpus focuses on subjectivity exclusively based on polarity.

Table 1. Computed p-values using Wilcoxon test

Corpus: Feature:	Mpqa	Rotten/Imdb	Chesley	Wiki/Blog
Affective words	< 0,0001	< 0,0001	< 0,0001	< 0,0001
Dynamic adj.	< 0,0001	< 0,0001	0,014	< 0,0001
Semantic adj.	< 0,0001	< 0,0001	0,045	< 0,0001
Conjecture verbs	0,00024	< 0,0001	0,021	< 0,0001
Marvel verbs	< 0,0001	< 0,0001	0,44	< 0,0001
See verbs	< 0,0001	< 0,0001	0,006	< 0,0001
Positive verbs	< 0,0001	0,00011	0,075	0,00061
Level of abstraction	0,003	< 0,0001	< 0,0001	< 0,0001

4.3 Multidimensional Scaling

In this subsection, we propose a visual analysis of the distribution of the datasets in the space of high-level features.

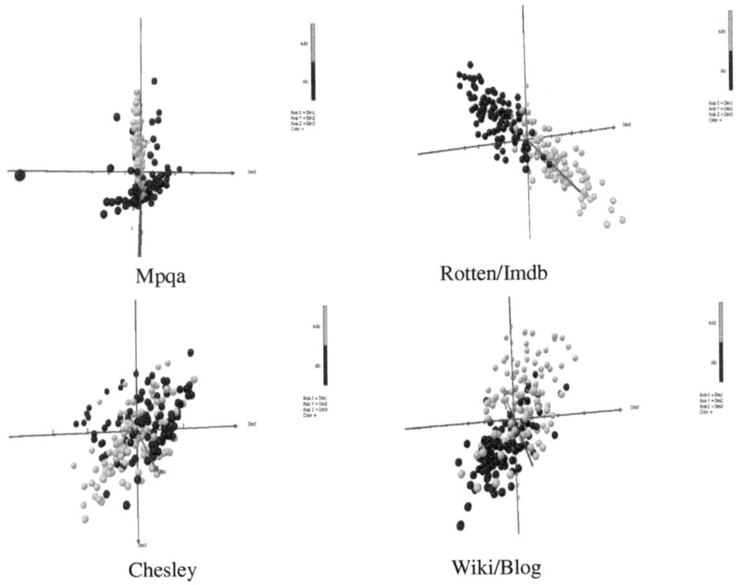

Fig. 1. MDS over all training datasets

The goal of this study is to give a visual interpretation of the data distribution to assess how well classification may perform. If objective and subjective texts can be represented in a distinct way in the reduced space of features, one may expect good classification results. To perform this study, we use a Multidimensional Scaling (MDS) process which is a traditional data analysis technique. MDS [19] allows to displaying the structure of distance-like data into an Euclidean space. In practice, the projection space we build with the MDS from such a distance is sufficient to have an idea about whether data is organized into classes or not. For our purpose, we perform the MDS process on all corpora trying to visualize subjective texts from objective ones. The obtained visualizations (Figures 1) show distinctly that a particular data organization can be drawn from the data. This visualization clearly shows that exclusively objective and subjective texts (i.e. Mpqa and Rotten/Imdb) may lead to improved results as data is well separated in the reduced 3-dimension space. In the case of Chesley's corpus and Wiki/Blog separating data in the space seems more difficult. Indeed, as these texts are not composed exclusively of subjective or objective sentences, the overlap in the space is inevitable. As [9] state, 75% (resp. 56%) of the sentences in subjective (resp. objective) texts are subjective (resp. objective)[7]. However, a pattern in the space seems to emerge comforting us in the choice of our high-level features for our classification task.

[7] These data are extracted from the Wall Street Journal.

5 Experiments

In this section, we report the results of machine learning experiments for which we used Support Vector Machines (SVMs) to learn models of subjectivity over four different domains. SVMs have consistently shown to perform better than other classification algorithms for topic text classification in general [20], and for sentiment classification in particular [8]. All experiments have been performed on a leave-one-out 5 cross validation basis. In particular, we used Joachim's SVMlight package[8] [20] for training and testing with SVM. As part-of-speech tagger we used the MontyTagger module of the free, common sense-enriched Natural Language Understander for English MontyLingua[9] [21].

5.1 Results for In-Domain Data

In order to evaluate the difference between high level features with low level ones, we performed a comparative study on our four test sets. For the high level features, we took into account 7 features (affective words, dynamic and semantically oriented adjectives, conjuncture verbs, see verbs, marvel verbs and level of abstraction of nouns)[10]. For the Unigram and Bigram models, we used all the lemmas inside the corpora withdrawing their stop words. The results of these experiments are shown in Table 2 and 3 and evidence an important gain with low level features compared to

Table 2. Results for High Level Features – In Domain (in percentage)

		All	Subjective		Objective	
		Accuracy	Precision	Recall	Precision	Recall
High-Level Features	Mpqa	71,2	81,1	55,2	66	87,2
	Rotten/Imdb	86,8	84,3	90,4	89,6	83,2
	Chesley	64,4	64,8	62,8	63,9	66
	Wiki/Blog	76,2	93,9	56	68,6	96,4

Table 3. Results for Low Level Features – In Domain (in percentage)

		All	Subjective		Objective	
		Accuracy	Precision	Recall	Precision	Recall
Unigrams	Mpqa	80,6	100	61,2	72	100
	Rotten/Imdb	97	97,9	96	96	98
	Chesley	72,6	64,7	99,2	98,3	46
	Wiki/Blog	94,6	90,2	100	100	89,2
Bigrams	Mpqa	67,8	100	35,6	64,6	100
	Rotten/Imdb	98	97,9	96	96,1	100
	Chesley	70,6	62,9	100	100	41,2
	Wiki/Blog	80	74,7	90,8	88,3	69,2

8 http://svmlight.joachims.org/

9 http://web.media.mit.edu/~hugo/montylingua/

10 An exhaustive study of the level of abstraction is made in the next section.

high level features. Indeed, as it has already been stated in other works, objective language and subjective language hardly intersect which means that one word, specific to one domain (i.e. which does not represent any subjective value outside it) can easily distinguish between objective and subjective texts.

5.2 Results for Cross-Domain Data

In order to test models across domains, we propose to train different models based on one domain only at each time and test the classifiers over all domains together. Before doing the experiments it is important to visualize the data to understand how difficult the task may be. Indeed, when gathering texts from different domains, the best case is when all subjective texts represent one unique cloud in the space which does not intersect with a unique cloud formed by objective texts. However, it is not usually the case. In Figure 2, we show two different situations which illustrate that positive results may be obtained (e.g. Rotten/Imdb and Wiki/Blogs) and other cases where results may not be expected (e.g. Rotten/Imdb and Mpqa) when using high level features to characterize each text. Indeed, in the first picture in Figure 2 (Rotten/Imdb and Wiki/Blogs), we can see that subjective texts (blue and red) and objective texts (green and yellow) form two clouds separated by the axe *Dim 1* although many blogs (blue) are spread over the space. Unlikely, the second picture (Mpqa and Rotten/Imdb) evidences four clouds with almost no intersection which clearly indicates that subjectivity can be expressed in different ways from domain to domain, thus complicating the learning process. We do not present the visualization results based on the vector space model representation of texts (i.e. low level features) as they evidence highly intersected clouds. As a consequence, unreliable results may be expected for low level feature across domains. So, in Table 4 and 5, we present the results for domain transfer for high level features and low level features. Each percentage can be expressed as the average results over all datasets. Best results overall are obtained for high level features for the Chesley dataset with accuracy of 71.2% .

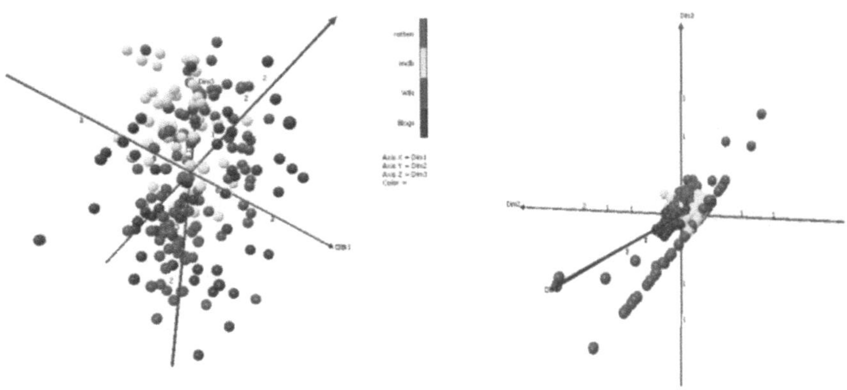

Rotten/Imdb and Wiki/Blogs Mpqa and Rotten/Imdb

Fig. 2. MDS over mixed datasets

Table 4. Results for High Level Features – Cross Domain (in percentage)

		All	Subjective		Objective	
		Accuracy	Precision	Recall	Precision	Recall
High-Level Features	Mpqa	58,8	47,7	81,9	33,9	35,8
	Rotten/Imdb	68,9	81	49,7	66,1	88,1
	Chesley	71,2	79,4	59,6	68	82,8
	Wiki/Blog	69,3	76,5	61,8	71,1	76,8

Table 5. Results for Low Level features – Cross Domain (in percentage)

		All	Subjective		Objective	
		Accuracy	Precision	Recall	Precision	Recall
Unigrams	Mpqa	53,8	25,9	15,6	53,2	92
	Rotten/Imdb	63,9	66,2	28,6	63,3	99,3
	Chesley	59,9	68,9	97,3	46	22,5
	Wiki/Blog	61,1	60	100	25	22
Bigrams	Mpqa	54,4	25	8,9	53,6	100
	Rotten/Imdb	67,1	66,3	90,3	65,2	44
	Chesley	55	53,2	99,8	25	10,3
	Wiki/Blog	57,5	56,2	97,7	22	17,3

5.3 Cross-Domain and Level of Abstraction

In order to evaluate the importance of the level of abstraction of nouns as a clue for subjectivity identification, we propose to study the six state-of-the-art features without the level of abstraction of nouns and then compare with the full set of seven features. Then, we present the importance of each class of features individually to assess how discriminative each class of features is. For that purpose, we defined four classes of features: affective words, adjectives (semantically oriented and dynamic), verbs (conjecture, marvel and see) and level of abstraction of nouns. The results are illustrated in Table 6 for leave-one-out 5 cross validation for cross-domain and evidence that the level of abstraction of nouns is the best feature to cross domains except for the case of the Mpqa dataset. This is mainly due to the over-evaluation of strong features by the SVM. Indeed, in Table 6, as affective words are the best feature for the Mpqa dataset, best results are obtained without the level of abstraction. In the other cases, the level of abstraction of nouns is the best feature thus implying best results with seven features.

Table 6. Results for High-Level Features – Cross Domain (in percentage)

	Mpqa	Rotten/Imdb	Chesley	Wiki/Blog
7 features	58,8	68,9	71,2	69,3
6 features	64,4	67,7	67,4	68,7
Affective words only	66,2	59,9	67,1	66,2
Adjectives only	60,1	67,2	65,3	68,5
Verbs only	64,8	69,3	59,9	68,1
Level of Abstraction only	51,7	70,9	72	71

6 Conclusions

Sentiment classification is a domain specific problem i.e. classifiers trained in one domain do not perform well in others. At the same time, sentiment classifiers need to be customizable to new domains in order to be useful in practice. In this paper, we proposed new experiments based on high-level features to learn subjective language across domains. Best results showed accuracy of 71.2% across domains. Indeed SVM steadily perform best for high-level features than for low-level features. Moreover, our experimental results show that using levels of abstraction of nouns as a feature leads to improved performance on subjectivity classification tasks. Also, the results produced via automatic construction of data sets (Wiki/Blogs) get near, on average, to the best cross-domains classifiers reaching accuracy levels of 69.3% compared to 71.2% for manually annotated texts. A direct application of this study is to automatically produce data sets for other languages than English and allow classification of multilingual opinionated texts. Indeed, building data sets for the classification of opinionated texts can be done automatically, at the document level, just by downloading Web Blogs for the subjective part and Wikipedia texts for the objective part. Thus labor-intensive and time-consuming work can be leveraged.

Acknowledgments. This work is supported by the VIPACCESS project funded by the Portuguese Agency for Research (Fundação para a Ciência e a Tecnologia) with the reference PTDC/PLP/72142/2006.

References

1. Blitzer, J., Crammer, K., Kulesza, A., Pereira, F., Wortman, J.: Biographies, Bollywood, Boom-boxes, and Blenders: Domain Adaptation for Sentiment Classification. In: Proceedings of Association for Computational Linguistics (2007)
2. Finn, A., Kushmerick, N.: Learning to Classify Documents According to Genre. J. American Society for Information Science and Technology, Special issue on Computational Analysis of Style 57(9) (2006)
3. Aue, A., Gamon, M.: Customizing Sentiment Classifiers to New Domains: a Case Study. In: Proceedings of International Conference on Recent Advances in Natural Language Processing, Borovets, Bulgaria (2005)
4. Boiy, E., Hens, P., Deschacht, K., Moens, M.-F.: Automatic Sentiment Analysis of On-line Text. In: Proceedings of the 11th International Conference on Electronic Publishing, Openness in Digital Publishing: Awareness, Discovery & Access, June 13-15 (2007)
5. Engström, C.: Topic Dependence in Sentiment Classification. Master Thesis. University of Cambridge (2004)
6. Hatzivassiloglou, V., McKeown, K.R.: Predicting the Semantic Orientation of Adjectives. In: Proceedings of the 35th Annual Meeting of the Association for Computational Linguistics and the 8th Conference of the European Chapter of the Association for Computational Linguistics (1997)
7. Yu, H., Hatzivassiloglou, V.: Towards Answering Opinion Questions: Separating Facts from Opinions and Identifying the Polarity of Opinion Sentences. In: EMNLP (2003)

8. Pang, B., Lee, L.: A Sentimental Education: Sentiment Analysis Using Subjectivity Summarization Based on Minimum Cuts. In: Proceedings of the 42nd Annual Meeting of the Association for Computational Linguistics (2004)
9. Wiebe, J., Wilson, T., Bruce, R., Bell, M., Martin, M.: Learning Subjective Language. Computational Linguistics 30(3), 277–308 (2004)
10. Chesley, P., Vincent, B., Xu, L., Srihari, R.: Using Verbs and Adjectives to Automatically Classify Blog Sentiment. In: Proceedings of AAAI Spring Symposium (2006)
11. Strapparava, C., Mihalcea, R.: Learning to Identify Emotions in Text. In: Proceedings of the Symposium on Applied Computing, pp. 1556–1560 (2008)
12. Strapparava, C., Valitutti, A.: WordNet-Affect: An Affective Extension of WordNet. In: Proceedings of the Language Resources and Evaluation International Conference (2004)
13. Hatzivassiloglou, V., Wiebe, J.: Effects of Adjective Orientation and Gradability on Sentence Subjectivity. In: Proceedings of International Conference on Computational Linguistics (2000)
14. Srihari, R., Li, W., Niu, C., Cornell, T.: InfoXtract: A Customizable Intermediate Level Information Extraction Engine. In: Proceedings of the HLT-NAACL 2003 Workshop on Software Engineering and Architecture of Language Technology Systems (2003)
15. Levin, B.: English Verb Classes and Alternations. University of Chicago Press (1993)
16. Osgood, C.E., Suci, G.J., Tannebaum, P.H.: The Measurement of Meaning. University of Illinois Press (1971)
17. Miller, G.A.: Wordnet: A Lexical Database. Communications of the ACM 38 (1995)
18. Bauer, D.F.: Constructing Confidence Sets Using Rank Statistics. Journal of the American Statistical Association 67, 687–690 (1972)
19. Kruskal, J.B., Wish, M.: Multidimensional Scaling. Sage Publications, Beverly Hills (1977)
20. Joachims, T.: Learningto Classify Text Using Support Vector Machines. In: Dissertation. Kluwer, Dordrecht (2002)
21. Liu, H.: Montylingua: An End-to-End Natural Language Processor with Common Sense (2004), http://web.media.mit.edu/~hugo/montylingua

Comparing Different Properties Involved in Word Similarity Extraction*

Pablo Gamallo Otero

Universidade de Santiago de Compostela, Galiza, Spain
pablo.gamallo@usc.es

Abstract. In this paper, we will analyze the behavior of several parameters, namely type of contexts, similarity measures, and word space models, in the task of word similarity extraction from large corpora. The main objective of the paper will be to describe experiments comparing different extraction systems based on all possible combinations of these parameters. Special attention will be paid to the comparison between syntax-based contexts and windowing techniques, binary similarity metrics and more elaborate coefficients, as well as baseline word space models and Singular Value Decomposition strategies. The evaluation leads us to conclude that the combination of syntax-based contexts, binary similarity metrics, and a baseline word space model makes the extraction much more precise than other combinations with more elaborate metrics and complex models.

1 Introduction

Most of the existing work on word similarity extraction has in common two properties: the observation that semantically related words will appear in similar contexts and the use of word space models built on the basis of such co-occurrence observations. Yet, the underlying methods can differ in four different aspects: their definition of context, the way they calculate similarity from the contexts each word appears in, the way they modify the word space model (singular value decomposition, association values, etc.), and finally, the algorithm used to perform pairwise word comparisons.

There are many interesting works comparing the accuracy of different approaches on word similarity extraction. However, most of them are focused only on one parameter of variation. Some compare systems on the basis of the type of context, namely window and syntactic-based methods [10]. Other compare several similarity measures [5]. Some are interested in testing whether changes in the word space model can improve the results [13]. And, there is also some work comparing the computational efficiency of the underlying algorithm [20].

The main contribution of this paper is to compare word similarity systems on the basis of several parameters or ranges of variation, and not only considering one of them as it was usual in the literature. For this purpose, four parameters will be taken into account: types of contexts (C), similarity measures (S), strategies to build word space models (M), and algorithms to compute similarity between pairwise words (A).

* This work has been funded by the Galician Government (*Consellaría de Industria e Innovación* and *Consellaría de Educación e Ordenación Universitaria*).

L. Seabra Lopes et al. (Eds.): EPIA 2009, LNAI 5816, pp. 634–645, 2009.

A system is defined as a tuple of 4 elements, (c, s, m, a), where c is a type of context, s a similarity measure, m a word space model, and a an algorithm. So, according to this range of variation, we will define the cartesian product of all possible 4-tuples:

$$C \times S \times M \times A =$$
$$\{(c, s, m, a) | c \in C \text{ and } s \in S \text{ and } m \in M \text{ and } a \in A\}$$

where each 4-tuple is an evaluable system. In this paper, we will define 3 contexts, 10 similarity coefficients, 3 word space models, and 1 algorithm. As all systems share the same algorithm, all comparisons will be made among the remaining 3 parameters. As far as we know, up to now, no work has attempted to compare more than two parameters of variation against the same corpus. So, the main contribution of this paper is to compare 65 different systems, built from much of all possible triplets (90) containing C, S, and M.

Another contribution of the paper is to describe a large-scale evaluation including a new kind of gold standard. In addition to WordNet [7], we will also use as reference for evaluation a closed terminology, namely a list of proper names annotated with three sharp categories: countries, capitals, and English towns. The use of such a closed list as gold standard tries to overcome some of the problems associated with standard thesaurus, namely the fact that an extraction system can compute many correct word pairs which are all counted as wrong since they are not in the thesaurus. With the use of a closed list of all countries, capitals, and English towns, this problem does not arise. For instance, given a word tagged as being a country, and given the most similar word extracted by the system, if it this word is not tagged as a country, it is sure that it is not a country. All words correctly proposed by the system must be in the gold standard and, therefore, will always be correctly evaluated.

The evaluation described in this paper will lead us to conclude that, on the one hand, the systems based on syntactic contexts tend to be better than the windowing techniques, and on the other, it is very difficult to perform better than the simplest metrics and the baseline word space models.

The remainder of the paper is organized as follows. Section 2 enumerates some works comparing different similarity extraction systems according to only one parameter. In Section 3, we describe the different parameters of variation that will be used in our experiments. And finally, in Section 4, we will introduce some corpus-based experiments, define the evaluation protocol and analyze the results performed by 65 systems against the same corpus (BNC).

2 Related Work

There are much previous work aimed to evaluate and compare different strategies to extract word similarity. Some compare the influence of different types of contexts. In [10], a syntax-based method is carefully compared to a windowing technique. The former is shown to perform better for high-frequency words, while the windowing method is the better performer for low-frequency words. The experiments performed made use of very small text corpora, probably due to the low efficiency of the syntactic techniques available at that time. Similar experiments were performed more recently [16,17,21].

All of them state that syntax-based methods outperform windowing techniques thanks to a drastic reduction of noise.

Other works compare the performance of different similarity measures. However, no agreement has been achieved concerning the best coefficients. In [14], the best performance was reached by the metric defined by the author. In [5], the best one was a specific version of Dice, and in [2], the best results were obtained by the simplest metrics, namely those based on merely counting contexts with non-zero values (i.e., binary measures).

There exists a large family of experiments comparing standard word space models to models previously reduced by Singular Value Decomposition (SVD). In [13], the best results are achieved using SVD, combined with large word contexts defined at the level of the document. In [22], SVD is outperformed by a more basic word space model. However, in [19,15,3], SVD combined with small window-based contexts outperform other approaches. In all these experiments, the evaluation uses as gold standard popular tests as TOEFL where the system has to choose the most appropriate synonym for a given word given a restricted list of four candidates. To compare the accuracy of two (or more) methods, it is assumed that the system makes the right decision if the correct word is ranked highest among the four alternatives. The main drawback of such an evaluation derives from the size of the test itself. Each word is compared to only other three words, and not to many thousands as in more reliable large-scale evaluations.

In addition, there are other works comparing word space models with regard to the type of association value (or weight) defining word-by-context co-occurrences [5,2]. Like in the case of similarity metrics, there is no agreement concerning the best weight function for word similarity extraction.

Finally, we also can find some work measuring both the complexity and computational efficiency of the algorithm implemented to make pairwise comparisons [9,20]. As the accuracy of any extraction system does not depend on the chosen algorithm, we will not compare systems with regard to this specific parameter.

Unlike the studies sketched above which make comparisons according to one or in some cases two parameters of variation, in this paper, we will compare different extraction systems with regard to 3 parameters.

3 Systems and Range of Variation

As has been said above, a system to extract word similarity can be defined as a 4-tuple consisting of:

- a type of context,
- a similarity measure,
- a word space model defined as a word-by-context co-occurrence matrix,
- an algorithm to compare pairs of words in an efficient way.

3.1 Types of Contexts

The systems we will compare were implemented according to 3 different types of word contexts. Two types of windowing strategies and one syntax-based method. As far the

Table 1. 10 similarity measures

$$\mathrm{OverBin}(w_1, w_2) = \parallel \mathrm{BIN}(w_1) \cap \mathrm{BIN}(w_2) \parallel$$

$$\mathrm{DiceBin}(w_1, w_2) = \frac{2 \parallel \mathrm{BIN}(w_1) \cap \mathrm{BIN}(w_2) \parallel}{\parallel \mathrm{BIN}(w_1) \parallel + \parallel \mathrm{BIN}(w_2) \parallel}$$

$$\mathrm{JaccBin}(w_1, w_2) = \frac{\parallel \mathrm{BIN}(w_1) \cap \mathrm{BIN}(w_2) \parallel}{\parallel \mathrm{BIN}(w_1) \cup \mathrm{BIN}(w_2) \parallel}$$

$$\mathrm{CosBin}(w_1, w_2) = \frac{\parallel \mathrm{BIN}(w_1) \cap \mathrm{BIN}(w_2) \parallel}{\sqrt{\parallel \mathrm{BIN}(w_1) \parallel}\sqrt{\parallel \mathrm{BIN}(w_2) \parallel}}$$

$$\mathrm{City}(w_1, w_2) = \sum_j |A(w_1, c_j) - A(w_2, c_j)|$$

$$\mathrm{Eucl}(w_1, w_2) = \sqrt{\sum_j (A(w_1, c_j) - A(w_2, c_j))^2}$$

$$\mathrm{Cosine}(w_1, w_2) = \frac{\sum_j A(w_1, c_j) A(w_2, c_j)}{\sqrt{\sum_j (A(w_1, c_j))^2}\sqrt{\sum_k (A(w_2, c_k))^2}}$$

$$\mathrm{DiceMin}(w_1, w_2) = \frac{2\sum_j \min(A(w_1, c_j), A(w_2, c_j))}{\sum_j A(w_1, c_j) + \sum_k A(w_2, c_k)}$$

$$\mathrm{JaccardMin}(w_1, w_2) = \frac{\sum_j \min(A(w_1, c_j), A(w_2, c_j))}{\sum_j \max(A(w_1, c_j), A(w_2, c_j))}$$

$$\mathrm{Lin}(w_1, w_2) = \frac{\sum_{c_i \in C_{1,2}} (A(w_1, c_j) + A(w_2, c_j))}{\sum_j A(w_1, c_j) + \sum_k A(w_2, c_k)}$$

windowing strategies are concerned, contexts can be defined using the immediately adjacent words, within a window of n words. Two different techniques can be applied: one defining contexts as bag of words, called *BOW*, and the other taking into account word order (*WO*). The technique based on bag of words builds context vectors considering simple words as dimensions, regardless of their positions within the window. By contrast, the *WO* technique uses word order to define context vectors, which is considered to be useful to simulate syntactic behavior. According to Rapp [18], this window technique is, then, closer to the syntax-based approach.

Our syntactic strategy (*SYN*) relies on dependency-based robust parsing. Dependencies are generated by means of *DepPattern*[1], a rule-based partial parser which can process

[1] *DepPattern* is a linguistic toolkit, with GPL licence, which is available at: `http://gramatica.usc.es/pln/tools/deppattern.html`

5 languages: English, Spanish, Galician, Portuguese, and French. The 5 grammars are very generic, they are constituted by about 20-30 rules each. To extract syntax-based contexts from dependencies, we used the co-compositional methodology defined in [8]. The *DepPattern* toolkit also includes a script aimed to extract co-compositional contexts from the dependencies generated by the parser.

3.2 Similarity Measures

The systems are built using 10 similarity coefficients, which represent much of the metrics defined in [14,5,2]. The simplest measures (suffix "Bin") transform all vectors into binary values: binary overlapping (OverBin), binary Dice (DiceBin), binary Jaccard (JaccBin), and binary Cosine (CosBin). By contrast, Cosine (Cos), Euclidian distance (Eucl), City-Block (City), Dice (DiceMin), and Jaccard (JaccMin) use vectors with co-occurrence (or weighted) values. The 10 similarity metrics between two words, w_1 and w_2, are defined in Table 1, where $BIN(w_1)$ stands for a set representation of the binary vector defining word w_1. This vector is the result of transforming the real-valued vector with co-occurrences or log-likelihood scores into a vector with binary values. The length $\| BIN(w_1) \|$ of a binary vector $BIN(w_1)$ is the number of non-zero values. On the other hand, $A(w_1, c_j)$ is an association value of a vector of length n, with j, i, and k ranging from 1 to n. In our experiments, the association value stands for either the simple co-occurrences of word w_1 with a contextual expression c_j, or a weight computed using the log-likelihood ratio between the word and its context. For Cosine, the association values of two words with the same context are joined using their product, while for JaccardMin [11,12] and DiceMin [5,23] only the smallest association weight is considered (in those works, they are noted as Jaccard† and Dice†, respectively). For the Lin coefficient, the association values of common contexts are summed [14], where $c_j \in C_{1,2}$ if and only if $A(w_1, c_j) > 0$ and $A(w_2, c_j) > 0$. Finally, in City, $|x - y|$ represents an absolute value. In sum, we use two types of similarity coefficients: those based on binary vectors (baseline metrics) and those relying on association values.

3.3 Word Space Models

In our experiments, we evaluate the performance of three different types of word space models. First, we call COOC the simplest method that takes as input a sparse matrix containing only word-by-context co-occurrences. This is the baseline model. No further operation was applied on the baseline matrix before computing word similarity.

The second method, called SVD, requires a dense matrix reduced by Singular Value Decomposition. Dimensionality reduction was performed with SVDLIBC.[2]. Before reduction, co-occurrence values were transformed into log-likelihood scores, as in most approaches to Latent Semantic Analysis [13].

The third method, called BORDAG, was defined in [2], and consists of the following tasks: all co-occurrences are weighted values (log-likelihood) and are ranked by decreasing significance. Then, only the N best ones are selected (where $N = 200$ in our experiments). This way, each word is associated, at most, with 200 non-zero weighted

[2] `http://tedlab.mit.edu/~dr/svdlibc/`

values. Given that corpus frequency follows the power-law distribution, only very frequent words co-occur with more than 200 other words. Even if such a filtering strategy only affects very frequent words, it allows us to reduce the number of pairwise comparisons (and thus runtime) significantly, while hopefully not decreasing accuracy with regard to the baseline model.

3.4 Algorithm

The naive algorithm to extract word similarity looks at each word and compares it with each other word, checking all contexts to see if they are shared. Complexity is quadratic. Yet, it is possible to make the algorithm simpler. Because of the power-law distribution of word-context co-occurrences, most word pairs have nothing in common. So, there is no reason to check them. Following [9,20], we implemented an algorithm that only compares word pairs sharing at least one context. As the list of words sharing a context is small (in general, less than 1000), the quadratic complexity of the entire algorithm turns out to be manageable.

4 Experiments and Large-Scale Evaluation

Given the parameters of variation described in the last section and the cartesian product of all possible 4-tuples, we could evaluate $3 \times 10 \times 3 \times 1$ systems, that is, 90 different strategies to extract word similarity. However, because of the computational complexity derived from SVD reduction, we only combined this word space model with one type of context, namely BOW (Bag Of Words). Moreover, as the matrices reduced with SVD do not allow similarity computation with binary metrics, at the end, we evaluate just 65 extraction systems. For instance, SYN-DiceBin-COOC stands for a system constituted by a syntactic-based context (SYN), a binary dice metric (DiceBin), and a simple word-by-context coocurrence matrix (COOC). To simplify, the name of each system is not provided with the specific algorithm, since it will not be evaluated. We also can use names to refer to sets of systems. For instance, SYN-COOC represents all systems made of syntactic contexts and co-occurrences, while SYN represents the more abstract set containing all syntax-based systems.

4.1 Corpus and Gold Standards

The experiments were performed on the British National Corpus (BNC)[3] corpus, containing about 100 million word tokens. For evaluation, we selected the $15,000$ most frequent proper names, on the one hand, and the $10,000$ most frequent common nouns, on the other. These are the target words to be evaluated. Proper names are evaluated taking as gold standard a closed list of countries, world capitals, and English towns[4]. This list contains 1610 names, each with a specif tag. Some (very few) contain more than one tag. For instance, *London* is both a world capital and an English town. Let's

[3] `http://www.natcorp.ox.ac.uk/`

[4] AUTHOR-URL

note that here the similarity relation is quite narrow. It is restricted to the relation of direct co-hyponymy, e.g., *England* is similar to *China* because they are both countries. By contrast, *England* is not related to *London*. 749 out of 1610 terms of the list are among the 15, 000 most frequent proper names in the BNC corpus. With the use of a closed list of related terms, we are sure that all similar words correctly proposed by a system are in the gold standard and, then, are correctly evaluated. Using Wordnet, however, many similar words that were correctly proposed by the system may not be in the gold standard, and consenquently, may be incorrectly considered as wrong.

To evaluate the common nouns, we take as gold standard WordNet [7]. Here the notion of similarity is larger than in the previous gold standard. The set of similar words of a given word is constituted by all those related to it by any direct semantic relationship (synonymy, meronymy, hyperonymy, ...), and indirectly, by those co-hyponyms selected from its hyperonyms at the first level. 6, 943 common nouns from WordNet were found among the 10, 000 most frequent ones in the corpus.

Given the 15, 000 most frequent proper names and the three types of contexts defined above, we build three 15, 000-by-15, 000 word-by-context co-occurrence matrices with proper names and contexts of proper names. Contexts are also the 15, 000 most frequent ones. They change according to the type of context selected to build the system. For instance, if the type of context is defined from syntactic dependencies, the matrix contains the 15, 000 most frequent syntactic contexts of proper names. So, the generated matrices are constituted by the same target words (the most frequent proper names), but they differ in the contexts: syntax-based, word order or bag of words. The same is done with the 10, 000 most frequent common nouns: we build three 10, 000-by-10, 000 word-by-context co-occurrence matrices with common nouns and contexts of common nouns. All these matrices represent the baseline word space model (COOC), from which BORDAG and SVD are derived. Previous tests led us to select 15, 000-by-300 and 10, 000-by-300 as those reduced matrices giving the optimal results for SVD-based systems.

4.2 Evaluation

To evaluate the quality of all tested extraction systems, we elaborate an automatic and large-scale evaluation protocol with the following characteristics. Each system provides for each target word (proper name or common noun of the input matrix), a ranked list with its top-10 most similar words. A similar word of the ranked list is considered a true positive if it is related in the gold standard to the target word. For instance, if *China* is in the top-10 ranked list of *England*, and both proper names are tagged with the same tag (country) in the gold standard, then *China* is counted as a true positive. To measure the quality of each system, we use "mean Average Precision" (mean-AP) [4]. Average Precision (AP) consists in evaluating the average quality of the ranking produced for each test word. More precisely, it is the average of the precision scores at the rank locations of each true positive. Assuming a word contains N similar words extracted by the system, in which K are true positives, and p_i the rank of i-th positive, AP is:

$$AP = \frac{1}{N}\sum_{i=1}^{k}\frac{i}{p_i}$$

Note that i/p_i is just the precision value at the i-th positive in this iterative process. Let's see an example. If 2 out 10 ranked words were found at ranking positions 2 and 5, the AP in percent in this case is: $1/10 * (1/2 + 2/5) * 100 = 9\%$. 100% is achieved when the 10 ranked words are related to the test word in the gold standard. Mean Average Precision is the sum of average precisions divided by the number of evaluable words (i.e., words occurring in both the gold standard and the training corpus):

$$mean\text{-}AP = \frac{1}{n}\sum_{i=1}^{n} AP_i$$

where n, the number of evaluable words, is 749 in the case of proper names, and $6,943$ for common nouns.

4.3 Results

Tables 2 and 3 shows the mean-AP scores obtained for all systems using respectively the $15,000$ most frequent proper names and the $10,000$ most frequent common nouns. Each column represents a combination between a type of context and a word space

Table 2. Mean-AP of Proper Names using as gold-standard a list of countries, capitals, and towns

METRIC	SYN-COOC	WO-COOC	BOW-COOC	SYN-BORDAG	WO-BORDAG	BOW-BORDAG	BOW-SVD
CityBlock	5.24	2.7	17.77	4.17	1.88	5.58	3.01
CosineBin	50.06	50.62	47.62	47.85	39.25	38.96	
Cosine	36.50	10.55	39.08	32.67	11.09	34.77	3.56
DiceBin	50.68	46.68	46.58	49.25	38.66	38.97	
DiceMin	47.55	18.31	43.40	45.77	15.54	43.69	2.88
Euclidean	16.92	7.63	17.93	18.73	6.91	18.99	2.96
JaccBin	50.68	46.68	46.58	49.25	38.66	38.97	
JaccMin	47.55	18.31	43.40	45.77	15.54	43.69	3.20
Lin	23.57	8.86	25.48	24.51	8.11	25.34	
OverBin	46.52	28.39	30.43	**59.04**	41.86	38.99	

Table 3. Mean-AP of common nouns using WordNet as gold-standard

METRIC	SYN-COOC	WO-COOC	BOW-COOC	SYN-BORDAG	WO-BORDAG	BOW-BORDAG	BOW-SVD
CityBlock	2.53	0.56	3.78	0.90	0.33	1.45	3.79
CosineBin	15.18	11.50	8.74	**16.54**	3.74	12.83	
Cosine	7.86	1.26	11.32	6.99	1.4	10.98	7.00
DiceBin	12.97	10.14	8.11	16.22	3.74	12.83	
DiceMin	11.23	2.76	7.28	12.65	1.80	11.76	4.84
Euclidean	2.64	0.98	2.78	2.71	0.91	3.63	3.37
JaccBin	12.97	10.14	8.11	16.22	3.74	12.83	
JaccMin	11.23	2.76	7.28	12.65	1.80	11.76	5.76
Lin	5.88	2.71	6.29	5.68	1.27	10.61	
OverBin	5.97	4.07	4.32	16.42	3.69	12.83	

model, while rows stands for the 10 similarity metrics introduced above in 3.2. The best score in Table 2 is 59.04%, achieved by the system SYN-OverBin-BORDAG. In Table 3 the best mean-AP value merely achieves 16.54%, obtained by SYN-CosineBin-BORDAG. Even if the two tables differ significantly in the scale of their values, most systems have a similar behavior across the two evaluations. The main exception corresponds to the SVD-based systems (BOW-SVD), which are the only systems whose mean-AP scores improve when they are evaluated using WordNet (Table 3).

4.4 Ranking of Systems

To interpret the results, instead of using test of significance looking for statistically different and similar groups of systems, we prefer ranking them using the mean of the two evaluations. For this purpose, mean-AP values are first normalized. Table 4 shows a sample of the 65 systems ranked by the mean of the normalized values. Notice that the best systems in the ranked list are based on syntactic contexts, binary similarity metrics, and the BORDAG word space model. Surprisingly, the system with the best score uses the simplest similarity metric (OverBin), which merely counts the number of contexts shared by the compared words. Systems with window-based contexts and metrics with association values appear at the bottom of the list.

It is also possible to rank separately the different parameters of variation underlying the evaluated systems. Table 5 shows the mean and variance of each metric. Given a

Table 4. Ranking of systems

Rank	System	Mean
1	SYN-OverBin-BORDAG	0.99
2	SYN-DiceBin-BORDAG	0.90
3	SYN-JaccBin-BORDAG	0.90
4	SYN-CosineBin-BORDAG	0.90
5	SYN-CosineBin-COCC	0.88
6	SYN-JaccBin-COCC	0.82
7	SYN-DiceBin-COCC	0.82
8	WO-CosineBin-COCC	0.77
9	SYN-DiceMin-BORDAG	0.76
10	SYN-JaccMin-BORDAG	0.76
...	...	...
20	WO-JaccardBin-COCC	0.69
25	BOW-Cosine-BORDAG	0.62
30	BOW-Lin-BORDAG	0.53
35	BOW-Lin-COOC	0.43
40	WO-OverBin-COCC	0.35
45	BOW-Cosine-SVD	0.22
50	BOW-JaccardMin-SVD	0.18
55	WO-Cosine-BORDAG	0.11
60	WO-Euclidean-COCC	0.07
65	WO-CityBlock-BORDAG	0.02

Table 5. Ranking of metrics, contexts, and models

Metric	**Mean**	σ
CosineBin	0.72	0.07
DiceBin	0.70	0.09
JaccBin	0.70	0.09
OverBin	0.58	0.18
JaccMin	0.48	0.26
DiceMin	0.47	0.27
Cosine	0.39	0.37
Lin	0.31	0.47
Euclidean	0.16	0.70
CityBlock	0.08	0.80
Context	**Mean**	σ
SYN	0.60	0.48
BOW	0.46	0.96
WO	0.28	0.90
Model	**Mean**	σ
BORDAG	0.48	0.94
COCC	0.47	0.64
SVD	0.15	0.71

metric, we compute the average score obtained across all systems based on this metric. From this point of view, the best metric is now CosineBin. Let's note that the four binary metrics are at the top of the ranked list. This is in accordance with the evaluation described by Bordag [2], but not with other related work, such as [5], where DiceMin was considered as the best coefficient. In [14], no binary metric was evaluated. We think, however, that the evaluation described by Curran and Moens [5] is not entirely reliable. In their work, equivalent metrics, like DiceMin and JaccMin or DiceBin and JaccBin, achieved very different precision scores. This is not in accordance with the fact that Jaccard and Dice coefficients should tend to yield the same similarity performance for any word. The Dice and Jaccard measures are fully equivalent, i.e., there is a monotonic transformation between their scores [6]. Notice that in our evaluation this pair of metrics produces almost always the same scores. It follows that our results are close to those expected by the theory. As far as the standard deviation (σ) is concerned, the table also shows how it increases from the top to the bottom of the list. The best metrics are then more stable across the different systems since they behave in the same way regardless of the context or model being used. Finally, Euclidean and CityBlock distances are not suited at all to deal with word similarity extraction.

Table 5 also shows the ranking of contexts and models. Whereas syntax-based contexts (SYN) perform clearly better than the two types of window-based contexts, the difference between BORDAG and the baseline model (COCC) is very small. Even if the best systems are based on the BORDAG model, its high standard deviation makes it quite instable. In particular, when it is combined with contexts of type WO the performance decreases in a significant way. By contrast, the word space model based on simple co-occurrences is more regular and stable, as we can infer from its low standard deviation.

Very far from the scores achieved by these two models, we find SVD. Latent information resulting of factorization by Singular Value Decomposition, such as high-order co-occurrences, do not help to improve the task of word similarity extraction.[5]

5 Conclusions

The main contribution of this paper is to compare 65 different systems to extract word similarity under controlled circumstances by means of a large-scale evaluation, and by taking as gold-standard, both WordNet and a large list of proper names classified in three semantic categories.

The results of the experiments leave no doubt that, at least, for the task at stake and for the most frequent words of a corpus, the simplest similarity coefficients, based on binary values, are much more precise than more complex metrics requiring association values. This is not far from the main conclusions drawn by Bordag [2] from different experiments. In addition, syntactic contexts perform better than those based on windowing techniques (with or without taking into account word order). This is also in accordance with most experiments comparing both types of contexts. Regarding the word space model, it seems that Bordag-based systems performs slightly better than those based on basic co-occurrences, but differences are actually very small. SVD-based models, however, are much less precise in their results. So, to compute word similarity, it turns out to be difficult to overcome those systems relying on baseline strategies, namely those using binary metrics and simple co-occurrence matrices. Only dependency-based information seems to be more precise than more basic contexts based on windowing techniques.

Given that the syntactic parser used in our experiments only was constituted by very few rules (about 20), there is still room for improvement. In future work, we will compare the efficiency of different sets of syntactic-based contexts by integrating them in baseline systems with basic metrics and basic word space models. A different strategy to improve results would be to explore other theoretical paradigms for modeling new types of contexts and different word spaces, such as the proposal described in [1].

References

1. Baroni, M., Lenci, A.: Concepts and properties in word space. Italian Journal of Linguistics 20(1) (2008)
2. Bordag, S.: A comparison of co-occurrence and similarity measures as simulations of context. In: 9th CICLing, pp. 52–63 (2008)
3. Budiu, R., Pirolli, P.: Navigation in degree-of-interest trees. In: Advance Visual Interface Conference (2006)

[5] To be sure that our SVD-based systems were well implemented, we made a comparison with the LSA strategy underlying Infomap (`http://infomap-nlp.sourceforge.net/`). We used as training corpus a small sample of proper names from BNC. There were no significant differences between the results achieved with our systems and those obtained with Infomap.

4. Chen, Z.: Assessing sequence comparison methods with the average precision criterion. Bioinformatics 19 (2003)
5. Curran, J.R., Moens, M.: Improvements in automatic thesaurus extraction. In: ACL Workshop on Unsupervised Lexical Acquisition, Philadelphia, pp. 59–66 (2002)
6. Stefan E.: The Statistics of Word Cooccurrences: Word Pairs and Collocations. PhD thesis, Institut fr maschinelle Sprachverarbeitung, University of Stuttgart (2005)
7. Fellbaum, C.: A semantic network of english: The mother of all wordnets. Computer and the Humanities 32, 209–220 (1998)
8. Gamallo, P., Agustini, A., Lopes, G.: Clustering syntactic positions with similar semantic requirements. Computational Linguistics 31(1), 107–146 (2005)
9. Gorman, J., Curran, J.R.: Scaling distributional similarity to large corpora. In: 44th annual meeting of the Association for Computational Linguistics, Sydney, Australia, pp. 361–368 (2006)
10. Grefenstette, G.: Evaluation techniques for automatic semantic extraction: Comparing syntactic and window-based approaches. In: Workshop on Acquisition of Lexical Knowledge from Text SIGLEX/ACL, Columbus, OH (1993)
11. Grefenstette, G.: Explorations in Automatic Thesaurus Discovery. Kluwer Academic Publishers, Dordrecht (1994)
12. Kaji, H., Aizono, T.: Extracting word correspondences from bilingual corpora based on word co-occurrence information. In: 16th Conference on Computational Linguistics (Coling 1996), Copenhagen, Danmark, pp. 23–28 (1996)
13. Landauer, T.K., Dumais, S.T.: A solution to plato's problem: The latent semantic analysis theory of acquision, induction and representation of knowledge. Psychological Review 10(2), 211–240 (1997)
14. Lin, D.: Automatic retrieval and clustering of similar words. In: COLING-ACL 1998, Montreal (1998)
15. Matveeva, I., Levow, G., Farahat, A., Royer, C.: Terms representation with generalized latent semantic analysis. In: RANLP 2005 (2005)
16. Padó, S., Lapata, M.: Dependency-based construction of semantic space models. Computational Linguistics 33(2), 161–199 (2007)
17. Peirsman, Y., Heylen, K., Speelman, D.: Finding semantically related words in dutch. co-occurrences versus syntactic contexts. In: CoSMO Workshop, Roskilde, Denmark, pp. 9–16 (2007)
18. Rapp, R.: Automatic identification of word translations from unrelated english and german corpora. In: ACL 1999, pp. 519–526 (1999)
19. Rapp, R.: A freely available automatically generated thesaurus of related words. In: LREC 2004, Lisbon, Portugal, pp. 395–398 (2004)
20. Pavel, R., Adam, K.: An efficient algorithm for building a distributional thesaurus (and other sketch engine developments). In: 45th Annual Meeting of the Association for Computational Linguistics, pp. 41–44, Czech Republic, Prague (2007)
21. Seretan, V., Wehrli, E.: Accurate collocation extraction using a multilingual parser. In: 21st International Conference on Computational Linguistics and the 44th annual meeting of the ACL, pp. 953–960 (2006)
22. Turney, P.: Mining the web for synonyms: PMI-IR versus LSA on TOEFL. In: 12th European Conference of Machine Learning, pp. 491–502 (2001)
23. van der Plas, L., Bouma, G.: Syntactic contexts for finding semantically related words. In: Meeting of Computational Linguistics in the Netherlands CLIN 2004 (2004)

A Document Descriptor Extractor Based on Relevant Expressions*

Joaquim Ferreira da Silva and Gabriel Pereira Lopes

DI/FCT Universidade Nova de Lisboa
Quinta de Torre, 2829-516 Caparica, Portugal
{jfs,gpl}@di.fct.unl.pt

Abstract. People are often asked to associate keywords to documents to enable applications to access the summarized core content of documents. This fact was the main motivation to work on an approach that may contribute to move from this manual procedure to an automatic one. Since Relevant Expressions (REs) or multi-word term expressions can be automatically extracted using the LocalMaxs algorithm, the most relevant ones can be used to describe the core content of each document. In this paper we present a language-independent approach for automatic generation of document descriptors. Results are shown for three different European languages and comparisons are made concerning different metrics for selecting the most informative REs of each document.

1 Introduction

Keywords/Key Terms — generically Keywords — provide efficient and sharp access to documents concerning their main topics, that is their core content. However, typically these *semantic tags* are manually introduced in documents.

Keywords are semantically relevant terms, usually being relevant noun-phrases rather than full phrases. Full phrases such as "Dow Jones significantly increases operating income again in third quarter 2007" or "Michael Phelps wins gold medals in Olympics" among others, can be extracted by summarization approaches, but they would not be efficient if used as keywords. In other words, one wouldn't declare these full phrases as Keywords of a document. On the other hand, by using LocalMaxs algorithm [10] it is possible to extract REs from documents and, as will be shown in this paper, the most relevant ones relatively to each document can be used as that document's descriptor, given their semantic relevance and sharpness, making them similar to keywords, as would be the case of "biological agriculture", "global financial crisis", "United Nations", among others.

Although REs extracted using LocalMaxs algorithm are semantically relevant, most of them has not the semantic relevance and sharpness that keywords require. For example, REs "staff member" or "command and control" have some relevance but they are too vague to be considered as strong REs pointing to

* Research supported by project VIP ACCESS, ref. PTDC/PLP/72142/2006.

L. Seabra Lopes et al. (Eds.): EPIA 2009, LNAI 5816, pp. 646–657, 2009.

sharp or meaningful topics such as, say, "United Nations" or "computer science". Thus, this implied a new challenge because after extracting REs from documents, the most *informative* ones had to be selected in order to obtain the REs that might be Keywords.

In this work we present a metric we created (*LeastRvar*) to measure the relevance of each RE, and consequently its relevance score in each document.

So, this paper proposes a statistical and language-independent approach to generate document descriptors based on the automatic extraction of the most informative REs taken from each document. Next section analyzes related work. A brief explanation of the LocalMaxs algorithm is presented in section 3. In section 4 we propose the $LeastVar$ metric and consider other measures to calculate the relevance of each RE. Results are presented in section 5 and conclusion are presented in the last section.

2 Related Work

In [3] authors focused on the automatic selection of noun phrases as document descriptors to build an FCA-based IR framework – FCA means Formal Concept Analysis. Results are interesting but, however, this can not be considered a language-independent approach as it uses some language-dependent tools such as stop-words removing, lemmatization, part-of-speech tagging and syntactic pattern recognition.

In [4], authors address the issue of Web document summarization by context. They consider the context of a Web document by the textual content of all documents linking to it. According to the authors, the efficiency of this approach depends on the size of the content and context of the target document. However, its efficiency also depends on the existance of links to the target documents; and their quantity and quality.

In [1] a generic summarization method is proposed. It extracts the most relevance sentences from the source document to form a summary. The summary can contain the main contents of different topics. This approach is based on clustering of sentences and, although results are not shown, it does not use language-dependent tools.

Other Information Extraction methods rely on predefined linguistic rules and templates to identify certain entities in text documents [5,6]. Again, these are not language-independent approaches, despite the good results that they give rise to.

In other related work, there are approaches addressing specific-domain problems. In [7], the extraction of personal information is focused. The authors propose a method to extract artist information, such as name and date of birth from documents and then generate his or her biography. It works with meta-data triples such as (subject-relation-object), using ontology-relation declarations and lexical information. Clearly, this approach is not language-independent. Besides, web pages often include free texts and unstructured data. A supervised approach [12] extracts Keywords by using lexical chains built from the WordNet ontology

[13], a tool which is not available for every language. In [8], a specific-domain is also addressed: extraction of personal information such as name, project, among other information. Although it extracts various personal information, it does not consider the relevance of the extracted information. In [9], a method to extract a domain terminology from available documents such as the Web pages is proposed. The method is based on two measures: Domain Relevance and Domain Consensus that give the specificity of a terminological candidate. In [2] the News specific-domain is addressed; this approach is not language-independent.

Rather than being dependent on specific languages, structured data, or domain, we try to find out more general and language-independent features from free text data.

3 Using LocalMaxs Algorithm to Extract REs from Text

Three tools working together were used in this approach for extracting REs from document *corpora*: the LocalMaxs algorithm, the Symmetric Conditional Probability (SCP) statistical measure and the Fair Dispersion Point Normalization (FDPN). A full explanation of these tools is given in [10]. However, a brief description is presented in this section for paper self-containment.

Although this algorithm may be used to extract other multi element units from text, such as characters or morpho-syntactic tag patterns, now we are interested just in words. Thus, let us consider that an n-gram is a string of words in any text[1]. For example the word *president* is an 1-gram; the string *President of the Republic* is a 4-gram. LocalMaxs is based on the idea that each n-gram has a kind of "glue" or cohesion sticking the words together within the n-gram. Different n-grams usually have different cohesion values. One can intuitively accept that there is a strong cohesion within the n-gram (*Giscard d'Estaing*) i.e. between the words *Giscard* and *d'Estaing*. However, one cannot say that there is a strong cohesion within the 2-grams (*or uninterrupted*) or within the (*of two*). So, the $SCP(.)$ cohesion value of a generic bigram $(x\ y)$ is obtained by

$$SCP(x\ y) = p(x|y) . p(y|x) = \frac{p(x\ y)}{p(y)} . \frac{p(x\ y)}{p(x)} = \frac{p(x\ y)^2}{p(x) . p(y)} \tag{1}$$

where $p(x\ y)$, $p(x)$ and $p(y)$ are the probabilities of occurrence of bigram $(x\ y)$ and unigrams x and y in the corpus; $p(x|y)$ stands for the conditional probability of occurrence of x in the first (left) position of a bigram in the text, given that y appears in the second (right) position of the same bigram. Similarly $p(y|x)$ stands for the probability of occurrence of y in the second (right) position of a bigram, given that x appears in the first (left) position of the same bigram.

However, in order to measure the cohesion value of each n-gram of any size in the corpus, the FDPN concept is applied to the $SCP(.)$ measure and a new cohesion measure, $SCP\_f(.)$, is obtained.

$$SCP\_f(w_1 \dots w_n) = \frac{p(w_1 \dots w_n)^2}{\frac{1}{n-1} \sum_{i=1}^{n-1} p(w_1 \dots w_i) . p(w_{i+1} \dots w_n)} \tag{2}$$

[1] We use the notation $(w_1 \dots w_n)$ or $w_1 \dots w_n$ to refer an n-gram of length n.

where $p(w_1 \dots w_n)$ is the probability of the n-gram $w_1 \dots w_n$ in the corpus. So, any n-gram of any length is *transformed* in a pseudo-bigram that reflects the *average cohesion* between any two adjacent contiguous sub-n-gram of the original n-gram. Now it is possible to compare cohesions from n-grams of different sizes.

3.1 LocalMaxs Algorithm

LocalMaxs [11,10] is a language independent algorithm to filter out cohesive n-grams of text elements (words, tags or characters), requiring no threshold arbitrarily assigned.

Definition 1. *Let $W = w_1 \dots w_n$ be an n-gram and $g(.)$ a cohesion generic function. And let: $\Omega_{n-1}(W)$ be the set of $g(.)$ values for all contiguous $(n-1)$-grams contained in the n-gram W; $\Omega_{n+1}(W)$ be the set of $g(.)$ values for all contiguous $(n+1)$-grams which contain the n-gram W, and let $len(W)$ be the length (number of elements) of n-gram W. We say that*

W is a Multi Element Unit (MEU) if and only if,

$$\text{for } \forall x \in \Omega_{n-1}(W), \forall y \in \Omega_{n+1}(W)$$
$$(len(W) = 2 \wedge g(W) > y) \quad \vee$$
$$(len(W) > 2 \wedge g(W) > \frac{x+y}{2}) \ .$$

Then, for n-grams with $n \geq 3$, LocalMaxs algorithm elects every n-gram whose cohesion value is greater than the average of two maxima: the greatest cohesion value found in the contiguous $(n-1)$-grams contained in the n-gram, and the greatest cohesion found in the contiguous $(n+1)$-grams containing the n-gram. Thus, in the present approach we used LocalMaxs as an REs — REs are MEUs where the elements are words — extractor, and used $SCP\_f(.)$ cohesion measure as the $g(.)$ function referred in the algorithm definition above. This enables the extraction of REs having very low cohesion values but locally maximal.

4 Selecting the Most Informative REs

Thus, by using LocalMaxs it is possible to obtain REs from a *corpus* of documents. However, not every RE has equal relevance or sharpness. In fact, concerning the relevance, some types of REs may be considered: strongly informative REs such as "United Nations" or "road traffic" as they point to important and not too specific topics; other REs being more vague in terms of semantic sharpness, such as "administrative cooperation" or "structural reforms"; and other REs being more specific in terms of the topic they point to, for example "periodic training of drivers" or "Lisbon strategy for growth and jobs". Besides, LocalMaxs is not a 100% Precision and Recall extractor and so, a percentage of the multi-words extracted by this algorithm are not really REs under the Information Retrieval (IR) point of view: for example locutions "in case of" or "according to" may be interesting to populate lexicons for NLP purposes, but not for IR. Furthermore, other multi-words extracted by the same algorithm are simply errors under the IR point of view; although they may be important for other purposes such as multi-word term translation: for example "adopted by" or "set as an alternate".

As a consequence, we felt the need to use an adequate metric to value and privilege the strongly informative REs and penalize the other REs and the errors.

4.1 The *Tf–Idf* Metric

Tf–IDF (Term frequency–Inverse document frequency) is a statistical metric often used in IR and text mining. Usually, this measure is used to evaluate how important a word is to a document in a document *corpus*. The importance increases proportionally to the number of times a word appears in the document but is offset by the frequency of the word in the *corpus*. Thus, we considered this as one of the metrics to try to privilege the most informative REs of each document.

$$Tf\text{–}Idf(RE_i, d_j) = p(RE_i, d_j)\,.\,Idf(RE_i) \ , \tag{3}$$

where

$$p(RE_i, d_j) = \frac{f(RE_i, d_j)}{N_{d_j}} \qquad Idf(RE_i) = \log \frac{\|\mathcal{D}\|}{\|\{d : RE_i \in d\}\|} \ . \tag{4}$$

In this work we used a variant of the *Tf–Idf* measure: we preferred the relative frequency (probability) of the RE_i in the document d_j instead of the absolute frequency, as we want to prevent a bias towards longer documents (which may have a higher absolute frequency regardless of the actual importance of that RE in the document). So, $p(RE_i, d_j)$ will give a measure of the importance of RE_i within the particular document d_j; $f(RE_i, d_j)$ stands for the frequency of RE_i in document d_j, N_{d_j} means the size (number of words) of that document, and $\|\mathcal{D}\|$ is the number of documents. By the structure of the term $Idf(.)$ we can see that it privileges the REs occurring in less documents, particularly those occurring in just one document.

4.2 The *LeastRvar* — A New Metric

As we will show in section 5, *Tf–Idf* is not really adequate to privilege the strong informative REs. Thus we worked on a new measure in order to obtain better results.

Then, we noticed that most of the times, weakly relevant multi-word expressions and errors extracted by LocalMaxs begin or end with a so called stop-word, that is a highly frequent word appearing in most documents. However, stop-words may exist in the middle of an informative RE, for example "United States of America" or "carriage of passengers"; but in fact, usually not in the leftmost or rightmost word of an RE. Then we propose the *LeastRvar*(.) measure:

$$LeastRvar(RE_i) = least(Rvar(lmostw(RE_i))\, ,\, Rvar(rmostw(RE_i))) \tag{5}$$

where

$$Rvar(W) = \frac{1}{\|\mathcal{D}\|} \sum_{d_i \in \mathcal{D}} \left(\frac{p(W, d_i) - p(W, .)}{p(W, .)}\right)^2 \tag{6}$$

and $p(W, .)$ means the average probability of the word W considering all documents — $Rvar(.)$ will be applied to the leftmost or the rightmost word of each RE, that is $lmostw(RE_i)$ or $lmostw(RE_i)$:

$$p(W, .) = \frac{1}{\|\mathcal{D}\|} \sum_{d_i \in \mathcal{D}} p(W, d_i) \ . \tag{7}$$

By using $Rvar(W)$ we wanted to measure the variation of the probability of the word W along all documents. Apparently the usual formula of the variance (the second moment about the mean), would measure that variation; however, it would wrongly benefit the very frequent words such as "of", "the" or "and", among others. In fact, as we experienced, this happens because the absolute differences between the occurrence probabilities of any of those frequent words along all documents is high, regardless of the fact that they usually occur in every document. These differences are captured and over-valued by the variance since it measures the average value of the quantity $(distance\, from\, mean)^2$, ignoring the *order of magnitude* of the individual probabilities. Then, we introduced a small change in the variance formula by dividing each *individual distance* by the order of magnitude of these probabilities, that is, the mean probability, given by $p(W, .)$; see equations 6 and 7. In other words, $Rvar(.)$ (Relative Variance) in equation 6 reflects that change if compared to the formula of the variance which we can recognize as being the same as $Rvar(.)$ but without $p(W, .)$ in the denominator.

Then, $LeastRvar(RE_i)$ is given by the least $Rvar(.)$ values considering the leftmost word and the rightmost word of RE_i. This way, we tried to privilege informative REs and penalize those multi-word expressions having semantically meaningless words in the begin or in the end of it.

Valuing the Words' Length. Considering that most of the semantically meaningless words are small, and long words usually have sharp meaning, we took into account the average length of the words in each RE to help on selecting the most informative REs. Thus, we created the following variant of the $LeastRvar(.)$ measure:

$$LeastRvarLen(RE_i) = leastRvar(RE_i) \, . \, avgLen(RE_i) \tag{8}$$

where $avgLen(RE_i)$ stands for the average length of each word (number of characters) of RE_i.

5 Results

In this section we analyze the quality of the document descriptors obtained after applying the LocalMaxs extractor followed by each of the three different statistical measures (*Tf–Idf*, *LeastRvar* and *LeastRvarLen*) to three different *corpora*: one having English documents, another one with French documents and another one for Spanish ones.

5.1 The Document Descriptor

We decided to represent the core content of each document by using the ten most informative REs in the document.

Unfortunately, sometimes there is no absolute consensus about which REs are the strong informative ones and which are not. We consider that, for example, "Head of Mission" and "17 November 2003" are not strong REs, as the first one is a too vague noun phrase and the second one, being a simple date, is just too specific; but we also consider that "United Nations" and "road traffic" are strong informative REs as they point to important topics, not being too vague nor too specific. However this may not be a consensual classification.

Thus, for each document, the extracted REs are sorted according to each statistical measure and the top ten REs are taken as the document's descriptor. Needless to say that, by ignoring the other REs, there is always document information *lost* by these descriptors, but it must be taken as a core content descriptor, not as a complete and detailed report about the document. Here is an example of a document descriptor extracted by the LocalMaxs and one of the measures mentioned above:

5.2 The Multi-language *Corpora* Test and Other Criteria

In order to test how language-independent is our approach, we used the *EUR-Lex corpora* which provides direct free access to European Union law about several topics in several European languages.

It is available by http://eur-lex.europa.eu/en/index.htm. From this large *corpora* we took 50 documents written in English, 50 documents in French and 50 in Spanish to form three different *sub-corpora*. The only restriction of this selection was to avoid too short documents (less than half a page), as we need to prevent

Table 1. Example of an English document descriptor. Application of the *LeastRvar* measure.

zoonotic agents
borne zoonotic agents
Iceland and Liechtenstein
phytosanitary matters
salmonella and other specified food
JOINT COMMITTEE
notifications under Article 103
monitoring of zoonoses and zoonotic agents
repealing Council Directive 92 / 117
Veterinary and phytosanitary

biases on some relative frequencies of the n-grams of each document, caused by the document's size.

To evaluate the approach performance in these three languages, we used the Precision and Recall concepts. In this case, precision was given by the number of strong informative REs in the set of the multi-word expressions proposed to be the document's descriptor, by the combination LocalMaxs–metric used, divided by ten.

The recall was given by the number of strong informative REs that are simultaneously in the document's descriptor proposed and in the set of the correct ten most informative REs of the document, divided by ten.

Some proposed document descriptors contain multi-word expressions which are not noun phrases but still they are not weakly informative expressions. For example, "Veterinary and phytosanitary" in table 1 is an expression having a well formed morpho-syntactic tag being also a highly informative conjunction of adjectives. We call these cases the *near miss* REs and they were considered separately in the results, as it is shown in the next subsection.

According to our criterion, this is the evaluation of the descriptor shown in table 1, considering Precision: 7 informative REs (1st, 2nd, 3rd, 4th, 5th, 7th and 8th); 1 *near miss* RE (10th); and 2 weak or wrong REs (6th and 9th). So, precision is .70 or .80 if considering the *near miss* RE. Concerning Recall, the document this descriptor represents has 3 informative REs which should be in the top 10 ones, but they are not in the descriptor proposed: "control of salmonella", "Council Directive 92 / 117 / EEC" and "Norwegian language". However, these missing REs were also extracted by the same combination (LocalMaxs–*LeastRvar*) but their scores were above 10th position, that is 11th, 12th,..., and then, they were not included in the descriptor. Thus, Recall is .70 for this case.

5.3 Results for Different Languages and Metrics

By tables 2, 3 and 4 we may see that for the same statistical measure, Precision or Recall values are similar for English, French and Spanish. So, we may say that

Table 2. Precision and Recall average values for the English document descriptors

Measure	Precision	*near-miss* Precision	Total Precision	Recall
Tf–Idf	0.41	0.12	0.53	0.35
LeastRvar	0.57	0.15	0.72	0.68
LeastRvarLen	0.51	0.27	0.77	0.62

Table 3. Precision and Recall average values for the French document descriptors

Measure	Precision	*near-miss* Precision	Total Precision	Recall
Tf–Idf	0.40	0.12	0.52	0.34
LeastRvar	0.58	0.13	0.73	0.67
LeastRvarLen	0.52	0.26	0.77	0.61

Table 4. Precision and Recall average values for the Spanish document descriptors

Measure	Precision	*near-miss* Precision	Total Precision	Recall
Tf–Idf	0.41	0.13	0.54	0.34
LeastRvar	0.58	0.14	0.72	0.67
LeastRvarLen	0.51	0.26	0.78	0.62

Table 5. Example of a French document descriptor. Application of the *LeastRvar* measure.

protoxyde d'azote
postes de travail
main-d'oeuvre qualifie
dioxyde de carbone
stockage du carbone
biomasse produite
victime du changement climatique
Rapports entre changement climatique
livre vert
changements climatiques

Table 6. Example of a Spanish document descriptor. Application of the *LeastRvar* measure.

Sistema Nacional de Salud
Sistema Nacional de Salud español
tratamiento hospitalario
equilibrio financiero
Comunidades Europeas
nivel de cobertura
articulo 22
necesarias para evitar
legislación española
asistencia sanitaria

Table 7. Example of an English document descriptor. Application of the *Tf–Idf* measure.

zoonotic agents
Parliament and of the Council of 17 November
Council of 17 November 2003
Council Directive 92 / 117 / EEC
92 / 117 / EEC
17 November 2003 on
No 2160
Directive 2003 / 99 / EC
2003 / 99 / EC
Directive 92 /

this approach does not seem to privilege any of these languages. And we believe that probably this happens for many other languages, as no specific morpho-syntactic information was used. Even the small differences shown by the tables, such as 0.13 and 0.15 (near-miss Precision of *LeastRvar* measure for English and French documents), would probably decrease if the test *corpora* had more documents.

On the other hand, we can see that *LeastRvar* measure presents the highest Precision (0.57, 0.58 and 0.58 for English, French and Spanish). However if we consider the near-miss cases, *LeastRvarLen* presents the highest precision performance; see Total Precision: about 0.77, 0.72 and 0.53 for *LeastRvarLen*, *LeastRvar* and $Tf\text{–}Idf$ measures respectively and considering the three languages. However, the highest Recall values are obtained for *LeastRvar* measure: about 0.67. Thus, this means that the introduction of the RE word's average length in the *LeastRvar* metric, that is *LeastRvarLen*, privileged some more specific REs (due to their larger length) and so, the number of near-miss REs. But this implied some decreasing on the Recall, once the more informative and not too specific REs were not selected by *LeastRvarLen* to be in the top ten score REs.

Tables 2, 3 and 4 also show that $Tf\text{–}Idf$ presents the poorest results. In fact, due to its structure — see equation 3 — we can see that REs that occur in just one document are the most valued/privileged ones. This explains why the descriptors made by this measure tend to include too specific REs, regardless of some important ones. Table 7 shows a document descriptor generated by the combination LocalMaxs–$Tf\text{–}Idf$; it is the descriptor of the same document from where another descriptor, the one shown in table 1, was generated by the combination LocalMaxs–*LeastRvar*.

Thus, considering the three statistical metrics, we chose *LeastRvar* as being the most adequate one to select the informative REs to generate document descriptors, due to its more equilibrated Recall and Precision vales. Tables 1, 5 and 6 shows examples of document descriptors for the three languages, selected by the combination LocalMaxs–*LeastRvar*.

6 Conclusions

Keywords are semantic tags associated to documents, usually declared manually by users. Somehow, these tags form small document descriptors and enable applications to access to the summarized documents' core content. This paper proposes an approach to automatically generate document descriptors, as a language-independent and domain-independent alternative to related work from other authors.

This approach is based on LocalMaxs algorithm to extract REs, and a new statistical measure, *LeastRvar*, to select the ten most informative REs from each document in order to form document descriptors.

Results showed that this new measure presents better Precision and Recall values (0.72 and 0.68) than $Tf\text{–}Idf$. In fact, $Tf\text{–}Idf$ does not seem to be adequate to deal with this type of selection, as it privileges the too specific REs and penalizes most of the strong informative ones.

On the other hand, the introduction of the word's average length to help on selecting the most informative REs, showed to extract some more near-miss REs; however it presents lower Recall.

Results also showed that Precision and Recall values are similar for the three languages tested (English, French and Spanish), which enable us to expect similar performance to other languages.

Apart from the Precision and Recall values, document descriptors made by this approach does indeed capture the core content of each document. However, in order to increase the Recall values, in future research we will work to include the relevant single words in this approach.

References

1. Aliguliyev, R.M.: A Novel Partitioning-Based Clustering Method and Generic Document Summarization. In: Proceedings of the IEEE/WIC/ACM International Conference on Web Intelligence and Intelligent Agent Technology (WI-IAT 2006 Workshops)(WI-IATW 2006) (2006)
2. Martínez-Fernández, J.L., García-Serrano, A., Martínez, J.: Automatic keyword extraction for news finder. In: Nürnberger, A., Detyniecki, M. (eds.) AMR 2003. LNCS, vol. 3094, pp. 99–119. Springer, Heidelberg (2004)
3. Cigarrán, J.M., Penhas, A., Gonzalo, J., Verdejo, F.: Automatic selection of noun phrases as document descriptors in an FCA-based information retrieval system. In: Ganter, B., Godin, R. (eds.) ICFCA 2005. LNCS (LNAI), vol. 3403, pp. 49–63. Springer, Heidelberg (2005)
4. Delort, J.-Y., Bouchon-Meunier, B., Rifqi, M.: Enhanced Web Document Summarization Using Hyperlinks. In: Proceedings of the fourteenth ACM conference on Hypertext and hypermedia, Nottingham, UK, August 26-30 (2003)
5. Yangarber, R., Grishman, R.: Machine Learning of Extraction Patterns from Unanotated Corpora: Position Statement. In: Workshop Machine Learning for Information Extraction, pp. 76–83. IOS Press, Amsterdam (2000)
6. Christian Jacquemin, C.: Spotting and discovering terms through natural language processing. MIT Press, Cambridge (2001)
7. Alani, H., Kim, S., Millard, K., Weal, D.E., Lewis, M.J., Hall, P.H., Shadbolt, W.: Automatic Extraction of Knowledge from Web Documents. In: Workshop of Human Language Technology for the Semantic Web and Web Services, 2nd International Semantic Web Conference, Sanibel Island, Florida, USA (2003)
8. Dingli, A., Ciravegna, F., Guthrie, D., Wilks, Y.: Mining Web Sites Using Unsupervised Adaptive Information Extraction. In: Proceedings of the 10th Conference of the European Chapter of the Association for Computational Linguistics, Budapest, Hungary (2003)
9. Velardi, P., Missikoff, M., Basili, R.: Identification of relevant terms to support the construction of Domain Ontogies. In: ACL-EACL Workshop on Human Language Technologies, Toulouse, France (2001)
10. Silva, J.F., Dias, G., Guilloré, S., Lopes, G.P.: Using localMaxs algorithm for the extraction of contiguous and non-contiguous multiword lexical unit s. In: Barahona, P., Alferes, J.J. (eds.) EPIA 1999. LNCS (LNAI), vol. 1695, pp. 113–132. Springer, Heidelberg (1999)

11. Silva, J.F., Lopes, G.P.: A Local Maxima Method and a Fair Dispersion Normalization for Extracting Multi-word Units. In: Proceedings of the 6th Meeting on the Mathematics of Language, Orlando, pp. 369–381 (1999)
12. Ercan, G., Cicekli, I.: Using lexical chains for keyword extraction. Information Processing and Management: an International Journal archive 43(6), 1705–1714 (2007)
13. Fellbaum, C. (ed.): WordNet: An Electronic Lexical Database. MIT Press, Cambridge (1998)

Topic-Related Polarity Classification of Blog Sentences

Michael Wiegand and Dietrich Klakow

Spoken Language Systems, Saarland University, Germany
{Michael.Wiegand,Dietrich.Klakow}@lsv.uni-saarland.de

Abstract. Though polarity classification has been extensively explored at various text levels and domains, there has been only comparatively little work looking into topic-related polarity classification. This paper takes a detailed look at how sentences expressing a polar attitude towards a given topic can be retrieved from a blog collection. A cascade of independent text classifiers on top of a sentence-retrieval engine is a solution with limited effectiveness. We show that more sophisticated processing is necessary. In this context, we not only investigate the impact of a more precise detection and disambiguation of polar expressions beyond simple text classification but also inspect the usefulness of a joint analysis of topic terms and polar expressions. In particular, we examine whether any syntactic information is beneficial in this classification task.

1 Introduction

Though polarity classification has been extensively explored at various text levels and domains, there has only been comparatively little work examining topic-related polarity classification. This paper takes a detailed look at how sentences expressing a polar attitude towards a given topic can be retrieved from a blog collection. This means that for a specific topic, we do not only extract opinionated sentences but also distinguish between positive and negative polarity. For example, an appropriate positive opinion for a topic, such as *Mozart*, is Sentence (1) and an example of a negative opinion Sentence (2). Traditional *factoid* retrieval is inappropriate for this task, since arbitrary sentences regarding a specific topic are retrieved. On a query, such as {*topic:* ***Mozart***, *target polarity:* ***positive***} a state-of-the-art method would probably highly rank Sentences (1)-(3), thus failing to single out mere factual statements, such as Sentence (3), and subjective statements with opposing polarity, such as Sentence (2).

(1) **positive statement:** My argument is that it is *pointless*$^-$ to ordinary mortals like you and me to discuss why <u>Mozart</u> was a ***genius***$^+$.
(2) **negative statement:** I have to say that I [don't ***like***$^+$]$^-$ <u>Mozart</u>.
(3) **neutral statement:** Wolfgang Amadeus <u>Mozart</u>'s 250th birthday is coming up on the 27th of this month.

We show that though simple text classification can enhance the performance of factoid retrieval a more sophisticated approach is preferable. For example, Sentence (1) is ambiguous judged by the presence of polar expressions, i.e. words

L. Seabra Lopes et al. (Eds.): EPIA 2009, LNAI 5816, pp. 658–669, 2009.

containing a prior polarity, since there is both a positive and a negative polar expression, i.e. *pointless* and *genius*. Bag-of-words classifiers might therefore mislabel this sentence. A classification which jointly takes topic term and the polar expressions into account, on the other hand, results in a correct classification. For example, the closest polar expression, i.e. *genius*, is the expression which actually relates to the topic. Not only spatial distance but also syntactic information can resolve this ambiguity. In the current example, there is a direct syntactic relationship, i.e. a *subject-of* relationship, between the topic term and the polar expression relating to it. Usually syntactic relation features are more precise but also much sparser than proximity features.

Not only is it important to identify the polar expression within a sentence which actually relates to the polar expression but also to interpret a polar expression correctly in its context. In Sentence (2), the only polar expression has a positive prior polarity but since it is negated its contextual polarity is negative.

All these observations suggest that there are several sources of information to be considered which is why we examine features incorporating polarity information extracted from a large polarity lexicon, syntactic information from a dependency parse and surface-based proximity. In particular, we address the issue whether syntactic information is beneficial in this task.

2 Related Work

The main focus of existing work in sentiment analysis has been on plain polarity classification which is carried out either at document level [1], sentence level [2], or expression level [3]. There has also been quite some work on extracting and summarizing opinions regarding specific features of a particular product, one of the earliest works being Hu and Liu [4]. Unlike our paper, the task is usually confined to a very small domain. Moreover, the plethora of positively labeled data instances allow the effective usage of syntactic relation patterns.

Santos et al. [5] show that a Divergence From Randomness proximity model improves the retrieval of subjective documents. However, neither an evaluation on sentence level and nor an evaluation of polarity classification is conducted.

The work most closely related to this paper is Kessler and Nicolov [6] who examine the detection of targets of opinions by using syntactic information. Whereas Kessler and Nicolov [6] discuss how to detect whether two entities are in an opinion-target relationship – already knowing that there is such a relationship in the sentence to be processed – we do not conduct an explicit entity extraction but classify whether or not a sentence contains an opinion-target relationship. Unlike Kessler and Nicolov [6], we also restrict the opinion-bearing word to be of a specific polarity. Thus, we can use knowledge about polar expressions in order to predict an opinion-target relationship in a sentence. This change in focus raises the question whether for a sentence-level classification a similar amount of syntactic knowledge is necessary or whether sufficient information can be drawn from more surface-based features and lexical knowledge of prior polarity. Moreover, we believe that our results are more significant for realistic scenarios like *opinion question answering*, since our settings are more similar to such a task than the ones presented by Kessler and Nicolov [6].

3 The Dataset

The dataset we use in this paper is a set of labeled sentences retrieved from relevant documents of the TREC Blog06 corpus [7] for TREC Blog 2007 topics [8]. The test collection contains 50 topics. For each topic we formulate two separate queries, one asking for positive opinions and another asking for negative opinions. In the final collection we only include queries for which there is at least one correct answer sentence. Thus, we arrive at 86 queries of which 45 ask for positive and 41 ask for negative opinions. The sentences have been retrieved by using a language model-based retrieval [9]. Each sentence from the retrieval output has been manually labeled. An annotator judged whether a sentence expresses an opinion with the target polarity towards a specific topic or not. Difficult cases have been labeled after discussion with another annotator. The annotation is strictly done at sentence level i.e. no information of surrounding context is taken into consideration. This means that each positively labeled sentence must contain some (human recognizable) form of a polar expression and a topic-related word. Our decision to restrict our experiments to sentence level is primarily to reduce the level of complexity. We are aware of the fact that we ignore inter-sentential relationships, however, Kessler and Nicolov [6] state that on their similar dataset 91% of the opinion-target relations are within the same sentence.

The proportion of relevant sentences containing at least one topic term is 97% which is fairly high. Although 71% of the relevant sentences contain a polar expression of the target polarity according to the polarity lexicon we use, in 50% of the sentences there is also at least one polar expression with opposing polarity. The joint occurrence of a polar expression matching with the target polarity and a topic term is no reliable indicator of a sentence being relevant, either. Only approximately 17% of these cases are correct. The entire dataset contains 25651 sentences of which only 1419 (i.e. 5.5%) are relevant indicating a fairly high class imbalance. This statistical analysis suggests that the extraction of correct sentences is fairly difficult.

4 Features

4.1 Sentence Retrieval, Topic Feature and Text Classifiers

Our simplest baseline consists of a cascade of a sentence-retrieval engine and two text classifiers, one to distinguish between objective and subjective content, and another to distinguish between positive and negative polarity. We employ stemming and only consider unigrams as features. The two text classifiers are run one after another on the ranked output. Rather than combining the scores of the classifiers with the retrieval score in order to re-rank the sentences, we maintain the ranking of the sentence retrieval and delete all sentences being objective and not matching the target polarity. This method produces better results than combining the scores by some form of interpolation and does not require any parameter estimation. This hierarchical classification (subjectivity detection followed by polarity classification) is commonly used in opinion mining [3,10].

We also consider a separate topic feature which counts the number of topic terms within a sentence since this feature scales up better with the other types of features we use for a learning-based ranker than the sentence retrieval score.

4.2 Polarity Features

For our polarity features, we mainly rely on the largest publicly available subjectivity lexicon [3]. We chose this lexicon since, unlike other resources, it does not only have part-of-speech labels attached to polar expressions, thus allowing a crude form of disambiguation[1], but also distinguishes between *weak* and *strong* expressions. As a basic polarity feature (`PolMatch`), we count the number of polar expressions within a candidate sentence which match the target polarity. Since this basic polarity feature is fairly coarse, we add further polarity features which have specific linguistic properties. We include a feature for strong polar expressions (`StrongPolMatch`) and a feature for polar expressions being modified by an intensifier (`IntensPolMatch`), such as *very*. We suspect that a strong polar expression, such as *excellent*, or an intensified polar expression, such as *very nice*$^{+}$, might be more indicative of a specific polarity than the occurrence of any plain polar expression. We use the list of intensifiers from Wilson et al. [3]. Furthermore, we distinguish polar expressions with regard to the most frequent part-of-speech types (`Pol`*POS*`Match`), being *nouns*, *verbs* and *adjectives*[2]. Some parts of speech, for instance adjectives, are more likely to carry polar information than others [1]. Table 1 lists all polarity features we use. It also includes some combined features of the features mentioned above, i.e. `StrongPol`*POS*`Match`, `IntensPol`*POS*`Match`, and `StrongIntensPol`*POS*`Match`.

4.3 Negation Modeling

A correct contextual disambiguation of polar expressions is important for topic-related sentence-level polarity classification since the instances to be classified are rather sparse in terms of polarity information. Therefore, we conduct negation modeling. Our negation module comprises three steps. In the first step, all potential negation expressions of a sentence are marked. In addition to common negation expressions, such as *not*, we also consider *polarity shifters*. Polarity shifters are weaker than ordinary negation expressions in the sense that they often only reverse a particular polarity type[3]. In the second step, all the potential negation expressions are disambiguated. All those cues which are not within a

[1] e.g. thus we can distinguish between the preposition *like* and the polar verb *like*
[2] We subsume *adverbs* by this type as well.
[3] e.g. the shifter *abate* only modifies negative polar expressions as in *abate the damage*

negation context, e.g. *not* in *not just*, are discarded. In the final step, the polarity of all polar expressions occurring within a window of five words[4] after a negation expression is reversed. We use the list of negation expressions, negation contexts and polarity shifters from Wilson et al. [3].

Table 1. List of polarity features

Feature	Abbreviation
Number of polar expressions within sentence with matching polarity *(basic polarity feature)*	`PolMatch`
Number of strong polar expressions within sentence with matching polarity	`StrongPolMatch`
Number of intensified polar expressions within sentence with matching polarity	`IntensPolMatch`
Number of strong and intensified polar expressions within sentence with matching polarity	`StrongIntensPolMatch`
Number of polar nouns/verbs/adjectives within sentence with matching polarity	Pol*POS*Match
Number of strong polar nouns/verbs/adjectives within sentence with matching polarity	StrongPol*POS*Match
Number of intensified polar nouns/verbs/adjectives within sentence with matching polarity	IntensPol*POS*Match
Number of strong and intensified polar nouns/verbs/adjectives within sentence with matching polarity	StrongIntensPol*POS*Match

4.4 Spatial Distance

Textual proximity provides additional information to the previously mentioned features, as it takes the relation between polar expression and topic term into account. In Sentence (1), for example, the positive polar expression *genius* is closest to the topic term *Mozart*, which is an indication that the sentence describes a positive opinion towards the topic.

We encoded our distance feature as a binary feature with a threshold value[5]. This gave much better performance than encoding the explicit values in spite of attempts to scale this feature with the remaining ones. Since we do not have any development data, we had to determine the appropriate threshold values on our test data. The threshold value is set to 8.[6] Since all feature sets containing this distance feature supported the same threshold value, we have strong reasons to believe that the value chosen is fairly universal. We also experimented with a more straightforward distance feature which checks whether the closest polar expression to the topic term matches the target polarity. However, we did not measure any notable performance gain by this feature.

---

[4] This threshold value is taken from Wilson et al. [3].

[5] i.e. the feature is active if a polar expression and topic term are sufficiently close

[6] The threshold may appear quite high. However, given the fact that the average sentence length in this collection is at approx. 30 tokens and that there is a tendency of topic terms to be sentence initial or final, this value is fairly plausible.

4.5 Syntactic Features from a Dependency Path

In addition to polarity and distance features we use a small set of syntactic features. By that we mean all those features that require the presence of a syntactic dependency parse. This set of features supplements both of the other feature types.

Similar to the polarity features are the two *prominence features* we use. Their purpose is to indicate the overall polarity of a sentence. On the news domain, they have already been shown to improve plain polarity classification [2]. Each polar expression can be characterized with its depth within the syntactic parse tree. Depth is defined as the number of edges from the node representing the polar expression to the root node. Usually, the deeper a node of a polar expression is, the less prominent it is within the sentence [2]. Similar to the distance feature, we define a binary feature (`LowDepth`) which is active if a polar expression has a sufficiently low depth. The threshold value is set to 5.[7] The main predicate (`MainPred`), too, is usually very indicative of the overall polarity of a sentence. Sentence (2) is a case where the main predicate coincides with the correct polarity.

The shortcoming of the prominence features is that they do not consider the relation of a polar expression to a mentioning of a topic but just focus on the overall polarity of a sentence. The overall polarity, however, does not need to coincide with the polarity towards a topic term as Sentence (4) illustrates:

(4) The strings $[\textit{screwed up}]^{-}_{mainPred}$ the concert, in particular, my ***favorite***$^{+}$ scores by <u>Mozart</u>. *(overall polarity: negative, polarity towards Mozart: positive)*

Moreover, textual proximity is sometimes misleading as to discover the correct relation between polar expression and topic term as illustrated by Sentence (5) where the polar expression with the shortest distance to the topic term is not the polar expression which relates to it.

(5) <u>Mozart</u>, it is *save*$^{+}$ to say, ***failed***$^{-}$ to bring music one step forward.

That is why we use a set of features describing the dependency relation path between polar expression and topic term. Unlike previous work [6], we do not focus on the relation labels on the path due to a heavy data-sparseness we experienced in initial experiments. Instead, we define features on the configuration of the path. The advantage of this is that these features are more general.

We use one feature that counts the number of paths with a direct dominance relationship (`ImmediateDom`), i.e. the paths between polar expressions and topic terms which are directly connected by one edge. All common relationships, such as *subject-verb*, *verb-object* or *modifier-noun* are subsumed by this feature. We also assume that, in general, any dominance relationship (`Dom`) is more indicative than other paths[8]. Furthermore, we distinguish between the two cases that

[7] The large value for the depth feature can be explained by the fact that MINIPAR uses auxiliary nodes in addition to the nodes representing the actual words.

[8] i.e. paths which go both up and down a tree

Table 2. List of syntactic features

Feature	Abbreviation
Syntactic Prominence Features	
Number of matching polar expressions with low depth within the syntactic parse tree	LowDepth
Is the main predicate of the sentence a matching polar expression?	MainPred
Syntactic Relation Features	
Feature	**Abbreviation**
Number of paths with an immediate dominance relationship between topic term and matching polar expression	ImmediateDom
Number of paths with a dominating relationship between topic term and matching polar expression	Dom
Number of paths where topic term dominates matching polar expression	TopicDomPol
Number of paths where topic term is dominated by matching polar expression	PolDomTopic
Number of paths between matching polar expression and topic term which are contained within the same event structure	SameEvent
Number of paths between matching polar expression and topic term which do not cross the root node	NoCrossRoot

the topic term dominates the polar expression (`TopicDomPol`) and the reverse relation (`PolDomTopic`).

Often a sentence contains more than one statement. A polar expression is less likely to refer to a topic term in case they appear in different statements. We account for this by two additional features. The first counts the number of paths within a sentence between polar expressions and topic terms which are within the same event structure (`SameEvent`). For this feature, we exclusively rely on the event-boundary annotation of a sentence by the dependency parser we use, i.e. Minipar [11]. Two nodes are within the same event structure, if the they have the same closest event-boundary node dominating them[9]. Additionally, we define a feature which counts the number of paths which do not cross the root node (`NoCrossRoot`). The root node typically connects different clauses of a sentence.

Table 2 summarizes all the different syntactic features we use. In order to familiarize yourself with the features, Figure 1 illustrates a sentence with two candidate paths and the feature updates associated with both paths.

5 Experiments

We report statistical significance on the basis of a paired t-test using 0.05 as the significance level on a 10 fold crossvalidation. For sentence retrieval, we used the language model-based retrieval engine from Shen et al. [9]. The text classifiers were trained using SVMLight [12] in its standard configuration. The subjectivity classifier was trained on the dataset presented by Pang et al. [10]. The polarity classifier was trained on a labeled set of sentences we downloaded

[9] We assume the dominance relationship to be reflexive.

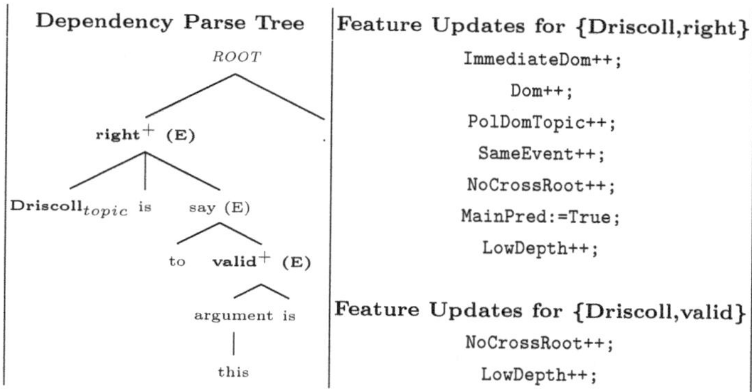

Fig. 1. Illustration of a (simplified) dependency parse tree of the sentence: *Driscoll is right to say this argument is valid* and corresponding updates for syntactic features. Target polarity: *positive*. Nodes which present an event boundary are marked with *(E)*. Note that the pair {*Driscoll,right*} expresses a genuine opinion-target relationship. Consequently, much more features fire.

from *Rate-It-All*[10]. Both datasets are balanced. The former dataset comprises 5000 sentences and the latter of approximately 6800 sentences per class. Unlike the standard dataset for polarity classification [1], our dataset is not at document level but sentence level[11] and also comprises reviews from several domains and not exclusively the movie domain. Thus, we believe that this dataset is more suitable for our task since we use it for multi-domain sentence-level classification. We use the entire vocabulary of the data collection as our feature set. Feature selection did not result in a significant improvement on our test data.

For ranking we use *Yasmet*[12], a Maximum Entropy ranker. Maximum Entropy models are known to be most suitable for a ranking task [13]. We trained the ranker with 1000 iterations. This gave best performance on all feature sets. For part-of-speech tagging we employ the *C&C tagger*[13] and for dependency parsing Minipar [11]. We evaluate performance by measuring *mean average precision (MAP)*, *mean reciprocal rank (MRR)*, and *precision at rank 10 (Prec@10)*.

Due to the high coverage of topic terms within the set of positive labeled sentences (97%), we discard all instances not containing at least one topic term. This means that the topic feature counting the number of topic terms (see Section 4.1) is no longer an obligatory feature. In fact, we even found in our initial experiments that this gave much better performance than taking all data instances into account and always adding the topic feature.

5.1 Impact of Sentence Retrieval Combined with Text Classification

Table 3 displays the results of sentence retrieval with an opinion and a polarity filter. The results show that both text classifiers systematically increase performance

[10] `http://www.rateitall.com`

[11] We only extracted reviews comprising one sentence.

[12] `http://www.fjoch.com/YASMET.html`

[13] `http://svn.ask.it.usyd.edu.au/trac/candc`

Table 3. Performance of factoid sentence retrieval in combination with text classifiers

Features	MAP	MRR	Prec@10
sentence retrieval	0.140	0.206	0.088
sentence retrieval + opinion classifier	0.179	0.247	0.118
sentence retrieval + opinion classifier + polarity classifier	0.220	0.267	0.114

of the retrieval. Only the increase in Prec@10 is marginal and slightly decreases when polarity classification is added to opinion classification.

5.2 Comparing Basic Polarity Feature and Text Classifiers

Table 4 compares the baseline using sentence retrieval and text classifiers with the basic polarity feature (i.e. `PolMatch`) using polarity information from the polarity lexicon. The polarity feature outperforms the baseline on all evaluation measures, most notably on MRR and Prec@10. We assume that the text classifiers suffer from a domain mismatch. The polarity lexicon is more likely to encode domain-independent knowledge. Unfortunately, combining the components from the baseline with the polarity feature is unsuccessful. Only the addition of the topic feature (which encodes information similar to the sentence retrieval) to the polarity feature results in a slight (but not significant) increase in MAP. Apparently, the precise amount of word overlap between topic and candidate sentence is less important than in factoid retrieval. Neither do the text classifiers contain any more additional useful information than the polarity feature.

Table 4. Performance text classifiers and basic polarity feature

Features	MAP	MRR	Prec@10
sentence retrieval with text classifiers	0.220	0.267	0.114
basic polarity feature	0.236	**0.420**	**0.212**
basic polarity feature + topic	**0.239**	0.394	0.200
basic polarity feature + text classifiers	0.227	0.380	0.188
basic polarity feature + topic + text classifiers	0.222	0.390	0.179

5.3 Comparing Polarity Features and Syntactic Features

Table 5 displays the performance of various feature combinations of polarity and syntactic features. Each feature set is evaluated both without negation modeling (*plain*) and with negation modeling (*negation*). When syntactic features are added to the basic polarity feature, there is always an increase in performance. With regard to MAP the improvement is always significant. With regard to Prec@10, only the presence of the relation features results in a significant increase. When the syntactic features are added to all polarity features the increase in performance is similar. The best performing feature set (on average) is the set using all polarity scores and the syntactic relation features. It significantly outperforms the basic polarity feature on all evaluation measures. We,

Table 5. Performance of polarity features and syntactic features. Each feature set is evaluated without negation modeling (*plain*) and with negation modeling (*negation*).

Features	MAP		MRR		Prec@10	
	plain	negation	plain	negation	plain	negation
basic polarity feature	0.236	0.245	0.420	0.441	0.212	0.215
basic pol. feat. + syntactic prominence feat.	0.258	0.266	0.477	0.473	0.214	0.216
basic pol. feat. + syntactic relation feat.	0.256	0.269	0.444	0.481	0.237	0.249
basic pol. feat. + all syntactic feat.	0.262	0.278	0.475	0.509	0.237	0.244
all polarity features	0.245	0.257	0.466	0.489	0.207	0.215
all pol. feat. + syntactic prominence feat.	0.261	0.269	0.477	0.474	0.210	0.222
all pol. feat. + syntactic relation feat.	**0.273**	0.281	**0.509**	0.518	**0.240**	**0.249**
all pol. feat. + all syntactic feat.	0.272	**0.284**	0.502	**0.526**	0.231	0.242

therefore, assume that the syntactic relation features are much more important than the syntactic prominence features. With the exception of very few feature sets, adding negation modeling increases performance as well. However, the improvement is never significant.

5.4 Impact of Distance Feature

Table 6 displays in detail what impact the addition of the distance feature has on the previously presented feature sets. On almost every feature set, there is an increase in performance when this feature is added. However, the degree of improvement varies. It is smallest on those feature sets which include the syntactic relation features. We, therefore, believe that these two feature types encode very much the same thing. Many of the syntactic relation features implicitly demand the topic word and polar expression to be close to each other. Therefore, when a syntactic relation feature fires, so does the distance feature. Unfortunately, our attempts to combine the syntactic relation features with the distance feature in a more effective way by applying feature selection remained unsuccessful. Moreover, we assume that the parsing accuracy upon which the syntactic features rely is considerably degraded by the less structured sentences from the blog corpus. Table 6 even suggests that syntactic features are not actually required for this classification task since the best performing feature set only comprises all polarity features and the distance feature. The improvement gained by this feature set when compared to the basic polarity feature is larger than the sum of improvements gained when the two feature subsets are evaluated separately[14]. We assume that in the feature spaces representing the two separate feature sets the decision boundary is highly non-linear. The *combination* of the two sets provides the feature space with the best possible class separation, even though there are other feature subsets, such as the basic polarity feature & the syntactic features,

[14] i.e. the improvement from the basic polarity feature to the optimal feature set is greater than the sum of improvements of the feature set comprising the basic polarity feature & the distance feature and the feature set comprising all polarity features

Table 6. Impact of distance feature. All feature sets – with the exception of *sentence retrieval with text classifiers* – include **negation** modeling.

Features	MAP		MRR		Prec@10	
		+distance		+distance		+distance
sentence retrieval with text classifiers	0.220	–	0.267	–	0.114	–
basic polarity feature	0.245	0.266	0.441	0.491	0.215	0.226
basic pol. feat. + syntactic prominence feat.	0.266	0.276	0.473	0.499	0.216	0.235
basic pol. feat. + syntactic relation feat.	0.269	0.270	0.481	0.498	0.249	0.253
basic pol. feat. + all syntactic feat.	0.278	0.271	0.509	0.521	0.244	0.256
all polarity features	0.257	**0.302**	0.489	**0.596**	0.215	**0.257**
all pol. feat. + syntactic prominence feat.	0.269	0.285	0.474	0.532	0.222	0.256
all pol. feat. + syntactic relation feat.	0.281	0.285	0.518	0.569	**0.249**	0.256
all pol. feat. + all syntactic feat.	**0.284**	0.281	**0.526**	0.555	0.242	0.252

which are *individually* more discriminative than the feature set comprising all polarity expressions or the feature set comprising the basic polarity feature & the distance feature.

Accounting for different types of polar expressions is important and, apparently, this is appropriately reflected by our set of different polarity features. Furthermore, polar expressions within the vicinity of a topic term seem to be crucial for a correct classification, as well. Obviously, defining vicinity by a fixed window size is more effective than relying on syntactic constraints.

Despite its lack of syntactic knowledge, the optimal feature set shows a considerable increase in performance when compared with the baseline ranker relying on text classification with an absolute improvement of 8.2% in MAP, 32.9% in MRR, and 14.3% in Prec@10. There is still in improvement by 6.6% in MAP, 17.6% in MRR, and 4.5% in Prec@10 when it is compared against the simplest ranker comprising one polarity feature (without negation modeling).

6 Conclusion

In this paper, we have evaluated different methods for topic-related polarity classification at sentence level. We have shown that a polarity classifier based on simple bag-of-words text classification produces fairly poor results. Better performance can be achieved by classifiers based on lexicon look-up. Obviously, the polarity information encoded in polarity lexicons is more domain independent. Optimal performance of this type of classifier can be achieved when a small set of lightweight linguistic polarity features is used in combination with a distance feature. Syntactic features are not necessary for this classification task.

Acknowledgements

The authors would like to thank Sabrina Wilske for interesting discussions and, in particular, Joo-Eun Feit and Saeedeh Momtazi for annotating the TREC

Blog06 data. Michael Wiegand was funded by the German research council DFG through the International Research Training Group between Saarland University and University of Edinburgh.

References

1. Pang, B., Lee, L., Vaithyanathan, S.: Thumbs up? Sentiment Classification Using Machine Learning Techniques. In: Proc. of EMNLP (2002)
2. Wiegand, M., Klakow, D.: The Role of Knowledge-based Features in Polarity Classification at Sentence Level. In: Proc. of FLAIRS (2009)
3. Wilson, T., Wiebe, J., Hoffmann, P.: Recognizing Contextual Polarity in Phrase-level Sentiment Analysis. In: Proc. of HLT/EMNLP (2005)
4. Hu, M., Liu, B.: Mining and Summarizing Customer Reviews. In: Proc. of KDD (2004)
5. Santos, R.L., He, B., Macdonald, C., Ounis, I.: Integrating Proximity to Subjective Sentences for Blog Opinion Retrieval. In: Proc. of ECIR (2009)
6. Kessler, J.S., Nicolov, N.: Targeting Sentiment Expressions through Supervised Ranking of Linguistic Configurations. In: Proc. of ICWSM (2009)
7. Macdonald, C., Ounis, I.: The TREC Blog06 Collection. Technical Report TR-2006-226 (2006)
8. Macdonald, C., Ounis, I., Soboroff, I.: Overview of the TREC-2007 Blog Track. In: Proc. of TREC (2007)
9. Shen, D., Leidner, J.L., Merkel, A., Klakow, D.: The Alyssa System at TREC 2006: A Statistically-Inspired Question Answering System. In: Proc. of TREC (2006)
10. Pang, B., Lee, L.: A Sentimental Education: Sentiment Analysis Using Subjectivity Summarization Based on Minimum Cuts. In: Proc. of ACL (2004)
11. Lin, D.: Dependency-based Evaluation of MINIPAR. In: Proc. of the Workshop on the Evaluation of Parsing Systems (1998)
12. Joachims, T.: Making Large-Scale SVM Learning Practical. In: Advances in Kernel Methods - Support Vector Learning (1999)
13. Ravichandran, D., Hovy, E., Och, F.J.: Statistical QA - Classifier vs. Re-ranker: What's the Difference. In: Proc. of the ACL Workshop on Multilingual Summarization and Question Answering (2003)

Chapter 12

WNI – Web and Network Intelligence

Item-Based and User-Based Incremental Collaborative Filtering for Web Recommendations*

Catarina Miranda[1] and Alípio Mário Jorge[2,3]

[1] Faculty of Economics, University of Porto
[2] Faculty of Science, University of Porto
[3] LIAAD - INESC Porto L.A., Portugal

Abstract. In this paper we propose an incremental item-based collaborative filtering algorithm. It works with binary ratings (sometimes also called implicit ratings), as it is typically the case in a Web environment. Our method is capable of incorporating new information in parallel with performing recommendation. New sessions and new users are used to update the similarity matrix as they appear. The proposed algorithm is compared with a non-incremental one, as well as with an incremental user-based approach, based on an existing explicit rating recommender. The use of techniques for working with sparse matrices on these algorithms is also evaluated. All versions, implemented in R, are evaluated on 5 datasets with various number of users and/or items. We observed that: Recall tends to improve when we continuously add information to the recommender model; the time spent for recommendation does not degrade; the time for updating the similarity matrix (necessary to the recommendation) is relatively low and motivates the use of the item-based incremental approach. Moreover we study how the number of items and users affects the user based and the item based approaches.

1 Introduction

Collaborative Filtering (CF) algorithms are the best known type of recommender systems [9]. These provide advice to users about products they might wish to purchase, Web pages they are potentially interested in, or about any item that is likely to be of use to someone with a very large number of options. In the case of Collaborative Filtering, items are recommended based upon values assigned by other people with similar taste [12].

In particular, recommender systems can be used to facilitate navigation in a Web site. However the Web is a very dynamical environment, where new users keep appearing, new items are introduced and preferences changing. This implies that recommender models must be constantly updated. The core of a collaborative filtering algorithm is a similarity function, typically between users or between

* FEDER, Fund. Ciência e Tecnologia (SFRH/BD/22516/2005) and grants QREN-AdI Palco3.0/3121 PONORTE and PTDC/EIA/81178/2006 Rank!.

L. Seabra Lopes et al. (Eds.): EPIA 2009, LNAI 5816, pp. 673–684, 2009.

items. This function is mathematically represented by a matrix. One way to keep the recommendations up to date with the Web activity is to refresh periodically the similarity matrix to reflect the changes. The obvious disadvantage is to have to rebuild the whole matrix every time. Besides, if we delay the incorporation of new information, we are not using the latest information for recommendations. The alternative is an incremental continuous approach. For every new session, the similarity matrix is updated according to the new data. Depending on what similarity is measured, recommender systems can be item-based (similarity between items) or user-based (similarity between users) [11]. In any of the cases, CF algorithms are built on the basis of ratings (values in a fixed range) given by users to certain items. In the context of recommender systems for the Web, rating information is typically limited. We only know whether a given user has accessed this or that item (e.g. Web page). These data are processed as binary implicit ratings. In this paper we are dealing only with this binary setting.

An incremental user-based CF method for continuous explicit ratings has been proposed by Papagelis et al. [7]. This method is based on incremental updates of user-user similarities. What we propose here is an item-based incremental algorithm for binary implicit ratings. We empirically evaluate non-incremental and incremental item-based binary algorithms as well as an incremental user-based binary algorithm, both in terms of time spent and predictive performance. We also measure the effect of the use of sparse matrices. All the variants are implemented in R [8] using 3 different packages to deal with sparse matrices, which are also indirectly assessed. With respect to our previous work presented in [5] this paper provides more and better experimental evidence of the advantage of our item-based incremental proposal. Here, we also study the relationship between the number of users and items in the datasets and the performance of the incremental item-based and user-based approaches.

2 Recommendation with Collaborative Filtering

Collaborative Filtering requires a database of ratings for items by users in order to perform recommendations. In the case of Web recommendation, the ratings we have are implicitly provided by accesses. Therefore, we assume that these ratings are binary, 1 if the user has seen the item, 0 otherwise. Information on Web accesses can be given by access logs or equivalent. We use this information as a proxy for preference. Thus, given a new session $s_j = \{< u, i_{j,1} >, ..., < u, i_{j,k} >\} >$, a set of pairs $< user, item >$ for the same user, to a CF algorithm, the aim is to recommend items to u. For that, the new session is directly or indirectly matched against the historical database D, containing sessions of the same form, to obtain items that are likely to be preferred by u.

There are two main approaches to collaborative filtering: user-based and item-based.The user-based approach proceeds by looking for N users in D that are most similar to u. The items preferred by these neighbors are the recommendations to make. In the item-based approach we look for N items which are similar, in terms of users that preferred them, to the items in the session. This subtle difference carries important computational consequences. Item-based algorithms may be able to provide the same quality as the user-based algorithms but with less online computation [11] [4]. Similarity between users/items can be defined in different ways. Here we have adopted the cosine distance measure.

Let n be the number of items in the database and m the number of users.

- **User-based similarity:** Users u and w are two vectors in the n dimensional product-space. The similarity between them is measured as the cosine of the angle between them [10]. We can simplify and obtain:

$$sim(u, w) = cos(\overrightarrow{u}, \overrightarrow{w}) = \frac{\#(U \cap W)}{\sqrt{\#U} \times \sqrt{\#W}} \tag{1}$$

  where U and W are the set of the items that user u or w evaluated.
- **Item-based similarity:** The similarity between items i and j [11] can also be simplified for the special case of binary ratings. If I and J are the set of users that evaluated i and j, we have:

$$sim(i, j) = cos(\overrightarrow{i}, \overrightarrow{j}) = \frac{\#(I \cap J)}{\sqrt{\#I} \times \sqrt{\#J}} \tag{2}$$

2.1 Computational Issues

There are some important computational differences between the user-based and the item-based approaches. Whereas in the user-based approach, recommendations for a new session are generated by analyzing the whole database D of user-item interaction, in the item-based approach, we only need to keep the similarities between each pair of items $< i_j, i_k >$. These similarity values are kept as the matrix S, where $S_{j,k} = similarity(i_j, i_k)$. Since, typically the number of items is orders of magnitude smaller than the number of users, this results in an important memory and computational reduction [11][4].

In the user-based approach, we could discard the database D if we kept the user-user similarity matrix. The problem would be that, given a new session with an unknown user (which is a very common situation in practice) we would not be able to relate this new user with previously seen ones.

Another issue is on the choice of the data structures that store the similarity matrices. In realistic applications, the matrices are very large and sparse. The data structures must be adequate to spare space in memory, although possibly with the cost of taking more computational time.

3 Incremental Collaborative Filtering

The above described problem of dealing with unknown users is reduced in [7], where an incremental user-based CF method is presented. It is based on incremental updates of the user-to-user similarity matrix. Although this matrix is kept and updated, it is also necessary to keep the whole database D. The authors claim that the update of the similarity matrix is made with relatively low computational cost.

Our proposal is an incremental item-based CF approach for binary/implicit ratings. Thus, we benefit from the incrementality facility, maintaining fresher models (matrices) as much as possible, and of the computational advantages of the item-based approach. With respect to the user-based approach, the item-based does not require the storage of the whole historical database D. With respect to the non-incremental approach, where the similarity matrix is reconstructed periodically from scratch, the incremental algorithm updates the similarity matrix after each new session.

4 Algorithms

In this section we present the four algorithms under study: two non-incremental and two incremental. The first non-incremental uses plain matrix structures and serves as the baseline. The other non-incremental is the first one but using sparse matrix structures. The two incremental algorithms are the item-based and the user-based. These also use sparse matrices. All of them start with a database D of pairs $< u, i >$ (user u saw the item i). All the algorithms require the computation of either the distance between pairs of items or users. In either case, such information is kept as a similarity matrix, S. All the algorithms start by constructing S and take parameters $Neib$ (the number of neighbors to be found for a given user/item) and N (number of recommendations to be made), and maintain a set of known $Users$ and a set of known $Items$.

Algorithm A1: This is the baseline non-incremental item-based recommender.

- Given a new session (of active user, u_a)
  - Determine the activation weight of each item never seen by u_a
  - Recommend to u_a the N items with higher activation weight

The activation weight of an item is calculated by determining the $Neib$ items most similar (neighbors) to i. The activation weight of i is:

$$W(i) = \frac{\sum_{\text{items in the neighborhood that was evaluated by the active user}} S[i,.]}{\sum_{\text{items in the neighborhood}} S[i,.]} . \quad (3)$$

Algorithm A2: Similar to A1 but using data structures that spend less memory when storing sparse matrices. This is motivated by the need for scalability. This is the baseline assuming the use of sparse matrices.

Algorithm A3: This is our central proposal. It is the incremental version of A2. In the incremental algorithm, besides S we also save in memory the matrix Int with the number of users that evaluate each pair of items. The principal diagonal gives us the number of users that evaluate each item. This auxiliary matrix is necessary for updating S.

- Build the matrix with the frequencies of the pairs of items Int
- For each test user (active user, u_a)
  - Determine the activation weight of each item never seen by u_a
  - Recommend to u_a the N items with highest activation weight
  - Update the similarity matrix and the matrix Int

The updating of S and Int is done as follows:

- Let I be the set of items that u_a evaluated in the active session.
- Add u_a to the list of $Users$
- Add new items in I to $Items$
- Add, for each new item, a row and column to Int and to S
- For each pair of items in I, (i,j), update $Int_{i,j}$ to $Int_{i,j}+1$
- For each item i_a in I update the corresponding row (column) of S:

$$S_{i_a,.} = \frac{Int_{i_a,.}}{\sqrt{Int_{i_a,i_a}} \times \sqrt{Int_{.,.}}} \tag{4}$$

Algorithm A4: The fourth algorithm is user-based and incremental. This is a binary version of the algorithm proposed in [7], originally meant for non-binary ratings. It also uses sparse matrices. Besides S we also keep in memory the matrix $Int.u$, with the number of items evaluated by each pair of users, and the database D. Similarly to A3, the principal diagonal of $Int.u$ gives us the number of items that were evaluated by each user.

- Build the matrix $Int.u$
- Given a new session (of active user, u_a)
  - Update D, $Int.u$ and the similarity matrix S
  - Determine the activation weight of each item never seen by u_a
  - Recommend to u_a the N items with highest activation weight

The updating of $Int.u$ and S is done as follows:

- Let I be the set of items in the active session
- Add u_a to $Users$
- Add the session to D
- If u_a is a new user, a row and a column are added to $Int.u$ and to S
- The row/column of $Int.u$ corresponding to u_a are updated using the new D.
- Add new items in I to $Items$
- Update the row (column) of S corresponding to user u_a:

$$S_{u_a,.} = \frac{Int.u_{u_a,.}}{\sqrt{Int.u_{u_a,u_a}} \times \sqrt{Int.u_{.,.}}} \tag{5}$$

The activation weight of an item for the user-based algorithm is [6]:

$$W(i) = \frac{\sum_{\text{users in the neighborhood of } u_a \text{ that evaluated } i} S[u_a,.]}{\sum_{\text{all the users in the neighborhood of } u_a}} . \tag{6}$$

Implementation: All the algorithms were implemented for the R Statistical Package [8]. For sparse matrices we have tried 3 different available R packages: *SparseM*, *spam* [3] and *Matrix*. We only show the results obtained with the package *spam*, since it was the one with the shortest processing time.

Complexity: The computational complexity for the recommendation phase of all the item-item algorithms (A1, A2 and A3) is $O(n.k)$, where n is the number of items and k is the size of the session. For each of the k items in the active session, the activation weight for each item is calculated. The recommendation of algorithm A4 (user-user) is $O(max(m, n))$, where m is the number of users. Given a user, we process the m users to locate neighbors and then process the n items for calculating their activation weight. So the process has complexity $O(m + n)$ which is dominated by the larger of the two. With respect to update time, in the item-item approach, to update Int, it must make $O(k^2)$ operations. Then, it updates the distance between each of the k items in the active session and each of the n items. This yields $O(k(k + n))$ which is $O(n.k)$ if we assume that $k << n$, which is reasonable. To update the user-user similarity matrix, we update D with the information of the new session ($O(m.k)$) and $Int.u$. To update this last matrix we have to consider each user, and update the intersection frequency with respect to the active user. This operation is again $O(m.k)$.

5 Experimental Evaluations and Results

In our experiments we intend to assess both the computational time and the predictive performance of the 4 algorithms. We want to draw conclusions about the impact of incrementality, user-based vs. item-based and the use of sparse matrices. We have used, from our projects, 5 datasets with web accesses. These data come from 4 sources: a portal for professionals with interest in economics and management (PE), a basic e-learning site of an university computer course (ZP), a Portuguese site that promotes the development of human resources (EGOV); and a site of a Portuguese computer online store (ECOM) [2]. The characteristics of each dataset are shown in Table 1. The datasets chosen have different proportions of items and users, which will help us to identify important differences between the item-based and the user-based proposals. From the PE data we have built 2 smaller datasets with different proportions of users and items. The ZP data has 509 users/sessions and 295 items, after filtering out sessions with less than 1 access and more than 20. The datasets EGOV and ECOM are also samples of the original datasets. On these datasets, similarly to ZP, we remove the sessions with only one access and more than 20. The singleton sessions are not usable for prediction (we assume there is no attempt to predict without information). Very long sessions significantly increase the time for carrying out experiments and do not add much knowledge on incrementality.

5.1 Methodology of Evaluation

For the experimental evaluation we follow the all-but-one protocol [1]. We separate the database in training set, test set and hidden set. We have conducted different experiments using different proportions (splits) of the training and the test sets. The splits used were 0.8 (80 % of the sessions go to the training set, 20 % are test sessions), 0.6, 0.4 and 0.2. The choice of the training sessions is random and does not take into account the original sequential or chronological order. From each test session 1 item is hidden. Again, the choice of this hidden

Table 1. Description of the data sets

Data set	# Users	# Items	# Transactions
ZP	509	295	2646
PE200	200	199	2042
PE802	802	100	6070
EGOV	1244	133	4047
ECOM	413	335	1409

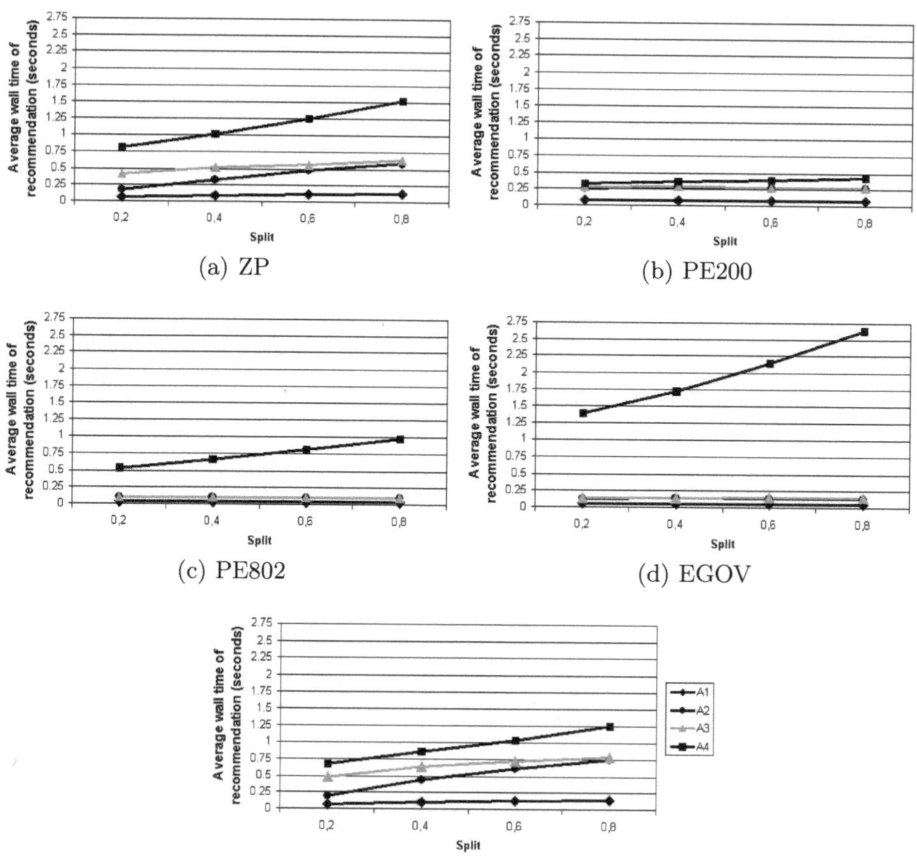

(a) ZP (b) PE200 (c) PE802 (d) EGOV (e) ECOM

Fig. 1. Recommendation time of each dataset for Split and algorithm item is random. Testing is done by comparing produced recommendations with the hidden items. The number of neighbors used in CF was 3, 5 and 10.

5.2 Evaluation Measures

To compare the computational efficiency of the algorithms, we have measured the average wall time of recommendation. To compare the predictive ability we have used the measure of *Recall*. For the experiments, we do not show values of *Precision* because, in our case, they are redundant. Due to the characteristics of the algorithms and of the evaluation methodology (described below), given a data set and a value for N, *Precision* can be calculated from *Recall*.

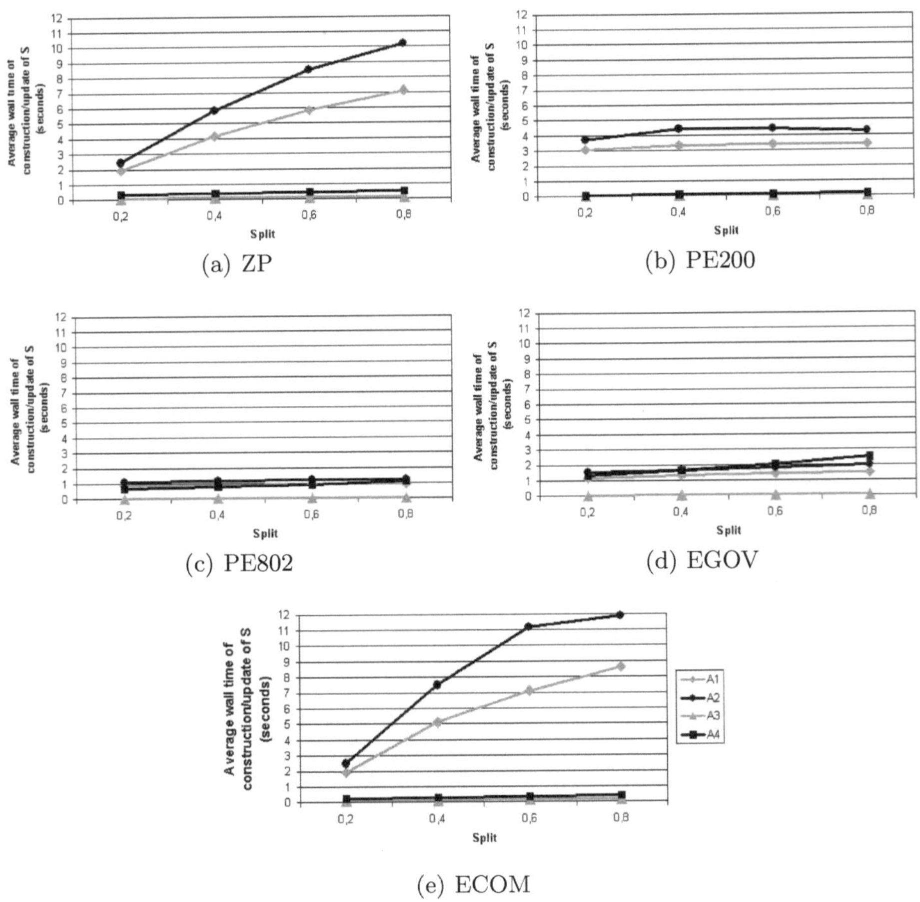

Fig. 2. Time of update/construction of similarity matrix of each dataset for Split and algorithm

Let *hit set* be the set with the hits of the recommendation system; *hidden set* be the set with the pairs $< u, i >$ that are hidden; and *recommendation set* the set with all the recommendations done by the recommendation system.

- **Recall** $= \frac{\text{size of hit set}}{\text{size of hidden set}}$ measures the ability to recommend the items that are relevant to the user.
- **Precision** $= \frac{\text{size of hit set}}{\text{size of recommendation set}}$ measure the ability to recommend only what is relevant, leaving out what will probably not be seen.
- **Time:** We measure the time needed to construct the similarity matrix in each method and, per user, the average wall time of recommendation and the average time to update the matrix and other supporting data structures.

5.3 Results

Time: Results are shown for the recommendation time (Figure 1), as well as for the update time (or construction time in the case of the non incremental algorithms) (Figure 2). These results are shown for all the datasets and for different values of split. Different splits help us to study how the algorithms evolve as the initial matrix grows, since lower values of split imply starting up the process with a smaller matrix.

As can be observed, the use of sparse matrices has a high cost in terms of recommendation time. The lowest line across datasets and values of split is the one of A1 (the fastest), which does not use sparse matrices. This is a necessary price to pay, due to the scalability limitations of full matrices. Besides, better implementations of sparse matrices could reduce these differences. In terms of construction time this is not as visible (Figure 2) when we compare A1 with A2, although A1 tends to be faster.

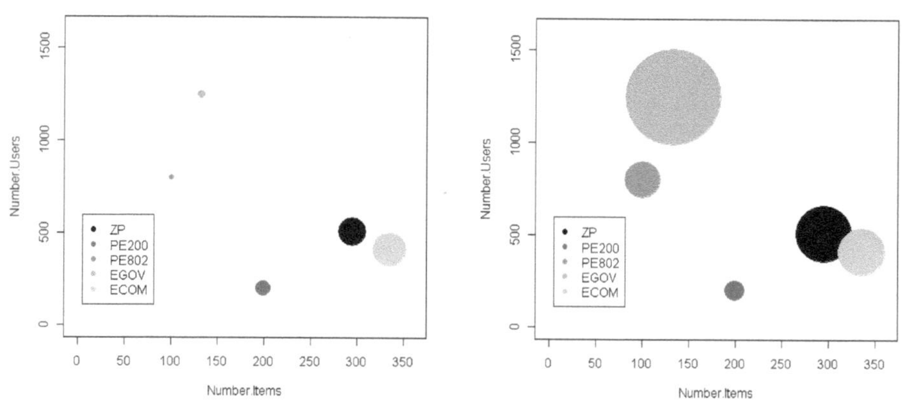

(a) A3 (item based) (b) A4 (user based)

Fig. 3. Time of recommendation shown as the radius of the circles for the different datasets. Coordinates give the characteristics of the datasets.

From the comparison of incremental (A3) and non-incremental (A2) item-based algorithms, we can see that the impact of incrementality on recommendation time is unnoticeable for higher values of split. However, for lower values of split, the original matrix of the incremental algorithm grows as more information is provided and this degrades recommendation time. This has a predictive counterpart: the incremental algorithm tends to have higher values of recall for lower values of split. This is explained by the fact that the incremental algorithm is able to incorporate new information into the model, and that this is more visible when the starting matrix has less information. When we compare the time for building a whole model (A2) with the time for updating it (A3), we can see the difference is huge. This shows that incrementality has a high computational

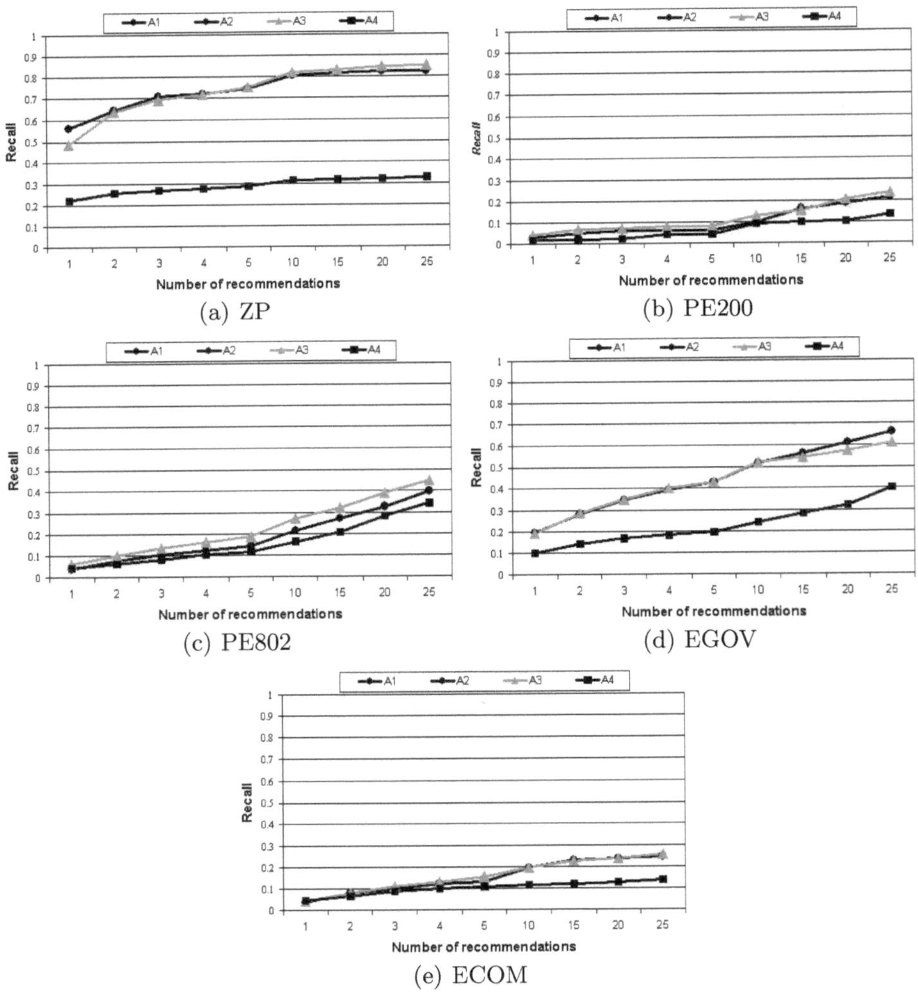

(a) ZP (b) PE200 (c) PE802 (d) EGOV (e) ECOM

Fig. 4. Value of Recall for Split=0.2 and Neib=5

return. Moreover, construction time significantly increases with the size of the matrix (value of split), whereas update time is kept low across splits.

The user based incremental approach revealed some limitations. A4 (the user based incremental algorithm) tends to be much slower when recommending, as compared with A3 (the item based one). The only exception is for dataset PE200. However this dataset has the special feature that the number of users is almost the same as the number of items. This is not the common situation. In reality, the number of users tends to be much larger than the number of items. Update time of the item based algorithm (A3) is also lower than the update time of the user based one (A4). These differences are more visible in Figure 3 where the radius of each circle represents the recommendation time of algorithms A3 (item-based) and A4 (user-based). Here we can also see that the user based approach deals poorly with the increase in the number of users. This supports the hypothesis that our item-based incremental approach deals better with data sets where the number of users is much larger than the number of users. This is also justified by the complexity analysis we show in Section 4.

Predictive Ability. Figure 4 shows the curves of recall for increasing values of N (the maximum number of recommendations allowed to the algorithms). We just show the results for Split=0.2 and Neib=5, since the other possible combinations of Split and Neib get very similar results. The value of recall naturally increases with the number of recommendations (N). A1 and A2 give exactly the same results since they differ only in the data structures for storing the matrices.

We can see that the incremental item-based algorithm has better or equal values of recall when compared with the non-incremental ones, so the incrementality doesn't decrease the predictive ability of the item-based algorithm. Concerning the user-based (incremental) approach, it shows the worst results.

6 Conclusions and Future Work

We have described an incremental item-based Collaborative Filtering algorithm for data with implicit binary ratings. We have empirically evaluated our approach by comparing it with a non-incremental item-based approach and with an incremental user-based approach. Results on 5 datasets further demonstrate (with respect to [5]) the advantages of item-based incrementality in terms of computational cost, with low similarity matrix update times and recommendation times. The advantages of the incremental approach are more visible when we start with a smaller model and more information is incorporated into the similarity matrix. The incremental item-based approach also had better results than the user-based, both in terms of time and predictive accuracy. The update of similarities between items is faster than between users because it doesn't need to revisit the usage database. We have also used sparse matrices to cope with scalability. We conclude that the package *spam* yields faster R programs and that there is a relatively high price for using sparse matrices, as expected.

These results are very relevant for the application of incremental item based collaborative filtering to Web navigation, where we have only binary information (accessed, didn't access). In particular, these algorithms can be applied to data from Web access logs. As future work we need to investigate the behavior of the algorithms with larger datasets and in a continuous setting. We may extend this study to explicit ratings (rates given by the user to a certain item). The incremental algorithm will be included in an adaptive web platform, and the impact of incrementality in the accurate response of CF will be studied on a live setting. Another line of research is the ability of the incremental algorithms to forget old data and to better adapt to changing environments.

References

1. Breese, J.S., Heckerman, D., Kadie, C.M.: Empirical analysis of predictive algorithms for collaborative filtering. In: Cooper, G.F., Moral, S. (eds.) UAI, pp. 43–52. Morgan Kaufmann, San Francisco (1998)
2. Domingues, M.A., Jorge, A.M., Soares, C.: The impact of contextual information on the accuracy of existing recommender systems for web personalization. In: Proc. of the 2008 IEEE/WIC/ACM Int. Conf. on Web Intelligence and Intelligent Agent Technology, December 2008, vol. 1, pp. 789–792 (2008)
3. Furrer, R.: spam: SPArse Matrix. R package version 0.12
4. Linden, G., Smith, B., York, J.: Industry report: Amazon.com recommendations: Item-to-item collaborative filtering. IEEE Distributed Systems Online 4(1) (2003)
5. Miranda, C., Jorge, A.M.: Incremental collaborative filtering for binary ratings. In: Proceedings of the 2008 IEEE/WIC/ACM International Conference on Web Intelligence and Intelligent Agent Technology, vol. 1, pp. 389–392, Sydney, Australia (December 2008)
6. Papagelis, M.: Crawling the Algorithmic Foundations Of Recommendation Technologies. Master's thesis, University of Crete, School of Sciences and Engineering, Computer Science Department, Greece (March 2005)
7. Papagelis, M., Rousidis, I., Plexousakis, D., Theoharopoulos, E.: Incremental collaborative filtering for highly-scalable recommendation algorithms. In: Hacid, M.-S., Murray, N.V., Raś, Z.W., Tsumoto, S. (eds.) ISMIS 2005. LNCS (LNAI), vol. 3488, pp. 553–561. Springer, Heidelberg (2005)
8. R Development Core Team. R: A Language and Environment for Statistical Computing. R Foundation for Statistical Computing, Vienna, Austria (2007)
9. Resnick, P., Varian, H.R.: Recommender systems - introduction to the special section. Commun. ACM 40(3), 56–58 (1997)
10. Sarwar, B.M., Karypis, G., Konstan, J.A., Riedl, J.: Analysis of recommendation algorithms for e-commerce. In: ACM Conf. on Electronic Commerce, pp. 158–167 (2000)
11. Sarwar, B.M., Karypis, G., Konstan, J.A., Riedl, J.: Item-based collaborative filtering recommendation algorithms. In: WWW, pp. 285–295 (2001)
12. Shardanand, U., Maes, P.: Social information filtering: Algorithms for automating "word of mouth". In: Human Factors in Computing Systems, CHI 1995 Proceedings, pp. 210–217 (1995)

Author Index

FSC
www.fsc.org
MIX
Papier | Fördert gute Waldnutzung
FSC® C083411

Kolibri 360 GmbH
Ferdinand-Jühlke-Straße 7
99095 Erfurt, Deutschland
produktsicherheit@kolibri360.de